Equity Cases
in the
Court of Exchequer
1660 to 1714

MEDIEVAL AND RENAISSANCE
TEXTS AND STUDIES

VOLUME 313

Equity Cases
in the
Court of Exchequer
1660 to 1714

Edited by
W. H. Bryson

ACMRS
(Arizona Center for Medieval and Renaissance Studies)
Tempe, Arizona
2007

© Copyright 2007
Arizona Board of Regents for Arizona State University

Library of Congress Cataloging-in-Publication Data

Equity cases in the Court of Exchequer, 1660 to 1714 / edited by W.H. Bryson.
   p. cm. -- (Medieval and Renaissance texts and studies)
 Includes index.
 ISBN 978-0-86698-358-7 (alk. paper)
 1. Equity--England--Cases. 2. Equity pleading and procedure--England--Cases. 3. England and Wales. Court of Exchequer--History--Sources. 4. Equity--England--History--Sources. I. Bryson, William Hamilton, 1941-

KD236.5.E68 2007
346.42'004--dc22

2007013634

∞
This book is made to last.
It is set in Adobe Caslon Pro,
smyth-sewn and printed on acid-free paper
to library specifications.
Printed in the United States of America

Table of Contents

Preface   ix

Introduction   xi

Table of Cases Reported   xxi

Cases   1

Index of Persons and Places   687

Subject Index   697

In recognition of a great debt for many years of learned assistance, wise advice, and friendly encouragement, this volume is dedicated to David E. C. Yale, Q.C., F.B.A.

Preface

This publication was generously aided by a major grant from the American Council of Learned Societies and by summer research grants to the editor from the University of Richmond and from the law firm of Hunton and Williams in Richmond, Virginia.

    We would like to thank the following for their permission to reproduce reports from manuscripts in their possession: the British Library; the Masters of the Bench of Lincoln's Inn; the Masters of the Bench of Gray's Inn; the Masters of the Bench of the Inner Temple; the Masters of the Bench of the Middle Temple; Harvard University School of Law; Georgetown University School of Law; The Lilly Library of Indiana University; and the Folger Shakespeare Library, Washington, D.C. I, personally, would like to thank the librarians and archivists at those institutions, the School of Law of the University of Richmond, and the School of Law of the University of Virginia for their numerous courtesies and kindnesses to me.

Introduction:
The Court of Exchequer

The high court of exchequer evolved within the exchequer department in the middle ages in order to determine legal disputes over the royal revenue.[1] Later, the court of exchequer began to hear common law disputes between private persons where this would assist in the collection of the royal revenue.[2] In the middle of the sixteenth century, the court of exchequer developed an equity side of its jurisdiction so that it could grant equitable remedies as long as there was some connection to the crown and its revenue.[3] In 1649, by means of fictitious allegations of jurisdiction that could not be challenged in court, the exchequer extended its jurisdiction to all civil cases of common law and equity without limitation.[4]

The court of exchequer was presided over by the chief baron and three puisne barons. When the court sat to hear equity cases, the four barons were joined on the bench by the lord treasurer of England and by the chancellor of the exchequer; however, in practice, the latter two officers sat only infrequently.[5]

The court of exchequer had concurrent equity jurisdiction with the court of chancery. However, the exchequer was a collegial court of four to six judges, but the lord chancellor decided cases as a single judge. Although the court of exchequer heard revenue, common law, and equity cases, these three jurisdictions were kept separate procedurally and clerically. The barons heard common law cases one day and equity cases another, as did the court of chancery. The court of common pleas and the court of king's bench had no equity jurisdiction.

---

[1] See generally J. Manning, *Practice of the Court of Exchequer, Revenue Branch* (2nd ed. 1827).

[2] See generally H. Wurzel, 'The Origin and Development of *Quo Minus*', *Yale Law Journal*, vol. 49, pp. 39–64 (1939); P. Burton, *Practice of the Office of Pleas in the Court of Exchequer* (1791).

[3] See generally W. H. Bryson, *The Equity Side of the Exchequer* (1975); H. Horwitz, *Exchequer Equity Records and Proceedings* 1649–1841 (2001); D. B. Fowler, *Practice of the Court of Exchequer upon Proceedings in Equity* (2nd ed. 1817).

[4] Bryson, *The Equity Side of the Exchequer*, pp. 25–27.

[5] Bryson, *The Equity Side of the Exchequer*, pp. 34–63, 170–186.

The courts of equity grant equitable remedies, such as injunctions, and allow equitable defenses, such as laches. Equitable remedies are available only when common law remedies are inadequate, incomplete, or unjust. Common law remedies can be supplemented by equitable ones in matters of procedure, evidence, substantive rights, and remedies to enforce rights. Equity jurisdiction is extraordinary in the sense that, if the common law remedy is adequate and complete, then the courts of equity will not take jurisdiction over the case but will leave the litigants to pursue their common law remedies. Although there is consistency among the principles and procedures of equity, equity exists against the specific background of the common law of England. But, since equity arose expressly to supplement and to complement the common law, when the principles of common law and equity conflict, the equity result will prevail. This is the very origin and purpose of equity, that is, to correct and modernize the common law. But, if, as between the litigants, their equities are equal, the common law results will be applied by the courts of equity.[6]

Although a small handful of equity cases appear in the yearbooks,[7] the medieval tradition of law reporting centered on the common law courts and this tradition continued in the sixteenth and seventeenth centuries. This was so because, until the early modern period, the substantive law of England was, primarily, developed in the common law courts and the equity courts provided, primarily, more modern and sophisticated remedies to enforce common law rights. Thus, law students spent their time in the courts of common law rather than in the courts of equity, and the notes they took there were revised and reworked into law reports. For many lawyers, the habits of reporting cases they developed as students were continued after their admission to practice law, and in some cases, such as Edward Ward,[8] after they became judges. As a result, reports of equity cases are scarce before the middle of the seventeenth century.[9] Therefore, this collection of equity reports adds substantially to the number of seventeenth century equity reports in print.

---

[6] See generally W. H. Bryson, 'Introduction', *Cases Concerning Equity and the Courts of Equity 1550–1660*, Selden Society, vol. 117, pp. xviii–lii (2001); F. W. Maitland, *Equity* (2nd ed. 1936); J. N. Pomeroy, *A Treatise on Equity Jurisprudence in the United States* (5th ed. reprint 1994); E. H. T. Snell, *Principles of Equity* (30th ed. 2000); J. Story, *Commentaries on Equity Jurisprudence as Administered in England and America* (13th ed. reprint 1988).

[7] These can be found through R. Brooke, *La Graunde Abridgement* (3rd ed. 1586), titles 'Conscience & Subpoena & Injunctions' and 'Feffements al Uses.'

[8] See below.

[9] See M. Macnair, 'The Nature and Function of the Early Chancery Reports', in C. Stebbings, *Law Reporting in England* (1995), pp. 123–132; Bryson, 'Introduction', *Cases Concerning Equity and the Courts of Equity 1550–1660*, pp. xiii–xviii.

Reports of Exchequer Cases

The court of the exchequer had the smallest case load of the four high courts at Westminster. Therefore, one should not be surprised to learn that the number of law reports of cases there was the smallest. Indeed, it was the smallest by far. The first collection[10] of exchequer cases is that attributed to Richard Lane;[11] it was published posthumously in 1657, and it covers the period 1605 to 1612.[12] The next collection was by Robert Paynell; the cases date from 1627 to 1631; they are presently in manuscript only, except for the equity cases, which are published in the Selden Society series, volume 118. An edition of Paynell's reports is currently being prepared for publication. The third set of exchequer reports was made by Thomas Hardres; this book covers the period 1655 to 1669; the first edition was published posthumously in 1693.[13] Hardres' reports include sixty-eight equity case reports dating from 1660 to 1669. Samuel Dodd's reports date from 1678 to 1713, but they were not printed until the year 2000.[14] Edward Ward's extensive exchequer reports date from 1660 to 1713. Ward reported numerous equity exchequer cases, and they are printed here for the first time; they constitute a significant increase in the quantity and quality of the case law from the exchequer in the seventeenth century.

Edward Ward

Edward Ward was born in June 1638; he was the second son of William Ward of Preston, Rutland. Edward Ward was a student at Clifford's Inn, and then in June 1664, he was admitted a student at the Inner Temple. He was called to the bar in 1670 and quickly developed a substantial practice in the court of exchequer. He was politically connected with the Whigs. In 1687, Ward was elected a bencher of the Inner Temple, and Treasurer in 1693.

---

[10] There are several miscellaneous exchequer cases reported here and there among the general law reports.

[11] J. Campbell, *Lives of the Lords Chancellors*, vol. 3, pp. 292–303 (1874); E. Foss, *A Biographical Dictionary of the Judges of England* (1870), pp. 392–393.

[12] G. D. G. Hall, 'Bate's Case and "Lane's" Reports: The Authenticity of a Seventeenth-Century Legal Text', *Bulletin of the John Rylands Library*, vol. 35, pp. 405–427 (1952); J. W. Wallace, *The Reporters* (4th ed. 1882), pp. 237–241.

[13] Wallace, *The Reporters*, pp. 291–294.

[14] *Samuel Dodd's Reports 1678–1713 and Miscellaneous Exchequer Cases 1671–1713* (2000). This book also publishes new editions of the few miscellaneous exchequer cases printed in the other reports of the period. This is with a view to having in one place all of the printed exchequer cases between the exchequer reports of Thomas Hardres and those of William Bunbury.

Upon the accession of William and Mary, he was offered a seat in the court of common pleas, but he declined this honor. On 30 March 1693, he was appointed attorney general, and he was knighted on 30 October 1693. On 8 June 1695, he was made chief baron of the court of exchequer. In May 1700, he was one of the commissioners to hold the great seal during the temporary vacancy in the office of the lord chancellor.

Ward was married to Elizabeth Papillon of London in 1676, and they had ten surviving children. His eldest son, Edward, became a distinguished barrister. Sir Edward Ward died at his house in Essex Street, Strand, London, on 14 July 1714,[15] and he was buried at Stoke Doyle, Northamptonshire.[16]

The manuscripts of Ward's case reports are all in the library of Lincoln's Inn.[17] The earliest and the neatest in appearance are in two volumes now labeled as Misc. 499 and Misc. 500. Ward, himself, called them Book 1 and Book 2, or L.1 and L.2. These two volumes include exchequer cases from 1660 to Trinity term 1673. Actually the first thirty-eight pages of Misc. 499 are a collection of reports from Mr. Weston of Gray's Inn and of cases in the court of common pleas in the years 1654 and 1655; the last part of Misc. 500 are reports from the king's bench, which seem to have come from Holt. These groups of cases appear to have been copied *en bloc* by Ward. The earliest cases were probably copied at the beginning of his law studies before he began collecting his own reports.

The cases in Misc. 499, pp. 41 to end, and Misc. 500, ff. 1–220, were collected by Ward himself from the courts of the exchequer and the king's bench from 1660 to 1673. On page 112 of Misc. 499 is a reference to 'L.A. fo. 1'; it is next to a case heard in Michaelmas term 1664. The last such reference is on folio 220 of Misc. 500 to 'F.192'. These notebooks of Ward, which he numbered A through F, are not in Lincoln's Inn. Perhaps Ward himself discarded them after having transcribed or rewritten the reports he wanted from them into his books one and two (Misc. 499 and 500).

However, notebook G, which begins in Michaelmas term 1673, is Lincoln's Inn Misc. 555. Note that it begins the very next term after the exchequer cases in Misc. 500 (Ward's Book 2) end. From this, similarity of handwriting, and cross-references,[18] it can be seen that Misc. 499 and 500 are indeed Ward's reports.

---

[15] *Samuel Dodd's Reports*, Note, No. 305, gives the date of death as 16 July.

[16] *Dictionary of National Biography*; E. Foss, *Judges of England*, vol. 7, pp. 406–408 (1864).

[17] See generally J. H. Baker, *English Legal Manuscripts*, vol. 2, pp. 118–124 (1978); J. H. Baker, 'The Dark Age of English Legal History, 1500–1700', *The Legal Profession and the Common Law* (1986), p. 456.

[18] E.g. the cross-references back and forth between LI MS. Misc. 500 (L.2), f. 220, and LI MS. Misc. 557 (L.K), f. 83.

The notebooks which Ward labeled G through M are now Lincoln's Inn Misc. 555 through 559. Book J, which covered the period 1680 to 1683, was lost before the collection came to Lincoln's Inn.[19] There was never a Book I. Folios 71–102 of Book L (Misc. 558) are missing; they covered the period from Easter term 1689 to Hilary term 1691. Ward was attorney general from 1693 to 1695; he does not seem to have kept notebooks during this period.

These notebooks seem to have been used in the courtroom for taking notes. Misc. 555 consists mainly of jottings of points made during arguments with here and there an occasional report suitable for editing. He leaves spaces at the end of most cases for future personal comments and cross-references. As time goes by, the notes become fewer and the reports become more frequent, longer, and much better. It is interesting to watch Ward's abilities as a reporter grow with experience. By 1683, when Book K is begun, the notes of arguments are very infrequent; also, by this time, Ward rarely notes a case that was not in the exchequer except for the notable state trials of his day. He has become a specialist in exchequer practice, handling equity, common law, and revenue litigation there.

Perhaps the reason that these cases were not transcribed into a book three was that, by 1673, his practice was such that he did not have the time to do it. Perhaps his skill as a reporter had become such that it was no longer necessary to rewrite his reports

In Trinity term 1695, Ward was raised to the position of chief baron of the exchequer. In this same term, he began a new notebook, M, which is exactly the same in form as the earlier ones except that Ward switched over from law French to English. Book M (Misc. 559) ends with Michaelmas 1697.

The next set of Ward's manuscripts to be considered are his 'judicial notebooks', Lincoln's Inn Misc. 531 through Misc. 539. Ward himself referred to them as his 'papers'. They cover the period of Michaelmas term 1696 to Trinity term 1714, when he died. These are long, narrow books consisting of careful notes of the evidence and arguments produced at the trials which took place before him. There are a few reports here and there; in these nine books there are less than three dozen equity reports. These papers were bound after Ward's death and are not in strict chronological order. This set of manuscripts appears to have superseded the notebooks in being the last he made.

Lincoln's Inn also has Ward's cause papers, Misc. 510 through 530, and an index to them, Misc. 540. Ward called this material his 'arguments'. They cover the period 1674 to 1714, thus paralleling the books which contain his reports. These miscellaneous papers consist of arguments and notes; perhaps these were the notes used when addressing the court. None have been transcribed but they are referred to in the notes to the transcribed reports.

---

[19] Book J is referred to, *inter alia*, at LI MS. Misc. 557, f. 8, and LI MS. Misc. 558, f. 18. The cases in Book J were copied in the Georgetown manuscript; see below.

By way of summary, Ward's reports have been transcribed from his books one and two (1660–1673), books G through M (1673–1697), and from his papers (1696–1714). His reports constantly improve in quantity and quality until a year after he becomes chief baron, 1697, and then he is unable to keep up the volume of this part of his legal career. The importance of Ward's reports is that they neatly fill with a good selection of well-reported equity exchequer cases the gap between the reports of Hardres (1655–1669) and Bunbury (1713–1741).

An eighteenth-century copy of Ward's manuscripts is in the Georgetown University Law Library. GUL MS. B88–7 is a copy of LI MS. Misc. 556 [Ward Book H], Ward Book J which was lost before the Ward manuscripts came to Lincoln's Inn, and the first part of LI MS. Misc. 557 [Ward Book K]; these reports date from 1677 to about 1685. GUL MS. B88–8 copies the second part of LI MS. Misc. 557 [Ward Book K], LI MS. Misc. 558 [Ward Book L], and LI MS. Misc. 559 [Ward Book M]; these reports date from about 1685 to 1697. GUL MS. B88–9 is a copy of Chief Baron Ward's judicial notebooks, including cases from 1698 to 1707, copying LI MSS. Misc. 532, Misc. 533, and Misc. 536. The copies of the judicial notebooks are continued in GUL MS. B88–10, which copies LI MSS. Misc. 538 and Misc. 539, which have reports and notes from 1708 to 1714, when Ward died. It is clear that the Georgetown manuscripts are copies of the Lincoln's Inn manuscripts because the former copy the cross-references in and to the latter, e.g. GUL MS. B88–7, p. 365, refers to a case on page 75, which is on page 348 of the Georgetown manuscript.[20]

Indiana University Lilly Library Parker MS. 'Cases in the Exchequer, vol. 6', pp. 120–150, copies twenty-seven cases from Ward's manuscripts; these cases date from 1677 to Trinity term 1680. On page 120 is written 'the following cases, to folio 150 inclusive, were transcribed from and examined with the late Lord Chief Baron Ward's original manuscripts, whose manuscripts are at the family seat of Stoke Doyle near Oundle in Northamptonshire.'

Robert Price reported many exchequer cases from the time when he sat as a baron of this court. His manuscript reports have not heretofore been printed, and those cases from the equity side of the court are now published herein.

Robert Price

Robert Price was born on 14 January 1655 in Cerrig-y-Druidion, Denbighshire; he was the second son of Thomas Price and Margaret Vynne Price. He was a student at St. John's College, Cambridge, having been admitted on 28 March 1672. On 8 May 1673, he was admitted to Lincoln's Inn, and he was called to the bar in July 1679.

---

[20] See generally J. H. Baker, *English Legal Manuscripts in the United States of America*, part 2 (1990), pp. 93–94, nos. 474–479.

In politics, he was a member of the Tory party, serving in Parliament from 1690 to 1700 and in 1701. Among his numerous public offices were those of recorder of Radnor, attorney general for South Wales, and king's counsel at Ludlow. He achieved a reputation as a good lawyer and was active in several high-profile cases.

Price was made a baron of the exchequer on 24 June 1702, and on 16 October 1726, he was moved to the court of common pleas, where he sat as a justice until his death on 2 February 1733. He married Lucy Rodd of Foxley, Herefordshire, and they had two sons, Thomas and Uvedale, and a daughter Lucy. In 1717, Price built a house at Foxley which remained in his family until 1855. He died at Kensington at the age of 78 and was buried at Yazor, Herefordshire.[21]

Robert Price's reports have survived in an eighteenth-century copy that is now in the Lilly Library of Indiana University. These three volumes, 'Cases in the Exchequer', vol. 3, vol. 4, and vol. 5, belonged to Sir Thomas Parker (d. 1784), who was a baron of the exchequer from 1738 to 1740, justice of the court of common pleas from 1740 to 1742, and chief baron from 1742 to 1772. These copies were made from the original in Price's own hand by Uvedale Price, his son and heir, or by John Castle, his clerk, when they were in the possession of Uvedale Price at Foxley, Herefordshire. Perhaps Parker himself commissioned this copy. The original manuscript was subsequently given to the Hon. Heneage Legge (d. 1759), baron of the exchequer, and its present location is unknown.[22]

The scope of this volume of reports of cases includes all heretofore unpublished equity case reports from the court of exchequer that I have been able to locate. They date from the period 1660 to 1714, the time of the later Stuart monarchs of England. Thus the four hundred and sixty-nine equity exchequer cases printed here fill a major gap in the exchequer reports, that between those of Thomas Hardres, which end in 1669, and those of William Bunbury, which begin in 1713.

This book includes reports of the judges' opinions but not orders and decrees. The formal written orders and decrees of the court were drafted by the attorneys for the parties not by the judges, and thus they do not often give the reasons for the decision. Although the orders may give additional information about the case, for the numerous anonymous cases and for many others, the orders cannot be located; when they can be, they are often so bulky that it is impractical to print them. However, numerous exchequer decrees have been published in Hutton Wood, *A Collection of Decrees by the Court of Exchequer in Tithe Causes* (1798), which covers the period 1650 to 1798. These have been reprinted in F. K. Eagle and E. Younge, *A Collection of the Reports of Cases . . . Relating to Tithes* (1826).

---

[21] *Dictionary of National Biography*; E. Foss, Judges of England, vol. 8, pp. 149–153 (1864).

[22] Baker, *English Legal Manuscripts in the United States of America*, part 2, p. 279, nos. 1139–1141.

Editorial Principles and Practices

Because of the great disparity of style, format, and language of the original texts, the decision has been made to translate all of the cases in law French into modern idiomatic English and not to print any of the original cases *literatim*. Law French, by the time of the cases in this volume, was a language in a moribund condition. The reporters were obviously thinking in English though writing in law French; this is clear from both the vocabulary and the syntax of the sentences. This is universally true, not merely that some lawyers were linguistically superior to others in law French. In many cases, the precise English words in the mind of the writer are transparently obvious. The difficulties of translation (and they were numerous) came from the law and not the language, from elliptical writing, from poor handwriting, poor copying, and the bad state of the manuscripts. The problems would have been as difficult had the original been in English. Where there were serious doubts as to the meaning of the law French, a transcription of the original has been given in a footnote.

A transcription of the law French original in addition to the translation has not been given for several reasons. Primarily, the law French of the seventeenth century is linguistically artificial in that the writers were thinking in English and the quirks of their French are matters of legal jargon, not of linguistics. Thus, the true original language is English. Second, several reporters alternated law French and English sentences within a single case without any discernible logic or system. All the reporters used English words when they did not know the French one. Third, to publish the law French original would substantially increase the costs of this volume. Fourth, many of the original manuscripts are available in microfiche copy.

Those reports that were originally in English have been transcribed using modern spelling and punctuation. As a matter of law, a word is a spoken thing not a written thing, and thus spelling is of no legal significance so long as the word sounds correctly. This is the rule of *idem sonans*. In the seventeenth century, writers were careful to spell Latin words according to the standard conventions, but the same writer felt no such constraints when writing in English and quite happily would spell the same English word, even proper nouns,[23] differently within the same sentence. Thus, to transcribe the English cases *literatim*

---

[23] The printer Richard Tottell spelled his own surname at least eleven different ways in the books printed by himself: J. H. Beale, *A Bibliography of Early English Law Books* (1926), p. 196, note also pp. 52–104; Valentine Simmes, the Elizabethan printer, occasionally printed his own surname with different spellings: W. C. Ferguson, *Valentine Simmes* (1968), p. 80; see also R. Munter, *Dictionary of the Print Trade in Ireland 1550–1775* (1988), p. 6.

instead of using modern, standard orthography is useless. Even after this has been done, this book of reports lacks a uniformity of style and appearance, but no more can be done in this direction without compromising the integrity of the substance of the original reports.

The modern forms of i, j, u, and v have been used, as this is a matter of calligraphy and typography rather than orthography.[24]

Since modern usage in spelling, paragraphing, capitalization, and other punctuation has been used for the material translated into English from law French, names of persons and of places have been put into modern spelling unless there is some doubt or uncertainty. In the original, frequently the same name was spelled differently in the same report. Where the true name of a party has been found from the official record of the case, this has been used instead of a garbled version as frequently found in the manuscript report.

Each case is a transcription (of a case originally in English) or a translation (of a case originally in law French) of a single manuscript rather than a composite of several versions of the report. The manuscript used is noted after the style of the case, and after the citation to the manuscript is a note in square brackets of whether it was originally in law French or in English. Significant variations in other manuscripts are given in footnotes, but minor verbal variations are not noted.

The headnotes, or syllabi, which are in italics at the beginning of each case, are the product of the present editor. The purpose of these headnotes is not to provide a complete legal analysis of the reports which they accompany, but, rather, they are intended to serve as an indication of the general subjects of the case.

Square brackets have been used to enclose matter added by the editor; such matter are words added where there has been a deterioration in the original manuscript or a blank left in a citation. Most frequently, however, they are words added to aid the flow of the text or to make an abbreviated note into a grammatical sentence. Ellipses set off by square brackets indicates that the editor could not decipher a word or several words in the manuscript but declined to speculate on what is missing. A question mark between square brackets warns the reader that the editor was unsure of the correctness of the preceding word.

Marginalia, endorsements, erasures, and cancellations have not been transcribed as a general rule. Those erasures that have been transcribed are enclosed within angle brackets.

Dates are all given in Old Style since New Style was not adopted in England until 1752.[25]

---

[24] H. Maxwell Lyte, ' "u" and "v", a Note on Palaeography', *Bulletin of the Institute of Historical Research*, vol. 2, pp. 63–65 (1925).

[25] Stat. 24 Geo. II, c. 23, s. 1.

Since the method of citation to the English cases and statutes has been established and consistently followed for several centuries, the modern scholarly conventions for footnotes have not been used. The cases are cited as follows: the name (style) of the case followed by the date of its decision by the court, if known, then the volume number, the name of the printed book of reports, and the page number. I have also given the parallel references to the nineteenth-century *English Reports Reprint* since this is the edition that is most widely available today. The yearbook (YB) cases are cited by the legal term, the regnal year, the folio number, the placitum number, and the date of the case. The statutes are cited by the regnal year followed by the chapter of the statute, and then the reference to the printed edition is given in parentheses with the volume and then the page numbers. *SR* refers to the edition used, i.e. *The Statutes of the Realm* (London, 1810–1828). Where a case or a statute is referred to more than once in a particular case, only the first reference has been identified in a footnote.

I have attempted to locate the official written order that corresponds to the unofficial report published here. In those cases where one cannot be sure which order is the exact one, I have noted all possible ones that I was able to identify. In many cases, there were no orders for the term of the report (where the term is known), and so references to orders from preceding or following terms have been noted where possible.

The general problem is that equity cases normally took several years from filing to final decree. During the pendency of the litigation, numerous interlocutory orders would be entered; some were orders of course, others followed interlocutory hearings. The reports could have been of proceedings at interlocutory or final hearings; in most cases, one cannot know which.

On the other hand, the parties may not have ever had a formal order drafted and entered in the order books following an oral ruling delivered from the bench. Where a final decision was for the defendant or where the parties settled the case out of court, for example, money was to be saved by omitting this formality.

Table of Cases Reported

Cases are organized in this book chronologically by case number. The following list shows each case alphabetically, its case number, and the corresponding page number where the case appears.

No.	Case	Page
331	Abbot v. Hicks (1696)	407
260	Abergavenny, Lord ads. Bathurst (1688)	293
244	Acton v. Smith (1687)	277
378	Adams v. Rogers (1702)	471
413	Agates ads. Constable (1707)	559
344	Ainge ads. Wyrley (1697)	425
173	Alcock v. Alcock (1683)	181
257	Allen ads. Masters (1687-89)	290
259	Andrews v. Child (1688)	292
390	Anger ads. Lennard (1705)	513
90	Anglesea, Earl of, relator v. Mayor of Rochester (1678)	96
4	Anonymous (1665)	5
14	Anonymous (1666)	10
15	Anonymous (1666)	10
38	Anonymous (1669)	42
39	Anonymous (1669)	42
41	Anonymous (1669)	42
42	Anonymous (1669)	42
43	Anonymous (1670)	44
441	Anonymous (1709)	642
449	Anonymous (1710)	662
450	Anonymous (1710)	662
13	Anonymous v. Baker (1666)	10
358	Appreece ads. Seaman (1697)	443
114	Ashfordby v. Newcomen (1681)	121
60	Athy ads. Stevens (1673)	69
433	Atkins v. Wayland (1709)	601
298	Atkinson ads. Cumber (1695)	351
262	Atkyns v. Savage (1688)	295

No.	Case	Page
194	Atterbury v. Stafford (1684)	209
227	Attorney General v. Barnardiston (1686-87)	252
415	Attorney General ads. Bartlett (1707-09)	561
373	Attorney General v. Basnett (1700)	465
301	Attorney General v. Broadbridge (1695)	354
276	Attorney General v. Brown (1689)	318
395	Attorney General v. Burdett (1705)	521
250	Attorney General v. Calvert (1687)	283
143	Attorney General v. Carrington, Lord (1682)	150
458	Attorney General ads. Cary (1711)	669
419	Attorney General v. Croft (1707)	567
53	Attorney General v. Fitzjames (1672)	51
92	Attorney General v. Fitzmaurice (1678)	98
140	Attorney General v. Flatman (1682)	146
261	Attorney General v. Galliard (1688)	294
421	Attorney General v. Herring (1707)	568
220	Attorney General v. Honiwood (1686)	241
386	Attorney General v. Jeffreys (1704)	501
84	Attorney General v. Jenkinson (1678)	91
269	Attorney General v. Gaynor Jones (1688-90)	304
28	Attorney General v. Jones (1667-68)	33
427	Attorney General v. Mason (1708)	577
52	Attorney General ads. Morgan (1671)	50
328	Attorney General v. Orsell (1696)	400
370	Attorney General v. Oxford, City of (1699)	463
23	Attorney General ads. Pawlett (1667-68)	23
3	Attorney General v. Plymouth, Mayor of (1664)	4
284	Attorney General v. Price (1691)	329
16	Attorney General v. Sandys (1666-69)	11
138	Attorney General v. Sharpe (1682)	145
196	Attorney General ads. Shish (1684)	212
399	Attorney General v. Smith (1705)	527
176	Attorney General ads. Sowton (1683)	184
270	Attorney General v. Spooner (1688)	309
359	Attorney General ads. Tilson (1697)	444
101	Attorney General v. Waller (1679)	107
422	Attorney General v. Weeks (1707)	570
338	Attorney General ads. Williams (1696)	420
90	Attorney General ex rel. Anglesea, Earl of v. Mayor of Rochester (1678)	96
457	Attorney General ex rel. Barnardiston v. Butterworth (1711)	666

No.	Case	Page
254	Attorney General ex rel. Barnwell v. Baker (1687)	288
322	Attorney General ex rel. Bennet v. St. John (1696)	392
291	Attorney General ex rel. Boucher v. Portington (1694)	338
445	Attorney General ex rel. Burton v. Bishop of London (1710)	645
362	Attorney General ex rel. Chicheley v. Laycock (1697)	447
341	Attorney General ex rel. Chubb v. Corning (1697)	421
349	Attorney General ex rel. Dongworth v. Tathwell (1697)	431
265	Attorney General ex rel. Duppa v. Dean of Winchester (1688)	299
198	Attorney General ex rel. Frowd v. Whitley (1684)	213
420	Attorney General ex rel. Gwyn v. Prytherch (1707)	568
320	Attorney General ex rel. Huntington, Mayor of v. Mercers Co. (1696)	388
63	Attorney General ex rel. Italian Merchants v. Blake (1675)	72
167	Attorney General ex rel. Knatchbull v. Loving (1683)	176
248	Attorney General ex rel. Lloyd v. Clopton (1687)	281
106	Attorney General ex rel. Lowther v. Fletcher (1680)	113
133	Attorney General ex rel. Maidenhead, Mayor of v. Jeffs (1682)	141
302	Attorney General ex rel. Maidenhead, Mayor of v. Rose (1696)	354
405	Attorney General ex rel. Marriot v. Lord Wharton (1706-08)	536
214	Attorney General ex rel. Moneyers of the Mint v. Slingsby (1685)	236
336	Attorney General ex rel. Newcastle, Mayor of v. Hemings (1696)	418
79	Attorney General ex rel. Oxley v. Partridge (1678)	87
104	Attorney General ex rel. Powell v. Corp. of Ludlow (1680)	110
94	Attorney General ex rel. Rookeby v. Sanderson (1679)	99
303	Attorney General ex rel. Shaw v. Bowater (1696)	357
31	Attorney General ex rel. Skelton v. Doughty (1668)	37
202	Attorney General ex rel. Smith v. Pollard (1685)	223
264	Attorney General ex rel. Sowerby v. Whitaker (1688)	298
46	Attorney General ex rel. Steers v. Hale (1670)	46
356	Attorney General ex rel. Strode v. Birl (1697)	441
132	Attorney General ex rel. Talbot v. Price (1681)	140
62	Attorney General ex rel. Thistlethwaite v. Wilson (1675)	71
74	Attorney General ex rel. Waller v. Mayor of Bristol (1676)	83
267	Attorney General ex rel. Warnham Churchwardens v. Michell (1688)	300
383	Attorney General ex rel. Wells v. Brewster (1703-05)	476
247	Attorney General ex rel. White v. Lord Bulkely (1687-90)	279
166	Audley v. Scroggs (1683)	175
209	Aunesly v. Lort (1685)	231
164	Awborne v. Windebank (1682)	174
161	Aynsworth ads. Sheen (1682)	171
440	Bagnall v. Yates (1709)	641
254	Baker ads. A.G. ex rel. Barnwell (1687)	288

No.	Case	Page
13	Baker ads. Anonymous (1666)	10
215	Baker v. Howland (1685)	236
57	Banister v. Brooke (1672)	67
224	Bankes v. Rye (1686)	247
64	Barker ads. Widdrington (1675)	73
227	Barnardiston ads. Attorney General (1686-87)	252
457	Barnardiston, relator v. Butterworth (1711)	666
254	Barnwell, relator v. Baker (1687)	288
447	Barret ads. Dummer (1710)	657
145	Barrow ads. Burton (1682)	153
415	Bartlett v. Attorney General (1707-09)	561
373	Basnett ads. Attorney General (1700)	465
260	Bathurst v. Lord Abergavenny (1688)	293
180	Bax ads. Inder (1683)	190
78	Baynes v. Moor (1677)	87
234	Beacon ads. Berriff (1687)	265
27	Beake ads. Croke (1667)	31
466	Beale v. Hacking (1713)	682
435	Beamont ads. Lay (1709)	604
400	Beene ads. Frampton (1705-06)	528
318	Beer v. Caswell (1696)	386
210	Beilby ads. Mayor of Hull (1685)	232
456	Bendlowes ads. Collingwood (1711)	666
404	Bendlowes' Case (1706)	535
322	Bennet, relator v. St. John (1696)	392
287	Bennett v. Golding (1693)	334
452	Bernard v. Jenkins (1711)	664
234	Berriff v. Beacon (1687)	265
5	Berringer ads. Wheeler (1665)	5
360	Berry v. Ladbrooke (1697)	445
396	Betts ads. Humphrey (1705)	521
89	Bickerton v. Bickerton (1678)	94
134	Biggs ads. Cartwright (1682)	142
339	Bigs ads. Nicholls (1697)	420
179	Birch ads. Price (1683)	189
271	Bird ads. Earl of Chesterfield (1688)	310
356	Birl ads. A.G. ex rel. Strode (1697)	441
232	Birt v. Humfreys (1687)	261
221	Blacket ads. Squire (1686)	243
241	Blagrove ads. Chamberlain (1687)	274
63	Blake ads. A.G. ex rel. Italian Merchants (1675)	72

Table of Cases Reported xxv

No.	Case	Page
355	Blanchard ads. Veel (1679)	439
51	Bland's Case (1671)	49
268	Blaythorne ads. Hornely (1688-90)	302
59	Blucke ads. Elliott (1673)	69
426	Boomer ads. Lord Howard (1708)	576
291	Boucher, relator v. Portington (1694)	338
303	Bowater ads. A.G. ex rel. Shaw (1696)	357
285	Bowater v. Hartley (1692)	332
310	Bowyer v. Gibbs (1696)	365
203	Bradbury ads. Warner (1685)	224
171	Bradshaw ads. Hillingham (1683)	179
334	Bradshaw ads. Sutton (1696)	413
102	Bradshaw v. Clifton (1679)	108
201	Brage v. Heninge (1685)	222
295	Bramly v. Philips (1695)	343
155	Brand ads. Husbands (1682)	163
218	Brewer ads. Parker (1686)	239
383	Brewster ads. A.G. ex rel. Wells (1703-05)	476
380	Bridges ads. Ekins (1703)	472
387	Bridges v. Jeffreys (1704)	506
323	Briggs ads. Chambers (1696)	393
7	Briggs ads. Tully (1666)	7
74	Bristol, Mayor of ads. A.G. ex rel. Waller (1676)	83
301	Broadbridge ads. Attorney General (1695)	354
385	Brockman v. Randolph (1704)	500
57	Brooke ads. Banister (1672)	67
258	Brookes v. Hart (1688)	291
87	Brookesby v. Coppin (1678)	93
109	Brooks v. Hill (1680)	116
204	Broune ads. Okeham Hospital Governors (1685)	226
276	Brown ads. Attorney General (1689)	318
306	Browne v. Chaplin (1696)	360
363	Browne v. Culworthy (1697)	447
337	Browne ads. Goate (1696)	419
33	Browne ads. Lucas (1668)	39
12	Browne v. Moody (1666)	9
226	Brownlow ads. Heron (1686)	250
309	Buckingham ads. Clay (1696)	365
467	Buckingham v. Pycroft (1713)	682
468	Buckly, Lady ads. Lady Campbell (1714)	683
247	Bulkely, Lord ads. A.G. ex rel. White (1687-90)	279

No.	Case	Page
395	Burdett ads. Attorney General (1705)	521
446	Burton ads. Hutchinson (1710)	652
145	Burton v. Barrow (1682)	153
445	Burton, relator v. Bishop of London (1710)	645
122	Burwell v. Newton (1681-83)	130
124	Butcher ads. Margets (1681)	134
424	Butterfield v. Perkins (1707)	572
457	Butterworth ads. A.G. ex rel. Barnardiston (1711)	666
250	Calvert ads. Attorney General (1687)	283
172	Cambridge, City of v. Gonville and Caius College (1683)	180
125	Camell v. Ward (1681)	135
468	Campbell, Lady v. Lady Buckly (1714)	683
429	Campbell, Lady v. Lort (1708)	583
451	Canning v. Clark (1710)	663
300	Capon ads. Cutlove (1695)	353
381	Carmarthen, Marquess of v. Lord Halifax (1703)	473
22	Carr ads. Heaton (1667)	22
143	Carrington, Lord ads. Attorney General (1682)	150
430	Carter ads. Streper (1708)	587
134	Cartwright v. Biggs (1682)	142
458	Cary v. Attorney General (1711)	669
423	Cary v. Machan (1707)	571
347	Castle v. Cullen (1697)	428
318	Caswell ads. Beer (1696)	386
263	Cave's Case (1688)	297
316	Chaffin v. Frampton (1696)	384
408	Chamberlain ads. Newt (1706)	552
241	Chamberlain v. Blagrove (1687)	274
40	Chamberlaine ads. Raleigh (1669)	43
323	Chambers v. Briggs (1696)	393
306	Chaplin ads. Browne (1696)	360
137	Chapman v. Hale (1682)	144
252	Chapman ads. Speccol (1687-88)	286
189	Chappell ads. Hopkins (1684)	199
235	Charlett ads. Fox (1687)	267
271	Chesterfield, Earl of v. Bird (1688)	310
255	Chesterfield, Earl of v. Lord Holles (1687)	289
391	Chetham v. Lamplugh (1705)	514
362	Chicheley, relator v. Laycock (1697)	447
259	Child ads. Andrews (1688)	292
49	Chislett v. Morrice (1670)	48

No.	Case	Page
304	Chittle ads. Hawkins (1696)	358
242	Chitty v. Reeve (1687)	274
147	Cholmly ads. Hewley (1682)	155
341	Chubb, relator v. Corning (1697)	421
376	Clargies ads. Sherwin (1701-02)	468
451	Clark ads. Canning (1710)	663
327	Clarke ads. Tayes (1696)	399
309	Clay v. Buckingham (1696)	365
157	Clements v. Downes (1682)	165
107	Cliff ads. Harris (1680)	115
102	Clifton ads. Bradshaw (1679)	108
248	Clopton ads. A.G. ex rel. Lloyd (1687)	281
10	Clothworkers Co. ads. Joyce (1666)	8
9	Clothworkers Co. ads. Staughton (1666)	8
345	Cogger v. Randall (1697)	425
236	Coles v. Eyans (1687)	267
136	Collard v. Newton (1682)	143
434	Collet ads. Robinson (1709)	602
456	Collingwood v. Bendlowes (1711)	666
47	Collop v. Foster (1670)	47
103	Colson ads. Turner (1680)	110
67	Colwall v. Vyner (1675)	77
160	Coney v. Dorrington (1682)	170
332	Coney v. Horne (1696)	412
464	Conning v. Menzies (1712)	678
413	Constable v. Agates (1707)	559
152	Cook v. Fountain (1682)	160
205	Cooke ads. Croxall (1685)	227
174	Cooke ads. Haslehurst (1683)	182
126	Cooke ads. Toller (1681)	135
319	Cooke v. Haynes (1696)	387
87	Coppin ads. Brookesby (1678)	93
389	Coppleston ads. Scamell (1705)	510
393	Corbet ads. Walker (1705)	518
162	Corbett ads. Kettleby (1682)	171
54	Cornbury, Lord ads. Cottington (1672)	54
341	Corning ads. A.G. ex rel. Chubb (1697)	421
54	Cottington v. Lord Cornbury (1672)	54
283	Coventry, Mayor of v. King (1691)	329
372	Cowper ads. Wyne (1700)	465
297	Crane v. Hill (1695)	347

No.	Case	Page
153	Creamer ads. Robinson (1682)	161
274	Crew ads. Haselrig (1688)	314
436	Crispe v. Mickleburgh (1709)	605
419	Croft ads. Attorney General (1707)	567
225	Croke ads. Leach (1686)	248
27	Croke v. Beake (1667)	31
48	Crouch ads. Risden (1670)	48
371	Crow v. Crow (1700)	464
187	Crowther v. Lee (1684)	197
205	Croxall v. Cooke (1685)	227
347	Cullen ads. Castle (1697)	428
127	Cullier v. Mead (1681)	136
131	Culpeper, Lord ads. Curtis (1681)	139
363	Culworthy ads. Browne (1697)	447
298	Cumber v. Atkinson (1695)	351
25	Currer ads. Countess of Pembroke (1667)	28
131	Curtis v. Lord Culpeper (1681)	139
300	Cutlove v. Capon (1695)	353
98	Dacres, Lady v. Walter (1679)	104
197	Daffy ads. Wright (1684)	212
425	D'Allone v. Hart (1708)	575
245	Daniell v. Gore (1687)	278
181	David ads. Griffith (1683)	191
397	Davies ads. Snag (1705)	523
115	Dean ads. Walker (1681)	123
182	Dearsly v. Kemp (1683)	192
56	De la Fountain v. Dean of Lincoln (1672)	65
228	Delaval v. Delaval (1687)	255
442	Devonshire, Duke of ads. Kempen (1709)	643
418	Devonshire, Duke of v. Jackson (1707)	566
177	Deye v. Thwaits (1683)	185
237	Dingly ads. Lechmere (1687)	268
292	Dod v. Hesketh (1694)	340
100	Dodd v. Ingleton (1679)	106
278	Doddridge v. Startop (1690)	324
349	Dongworth, relator v. Tathwell (1697)	431
160	Dorrington ads. Coney (1682)	170
31	Doughty ads. A.G. ex rel. Skelton (1668)	37
130	Dowdeswell ads. Windsor (1681)	139
157	Downes ads. Clements (1682)	165
273	Drake v. Young (1688)	313

No.	Case	Page
325	Draper ads. Poole (1696)	398
81	Drax v. Sedgwick (1678)	89
412	Droitwich, Bailiffs of ads. Packington (1706-07)	557
447	Dummer v. Barret (1710)	657
282	Dummer v. Wingfield (1690)	328
265	Duppa, relator v. Dean of Winchester (1688)	299
377	Earle's Case (1702)	470
86	Eaton v. Gregson (1678)	92
410	Edge v. Warburton (1706)	556
154	Edwards ads. Paul (1682)	161
380	Ekins v. Bridges (1703)	472
448	Elderton ads. Wright (1710)	659
59	Elliot v. Blucke (1673)	69
384	Elliot v. Pearne (1703-05)	495
11	Ely, Bishop of, Case of (1666)	9
365	Entiknapp ads. Layfield (1698)	457
168	Epworth Commoners ads. Redding (1683)	177
175	Evans ads. Lloyd (1683)	183
230	Eve ads. Stracy (1687)	258
299	Ewen ads. Twitty (1695)	352
236	Eyans ads. Coles (1687)	267
113	Eyre ads. Skinner (1680)	119
6	Falkener v. Mottenshead (1666)	6
335	Fanshawe v. Fowles (1696)	416
353	Fawcet v. Wright (1697)	438
469	Fellon's Case (1714)	684
343	Fifield v. Squire (1697)	423
171	Fillingham v. Bradshaw (1683)	179
431	Filts ads. Hall (1708)	589
185	Fish v. Wimberly (1684)	195
364	Fitch v. Commissioners of the Navy (1697)	450
53	Fitzjames ads. Attorney General (1672)	51
92	Fitzmaurice ads. Attorney General (1678)	98
346	Fitzwilliam v. Pitt (1697)	426
140	Flatman ads. Attorney General (1682)	146
357	Fleming v. Webb (1697)	442
106	Fletcher ads. A.G. ex rel. Lowther (1680)	113
401	Floyd v. Goldsmith (1705 x 1706)	530
47	Foster ads. Collop (1670)	47
208	Foster v. Hall (1685)	229
152	Fountain ads. Cook (1682)	160

No.	Case	Page
73	Fountain v. Guavas (1676)	82
233	Fountain ads. Gwavas (1687)	262
335	Fowles ads. Fanshawe (1696)	413
235	Fox v. Charlett (1687)	267
400	Frampton v. Beene (1705-06)	528
316	Frampton ads. Chaffin (1696)	384
342	Frankland v. Mason (1697)	422
216	Franklyn v. Jones (1686)	237
454	Freke v. Sundry (1711)	665
198	Frowd, relator v. Whitley (1684)	213
222	Gaell ads. Thrumpton (1686)	244
261	Galliard ads. Attorney General (1688)	294
246	Gallop v. Larder (1687)	279
409	Gardner v. Pole (1706)	555
229	Gerard v. Woodward (1687)	256
310	Gibbs ads. Bowyer (1696)	365
455	Gibson v. Taylor (1711)	665
212	Gifford ads. Wightwick (1685)	234
32	Gill v. Thompson (1668)	38
192	Gloucester, Dean of v. Stoodly (1684)	208
337	Goate v. Browne (1696)	419
287	Golding ads. Bennett (1693)	334
314	Golding ads. Harding (1696)	383
401	Goldsmith ads. Floyd (1705 x 1706)	530
95	Gonning ads. Whittington (1679)	100
172	Gonville and Caius College ads. City of Cambridge (1683)	181
17	Goodyear ads. Huxley (1666)	18
245	Gore ads. Daniell (1687)	278
135	Goter ads. Williams (1682)	143
163	Gower v. Howard (1682)	172
193	Grainger ads. Greenwood (1684)	209
219	Grantham ads. Kemp (1686)	240
251	Grascomb v. Jeffreys (1687-88)	285
407	Greenway v. Earl of Kent (1706)	546
444	Greenway v. Marquess of Kent (1709)	644
193	Greenwood v. Grainger (1684)	209
207	Gregory v. Loving (1685)	228
294	Gregory ads. Sherrington (1695)	342
86	Gregson ads. Eaton (1678)	92
181	Griffith v. David (1683)	191
73	Guavas ads. Fountain (1676)	82

No.	Case	Page
233	Gwavas v. Fountain (1687)	262
105	Gwavas v. Teage (1680)	111
420	Gwyn, relator v. Prytherch (1707)	568
414	Haanan v. King (c. 1707)	560
266	Hacker ads. Mullington (1688)	300
466	Hacking ads. Beale (1713)	682
195	Haffenden v. Sharpe (1684)	210
46	Hale ads. A.G. ex rel. Steers (1670)	46
137	Hale ads. Chapman (1682)	144
381	Halifax, Lord ads. Marquess of Carmarthen (1703)	473
431	Hall v. Filts (1708)	589
208	Hall ads. Foster (1685)	229
368	Hall v. Moore (1698)	462
311	Hall ads. Tucker (1696)	367
293	Halsey ads. Ode (1695)	342
314	Harding v. Golding (1696)	383
460	Harding v. Hoblyn (1711)	671
417	Harris ads. Moulder (1707)	565
211	Harris ads. Wimberley (1685)	233
107	Harris v. Cliff (1680)	115
119	Harrison ads. Thornhill (1681)	128
117	Harrison v. Houblon (1681)	126
258	Hart ads. Brookes (1688)	291
425	Hart ads. D'Allone (1708)	575
88	Hart v. Weeks (1678)	94
285	Hartley ads. Bowater (1692)	332
188	Harvey v. Juxon (1684)	198
191	Harvey ads. Ward (1684)	208
274	Haselrig v. Crew (1688)	318
174	Haslehurst v. Cooke (1683)	182
375	Hawes v. Mayor of Liverpool (1700)	467
304	Hawkins v. Chittle (1696)	358
374	Hawson ads. Duke of Leeds (1700)	466
99	Hawys v. Kett (1679)	105
319	Haynes ads. Cooke (1696)	387
462	Hayter ads. Mathews (1712)	676
22	Heaton v. Carr (1667)	22
336	Hemings ads. A.G. ex rel. Mayor of Newcastle (1696)	418
201	Heninge ads. Brage (1685)	222
150	Hepburne ads. Trinity College (1682)	158
83	Herbert ads. Williams (1678)	90

No.	Case	Page
226	Heron v. Brownlow (1686)	250
421	Herring ads. Attorney General (1707)	568
292	Hesketh ads. Dod (1694)	340
329	Hesketh ads. Spencer (1696)	406
367	Hewett ads. Johnson (1698)	461
147	Hewley v. Cholmly (1682)	155
281	Hibbett ads. Leach (1690)	327
331	Hicks ads. Abbot (1696)	407
253	Hicks v. Littleton (1687)	287
206	Hicks v. Snelling (1685)	228
289	Hilder ads. Ward (1693)	336
109	Hill ads. Brooks (1680)	116
297	Hill ads. Crane (1695)	347
171	Hillingham v. Bradshaw (1683)	180
213	Hills v. Hills (1685)	235
463	Hilton v. Lambton (1712)	677
305	Hobby ads. Stanly (1696)	360
460	Hoblyn ads. Harding (1711)	671
352	Hockerston ads. Pierson (1697)	437
29	Hodgson v. Wilshaw (1668)	34
149	Holland ads. Duke of Newcastle (1682)	157
116	Holland v. Stephens (1681)	125
255	Holles, Lord ads. Earl of Chesterfield (1687)	289
369	Hollingsworth ads. Trevor (1699)	462
220	Honiwood ads. Attorney General (1686)	241
288	Hooke ads. Shaftoe (1693)	335
361	Hopkins ads. Knight (1697)	445
189	Hopkins v. Chappell (1684)	199
332	Horne ads. Coney (1696)	412
268	Hornely v. Blaythorne (1688-90)	302
117	Houblon ads. Harrison (1681)	126
163	Howard ads. Gower (1682)	172
426	Howard, Lord v. Boomer (1708)	576
215	Howland ads. Baker (1685)	236
210	Hull, Mayor of v. Beilby (1685)	232
232	Humfreys ads. Birt (1687)	261
396	Humphrey v. Betts (1705)	521
320	Huntington, Mayor of, relator v. Mercers Co. (1696)	388
26	Huntington ads. Wise (1667)	30
155	Husbands v. Brand (1682)	163
446	Hutchinson v. Burton (1710)	652

No.	Case	Page
17	Huxley v. Goodyear (1666)	18
406	Hyde v. Tenison (1706)	545
180	Inder v. Bax (1683)	190
178	Infield v. Infield (1683)	188
100	Ingleton ads. Dodd (1679)	106
63	Italian Merchants, relators v. Blake (1675)	72
418	Jackson ads. Duke of Devonshire (1707)	566
340	Jackson ads. Latus (1697)	420
286	Jackson ads. Wilbraham (1693)	333
91	Jacob ads. Thomas (1678)	97
112	James v. Killigrew (1680)	118
354	James ads. Knowles (1697)	439
69	James ads. Winford (1675)	79
386	Jeffreys ads. Attorney General (1704)	501
387	Jeffreys ads. Bridges (1704)	506
251	Jeffreys ads. Grascomb (1687-88)	285
200	Jeffreys ads. Williams (1685)	220
133	Jeffs ads. A.G. ex rel. Mayor of Maidenhead (1682)	141
452	Jenkins ads. Bernard (1711)	664
85	Jenkins v. Millbanke (1678)	91
84	Jenkinson ads. Attorney General (1678)	91
123	Jessup ads. Twistleton (1681)	132
146	John v. Watkins (1682)	154
367	Johnson v. Hewett (1698)	461
437	Johnson ads. Smith (1709)	606
28	Jones ads. Attorney General (1667-68)	33
269	Jones, Gaynor ads. Attorney General (1688-90)	304
216	Jones ads. Franklin (1686)	237
10	Joyce v. Clothworkers Co. (1666)	8
188	Juxon ads. Harvey (1684)	198
411	Keble v. Onley (1706)	556
465	Keddington v. Simpson (1713)	681
182	Kemp ads. Dearsly (1683)	192
219	Kemp v. Grantham (1686)	240
442	Kempen v. Duke of Devonshire (1709)	643
407	Kent, Earl of ads. Greenway (1706)	543
444	Kent, Marquess of ads. Greenway (1709)	644
99	Kett ads. Hawys (1679)	105
162	Kettleby v. Corbett (1682)	171
112	Killigrew ads. James (1680)	118
283	King ads. Coventry, Mayor of (1691)	329

No.	Case	Page
414	King ads. Haanan (c. 1707)	560
158	Kingsmill v. Bishop of Rochester (1682)	166
210	Kingston upon Hull, Mayor of v. Beilby (1685)	232
432	Kirton v. Manwaring (1708-10)	590
167	Knatchbull, relator v. Loving (1683)	176
361	Knight v. Hopkins (1697)	445
354	Knowles v. James (1697)	439
360	Ladbrooke ads. Berry (1697)	445
71	Lambert ads. Scudamore (1676)	81
463	Lambton ads. Hilton (1712)	677
391	Lamplugh ads. Chetham (1705)	514
403	Landon v. Sheffield (1706)	533
110	Landy ads. Pomfret (1680)	116
246	Larder ads. Gallop (1687)	279
340	Latus v. Jackson (1697)	420
184	Laurence v. Watts (1684)	194
435	Lay v. Beamont (1709)	604
362	Laycock ads. A.G. ex rel. Chicheley (1697)	447
365	Layfield v. Entiknapp (1698)	457
225	Leach v. Croke (1686)	248
281	Leach v. Hibbett (1690)	327
237	Lechmere v. Dingly (1687)	268
187	Lee ads. Crowther (1684)	197
374	Leeds, Duke of v. Hawson (1700)	466
390	Lennard v. Anger (1705)	513
56	Lincoln, Dean of v. De la Fountain (1672)	65
253	Littleton ads. Hicks (1687)	287
375	Liverpool, Mayor of ads. Hawes (1700)	467
175	Lloyd v. Evans (1683)	183
18	Lloyd ads. Smith (1666)	19
248	Lloyd, relator v. Clopton (1687)	282
445	London, Bishop of ads. A.G. ex rel. Burton (1710)	645
65	London, Mayor of v. Thody (1675)	76
209	Lort ads. Aunesly (1685)	231
429	Lort ads. Lady Campbell (1708)	583
169	Lovell ads. Page (1683)	178
432	Lovell, Baron, Case of (1708-10)	590
167	Loving ads. A.G. ex rel. Knatchbull (1683)	176
207	Loving ads. Gregory (1685)	228
120	Loving ads. Whittle (1681)	129
106	Lowther, relator v. Fletcher (1680)	113

No.	Case	Page
33	Lucas v. Browne (1668)	39
459	Lucas ads. Corporation of Warwick (1711)	671
249	Luck v. Luck (1687)	282
317	Luckin, Lady ads. Panton (1696)	385
243	Lucy v. Newton (1687)	276
104	Ludlow, Corp. of ads. A.G. ex rel. Powell (1680)	110
423	Machan ads. Cary (1707)	571
133	Maidenhead, Mayor of, relator v. Jeffs (1682)	141
302	Maidenhead, Mayor of, relator v. Rose (1696)	354
118	Manning ads. Shorter (1681)	127
432	Manwaring ads. Kirton (1708-10)	590
124	Margets v. Butcher (1681)	134
405	Marriot, relator v. Lord Wharton (1706-08)	536
402	Marshall v. Martin (1705 x 1706)	532
402	Martin ads. Marshall (1705 x 1706)	532
308	Martin ads. Stevens (1696)	362
111	Marwood ads. Morrell (1680)	117
272	Marwood v. Lord Tiveot (1688)	312
19	Masham ads. Duke of York (1667)	19
427	Mason ads. Attorney General (1708)	577
342	Mason ads. Frankland (1697)	422
257	Masters v. Allen (1687-89)	290
159	Masters ads. Walsingham (1682)	168
462	Mathews v. Hayter (1712)	676
165	Mathews ads. Paris (1683)	174
127	Mead ads. Cullier (1681)	136
464	Menzies ads. Conning (1712)	678
320	Mercers Co. ads. A.G. ex rel. Mayor of Huntington (1696)	388
108	Meservy v. Pritchard (1680)	115
129	Metcalf v. Palmer (1681)	138
348	Metcalfe v. Preston (1697)	430
267	Michell ads. A.G. ex rel. Warnham Churchwardens (1688)	300
436	Mickleburgh ads. Crispe (1709)	605
85	Milbanke ads. Jenkins (1678)	91
139	Millington ads. Warnford (1682)	145
214	Mint, Moneyers of, relators v. Slingsby (1685)	236
312	Monck ads. Pride (1696)	368
35	Monday ads. Poeton (1668)	40
144	Monkes v. Worden (1682)	152
68	Monmouth, Duke of v. Countess of Northumberland (1675)	78
394	Montague, Earl of v. Weddall (1705)	520

No.	Case	Page
12	Moody ads. Browne (1666)	9
78	Moor ads. Baynes (1677)	87
368	Moore ads. Hall (1698)	462
52	Morgan v. Attorney General (1671)	50
315	Morgan v. Tevell (1696)	384
111	Morrell v. Marwood (1680)	117
49	Morrice ads. Chislett (1670)	48
238	Morrice ads. Morse (1687)	270
238	Morse v. Morrice (1687)	270
36	Mott ads. Spencer (1668)	40
6	Mottenshead ads. Falkener (1666)	6
417	Moulder v. Harris (1707)	565
8	Mounson ads. Place (1666)	7
266	Mullington v. Hacker (1688)	300
97	Nappier v. Lord Pawlet (1679)	102
364	Navy Commissioners ads. Fitch (1697)	450
183	Newburgh, Earl of ads. Wren (1683)	193
149	Newcastle, Duke of v. Holland (1682)	157
388	Newcastle, Duke of ads. York, Archbishop of (1704)	507
336	Newcastle, Mayor of, relator v. Hemings (1696)	418
114	Newcomen ads. Ashfordby (1681)	121
307	Newsom ads. Wilkinson (1696)	361
408	Newt v. Chamberlain (1706)	552
122	Newton ads. Burwell (1681-83)	130
136	Newton ads. Collard (1682)	143
243	Newton ads. Lucy (1687)	276
339	Nicholls v. Bigs (1697)	420
75	Nichols v. Smith (1676)	84
55	Northey ads. Pinfold (1672)	57
68	Northumberland, Countess of ads. Duke of Monmouth (1675)	78
45	Northumberland, Earl of v. Radcliffe (1670)	45
2	Noseworthy ads. Seymour (1664-65)	1
1	Note (1662)	1
21	Note (1667)	22
275	Note (c. 1688)	318
293	Ode v. Halsey (1695)	342
204	Okeham Hospital Governors v. Broune (1685)	226
411	Onley ads. Keble (1706)	556
37	Onslow ads. Stoughton (1669)	41
256	Ormerod v. Wharton (1687)	290
328	Orsell ads. Attorney General (1696)	400

Table of Cases Reported xxxvii

No.	Case	Page
20	Overbury ads. Bishop of Oxford (1667)	21
20	Oxford, Bishop of v. Overbury (1667)	21
370	Oxford, City of ads. Attorney General (1699)	463
79	Oxley, relator v. Partridge (1678)	87
412	Packington v. Bailiffs of Droitwich (1706-07)	557
438	Packington v. Wyche (1707-09)	619
169	Page v. Lovell (1683)	178
279	Paine v. Tape (1690-91)	324
129	Palmer ads. Metcalf (1681)	138
317	Panton v. Lady Luckin (1696)	385
165	Paris v. Mathews (1683)	174
218	Parker v. Brewer (1686)	239
34	Parry v. Parry (1668)	39
79	Partridge ads. A.G. ex rel. Oxley (1678)	87
379	Pate ads. Pierson (1703)	471
154	Paul v. Edwards (1682)	161
58	Paul v. Reeves (1673)	68
97	Pawlet, Lord ads. Nappier (1679)	102
23	Pawlett v. Attorney General (1667-68)	23
384	Pearne ads. Elliott (1703-05)	495
25	Pembroke, Countess of v. Currer (1667)	28
424	Perkins ads. Butterfield (1707)	572
77	Pesier ads. Speed (1677)	86
295	Philips ads. Bramly (1695)	343
290	Phillips ads. Webb (1694)	337
128	Phrip ads. Strickland (1681)	137
296	Pickering ads. Werden (1695)	345
352	Pierson v. Hockerston (1697)	437
379	Pierson v. Pate (1703)	471
280	Pigott ads. Sandys (1690)	326
55	Pinfold v. Northey (1672)	57
346	Pitt ads. Fitzwilliam (1697)	426
8	Place v. Mounson (1666)	7
66	Player ads. Robinson (1675)	76
3	Plymouth, Mayor of ads. Attorney General (1664)	4
35	Poeton v. Monday (1668)	40
141	Pointz, Lady v. Porter (1682)	147
409	Pole ads. Gardner (1706)	555
202	Pollard ads. A.G. ex rel. Smith (1685)	223
110	Pomfret v. Landy (1680)	116
325	Poole v. Draper (1696)	398

No.	Case	Page
428	Poole v. Wilshaw (1708)	582
141	Porter ads. Lady Pointz (1682)	147
291	Portington ads. A.G. ex rel. Boucher (1694)	338
330	Portman v. Snow (1696)	407
50	Potts ads. Spelman (1671)	49
104	Powell, relator v. Corporation of Ludlow (1680)	110
348	Preston ads. Metcalfe (1697)	430
284	Price ads. Attorney General (1691)	329
132	Price ads. A.G. ex rel. Talbot (1681)	140
179	Price v. Birch (1683)	189
416	Price v. Watkins (1707)	563
312	Pride v. Monck (1696)	368
108	Pritchard ads. Meservy (1680)	115
420	Prytherch ads. A.G. ex rel. Gwyn (1707)	568
151	Pulford ads. Sawbridge (1682)	159
467	Pycroft ads. Buckingham (1713)	682
333	Pyot v. Trafford (1696)	413
30	Queen Mother ads. Savile (1668)	35
217	Rackett ads. Whitfield (1686)	239
45	Radcliffe ads. Earl of Northumberland (1670)	45
40	Raleigh v. Chamberlaine (1669)	43
96	Ramsden v. Smith (1679)	102
345	Randall ads. Cogger (1697)	425
385	Randolph ads. Brockman (1704)	500
72	Raymond ads. Umfrevile (1676)	81
156	Raynsford v. Raynsford (1682)	164
168	Redding v. Epworth Commoners (1683)	177
439	Redwell ads. Ringstead (1709)	639
242	Reeve ads. Chitty (1687)	274
58	Reeves ads. Paul (1673)	68
44	Rex v. Skinner (1670)	44
223	Ridges v. Ridges (1686)	246
76	Ridley v. Skipwith (1677)	86
439	Ringstead v. Redwell (1709)	639
48	Risden v. Crouch (1670)	48
434	Robinson v. Collet (1709)	602
153	Robinson v. Creamer (1682)	161
66	Robinson v. Player (1675)	76
158	Rochester, Bishop of ads. Kingsmill (1682)	166
90	Rochester, Mayor of ads. A.G. ex rel. Earl of Anglesea (1678)	96
231	Rockingham, Lord v. Sawyer (1687)	258

No.	Case	Page
321	Rockingham, Lord v. Vyner (1696)	391
378	Rogers ads. Adams (1702)	471
94	Rookeby, relator v. Sanderson (1679)	99
302	Rose ads. A.G. ex rel. Mayor of Maidenhead (1696)	354
224	Rye ads. Bankes (1686)	247
322	St. John ads. A.G. ex rel. Bennet (1696)	392
351	St. Mary's, Vicars of ads. Williams (1697)	433
382	Saladine v. Seigmoret (1703)	475
148	Salisbury v. Whitby (1682)	157
366	Salisbury, Dean of ads. Terry (1698)	460
324	Salter v. Salter (1696)	397
240	Sambrooke v. Squibb (1687)	272
94	Sanderson ads. A.G. ex rel. Rookeby (1679)	99
16	Sandys ads. Attorney General (1666-69)	11
280	Sandys v. Pigott (1690)	326
262	Savage ads. Atkyns (1688)	295
30	Savile v. Queen Mother (1668)	35
151	Sawbridge v. Pulford (1682)	159
231	Sawyer ads. Lord Rockingham (1687)	258
389	Scamell v. Coppleston (1705)	510
166	Scroggs ads. Audley (1683)	175
71	Scudamore v. Lambert (1676)	81
70	Scudamore v. Win (1675)	80
358	Seaman v. Appreece (1697)	443
81	Sedgwick ads. Drax (1678)	89
382	Seigmoret ads. Saladine (1703)	475
2	Seymour v. Noseworthy (1664-65)	1
288	Shaftoe v. Hooke (1693)	335
138	Sharpe ads. Attorney General (1682)	145
195	Sharpe ads. Haffenden (1684)	210
303	Shaw, relator v. Bowater (1696)	357
161	Sheen v. Aynsworth (1682)	171
403	Sheffield ads. Landon (1706)	533
294	Sherrington v. Gregory (1695)	342
376	Sherwin v. Clargies (1701-02)	468
196	Shish v. Attorney General (1684)	212
118	Shorter v. Manning (1681)	127
313	Shrewsbury, Duke of v. Steynor (1696-97)	373
80	Sibley ads. Squibb (1678)	88
465	Simpson ads. Keddington (1713)	681
31	Skelton, relator v. Doughty (1668)	37

No.	Case	Page
113	Skinner v. Eyre (1680)	119
44	Skinner ads. Rex (1670)	44
76	Skipwith ads. Ridley (1677)	86
398	Skipwith ads. Sturmy (1705)	524
350	Skrine ads. Tyndale (1697)	432
214	Slingsby ads. A.G. ex rel. Moneyers of the Mint (1685)	236
244	Smith ads. Acton (1687)	277
399	Smith ads. Attorney General (1705)	527
437	Smith v. Johnson (1709)	606
18	Smith v. Lloyd (1666)	19
75	Smith ads. Nichols (1676)	84
96	Smith ads. Ramsden (1679)	102
277	Smith v. Smith (1689)	319
199	Smith v. Steel (1684)	219
326	Smith ads. Wade (1696)	399
93	Smith v. Walker (1679)	99
202	Smith, relator v. Pollard (1685)	223
397	Snag v. Davies (1705)	523
206	Snelling ads. Hicks (1685)	228
330	Snow ads. Portman (1696)	407
264	Sowerby, relator v. Whittaker (1688)	299
176	Sowton v. Attorney General (1683)	184
252	Speccol v. Chapman (1687-88)	286
77	Speed v. Pesier (1677)	86
50	Spelman v. Potts (1671)	49
329	Spencer v. Hesketh (1696)	406
36	Spencer v. Mott (1668)	40
270	Spooner ads. Attorney General (1688)	309
240	Squibb ads. Sambrooke (1687)	272
80	Squibb v. Sibley (1678)	88
343	Squire ads. Fifield (1697)	423
221	Squire v. Blacket (1686)	243
194	Stafford ads. Atterbury (1684)	209
305	Stanly v. Hobby (1696)	360
278	Startop ads. Doddridge (1690)	324
9	Staughton v. Clothworkers Co. (1666)	8
199	Steel ads. Smith (1684)	219
46	Steers, relator v. Hale (1670)	46
60	Stephens v. Athy (1673)	69
116	Stephens ads. Holland (1681)	125
308	Stevens v. Martin (1696)	362

No.	Case	Page
461	Stewart v. Worsely (1711)	673
313	Steynor ads. Duke of Shrewsbury (1696-97)	373
190	Stokes v. Wells (1684)	207
192	Stoodly ads. Dean of Gloucester (1684)	208
37	Stoughton v. Onslow (1669)	41
230	Stracy v. Eve (1687)	258
430	Streper v. Carter (1708)	587
128	Strickland v. Phrip (1681)	137
356	Strode, relator v. Birl (1697)	441
398	Sturmy v. Skipwith (1705)	524
454	Sundry ads. Freke (1711)	665
334	Sutton v. Bradshaw (1696)	413
132	Talbot, relator v. Price (1681)	140
279	Tape ads. Paine (1690-91)	324
349	Tathwell ads. A.G. ex rel. Dongworth (1697)	431
327	Tayes v. Clarke (1696)	399
455	Taylor ads. Gibson (1711)	665
105	Teague ads. Gwavas (1680)	111
406	Tenison ads. Hyde (1706)	545
366	Terry v. Dean of Salisbury (1698)	460
315	Tevell ads. Morgan (1696)	384
453	Theedam ads. Wall (1711)	664
62	Thistlethwaite, relator v. Wilson (1675)	71
65	Thody ads. Mayor of London (1675)	76
91	Thomas v. Jacob (1678)	97
32	Thompson ads. Gill (1668)	38
443	Thomson ads. City of York (1709)	643
119	Thornhill v. Harrison (1681)	128
61	Thorowgood ads. Lady Wentworth (1674)	70
222	Thrumpton v. Gaell (1686)	244
177	Thwaits ads. Deye (1683)	185
359	Tilson v. Attorney General (1697)	444
272	Tiveot, Lord ads. Marwood (1688)	312
126	Toller v. Cooke (1681)	135
392	Townley v. Wilson (1705)	517
333	Trafford ads. Pyot (1696)	413
369	Trevor v. Hollingsworth (1699)	462
150	Trinity College v. Hepburne (1682)	158
186	Trinity College v. Wrottesley (1684)	196
311	Tucker v. Hall (1696)	367
7	Tully v. Briggs (1666)	7

No.	Case	Page
103	Turner v. Colson (1680)	110
123	Twistleton v. Jessup (1681)	132
299	Twitty v. Ewen (1695)	352
350	Tyndale v. Skrine (1697)	432
72	Umfrevile v. Raymond (1676)	81
355	Veel v. Blanchard (1697)	439
67	Vyner ads. Colwall (1675)	77
321	Vyner ads. Lord Rockingham (1696)	391
326	Wade v. Smith (1696)	399
393	Walker v. Corbet (1705)	518
115	Walker v. Dean (1681)	123
93	Walker ads. Smith (1679)	99
453	Wall v. Theedam (1711)	664
101	Waller ads. Attorney General (1679)	107
74	Waller, relator v. Mayor of Bristol (1676)	83
159	Walsingham v. Masters (1682)	168
98	Walter ads. Lady Dacres (1679)	104
410	Warburton ads. Edge (1706)	556
125	Ward ads. Camell (1681)	135
191	Ward v. Harvey (1684)	208
289	Ward v. Hilder (1693)	336
203	Warner v. Bradbury (1685)	224
139	Warnford v. Millington (1682)	145
267	Warnham Churchwardens, relators v. Michell (1688)	300
459	Warwick, Corporation of v. Lucas (1711)	671
146	Watkins ads. John (1682)	154
416	Watkins ads. Price (1707)	563
239	Watkins v. Webster (1687)	271
184	Watts ads. Laurence (1684)	194
433	Wayland ads. Atkins (1709)	601
357	Webb ads. Fleming (1697)	442
290	Webb v. Phillips (1694)	337
239	Webster ads. Watkins (1687)	271
394	Weddall ads. Earl of Montague (1705)	520
422	Weeks ads. Attorney General (1707)	570
88	Weeks ads. Hart (1678)	94
190	Wells ads. Stokes (1684)	207
383	Wells, relator v. Brewster (1703-05)	476
121	Wem, Tenants of v. Wicherly (1681)	130
170	Wem, Tenants of v. Wicherly (1683)	178
61	Wentworth, Lady v. Thorowgood (1674)	70

No.	Case	Page
296	Werden v. Pickering (1695)	345
256	Wharton ads. Ormerod (1687)	290
405	Wharton, Lord ads. A.G. ex rel. Marriot (1706-08)	536
5	Wheeler v. Berringer (1665)	5
142	Whitaker v. Whitaker (1682)	149
148	Whitby ads. Salisbury (1682)	157
247	White, relator v. Lord Bulkely (1687-90)	279
217	Whitfield v. Rackett (1686)	239
198	Whitley ads. A.G. ex rel. Frowd (1684)	213
264	Whittaker ads. A.G. ex rel. Sowerby (1688)	299
95	Whittington v. Gonning (1679)	100
120	Whittle v. Loving (1681)	129
121	Wicherly ads. Tenants of Wem (1681)	130
170	Wicherly ads. Tenants of Wem (1683)	178
64	Widdrington v. Barker (1675)	73
212	Wightwick v. Gifford (1685)	234
286	Wilbraham v. Jackson (1693)	333
307	Wilkinson v. Newsom (1696)	361
338	Williams v. Attorney General (1696)	420
135	Williams v. Goter (1682)	143
83	Williams v. Herbert (1678)	90
200	Williams v. Jeffreys (1685)	220
351	Williams v. Vicars of St. Mary's (1697)	433
82	Williams ads. Worcester, Marquess of (1678)	89
29	Wilshaw ads. Hodgson (1668)	34
428	Wilshaw ads. Poole (1708)	582
62	Wilson ads. A.G. ex rel. Thistlethwaite (1675)	71
392	Wilson ads. Townley (1705)	517
211	Wimberley v. Harris (1685)	233
185	Wimberly ads. Fish (1684)	195
70	Win ads. Scudamore (1675)	80
24	Winchester, Bishop of, Case of (1667)	27
265	Winchester, Dean of ads. A.G. ex rel. Duppa (1688)	299
164	Windebank ads. Awborne (1682)	174
130	Windsor v. Dowdeswell (1681)	139
69	Winford v. James (1675)	79
282	Wingfield ads. Dummer (1690)	328
26	Wise v. Huntington (1667)	30
229	Woodward ads. Gerard (1687)	256
82	Worcester, Marquess of v. Williams (1678)	89
144	Worden ads. Monkes (1682)	152

No.	Case	Page
461	Worsely ads. Stewart (1711)	673
183	Wren v. Earl of Newburgh (1683)	193
197	Wright v. Daffy (1684)	212
448	Wright v. Elderton (1710)	659
353	Wright ads. Fawcet (1697)	438
186	Wrottesley ads. Trinity College (1684)	196
438	Wyche ads. Packington (1707-09)	619
372	Wyne v. Cowper (1700)	465
344	Wyrley v. Ainge (1697)	425
440	Yates ads. Bagnall (1709)	641
388	York, Archbishop of v. Duke of Newcastle (1704)	507
443	York, City of v. Thomson (1709)	643
19	York, Duke of v. Masham (1667)	19
273	Young ads. Drake (1688)	313

1
Note (Ex. 1662)

Leases and mortgages can be set aside as fraudulent conveyances.

BL MS. Lansd. 1077, f. 60, pl. 69 [Fr.] (Leving's Reports)

Note [that] HALE, chief baron of the exchequer, was of the opinion and said that it had been adjudged that if a man made a lease for years rendering rent, that this is an estate within the Statute of 27 Eliz. made to avoid fraudulent conveyances,[1] and this was a case between Coke and Woodroffe, Hilary [term] 1652.[2] And he further said that it had been adjudged that if a creditor accepted a mortgage and still continued upon the first security by bond where etc., that this is also within the aforesaid statute for fraud.

2
Seymour v. Noseworthy (Ex. 1664–1665)

A later will does not ipso facto revoke a former will.

LI MS. Misc. 499, p. 113 [Fr.] (Ward's Reports)

Upon an issue directed out of the exchequer chamber *ad informandam conscientiam* whether Sir Henry Killigrew had revoked his will made in 1644, this special verdict was found, *scil.* the jury found the will in 1644 *prout* etc. And also they found that Sir Henry Killegrew *condidit subsequens testamentum suum in scriptis in 1645 sed non reperiunt quod terrae devisatae per dictum testamentum in 1644 fuerint devisata per dictum subsequens testamentum in 1645*. And whether this subsequent will thus found should be taken for a revocation of the former was the question, and of what validity is this non finding in the special verdict.

Sir R[obert] Atkyns for the plaintiff argued that those words '*non reperiunt*' were not any part of the verdict, and that then there was a subsequent will found that in itself revoked the former, and that [it] should be understood that the subsequent will was of the lands, since it was in writing, and of the same lands

---

[1] Stat. 27 Eliz. I, c. 4 (*SR*, IV, 709–711).
[2] *Coke v. Woodroffe*, PRO C.33/197, ff. 349, 359v [these orders are uninformative].

contained in the former will, since it was not found that the testator had any other lands but those that were contained in the former will.

Sir H[eneage] Finch for the defendant urged that matters of fact should not extend beyond what the jury found, as in Duncombe and Wingfield's Case, Hobart 254, 262;[1] [where] the jury found a fine but did not find proclamations, [it] should be taken to be without proclamations. Thus here the jury did not find anything that [would] defeat the first will, because though there be a subsequent will, it is not a revocation absolutely in itself, because a man can have ten wills and each of them be good and taken for his last will, because a man can devise White Acre by one, Black Acre by another, his lands in one county or town by one and other lands in another county by another will, his lands by one and his goods by other wills. And there is no inconsistency between them, being of different things. And [just] as at the making of a will there must be an *animus testandi*, so at the revocation there must be an *animus revocandi*, Eyres v. Eyres, 1 Croke 51.[2] And there cannot be any revocation except by the party or by the law. And if the party revoked it, the jury must find it. And if the law revoked it, the jury must find something that amounted to a revocation in law, but here notwithstanding the latter will was found, the former can be a good will, because perchance only goods were devised by it or other lands. And he cited Coward and Marshall's Case, 1 Croke 24,[3] where lands were devised to a younger son in fee and by a second will the devisor devised the same lands to his wife for her life, and it was adjudged to be a good devise to both, *scil.* to the wife for her life and the son to take the fee.

Jones for the plaintiff [argued that] the non finding of the jury is a mere ignoramus and nothing is to be concluded by this one way or another. And he observed that the same words were in the verdict that were in the first will, *scil. testamentum* etc., thus the point by this verdict, which was submitted to the court, is whether a subsequent will shall revoke a former, and for this he cited 2 Hen. V, 8b.[4] And he also insisted that the jury's not finding that the testator had any other lands except those that were contained in the first will should be understood as that those lands were devised by the subsequent will. And the oral will implied a complete will and not a codicil as the civilians observed. Lit. sect. 58b, 167.[5] And he said that it is harsh to suppose that if a man makes his will and devises his land and goods and afterwards he has a son born and then he makes

---

[1] *Duncombe v. Wingfield* (1617), Hobart 254, 80 E.R. 400.
[2] *Eyres v. Eyres* (1626), Cro. Car. 51, 79 E.R. 648.
[3] *Coward v. Marshal* (1599), Cro. Eliz. 721, 78 E.R. 955.
[4] YB Trin. 2 Hen. V, f. 8, pl. 3 (1414).
[5] T. Littleton, *Tenures*, sect. 167.

another will of his goods only, that the latter will would not be a revocation of the former, since it is not a revocation *de omnibus in eadem subjecto*, and by this the mind of the testator was altered.

Serjeant *Glyn* [argued] for the defendant. And he said that there is not any authority for debating whether a subsequent will will revoke a first, because in this case it is not known what the latter will is, and on account of that it can be or not be a revocation. And it is dangerous for the court to presume that the latter is a revocation of the former, because if afterwards the latter will should be produced and be consistent with the former, then the jury by the presumption of the court is liable to an attaint. And he agreed that a will by its nature is revocable notwithstanding a clause of non revocation, but it should be revoked in fact or in law, 2 Croke 115.[6] And the latter will is no revocation of the former, if by any possibility they can be consistent, Hodgkinson and Wood's Case, 1 Croke [691].[7] And the jury did not find any revocation, and the court will not presume one, and the court can not be judge and jury also, because the jury should find sufficient matter in fact or in law (which the jury has not) and the court should judge matters of law.

And afterwards in Easter [term] 1665, the barons dismissed the plaintiff's bill, being satisfied that, as this special verdict was found, there is not any reason to suppose that this last will is any revocation of the former, except it appear to the court that this will was which did not appear thus far.[8]

Note that a verdict passed upon a first trial for the plaintiff. They had inquired of Baron Turnor, who came to take the private verdict, whether a later will would in all things revoke a former, which he said it would. Otherwise the jury had concluded to find for the defendant. But the court, not being satisfied with this verdict, awarded another trial, which gave the special verdict aforesaid.

[Other reports of this case: Hardres 374, 145 E.R. 504.]

[Order of 22 Nov. 1666: PRO E.126/9, f. 164.]

[This case is cited in Attorney General v. Penn (1686), Samuel Dodd's Reports, p. 67.]

[Related cases: Basset v. Noseworthy (1670–1674), Rep. temp. Finch 102, 23 E.R. 55, Nelson 135, 21 E.R. 809, Cases 76, 107, Nottingham's Chancery Cases, 73 Selden Soc. 37, 62, *White & Tudor's Leading Cases in Equity*, II (9th ed. 1928), pp. 136–139; Noseworthy v. Basset (1685), 1 Vernon 351, 23 E.R. 516; Hitchins v. Basset (1688), Case 125, 3 Modern 203, 87 E.R. 131, Comberbach 90, 209, 90 E.R. 362, 433, 2 Salkeld 592, 91 E.R. 495, 1 Shower K.B. 537, 89 E.R. 738; Hungerford v. Nosworthy (1694), Shower 146, 1 E.R. 99.]

---

[6] *Symson v. Kirton* (1606), Cro. Jac. 115, 79 E.R. 99.
[7] *Hodgkinson v. Wood* (1624), Cro. Jac. 691, 79 E.R. 599.
[8] adhuc *MS*.

3
Attorney General v. Mayor of Plymouth (Ex. 1664)

Land where the tides ebb and flow within a port belong to the crown, and houses built upon such land are nuisances.

LI MS. Misc. 499, p. 116 [Eng.] (Ward's Reports)

There was a trial at law by information of intrusion at the bar by a Devonshire jury directed and had touching the right of the soil of Sutton Poole within the port of Plymouth between the attorney general and the corporation, and [there was] a verdict for the king. There were also defendants to the bill who claimed title to several houses standing upon the soil in question, who were lessees for years under the corporation by leases made several years before and to endure for many years after under reserved rents to the corporation. And upon that verdict, the court awarded an injunction and established the possession of all with the crown and against the lessees as well as the corporation though the lessees were not parties to the information of intrusion but were so to the English bill. And costs went against all the defendants generally.

Note by this bill the attorney general charged that the crown was seised in its demesne as of fee of the ground and soil of the coasts and shores of the seas belonging to the kingdom of England and of the ground and soil of every port, haven, arm of the sea, creek, pool, and navigable rivers thereof into which the sea does or has used to ebb and flow and particularly of the soil and ground of Sutton Poole near the port and town of Plymouth and of the fishing upon that pool, wreck of sea, anchorage, moorage, and ballasting of ships, measurage of corn and coals and salt shipped or unshipped upon the pool, wharfage and groundage of all ships and goods landed or coming on the banks and shores there that the freedom of trade and safety of ships anchored there ought not to be straitened or hindered nor course of water to the nuisance or destruction of trade to the town and port of Plymouth where His Majesty has a custom house and lawful places for the service thereof etc.

The defendants insisted upon their rights to the soil and all other the premises.

[The] court declared themselves fully satisfied with the verdict and that all the soil of the said pool lying within the barbican and causeway within the flux and reflux of the sea at ordinary tides, but as to the extent of the port other than as to the houses built within the flux and reflux of the sea, the court does not determine one way or the other.

The two issues tried were first whether such buildings (describing them) were nuisances to the straitening and damage of the port of Plymouth, secondly whether the soil of the place [?] within the causeway and barbican there between the high and low water mark [was] the inheritance of the crown or not.

Then [it was] ordered that a commission issue to commissioners to be named by the court to enquire of certain articles of instructions to be annexed to be agreed by counsel on both sides concerning the nuisances to the port. But by this decree, [it was] not known what was done upon it.

[Order of 21 Nov. 1664: PRO E.126/9, f. 41.]

4
Anonymous (Ex. 1665)

Where a plaintiff pleads a privilege to sue in the exchequer, supersedeas *does not lie unless the defendant proves that the claim of privilege is false and the court of exchequer fails to dismiss the case.*

LI MS. Misc. 499, p. 123, pl. 2 [Fr.] (Ward's Reports)

In this term one of the cursitors of the chancery brought a *supersedeas* into the court of exchequer with the intent of staying a suit in the office of pleas of this court between two persons because the plaintiff was not a debtor of the lord king as he had alleged himself to be. And he prayed allowance of it.

Chief Baron HALE said to him that he was a half cursitor and did not understand his office because no *supersedeas* lies in such a case before the defendant has pleaded that the plaintiff was not a debtor to the king. And when it appears upon an issue tried that he is not a debtor, if the court proceeds, a *supersedeas* lies, but not before.

5
Wheeler v. Berringer (Ex. 1665)

In this case, the tenants of a manor were required to disclose what quit rents were payable out of which lands, and commissioners were appointed to aid the court in the determination of this matter.

LI MS. Misc. 499, p. 139, pl. 2 [Fr.] (Ward's Reports)

The plaintiff before this time (being an infant) exhibited his bill against the defendant to discover what quit rents were payable by the defendant to the plaintiff as lord of the manors of Datchet and Datchet St. Helens in the County of Buckingham[1] and out of which particular lands they arose and to have the decree of this court for the enforcement of the payment of the arrears and to charge

---

[1] V.C.H., *Buckinghamshire*, III (1925), p. 252.

particular lands of the defendant to pay the said rents for the future and to have those particular lands set out by a commission of this court so that they may be known.

And the cause coming to a hearing, a trial at bar was directed. And upon full evidence it was found that there was annually due and payable to the plaintiff as lord of the manors by the defendant for the freehold and copyhold lands of the defendant held of the said manors and which have been paid within forty years by the owners of the said lands to the lord of the said manors £11 *per annum*, upon which the court decreed the arrears of those rents to be paid from the time of the defendant's purchase and referred it to the auditor to cast up the arrears. And [the court] also decreed a commission to issue to commissioners to be nominated by the plaintiff and defendant to ascertain the lands liable to those rents and to inquire which lands were the most probable to be liable to them and to distinguish the freehold and copyhold [lands] and out of which particular lands the particulars of the said £11 rents issued and to settle and to proportion them so that the plaintiff for the future can know to which lands to resort for payment of the said rents. And such lands which the commissioners shall set out by virtue of this commission shall be chargeable for the future with these said rents according to the proportions certified by the said commissioners.

And the auditor certified that the said rents were in arrears for thirty-three years to Lady Day 1664 and amounted to £363, of which the plaintiff admitted to have received £121 10s. 1d., so that there remained due £241 9s. 11d. to the plaintiff, which was decreed to be paid to the plaintiff with exemplary costs.

And the commissioners returned the commission executed according to the effect [of the decree], distinguishing the freehold and copyhold [lands] and the particulars of them and the particular sums by them thought reasonable to be charged upon the particular parcels and showed them in certain. And upon exceptions to the commissioners' certificate, it was confirmed, and the lands were decreed to be charged thereafter according to the proportions certified by the commissioners.

[Order of 20 Apr. 1665: PRO E.126/9, f. 82.]

6
Falkener v. Mottenshead (Ex. 1666)

Where there is a custom to grind at a particular mill, the miller must grind within thirty-four hours or lose his right.

LI MS. Misc. 499, p. 207, pl. 1 [Fr.] (Ward's Reports)

Note that it was said by the court that when a bill is preferred to compel inhabitants to grind their grain at the mill of the lord according to a custom, if the grain lie at the mill unground for thirty-four hours, the court will make a decree that the party may carry his grain to another mill.

[Order of 10 Feb. 1662: PRO E.126/8, f. 89v.]

7

Tully v. Briggs (Ex. 1666)

Tithes of minerals are not due of common right but only by custom.

LI MS. Misc. 499, p. 208, pl. 1 [Fr.] (Ward's Reports)

Note that tithes of lead ore or minerals are not due of common right but only by custom. And though the defendant was lessee for eight years [and] the reversion [was] in the king, still the decree was made against the lessee upon this custom, but it will not conclude the king when his estate or interest begins, because there is no other remedy to relieve the plaintiff.

[The order of 17 May 1666, PRO E.126/9, f. 109, is printed at 1 Wood 74; see also order of 26 Nov. 1666: PRO E.126/9, f. 164.]

8

Place v. Mounson (Ex. 1666)

Depositions taken without notice to the other party will be quashed.

LI MS. Misc. 499, p. 212, pl. 1 [Fr.] (Ward's Reports)

Note that upon a motion by *Wilmot*, depositions of witnesses taken and examined at Lincoln before Baron Turnor in his assize circuit were quashed because [neither] the plaintiff nor his attorney in court had notice of this examination in order to be able to cross-examine them.

[Order of 21 June 1666: PRO E.126/9, f. 131v.]

[This case is cited in Dummer v. Barret (Ex. 1710), below, No. 447.]

9

Staughton v. Clothworkers Company (Ex. 1666)

A judge of a court of equity will not adjudicate the validity of a custom or by-law of the City of London.

LI MS. Misc. 499, p. 212, pl. 2 [Fr.] (Ward's Reports)

The plaintiff being an alderman of London was elected by the defendants to be one of the livery of this company. And for not attending upon the lord mayor as a liveryman (though he attended as an alderman), he was according to the custom and by-laws of the city and company fined £20. And for not paying this, an action of debt was brought and the £20 recovered by judgment, and this judgment was affirmed upon a writ of error. And the plaintiff preferred his English bill to be relieved against this fine. And *Smith* prayed that, upon bringing the said £20 into court, they should have an injunction.

But the court denied it because this injunction will determine the validity of the custom and by-laws of the city, which the court will not intermeddle with. And Chief Baron HALE said if this custom or by-law is not good, this court will not help or supply it, and if it is good, this court will not weaken it, and if the city proceeding should be stayed, a great clamor and noise will ensue.

10

Joyce v. Clothworkers Company (Ex. 1666)

A defendant can open his records to a plaintiff in lieu of responding to interrogatories in a bill of complaint where the records contain the answers sought.

LI MS. Misc. 499, p. 216, pl. 4 [Fr.] (Ward's Reports)

The defendants recovered a judgment of £10 imposed on the plaintiff for refusing to be a budge bachelor of this company and to attend Robinson, lord mayor of London, being of the same company. And the plaintiff exhibited his bill against the defendants to be relieved, and in his bill he charged the defendants to show all the orders of the company that empowered them to impose such penalties. The defendants showed some and said that the plaintiff could have recourse to their books in the hands of the master and assistants of this company and see all of these orders. And exception was taken that the defendants should show them, but it was not allowed because, if the plaintiff can have recourse and view of them, he can satisfy himself without stuffing an answer with a great company of orders.

[Order of 1 June 1668: E.126/9, f. 352v.]

11
Bishop of Ely's Case (Ex. 1666)

The office of pleas in the exchequer cannot issue subpoenas.
A letter, and not a subpoena, issues to a peer to compel an appearance.

LI MS. Misc. 499, p. 221, pl. 3 [Fr.] (Ward's Reports)

The bishop of Ely was served with a subpoena out of the office of pleas. And [Arthur] Sparke, the deputy king's remembrancer, complained to the court that no subpoena should be made in the office of pleas but all [should be] in the office of the king's remembrancer, upon which the court ordered:

1. That all subpoenas should be made in the office of the king's remembrancer,
2. That no more printed tickets (especially those that have the arms of the king in the first letter) should be used in the office of pleas,
3. That no bond shall be sued on behalf of the king in the office of pleas without a special warrant of the attorney general. Winckworth's Case.[1]

Note [that] when a peer is sued in the office of the king's remembrancer, the first process is a letter on the English side [and] a *distringas* on the Latin side. And in the office of pleas, the first process against a peer is a *venire facias*, the second a *distringas*, and upon the *distringas*, issues [a]re returned which affect goods and profits of lands, and [it] is thought [?] the most expeditious and effectual process against peers to compel appearances. And no other court has such process.

[Perhaps Bishop of Ely v. Clare College, orders of 8 and 22 Nov. 1666: PRO E.126/9, ff. 154v, 155.]

12
Browne v. Moody (Ex. 1666)

A subcollector can sue his principal for imposing a false super upon him in the exchequer.

LI MS. Misc. 499, p. 223, pl. 1 [Fr.] (Ward's Reports)

Moody being a high collector of the assessment in Suffolk and Browne being a subcollector, Moody made an account and imposed a super of [*blank*] on Browne, who upon process came in and accounted, upon which account it

---

[1] *Winckworth's Case* (Ex. 1665), LI MS. Misc. 499, p. 159, pl. 1.

appeared that Browne was not in super but in surplussage £169 and more, *quas ipse domino regi remittere voluit*. And this account was sworn and declared and a *quietus est* was had upon it.

And afterwards Browne endeavored [to have] a remedy against Moody for his false super and thus preferred his English bill against him. And the court, on the motion of Browne at the side bar and [on] examination of the matter, ordered that the remission for so much of the surplussage that concerned the king should stand, and as to the residue, that Moody should answer. The court will give relief on the bill. And the account and record in the pipe [roll] was thus marked.

13

Anonymous v. Baker (Ex. 1666)

A court of equity can award a subpoena in the nature of a writ of scire facias.

LI MS. Misc. 499, p. 223, pl. 2 [Fr.] (Ward's Reports)

A subpoena in the nature of a scire facias upon a decree made in 9 Car. I [1633] for the payment of £20 *per annum* to the vicar of [*blank*] in Lincolnshire was awarded against one Baker, who had married the Lady Saunderson, who had the estate liable to pay it by the decree.

14

Anonymous (Ex. 1666)

Tithes due from a tinner of the stannaries in Cornwall can be sued for in the court of exchequer.

LI MS. Misc. 499, p. 223, pl. 4 [Fr.] (Wards Reports)

A vicar preferred his bill for tithes against a tinner in the stannaries in Cornwall, who pleaded the charter of Edward I granted to the stannaries[1] and on account of that he should not be sued here. But the plea was overruled, and the defendant was ordered to answer.

---

[1] *Calendar of the Charter Rolls*, III (1908), p. 53.

15
Anonymous (Ex. 1666)

The right to sue for tithes arises during the year they are due, not only at the end of the year.

<blockquote>LI MS. Misc. 499, p. 223, pl. 5 [Fr.] (Ward's Reports)</blockquote>

[A] vicar preferred his bill for tithes for wool for one year. And by his bill, it appeared that one year was not totally run, on account of which the defendant demurred. But it was overruled, inasmuch as the duty arose during the time, though it was not a complete year.

16
Attorney General v. Sandys (Ex. 1666–1669)

A person will not be compelled to make discovery of matters that might lead to a forfeiture.
A defendant against whom other suits for the same matters are pending may appear and plead without having been served with process.
The lands of a convicted felon go to his lord by escheat and not to the crown by forfeiture.
Where a beneficiary of a trust is convicted of a felony, there is neither an escheat nor a forfeiture to the crown.

<blockquote>LI MS. Misc. 499, pp. 253, 423, 485 [Fr.] (Ward's Reports)</blockquote>

Sir John Stowell being the purchaser for valuable consideration of lands from Sir George Sandys, the attorney general preferred an information of intrusion against the said Sir George Sandys for the same lands, and being at issue Sir John Stowell was sworn a witness to prove the value of the lands. And when the interrogatory was read to him, he refused to answer to it, of which it was complained to the court. And the court said that they would not compel such a purchaser to answer to such interrogatories that concerned the title or value of lands purchased by him.

The attorney general preferred an English bill against the defendant and others. The defendant not being served with process appeared and pleaded the pendency of four bills for the same matter. The attorney in court for the plaintiff accepted the plea, and afterwards [it] was moved that this plea [was] worth nothing because the defendant was not served with process.

But the court said that when a defendant in such a case is in jeopardy, he can appear *gratis* without being served. And in the principal case (for the reason of acceptance) the plea should stand.

Sir Ralph Freeman, possessed of a term for ninety-nine years of lands held of the king, purchased the inheritance of them in the name of the defendant (who married Jane the daughter of the said Sir Ralph) in trust for himself and his heirs. The said defendant having issue by his said wife, two sons, namely Freeman and George, the said Sir Ralph made his will in writing and his nephew Ralph Freeman [was made] executor of it and devised the said lands to the said Freeman and George and to all other sons that the said Jane should have living at the time of the death of the said Sir Ralph Freeman and to their heirs and assigns. And by the same will, he appointed the said defendant and his said executor to convey the said lands accordingly. Sir Ralph Freeman died, the said Jane not having any other sons living at the time of his death but the said Freeman and George. The executor refused [to act] and administration was committed to the defendant and his said wife *cum testamento annexo*. Freeman the older son died without issue. After this, the defendant had issue by his said wife, another son called Freeman, who afterwards murdered his brother George and for it was attainted and executed, no conveyance being made according to the will.

The defendant was [made] administrator to George, upon which an English bill was exhibited by the attorney general against the said Sir George Sandys in the exchequer to compel him to answer for the profits of the lands from the time of the attainder and to convey them to the king. The defendant pleaded all the matter as above. And the general question was whether any of those estates that the defendant had were forfeited to the king by the said attainder or who should have them.

This case was argued in Easter [term] 17 Car. II [1665] by Maynard, king's serjeant, and Palmer, the attorney general, on behalf of the king and by Mountagu, Sir Robert Atkyns, and Ellys on behalf of the defendant. And afterwards a case was agreed as above and this term argued by Winnington on behalf of the king and Ellys on behalf of the defendant, which considered these points:

1. Whether the trust of this lease should attend the inheritance.
2. Whether the trust of the inheritance should be forfeited for felony.
3. Whether the trust of this lease should be forfeited for felony.

Maynard and the attorney general [*Palmer*] argued that the lease should attend the inheritance and both made but one estate, which descended to Freeman, the party attainted, which estate the king should have in as large a manner as Freeman should have it if he had not been attainted, and without doubt in such a case after the death of George without issue (as here), all of the estate should have descended to Freeman as heir to George, and in such a case Freeman could compel the defendant to execute his trust. And here the king should have the same remedy against the defendant as Freeman could have had if he had not been attainted.

But *Winnington* argued that [they] are distinct estates and the lease [is] substantive of itself and not attendant upon the inheritance nor consolidated or confounded in it but is liable to pay debts as assets in his hands and can be granted separately. And thus the king is entitled to have the trust of this term executed. And he should have preference before the administrator. 5 Rep. 56, Knight's Case.[1]

But the court [was] against him here inasmuch as this term never was in Freeman, [who was] attainted, to be forfeited.

And that the trust of a lease for years is forfeited by attainder for felony, they cited and relied upon Sir John Daccomb's Case in 2 Croke 512 and Hobart 214;[2] Ford and Sheldon's Case, 12 Rep. 1–3;[3] 1 Anderson 294, Sir Francis Englefield's Case.[4] And Winnington said that the trust of an inheritance is also forfeited by attainder for felony upon the reason of the privity that exists between the trustee and the beneficiary, inasmuch as the law takes notice of trusts, that they are grantable and the trustee compellable to execute it. And for this he cited Littleton, [*Tenures*], sect. 464; 5 Edw. IV, 7;[5] 1 Rep. 21.[6] And the difference hangs[7] between a nude trust of a thing purely personal, as in the Marquess of Winchester's Case, 3 Rep. 2, 3,[8] and the case here, which is a trust annexed to an estate. But he confessed as to this point the cases[9] cited above in Croke, Hobart, and Anderson are otherwise, but he submitted to the reason of them.

On the other side, it was argued, and principally by *Ellys*, that none of these trusts or estates are forfeited by the said attainder. And they agreed that the lease and the inheritance are distinct estates. And though they agreed that a trust of a lease can be forfeited for felony, as [in] Sir John Daccomb's Case and the other authorities cited above, which authorities also prove that a trust of an inheritance should not be forfeited in such a case, yet it is impossible that the trust of the lease here should be forfeited inasmuch as Freeman was not born at the time of the limitation or taking effect of the trust nor included within the will as to the term,

---

[1] *Knight's Case* (1588), 5 Coke Rep. 56, 77 E.R. 137.
[2] *Rex v. Exors. of Sir John Daccombe* (1618), Cro. Jac. 512, 79 E.R. 437, *sub nom. Earl of Somerset's Case* (1618), Hobart 214, 80 E.R. 361; *Attorney General v. Carr* (Ex. 1618), 118 Selden Soc. 475.
[3] *Rex v. Ford and Sheldon* (1606), 12 Coke Rep. 1, 77 E.R. 1283; also *sub nom. Attorney General v. Hoord*, 117 Selden Soc. 345.
[4] *Inglefield's Case*, Pl. 302, 1 Anderson 293, 123 E.R. 480.
[5] YB Mich. 5 Edw. IV, f. 7, pl. 16, 17, 18 (1465).
[6] *Attorney General v. Porter* (1592), 1 Coke Rep. 16b, 76 E.R. 36.
[7] depend *MS*.
[8] *Marquess of Winchester's Case* (1583), 3 Coke Rep. 2, 76 E.R. 621.
[9] livers *MS*.

because when the elder Freeman died, the entire trust survived for George. And when George died the trust of the term should go to the defendant either as administrator of George or should extinguish in him inasmuch as there is not any person to whom [it] can be executed. And *eo potius* inasmuch as the defendant is administrator to Sir Ralph Freeman. And though Freeman, who was attainted, took the trust of the inheritance, yet it was as heir of George by way of limitation only in the will and not directly by the will.

And *Ellys* said that a trust of an inheritance is not forfeitable for felony because there is not any tenure in the case because in all escheats (which this is) a tenure is requisite, though in the case of the king, as 3 *Institutes* 21.[10] And he said that Judge Hutton assigned the reason that a trust of a term is forfeited for felony by virtue of the Statute 3 Hen. VII, c. 4.[11] And he argued that a beneficiary did not have *jus in re* nor *[jus] ad rem*, as 1 *Institutes* 272,[12] nor is such a trust grantable as Winnington said, as appeared by Sir Moyle Finch's Case, Moore 339,[13] but it is purely a confidence and compellable to be executed in chancery. And on account of that he said if the trust of this lease should attend the trust of the inheritance, it would be of the same fate as the inheritance, but the trust of the inheritance is not forfeited. And if it is not attendant, it should go to the defendant as administrator either of Sir Ralph Freeman or of George, inasmuch as [it] was never in Freeman to be forfeited. Thus whichever way is given, it is for the defendant.

Note that afterwards in Easter [term] 21 Car. II [1669], judgment was given by Chief Baron HALE and Baron TURNOR for the defendant, Atkyns being ill and Rainsford removed to the king's bench. And the argument of HALE was as follows, in which he declared his opinion that neither the inheritance nor the term is forfeited by this attainder on these grounds.

Though the lands are held of the king, yet this trust is not forfeited by the felony inasmuch as the king is entitled to the forfeiture (if there were any) as lord by escheat and not by prerogative, in which case by escheat he shall not have a trust inasmuch as he shall have a tenant. And he agreed that in some cases trusts of inheritances are forfeitable, as

(1) If at this day a beneficiary commits treason, the trust is forfeited by 33 Hen. VIII, c. 20,[14] as the Marquess of Winchester's Case, 3 Rep. 2, 3, but it was not by the common law;

---

[10] E. Coke, *Third Institute* (1644), p. 21.
[11] Stat. 3 Hen. VII, c. 4 (*SR*, II, 513).
[12] E. Coke, *First Institute* (1628), f. 272b.
[13] *Finch v. Finch*, Pl. 459 (1590), Moore K.B. 339, 72 E.R. 615.
[14] Stat. 33 Hen. VIII, c. 20, s. 3 (*SR*, III, 857).

(2) If an alien is a beneficiary, at this day, of an inheritance, the trust shall be executed in a court of equity for the king and afterwards the estate will be seized, as it was in the case of Rex v. Holland in the king's bench, Trinity [term] 23 Car. I [1647], q.v. 1 Rolle's [Abridgment] 194, [sect.] 8, and Style 20, 40, 75, 84, 90, 94,[15] inasmuch as the alien did not have the capacity to purchase but only for the king. And this point, though it was not judicially in question, yet was admitted by all in this case of Holland, in which he was of counsel;

(3) By the common law and the practice of this court, which is a part of the common law, if the debtor of the king is a beneficiary of a trust, the debt is leviable upon the lands in trust, and this is the true reason of Chirton's Case 24 Edw. III [1350], cited in 12 Rep. 3,[16] and of Ford and Sheldon, 12 Rep. 1–3, and of Babington's Case 3 Car. [I, 1627][17] and of Sir Edward Coke's Case,[18] and it was before the statutes of 4 Hen. VII, c. 17, and 19 Hen. VII, c. 15,[19] which are the lands of beneficiaries of uses liable to their debts. But he said that those cases did not get to the reason of this case, because the reason that lands escheat to the lord is *pro defectu tenentis* and here the king had his tenant continuing because the defendant and not the beneficiary was the tenant and thus remained and should pay the rents and services reserved and due. And this case is the same as escheats in such cases between common persons. And here the attainder of Freeman, who was the beneficiary of the trust of the inheritance, did not cause an escheat. And this appeared to be the law at the time of the statutes 19 Hen. VII, [c.] 15, [and] 27 Hen. VIII, [c.] 10,[20] the first of which supposes lords [to be] remediless where uses were limited to villeins, and the second that tenants defraud their lords of escheats by [means of] secret uses.

And if anyone inquire what shall become of this trust if it is not forfeited to the king because the heir of Freeman shall not have it by reason of the attainder, and [it] had been objected that it is unreasonable that the defendant should have it, being against all intention, he answered and said that the defendant shall have it *ex necessitate*, inasmuch as the lands are discharged of the trust there not being any person *in esse* to take advantage of it. And it is similar to the case in 1 *Institutes* 318, where a joint tenant made a lease for years reserving a rent and died, the survivor shall not have it, but the lessee shall hold it discharged of the rent during the term.

---

[15] *Rex v. Holland* (1647), 1 Rolle, Abr., *Alien*, pl. A, 8, p. 194, Style 20, 40, 75, 84, 90, 94, 82 E.R. 498, 513, 542, 549, 554, 557.
[16] 12 Coke Rep. 3, 77 E.R. 1286.
[17] *Attorney General v. Abington* (Ex. 1613), 118 Selden Soc. 408.
[18] *Coke's Case* (1623), Benloe 108, 117, 73 E.R. 976, 983, Godbolt 289, 78 E.R. 169.
[19] Stat. 4 Hen. VII, c. 17 (*SR*, II, 540–541); Stat. 19 Hen. VII, c. 15 (*SR*, II, 660).
[20] Stat. 19 Hen. VII, c. 15 (*SR*, II, 660); Stat. 27 Hen. VIII, c. 10 (*SR*, III, 539–542).

And he said that forfeitures of trusts of terms for felony depend upon this difference, whether the term is assigned over in gross without fraud for my son and [the] beneficiary of the trust is outlawed in a personal action or for felony, the trust is forfeit inasmuch as, if the lease is a chattel, thus the trust is a chattel also, as in Sir John Daccomb's Case, cited above, and Babington's Case and Sir Walter Raleigh's Case.[21] And in such a case, if a term is assigned over in trust for a man and his heirs, it will go to the executor or administrator, Moore 807,[22] and thus a trust of a term in gross is that by the same law as[23] the term. But in some cases [there] is a difference between the rules of [common] law and courts of equity, because if a woman possessed of a term takes a husband and dies, the husband shall have it, but if she had granted it over to her own use and afterwards took a husband and died, the husband would not have the trust but the executor or administrator of the wife, as 1 Institutes 351. And such difference is warranted by the usage of the court, of which all take notice. Thus if a man convey lands in fee in trust for himself and his heirs, they are not assets to charge the heir, but an assignment of a term in trust for himself will be assets in equity and in law also when the trust is executed. But the trust of a term that attends the inheritance (as this in question does) is not governed by rules of [common] law, but by equitable construction [it] will go with the inheritance. Charters sealed in a chest that concern the inheritance shall go with the inheritance, but if granted over to a stranger, they will go to the executor. 8 Edw. IV, 3, and 4 Hen. VII, [10].[24]

And his reasons why the trust of the term in question was not forfeited were as follows:

1. That if it were forfeited in Freeman, it must be a chattel in Freeman. But it was never a chattel in Freeman, because if it was a chattel in Freeman, it was a chattel in George, and if it was a chattel in George, it could never come to Freeman but appertained to the administrator of George (who is the defendant) because a chattel never comes to the heir. And if it was not a chattel in George, it cannot be a chattel in Freeman, because nothing shall come to Freeman that was not devised to George (because Freeman the elder being dead without issue and there not being any sons at the time of the death of Sir Ralph Freeman, the case is not other than if the devise had been to George and his heirs). Thus whichever way is taken, if it is not a chattel, it is not forfeitable, if it is a chattel, Freeman did not have it to forfeit.

---

[21] *Attorney General v. Raleigh* (Ex. 1609), 117 Selden Soc. 364.
[22] *Cole v. Moore* (1607), Moore K.B. 806, 72 E.R. 917.
[23] ove *MS*.
[24] YB Pas. 8 Edw. IV, f. 3, pl. 7 (1468); YB Trin. 4 Hen. VII, f. 10, pl. 4 (1489).

2. It is apparent by the will itself that [it] never was intended that the inheritance and the term should be separate but consolidated together[25] to be conveyed to George and his heirs. And if it was thus, there was not any trust to convey the lease to Freeman. And though there is no doubt but that if the inheritance had been conveyed to George according to the will, the term can be kept on foot if he had desired it. But though it can be made, yet the trustees were not obliged to make it, nor is it any consequence to say that inasmuch as Freeman by any possibility and means could have disposed of the trust of the term for the same reason he had it to forfeit. He said that Freeman could not have disposed of it without disposing of the inheritance, which did not prove that it rested in him but only that it attended the inheritance. And the inheritance not being disposed of, the term must continue as security for the inheritance.
3. This Freeman Sandys was not the first person to whom the trust was limited, nor could he entitle himself otherwise than as heir to George. And thus his claim is by descent and the term only as a consequent of it. Thus that is to be admitted either that Freeman did not have a right to the term or that this trust so greatly partakes of the nature of the inheritance that it descends with the inheritance, and on account of that [it] could not be a chattel and thus not forfeited without a forfeiture of the inheritance. And if it should be otherwise, a great inconvenience would ensue, because suppose that upon the settlements of great estates upon families, there should be long leases to protect them from encumbrances; if those leases should be chattels, they would be irrecoverably lost by outlawry in personal actions, and by such an accident, the entire design of the settlement is destroyed.

And our case greatly differs from Sir Walter Raleigh's (upon which the counsel for the king greatly relied), which was in this court [in] 7 Jac. [1609] and was thus, Queen Elizabeth having a lease assigned it to Sir Walter Raleigh; afterwards the queen had the inheritance of the same land given to her by an Act of Parliament; after this Sir Walter Raleigh assigned over this lease in trust for his son, who was seven years of age, and took the profits himself and renewed it with the queen. After this the queen conveyed the inheritance of the same premisses to Sir Walter Raleigh and Sir Walter Raleigh conveyed this over to another in trust (but [there] was a defect in the conveyance). And afterwards Sir Walter Raleigh was attainted for treason. And [it] was adjudged in this court that the

---

[25] insement *MS*.

inheritance was forfeited to the king and that the assignment of this lease was fraudulent and in truth in trust for Sir Walter Raleigh himself and on account of that was decreed to be cancelled. But it is to be observed that it was in a case of treason, and in such a case, if it was a term in gross, it pertained to the king as a chattel, and if it attended the inheritance, it pertained to the king to whom the inheritance was forfeited. But our case is a case of felony, in which the inheritance is not forfeited, but the defendant shall have it and the term also as attendant upon it.

Judgment [was given] for the defendant.

[Other reports of this case: Hardres 405, 488, 145 E.R. 520, 561, 2 Freeman 129, 22 E.R. 1106, 3 Chan. Rep. 33, 21 E.R. 720, Nelson 130, 21 E.R. 808, Pl. 10, 1 Siderfin 403, 82 E.R. 1182.]

[Order of 17 June 1669: PRO E.126/10, f. 56v; E.159/512, recorda Trin. rot. 55.]

[This case is cited in Smith v. Smith (Ex. 1689), below, No. 277; Kirton v. Manwaring (Ex. 1708), below, No. 432; Attorney General v. Duplessis (1752), Parker 144, 156, 145 E.R. 739, 743; Burgess v. Wheate (1759), 1 Eden, 177, 199, 28 E.R. 652, 661, 1 W. Bl. 123, 96 E.R. 67; Rittson v. Stordy (1855), 3 Sm. & Giff. 230, 239, 65 E.R. 637, 641; Barrow v. Wadkin (1857), 24 Beavan 1, 13, 53 E.R. 257, 261; Sharp v. St. Sauveur (1871), L.R. 7 Ch. 343, 353, 354.]

17
Huxley v. Goodyear (Ex. 1666)

A covenant of clear title made by an administrator will not bind him personally.

LI MS. Misc. 499, p. 260, pl. 2 [Fr.] (Ward's Reports)

The father of the defendant fifty years ago entered into a statute of £600 to one Duncombe for money. This statute was assigned to Sir W. Turnor. And then the said father of the defendant mortgaged his lands to the plaintiff for ninety-nine years. And after [he] sold the inheritance to A., B., and C., the mortgage was forfeited. The plaintiff purchased the estate from A., B., and C. Goodyear, senior, the conusor of the statute, died, and the defendant was his administrator. And afterwards the plaintiff for £100 procured the defendant and his wife to acknowledge a fine to him, which was done accordingly, of the same lands in fee. And the defendant covenanted that they were clear of all encumbrances made by him. Then the defendant with his own assets purchased the said statute, it not being satisfied, and then set it up against the title of the plaintiff. And the plaintiff exhibited his English bill for setting aside or to be relieved against the said statute.

But the court agreed that [it] could not be because the statute was not purchased with the assets of Goodyear's estate.

[Order of 19 Nov. 1666: PRO E.126/9, f. 154.]

18

Smith v. Lloyd (Ex. 1666)

A grant of goods, debts, etc. includes copyhold lands that secure the repayment of a loan.

LI MS. Misc. 499, p. 395 [Fr.] (Ward's Reports)

John Lloyd lent[1] £50 to Winchester, who for security for the repayment of it surrendered copyhold lands in fee conditioned for the payment of the principal and interest to the said Lloyd, his heirs, executors, or administrators. The mortgage was forfeited. And Lloyd for valuable consideration granted all of his plate, goods, bonds, bills, debts, and sums of money to the plaintiff. John Lloyd died, and Lloyd his heir claimed the lands mortgaged and the money due upon them. The plaintiff preferred his English bill against Winchester and Lloyd and the administrator of John Lloyd. And upon a demurrer, [it was] adjudged that the plaintiff should be relieved in equity for the money lent by John Lloyd.

[Order of 11 Nov. 1667: PRO E.126/9, f. 287.]

19

Duke of York v. Masham (Ex. 1667)

Copyhold lands are not forfeited to the crown for treason.

LI MS. Misc. 499, p. 276, pl. 2 [Fr.] (Ward's Reports)

Isaac Penington,[1] [who was] seised of copyhold lands held of a manor of the defendants in Kent, was attainted of high treason by Act of Parliament, 12 Car. II, c. 30.[2] And all of his manors, lands, tenements, hereditaments, and other things of whatever nature they were were given to the king, but copyhold lands were not expressed. And in the said Act there was a proviso that no grant and surrender by copy of court roll made by the said Isaac Penington before such a

---

[1] mutuate *MS.*

---

[1] Died 1660, *D.N.B.*, s.v. Penington, Isaac.
[2] Stat. 12 Car. II, c. 30 (*SR*, V, 288–290).

day should be impeached. The king by his letters patent granted all the lands etc. of the said Isaac Penington to the plaintiff in as ample a manner as the said Act gave to him. And upon a bill preferred against the defendant in this court, he showed his title as lord by escheat. And upon this these two questions were moved.

1. Whether the general words of manors, lands, tenements or hereditaments or other words expressed in the said Act include copyhold lands to be forfeited to the king for treason.
2. If copyhold lands were not included in the general words, then whether the proviso that saved grants and surrenders of copyhold lands should not be extended by implication [so] that copyholds were forfeited except those that were saved by this proviso.

Thurland for the plaintiff argued as to the first point [that] the copyholds were included within the general words. And he observed the same reasons that Yelverton had in his argument of the case of Rowden and Malster, Cro. Car. 42, 43,[3] where several statutes and cases are enumerated that copyholds should be included within [the] general words. And he cited also the case of Crisp and Pratt, Cro. Car. 549, 550,[4] where it was adjudged that copyholds are within the Statutes of Bankrupts,[5] and Heydon's Case also, 3 Rep. f. 8.[6] And he said that in this case, copyholds were forfeited *ex vi termini* because no estate or title to anything can exist which is not enumerated in the act of attainder. And copyholds can be surrendered to the king, and thus they can be forfeited to the king also. But query this.

[As to the] second point, he observed that this negative clause that saved any copyholds explained the intention of Parliament, that all others that were not saved should be forfeited to the king by necessary implication, because otherwise there was no use of the proviso, and it should not be taken to be vain.

Hardres [argued] for the defendant. And he insisted upon this difference that when any alteration of the tenant without the consent of the lord is introduced, in such a case copyholds are not within any statute without being named. And for this reason they are not within the statutes of extent, elegit, and similar. But when a statute is made for the public good without a wrong to anyone, in such a case copyholds are within this statute by the general name, as the statute of limitations.

---

[3] *Rowden v. Maltster* (1626), Cro. Car. 42, 79 E.R. 641.

[4] *Crisp v. Pratt* (1639), Cro. Car. 549, 79 E.R. 1072.

[5] Stat. 13 Eliz. I, c. 7 (*SR*, IV, 539–541); Stat. 1 Jac. I, c. 15 (*SR*, IV, 1031–1034); Stat. 21 Jac. I, c. 19 (*SR*, IV, 1227–1229).

[6] *Heydon's Case* (1584), 3 Coke Rep. 8, 76 E.R. 637, also Moore K.B. 128, 72 E.R. 485.

And for this he cited Heydon's Case, 3 Rep. 8, and in Moore 128;[7] Rowden and Malster's Case, Cro. Car. 44; Margaret Podger's Case, 9 Rep. [104].[8] And in the case at bar, if there should be a forfeiture, the lord will lose his tenure, because the king cannot be admitted to be tenant to any subject.

As to the second point, he said that if there could not be a forfeiture by general and extensive words, there could not be a forfeiture by implication. And he said that this proviso could have this reasonable construction to extend only to surrenders made by copyholders between 1646 and 1659 which without such a proviso would have been forfeited to the lord. Also he said that the said Act of Attainder saved every right to every person except to the offenders and their wives and heirs. And if copyholds should be forfeited to the king, the lord would lose his right, rent, and tenure, which cannot be thought to be the intention of Parliament, *perdere innocentem cum impio*.

And the entire court inclined that copyholds were not forfeited to the king neither by the general words nor by implication upon the proviso.

And Chief Baron HALE said that [?] if a copyhold comes to the king in that manner the king will take and grant it. And he also said that in the former times it was ruled that copyholds were not forfeited except to the lord of the manor, because copyholds should pass by surrender only and because the grant of the plaintiff was not sufficient to pass copyhold lands (if they were forfeited to the king) to the plaintiff, because it should be by surrender. And the plaintiff ceased his suit. And HALE said that the proviso could be satisfied where copyholds were held of a manor of the king and surrenders and grants of them had been made, which without such a proviso could be endangered.

[Other reports of this case: Hardres 432, 145 E.R. 533.]

20

Bishop of Oxford v. Overbury (Ex. 1667)

A successor party to litigation can use his predecessor's depositions.

LI MS. Misc. 499, p. 299, pl. 2 [Fr.] (Ward's Reports)

The plaintiff exhibited his English bill with the intent to revive a suit commenced by his predecessor in the right of the Church. And it was moved on the part of the plaintiff that he should have the benefit of the depositions of witnesses taken in this cause upon the hearing of the cause now in question. And by the

---

[7] *Heydon's Case* (1584), *ut supra*.
[8] *Podger's Case* (1612), 9 Coke Rep. 104, 77 E.R. 883.

court, he should because the successor comes in in privity with the predecessor, as the heir with the ancestor.

[Order of 4 Feb. 1669: PRO E.126/9, f. 397v.]

21
Note (Ex. 1667)

A person sued for tithes must show the certainty of the tithes in his answer.

LI MS. Misc. 499, p. 299, pl. 3 [Fr.] (Ward's Reports)

Note that it is the constant practice of the exchequer that if an English bill is exhibited to be relieved for tithes, though the defendants plead or show a *modus decimandi* or other discharge or otherwise deny the plaintiff's title, still the defendants should show the certainty of their tithes charged in the bill, or otherwise it is a good cause for exception.

22
Heaton v. Carr (Ex. 1667)

A defendant who is incompetent will not be required to put in an answer, and the guardian of his estate can answer separately.

LI MS. Misc. 499, p. 310, pl. 1 [Fr.] (Ward's Reports)

The plaintiff preferred an English bill against the defendants. And in this bill it was suggested that the sole management of the estate of Sir Robert Carr was committed to the said Mary and the earl of Northumberland and others. *Ellys* prayed a commission to take the answer of the said Mary only omitting the said Sir Robert because he was naturally disabled to manage his estate and by a private Act the management of it was committed as above. And the commission was awarded accordingly, and the said Mary put in her answer separately and without the said Sir Robert. And an attachment against the said Sir Robert was spared for not responding.

23
Pawlett v. Attorney General (Ex. 1667–1668)

An equity of redemption survives the escheat or forfeiture to the crown of the mortgagee's interest in the mortgaged land.

LI MS. Misc. 499, pp. 312, 394 [Fr.] (Ward's Reports)

The plaintiff preferred his English bill to be relieved against the king and the other defendants. And the case was thus, the plaintiff borrowed money from one Ludlow and for security mortgaged the manor of Tarrant in the County of [Dorset] to the said Ludlow in fee (the said manor being held of the king *in capite*) upon a condition for redemption [on] such a day and also entered into a recognizance and statute to the said Ludlow [with a] defeasance upon payment of the same sum. The mortgage was broken, and afterwards the mortgagee accepted the interest money and so continued receiving it as [it] became due. And afterwards the said mortgagee devised all of his debts and personal estate to his executors and died, after whose death the estate in law of the forfeited mortgage descended to Edmund Ludlow[1] (who was attainted for treason by Act of Parliament 12 Car. II, c. 30[2]) as heir and nephew of the mortgagee. And by the attainder of the said Ludlow, the estate came to the king.

And to this bill, the attorney of the king demurred in law generally, but the executors answered. And the sole question was whether any equity of redemption lay in this case against the king in this court in such a manner as was demanded, because the executors sued upon the recognizance and thus the plaintiff would not only lose his lands mortgaged to the king but also would answer the debt to the executors upon the recognizance, and thus [there would be] a double charge.

As for the equity of redemption against the king, this point was argued by Sawyer for the king. And he insisted that before the Statute of 33 Hen. VIII, c. 39,[3] no equity in this court lay against the king. And this case [is] outside of the statute, because the case in question is only a trust and the king is not liable to the executor [for] a trust. And he also insisted that the king is in by escheat of his title paramount, and [asked] whether relief should be [had] against him in such a case. In both cases, as well when a mortgagor as a mortgagee dying without heirs, the king would lose his escheat, if relief were allowed.

---

[1] Died 1692, *D.N.B.*
[2] Stat. 12 Car. II, c. 30 (*SR*, V, 288–290).
[3] Stat. 33 Hen. VIII, c. 39 (*SR*, III, 879–892).

And the attorney general said that the king is not compellable in equity, because no subpoena lies against him. And if the king is not compellable to execute a use, he should not be compelled to execute a trust. And he said that though he is compellable to answer, yet the king is not compellable to convey. And he seemed to insist on the said Act of Attainder, which the words trust and equity are here saved. And if he was relievable by the ordinary course, [there was] no need to be expressed in the said Act. But they said that a petition of grace was the plaintiff's sole remedy.

Sir Robert Atkyns, Stephens, and *Winnington* [were] for the plaintiff. And they argued that the king is in by escheat and against a lord there should be relief in such a case and that there was relief against the king in this court before the Statute of 33 Hen. VIII. And Winnington cited the case of 3 Edw. III, [4],[4] in which the king was lord paramount and [there] was a mesne [lord] and a tenant. The tenancy escheated by which the mesnalty was extinct, yet this yearbook is according to the course of the exchequer; allowance should be made to the mesne [lord] proportionable to the rent that he lost. And this remedy is warranted by the common law.

Chief Baron HALE: In the case of the mesne [lord], it is a rent by surplusage, and [there is a] remedy by the common law. 13 Edw. III, Fitzherbert [Abridgment], *Petition*.[5] And he inclined that the attorney general should answer because the king is in purely by escheat and not by prerogative, as a forfeiture. And though a wife of a mortgagee in fee will be endowed, yet there will be relief against her. And so also against a free bench of the wife of copyhold lands surrendered to her husband in trust. And he remembered the case of Sir Francis Popham and Huckmore in the exchequer chamber and by petition in Parliament to be relieved against an outlawry, by which a lease in trust was forfeited. [The case] was adjourned.

This case was debated again.

And *Mountagu*, attorney for the queen, *North*, and *Sawyer* for the attorney general [argued] that no relief can be [had] in this case against the king in this court. And *Mountagu* cited the Case of the Earl of Cleveland,[6] which was to the same effect as it, but [he] could not be relieved here but was constrained to go into parliament. Thus the plaintiff must resort to a petition of grace because a petition of right does not lie. And he said that there is not any relief in equity against a disseisor.

---

[4] YB 3 Edw. III, Lib. Ass., p. 4, pl. 1 (1329); or YB Mich. 3 Edw. IV, f. 24, pl. 18 (1463).

[5] Perhaps Hil. 46 Edw. III, Fitzherbert, Abr., *Peticion*, pl. 19.

[6] *SR*, V, 303, 320, 622.

And *North* cited the case of Nash and Preston, 1 Cro. 190,[7] in which relief against a tenant in dower was denied. And this rule [was] taken that when there is not any fraud or covin, a court of equity will not relieve. And he said that before the Statute of 33 Hen. VIII, c. 39, [there was] no equity against the king in this court, and this statute gave [it] only in personal things, and the case in question is real. And he held that the case in question is a trust in the king and for this trust [there is] no remedy.

Sawyer said that the king is in his original[8] estate and by title paramount, and on account of that he is not liable to the collateral rights of a mortgagor and mortgagee, but inferior estates as dower, curtesy, occupancy, etc., which are carved out of the general estate, can be liable to encumbrances, and on account of that the courts of equity relieve against them. And all these cases hold in the case of a subject and then in the case of the king *a fortiori* for the reason of his pre-eminence and prerogative. And he cited Wike's Case, Lane 54; Dyer 155, 283; Yelverton 150, Poole's Case[9] upon a lease made by a tenant in tail the reversion in the crown, if a tenant in tail is attainted of treason, all leases made by him are gone, which does not hold in the case of a common person. But his great objection was that if the mortgagor dies after forfeiture without heirs, the land will not escheat. And if the mortgagee dies after forfeiture without issue, if relief may be against him in equity, then in both cases the lord will lose his escheat, which is harsh, and in this case in question, the court cannot decree relief against the king, by which etc.

Sir Robert *Atkyns*, solicitor of the queen, Serjeant *Newdigate, Lechmere, Stevens, Winnington*, and *Smith* [were] for the plaintiff. And they first insisted that it is not the present question whether there should be relief against the king, but the sole point is whether the attorney general should answer or not, because if the demurrer stands, the cause is stifled at the beginning. And the merits of it can be easily reserved to the hearing of the cause, and then it easily will come into dispute whether any and what relief [should be had] in the case.

And *Lechmere* said that the person of the king in this case does not matter, because he is in by escheat as Nichol's Case, Plowden 481; 1 *Institutes* 13.[10] And he said that equities of redemption are greatly enlarged just as they were in earlier times. And the equity of redemption is taken notice of by all courts. And he cited

---

[7] *Nash v. Preston* (1630), Cro. Car. 190, 79 E.R. 767.
[8] veiel *MS*.
[9] *Wike's Case* (1609), Lane 54, 145 E.R. 294; *King v. Boys* (1569), 3 Dyer 283b, 73 E.R. 636; *Poole v. Nedham* (1608), Yelverton 145, 80 E.R. 100.
[10] *Nichols v. Nichols* (1576), 2 Plowden 477, 75 E.R. 711; E. Coke, *First Institute* (1628), f. 13.

the case of Lady Thynne,[11] that relief was of the tenant in dower, and the case of James and Draper, that relief would be against the occupant.

Newdigate: As to Wick's Case, there is not any resolution nor [does it] reach the case in question. And he observed that, if the mortgagor had paid the money at the day, the king would not have any title. And it is harsh that such default should be remediless.

Sir Robert Atkyns cited the Case of Ford and Sheldon, 12 Rep. [1],[12] and said that the common law took notice of mortgages and favored them before all conditions annexed to estates. And it was against the intention of the mortgagor and mortgagee that the plaintiff should be in so bad a condition to lose his land and to pay the money also.

Stephens observed that this court relieved against a dean and chapter as in the Case of the Deans of Canterbury and Windsor, yet they could not be seised to one so well as the king could. Also he said that accident (especially such as this in question) is as proper to be relieved as a fraud. And as to the objection of the extinction of the seignory, he cited the case of Littleton[13] and the rent by surplusage. And that the king can grant the same land under the same tenure as before. Sir John Molin's Case, 6 Rep. [5b].[14] And as to the objection that the king cannot be decreed to convey, he agreed [with] it but said that the court can award an *amoveas manus* and recommend the plaintiff to the grace of the king. And he cited the Case of the Tenants of Bromfield and Yale in this court, in which a decree was made, which afterwards passed into an Act of Parliament, and the decree was recited in the Act.

Winnington observed that there is a right and a remedy for it. As to the right, he said that it was held in the case of Marshall and Keys, Hobart [63],[15] that chancery is part of the common law. And he observed the reviver of the tenures and services by the grant of the king, which cannot be in the case of a subject, and [it is] even more strong in the case of the king than a subject. And as for the remedy, he said that this court has a jurisdiction as the king's council and can decree possessions against the king by *amoveas manus*, and on account of that the plaintiff had pursued his proper remedy to commence his suit here, by which the king can be informed that the plaintiff had a right in equity, and afterwards he will make his application to the king.

---

[11] *Thynn v. Thynn* (1647 x 1648), Style 67, 77, 91, 98, 101, 143, 82 E.R. 535, 543, 555, 560, 562, 596.

[12] *Rex v. Ford* (1606), 12 Coke Rep. 1, 77 E.R. 1283, also 117 Selden Soc. 345.

[13] Perhaps *Sir John Littleton's Case*, Lane 56, 145 E.R. 295.

[14] *Molyn's Case* (1598), 6 Coke Rep. 5b, 77 E.R. 261.

[15] *Martin v. Marshal and Key*, Hobart 63, 80 E.R. 211.

Smith cited the case in Dyer 369, Manningham's Case,[16] in the court of wards, in point.

Chief Baron HALE: There is a great difference between trusts and rights of redemption. And he thought that there should be relief against all who come in in the post. And he said that the same equity that will give relief should make compensation for the extinction of the seignory. But he said that the great question was in respect of the person of the king. And he said when the king is entitled by a single matter of record, it is not any entry upon him, but when it is granted over, that entry can be [made] upon the grantee, and thus he thought that if the king would grant over the lands in question that relief should be against the grantee. And in the Case of the Earl of Cleveland (1666) (as I believe), it was resolved by the judges that, if mortgaged lands come to the king, there is a right of equity against the king, but as for the remedy, he in this case asked to be excused because it was pending before him in judgment. But he said that an *amoveas manus* savored too much of a legal proceeding. And he said that the first equity is for the executors and afterwards the heir should be admitted.

And afterwards in Easter [term], 20 Car. II [1668], the whole court declared their opinions that there is an equity of redemption in the case and that the attorney general should answer without prejudice to the executors.

Note [that] afterwards this case was ended among the parties themselves. And the plaintiff had a grant of the estate from the king.

[Other reports of this case: Hardres 465, 145 E.R. 550.]

[This case is cited in Reeve v. Attorney General (1741), 2 Atkyns 223, 26 E.R. 538, 539; Burgess v. Wheate (1757–1759), 1 Eden 177, 255, 28 E.R. 652, 682; Dyson v. Attorney General, L.R. [1911] 1 K.B. 410, 415, 521.]

24
Bishop of Winchester's Case (Ex. 1667)

A bishop answers a bill in equity upon his honor and not on his oath.

LI MS. Misc. 499, p. 321 [Fr.] (Ward's Reports)

Note [that] on a question among the clerks of the king's remembrancer whether the answer of the said bishop to an English bill should be taken upon his honor or on his oath, I searched and found this order of the House of Peers following: (and it is entered in this office Hilary 16 Car. I [1641] rotuli 24[1]):

---

[16] *Bruerton's Case* (1577), 3 Dyer 359, 73 E.R. 806.

[1] PRO E.159/480, recorda Hil. rot. 24.

Thursday 31 December 1640

Ordered upon the question (*nemine contradicente*) that the nobility of this kingdom and lords of the upper house of Parliament are of ancient right to answer in all courts as defendants upon protestation of honor only and not upon the common oath, and that the said order and this explanation does extend to all answers and examinations upon interrogatories in all causes as well criminal as civil and in all courts and commissions whatsoever and also to the persons of the widows and dowagers of the temporal peers of this land, and that the lord keeper of the great seal of England for the time being or the speaker of the Lords' House for the time being do forthwith give notice of it together with this explanation to be recorded in all courts, and that all orders, constitutions, or customs entered or practiced to the contrary whatsoever may be abolished and declared void, and the lord keeper of the great seal for the time being or commissioners of the great seal out of Parliament time shall see all practice to the contrary hereafter to be punished with exemplary severity to deter others from the like attempts.[2]

And the answer was upon the protestation of honor of the bishop in this case, and thus is the practice, because [?] some doubt about it was made.

25

Countess of Pembroke v. Currer (Ex. 1667)

Only the original parties to a suit can bring a bill of review.
Only depositions that can be read against all parties are admissible in evidence.

I
MT MS. 'Maynard's Repts. t. Car. I & II, G.4', f. [300] [Fr.]

In Michaelmas [term] 12 Car. II [1660], the countess of Pembroke and others, her tenants, brought a bill in the exchequer.[1] And the case was [that] Currer and others exhibited a former bill here against Rayner and others and obtained a decree that the defendants and all of the tenants and inhabitants within the manor of Selsden should do suit at the mill of Boulton. The decree was founded upon a custom that all of the inhabitants and tenants within Selsden should do and have done their suit at the mill of Boulton. The countess, being lady of the manor and she and her tenants [being] prejudiced by it because by covenants they are bound to grind at the mill of the countess, brought this new bill against the

---

[2] This order is in English.

[1] Orders of 12 and 30 Nov. 1660: PRO E.126/8, ff. 24v, 25v.

plaintiffs and the defendants in the former bill and alleged that there is no such custom and that the former decree was made by color of an agreement with the lord of Cumberland, tenant in tail and now dead without issue the remainder to the countess, so that she is not bound by it. And she prayed that the decree be reviewed and reversed and that 'they may be freed from the decree'.

Sir J[effrey] Palmer, attorney general, at the hearing took exception, that this bill did not lie at all because it is a bill of review and none of the defendants in the first suit were plaintiffs.

To this, it was answered that true it is that no one except the party, his heirs, or executors or [those] privy to the decree can have a bill of review and so that to this intent the bill is not good, but although the plaintiffs prayed for that which they cannot have, as here they prayed for a review, yet if the matter of the bill be such that it should in equity maintain their prayer in another respect, the prayer for that which they should not have should not do them prejudice in that which in justice they should have. And here the first decree was made against all of the inhabitants so that the plaintiffs, as inhabitants, being comprised within the words of the decree and being poor and ignorant men, did not know but that they were also legally and effectually bound, and on account of the terror and mischief arising by the decree of the court, it is just for them, and respectful, to apply themselves to the court for a remedy. And the countess is at a great prejudice because her tenants are doubtful and will not take leases with the covenants to grind at her mill etc. And the fear of being vexed, [or] where there is such color of vexation as this decree, is good ground to ask the remedy of the court.

Chief Baron HALE and the others dismissed the bill because in effect it was only to review the former bill and here there was no party enabled to do it, and it is not a sufficient ground for the bill that the plaintiffs imagined themselves bound by the decree or dream [?] they are not bound because though the words are comprehensive and general, [it is] not [against] all of the inhabitants [and] no process of attachment shall be ever made upon the general clause but only [?] the particular persons, which also was affirmed by the clerks in the court when the question was asked them. And on account of that, the court cannot do more than the counsel can do in the case, *viz.* declare that the plaintiffs are not bound by the decree.

Maynard: It is sufficient to us if you declare, but your declaration is authoritative, and thus [it is] shown [?] to us, and on account of that if it pleases [you] to declare [that] the reason of the dismission [is] that because we are [?] not parties [is] because we are not bound by the decree.

HALE: This by chance would give countenance to the plaintiffs to oppose the plaintiffs in the former decree, and we do not know if [?] the right be with the one or the other, and so we will not declare any other reason for the dismission but that here there are not good parties to [the bill of] review etc. 30 November 1660.

II
LI MS. Misc. 499, p. 336, pl. 2 [Fr.] (Ward's Reports)

Lechmere moved for a new trial because the depositions taken in a cause between the old tenants of the plaintiff and one Currer (under whom the defendant claims) upon the same matter in variance between the now plaintiff and defendant were not allowed to be read in evidence by Baron Turnor upon the trial of the cause in question, by reason of which the verdict passed for the defendant. And this appeared by affidavit, and Baron Turnor said the same.

And by the court [it was said that] all depositions should be reciprocal or should not be read. And afterwards upon hearing counsel of both sides, the court was of the opinion that they should be allowed to be read.

And Chief Baron HALE said that it was resolved in the king's bench that depositions taken in a cause between one who claims title and a tenant for life (an infant being in the reversion and not made a party), could not be read by the one in reversion. And [it was] resolved upon great debate.

Note that this case concerned a suit of mill and that there was contained much good matter touching suit of mill and the quality of the mill and suit at it and quantity of the toll.

[Orders of 2 July 1667 and 6 and 10 Feb. 1668: PRO E.126/9, ff, 247v, 300, 305.]

[Related cases: Rushworth v. Countess of Pembroke and Currier (1668), Hardres 472, 145 E.R. 553.]

26

Wise v. Huntington (Ex. 1667)

A writ of sequestration lies to force a defendant to proceed in a case after he has answered.

LI MS. Misc. 499, p. 336, pl. 3 [Fr.] (Ward's Reports)

The plaintiff preferred his English bill to be relieved for a lease made by the bishop of Oxford. The defendant answered, upon which answer [it] appeared to the court that a trial at law was necessary to be had before a decree could be made. And on account of that an interlocutory order was made that the defendant should name his attorney in court for the said trial at law, which the defendant refused [to do]. And upon this an attachment, afterwards a commission of rebellion, and afterwards a sergeant at arms were returned [unexecuted].

And the question was whether a sequestration could be awarded in such a case. And a precedent out of the chancery, Logger and Logger 16 Car. II [1664], was produced where a bill was preferred and the defendant did not answer but stood out all contempts. And upon this the bill was taken *pro confesso*, and sequestration was awarded. But this difference was taken between the case in question and the precedent because in one there is an answer but not in the other. And when there is no answer, then the bill can be taken *pro confesso*, but not when there is an answer, because in such a case the plaintiff can procure the cause to be heard on the bill and answer and thus obtain a decree and afterwards a sequestration on it (and of such opinion was Edwards, a deputy register in chancery, as he told me).

But Chief Baron HALE strongly inclined [to the view] that a sequestration should go in the principal case because it is harsh that the putting in of an answer should delay the plaintiff. And he said that there is not any difference when the defendant refuses a trial before or after the hearing of the cause, because if a trial at law should be necessary, no decree can be made before it.

And Baron TURNOR put this case that, if a criminal person upon his trial pleads not guilty and afterwards refuses to put himself upon the country for his trial, he shall be punished as a mute.

And sequestration was awarded *nisi causa*. And then the defendant complied and named his attorney and paid full costs. And a trial [was] awarded at the bar, which passed for the defendant. And the plaintiff's bill was dismissed with costs.

[Order of 8 Feb. 1669: PRO E.126/9, f. 404.]

27
Croke v. Beake (Ex. 1667)

A naturalized subject cannot inherit from another naturalized subject where the descent is through an alien.

LI MS. Misc. 499, p. 349 [Fr.] (Ward's Reports)

The case upon a plea to an English bill appeared to be thus, Sir Peter Vanlore, a naturalized alien, had issue, Sir Peter Vanlore, Junior, who had issue, three daughters, to wit Susanna, Jacoba, and Mary. John Vanlore, the brother of Sir Peter Vanlore the father, was an alien and had issue John, his son an alien, who had issue Maurice and Jane, aliens. Maurice was naturalized and purchased lands in fee and died without issue. And the sole question was whether the said Susanna, Jacoba, and Mary should be heirs to Maurice or whether the lands should escheat. The plaintiff claimed under the three daughters; the defendant under the escheat.

Ellys for the plaintiff argued that though John and John were aliens, yet they did not hinder the conveyance of the title to the three daughters inasmuch as no estate was claimed under the said John and John, and on account of that there is no use of their blood to make a descent to the plaintiffs because the estate was derived from Maurice and his naturalization made him inheritable from the three daughters, and on account of that they are inheritable from him, because heir and ancestor are correlatives. And he admitted that if the said John and John had been attainted, which was a disability, [it] could be otherwise, but here it was only an alienship, which is a nonability, and thus not so strong as a disability. Also the words of the naturalization were violent [sic] and had a strong operation and made him heir to lineal and collateral ancestors and enured as a restitution. And he cited Godfrey and Dixon's Case, 2 Cro. 539, Dyer 274, 3 *Inst.* 241.[1] Also he said that the estate in question was only a trust and the plaintiff [was] capable of a trust. Also the defendant denied the act of naturalization, which was proved, and thus it was similar to an outlawry, which when it is pleaded and comes to issue determines the cause, so here.

Weston [argued] for the defendant. And he insisted that the descent between the said Maurice and the three daughters was a mediate descent and that the ancestors of the said Maurice in the conveyance of the descent must be recounted and then by their alienship the bridge of the conveyance of this descent is broken and the plaintiff never could make title by reason of their nonability. And he denied that Maurice could be heir to the three daughters, and thus they never would be heirs to him, because they are mutual and equal in a collateral line. But he admitted that this rule sometimes did not hold in a lineal descent, as in Godfrey and Dixon's Case, cited by Ellys. But here med. proximate and med. remote both break the descent, lineal and collateral; Fitzherbert, Abridgment, *Cosinage* 5; Dyer 274; Hobart 343;[2] Heard and Baskervile's Case.[3] Also he said that if Maurice had been born in England, the three daughters could not inherit [from] him. And naturalization, which is a privilege *datum*, is not more strong than birth, which is a privilege *natum*. And he denied that a naturalization had the effect of a restitution, and for this he relied upon the authority of 3 *Inst.* 241 and that the disability in this case of the marquess of Exeter[4] was solely in the father. And he said that Maurice had two disabilities in him, one was tolled by the naturalization, the other remained.

Chief Baron HALE said that if A. and B. are brothers, A. natural born, B. an alien, B. had issue the one natural born subject C. [he] never shall be heir to A., because it is a descent *mediante patre*, but [it is] otherwise among brothers, because this is an immediate descent among them and not *mediante patre*. And as to this case [cited] by Ellys that the naturalization will enure as restitution, he

---

[1] *Godfrey v. Dixon* (1619), Cro. Jac. 539, 79 E.R. 462; *Grey's Case* (1568), 3 Dyer 274a, 73 E.R. 612; E. Coke, *Third Institute* (1644), f. 241.
[2] *Lord Sheffield v. Ratcliffe* (1615), Hobart 334, 343, 80 E.R. 475, 483, 484.
[3] *Heard v. Baskervile* (1614), Hobart 232, 80 E.R. 378.
[4] E. Coke, *Third Institute* (1644), f. 241.

doubted it, because if A. is attainted and had issue, an alien though the issue is naturalized, yet the disability of the attainder remains and is not tolled. And the court inclined for the defendant. [The case] was adjourned. And afterwards the plaintiff surceased.

[Orders of 28 and 31 Oct. and 14 and 21 Nov. 1667: PRO E.126/9, ff. 281, 281v, 187v.]

28

Attorney General v. Jones (Ex. 1667–1668)

An acquittance from the exchequer does not bar the rights of the crown.

Whether one collector of the king's estate appointed by an ordinance can be held liable for money received by a co-collector.

MT MS. 'Maynard's Repts. t. Car. I & II, G.4', f. [409] [Eng.]

Hunt and Jones were by ordinance[1] appointed treasurers of the money arising by sale of the king's goods. The Act of Oblivion[2] pardons all debts, etc., accounts, except treasurers of sequestrations of the king's estate etc., *inter alia*, provided they be sued within two years. They were not sued within two years, but Jones came voluntarily and made account in the exchequer, wherein he charges himself with a great sum and by his account makes a supra or rest of £3000 *unde* etc. demands two sums, *viz*. £1400 and £400 *inter alia*, as paid by him for fees of the commissioners and the contractors for sale of the goods, which sums appear by the same account on [the] true casting of them to be overpaid and so unduly paid, yet the said account was allowed by the chancellor of the exchequer, and the said Jones had thereon a *quietus est*.

The king's attorney [general] exhibited his bill to set aside the allowance of these two sums and the quietus est as to them. The defendant pleaded by Act of Oblivion and set forth also that the other treasurer, *viz*. Hunt, received the money and that [he] himself was not sued within the two years. The attorney general replied, and the cause [was] heard at Serjeants' Inn.

Chief Baron HALE: Seizing and selling the goods is a sequestration within the Act of Oblivion, and the defendants [were] treasurers within the Act. The information or bill now brought, *viz*. after the two years, is well brought for it is grounded on the defendant's account itself and then there needed [to be] no suit for he has charged himself. The *quietus est* bars not the king, which is always *salvo jure regis* when a judgment is given against the king or a *quietus est* [is] given.

---

[1] C. H. Firth and R. S. Rait, *Acts and Ordinances of the Interregnum 1642–1660*, II (1911), 166.

[2] Stat. 12 Car. II, c. 11 (*SR*, V, 226–234).

The king shall never question the fact therein adjudged, though there be a *salvo jure* and though the judgment be grounded on confession or verdict, but that is not here, for the account appears. He said it was a hard case to charge Jones with Hunt's receipts, they not being joined in the employment by contract but by force of authority imposing the service on them, and [he] seemed to be of opinion that, in such case, the one should not be charged with the receipts of the other. He said that the king was not to recover the money in this suit, but by this suit [he] may set aside the allowance of the account and the *quietus est* and afterwards bring a *scire facias* to recover the money. But in the end, direction was given that a case be drawn and the court attended therewith.

[Orders of 4 Dec. 1667, and 3 Feb. and 12 Nov. 1668: PRO E.126/9, ff. 299, 299v, 382v.]

29

Hodgson v. Wilshaw (Ex. 1668)

In this case, the land in question was discharged from the payment of tithes by a statute.

GI MS. 35, p. 596 [Eng.]

The plaintiff's bill was for tithes [of] corn, hay, etc. due to the plaintiff from the defendant in Uttoxeter in the County of Stafford, the plaintiff being farmer to the dean and chapter of the rectory.

The defendant sets forth his seisin in fee and that it was parcel of the monastery of Croxden of the Cistercian Order and that Thomas Challinor, late abbot, in the year 1538 (29 Hen. VIII) 17th September surrendered it to Henry VIII under the convent's seal and by it and the Statute of 31 Hen. VIII[1] it was enjoyed free etc.

A trial was ordered at law, but afterwards the plaintiff's counsel, stating the point to be whether the lands came to the crown by 27 Hen. VIII[2] or 31 Hen. VIII and producing a record out of the Augmentation Office, that in the year 30 Hen. VIII, a rent was answered out of these lands to the king, the court ordered for [the] plaintiff *nisi causa* etc. on Monday following.

At that day a proviso in the Statute 27 Hen. VIII which is not in the printed book was shown, *viz.*:

> Provided always that the king's highness at any time after the making of this Act, may at his pleasure ordain and declare by his letters patents under the great seal that such of the said religious houses, which His Highness

---

[1] Stat. 31 Hen. VIII, c. 13 (*SR*, III, 733–739).
[2] Stat. 27 Hen. VIII, c. 28 (*SR*, III, 575–578).

shall not be disposed to have suppressed nor dissolved by authority of this Act, shall still continue, remain, and be in the same body corporate and in the said essential estate, quality, and condition as well in possession or otherwise as they were before the making of this Act, without any suppressing or dissolution thereof, or of any part of the same by authority of this Act and that every such ordinance and declaration so to be made by the king's highness shall be good and effectual to the chief governors of such religious houses which His Majesty will not have suppressed and to their successors according to the tenors and purports of all the letters patents to be made thereof, any thing or things contained in this Act to the contrary hereof notwithstanding.

[On] 2d July 29 Hen. VIII, the king, reciting the said Act of Parliament and the power therein given him, does by his letters patent confirm the Monastery of Croxden as a body corporate as it was before the Act and confirm the abbot and convent[3] to all intents etc. and grants them their manor for future security to hold of him and his successors *in puram et perpetuam eleemosinam* of his foundation and not otherwise.

[In] 31st Hen. VIII, all abbeys etc. that came to the crown since 27th Hen. VIII are vested in the crown and discharged from payment of tithes. [On] 17 September 29 Hen. VIII, the abbot surrendered to the king, so that though this be a lesser abbey and suppressed yet being restored etc. was suppressed by 31 Hen. VIII and so discharged. And [it was] so held by the court, and the plaintiff's bill [was] dismissed, with four marks costs to the defendant.

See 2 Cro. 559, Porter v. Bathurst, Cistercians,[4] though in lease at the time of the dissolution, yet *quoad* the inheritance and in the lands of the patentee are discharged.

[The order of 18 Nov. 1667, PRO E.126/9, f. 293v, is printed at 1 Wood 88; see also orders of 3 and 19 Feb. 1668: PRO E.126/9, ff. 299v, 310, 320.]

30
Savile v. Queen Mother (Ex. 1668)

A bill in equity lies in the exchequer for relief for arrears of rent due to the crown even though the same matter could be pleaded in bar to an action at common law on the revenue side of the court.

---

[3] covenant *MS*.

[4] *Porter v. Bathurst* (1620), Cro. Jac. 559, 79 E.R. 479, also 1 Eagle and Younge 312, 1 Gwillim 373, 2 Rolle Rep. 142, 81 E.R. 712.

LI MS. Misc. 499, pp. 313, 479 [Fr.] (Ward's Reports)

There was a seizure of the lands of the defendant by virtue of an extent upon the *schedula auditorum* for rent in arrears for divers years in the former times to the queen mother, to which extent the defendant pleaded a Latin plea of equity. And divers exceptions were taken upon it. And it was said and argued by Sawyer for the king that this plea should be as certain as a plea in any other action is. And being argued, it appeared that it was not good, but the court did not give judgment immediately. And Stephens said that an immediate extent could not regularly go upon a super set by a deputy auditor.

But [it was ruled] by the court [that] when a super is set by a receiver upon the tenant, it is a debt, and, on the *schedula auditorum*, the long writ shall issue out of the lord treasurer's remembrancer's office, but, upon a super set by a receiver upon an accountant or other inferior officer, a distringas [is] to issue for so much only. And this is the difference and practice.

Upon a schedule of the auditor, the long writ issued, upon which the lands of the defendant were seized for arrears of fee farm rents due to the queen mother from Michaelmas 1647 amounting to £437. The defendant pleaded a Latin plea to the said seizure according to the Statute of 33 Hen. VIII, c. 39,[1] in which plea he pleaded the acts of oblivion of 24 February 1651[/52][2] and 25 April 1660.[3] But this Latin plea as pleaded was not good in law to discharge the defendant.

And before the allowance or disallowance of this Latin plea, the defendant exhibited his English bill against the king to be relieved for those arrears of rents against the seizure.

And the attorney general demurred to this English bill. And *Sir Peter Ball*, attorney general for the queen mother, and *Sawyer*, for the king, argued that the defendant had pleaded a Latin plea for the same matter contained in his bill and that this plea was depending [and] not determined. Also the substance of his bill was pleadable at law, and when anything is well pleadable at law, the party will not be relieved in equity by the Statute of 33 Hen. VIII, c. 39, because upon a Latin plea and judgment upon it, a writ of error can be brought, which cannot be if the party should be relievable in equity upon his English bill.

But the court inclined for the defendant that his English bill was well preferred and that if it contained sufficient matter, he should be relieved upon it by virtue of the Statute of 33 Hen. VIII, c. 39, notwithstanding that the matter contained in it is pleadable in a Latin plea.

---

[1] Stat. 33 Hen. VIII, c. 39 (*SR*, III, 879–892).
[2] Firth and Rait, eds., *Acts and Ordinances of the Interregnum, 1642–1660*, II (1972), pp. 565–577.
[3] Stat. 12 Car. II, c. 11 (*SR*, V, 226–234).

And as to the objection of the writ of error, Chief Baron HALE said that in the court of augmentations, which was a court of record, there were pleas at law but no trials or writs of error but the remedy was by bill. And he said that he had known many such Latin pleas but never known any good as to form and substance upon which the court could give judgment for the pleader, because he said that it is almost impossible to plead such a good plea. And precedents were to be searched for, and it was adjourned.

And afterwards upon the hearing of the cause, the plaintiff was relieved.

[Other reports of this case: Hardres 502, 145 E.R. 568.]

[Related case: Attorney General v. Norton (1668), PRO E.126/9, f. 321.]

31

Attorney General ex rel. Skelton v. Doughty (Ex. 1668)

In this case, a release was pleaded to a suit for fraud, and the defense of release was sustained, and the defendant was not required to make discovery.

LI MS. Misc. 499, p. 391, pl. 1 [Fr.] (Ward's Reports)

Doughty was a farmer of the excise in the County of Norfolk for divers years in the time of the late usurped powers. And his charge came to £80,000. When the king returned, a commission under the great seal was made to Sir George Benion and others to state the debt and account of Doughty, in which these two sums of £11,000 and £9,000 were in question and part of the £80,000, and to compound with him and make allowances. The commissioners made their report that they had examined the accounts of the said Doughty for the excise for all of the time in which he was farmer and certified that they thought that if Doughty paid £1,900 to the use of the king, that it would be a greater advantage to the king than could be recovered. And this report and composition was confirmed by the lord treasurer according to the said commission. And the £1,900 was paid accordingly.

And afterwards Doughty preferred his English bill against the attorney general, and a decree of the court was obtained, by which the said Doughty was acquitted and discharged of the whole £80,000. And after this Doughty made his account in the court, which was declared and entered in some offices. But before the quietus was obtained, an order was procured from lord Ashley, chancellor of the exchequer, for staying the making of the said quietus.

And afterwards the attorney general preferred his English bill against the said Doughty showing that the said Doughty had not discovered all of his charge to the commissioners because he had concealed the £11,000 and no notice of it was taken by the commissioners, but the rise of the said account was in regard to the £9,000. And so he prayed relief for the £11,000 concealed by fraud.

To this bill Doughty pleaded all of the matter [above] and prayed the judgment of the court whether he should be compelled to give any other answer.

And because it appeared and was agreed by all that the total charge was only £80,000 and that the commissioners had taken notice of it, the court inclined for Doughty, that his plea was good. Otherwise he never could be discharged.

And afterwards in Easter term 21 Car. II [1669] upon the hearing of this last bill and plea, it was agreed and adjudged that Doughty was totally discharged by force of the said composition and decree and that no retrospect should be in his account for the great mischief that would ensue if such compositions thus made should be invalidated. And though it was objected and insisted upon that the commissioners did not have the power to discharge farmers of the excise but only accountants, yet the commission was to hear and determine the accounts of all of the farmers and to make allowances to them, which [is] tantamount to a parol discharge. And the bill was dismissed with costs to be paid by the relator.

[Order of 25 May 1669: PRO E.126/9, f. 422v, E.126/10, 39v.]

32

Gill v. Thompson (Ex. 1668)

Dilapidations are not debts to be paid by the executors of a deceased vicar.

LI MS. Misc. 499, p. 421 [Fr.] (Ward's Reports)

The plaintiff preferred his English bill against the defendants and showed that he is vicar of A. and that the defendants are executors of B., who was the plaintiff's predecessor in the vicarage, and that B. had permitted dilapidations and had devised lands to the defendants on condition to pay his debts within three years. And the sole question was whether dilapidations are debts to be paid by the executors.

And by Chief Baron HALE, it seemed to him that they are not because by the Statute of 13 Eliz., c. 5,[1] fraudulent conveyances for avoiding debts are made void but at the same Parliament, that is to say [the Statute] 13 Eliz., c. 10,[2] a remedy is given for dilapidations, which is an argument that dilapidations are not debts within the first statute because if they were, there would not be any use for the second statute, to which the court inclined. Also the heir was not made a party,

---

[1] Stat. 13 Eliz. I, c. 5 (*SR*, IV, 537–538).
[2] Stat. 13 Eliz. I, c. 10 (*SR*, IV, 544–545).

and if any decree can be made, it will bind only the estate of the executors, which is conditional and can be avoided.

[Order of 1 June 1668: PRO E.126/9, f. 346v.]

33
Lucas v. Browne (Ex. 1668)

Where a defendant dies after a final decree but before performance of it, the suit is continued by a bill of revivor if the decree is for an uncertain payment but by a subpoena in the nature of a scire facias *if the decree orders that which is certain.*

LI MS. Misc. 499, p. 437, pl. 2 [Fr.] (Ward's Reports)

Note [that] it was resolved by the court that where a decree was made that an executor should make an assignment of the lease and should answer for the mesne profits, if he die, there should be a bill of revivor against his executor and not a subpoena in the nature of a *scire facias* for the performance of the decree. And the difference is[1] where the thing demanded was certain, there a subpoena [is appropriate], where uncertain, there a bill of revivor. And here it did not appear to the court what the mesne profits were, and they are not examinable by interrogatories upon contempt. And HALE, the chief baron, compared this to a writ of account where the first judgment makes the party chargeable in account but the second judgment gives the remedy.

34
Parry v. Parry (Ex. 1668)

'Mortgaged lands' is a good and sufficient description of land in a devise.

LI MS. Misc. 499, p. 466, pl. 1 [Fr.] (Ward's Reports)

A., the uncle of B., mortgaged lands in fee simple to B., which B. enjoyed as mortgaged lands. And after forfeiture A. released his right of equity [of redemption] to B., and afterwards B. (being the heir at law of A.) devised all his mortgaged lands to the defendant. And notwithstanding the release, yet when the devisor devises his mortgaged lands, it is a good description of which lands shall pass. And upon a verdict before Justice Wyld at the Shrewsbury assizes for the plaintiff, a new trial was awarded upon the motion of *Williams* of Gray's Inn.

---

[1] consist *MS*.

35
Poeton v. Monday (Ex. 1668)

Parishioners sued for tithes can defend by proving that the plaintiff is not the rector and need not answer to the allegation of tithes being due.

LI MS. Misc. 499, p. 477, pl. 1 [Fr.] (Ward's Reports)

Upon a trial at the bar,[1] the defendant Monday was found to be the legal rector and incumbent of Ashbury in Berkshire.[2] And after this the plaintiff pretending that he was the rector there (notwithstanding that the verdict and judgment was against him) preferred his English bill against the said Monday and the other inhabitants of Ashbury being defendants for tithes, some of which were due before Monday's title and some after. All of the defendants pleaded the verdict and the recovery of the rectory by the said Monday and did not show their tithes, as the practice of this court is. And upon the argument of this plea, it was said that the inhabitants should not be able[3] to plead this verdict, but [should] show their tithes, and so referred it to the judgment of the court.

But by the entire court, the plea as it is stands for an answer, because we do not wish to try the title to the rectory again. And thus the plea was held good.

36
Spencer v. Mott (Ex. 1668)

The issue in this case was whether a rent reserved out of a liberty is like a contract so that the assignee of the grantor cannot be sued.

LI MS. Misc. 499, p. 479, pl. 2 [Fr.] (Ward's Reports)

King Charles I [in] 14th *regni sui* [1638] granted to Arnold Spencer in fee the rivers of Stour and Ouse (the first in Essex and Suffolk, the second in Huntingdonshire and Bedfordshire) reserving two distinct rents by two distinct reddendums. Arnold Spencer granted the River Stour to the defendant in fee and died, and the River Ouse descended to Luke Spencer, the plaintiff, in fee. And the rent for the Ouse was continually duly paid, but the rent for the Stour was in arrear for divers years. And the defendant lived obscurely, and the said River Stour was in great decay. And because the rent for the said River Stour was not paid, process issued against the plaintiff for the rents of both rivers. And upon

---

[1] *Billingsly v. Poeton* (Ex. 1667), LI MS. Misc. 499, p. 299, pl. 1.
[2] V.C.H., *Berkshire*, IV (1924), p. 511.
[3] ne doient aver *MS*.

this Ellys and Wingfield prayed an apportionment and that the rent of the Stour should be made chargeable on the defendant solely.

But the court doubted if the defendant being only an assignee of the grantee of the king should be chargeable to the king for the rent, because the rent that is reserved out of a liberty is only like a contract that will not charge the assignee. And the rule was that the defendant should appear and show cause to the contrary.

37
Stoughton v. Onslow (Ex. 1669)

The Statute of Limitations bars trusts.
When a fine and nonclaim will bar an equity or a trust.
When lands are devised to be sold for payments of debts generally, debts for a simple contract are included, and no preference of payment of debts of a superior nature can be compelled.

LI MS. Misc. 500, f. 39, pl. 1 [Fr.] (Ward's Reports)

Upon a plea to an English bill, it was agreed that the Statute of Limitations[1] should bar a trust, as was adjudged between Lord Parmarino and Sir Robert Heath cited by HALE, and that a fine upon 4 Hen. VII[2] and nonclaim would bar an equity and a trust as well as a right. And this difference was taken, when by the fine the trust is carried over to the cognizee, there this fine should not bar the trust or equity of redemption; [it is] otherwise where the trust is not thus carried over. And it was also agreed that a fine levied by a *cestui que trust* would bar the heirs of his body but not the estate, trust, or equity of redemption of a stranger. Also it was said by the court that lord Coventry, the chancellor, gave relief to an heir who was sued upon the bond of his ancestor against the executors who had assets, but the chancellor in such a case would not impede the remedy of an obligee against the heir but would relieve the heir against the executors, inasmuch as testamentary things are properly liable to the payments of debts.

Also HALE said that when a legacy of £1000 is given to a younger son to be paid on such a day or, in default of the payment, such a farm, there is not any equity for redemption of the farm if the £1000 is not paid at the day. And when there is a special provision for the payment of a debt and another provision in the same will for payment of debts generally, the first debt is not included within the

---

[1] Stat. 21 Jac. I, c. 16 (*SR*, IV, 1222–1223).
[2] Stat. 4 Hen. VII, c. 24 (*SR*, II, 547–548).

second provision. *Clausula generalis non nefasta [est] ad ea quae specialiter sunt expressa.*[3] And when lands are devised to be sold for payments of debts generally, there debts for a simple contract are included, and no preference of payment of debts of a superior nature can be compelled.

[Other reports of this case: *sub nom.* Wolston v. Aston (1669), Hardres 511, 145 E.R. 573.]

[Orders of 11 and 18 Nov. 1669: PRO E.126/10, ff. 86, 92.]

[Appealed but no judgment given: *Lords' Journal*, XIII (n.d.): pp. 28, 32, 537.]

38
Anonymous (Ex. c. 1669)

A defendant is not bound to accuse himself.

BL MS. Hargr. 62, f. 9v, pl. 1 [Eng.]

A bill was preferred for 3s. chimney money and 1s. 6d. for distraining and to discover etc. To this it was demurred and three causes [were] shown:

1. For if that Act[1] prescribes a way to levy it and [there are] severally penalties and imprisonment for disturbing the collector, and the defendant is not bound to accuse himself.
2. The smallness of the sum [is] not worthy [of] the bringing [of it] into this court.
3. [*blank*]

39
Anonymous (Ex. c. 1669)

A defendant cannot be compelled to disclose anything that might result in a penal forfeiture.

BL MS. Hargr. 62, f. 9v, pl. 2 [Eng.]

[An] obligation [of] £200 [with a] condition that the defendant shall pay so much yearly so long as he shall continue in the office of exigenter [was sued upon at common law]. And judgment [was given] for the plaintiff.

---

[3] A general clause is not contrary to that which is expressed specially; cf. *clausula generalis non refertur ad expressa* (a general clause does not refer to things expressed): *Black's Law Dictionary* (5th ed. 1979), p. 226; *Altham's Case* (1610), 8 Coke Rep. 150, 154, 77 E.R. 701, 708–709.

---

[1] Stat. 14 Car. II, c. 10 (*SR*, V, 390–393).

The defendant [then] preferred a bill to discover etc. [. . .] and that the same was a void bond, being given for the enjoying [of] an office. To this bill the defendant [in equity] demurred [as] being not bound to discover a forfeiture against a penal law.[1] And the court was in accord.

40

Raleigh v. Chamberlaine (Ex. 1669)

In this case, relief was granted against a survivorship in a financial agreement, since the plaintiff would otherwise lose his investment and the defendant would receive a windfall.

BL MS. Hargr. 62, f. 12 [Eng.]

In the case of Mr. Raley against Chamberlaine to be relieved against a survivorship of a lease taken in the name of the plaintiff's son and the defendant, the plaintiff's son being named in trust for his father and died before the end of the term [of] the lease of the farm of [the] excise of beer, ale, etc. in the County of Gloucester and City of Bristol and by articles of agreement the defendant to have the profits of the lease as to Bristol and the plaintiff's son as to Gloucester, the trust being fully proved and the plaintiff being administrator to his son, [it was] agreed by the Lord Chief Baron HALE and [the] court [?], the defendant insisting upon the survivorship and that he had no notice of the trust for the father, that the matter was not material otherwise than as an evidence but the agreement that each should take the profits of his part for the term was a guidance in itself of the jointure upon the reason of the case of merchants trading [?] together especially nothing of interest in land being in question but a mere taking of profits, for otherwise the plaintiff, having advanced £1000 for the rent of the last quarter of the term, should [lose] his money and the defendant have the same to himself and pay but half the rent paid [?]. So [?] the plaintiff had a decree to be relieved and the defendant to account.

[Orders of 28 June 1669 and 29 Apr. and 22 June 1672: PRO E.126/10, f. 71v, E.126/11, ff. 62v, 108.]

41

Anonymous (Ex. 1669)

The issue in this case was whether a bill of discovery must allege a pending action.

---

[1] Stat. 5 & 6 Edw. VI, c. 16 (*SR*, IV, 151–152).

BL MS. Hargr. 62, f. 12v, pl. 1 [Eng.]

A bill [was filed] to discover assets against an executor. And [it was] demurred to because the plaintiff did not allege any action pending. The court [inquired] how are the precedents and adjourned.

42

Anonymous (Ex. c. 1669)

A defendant must put in his answer under oath.

BL MS. Hargr. 62, f. 13, pl. 3 [Fr.]

Upon a bill exhibited for tithes, the defendant was taken and imprisoned for contempt for not answering. And it was moved by *Lechmere* that the plaintiff was willing to accept the answer without oath [but] upon [his] word only, which the defendant was willing also to put in but would not be sworn. And he prayed that the answer be accepted. And the court would not make any order because it would happen [?] often to do thus but left the defendant and plaintiff to agree and accept it, if they wished to. And it was alleged that it was ordinary to make an order that a married woman should be permitted to answer without her husband.

43

Anonymous (Ex. 1670)

A defendant objecting to the jurisdiction of the exchequer must allege that the plaintiff was not a debtor to the king at the time of the subpoena.

BL MS. Hargr. 62, f. 13v, pl. 1 [Fr.]

[To an] English bill, the defendant pleaded that the plaintiff was not a debtor to the king. And it was overruled because it was not said that he was not a debtor at the time of the subpoena etc.

44

Rex v. Skinner (Ex. 1670)

The issue in this case was whether a defendant can be compelled to accuse himself so as to be liable for penalties.

BL MS. Hargr. 62, f. 13v, pl. 2 [Fr.]

[There was an] information against the defendant and others for defrauding the king in the payment of custom dues for corn exported and to discover the particular[s] of the corn and of the values and to have the true duty and the sums of the pains and penalties for such frauds etc. The defendant pleaded that the effect of the bill was to make him betray himself and to draw him into the penalties, and he demurred. And he demanded whether he should be compelled to answer.

And [. . .] moved for the defendant:

1. That it could be perhaps a question only for discovery and [the] attorney for the king should waive the [. . .] advantage of the penalty.
2. But upon that, as the case is, he will not be compelled to answer.

Sir Heneage Finch, attorney general, [argued] *contra*, and he cited Greenway's Case, a case where [. . .] was put to answer etc.

The court thought [?] that he should not be compelled to answer to accuse himself or to give advantage to another to proceed against him for the penalties.

Smith cited one Johnson's Case of recent time in this court where, by the barons (Chief Baron Hale being absent), in [a] case of the same nature, the demurrer was overruled and the defendant put to answer.

But Chief Baron HALE [ordered a] search for precedents and argument of counsel on both sides because [the point] is considerable.

45
Earl of Northumberland v. Radcliffe (Ex. 1670)

The owner of a rent seck can sue in equity the descendant of a covenantor to pay the rent even though there is a common law remedy sounding in property available.

LI MS. Misc. 500, f. 87, pl. 2 [Fr.] (Ward's Reports)

The plaintiff preferred his English bill to be relieved against the defendant and showed that Edward VI, seised in fee by right of the crown of a rent service of £6 19s. 3d. issuing out of the barony of Langley, granted the said rent without the services (by which it became a rent seck) to the plaintiff's ancestors in tail male, the barony came back to the crown by attainder, and King James granted the barony to the earl of Annandale in fee, who covenanted with the king to pay the said rent to the earls of Northumberland and to save the king harmless, the plaintiff's grandfather was seised of the rent (but not within thirty years), and the earl of Annandale conveyed to the ancestor of the defendant. And to discover the estate and whether such a covenant was made and to be relieved was the scope of the bill.

And the defendant demurred generally for want of equity. But though the plaintiff could have an assize, yet the defendant must answer to the covenant. And for this the demurrer was overruled.

46

Attorney General ex rel. Steers v. Hale (Ex. 1670)

Tenants in ancient demesne are not free of tolls on their trade.

LI MS. Misc. 500, f. 87, pl. 3 [Fr.] (Ward's Reports)

The plaintiffs exhibited their English bill against the defendants and showed that the king and his ancestors [for] time of which etc.[1] have had a toll of so much for each boat passing on the river under Staines Bridge, which was confirmed by two acts of parliament,[2] and that the relators were made bridge masters and collectors of this toll and [were required] to give an account of it to the lord chancellor etc. for the time being and that the defendants being common bargemen had divers times passed with their barges under the said bridge and had not paid the toll. And to discover how many times they had thus passed and to be relieved was the scope of the bill.

The defendants pleaded in bar that they were tenants in ancient demesne of Sir Bulstrode Whitelocke[3] of his manor of Henley in Oxfordshire, which is ancient demesne, and by reason of this their tenure are, have [been], and should be free and discharged of the toll demanded and all other tolls.

But the court overruled the plea inasmuch as everyone in ancient demesne should not be discharged from tolls for their merchandise nor in their trade by which they acquire their livelihood by buying and selling, contrary to Fitzherbert, *Natura Brevium*, 228 E, and the defendants here are not more privileged than a common carrier. And the prejudice would be great if he who had a small part of land in ancient demesne should have such a large privilege, which is to be extended only with respect to his person, his land, and the things used on the land and for his family, as was resolved in 1 Rolle's [Abridgment] 321 g; Cro.

---

[1] 'Time of which the memory of man runneth not to the contrary' were the words used to assert a right based on prescription.

[2] Stat. 1 Hen. VIII, c. 9 (*SR*, III, 5–6); Private Act 39 Eliz. I, c. 11 (*SR*, IV, 890) (not printed).

[3] Died 1675, *D.N.B.*

Eliz. 227; and the yearbook of 19 Hen. VI, 66b,[4] which made [. . .] query was considered.[5] Thus were 7 Hen. IV, 44b, 43; 11 Hen. IV, 86; 9 Hen. VI, 25b; 9 Hen. VIII, 25. See 1 Leon. 231–233; 2 Inst. 221; 4 Inst. 269.[6]

[Order of 10 July 1671: PRO E.126/11, f. 23.]

[This case is cited in Attorney General ex rel. Mayor of Maidenhead v. Jeffs (Ex. 1682), below, No. 133.]

47
Collop v. Foster (Ex. 1670)

A co-heiress can take by devise as a joint tenant with right of survivorship.

LI MS. Misc. 500, f. 91, pl. 3 [Fr.] (Ward's Reports)

The plaintiff entitled himself as heir of one who was one of the coheirs of J.S. with the defendant and showed that the plaintiff had enjoyed (and should by virtue of coparcenership enjoy) the moiety of such lands with the defendant for thirty years past. And to discover the evidences and to lodge them in safe hands was the scope of the plaintiff's bill.

The defendant answered and denied part of the pedigree and the confederacy etc., and as to the other pleaded that J.S. devised the land in question to the mother of the plaintiff and to the defendant (being his heirs at law) in fee simple and that they were joint tenants and that the mother of the plaintiff died and the defendant claimed and should have all by survivorship, and did not answer anything to the evidences, though in so long a time it can be inferred that there was a partition, but this not being charged, the court held this [to be a] good plea, inasmuch as the plaintiff's pretenses were evicted by the plea. And if the will is denied, the plaintiff can reply, but no costs [were awarded], nor anything except the probate of the will was produced.

---

[4] 1 Rolle, Abr., *Auntient Demeasne*, B, p. 321; *Ward v. Knight* (1588), Cro. Eliz. 227, 78 E.R. 483; YB Pas. 19 Hen. VI, f. 66, pl. 9 (1441).

[5] que fait ter [? or ser or ceo] Quer fuit consider *MS*.

[6] *Birmingham v. J.M.*, YB Pas. 7 Hen. IV, f. 44, pl. 11 (1406); *Lord Fitz-Hugh v. Anonymous*, YB Trin. 11 Hen. IV, f. 85 at 86, pl. 36 (1410); YB Trin. 9 Hen. VI, f. 25, pl. 20 (1431); *Ward v. Knight* (1588), 1 Leonard 231, 74 E.R. 212; E. Coke, *Second Institute* (1642), p. 221; E. Coke, *Fourth Institute* (1644), p. 269.

48
Risden v. Crouch (Ex. 1670)

Hops growing in fields are small tithes.

LI MS. Misc. 500, f. 114v, pl. 1 [Fr.] (Ward's Reports)

Note that it was ruled by Chief Baron HALE and all the court upon a demurrer to the English bill for tithes by a vicar that hops growing on a great quantity of ground and not in gardens are small tithes and that the omission of the clause in the bill by which the plaintiff waives the treble value[1] is not cause for a demurrer, because after answer the plaintiff can waive his bill and proceed for the tithes otherwise. 3 Leonard 204.[2]

[The final decree of 26 Oct. 1671, PRO E.126/11, f. 19v, is printed at 1 Wood 117, 2 Gwillim 522, 1 Eagle & Younge 495.]

[This case is cited in Knight v. Halsey (1800), 4 Gwillim 1531 at 1554.]

[Related cases: Crouch v. Risden (1670), 2 Keble 612, 84 E.R. 385, 1 Ventris 61, 86 E.R. 43, pl. 17, 1 Siderfin 443, 82 E.R. 1207, 1 Eagle and Younge 481.]

49
Chislett v. Morrice (Ex. 1670)

Where a defendant in equity has been sued at common law by the same plaintiff for the same matter, he can compel the plaintiff to elect which suit he will pursue before the defendant will be compelled to answer.

LI MS. Misc. 500, f. 118, pl. 2 [Fr.] (Ward's Reports)

It was ruled in this case that Chislett, who had brought his action on the case in the office of pleas and also had preferred his English bill for the same matter (as appeared by the declaration and bill), should make his election which way he will proceed before any answer made to the bill by *Morrice, ex motione unica*. And [there was] a hearing of *Stephens* for the plaintiff, who said that no such election was ever compelled in this court or [in] chancery before answer. But Chief Baron HALE and the entire court thought the election before answer was reasonable, otherwise a man would be molested in two ways for one and the same thing. And thus it was ruled here; *quod nota*.

---

[1] Treble damages for the non-payment of tithes was provided for by Stat. 2 & 3 Edw. VI, c. 13, s. 1 (*SR*, IV, 56).

[2] *Anonymous* (1588), 3 Leonard 204, 74 E.R. 634.

But it seems that the constant practice afterwards was opposite to this resolution, because the answer can be necessary evidence for the plaintiff at [common] law. And thus after the answer, he can dismiss his bill and proceed at law.[1]

50
Spelman v. Potts (Ex. 1671)

The Statute of Limitations can be pleaded to a suit in equity for an account and payment but not to a suit for an account and discharge or exoneration of the defendant's claims against the plaintiff.

LI MS. Misc. 500, f. 137, pl. 1 [Fr.] (Ward's Reports)

It was ruled in this case by Chief Baron HALE and all the barons that where the plaintiff exhibited a bill in equity to have an account and payment of money received for rents due to him six years before, the Statute of Limitations[1] is a good plea, and no relief will be given. But when the plaintiff endeavors by his bill to have an account of such money due to him six years before and to apply it to the discharge or exoneration of a debt or duty claimed by the defendant that became due to the defendant by reason of anything within this account or relating to it, there it is not a good plea, but he should answer further.

[Orders of 20 Feb., 19 June, and 21 Nov. 1672 and 6 Feb. 1673: PRO E.127/7. ff. 45v, 150v, 217v, E.126/11, f. 197.]

51
Bland's Case (Ex. 1671)

When lands are seized into the king's hands for a debt originally due to the king, if the lessee of the king is disturbed in his possession, he shall have an injunction and will not be compelled to bring ejectment. But when the seizure is in aid of the subject, the lessee must resort to his remedy by ejectment and will not have an injunction.

LI MS. Misc. 500, f. 141, pl. 1 [Fr.] (Ward's Reports)

Bland being a receiver of the revenues of the king in Yorkshire and one J.S. being indebted to him by an obligation, Bland assigned this obligation and debt to the king, upon which an extent issued by virtue of which a house and lands

---

[1] If discovery of evidence is the object of the suit in equity, the bill should not pray for relief, and if it does not, then the plaintiff will not be put to an election. [Editor's Note]

[1] Stat. 21 Jac. I, c. 16, s. 3 (*SR*, IV, 1222).

were seised into the hands of the king. And a lease of these [were] made to Bland under the exchequer seal reserving a rent. And Montagu, attorney for the queen and king's counsel, producing this lease in court prayed an injunction for quieting possession of the said house and lands in Bland.

But this was denied by Chief Baron HALE (from whom the other barons did not dissent) upon this difference, *viz.* when the lands are seized into the king's hands for a debt originally due to the king, there, if the lessee of the king is disturbed in [his] possession of the lands, he shall have an injunction and will not be compelled to bring ejectment. But when the seizure is in aid of the subject, as it is here, there the lessee must resort to his remedy by ejectment and will not have an injunction; which note.

And the reason for such injunctions seems to be that when the king is entitled by inquisition, that no person may traverse nor amove the hands of the king by any plea of title, which is reasonable that the king or his lessee shall be put into possession there being title upon record not controverted or avoided by anyone. And thus no one can pretend title or right to possession who does not show his title by plea.

52
Morgan v. Attorney General (Ex. 1671)

Robbery of an accountant of the king without fraud is a good discharge before the auditors.

In this case, an indemnity bond was discharged because the indemnitee did not suffer the loss covered by the bond.

LI MS. Misc. 500, f. 180, pl. 3 [Fr.] (Ward's Reports)

The defendant Lloyd was appointed by the last lord treasurer [to be] receiver general of the royal and additional aids in the County of Monmouth and other counties. And he was directed by the said lord treasurer and the lord Ashley[1] to observe such directions for returning and paying the money to the king that he would receive from Sir William Doyly, Scawen, and others appointed for this purpose and to pay it to the carriages of the king, which for convenience and security would be sent for it. When he received directions from the said persons, the said Lloyd appointed the plaintiff Morgan his deputy for the said aids in Monmouthshire and directed him to observe all matters which concerned the returns and payment of the moneys to the carriages and otherwise. The said Sir William Doyly and others from time to time gave direction to provide money,

---

[1] Chancellor of the exchequer and undertreasurer. This was Anthony Ashley Cooper, later to be earl of Shaftesbury and lord high chancellor. *D.N.B.*

and to have it ready accordingly at such a time, and to pay it to the carriages sent for this purpose. And the said Lloyd gave similar directions to the plaintiff. The plaintiff having received £600 for part of those aids conserved it in the house of his father-in-law, where the plaintiff lived, in expectation of the carriages. And after some time, the carriages not coming, the plaintiff resolved to carry it to Bristol for return. And the night before, the house where the £600 was conserved was broken into and the said £600 stolen.[2]

And upon an English bill exhibited by the plaintiff to be relieved against an obligation entered into by him to the said Lloyd for his receipt, which was put in suit against the plaintiff, and upon a trial at law directed to be tried in Monmouthshire where the robbery was, upon an issue whether the robbery was real and not feigned, and upon a verdict for the said Morgan, he was discharged of the said £600 by decree of the court. And upon payment of the residue due from him, his obligation was delivered up. And the said Lloyd in his account to the king was allowed the said £600.

Note [that] the attorney general in this case admitted that robbery of the accountant of the king without fraud is a good discharge before the auditors.

Lechmere, Sawyer, and Ward [were] of counsel with Morgan.

[Orders of 10 July, 27 Nov., and 4 Dec. 1671: PRO E.126/10, f. 251v, E.126/11, ff. 7, 18.]

53
Attorney General v. Fitzjames (Ex. 1672)

A trust is forfeited by an outlawry not by the inquisition upon the outlawry.

An issue in this case was whether a trust for the separate maintenance of a wife is liable for the debts of her husband.

LI MS. Misc. 500, f. 197v [Fr.] (Ward's Reports)

The case was thus. One Tufton in 1645, being seised in fee of divers houses etc. in Westminster, and which were now in question, in consideration of marriage with Frances (now the wife of Fitzjames) and for her provision after his death in the nature of a jointure made a lease of them to Thurland, Salter, and Chute, the defendant, for ninety-nine years under a peppercorn rent in trust that they, after the death of Tufton, should pay to the said Frances for the term of her life £150 *per annum* and £50 *per annum* further after the death of one Chrysagon Jowles. And in the same lease, there were other trusts for Tufton and his heirs. Tufton died in 1649, and within a short time afterwards, Frances his wife intermarried with the defendant Fitzjames, by which he was possessed of this trust

---

[2] emblea *MS*.

in the right of his wife. Salter died, and Thurland released to Chute, by which Chute alone was possessed of the trust.

Fitzjames, being indebted to one French for £180 by a judgment recovered in Trinity term 1669, was outlawed after this judgment 3 November 1670. And afterwards in the same month of November, the said Chute upon his bill exhibited in chancery to be discharged of this trust was decreed to assign the said lease to such persons as the heir of Tufton and the said Fitzjames and Frances his wife should appoint, in pursuance of which the said Chute in January 1670 assigned to Newman, senior, and Higgs. And this was subject to the first trust.

And afterwards in February 1670[/71] by a quadripartite deed between Newman, senior, and Higgs and Hoare and Newman, junior, of the first part, the defendant Fitzjames and Frances his wife and her daughter of the second part, the heir of Tufton and others of the third part, and divers tenants of the premises of the fourth part, the said premises were assigned for the residue of the said term of ninety-nine years to the said Hoare and Newman, junior, in trust for raising and paying to the said Frances, wife of Fitzjames, £250 *per annum* for her life and for allowing him to receive the rents and profits of the house in which Fitzjames inhabited. And in this indenture it was provided that the said £250 *per annum* and the said rents and profits of the said house of Fitzjames should be paid and disposed in such a manner as the said Frances by some writing under her hand should limit and appoint and that the said acquittance of Frances should be a good discharge to the trustees and tenants notwithstanding her coverture. In pursuance of those powers, the said Frances [on] 26 March 1671 limited and appointed the said £250 *per annum* and the said rents and profits of the said house to the defendant Hoare for satisfaction of a debt of £363 18s. justly due to him by the said Fitzjames, the husband, who received the said annuity and profits accordingly.

In April 1671 an inquisition was taken upon a special *capias utlagatum* which found the seisin of the said Fitzjames in the right of the said Frances for her life, to which inquisition the said Hoare and Newman pleaded the assignment of the said original lease to them, upon which the attorney general on behalf of the king (there not being any grant or privy seal in the case, but French was ordered to pay costs in case the defendants should be unjustly vexed) exhibited an English bill for discovery of the trusts for the said Fitzjames or his wife. And in their answers to this bill, the entire matter appeared to be as above.

And the entire court, that is to say Chief Baron TURNOR, TURNOR and LITTLETON, barons, (Wyndham being in chancery) were of the opinion that by the outlawry, which was before the title of the defendant Hoare, the said trust of the term was forfeited. And Hoare was decreed to answer for the profits received by him by virtue of the trust and deed of the said Frances notwithstanding that it was strongly objected by Stephens and Philips, of counsel with the defendants, that here Hoare had not only an equity but also the estate in law in him. And on account of that, the king, who also had only an equity, should not be preferred before one who had an equity and also the legal estate, because by all the rules in equity, there shall not be relief upon an equity against one who has an equity and the estate in law in himself also.

But the court did not regard this reason in this case inasmuch as by the outlawry the trust was forfeited, and Hoare came in subsequent to it though before the inquisition. And in the debate of this case, the case in this court, the Attorney General *ex rel.* Goswell, plaintiffs v. Sydenham, his wife, *et al.*, defendants, was remembered, which was such, that one Sydenham, who had married one of the daughters of Porter, was in 1660 outlawed after judgment at the suit of Goswell, and an inquisition was found that Sydenham was seised of certain lands in the right of his wife and seized them into the hands of the king. And upon a plea of the terre tenants, the attorney general exhibited his English bill against Sydenham, his wife, and others. And upon the hearing it appeared that Porter was seised in fee of the lands in question and bargained and sold them to certain persons and this bargain and sale was in trust for Porter and his heirs and that before the said outlawry Porter died, upon which this trust descended to the wife of Sydenham and her sister as heirs to Porter, and that by a decree in chancery this trust was declared accordingly and a moiety decreed to be conveyed to such persons which the wife of Sydenham shall nominate in trust for her and her heirs and the other moiety to the other sister and her heirs, and a fine [was] levied accordingly. And as for the moiety of the wife of Sydenham, it was made liable by the decree of this court to the said outlawry, and process of *levari* upon it [was] awarded accordingly. But inasmuch as it was alleged that by an agreement before the marriage of Sydenham with his wife, the said moiety of his wife was to remain with the said wife for her separate maintenance in regard that she did not have a jointure nor was she entitled to dower, it was referred to a trial [at law] whether there was any such agreement before marriage. And though it was mentioned in the indenture [of] 19 Car. II [1667], yet Sydenham did not insist [?] to go to trial upon it. And this case was ruled by Chief Baron Hale and the other barons in the exchequer chamber in Michaelmas [term] 22 Car. II, Thursday 10 November 1670.[1] And for a great time afterwards, Goswell the lessee of the king by force of the process of *levari* and injunction from this court received the profits, and when the lands lay fresh, the rents of those lands pertained to the wife of Sydenham.

And afterwards in the principal case, French obtained a lease from the king for the houses seized upon the inquisition. And Hoare paid French his entire

---

[1] PRO E.126/10, f. 194v.

debt and costs of suit, and French assigned this lease to Hoare for his further security for his debt and [for] reimbursing himself for the money paid to French.

Sawyer and Ward [were] of counsel with French.

Note [that] the court here as well as in Sydenham's Case inclined that a separate maintenance for a wife or a trust of it made before marriage is not forfeited by the outlawry of the husband.

[Orders of 7 and 20 May 1672: PRO E.127/7, ff. 91v, 117.]

54
Cottington v. Lord Cornbury (Ex. 1672)

In this case, the conveyance in issue was found to be a mortgage. However, a subsequent purchaser had no notice of the proviso and was not bound by the right of redemption.

I
LI MS. Misc. 500, f. 198v [Fr.] (Ward's Reports)

The case was thus. In 1635 the lord Cottington (afterwards high treasurer of England)[1] purchased the interest of a lease made in 1592 to Queen Elizabeth by the bishop of Winchester of the manor of Knoyle in the county of Wiltshire[2] (at this day of the annual value of £500) for the residue of the term of seventy-nine years (which by computation ended at Michaelmas 1671) and gave for the purchase £5000. And in the same year, the said lord Cottington borrowed from Sir Roger Palmer £5000 and for security assigned to him the said lease. And there was a proviso in it that if the lord Cottington, his executors, administrators, or assigns paid the said sum of £5000 at the end of seven years, that the said assignment would be void, but there was not any provision for interest nor covenants usual in mortgages. But the lord Cottington continued [in] the possession during the seven years and afterwards and received the profits to his own use. And he paid £2500 in 1640, part of the £5000. And afterwards in 1645, the said Sir Roger Palmer entered for non payment of the residue, the lord Cottington being disabled by his loyalty from paying it. And afterwards Sir Roger Palmer compounded for this lease as part of his own estate and made a lease in 1649 to one Manning (who had been a servant to lord Cottington, and as the plaintiff thought, that it had been a trust for the said lord and that Manning had had notice of the proviso, but all [was] denied by Manning) for a £250 fine and £250 annual rent, beyond the rent reserved upon the large lease, for the entire old term except three days. And presently afterwards he sold the said £250 rent

---

[1] Died 1652, *D.N.B.*
[2] V.C.H., *Wiltshire*, XI (1980), p. 86.

and the said reversion of three days to Ludlow,[3] who was afterwards attainted of high treason. And thus this estate came to the king, who granted it to the defendant the lord Cornbury, who surrendered this old lease and accepted a second from the bishop of Winchester in 1661. But there was not any proof that Ludlow had any notice of the proviso except by presumption inasmuch as it was included within the deed that conveyed to Sir Roger Palmer and thus showed his title to convey to Ludlow.

But after the return of the king and before any renewal with the bishop, Sir Francis Cottington, son of lord Cottington and father to the plaintiff, took administration to lord Cottington and entered and received some rents. And notice was given to the bishop of this title and claim, who promised to use him kindly, but there was not any enrollment according to the Statute of Attainder [of] 12 Car. II [1660], ca. 30,[4] within two years after 1 January 1660[/61]. And now the plaintiff being administrator *de bonis non* of the said lord Cottington exhibited his bill to have an account of the profits and the equity of redemption.

Manning denied any trust for lord Cottington and denied any notice of the proviso and that lord Cottington had any estate in it. And the lord Cornbury answered to the same effect and also pleaded that he was a purchaser for valuable consideration without notice. But it was not proved what sum he paid or with certainty what sum Ludlow paid.

And upon the hearing of this cause, the barons, that is to say Chief Baron TURNOR, TURNOR and LITTLETON, barons, (Wyndham being in chancery), considered these three points.

1. Whether it was a mortgage redeemable after the day of payment or not, inasmuch as there was not any provision for interest or the usual covenants in mortgages. And it was urged by Attorney General *Finch*, Solicitor General *North*, *Mountagu*, *Stephens*, *Calthrop*, and *Sawyer* for the defendants that there was not any mortgage. And the case of Sir Anthony Cage and Sir Ralph Bovey[5] was remembered that where[6] a man sells his lands under a proviso that the vendor upon the payment of such a sum on such a day shall have them back, it was adjudged [to be] no mortgage nor [was] the vendor relievable

---

[3] Died 1692, *D.N.B.*

[4] Stat. 12 Car. II, c. 30 (*SR*, V, 288-290).

[5] *Jennet v. Cooles* (1666 x 1667), 1 Siderfin 223, 262, 344, 82 E.R. 1070, 1094, 1147, *sub nom. Sir Ralph Bovy's Case*, 1 Ventris 193, 211, 217, 86 E.R. 131, 142 146, *sub nom. Jemot v. Cooly*, T. Raymond 135, 158, 83 E.R. 73, 84, 1 Levinz 170, 83 E.R. 353, 1 Keble 784, 915, 83 E.R. 1241, 1318, 2 Keble 20, 184, 270, 295, 84 E.R. 13, 115, 168, 184, *sub nom. Jemott v. Cowley*, 1 Wms. Saunders 112, 85 E.R. 122.

[6] si *MS*.

after the day. But the court took a difference because when in such a case the vendor gives possession to the vendee in the meantime without question, it is no mortgage but only a contract between the parties which does not extend beyond the time limited, and this was Sir Ralph Bovey's Case. But here the lord Cottington continued in possession notwithstanding the conveyance and received the profits to his own use, which in itself is a badge and evidence of a mortgage. And though no interest was reserved, this does not alter the case. Also the account and payment of money, part of the money borrowed, alters the case and is a badge of a mortgage. And all of the barons were of such opinion, that it was a mortgage.

2. But the barons were of the opinion that inasmuch as Manning did not have any notice of the proviso, he was not bound. And though it was insisted by *Maynard*, king's serjeant, *Lechmere, Wallop, Thomas*, and *Ward* of counsel with the plaintiff that Ludlow by his purchase of the reversion and rent should be presumed to have notice of the proviso inasmuch as it was contained within the mortgage made to Sir Roger Palmer and without which he did not have title and it should not be inferred that one [would] purchase an estate without a view of the title (though one could accept a lease without such a view as Manning had done), yet it was resolved [that] this notice should go only to the reversion of the three days, and there is not any such thing as a tenant [by] right of the church, neither in law nor in equity, where it is not a parcel of the tenure as it is in the northern parts. And thus the renewal of the lease by the lord Cornbury was good and will not be set aside, nor [is there] any equity of redemption of it. And if there was notice to Ludlow, it does not bind the king.

3. It was agreed by all of the barons aforesaid that if there was an equity of redemption or trust for the plaintiff in Ludlow (which should be, if the plaintiff had any by reason of the words in the Act of Attainder which saved all trusts in the offenders for others), that the plaintiff should have enrolled this claim and pretense of his before the first of January 1662[/63], because without this saving, all trusts in the offenders for others would have been forfeited. And if the plaintiff will have the benefit of the saving, he must follow the direction of it, that is to say enroll his claim, because the purpose of this clause of enrollment was to make all pretenses public within a short time so that the king can afterwards know certainly the residue of the offenders' estates to be free of all claims and thus all will be barred in the nature of the Statute of Limitations,[7] as *North* said, notwithstanding that it

---

[7] Stat. 21 Jac. I, c. 16, s. 3 (*SR*, IV, 1222).

was objected by the plaintiff's counsel that Ludlow was never possessed of any trust for him but claimed all in his own right and thus [was] not within the meaning of this saving [clause].

And upon the entire matter, the plaintiff's bill was dismissed without costs. And afterwards in the same term, the motion of *Lechmere* for a rehearing was denied, and the plaintiff was put to a bill of review, if he thought it reasonable.

II
IU Lilly MS. Parker, 'Attorney's Reports, 1707/8–1760', p. 422 [Eng.]

Lord Cottington purchased a long lease for £5000 and assigns it to Sir Roger Palmer for £5000 [with a] proviso that if he pays it within seven years, he shall have his term again. Sir Roger Palmer assigns it to Maulle [?], all except three days, who assigns it to Ludlow, upon whose attainder, the Lord Cornbury begged the term. And now the heir of Lord Cottington would redeem it as a mortgage.

1. [It was] resolved that this was not a mortgage but a collateral covenant, which being not performed, he is barred.
2. The assignee of part has not presumptive notice.
3. Admit he had notice, yet because the deed of claim was not enrolled, it shall not avail against my Lord Cornbury, grantee of the forfeiture.

[Orders of 5 Feb. and 3, 18, and 22 May 1672: PRO E.126/11, ff. 34v, 67, E.127/7, ff. 83, 104.]

55
Pinfold v. Northey (Ex. 1672)

There should not be restitution, neither of the things themselves sold upon venditioni exponas *nor other goods nor of their value, upon a reversal of an outlawry, because it is a thing executed and irrevocable.*

A debtor can prefer one creditor over another at will.

LI MS. Misc. 500, f. 199 [Fr.] (Ward's Reports)

The case upon the hearing in the exchequer chamber appeared to be thus. Sir William Bateman of the City of London had a venture[1] of £500 stock in the East India Company, where all the security that he (and all other adventurers in the same nature) had for it was the entry of his name for such sum in their book, and by virtue of it he was entitled to all the produce and benefit of the said £500.

---

[1] adventure *MS*.

And the nature of this security and venture was that the money paid to the company could not afterwards be paid out of the company but the adventurers would receive the benefit and produce of it as they arose according to the proportionable dividends. And when anyone wished to transfer his interest to another, it was done solely by alteration of the names, that is to say, striking out of the name of the party who had the title and inserting the name of the party to whom it should be transferred.

Sir William Bateman was outlawed in debt at the suit of Northey and also at the suit of Boothby, and both of those outlawries were before judgment. And upon an inquisition taken in London by virtue of two extents upon those outlawries, this venture of £500 was found and seized into the hands of the king, after which the king by privy seal granted it to Northey and Boothby in and against satisfaction of their debts and demands from Bateman. And inasmuch as the East India Company refused to strike out the name of Bateman and insert the names of Northey and the other persons without direction or decree for their indemnity, Northey and the other person exhibited their English bill to such purpose comprehending all the matter aforesaid against the attorney general, The East India Company, and Bateman. And it was decreed accordingly by the court.[2]

But Bateman, though he was made a party to the said bill, he never answered being a prisoner in the king's bench, nor was he a part[y] to the judgment, after which decree and the alteration of the names accordingly, Bateman brought a writ of error and reversed the outlawry. And this reversal was pleaded in this court and confessed by the attorney general, and judgment was entered upon it that the hands of the king should be removed from the possession of the said £500 and that Bateman should be restored to all that he lost by the said outlawry, *unde dicto domino regi nondum est responsum*, and restitution [was] awarded accordingly, after which the said Sir William Bateman was outlawed after judgment in debt at the suit of the plaintiff Pinfold.

And by inquisition upon a *capias utlagatum* upon this outlawry, this £500 was found as the estate of Bateman and seized into the hands of the king, after which Pinfold obtained a grant of it by privy seal from the king (without mention of [its] being a part[3] of his debt due from Bateman) and exhibited his English bill in this court against the attorney general, Northey, and the other defendants comprehending all the matter [above]. And the effect of it was to set aside this decree inasmuch as Bateman was not brought to judgment upon it and inasmuch as the first outlawries were reversed and Bateman restored and to compel the East India Company to strike out the names of Northey and the other person

---

[2] *Northey v. East India Co.* (Ex. 1668), PRO E.126/9, f. 353.
[3] in payment [?].

and to insert the name of Pinfold in their books for this £500 and all of the growing benefit so that he could have it according to his grant by privy seal.

And this case was heard in the exchequer chamber Friday 9 May 1672. And Sawyer for the plaintiff solemnly argued it, that the plaintiff in this case should be relieved. And he argued upon these things.

1. He admitted that by the outlawry the ownership of the £500 was vested in the king without office and that by the privy seal the ownership was vested in Northey and Boothby and that the decree was well founded at the time of making, the outlawry at this time being in force and not reversed.

2. But he argued that upon reversal of the first outlawry and judgment and restitution upon it, Bateman was restored to the said £500 notwithstanding the decree, privy seal, and alteration of the name in the book of the East India Company accordingly, because the title here to the £500 is by the outlawry and not by the decree. And the outlawry being reversed, the entire title is gone, and *nul tiel record* is a good plea. And he insisted that the alteration of the name is not such an execution as if the East India Company had paid the £500 to Northey and Boothby according to the privy seal (in which case it was admitted that there should be no restitution nor if it had been paid to the king himself), but the absolute ownership remained in Bateman, which was restored upon the reversal of the outlawry. And he argued on these grounds, when a thing that is principal is seized and forfeited by outlawry, there, upon reversal of the outlawry the same principal shall be restored but not the accessory (as the mesne rates, etc.) that is paid to the king. And for this he cited and relied on Beverley and Cornwall's Case, Moore fo. 241, 269,[4] in point. And he greatly relied on Eyre and Woodfine's Case, Cro. Eliz. 278 and 1 Anderson fo. 277,[5] where the case was that, a termor being outlawed, his term was sold and afterwards the outlawry was reversed, and, on a special verdict upon argument and consideration, it was adjudged by Anderson and Walmsley (Periam not being resolved) that the termor should be restored, and judgment was given accordingly in ejectment. And he insisted upon the reasons put in this case and said that it was a stronger case than this in question, because if a sale by process of this court should not conclude the party, *a fortiori* a privy seal and alteration of the name by force of a decree to which Bateman was not a party should not conclude him. And he cited the case of 7 Edw. IV, 2,[6] mentioned in Hoe's Case, 5 Rep. 90b,[7] and the opinion of Lord Coke there, that if a debtee is outlawed and the debtor pays his debt to the king,

---

[4] *Beverley's Case* (1588), Moore K.B. 241, 269, 72 E.R. 555, 573.
[5] *Eyre v. Woodfine* (1592), Cro. Eliz. 278, 78 E.R. 533, 1 Anderson 277, 123 E.R. 471.
[6] YB Pas. 7 Edw. IV, ff. 1, 2, pl. 3 (1467).
[7] *Hoe v. Boulton* (1600), 5 Coke Rep. 90, 77 E.R. 191.

after the reversal of the outlawry, the debtee should recover it against the debtor, and that restitution should be made of goods sold by the sheriff by a writ of capias utlagatum upon reversal of the outlawry. And he observed [that] the judgment is the reversal, that the party shall be restored to all that he lost, as 1 Rolle's [Abridgment] 805, 11 Hen. VII, 53b,[8] that such restitution though in a case of outlawry for felony, shall be at common law. And he also cited 7 Hen. IV, 1,[9] and Brooke [Abridgment], *Restitution* 21,[10] that grantees of the liberties of the king, who have *bona et catalla utlagati*, should make such restitution and such grantees have as good title to them as grantees by privy seal have. And such restitutions in the case of liberties is the constant practice of this court. And he admitted some difference between a sale made by process of the court by an officer in a compulsory manner and when by a grantee of the king or his act. The first can be bound but not the second. And he also admitted that a pardon of the outlawry is not restitution according to 29 Ass. 34; Brooke [Abridgment], *Restitution* 18; and 7 Hen. IV, 5,[11] because it is an act of grace, but reversal is restitution, it being an act of justice and right. And he cited Garrett's Case in the common pleas, Michaelmas [term] 23 Car. II [1671], where it was said that the case was that Garrett had judgment against the earl of Holland in debt and was outlawed; the king granted this judgment and all of the benefit of it to Mr. Progers, who released to the earl of Holland, and afterwards the outlawry was reversed and [it was] adjudged that Garrett should be restored. And thus he concluded that the £500 should be restored to Bateman, the property[12] itself not being altered. And in this case he greatly insisted that the decree should not be objected against Bateman but was void as to him, he not being a party to it. And he observed that, if payment to a grantee upon a privy seal should not be avoided upon reversal, each person could be outlawed and a grant of his goods obtained before he might know of it, which would be inconvenient.

The attorney general [*Finch*] and *Stephens* for the defendants Northey and Boothby argued to the contrary and insisted upon these things.

1. That when any money or thing is forfeited by outlawry be it principal or accessory, it is paid to the king or to the grantee of the king (which is the same), though the outlawry is afterwards reversed, yet there should not be any restitution, it being a thing executed. And though after a reversal *nul tiel record* is a good plea, yet it can be replied to and

---

[8] 1 Rolle, Abr., *Error*, pl. O, 5 (11 Hen. IV, 53b).
[9] YB Mich. 7 Hen. IV, f. 1, pl. 2 (1405).
[10] 6 Hen. VII, 9, Brooke, Abr., *Restitution*, pl. 21.
[11] YB 29 Edw. III, Lib. Ass., f. 164, pl. 34 (1355); Brooke, Abr., *Restitution*, pl. 18; YB Mich. 7 Hen. IV, f. 4, pl. 27 (1406).
[12] I.e. ownership.

shown that *habebatur tale record*, and it suffices for the profits to answer to the king. And in the case of the Viscountess of Baltinglass v. Sir Richard Temple,[13] where the lessee for life suffered a common recovery and the reversioner entered for the forfeiture, and afterwards the recovery was reversed by the lessee for life, who pleaded *nul tiel record* as the recovery, yet it was adjudged lately in the king's bench that *habebatur tale record* was a good replication, thus here [also]. And in the Case of Ellison and Van Vanghenberg in this court, Friday 1 May 1651, in the lord treasurer's remembrancer's office, it was adjudged by the whole court that a term sold by a *venditioni exponas* upon an outlawry and the money paid to the king was irrevocable and there should be no restitution. But it was agreed in this case as well as in the principal case that, if the money remained in the hands of the sheriff or other officer not paid to the king or his grantee before reversal, that in such case restitution of the money should be made. And it is the true difference between things executed and not executed before reversal.

2. That the alteration of the name of Bateman and inserting the names of Northey and Boothby in the book of the East India Company was an absolute alteration of the ownership of the £500 and a vesting of it absolutely in the grantees, which could not be avoided by a reversal of the outlawry. And it is tantamount to the £500 having been paid to the king and given by him in specie to Northey and Boothby, because this forfeiture, privy seal, and alteration is *novatio contractus* and made it the stock of Northey and Boothby and not of Bateman.

3. They insist that it is not necessary to carry Bateman to judgment on this decree, because it is only to compel the East India Company to alter the name and Bateman cannot deny the outlawry by which the £500 was forfeited.

Upon the hearing of those arguments, the court took [them under] advisement until this day. And WINDHAM, LITTLETON, and Chief Baron TURNER argued for the defendants. And only Baron TURNER [was] for the plaintiff, and these were [his] reasons:

1. That here there was not any binding decree, Bateman not being a party, and if [there were] no decree, the plaintiff should have the £500 by the reversal of the first outlawry and his second grant, because the

---

[13] *Viscountess Baltinglass v. Temple* (Ex. 1669), LI MS. Misc. 500, f. 60v, pl. 1. Note the connected case of *Tustian v. Roper* (1668), T. Jones 27, 84 E.R. 1130, Vaughan 28, 124 E.R. 954; *sub nom. Lady Baltinglass's Case*, 1 Freeman 23, 89 E.R. 21.

decree did not alter the case, the alteration of the name being only a manifestation of the stock but not an alteration of the ownership, because by the first outlawry the king only was entitled and the £500 remained in the same hands at the reversal, which was at the time of the outlawry by the reversal the first owner was restored, and it does not matter which name was in the book, inasmuch as all that was lost should be restored.

2. The inconvenience would be great if there should not be such restitution, because [in] a case [where] a man is outlawed privately and a privy seal obtained in a secret manner (which can be), it is harsh that the party should be remediless upon a reversal though innocent. And he considered the authorities and cases to [be of the] same effect as the plaintiff's counsel.

3. The ground of the plaintiff's bill grew out of matter emerging after the decree, and it is proper for relief in equity in this court by an original bill grounded upon the whole matter.

But the chief baron and the other barons [were] resolved [to] the contrary. And they went upon these grounds.

1. If anything, be it goods or profits of lands, that are answered to the king or his grantee (which is the same), there should not be restitution, neither of the things themselves (as a term) sold upon *venditioni exponas* or other goods nor of the value upon a reversal of the outlawry, because it is a thing executed and irrevocable. And this holds in all cases where the sale was made by compulsory process by an officer, and on account of that they distinguished the case of Eyre and Woodfine cited by Sawyer, because there the sale was by the treasurer and barons, which was not good but should have been by *venditioni exponas* by the proper officer, and in this case [it] had been good. And they agreed with the opinion of Periam in this case and well approved the precedent of Ellison and Van Vanghenberg in this court in 1651 cited by the defendant's counsel and the reason of it. And though in this case there was restitution, yet it was of the money only that remained in the hands of the sheriff not answered to the king or his grantee. And they fully admitted that where the sale is not good as not being made by due process and in a legal manner, as if a sheriff sold goods upon a *capias utlagatum* or similar, there should be restitution upon a reversal according to Dr. Drury's Case, 8 Rep. 143,[14] and Procter's Case, Dyer 223.[15] And [it is] the same in the sale

---

[14] *Drury's Case* (1610), 8 Coke Rep. 141, 77 E.R. 688.
[15] *Proctor's Case* (1563), 2 Dyer 222b, 73 E.R. 493.

above mentioned by the treasurer and barons, because such sales are not compulsory nor in a judicial manner: Dyer 363;[16] Hoe's Case, 5 Rep. 90. And the judgment here upon the reversal makes it plain, because it belongs to the whole that he lost *unde domino regi nondum est responsum*, and this which was paid to the grantee of the king was paid to the king himself. And all judgments by restitutions should be understood of those things that are not answered to the king, and *unde domino regi nondum est responsum* is in reversals for goods as well as for lands.

And WYNDHAM held clearly that if the debtor of an outlawed person paid the debt according to the grant of the king or by process of the law that is compulsory or gives other security for it in discharge of the first, that upon reversal of this outlawry the debtee should not be restored to it, notwithstanding the opinion of Lord Coke in Hoe's Case, 5 Rep. 90b, which was not by any means warranted by the yearbook at large in 7 Edw. IV, 2, there cited, with which the said chief baron [TURNER] and Baron LITTLETON agreed.

And the chief baron insisted upon the difference of the privy seals, because Northey's was in part[17] of his debt, which is to be preferred before the plaintiff's which did not have such a mention but was general. And he also said that he had a private report of Beverley and Cornwall's Case, cited by Sawyer out of Moore's *Reports*, by which it appeared that the presentation was by the queen *pleno jure* and not by the outlawry and Cornwall was reproved for his abuse of the court

And as for Garrett's Case, the barons who argued for the defendants received information of it from the judges of the common bench. And it was thus, Garrett obtained judgment against the lord Holland and afterwards was outlawed and the king granted this judgment to Progers of the bedchamber who gave a power of attorney[18] to acknowledge satisfaction upon it, but before satisfaction was acknowledged, the outlawry was reversed, and the court was moved that the attorney could acknowledge and enter his satisfaction, and the motion was denied by the court, but [it] was held that if [it] had been made before the reversal, it would have been binding at all times.

---

[16] *Anonymous* (1578), 3 Dyer 363a, 73 E.R. 815.
[17] payment [?].
[18] garrant al attorney *MS*.

2. It was resolved that the alteration of the names in the book of the Company before reversal and in pursuance of the decree was an alteration of the ownership of the £500 and vested it absolutely in Northey and Boothby and their title should not be impeached by the reversal, because it was tantamount to having been paid to the king and the king had given it to them. And the said £500 is not capable of other alteration of the ownership than by alteration of the names, it being the nature of all such ventures and securities for them. And inasmuch as Northey and Boothby have just debts due to them from Bateman though before judgment and though they have other security for them, yet they having done all that can be to obtain it and the court having made a decree accordingly, there should not be restitution.
3. Here is a decree in the case, which should not be set aside by this original bill, though a decree can be in any case set aside by an original bill, as was admitted in the Earl of Carlisle's Case,[19] if [there is] discovery of new papers in the case of the redemption of a mortgage, which contradicts the decree, by the earl of Clarendon, in which case the chief baron was of counsel. But here the court did not see any reason to take away the benefit to Northey and Boothby and to give it to the plaintiff, who are creditors. And there is no difference upon a forfeiture in outlawry before or after judgment. And if Pinfold should be relieved against Northey and Boothby, it would arise for all of the creditors of Bateman, because by the same reason other creditors could reverse this outlawry and thus there would not be any end. And if by the reversal the plaintiff had title in law, he could resort to his remedy there, but there is not any equity in the case for one creditor against others. And thus it lies in the power of Bateman to gratify which creditor he pleases. And upon the whole matter, the plaintiff's bill was dismissed.

And the defendants Northey and Boothby having a cross-bill heard at the same time (the intent of which was to corroborate and establish the first decree and their title), [it] was dismissed also inasmuch as there was a sufficient remedy and relief by this former decree for the defendants Northey and Boothby.

Note [that] afterwards Northey's outlawry was reversed and Pinfold obtained a grant by privy seal of the whole sum and brought his action upon the case against Northey, who received a dividend after the privy seal, for as much

---

[19] *Earl of Carlisle v. Gober* (Ch. 1660), Nelson 52, 21 E.R. 787, *sub nom. Earl of Carlisle v. Goble*, 3 Chan. Rep. 94, 21 E.R. 739, *sub nom. Earl of Carlisle v. Globe*, 2 Freeman 148, 22 E.R. 1121, also 118 Selden Soc. 736.

money as received to his use. And upon it [there was] a special verdict, Chief Justice HALE inclining towards Pinfold, upon which Northey exhibited an original bill to establish his decree and to be relieved against this action. Pinfold answered, pleaded, and demurred, showing his case and title and that he had a remedy by the law upon a good title, which equity [should] not alter or prejudice. But it was overruled upon arguing it (which seems harsh).

And afterwards *Lechmere* for Northey and myself [*Ward*] for Pinfold ended the case by compromise in obedience to the direction of the court. And Northey assigned to Pinfold £150, part of the venture, and all of the growing duty and dividends of it. And thus this case was ended.

[Orders of 31 Jan., 26 Apr., 13 June, and 23 Oct. 1672: PRO E.126/11, ff. 105, 125v, E.127/7, ff. 26v, 78v, 222.]

56
Dean of Lincoln v. De la Fountain (Ex. 1672)

In this case, a payment of a pension issuing out of a rectory was ordered pursuant to a former decree.
An alienation in prejudice of the church will not be presumed.

LI MS. Misc. 500, f. 201v [Fr.] (Ward's Reports)

The plaintiffs exhibited their bill against Sir Erasmus De la Fountain (now dead), father of the defendant, which being revived against the defendant, his heir, the case upon the proofs and hearing appeared to be thus. For many years before the dissolution of the monasteries in the time of King Henry VIII, a pension of 13s. 4d. *per annum* was issuing out of the rectory of Kirkby Bellars in the county of Leicester and continually paid to the plaintiff's predecessors for the time being as appeared by the books of their receivers and ministers of this time. And after the dissolution, *viz.* 34th Hen. VIII [1542], there was a decree of the court of augmentations that this pension in particular (among divers others there mentioned) was droiturally due and payable out of this rectory to the plaintiffs' predecessors and that for the future it should be duly paid to them and their successors by the king (who at this time had this rectory in his hands) and the owners for the time being. And this decree was exemplified under the exchequer seal, after which decree, this rectory (being leased for years) was sold to one under whom the defendant claimed. And a reprise of this pension was allowed in the sale of it. But it did not appear by any book or proof that this pension was ever paid to the plaintiffs' predecessors from this time of sale until this day. But the father of the defendant, who purchased it in 1625, swore in his answer that he never had paid it nor known or heard anything about it until the plaintiffs' demand of it in 1664. (But a pay book in the handwriting of several persons relating to the cathedral was produced in which mention was made of this pension in 1641 and that the receiver charged himself with it for this year, but little or no credit was given to this book.)

And it was strongly urged by *North*, king's solicitor, *Mountagu*, attorney for the queen, and *Dolben* for the defendant that the defendant or this rectory of Kirkby Bellars should not be charged with this pension, because there did not appear to be any seisin within sixty years and thus [it was] barred by the express words of the Statute of Limitations, 32 Hen. VIII, c. 2.[1] And this statute is a good bar in equity as well as at [common] law. And [it] can be inferred that before the restraining statutes in the time of Queen Elizabeth that the plaintiffs' predecessors had granted or released this pension to the owner of the rectory. And non payment for such a long time is strong evidence against the plaintiffs.

And of such opinion was Baron TURNOR. And on account of that [it was] moved to refer it to a trial at law.

But Chief Baron TURNOR, Baron LITTLETON, and Baron WYNDHAM were clear of the opinion for the plaintiffs and decreed the arrears of this pension from the time of the restoration of the king, which was 1660, to be paid by the defendant to the plaintiffs and denied a trial at law in the case. And their principal reasons were:

1. That by the decree in 34 Hen. VIII [1542] the right of the pension sufficiently appeared, and it is proper for this court to compel execution of their own decrees (because the court of augmentations was annexed to this court), and if this pension was decreed to be paid [while] in the hands of the king, *a fortiori* in the case of a subject who claims under him.
2. Inasmuch as there was a reprise in the purchase of the rectory.
3. The Statute of Limitations does not extend in this case to an English bill as it is not one of the actions enumerated there and the decree here is only an execution of the first decree.
4. An alienation in prejudice of the church will not be presumed.
5. By the malignity of the former times, all the books and evidences of the plaintiffs had perished and were gone, and if there should not be a remedy here, it would be harsh.

And upon all of the matter, a decree was [ordered] for the plaintiffs.

Ellys, king's serjeant, Bigland, Wingfield, and Ward [were] of counsel with the plaintiffs.

[Order of 20 June 1672: PRO E.126/11, f. 132.]

---

[1] Stat. 32 Hen. VIII, c. 2, ss. 1, 6 (*SR*, III, 747).

57
Banister v. Brooke (Ex. 1672)

Money received in redemption of a mortgage that was in default passes upon the death of the mortgagee as real property does.

LI MS. Misc. 500, f. 206, pl. 2 [Fr.] (Ward's Reports)

Sherborne, [who was] seised in fee of lands, borrowed from the plaintiff's ancestor £1000 in 1637. And for security for repayment with interest in five years, he mortgaged those lands to certain persons in fee in trust for the said ancestor and his heirs with the proviso [for it] to be void if the said principal and interest were paid at the day to the said ancestor, his executors, administrators, or assigns. And this not being paid accordingly, an entry was made. And afterwards the surviving trustee with the said ancestor for the provision of the ancestor's wife conveyed and assured the said lands to other persons and their heirs in trust for the said ancestor and Joan his wife for their lives to have the benefit of them and afterwards for the benefit of such persons that the said ancestor by his deed or will in writing should appoint and in default of it for the next heirs of the ancestor. The ancestor died having made a nuncupative will by which he gave everything to his wife. And the wife proved the will and took administration *cum testamento annexo*. And afterwards by compulsion of the powers in 1647, she was compelled with the trustees to take £1300 for interest and principal (there being more due) and to convey the land, the plaintiff being heir to the mortgagee and under age. And afterwards Joan the wife died having made the defendant executor with sufficient assets to him for payment of debts and legacies. And when the plaintiff became of full age, he exhibited his bill in this court against the defendant to compel him to pay the said £1300 to the plaintiff.

And upon the hearing of the cause, it was decreed by the whole court that the defendant should pay to the plaintiff two parts of the £1300 and should retain the third part to himself, this being the proportionable division according to the interests and estates limited by the plaintiff's ancestor in trust as above, and the court was clear that, in this case, the mortgage money appertained to the heir, the mortgage being broken and the mortgagee leaving assets for payment of debts and legacies, but the plaintiff's ancestor having limited the benefit of the mortgaged lands to Joan for her life, the remainder to his next heir, the executor of Joan should have the third part and the heir two parts.

[Order of 3 Dec. 1672: PRO E.126/11, f. 141.]

58
Paul v. Reeves (Ex. 1673)

Exemption from prisage duties on wines in London apply to residents and inhabitants not to citizens and freemen nor to resident servants of citizens.

LI MS. Misc. 500, f. 220, pl. 1 [Fr.] (Ward's Reports)

The plaintiff being grantee of the prisage [for] wines in London etc. exhibited his bill to discover certain wines imported by the defendants into the port of London and to be relieved for the duty of prisage.

The defendants answered and also pleaded the Charter of Edward III by which the citizens and freemen of London are exempt from prisage for their wines. And the defendants averred themselves to be citizens and freemen and that the defendant Reeves was at the time of the importation sheriff of the county of Hertford and resident in his bailiwick but had servants and family resident in Spitalfields near London. And Stephens and Jeffreys endeavored to maintain the plea inasmuch as the defendants are, within the words of the charter, to be exempt.

But it was ruled by the court upon hearing the attorney general, *Sir Peter Ball*, and *Lechmere* for the plaintiff that the plea is not good it not being averred that the defendants at the time of the importation were residents and inhabitants and paid scott and lott in London according to the cases in Moore 833;[1] *Rotuli Parliamentorum*, 9 Hen. IV, m. 73;[2] 3 Bulstrode 1 and 26.[3] And this [was] notwithstanding that this distinction can more aptly come from the side of the king by replication the defendants having made their case within the words of the charter. Still the plea was overruled and the defendants ordered to answer.

And afterwards the cause came to a hearing at Serjeants' Inn after Trinity [term] 1674, where Ward of counsel with the defendants insisted on the discharge. But it was overruled on the differences aforesaid. And the plaintiff had a decree for the value of the wines imported that were due for prisage. See Calthrop's *Reports of Customs of London* in the case of prisage there.[4]

[Order of 26 June 1674: PRO E.126/12, f. 26.]

---

[1] *Walter v. Hanger* (1602), Moore K.B. 832, 72 E.R. 935.
[2] I.e. 11 Hen. IV; *Rotuli Parliamentorum*, III (1832), p. 646.
[3] *Rex and Waller v. Hanger* (1615), 3 Bulstrode 1, 81 E.R. 1.
[4] *Waller v. Hanger* (1615), Calthrop's Reports, 80 E.R. 656.

59
Elliot v. Blucke (Ex. 1673)

The issue in this case was whether a six clerk in the chancery has the privilege to be sued only in chancery.

LI MS. Misc. 555, f. 3, pl. 1 [Fr.] (Ward's Reports)

The plaintiff by an English bill sued the defendant and two others, his tenants, as occupiers of land, and [. . .] of a *modus* [?] for tithes. The defendant being a six clerk in chancery pleaded his privilege in chancery as a six clerk.

[These] precedents for decrees for tithes in the chancery [were cited] for the defendant: Moore and Bond, 20 November 38 Eliz. [1595]; Windham and Norris 17 Eliz. [1575] in chancery; 30 January 8 Jac. [1611], Hope and Holditch,[1] was for a pension and tithes, and the demurrer [was] overruled, but it was not to the purpose [. . .].

[These precedents were cited] for the plaintiff: Cartwright and Massam [was] in point, and a writ of privilege [was] annexed and disallowed, and [there was a] decree upon it; Baker and Lenthall[2] [was] also in point; in which cases upon debate, the defendant's privilege [was] overruled. And also there were here several defendants. The court of chancery [has] no jurisdiction of tithes. And no writ of privilege [was] annexed and thus bad.

See Trinity [term] 12 Car. I [1636] where a debtor to the king had [his] privilege in an English bill in the exchequer against an examiner in chancery: R. Crompton, *Jurisdiction [des Courts]*, 112.

[Orders of 26 Apr. and 21 June 1675: PRO E.126/12, ff. 116, 177v.]

60
Stephens v. Athy (Ex. 1673)

In this case, there was no custom requiring certain persons to grind their grain at a certain mill.

LI MS. Misc. 555, f. 6 [Fr.] (Ward's Reports)

The plaintiff exhibited a bill to compel the defendants, some of whom were inhabitants of South Molton in the county of Devon, to grind their grain spent in their [own] houses at Molemills in the said parish, which were formerly mills of the crown granted out in fee farm to Sir Lewis Pollard, suggesting a custom for

---

[1] *Hopes v. Holditche* (1611), PRO C.33/119, f. 473.
[2] *Baker v. Lenthall* (1658), Hardres 117, 145 E.R. 409.

such grinding and also a decree made 28 January 1635[/36] upon a bill exhibited by Sir Lewis Pollard against some foreign mills and loaders who fetched the corn of the inhabitants and ground it. And though there was a second decree, yet as alleged it had not been obeyed for divers years.

The court upon the hearing put it to a trial at law upon the custom, which went for the defendants.

I was for the defendants.

[Order of 24 Nov. 1673: PRO E.126/11, f. 290.]

61
Lady Wentworth v. Thorowgood (Ex. 1674)

In this case, a mortgagor in default was allowed to redeem although several deadlines had expired.

LI MS. Misc. 555, f. 17 [Fr.] (Ward's Reports)

The 28th of November 1635 Sir John Thorowgood lent to the earl of Cleveland £3000 and took a mortgage of the Manor of Harlington in the County of Bedford[1] with the condition to be void upon the payment of the principal and interest within a short time, which not being paid, Sir John exhibited a bill in chancery to conclude the plaintiff of the equity of redemption, which was decreed in December 1639 to be absolute if the earl did not pay the principal and interest which was computed for divers days to come, the last of which was in 1642 and some in 1641, which was the time of the peace and [. . .] absolute which was not paid accordingly. But the troubles came before the said 1642 and the earl went with the king and was sequestered and disabled by his loyalty to pay the money. At the return of the king in 1660, there was a private act[2] which recited the sufferings and debts of the earl and his mortgages and declared and enacted that all of the mortgages of the earl (of which this in question was one) not excepted in the Act 'are and ought to be still redeemed and redeemable by the said earl and his son and their heirs as forfeited mortgages redeemable in [the] course of equity. And for the effecting thereof, the barons of the exchequer during seven years are empowered in a summary way for the uses in the Act to hear and determine all things in relation to the redemption of the mortgages according to the provisoes and intent of the Act, provided that nothing in the Act extend to avoid any estate or estates made absolute by any decree in any court of equity before the 25th of March 1641'. By another act[3] made [in] 18 Car. II [1666],

---

[1] V.C.H., *Bedfordshire*, III (1912), p. 380.
[2] *SR*, V, 303, 320.
[3] *SR*, V, 622.

reciting that by the multiplicity of persons claiming under the original mortgages and the intricacy of the accounts, the time allowed for the first Act was almost elapsed and the benefit intended for the earl like to be lost, it was enacted that the time allowed by the first Act and the powers and authorities should be enlarged until 8 May 1670.

After that, the plaintiff[4] exhibited a bill for redemption in the usual course, to which the defendants pleaded all the matter [above], which was overruled as a plea, but the equity was reserved. And the sole question was whether the mortgage in question was redeemable in the usual manner as in courts of equity.

And afterwards it was resolved by the court here that it was, and it was decreed accordingly in which interest was deducted for the mesne profits received after the entry and no interest was allowed for the growing interest of the principal sum lent, which seemed harsh, but [it was] said to be made [by] consent. Query.

[Order of 5 Feb. 1673: PRO E.126/11, f. 301.]

62

Attorney General ex rel. Thistlethwaite v. Wilson (Ex. 1675)

A bill for discovery and payment of duties is good where the penalties are waived.

LI MS. Misc. 555, f. 58 [Fr.] (Ward's Reports)

[There was an] English bill for discovery and payment of duties of excise, waiving the penalties and claiming the duty. The defendants pleaded that, by the statutes of the excise,[1] the right[2] of excise was annexed to the commissioners only. And as for the discovery of the not making of entries and non payment of the duty, the defendants demurred and for cause showed that there are penalties annexed for the not making of entries, and on account of that they should not be obliged to make discovery which would expose them to the penalty.

As for the plea, it seems that it is not exclusive of this court.

As to the demurrer, *Lechmere* cited Wadlowe's Case,[3] Michaelmas [term] 1672, and Mico's Case,[4] where the demurrers in those cases were allowed in cases of the king. And there was a waiver of penalties in Mico's Case. And the

---

[4] Henrietta, lady Wentworth, daughter and heir of lord Wentworth, son and heir of the earl of Cleveland.

---

[1] Stat. 15 Car. II, c. 11, s. 2 (*SR*, V, 489); note also Stat. 16 & 17 Car. II, c. 4 (*SR*, V, 554).
[2] Jur *MS*.
[3] *Wadlowe's Case* (1672), PRO E.126/11, f. 144.
[4] *Attorney General v. Mico* (1658), Hardres 137, 145 E.R. 419.

waiver of the penalty by the attorney general was not conclusive to the king or the informer.

The attorney general [*Jones*] and *Sawyer* [argued] for the king [that] only the duty [was] demanded. Where the act placed [?] a duty and had a small penalty for payment, the king is not deprived of his remedy for the duty; [it is] otherwise where the offense is purely penal. But the penalty here is *nomine pene*, and the king is not deprived of discovery by reason of [being] *nomine pene*. Where the act gives [. . .] it is a penalty, [. . .] and remedy purely penal, there the demurrer [is] good; [it is] otherwise where [there is a] duty. [In the] case of tithes, [there are] treble damages, yet [there is] discovery, and an injunction [will be] awarded if [?] proceeding to the king. £12 [is due] by the intent [?] of the Act, yet [there should be a] discovery; and the waiver of the penalty [is] considerable.

Lechmere [argued] for the defendant [that the] penalty [is] given to the informer [. . .] and the king by three parts.

The court [ruled] the demurrer [to be] good as to the penalties for things for which no duty [is] given, and [there is] no duty for mingling, and it seems where [there is] no duty but a penalty, it is harsh.

Baron TURNOR [said that it was] scandalous for merchants etc. not to make entries.

Precedents were to be searched for by the defendants and notes given to the attorney general. Afterwards, though no precedents of such bills were produced, the demurrer was overruled as to the things for which [there was a] duty, and the plea [. . .] as to the jurisdiction.

[This case is cited in Attorney General v. Smith (Ex. 1705), below, No. 399.]

63
Attorney General ex rel. Italian Merchants v. Blake (Ex. 1675)

A relator action lies where the king's honor is involved, even though his financial interest is not.

LI MS. Misc. 500, f. 259 [Fr.] (Ward's Reports)

The defendants in the former times of the usurpation had been commissioners for prizes, and the relators had certain goods taken as prizes in those times that should not have been but were condemned by sentence in the admiralty as prize, against which sentence the relators appealed and obtained sentence for restitution. After the restoration of the king in 1660, there was an Act made for Confirmation of Judicial Proceedings.[1] And in the Act of Oblivion in the same

---

[1] Stat. 12 Car. II, c. 12 (*SR*, V, 234–236).

Act, prize goods not accounted and answered were excepted,[2] and afterwards in the same Act, they were vested in the king. The defendants obtained a general pardon [with the] proviso that they should save the king harmless against the relators. And now the relators prosecute an English information in the name of the attorney general to compel the defendants to account and answer for the prize goods to the benefit of the king and the relators.

The defendants demurred to this bill inasmuch as the king is not concerned in interest and, if the relators have a cause of suit, they should sue in their own names.

But the demurrer was overruled inasmuch as the king is concerned in honor though not in interest. And it is the common practice that such bills are exhibited by the attorney general in the name of the king and prosecuted as *pater patriae* and for the public good. And the public justice of the nation and the proviso in the pardon are good causes for this bill. And the case of Dr. Gurdon[3] touching the mint or ordnance was remembered to be in this court five or six years past to the same purpose and on the same ground.

64
Widdrington v. Barker (Ex. 1675)

Tithes of coleseed are payable to the parson and not to the vicar.

I
LI MS. Misc. 555, ff. 59, 64 [Fr.] (Ward's Reports)

The plaintiff [was the] parson of Terrington[1] in Norfolk in the right of the [Lady] Margaret Professor[ship of] Divinity in Cambridge.[2] The defendants [were the] vicar and inhabitants. [The] bill [was] for tithes of coleseed, and the question [was] between the parson and vicar.

The attorney general [*Jones*], for the plaintiff, cited and relied upon Udall and Tindall, Cro. Car. 28 and Hutton,[3] 2 Rolle's [Abridgment] 334, 335,[4] for woad; the reason of it [was] that the vicar should have all tithes except corn and

---

[2] Stat. 12 Car. II, c. 11, s. 10 (*SR*, V, 228–229).
[3] *Attorney General v. Guerdian* (1664), PRO E.126/9, ff. 1v, 4v, 44v (re the mint).

[1] Tyringham *MS*.
[2] Ralph Widdrington held this professorship from 1672 until his death in 1688: J. Peile, *Biographical Register of Christ's College*, I (1910), pp. 421–422.
[3] *Udall v. Tindall* (1626), Cro. Car. 28, 79 E.R. 629, Hutton 77, 123 E.R. 1112, also 1 Eagle & Younge 339.
[4] See generally 2 Rolle, Abr., *Parson, Patron*, pp. 334–335.

hay. But here [there was] no such endowment. And in this case, first coleseed is not a small tithe, secondly if it is in its nature small, yet by the greatness of the quantity, it is established with the parson as a large tithe and [stays] not with the vicar as small. And the constant payment of tithes [at] all times from the first sowing of coleseed was to the parson, and it [was paid] for forty years. And common right [is] with the parson.

Lechmere [argued] for the defendant. Here the rectory and parson [are] presentative, and the vicar also [was] endowed, but the endowment is lost. The parson [holds] exclusive of all tithes except corn and hay; woad, hops, and saffron [are] all small tithes; if *inter majores proventus ecclesie*,[5] [they are] large but not small. This distinction [was] disclaimed, and [it was argued that] the kind and nature and not the quantity give right to the parson or [to the] vicar. Feake and Beddingfield, Cro. Eliz.,[6] [was an] instance in a case of an arable parish converted into in pasture, the parson lost the tithes of corn and hay and the vicar gained the tithes of pasturage.

The value of the coleseed in question [was] not greater than £6 *per annum*.

The inheritance should not jump from the parson to the vicar or from the vicar to the parson by reason of the quantity of the harvest [?].

Rapeseed for thirty years [was] paid to the vicar and [there was] no coleseed, but [. . .] thirty years ago coleseed [was] reputed for thirty years [to be] small tithes and for ten years [was] paid to the vicar.

For the plaintiff, [it was argued that] the land sown with coleseed was formerly [?] sown with corn, which paid tithes to the parson [for] thirty-nine acres sown. [For] forty years, coleseed [was] sown and tithes of it [were] constantly paid to the parson until twelve years ago.

For the defendant, [it was shown that there was] no vicar from 1638 until 1660; this interval responds to the payment to the parson.

Upon the question whether coleseed, being sown in open fields, should be large or small tithes and belong to the rector or the vicar [and] whether the nature or quantity distinguished it as large or small tithes, the cases of Udall and Tyndall, Cro. Car. and Hutton, and Feake and Beddingfield, Cro. Eliz., [were cited].

[Baron] THURLAND [said that the] vicar derived out of the parsonage and the endowment did not extend to coleseed, no such tithes being *in esse* at the time of the endowment. 1 Rolle's [Abridgment] 643 expounds small tithes, Reynolds and Green.[7]

---

[5] among the greater crops of the church.

[6] *Beddingfield v. Feake* (1596), Cro. Eliz. 467, 78 E.R. 719; also Moore K.B. 909, 72 E.R. 989, 1 Eagle & Younge 118, 1 Gwillim 166, Owen 74, 74 E.R. 911.

[7] *Reynolds v. Green* (1612), 1 Rolle, Abr., *Dismes*, pl. U, 2, p. 643, also 2 Bulstrode 27, 80 E.R. 931, 1 Eagle & Younge 213, 4 Gwillim 1573.

The tithes of coleseed [were] £5; the parsonage [was] greater than 200s. *per annum*.

No endowment of the vicarage [was] produced, but proof of small tithes [was] general [?] but not this in general, and the usage of payment to the parson [was] considerable.

The decree for the parson was referred to the auditor, and afterwards [on] 17 June 1675, the auditors report was confirmed.

II
GI MS. 35, p. 773, pl. 3 [Eng.]

Doctor Witherington, parson, [sued] Henson, vicar of Terrington in Marshland in Norfolk; the parsonage is annexed to the [Lady] Margaret Professor's place in Cambridge. Dr. Witherington exhibited his bill for tithe [of] coleseed.

The proof was that the parson had enjoyed it for forty years till interrupted by the vicar for eight or nine years.

Note [that] it is a seed brought from the Netherlands into England and there sown within one hundred years and not sown in this town for so long time.

[It was ruled] by the court, *viz*. Chief Baron TURNER, Baron TURNER, Baron LITTLETON, and [Baron] THURLAND, that all predial tithes may be *majores* or *minores*, if within gardens or small places or if in fields and great profit arising, and so turnips sown in great fields are great tithes, and so hops and so wool and lamb, and so it may be one one year, otherwise another year. Rolle 643 of woad.

And these differences were taken by the chief baron:

1. Where the parson is stinted by his reservation on the endowment, all cole [is] a small tithe or belongs to the vicar, that reservation and endowment appearing.
2. Where the vicar has endowment of small tithes generally and thereby stinted, he has only small [tithes] in value, as [in] gardens and small places etc.
3. Where there is no endowment but at large great or small [tithes], in construction of law, there usage shall regulate, and here it being in proof forty years for the parson and but eight or nine since for the vicar, the usage shall carry it to the parson as great [tithes] from the great quantity and so *pro hic et nunc*, one or other.

And coleseed was not sown at [the time of] the endowment and is sown after the plow like corn, and perhaps as to [the] impropriator, a difference may be, but here both parson and vicar have *curam animarum*. For the argument of inconvenience, from compact, or will of the parishioner to sow or not, it is answered as to the last as equal, not as to the former, and where both have cure of souls, the parson is preferred though not enjoined residence. See Shepherd [Abr.], title *Agreement*.

[The order of 11 Feb. 1675, PRO E.126/12, f. 98v, is printed at 1 Wood 145, 1 Eagle & Younge 504. See also the order of 29 Apr. 1675: PRO E.126/12, f. 117.]

65
Mayor of London v. Thody (Ex. 1675)

A grant of bona et catalla felonum *does not pass a trust.*

LI MS. Misc. 555, f. 60, pl. 2 [Fr.] (Ward's Reports)

The plaintiffs having *bona et catalla felonum* granted by charter exhibited their English bill to discover a trust for a felon of a bond for £800 due to the felon but in another's name. And upon the hearing, it was referred to a trial whether [there was] a trust or not. And *Lechmere* insisted that a grant of *bona et catalla felonum* does not pass a trust. But query. And afterwards the plaintiff's bill was dismissed.

[Orders of 25 Feb. and 7 Dec. 1675: PRO E.126/12, ff. 99, 197v.]

66
Robinson v. Player (Ex. 1675)

Where a will directs the redemption of a mortgage secured by land owned by another, this is a devise by implication.

LI MS. Misc. 555, f. 64 [Fr.] (Ward's Reports)

Sir Martin Noel and his wife [were] possessed of a term for years. Sir Martin mortgaged it for £300 and interest; the mortgage was broken. Sir Martin made his will reciting the lease and the mortgage [and] directed the payment of the £300 and interest out of his general estate and that his wife should not be charged with it.

The question [was] whether this was a devise by implication to the wife, it being found by a verdict that the plaintiff, who was executor to Sir Martin, had assented and agreed to it.

And the plaintiff exhibited his bill to be relieved against a recognizance entered [into] for [. . .] inventory of the personal estate of Lady Noel, to whom the plaintiff was executor also.

It seemed to the court that it was a devise to the wife by implication upon the reason of devises by implication, but it seemed harsh that the plaintiff who was executor to both and one survived [. . .] two days should be liable to a *devastavit* by this assent, and [*blank*].

But the estate was sold for £1100 as the estate of the lady, the plaintiff [...] himself only as executor of the lady. And afterwards [it was] adjudged a *devastavit* by the assent to the legacy, and the cause ended by agreement, but Robinson paid £1000.

[Orders of 29 June and 7 Dec. 1674 and 3 and 10 May and 7 Dec. 1675: PRO E.126/12, ff. 21 bis, 58, 116, 118v, 196v.]

67
Colwall v. Vyner (Ex. 1675)

The issue in this case was when an escheator can be sued in the court of exchequer as an accountant of the crown.

I
LI MS. Misc. 555, f. 65 [Fr.] (Ward's Reports)

The plaintiff filed a bill against the defendant as accountant, being an escheator *super visum compoti*, and pressed for a plea or judgment. *Sawyer* moved against it, [the defendant] not being an accountant until his acc[ount] expires, which is not [the case] here, nor [there being] any view of his account, nor there being anything[1] for which he was accountable, nor having any deputy in court, as a sheriff has, nor [having] given any security for accounting, as a sheriff does.

Williams, on behalf of the plaintiff, produced these precedents out of the office of pleas.

Trinity [term], 20 Edw. IV [1480], rotulo 3: *Agnes Baynar queritur versus Adelinum Hungerford escaetorem domini regis comitatu Southampton et Wiltshire present hic in curia super visum compoti sui de exitibus et proficiis officii sui, pro cus. et assault, exi*[...] *venire facias* was awarded.

Easter [term], 7 Jac. I [1609], rotulo 75, *Edwardus Farmeden queritur versus Henricum R[...]ve militem nuper major et escaetorem Londoniae present hic in curia super compositum suum ratione officii sui escaetoris ad hoc scaccarium reddendum.*

See the breviate among the special breviates. And afterwards the plaintiff proceeded upon it in his suit.

II
LI MS. Misc. 496, p. 325, pl. 1 [Fr.]

It was debated in the exchequer whether a bill could be filed there against the lord mayor of London before his year expires. At first the court made a distinction between the mayor and the sheriffs. A sheriff is an accountant before his

---

[1] nec ou fuit esteant ascun *MS*.

year expires because each Easter term when he makes the proffers, he enters upon his accounts and from this time, being an accountant to the king, has the privilege of the exchequer, but the mayor of London, being escheator of the city and thus accountable to the king, is not upon his account until after his year expires, because he is sworn to account at that time and not before.

Williams [argued] at the bar: The lord mayor makes his proffers also each Easter but this will not make him an accountant if he does not at that time enter upon his account.

But I relied upon this that he at that time makes an attorney in this court then to appear for him, and I am informed by the clerks that, after he has made his proffers, he can plead the privilege of the exchequer in any other court.

It was doubted then by the court whether the attorney made by the mayor was not for the corporation only. But upon examination, it appeared that the same person who is attorney for the city of London in each Easter term when the mayor makes his proffers is a personal attorney, the attorney for the lord mayor himself. The clerks reminded the court of the Statute 1 Ric. III, c. 14,[2] which proved the course of the exchequer in such cases at common law. And it was said by them that after an escheator has made an attorney, that the attorney himself would have the privilege of the exchequer for his own debt.

It is to be remembered that upon the debate of the return of Sir Robert, *quod vide supra* 317,[3] Chief Justice Hale said that the lord mayor was always present in the exchequer and a bill could be filed against him.

68

Duke of Monmouth v. Countess of Northumberland (Ex. 1675)

The issue in this case was when counsel are required to reveal information communicated by their clients and when not.

LI MS. Misc. 496, p. 325, pl. 2 [Fr.]

Upon a motion made in this cause in the exchequer, it was debated when[1] counsel are obliged to conceal and when the court will oblige them to discover the causes of their clients. Chief Baron TURNER remembered a case in the time of Sir Orlando Bridgman, lord keeper of the great seal, where a term for years was devised to a married woman if she so long live. The words 'if she so long

---

[2] Stat. 1 Ric. III, c. 14 (*SR*, II, 497–498).
[3] *Neighbour v. Adams* (K.B. 1675), LI MS. Misc. 496, p. 317, pl. 4.

[1] coment *MS*.

live' were erased. The question was whether the devise was absolute or determinable upon her life. The counsel of the husband of the devisee who had made this erasure were required to depose whether they had not seen the will well written without any erasure. The lord keeper took the advice of all of the judges touching it, and after several arguments before them, it was agreed that they should be forced to discover whether they had seen it or not. This can appear to be a hard case, because it was the very[2] secret of the cause, and it has been commonly held that a counsellor should not be compelled to disclose the secrets of the cause of his client. But to some questions relating to the cause of his client in general, he will be forced to give an answer, as whether he had seen such a deed or whether it was not of such a date and such like. But the case of the will was an odious cause. If a title appears upon the record in this court for the king, we will force anyone who is supposed to have any deeds in his custody which in any way concern the title of the king to produce them. But if a subject controvert the title of the king, neither he nor his counsel will be forced to show any deeds or to discover their cause any more than in the case of a common person.

[Other copies of this report: IT MS. Misc. 49, p. 918.]

69
Winford v. James (Ex. 1675)

In this case, a contract to pay rents to the lord of the manor was specifically enforced.

LI MS. Misc. 555, f. 71 [Fr.] (Ward's Reports)

The plaintiff, lord of the manor of Astly in the County of Worcester,[1] exhibited a bill against the tenants for counterparts of grants and to have rents reserved on grants in tail from the copyholders. The case [was that] Sir Robert Sadler, seised in fee of the manor, enfeoffed a copyholder in tail male, reserving a rent with [right of] distress, and afterwards the grantees [. . .] agreed the rent remain. The question [was] what remedy [was there]. Pemberton [said that it was] distress, being a rent service [. . .] by the clause of distress.

[In the case in] 3 Leonard 261,[2] the tenant in tail with rent reserved suffered a recovery, [and] the rent was gone forever according to some, and according to others it was converted into a rent seck.

---

[2] meer *MS*.

---

[1] V.C.H., *Worcestershire*, IV (1924), pp. 232–233.
[2] Case 349 (1590), 3 Leonard 261, 74 E.R. 672.

The question [was] whether those rents passed to the plaintiff by the grant of the manor and rents.

The grantee in tail levied a fine which discontinued the [en]tail and severed it from the reversion, and on account of that [there is a] right in equity though there can be a remedy upon the clause of distress.

The court [said that the] act of the party does not prejudice the lord, and here there is an agreement of the party upon which the decree [is] good so to compel all other things found the agreement and covenant in specie and held also to suit of court, which was covenanted to be also performed, which *Pemberton* denied, there not being any tenure between the parties. And a court of equity cannot create or continue a tenure that is gone and destroyed in law, and the lord and the tenant are relatives and as it comes no duty to perform there, and further he said that [there was] no suit of court except to be sworn on juries which cannot be after a tenure [is] destroyed. And the [. . .] is idle here to restrain parties to do an illegal thing.

If a lord enfranchise a copyholder, he does not become a freeholder of the manor, but he holds outside[3] and does not have any tenure of the manor. The chief baron [TURNOR] thought not; *Pemberton* thought so and was of the opinion [?] he belongs to the manor and the tenants [are] subject to the tenures in capite when they were.

The chief baron put the case of the tenants of Clitheroe in Lancashire when the king sold it in fee, the tenants covenanted to grind corn at the mills of the king [that were] not sold, and it was held good, [and] so here.

[There was a] decree for the plaintiff, and a commission was awarded.

[Order of 21 June 1675: PRO E.126/12, f. 156v.]

70

Scudamore v. Win (Ex. 1675)

The issue in this case was whether tithes in London can be sued in the court of exchequer.

MT MS. 'Maynard's Reports t. Car. I & II, G.4', f. 198 [Eng.]

Scudamore, parson of St. Dunstan's in the West, London, sues the defendant Win and others for tithes according to the rates in the Statute [of] Hen. VIII[1] in the exchequer by English bill. The question was might [it] be here or must of necessity [it] be before the mayor etc., for it is a new duty appointed by

---

[3] ouster *MS*.

---

[1] Stat. 37 Hen. VIII, c. 12 (*SR*, III, 998–1000).

the Statute and was not due before and therefore the remedy appointed by the Statute must be pursued, especially because the Statute gives an appeal from the mayor which will be lost if the suit should lie in the exchequer. To the contrary a precedent of a decree in King James's time was shown and the plaintiff here sues as debtor to the king so as the privilege is the king's and in right of the king he may sue in any court, and if the king had the parsonage he might sue here for the tithes, and the Statute is not in the negative, and not nowhere else. D. R. 51. At last the court directed that precedents be shown, and [they] adjourned.

[Order of 10 June 1675: PRO E.126/12, f. 173v.]

[Note the same or related case of Scudamore v. Lambert (Ex. 1676), below No. 71.]

71
Scudamore v. Lambert (Ex. 1676)

Tithes for rent in London can be sued for in the court of exchequer.

LI MS. Misc. 555, f. 105 [Fr.] (Ward's Reports)

The plaintiff exhibited a bill for tithes of houses in Fleet Street according to the decree of 37 Hen. VIII for 2s. 9d. in the pound.[1] The cause [was] at issue, and the court took exception to the jurisdiction, whether the court should hold the plea of it and [the parties should] not resort to the remedy before the mayor etc. according to the statute for the jurisdiction: Jual and Warren, Pas. 16 Jac. [1618], f. 408, in the king's remembrancer's memoranda roll, a bill for 2s. 9d. The plea to the jurisdiction was overruled, and it was decreed for 2s. 9d.

[Orders of 7 Dec. 1675 and 27 Nov. 1676: PRO E.126/12, ff. 203, 327v.]

[Scudamore v. Win (Ex. 1675), above No. 70, is a related or the same case.]

72
Umfrevile v. Raymond (Ex. 1676)

Notice to take depositions cannot be given before issue is joined.

LI MS. Misc. 555, f. 79 [Fr.] (Ward's Reports)

The plaintiff gave notice before replication of certain witnesses to be examined. Afterwards the replication was filed and the witnesses [were] examined without [any] other notice. And [the depositions] were suppressed because the

---

[1] Stat. 37 Hen. VIII, c. 12 (*SR*, III, 998–1000).

notice was not good being before issue was joined nor were they cross-examined. And this [was done] upon the opinion of all of the clerks.

I [was] of counsel with the defendant.

[Orders of 10 Feb. and 18 Apr. 1676: PRO E.126/12, ff. 229, 280v.]

73
Fountain v. Guavas (Ex. 1676)

In this case, the defendant pleaded a pending suit by the plaintiff's predecessor in interest for the same matter as a bar to the present suit.

LI MS. Misc. 555, f. 97 [Fr.] (Ward's Reports)

The plaintiff exhibited a bill against the defendant to have discovery of divers things, and particularly touching divers sums of money in a bill and schedule mentioned, as appertaining to him and to be relieved.

The defendant pleaded that a bill in Trinity term 1673 was exhibited in this court in the name of Sir Thomas Chichele (the daughter of whom the plaintiff married) during a suit between one Coke and others, plaintiffs, plaintiff here and others, defendants, for relief touching the money in question and of which suit Sir Thomas Chichele had notice showing that the plaintiff upon his marriage with the daughter of Sir Thomas Chichele had made some contract or conveyance to or with Sir Thomas Chichele for the same moneys in question, as a result of[1] which bill of Sir Thomas Chichele, discovery and relief was prayed for the same moneys to be applied to the marriage agreement and for the same things that the plaintiff's bill here contained, to which bill the defendant here pleaded and demurred inasmuch as a transaction of such nature was against the laws provided against maintenance and pretended titles.[2] This plea and demurrer was overruled. And afterwards exceptions were taken to the answer, and the answer was adjudged good in several parts, and as to others the defendant here, and there, gave a further answer, which was adjudged good. And he averred that Sir Thomas Chichele's bill, though countenanced by him, was exhibited and prosecuted by the plaintiff here or for him or on his behalf and at his charge and for the same end for which the plaintiff's bill here is and managed by the same counselor's clerk and solicitors, whence, inasmuch as this bill of Sir Thomas Chichele was pending and [was] to the same effect as the present bill and inasmuch as proceedings of this nature were of ill consequence and tended to double prosecution

---

[1] per *MS*.
[2] Stat. 32 Hen. VIII, c. 9 (*SR*, III, 753–754).

and vexation for the same things, which is against the rules of equity, the defendant pleaded the pendency of Sir Thomas Chichele's bill and the proceedings in it in bar of the present plaintiffs.

[Related cases: Guavas v. Fountain (1687), 2 Freeman 99, 22 E.R. 1083, 2 Eq. Cas. Abr. 281, 710, 22 E.R. 237, 597, and below, No. 233; Cook v. Fountain (Ch. 1672–1676), 3 Swanston 585, 36 E.R. 984, Cases 273, 500, Nottingham's Reports (73 Selden Soc. 185, 362); Gwevers v. Earl of Danby (1688), 3 Chan. Rep. 216, 21 E.R. 771.]

74
Attorney General ex rel. Waller v. Mayor of Bristol (Ex. 1676)

Prisage is due when bulk is broken.

LI MS. Misc. 555, f. 105 [Fr.] (Ward's Reports)

The bill was for prisage of wines imported into Bristol in Whitsun week, Sir William Waller being farmer of the prisage there. The defendants admitted that the wines in question were imported in Whitsun Week but did not mention that bulk was broken within this week. And the truth was that bulk was not broken in this week, before which prisage is not due. The defendants insisted on a grant made by the earl of Gloucester in the time of Henry II that granted to the Church of St. James in Bristol the Whitsun Week Fair that he held at Bristol and the prisage of wines, which grant was afterwards confirmed by divers grants of divers succeeding kings of England. After that the Priory of St. James came to the crown by the dissolution of the monasteries etc. in the time of Henry VIII, who on 2d January 35th of his reign [1536] granted the site of the priory and all tolls and customs in as large a manner as the prior had them to one Brown in fee, under the title and estate of whom [it] was demised to some of the aldermen of Bristol, defendants, in trust for the city. And it was admitted that the defendants under whom they claim had held a court in Bristol, called the Whitsun court, during the time of the fair, which commenced at twelve o'clock on Whitsun Eve and finished at twelve o'clock the Saturday in Whitsun week. And during this time they received the prisage of all wines imported into the port of Bristol during Whitsun week. And the defendants showing that the wines the prisage of which are in question were imported within Whitsun week and that the officer of the city within this week and at the Whitsun court made entry of the said ships and wines and went aboard and demanded the prisage and afterwards received them, which were disposed to the use of the city. But the defendants did not know what bulk of the ships were broken within Whitsun week but in a short time afterwards.

And upon consideration of this case, the whole court was of the opinion and declared that the defendants did not have title to the prisage of wines in question and that there was not any prisage due within the time that the city claimed it by their answer. (It seems the reason was inasmuch as bulk was not broken; otherwise their grant and usage seemed good.) And the defendants, the merchants, were decreed severally to pay their prisage to the relator, Sir William Waller.

I was for the plaintiff.

[Orders of 16 and 29 Nov. 1676: PRO E.126/12, ff. 325v, 327v.]

[Related cases: Attorney General v. Waller (Ex. 1679), below, No. 101.]

75

Nichols v. Smith (Ex. 1676)

In this hotly contested case, the court of equity granted relief against a final judgment at common law.

LI MS. Misc. 555, f. 106 [Fr.] (Ward's Reports)

The father of Mayne, being possessed of a lease for years of the rectories of Haddenham and Cuddington in the County of Buckingham, was attainted for treason by the Act of 12 Car. II[1] for the murder of the king, by which his estate was forfeited to the king, who granted the lands in question to the defendant, Sir William Smith, and Mr. Lane, who made a lease of the Cuddington tithes to the plaintiff for twenty-one years for a £70 fine and £26 annual rent, who enjoyed them for ten years and more without paying the rent, so that £286 was due for rent. After this lease was made, Mayne, the defendant, recovered at law two parts of three of the original lease. And Sir William Smith and Lane exhibited their bill in chancery to be relieved, but it was dismissed with direction to pay to the defendant Mayne two parts of the arrears of the rent with his costs, upon which Mayne agreed and purchased the third part, and upon this Mayne entered, the plaintiff's lease being avoided before this for non payment of rent. And for Mayne's satisfaction, the defendant Sir William Smith, who had all of the estate in himself, by his deed in December 1672 assigned all of the arrears of the rent due from the plaintiff to one in trust for Mayne with covenants and powers usual in such cases. But in the recital of the plaintiff's lease, the date was mistaken, being recited to be 12th where it was the 20th of May, but there were general words otherwise which aided it, and the consideration of the assignment was mentioned to be 10s. though in truth there was due to Mayne more

---

[1] Stat. 12 Car. II, c. 30 (*SR*, V, 288–290).

than £500, for which he had nothing except this assignment. After this assignment and notice of it to the plaintiff, the defendant Sir William Smith (as it was proved at the trial at law directed in this case) agreed with the plaintiff for £50 to discharge him from all the arrears of the rent, and this agreement was made 12 May 1673, almost a half a year after the assignment and notice. Forty pounds was paid to Sir William Smith (and the other £10 was not). After that, Mayne in the name of Sir William Smith brought [a common law action of] debt for £286 arrears of rent on his lease and had a verdict and judgment, and the plaintiff [was] taken in execution, after which he exhibited his bill against the defendants to be relieved upon payment of the £10 according to the agreement. And upon the bill, answers, and proofs, the case appeared to be as above.

And the court relieved the plaintiff upon this agreement and decreed Sir William Smith upon payment of £10 to acknowledge satisfaction upon the judgment notwithstanding that it was strongly urged for Mayne that no agreement made by Sir William Smith would bind or affect Mayne, and after this assignment and notice to the plaintiff, Sir William Smith was only trustee for Mayne and could not affect [?] anything without a breach of trust. And this decree was against the usages in courts of equity, being to compel Sir William Smith to break his trust where equity enforces performance of trusts. And it was also against the rule and maxim of law that *res acta inter alios alteri nocere non debet*, and there was not a shadow of proof that Mayne entrusted Sir William Smith or was cognizant of the agreement made by him. And in truth Mayne was a purchaser *bona fide* and for valuable consideration. And it was proved that after this pretended agreement, the plaintiff applied himself to Mayne and offered terms of £120 by Sergeant.

And it was urged on the other part that this agreement was with the consent of Mayne or at least that the assignment was not *bona fide*. But there was no shadow of proof of it. And it was for the plaintiff insisted that he lost the benefit [of the] lease, which was worth £12 *per annum* more than the rent, and the fine was also consideration, and Mayne was the person who recovered by a prior title. And it was alleged that he should not take advantage of his prior title and also of the arrears. But it was answered that the plaintiff had quiet possession and thus [. . .] for all times upon the arrears of which the suit was. And as to the fine, at most there could be but a proportionable abatement. But it was decreed as above, and Mayne [was] dismissed with his costs. Query.

[Order of 16 Nov. 1676: PRO E.126/12, f. 325.]

76
Ridley v. Skipwith (Ex. 1677)

A bill of review cannot assign error against the decree as not being supported by the evidence.

LI MS. Misc. 555, f. 112 [Fr.] (Ward's Reports)

[To a] bill of review, the defendant pleaded and demurred. Part of his plea was that the plaintiff had not given security for costs, which upon motion and payment of 20s. costs was admitted to be given. And the other part of the plea was that the plaintiff had not recited the decree *in haec verba*, but though there were some small omissions in the recital of the decree, yet inasmuch as it referred to the decree and the proceedings entered and enrolled, the court held it good enough. And the practice in chancery is in both points as above.

But inasmuch as the principal error assigned was that the court did not have any proof to make the decree for so many acres as it had, the question being whether 12d. per acre [is] per customary acre as the defendant wishes to have had it or per acre according to the Statute *De Terris Mensurandis*[1] as the plaintiff wishes to have had it was due for tithes, and the defendant in his answer not having confessed but mentioned the number that the decree had charged and [there being] no proof for more, the court held it to be error assigned against the judgment of the court, which could not be assigned. And on account of that the demurrer [was] allowed without costs, the court holding that no error can be assigned but in the proceedings or matter afterwards and not in the judgment. And it was upon this ground, that a trap of the decree was alleged, that 'forasmuch as it appears to the court that 12d. per acre after the rate of statute acres is due' therefore they decreed it and that intimates the judgment of the court.

[Orders of 23 Jan. and 15 Feb. 1677: PRO E.127/10, ff. 10v, 25v.]

77
Speed v. Pesier (Ex. 1677)

Neither conies nor their herbage are tithable in the absence of a custom.

LI MS. Misc. 555, f. 113, pl. 1 [Fr.] (Ward's Reports)

The defendant had a warren by charter, and afterwards he stocked two hundred acres of land, which before yielded a vicarage tithes, with conies. The plaintiff sued for satisfaction of the herbage and loss of the vicarage rights. The court

---

[1] *SR*, I, 206–208.

dismissed the bill without costs because the conies being *ferae naturae* were not tithable (there not being any custom). And their herbage is no more tithable than the herbage of deer. And in this respect [there is] a difference from the herbage for dry cattle.

78
Baynes v. Moor (Ex. 1677)

In this case, the defendant was ordered to pay a debt owed by his testator as an executor in that he and his testator had received assets from the original debtor.

LI MS. Misc. 555, f. 113, pl. 2 [Fr.] (Ward's Reports)

The plaintiff exhibited a bill for tithes for thirteen years beginning in 1643 against the defendant as executor of the executor of the executor of the occupier. The plaintiff proved the assets of the first testator had come to the hands of the defendant's testator. And the defendant having assets from his testator but nothing in specie [?] of the first testator or from the mesne executor but to the value of £6, the court decreed the defendant to pay the duty besides[1] the £6 being less[2] than the assets to the defendant's testator, inasmuch as it appeared that the defendant's testator's estate was increased by this accession of assets to his estate, but no costs on account of the length of time.

79
Attorney General ex rel. Oxley v. Partridge (Ex. 1678)

The grant of a fair and market includes the rights to set up stalls and pens in the market place.

LI MS. Misc. 556, f. 9 [Fr.] (Ward's Reports)

Note in this case it was the opinion of Chief Baron MOUNTAGU that if the king grant a fair and market to the inhabitants within his own manor with all profits appertaining to the fair and market, that by those words liberty to set up stalls and pens on the soil of the king in the market place passes to the grantees and that they shall have the profits of them. And he said that liberty to dig the soil for erecting such stalls and pens on the market and fair day passes also to them being necessary ingredients to the fair and markets. And it was said to be

---

[1] ouster *MS*.
[2] mener *or* mender *MS*.

thus agreed by Chief Justice North in the case of Borrow Brig[1] upon a contest between the grantee of a fair and market with such words and a grantee of them by express words afterwards. And in this case on this reason, the plaintiff's bill was dismissed.

I was for the king.

[Other copies of this report: GUL MS. B88–7, p. 23.]

[Order of 13 Feb. 1678: PRO E.126/13, f. 27v.]

80

Squibb v. Sibley (Ex. 1678)

A debt due to the administrator of a decedent's estate cannot be attached by a creditor of the decedent.

LI MS. Misc. 556, f. 18, pl. 2 [Fr.] (Ward's Reports)

The defendant being administratrix to her husband sold a term of his estate to the plaintiff for £600, who paid £400 and gave a bond for £400 to the defendant herself for the other £200, which not being paid, one Thompson, a creditor of the defendant's husband by a simple contract, attached the £200 in London in the hands of the plaintiff as the proper monies of the intestate. And upon the proceedings there was a judgment and execution against the plaintiff and the money paid to Thompson upon security to be repaid upon disproof of the debt within a year and a day according to the custom. The defendant sued [on] the bond in this court. The plaintiff exhibited his bill to be relieved upon all of the matter [above].

And upon the hearing of the cause (which was within the year in which the debt could be disproved), [it] was insisted by myself as counsel for the defendant that this debt was not attachable for a debt of the intestate, because it should go to the executors or administrators of the obligee and not to the administrators *de bonis non* of the intestate and could be attached for the obligee's debt and for this [it was] not attachable in two several capacities. And upon enquiry made by the barons of the other judges and of the recorder and judges of the city [of London], they all agreed that for those reasons [it] was not attachable for the intestate's debt.

And afterwards the plaintiff agreed with the defendant [out of court].

[Other copies of this report: GUL MS. B88–7, p. 48.]

[Order of 5 Feb. 1678: PRO E.127/10, f. 259.]

---

[1] Perhaps Burrow Bridge, Somerset, or Boroughbridge, Yorkshire.

81
Drax v. Sedgwick (Ex. 1678)

In this case, a purchaser of land, whose predecessor in title had been defrauded partly through the mortgagee's negligence, was required to redeem the mortgage in order to have relief against a judgment in ejectment.

LI MS. Misc. 556, f. 18, pl. 3 [Fr.] (Ward's Reports)

Clegatt [who was] possessed of a term mortgaged it for £300 to the defendant and two years afterwards borrowed the original lease from the defendant and gave a note to restore it but did not restore it and afterwards mortgaged it for £250 to one who afterwards with Clegatt conveyed it absolutely to one under whom the plaintiff claims. And the plaintiff purchased it for £600 and enjoyed it for many years. Clegatt continued payment of the interest for many years but afterwards failed and died. And upon this the defendant brought ejectment and had a verdict.

And the plaintiff exhibited a bill to be relieved. And the defendant proved his debt and the conveyance.

And though the plaintiff was cheated by Clegatt and partly by means of the defendant's parting with the original lease, still the court refused to relieve the plaintiff without [his] paying the defendant principal, interest, and charges.

[Other copies of this report: GUL MS. B88–7, p. 48.]

[Orders of 14 May and 10 June 1678: PRO E.126/13, ff. 38v, 59v.]

82
Marquess of Worcester v. Williams (Ex. 1678)

Suit of mill within a manor cannot be compelled in respect of a purchased mill. An objection to the jurisdiction of the court must be raised before the hearing.

LI MS. Misc. 556, f. 22, pl. 1 [Fr.] (Ward's Reports)

The plaintiff exhibited his bill against the defendant to compel him being a tenant to do suit of mill at the plaintiff's mill within his manor and hundred of Cricklewell in the County of Brecon and alleged the tenure and duty of the defendant so to do.

The defendant showed himself to be a freeholder of lands held of the manor but said that they were not a parcel [of the manor] and the title went only to the tenants. And [he] further showed that the plaintiff's mill was not the old mill but one that he [had] purchased from another person, and so [he was] not liable.

And upon the first hearing, the plaintiff was dismissed. And upon a rehearing this day, he was dismissed also upon this reason specially, that the defendant was not held to grind at this purchased mill, notwithstanding the reason in Luttrel's Case, 4 Rep. 88b,[1] the Chief Baron MOUNTAGU doubting the authority of the old yearbook of 19 Edw. II, Ass. 399,[2] and all that in that case tending to the same purpose. And if the law was so for a mill newly built, yet it did not extend to a mill purchased. Also he inclined that the defendant was not a tenant within the law to be compelled.

Also it was objected that the plaintiff was not a fee farmer, not did it so appear, and then he did not have the privilege to sue here, this privilege only extending to mills for which fee farm rents [were] paid to the king or his grantee. But inasmuch as the defendant did not object [to] it before the hearing, he inclined that he could not object now.

I was for the plaintiff.

Hardres f. 21.[3] It seems that a custom to grind at a mill (without a rent reserved) when proved can be decreed.

[Other copies of this report: GUL MS. B88–7, p. 57.]

[Order of 13 June 1678: PRO E.126/13, f. 64.]

83
Williams v. Herbert (Ex. 1678)

A court of equity will order a specific recovery of chattels in the case of a pretium affectionis.

LI MS. Misc. 556, f. 22, pl. 2 [Fr.] (Ward's Reports)

[There was a] decree for jewels in specie, even though it was objected that detinue or trover lay, because they could be more valuable to the plaintiff than the jury thinks them [to be]. But it was without costs.

I was for the plaintiff.

[Other copies of this report: GUL MS. B88–7, p. 58.]

[Order of 12 June 1678: PRO E.126/13, f. 72.]

---

[1] *Luttrel's Case* (1601), 4 Coke Rep. 88b, 76 E.R. 1063, 1070.

[2] This garbled citation comes from Coke's report; *cf.* YB 9 Edw. III, Lib. Ass., p. 23, pl. 19 (1335).

[3] *Currier v. Cryer* (1655), Hardres 21, 145 E.R. 360.

84
Attorney General v. Jenkinson (Ex. 1678)

A bond with the penalty blank but with the sum due stated in the condition is enforceable.

LI MS. Misc. 556, f. 22, pl. 3 [Fr.] (Ward's Reports)

Relief [was prayed] for the king against a blank bond entered to him, no penalty being inserted, but the sum due appeared in the condition. And the court decreed the defendants being sureties only (the principal standing out all contempts and a sergeant at arms returned) to pay the money due by the condition and interest for it. And Dovell, the principal, was bankrupt. And the court went on this reason, that the sureties signed and sealed the writing, though the penalty [was] omitted by the default of the officer, and the money being due to the king for duties on wines, it is a sufficient agreement to pay the money, which equity will enforce.

[Other copies of this report: GUL MS. B88–7, p. 58; IU Lilly MS. Parker, 'Cases in the Exchequer, vol. 6', p. 121.]

[Orders of 24 Jan. and 18 Apr. 1678: PRO E.126/13, ff. 25, 37.]

85
Jenkins v. Milbanke (Ex. 1678)

A trustee who has notice of another person's interest in land and who later acquires that land holds it subject to that other person's interest.

LI MS. Misc. 556, f. 23, pl. 1 [Fr.] (Ward's Reports)

Bradford and his trustee being seised in fee of lands in Northumberland made a lease of them to Milbanke for thirty-one years. Milbanke the next day redemised them to Bradford and Thompson for thirty years and eleven months conditioned for payment of £40 *per annum* to Milbanke for eight years. Bradford, being in possession for marriage to be had with the now plaintiff's wife and for a great marriage portion, settled the lands in jointure upon himself and his wife for life [with] remainders over. And afterwards Bradford became indebted to Thompson in £120 by a simple contract, and for security of this money Bradford covenanted that Thompson should hold the lands after Milbanke's debt [was] paid until satisfaction of his debt and afterward died. Thompson survived. Milbanke, not being paid his £40 *per annum*, brought [a common law action of] ejectment and recovered against the jointress's title, who did not have any notice of the title of Milbanke.

The plaintiff Jenkins, having married the jointress, for £350 bought in Milbanke's title. Thompson being dead, his executrix brought [an action of] ejectment, inasmuch as Milbanke's redemise to Bradford and Thompson was never avoided by any demand of the £40 *per annum* and thus Thompson's executor [had] good title to the redemise by survivorship of his testator, to be relieved against which, the plaintiffs exhibited their bill.

And [they] were relieved, and an injunction [was] granted until the death of the jointress and satisfaction of the £40 *per annum* for eight years. And the reasons were inasmuch as Thompson being only trustee for Bradford in the redemise and had notice of the settlement upon the jointress before he took the covenant from Bradford should not defeat the jointress's estate or the security of Milbanke, because by the jointure Bradford passed all of his estate and also the trust of Thompson. And for this, Bradford's covenant afterwards should not prejudice the jointress or aid the covenantee in equity to hold the land by virtue of his title in law, inasmuch as by such pretending, all jointures could be encumbered by the husband after jointures made. And though law and equity concur in the same person, yet it will be subject in this case to the prior estates.

I was for the plaintiff.

[Other copies of this report: GUL MS. B88–7, p. 58.]

[Order of 17 June 1678: PRO E.126/13, f. 78v.]

86
Eaton v. Gregson (Ex. 1678)

Where a person dies overseas, the probate of his will should be in the prerogative court of Canterbury, even though he had goods only in one inferior diocese.

LI MS. Misc. 556, f. 23, pl. 2 [Fr.] (Ward's Reports)

The plaintiff exhibited his English bill against the defendant to have a bond in his custody entered into by Matthew Smith to Edward Smith, to which Edward the plaintiff was executor, and entitled himself in his bill by probate in the prerogative court. The defendant confessed to having the bond and undertook to deliver [it] as the court directed being saved harmless.

At the hearing he produced the probate of an inferior ordinary only. And the proof was that the testator died in Holland. And upon an exception to the title, it was held by the court that the party dying overseas though he did not have any goods but in this inferior diocese that the probate should be in the prerogative [court of Canterbury], and thus is the practice. And for authority, see 1 Rolle's Abridgment, f. 908, sect. 30, and f. 909, sect. 30.[1]

But by the consent of the defendant and the plaintiff paying £5 costs to him, he was decreed to deliver the bond to the plaintiff (who was to prove the will in the prerogative [court]) and the defendant [was] indemnified.

I was for the defendant.

[Other copies of this report: GUL MS. B88–7, p. 60.]

[Order of 20 June 1678: PRO E.126/13, f. 72.]

87

Brookesby v. Coppin (Ex. 1678)

Tithes of pigeons are due only by custom and not by common right; where there is such a custom, tithes shall be paid for those spent in the house.

LI MS. Misc. 556, f. 27 [Fr.] (Ward's Reports)

Upon the hearing, the court seemed to be of the opinion that tithes of pigeons were due only by custom and not by common right, and where there is such a custom, tithes shall be paid for those spent in the house. And in this case, the defendant having paid tithes for those which were sold but insisting on exemption for those spent in the house, the court decreed tithes to be paid for those spent in the house also, inasmuch as it is apparent by the defendant's paying for those sold that tithes of pigeons were payable by custom. And in this case no distinction [was made] between those spent in the house and those sold, because then there could be an exemption for the same reason for other small tithes spent in the house. And in this case the authorities 1 Rolle, Abridgment, title *Dismes*, f. 642, letter S, sect. 5, and f. 644, letter Z, sect. 4, and f. 635, letter C, sect. 2; and 2 Rolle's *Reports*, f. 2,[1] were considered.

[Other copies of this report: GUL MS. B88–7, p. 67; IU Lilly MS. Parker, 'Cases in the Exchequer, vol. 6', p. 121.]

[Orders of 26 Jan. and 9 Feb. 1678: PRO E.127/10, ff. 251, 270.]

---

[1] 1 Rolle, Abr., *Executor*, pl. F, 3, p. 908; pl. H, 7, p. 909.

---

[1] *Watley v. Hamberry* (1616), 1 Rolle, Abr., *Dismes*, pl. S, 5, p. 642, pl. Z, 4, p. 644, pl. C, 2, p. 635; *Jones v. Gastrill* (1618), 2 Rolle Rep. 2, 81 E.R. 620.

88
Hart v. Weeks (Ex. 1678)

There is no equitable right of relief against distress for a rent charge where the owner could have rented the land for a sum sufficient to pay it.
A grantee of a rent charge is not responsible for maintaining the land.

LI MS. Misc. 556, f. 28, pl. 1 [Fr.] (Ward's Reports)

The case upon the hearing was this. One Hart seised in fee of divers houses granted three several rent charges out of them to three grandchildren, of whom the plaintiff was one, of £4, another of £6, and another of £4 *per annum* in fee. The inheritances of the houses came [?] to Michael Hart in fee, who mortgaged them for £350. The plaintiff purchased the rent of £6 *per annum* and the mortgage and inheritances. The three houses became ruinous. The plaintiff rebuilt them at a great charge, and two of them stood empty for seven years and more and *ad huc* remain empty for default of tenants, and all was let only for £13 *per annum*, which was not sufficient to pay the rent charges. And to have apportionment for the vacant times with respect to the other two rents and to be relieved against distress for it, the plaintiff exhibited his bill.

And the court dismissed it inasmuch as it is not equity to have apportionment, because though the plaintiff cannot let the two vacant houses for as much as he desires, yet he can let them for more than all the rent charges amount to. And as to the charges for rebuilding them, they are not to be considered, because it is the care and charge of the inheritance. And if the grantee had the right or means in law to recover, equity does not stop it.

I was for the plaintiff.

[Other copies of this report: GUL MS. B88–7, p. 68.]
[Order of 28 Oct. 1678: PRO E.126/13, f. 101v.]

89
Bickerton v. Bickerton (Ex. 1678)

The question in this case was whether an equity court will grant possession or only set up a deed of settlement that had been destroyed in order to defeat the claimant's title.

LI MS. Misc. 556, f. 28, pl. 5 [Fr.] (Ward's Reports)

The plaintiff exhibited his bill to be relieved against the destruction of a deed of settlement made by George Bickerton, the grandfather, who was seised in fee of divers lands in Cheshire. And by this settlement made upon his marriage, he made himself tenant for life, remainder to [his] wife for life, remainder to the first son and thus to the tenth son in tail male and died leaving George, his oldest son, and three other sons. The wife of George, the oldest, died, and afterwards George, the son, died, leaving issue only a daughter, the defendant, who was an infant. The other defendant was his wife, who claimed the jointure. The plaintiff claimed as heir in tail male to one under [. . .].[1] The defendant denied this settlement and showed a fine by George, the son, and articles before his marriage, by which the lands were settled in George in tail, remainder to his right heirs.

The court at first directed a trial in ejectment with directions that the fine that discontinued the estate tail should not be given in evidence, because it destroys the possessory action and drives the plaintiff to formedon. Upon this trial, a verdict was [found] for the plaintiff's title, which was such a settlement. But upon importunity another trial in a feigned action was directed, whether there was such a settlement and to the uses above, which was found for the plaintiff which was, and it was proved in the cause, that George, the son, tenant in tail, destroyed the deed of settlement. And the question was what relief the court can give to the plaintiff who was heir male of this entail.

The plaintiff's counsel prayed for an injunction for possession and an account of the profits, having no remedy at [common] law, because without this deed of settlement (which was voluntarily destroyed by George) no formedon is maintainable, being in remainder which this case did not create without a deed, and if the court only should set up the deed and enjoin the defendants to admit it upon a formedon without producing the deed of settlement, it is in the power of the defendant either to refuse to admit such a deed and thus only contempt lies against him, or it is questionable whether the court of common bench can or will admit the plaintiff to maintain the formedon without producing the deed, and on account of that the relief [would be] vain and fruitless without possession and for such a delay whether any remedy ensue, yet it is a loss of the mesne profits. And it was compared to the case when an obligation is destroyed or lost. The court upon proof that there was such an obligation decrees the debt without question, and there is a difference between the loss of a deed by fire or other accident which is not the fault of the defendant nor any other [person] under whom he claims and the loss of it by the willful act of the party who claims under it, as here, because in the first it can be reasonable only to set up the deed without more, but in the latter it is reasonable to decree possession, especially as [in] this case that the defendant though an infant *pendente lite* had made a feoffment by her own hands and altered the tenancy so greatly and made a deed of vouchers with divers warranties so that by reason of several vouchers and divers of them foreign to the

---

[1] est entail: GUL *MS*.

remedy by formedon where [?] though [?] it is not taken away yet [it is] greatly delayed without default of the plaintiff who could have prevented it.

On the defendant's part it was insisted that as to the mesne profits, the court should not decree them inasmuch as they are not recoverable in formedon and equity will not give a better remedy than the law, and as for possession, that the Court should not intermeddle with it especially inasmuch as the plaintiff had not filed a formedon nor the defendant taken advantage of the want of the deed, until which the court cannot give nor is the plaintiff entitled to any relief. And a court of equity will not alter possession settled by law nor take away any advantage that the law gives to the defendants by discontinuance, warranty, voucher, or otherwise.

The court decreed relief for the plaintiff and denied a new trial, there not being any fault found with the verdict, but took time to view precedents [as to] whether it could give possession or only set up the deed.

The attorney general Sir Robert Sawyer [and] myself [were] for the plaintiff; Lechmere and Williams [were] for the defendant.

See for the plaintiff Hobart 109, Rex v. Lord Hunsdon,[2] [where it was] decreed for enjoyment until producing the deed and the court gives further order, and the precedents in chancery, Wednesday 18 November 15 Car. II [1663], Moreton et al. v. Wordsworth et al.[3] and [*blank*].

[Other copies of this report: GUL MS. B88–7, p. 70.]

[Orders of 10 June and 31 Oct. 1678: PRO E.126/13, ff. 70v, 93.]

[An appeal was taken but no judgment was given: *Lords' Journal*, XIII (n.d.): p. 753.]

90
Attorney General ex rel. Earl of Anglesea v. Mayor of Rochester (Ex. 1678)

A corporation can make discovery without swearing to it.
A prayer for process is sufficient even if it prays for the wrong process.

LI MS. Misc. 556, f. 29 bis [Fr.] (Ward's Reports)

The plaintiff exhibited an English bill against the defendants and divers others and prayed process of subpoena by the bill, but the defendants were served with a *distringas*. And upon an appearance, [there was] a demurrer to the bill:

---

[2] *The King and Lord Hunsdon v. Countess Dowager of Arundel* (1616), Hobart 109, 80 E.R. 258.

[3] *Moreton v. Wordsworth* (1663), PRO C.33/222, f. 279.

1. Because [there was] no charge against them, but this was not allowed because there was a good charge;
2. Because it prayed discovery under oath, which a corporation cannot make, but it was not allowed because discovery is good enough and the oath [is] surplus;
3. Because [there was] no prayer of process of *distringas* but of subpoena, which does not lie against a corporation. And for this reason, the court ordered an amendment of the bill upon the payment of 20s. costs because proper process should be prayed though it was urged that the appearance aided this and all process is ended by the appearance. And though the word is subpoena, yet it is process of subpoena, which can include [within] it *distringas*, which is a pain and penalty to appear and answer.

I was for the plaintiff.

Note [that] prayer for process [is] sufficient and the words of subpoena surplusage. And appearance cures all.

[Other copies of this report: GUL MS. B88–7, p. 76; IU Lilly MS. Parker, 'Cases in the Exchequer, vol. 6', p. 122.]

91

Thomas v. Jacob (Ex. 1678)

In this case, various ecclesiastical fees and tithes were ordered to be paid.

LI MS. Misc. 556, f. 31, pl. 1 [Fr.] (Ward's Reports)

The court decreed 6s. 8d. for a burial place in the chancel according to the custom, though [there was] disputable proof, upon reason of common right, and also sums for offerings, and also recompense for tithe lambs, though [there was] no proof that [he] had more than six of his own having eleven others fallen on his land and did not show whose they were.

[Other copies of this report: GUL MS. B88–7, p. 79; IU Lilly MS. Parker, 'Cases in the Exchequer, vol. 6', p. 124.]

[Order of 25 Nov. 1678: PRO E.126/13, f. 101.]

92
Attorney General v. Fitzmaurice (Ex. 1678)

A final decree based upon a final account in the exchequer will not be reviewed in the absence of proof of any surprise resulting in prejudice to the crown.

LI MS. Misc. 556, f. 33 [Fr.] (Ward's Reports)

Note [that] the court having heard this cause at the setting down of causes by order continued it divers days afterwards. And this day (being after the sealing day) the court delivered their opinion seriatim and dismissed the bill.

The cause concerned the victualling of the Navy in the time of Sir Dennis Gawdey. And the purpose of the bill was to unravel a decree in this court by which Sir Dennis Gawdey was decreed to pay to Fitzmaurice £3100 upon pretense that though it was allowed to Sir Dennis Gawdey in his account by the king and this account [was] declared and allowed by the lord treasurer and the chancellor of the exchequer and in respect of it Fitzmaurice, who was the trustee only for the children of Amory, who was victualler in Ireland under Sir Dennis Gawdey, [was] entitled to the entire profit of the victualling in Ireland in respect of which this £3100 became due, yet this money became due for the victualling of Sir Jeremy Smith's squadron there which was not within the victualler's declaration for this year, and because this navy was victualled with money of the king delivered by Sir Jeremy Smith to the victualler's agent out of the prizes of the king, that the profit of this victualling belonged to the king and not to the victualler of the Navy, and on account of that the allowance to Sir Dennis Gawdey in his account was an injury to the king.

But the court upon consideration of the proofs and the nature of the case and the danger of unravelling the account declared and settled by the lord treasurer and the chancellor [of the exchequer] without proving any surprise in damage to the king (because it did not appear in the proof if all the allowances were allowed whether any profit would emerge to the king by the victualling) and upon perusal of some precedents in point and proof that the money was imprested to the victualler's agent in Ireland by Sir Jeremy Smith by warrant of the duke of York, at that time lord admiral, and that it was implied accordingly by the agent (who acted for the victualler and not otherwise) and appearing in Sir Dennis Gawdey's account that it was imprested to the victualler, the court dismissed the bill and ordered [. . .] Sir Robert Sawyer (who in this case had a dispensation).

I [was] for the defendant; the attorney general, solicitor, Jeffreys recorder [were] for the plaintiff.

[Other copies of this report: GUL MS. B88–7, p. 87.]

[Orders of 5, 9, and 18 Dec. 1678: PRO E.126/13, ff. 86, 86v, 95.]

93
Smith v. Walker (Ex. 1679)

A debtor to the crown can sue in the court of exchequer for matters concerning land in Cheshire.

LI MS. Misc. 556, f. 37, pl. 1 [Fr.] (Ward's Reports)

The plaintiffs exhibited a bill as debtors to the king against the defendant to discover writings and title and mesne profits concerning lands in Cheshire. The defendant pleaded the jurisdiction of the county palatine and that all matters arise within it and that the person lives and the lands lie within it, but he did not plead that there are courts within the county palatine that can give relief.

Levinz and *Williams* [argued] for the defendant. 'County palatine' implies the court. They admit ejectments, trover, and transitory actions but not real [actions], and they cite Starkey and Starkey's Case in chancery, 26 January 1619, a certificate of the master of the rolls and Chief Justice Mountagu: 4 [Coke] *Inst.* 212, 3 Bulstrode [*blank*], 2 Rolle's [*blank*].

Sawyer [argued] for the plaintiff. [There is] constant usage for ejectments. And this court exceeds the jurisdiction in chancery, and no privilege holds against a debtor of the king. And so it was ruled in the time of Hale, etc.

The plea [was] overruled by the entire court.

[Other copies of this report: GUL MS. B88–7, p. 96.]

94
Attorney General ex rel. Rookeby v. Sanderson (Ex. 1679)

In this case for aulnage duty and fees, the money was ordered to be paid to the crown because the grantees thereof failed to prove their grant.

Woolen stockings are clothes for the purposes of the statutes granting aulnage duty.

LI MS. Misc. 556, f. 38, pl. 2 [Fr.] (Ward's Reports)

The attorney general *ut supra* exhibited an English bill against the defendant, being a dealer in Yorkshire in woolen stockings, for aulnage of them and showed the title of the king (and a lease and grant made by the king to the duke of Lennox and under him title to the relators) to the subsidy of aulnage and to the aulnager's fee.

And upon the hearing, these things [were] resolved by the court:

1. That though good title [was] shown in the bill under the king to the relators and that the duty was granted out of the crown, yet [it] not

being proved at the hearing, the court will decree for the king, which note and query.
2. That woolen stockings were within the equity of the statutes of 27 Edw. III[1] and especially 17 Ric. II, c. 2,[2] notwithstanding the words are clothes, because all manufacture of wool are within it and because it had been decreed for monmouth caps, and [there was a] 6 Car. I [1630] decree in point for woolen stockings until eviction by action in the office of pleas, though [they] are not like assurable commodities.
3. That the king being in possession should be established by decree until eviction and that the duty is for sixty-four pounds weight of stockings 4d. subsidy and ½d. aulnager's fee. And as to it, [it] followed the Statute of 4 Jac. I.[3]

[Other copies of this report: GUL MS. B88-7, p. 99.]

[Order of 13 Feb. 1679: PRO E.126/13, f. 121v.]

95
Whittington v. Gonning (Ex. 1679)

In this case, the rents in question were payable in full by the defendant according to the conveyances of the common grantor, and the payment thereof for a long time was further evidence of the parties' intention.

LI MS. Misc. 556, f. 39 [Fr.] (Ward's Reports)

The case [was thus]. John Pepwall [was] seised in fee of the manors of Hamswell, Tatwick, and Cold Ashton in the County of Gloucester out of which a fee farm rent of £4 2s. 8d. was issuing payable to the king. In 20 Jac. [1622] he sold and conveyed the manor place of Hamswell and some lands, part of the premises, to the plaintiff's grandfather in fee and covenanted for himself and his heirs that the purchaser and his heirs enjoy this manor place etc. clearly acquitted, exonerated, and discharged or otherwise sufficiently saved harmless of all former bargains, sales, gifts, grants, leases, annuities, jointures, dowers, etc. and divers other particulars among which were these, *viz.* 'rents, arrearages of rents, and debts to the king's majesty, and of and from all other titles, troubles, charges, encumbrances, and demands whatsoever had, made, suffered, or done or to be had,

---

[1] Stat. 27 Edw. III (*SR*, I, 330-331).
[2] Stat. 17 Ric. II, c. 2 (*SR*, II, 88).
[3] Stat. 4 Jac. I, c. 2 (*SR*, IV, 1137–1140).

made, suffered, or done by the said John Pepwall or by any other person or persons whatsoever'. And after[wards in] 5 Car. I [1628], the said Pepwall sold and conveyed the residue of the said manors to the grandfather and father of the defendant in fee and covenanted with him that the premises then were and all times after should remain to them and their heirs clearly acquitted and discharged or otherwise by the vendors their heirs etc. 'save harmless of and from all former and other bargains' etc., and thus enumerated many things, among which are the words 'rents charge, rents seck, arrearages of rents, titles, troubles, charges, and encumbrances made or done or to be made or done by the vendors, their heirs, or assigns' or by certain of their ancestors there enumerated 'or any other lawfully claiming or to claim by, from, or under them or any of them'. The said Pepwall and the ancestors of the defendant and the defendant himself at all times after the sale [in] 20 Jac. [1622] to the plaintiff's grandfather paid all of the fee farm rent without any charge or demand upon the plaintiff or his ancestors until three years past when the vendee of the fee farm rent by means of the defendant distrained upon the plaintiff for the rent for one year, to be relieved against which and to make the defendant and the owners and occupiers of the defendant's lands liable to pay all of the rent for the future, the plaintiff exhibited his English bill.

And the defendant by answer insisted that the plaintiff should pay his ratable proportion, and though such continual payment had been made by the defendant's ancestors and the defendant, in that it was during his infancy, yet this does not bind him nor discharge the plaintiff's land, which is chargeable in law.

And the case appearing thus, all the barons, *scil.* Chief Baron Mountagu, Littleton, Thurland, and Bramston, being attended with the conveyances of the plaintiff and defendant were of the opinion and thus decreed that all of the rent should be paid by the defendant, his heirs, and assigns, and that the defendant, his heirs, and assigns should save the plaintiff, his heirs, and assigns harmless from it and reimburse the plaintiff the rent and charges of the distress paid by him with directions to the purchaser of the fee farm rent upon notice of this decree to levy all [of it] on the defendant, his heirs, and assigns. And the reasons of the barons were that the words 'rents, arrearages of rents, debts to the king's majesty, encumbrances, and demands' made by Pepwall or any other can well extend to discharge the lands sold to the plaintiff's ancestor from payment of fee farm rent. And the constant payment is evidence that thus was the intention of the parties. And after so long a time, it can be inferred that the plaintiff's ancestor in their purchase gave consideration for such exemption or at least that the defendant's ancestors in their purchase had an abatement in respect of their payment of it, or otherwise they would not have been willing to pay it so long to their wrong. And the words of the covenant in the defendant's ancestors' purchase are not so large or extensive as those in the plaintiff's ancestor's purchase are. And though the court cannot discharge the plaintiff's lands from payment of the rent, yet they can and will decree the defendant, his heirs, and assigns to pay all of the rent and to save harmless the plaintiff, his heirs, and assigns from it.

Note [that] the purchaser of the rent was not a party.

Serjeant Maynard, Sir Robert Sawyer, and I [were] for the plaintiff. The attorney general, Jones, and Lechmere and another [were] for the defendant.

[Other copies of this report: GUL MS. B88-7, p. 101.]

[Orders of 13 and 24 Feb. 1679: PRO E.126/13, ff. 115, 117.]

96
Ramsden v. Smith (Ex. 1679)

The issue in this case was when the administrator of the assignee of a mortgagee should be a party to a suit in equity to redeem.

LI MS. Misc. 556, f. 45, pl. 2 [Fr.] (Ward's Reports)

Note [that] upon a demurrer to the plaintiff's bill for not making the administrators of the Lady Duncomb, who was the administrator of the assignee of the mortgage, a party, it was held and resolved by the court that if there be a mortgagor and a mortgagee for years, and the mortgage is forfeited and assigned over to others, who take the profits, and the heir of the mortgagee[1] prefers a bill to redeem, that it is not necessary to make the administrator of the first assignee a party, if it is not endeavored to call him to account and to have relief for the surplus profits. But if the heir exhibits his bill against the last and present assignee, he can in this suit suck the profits received by the first assignee in discharge of the entire mortgage without making the administrator of the first assignee a party. [It is] otherwise, if he seeks relief for the surplus profits.

[Other copies of this report: GUL MS. B88-7, p. 114.]

[Order of 14 July 1679: PRO E.127/11, f. 228.]

97
Nappier v. Lord Pawlet (Ex. 1679)

In this case, the lessee was not required to pay fee farm rents, which were real charges on the land in question and payable by the lessor.

---

[1] Sic in MS. for mortgagor.

LI MS. Misc. 556, f. 45, pl. 3 [Fr.] (Ward's Reports)

The case was thus upon the hearing. Henry VIII granted divers manors and lands, among which were the two farms of Whaddon and Ashley, to the marquess of Winchester in fee rendering rent of £21 12s. 11d. By an old usage or agreement, this fee farm rent was apportioned, and £8 2d. lay upon the said two farms and the residue upon the other manors etc. And in such manner the said apportionment answered for a long time. [In] 36 Eliz. [1593 x 1594], the marquess of Winchester for £1000 paid by a base son called William Lambert *alias* Pawlet by indenture demised Whaddon farm to him for ninety-nine years to commence after two lives rendering £40 rent *per annum*.

The inheritance of both farms descended to John, marquess of Winchester, who died in 1675, having in 1657 in his life for valuable consideration sold Ashley farm to Hurding and covenanted that it should be discharged of the £8 2d. *per annum* and if demanded of him, then that should be distrained in Whaddon farm, and if not liable to the distress, then that should be indemnified out of the £40 rent.

The reversion of Whaddon and the £40 rent after the death of John, marquess of Winchester, came to the defendant Francis, lord Pawlet.

A great part of the fee farm rent was from time to time after the year 1660 levied upon Sir Nathaniel Nappier, who was the purchaser of the lease for ninety-nine years for valuable consideration without notice of the rent, and upon Mr. Hurding, to be relieved against which, the plaintiffs exhibited their bills.

And it was proved in the causes that this rent of £8 2d. was always until 1660 paid and allowed by the owner of the inheritance of Whaddon and Ashley.

And in this case, the court decreed:

1. That the plaintiff Sir Nathaniel Nappier should be satisfied [for] all arrears paid by him out of the £40 rent *per annum* and that the lease should be discharged of all fee farm rents for the future, the court being of the opinion that it was a real charge and payable by the reversioner and not the lessee.
2. That Hurding should be reimbursed all of the rent that he had paid out of the £40 rent as well in the life of Marquess John as afterwards, his farm of Ashley being discharged in equity and the £40 rent charged with it and the lord Pawlet claimed under Marquess John and that the £40 *per annum* lasted for the lease. And Whaddon farm afterwards should discharge Ashley. Nappier had upon this[1]

[Other copies of this report: GUL MS. B88–7, p. 115.]

[Order of 24 Nov. 1679: PRO E.126/13, f. 186v.]

---

[1] The report in the manuscript stops here in mid-sentence.

98
Lady Dacres v. Walter (Ex. 1679)

A promise to make conveyances and a will that is oral and not in writing is unenforceable.

LI MS. Misc. 556, f. 47, pl. 1 [Fr.] (Ward's Reports)

The plaintiff exhibited her bill against the defendant showing that before the marriage of the plaintiff and the testator and in consideration that the plaintiff would marry him, the testator promised and agreed to make her a jointure of the manors of A and B which he had *in presenti* and to settle and leave to her all other lands that he might purchase during the marriage and also all his personal estate which he would have at his death, and showed that he left at his death a great personal estate which the defendant had as executor of the will of the testator. And to discover this promise and the personal estate and to be relieved was the scope of the bill.

The defendant demurred because the promise was not sufficient to charge the defendant being only by parol, and a courtly and amorous expression and not a solid or considerate agreement, because if it was thus, it was strange that a jointure being made before marriage of the testator's lands that no covenant of it or other provision in writing for the other lands and the personal estate that he should leave at his death should be made, on which reason the court principally relied.

And there was another reason for the demurrer also assigned inasmuch as by the agreement the testator was to settle and leave and the settling must be the act of the testator to which he should be compelled during his life. And it was touched by some of the defendant's counsel that the intermarriage discharged the promise according to Smith and Stafford's Case, Hobart 216.[1]

But the plaintiff's counsel insisted that the promise here is not to be performed until the death of the husband and thus not discharged by intermarriage, and for this I cited Hutton 17, 18,[2] 2 Cro. 571,[3] 1 Rolle's Abridgment 343.[4]

But on this point the court inclined against the defendant, but for the other admitted the demurrer without costs.

I [was] for the plaintiff.

[Other copies of this report: GUL MS. B88–7, p. 118.]

---

[1] *Smith v. Stafford* (1618), pl. 280, Hobart 216, 80 E.R. 363.
[2] *Smith v. Stafford* (1618), Hutton 17, 123 E.R. 1069.
[3] *Clark v. Thomson* (1620), Cro. Jac. 571, 79 E.R. 489.
[4] 1 Rolle, Abr., *Baron & Feme*, pl. F, 10, p. 343.

99
Hawys v. Kett (Ex. 1679)

A writ of sequestration lies to enforce a final decree in equity.

LI MS. Misc. 556, f. 54 bis, pl. 2 [Fr.] (Ward's Reports)

The plaintiff had a decree against the defendant for £1200 on an account for the excise [tax], in which they were partners in the farm. And the money not being paid, the defendant was taken upon an attachment and by habeas corpus brought to the bar and charged with the decree and put in execution for it into the Fleet [Prison] where he lay several years. And for his greater ease, he removed himself into the prison of the king's bench where he lay and sometimes enjoyed liberty and defied the plaintiff having an estate sufficient [to pay the decree], upon which the court, upon the consideration of precedents in chancery, granted a sequestration, notwithstanding that it was objected that this court never granted a sequestration after a decree and rarely before. But it was granted in the case of Walker and Deane, which was for default of an answer, and the reason is similar after as before the decree. And the entire court, *scil.* MOUNTAGU, RAYMOND, ATKYNS, and GREGORY, agreed that it should be granted both after and before and it is as legal and reasonable as in chancery and that without it decrees here would be fruitless. And it was granted accordingly, as a result of which the plaintiff obtained his debt.

I [was] for the plaintiff.

See Liber J, f. 75,[1] [for] the contrary opinion by three of the same judges. See Liber K, ff. 150, 151.[2]

And note [that] here sequestration was awarded notwithstanding that the person of the defendant was in execution in prison for the same debt and cause.

[Other copies of this report: GUL MS. B88–7, f. 136; IU Lilly MS. Parker, 'Cases in the Exchequer, vol. 6', p. 132.]

[Orders of 5 June and 1 and 9 July 1679: PRO E.127/11, ff. 187, 206, 326.]

[This case is cited in: Coke and Gwavas v. Fountain (Ex. 1682), below, No. 152; Hall v. Moore (Ex. 1698), below, No. 368.]

---

[1] *Cook and Gwavas v. Fountain* (Ex. 1682), below, No. 152.
[2] *Gwavas v. Fountain* (Ex. 1687), below, No. 368.

100
Dodd v. Ingleton (Ex. 1679)

Tithes of milk are to be delivered to the church porch.

LI MS. Misc. 556, f. 63, pl. 2 [Fr.] (Ward's Reports)

The plaintiff exhibited his bill against the defendant being the inhabitant and occupier of divers lands in Chigwell in the County of Essex to have his tithe milk paid. And on the bill and answer the sole question that was referred to the court was if a parishioner as of common right (because it was admitted in the cause that there was not a custom of fetching or carrying the tithe milk in this parish) should carry his tithe milk to the vicarage house or the church porch, or whether the vicar should fetch it from the place of milking or the house of the inhabitant. And upon the hearing of Dr. Raynes, a civilian, who cited the text of Malachi, chapter 3, verse 10, by which tithes are commanded to be brought into the storehouse and that the opinion of all the civilians and thus the common law holds that tithes should be brought *in horreum sacerdotis*, and upon the hearing of myself for the plaintiff in the last Easter term, the court took time to deliver their opinion.

And thus this day the entire court delivered their opinions seriatim that because there is not any custom in the case for the plaintiff's fetching the milk, the inhabitants should carry it to the church porch each tenth meal, and that it is more reasonable thus to do than for the plaintiff to fetch it, which would impose such trouble on him and the clergy that if otherwise it would be that the tithes of milk, in place of profit, they would be a burden to ministers, and that the tenth meal and not the tenth part of each meal are the tithes.

[Other copies of this report: IU Lilly MS. Parker, 'Cases in the Exchequer, vol. 6', p. 133.]

[Other reports of this case: T. Raymond 277, 83 E.R. 143; Case 409, 1 Freeman 329, 89 E.R. 244, 1 Rayner 54.]

[The decree of 24 Feb. 1679, PRO E.126/13, f. 119, is printed at 1 Wood 188, 2 Gwillim 527, 1 Eagle & Younge 516. See also the orders of 15 and 22 May and 10 Nov. 1679: PRO E.126/13, ff. 133, 135v, 192.]

[This case is cited in Hill v. Vaux (1698), Holt K.B. 672, 90 E.R. 1271, 1 Lord Raymond 358, 91 E.R. 1136, 1 Eagle & Younge 629; Bosworth v. Limbrick (1777), 2 Rayner 809, 842, 3 Gwillim 1101, 1114, 2 Eagle & Younge 310, 314; Cullimore v. Bosworth (1779), 3 Rayner 934, 938, 2 Eagle & Younge 315, 316.]

101
Attorney General v. Waller (Ex. 1679)

The issue in this case was how the duty of prisage of wine is to be assessed and paid.

LI MS. Misc. 556, ff. 63, 66 [Fr.] (Ward's Reports)

[The] attorney general by his [English] bill showed that the duty of prisage was an ancient duty to the kings of England and was leased for several years to the defendant Waller and that, by the ninth article of the book of rates annexed to the Act of Tonnage and Poundage,[1] each hogshead of wine run out to seven inches and each butt or pipe run out to nine inches should be outs and no subsidy [should be] paid for them to the king. And he complained that though the officers should take the prisage wines, and that though[2] they have time out [of] mind been taken by outward view and canting not by tasting or filling up in port, yet [?] that by confederacy between the prisage officer and the merchants with intent to prejudice the king in his subsidy for wines, they chose the emptiest vessels in port for the prisage and filled them up in the port with other of the more empty vessels near to outs and by this means rendered divers of the vessels of wine outs and not liable to pay the subsidy to the king that otherwise and without such filling up they should pay. And the decree was in this case for the regular taking of prisage so that the customs would not be prejudiced and that the prisage should not be by filling up to the prejudice of the customs.

I was for the king.

See the decree of 12 June 16 Eliz. [1574] where the prisage of the wines brought into the port of Bristol in the Whitsun week should be paid to the grantees of the crown, *viz.* Sir Charles Somerset and George Winter in right of their wives, [the] daughters and heirs of Henry Brain, Esq., grantee in fee from King Henry VIII.

Note [that] in the principal case here above, the attorney general by his bill sets forth the right of taking prisage by outward view, canting, and knocking, but not by tasting. And Sir William Waller by his answer says that as to the taking prisage by view, canting, and knocking and not to taste or fill up he knows not nor believes but rather the contrary. The farmer under Waller says he received direction from Waller to take the prisage before and behind mast and of the best wines and to taste, choose, and fill up, which he did accordingly when not compounded for. The defendants, the merchants, deny tasting and [?] filling up. The king's counsel, declaring they would not controvert the canting or tasting but only the filling up, to regulate which filling up they desire the decree of

---
[1] Stat. 12 Car. II, c. 4 (*SR*, V, 181–205).
[2] soe [?] *MS*.

the court, it is declared, ordered, and decreed that the prisage officers in Bristol shall and may make choice of wines for the said duty by outward view of the cask by canting and knocking the vessels and to have liberty to taste the wines in any vessels and to take the fullest vessels for prisage, but not to fill up any vessels of wines taken for prisage. And the court orders and directs that prisage wines in all other ports of England and Wales and Berwick shall be taken in the same manner and form and under same restrictions and directions as before in the port of Bristol and not otherwise. And all officers for prisage in all the ports are required to act and conform themselves accordingly.[3]

[Other copies of this report: GUL MS. B88–7, p. 157; IU Lilly MS. Parker, 'Cases in the Exchequer, vol. 6', p. 135.]

[Orders of 9 July and 6 Nov. 1679: PRO E.126/13, ff. 151v, 180.]

[Related cases: Attorney General ex rel. Waller v. Mayor of Bristol (Ex. 1676), above, No. 74.]

[This case is cited in Paul v. Edwards (Ex. 1682), below, No. 154.]

102
Bradshaw v. Clifton (Ex. 1679)

In this case for tithes, the court disallowed a defense that the land was discharged as formerly belonging to the Premonstratensian Order.
Papal bulls of privilege not to pay tithes are not valid in England.

I
LI MS. Misc. 556, f. 65 [Fr.] (Ward's Reports)

The plaintiff exhibited his bill as proprietor of the tithes in Forton in the County of Lancaster[1] against the defendants as occupiers of lands there for predial tithes of grains. The defendants in their answer showed and insisted that their lands were parcel of the manor of Forton, part of the possessions of the dissolved monastery of Cockersand, which was of the order of Premonstratensians or some other order and dissolved by virtue of the Statute 31 Hen. VIII[2] (though it was of the lesser sort, being preserved by the clause in the Statute of 27 Hen. VIII[3]), and that the abbot and convent of this monastery or some other religious house

---

[3] This last paragraph was in English.

[1] V.C.H., *Lancashsire*, VIII (1914), p. 107, n. 20.
[2] Stat. 31 Hen. VIII, c. 13 (*SR*, III, 733–739).
[3] Stat. 27 Hen. VIII, c. 28 (*SR*, III, 575–578).

of the Premonstratensian Order or some other order were seised of this manor and by bull, order, privilege, grant, prescription, or some other good way held the premises discharged of the payment of tithes *quamdiu in propriis manibus excolebantur*, that this monastery came to the crown thus discharged by the Statute of 31 Hen. VIII and the abbot and convent [in] 30 Hen. VIII [1538] made a lease of the manor for ninety-nine years rendering rent, that Henry VIII [in] the 35th [year] of his reign [1543] granted the reversion to Thomas Holt in fee, the heir of whom [in] 18 Car. II [1666] sold the lands, the tithes of which the plaintiff claims, to the defendant in fee, and by reason of this they should be discharged of payment of tithes, being *in propriis manibus*, and though it was admitted that the tithes had been paid for a long time, yet it was when the lands were enjoyed under the said lease for ninety-nine years or other subsequent leases made by the owner of the inheritance. And [there was] no proof that tithes [were] paid by any owner of the inheritance.

And though at the first hearing of this cause 26 June 1678, the defendants insisted solely for their discharge by some bulls of the pope and the order of the Premonstratensians, both of them were disallowed by the court.

[Other copies of this report: IU Lilly MS. Parker, 'Cases in the Exchequer, vol. 6', p. 134.]

II
MT MS. 'Maynard's Reports t. Car. I & II, G.4', f. [446] [Eng.]

[It was held] that the tenants of the manor of Cockerham, parcel of the possessions of the abbey of Cockerham of the Order of the Premonstratensians, were not discharged of the payment of tithes *quamdiu [in] propriis manibus* etc., although the said monastery came to the crown by the Statute of 31 Hen. VIII as it truly[4] did, and was admitted, for though it was one of the lesser monasteries and so pretended, therefore, to be dissolved by the Statute 27 Hen. VIII, yet there is a clause in 27 Hen. VIII not printed that continues such monasteries as it pleased the king to continue, whereof this was one.

The reason of the decree was grounded on the Statute 2 Hen. IV and 4 Hen. IV and 28 Hen. VIII,[5] which makes all bulls of the popes of privileges void, so that they could not be exempted by bull, and the discharge by order extend[s] only to [the] three orders of Cistercians, Hospitalers, etc.

[The decree of 17 Nov. 1679, PRO E.126/13, f. 168, is printed at 3 Gwillim 1014, 3 Eagle & Younge 1231.]

[This case is cited in Townley v. Tomlinson (1762), 3 Gwillim 1004, 1008, 2 Eagle & Younge 189, 193.]

---

[4] revera *MS*.
[5] Stat. 2 Hen. IV, c. 4 (*SR*, II, 121–122); Stat. 7 Hen. IV, c. 6 (*SR*, II, 152); Stat. 28 Hen. VIII, c. 10 (*SR*, III, 663–666).

103
Turner v. Colson (Ex. 1680)

In this case, tithes of hornbeams were ordered to be paid.

LI MS. Misc. 556, f. 78, pl. 1 [Fr.] (Ward's Reports)

The plaintiff, the rector of Stapleford Tawney[1] in Essex, exhibited his bill for tithes of wood. And upon the hearing, the court decreed that tithes should be paid for hornbeams though of the age of thirty years not being timber by the custom of the country as proved by divers witnesses, notwithstanding 2 *Inst.* 643,[2] which was denied in this case.

[Other copies of this report: GUL MS. B88–7, p. 181; IU Lilly MS. Parker, 'Cases in the Exchequer, vol. 6', p. 143.]

[Order of 5 Feb. 1680: PRO E.126/13, f. 195.]

[This case is cited in Ashfordby v. Newcomen (Ex. 1681), below, No. 114.]

104
Attorney General ex rel. Powell v. Corporation of Ludlow (Ex. 1680)

The issue in this case was whether a person can have a subpoena to enforce a decree that has not been observed for forty years.

LI MS. Misc. 556, f. 82, pl. 2 [Fr.] (Ward's Reports)

The plaintiff brought a subpoena in the nature of a *scire facias* to have execution of a decree in this court made forty years past, *scil.* 14 Car. I [1638], by which the said corporation and inhabitants [of Ludlow] were decreed to grind their corn at the mills of the king and that the stream of the river should be made as deep and wide as before and that three mills of Aldwells belonging to the corporation, being formerly fulling mills, should be demolished as corn mills and that all hand mills and querns within Ludlow should be abated.

The defendants came in and put in a plea in bar in English without oath showing their title, and that there had been enjoyment against the decree [at] all times afterwards, and that this decree was obtained by fraud and surmise, and that the relator's testator Gretton had released his benefit from the decree to the corporation [of Ludlow] before their sale to Sir Job Charlton etc.

---

[1] Stapleton Tawney *MS*.
[2] E. Coke, *Second Institute* (1642), p. 643.

And upon debate and long consideration, the court abated and quashed the subpoena in the nature of a *scire facias* and put the relator to prefer his bill to have execution of the decree if he wished, being of dangerous consequence for the court in such a case to compel execution of a decree that was never observed for more than forty years. And in such a new suit, but not here, the matter of the acts[1] of both parties and the matters subsequent to the decree can be examined.

But note that after Trinity term 1690, that is to say [*blank*] July 1690, this plea, being upon motion the last term ordered to be reheard, was overruled and process awarded upon the decree on the reason that nothing appeared after the decree of an [?] act that can enervate the decree and that the decree should stand in force and should be observed until a reversal by bill of review or appeal.

But note that it is an unusual thing to rehear a plea after ten years and to revive a subpoena in the nature of a *scire facias* which was abated by a judgment ten years past.

[Other copies of this report: GUL MS. B88–7, p. 194; IU Lilly MS. Parker, 'Cases in the Exchequer, vol. 6', p. 143.]

105
Gwavas v. Teage (Ex. 1680)

The right to tithes of fish is not affected by the method of catching them.

GUL MS. B88–7, p. 206 [Fr.] (Ward's Reports)

The plaintiff, as impropriator of Paul in the County of Cornwall, sued the defendants being fishermen for the tithes of pilchards and other fish taken in the sea and entitled himself by custom (as he should in such a case) to those tithes. And the case upon the hearing appeared to be thus. Formerly, and until [this] case where twelve years passed the way for the taking of pilchards in the sea was with nets called seines which have [*blank*] and a large cod in the middle of the [*blank*] of the sleeves were larger than the meshes of the cod but the bulk and fish taken was in the cod, but some were taken by the [. . .][1] in the mesh of the sleeves, which were called mesh fish, and being few were given to the seamen for cleansing the net, but of those taken in the cod, tithes were at all times paid either in kind or satisfaction [was made] in money. And driving nets formerly were not used except to take bait for hook fish and at [. . .][2] fisher boat there was

---

[1] fait *MS*.

---

[1] fuit *MS*.
[2] ou *MS*.

only one driving net *circa* ten fathoms long and all were preserved and used for bait and not more than twenty driving nets [were] used. But afterwards driving nets that were prohibited by the Statute of 14 Car. II, chap. 28,³ became generally in use for the taking of pilchards, and the number of the boats increased to 140, each of which carried three or four driving nets each net one hundred fathoms long, with which they took large quantities of pilchards and lobsters. The plaintiff demanded tithes of all taken in driving nets (except those used for bait for hook fish) either in kind or the tenth part of the money for which they were sold or could be sold when fresh because the usage now is not to sell the pilchards fresh but to make them into fumathoes and thus to sell them to the merchants in barrels to carry into parts beyond the sea.

The defendants insisted that even though tithes of fish in the sea are due only by custom and not of common right, that the custom should direct [?] in [*blank*] case and on account of that, no tithes are due for the [...]⁴ fish taken in the sleeves of the net but only the tenth part of the money for those taken in the cod of the seine nets. Secondly, that no tithes are due for any pilchards taken in the driving nets though sold and it was in fumathoes and not used for bait because the custom extends only to pilchards and fish taken in the cod of the seine nets and not to the fish taken in the driving nets, which sort of nets have been used several [?] years [...]. So much and so great as now are, and great quantities of pilchards was proved to be taken by them and was in fumathoes and sold and yet no tithes [were] ever demanded [?] and paid and for this it is the particular way of tithing. For suppose a special agreement to such effect and for the manner of taking is the ingredient of the custom and further the custom [is] no tithe given.

But the court, upon consideration and advice, decreed for the plaintiff principally upon this reason that the custom of having tithes of fish cannot or should not in construction of the law be restrained by the manner of the net or the form of the taking that can be varied at the pleasure of the parties and that alteration of the net or instrument with which the fish are taken will not be [to the] destruction of the right or substance it being only the form. And the decree extended to all [...]⁵ fumathoes but not to [*blank*] taken for [...].⁶

[The order of 14 June 1680, PRO E.126/13, f. 225v, is printed at 1 Wood 203, 1 Eagle & Younge 528. Other orders: 6 May and 9 Dec. 1680: PRO E.126/13, ff. 219, 248.]

[Other reports of this case: *sub nom.* Gwavas v. Kelnack (1680), 1 Rayner 61.]

---

³ Stat. 14 Car. II, c. 28 (*SR*, V, 423–424).
⁴ meas^d *MS*.
⁵ meas^d in sole use *MS*.
⁶ fait *MS*.

[Later proceedings in this case: 1 Rayner 240, 247, 251, Bunbury 239, 256, 145 E.R. 660, 665, 2 Wood 284, 2 Eagle & Younge 1 (Ex. 1727–1729); 2 Gwillim 691, 2 Brown 446, 1 E.R. 1054 (H.L. 1729).]

[This case is cited in Nicholas v. Elliott (Ex. 1711), Samuel Dodd's Reports, p. 227, 4 Gwillim 1581, 1 Eagle & Younge 698; Chapman v. Bishop of Lincoln (1730), Mosely 266, 267, 25 E.R. 387, 388, 2 Eagle & Younge 11, 2 Gwillim 679, 680.]

106
Attorney General ex rel. Lowther v. Fletcher (Ex. 1680)

A person cannot erect a pier between high water and low water marks without a license from the crown.

GUL MS. B88–7, p. 207 [Fr.] (Ward's Reports)

The defendant was lord of Parton Manor in Cumberland adjoining to the sea, within which anciently there was a pier erected for the shelter and reception of ships. But it being demolished many years past and the place where it stood not being now commodious or convenient for rebuilding another there, he proceeded to erect another pier newly between the high water and low water marks within his manor. The relator had a convenient pier at Whitehaven next adjoining, and he was also the grantee of the title of the king of the soil between the high and low water marks within the defendant's manor, which land was thought to belong to the king under rent.

And the bill was exhibited to restrain the defendant from erecting the new pier and for demolishing so much as he did [*blank*] being as well to the damage of the king and his port, Whitehaven, as of the [*blank*] defendant insisted upon his freehold and that he could erect any pier or building upon it at his pleasure.

The court granted an injunction [*blank*] hearing. And at the hearing, it was clear of the opinion that no subject without license of the king, which the defendant did not have, could not erect any pier or shelter or receptacle for ships in the sea or navigable river between the high and low water marks though it be and is his own soil because the king only, in virtue of his prerogative, has the sole care and power for such things and it could be greatly prejudicial to navigation and safety of the [. . .] if anyone could at his pleasure erect such things in fair ports or the sea that could be receptacles for pirates or enemies or means to deprive the king of his customs and duties. And on account of that, the court decreed a perpetual injunction and also that the defendant abate all of the pier that was erected.

And in the debate of this case, these cases in this court of exchequer were remembered.

26 October 2 Car. I [1626], Town of Newcastle v. Errington;[1] buildings upon waste ground next to the river anciently used for mooring and building ships and by which buildings the port was prejudiced [were] decreed to be abated.

Town of Newcastle v. Johnson, 23 April 5 Car. I [1629];[2] a brew house erected at North Shields that sold beer to the masters of ships and others to the prejudice of the trade of Newcastle and of the port there, though seven miles from Newcastle and the party licensed by the justices, [was] decreed to be suppressed [as] being forestalling of the trade of Newcastle and tending to the impoverishment and depopulation of Newcastle, an ancient port. Note [that] in this case, a custom was suggested [that] no one could erect a brew house within the liberties of the port of Newcastle but only within the town and that North Shields is within those liberties.

Town of Bristol v. Morgan et al., 8 June 11 Car. I [1635][3] [*blank*] houses, accommodation for mariners etc., erected upon the east ground adjoining to the rivers Severn and Avon which flow together at Bristol, which ground was anciently used for the mooring of ships trading at Bristol anticipated were decreed to be demolished. And there [it was] declared that all purprestures, erections, and encroachments to the prejudice of the ports of the king are removable by this court. And in this case, the allegation that Crocherne Pill, the place where the houses were erected, was more convenient for passengers etc. than Bristol was rejected and not regarded that.

July 22 Car. II [1670], Exeter City v. Browning et al.,[4] the defendants having cut a small rivulet (for the service of his fulling mills erected upon his own soil) out of the public river which goes to Exeter as being to the prejudice of the trade at Exeter and of the port there by making the river the less navigable, the defendants were decreed to repair the banks back at his own charge. And in this case, the suppression of annoyances to the public ports was declared to belong to the jurisdiction of this court of exchequer.

See Liber G, 76, Case of Boston,[5] 15 November 1675, Newcastle and [. . .] Durham. See Rolle's [Abr.] *Prerogative*, 171,[6] where persons [were] fined for taking a toll without license in their own land. See Statute 4 & 5 Anne, chap. 18, which establishes Parton Pier.[7]

[Order of 17 June 1680: PRO E.126/13, f. 224v.]

---

[1] *Mayor of Newcastle v. Errington* (1626), PRO E.126/3, f. 106.
[2] *Mayor of Newcastle v. Johnson* (1629), PRO E.126/3, f. 300.
[3] *Mayor of Bristol v. Morgan* (1635), PRO E.125/17, ff. 361, 404v.
[4] *Mayor of Exeter v. Browning* (1670), PRO E.126/10, f. 177.
[5] *Case of Boston*, LI MS. Misc. 555, f. 76, pl. 1.
[6] *Rex v. Morgan* (1635), 2 Rolle, Abr., *Prerogative le Roy*, pl. D, p. 171.
[7] Stat. 4 & 5 Anne, c. 5 (*SR*, VIII, 465–468).

107
Harris v. Cliff (Ex. 1680)

In this case, the executors were executors in trust only and could not claim any surplus of the estate to their own use.

GUL MS. B88–7, p. 217 [Eng.] (Ward's Reports)

Anne Dallum, the plaintiff Anne's grandmother, gave her by will a house and some money and gave her father a workhouse paying £20 rent for it during his life and made two executors giving each £5 apiece, and after her debts and legacies [be] paid, she willed that the overplus of her rents should be paid to the plaintiff Anne and to such other good uses as her executors should think fit. And it was proved in the cause that the testatrix intended that the plaintiff Anne should have all her personal estate not otherwise disposed and declared it so at the time of her making the said will though it was not so expressed.

And upon [the] hearing [of] the cause in regard [that] the executors had not any ways given or disposed of any part of the overplus of her rents which they had power to do to such good uses as they should think fit nor insisted upon any title to it by their answer, the court was of opinion and did decree that all the overplus of the rents should be paid to the plaintiff and that she had a right to a moiety by the express words of the devise and the other was a trust for her as residuary legatee not being otherwise disposed in convenient time by the executors and that by the executors having particular directions given to them and the proof of the testator's intentions that the plaintiff should have all, the court was satisfied that the executors were executors in trust only and could not claim to their own use. And the decree was made and observed and executed by the executors accordingly.

I [was] for the plaintiff, and it seems [that the] decree was [made] afterwards in Easter term 1682.

[Order of 21 June 1680: PRO E.126/13, f. 229.]

108
Meservy v. Pritchard (Ex. 1680)

A release obtained in order to defeat an assignment of the bond to a third party will not be allowed in equity where the debtor had knowledge of the assignment.

GUL MS. B88–7, p. 220 [Eng.] (Ward's Reports)

The case upon the hearing was this. Booth was indebted by two bonds in above £100 to the plaintiff, and Pritchard, the defendant, was indebted by bond of £200 for [the] payment of £100 and interest to Booth at a certain day. Booth, for [the] securing [of] his debt to the plaintiff, assigns and delivers the defendant's bond to him with [a] letter of attorney to sue and [a] covenant not to revoke. Of this, [the] defendant had notice, as he confessed by [his] answer. And yet afterwards without [the] plaintiff's privity (and as Booth by answer said by surprise), [he] got a release from Booth of his bond assigned to [the] plaintiff under [the] pretense that Booth was indebted to the defendant and had no other way to satisfy that debt.

In this case, the court relieved the plaintiff against the release and decreed the defendant to pay the money, principal and interest, with costs, for after Booth had assigned and the defendant had notice of it, he was bound, and the defendant could not nor ought to get any discharge of the bond or debt without the plaintiff's privity and his being heard to controvert it. And the defendant not having any other way to secure his debt from Booth alters not the case.

I [was] for the plaintiff.

[Order of 28 June 1680: PRO E.126/13, f. 228.]

109

Brooks v. Hill (Ex. 1680)

Tithes of madder are due in kind.

GUL MS. B88-7, p. 223, pl. 1 [Fr.] (Ward's Reports)

[There was a] decree for tithes of madder in kind though madder is a plant and does not renew annually but yields the profit only the third year and compares to the case of liquorice.

I was for the plaintiff. An Isle of Ely case.

110

Pomfret v. Landy (Ex. 1680)

Clover made into animal feed is tithable. Such tithes are payable to the vicar.

GUL MS. B88-7, p. 224, pl. 1 [Eng.] (Ward's Reports)

Tithe of clover grass threshed and made into horse bread and hogs' feed with seed yet [was] adjudged to be hay and tithable to the vicar, who was [endowed] with hay and not to the impropriator as a new and different tithe from hay.

See Standfast's case, Liber H, 85.[1]

[Order of 15 Nov. 1680: PRO E.126/13, f. 245v.]

---

[1] *Woodford v. Standfast* (Ex. 1680), LI MS. Misc. 556, f. 85, 1 Rayner 59, 1 Eagle & Younge 527.

111
Morrell v. Marwood (Ex. 1680)

A penal bond to give a just account will not be relieved against where the party bound by it has deliberately disabled himself from giving a true account by burning his records.

GUL MS. B88–7, p. 224, pl. 2 [Eng.] (Ward's Reports)

[The] plaintiffs exhibit their bill to be relieved against a bond of £1,000 entered into by Loftus, undersheriff to the deputy sheriff of Yorkshire. [The] plaintiff Morrell was servant to Loftus and afterwards married his widow and executrix. The bond [was] conditioned for Loftus' performance of [the] covenants in an indenture whereby Loftus was enabled to receive to his own use the undersheriff's fees without account and to receive the high sheriff's fees to the defendant's use (they being all distinguished) except £80 which he was to have for executing the place and £30 towards passing the account. And thereby Loftus covenants that he or his executors upon request would give unto the defendant just accounts of all the fees and profits due and received for the defendant's use (the undersheriff's fees excepted) and to procure a quietus by such a time. Loftus dies in his office executing it for near three-quarters of a year. [The] defendant requires an account but can get none that is satisfactory. He desires to see the books that Loftus kept and offers to be bound by them. Morrell dissuades the evidence from gratifying the plaintiff[1] so that the defendant could get no other account than a confused paper book of several kinds of paper and different hands writing, part being of Loftus's and [the] rest of Morrell's writing. The papers produced seemed very suspicious to be torn and stuck together and for part of the time no account at all [was] entered of the receipt of [the] defendant's fees. [The] defendant to obtain [a] true account put his bond in suit, and [the] defendants, to be relieved, exhibited their English bill. And at [the] first hearing [they] were referred to an account pretending they could give no other than that delivered, but upon a second hearing in respect [that] it appeared in proof and was insisted on for the defendant that Loftus had other books or papers wherein the fees were contained and that his wife desired Morrell to produce them to [the] defendant, but Morrell dissuaded her from so doing and said Loftus had caused him to burn them after they were written out.

The court was divided. Chief Baron Mountagu and Atkyns were to relieve against the penalty and refer to account for it would be hard to let the penalty run where the subject matter was an account only and no clause to compel Loftus to keep an account though he was to give one which is satisfied by the account to be given by the plaintiffs and the defendants power to surcharge

---

[1] Sic in MS.

which may be done in a great measure by taking an account of the writs issued, executed, and returned, which may be easily come by. But Gregory and Weston were not for relieving the plaintiffs in regard, by the burning [of] the true books, they were disabled from giving a true account and no favor ought to be shown *in odium spoliatoris* and no man shall take advantage of his [*blank*] and though it is not mentioned that Loftus should keep accounts, yet he is bound to give just accounts, which cannot be done unless [they are] kept by him. And it appears [that] accounts were kept but burnt. And Sir Thomas Chamberlayne's Case in chancery was vouched, who because he burnt books was charged with all that could be laid upon him and it would be injurious to the defendant to be put to charge the defendant [?] and cost him more than the fees received.

The court being divided, the opinion of SIR JOHN [ERNLE], chancellor of the exchequer, was desired, who was of opinion with GREGORY and WESTON, the plaintiff having refused some overtures and treaties. And so the bill was dismissed.

I [was] for the defendant.

Note the case of mingling coin or money that the others can [*blank*].

[Order of 29 Apr. 1680: PRO E.126/13, f. 215v.]

112

James v. Killigrew (Ex. 1680)

An oral contract to pay a pension that has been partially performed will be ordered to be specifically performed in full.

GUL MS. B88–7, p. 226 [Fr.] (Ward's Reports)

The plaintiff by bill which showed [that] by his industry he had attained to [. . .] to improve the revenue of the king from the excise and by advance of the farm of it and being assured that the king would graciously recompense such service and make choice of the defendant, being vice chamberlain of the queen and brother-in-law to the plaintiff and one who had interest, and the king and to whom the king had respect to discover a way for this improvement to the king and his great ministers that had such effect that by it the excise farm was advanced to the king £40,000 *per annum* pension for his life out of the excise,[1] and the plaintiff suggested an agreement with [?] the defendant that the plaintiff shall have one fourth part of such recompense that the king will give to the defendant and the defendant's assent to it, and then [he] showed the grant of the pension and that the plaintiff was put [to] the fourth part of the charges for

---

[1] Sic in MS.

levying tallies and otherwise in receiving the £500, and for divers years he had received the fourth part of the £500 to his own use pursuant to the said agreement, but that now the defendant denies it to the plaintiff, and it being in arrears for some time, to have these arrears paid and the future growing fourth part was the scope of the bill.

And the attorney general and the commissioners of the excise that were to pay the pension were named parties defendant. Killegrew at first demurred and assigned for cause that the plaintiff through default of a good consideration did not have any cause for suit, and, if he had any, yet an action at law upon a *quantum meruit* and not a remedy in equity [lay]. But the demurrer being overruled and the defendant having by his answer in effect denied the merits of the plaintiff's cause, the plaintiff made proof of the agreement and produced letters by which the defendant desired the plaintiff to procure writings to secure his part of the offer, his willingness to seal them, and [it] being fully in proof that the plaintiff had been in possession [?] of his fourth part for divers years, which was an execution of the agreement in part, the court decreed [to] the plaintiff his arrears and growing duty and that the defendant execute an assignment of the fourth part *nisi causa*[2] next term. And this decree was made absolute.

But Baron WESTON seemed to doubt whether a plaintiff is relievable in equity. But the other barons [were] clear that there was full proof of an agreement and [it was] executed in part, and on account of that, [it is] proper only in a court of equity to have execution of all specifically.

I [was] for the plaintiff.

Note that the first agreement was before the Statute of Frauds and Perjuries.[3]

[Orders of 7 July and 25 Oct. 1680: PRO E.126/13, ff. 230v, 244.]

113

Skinner v. Eyre (Ex. 1680)

In this case, the issue was whether recompense for a modus should be paid if the modus was not possible or whether tithes in kind should be paid.

GUL MS. B88–7, p. 234 [Fr.] (Ward's Reports)

The plaintiff, being rector of Hartlebury in the County of Worcester, sued the defendants, being farmers of Hartlebury Park, part of the demesne of the bishop of Worcester, for tithes of corn and grain growing there. The defendants alleged and proved that it was an ancient park belonging to the bishops of

---

[2] Unless cause [be shown to the contrary].
[3] Stat. 29 Car. II, c. 3 (*SR*, V, 839–842).

Worcester and that, until the last wars in England, it was impaled and stocked [with] deer and that a shoulder of each deer killed there was, time of which etc., paid as a *modus decimandi* for all of the tithes of the said park to the parson of Hartlebury until the destruction of the deer and pulling down of the pales of the said park in the said last wars, that it was not a park stocked with deer, there were corn and grass growing there and cattle of the keeper and bishop pastured, but no tithes [were] ever paid except the said shoulder of the deer. And even though during the time of the bill, there were not any deer but tenders of 20s. *per annum* in lieu of the shoulders, which was the full value of them, whether tithes in kind were due to be paid or recompense for the *modus* was the question.

And the court seemed to incline after several hearings of the cause and counsel for both parties that tithes in kind were not due to be paid but recompense for the shoulders and the shoulders again when the park [is] stocked. And this difference was observed between parks legally disparked as adjudged [?] in *quo warranto* etc. and a park not legally disparked but the deer and pales destroyed by disseisors which does not amount to a disparking in law, Cro. Car. 59, Sir Charles Howard's Case,[1] Hobart 39, 40,[2] etc., because in the first case where the park is legally disparked and the deer [are] gone, there the *modus* of the shoulders (if it is of the deer in the park but[3] not generally a shoulder of venison that can be furnished otherwise possibly is discharge and tithes in kind restored according to the doubt of Lord Hobart in Cooper and Andrews' Case, f. 40, and the opinion of Popham in Bedingfield and Feake's Case, Cro. Eliz. 467,[4] but where [?] there is not any legal disparking but a temporary suspension of the privilege of park, there it seems that recompense for the *modus* that cannot be paid in kind) will be paid and not tithes in kind result according to Hobart 44, and the case of Dryer[5] there, but the court did not [make] any judicial determination of this cause but concluded as above.

Note that between the same plaintiff and one Smith, defendant,[6] Trinity [term] 8 June 28 Car. II [1676], the plaintiff had a decree for tithes in kind, but the court did not regard this here inasmuch as the reason of the destruction as above was not observed nor a similar defense made as here.

---

[1] *Sir Charles Howard's Case* (1627), Cro. Car. 59, 79 E.R. 655.

[2] *Cowper v. Andrews* (1612), Hobart 39, 80 E.R. 189, also Moore K.B. 863, 72 E.R. 957, Godbolt 237, 78 E.R. 138, 1 Gwillim 275, 1 Eagle & Younge 240, *sub nom. Hooper v. Andrews*, 1 Rolle Rep. 120, 81 E.R. 372.

[3] per *MS*.

[4] *Bedingfield v. Feak* (1596), Cro. Eliz. 467, 78 E.R. 719, also 1 Gwillim 166, 1 Eagle & Younge 118, Moore K.B. 909, 72 E.R. 989, Gouldesborough 149, 75 E.R. 1057.

[5] *Parson of Peykirke's Case* (1576), 3 Dyer 349, 73 E.R. 784, 1 Gwillim 136, 1 Eagle & Younge 66.

[6] *Skinner v. Smith* (1676), 1 Wood 161, 2 Gwillim 526, 1 Eagle & Younge 510.

114
Ashfordby v. Newcomen (Ex. 1681)

A modus decimandi *that is not limited to a certain person or place is invalid.*

GUL MS. B88–7, p. 238 [Fr. & Eng.] (Ward's Reports)

The plaintiff, being parson of Mablethorpe St. Mary's cum Stain in the County of Lincoln, exhibited his English bill for tithes of wool, lamb, and pasturage tithes against the defendants. And upon the hearing, the court [*blank*] term ordered a case to be made. And [it was] agreed for counsel of both parts [to hear it], and in case of disagreement [it was] to be settled by the chief baron. And the case was settled and agreed by Pollexfen for the defendant and myself [Edward Ward] for the plaintiff in the presence and by the direction of the chief baron. And it was thus.

The plaintiff, during the years 1677 and 1678, was and still is rector of Mablethorpe St. Mary's in the County of Lincoln. And the defendants, dwelling out of that parish, farmed and occupied divers closes and pasture lands there during those years, some called by the name of ancient pasture and some new converted ground, whereupon they kept and had many sheep and other tithable matters. The plaintiff exhibits his bill to be relieved for the tithes thereof. The defendants allege a custom within the parish that any person or persons living out of the parish occupying or taking to farm any pasture ground within the parish have time out of mind paid and used to pay to the rector of the parish 12d. per acre for the tithes of every acre of pasture ground within the parish called new converted ground when not in tillage and 4d. per acre for ancient pasture and that the proofs extend to foreigners. But it was proved and agreed that all inhabitants in Mablethorpe St. Mary's whether owners or farmers that shall hold the same or any pasture lands there have and ought to pay tithes in kind for the same and stock thereon as also that tithes in kind have and ought to be paid as well by foreigners as inhabitants for the same and all other pasture ground there when turned into tillage.

The question is whether the custom alleged be reasonable and consistent with the rules of law so as to bar the plaintiff from his tithes in kind or whether tithes in kind ought not to be paid to the plaintiff for the lands and tithable matters in question notwithstanding such pretense of custom.

And this day[1] by the uniform opinion of all the court, that is to say, Chief Baron MOUNTAGU, ATKINS, GREGORY, and WESTON, barons, they resolved that the pretended custom is unreasonable and inconsistent with the rules of the law because it is not confined to a certain person or place as all customs must [be]

---

[1] 27 January 1681.

and it cannot in judgment of the law have any reasonable beginning. Inasmuch as the same land, as the owners hold it and live in the parish, will pay tithes as to his leases, not living in the parish, will pay a certain small sum in place of tithes and thus for the variousness of the pretenses that the lessee will have a greater privilege than the owner and that living within or out of the parish will change the course of the law, it is a more feeble foundation for a custom, especially as to the same land and any case, and in any person's tenure it will pay tithes.[2]

And the plaintiff had a decree.

But see Liber K, 1679/[80], 5 February;[3] [in] 1684[/85], 9 February, [it was] otherwise resolved[4] by the same judges, except for Baron Wright in the place of Weston.

[On] November 24, 1690, in the case between Langton and Claxton[5] for the same rectory, it was resolved [that] the custom [was] good and the bill [was] dismissed with costs. I [was] for the defendant there.

The case of Uppingham and Oakham Schools and Brown.

Blake v. Horne, after, another [on the] same point as Slater and Weeks[6] upon a special verdict and [it was] thus resolved. See folio 8.

[Order of 27 Jan. 1681: PRO E.126/13, f. 262v.]

[For earlier decrees in this case, see 1 Wood 166, 183, 207, 1 Eagle & Younge 511.]

[This case was cited in Governors of Oakham Hospital v. Broune (Ex. 1685), below, No. 204; Chapman v. Bishop of Lincoln (1730), 2 Gwillim 679, 688, 3 Rayner 1120, 1123, 2 Eagle & Younge 11, 16.]

---

[2] entant que mesme le terre quant [*or* quant al] owners tene ceo et vive en le parish payeta [sic] dismes quant [*or* quant al] son lesses [*or* lessee] ne vivant en le parish payera certain petit summe en lieu de dismes et sic pur le variousness del pretences que lessee avera greinder priviledge que les owner et que vivant deins ou hors del parish altera le course del ley est pluis feeble foundation pur custome especialment quant mesme le terre et ascun case et en ascun persons tenure payera dismes *MS*.

[3] *Turner v. Colson* (Ex. 1680), above, No. 103.

[4] *Governors of Okeham Hospital v. Broune* (Ex. 1685), below, No. 204.

[5] *Claxton v. Langton* (1690), 1 Wood 283, 1 Eagle & Younge 567.

[6] *Slatter v. Weeks* (Ex. 1680), GUL MS. B88–7, p. 221.

115
Walker v. Dean (Ex. 1681)

A limitation of a term for years in tail is void.

GUL MS B88–7, p. 241 [Fr.] (Ward's Reports)

The case upon the hearing appeared to be thus. William Dean, possessed of a term for 200 years of lands in Norfolk and Suffolk, conveyed this term to his son and heir, Sir Drue Dean, who, upon his marriage with Lucy, his wife, in 4 Car. I [1628], conveyed this term to Lord Goring as trustee in trust for Sir Drue Dean during his life and afterwards in trust for Lucy during her life and afterwards in trust for the heirs male of the body of Sir Drue Dean. Lucy died. Sir Drue died having made his will and three persons executors, the survivor of whom died in 1637, but there was not any disposition of the term of his will. Afterwards in 1648 upon the marriage of Anthony Dean, son and male heir of Sir Drue Dean, with the defendant Jane, daughter of Sir Edward Barkham, the Lord Goring, the surviving trustee, and the said Anthony [in] consideration of the said marriage and £1500 portion paid to Anthony and for settling a jointure for the said Jane, conveyed the said term to Sir Edward Barkham and others in trust for the said Anthony during his life and afterwards in trust that the said Jane should have £350 *per annum* out of it for her life for her jointure and afterwards in trust for the heirs male of the body of Anthony engendered upon Jane and for default of such issue male, as much for raising portions for daughters of their bodies. And the possession constantly went with this settlement and the settlement of Sir Drue Dean without any claim by the executors of Sir Drue Dean or others.

On May 1673, Anthony, for £1500 borrowed from Walker, the plaintiff, mortgaged part of the premises in the said term for forty-one years and the other part for ninety-nine years to confirm the said forty-one years to begin after the death of Anthony to the plaintiff for payment of the said £1500 and interest. Anthony died. Jane was made his executrix, and the defendant John, his son and male heir engendered upon Jane, [on] 5 October 1676, John, for payment of the said £1500 and also more, which the plaintiff lent Anthony, and for £600 lent by the plaintiff to the said John, in all £2450, mortgaged all of the premises [?] for ninety-nine years to the plaintiff to be void upon payment of the said £2450 and interest, after which, *viz*. [on] 29 October 1676, John Dean, Jane Dean, and Barkham, the surviving trustee, conveyed to Curtis and [*blank*] upon trusts and under this, it came to Sir Nicholas and Sir John Pelham for security for £600 and interest. And in this case, these points were resolved:

1. That the residue of the term of two hundred years will be understood to be well vested in the Lord Goring and Anthony Dean in 1648, notwithstanding the will and executors of Sir Drue Dean, in whom the trust of the estate after the death of Sir Drue Dean vested, inasmuch as possession at all times went accordingly, in which case, the court will imply an assignment in another conveyance.
2. That by the settlement in 1648, there was a trust created for Anthony for life and afterwards to Jane for life and that the remainder of the term after the death of Anthony and not by him conveyed to the plaintiff vested in Jane, his executrix, and John, the male heir, took nothing by it and consequently his conveyance to the plaintiff for the said £350 and £600 was void, and thus the plaintiff had security only in 1673 who had the disposing power of it, and the court held it to be a plain case that John took nothing by the settlement in 1648 because there being a limitation of the term for years in tail, this is void and it will go to the executors of the limitor; [it is] otherwise if it had been limited to the first or second son or anyone by particular name who should take it as purchaser.

But *Sir Francis Pemberton* was of the other opinion, that the equity of the term was vested in John after the death of Anthony and Jane.

But it was decreed as above, and upon payment of the £1500 and interest, the plaintiff conveyed to Sir Harbottle Grimstone, master of the rolls, who furnished the money. And it was said and held in this case that when a man by such a settlement of a term has a trust limited to him for life and afterwards to others for life and afterwards for the heirs male or for the heirs of his body, that it will be an estate tail in him if it was a settlement of [*blank*] tenement, that in such a case of disposition of the said trust in tail of the term, it is as well and as strongly in the tenant in tail and he has as great a power over it as a tenant in tail has over his estate tail, that it can be barred by him by a fine or recovery, and on account of that, the law permits him that has the [*blank*] of such in tail to give or dispose of it in his lifetime, and if it be not done, then that it will come to the executor of him, and it will not go to the heirs male or the heirs of his body, that if thus peradventure it will establish a perpetuity of a term that the law rejects as void, the trust of the term will go to the executors.

See Siderfin 37; Child and Bayly, 2 Cro. 459, etc.[1]

See the argument of Lord Chancellor Nottingham in the case between Mr. Howard and the Duke of Norfolk, 1683, among my arguments where a remainder

---

[1] *Grig v. Hopkins* (1661), 1 Siderfin 37, 82 E.R. 955; *Child v. Bayly* (1618), Cro. Jac. 459, 79 E.R. 393, also Palmer 48, 333, 81 E.R. 972, 1109, W. Jones 15, 82 E.R. 9, 1 Eq. Ca. Abr. 192, 21 E.R. 982, 2 Rolle Rep. 129, 81 E.R. 704.

of a term after an estate tail was decreed [to be] good, but afterwards [it was] reversed upon the point in law, but after this reversal, [it was] reversed in Parliament in June 1685.[2] But it seems that this case is not similar to the case in question.

116
Holland v. Stephens (Ex. 1681)

In intestate distributions between collaterals, representatives will not be admitted after cousins german.

GUL MS. B88–7, p. 229–E [Fr.] (Ward's Reports)

Parker died intestate. The defendant was his cousin german. The plaintiffs were the children of another cousin german, who died in the lifetime of the intestate.

And upon a demurrer, it was the clear opinion of the court that the plaintiffs are not entitled to have any proportion of the intestate's estate inasmuch as the defendant at the time of the intestate's death was the next of kin to the intestate and [there were] no others in equal degree with him and the representatives of the other cousin german who died in the lifetime of the intestate will not be admitted, they not being in equal degree with the defendant, also for the reason of the clause[1] that between collaterals there will not be any representatives admitted after cousins german.

I [was] for the defendants.

See Raymond's Reports, Carter and Crawley's Case,[2] the argument of Chief Justice North against the other justices of the common pleas, ff. 496, 497, 501 etc., agrees with the case above, and it was in 34 & 35 Car. II [1683].

The words of the Act [are] 'The residue of the . . . estate to be distributed equally to every of the next of kindred of the intestate who are in equal degree and others[3] who legally represent them', but 'no representations to be admitted amongst collaterals after brothers' and sisters' children'. And in that case of Carter and Crawley, it was held by Chief Justice North that the words brothers and sister[s] relate to the intestate and not to the collaterals.

---

[2] *Howard v. Duke of Norfolk* (1683), 2 Chan. Rep. 229, 21 E.R. 665 (1683); 2 Freeman 72, 80, 22 E.R. 1066, 1070 (1681); 2 Swanston 454, 36 E.R. 690 (1681); 3 Chan. Cas. 1, 22 E.R. 931; 1 Eq. Cas. Abr. 192, 21 E.R. 982; 1 Vernon 163, 23 E.R. 388 (1683); Pollexfen 223, 86 E.R. 568; Cases 1145, 1155, Nottingham's Chancery Cases, 79 Selden Soc. 904, 922; Samuel Dodd's Reports, p. 42; *Lords' Journal*, XIV (n.d.), pp. 49–50.

---

[1] Stat. 22 & 23 Car. II, c. 10, ss. 3, 4 (*SR*, V, 720).
[2] *Carter v. Crawley* (1681), T. Raymond 496, 83 E.R. 259.
[3] those *MS*.

117
Harrison v. Houblon (Ex. 1681)

Contraband goods can be insured but it should be by express terms and not within the general words of the policy or of the endorsements.

GUL MS. B88–7, p. 230–F [Fr.] (Ward's Reports)

Upon the arguing of exceptions to the defendants' answer, the case appeared to be thus. Fountain, being a Frenchman and [*blank*] in France and having shipped divers goods to Cadiz in Spain to be brought to Vera Cruz in the Spanish West Indies in a Spanish ship, caused himself to be secured for divers sums upon bottomry upon the said goods. He sent to the defendant Houblon, his correspondent in England, to take insurance for those goods, who took insurance from the plaintiffs and others by a common policy. But Houblon, thinking it not to be insufficient to exclude[1] the insurers to have an account of the qualities and values of the goods if a loss should happen and by the direction of Fountain and with the consent of the plaintiffs, insurers, caused two endorsements to be made upon the policy to this effect, that if a loss should happen, the goods insured will be taken to be of such value in certain and that no account will be made of the natures, kinds, or qualities of the goods. And without such endorsements Houblon and Fountain swore that he would not have taken the insurance. And the plaintiffs subscribed both endorsements.

And afterwards, in the voyage, the ship and goods were taken by the governor of Puerto Rico (being in the Spanish territories and a Spanish governor) to which place the ship and the policy was to pass by and to land soldiers there. And all of the defendant's goods in the ship were taken by the governor. Upon this the defendant brought an action upon the case upon the policy in the [court of] king's bench. And against some of the plaintiffs, he had judgment by default, and against others, he was proceeding in [common] law.

To be relieved against this, the plaintiffs exhibited their bill in chancery suggesting that the goods insured were contraband goods, that is to say such that should not be carried from Cadiz to Vera Cruz, and that none except only Spaniards should trade from Cadiz to the Spanish West Indies, and thus the goods, in respect of their nature and also in respect of the owner, were contraband, and thus for these causes seized by the governor of Puerto Rico as a transgression of the law of the country, against which neither the policy of insurance itself nor any of the memorandums endorsed extended, but inasmuch as the plaintiffs could not disprove those things without the oaths of the defendants, they exhibited their bill for discovery.

---

[1] Sic in MS. for 'sufficient to preclude' perhaps.

And the sole question was whether the defendants, notwithstanding the said policy and endorsements, should reveal the kinds, qualities, and values of the goods. And in chancery upon the same exceptions to the answer, the lord chancellor held clearly that the defendants were not to be compelled to reveal them:

1. By reason of the endorsements which settled the value and excluded the insurers from demanding any account of the goods in case of loss.
2. To [. . .] of the nature of the trade from Cadiz to Vera Cruz, which was shown by the defendants' answer to be driven more by others than by Spaniards though prohibited and that it is [blank] held to all merchants that the several goods shipped there are contraband and of necessity he must take notice of it.

And the plaintiffs dismissed their bill in chancery and preferred a bill here. And upon the same answer in effect, they presented the same exceptions. And upon argument and reference [and] hearing of merchants in court, the court ordered the defendants to reveal the qualities and values of the goods.

And the reason principally was that [blank] the policy [blank] the endorsements extended to weigh[2] against the laws of the country, for which reason, as it was said, the goods were seized. But on the defendants' part, it was said the cause of the seizure was piracy and if not, still it was denied [that] the words of the policy and the construction would oust him nor the insured of any advantage.

And in this case, it was agreed by all that contraband goods can be insured but that it should be by express terms and not within the general words of the policy or of the endorsements.

I [was] for the defendants.

It seems a hard case not to be enquired in equity inasmuch as the debtor must make title at [common] law before he can recover.

118

Shorter v. Manning (Ex. 1681)

Tithes are not due for after-pasture of sheep or other cattle if the parson had tithes of the hay. The second crop of hay in the same year pays tithes in kind.

GUL MS. B88–7, p. 232–H, pl. 1 [Fr.] (Ward's Reports)

[It was] resolved by all of the court that, by the law of the realm (without a particular custom), tithes are not due for after-pasture of sheep or other cattle when the parson had tithes of the hay, and the plaintiff's bill [was] dismissed.

I [was] for the defendant.

---

[2] pur ensuere [?] *MS.*

And there is no difference whether the [tithe of] hay belongs to the parson and the pasturage tithes to the vicar because in this case also one sort of tithe only will be paid [*blank*] but it is settled in law that the second crop of hay in the same year pays tithes in kind without anything that will discharge it which [is the] reason of the difference after 30.

[Order of 7 Feb. 1681: PRO E.126/13, f. 267.]

119
Thornhill v. Harrison (Ex. 1681)

A grazier who earns his living by buying and selling can be a bankrupt, but not a farmer who buys and sells his own stock.
In this case, relief was granted against a fraudulent transfer.

GUL MS. B88–7, p. 232–H, pl. 2 [Fr.] (Ward's Reports)

The case was thus. Harrison being a grazier became bankrupt, but before he so became, he made a bargain and sale of his goods to the value of £2400 to one Perkins, who, it was said, paid him £500, and for the other £1900, Perkins, with the consent of Harrison, assigned and sold the goods to Rucke, the defendant Harrison's housekeeper, but [in] truth Rucke did not pay any money for them. Videan and Hooke also bought divers goods of Harrison before he became bankrupt and for payment gave notes or bonds to Rucke by Harrison's directions. Harrison's goods and personal estate were assigned to the plaintiff, being a creditor of Harrison, by the commissioners of bankrupts. Rucke sued Videan and Hooke for the moneys due for Harrison's goods.

The plaintiff exhibited his bill [for] discovery and to be relieved for Harrison's estate surmising Rucke to be only trustee for Harrison and to stay the actions against Videan and Hooke. And it was clearly in proof that Harrison was a grazier and that he became bankrupt. And it appeared that Rucke was only trustee for Harrison.

And the court resolved these things:

1. That a grazier who lives by selling and buying can be a bankrupt, [but] contrarily if [he is] only a farmer and sells and buys his stock only.
2. That the plaintiff in this case was relievable against the defendants inasmuch as the sale by Harrison was before his bankruptcy and, on account of that, it was proper for a court of equity to set aside the notes or securities given to Rucke and the bargain and sale to him by Perkins being only a trust by the bankrupt. But it was agreed that it would be otherwise if the sales of the goods had been after the

bankruptcy inasmuch as in such cases the sales would have been void and the plaintiff, as assignee of the commissioners [of] bankrupt[cy], had a proper remedy at [common] law for the goods. But in this case, he had no such remedy, but he was relievable for the trust only in equity. And on account of this, he was relieved, and an injunction [was] granted to stay the suits against Videan and Hooke, who submitted to pay according to the court's direction.

3. That if the case of the bankruptcy appeared in proof clearly, the court can make a decree without a trial at [common] law, especially in this case where no one opposed the matter except for the bankrupt himself and his trustee.

And on account of that, the plaintiff was relieved.
I [was] for the plaintiff.

[Order of 10 Feb. 1681: PRO E.126/13, f. 269.]

120
Whittle v. Loving (Ex. 1681)

A judgment creditor can redeem a mortgage made by his debtor where the equity of redemption was afterwards conveyed to a third person.

GUL MS. B88–7, p. 238–O, pl. 1 [Fr.] (Ward's Reports)

The case upon the hearing was thus. Oliver Gregory, seised of the Talbott Inn in Southwark, mortgaged it to Hutchins and his trustees for £1000 in April 1678. And in July 1678 he gave a statute staple of £2000 defeasible [?] for payment of the £1000 and interest. And in Trinity term 1678, Whittle, the plaintiff, recovered a judgment against Gregory for £147 10s., after which Gregory being in debt (as it was alleged), he acknowledged to Loving in £3000, and further, in February 1679[/80] for the securing of [it], he conveyed the equity of redemption to Sir Francis Winnington by the direction of Loving in trust for securing £1500 lent by Winnington to Loving and afterwards in trust for Loving for the residue of the £3000. The plaintiff, as creditor upon a judgment against Gregory, exhibited his bill to redeem the first mortgage upon payment of the £1000 and interest to Hutchins (Gregory being dead). Hutchins *[pendente] lite* conveyed to Winnington by direction for his money.

But upon the hearing, the court was of opinion that, by the judgment (which was before the conveyance to Winnington by Gregory), the plaintiff was entitled to the equity of redemption and should have it discharged [as to the] conveyance made by Gregory after the judgment. And upon this, Loving paid [to] the plaintiff his judgment.

I [was] for the plaintiff.

Note that in this case, the plaintiff, who had only an equity, was preferred before others who had also a subsequent equity and had obtained the statute in [common] law also but it [was] *pendente lite*.

121
Tenants of Wem v. Wicherly (Ex. 1681)

The issue in this case was the certainty of fines in a particular manor.

GUL MS. B88–7, p. 240–Q [Fr.] (Ward's Reports)

[There was a] decree upon a trial for settling a fine certain in copyholds not [to] exceed one year's ancient rent to the lord but being until eviction afterwards.

Upon another trial at the bar and full evidence of the uncertainty of the fine, the tenants' bill was dismissed without costs after great agitation in this court by English bill and trials endeavoring to prove and settle the certainty of the fines to be not in any sum certain but some sum at the pleasure of the lord not [to] exceed two years ancient rent.

[Order of 21 June 1680: PRO E.126/13, f. 225v.]

[Affirmed on appeal: *Lords' Journal*, XIII (n.d.), p. 714.]

122
Burwell v. Newton (Ex. 1681–1683)

The benefit of a mortgage, though it be in fee, is the personal estate of the mortgagee and goes to his administrator and is liable for his debts.

In this case, the issue was whether an heir who administers his father's estate takes as at common law or upon the Statute of Distributions.

I

GUL MS. B88–7, p. 247 [Fr.] (Ward's Report)

The case upon the hearing appeared to be thus. Dr. Burwell, chancellor of Durham, lent to one Johnson £600, and he, for the security of it, mortgaged lands in Suffolk to Dr. Burwell, the younger, and Francis Burwell in fee in trust for the doctor, the chancellor, who died intestate in 1671. And the doctor, the younger, took administration, to whom Francis released his right in the lands. After this, the doctor, the administrator, died in 1676 having made the defendant Newton his executor, to whom he devised 'all the rest of his estate in Suffolk, Durham, or anywhere else'. Francis Burwell, heir at law to the old and young doctors, took administration *de bonis non* to the old doctor and died, and by his will he devised all to Charles Burwell, who took administration *de bonis non* to the old doctor. And he exhibited his bill for relief.

And in this case, these things were resolved by the court:

1. That the benefit of the mortgage, though it was in fee, should be accounted [to be] the personal estate of the old Dr. Burwell and go to his administrator.
2. That the release of Francis to the young Dr. Burwell of the land did not[1] alter the case, nor was the mortgage, estate, or remedy of the other nature, but that it remained part of the personal estate of the old doctor.
3. That the devise to the defendant was worth nothing, and the devisor was entitled only as administrator to the old doctor, and thus [it was] not devisable.
4. (and this was not a principal question) That the Statute for Settling Intestates' Estates, 22 & 23 Car. II,[2] as it was made before the mortgage of the old doctor and because the old doctor did not have any other child than the young doctor, to whom administration and distribution of the estate belonged as of right, did not aid the defendant in this case nor give any interest or disposition to the young doctor so as to entitle him to have the benefit of the mortgage, and his own right was barred, [and the] reasons were:

1. That the Statute does not extend to this case because[3] it is a person only who shall have the residue, but distribution was intended to be made to several [rather] than one, and to those cases the Statute extends only.
2. That the benefit of the mortgage remains part of the personal estate of old Dr. Burwell, and it will be liable to his debts; otherwise, it would be mischievous and cheating of creditors because there is not any privity between the defendant and old Dr. Burwell, and on account of this [there is] no remedy, and the Statute does not make dispositions without ceremonies of the law that is administration.

And the plaintiff had a decree.

I [was] for the plaintiff.

---

[1] de *MS*.
[2] Stat. 22 & 23 Car. II, c. 10 (*SR*, V, 719–720).
[3] bon *MS*.

See above,[4] the argument upon the bill of review, but the court held [to] their former opinion and dismissed the bill of review.

II

BL MS. Hargr. 71, f. 45 [Fr.] (Dodd's Reports)

Upon an English bill in the exchequer, [it was] resolved in Trinity [term] 35 [1683] that if a man die having a son who administers [his estate] that he should have it as at common law and not upon the Statute of Distributions[5] to have a settled interest because it is out of the Statute and not [. . .].[6] This opinion was resolved and affirmed again upon the rehearing upon the point in law. And thus also was the opinion of the judges delegates (five judges) in other cases. But this term in a case in the king's bench, the whole court thought to the contrary and gave judgment *nisi*.

[Other copies of this report: HLS MS. 537(b), p. 10, pl. 1; Oxford Brasenose MS. 59, p. 11, pl. 2.]

[Order of 7 May 1681: PRO E.126/13, f. 288.]

123

Twistleton v. Jessup (Ex. 1681)

The nonpayment of tithes is not a disseisin of the right to receive tithes because a nonfeasance does not create an estate or displace an estate.

GUL MS. B88-7, p. 251 [Fr.] (Ward's Reports)

The plaintiff exhibited a bill as impropriator of the rectory of Drax in Yorkshire for tithes of hay, agistment, and herbage. The defendant by answer showed that he held a farm called Brockhalls consisting of 180 acres of pasture within that rectory but denied to pay tithes upon these pretenses:

1. That the farm was anciently part of the possessions of the priory of Drax of the grant of Payanell, and the prior of Drax was also seised of the rectory of Drax, and thus [there was] unity of possession of the lands and tithes [in the] time of Henry II.

---

[4] GUL MS. B88-7, p. 246.
[5] Stat. 22 & 23 Car. II, c. 10 (*SR*, V, 719-720).
[6] null Deved[t] *MSS*.

And it appeared that the priory of Drax came to [*blank*] in 27 Hen. VIII [1535],[1] being [one] of the lesser monasteries, and the farm was granted to one and the rectory to another, that the plaintiff's ancestor was seised of the farm, and [in] 10 Jac. [1612] he sold it to Grimsditch, who sold it to one Hatfield, who sold it to the defendant [in] 17 Car. II [1665], and that, in the conveyance of it [in] 10 Jac. [1612], the farm was conveyed to Grimsditch 'together with all such lawful exoneration and discharge from payment of tithes as the same were thentofore held and not otherwise', after which the plaintiff's ancestors purchased the rectory, and that, upon the sale to the defendant, there was a fine [levied] of the lands and the tithes of it, the uses of which fine were declared [in] 31 Car. II [1679] (after the plaintiff's bill [was] exhibited) to the defendant in fee, and it was admitted that no tithes be paid to the plaintiff or others. And the defendant insisted upon the fine and nonclaim for five years before the bill.

And it was held by the court that the defendant should pay his tithes in this case because the fine did not operate in this case to bar the plaintiff inasmuch as the defendant nor any others [held][2] the tithes in pernancy but only claimed exoneration and discharge of them, and he did not have any title in which this fine and nonclaim is[3] a bar to the plaintiff, who claims the tithes, according to the reason of Saffyn's Case, 5 Rep. 124,[4] and Stowell, Plowden 373,[5] there cited, because the estate of the plaintiff was not divested [any] more than in the case of common [. . .] rent, and thus it was held in Pace and Risley's Case,[6] in this court about two or three years past, and the defendant was decreed to pay tithes without any trial at law.

And it was held by all of the court that the defendant's not putting out of his tithes was not a disseisin of the plaintiff's title of tithes upon which a fine could operate because it was only a nonfeasance and did not create an estate in the defendant or displace the plaintiff's estate.

[Orders of 9 June and 1 July 1681: PRO E.126/13, ff. 292, 296.]

---

[1] Stat. 27 Hen. VIII, c. 28 (*SR*, III, 575–578).
[2] de *MS*.
[3] ne *MS*.
[4] *Saffyn's Case* (1605), 5 Coke Rep. 123b, 77 E.R. 248.
[5] *Stowel v. Lord Zouch* (1569), 1 Plowden 353, 75 E.R. 536.
[6] *Payce v. Risley* (1678–1679), PRO E.126/13, ff. 38v, 134v, 151v, 165.

124
Margets v. Butcher (Ex. 1681)

Tithes for a second crop of grass are due as a matter of right.

GUL MS. B88–7, p. 253 [Fr.] (Ward's Reports)

The plaintiff[1] exhibited a bill to be relieved for tithes of the second moath or after moath of grass. The defendants insisted upon discharges inasmuch as they spent the first crop upon their farms and in truth the tithes of the first moath were only made into grass cocks and not into hay.

And upon the question [being] raised, it was held that tithes of after moath, *scil.* second crop of grass, are due of common right without a prescription to do something that can be satisfaction, as making the first crop into hay cocks, and that making the first crop into grass cocks is not sufficient inasmuch as it is not more than the law requires and makes necessary for division. And [it was held] by all of the court [that] the spending of the first crop upon the farm is not any reason [or] cause to discharge notwithstanding Baxter and Hopes' Case, 2 Brownlow 30, 31, etc.[2] See Rolle's [Abr.] *Dismes* 650, 13.[3] And the court upon consideration of the cases [in] 1 Rolle's Abridgment 640, 11; Moore 758; Cro. El. 660; Cro. Car. 403; Hobart 250; Godolphin, title 'tythes' L.[4] A and after moath; 2 Cro. 116;[5] and the reason of the law and authorities that after moath was [at] all times discharged by prescription or by making or giving something for it and never otherwise, as the author above-mentioned, they decreed for the plaintiff without any tri[al] notwithstanding the opinion of Popham [in] 2 Cro. 42, in Hall and Fettyplace,[6] the reason of the other cases being against it, and if tithes of after moath be not due *de jure* why[7] [are] such prescriptions [at] all times alleged and [there be] no discharge without them, and tithes of after moath

---

[1] Margets, tenant of Sir John Elwes, impropriator of the rectory of King's Sutton, Northamptonshire.

[2] *Baxter v. Hopes* (1611), 2 Brownlow 30, 123 E.R. 797, 1 Eagle & Younge 200.

[3] *Anonymous* (1605), 1 Rolle, Abr., *Dismes*, pl. D, 13, p. 650.

[4] *Parson of Stanfield's Case* (1599), 1 Rolle, Abr., *Dismes*, pl. Q, 11, p. 640; *Hall v. Fettiplace* (1604), Moore 758, 72 E.R. 887; *Johnson v. Awbrey* (1599), Cro. Eliz. 660, 78 E.R. 899; *Anonymous* (1635), Cro. Car. 403, 79 E.R. 951; *Hide v. Ellis* (1619), Hobart 250, 80 E.R. 397, also Hetley 133, 124 E.R. 401; *Hall v. Simonds* (1604), J. Godolphin, *Repertorium Canonicum* (1680), p. 374, pl. 50.

[5] *Green v. Austen* (1606), Cro. Jac. 116, 79 E.R. 100, also 1 Eagle & Younge 164, Yelverton 86, 80 E.R. 59.

[6] *Hall v. Fettyplace* (1604), Cro. Jac. 42, 79 E.R. 34, 1 Eagle & Younge 157, also 1 Gwillim 222, Moore K.B. 758, 72 E.R. 887.

[7] quare *MS*.

here [are] reasonable, as tithes of second or third crop[s] of woad, saffron, clover, grass, and similar.

I [was] for the plaintiff. See above f. 21.

[Other reports of this case: 2 Gwillim 531.]

[The decree of 13 June 1681, PRO E.126/13 f. 310, is printed at 1 Wood 210, 1 Eagle & Younge 530.]

125
Camell v. Ward (Ex. 1681)

Wild fowl in a decoy and duck eggs and chicks for the king's use are not tithable.

GUL MS. B88–7, p. 256 [Fr.] (Ward's Reports)

[It was] resolved by the court that tithes for wild fowl in a decoy are not due without a custom and that no tithes should be paid for eggs or young ducks coming from tame ducks taken within the decoy for use and service of the king. And the plaintiff's bill was dismissed.

[This] was a Suffolk case. I [was] for the defendant.

[The decree of 21 June 1681, PRO E.126/13, f. 306, is printed at 1 Wood 209, 2 Gwillim 531, 1 Eagle & Younge 530.]

126
Toller v. Cooke (Ex. 1681)

In this case, the defendants, who were bakers living in another place, did not owe suit of mill where they sold their bread.

GUL MS. B88–7, p. 257, pl. 1 [Eng.] (Ward's Reports)

The plaintiffs were fee farmers to the king of four ancient corn mills in Ottery St. Mary's under a rent, to which all the tenants and inhabitants of Ottery St. Mary's owed suit of mill and ought to grind all their corn spent ground in their houses at those mills. The defendants were bakers, who lived at Honiton four or five miles from Ottery and ground their bread corn at Honiton mills and made the same into bread and sold the same on market days and other days at Ottery St. Mary's and for that purpose paid for standings or stalls there, and one rented a shop which he held the year round.

And the court was of opinion that the bakers were not within the custom or to be restrained from selling their bread in Ottery though the corn was ground at Honiton and the bread sold to the tenants or inhabitants of Ottery, though in this case there was no proof made of the bread sold to the inhabitants or tenants of Ottery. And the plaintiff's bill [was] dismissed.

The custom and right of grinding by the inhabitants and tenants was settled by several former decrees.

I [was] for the plaintiffs.

See 24 February 1713 setting down of causes, Nichols v. Inhabitants.

[Order of 21 June 1681, *sub nom.* Toller v. Bawden et al.: PRO E.126/13, f. 304.]

127
Cullier v. Mead (Ex. 1681)

In this case, the defendants were ordered upon very weak evidence to pay certain ancient pensions to the plaintiff.

GUL MS. B88–7, p. 261 [Fr.] (Ward's Reports)

The case upon the hearing was thus, [on the] 4th October 30 Eliz. [1588], Edmund, then bishop of Norwich, made a lease for eighty years to Queen Elizabeth of all pensions in Norfolk and Suffolk due and payable to the bishopric of Norwich, paying £45 9s. 10d. rent *per annum*, none of them being particularized in the lease. [On] 3 January 31 Eliz. [1589], the queen assigned this lease to Sir Thomas Heneage for the residue of the term. [On] 9th October 11 Car. I [1635], this lease by assignment came to Augustine Cullier. The plaintiff, as executor of Robert Cullier, who was executor of Augustine, demanded the arrearages of a pension of £3 6s. 8d. against the defendants Mead and Stephens and of a pension of 10s. *per annum* against the defendant Garlick for thirty-three years, *scil.* from the time of the assignment to Augustine Cullier until 1668 when the lease ended. And notwithstanding that there was not any proof that there were any such pensions except a record of the court of augmentations from the time of Henry VIII nor that those pensions were ever paid except for a book alleged to be a ledger belonging to the bishop of Norwich and made in the year 1613 during the existence of the lease, in which book, it was entered that those pensions (among others) were paid without contradiction, and notwithstanding that, after 1613, there was not a shadow of any payment or demand until the exhibiting of this bill, which was twelve years after the lease expired, and notwithstanding that the defendants Mead and Stephens were only executors of the lessee for years in trust for an infant now come of age and the title under the dean and chapter of Westminster, who were disseised of their revenue during the late troubles until the restoration of the king, and the defendant Garlick was not instituted into his rectory until 1670, which was two years after the lease expired, yet the court decreed the defendants to pay the pensions. They were charged with the possession according to the Case of Trinity College and [Tunstal], Cro. Eliz. 810,[1] and 5 Rep. 41, Downer's Case.[2]

Query the law because it seems a hard case against the defendants after Ognel's Case, 4 Rep. 49,[3] and the reason of it.

Liber K, f. 61,[4] ac[cord] with this case. See Liber J, f. 202, 6, and afterward here [ff.] 44, 45.

[This case is cited in Dean of Gloucester v. Stoodly (Ex. 1684), below, No. 192.]

128
Strickland v. Phrip (Ex. 1681)

In this case, the court refused to give the terms of a contract a strict interpretation that would defeat the expectations of the defendant.

GUL MS. B88–7, p. 262 [Fr.] (Ward's Reports)

The case upon the hearing was thus. In 1665, the plaintiff took a lease from the king of the duties upon foreign and Scottish salt for twenty-one years beginning [in] Michaelmas 1667 under the rent of £1800 *per annum*, which was more than the duties amounted unto. And the plaintiff by a deed covenanted to pay £100 *per annum* during the twenty-one years to the defendant's testator for being surveyor of those duties if the defendant's testator so long live. After this, that is to say around 1670, the plaintiff by consent of the defendant's testator surrendered the lease and took another for the residue of the twenty-one years under a rent of £1000 *per annum*. And the £100 *per annum* being in arrears for six years after the new lease, the defendant brought [an action of] covenant against the plaintiff. To be relieved against this, the plaintiff exhibited his bill. And his equity depended upon this, that the words of the covenant were to pay £100 *per annum* during the twenty-one years where the intention was to be during the term, and thus, the first term being surrendered by consent of the defendant's testator, the covenant should not be sued against him.

But the court held that the plaintiff did not have a cause for relief because, though there is a difference between *tempus* and *terminus 21 annorum*, yet in this case, as the plaintiff took the new lease not more or less than for the residue of the first twenty-one years, [there is] not. And the plaintiff, by no construction, shall

---

[1] *Trinity College v. Tunstal* (1601), Cro. Eliz. 810, 78 E.R. 1037.
[2] *Dormer's Case* (1593), 5 Coke Rep. 40a, 77 E.R. 115.
[3] *Ognel's Case* (1587), 4 Coke Rep. 49, 76 E.R. 1000.
[4] *Dean of Gloucester v. Stoodly* (Ex. 1684), below, No. 192.

avoid his covenant, but it will be construed to be the same term that was originally granted, and on account of that, the covenant [is] in full force. And if it had been 'term' and not *'tempus'* in the covenant so that strictly the legal remedy was gone by the surrender, still the [court] held that the covenantee[1] in such case shall be relieved in equity for the £100 *per annum*, if nothing appears to the contrary, that the intention was to determine the covenant by the surrender.

And note that the consent to the surrender by the defendant's testator was not well proved. And it is not reasonable to construe that the plaintiff, by reducing his rent to £1000 *per annum* by which he gained £800 *per annum*, will be in a better case than he was when he was bound to pay £1800 *per annum* and thus had a loss.

And by mediation of the court and the plaintiff's offer to pay 500 marks, the court decreed it by consent.

I [was] for the defendant.

[Order of 4 July 1681: PRO E.126/13, f. 303v.]

129
Metcalf v. Palmer (Ex. 1681)

Where a seller of land has beforehand contracted to pay a sum certain in lieu of tithes, the buyer takes free of the obligation to pay tithes.

GUL MS. B88–7, p. 273, pl. 1 [Fr.] (Ward's Reports)

[This was a] bill for tithes, and the case upon the hearing was thus. The defendant was impropriator, and one J.S. [was] owner and occupier of the land sown. And in July, before harvest, the plaintiff and J.S. agreed for the tithes for such a sum certain, after which and before harvest, J.S. sold the crop to the defendant tithe free. And the defendant did not set out any tithes. And for the recovery of the tithes, the plaintiff exhibited his bill against the defendant, and J.S. was not a party, but he refused to pay the composition.

And the court dismissed the bill inasmuch as the defendant should have the benefit of the composition and agreement made between the plaintiff and J.S., and the plaintiff must resort in this case to J.S. for the composition money.

I [was] for the plaintiff at the bar.

It seems upon the reason that, by the composition, the obligation to set out the tithes in kind was discharged and the right of the tithes converted into the composition.

---

[1] Covenanted *MS*.

130
Windsor v. Dowdeswell (Ex. 1681)

In this case, the defendant's proportion of a rent was clearly proved and decreed to be paid.

GUL MS. B88–7, p. 278 [Fr.] (Ward's Reports)

The plaintiffs exhibited their bill against the defendant to compel him to pay his proportion of a fee farm rent already apportioned. And in this case, the court gave great respect and credit to the former payments of the proportions and understood the rent to be apportioned, but as the proportion of the rent appeared in some conveyances, there the court decreed the payment accordingly without doubt or question.

[Order of 2 Dec. 1681: PRO E.126/13, f. 332v.]

131
Curtis v. Lord Culpeper (Ex. 1681)

A continuous course of payments in the past is evidence of the correctness thereof and can constitute proof of an apportionment of rents.

GUL MS. B88–7, p. 279 [Fr.] (Ward's Reports)

In the time of Queen Elizabeth some fresh and salt marshes in Kent and Sussex were granted under the fee farm rent of £122 0d. money. The lands were afterwards divided among the heirs general and special of one Smith who for some time, as it was said, paid this rent equally among them. One moiety was purchased from[1] them, under which the plaintiff claimed, and the other moiety was purchased by the father of lord Culpeper. And for some years this rent was paid by moieties to the officer of the king in 1639, 1640, and 1641. And one had a moiety of the fresh marsh and the other the other. Afterwards the salt marsh, by great charges, were improved and became profitable. Sir John Austin purchased the fresh marsh from lord Culpeper and paid £40 *per annum* for his moiety and Culpeper the residue. Lord Culpeper was in arrears, and the purchaser compelled the plaintiff to pay the arrears. And to have relief, the plaintiff preferred a bill.

And in this case, the court, upon a hearing and rehearing, were of the opinion that the payment of the moieties in 1639, 1640, [and] 1641 and afterwards was good evidence of an apportionment, especially as to the lord Culpeper. The

---

[1] per *MS*.

defendant here in a suit between him and the plaintiff took notice that the plaintiff paid £62 *per annum* and agreed to pay part of it. And the court did not regard the improvement of the salt marsh but seemed to incline that the rent, in judgment of the law, issued out of the fresh marsh and the profitable land at the time of the grant.

I query [this] because it seems clear that it issued out of all, as well the salt as the fresh [marsh]. But the court [held] those constant payments implied apportionment, and so it was decreed between the plaintiff and defendant lord Culpeper. But as to the defendant Austin, the Court would not meddle [. . .] proportion between him and lord Culpeper, there being nothing in the bill for it. But the decree was general against both of the defendants.

And afterwards Sir John Austin exhibited a bill against the lord Culpeper to have his proportion decreed. See the decree [in] 16 February 1682/3.[2]

132

Attorney General ex rel. Talbot v. Price (Ex. 1681)

An officer of the crown who received money from the crown to pay to others but does not pay it is a debtor to the crown.

The crown, as creditor, has priority over others creditors of the same debtor.

GUL MS. B88–7, p. 282 [Eng.] (Ward's Reports)

The relator being a colonel of the late raised forces and since disbanded received pay for his regiment from the king which, as the use was, he ordered to be paid to every captain for his own troop for the use of the soldiers. And for the colonel's troop, that was paid to one Captain Townly, who was his captain brevet. And the money was paid accordingly. Captain Townly had received for that troop about £80 more than he had paid and, being so indebted to the troop, died at Oxford, whereupon the relator, Colonel Talbot, caused all his money, apparel, horses, arms, and other goods to be seized upon and sold to satisfy the debt to the troop and which did not fully extend to do it at the rate they were sold. Townly being indebted to the defendant by bonds in about £50 or £60, the defendant [took] administration to Townly, who died suddenly and intestate (his wife having renounced), and brought his action of trespass against the relator for the goods and things so seized and sold in the [court of] king's bench.

To be relieved against [this], the relator procured Mr. Attorney General to prefer an English information against the defendant as well on the behalf of the king as of the relator and set forth the whole matter laid for equity that Townly,

---

[2] PRO E.126/14, f. 34.

being indebted to the king at the time of his death and the king being willing that his estate which was and ought to be liable to his debt should be applied to the payment of the troop, and therefore [etc.] and to avoid circuity and multiplicity of suits, prayed that the defendant's proceedings upon his action might be stayed and the matter determined in this court, and added a charge that [the] defendant had got many of Townly's goods into his hands which ought to be liable to the king's debt and to satisfy what the other goods seized and sold by the relator did not extend to [*blank*].

The defendant answered [and] set forth his just debt and administration and his ignorance of Townly's being indebted to the king but, if [the] troop [were] not paid, the relator [is] the debtor etc., and, if [the] fact [be] true as per [the] bill, it is a good defense against the action by plea or evidence.

The court, upon hearing the cause, sent it to a trial upon a feigned issue whether Townly, at his death, was debtor to the king and how much, which coming to a trial the latter end of the term and it being proved that Townly did receive the very money appointed to pay off that troop (though the relator gave the acquittance to the king's officers that paid it), the Lord Chief Baron Mountagu directed that that was the king's money though received for the use of the troop as aforesaid and that it not being paid to the troop, Townly remained debtor for it to the king at his death and so directed the jury, who found accordingly. And afterwards, at the setting down of causes after the term, it was decreed, *viz.* a perpetual injunction against that and all other actions by the defendant and that the defendant account for what goods of Townly's came to his hands and [they] to be applied to pay the residue of the debt due to the troop not paid by Townly's goods seized on by [the] relator.

I [was] for the defendant.

[Order of 3 Dec. 1681: PRO E.126/13, f. 327.]

133

Attorney General ex rel. Mayor of Maidenhead v. Jeffs (Ex. 1682)

Ancient demesne does not privilege any goods of merchandise but only the goods growing upon the ancient demesne lands.

GUL MS. B88–7, p. 297, pl. 1 [Fr.] (Ward's Reports)

[The plaintiffs sued] by English bill for tolls for boats passing under Maidenhead Bridge. The defendant pleaded that he is a tenant in ancient demesne in Henley and on account of that [is] discharged of this toll. And [it was] ruled [to be] no plea because ancient demesne does not privilege any goods of merchandise but only the goods growing upon the ancient demesne lands. 2 *Inst.* 221; *Liber 2*, 87, accord.[1]

And the defendant [was ordered to] pay costs.

I [was] for the plaintiff.

134

Cartwright v. Biggs (Ex. 1682)

Where a common is enclosed and turned from a sheep down to farm land and the vicar's glebe is increased as compensation for the loss of tithe of sheep, the vicar does not pay tithe for this additional land.

GUL MS. B88–7, p. 298 [Eng.] (Ward's Reports)

The defendant Biggs is vicar of Shrewton in Wiltshire, and the plaintiff [is] impropriator. A great down in that parish called Pet Down, being constantly till within two or three years used as a sheep down, the soil not worth above 6d. an acre, was now plowed up and sown with corn. The vicar, while [it was] a sheep down, had the tithes of the sheep. And the vicar in [the] right of his glebe and the other defendants in right of their lands had common for their sheep there. And now upon [its] plowing up, [it was] agreed to lay out two acres for a yard land in lieu of common, which each party plowed and sowed. The vicar had his proportion for his glebe and an acre more set out for him. And for the tithes of the vicars and [the] other inhabitants [that were] come upon the down, the plaintiff exhibits his bill.

The court upon [the] hearing agreed [on] these points:

1. That the ground allotted to the vicar, coming in lieu of his common which was part of his glebe though it something exceeded the common proportion to [the] others, yet should be taken and accepted for and as part of his glebe and a recompense for the loss of the tithe of sheep and so pay no tithes to the plaintiff. And so the bill was dismissed as against the vicar but without costs.

2. That though the down was not before the plowing worth above 6d. an acre, yet in regard [that] it had yielded a tithe, it could not nor ought to be taken for or as barren ground within the Statute of 2 Edw. VI[1] and be exempt from payment of tithes for seven years, though it was proved that [the] defendants had been at great charge in making the ground fertile for corn by manuring it. And it was proved that wheat growing there was worth £3 10s. an acre.

---

[1] E. Coke, *Second Institute* (1642), p. 221; *Attorney General ex rel. Steers v. Hale* (Ex. 1670), above, No. 46.

---

[1] Stat. 2 Edw. VI, c. 13, s. 5 (*SR*, IV, 56).

And the court denied a trial and decreed against all the defendants.
I [was] for the plaintiff.

[Order of 20 Feb. 1682: PRO E.126/13, f. 347v.]

135
Williams v. Goter (Ex. 1682)

In this case, a pension issuing out of a rectory was ordered to be paid.

GUL MS. B88–7, p. 299, pl. 1 [Eng.] (Ward's Reports)

[The] plaintiff, being vicar of Thorley in the Isle of Wight, had a decree against the defendant, being impropriator, for a pension of 40s. issuing out of the rectory though [there was] no proof or footsteps of any payment. But in regard [that] it stood fairly in charge upon the dissolution of a monastery whereof the rectory was part and appeared to be allowed by the bailiffs' accounts for a year when in the king's hands and, upon the conveyances of the rectory in King James's time, mention is made of it and some covenants to be saved harmless against it, the court decreed the duty and arrears for fifteen years without costs and denied a trial at law.

I [was] for the defendant.

[Order of 21 Feb. 1682: PRO E.126/13, f. 345v.]

136
Collard v. Newton (Ex. 1682)

The issue in this case was whether the Cistercian Order could have a prescriptive right not to pay tithes.

GUL MS. B88–7, p. 299, pl. 2 [Eng.] (Ward's Reports)

[The] plaintiff exhibited [a] bill for tithes. [The] defendant shows that the lands are of the Cistercian Order and of the greater monasteries and that he is [a] lessee for years but that neither he nor any other ever paid tithes but believes they were discharged by prescription, order, or some other way. The question was whether the Cistercian Order had or can have any other discharge than *quamdiu [in] manibus propriis* or whether they could prescribe in *non decimando*. To me it seemed at first [that] no such prescription can be, for the Council of Lateran, which gave the Cistercians that privilege,[1] was in the time of King John, which is

---

[1] X, 3. 30. 10.

within [legal] memory, and so [there can be] no prescription. And the books take no notice of any other discharge from that Order but that Council and for those lands only that they then had and not for any others acquired after.

Baron ATKYNS said [that] Lord Chief Baron Hale was of opinion [that they] might have lands for which they might so prescribe.

And Serjeant *Strode* said it might be that they had lands conveyed to them from other ecclesiastical persons who could so prescribe.

But Chief Baron MOUNTAGU inclined that the Cistercians had no other discharge but their Order's *quamdiu [in] manibus propriis* whereof the now defendant being lessee for years could not take advantage. But this being a matter of law, they directed an action of debt upon the Statute[2] and saved the equity till the event of that trial should appear, and, if doubtful, it might be found specially.

Note [that] about two years after in the like question upon another case,[3] the whole court seemed to incline that the Cistercians, being spiritual persons, might prescribe in *non decimando* and might have lands discharged for the reason given by Strode, *supra*. And so it has since been held in the court.

[Other reports of this case: 1 Rayner 58, 2 Gwillim 530, 1 Eagle & Younge 526.]

[This case is cited in Hankin v. Gay (1718), Bunbury 37, 145 E.R. 587, 1 Rayner 145, 1 Eagle & Younge 744.]

137

Chapman v. Hale (Ex. 1682)

Where sheep are wintered in one parish and shorn in another, each parson should receive a moiety of the tithes of wool.

GUL MS. B88–7, p. 300 [Eng.] (Ward's Reports)

In this case, the court decreed that the defendant should pay the plaintiff the moiety of the tithes of wool of ewes and other sheep wintered in the plaintiff's parish or kept there from St. Thomas [day] or before until St. Mark's day and after and then driven into and kept in other parishes and shorn there notwithstanding the plaintiff had the tithes of the lambs that fell in his parish from those sheep so kept and driven out.

A Sussex case. I [was] for the plaintiff.

[Order of 20 Feb. 1682: PRO E.126/13, f. 341v.]

---

[2] Stat. 2 Edw. VI, c. 13 (*SR*, IV, 55–58).
[3] Note *Wright v. Daffy* (Ex. 1684), below, No. 197.

138
Attorney General v. Sharpe (Ex. 1682)

In this case, a special jury found that certain proposed buildings would not create a nuisance to the Tower of London.

GUL MS. B88–7, p. 301, pl. 2 [Eng.] (Ward's Reports)

Attorney General Levinz exhibited on English information against Captain Sharpe to restrain him from proceeding to finish certain houses upon Little Tower Hill, some whereof were one story high and foundations of others laid, alleging they would be nuisances to endanger the Tower of London. And thereupon after answer setting forth the defendant's title to the inheritance and the distance to be above 300 feet from the outside of the Tower ditch and that others were built nearer, yet upon an affidavit of some of the Tower officers expressing their belief [that] it might be a nuisance to the Tower both in case of fire and war, the court granted an injunction to stay the further building without any office found [?] or other matter than the affidavit. And upon hearing the cause, the court sent it to a trial at law whether the buildings would be a nuisance to the Tower or not. And after a view by a special jury of Middlesex and a long evidence[1] at the bar, a verdict passed for the defendant. But because the defendant offered at the trial not to build above the second rate of buildings, the court would not allow him to build higher. And so the order is entered by the attorney general's consent.

I [was] for Sharpe.

[Order of 20 Feb. 1682: PRO E.126/13, f. 341.]

139
Warnford v. Millington (Ex. 1682)

The executors of an obligor are liable to pay his contractual obligations.
Where rents are charged upon land, the obligee can go against the personal estate of the deceased obligor or the land itself.

GUL MS. B88–7, p. 302 [Eng.] (Ward's Reports)

The plaintiff, being entitled to a moiety of certain lands in Kent, and Mr. King, the defendant, then Lady Millington's former husband, being entitled to the other moiety, and the plaintiff, because of the relation between them, being willing [that] Mr. King should have all after her death but she to have the

---

[1] Sic in MS.

profits of her moiety during her life, conveys her moiety to Mr. King in fee, Mr. King covenanting for himself, his heirs, executors, and administrators (but not for his assigns) to pay the plaintiff the moiety of the rents and profits during her life, the lands being then esteemed to be in all [worth] £500 *per annum* or thereabouts. Mr. King dies leaving the defendant, the Lady Millington, executrix and £10,000 assets. And the lands being gavelkind, she enjoyed the moiety during her widowhood.

The plaintiff exhibits her bill against the defendant as executrix to make good and execute in specie her husband's covenant and made not the heir at law [a] party. And in that case, [it] arising whether Mr. King had made any addition to the plaintiff's £200 *per annum* by his will, which the court held he had not, they resolved these two things:

1. That the defendants were bound by the covenants out of Mr. King's personal estate to make the covenant good and to execute it in specie notwithstanding [that] the covenant was made in respect of the [*blank*], and
2. It was not necessary for the plaintiff to make the heir at law or [the] devisee of the land a party, but [she] had an election to charge the executors or lay it upon the land, which without doubt was charged with it.

And that point of the parties was settled upon a plea put in by the defendants to the plaintiff's bill.

And a decree with costs passed upon this.

I [was] for the plaintiff.

[Order of 6 and 20 Feb. 1682: PRO E.126/13, ff. 339v, 350v.]

140

Attorney General v. Flatman (Ex. 1682)

A defendant must answer and make discovery under oath where any penalties to the crown have been waived and no one else can make a claim against him.

GUL MS. B88–7, p. 303, pl. 1 [Eng.] (Ward's Reports)

It was, upon a plea and demurrer to Mr. Attorney General's bill to have a discovery of what sums for law duty the defendant[1] had received and not accounted for, resolved by the court [that] the defendant ought to answer, Mr. Attorney General having waived the penalties, which are wholly [due] to the king. And

---

[1] One of the sworn attorneys in chancery.

though the six clerks are made the receivers from the under clerks, yet if they never pay the six clerks, it is no reason [that] the king should lose it when they have received it from the clients; besides the six clerks are not appointed receivers of the money.

[This case is cited in Attorney General v. Herring (Ex. 1707), below, No. 421.]

141
Lady Pointz v. Porter (Ex. 1682)

In this case, the intent of the testator was construed by the court.

GUL MS. B88-7, p. 303, pl. 2 [Fr.] (Ward's Reports)

The case upon the hearing was thus. Sir John Pointz, seised in fee of the manor of Iron Acton and three others in the County of Gloucester, mortgaged and encumbered these lands. And he was also indebted to divers persons. And [on] 23 April 1680 by his will in writing, he devised all of his estate and equity of redemption in the premises to the plaintiff and her assigns forever, and after a legacy of £500 devised to one Smith, he devised all of the residue of his estate, real and personal, after debts and funerals [were] paid, to the plaintiff. And he made her sole executrix. In this will, a proviso ensued that if the defendant Porter, who was his nephew, within two years after his death should pay the mortgages and redeem the premises and settle upon the plaintiff £300 *per annum* to be issuing out of the premises or other lands for her life, in such case he devised the premises to the defendant Porter in tail male, remainder to the joint and equal use of the duke of Ormond and George Penn and their heirs. And in such case, he devised to the said Porter all of his personal estate for the execution of his will.

In October afterwards, Sir John, by lease and release, conveyed the premises to Baker and Hawkins and their heirs in trust that they, with convenient speed, should sell the premises for the best price and with the money and rents pay the money due upon the mortgage, *viz.* to Sir James Smith and Simon Bennet, and afterwards a debt of £160 to Hawkins, and £83 to Penton, and £40 to Lewis, and £250 to Brereton, and after all other debts that he should declare by any writing to be owing by him, and in the fifth place to pay to the plaintiff £2000, and lastly to pay the residue of the money to be raised by the sale and rents to such persons and in such manner as Sir John by his last will or any other writing to be by him signed and sealed shall give or appoint. Sir John died without making another will or writing, and the plaintiff proved the will and had administration.

The defendant Porter contested because Sir John, at the time of the making of the lease and release, was *non compos mentis*. But upon a trial at the bar, he was proved to be *compos mentis*, and there was a verdict for it.

And now the single question was who should have this residue or surplus after the performance of the trusts in the release because it was agreed by all that the lease and release as to the real estate was a revocation of the will as to it. The heirs at law, who were the duke of Ormond and Mr. Penn, did not contest the point. But the sole contest was between the plaintiff and the defendant Porter.

And the counsel for the defendant endeavored to entitle him to the residue upon these reasons:

1. That as to it, the will and release are or in judgment of the law only a conveyance, for, as the matter stands upon the will, the plaintiff should have only £300 *per annum* by the intent of the devisor by the devise to the plaintiff of the lands, and the making her executrix was only security for it, and this being well made to the plaintiff, the defendant should have all beyond, and if he pretermitted the two years limited in the will, still it is equity for her afterwards (but the two years have not expired).
2. Though the deeds revoked the will as to the lands, yet by them the plaintiff can have only £2000 which is recompense and comes in place of the £300, and if by the will, the plaintiff can have only the £300 *per annum* or the benefit of the devise as personalty, thus having satisfaction for this £300 *per annum* by the £2000 in the release, she cannot claim more, but all of the residue should go to the defendant, and the residue limited to the plaintiff by the will was in reality only in the nature of a mortgage or security for the £300 *per annum*, as to the £300 *per annum* being recompense and satisfied by the £2000, the residue by the deeds will go as the residue must by the will which is to the defendant subject to the £300 *per annum*, and the deeds are only better provision for payment of the debts.

And upon these reasons, Chief Baron MOUNTAGU declared his opinion for the defendant. But the other three barons, *scil.* ATKYNS, GREGORY, and STREET, declared their opinion for the plaintiff upon these reasons:

1. That when the will was made, Sir John intended the lands to be preserved and that the defendant Porter should have them upon the terms in the will, but at the time of the making of the deeds, his intent was changed, and he intended the lands to be sold.
2. The defendant cannot have the residue without entitling himself to the lands, but his claim to the lands was by the will only, that as to them it is totally revoked by the deeds, and on account of that, he

cannot have the residue, so that the question must be determined as if no devise or proviso had been [made] for the defendant.

3. The law that is executor [. . .] entitled to Sir John's personal estate to be to have the residue[1] in the release because, as it was said, Porter without having the lands cannot have the residue, and on account of that inasmuch as Sir John, after the deeds, did not make any will or writing otherwise directing this residue, it must go to the executors appointed in his will made before, who is the plaintiff, and it is as reasonable to make such a construction upon it, that it is to dispose of the residue by the release respecting a will or writing to be made (as no such was made) it will apply to the will made before as the word *procreandis* respects issue procreated; as 1 *Inst.* 20, 6.[2]

The attorney general, Williams, and others [were] for [*blank*]. The solicitor general, myself, and others [were] for [*blank*].

The right of the heir at law to the residue [is] because it seems in all cases when lands are to be sold for the payment of debts the remainder to the heir without other [words is a] full disposition because it is as part of the [. . .] and it will go as the land should.

[Orders of 11 and 18 May 1682: PRO E.126/13, ff. 365v, 366.]

142
Whitaker v. Whitaker (Ex. 1682)

Lancashire clothes pay same subsidy of aulnage as the others pay.

GUL MS. B88–7, p. 319 [Eng.] (Ward's Reports)

[It was] resolved by the court that Lancashire clothes shall pay the king's subsidy of aulnage after the same rate that others pay, that is by weight without regard to the coarseness of the clothes, and this over and besides the 3d. per pack and half penny per piece appointed for the aulnagers fee by the Statute of 8 Eliz., c. 12,[1] and that short Statute in no sort extends the subsidy. And the plaintiff's bill brought for relief that they might pay no more in all, both for subsidy and aulnage, than 3d. per pack and ½d. a piece [was] dismissed with £20 costs.

I [was] for the plaintiffs.

---

[1] ley q est exec^r ou entitle al Sr Johns personall Estate dee aver le residue *MS*.
[2] E. Coke, *First Institute* (1628), f. 20b.

---

[1] Stat. 8 Eliz. I, c. 12 (*SR*, IV, 495–496).

143
Attorney General v. Lord Carrington (Ex. 1682)

Land conveyed in trust to superstitious uses is forfeited to the crown.

GUL MS. B88–7, p. 320 [Eng.] (Ward's Reports)

[In] Trinity Term 31 Car. II [1679], the attorney general, Sir William Jones, exhibited an English information into the exchequer on behalf of His Majesty against Sir Thomas Preston, baronet, lord viscount Molineux, lord Carrington, Robert Dalton, and Humphrey Weld, esq., and others thereby charging that Sir Thomas Preston was a Romish priest of the order and college of Jesuits and in May 1674 was seised in fee of divers manors, lands, and tenements in the counties of Lancaster, Westmoreland, Northampton, Warwick, and elsewhere in England and, being minded to settle the same in such manner that the rents and profits thereof should privately be applied for the support of the order or college of Jesuits or some such like unlawful or superstitious use, did, by indentures of lease and release of the 5th and 6th of May 1674, convey the soil of the late dissolved monastery of Furness in the County of Lancaster and divers other lands and hereditaments in that county to the defendants, the lord Carrington and Richard Walmesly, and their heirs; and by deed poll of the said 6th of May reciting the said lease and release, Sir Thomas Preston declared they were so made with a power of revocation; and by another indenture of the same date made between Sir Thomas Preston, lord Carrington, and Walmesly of the one part and [the] defendant Weld of the other part, it was declared that the lord Carrington and Walmesly and their heirs should stand and be seised of the premises in trust and for the only use of such persons and estates as the defendant Weld should appoint and for want of such appointment and until such appointment for the use and benefit of the said Weld, his heirs, and assigns forever; that by deed poll of the 11th of May 1674, Weld appointed that the lord Carrington and Walmesly and their heirs should thenceforth stand and be seised of the premises in trust for Weld for his life and after for the use of such persons as Edmund Plowden, esq., should direct and for want of such direction then in trust for the only use and benefit of the said Plowden, his heirs, and assigns forever; and further charges that by indenture of the 30th of May 1674, Sir Thomas Preston leased other lands in Lancashire, Westmoreland, Cumberland, Warwick, Northampton, [and] Coventry for forty years to the defendants, lord Molineux, lord Carrington, Dalton, and Walmesly, which by deed poll of that date were declared to be under power of revocation; that soon after the execution of these deeds, Sir Thomas Preston went to the College of Jesuits at St. Omers where he remained a Romish priest of that order; that the inheritance of the premises in the lease and release vested in the said lord Carrington and Walmesly and the term of forty years in the lessees notwithstanding the declarations and powers of revocation; and that all the said conveyances were construed and executed only for unlawful and superstitions uses appointed and designed by Sir Thomas Preston; and that the rents and profits received out of all the premises have been and the growing rents and profits are designed to be applied to unlawful and superstitious uses though defendants know they ought to be answered to His Majesty; and to have a discovery of the premises and of the rents and profits and how applied; and that the said premises may be conveyed to the king; and the attorney general relieved in the premises was the bill.

The lords Molineux and Carrington, Dalton, and Weld (Walmesly and Plowden being dead), by answer, say they know not that Sir Thomas Preston was a priest or Jesuit, believe he was seised in fee of the lands in the bill and that he made the lease for forty years charged with debts, fee farms, and other payments, but know not that he made the lease and release [alleged] in the bill. The lord Carrington and Mr. Weld own it and other the deeds [mentioned] in [the] bill but deny that they know or believe they were made to any unlawful or superstitious or to any other uses than what are therein expressed.

After examination of witnesses the 14th [of] February 1681, when it was referred to a trial at law at the bar of the court upon a feigned issue between the attorney general and lord Molineux and Carrington, Dalton, and Weld first whether the indentures of lease and release were made to or for any and what unlawful or superstitious use or uses and the second issue to be the same as to the lease for forty years, the trial was had in Easter term 1682 by a special jury of Middlesex, who found the first issue for the king and that the lease and release were made to and for unlawful and superstitious uses (but [it was] not mentioned in particular what they were). And the second issue was found for the defendants.

And the cause coming this day[1] to be heard, the court declared themselves satisfied that the lease and release were made for unlawful and superstitious uses (not saying what) and decreed that the king, his heirs, and successors shall forever hereafter hold and enjoy the premises conveyed by the said lease and release against the defendants and all claiming under them and further decreed the lord Carrington and Weld being but trustees to bring in their deeds and evidences and convey their whole estate therein to the king and his heirs and successors freed from all incumbrances done by them and deliver the possession to the king or such as he shall appoint. And an injunction is awarded for that purpose and an account [is] to be taken of the rents and profits since the bill and lord Carrington and Weld to be indemnified for what they shall do pursuant to that decree. And as to the lease for forty years, the defendants are dismissed.

---

[1] 30 May 1682.

Entered in the decree book at folios 370, 371, 372.[2] See Liber L, f. 34.[3]

Query what was done pursuant to this decree which was never altered or reversed that I know or heard of after 72.[4]

The estate was conveyed to the king, his heirs, and successors by those that had the legal estate in them and enjoyed by the crown.

[Orders of 14 Feb. and 30 May 1682: PRO E.126/13, ff. 344v, 370v.]

[This case is cited in Attorney General v. Gaynor Jones (Ex. 1688), below, No. 269; Attorney General ex rel. Boucher v. Portington (Ex. 1694), below, No. 291; Attorney General v. Burdett (Ex. 1705), below, No. 395.]

144

Monkes v. Worden (Ex. 1682)

Property settled absolutely on a wife is part of her estate and is to be administered by her executors.

GUL MS. B88–7, p. 325 [Eng.] (Ward's Reports)

The case upon the bill and answer appeared to be thus. Edmund Worden having married Elizabeth Blondell, with whom he was to have a portion and upon whom he was to settle a provision or jointure if she survived, prevailed to have the portion upon security for the provision or settlement. And he being tenant for life remainder to his brother James, [the] defendant, for life or in tail, Edmund and James, made a lease of the lands to some of the defendants for forty years in trust that they should receive the rents and profits after the decease of Edmund until they should receive £196 10s. for the use, benefit, and behoof of the said Elizabeth and her assigns if she be living at Edmund's death and, if she be dead, then for the use of Mary, Edmund's daughter by Elizabeth, provided that if Elizabeth survive Edmund and die before £196 10s. be raised, that the residue unraised should go to Edmund's daughter then living. Edmund dies. Mary, the daughter, dies, no other children of Edmund being living. Then Elizabeth, the wife, dies, who by her will devised the £196 10s. for payment of her debts, and [she] made the plaintiffs her executors, who sue for it.

And the question was, it not being raised in her life, whether it shall go to her.

And the opinion of the court was [that] it should go to the plaintiffs. And so it was decreed, for it was originally intended to be a provision for the wife and it

---

[2] Order of 30 May 1682: PRO E.126/13, f. 370v.
[3] *Attorney General v. Gaynor Jones* (Ex. 1688), below, No. 269.
[4] Sic in *MS.* for 1692 perhaps.

was limited to her and her assigns, and the first limitation to her being absolute, the proviso takes it not out of her but in case she die leaving Mary or any other issue by Edmund living, but that contingency not happening, it ought to go to the executors of Elizabeth.

I [was] for the plaintiffs. The attorney general, Serjeant Rigby, Birch, and others [were] for the defendants.

145

Burton v. Barrow (Ex. 1682)

Where sheep are wintered and shorn in one parish but pastured in another for part of the year, the parson of the former parish receives the tithes of lamb and wool, and the parson of the latter pro rata tithes of pasturage.

GUL MS. B88–7, p. 326 [Eng.] (Ward's Reports)

[It was] resolved by the court and so decreed that if sheep be wintered in the parish of A. and be kept there for half a year or any other time and then are agisted in any other parish for the other part of the year and brought thence into the parish of A. and there shorn and carried again to agistment in the other parish, in regard [that] the owner of the sheep lives in A. and the sheep were shorn there, that the tithe wool is all due to the parson of A. and that the parson of the other parish, where they were agisted part of the year, shall only have a pasturage tithe *pro rata temporis* and not part or share of the wool as formerly had been constantly used.

And so it was the same term decreed between Jones and Townam[1] about the Rectory of [*blank*], a Welsh cause, where sheep intercommoned in two separate parishes and the owner had right of common in both, that the tithe of wool and lamb should be paid in that parish only where the lambs fell or [the] wool shorn and the other minister to have recompense for pasturage tithe, as above.

But I query against whom. It seems [it would be] the minister of the other parish that had the wool.

I query in those two cases whether anything be due above tithe wool for pasturage, and, if due, against whom; the parson of the agisting or commoning parish shall recover his tithe of pasturage; and after what rate; the inhabitant that pays wool and lamb in kind shall be liable or deduct to the minister, for it is not reasonable that he should pay tithe in kind to one minister both of wool and lamb and yet be liable to the other for a ratable tithe after the pasturage.

---

[1] Probably *John v. Watkins* (Ex. 1682), below, No. 146.

146
John v. Watkins (Ex. 1682)

In this case, tithes of wool were due to the owner of the tithes where the sheep were shorn.

GUL MS. B88–7, p. 327 [Eng.] (Ward's Reports)

The rectory of Talgarth, wherein there have used to be several tithings and hamlets, *viz.* A. and B., was leased to Gunter, who demises all tithes arising in the tithing of A. to the plaintiff and in the tithing of B. to the defendant under distinct leases and several rents. There are several distinct commons usually enjoyed severally [by the] inhabitants of A. and B. and reputed as their distinct commons, all lying in the same parish contiguous one to the other. And in truth, [they] did really intercommon one with the other, as the defendant's witnesses swore. The defendant was an inhabitant in the hamlet or tithing of B. but had sheep that went on the common of A. all the year except at shearing time when they were fetched five miles from the common of A. to be shorn at B. and when shorn then in a week's time driven back to A. And for the tithe wool of these sheep, the plaintiff exhibited his bill. And his counsel insisted that [the] distinction of the tithings and rights were as much as if they had been separate parishes (especially the lessee of the tithing of B. being in combination with the occupier), and then it is the common case that such driving and shearing in another parish is fraudulent[1] and hurts not.

But the court was of opinion that in regard [that] all the commons lay in one parish and that the sheep did or might promiscuously feed on both, that the tithe wool should be paid to the owner of the tithes where the sheep [were] shorn and no recompense for that or any pasturage tithe [was due] to the farmer of the other tithing where they were kept almost all the year. And so [they] dismissed the plaintiff's bill with costs.

Query how this [case] and that of Nantmellin, *supra*,[2] do agree; see above. See for these cases: Brooke [Abr.] *Dismes* 16; Lane 16; Degge 245–253; Godolphin, title 'wool and sheep'.[3] See above, f. 53, Chapman v. Hale.[4]

[Order of 10 July 1682: PRO E.126/13, f. 388.]

---

[1] Sic in MS.
[2] Probably *Burton v. Barrow* (Ex. 1682), above, No. 145.
[3] Brooke, Abr., *Dismes et Tenthes Spirituelles*, pl. 16; *Huddleston v. Hill*, Lane 16, 145 E.R. 262; S. Degge, *Parson's Counsellor* (1681), pp. 249–253; *Anonymous*, J. Godolphin, *Repertorium Canonicum* (1680), p. 359, pl. 15.
[4] *Chapman v. Hale* (Ex. 1682), above, No. 137.

147

Hewley v. Cholmly (Ex. 1682)

In this case, arrears of rent were ordered to be paid to the lessor, who was the mortgagee.

GUL MS. B88–7, p. 331 [Fr.] (Ward's Reports)

The case upon the hearing was thus. Sir William Darcy and his son, George Darcy, mortgaged certain alum mines in the County of York *inter alia* [to] Mr. Woodrick. The money not being paid, they and the plaintiff and his [wife], administratrix to Woolwrick,[1] in 1665 leased the mines to the king paying £400 annually generally. In a small time afterwards [?], the king, under the great seal, leased the mines [to] *inter alia* Sir Nicholas Crispe and others, under whom the defendants claim, for certain years reserving a rent of £400 *per annum* to be paid to Sir William Darcy and George, his son (not mentioning the plaintiff [or] his wife). Sir William Darcy, being satisfied that his mortgage money was not paid, by a note under his hand, directed Cowardsley [?], the farmers' agent, to pay a third part of the £400 *per annum* rent to Sir John Hewley, the plaintiff, until further order, which was paid in 1666 until Midsummer 1672,[2] after which, Sir William thinking that all of the mortgage money was paid, he discharged Coward from further payment of the third part. And in Trinity term 1673, Sir William Darcy and his son exhibited their bill against the now plaintiff to have a reconveyance supposing that all of the money due was paid with a surplus, which bill Sir John and [his] wife answered.

And afterwards [in] Michaelmas [term] 1674, they exhibited their cross-bill against Sir William Darcy and [his] son for payment of the money due upon the mortgage or to foreclose them of the equity of redemption and against the now defendants to have the third part of the £400 *per annum* rent to be paid against satisfaction of the mortgage alleging that the reservation should have been made [?] to him as well as to Sir William and [his] son inasmuch as Sir John and [his] wife had the estate in [common] law in them, out of which the lease to the king was created and derived.

Sir William Darcy, his son, and the farmers, defendants, all joined in an answer. Sir William and [his] son denied the equity of the bill. The farmers offered to pay as the court should direct and prayed to be indemnified.

Both causes were heard together on 8 November 1677 and referred to accounts between Sir William Darcy, his son, and Sir John Hewley. And no notice [was] taken at the hearing or in the order of the arrears of the third part to Midsummer 1672 until this time, but this third part for the time to come was ordered

---

[1] Sic in MS.
[2] jesque ad et pro Midsomer 1672 *MS*.

to be paid into the court, which was paid accordingly. [On] the 3 May 1679, the farmers surrendered their lease, by which the rent of £400 *per annum* ceased. [On] 6 May 1680 upon the auditors' report, Sir William Darcy and [his] son were reported £580 in debt to Sir John Hewley, which was decreed to be paid by Sir William Darcy and [his] son by Lady Day next or their bill to be dismissed.[3]

Sir John Hewley received the money out of the court amounting to £200 towards [the] payment of his £580, and the lease being surrendered and thinking Sir William Darcy and his son not sufficient, he prosecuted the farmers, the defendants, for the arrears of the third part of the rent from Midsummer 1672 until November 1677, the time of the first order and decree.

And [on the part] of the farmers, it was urged:

1. That there was not any privity between them and the plaintiff but that they must pay to Sir William Darcy and [his] son.
2. They cannot pass their account with the king, who was entitled to the surplus, and they refused to give an acquittance without receipt of all the rent.
3. That Coward's authority was only a private order and in the nature of a bill of exchange, and it was revoked.
4. That the order upon the hearing [of] 8 November [. . .] all past, no notice being taken of the arrears then incurred nor [was there] any provision for them but only prospect[ive] for the future, which the defendants obeyed. And if it had been the judgment of the court at this time that the defendants should have answered for the past arrears, they could and would have stopped the money out of the rent after and before the surrender notwithstanding that none of the court decreed that the defendants should satisfy Sir John Hewley for the arrears after his bill and before the hearing [of] 8 November inasmuch as the first bill was sufficient notice to the defendants of the plaintiff's title and they offered to pay as the court directed, without their direction, they should not have paid, and this was a gross and supine neglect to pay without an order.

And though the order upon the hearing [of] 8 November did not mention the arrears incurred without, yet it did not discharge them. And on account of that, they should pay out of their own estates without costs.

But the court held that the notice of the lease to the king nor the note of [*blank*] were not any good notice.

I [was] for the defendants.

[Order of 11 May 1682: PRO E.126/13, f. 368.]

---

[3] PRO E.126/13, f. 219.

148
Salisbury v. Whitby (Ex. 1682)

A suit for dilapidations cannot be brought in the court of exchequer.

GUL MS. B88–7, p. 334, pl. 4 [Fr.] (Ward's Reports)

An English bill for relief [for] dilapidations [was] dismissed with costs inasmuch as the court did not have jurisdiction of the cause. It was held a good bill for discovery of assets but not for relief. A similar [result] was declared spoken in the Case of Dr. Barker upon a plea two terms past and that because [?] the court will not hold a plea of dilapidations [*blank*] of tithes, procurations, and other ecclesiastical things. [An allegation of] debtor of the king gives privilege [to the court].

[Order of 29 June 1682: PRO E.126/13, f. 376v.]

149
Duke of Newcastle v. Holland (Ex. 1682)

Persons with separate titles to separate mills all of which are ancient crown mills in the same place can join as co-plaintiffs where the defendants are alleged to be compellable to grind at any one of them.
In this case, the plaintiffs were unable to prove their alleged right.

GUL MS. B88–7, p. 345 [Fr.] (Ward's Reports)

The plaintiffs all join in one English bill to compel the defendants to grind their corn at the mills of the plaintiffs or any one of them. And for title, the duke claimed the mills called Mansfield Mills and Mansfield Woodhouse Mills, and the other defendants[1] claimed another mill called Sutton Mills. And they showed that all of these mills were ancient crown mills and that all of the inhabitants and residents of Mansfield, by tenure, custom, or otherwise, must grind their corn spent [or] ground in their houses at these mills or any of them and that Queen Elizabeth granted [them] (but no fee farm rent was shown to be reserved) and that afterwards, in the time of King James, Sutton Mills were granted under a fee farm rent to others [?], under whom the [plaintiffs] Linley and Holmes claimed as tenants in common, one of a fourth part, the other of three fourths. And the purpose and prayer of the bill was that the defendants should be enjoined to grind their corn at the mills of all of the plaintiffs or any of them and that loaders should be restrained from fetching or carrying to the other mills.

---

[1] Sic in MS. for plaintiffs.

The defendants demurred to this bill, and for cause they showed that the plaintiffs, having distinct titles and distinct interests in distinct mills, should not join in one suit inasmuch as the court could not know for whom to make a decree if the defendants should be compelled to grind at any of their mills.

Secondly, it was insisted that the duke did not have privilege to sue here inasmuch as no fee farm rent was reserved.

But the court overruled the demurrer without costs for this reason, that though the plaintiffs have now distinct titles to these distinct mills, yet inasmuch as it was laid in the bill that they were all the ancient crown mills and that the tenants and inhabitants of Mansfield owe suit and service to them, the making of separate grants of them to separate persons did not destroy this service, but the defendants should be compelled to grind their corn at any of the mills, and on account of that, none of the plaintiffs can sue separately to compel suit at his mill distinct from the others. They must join *ex necessitate*. And inasmuch as a fee farm rent was reserved upon one grant, though none upon the others, yet the privilege remains.

But afterwards, [on] 14 June 1683, the cause came to a hearing, and the defendants' counsel insisted upon the same exceptions. But inasmuch as the plaintiffs did not make full proof of the usage of grinding and that it was proved that Mansfield Woodhouse Mill did not stand in the same place as before but a furlong distant, the plaintiffs' bill was dismissed.

I [was] for the defendants.

As to the matters of law, see Coriton and Lisbie's Case, Liber H, f. 43, in the [court of] king's bench, where it was held that [where] such tenants claim by distinct interests, they can join in [one] action or suit. Ventris and Saunders reports [show] that they can join; 2 Levinz 27, they can join.[2]

150
Trinity College Cambridge v. Hepburne (Ex. 1682)

In this case, various pensions payable out of various rectories were found due to the plaintiff.

GUL MS. B88–7, p. 347 [Eng.] (Ward's Reports)

The plaintiff sues for several pensions issuing out of the three several rectories in Bill and entitle themselves to the said pensions by a grant of King Henry VIII, and to be paid the arrears and for settling future payments was the bill.

---

[2] *Coriton v. Lithby* (1671), 1 Ventris 167, 86 E.R. 114, 2 Wms. Saunders 115, 85 E.R. 823, *sub nom. Lithebury v. Coriton*, 2 Levinz 27, 83 E.R. 437.

The defendants, rectors of the three rectories, each answer for themselves and severally deny their several knowledge of the several and respective pensions issuing out of and or payable for their respective rectories. But upon reading the surveys, ledger books, and evidence of the College for the plaintiff, the court decreed the arrears for divers years and the future payments so long as the defendants respectively are rectors of the rectories. And also the decree extends to the successors of the rectors for their times. [This was] entered in the Book of Decrees, folio 214.[1]

151
Sawbridge v. Pulford (Ex. 1682)

A court of equity does not have the power to make a distribution of an intestate's estate.

GUL MS. B88–7, p. 348, pl. 2 [Fr.] (Ward's Reports)

The entire court, that is to say MOUNTAGU, chief baron, ATKYNS, GREGORY, and STREET, barons, declared their opinion that this court does not have the power to make distribution of intestates' estates and dismissed the plaintiff's bill upon this point notwithstanding that it was urged by the plaintiff's counsel that the court of chancery gives relief in such cases and see[1] the precedent in chancery, Winnington *et al.* v. Winnington *et al.*, 28 January 32 Car. II [1681], where the court relieved the plaintiffs being children of the brother and sister of the intestate against the intestate's wife who took administration and [the court] decreed an account and distribution. And another precedent was there also cited to the same purpose. But the court here went upon this reason that this Statute[2] though it is in the affirmative yet *est introductio novi juris* because before it, the chancery or this court did not have any power to make distribution and when the Statute created and gave this power to distribute to the ecclesiastical court and prescribed the form and method to be pursued in making this distribution and that that which is to be distributed is only the foot of the account after debts and funeral [expenses] paid as appears by the condition of the bond in the act, no authority emerged or resulted out of this Statute to a court of equity to make distribution, and before the act, there was not any such authority.

But it was admitted for discovery of the estate liable to be distributed, or for decreeing trusts to be part of the personal estate and executing those trusts, courts of equity can intermeddle there.

---

[1] Order of 10 May 1680: PRO E.126/13, f. 213.

---

[1] non *MS.*
[2] Stat. 22 & 23 Car. II, c. 10 (*SR*, V, 719–720); Stat. 30 Car. II, c. 6 (*SR*, V, 890).

I [was] for the defendant.

Afterwards [in] 1682, Walsingham v. Masters;[3] but after this case, the court of exchequer decreed accounts and distributions of intestates' estates in all cases, as well merely personal things, as debts and goods, as of trusts and chattels real exercising the same jurisdiction as at first [they were] squeamish.

Note a debtor of the king carries the privilege [of the court of exchequer].

[Order of 6 Nov. 1682: PRO E.126/14, f. 4v.]

[This case was cited in Walsingham v. Masters (Ex. 1682), below, No. 159.]

152
Cook and Gwavas v. Fountain (Ex. 1682)

Sequestration for disobedience to a final decree does not lie unless land or a trust of land was in issue.

GUL MS. B88–7, p. 349 [Fr.] (Ward's Reports)

Sequestration was denied by MOUNTAGU, ATKINS, and GREGORY (STREET inclining to the contrary) for sequestering the estate of the defendant for not performing the decree of the court made for payment of money, no land nor trust of land being in question.

And this was contrary to the resolution and order of the court in Hawys and Kett's Case, Thursday 10 July 1679, where such a sequestration was awarded; see Liber H, f. 54,[1] but [*blank*] this case; the exchequer granted sequestration in this and other case[s].

[Order of 22 June 1682: PRO E.126/13, f. 386.]

[There are notes of further proceedings in this case in GUL MS. B88–7, pp. 380–383; reversed on appeal: *Lords' Journal*, XIV (n.d.), pp. 449, 462. Note also the connected cases of Fountain v. Gwavas (Ex. 1676), above, No. 73, and Gwavas v. Fountain (Ex. 1687), below, No. 233.]

[This opinion is cited in Hawys v. Kett (Ex. 1679), above, No. 99.]

---

[3] *Walsingham v. Masters* (1682), below, No. 159.

[1] *Hawys v. Kett* (Ex. 1679), above, No. 99.

153
Robinson v. Creamer (Ex. 1682)

An executor cannot sue before proving the will.
An inadvertent omission in a pleading can be cured by an amendment thereto.

GUL MS. B88–7, p. 350 [Fr.] (Ward's Reports)

The plaintiff exhibited his English bill against the defendant. And the plaintiff's demands were only as executor and did not say in all his bill that he had proved the will. The defendant demurred specially and showed this for the cause and that, before probate, the plaintiff does not have the right to sue because it is not [*blank*] him executor, which gives right before probate inasmuch as the plaintiff can renounce, and it is the same reason in equity that it is in [common] law, without profert in court of letters testamentary *per quas satis liquet curia hic se esse executorem et inde haberi ad[ministrat]ionem*, that without doubt it is a good cause to demur showing this for cause. And the demurrer was ruled good. But inasmuch as the plaintiff in truth had proved the will and it was only an omission of putting it into the bill, the court gave leave to amend the bill in this point.

I [was] for the defendant.

154
Paul v. Edwards (Ex. 1682)

An exemption from prisage applies only to wine imported into the place where the exempted importer lives.

GUL MS. B88–7, p. 353 [Fr.] (Ward's Reports)

The plaintiff [Sir William Paul], executor of Anthony Paul, his father, who was lessee of the duty of prisage of wines in all [of the] ports in Kent under Sir Thomas Waller, lessee of King James of all the duty of prisage within England etc., for a term of years in being under an annual rent of £500 reserved to the crown, exhibited his English bill against the defendant for the duty of prisage of two large quantities of wine imported by the defendant within the port of Rochester in Kent and the bulk first broken, for which three tuns were given to the plaintiff for prisage. The defendant being an inhabitant of Faversham,[1] a member of Sandwich, one of the Cinque Ports, at first by plea and this being overruled, afterwards by answer, insisted upon the privilege of the Cinque Ports to be discharged of prisage. And he showed himself to be a member of it and claimed

---

[1] Feversham *MS.* throughout.

exemption for the Cinque Ports by prescription (and this [was] confirmed by charter) for all their wines imported both within the Cinque Ports and within other places.

But the court (upon the sight of a precedent on the point between Sir John Swinnerton and Thornhill,[2] 6 July 1609, 7 Jac., which declared and decreed that the exemption of the Cinque Ports' men from prisage extends only to the wines imported into this particular port or member where they lived and not into other places, and upon consideration also of the case between Sir William Waller and Traverse, 27 November 14 Car. II [1662], (both of them precedents in this court) where it was declared and decreed by Chief Baron Hale and all of the court upon the case and argument that a citizen of London importing wines into the port of Bristol should pay prisage for them notwithstanding their grant was general *quod de vinis eorum nulla prisa fiet*) decreed the defendant here to pay the duty of prisage with costs upon the reasons in those two cases being principally that the general words of the grant of the king should have a reasonable construction, and on account of this, he shall be restrained to that port only where the party lives and imports the wines. And if the contrary should be admitted, such privileged persons could and would in a short time be the sole importers of wine if they could import cheaper than others in other ports, and the general words of the grant to the citizens of London are not only restricted to the place but to the persons, also because every freeman of London who in any meaning is a citizen will not have the privilege if he is not a citizen *in re facto et nomine*, as in Hanger's Case, which [was in the time of King] James, Calthorp's Reports 32, a case of prisage, and 3 Bulstrode 1, and Moore 832, 1 Rolle's Rep. 145,[3] and note this case, as Rochester is a member at large of the port of Sandwich as well as Faversham is, where the defendant lived at the time of the importation, yet it is not a member of Sandwich as one of the Cinque Ports, as [is] Faversham, because none of the privileges of the Cinque Ports extends into Rochester [*blank*] extends to Faversham. See Liber G, 4, 75;[4] Rolle's [Abr.] *Prerogative* 162, 163;[5] and the Statute of 1 Hen. VIII, c. 5;[6] L.G.; and 2 [&] 3 Edw. VI, [c.] 22.[7]

---

[2] *Swinnerton v. Thornhill* (Ex. 1609), 117 Selden Soc. 360.
[3] *Waller v. Hanger* (1611–1614), Calthrop 33, 80 E.R. 656, 3 Bulstrode 1, 81 E.R. 1, Moore K.B. 832, 72 E.R. 935, 1 Rolle Rep. 138, 81 E.R. 386.
[4] *Roberts v. Whitwood* (Ex. 1673), LI MS. Misc. 555, f. 4; *Attorney General v. Blofield* (Ex. 1675), LI MS. Misc. 555, f. 75.
[5] 2 Rolle, Abr., *Prerogative le Roy*, sect. R 'Prisage', pp. 162–163.
[6] Stat. 1 Hen. VIII, c. 5 (*SR*, III, 3).
[7] Stat. 2 & 3 Edw. VI, c. 22 (*SR*, IV, 67–68).

The charters of the Cinque Ports pleaded were 17 June 6 Edw. I [1278], 28 April 26 Edw. I [1298], 5 February 1 Ric. II [1378]. See Hardres 477.[8] See the decree [of] 6 November 31 Car. II [1679], Liber H, 63,[9] which settles the taking of [*blank*] by view, canting, and taking throughout England.

[Order of 13 Nov. 1682: PRO E.126/14, f. 4v.]

155
Husbands v. Brand (Ex. 1682)

Tithes due to a lay impropriator cannot be sequestered for the failure to provide the parish with a vicar.

GUL MS. B88–7, p. 357 [Fr.] (Ward's Reports)

The plaintiff being impropriator of Little Hockesly by title derived under the crown and there not being at the vicarage a spiritual person to [serve] the cure there so that, in default of it, there was not any divine service or preaching nor anyone to baptize the infants or to bury the dead, a complaint was made to the bishop of London of this, who admonished the plaintiff to provide to have the cure served. And upon neglect and contempt, he awarded a sequestration of the tithes of the parishioners for defraying the charge of the cure. And in truth all of the parishioners' tithes did not exceed £25 *per annum*. And upon publication of this sequestration, the defendants did not pay their tithes to the plaintiff nor in truth to the sequestrators but held them in their [own] hands but procured the cure to be served at their [own] charges intending to be reimbursed out of the value of their tithes.

The plaintiff exhibited his bill to be relieved in an ordinary manner for his tithes. The defendants showed all this matter in their answers and also that it was fully proved in the cause that all of the owners of the impropriation for fifty years and more had provided for the cure at their own charge and [there was] no neglect until three or four years past.

And upon the hearing of the cause, all of the court was of the opinion that the sequestration in this case was worth nothing, it not being in the power of the bishop to sequester the tithes of the impropriation that had now become a lay fee by statute, and on account of that [it was] no excuse for the defendants for not paying their tithes. And the plaintiff had a decree for the tithes, but the court moderated the costs to £5.

I [was] for the defendants.

---

[8] *Attorney General v. Horsham* (1668), Hardres 477, 145 E.R. 555.
[9] *Attorney General v. Waller* (Ex. 1679), above, No. 101.

Note in the case in the term [*blank*] in the [court of] common pleas [*blank*] Chief Justice North and all the court was of the opinion that if an impropriator was sued in the ecclesiastical court for not repairing the chancel which he of right should do and [he did] not repair it [*blank*].

Query the difference, whether there is any between non procuring the cure to be served and non repairing the chancel, both being of spiritual cognizance [*blank*] but it, that difference [with] the case *supra*, was that, in the principal case, the defendants' being parishioners and not having set out their tithes could not be excused if they had set out their tithes and the sequestrators had received them; this was thought to be a good excuse against the suit of the plaintiff as to the parishioners who had put those tithes out, and in such case [*blank*] plaintiff [is] provided with his remedy against those who took them away.

[Order of 16 Nov. 1682: PRO E.126/14, f. 6.]

156
Raynsford v. Raynsford (Ex. 1682)

In this case to have money allegedly due pursuant to a marriage settlement, the court held that the plaintiff's claim was not warranted by the terms of the settlement.

GUL MS. B88–7, p. 358 [Fr.] (Ward's Reports)

Sir Richard Raynsford, former chief justice of the king's bench, and baron Littleton, during his life, and his lady, after his death, made an agreement for a settlement and portion upon the marriage of Sir George Raynsford, the younger son of the chief justice, with Ayliffe Georges, niece of lady Littleton. Upon this agreement, the said Ayliffe was to have £1500 for her portion, and the chief justice was to settle £6000 upon his son, one moiety in lands, the other in money, the lands to be settled before marriage and the money by both parties at certain times, and the money was agreed to be for the purchase of other lands. And Ayliffe was to give a jointure in the first lands settled and an additional jointure in the other lands which [were to be] purchased and settled. And this agreement was reduced into articles in writing. And the chief justice by lease and release for £3000, part of the £6000, settled divers lands to the use of himself and his heirs until the said marriage and afterwards to the use of Sir George for ninety-nine years if he live so long, afterwards to Ayliffe for life, and afterwards, as to first and other sons of Sir George and Ayliffe, [in] tail male with an estate to preserve contingent remainders and afterwards to the daughters of their bodies and afterwards to the heirs of the body of Sir George and afterwards to the chief justice and his wife for their lives and afterwards to the use of the plaintiff Francis Raynsford in tail and afterwards to the use of Sir George in fee with a proviso and power of revocation to Sir George in some cases, none of which ever happened.

And by the said articles, it was agreed that £2000, another part of the portions agreed to, should be laid out in lands to be settled to the use of Sir George for ninety-nine years if he live so long and afterwards to the use of the first and other sons of Sir George and Ayliffe in tail male successively in such manner and form and with such provision for preserving the contingent remainders and with such powers of revocation as in and by the said deeds of lease and release are contained, with [a] remainder to the right heirs of Sir George.

The plaintiff exhibited his bill (Sir George being dead without issue) to have the £2000 laid out in lands to be settled according to the articles, as above. The defendant, Dame Ayliffe, demurred, and she showed for cause that the plaintiff did not have any right by the articles to the £2000 or the lands to be purchased inasmuch as there was not any provision for him by the said articles because all the appointments by the articles as to this £2000 and lands to be purchased do not extend further than to Sir George and his issue, remainder to his right heirs, and that the words 'in such manner and form', as above, do not carry any provision beyond the issue of Sir George nor extend to the plaintiff.

And of such opinion was the court. And afterwards the plaintiff dismissed his bill.

I [was] for the plaintiff.

157
Clements v. Downes (Ex. 1682)

A discharge of tithes by prescription can extend to copyholders in fee.

GUL MS. B88–7, p. 360 [Fr.] (Ward's Reports)

The plaintiff, as vicar of East Meon and Steep in the County of Southampton, exhibited his bill for tithes of wood within that parish. The defendant showed himself by [his] answer to be a copyholder in fee of lands where the wood grew and was cut and that those lands are part or held of the manor of East Meon, of which the bishop of Winchester is and his predecessors were seised in the right of the said bishopric, and that by prescription in the said bishops, being spiritual persons, they for themselves and their copyhold tenants in fee of the said manor have been discharged from payment of the tithe wood.

The court, at the last term, put the case to a trial at law, and the plaintiff upon full evidence was nonsuited and afterwards, this day,[1] [was] dismissed with £20 costs.

---

[1] 20 November 1682.

For the prescription and discharge, see 1 Rep., Bishop of Winchester's Case;[2] Moore 618, 619; Rolle's [Abr.], title *Dismes* 653; Yelverton 2.[3]

And [it was] held by the court that the discharge of the tithes by prescription can well extend to the copyholders in fee, tenants of the said manor, according to the authorities above [cited].

I [was] for the defendant.

158
Kingsmill v. Bishop of Rochester (Ex. 1682)

If the almoner made a grant of the goods of a suicide before he had notice of the pleasure of the king to have them otherwise given, this disposition by the almoner is good and will bind the king and his grantee.

The warrant of the king is a sufficient countermand of the authority of the almoner, and it makes his subsequent sale void where the purchaser had notice.

GUL MS. B88–7, p. 361 [Fr.] (Ward's Reports)

The case upon the hearing appeared to be thus. [On] 6 September 1676, one Richard Withers became a suicide by hanging himself. Afterwards and before any inquisition, there were applications to the king by the plaintiff and Sir Edmond Wyndham separately for a grant of the goods of the said suicide, and the king ordered a warrant to the plaintiff, and Wyndham entered a caveat against it. [On] 20 September an inquisition was found of the suicide, and the plaintiff and Sir Edmond Wyndham continued their separate applications for obtaining grants of the goods of the suicide. And Wyndham afterwards applied to the bishop of Rochester, lord almoner, for his title, who [on] 30 September gave authority to one Blackford under his hand and seal for seizing and inventorying all of the goods of the suicide and to bargain and sell a messuage and several acres of land which the suicide held by a lease for years.

And the defendants alleged an agreement between Sir Edmond Wyndham and the bishop of Rochester after the inquisition and before the authority to Blackford for all of the goods of the suicide for £200, after which, *viz.* 3 October 1676, the king made a warrant for passing a privy seal containing a grant of all the goods of the suicide to the plaintiff, against which grant a caveat was entered in the name of the bishop of Rochester, almoner, [on] 5 October, and [it

---

[2] *Wright v. Wright* (1596), 2 Coke Rep. 38a, 76 E.R. 501 (1596); note also 1 Rolle, Abr., *Dismes*, pl. H, 1–4, p. 653.

[3] *Crowcher v. Fryar* (1599–1602), Moore K.B. 618, 72 E.R. 796; 1 Rolle, Abr., *Dismes*, pl. H, 3, p. 653; Yelverton 2, 80 E.R. 2, also 1 Eagle & Younge 149, 1 Gwillim 218, Cro. Eliz. 704, 784, 78 E.R. 940, 1014.

was] proved by the depositions that he insisted and justified the caveat and had notice of the said warrant of the king for the privy seal, after which, *scil.* the 10th October, Blackford sold all of the goods of the suicide to the defendant Withers, who was next of kin to the suicide, for £230, after which the said lord almoner, by writing under his hand and seal dated 21 October, confirmed the sale of Blackford to the defendant Withers and for the said £230 paid and secured to him, bargained and sold the goods to the defendant Withers.

And afterwards, *viz.* 30 November 1676, the privy seal pursuant to the warrant of 3 October passed to the plaintiff. And the bishop received £100, which he disposed in alms. And Sir Edmond Wyndham had the other £130, but the bishop gave a receipt for all. And in this case, these points were resolved:

1. That the almoner did not have any interest by his patent but only an authority for disposing the alms of the king, according to the opinion [in] 1 Rep. 50, Alton Woods Case, and Dyer 107, 108.[1]
2. That if the almoner made a grant of the goods of the suicide before he had notice of the pleasure of the king to have them otherwise given or disposed, that this disposition by the almoner was good and will bind the king and his grantee.
3. That the warrant of the king in this case was a sufficient countermand of the authority of the almoner, and it made his subsequent sale or disposition void and ineffectual, especially in this case where the bishop himself and Sir Edmond Wyndham and the defendant Withers, who purchased the goods, had notice of the pleasure of the king by his warrant, and this [was] before any money [was] paid or conveyance sufficient in law was executed.
4. It was held by Chief Baron MOUNTAGU and barons ATKYNS and GREGORY that notice to Blackford of the said warrant or pleasure of the king was not necessary because he was only the attorney of the bishop and nominated by Wyndham and came in with the privity of Withers, and they having notice, it was not necessary that he should have it, not having any interest but only an authority. But as to this point, Baron STREET differed and upon this reason he was of the opinion that his sale was good, *quod fieri non debuit, [sed] factum valet*,[2] and for this reason that the plaintiff should not be relieved. (But the other three [were] against him.)

---

[1] *The Case of Alton Woods* (1595–1600), 1 Coke Rep. 26b, 50, 76 E.R. 64, 113; *Bishop of Chichester v. Webb* (1554), 2 Dyer 107b, 73 E.R. 238.

[2] It ought not to be done, but [if] done, it is valid. *Black's Law Dictionary*, p. 755 (4th ed. 1968).

5. That the authority to Blackford extended only to sell the messuage and lease of the said acres of land and not to the other goods, and as to it, all that he did beyond was void within the rules of authorities and the express words in this case, and this the rather inasmuch as the words of the almoner's grant was seizure *levare [per] se vel deputatum suum et, sic seisit[us], levat., etc. per se disponendum [est]*, so that no deputy of the almoner can dispose.
6. That if the almoner disposed after a grant or warrant for a grant from the king with notice of it, that such disposition is void because though the grant of the king, which must go by steps, passed after the grant of the almoner, yet by the relation that he had by the warrant of the king and notice and the countermand, it will be preferred.

And in the principal case, the court decreed the defendant Withers to account for all of the estate of the suicide having a deduction for the £230 paid to the bishop. And as to the bishop, they decreed that he should be discharged of the £230 upon his oath that he had disposed [of the] £100 in alms and £130 to Sir William[3] Wyndham, who was really an object of charity.

I [was] for the plaintiff.

[Order of 20 Nov. 1682: PRO E.126/14, f. 2v.]

159
Walsingham v. Masters (Ex. 1682)

Where discovery is needed, a court of equity can order the distribution of a decedent's estate. The issue in this case was whether a release was voluntary, fraudulent, or valid.

GUL MS. B88–7, p. 365, pl. 2 [Fr.] (Ward's Reports)

The plaintiff and divers others were entitled to the distribution of one Richard Masters' estate, who died intestate, from the defendant [James Masters], his brother of the whole blood, [who] was administrator.

The defendant at first demurred generally upon the point of jurisdiction of the court, whether this court can make distribution, having resolved against it this term in the case of Sawbridge and Pulford,[1] but inasmuch as the bill required discovery, the demurrer was overruled.

And afterwards the defendant, in bar of the plaintiff's right, pleaded a contract and agreement between the intestate and himself thirty years past, that the

---

[3] Sic in MS.

[1] *Sawbridge v. Pulford* (Ex. 1682), above, No. 151.

defendant shall have £2091 [of the] intestate's in the Chamber of London to his own use and that the defendant shall maintain him as a gentle[man] during his life and make provision [*blank*] will to allow him £120 *per annum* during his life if the defendant should die first. And [the] defendant pleaded that he had maintained him accordingly for twenty-eight years and had spent in this [matter] £120 *per annum* and that this agreement was made with the advice of the intestate's mother, the intestate being a man addicted to company and vain expense but of sane memory. And also he pleaded a release under the hand and seal of the intestate in 1676, being six years before his death, of all debts, accounts, and demands and to have it in good faith and without fraud or any indirectness and with the intention to quiet the possession of the defendant in the intestate's estate and that the £2091 was received by the defendant twenty-six years past, and then he claimed it as the proper estate of the defendant, and that the defendant did not receive any of the intestate's estate within twenty-six years past, and he showed the inventory of the intestate's estate, which amounted to £20 [for] his funeral charges, and so he claimed all except the £20 spent on funerals, and that he was next of kin, being brother by the whole blood, and the plaintiffs [were] only nephews and nieces and some [were] of the half blood.

And upon the argument, the court overruled the pleas upon these reasons:

1. Inasmuch as this release was impeached[2] by the plaintiffs in their bill and objected to be obtained by fraud and circumvention notwithstanding that it was denied altogether by the defendant and this upon the rule *non competit exceptio eiusdem rei cuius dissolutio petitur*.[3]
2. Inasmuch as the release was voluntary and without good consideration, because [?] there is not good provision for the will inasmuch as it was in his power to make it or not and the mesne maintenance did not aid it notwithstanding that it was objected by myself or the defendant that the plaintiffs were not creditors or purchasers and on account of that, though the defendant's title was voluntary, it is not examinable by others who come in upon a voluntary provision or at least not as creditors or purchasers.

And it is harsh if a brother's disposition not be observed against those who claim under him. And as to the objection that the plaintiffs impeached the release and on account of that, it cannot be pleaded against them, the reason and practice is otherwise because this rule *non competit exceptio* etc. does not hold in

---

[2] quarrel *MS*.
[3] Also: *Non potest adduci exceptio eiusdem rei cuius petitur dissolutio.* A matter, the validity of which is at issue in legal proceedings, cannot be set up as a bar thereto. H. Broom, *Maxims* (10th ed. by R. H. Kersley, 1939), p. 101.

this case; it is to reverse the outlawry, it cannot be pleaded against him, and similar cases. And the mischief here is great if an allegation from wherever against a release or other thing, that this deed [was] obtained by fraud or similar, should take away the benefit of the plea as to all of the fraud etc., and [it was] utterly denied by the answer. And in such a case, fraud or not fraud is only in question because if it is not fraud, the release is a good bar, and the release here operates in the nature of a will, which is purely voluntary, and still [there is] no equity against it.

160

Coney v. Dorrington (Ex. 1682)

In a case of account, there must be proof of some duty that arose before the filing of the bill.

GUL MS. B88–7, p. 367 [Fr.] (Ward's Reports)

Note [that] the plaintiff exhibited his bill to discover what judgments and encumbrances and for what causes the defendant had and claimed against the plaintiff and his estate and, upon satisfaction of them, to have them vacated. The defendant, among other [things], showed that he had a [confessed] judgment for £1000 against the plaintiff defeasible upon the plaintiff's performance of articles. It was held a [*blank*] estate to the part of which the plaintiff was entitled, and for £300 he had sold his part to the defendant, and there were covenants on the plaintiff's part that he had not received nor would receive any part of the said estate. And the defendant in his answer showed that he [. . .] and [. . .] to prove[1] for the plaintiff had broken his covenant for receiving part of the said estate to the defendant's damage of £500 or £600.

The cause descended to the hearing. And the defendant, thinking that he should make proof of this receipt and breach as well after as before the hearing, [it] being matter of account, did not make[2] any proof of it. And upon the argument touching the settling of the decretal order, which was drawn to vacate this judgment and [to] rehear the cause, all of the court, that is to say MOUNTAGU, ATKYNS, GREGORY, and STREET, by order restrained the defendant to make any proof of any breach or receipt before the plaintiff's bill [was filed] inasmuch as he was[3] made to prove some breach before the hearing.

Note this, and [I] query if this was never done or heard of before.

[Order of 19 June 1684: PRO E.126/14, f. 179.]

---

[1] approve [?].
[2] full *MS*.
[3] ad *MS*.

161
Sheen v. Aynsworth (Ex. 1682)

A mortgage cannot be redeemed after a long period of time after default because a release or other estate will be presumed.

GUL MS. B88–7, p. 368, pl. 1 [Fr.] (Ward's Reports)

Note that the plaintiff's bill was to redeem a mortgage for years made in 7 Jac. [1609] of lands in Worcestershire mortgaged for £100 redeemable in three years after, the money then being at £10 *per centum* interest, which £100 not being paid and the parties being relations, the £10 *per annum* was at all times afterwards paid at the days designated in the mortgage deed. And the mortgagor or those claiming under him, and not the mortgagee, continued the possession paying the £10 *per annum*. And the mortgagor and those claiming under him and not the mortgagee[1] were taxed in the parish, and no deduction or defalcation out of the £10 *per annum* was ever made though great taxes had been paid and the land [was] worth little more than £10 *per annum*, but the mortgagor a little time before the mortgage had purchased the land for and paid £200 or about that on account that it was an open field and not worth £10 *per annum* and yet [he] paid £10 [at] all times after the mortgage. The plaintiff's equity consisted [?] to have redemption upon the proviso in the deed and the contin[uance] of the payment of £10 *per annum* as interest, and thus an abatement of the interest so as the law reduced it first to 8 and afterwards to £6 *per centum* of the mortgage money,[2] and interest was paid.

But the court, that is to say MOUNTAGU, ATKYNS, GREGORY, and STREET, dismissed the bill, with moderate costs only, upon the reason of the length of time being sixty years and the danger [of] putting the defendant to a long account and that in such long time a release or other estate will be presumed.

I [was] for the plaintiff.

[Order of 27 Nov. 1682: PRO E.126/14, f. 5v.]

162
Kettleby v. Corbett (Ex. 1682)

In this case, a person was ordered to rebuild for a vicar a house that had been wrongfully destroyed.

---

[1] Mortgager *MS*.
[2] Stat. 13 Eliz. I, c. 8, s. 2 (*SR*, IV, 542); Stat. 21 Jac. I, c. 17, s. 1 (*SR*, IV, 1223); Stat. 12 Car. II, c. 13, s. 1 (*SR*, V, 236).

GUL MS. B88-7, p. 370, pl. 1 [Fr.] (Ward's Reports)

The plaintiff exhibited his bill against the defendant to have relief for a vicarage house destroyed by the defendant or his ancestor [?] and for divers other things due to him as vicar. The defendant admitted the destruction of the house and justified [it] as his freehold and part of the rectory. But inasmuch as upon the proof [it] sufficiently appeared that there was a house that belonged to the vicarage and that that which was destroyed was [from the] beginning esteemed to be that house, the court decreed the defendant to rebuild a convenient house with an outhouse suitable to those destroyed for the vicar and to expend such a sum in building those things. And inasmuch as the extent and certainty of the ground where the prior house stood was not clear to the court, a commission was awarded to set it out and to know what sum will suffice for the erecting of such a house. And [the court] decreed the defendant to do it.

[Orders of 10 July and 20 Nov. 1682: PRO E.126/13, f. 376, E.126/14, f. 10.]

163
Gower v. Howard (Ex. 1682)

The officers of the exchequer cannot issue tallies without a treasury warrant. The amount of money in the exchequer is privileged from discovery.

GUL MS. B88-7, p. 375, pl. 2 [Fr.] (Ward's Reports)

The plaintiff was an assignee of one of the bankers and goldsmiths, to which banker, his heirs, and assigns the king by letters patent had granted an annual perpetual interest (for a large sum due to the banker) issuing and charged out of and upon his hereditary revenue [of the] excise with power to the banker to make assignments to his creditors and power to command to all officers to pay the annuity and to levy tallies for it as the case required, and the letters patent directed with divers advantageous clauses for the sure payment of the money and levying [of the] tallies accordingly by the patent. And the plaintiff and divers others of the bankers and their assignees not being able to procure their money or tallies for it, though the Lord Danby as treasurer and, after him, the present commissioners of the treasury have made a warrant for levying those tallies (but this last warrant was revoked by a subsequent warrant to the commissioners of the treasury, by which the officers were directed to forbear levying tallies until the tallies levied before should be paid and further order given), the plaintiff, in order to compel payment of the money or levying of the tallies according to the letters patent, exhibited his English bill (which was in the nature of a petition of right) against the attorney general and the defendant [Sir Robert Howard],[1] being an auditor and writer of the tallies who must make the first act in order for the levying of tallies, *scil.* to give the sum or debet to the tally cutter to the other officers of the [exchequer of] receipt concerned in levying tallies, and also against the commissioners and officers of the excise to be relieved either for payment of the money or by levying tallies according to the letters patent.

The officers of the excise demurred inasmuch as, by the laws and statutes, they must pay the excise [money] into the exchequer and inasmuch as, the plaintiff not having any tally, they are not chargeable to the plaintiff nor can they detain money in their hands for such satisfaction nor were they bound to discover whether there was ancient money in their hands to satisfy tallies if any were levied.

And the defendant and officers of the receipt pleaded the revocation of the warrant for levying tallies and that, by the ancient course and practice there, they cannot levy any tallies without a warrant in the treasury and that the last warrant must be obeyed. And some of them demurred to the charge of the bill for discovery of the money that came into the exchequer inasmuch as, to allow entrance into [their] offices, they took an oath not to discover[2] the money in the exchequer.

And those pleas and demurrers for the reasons contained in them were allowed without defense by the plaintiff except for the demurrer of the officers of excise.

I [was] for the plaintiff.

[See] above [page] 78, whether such a warrant is absolutely necessary or the letters patent are not sufficient warrant to levy and discharge if levied without other warrant and that thus if [there is] any use of another warrant after an issue that directs levying tallies, it being an intimation that the letters patent are approved at the treasury and that thus, if such warrant [is] once issued, whether it can be revoked or superseded inasmuch as it passed an interest to a third person as a power of attorney to acknowledge a judgment is not revokable for this reason. And it seems that letters patent entered and enrolled in the receipt are a sufficient warrant to levy tallies without another warrant for this purpose, especially as the letters patent have been approved and allowed to be good in law. But see above [page] 78, where it was held by the court [that] the treasury warrant is necessary in such cases. [See] below [page] 109.

---

[1] L. Squibb, 'A Book of All the Several Officers of the Court of Exchequer . . . 1641', *Camden Miscellany*, No. 26, Camden Soc., 4th ser., vol. 14, pp. 130–132 (W. H. Bryson ed. 1975).

[2] I.e. reveal.

164
Awborne v. Windebank (Ex. 1682)

A court of equity cannot alter the terms of a trust.

GUL MS. B88–7, p. 378 [Fr.] (Ward's Reports)

The case upon the hearing was thus. The plaintiffs intermarrying, the portion of the wife was settled in trust for both of them during coverture and afterwards the surviving wife and the issue of her body. And the husband at the time of the marriage being a practicing attorney did not make any settlement or provision out of his estate. And divers years afterwards, the husband became poor and was not able to sustain the wife and children, but they were in effect put onto the parish, upon which the defendants, being trustees of the wife's portion, which was in money upon a mortgage and annuity for the necessary sustenance of the wife and[1] children, paid the profits for their maintenance, the husband being in jail and furthermore insolvent. And now being out of prison, he exhibited this bill in the name of himself and [his] wife against the trustees to have the growing duty paid to himself during the coverture (voluntarily remitting that which was past).

The trustees admitted the trust but showed the poverty and inability of the husband to maintain himself and wife and children and prayed that there could be a maintenance assigned for the wife and children.

And upon the hearing of the cause, all of the court declared that they could not do thus but decreed the trustees to pay all to the husband for the future though there was not anything out of which the wife and children could be maintained because they [*blank*] that they could not alter the agreement and settlement that limited the trust for the husband and wife during the coverture, and on account of that all said [that] it is his power and disposition during the coverture that no court of equity can or should alter in such a case.

I [was] for the trustees, the defendants.

165
Paris v. Mathews (Ex. 1683)

In this case, the court construed the terms of a legacy in a will.

---

[1] fame al *MS*.

GUL MS. B88-7, p. 384, pl. 1 [Fr.] (Ward's Reports)

[It was] decreed for the plaintiff upon such a devise of a legacy, 'I give to A. and B. £90 apiece to be paid to them as they shall respectively attain their ages of 21 years', that though B. died before twenty-one, that the legacy will be a charge to his administrator. Swinburne 313.[1] And in this case, the court admitted the administration and twenty-six years absence [*blank*] proof of death and made a decree for the plaintiff.

I [was] for the plaintiff.

[Order of 25 Feb. 1683: PRO E.126/14, f. 24.]

166
Audley v. Scroggs (Ex. 1683)

In this case for specific performance of a contract to account, the plaintiff could not prove his case, and the case was dismissed to the common law.

GUL MS. B88-7, p. 384, pl. 2 [Fr.] (Ward's Reports)

The plaintiff exhibited his bill against the defendant to be relieved upon an agreement alleged to be made by the defendant when he was lord chief justice of the king's bench[1] with the plaintiff, who was the defendant's crier in London and Middlesex and had given the defendant four hundred guineas for this place, that the defendant should restore to the plaintiff so much of the said sum as the plaintiff should not receive in his office if the defendant should be removed from his place of chief justice before the plaintiff should be reimbursed all of the said four hundred guineas. And this agreement to have four hundred guineas and the receipt of them for the said place was admitted by the defendant, but he positively denied any agreement to restore any part in case of [his] removal.

The plaintiff examined two witnesses who proved that Whorewood, the defendant's servant who transacted and negotiated the said affair with the plaintiff's father and friends, said that he had authority from the defendant to make the contract and that he would make allowance in case of removing and whether to give this under his [*blank*] and seal. The defendant utterly denied any such authority. And Whorewood, being examined, remembered it. And it appeared that the contract was completed with the defendant himself and [there was] no pretense to be mentioned to the defendant of any such allowance in case of [his]

---

[1] H. Swinburne, *Brief Treatise of Testaments* (1590), f. 173.

[1] Sir William Scroggs was chief justice of the king's bench from 1678 to 1681; he died 25 October 1683.

removal. And upon evidence of one witness examined for the defendant, who was said and agreed to be the prime mover of the matter and by the plaintiff's witnesses admitted to be the prime mover of the allowance in case of removal and that was to have advanced part of the money for the plaintiff and to have part of the profits, who swore that he did not remember any[thing] of the said allowance in case of removal and [there being] no pretense of an account appearing in this case, the court dismissed the plaintiff to [the common] law without costs, in commiseration with the plaintiff.

I [was] for the defendant.

[Order of 25 Jan. 1683: PRO E.126/14, f. 23.]

167
Attorney General ex rel. Knatchbull v. Loving (Ex. 1683)

In this case, certain money in the hands of the deceased clerk of one of the tellers of the exchequer was held not to be part of the clerk's accounts with the teller, it having been received from another source.

GUL MS. B88–7, p. 406 [Eng.] (Ward's Reports)

The case upon the hearing was thus. The defendant was one of the four tellers in the exchequer, and Oliver Gregory was his chief clerk and transacted the affairs in the office and kept the keys of the chests where the money was and [was] looked upon to have the sole care and management thereof under the defendant, who seldom came there or intermeddled therein. One Mr. Knatchbull was in April 1678 appointed receiver of the peers' poll money, who was to pay it into the exchequer. And as for his ease as security in that behalf upon agreement between him and Gregory, he directs those persons that were to pay the peers' poll money to pay it into Loving's office in the exchequer to Gregory there, with whom Knatchbull had left blank acquittances signed by him, which upon payment were filled in by Gregory and delivered to the payors of the money. And by [the] direction of Knatchbull, Gregory was to cause tallies to be struck for the money so paid in as often as it came to £500 or above, but there was no entry or charge of any [of] the money made in the office or any [of] the books of it until bills came to be thrown down in order to have [the] tallies levied, which matter was transacted solely by Gregory and his direction. And it did not appear that Loving was consenting to or knew of any [of] the transaction or agreement between Knatchbull and Gregory or the paying in [of] the peers' poll money there save what he found by the bills thrown down and entries in his office and the tallies levied.

It fell out that £7600 was in [the] manner aforesaid actually paid in to Gregory in the defendant's office, for £7100 whereof bills were thrown down and the office charged and tallies levied. But for the £500 residue, no such thing was done, but Gregory owned the receipt of the £500; and promised to throw down a bill for it in order to have a tally and wrote and spoke to [the] defendant and Barcroft, his other clerk, to do it telling and showing Barcroft where the money lay in the office and affirmed that part of it was paid out in discharge of orders upon the office. But Gregory died insolvent before anything was done. The defendant claim[ed] his estate in [the] mortgage and under security for his fidelity, which, as was alleged, was not nearly sufficient to satisfy the defendant's other just demands against Gregory.

But the court upon [the] hearing decreed the defendant to pay the £500 to His Majesty in regard [that] it was paid into his office and to his chief clerk there, and the defendant by his books etc. must take notice of the dealings between parties in his office and so [it is] to be esteemed [to be] the king's money though no entry or charge appeared in the office, nor [was] any bill thrown down until which time the defendant insisted he was or ought to be charged and further insists that Gregory acted not in this case as his agent but as a private correspondent of Knatchbull. And Gregory's letters and acknowledgment of the receipt of the £500 and his promises to throw down a bill for it were the principal evidence against the defendant.

I [was] for the king.

[Order of 3 May 1683: PRO E.126/14, f. 46.]

168

Redding v. Epworth Commoners (Ex. 1683)

Where a commons was enclosed fifty years before, the court will presume that all of the commoners consented to the enclosure unless any can prove lack of consent by himself or his predecessor in title.

GUL MS. B88–7, p. 413 [Fr.] (Ward's Reports)

Where 370 commoners by grant subscribed their consent to the enclosure of a commons in 1636 and [there was] enjoyment for three years, and afterwards [there was] no enjoyment for forty years, but [it was] held by all of the court that all the commoners, being more than 1000 who did not give consent and all claiming under them, will be bound by this decree under the presumption that they consented. And the commoners and their heirs and assigns who did not consent were enjoined to obey the decree until by another bill they made it to appear that they were not parties nor bound by the first decree.

Note and query because it seems hard inasmuch as, if they were parties, they are bound by the decree and a remedy upon it lies, and if they are not parties and on account of that not bound by the decree, they cannot have a bill of review, nor can they exhibit a bill to be relieved against a decree to which they were parties.

169
Page v. Lovell (Ex. 1683)

This was a suit for mortuaries; it was sent to commissioners to hear the evidence.

GUL MS. B88-7, p. 472, pl. 1 [Fr.] (Ward's Reports)

The plaintiff as vicar of Bloxham in Oxfordshire[1] exhibited his bill against the defendants as executors and administrators of divers parishioners for mortuaries suggesting them to be due by custom and prayed discovery of assets and relief for the mortuaries. The defendants denied the custom and insisted upon the Statute 21 Hen. VIII, c. [6].[2]

And upon the proof for the plaintiff by several witnesses of payment (but [it was] not very full), the court directed a reference [to commissioners] but inclined to send [the case] to a trial at law.

Note there was not any exception taken that the bill was for mortuaries and for them only.

I [was] for the plaintiff.

170
Tenants of Wem v. Wicherly (Ex. 1683)

Burgage tenements can be alienated according to the custom of the borough.

GUL MS. B88-7, p. 490 [Fr.] (Ward's Reports)

The only question [was] whether burgage tenements in Wem can be alienated otherwise than by surrender. And for the defendant, it was insisted by Maynard, Pemberton, and others that they cannot be because they are only and purely, as they said, copyholds, and it is contrary to the nature of copyholds to be alienated otherwise than by surrender and copy. And divers copies of court rolls and some proceedings in courts in the time of Queen Elizabeth were produced to the same purpose.

---

[1] V.C.H., *Oxfordshire*, IX (1969), p. 74.
[2] Stat. 21 Hen. VIII, c. 6 (*SR*, III, 288–289).

But on the other part, it was insisted for the plaintiffs, and thus resolved and decreed by the court upon sight and perusal of divers ancient feoffments before and in the reign of Queen Elizabeth and all times afterwards and upon sight of an ancient roll containing the customs of the manor, [that] those burgage tenements could be alienated as well by feoffment as by surrender and that they were not purely copyholds but customary estates that depend upon custom only and this can regulate the alienation, and such alienations being always allowed by the lords and officers of the manors that were privy to them, divers entered in the courts, and livery in all made by the lord's bailiffs and the tenure being according to the custom of the borough and not by copy of the court roll according to the custom of manors, all the court held that the tenants had the election to alienate either by feoffment or by surrender. And thus [it was] decreed.

See the Decree Book of Hilary [term] 35 & 36 Car. II, ff. 125, 126.[1]

[Orders of 6 Dec. 1683 and 13 and 20 Feb. 1684: PRO E.126/14, ff. 112, 125v, 153.]

171
Hillingham[1] v. Bradshaw (Ex. 1683)

In this case, the court enforced a treasury bill, since it was an assignable interest in equity.

LI MS. Misc. 557, f. 1, pl. 1 [Eng.] (Ward's Reports)

The case upon hearing was this. In the year 1666 part of the royal aid and assessment money was ordered to be paid into the chamber of London by the receivers general of some counties, and tallies were struck for that purpose and left with the chamberlain to deliver out to the receivers who paid their money. And the money was ordered to be paid out by the chamberlain to such persons who should produce bills for the same signed by the treasurer or undertreasurer of the Navy for goods and stores by them sold and furnished to the use of the Navy. In May 1666 one Pidgeon, the father, having furnished to the Navy goods to the value of £266 had a bill for the same under the hand of John Fenne, undertreasurer of the Navy, to Sir George Carteret, then treasurer, directed to old Sir Thomas Player, then chamberlain, but money not coming in to pay it, Pidgeon for the value received assigned that bill by endorsement to Sir Robert Vyner in the same month. And it was proved that the chamberlain's servant or agent in that affair had and took notice of that assignment. And in 1671 or thereabouts, old Pidgeon being then dead, young Pidgeon, his son, took administration to

---

[1] PRO E.126/14, f. 125v.

---

[1] Or Fillingham.

him and obtained a second bill from the undertreasurer of the Navy for the same money taking notice that a former had been given and this second bill was for about £100 assigned by the administrator to the defendant Bradshaw, and he procures the same to be satisfied. But the chamberlain refused to do it unless he might be indemnified from the first bill, which Bradshaw agreed to do and gave him security for that purpose.

And about 1673 Sir Robert Vyner being indebted to the plaintiff in a great sum assigned the first bill to him in part of his satisfaction, who exhibited his bill against Bradshaw and the administrator of the chamberlain and Sir Robert Vyner and had a decree by the uniform opinion of the whole court against Sir Thomas Player the administrator for the money, who was left to his remedy upon his security. For the court was clear that the first bill was an assignable interest in equity and that the chamberlain had notice of the assignment to Vyner, which bound him and his administrator, and that the defendant Bradshaw had also sufficient notice of the first bill, it being mentioned in the second, and that he bought the second without any other cause but to make profit, and it was at his peril, and he gave security against the first without which the second would not have been paid, and that the first in equity and justice ought to be paid. And it was so decreed.

But upon a rehearing, an issue was directed whether Sir Thomas Player or any [of] his agents had notice of the assignment to Vyner before the second bill was paid to Bradshaw, which was found that he had, and the decree [was] confirmed afterwards.

[Other copies of this report: GUL MS. B88–7, p. 422.]

[Orders of 5 July and 6 Dec. 1683: PRO E.126/14, ff. 81, 115.]

172

City of Cambridge v. Gonville and Caius College (Ex. 1683)

In this case, a contract regulating the use of water by two neighboring mills was specifically enforced.

LI MS. Misc. 557, f. 1, pl. 2 [Eng.] (Ward's Reports)

The Corporation of Cambridge and Townshend and others their tenants exhibit their bill against the master and fellows of Caius College there and Drury and others their tenants to have an agreement in Henry VII's time between the Corporation and the College in relation to their mills executed in specie and to restrain the College's mill called Newnham Mill from grinding with more than one wheel at a time. And the case upon hearing was this. The plaintiffs and their predecessors time out of mind have been seised in fee of a water corn mill called the King's Mill in Cambridge under a fee farm rent to the crown and the defendants of a mill called Newnham Mill (situate upon a cut out of the same stream but above the King's Mill) held of the plaintiffs as of their high gable by a yearly rent, that either or as well by custom time out of mind as by indenture of the 24 January 22 Hen. VII [1507] between the Corporation and College King's Mill had these rights and customs belonging to it and which the owners and occupiers thereof ought still to enjoy and have performed to them, *viz.*:

1. That the occupier of Newnham Mill ought not to begin to grind any corn till the occupier of the King's Mill has set his mill to work and blown his horn except in time of reparation or that the miller of King's Mill set to work and blow not his horn in the time that a man may go from King's Mill to Newnham (in which cases Newnham miller may work);
2. When King's Mill wants water to grind and blows an horn, Newnham Mill [is] to leave off;
3. That Newnham Mill had anciently but one wheel and though of late it has had two, yet it ought to use but one at a time;
4. Fourth, that Newnham Mill ought to shut up the water gates and not suffer the water to run waste.

And the plaintiffs by their bill complained of the breach of the said several matters by the tenants of Newnham Mill and prayed that the defendants might be compelled to perform the same in specie. The defendants by their answer admitted part but contested other part[s], and two issues were directed and both found for the plaintiffs, who had a decree accordingly and recompense of £20 found by the jury for the loss they sustained.

I [was] for the plaintiffs.

Note there was in the year 1700 another decree conformable to this in the exchequer in another suit and I think the same parties.

[Other copies of this report: GUL MS. B88–7, p. 423.]

[Orders of 8 Feb. and 22 May 1683: PRO E.126/14, ff. 24v, 46v.]

173

Alcock v. Alcock (Ex. 1683)

In this case, a trust was enforced against the heiress of the settlor.

LI MS. Misc. 557, f. 2, pl. 2 [Eng.] (Ward's Reports)

The case upon hearing was this. Edward Alcock seised in fee of freehold and copyhold lands in Lancashire and upon his marriage with the defendant, Mary Alcock, according to articles, settles his said lands by lease and release (the copyhold being contained therein though not mentioned to be copyhold) upon trustees to the use of himself for life, remainder as far as £50 *per annum* rent to the defendant, Mary, for her life, the remainder to the heirs male of his body, the remainder to his brother, Stephen Alcock, the now plaintiff, in tail male, the remainder to his own right heirs, under a power that, if Edward died without issue male, that he might by any deed charge the lands not limited in jointure to Mary with any sum not exceeding £1500 for his daughter or daughters' portions. Edward Alcock died leaving issue only one daughter, Margaret, one of the defendants and an infant of about ten years old, having by his deed pursuant to his power charged all his said lands with £1200 for his said daughter's portion to be paid unto her when she should attain the age of sixteen years, and died, but in his sickness whereof he died surrendered all his copyhold lands except those in Widnes to the uses above. But before the tenants of Widnes manor could come to take his surrender of those lands (which was prepared), he died whereby the copyhold lands in Widnes descended to his daughter, Margaret, the infant. So the plaintiff exhibited his bill against the widow and infant to have a surrender of the copyhold lands in Widnes when the infant came of age and that he might hold the same in the meantime by the decree of the court or otherwise, that he might have an abatement of the value of Widnes lands out of the £1200 portion when payable, and might hold them in the meantime.

And the court in this case resolved that the plaintiff had an equity against the infant and to be relieved against the descent of law, notwithstanding it was a voluntary settlement by the father, and that the plaintiff should pay the £1200 when sixteen according to the deed, and that the infant at twenty-one years of age should surrender the lands to the plaintiff and his heirs and should in the meantime hold and enjoy them subject and liable to the said £1200. And the court declared that the £1200 should go to the infant's executors or administrators if she died before sixteen, being an interest and to be paid when sixteen. No costs [were awarded].

I [was] for the defendant.

[Other copies of this report: GUL MS. B88–7, p. 426.]

[Orders of 7 and 22 May 1683: PRO E.126/14, ff. 44, 51.]

174

Haslehurst v. Cooke (Ex. 1683)

In this case, a trust was enforced even though the plaintiff's predecessor had not claimed his own interest under it for thirty years.

LI MS. Misc. 557, f. 8 [Eng.] (Ward's Reports)

Haslehurst, the father, in 1651 put £130 into the testatrix Mrs. Warren's hand who by deed declares the trust to be that the money shall be put out to interest and Haslehurst, the father, shall receive the interest during his life and his wife (who is one of the plaintiffs and his executrix) for her life and after both their deaths the principal money to remain to such of their children by name successively when they should come to [the age of] twenty-one, whereof another of the plaintiffs was such child as was entitled to it after the wife's death, and this and the interest due since 1651 the plaintiffs claim by their bill, pretending a great kindness from the testatrix Mrs. Warren to whom by a will in 1641 she gave the residue of her estate, but was afterwards overpersuaded to revoke that and other wills and gave them nothing.

The defendant by answer insisted that he was a stranger and executor only and upon the length of time and that never any interest or claim was paid or demanded for thirty years and so by presumption was paid or discharged, and when he first claimed it (which was after the deed and counterpart which were both found together in a 3d. hand and after Mrs. Warren's death) being asked why he never claimed it before said because he had forgot it (though he was but a mean man and often paid Mrs. Warren interest money).

But MOUNTAGU, chief baron, GREGORY and STREET, barons, were of opinion for the plaintiffs, *viz.* the widow and child notwithstanding the length of time upon the reason that after the trust was created for a feme covert and children (though by the voluntary provision of the father) that trust could not be destroyed by the husband or any other, and though length of time was a great objection against the husband, yet it is now against [the] wife and child, whose interest commenced but after the husband's death, which was shortly before the bill, and so decided it for the plaintiffs as to the principal £130 and interest for the same from the husband's death, Baron ATKYNS not being of that opinion.

[Other copies of this report: GUL MS. B88–7, p. 434.]

[Order of 14 June 1683: PRO E.126/14, 80v.]

175
Lloyd v. Evans (Ex. 1683)

In this case, a decree in equity from the council of the marches of Wales was reviewed in the court of exchequer and affirmed.

LI MS. Misc. 557, f. 9, pl. 1 [Fr.] (Ward's Reports)

The defendant here had exhibited his English bill and obtained a decree against the plaintiff here in the court of Ludlow. And the plaintiff here thinking himself aggrieved by this decree exhibited his English bill in this court in the nature of an appeal to this decree comprising all the matter and the decree and showing in which things the decree was erroneous and should be reversed, which was prayed accordingly. The defendant here by his answer insisted upon the justice of the decree and the jurisdiction of the court below, that it was a competent judicature, and the decrees of it [are] not examinable or reversible in this court. And the cause descended to the issue. And upon the hearing of it, the first decree was confirmed as a just decree upon the merits.

I [was] for the plaintiff here.

[Other copies of this report: GUL MS. B88–7, p. 436.]

[Order of 5 July 1683: PRO E.126/14, f. 89.]

176

Sowton v. Attorney General (Ex. 1683)

In this case, the court of equity took jurisdiction to hear an allegation of perjury resulting in an adverse verdict at common law. However, in the suit in equity, the alleged perjury was not fully proved and the equity case was dismissed.

LI MS. Misc. 557, f. 12 [Fr.] (Ward's Reports)

The defendant Breedon having obtained a presentation from the king to the rectory of Fowlston in the County of York, supposing it vacant by the simony or simoniacal promotion of the plaintiff, the incumbent there, prosecuted in the name of the attorney general a *quare impedit* against the plaintiff concerning all of the matter of simony. And upon the issue, the jury at the assizes at York gave a verdict for the king, upon which the assize judge gave judgment immediately and awarded a letter to the bishop. But the plaintiff suspecting the event had a writ of error in his hands, which was delivered and allowed and execution was stayed.

And now he brought his English bill in the exchequer against the attorney general and Breedon, the presentee of the king, and Toune, his solicitor and a witness upon the sole evidence of whom the verdict passed, principally to have a new trial, suggesting that he did not come in by simony but justly and that the verdict passed against him only upon the testimony of Toune, that he had [been] indicted for perjury and had a [true] bill found and that he absented himself and absconded and against whom there was a proceeding to outlawry and that the evidence was not true upon which he was convicted of simony supposed to have been done ten years past and he had quiet enjoyment and that after this trial he had made discovery of other things that will clear him of any simony, and because there was not any power or any court to grant a new trial except here, inasmuch as the writ of error had taken it from the court of common pleas and yet the king's bench where it was depending did not have the power to grant a new trial but only to affirm or reverse the judgment, it is only relievable here in this court, [it] being harsh to be concluded in his right by a trial solely upon the sole testimony of a perjured person.

The defendant Breedon in his own name and in the name of Toune demurred to the bill [as] being matter determinable solely and duly determined at law upon full evidence, which can not be arraigned or reexamined in a court of equity. But the court overruled the demurrer upon the reason that if the plaintiff can show that Toune was perjured, which shall be presumed if he should be outlawed and refuse to appear, or that there was any other mistake touching the purchase of the next avoidance, upon which the plaintiff was presented, or other equitable matter shown that could induce the court to grant a new trial, that they declared they could and should upon reasonable matter proved, it is harsh to conclude the plaintiff.

And afterwards the cause descended to issue, and divers witnesses [were] examined, but none of them fully contradicted the evidence of Toune, who at this time was actually outlawed for the perjury. Though there were circumstances that there was no simony but there being a verdict and judgment and this was affirmed by leave of court during the suit, the court dismissed the plaintiff's bill without any relief.

[Other copies of this report: GUL MS. B88–7, p. 443.]

[Order of 20 Feb. 1684: PRO E.126/14, f. 124.]

177

Deye v. Thwaits (Ex. 1683)

In this case, a conveyance that had been altered after execution was enforced according to its original terms without any proof as to who made the alteration.

Where a decree is made against an infant, he must be given an opportunity to show cause against it after he comes of age.

LI MS. Misc. 557, ff. 14, 16 [Fr.] (Ward's Reports)

The case upon the hearing was thus. Captain William Thwaits, [who was] seised in fee of Varnish Hall and lands in Essex valued [at] £200 *per annum*, made a settlement of them by lease and release 11 and 12 December 1678, by which he settled them to the use of himself and Frances his wife for their lives, afterwards to such of their children that the captain by some writing under [his] hand and seal should appoint, and by default of such appointment to the use of Thomas, his second son, and Frances, the daughter of the captain, and their heirs. And this limitation appeared by the draft of the conveyance by the clerk of Mr. Jenner of the Inner Temple, who was a counsel in the case, who left a blank in the draft for the names of Thomas and Frances to be filled up by direction of the captain, who afterwards and before engrossment gave directions to Jenner to put in their names, who did it accordingly with his own hand in their presence. And afterwards they were engrossed by Jenner's clerk who made the draft, and [he] examined the intent and executed [it]. And the captain took them with him and delivered them to Heath, one of the trustees. And after the death of the captain, Heath delivered them to Porter and Strutt. The captain and [his] wife died; Thomas the second son died without issue; Frances the daughter, having married the plaintiff Deye, insisted to have the premises. Upon inspection and perusal of the writings, there appeared an erasure in the place where the name of Frances the daughter was and in the place of it the name of James the now defendant (and who was the oldest son and heir of the captain but otherwise provided for) was inserted.

The plaintiffs exhibited their bill to have discovery and relief, complaining of the erasure but not charging it (it being a criminal thing and on account of that demurrable) to be made by the defendants. The matter of the draught and the testimony of the counsel and his son were satisfactory to the court that at the time of the sealing the name of Frances the daughter was in the conveyance and not of James, but upon the pressure of the defendants, the court detained the deed in court and put it to a trial at bar upon this issue, whether the deed of release 12 December 1678 was erased after execution of it or not. And after a long trial and full evidence of both parties, the jury found a verdict for the plaintiffs, that the said deed was erased after the execution of it. After that the court made a decree for the plaintiffs that they should enjoy the premises to themselves and the heirs of Frances the plaintiff, daughter of the captain, against the defendant and all others claiming under him and granted a perpetual injunction.

I [was] for the plaintiffs.

Note that the court having an erasure and more decreed for the plaintiffs without any proof of who made the erasure.

But after an appeal to Parliament, this decree was reversed for this reason only, that being made against an infant (though after a trial at law), there was no day given to the infant to show cause against the decree within six months or other time after he comes of full age. And this error being rectified, the lords directed that there should be a new trial after the infant comes of age. But the plaintiff Deye having mortgaged the lands recovered and decreed to Lady Bridgman for £2000, all of which money [was paid] on the credit of the trial and decree, the lady's executor after her death petitioned the lords in Parliament to terminate their order for a new trial if the defendant Thwaits does not try the same issue again within a convenient time to be prefixed for this purpose (he having attained his full age divers years ago). And the lords in Parliament by their order 25 March 1699[1] confined Thwaits to try the former issue within a limited time, which was done in Trinity term 1700 at the exchequer bar by a special jury of Middlesex knights and esquires. And after long and full evidence on both parts, the jury gave a verdict against the first verdict and that the deed was not erased after the execution of it but before. And afterwards in Parliament begun 6 February 1700[/01], Lady Bridgman petitioned the lords in Parliament for a new trial of the same issue upon the merits of the case, there being verdict against verdict and a mortgagee in the case for £2000 who had not any other security, and the court of exchequer could not grant a new trial without direction inasmuch as the last trial was only by their direction. And divers days were appointed to have the case heard at the lord's bar. And Tuesday 10 June 1701, the lords upon the hearing of counsel for Thwaits and Lady Bridgman, no one attending for Deye, ordered a new trial to be before the end of Michaelmas term next.[2]

Note that this trial was upon the sole petition of a mortgagee, who came in touching the remainder in the daughter and was not a party or at the original cause or at the issue tried. After that, *scil.* 19 November 1701, there was another or new trial upon the same issue by a special jury of knights, esquires, etc. of the County of Middlesex at the exchequer bar, which lasted twelve hours. And the jury, not being agreed, slept the entire night, and around 11 o'clock the next day in the morning, they found and returned a verdict for the plaintiff, that is to say, that the deed was erased after the execution, that they agreed with the first verdict (though against the last verdict, which was by the direction of the lords in Parliament, who ordered the third trial and confined Thwaits to try it before the end of Michaelmas term 1701). This last trial was established, and the decree stood, and thus the mortgage to Lady Bridgman became good security, which otherwise would have been avoided.

And this last trial was carried on by the executors of Lady Bridgman and not by Deye, whom they did not trust in this case.

Note that [there were] three trials at the bar of the exchequer by three Middlesex special juries to try and determine one and the same matter of fact only, *scil.* whether a deed was erased and new persons' names [were] inserted before or after the first execution of the deed:

---

[1] Order of 23 May 1698: *Lords' Journal*, XVI (n.d.), p. 294.
[2] *Lords' Journal*, XVI (n.d.), p. 734.

1. In 1683 by direction and for satisfaction of the court to make a decree, and [there was a] verdict for Deye.
2. In 1700 by direction of the lords in Parliament upon a reversal of the decree for the fault of [not] giving a day to the infant after age, and [there was a] verdict for Thwaits.
3. By direction of the lords in Parliament (not being satisfied by the last verdict), and then [there was a] verdict for Deye's title, which was conclusive.

[Other copies of this report: GUL MS. B88–7, pp. 448, 450.]

[Orders of 7 May and 18 June 1683: PRO E.126/14, ff. 43v, 90.]

[For notes of other proceedings in this case, see LI MS. Misc. 533, ff. [59–66], and LI MS. Misc. 535, ff. [57–67]. Modified and affirmed on appeal: Thwaites v. Deye (1701), Colles 179, 1 E.R. 238, *Lords' Journal*, XVII (n.d.), pp. 24, 64.]

[Connected case: Thwaytes v. Dye (1688), 2 Vernon 80, 23 E.R. 661, 1 Eq. Cas. Abr. 343, 21 E.R. 1090, affirmed on appeal: *Lords' Journal*, XIV (n.d.), p. 398.]

178
Infield v. Infield (Ex. 1683)

Where a plaintiff lacks standing to sue, as where a grant of administration has been suspended pending an appeal, the defendant need not answer to the merits.

LI MS. Misc. 557, f. 30, pl. 1 [Fr.] (Ward's Reports)

To be relieved for a lease for years, the plaintiff entitled himself by a remainder limited to him of this lease after an estate tail limited to another. And also (which was his better title, the court rejecting the first) he entitled himself as administrator to one who had the right of the lease in him at the time of his death.

The defendant pleaded that after administration [was] granted to the plaintiff and before the bill, *viz.* such a day and year, an appeal from the grant of the administration was, in the same court that granted the administration and within fifteen days after the grant of it, duly interposed directed to such judges delegates by virtue of a commission to them under the great seal on such a date, and that this appeal was duly entered, exhibited, and admitted and an inhibition upon it was granted and the plaintiff was served with it, who had appeared, and that this appeal remained indeterminate, by reason of which appeal all acts and proceedings upon the said administration were suspended and that pending it no action or suit could be brought or maintained in [common] law or equity by virtue or color of this administration. And so [he] prayed judgment whether the defendant should be compelled to make any answer to this bill pending this appeal and before the determination of it.

And the court ruled it a good plea *quousque*, etc., according to the resolution in Packman's Case, 6 Rep. 18,[1] notwithstanding [that] the defendant had not denied the combination nor shown any title to himself or another by the appeal or otherwise.

I [was] for the plaintiff.

[Other copies of this report: GUL MS. B88–7, p. 475.]

179
Price v. Birch (Ex. 1683)

In this case, the issue was whether a bill in equity lies to recover a sum certain due as rent out of land.

LI MS. Misc. 557, f. 31, pl. 1 [Fr.] (Ward's Reports)

The plaintiff exhibited his bill for discovery and relief for 8s. rent payable to him out of lands in a parish in the County of Hereford in the possession of the defendant. The defendant answered and showed his purchase from Sir Thomas Tomkins and that he was ignorant of any such rent and showed his reasons by which he conceived [that] no such rent was due or payable. The plaintiff proved payment of the rent within thirty-five years and for the same lands that the defendant had and of which the certainty sufficiently appeared. And those payments were [made] by direction of the owner of the inheritance, under whose title the defendant claimed.

And the question was upon the hearing whether the plaintiff should be relieved here in equity or should be dismissed to the [common] law, inasmuch as the certainty of the rent and of the lands appeared and for this the plaintiff had a full remedy at law by distress and it is not reasonable or usual in such a case to relieve in equity, especially when there was not any payment for thirty years. And of this opinion was Baron ATKYNS.

But Chief Baron MOUNTAGU and barons GREGORY and STREET declared the plaintiff [to be] relievable here, inasmuch as [he] had alleged by [his] bill that [he] did not know the lands out of which the rent issued (but it was proved clearly by his witnesses). And they were not satisfied that the 8s. was rent, for which [there] could be distress or other remedy in law, but only a pension (being originally payable to an ecclesiastical corporation, a monastery, under which the plaintiff claimed), though neither in the bill, proofs, or otherwise was there any mention of the name of a pension but only of rent and chief rent.

And the cause was afterwards finished by agreement, and the defendant purchased it.

---

[1] *Packman's Case* (1595), 6 Coke Rep. 18, 77 E.R. 281.

I [was] for the defendant.
[Other copies of this report: GUL MS. B88–7, p. 476.]
[Order of 19 Nov. 1683: PRO E.126/14, f. 104.]

180
Inder v. Bax (Ex. 1683)

Under the terms of the will at issue in this case, all of the legacies were ordered to be paid, but each was liable proportionately for the decedent's debts.

LI MS. Misc. 557, f. 33, pl. 1 [Fr.] (Ward's Reports)

The case upon the hearing was thus. Mary Bax, widow, by her will, taking notice that she was possessed of a lease[hold] called Dean and Chafont and had laid out divers sums in stocking it, which stock was on the farm, and that she had laid out £280 for renewing the lease and repairs upon the premises and that after her death those premises should go to the children of her daughter Hill, she for the greater ease of her executor and that it or [any] other [of] her estate should not be troubled or charged with the payment of any of her legacies to her daughter or any of the children of her daughter, she gave and disposed of the stock and goods that should be on the said farm at the time of her death to and among her executor and so many of her said daughter's children and in such proportions as is after mentioned, *viz.* to her executor £280 in the first place, and to her granddaughter Mary Hill £500 in the next place, and next after [that] £100 to her granddaughter Katherine Hill, and the residue and overplus of the said stock and goods to her two granddaughters Alice and Sarah Hill to be equally divided. And [she] willed that the legatees of the said stock should out of their legacies proportionably abate towards any charge or repair or breach of covenant she or her executor should be subject to about that farm. And she made the defendant sole executor and died a year and more afterwards. The wife of the plaintiff was executrix to Mary Hill, the legatee for £500. Katherine, the legatee for £100, was married to Butler, who were both defendants here. The value of the stock and goods at the time of the death of the testatrix was £726 13s. 10d. and not more, out of which repairs must be taken (because there was not any breach of covenant).

And in this case, the court decreed:

1. That the £280 to the executor was a legacy to him and liable to the repairs.
2. That notwithstanding her words in the will, that the £280 should be paid in the first place and the £500 in the next place and the £100 next, yet that there should not be any preference in this case,

inasmuch as the stock did not suffice to pay all, but that each legatee of the £280, £500, and £100 should have his proportion without any preference. And the reason was that it should be presumed that the stock at the time of the making of the will was sufficient to pay all of the legacies with an overplus (which was also disposed of [by the will]), and on account of that the intention of the testatrix was that the £100 should be paid as well as the precedent legacies though not as soon, but as the effects were diminished so that all could not be paid, it is reasonable that each should have a proportion and not some all and some nothing, and the first or next place in such a case should not take place.
3. That the legatees of the overplus are excluded, there not being any overplus.
4. That each legatee should pay a proportionable part of the repairs.

I [was] for the plaintiff.

[Other copies of this report: GUL MS. B88–7, p. 480.]

181
Griffith v. David (Ex. 1683)

In a suit in equity for discovery and common law relief, the court of equity will determine the prayer for common law relief unless there is a demurrer to the prayer for relief, and this rule applies also where the defendants are executors.

LI MS. Misc. 557, f. 34 [Fr.] (Ward's Reports)

The plaintiff exhibited his bill against the defendants showing that they were executors of one A.B. [*blank*] and that the said testator in his life, *scil.* 1676, in consideration that the plaintiff would marry the testator's daughter, who was a widow, promised and agreed to pay and give to the plaintiff with his daughter in marriage £60 and averred his marriage. And to discover assets and to be relieved was the scope of the bill.

The defendants answered that they were strangers to the promise and agreement and ignorant of it and they believed that no such promise was made and that the testator lived for three years after the promise and [there was] no demand or suit for it and [he] made [?] his will and the defendants executors and gave divers legacies and a part of his personal estate to the plaintiff's wife and they received this part and gave a discharge for it without any pretense of such a promise. And the other part was divided among the testator's other children. And they annexed to the answer an inventory of the personal estate and how it was disposed.

The plaintiff examined witnesses and by two [of them] proved the promise and that by the consent and desire of the testator this promise was to be concealed until the death of the testator.

And at the hearing the court directed an issue whether such an agreement was made or not and refused to relinquish the plaintiff to his action at [common] law, it being, as the defendants' counsel insisted, only an action at law upon a special promise that the testator in consideration that the plaintiff would marry his daughter would give him £60 and that it is not a cause relievable in equity because the plaintiff has his remedy at law as he has discovery of the personal estate and the £60 consisted in damages because the jury can give less in damages than £60 if it should wish to. But the court inasmuch as it had jurisdiction on the part for the discovery of the assets did not wish to dismiss or relinquish the plaintiff to [the common] law, inasmuch as the defendant had not demurred to the relief, which note and query.

Query whether by such means all executors and administrators who are compellable to discover assets should not be drawn into a court of equity for all actions upon the case against the testator because a demurrer to the relief is not usual nor allowable, inasmuch as the merits of the cause are not before the court upon a demurrer.

[Order of 26 Nov. 1683: PRO E.126/14, f. 122.]

182

Dearsly v. Kemp (Ex. 1683)

Where a seller contracts to sell land, it is presumed that the land is freehold land free of rents and services, and, if it is not, the buyer is entitled to an abatement in the price.

LI MS. Misc. 557, f. 36 [Fr.] (Ward's Reports)

Upon the hearing of the cause, the court was of the opinion and thus decreed that, if a man covenant upon payment of a sum certain to convey such lands, in certain, particularly named in the articles to another and his heirs in such a manner as the counsel of the purchaser shall advise, and there is not any mention made in the articles that any part of them are copyhold and liable for rent, nor that any rent or service is due for the other lands, that in such case these articles do not bind the purchaser to pay the money, but that there should be an allowance for the copyhold fines and rents and the other rents. Though the vendor was not bound to convey without encumbrances, because, by the court, where no mention is made in the articles, it shall be understood that all is franktenement and fee and free from all rents and services. And the decree was that the plaintiff shall be free from the defendant's articles and that the defendant deliver up the articles and stay the action, without costs.

I [was] for the defendant.

[Other copies of this report: GUL MS. B88–7, p. 488.]

183
Wren v. Earl of Newburgh (Ex. 1683)

Where a mortgagee is beyond the jurisdiction of the court, service of process in a suit to redeem can be served on the agent of the mortgagee.

LI MS. Misc. 557, f. 37, pl. 1 [Fr.] (Ward's Reports)

Mr. Wren exhibited an English bill against the countess and earl of Newburgh for the redemption of lands conveyed by Sir Henry Poole for security of the payment of £6000 to the countess, which not being paid the countess entered. And the lands were settled in the marriage of the countess and descended to the present earl, her son. And the plaintiff alleged an equity of redemption under Sir William Doyly, who alleged title from Sir Henry Poole to this redemption.

The earl before this bill [was] exhibited had gone to France for education and was an infant around eighteen or nineteen years. And the profits of the land were received by his bailiff.

And upon motion and debate and oath made that the earl was overseas, the court ordered that leaving the subpoena with the bailiff who received the profits should be good service to bring the earl into contempt for not answering notwithstanding that the earl was *bona fide* overseas before the bill [was] exhibited and it was not begun by him or on his behalf. And the reason that the court went on in this case was the mischief that otherwise would ensue, that no mortgagor could redeem if the mortgagee be overseas. And outlawry aids at common law, but [there would be] no relief in equity, if such a course should not be admitted, which [is] the practice in chancery.

I [was] for the defendant.

Note [that] it was denied that the chancery practice was such and afterwards this [. . .] in chancery by the lord keeper.

[Other copies of this report: GUL MS. B88–7, p. 489.]

184
Laurence v. Watts (Ex. 1684)

Even though a decedent's personal estate is insufficient to pay debts, funeral expenses, and money legacies, specific legacies of leases must be paid without any deduction or abatement.

LI MS. 557, ff. 37, 42 [Fr.] (Ward's Reports)

The case upon the hearing was that the defendants' testatrix, to whom they were executors, devised divers money legacies and also divers leases for years to several persons specifically, and she died. And her personal estate besides the leases for years did not suffice to pay her debts, funerals, and money legacies. And the court was of opinion that the specific legatees of the leases should pay and abate out of their legacies proportionally with the money legatees, and they took a difference between a specific legacy of an entire thing, as a horse, cup, or similar [thing], which will not endure division, and a lease for years, which can be divided. And thus they would not compel the executors to assent to the legacies of the leases without security to save them harmless against the money legatees.[1]

I [was] for the defendants.

See below f. 42 [where] the same case was otherwise resolved and decreed.

In this case, it was declared by the court and thus decreed that where the testatrix had devised leases for years to several persons in specie and also goods in specie and also legacies in money and all the personal estate except the leases and goods specifically devised did not extend to pay all the legacies in money, that yet the specific legacies of the leases and goods should be delivered and assented unto without any deduction or abatement and the defect of the personal estate should fall upon the money legatees proportionally among all. And the defendants being executors [were] decreed to assent to those specific legacies being indemnified for it by the decree. And no difference was conceived in this case to be between a specific legacy of a lease and of an entire thing, as a horse, cup, or similar [thing], though the court the last term in the same case was of a contrary opinion, as above, f. 37.

I [was] for the defendant.

[Other copies of this report: GUL MS. B88–7, p. 499.]

[Order of 13 Feb. 1684: PRO E.126/14, f. 138.]

---

[1] This first report was stricken out in the manuscript but is printed here because Ward refers back to it at the end of the report of the decree the following term.

185
Fish v. Wimberly (Ex. 1684)

Tithes of coleseed are small tithes that are included in an endowment of altarages.

LI MS. Misc. 557, f. 41, pl. 1 [Fr.] (Ward's Reports)

The plaintiff demanded by his suit as vicar of Gedney in the County of Lincoln tithes of coleseed, and his endowment was '*de toto alteragio et omnibus aliis obventionibus praeter decimam faeni de dominico*' without [any] other words. And his proof was that the vicars had received all the small tithes within Gedney and that the rector had only the tithes of corn. And there was some proof that his predecessors forty years ago had received tithes of coleseed. And also it was proved that they within the past twenty years had received such tithes from some persons and that the vicars in divers adjacent vills and not the rectors had the tithes of coleseed.

And Chief Baron MOUNTAGU [and] barons ATKYNS and GREGORY (Street being absent) decreed for the plaintiff without any trial at law, notwithstanding that it was proved that more than forty years ago tithes of coleseed had been answered to the right of the rector and that within the past twenty years the rector had divers times received them without molestation or claim and the vicar had surceased a suit that he had commenced for them upon advice that he did not have title to them by his endowment. And this proof was by several witnesses. And notwithstanding that it was urged that coleseed was a new tithe and recently (that is to say within the past sixty years) used in England and on account of that could not be inferred to be included within the word *alteragium* and the usage is not general for the vicar but as much for the rector as the vicar, and the common right is for the rector, and the coleseed in question was in great quantities, that is to say 250 acres, and the tithes worth £100, and in so doubtful a case a trial [is usually] prayed whether [they] belong to the vicar, as the plaintiff alleged, or to the rector, as the defendant alleged, and the rector had a bill for the same tithes depending against the defendants and the plaintiff, and it was not the defendant here as the defendants insist upon his title.

But it was decree as above. And the reasons given were first that coleseed was in its nature a small tithe notwithstanding the quantity of land sown with it, and on account of that it should go to the vicar though the rector had received them divers years, the vicars having received them also, secondly that the word *alteragium* with the usage is large enough to pass all small tithes, Hetley 135,[1] Degge 199 and 221, and though the tithe in question was not *in esse* at the time

---

[1] *Wood v. Greenwood* (1627–1632), Hetley 135, 124 E.R. 402, also 1 Eagle & Younge 368, Littleton 243, 124 E.R. 228.

of the endowment and though there were not any exclusive or restraining words to the right of the rector that he should have only such things, yet that this word can contain all small tithes, the construction of it with the usage will include all small tithes.

I [was] for the defendants.

[Other copies of this report: GUL MS. B88–7, p. 496.]

[The order of 4 Feb. 1684, PRO E.126/14, f. 137, is printed at 1 Wood 222, 2 Gwillim 532, 1 Eagle & Younge 540.]

186
Trinity College v. Wrottesley (Ex. 1684)

In this case, the defendant was ordered to pay a certain rent or pension payable out of his land though he was a purchaser without notice of it.

LI MS. Misc. 557, f. 42, pl. 2 [Eng.] (Ward's Reports)

Plaintiffs by grant from the crown 24 December 38vo *regni sui* [1546] entitled to a rent or pension of £5 *per annum* issuing out of Pirton Manor in the County of Stafford by dissolution of monasteries sue the defendant owner of that manor for twenty-two years arrears of that pension by English bill the defendant having been so long in possession of that manor by purchase from the earl of Dorset. Defendant by answer says he knows not of the right or grant of the crown nor of any rent or pension issuing out of or chargeable upon the said manor and that he is a purchaser thereof without notice and for a valuable consideration, only says that there was a flying report about the time of the purchase of some rent or pension out of the manor and that before his purchase he repaired to and acquainted the said earl with such report and desired to know whether any such was, who assured him he never heard of it nor ever paid it nor was it demanded, and thereupon defendant proceeded in the purchase without other notice or having any allowance or abatement for it, and insisted he ought not to be charged with that portion or arrears of it.

At the hearing, the records of the [court of] augmentations made it appear that such pension was due, and by the college books and bursar's accounts, it appeared to be paid till near the time of defendant's purchase. And the court decreed the payment of the arrears for twenty-two years and the future growing duty and this without trial at law.

I [was] for the plaintiffs.

[Other copies of this report: GUL MS. B88–7, p. 500.]

[Order of 7 Feb. 1684: E.126/14, f. 136.]

187
Crowther v. Lee (Ex. 1684)

A contract to convey is not a debt.
Where a purchaser enters land pursuant to the contract and remains in possession until his death, it will be presumed that the conveyance was duly executed.
An interested party cannot give evidence.

LI MS. Misc. 557, f. 51, pl. 1 [Fr.] (Ward's Reports)

The case upon the hearing was thus. Sir Gilbert Ireland seised in fee of copyhold lands in right of his wife by writing under his hand and the hand of his wife for £600 in hand paid to Sir Gilbert by Edward Aspinwall, who had married Eleanor, the sister of Sir Gilbert, promised and agreed to make a lease of those lands to Edward Aspinwall for 99 years if Eleanor and two sons of Edward Aspinwall or any of them so long live. And this agreement was made in 1652 and the lands were enjoyed by Edward Aspinwall until his death, which was in 1656, who by his will demised his estate and lease to the said Eleanor for her life and afterwards to the said two sons. And after the death of Aspinwall, the said lands were enjoyed all the lives of Sir Gilbert and his wife, both of whom died in 1675, Sir Gilbert having made provision in his will or lease to the defendants, his trustees, of divers lands for payment of his debts. And in truth after the death of the Lady Ireland, the lands were enjoyed by the plaintiffs, as it was alleged (but not proved) that the Lady Ireland, who survived Sir Gilbert, devised them to Eleanor, the widow of Aspinwall, for her life for advantage of her children. And in the debate of this case, the court resolved these points:

1. That this contract and payment of Aspinwall of the £600 to Sir Gilbert was an absolute contract and bargain for the said lease and not a debt of Sir Gilbert in the provision made by him by lease to the trustees for payment of his debts, because Aspinwall entered and enjoyed presently and the sum of £600 was a just purchase of the lease for three lives at twelve years purchase and not any security for the said £600. And enjoyment is a great evidence of it.
2. It is presumable that the lease was executed accordingly, there being constant enjoyment from 1652 to now pursuant to the contract without claim or interruption.
3. That Eleanor, the widow and demisee of Aspinwall, though she had released to the plaintiffs, the daughters and administrators of Edward Aspinwall *cum testamento annexo*, upon the refusal of Sir Gilbert Ireland, the executor could not be a witness in this case, being demisee of the term. And the length of time of the enjoyment by

Eleanor after the death of Aspinwall, her husband, which was almost twenty years is evidence of the assent of the executor to the said legacy, which was not divested by this release.

And the plaintiffs' bill was dismissed with costs.
I [was] for the defendants.

[Other copies of this report: GUL MS. B88–7, p. 512.]
[Order of 24 Apr. 1684: PRO E.126/14, f. 158.]

188
Harvey v. Juxon (Ex. 1684)

An assignee who has an equity by a power of attorney can sue in equity in his own name. Rent is payable even though the land has lost its value.

LI MS. Misc. 557, f. 51, pl. 2 [Fr.] (Ward's Reports)

Sir William Bateman was entitled to £12 10s. *per annum*, rent reserved on a building lease in London of houses burned there in the Great Fire. But they were not rebuilt by the lessee, and for not rebuilding the City of London entered and sold the land, and the money was divided. Sir William Bateman being indebted to the plaintiff in £80, for payment of this sum, he constituted the plaintiff his attorney and irrevocable assignee in the name of Bateman but to the use of the plaintiff to receive and sue for this rent in arrears from Christmas 1675. And for this rent incurred from this time until 1678, when the City sold the land, the plaintiff exhibited his bill.

And by the whole court:

1. The suit is well brought by the plaintiff in his own name (Bateman being a defendant) because he had an interest in equity by letter of attorney to receive for his own use. And [he] is also a purchaser of it.
2. Though the soil was unprofitable to the lessee, yet he must pay the rent, because it is his fault for not improving [it] and the plaintiff did not have any other remedy.

And the plaintiff had a decree for the rent.
I [was] for the plaintiff.

[Other copies of this report: GUL MS. B88–7, p. 514.]
[Order of 17 Apr. 1684: PRO E.126/14, f. 156.]

189

Hopkins v. Chappell (Ex. 1684)

In this case, an increased payment for an ecclesiastical position belonging to a prebendary was due to the vicar even though it had been paid to a curate.

I
LI MS. Misc. 557, f. 53 [Fr.] (Ward's Reports)

The case upon the hearing was thus. John Chappell before and at the time of the restoration of the king was a prebendary of the prebend of Comb and Harnham in the County of Wiltshire, and [on] 5 November 12 Car. II [1660] he demised the said prebend and parsonage to Vennard and Young for three lives under the old annual rent of £32 3s. 4d. to the prebendary and his successors, and also £30 *per annum* more, which by this lease was declared to be intended and appointed for the further augmentation, benefit, and endowment of the vicarage of Comb Bisset, according to the direction and declaration of the king (who in June before had written letters to all ecclesiastical persons, owners of impropriations, to make augmentations to all their vicarages) and for the better maintenance of the vicar there and his successors. And this lease was under a condition to be void upon the tender or payment of 6d. (because in truth it was a trust for the lessor and to be at his disposal). And in this lease there was a covenant on the lessees' part to procure the cure of West Harnham (being a curacy and chappelcy within the said prebend and parsonage) to be served at their own charge, after which, that is to say in January 1663[/64], this lease was avoided by the payment of 6d. and entry. And the next day after, a new lease was made for three lives to the defendant, being the son of the lessor, under the same rents of £32 3s. 4d. and £30 as above and the same covenant to serve the cure of West Harnham, after which, that is to say in July 1669, the same prebendary (upon surrender of the last lease) made another lease of the same prebend and parsonage to the defendant under the old rent to the prebendary and his successors and also reserving the rent of £30 *per annum* for the endowment of the church or chapel of West Harnham for the maintenance of the curate and his successors there for the discharging [of] the cure of the said chapel. And no mention or reservation was made in the same lease of the £30 *per annum* or any other thing for the augmentation of the said vicarage of Comb Bisset, the design being to transfer the said £30 *per annum* reserved in the first lease for the vicar of Comb Bisset to the curate of West Harnham, both being within the said prebend and parsonage. And in this lease, the covenant to preserve the cure of West Harnham was omitted, after which, that is to say in 1670, the same prebendary renewed the lease formerly mentioned under the same rents, reservations, and terms contained in the lease of 1669 and no reservation, revision, or augmentation was made by the vicar of Comb Bisset, after which, that is to say [by Statute] 29 Car. II, c. 8,[1] an act of parliament was made for the confirming and perpetuating [of] augmentations to vicarages and curacies made pursuant to the letters of the king 1 June 1660, by which all augmentations made by ecclesiastical persons and which then were reserved, declared, or intended or afterwards should be granted, reserved, or made payable to any vicar or curate should be continued as well during the estate and term upon which they were reserved or made payable as afterwards in whomsoever's hands they should come and though they should be reserved again or not. And it gave a remedy to vicars and curates by distress or action of debt, and it made all subsequent leases upon which there should be no reservation of such an augmentation void. The defendant paid the £30 to the curate of West Harnham constantly according to the reservation and nothing to the vicar. The vicarage became void by deprivation, and the plaintiff served the cure of it divers years and afterwards was instituted and inducted into it.

And he preferred his English bill in this court against the defendant to have the £30 *per annum* first reserved for the vicar and the arrears of it incurred after the deprivation of the last vicar. And whether the £30 *per annum* should be paid to the vicar or curate was the question.

And for the defendant it was urged that it was indifferent to the king and parliament whether the vicar or the curate should have it, [they] being both ecclesiastical persons and within the care and intention as well as the provision of the Act, because curacies were mentioned as well as vicarages, and thus the lessor had complied with the intention of the king by making the £30 by itself to be reserved for the curate. And the purpose of the Act was to confirm the reservation and augmentation *in esse* at the time of the Act. And the defendant, having paid and being bound by the lease to pay to the curate and this augmentation being vested in the curate by the Act, to compel the defendant to pay to the plaintiff is to subject him to a double charge of £30 *per annum*, one to the vicar, the other to the curate. And the first lease which created the title or pretense in the vicar is and divers years before the Act was avoided and another [was] made under which the defendant claims which obliges payment to the curate. Also the Act giving an express and new remedy by distress or debt and being introductive of a new right, the plaintiff, if he had a right, should take [as] his remedy one of those ways and not resort to equity.

But all of the barons, that is to say Chief Baron MOUNTAGU, ATKYNS, GREGORY, and STREET, barons, were entirely of opinion for the plaintiff, and resolved these points:

1. That the prebendary's complying with the letter of the king at first was an original equity in the vicar without the Act.

---

[1] Stat. 29 Car. II, c. 8 (*SR*, V, 849–850).

2. That the Act in this case confirmed the augmentation to the vicar and set it up again notwithstanding that there was not any reservation for the vicar *in esse* at the time of the Act, and this [was] both by the words and intent of the Act as by the nature and equity of this case because the words of the Act are both retrospective for those augmentations made before the Act and prospective for those that should be made after the Act, and the purpose was to confirm those made at first pursuant to the letters of the king. And in reason and justice the vicar and not the curate should have it, because the vicar had the cure of souls of his own not depending upon the prebendary and was obliged to serve the cure, but the curate is in effect the prebendary himself who is bound to provide for his own cure, and he took the covenant from the lessee to provide for this curacy as the vicar had the £30, and by translating the augmentation from the vicar to the curate, he is only easing himself or his son, his tenant, who was bound without any augmentation to provide for this curacy.
3. That it was not in the power of the lessor after he had made the augmentation to change it to another person. And the vicar was principally considered.[2]
4. That the lessee was not bound to pay the £30 to the curate but should be relieved in equity against it.
5. That the plaintiff had a good remedy in equity as well as by the means provided by the Act for the arrears and growing duty, and it is the proper remedy for the arrears.

And thus it was decreed for the plaintiff.
I [was] for the defendant.

[Other copies of this report: GUL MS. B88–7, p. 515]

II
BL MS. Hargr. 230, f. 15v [Eng.]

John Chappell, prebend of Comb Harnham in the Cathedral Church of Sarum, [on the] 5th November 12 of the king [1660] demises unto George Vennard and John Young and their heirs the prebend and parsonage of Comb Harnham for three lives rendering the ancient rent of £32 3s. 4d. and rendering the further improved rent of £30 *per annum* for an augmentation of the vicarage of Comb Bisset, which lease was made upon [a] condition to be void upon the tender of [*blank*] by the said John Chappell to the lessees.

---

[2] respect *MS*.

[On] 25th January 1663, John Chappell tenders six pence to the tenants to make void the lease and enters accordingly and then after other leases made and surrendered [on] 9th January 1670, he makes a lease of the premisses to the defendant, Charles Chappell, rendering the ancient rent of £32 3s. 4d. and an improved rent of £30 *per annum* for the [*blank*] of the Chapel of Harnham.

[In] 29 Car. II [1677] comes the Act for Augmentation of Small Vicarages and Curacies, *viz.* the Act [*blank*].[3] The query in general [is] whether the parsonage in the hands of the defendant, Charles Chappell, who claims the same by virtue of a lease made in the 22nd year of the king [1670] wherein there is no reservation of any rent nor any other agreement for any augmentation of Combe Bisster but the rent of £30 *per annum* which the lease in the 12th [year] of the king [1660] was reserved for the augmentation of the vicarage of Combe Bister transferred to the Chapel of Harnham whether Charles Chappell notwithstanding the determination of the said lease shall be liable to pay £30 *per annum* either in law or equity.

I think that at the common law in case there were no statute in the case neither the Statute of Charitable Uses[4] nor the Statute made [in] 29 Car. II [1677] for the Augmentation of Small Vicarages and Curacies there would be no question but that this rent of £30 *per annum* did cease when the lease upon which it was reserved and which upon the original reservation was to continue during the term did determine when the lease determined, then whether there be any reason in equity to revive or continue this rent as a charge upon the land for the benefit of the vicar, and I think with submission there is no reason.

I shall admit that the vicar shall have as good title in equity to the rent by the declaration of John Chappell, the lessor, as he should have had in law in case the lessor should have reserved the rent to himself and then granted it during the term to the vicar.

When the rent is determined, the foundation is gone, and the vicar was entitled to no more than the rent.

Objection: That this would be for the prebend to derogate from his own grant and by his own act by entering by virtue of the condition to avoid the interest of a third person that claims under him.

Answer: This is [in] no way derogatory from his own grant, taking this as a grant from the prebend to the vicar, but consistent and agreeable to the grant for the thing granted [*blank*] the rent was originally subject to this contingency to be defeated upon the determination of the lease. And I must observe that this lease did not determine by any act subsequent to the lease, as by surrender, which might, it may be, have made some difference but by virtue of a condition

---

[3] Stat. 29 Car. II, c. 8 (*SR*, V, 849–850).
[4] Stat. 39 Eliz. I, c. 6 (*SR*, IV, 903–904); Stat. 43 Eliz. I, c. 4 (*SR*, IV, 968–970).

originally annexed to the lease so that the lease which was the foundation of the rent and upon the continuance of which the rent was to depend from its [*blank*] did determine nor by any act subsequent of the lessee, but by a condition annexed to a lease, the lessor is in by a title superior to or at least commensurate with that of the lessee, and the lessee cannot therefore be liable to any rent reserved upon that lease which is ended by the entry or the performance of the condition.

If a man grants the office of parker of his park, yet he may dispark his park, or if a man grants his stewardship of his court, yet he may release his services and so frustrate his own grant. And yet this is not derogating from his own grant but doing that which was consistent with the nature of his own grant but only using the liberty reserved to himself upon the grant standing with the grant. Hobart 41.[5]

Then the next question is whether this charge of £30 *per annum* be preserved and continued by the Act of 29 Car. II [1677] for the Augmentation of Small Vicarages and Curacies.

This lease of 12 Car. II [1660], upon which this augmentation was reserved, determined sixteen years before the Act [was] made, and thereby the parsonage [was] wholly discharged of it for all that time. And if any person come to take a lease had asked the best advice that he could whether this £30 *per annum* was any charge upon the land or no, he certainly had been told no but that it was determined by the determination of the lease during which it was reserved.

Why then if this was so that this charge was determined in law so long before the Act and [a] new lease [was] made to the defendant, who is a purchaser upon a valuable consideration, nine years before the Act when at that time the land was discharged in law and equity, except the words of the Act of Parliament are very plain and express to have a retrospect so far as to revive augmentations that were determined before the Act and to charge purchasers by Act of Parliament that was not in being when they purchased nor any [*blank*] of its ever having a being, I say, except the Parliament has plainly declared their intention to be that the Act should have such a retrospect. Your Lordship will not by construction intend it but construe it in that sense which general words in an act of Parliament are taken in only to look forwards, for it was the design and intention of the Parliament that such augmentation that had a being when the Act was made to prevent their being defeated for the future. Now let us see what the words of the Act are.

The preamble, which is generally the best guide and direction for the true interpretation of the body of the act, that says whereby the said provision will depend upon the good pleasure of the successors and may in time be disappointed.

---

[5] *Cowper v. Andrews* (1612), Hobart 39, 41, 80 E.R. 189, 1 Eagle & Younge 240, also Moore K.B. 863, 72 E.R. 957, Godbolt 237, 78 E.R. 138, *sub nom. Hooper v. Andrews*, 1 Rolle Rep. 120, 81 E.R. 372.

So that what it seems the Act of Parliament seems to aim at and endeavor a prevention of is only a future disappointment and defeating of the said augmentation which was before the Act legally determined.

In the body or enacting part of the Act, I do find no express words that declare any such meaning that they would put upon it. The strongest words that they seem to rely upon are these, 'that all and every augmentation of what nature soever granted, reserved, or . . . made payable . . . since the first day of June which was in the twelfth year of his Majesty's reign . . . shall be deemed and adjudged to continue and be and shall hereafter forever continue and be as well during the continuance of the estate or term upon which the said augmentations were granted . . . as afterwards'.

Now these words stand indifferent in themselves where they shall extend to augmentations upon leases that were in being at the time of the Act only or to all augmentations made since the 12th January in the 12th [year] of the king [1661] though the leases whereupon augmentations were reserved had been determined before the Act. Therefore the words, being so general, must be expounded according to what is rationally to be presumed to have been the meaning of the Parliament, which certainly could not be to make a law with a retrospect to charge the interest of a third person who could not divine that such a law should be made, for that would be to punish a man for transgressing a law for what he did before any such law [was] made.

And general words in an act of Parliament are always expounded so as not to have a [blank]. And if they swear a [blank], yet [it] is not against a third person that is a purchaser. Moore 135.

And if we consider the Act together, the meaning of the Parliament does appear very plain that they intended to establish augmentations only for the future 'and the same shall forever hereafter be taken, received, and enjoyed by the said vicars and curates and their successors as well during the continuance of the term or estate upon which the said augmentations were granted . . . as afterwards'.

So that it is plain by the words 'hereafter shall enjoy' that the Parliament meant only to provide for the future. And these words 'as well during the continuance of the term . . . as afterwards' do plainly show that the Parliament supposed the lease had a continuance and were in being at the time of the Act. And then this Act established the augmentations reserved upon such leases as well during the continuance of the said term as after they shall expire for these words can in no sense be extended to a term that was determined before the Act, because the vicar, after the making [of] the Act cannot enjoy the augmentations reserved upon such leases during the continuance of those leases because they had no continuance at the time of the Act made nor [at] any time after. Then there is another clause in the Act which plainly expresses the meaning of the

Parliament 'Provided always . . . that if upon the surrender, expiration, or other determination of any lease wherein such augmentation as aforesaid hath been or shall be granted, any . . . lease of the premises or any part thereof shall hereafter be made without any express continuance of the said augmentation, every such new lease shall be utterly void to all intents and purposes'.

The next thing considerable is whether the clause in the Statute for the beneficial exposition of the Act that says that 'if any question shall hereafter arise concerning the validity of such grant or any other matter of thing . . . mentioned or contained such favorable constructions and . . . further remedy if need be shall be had and made for the benefit of the vicars and curates as heretofore hath been had and made or may be had for other charitable uses upon the Statutes for Charitable Uses', whether this clause gives any direction or any way authorize the court to make such an exposition of the Act as the counsel for the plaintiff do now press for.

All the cases I can find upon the Statute of Charitable Uses tend only to the supplying [of] the gift or devise to charitable uses according to the intention and meaning of the donor that where he makes any appointment to a charitable use, which appointment would not be good by the strict rules of law for want of some ceremony or circumstance to be done further than was done, there they have been so favorable in the interpretation of that Act of Charitable Uses as to construe it so to confirm and make good such charitable declarations and appointments.

So are the cases [in] Moore 890:[6] If a [*blank*] devise part of the goods of the intestate to charitable uses, this is good by the Statute.

If a copyholder devise his estate to charitable uses without any surrender, this is good by the Statute, Moore 890, for the Statute supplies the want of a surrender.

But in all these cases, the great guide and direction for the judges to expound this by has been the meaning and intention of the giver. They have not ever enlarged any charity for [a] longer time than the donor had appointed it to continue. And I think there is no case where ever any charity was actually determined before the Act of 43 Eliz. [1601][7] by virtue of the limitations made by the donor himself that ever that has been set up again by the relation. And [*blank*] of that Act, it is true that they have made good by construction of the Act goods and devises to charity which to the meaning and intention of the donors had a continuance at the time of the Act but not in strictness of law, for want of some ceremony to complete the conveyance.

---

[6] *Rivet's Case* (c. 1616), Moore K.B. 890, 72 E.R. 977.
[7] Stat. 43 Eliz. I, c. 4 (*SR*, IV, 968–970).

As a devise before 37 Hen. VIII [1545] to a charitable use has been good by that Statute:[8] Hobart 136, Collison's Case.[9] But it was a devise that was intended to be perpetual by the will of the donor, for he devised his land to [*blank*] for his life and afterwards that he should stand seised in [*blank*] to dispose [of] the profits for the reparation of the highways:

1. Not against the purchaser, but the [*blank*]
2. The charity was intended perpetual.

The Corporation of Bridgewater, Moore 131,[10] [*blank*] [in] 33 of his reign [1541] makes a lease to the Earl of Bath of the Rectory of Bridgewater [*blank*] [in the] 2d year of her reign [1560] makes a lease of the said rectory [*blank*] without reciting the former lease to the Earl of Bath, which was then in being, after Queen Elizabeth [in the] 3d [year] of her reign [1561] grants the rectory of Bridgewater to the Corporation of Bridgewater. In the 18th [year] of Queen Elizabeth [1576] comes the Statute of Non Recitals[11] which says against all patents made since the 2d day of November in the first year of Queen Elizabeth [1559] shall be good notwithstanding non-recitals. That though the Act by express words was to have a [*blank*] to the said year of the queen [1559], yet in respect [that] the queen has made a grant to the Corporation of Bridgewater [*blank*] between the first year of her reign [1559] and the 18th [1576], the Act should not affect their interest which 1 Rep. 24.[12] Statute 23 Hen. VIII for Suppressing Superstitious Uses[13] with an exception of some few charitable uses that were good uses and that therefore all other gifts and charitable uses that were not superstitious should not be within the Statute of 23 Hen. VIII. But it was resolved that that was but a flattering proviso made to satisfy some of the scruples of some of the members that were not very well skilled in the law.

So upon the Statute 5 Edw. VI[14] Against the Selling of Offices, the body of the Act speaks only of offices concerning the administration of justice and management of the king's revenue; [it] has an exception of the keeper of a park, which is neither. It did not follow that all other offices that were not excepted should be within the body of the Act because of the needless and frivolous exception.

The court of exchequer, Chief Baron MOUNTAGU and the rest of the barons, held that the Statute for Augmentation did revive all augmentations made since

---

[8] Stat. 43 Eliz. I, c. 4, s. 8 (*SR*, IV, 970); note also the Act for Dissolution of Colleges, Stat. 37 Hen. VIII, c. 4 (*SR*, III, 988–993).

[9] *Collison's Case* (1617), Hobart 136, 80 E.R. 286.

[10] *Bossevile v. Corporation of Bridgewater* (1583), Moore K.B. 131, 72 E.R. 487.

[11] Stat. 18 Eliz. I, c. 2 (*SR*, IV, 608–610).

[12] *Attorney General v. Porter* (1592), 1 Coke Rep. 16b, 22b, 76 E.R. 36, 50.

[13] Stat. 23 Hen. VIII, c. 10 (*SR*, III, 378).

[14] Stat. 5 Edw. VI, c. 16 (*SR*, IV, 151–152).

the first day of January 12th of the king [1661], though the leases upon which they were reserved were determined before the Act, [and] that in this case, there was a new augmentation of the same value reserved by the lease of 22d of the king [1670] to the Chapel of Harnham. Yet, because upon the first lease there was a covenant from the tenant to supply the Chapel of Harnham, which was an evidence that the charge of that cure lay upon the prebend so that this £30 *per annum* given to the curate there was but in ease of the prebend, they decreed that the £30 *per annum* [be] reserved upon the first lease for the augmentation of the vicarage of Comb Bisset and made perpetual by the 29th of the king [1677]. The prebend might supply the cure himself, and then the £30 *per annum* to the curate would be no charge to him.

[Order of 28 Apr. 1684: PRO E.126/14, f. 166.]

[This case is cited in Terry v. Dean of Salisbury (Ex. 1698), below, No. 366.]

190

Stokes v. Wells (Ex. 1684)

After a conveyance of land to a bona fide purchaser, a subsequent purchaser of the same land by a valid contract under seal cannot avoid the first conveyance.

LI MS. Misc. 557, f. 59, pl. 1 [Fr.] (Ward's Reports)

The case upon the hearing was thus. The defendant Tabor (who was not brought to the hearing) contracted with the defendant Wells to sell him a house for £100 and gave Wells a receipt under his hand testifying to the payment of 42s. in part [payment] of the bargain and sale, and this was 23 May 1683. And afterwards, the 25th day of the same month, the said Tabor contracted under [his] hand and seal with the plaintiff to sell and convey the same house to the plaintiff for £110. The said Wells obtained conveyances by fine, lease and release of the same house from the said Tabor executed 4 June 1683 and paid the residue of the £100 purchase money. And no notice was proved to be given to the defendant of the plaintiff's pretensions because in truth it was proved that the payment of the 42s. and the note of 23 May was before any treaty with the plaintiff.

And the court dismissed the plaintiff's bill that he had preferred to compel the defendant Wells to convey the house to the plaintiff under pretense that he had notice of the plaintiff's agreement and articles before he had paid any money, which was not proved. And the court went upon this reason, though the defendant's contract was not under seal and by chance[1] if he had endeavored to compel an execution in specie, the court would not have retained [a bill], yet having

---

[1] case *MS*.

obtained the legal estate and paid the money, they would not take the house away from him to serve the plaintiff, though he had articles under seal.

I [was] for the defendant.

[Other copies of this report: GUL MS. B88–7, p. 523.]

191
Ward v. Harvey (Ex. 1684)

Servants of a wife are also servants of her husband since he is liable to pay their wages.

LI MS. Misc. 557, f. 59, pl. 2 [Fr.] (Ward's Reports)

Sir Daniel Harvey two years before he went as ambassador to Constantinople made his will and bequeathed to all his servants that should be living with him at the time of his death £10 apiece and to his servant A.B. £10 during his life. And afterwards being designated ambassador to Turkey, he broke up housekeeping and discharged his servants except those who went with him and made provision for his wife and the education of his children in a liberal manner under certain sums. And divers years afterwards he died at Constantinople.

And it was decreed that both the servants that lived with the lady in England and whom she hired with [her] separate maintenance and the servants who lived with Sir Daniel at the time of his death were entitled to the £10 apiece and that A.B. should have the £10 notwithstanding the £10 *per annum*. And the court went on this rule, that, in the judgment of the law, the servants of the lady are the servants of Sir Daniel within the words and intention of the will and that Sir Daniel would have been compelled to pay their wages if they should be in arrears. And his will being made so long before he broke up housekeeping, [it] cannot be inferred that he meant those servants only who were with him at Constantinople at the time of his death.

[Other copies of this report: GUL MS. B88–7, p. 523.]

192
Dean of Gloucester v. Stoodly (Ex. 1684)

The current holder of land is liable for all arrears of payments issuing out of the land including payments that accrued before he became the holder.

LI MS. Misc. 557, f. 61, pl. 1 [Fr.] (Ward's Reports)

[It was] decreed that the defendant should pay the arrears of a pension of 53s. 4d. *per annum* issuing out of the defendant's rectory both during the time that the defendant was incumbent and in the time of his predecessors though the predecessors were alive and shown by name in the answer. And this [was ordered] for the reason that the rectory itself is charged with the pension and it is not a personal charge. Cro. Eliz. 810; Liber J, [f.] 34: Cullier v. Mead; 5 Rep. 41: Dormer's Case.[1]

And the case of Pilsworth and English in this court around 1680 [was cited] where a pension was decreed to be paid by English, who was the owner only of part of the land charged with it though the other owners were named. And English [was] put to his bill against the others for contribution. And this was thus ruled here.

I [was] for the plaintiffs.

[Other copies of this report: GUL MS. B88–7, p. 525.]

193
Greenwood v. Grainger (Ex. 1684)

A vicar's lessee is liable to the impropriator for tithes; however, in this case, it was presumed from past non-payment that the endowment of this vicarage was that the vicar's lessee was exempt from tithes.

LI MS. Misc. 557, f. 61, pl. 2 [Fr.] (Ward's Reports)

Note [that] it was ruled in this court this term that although ordinarily and by the law the lessee of the vicar shall pay tithes of the glebe to the impropriator [. . .] being proved in the cause that the vicar's predecessors having demised the glebe to tenants who never paid tithes of the glebe, that it will be understood in such a case that it was part of the endowment of the vicarage to have the glebe discharged of all tithes as well in the actual hands of the vicar as in the hands of the lessee. And the plaintiff's bill [was] dismissed without costs.

I [was] for the plaintiff.

[Other copies of this report: GUL MS. B88–7, p. 525.]

[This case is cited in Hawkins v. Chittle (Ex. 1696), below, No. 304.]

194
Atterbury v. Stafford (Ex. 1684)

An ancient enclosure and modus will not be set aside at the suit of a later parson even though the bishop did not consent to the enclosure.

---

[1] *Trinity College, Cambridge v. Tunstal* (1601), Cro. Eliz. 810, 78 E.R. 1037; *Cullier v. Mead* (Ex. 1681), above, No. 127; *Dormer's Case* (1593), 5 Coke Rep. 40a, 77 E.R. 115.

LI MS. Misc. 557, f. 62 [Fr.] (Ward's Reports)

In this case the plaintiff exhibited his bill as parson of Middleton Keynes in the County of Buckingham[1] for tithes and to have his glebe set out and an old enclosure of the manor made pursuant to an agreement in 1593 [. . .] between the parson and the patron but not the ordinary to be laid open. And during this suit Stafford sold the manor to the earl of Nottingham, who exhibited his bill to have the enclosure established and also a certain *modus decimandis*, for which there were three trials and verdicts at law for the moduses. And after divers hearings and the bishop of the diocese [was] made a party, who answered that he had issued his commission and that it was returned to him (but not under oath) that the enclosure was to the great prejudice of the parsonage, the court considering the great time that the enclosure had continued (though a third part of the lordship was enclosed only thirty or forty years past) and that the parson had neither glebe nor common, the court confirmed the enclosure and moduses making certain annual allowances to the parson for certain small prejudices that the rectory sustained by reason of the enclosure though it was proved in the cause that it was of as great a value at this day as it was before the enclosure. And the court gave small regard to the consent or non consent of the ordinary at this day. And divers precedents in chancery were produced by which ancient enclosures (though failing in some particulars) were not permitted to be laid open at the pleasure of the incumbent though the ordinary had not consented. And here Atterbury had for divers years contented himself with the enclosure and the allotment for the glebe and having plowed it out of the common[2] he now quarreled with the enclosure, and upon the entire matter the court decreed as above.

[Other copies of this report: GUL MS. B88–7, p. 526.]

[The order of 23 June 1684, PRO E.126/14, f. 94, is printed at 1 Wood 227, 1 Eagle & Younge 543.]

[This case is cited in Lechmere v. Dingley (Ex. 1687), below, No. 237.]

195

Haffenden v. Sharpe (Ex. 1684)

Where a female beneficiary of a trust dies, the assets of the trust are payable to the administrator of the beneficiary and not to her surviving husband or his administrator.

Where a decedent's estate is insufficient to pay debts and legacies, a gift made shortly before execution of the will will be taken to be an ademption of the legacy.

---

[1] V.C.H., *Buckinghamshire*, IV (1927), pp. 401–403.
[2] hors de coeur *MS*.

LI MS. Misc. 557, f. 63 [Fr.] (Ward's Reports)

The case upon the hearing was thus. The said Margaret [Peckham] before her marriage with Peckham, being possessed of a mortgage leased as security for £100, with the consent of Peckham, her intended husband, assigned it to [Thomas] Dunke in trust that Peckham should not intermeddle with it, but that Dunke, his executors, and assigns should permit the said Margaret during her life to have and enjoy it or any other to whom Margaret by some writing should give it, and if Margaret survive Peckham, then in trust that Dunke should regrant to Margaret; but no provision was made if Peckham should survive Margaret, the term not being disposed of.

Margaret died in the lifetime of Peckham, not having disposed of the term or trust nor the £100 received. Peckham died not having made any disposition. And afterwards, the plaintiff, Mary [Haffenden], took administration to Margaret [Peckham, her mother] and sued [John] Sharpe, the executor of Dunke, in equity for the £100 received by Dunke in his lifetime upon the mortgage. And she had a decree for it upon this ground, that though Margaret had not made any disposition of it during her lifetime, yet the trust was for him who at first had the estate in law, who was Margaret, and the husband was excluded by the assignment. And there not having [been] made any disposition in the lifetime of Margaret, it should go to the administrator of Margaret, and the marriage was not any gift in law to the husband, being a chose in action and a trust, to which the husband by survivorship was not entitled without administration to the wife. 1 *Inst.* 351; Lane's Reports 113, Clerk and Rutland.[1]

In this case, it was ruled upon another point that 200 guineas given by Dunke to the plaintiff in the lifetime of Dunke and a short time before he made his will should be accepted in part [payment] of the £300 legacy given by Dunke in his will to the plaintiff, and this [was ordered] upon the reason that Dunke without those 200 guineas did not leave enough to pay his debts and other legacies.

I [was] for the plaintiffs.

A decree absolute [was given] on both points Monday, 27 October 1684, and the deputy king's remembrancer's report was confirmed. But afterwards in Hilary term upon motion of the attorney general, suggesting that by this judgment, the defendant would be charged with the £100 and interest, which amounted in all to £200 and more, the defendant did not have assets to pay all of the plaintiff's legacy, the court directed the matter of the inventory to be examined by the deputy [king's] remembrancer and to make a deduction out of the money reported due to the plaintiff for so much as it should be proportionally paid, his

---

[1] E. Coke, *First Institute* (1628), f. 351; *Clerk v. Rutland* (1608), Lane 113, 145 E.R. 343.

legacy with the other legatees, reckoning [?] the 200 guineas aforesaid (though given before the will, but being included in the inventory) as part of his legacy, which was done accordingly, the final decree not being signed and enrolled, which note.

[Other copies of this report: GUL MS. B88–7, p. 527.]

[Orders of 26 June, 27 Oct., and 29 Nov. 1684: PRO E.126/14, ff. 190v, 204, 206.]

196
Shish v. Attorney General (Ex. 1684)

In this case, the plaintiff's bill was dismissed because he failed to prove the alleged fraud.

LI MS. Misc. 557, f. 67, pl. 1 [Fr.] (Ward's Reports)

The court, upon the hearing of the cause upon an English bill to be relieved against the same fraud alleged upon the plea to an extent, dismissed the bill on the reason that the debt from Surry and Stephenson to the king was before the time of the alleged bankruptcy of Hinton and because Hinton before his bankruptcy was justly indebted to Goft in £1200 and that Goft delivered up his securities for it to Hinton and upon it Hinton gave the four bonds for securing the said £1200 to the defendants (being debtors to the king) by direction of Goft, who had received wines for them at the value. And because there was not any fraud, Hinton not having contracted [for a] greater debt to the defendants than he owed to Goft, though the defendants happened to have a better remedy to receive the same debt than Goft had, and because Hinton was not charged with any fraud nor [was] party to the suit and also because no commission of bankruptcy was sued out against Hinton until after the extents and inquisitions, which found and seized the debts of Hinton's debtors into the hands of the king, the bill was dismissed.

I [was] for the defendants.

See above [f.] 44.[1]

[Other copies of this report: GUL MS. B88–7, p. 529.]

197
Wright v. Daffy (Ex. 1684)

The question in this case was who should pay court costs when a defendant answers and pleads an issuable plea.

---

[1] *Attorney General v. Thomas* (Ex. 1684), LI MS. Misc. 557, f. 44.

LI MS. Misc. 557, f. 69, pl. 1 [Fr.] (Ward's Reports)

The plaintiff exhibited a bill for tithes. The defendant answered and pleaded and by his answer showed the quantity, quality, and value of the tithes, and by his plea he showed a discharge of tithes by the Cistercian Order *quamdiu [in] propriis manibus* and showed himself [to be the] owner.

And the plea was held good but [with] liberty to the plaintiff to reply. And costs [were] awarded notwithstanding that this plea is not a bar as a plea any more than it was a bar by answer. And the plaintiff must reply to matter pleaded as well as [to what] was in an answer.

The attorney general [was] for the defendant. I [was] for the plaintiff.

Query because it seems contrary to the rule that the plaintiff shall be charged with costs in such a case, inasmuch as the matter of the plea was issuable and the defendant shall have the same advantage of it by answer as by plea and more aptly.

[Other copies of this report: GUL MS. B88–7, p. 535.]

198
Attorney General ex rel. Frowd v. Whitley (Ex. 1684)

This was a suit for a discovery and accounting of the profits of the post office.

LI MS. Misc. 557, ff. 71, 79 [Fr.] (Ward's Reports)

The case was thus upon the hearing. By an Act of Parliament made [in] 12 Car. II [1660] the post office was erected and vested in the king and his heirs.[1] The king made a lease or grant of the profits of this office to Daniel O'Neal, which by the passage of time expired at midsummer 1667. In 15 Car. II [1663] an Act of Parliament[2] was made that vested the profits of this office in the duke of York and his heirs male, but the nomination of the postmaster remained in the king and he would be able to charge those profits with the annual sum of £53821 10s. The 21 December 18 Car. II [1666] the king granted the office of postmaster to Henry, lord Arlington,[3] for ten years from midsummer 1667. And the next day the duke of York by indenture demised the profits of the post office to the said lord Arlington and lord Berkeley for ten years beginning midsummer 1667 under the annual rent of £25,000 including the £5382 10s. which the king had the power to charge upon the profits (and which in truth had been granted to the countess of Falmouth and others). And by the same indenture, the lords Arlington and Berkeley covenanted for themselves, their heirs, executors,

---
[1] Stat. 12 Car. II, c. 35 (*SR*, V, 297–301).
[2] Stat. 15 Car. II, c. 14 (*SR*, V, 495–498).
[3] G.E.C., *Complete Peerage*, I (1910), pp. 216–218; *D.N.B.*, s.v. Bennet, Henry.

administrators, and assigns with the duke, his heirs, and assigns 'that all letters, packets, and dispatches ordinary and extraordinary, directed or to be directed to or from His Majesty, his heirs, or successors, or to or from the lord admiral, lord chancellor, lord treasurer, commissioners of the treasury, lord warden of the cinque ports, both the secretaries of state for the time being, and all the single inland letters only of the members of the present parliament during the continuance of the sessions of parliament shall be conveyed either by the ordinary mail or other safe passage free from payment of any rate or postage or other charges'.

The first five years of this term Sir Henry Bennet (now the lord Ossulston and brother of lord Arlington)[4] was lessee of it and enjoyed the profits under this annual rent. And in 1672 the lords Arlington and Berkeley demised the said profits and premises to the defendant Col. Whitley for five years beginning from midsummer 1672 (being the residue of the ten years) under the same annual rent, who enjoyed them accordingly.

Second [?] the king by a privy seal 5 October 19 Car. II [1667] directed to the treasurer, chancellor, barons, and other officers of the exchequer and to both secretaries of state, reciting the grant of the postmaster's office to lord Arlington and the settlement of the profits by the Act upon the duke of York in tail, that His Majesty's affairs so requiring it, His Majesty had commanded by his secretaries that divers letters and packets above what were to be sent frank by the lord Arlington's covenant were to be sent free and that His Majesty might then after command other services to be done frank which His Majesty intended not that the lord Arlington or his assigns should be damaged by, His Majesty thereby directed that for better ascertaining what allowances should be made for services done or damages sustained by the said lord Arlington or his assigns during his term and thereby willed and authorized the two secretaries of state for the time being to examine and consider those demands and to certify under one or both of their hands to the lord treasurer or commissioners of the treasury what sums ought to be allowed his lordship or his assigns for any the causes aforesaid and willed that the lord treasurer or commissioners of the treasury should have power to allow or disallow the same or any part thereof and what was so allowed the said privy seal directed should be paid out of the receipt of the exchequer and that tallies should be levied and warrants issued for the same accordingly. And it was thereby further directed that while the lord Arlington continued [to be] one of the secretaries of state and no longer that those demands and allowances should be examined and considered by any three or more of the lords of the council (whereof the other secretary [was] to be one), who should certify the lord treasurer etc. as aforesaid, and proceed thereon as if the two secretaries had certified,

---

[4] Sir John Bennet (d. 1695): G.E.C., *Complete Peerage*, X (1945), pp. 189–190.

and that privy seal was to be a sufficient warrant and discharge for what should be done thereon.

After this privy seal, the constant method and practice was thus, that the clerks and officers in the post office from time to time made accounts and abstracts (in the name of lord Arlington) upon oath of all letters, packets, and dispatches that were carried frank by command of the king within those times, which abstracts and accounts were from time to time presented to three lords of the council (one of whom was the other secretary [of state], because for the greater part of the defendant's term, the lord Arlington continued [to be] secretary [of state]) by the defendant or the other officers in the post office according to the usage. And those three lords of the council considered and approved those accounts and abstracts that contained the sums due for the postage. And in truth the letters, packets, and dispatches that the lord Arlington had covenanted (as above) to carry frank were included within those accounts and abstracts, without any distinction, under the title and denomination of frank letters etc. And the lords of the council made certificates of their examination and approbation to the lord treasurer and commissioners of the treasury for the time being and that they thought those sums [ought] to be allowed and paid according to the privy seal. After that, those accounts, abstracts, and certificates were brought to the lord treasurer or commissioners of the treasury where they were again examined and approved and warrants were issued at the receipt for payment of all of the sums so certified, either in ready money or by levying tallies upon some parts of the revenue of the king. And the money was paid from time to time in the name of the lord Arlington, and the receipt and acquittance for it was given by and in the name of the lord Arlington, though in truth the entire affair was managed by the lord Ossulston during his time and by the defendant during his time, and both received the money paid to their own use. And in respect of those allowances and payments, they gave the greater consideration for their leases. And in truth the defendant received in the name and under the title and interest of the lord Arlington by virtue of the indentures [and] privy seal of those allowances and payments out of the exchequer during his time £28,835 13s. 7d.

After that, that is to say Easter [term] 35 Car. II [1683], the attorney general exhibited an English information against the defendant and the lord Arlington and the executor and heir of the lord Berkeley, Frances Ellys, executrix of Andrew Ellys (from whom the defendant had purchased part of his interest), Philip Frowd, son and executor of Sir Philip Frowd (who had an annual payment of £300 paid to him out of the money received for the allowances aforesaid) to have an account of all the money thus received for the frank letters, suggesting that it was received in fraud and deceit of the king for the letters etc. which the lords Arlington and Berkeley had covenanted to carry frank, as above. And he showed that the privy seal did not give any power to the lords of the council nor to the treasurer or commissioners of the treasury to make any allowance or to pay any money for those letters etc. thus covenanted to be carried frank but only for those letters etc. directed by the king to be carried frank and not contained within this covenant. And he charged the defendant with the actual receipt of the money out of the exchequer to his own use and, inasmuch as the defendant had received it without any legal authority (because the privy seal did not extend to letters covenanted to be carried frank but to others directed by the king) and on account of that, as to those, the allowances made by the lords of the council and the payments by the treasurer and commissioners of the treasury were without any legal power or warrant. The attorney general by his information prayed discovery, an accounting, and relief for all of the money thus received by the defendant.

The other defendants were not prosecuted beyond an answer, and some of them never answered. But the aim and design of the suit was leveled at the defendant Whitley, who at first answered to the several matters of fact suggested by the bill. And as for the accounting for the money received out of the receipt of the exchequer and relief for it, he pleaded the aforesaid privy seal and the abstracts and accounts by the officers of the post office upon oath and the examinations and allowances by the three lords of the council and the other examinations and warrants by the treasurer and commissioners [of the] treasury, and payments according to the purport of the privy seal, with other necessary averments that all was done by virtue and in pursuance of the privy seal, and on account of that and inasmuch as the matters for which relief was prayed by the bill had passed two examinations and judicatures, that is to say the three lords of the council and the treasury, more than six years ago, the defendant pleaded it and prayed judgment.

But this plea, upon argument, was overruled with costs, because the entire court held that the privy seal did not extend to any of those letters etc. that were covenanted by lords Arlington and Berkeley to be carried frank but only to the others directed by the king to be carried frank and that the import of the privy seal was thus, and on account of that the examinations, allowances, and warrants for payment of money were all without any legal authority, and on account of that the defendant, who had received the money, though in the name of the lord Arlington and under his title, was accountable to the king for it, as is everyone who receives the money of the king without legal warrant and authority, according to the reason of the Earl of Devonshire's Case, 11 Rep. 89,[5] and of the cases cited in it. And though the plea of the defendant, if it had distinguished between the allowances and payments for the other services not contained within the covenant, would have been good as to those not within the covenant, yet this plea, which went both to those within the covenant and to the others, cannot be good in all

---

[5] *Earl of Devonshire's Case* (1607), 11 Coke Rep. 89, 77 E.R. 1266.

things and, being pleaded entirely as to all of the accounting, must be overruled. (But note that the defendant could not make any such distinction, all of the abstracts, accounts, and certificates being of all letters etc. that were carried frank, both those within the covenant and those outside of it.)

And the defendant insisted upon the matter and substance of his plea in his answer.

And these things were proved on the part of the defendant, first that this practice and those allowances were at all times observed and done in the time of O'Neal and Sir John Bennet, predecessors of the defendant, and [in] all times afterwards until this day, notwithstanding that there was at all times such a covenant in force and that it was the constant and universal opinion of all of the officers that the king should make recompense for all frank letters etc. without regard to any covenant and that the defendant directed the officers in making the abstracts, accounts, etc. to pursue the ancient and droitural method and to do right to the king and [to] himself. Second the defendant swore that he did not have any notice of this covenant and, that in respect that he should have allowance for all letters carried frank, he gave a greater consideration for the lease.

The court upon the hearing of the cause decreed the defendant to account and [decreed] that the money received out of the exchequer, that is to say the £28,835 13s. 7d., should be the charge upon him and that it should be incumbent upon the defendant at his peril to distinguish between the sums and services within and outside of the covenant, notwithstanding that it was urged for the defendant that, he having allowances made for frank letters and being in possession of the money, the proof that the defendant had received more (and how much more) than was due to him was incumbent upon the plaintiff, because the defendant claimed all of the money allowed and it seemed to be the usual course in all cases. But the court distinguished the case of the king.

Secondly the court declared that the defendant was bound by the covenant of the lords Arlington and Berkeley, though he was a lessee and not an assignee, inasmuch as he received the benefit of the indenture.

Thirdly [the court declared] that notice of the covenant to the defendant was not necessary, and, if it were, it would be presumed (notwithstanding his answer), inasmuch as he derived his entire title under the indenture in which this covenant was.

Fourthly [the court declared] that the defendant was accountable alone and without the lord Arlington, notwithstanding that the said lord gave the receipt for the money and the entire transaction was in the name of lord Arlington, inasmuch as the defendant received the money to his own use under the title of lord Arlington.

Fifthly [the court declared] that the privy seal extended only to the allowances for frank letters not within the covenant.

And the account was referred to Philips and Done, auditors, before whom the defendant demanded divers large sums for letters carried frank not within the covenant, as the duke of Lauderdale's box, Irish letters, double and treble letters of parliament men, divers private letters conveyed under the covers of the secretaries [of state] and other great officers, and several others that were carried frank in all times, and the defendant could not, nor any of his predecessors, have disputed or refused to carry them. And he also demanded allowance of other sums paid by him upon the account of the post office for the services of the king, all of which allowances demanded amounted to more than £24,000. And it was insisted by the defendant (and thought by many) that the money received by the defendant for the letters etc. covenanted to be carried frank in his entire time (if they could be distinguished, and not franked by the secretaries [of state] and the great officers, but those only that were for the sole and true account of the king and his great officers enumerated in the covenant) would not amount to more than £5000.

But it being impossible for the defendant to make such a distinction (no distinct account having been kept), and the auditors refusing to make to the defendant any allowance for any letters not within the covenant carried frank without proof of an express order or direction from the king for this purpose, though it was clear that they were carried frank, and though it was also unreasonable to think that the defendant would not have elected (if it were in his power) rather to have taken the postage of those letters in the post office without doubt or trouble than to have expected his satisfaction for them from the king, which was chargeable and in some manner hazardous, and though it was impossible to produce a particular order or direction from the king for carrying them frank, those orders being only by parol to the secretaries [of state] and by them to the defendant and his officers, and it not being in the defendant's power to question the secretaries' [of state] etc. franking letters, and there being a constant allowance in times past for all such letters thus franked, and it not being in the power of the defendant to dispute the double, treble, or quadruple letters of the members of parliament, being also allowed in all times and the postmaster [being] reprimanded by the House of Commons for disputing it, the defendant, thinking that the greater part of his allowances would not be allowed to him, submitted himself by order of the court to the determination of the Lord Treasurer Rochester, who afterwards made an arbitrament and awarded the defendant to pay around £22,000, *viz.* two parts of it at several payments into the exchequer and the other third part to Philip Frowd (who now manages the post office for the king, being the informer and prosecutor and having a grant by privy seal of this third part), which payments were made accordingly and tallies [were] levied and receipts [were] given upon the privy seal and satisfaction was acknowledged by the attorney general upon the decree.

I [was] for the defendant.
[Other copies of this report: GUL MS. B88–7, p. 540.]
[Order of 3 Dec. 1684: PRO E.126/14, f. 214.]

199
Smith v. Steel (Ex. 1684)

A contract by a widow-administratrix to purchase an equity of redemption to herself after her second marriage is invalid.

In this case, the heir was allowed to redeem a mortgage upon paying for repairs and improvements that were made in good faith by the possessor during the term of his possession.

LI MS. Misc. 557, f. 70, pl. 1 [Fr.] (Ward's Reports)

The case upon the hearing appeared to be thus. William Smith, father of the plaintiff, was possessed for a long term of years of the Blue Boar Inn in Holborn and mortgaged it and all of his term to Avery in trust for Sir R. Clayton and John Morris for securing £500, which by a defeasance was made payable out of the profits by £100 *per annum* for seven years and half of a year. Smith died (having paid divers of the sums according to the defeasance) intestate, and Elizabeth his wife took administration to him. And within six months she married Malbon, her servant, which marriage was concealed for the entire life of Elizabeth. After the death of Smith, Elizabeth continued some payments as administratrix. And three years after the death of Smith and after her marriage with Malbon, a new agreement was made between Elizabeth, by the name of Elizabeth Smith, widow, administratrix of William Smith, her first husband, and the said Avery (with the consent of Clayton and Morris) touching the said mortgage and payment. And by this agreement reduced to writing by way of indenture between the said Elizabeth as widow and administratrix and the said Avery, Avery covenanted with Elizabeth that, if she, her executors, administrators, or assigns should pay £60 *per annum* for eight years then to come, that then Avery would assign all of the said term and estate to Elizabeth, her executors, administrators, or assigns. And by the said indenture Elizabeth covenanted to pay the said £60 *per annum* accordingly. And there was a proviso in the said indenture that, if the said £60 *per annum* and the rents reserved upon the lease and covenants in it were not paid and performed accordingly, that then the said indenture should be void. And the first defeasance for the £100 *per annum* for seven years and a half was delivered up to the said Elizabeth and cancelled. Elizabeth during her life and afterwards the said Malbon, her husband, who took administration to her, continued the payment of the £60 *per annum*. And after all was paid, Avery assigned to Malbon the entire term (Elizabeth being dead), who continued [in] possession of the house. And during the life of Elizabeth and afterwards, he expended great sums in building and repairs upon the premises. And Malbon died, having made the defendant Steel his executor, who for a fine and a greater rent, leased to Worthington, an undertenant.

The plaintiff took administration *de bonis non* to his father and exhibited his bill to have the equity of redemption. And whether he should have [it] was the question. And the point in question was whether there was any alteration in point of estate or equity of redemption by Elizabeth in her lifetime.

And the court was of opinion that [there was] not and on account of that decreed for the plaintiff that he should redeem and put it to an account. And the reason given by the court was that the indenture in which Elizabeth covenanted to pay the £60 *per annum* was made during her coverture and she [was] not bound by the covenant and also because all that she did was only as administratrix and in affirmance of the intestate's right and she had not done any meritorious thing that could entitle herself to the lease by way of retainer nor any election by her in such case, all the debts of Smith her husband which were paid being paid out of Smith's estate and as it came in and not otherwise. And though the £60 *per annum* was paid, yet in truth it was raised out of the intestate's estate as it came in, and [it was] paid, and receipts were taken by Elizabeth as administratrix. And the agreement upon the payment of the £60 to assign and after payment the actual assignment by Avery did not alter the equity of redemption, there not being any allocation of the estate made during the life of Elizabeth. And as for the repairs and improvements, there should be allowance for them made to the defendant in the account.

And afterwards the cause was finished by agreement, and the defendants gave £700 to the plaintiff and conveyed the term to the plaintiff. See the decree 29 January 1684/85.

[Other copies of this report: GUL MS. B88–7, p. 537.]

[Orders of 20 Nov. 1684 and 29 Jan. 1685: PRO E.126/14, ff. 211v, 229.]

200
Williams v. Jeffreys (Ex. 1685)

Debts to the crown are not dischargeable in bankruptcy.

An assignment of commissioners in bankruptcy after execution of a writ of extent is invalid.

LI MS. Misc. 557, f. 74, pl. 4 [Fr.] (Ward's Reports)

The case upon the hearing was thus. In 1674 and 1677 Luke Santen, a London merchant, with the plaintiff and another became bound to the king in several bonds for payment of customs for wines imported by Santen. And there being divers sums due to the king, extents issued for recovering them. And some of the goods of Santen and of the plaintiff, as his surety, were seized. And the plaintiff paid divers sums to the use of the king out of his own estate amounting to £240. And after discovering that one Planner was indebted to Santen in [the amount of] £100 and one Devon in £40, he prosecuted an extent by leave of the court for the recovering [of] those debts. And in August and October 1679, they were seized into the hands of the king. And in Hilary term 1679[/80] and Easter [term] 1680 upon *scire feci* to Planner and Devon returned, extents issued, and they were taken in execution for those debts, upon which they paid the money to the sheriff of London to be redeemed out of the execution. After that, the 24th of May 1680, upon motion for the plaintiff, the court ordered the £140 to be paid to the plaintiff, he satisfying the sheriff their fees, the court having received full satisfaction by certificate and affidavit that the plaintiff had paid more for Santen to the king out of the plaintiff's own estate.

After that, *scil.* 21 January 1680[/81], the defendant and other creditors of Santen prosecuted a commission of bankruptcy against him, upon which he was found bankrupt before any extent for the king, *scil.* in May 1679. And in July 1681 the commissioners assigned the said £100 and £40 due from Planner and Devon to the defendant in trust for himself and Santen's other creditors, upon which assignment the defendant brought his action at law in the king's bench.

And the plaintiff exhibited his English bill in this court to be relieved and to make the order of this court effectual to him for those sums. The court gave leave to the defendant here to proceed to trial and judgment but awarded an injunction to stay execution. The defendant here obtained judgment upon a special verdict in the king's bench (but it was said that the truth of the case was not found in it).

And this day,[1] the court here relieved the plaintiff and granted a perpetual injunction and decreed the defendant to acknowledge satisfaction of the judgment on the record, because it was held clearly that the king is not bound by the Statute of Bankrupts[2] and that execution being executed before any commission of bankruptcy [was] pursued, the assignment of the commissioners of bankruptcy came too late and was worth nothing, although Santen was bankrupt before the extent. And Crump's Case in this court, Easter [term] 22 Car. II [1670], in the time of Chief Baron Hale, Liber 2, f. 89,[3] was remembered where the extent was pursued the same day as the assignment of the commissioners of bankruptcy and [was] preferred before the assignment, which is a stronger case. And there is not any difference when the execution is for levying for the immediate use of

---

[1] 26 January 1684/85.
[2] Stat. 13 Eliz. I, c. 7 (*SR*, IV, 539–541); Stat. 1 Jac. I, c. 15 (*SR*, IV, 1031–1034); Stat. 21 Jac. I, c. 19 (*SR*, IV, 1227–1229).
[3] *Crump's Case* (Ex. 1670), LI MS. Misc. 500, f. 89.

the king and for reimbursing one who had paid money before to the king for the debtor of the king, because in both cases it is an execution for the king. And thus is the constant course in cases of aid, and it seems to be warranted by the eighth chapter of Magna Carta,[4] which provides [that], if sureties pay, they should have the debtor's lands and rents until satisfaction.

I [was] for the plaintiff.

[Other copies of this report: GUL MS. B88-7, p. 550.]

[Related cases: Santen v. Regem (1678), LI MS. Misc. 510, f. [81] (Ward's Reports), *Lords' Journal*, vol. 13, p. 167.]

201
Brage v. Heninge (Ex. 1685)

Specific performance of an oral contract for a lease of a house will not be compelled where part performance was de minimis.

LI MS. Misc. 557, f. 75 [Fr.] (Ward's Reports)

The plaintiff and the defendant signed an agreement, which was intended to be sealed but was not (and a guinea was given as part of the consideration), by which it was agreed that the plaintiff upon payment of £200 to him by the defendant should assign two leases of houses of £90 *per annum* to the defendant or to his assignees for the residue of the terms in them and the defendant was to be charged after Michaelmas 1683 with the rent and repairs. The defendant was importunate for the bargain, which he made for Mr. Aldworth, and the plaintiff was put to a loss of £20 in the disposal of goods in the houses and to remove others to make the houses ready at Michaelmas. And after the agreement [was] signed (which was September 10th and before Michaelmas), the defendant with Mr. Aldworth and workmen came into the house to consider alterations but none were made. And afterwards and before Michaelmas, Aldworth disliking the house, the defendant acquainted the plaintiff with it and offered to lose his guinea and restore the leases to the plaintiff, which the plaintiff refused and at Michaelmas sent the keys to the defendant's house which were not received but restored. And the house stood empty more than a year. And to have this agreement executed (in which nothing was mentioned to be done by the defendant but all by the plaintiff), the plaintiff exhibited his bill.

But the court refused to compel execution upon so small a payment as a guinea for so great an interest and upon such articles which were intended to be

---

[4] *Statutes at Large* (Runnington ed. 1786), vol. 1, pp. 3, 4; *SR*, I, 115.

sealed and thus mentioned but not sealed. And inasmuch as the defendant took the house for another who disliked it and the terms and the plaintiff had notice of it before Michaelmas, the court dismissed the bill without costs.

I [was] for the plaintiff.

[Other copies of this report: GUL MS. B88–7, p. 552.]

202

Attorney General ex rel. Smith v. Pollard (Ex. 1685)

A frank rent can issue out of copyhold lands.

LI MS. Misc. 557, f. 76, pl. 1 [Fr.] (Ward's Reports)

The relator, being the receiver of the chantry and other rents in Essex for the king, demanded an annual rent of 8d. as a chantry, frank, or other rent payable to the king out of or for certain lands in Belchamp St. Pauls in Essex, of which the defendant was owner. And this rent, being in arrears for sixteen years, he threatened to distrain for those arrears and his fees as messenger, which in all amounted to 51s. To prevent this distress, the defendant paid the money and brought *indebitatus assumpsit* for it as for so much money received to the defendant's use. To stay this suit and for settling the right of this rent and to have a commission to set out the certainty of the lands liable to this rent (which were not certainly known to the receiver) was the scope of the bill.

But on account of that it was alleged and proved by the records of the court that in the time of King Edward VI, Queen Elizabeth, James, and Charles I that there was a *liber redditus de 8d. per annum exiens de certis terris in Belchamp Sancti Pauli Comitatu Essex per antea parcelles reventionum Collegii de Stoke in Comitatu Suffolk*, but there was not any description of the lands nor in whose occupation nor by what account[1] until 9 Car. I [1633] when one Eccleston, the receiver of those rents, returned a rental into the exchequer, in which there was an entry to this effect, *De Roberto Pollard pro libero redditu exeundo de certis terris in Belchamp Sancti Pauli*[2] *per annum 8d.* And this rent in all the records was accounted for to the crown. And it appeared by the book of one Watts, who was receiver after the restoration of the king that now is, that this rent was paid until 1664. And it was suggested by the bill that the now defendant had the lands of the said Robert Pollard and the other lands chargeable with this rent.

---

[1] respond *MS*.
[2] from Robert Pollard for a frank rent issuing out of certain lands in Belchamp St. Pauls 8^d per annum.

The defendant confessed and justified the action and denied the having of any lands of the said Robert Pollard or that, to his knowing or hearing, there was any such person *in rerum natura* who had any lands in Belchamp St. Pauls. And also he denied that he had any frank lands or other than copyhold lands in Belchamp St. Pauls or any lands liable to this rent or that this rent was ever paid by any owner or occupier of the defendant's lands. And he showed the particulars of his copyhold lands, which he had as heir to John Pollard, his father, and to Peter Pollard, his uncle (but not to Robert Pollard). And the copies were read, in one of which there was an exception of a parcel called Longcroft.

And upon the hearing of the cause, the court was of opinion:

1. That there was a rent of 8d. issuing out of lands in Belchamp St. Pauls.
2. That a frank rent can issue out of copyhold lands (it being a chantry rent), because it can be inferred that the lord and tenant both joined in the creation of it or at least that the lord confirmed the grant of it, [it] being at all times thus called and paid.
3. That by presumption, it will be said to issue out of Longcroft (being an excepted parcel) and to be paid by the Pollards though the name of Robert Pollard can be mistaken.
4. That the defendant should not have brought his action [at law] but [should have] resorted to this court for his remedy.
5. That the court decreed payment for the future out of Longcroft and a perpetual injunction against the action [at law] with £5 costs beyond the 51s. received.

I [was] for the plaintiff, but [I] query this decree.

[Other copies of this report: GUL MS. B88–7, p. 553.]

[Order of 29 Jan. 1685: PRO E.126/14, f. 231v.]

203
Warner v. Bradbury (Ex. 1685)

A suit in equity lies for contribution for damages paid by an inhabitant of a vill for the destruction of fences.

It is not necessary to join all of the inhabitants of a vill as defendants in such a suit, but at least one inhabitant for each vill should be joined.

Commissioners will be appointed to determine the proportionate liability of each such defendant.

LI MS. Misc. 557, f. 78, pl. 1 [Fr.] (Ward's Reports)

The case upon the hearing was thus. Process upon the Statute of 13 Edw. I[1] was sued against the inhabitants of Mildenhall and six other adjacent vills to inquire what damage one Malabar and one Suckerman [had] sustained by their fences and hedges being pulled down in the night. And £53 were found and levied only upon the plaintiff, being an inhabitant of Mildenhall. And the other inhabitants of Mildenhall and the six other vills refused to pay their proportions, to compel which the plaintiff exhibited his bill against the defendants, being inhabitants only of three [of] the vills, and no one from the other vills were parties.

And in this case the court were of opinion:

1. That the plaintiff had good cause in equity to be relieved against the other inhabitants of Mildenhall and of the other six vills for reimbursing him their proportionable rate in the same manner as if issues [were] returned upon a vill for repairing highways or similar are levied upon one inhabitant only, he shall have equity against the others for reimbursing him their proportions. And the Statute of 27 Eliz., c. [13],[2] in the case of robbery and hue and cry directs the justices to make a rate. And this court should observe the same rule.
2. The court held that in such a case it is not necessary to make all the inhabitants of all the vills parties but some from each is sufficient.
3. That in this case though no one from four of the vills are parties, yet the court will award a commission to impartial commissioners for rating and assessing each of the vills to the said £53, though no one from four vills are parties, inasmuch as this commission is only for information and tending to the ascertaining of each vill's and party's proportion.

And such a commission was awarded. But afterwards the court directed some from the other vills to be made parties so that all the vills should be represented by one or more [persons], which was done accordingly.

[Other copies of this report: GUL MS. B88–7, p. 559.]

[Orders of 9 Feb. and 2 June 1685: PRO E.126/14, ff. 241, 253v.]

---

[1] Statute of Westminster II, s. 46 (*SR*, I, 94).
[2] Stat. 27 Eliz. I, c. 13, sect. 3 (*SR*, IV, 721).

204

Governors of Oakham Hospital v. Broune (Ex. 1685)

By custom, foreigners can pay tithes at rates that are different from parishioners.

LI MS. Misc. 557, f. 78, pl. 2 [Fr.] (Ward's Reports)

The plaintiffs as impropriators of Leake in the County of Lincoln sued for tithes of dry and barren cattle. The defendant insisted upon a custom that all foreigners holding pasture lands in this parish should pay only 4d. per acre for those tithes though the defendant admitted by answer that in such case the inhabitants of Leake for the same land and pasturage when held by them should pay tithes in kind, *scil.* 2s. in the pound. And it was also agreed that tithes in kind should be paid by the inhabitants and foreigners if plowed. And it was also proved in the cause that if mowed for hay, the inhabitants by custom should pay 2d. per acre and foreigners 4d. per acre. And whether this custom was good in law as to pasturage tithes for foreigners paying 4d. per acre when the inhabitants pay in the same case 2s. in the pound (and on account of that foreigners to have a greater privilege than inhabitants) was the question. And the plaintiffs ground their bill and cause of suit upon the case between Asfordby and Newcommen in this court 27 January 32 & 33 Car. II [1681] where upon a case made and argued by counsel and the court (being the same barons that now are except Baron Weston in the place of Baron Wright) *seriatim* delivered their opinion that such a custom was void, q.v. Liber J, f. 17, and the reasons there.[1]

But the court [now] said that it was a hasty resolution and deserved to be reviewed and, as they heard, created a great disturbance in this part of the country and caused lands to lie fresh and it could have had a reasonable beginning, inasmuch as the parishes there consisting of great numbers of acres more than the inhabitants could stock and for the encouragement of foreigners to take and to stock those lands, this custom could be well commenced and take effect. And this intendment reconciles the custom to the rules of the law. [And] in the case in question, it was observed by the court that there is a difference between the cases, because in Asfordby's Case there was not any benefit [to] the parishioner more than to the foreigner in any case or thing, but here there is inasmuch as a parishioner should pay only 2d. per acre when mowed and a foreigner should pay 4d., which is more than a parishioner. And the plaintiffs' bill was dismissed without any costs.

I [was] for the plaintiffs.

[Other copies of this report: GUL MS. B88–7, p. 561.]

---

[1] *Asfordby v. Newcomen* (1681), above, No. 114.

205
Croxall v. Cooke (Ex. 1685)

Oysters are not liable to pay tithes unless there is a custom to the contrary.

LI MS. Misc. 557, f. 79 [Fr.] (Ward's Reports)

The case upon the hearing was thus. The plaintiff by his bill sought relief for tithes in kind of oysters in oyster layings in the salt water in the sea and within this parish or 2s. in the pound profit made by the oysters taken and sold out of their layings. And the fact was that the defendants, being [pers]ons who deal in oysters, catch little oysters in the sea outside of the parish and lay them in the layings in question, being in salt water and two fathoms deep at low water, in which layings (admitting them to be within the parish, which was contested in this case) the said little oysters increase and become fat. And whether any tithes were due by law for those oysters was the question, because it was admitted by everyone that there was not any custom for them within this parish.

And all of the court were of the opinion that no tithes [*de*] *jure* without a custom were due in this case, because oysters taken in the sea (as other fish taken there or in a fresh river) are not tithable without a custom, and the feed and increase of them being also in the sea though in layings did not aid the matter because the feed was not something tithable, as the feed of cattle is, and on account of that not to be resembled to the [case] of dry and barren cattle which feed on grass that is in its nature tithable. And though in other adjacent parishes some oystermen there pay 2s. in the pound rent for their layings and a decree was produced by the plaintiff in this case made in this court [on] 27 January 23 & 24 Car. II [1672] between Sherrill, rector of Muchstandbridge[1] in Essex, and Asser,[2] where the defendant was decreed to pay 2s. in the pound of his rent for his layings, but the court did not give regard to it, the plaintiff refusing to produce the bill, answer, and proofs, by which it was not doubted but a custom was alleged and proved for it, [and] without such a custom this decree cannot be maintained.

And in the principal case, the plaintiff's bill was dismissed.

I [was] for the defendants.

[Other copies of this report: GUL MS. B88-7, p. 560.]

[Order of 9 Feb. 1685: PRO E.126/14, f. 247v.]

---

[1] I.e. Great Stambridge.
[2] *Sterrell v. Asser* (1672), PRO E.126/11, f. 38v.

206
Hicks v. Snelling (Ex. 1685)

Where an entire term is devised, any proviso afterwards is invalid.

LI MS. Misc. 557, f. 84, pl. 1 [Fr.] (Ward's Reports)

A term [of years] was devised to the defendant Snelling in trust that he shall permit the plaintiff to receive the profits during the whole term to her own use [with the] proviso that, if the plaintiff or her husband, which she may take, shall assign or grant the term to anyone, that then J.D. another defendant shall have it. And the court decreed the defendant to pass the whole term to the plaintiff holding that the devise being of the whole term the proviso afterwards was repugnant and void. See Moore 748[1] and 655.

I [was] for the defendants.

[Other copies of this report: GUL MS. B88–7, p. 571.]

[Order of 20 Feb. 1685: PRO E.126/14, f. 246.]

207
Gregory v. Loving (Ex. 1685)

Whether consideration recited in a contract must be proved or not.

LI MS. Hill 50, f. 79 [Fr.]

A man made a mortgage of his lands to another. And after other recitals, [there was written] 'and whereas I am and stand justly indebted unto the mortgagee in the sum of £3300 17s. 6d., now this indenture witnesseth that in consideration' etc. and for payment etc. The plaintiff exhibited his bill for redemption and that the defendant will go to attachment and there was a material dispute [. . .] the consideration for the deed should be proved or that it should stand impregnable because there did not appear [to be] any fraud nor any suspicion of deceit and the defendants are heirs etc. and the deed bore a date eight years past. And Lutwyche urged strongly that the consideration need not be proved, and he agreed that when there is any suspicion of fraud and if the deed be controverted and disputed, there the purchaser will be put to prove his consideration if the deed be of less time, but after the death of a purchaser [. . .] other to show it would be extremely harsh and inconvenient, and the mortgagor himself will be estopped to speak against the consideration, and so will be all who claim under him, as the plaintiffs did, as legatees.

---

[1] *Handall v. Brown* (1603), Moore K.B. 748, 72 E.R. 880.

And NEVILL and GREGORY held that the consideration must be proved. And he put a case which he said was before Lord Hale when [he was] chief justice of the king's bench. A bond was entered into by one that if he paid etc. to the master all such monies as the apprentice should embezzle etc. and it should be proved by lawful witnesses or by the testimony of the apprentice; the apprentice embezzled, and the master brought an action, and to prove it, he produced a bill of things embezzled signed and admitted by the apprentice. Still Hale put the master to prove each parcel; otherwise he would not recover.

Lutwyche said that the case was reasonable, because the master could bring and by coercion compel the apprentice by hardship and ill usage to sign it, but this case differed [from the case at bar].

ATKYNS and the lord chief baron [MOUNTAGU] held the contrary and that the consideration should be presumed [to be] *bona fide* paid and it would be harsh to put the defendants, who are strangers, to prove the payment of it. And ATKYNS said if a man brings an action upon the case for monies received and to prove it[1]

[Orders of 10 May and 7 Dec. 1686: PRO E.126/14, f. 333, E.126/15, f. 37v.]

208
Foster v. Hall (Ex. 1685)

A bond given for a gambling debt will be relieved against in equity as the consideration was illegal and thus void.

Several small bonds given for one large gambling debt will not avoid the operation of the statute against gambling, which excepts debts below a certain sum.

I
LI MS. Misc. 557, f. 84, pl. 2 [Fr.] (Ward's Reports)

The defendant [John] Hall won at backgammon £480 from the plaintiff on ticket or credit, for which the plaintiff gave several bonds to the other defendants to whom Hall was indebted *bona fide*. The other defendants accepted the bonds but did not discharge Hall nor were they aware that the money for which the bonds were given was won at play against the Statute 16 Car. II, c. 7.[1] Some of the bonds were put in suit and pleas of the statute [were] pleaded. And the replication [was] that the plaintiffs in those actions were not privy nor had any notice that the money for which the bonds were given was won at play and that Hall was *bona fide* indebted to them for the same sums for which the bonds were

---

[1] This report ends here in mid sentence.

---

[1] Stat. 16 Car. II, c. 7 (*SR*, V, 523).

taken. And upon the trial, the verdict and judgments were against the plaintiff here and to be relieved against those judgments and the other bonds not put in suit, the plaintiff exhibited his bill, which being after more than a year after the offense was committed, the defendants were forced to answer.

And the equity alleged and upon which the court went was that the plaintiff here did not have any way at law to force the defendants here, who were plaintiffs at law, to prove that Hall was *bona fide* indebted to them because at law the sole producing of the bonds makes the debt without other proof. And the case being an odious case of gaming and against the law, the court directed an issue to try whether the defendant Hall won from the plaintiff at one time or meeting on ticket or credit more than £100 for which the said bonds were given.

And upon full evidence it was proved that all of the £480 was won at one time on ticket, etc. And upon this verdict, in Michaelmas term the plaintiff had a decree *nisi* and this January absolutely to have the bonds delivered up and satisfaction upon the record to be acknowledged of the judgments, and a perpetual injunction [was] awarded no proof being made that Hall was really indebted to the other defendants at the time of the bonds.

I [was] for the plaintiff.

See Ellis and Warnes's Case, Moore's Reports 752, and Liber 2, f. 297.[2] See below f. 122,[3] a similar case.

[Other copies of this report: GUL MS. B88–7, p. 571.]

II
BL MS. Hargr. 71, f. 42 [Eng. & Fr.] (Dodd's Reports)

Sir Humphrey [Foster] played with Hall, and [after] every £100 won, they rose up and [a] bond [was] given, and then [they] sat down again. And thus Sir Humphrey lost £400 or £500. And the bonds were given to other persons who were not privy [to the fact] that they were for game money. And in actions brought upon these bonds, the defendant pleaded the Statute.[4] The plaintiffs replied that [they were] for a true debt etc. And [there was a] verdict for the plaintiffs.

And a bill in equity in the exchequer was brought. And it was resolved that, upon the matter, he should be relieved and that, [as to] the rising up to piss or sealing the bonds, such small intermission of time did not avoid the Statute. This was the opinion of a similar [case] in Michaelmas [term] 1684.

---

[2] *Ellis v. Warnes* (1603), pl. 1035, Moore K.B. 752, 72 E.R. 883; *Clayton v. Rawlins* (Ex. 1678), LI MS. Misc. 500, f. 297v.
[3] *Parker v. Brewer* (Ex. 1686), below, No. 218.
[4] Stat. 16 Car. II, c. 7 (*SR*, V, 523).

[Other copies of this report: HLS MS. 537(b), p. 7, pl. 5; Oxford Brasenose MS. 59, p. 9, pl. 3.]

[Orders of 26 Jan. and 20 Feb. 1685: PRO E.126/14, ff. 229, 241.]

[This case is cited in Parker v. Brewer (Ex. 1686), below, No. 218.]

209
Annesly v. Lort (Ex. 1685)

A tenant in tail who has the power to bar the remainder by a recovery can bar it by a feoffment that creates a discontinuance.

LI MS. Misc. 557, f. 88 [Fr.] (Ward's Reports)

The case was thus. Thomas White being heir in tail male upon a marriage settlement made upon his ancestor's marriage took as a wife one Jane Powell and after his marriage in 1669, he made a feoffment in fee of the lands in question lying in Pembrokeshire to the use of himself for life and afterwards to Jane his wife for her life for her jointure and afterwards to the use of the heirs of the body of Jane by Thomas, remainder to his right heirs. And in 1670 he died without issue living [by] Jane, and his right heir was Elizabeth Lort the defendant. After the death of Thomas, Jane waived and relinquished her jointure and agreed with the friends of Elizabeth Lort, who was an infant, to take such a sum annually for her life as her dower, being a third part. This feoffment being concealed and one John White an infant being heir in tail male in the same settlement, under whom Thomas the feoffor claimed (which was made [in] 9 Jac. I [1611]), no care was taken of him, but Elizabeth Lort enjoyed the lands until 1680 when John White having attained his majority and [obtained] the said settlement of 9 Jac. I [1611] made his entry and as heir in tail by it recovered at a trial at the bar of this court in 1680 and had judgment, execution, and possession, after which John White levied a fine and suffered a common recovery to the use of himself in fee. And for raising £4000 for the payment of his debts, he conveyed the premises by lease and release to the plaintiff, whose daughter he had married. The plaintiff paid £600 of the debts and undertook and became bound for the residue, after which White died without issue, having a brother called Griffith.

And in the last long vacation, the defendants brought ejectment in the [court of] great sessions and gave the feoffment in evidence by which the estate tail under which John White claimed was discontinued and on account of that his entry [was] taken away and tortious. And upon this a verdict passed for the now defendants, upon which the plaintiff exhibited his bill to be relieved in equity inasmuch as he was without a remedy at [common] law because he could not bring formedon or any real action in order to avoid the discontinuance, not being heir in tail, and he, having only a mere right in equity and not of entry or action, was only relievable in equity, being a purchaser for valuable consideration without notice of the feoffment and under the trial at bar and the recovery there. To this bill the defendants Lort and his wife pleaded the said feoffment of Thomas, who was tenant in tail, in bar of the bill.

And the court upon the arguing of this plea took time to advise. And afterwards in the same term, the plea was allowed by the entire court upon the reason that Thomas the feoffor was tenant in tail and had in himself power by a recovery to have barred the remainder in tail to John, under whom the plaintiff claimed, and though he had not suffered a recovery, yet having made a feoffment which created a discontinuance of the estate tail (which in this country is like a title) and by this feoffment the entry of John was taken away and he being dead without issue and the right of the tail (if any remained after the recovery) was descended to Griffith White, younger brother of John. And on account of that the court could not relieve against this discontinuance of him who had the legal power to bar the tail by recovery.

I [was] for the plaintiff.

[Other copies of this report: GUL MS. B88–7, p. 576.]

210
Mayor of Hull v. Beilby (Ex. 1685)

In this suit for discovery and accounting of various duties to the plaintiff city, the issues were tried by a jury, who found for the defendants.

LI MS. Misc. 557, f. 89, pl. 1 [Fr.] (Ward's Reports)

The plaintiffs by their English bill demanded discovery and relief for two several duties due to the corporation [of Kingston upon Hull] from the defendants and all others bringing any Yorkshire lead from the City of York or from the county of the same city to Kingston upon Hull. There was a duty that for all such lead so brought in any vessel to the port of Hull to be sold and the same unloaded, time of which etc.[1] this lead was and should be taken up and unloaded at the weigh house in Hull and be weighed at the common beam there after the sale of it, and for that there was and should be paid to the plaintiffs, proprietors of the said weigh house, and their farmers 2s. 4d. for each fother unloaded and sold at Hull and thereafter transported into ships and vessels for or because of a certain duty for the unloading and weighing thereupon at the said weigh house and

---

[1] 'Time of which the memory of man runneth not to the contrary' were the words used to assert a right based on prescription.

for houseroom and striking and carrying the said lead thereafter aboard a ship. And the other duty was 1s. 6d. for each fother of such lead, as above, brought to Hull from the City of York and the county of this city and unloaded at the weigh house in Hull and after this shipped off and not sold for or because of a certain duty for the unloading of the said lead at the said weigh house for houseroom, striking, and carrying aboard a ship.

The defendants denied altogether the duties demanded, and the court directed the cause to be tried at law at the bar of this court upon two issues, whether the duties were paid and were due.

And upon the trial by a Middlesex jury, the plaintiffs upon full evidence were nonsuited.

I [was] for the plaintiffs.

See the statutes of 27 Edw. III, c. 1, for the staple,[2] [and] 8 Hen. VI, c. 5,[3] and the case [in] Rolle's [Abridgment], *Prerogative*, f. 178, N, 29.[4]

Note that at Newcastle upon Tyne, there is an ancient office called the troner and peyser and an ancient weigh house and a beam belonging to the kings of England, and this office [was] granted and grantable for lives by the king. And [there was] a custom that all lead brought to this vill to be exported, before shipment thence, should be brought to the weigh house and the same weighed by this officer, who was required so to do, and on account of that he was entitled to the fee of 12d. for a fother, which he had and could recover in an action for this purpose but not to detain the lead until weighed and the fee paid. See such an action [in] Michaelmas [term] 2 Jac. II [1686] in the king's bench between Welinany [?][5] plaintiff and Blacket defendant. Query whether there is not any difference between exportation into foreign parts and coasters.

[Other copies of this report: GUL MS. B88–7, p. 578.]

[Orders of 26 June 1684: PRO E.126/14, ff. 199, 201v.]

211
Wimberley v. Harris (Ex. 1685)

A single commoner cannot be compelled by the other commoners to assent to the enclosure of their commons.

Where one commoner expends funds to defend the commons against claims and suits, he is entitled to a proportionate reimbursement by the other commoners.

---

[2] Stat. 27 Edw. III, c. 1 (*SR*, I, 332–333).
[3] Stat. 8 Hen. VI, c. 5 (*SR*, II, 241–242).
[4] 2 Rolle, Abr., *Prerogative le Roy*, Pl. G, 29, p. 178.
[5] Welwag: GUL MS. B88–7, p. 578.

LI MS. Misc. 557, f. 89, pl. 2 [Fr.] (Ward's Reports)

An English bill [was brought] by the plaintiffs for themselves and all of the other commoners except the defendants to compel the defendants to assent to the enclosure of eighty acres, part of 2400 acres of common in Long Sutton in the County of Lincoln for the term of eleven years [and] for raising money to defend all of the common against claims and suits brought and threatened to be brought and to reimburse the plaintiffs £105 borrowed by them for this occasion. And though the plaintiffs were only ten, yet 150 under their hands and seals had sealed the articles to enclose and none except the defendants refused.

And the court upon the hearing of the cause refused to conclude or compel the defendants to assent or be bound by the articles or enclosure they having each a distinct inheritance which is not bound by the act or consent of the majority. And a case was cited where a cottager alone obstructed the enclosure of a large vill and the court would not compel him though his estate by the enclosure would have been better. But the party there afterwards obtained an act of Parliament.

And the court here in the principal case inclined to dismiss the bill. But afterwards it was retained until a rate should be made for reimbursing the plaintiffs the money borrowed and expended. And if the defendants refuse to pay their proportions, the court by decree will compel them.

I [was] for the plaintiffs.

[Other copies of this report: GUL MS. B88-7, p. 579.]

[Order of 21 May 1685: PRO E.126/14, f. 262.]

212
Wightwick v. Gifford (Ex. 1685)

Lands belonging to the lesser abbeys that were not continued in existence by the crown are liable to the payment of tithes.

LI MS. Misc. 557, f. 89, pl. 3 [Fr.] (Ward's Reports)

In this case it was held by the entire court that lesser abbeys, *viz.* under £200 *per annum*, though they were surrendered after 4 February 27 Hen. VIII [1536], yet if they were not continued by the letters patent of the king according to the clause in the Act of 27 Hen. VIII[1] [to] this purpose (not printed) that they should be in the judgment of the law taken as given to the king by the Stat. 27 Hen. VIII and not by color of such surrender afterwards nor by the Stat. 31 Hen. VIII[2] and

---

[1] Stat. 27 Hen. VIII, c. 28, s. 13 (*SR*, III, 577).
[2] Stat. 31 Hen. VIII, c. 13 (*SR*, III, 733–739).

thus their lands and possessions liable to pay tithes and not discharged by any clause in the Statute of 31 Hen. VIII. And the plaintiff upon debate had a decree accordingly.

I [was] for the plaintiff.

See this clause and proviso for continuance by letters patent now mentioned and printed in Dr. Burnet's *History [of the] Reformation*, first part, among the collections f. 142, book 3, sect. 2.

[Other copies of this report: GUL MS. B88–7, p. 580.]

[Orders of 21 May and 17 July 1685: PRO E.126/14, ff. 260, 273.]

[This case is cited in Wilkinson v. Newsom (Ex. 1696), below, No. 307.]

[A decree of 1683 in a related case is printed at 1 Wood 221.]

213

Hills v. Hills (Ex. 1685)

In this case, the court construed the terms of a devise in a will.

LI MS. Misc. 557, f. 94, pl. 1 [Fr.] (Ward's Reports)

The case upon the hearing was thus. Weston, who was seised in fee of an annuity of £8 *per annum* defeasible upon payment of £150 at a day past, devised £3 *per annum* of this to Elizabeth, his daughter, for her life and the other £5 of this to Anne, his wife, and Anne, his daughter, for their several lives equally to be divided between them. And afterwards in the will, he devised the said annuity (if the £150 was not paid) after the death of all of the said parties to the defendant. Anne, the wife, and Anne, the daughter, both dying and the plaintiff as heir to Anne, one of the coheirs of the devisor, sued for the moiety of the £5, Elizabeth being alive, supposing that the defendant did not have title until after the death of all of the devisees, Elizabeth being alive.

But the court took the devise to Elizabeth, Anne, and Anne [to be] distributive during their respective lives and that, by the death of any of them, her share would go to the defendant as devisee of the whole and would not descend until the death of Elizabeth according to the reason of Justice Wyndham's Case, 5 Rep. 7.[1] And the plaintiff's bill was dismissed but without costs.

[Other copies of this report: GUL MS. B88–7, p. 590.]

---

[1] *Wyndham v. Debney* (1589), 5 Coke Rep. 7, 77 E.R. 58, also Moore K.B. 191, 72 E.R. 524.

214
Attorney General ex rel. Moneyers of the Mint v. Slingsby (Ex. 1685)

A corporation must sue in its correct name.

LI MS. Misc. 557, f. 99, pl. 2 [Fr.] (Ward's Reports)

An English bill was exhibited against the defendant in the name of the Provost and Corporation of the Moneyers of His Majesty's Mint in the Tower of London to have an accounting and relief touching great sums of money supposed to be due to the moneyers from the defendant.

The defendant pleaded in abatement and prayed judgment of the bill, inasmuch as the pretended plaintiffs in it sued and styled themselves by the name of the Provost and Corporation, as above, pretending to be a corporation and to sue by this name where in truth and as the defendant pleaded there was not any such corporation at the time of the exhibiting of the bill and that the plaintiffs were not entitled or enabled to sue by any such name nor ever were incorporated by this name nor had the capacity to sue by this name, but that if there is any corporation in which the moneyers are concerned, the name of such corporation is *Custos Cambiorum Domini Regis Operarii Monetarii et alii Ministri ad ea quae tangunt officia [sic] praedicta Deputati*,[1] for that etc. inasmuch as all suits should be in the correct name of the body politic or [of] natural persons, that this suit is not, and on account of that [there is] no remedy [and moved] for costs. The defendant demanded judgment of the bill and that it should be quashed.

And this plea was held good, and the plaintiff's bill was dismissed upon motion of their own counsel with costs.

I [was] for the defendant.

[Other copies of this report: GUL MS. B88-7, p. 605.]

[Orders of 24 and 29 Nov. and 5 Dec. 1687: PRO E.126/14, ff. 124v, 126v.]

215
Baker v. Howland (Ex. 1685)

In this case, a contract to receive a money payment in lieu of tithes was declared to be cancelled for lack of mutuality.

---

[1] The relators were incorporated by charter on 20 Feb. 1462 under the name of the warden of the mints [of the lord king], the workers, moneyers, and [other] ministers appointed to the duties of the said offices; see *Calendar of the Charter Rolls*, VI (1927), pp. 143-144.

LI MS. Misc. 557, f. 103 [Fr.] (Ward's Reports)

An agreement in May 1682 was made in writing under seal between the plaintiff as rector of Streatham in Surrey and the defendant Howland, being the patron and one of the parishioners there. And the effect of it was that the plaintiff by this covenant with Howland for accepting of all parishioners 18d. per acre for all land except woodland and 6d. per acre for woodland *per annum* in lieu of tithes quarterly and if [there were] default of payment by any[one] for twenty-one days that then the plaintiff should be at liberty to take his tithes in kind from each defaulter. But there was not any covenant or remedy created by this agreement for the plaintiff to recover the composition money, nor was the agreement mentioned to be made on the behalf of the inhabitants.

And for this reason, though the plaintiff had received the composition money for some years, yet having given notice before tithes for the year 1684 became due that he would not stand upon this agreement for the future but would take his tithes in specie, the court, upon the bill for the plaintiff to have his tithes in kind and to set aside this agreement and a bond given by the plaintiff for performance of it, relieved the plaintiff and declared the agreement void (it not being reciprocal) and decreed a perpetual injunction upon the bond and tithes in kind.

But by consent, the plaintiff agreed to accept the compositions for the times past and tithes in kind afterwards.

I [was] for the plaintiff.

[Other copies of this report: GUL MS. B88–7, p. 611.]

[Order of 26 Oct. 1685: PRO E.126/14, f. 293.]

[This case is cited in Metcalfe v. Preston (Ex. 1697), below, No. 348.]

216
Franklyn v. Jones (Ex. 1686)

Where standing timber is sold, the parson can charge for tithes either the vendor or the vendee who fells the trees.

LI MS. Misc. 557, f. 109 [Fr.] (Ward's Reports)

The plaintiff being rector of Llangibby in Monmouthshire sued the defendant for tithes of wood. And he showed in his bill that the defendant was the occupier of the wood and sold 2000 cords to one Hanbury which were felled, corded, and carried away by Hanbury who paid the defendant for them at the rate of 7s. per cord. And the sale, felling, cording, and charking by Hanbury was proved in the cause.

The defendant answered generally and did not take advantage in his answer of the plaintiff's bill which showed that Hanbury and not the defendant was liable for the tithes. But he denied that tithes of wood were due to the plaintiff, but he did not show any legal discharge.

And upon the hearing, I insisted that the plaintiff's bill should be dismissed inasmuch as it was shown by the bill that Hanbury and not the defendant was responsible for the tithes, because by the law the vendee who fells the wood or cuts the corn, etc., and not the vendor is chargeable for the tithes, because he should and can sever the tenth part from the ninth, and this is the common experience in all cases, which was not denied by the court.

But here Chief Baron MOUNTAGU, ATKYNS and GREGORY, barons, (Baron NEVILE dissenting) took this difference, that here *non constat* that the defendant sold all of the wood to Hanbury but such a number of cords, and in this case, though Hanbury cut and corded this number, yet the defendant who sold such a particular number of cords should be liable for all of the tithes of all of the wood. And the plaintiff at least had the election [as to] which person to charge, either the vendor or the vendee, as in the case of agistments where the parson has the election to charge either the owner of the land or the owner of the cattle. Godolphin 458 [and] Degge 239 were cited and relied on for this difference, because of Rolle's [Abridgment], *Dismes*, 656, L. 2; thus is Godolphin 458, 459.

Another point was insisted on for the defendant, that the woods cut were only the germins growing out of the roots of ancient timber trees cut divers years ago, and on account of that no tithes [were] due for those germins, Liford's Case, 11 Rep. 49, 2 *Inst.* 643,[1] [being] in point. As to it, the court at first thought that those are tithable notwithstanding those authorities. But afterwards upon consideration, they allowed the authorities, and [there] not being any proof of it (though in truth it was so), they decreed for the plaintiff without costs.

Another point was that a great part of the wood was timber, that is to say oak, etc., more than twenty years of age, but being converted into cordwood for fire, the court decreed tithes for them.

I [was] for the defendant.

[Other copies of this report: GUL MS. B88-7, p. 622.]

[Order of 28 Jan. 1686: PRO E.126/14, f. 315.]

[This case is cited in Acton v. Smith (Ex. 1687), below, No. 244; Buckle v. Vanacker (Ex. 1693), Samuel Dodd's Reports, p. 131; Taswell v. Athill (Ex. 1694), 2 Gwillim 537, 1 Rayner 75, 1 Eagle & Younge 590, Samuel Dodd's Reports, p. 147; Abbot v. Hicks (Ex. 1696), below, No. 331; Greenway v. Earl of Kent (Ex. 1706), below, No. 407.]

---

[1] *Stamp v. Clinton* (1614), 11 Coke Rep. 46, 77 E.R. 1206, also 1 Rolle Rep. 95, 81 E.R. 354; E. Coke, *Second Institute* (1642), f. 643.

217
Whitfield v. Rackett (Ex. 1686)

Where a decedent through fraud gives assets of an estate to a third party instead of to the legatees, the third party will be declared a constructive trustee for the benefit of the legatees without any administration of either decedents' estates.

LI MS. Misc. 557, f. 122, pl. 2 [Fr.] (Ward's Reports)

The case upon the hearing was this. Robert Gregory devised divers legacies to the plaintiffs to be paid within a year and made Jane, his wife, executrix and left assets to pay [them] with a great surplus. Before the legacies became due, by a combination between the executrix and Rackett, the defendant, the executrix gave and conveyed the assets to the defendant without any consideration and (as it was proved) with a declared intention to deceive the plaintiffs of the legacies. And afterwards the executrix died intestate within the year (and before the legacies were due). And no one took administration to her or administration *de bonis non* to Gregory. And the defendant confessed to have all the assets.

And the court decreed the defendant to pay the plaintiffs their legacies on the reason that the actions between the executrix and the defendant were fraudulent, and the defendant [was] a trustee for the legatees, and on account of that [there was] no use for administration to the testator or intestate.

I [was] for the plaintiffs. The attorney general, Serjeant Pemberton, and Mr. Whitlock [were] for the defendant.

And the court held it to be a plain case. And it was not greatly opposed by defendant's counsel.

[Other copies of this report: GUL MS. B88–7, p. 643, pl. 1.]

218
Parker v. Brewer (Ex. 1686)

A court of equity will grant relief against a bond given upon the illegal consideration of a gambling debt.

LI MS. Misc. 557, f. 122, pl. 3 [Fr.] (Ward's Reports)

The case upon hearing was thus. Richard Brewer one of the defendants won at play from the plaintiff at two separate times £30 at each time and at each of these two times the plaintiff lost more than £100 on credit to the said defendant and others. After the last time, the plaintiff was prevailed upon to give a bond and power of attorney[1] for the said £60 in the name of the other defendant

---
[1] garrant d'attorney *MS*.

Andrew Brewer, who pretended that Richard was indebted to him for £100 and that he accepted the said bond and power [of attorney] for judgment [to be entered] for so much of his debt to Richard. (But he did not say that he delivered up any security or released Richard for so much. And in truth it was a trust for Richard.)

Richard in his answer admitted [that] the money [was] won at play and [that it was] more than £100 at the same time on credit.[2]

And on this confession, the court upon hearing the cause on the bill and answer relieved the plaintiff against Andrew and decreed the bond and power for judgment to be delivered up and satisfaction of the judgment, if any, entered and this without costs. And the court took the confession of Richard against Andrew. And for the merits they relied on the case of Sir Humfrey Foster v. Hall *et al.*, q.v. *supra*, f. 84.[3]

I [was] for the plaintiff. Powys, solicitor general, and others [were] for the defendants.

[Other copies of this report: GUL MS. B88–7, p. 643, pl. 2.]

219
Kemp v. Grantham (Ex. 1686)

A court of equity will grant relief against a bond on the grounds of failure of consideration.

LI MS. Misc. 557, f. 124 [Fr.] (Ward's Reports)

The defendant having imported from the East Indies to London the said monster [Shackshoone] (being an Indian man having a child growing out of his body) in August 1684 proposed it [sic] to be sold by shares to divers persons for £150 each share and sixteen shares in it with intent to be exposed to view as a strange sight. The plaintiffs and defendants came to an agreement. And those who were plaintiffs here being eight in number with others gave a note under their hands, by which they each promised to pay £150 to the defendant for his share in the monster upon a conveyance thereof to be made and approved by counsel, and this was the 10th of August. And upon it the plaintiffs and the others who had shares (because the defendant reserved four shares to himself) took the monster into their custodies and exposed it to view. And afterwards, that is to say the 12th of August, articles were drawn and approved by the plaintiffs, and their names [were] subscribed to the draught, and directions were given to

---

[2] Note Stat. 16 Car. II, c. 7, s. 2 (*SR*, V, 523).
[3] *Foster v. Hall* (Ex. 1685), above, No. 208.

Ambrose, an attorney, who negotiated the matter for every part[y], to have it engrossed, *viz.* fourteen parts.

But after the first note for the money and before the approval and signing of the draught, a question arose what property the defendant had in the monster and by what manner this property should be transferred to the plaintiffs. And upon this, Ambrose proposed and directed that the defendant (being a mariner) should bind and enroll the said Shackshoone as his apprentice before the mayor of London, to which the defendant agreed, and that the plaintiffs shall not be bound by the articles to prepare [it] nor to pay their money upon their first note until and before the said Shackshoone should be bound and enrolled as before according to the Statute of 5 Eliz., c. 5, for mariners.[1] But the said Shackshoone being brought before the mayor utterly refused to be bound, upon which the plaintiffs refused to pay their £150 apiece.

The defendant sealed one part of the articles, but none of the plaintiffs sealed them, and upon this the defendant brought an action against the plaintiff Cary in the king's bench and upon a trial had a verdict on the note for £150 upon the allegation that the entire bargain was contained in the note and articles signed and approved. And though the defendant did not have title to the Indian, it was not examinable in this action, upon which the plaintiffs, that is to say eight of the parties who signed the note for the money and the draught of the articles, exhibited their bill to be relieved against their note (without the defendant's binding the Indian to him according to the agreement) and against multiplicity of suits.

And upon the hearing of the cause, it was insisted that the entire matter was determinable at [common] law and not examinable in equity, and of this opinion were Heath and Milton, barons.

But SIR JOHN ERNLE, chancellor of the exchequer, Chief Baron ATKYNS, and Baron JENNER held the matter relievable if the agreement was that the defendant should bind the Indian apprentice to him. And upon this, an issue was directed to be tried at law whether the defendant so agreed. And afterwards the parties agreed [to settle out of court].

[Other copies of this report: GUL MS. B88–7, p. 646.]

220
Attorney General v. Honiwood (Ex. 1686)
A plea of estoppel does not lie against the crown.

---

[1] Stat 5 Eliz. I, c. 5, s. 9 (*SR*, IV, 424).

LI MS. Misc. 557, f. 126, pl. 2 [Fr.] (Ward's Reports)

[On] 12 December 3 Car. I [1627] a contract was made by the great officers of the king with the six clerks in chancery for advancing and paying to the king £10,000, for which they had conveyed to them divers fee farm rents by name amounting to £797 18s. 4d. *per annum* (which was within 21s. 8d. of the interest for the money at the rate of £8 for rents, because the interest for the £10,000 at this rate amounted to £800 *per annum*). And the conveyances were to be in fee. And in this contract there was such a clause, that although it be intended and declared that the same is to be an absolute sale, yet if the king within a year pay the six clerks the £10,000 (they receiving the rents in the meantime), then they were to reconvey to the king.

[On] 13 February 3 Car. I [1628] the king's trustees of those rents for a term conveyed the rents to the six clerks, and [on] 15 March 3 Car. I [1628] the king confirmed this conveyance and granted the inheritance of those rents to the six clerks in fee, in none of those grants was any notice taken of this contract (otherwise than[1] in pursuance of the contract generally). The six clerks not being paid after 1640 made divers sales of those rents to divers persons absolutely who purchased them for good and valuable consideration without notice of the contract. And a rent of £200 *per annum* (part of the rents conveyed) issuing out of West Malling manor and other lands in Kent was purchased and lodged in Ferdinando Massonn in fee, who in 1669 sold it to the defendant for £3600 and £350, a full and valuable consideration, and the conveyances were in the name of trustees. And afterwards the defendant purchased the manors and premises, or part of them, charged with this rent in his own name for £1810 being full and valuable consideration.

[In] 25 Car. II [1673] the king granted this rent of £200 *per annum* (with the others in the first grant to the six clerks) to Bernard Greenville and his heirs and all his estate and equity of redemption.

The attorney general exhibited an English information in his name for the king against the defendant to have an account and redemption of the £200 *per annum* (not being granted by the acts[2] for the sale of fee farm rents). The defendant pleaded his purchase and the length of time and that he did not have notice of the contract nor [was there] any mention in the evidences under which he purchased (which were absolute), and he [was] an absolute purchaser without notice, and the contract [was] not on record.

But the court overruled the plea without costs and put the defendant to answer, upon which he could have the advantage of the entire matter, it not being

---

[1] ousterment que *MS*.
[2] Stat. 22 Car. II, c. 6 (*SR*, V, 657–660); Stat. 22 & 23 Car. II, c. 24 (*SR*, V, 743–745).

reasonable to stifle the equity of the king by a plea. And the court declared that length of time does not prejudice the king and that the six clerks having notice and [being] parties to the contract, all who purchased under them were affected with the contract and notice. And in this case there is not anyone who should or could give notice. And it was said that there was a decree against Pindar in the time of Chief Baron Hale upon the same question. And it was observed that the rents conveyed were only the interest of the £10,000.

I [was] for the defendant.

The grant to Greenville was not then discovered, and the rents were put out of the charge in the exchequer and never claimed nor answered. And after the overruling of this plea, the cause did not proceed further, and on account of that I conceive that an accord was [made] between the parties, but query this.

[Other copies of this report: GUL MS. B88–7, p. 651.]

221

Squire v. Blacket (Ex. 1686)

Where an importer of wine brings in slightly less than the minimum taxable amount in order to avoid the tax, this is fraud and the prisage tax is due.

LI MS. Misc. 557, f. 127 [Fr.] (Ward's Reports)

In this case upon the hearing, the plaintiff, lessee of the prisage, had a decree for two tuns of wine against Blacket, who imported only eighteen and a half tuns, and against the defendant Leman for one tun, who imported only nine tuns of wine. And the reason for this decree was the apparent fraud, design, and practice by those defendants for avoiding the payment of prisage in importing a small quantity under ten and twenty tuns, it being proved in the cause that the ships would have imported other great quantities and that in the same ships divers quantities of brandies and other goods were imported with the wines. And it was also proved that Leman declared [that] he would not import the full ten tuns because he did not want to pay prisage. And in this cause these decrees in this court, as precedents, were produced and read, *viz.* Easter [term] 5 Car. I [1629], Sir William Waller v. Deiricie [?] of Bristol,[1] where prisage was decreed for nine and a half tuns; Hilary [term] 8 Car. I [1633], Sir William Waller v. Atkins of Lynn[2] for nine and a half tuns; [in] Trinity [term] 18 Car. II [1666], Attorney General *ex rel.* Morrice v. Mayor of Plymouth,[3] it was decreed for less than ten

---

[1] *Waller v. Dericke* (1629), PRO E.125/5, f. 292.
[2] *Waller v. Atkins* (1633), PRO E.125/11, f. 425v.
[3] *Attorney General ex rel. Morrice v. Munion* (1666), PRO E.126/9, f. 133v.

tuns; Hilary [term] 19 & 20 Car. II [1668], it was decreed against Meering of Plymouth[4] for two tuns for less than twenty tuns. And in those decrees, as in the decree now made, it was declared to be apparent fraud to import wines in such a manner and in such quantities.

But in the case in question, as for Lee, though he imported more than eight tuns and less than nine and great quantities of other goods amounting to forty tuns, yet it being proved that the reason that Lee did not import more wine was that Stockton would not carry off or dispose of more and that he had no use or market for more and that it was never heard that so great a quantity as eight tuns was imported into Stockton, and on account of that there was no apparent fraud.

The court forbore to pronounce any decree against Lee but wished to consider the matter.

I [was] for the plaintiff.

And this was a Newcastle and Stockton cause.

[Other copies of this report: GUL MS. B88-7, p. 653.]

222

Thrumpton v. Gaell (Ex. 1686)

In this case, the executor of a will was given land to pay debts and legacies, but the land was not given in fee and did not become his estate, nor could it be reached by his creditors.

LI MS. Misc. 557, f. 128 [Fr.] (Ward's Reports)

The case upon the hearing was thus. John Ashton, brother of the plaintiff [Susan Thrumpton] and whose heir the plaintiff was, being seised in fee of divers tenements in Curriers Alley, London, and of a messuage and lands in Kingston super Thames, by his will charged all to his wife for [her] life with £50 *per annum* and devised Curriers Alley to John Monke, son of the plaintiff, but in case he die without issue, to the children of Thomas Hudson share and share alike and made John Monke his executor, to whom he gave his lands at Kingston and all other else whereof he had any right to, as leases, bonds, bills, [and] debts, wishing him to pay his wife duly and make good all other things, as debts, funeral charges, and the like, as his wife should be put to for his funeral. And afterwards he died, leaving personal estate sufficient to pay his debts, funerals, and legacies with a surplus. Monke proved the will and entered upon the lands devised, paying the £50 *per annum*. The tenements in Curriers Alley being burnt in 1666, Gillingham, the lessee of them, had a decree made by the judges in Clifford's Inn

---

[4] *Attorney General ex rel. Morrice v. Merringe* (1668), PRO E.126/9, f. 304.

for adding a greater term and lowering the rent. Monke and Gillingham came to an agreement for the absolute purchase of the tenements in Curriers Alley by Gillingham in fee. And it was thus contrived that Gillingham should have the tenements conveyed to his trustee and to be protected from the payment of the £50 *per annum* during the life of the wife in order to [accomplish] which, the plaintiff with John Monke by deed and fine conveyed Curriers Alley and the Kingston lands to Halsey and Gillingham to the use of them and their heirs forever, after which John Monke and Gillingham (Halsey being dead) declared the true meaning of the parties to the first deed and fine to be that Curriers Alley remain to Gillingham and his heirs and the Kingston lands should remain to Gillingham and his heirs in trust for John Monke and his heirs, Gillingham being indemnified against the £50 *per annum* and arrears. John Monke became bankrupt and the Kingston lands were assigned to Gaell under whom the defendant Gaell claimed.

And the plaintiff exhibited a bill to have the Kingston lands assigned to her by Gillingham (the £50 *per annum* being determined and the arrears paid). This conveyance was opposed by the defendant Gaell insisting that either by the will or by the deed and fine and declaration of the trust by John Monke and Gillingham there was a fee or trust of a fee vested in John Monke, the bankrupt, and under him vested in the defendant and that he should have the conveyance from Gillingham.

But it was held and thus decreed by all the barons that the plaintiff and not the defendant should have the Kingston lands, because without question John Monke did not have the fee by the devise, there being personal estate sufficient to pay the testator's debts and all charges imposed by the will upon John Monke, in which case it was not an inheritance but an estate for life only by lack of parol [?] heirs. Secondly, they all held that there was a resulting trust for the plaintiff upon the deed and fine levied by him and there not being any consideration for it and the entire design was, by this deed and fine and all of the conveyances, to make security for Gillingham against the £50 *per annum*. And the declaration of the trust by Gillingham and Monke for Monke, the bankrupt, did not affect the plaintiff, [she] not being a party to it. And thus the plaintiff should have the trust [as] against (from the deed and fine) as resulting upon[1] his first fee simple and under that if Halsey and Gillingham, to whom the use in fee was declared, had voided what remedy the plaintiff had.

[Other copies of this report: GUL MS. B88–7, p. 654.]

[Order of 28 June 1686: PRO E.126/15, f. 14v.]

---

[1] sur de *MS*.

223
Ridges v. Ridges (Ex. 1686)

A voluntary conveyance that settles land on family members is covered by the Statute of Frauds and cannot be varied by an oral agreement.

LI MS. Misc. 557, f. 130 [Fr.] (Ward's Reports)

The case upon the hearing was thus. The plaintiff Charles [Ridges] being seised in fee by the devise of his father of divers houses in London and being an extravagant person and seeming to consume all of his estate and [being] a single man and designing to go abroad, he was prevailed upon by the defendants James, Joseph, and John Ridges to settle his estate and to put it out of his power to consume and squander it. But the entire discourse and design was that, if he came back from [across the] sea, he should have his estate back. And upon advice with a counsel of the Middle Temple, the plaintiff by lease and release for 10s. (which was not paid) and natural affection settled those houses upon the defendants to the use of himself for life without waste, remainder to the use of the first and others of his sons successively in tail male, remainder to the daughters of his body in it, remainder to the defendants being the brothers and sisters of the plaintiff in fee. The plaintiff returned in 1684 from [across the] sea and married and prayed to have his estate back, being become a sober man. Two of the releasees, *scil.* John and Joseph, agreed to it, but James and the sisters dissented and insisted upon the settlement. And for setting aside this voluntary settlement, the plaintiff exhibited his English bill.

And the two brothers, John and Joseph, confessed in their answer, and, being examined in the case, they both and the counsel who made the settlement swore that the design of the settlement was only to preserve the estate from being consumed and that before and after that the settlement was engrossed that the plaintiff declared and the three brothers, the releasees, agreed that if the plaintiff came back from [across the] sea that he should have up this settlement and that it was intended only to be a means of preventing the disposing or encumbering of the estate for little or no consideration, though it was not mentioned in the release. And it was proved also in the case that the plaintiff was sober and married (but [had] no children) and [was] not in debt and the premises [were] out of repair that no one wished to repair nor take them for security, the plaintiff being only tenant for life.

And it was upon the hearing of the cause strongly insisted by the plaintiff that this settlement being voluntary and made upon such a design and agreement to be resigned and delivered up when the plaintiff returned from [across the] sea, it should be thus decreed, and that it is agreeable to reason that the plaintiff should be owner and disposer of his estate and that it is now in his power appeared inasmuch as, if the plaintiff sold it to a purchaser for valuable consideration, this should bar the defendants (which last matter was agreed by all at the bar and bench) and that this case is not within the Statute for Frauds and Perjuries[1] so that there should be [no] use for a note in writing, because where there is a resulting trust within this law or there is a parol agreement which being proved can defeat the deed and there is not any averment against the deed and if the plaintiff can sell to a purchaser (which was agreed by all), this conveyance should be delivered up and should not stand in the way. And of this opinion and for those reasons were Chief Baron ATKYNS and Baron MILTON.

But SIR JOHN ERNLE, chancellor of the exchequer, and Baron JENNER and Baron HEATH were of a contrary opinion, and that this parol agreement not being made a part of the conveyance nor in writing was worth nothing and that the plaintiff could not be admitted to have the benefit of the trust agreement by parol inasmuch as it was directly against the Statute of Frauds and Perjuries, by which it was enacted that no estates, interests, or trusts touching lands shall be good if they are not committed to writing. And they observed that this settlement though voluntary yet it was a prudent and family settlement and he and his issue should have the benefit of it and if he had not had issue, what persons [are] so proper to have the estate than his brothers and sisters and this way complied with the father's will. And to admit such parol agreements against deeds destroys all the benefit and design of the Statute Against Frauds, which was to reduce into writing all which concerned land. And if it was a trust for the plaintiff, it should be in fact or in law. If in fact, a writing [is] necessary, and in law it could not be here (and thus to result to the plaintiff) because the plaintiff had disposed of all of the estate. And a conveyance at common law without consideration was a trust for the feoffor, and after the Statute of Uses,[2] it was to the use of the feoffor, but it was never a trust or a use where the blood was, as it is in this case. And on account of this the bill was dismissed without costs.

[Other copies of this report: GUL MS. B88-7, p. 659.]

[Orders of 20 May and 25 June 1686: PRO E.126/14, f. 339, E.126/15, f. 18v.]

224
Bankes v. Rye (Ex. 1686)

A collector and sequestrator of tithes cannot sue for them in his own name.

---

[1] Stat. 29 Car. II, c. 3 (*SR*, V, 839–842).
[2] Stat. 27 Hen. VIII, c. 10 (*SR*, III, 539–542).

LI MS. Misc. 557, f. 140, pl. 1 [Fr.] (Ward's Reports)

The vicarage of [*blank*] in Suffolk was vacant before 1677 and thus continued vacant for this year and two years afterwards; the plaintiff had an instrument under the seal of the bishop, by which he had the cure of this parish committed to him *quousque* etc. And he by an instrument under the seal of the bishop had a sequestration of the tithes of this parish, and he was by it made collector of those tithes with a clause that *ita quod ille redderit verum et fidelem compotem de decimis praedictis* to the bishop.

And the plaintiff by color of this title exhibited an English bill in his own name as collector and sequestrator against the defendants, who were inhabitants, for their tithes in arrears for three years.

And upon the hearing of the cause, the plaintiff's bill was dismissed because he did not have any interest or estate in his own right but only an authority to collect and to make his account to the bishop, who (and not this court) should and can make allowance to the plaintiff for the service of the cure, because it is plain that by the Statute 28 Hen. VIII, c. 11,[1] the interest and right of the tithes was vested and given to the next incumbent.

The attorney general and others [were] for the plaintiff; myself and Duncombe [were] for the defendants.

And divers such bills have been dismissed for the like cause. See February 1712[/13], between Buchanan and Pycroft, the bill [was] retained and an issue [was] directed; see Michaelmas 1713, 16 November.[2]

[Other copies of this report: GUL MS. B88–7, p. 675.]

[Other reports of this case: 1 Rayner 65.]

[This case is cited in Berwick v. Swanton (Ex. 1692), 1 Eagle & Younge 574, Samuel Dodd's Reports, p. 123.]

225
Leach v. Croke (Ex. 1686)

Where there is no estate to preserve contingent remainders, a life tenant can give away his estate without valuable consideration and disinherit his unborn heir by destroying the contingent remainder.

---

[1] Stat. 28 Hen. VIII, c. 11 (*SR*, III, 666–667).
[2] *Buckingham v. Pycroft* (Ex. 1713), below, No. 467.

LI MS. Misc. 557, f. 141 [Fr.] (Ward's Reports)

The case upon a plea to the bill was thus. The plaintiff's father was tenant of divers lands in the counties of Devon and York of £500 or £600 *per annum* for life without impeachment of waste by the devise of his older brother, remainder to the first and thus to the tenth son of his body, the next remainder in tail to Sir Simon Leach, an infant, with other remainders over, but there was not any estate to preserve the contingent remainders to the first and other sons of the plaintiff's father. The plaintiff's father married with the daughter of the defendant Unton Croke and being a person of easy understanding and not being satisfied with his wife or her proceedings by which means he was involved in divers judgments and bonds for the payment of money without any valuable consideration, and not being well satisfied with the fidelity and honesty of his wife, he by the advice of the defendant and of other friends and relations of himself and with an intent to render ineffectual the said judgments and securities and to prevent the now plaintiff, who then was *en ventre sa mere*, from inheriting or taking this estate, in August before the November in which the now plaintiff was born, which was in the year 167[*blank*], surrendered his estate for life to Sir Simon Leach, who was the next remainderman in tail and an infant, and afterwards in the next November, the plaintiff was born. And three or four years afterwards when the said Sir Simon Leach became of full age, a settlement was made and a common recovery [was] suffered by him of all of the estate, to which settlement the plaintiff's father was a party. And the uses were by this settlement limited and declared to the said Sir Simon Leach, as to the Devonshire estate [it was] charged with some sums of money and his heirs and as to the Yorkshire estate to the use of the defendant Croke and his wife, who was the sister of the plaintiff's father, and their heirs charged and chargeable for raising some annual sums for the plaintiff's mother and the plaintiff for their lives. And the defendants pleaded payment of £300 by Sir Simon Leach to the plaintiff's father as consideration or part of it for this surrender and settlement. And when Sir Simon Leach became of full age and before said settlement and recovery, he declared his acceptance of this surrender made by him during his infancy. And the plaintiff with his mother exhibited this bill charging divers frauds and matters, which were denied by the answers, to have relief against this settlement and recovery by which he was disinherited.

But the plea was held good, as had been before in chancery before the now lord chancellor to a bill there for the same purpose. And it was admitted by all the bar and bench that the surrender had destroyed the contingent remainder to the plaintiff since the plaintiff's father had levied a fine or made a feoffment because his estate for life, upon which the plaintiff's contingent remainder depended, being destroyed by the surrender before the birth of the plaintiff, the plaintiff's contingent remainder was destroyed also. Also, it was so held that though the next man in tail was an infant, yet that the surrender was good without actual or other acceptance, inasmuch as the estate for life was by it extinguished and merged in the estate tail. See 1 *Inst.* 338b,[1] that if a life tenant surrenders to the cestui in reversion under age, that he would not have [it upon] age. And the plea was allowed.

I [was] for the defendant.

And it was said that though it was a harsh thing, yet the father can disinherit his issue in such a case if he pleased without any consideration. But afterwards upon a trial in ejectment brought by the infant for the lands in Yorkshire at the bar of the common bench in Trinity term 1687, the plaintiff's father was proved to be a natural fool and the settlement and the will [to have been obtained] by practice, and [there was a] verdict for the plaintiff upon long and full evidence and with direction of the court.

And afterwards in 1689 or 1690, the judgment of the court of the common bench, *scil.* Chief Justice Pollexfen, Powell, and Rokeby (Ventris dissenting),[2] [was] that the surrender to the remainderman being an infant and not agreeing or accepting the surrender until after issue was born was not good, and on account of that the estate came to the issue notwithstanding the surrender.

And afterwards this judgment was reversed in Parliament (see Easter term 1701), tried at the bar in this court.

[Other copies of this report: GUL MS. B88–7, p. 678.]

226

Heron v. Brownlow (Ex. 1686)

In this case, the court refused to grant a continuance so that the defendants could present their evidence, their commissioner having been accidentally prevented from giving them notice of the taking of depositions.

---

[1] E. Coke, *First Institute* (1628), f. 338b.

[2] *Thompson v. Leech* (C.P. 1690), Samuel Dodd's Reports, pp. 91, 125, 3 Modern 296, 301, 87 E.R. 196, 199; 2 Ventris 198, 86 E.R. 391, 1 Eq. Cas. Abr. 278, 21 E.R. 1044, 3 Levinz 284, 83 E.R. 691, Comberbach 438, 468, 90 E.R. 577, 596, Carthew 435, 90 E.R. 852, Holt K.B. 357, 623, 665, 90 E.R. 1097, 1244, 1267, 2 Salkeld 427, 565, 576, 618, 675, 91 E.R. 372, 477, 485, 523, 573, 3 Salkeld 300, 91 E.R. 836, 837, 1 Lord Raymond 313, 91 E.R. 1104, 1 Comyns 45, 92 E.R. 951, 12 Modern 173, 88 E.R. 1243, Carthew 211, 250, 90 E.R. 726, 749, 1 Freeman 502, 89 E.R. 377, 1 Shower K.B. 296, 89 E.R. 584, also Shower P.C. 150, 1 E.R. 102, *Lords' Journal*, vol. 15, p. 163.

LI MS. Misc. 557, f. 142, pl. 2 [Fr.] (Ward's Reports)

The defendants and their tenants, claiming common in a marsh in [*blank*] in Lincolnshire for all their commonable cattle, obtained verdicts in replevins in affirmance of their rights of commons. After issue was joined in those actions, the plaintiff exhibited his bill to be relieved and to have the benefit of a decree made in this court in the time of Charles I, by which it was decreed upon some compensation mentioned in it that the now plaintiff or he under whom the plaintiff claims, his heirs, and assigns enjoy all of this marsh freed and discharged of the common for the cattle of those under whom the defendants Brownlow and Hussey claim. And in truth enjoyment was had according to this decree for all time afterwards, but as the defendants alleged there was some allowance made to the tenants in respect of their common in this marsh.

But the defendants did not have any opportunity to prove it, inasmuch as the plaintiff having obtained an injunction to stay judgment and execution was obliged to have the cause heard this term. And in the last vacation, he executed his commission and gave notice to Fisher, one of the defendants' commissioners, who the same day as the notice went to London thinking to be back by the time appointed for execution, which was the 20th of October, but was detained in London by the occasion of the death of a friend so that the defendants did not have any notice of the execution of the commission nor have they examined any witnesses. And this commission was not returned until the 7th or 8th of November, and the cause was appointed for the 18th, six days before which day, I [moved] upon an affidavit that the defendants had not examined any witnesses nor had seen any of the depositions and the said Mr. Fisher accordingly [being] in court and affirming and offering to make an oath of this matter and my consenting to continue the injunction and praying time to examine witnesses, yet the court utterly refused to grant it or put off the cause without the consent of the other party (who refused), giving as a reason only that the defendants moved too late.

And the cause was heard on the day appointed, and a decree [was given] for the plaintiff, there being no proof for the defendants, which note and query whether such a motion was ever before denied in such a case and for such a reason.

[Other copies of this report: GUL MS. B88–7, p. 682.]

[Order of 25 Nov. 1686: PRO E.126/15, f. 34v.]

227

Attorney General v. Barnardiston (Ex. 1686–1687)

A bill of complaint can be taken pro confesso *against a defendant who had been served with process, imprisoned, and refuses to enter an appearance.*

In this case, a fraudulent and voluntary conveyance was set aside so that the crown could collect a fine. Also, other assets were seized to pay the fine due to the crown.

LI MS. Misc. 557, ff. 110, 143, 172 [Fr.] (Ward's Reports)

Sir Samuel [Barnardiston][1] was fined in the king's bench £10,000 upon an information preferred there against him by the attorney general and committed in execution for it and detained there and still remained a prisoner.[2] And upon a *mittimus* of the record of the fine into the exchequer, his lands were extended and seized into the hands of the king, and the profits were levied by [a writ of] *levari facias*. And notwithstanding this the attorney general exhibited an English information against Sir Samuel and divers persons who were thought to be debtors to him by mortgage and otherwise and also to have the estates in lands in trust for Sir Samuel. And the scope of the bill was to discover those estates, debts, etc. and to have them made liable in equity to the payment of this fine of £10,000. Sir Samuel, being in prison in the king's bench for this fine, was served with a subpoena to answer this bill and had a copy of it sent to him in prison, but he not responding was brought to the bar by [a writ of] *habeas corpus* and charged with this bill. And the title of the bill and a small part, but not all [of it], was read to him, and he was demanded and endeavored to be persuaded by the court to enter his appearance. But he refused and was remanded. And three days afterwards [he was] brought again to the bar by another *habeas corpus* and charged with the bill, and then all of the bill was read to him, but he declined and refused to enter his appearance and was remanded. And this day,[3] he was brought again by another *habeas corpus* and charged with the bill, which at this time was read to him, and he again refused to enter his appearance, upon which third refusal, the attorney general prayed that the bill should be taken against him *pro confesso*, which was ordered by the court accordingly. But this taking *pro confesso* was afterwards waived, and [there were] other proceedings.

Note [that] a year passed (q.v. above f. 110 and below f. 172). The bill was ordered to be taken against him *pro confesso* when he was a prisoner in the Marshalsea [Prison] and [was] brought to the bar three times and [the bill] was read to him and [he was] remanded, but the attorney of the king did not think [it]

---

[1] Died 1707, *D.N.B.*
[2] *Barnardiston's Case* (1684), *State Trials*, III (Hargrave ed. 1776), pp. 933–942.
[3] 3 February 1686.

reasonable to proceed upon it but removed Sir Samuel the last term by a *habeas corpus* out of the king's bench [prison] into the Fleet [Prison] (the proper prison of the exchequer) where he remained charged with his fine. And after the same term, he was brought to the bar two times by [writs of] *habeas corpus* and had the bill (that is to say part of it) read to him each time. And the first day of this term he was brought to the bar by another *habeas corpus*, and the bill [was] read to him, and each of the three times he refused to enter any appearance, but the court ordered an appearance for him to be entered without and against his consent. And this day,[4] the court ordered the bill to be taken against him *pro confesso*.

Note [that] it seemed to me to be a doubt whether any bill can be taken against one *pro confesso* without an appearance entered in the court by him by an attorney. But Serjeant Hutchins said to me that it is the practice in the chancery thus to do as here, because, as he said, if the party can be taken, his obstinacy should not hinder my remedy. And it had been attempted to take a bill *pro confesso* against one who [had] absconded and could not be taken, but it had not prevailed, and for that see 2 Chancery Reports (octavo) f. 28, Nodes and Allan and Battle, 35 Car. II, f. 106;[5] 2 Chancery Reports (in folio), Denny and Filmer,[6] f. 133, 35 Car. II; same book f. 237;[7] 1 Chancery Reports, Salmon and Hamborow Company,[8] f. 208, decree *pro confesso* without an appearance by the lord's order.

The defendant Sir Samuel being fined and prosecuted, as above, ff. 110 and 143, and he having lent £2200 to Langly upon a mortgage of the manor of Mould in the County of Flint for a term of years, which was assigned to the defendant Blackerly in trust for Sir Samuel, and the inheritance of the manor being conveyed to Sir Samuel in fee for the same security, and the defendant Sir Samuel being in execution for the same fine and refusing to appear to the plaintiff's information, the purport of which was to discover and subject the real and personal estate and the credits of Sir Samuel (in his own name or [in the] name of his trustees) to the payment of this £10,000 fine, and the court upon the refusal of Sir Samuel to cause any appearance to be entered for him, having made an order for the entry and recording [of] his appearance without his consent, and afterwards he being brought to the bar by three habeas corpuses and the information read three times to him and he further refusing to answer, the bill was decreed against him *pro confesso* the 24th of January last.

---

[4] 24 January 1687.
[5] *Nodes v. Batle* (1683 x 1684), 2 Chan. Rep. 283, 21 E.R. 679.
[6] *Denny v. Filmer* (1663, 1682), 2 Chan. Cas. 133, 22 E.R. 881, 2 Freeman 172, 22 E.R. 1138, Nelson 64, 21 E.R. 790, *sub nom. Dunny v. Filmore*, 1 Vernon 135, 23 E.R. 369.
[7] *Anonymous* (1677), 2 Chan. Cas. 237, 22 E.R. 925.
[8] *Salmon v. Hamborough Company* (1671), 1 Chan. Cas. 204, 22 E.R. 763.

The case upon the hearing this day[9] appeared to be thus, that in June 1683 a term for one thousand years before created for security for £3000 was conveyed to Blackerly in trust for Sir Samuel for securing the payment of £2200 and interest and that for further security the inheritance was conveyed to Sir Samuel in fee, that the 18th of March 1683, which was after the information and trial, which were in Hilary term last, but before the judgment and fine, which were in Easter [term] 1684, there were conveyances executed which mentioned that in consideration of £2200 paid by Jacob Reynardson to Sir Samuel Barnardiston (but in truth as confessed by Reynardson in his answer, no money [was] paid by him) Blackerly assigned and Sir Samuel ratified the said term for one thousand years to the defendant Robert Foot in trust for the said Reynardson. And, by lease and release at the same time for the same consideration of £2200, the inheritance was conveyed by Sir Samuel and Langly to the said Reynardson. And Foot by his answer claimed nothing but in trust for Reynardson, and Blackerly admitted the trust in him for Sir Samuel.

And the court upon the bill and answer, taking notice of this decree *pro confesso*, decreed the defendant Langly to pay the £2200 with interest from the 18th of March 1683, which was before the judgment and fine or any execution, (before which nothing was forfeited, nor are goods bound but from the time of the execution, according to Sir Gerard Fleetwood's Case, 8 Rep. 171[10]) to Sir John Ernle, chancellor of the exchequer, to the use of His Majesty by the first of November next. And also it decreed the defendants Blackerly, Reynardson, and Foot to convey to the said chancellor [of the exchequer] to the use of the king all of their estate, interest, and right to the mortgaged premises, and upon payment of the money, the chancellor [was] to reconvey to the defendant Langly, and Sir Samuel [was] to deliver up all of the writings to the said chancellor, and that the East India Company (who were also defendants) should bring into the court £35 due to Sir Samuel from this company, deducting their charges, the interest and charges to be computed by the deputy [king's] remembrancer. And the court decreed indemnity to all defendants for what they should do pursuant to this decree.

I [was] for Blackerly, Reynardson, and Foot.

And thus note that the king had a decree to have a remedy in equity against his debtor for a fine and his trustees and creditors to make his real and personal estate liable to the fine, notwithstanding that the debtor remained in execution upon the commitment for the fine. And his lands were also extended and seized and the profits levied for the same fine at the same time. See above, ff. 106, 110; Hardres 137–147[11] and 201[12] as to discovery. And it seems that the king has a

---

[9] 9 June 1687.
[10] *Fleetwood's Case* (1610), 8 Coke Rep. 171, 77 E.R. 731.

remedy for a fine imposed in a court of justice against the person fined and his lands and goods, notwithstanding the person when the fine was imposed was committed in execution for it and remained in execution, but when the fine is levied on the lands and goods, the person should be delivered, if there is not any other matter for his restraint except the fine.

[Other copies of this report: GUL MS. B88–7, p. 624; GUL MS. B88–8, p. 72.]

[Orders of 10 Feb., 14 and 28 Apr., and 9 June 1687: PRO E.126/15, ff. 69v, 75, 75v, 102v.]

[This case is cited in Attorney General v. Croft (Ex. 1707), below, No. 419.]

228
Delaval v. Delaval (Ex. 1687)

In this case, the court construed the terms of a devise in a will.

LI MS. Misc. 557, f. 122, pl. 1 [Fr.] (Ward's Reports)

The case upon the defendant's plea to the plaintiff's bill was thus. Robert Delaval seised in fee of lands of £400 annual value devised them to his brother William for life, remainder to the defendant, [George Delaval] another brother, for his life, he the said George paying £300 to the two plaintiffs [Mary and Dorothy Delaval] and Isabell, daughters of William, each of them £100 or to so many or each of them as should be living at their several accomplishments of sixteen years old, 'if William be then dead', together with consideration after £6 per cent *per annum*, and after the decease of George, then to John, the eldest son of George, and Edward, another son of George, successively and the heirs male of their bodies successively, the said John and Edward paying the said £300 to the two plaintiffs and Isabell at their ages of sixteen years. Isabell died before sixteen; the plaintiffs Mary and Dorothy attained sixteen in the lifetime of their father William. William died. George the defendant entered and possessed the lands, and not paying the plaintiffs their £200, the plaintiffs exhibited their bill for relief.

The defendant pleaded all of the matter and that the plaintiffs attained their ages of sixteen in the lifetime of their father William and on account of that the legacies never became due inasmuch as the will did not charge George the defendant to pay but under this condition, 'if William be then dead' (which he was not).

---

[11] *Attorney General v. Mico* (1658), Hardres 137–147, 145 E.R. 419.
[12] *Attorney General v. Anonymous* (1661), Hardres 201, 145 E.R. 452.

But the court overruled the plea and held the charge good upon George though the plaintiffs attained their ages in the lifetime of William, because this clause, 'if William be then dead' was not a condition but an explanation of his intention that George should not pay until the death of William as a result of which he came into the lands, but that he should pay after he came into the lands though the daughters attained sixteen in the lifetime [of] William, because it is plain that the testator meant the daughters (his heirs at law) should have their legacies, and William had an estate for life not charged with their legacies, and on account of that, if George should not pay, they would lose their legacies against the intent of the testator. And upon this reason, the court overruled the plea, notwithstanding [that] Serjeant *Shaftoe* objected the condition 'if William be then dead' and that it should be inferred that the testator had computed that if William lived until his daughters attained sixteen, he on account of that would raise money for their portions.

And this opinion of the court upon the plea was confirmed upon the hearing of the case Thursday 10 February 1686[/87] when the plaintiffs were relieved by a decree for the principal and interest.

[Other copies of this report: GUL MS. B88–7, p. 641.]

229

Gerard v. Woodward (Ex. 1687)

A common recovery by a tenant in tail bars remainders to charitable uses.

A common recovery by a cestui que trust *in tail bars the remainders in trust to the charitable uses.*

LI MS. Misc. 557, f. 143 [Fr.] (Ward's Reports)

The case upon the hearing was thus. One Thomas Martin, [who was] seised in fee of divers lands in Sussex and Kent in November 1684, devised them to the defendants and their heirs to the use of the defendants and their heirs in trust and confidence that if Lucy Cooke his niece should not marry or after marriage should die without heirs of her body and that all of her issue should die without issue so that there did not remain any child, issue, or posterity mediately or immediately proceeding from the body of the said Lucy, that then the defendants and their heirs, out of the rents, issues, and profits of the premises devised to them, should build a school house in Putney for a master, servants, and twenty scholars to teach mathematics to the watermen's sons in Putney or Wandsworth where the school was to be built, with divers limitations and directions for the establishment and support of this charity. And he died. Lucy Cooke married Mr. Gerard, and he received the rents and profits. And afterwards he and Lucy levied a fine with proclamations of the premises to two persons to make them tenants to the *praecipe* in order to have a common recovery, which was suffered accordingly, and in it Mr. Gerard and his wife were vouchees, and the uses [were] limited to them for their lives, remainder to the issue between them, remainder to the right heirs of the survivor. Lucy died without issue. And this bill was exhibited to have the defendants convey the estate to the plaintiff and his heirs and to have delivery of the title deeds.[1]

And the entire court was clear [in their opinion] and so decreed the defendants to do it accordingly, being indemnified for doing it by the same decree. And [there was cited] a precedent in chancery, 2 March 1681, between Sir Francis North, chief justice of the common bench, plaintiff, and Mary Champernoon and others, defendants,[2] in the point where the lord Nottingham, then lord chancellor, declared and so decreed that a common recovery suffered by a *cestui que trust* in tail would bar the estate tail and remainders over limited by a will of Addington, in which case it was held and declared as a general rule that any conveyance or assurance in law made by a *cestui que trust* will have the same effect and operation on the trust that it would have upon the estate in law if the trustees had executed their trust. Otherwise the trustees by refusing or not being capable to execute their trust would hinder the tenant in tail of this liberty that the law gives to him as incident to his estate, that is to say to bar the remainders and to dispose of his estate, which would be inconvenient and tend to the introducing of perpetuities so greatly odious in the law. And on account of that, the said lord chancellor decreed the trustees to convey the estate according to the uses of the recovery.

And in the case in question here, it was admitted by the defendants' counsel and clearly held by the court that a common recovery by a tenant in tail will bar remainders to charitable uses as well as other remainders at law, and by the same reason such a recovery by a *cestui que trust* in tail will bar the remainders in trust to the charitable uses, because *aequitas sequitur legem*.

And in the principal case, the defendants were decreed to convey to the plaintiff in fee. And it was held that it was not necessary to make the churchwardens or inhabitants of Putney or Wandsworth parties in regard to the charitable use, because the recovery barred the charitable use in equity.

I [was] for the plaintiff.

And afterwards the trustees conveyed according to this decree. And Mr. Gerard enjoyed the estate without question or pretense from anyone.

[Other copies of this report: GUL MS. B88–8, p. 2.]

[Order of 3 Feb. 1687: PRO E.126/15, f. 61.]

---

[1] evidences *MS*.
[2] *North v. Williams* (1681), 2 Chan. Cas. 63, 78, 22 E.R. 848, 855, 79 Selden Soc. 888, 1 Eq. Cas. Abr. 256, 21 E.R. 1029, *sub nom. North v. Way*, 1 Vernon 13, 23 E.R. 270.

230

Stracy v. Eve (Ex. 1687)

A plaintiff cannot sue for waste without alleging his own title.

LI MS. Misc. 557, f. 145, pl. 1 [Fr.] (Ward's Reports)

The plaintiff by his bill showed that the defendant was tenant for life by the surrender and will of her former husband remainder to the plaintiff and his heirs of copyhold lands in a certain vill in Essex and that the defendant cut timber and made waste to the prejudice of the plaintiff in remainder and on account of that prayed relief.

The defendant insisted on a custom within the parish that a tenant for life can cut and sell timber.

And at the hearing, I for the defendant prayed that the plaintiff's bill should be dismissed inasmuch as it had not shown any custom within the parish that copyholders in fee should have the timber and, without such a custom, the timber belongs to the lord of the manor, who was not a party, and on account of that, though the custom alleged by the defendant that a tenant for life can sell the timber, should not be good, as is the case of Rochey v. Huggins, Cro. Car. 220; Rolle's [Abridgment], *Customs* 560; Jones 245.[1] Yet inasmuch as the plaintiff had not lodged any title in himself to the timber by the custom of the manor in his bill, the court cannot relieve him against the defendant.

And of this opinion was the entire court, and [they] dismissed the plaintiff's bill with costs, inasmuch as the plaintiff without making good title to the timber (which cannot be without a custom in the copyhold estate) will not be relieved against a tenant for life who cuts down the timber though he had no right to it.

[Other copies of this report: GUL MS. B88-8, p. 5.]

[Order of 7 Feb. 1687: PRO E.126/15, f. 68.]

231

Lord Rockingham v. Sawyer (1687)

In this case, the plaintiff impropriator should have alleged his particular title in his bill of complaint.

---

[1] *Rockey v. Huggens* (1631), Cro. Car. 220, 79 E.R. 793, W. Jones 245, 82 E.R. 129, 1 Rolle, Abr., *Customes*, pl. E, 17, p. 560.

LI MS. Misc. 557, f. 145, pl. 2 [Fr.] (Ward's Reports)

The plaintiff having a long lease of the rectory and tithes of Kettering in Northamptonshire made by the parson, patron, and ordinary before the restraining statute of Queen Elizabeth[1] exhibited his English bill against the defendant as occupier of lands in Kettering for discovering and recovery of the tithes. And by his bill he showed that he was executor of the executor of the first lessee 'and as executor or other representative or assignee of the said lessee or by some other lawful ways and means for many years before and ever since Michaelmas 1685 was and still is the true and lawful farmer or proprietor and possessed of and interested in the rectory or parsonage of Kettering and of all the tithes thereof etc.' and showed that the defendant had occupied lands in this parish and had not paid the tithes to the plaintiffs or any of them and prayed relief.

The defendant pleaded that before Michaelmas 1685 he was duly presented, instituted, and inducted into the rectory or parish church of Kettering upon the presentation of the plaintiff, the lord Rockingham, and thus continued at all times after and now is the legal and droitural rector and incumbent of this parish church and rectory and, as he hoped to prove, duly entitled to the tithes for which the plaintiffs by their bill demand against him. And for further plea he pleaded that he had not ever made any lease or title to the tithes to the plaintiffs or any of them and did not know of any title that the plaintiffs or any of them had to the tithes in question and pleaded this matter in bar to the plaintiffs' demands and on account of that and inasmuch as the plaintiff, the lord Rockingham, who is his patron, had only made a bare allegation of his right and had not shown how he entitled himself, he demanded judgment whether he should be compelled to answer further.

And the defendant also demurred to the entire bill and for cause showed that it did not appear how the lord Rockingham, under whom the other defendant claimed, derived his title to himself to the tithes in question nor by what conveyance nor how or when [it was] made or that the rectory is or ever was impropriate or that he or anyone under whom he claimed was ever rector of this rectory.

And this plea and demurrer being argued this day, I myself for the plaintiffs alleged that they should not be allowed but overruled, because it is clearly the uniform practice of this court not to compel a plaintiff to show his particular title or derivation of it how he is entitled to tithes, but to say that he is farmer or proprietor of such a rectory or tithes at all times was admitted good in all English bills, and at law to say that the plaintiff is proprietor without more was at all times admitted in debt upon the Statute of 2 Edw. VI.[2] And here the lord

---

[1] Stat. 13 Eliz. I, c. 20 (*SR*, IV, 556); Stat. 14 Eliz. I, c. 11, s. 1 (*SR*, IV, 602).
[2] Stat. 2 Edw. VI, c. 13 (*SR*, IV, 55–58).

Rockingham had thus done, and all the specifications of the particulars of his right either as executor, assignee, or other representative or by other legal title terminated in this, that he was droitural farmer, proprietor, and interested in the rectory and tithes which are sufficiently certain in a bill. And at a hearing in equity and a trial at law, the plaintiff must prove his title and how he is proprietor, otherwise he will be dismissed or nonsuited, and on account of this this demurrer cannot be good. And the plea did not aid it nor could, because by the bill the defendant is solely charged as an occupier of lands and thus [is] in the same case with all other occupiers, nor is the defendant in the bill mentioned or admitted to be rector, and on account of this though the defendant pleaded himself to be rector etc., yet this plea is issuable and the plaintiff can reply to it, and on account of that this plea does not make nor can make the demurrer good, because it was never heard that a defendant can take advantage of an issuable plea to make his demurrer to the bill, which should arise upon the imperfection of the bill and not upon the matter of the plea, good, because if it were so, then the defendant here by pleading a title that is issuable and the plaintiff can reply to it, foreclose, and debar the plaintiff from such replication by the demurrer which goes to the entire bill, and thus it never would come into question whether the defendant was rector or not. Also the constant practice of this court [is] and at all times was that the defendant responding to quantities and values should [show] the title of the plaintiff or defendant whenever or rather if the defendant pleads a release or other sufficient discharge.

And of this opinion was Chief Baron ATKYNS clearly, and [he held] that the demurrer was not good nor the plea to bar the plaintiff to have discovery of the quantities and values.

But barons JENNER, HEATH, and MILTON (who all allowed that a proprietary [right] at law is good, and thus in equity, against a bare occupier) held the plea and the demurrer also good. And they endeavored to distinguish this case from the case of a parishioner or occupier inasmuch as the defendant had pleaded himself rector and induction to the rectory and thus title in law to the tithes and that though the plea by itself and the demurrer by itself were not good apart, yet *juncta juvant*, and thus they allowed it.

Quod mirum videtur, it being considered that in no case can a plea help a demurrer or a demurrer the plea for the reasons aforesaid. And also no title appeared in the defendant except by his plea (which is issuable), and [this] distinguished him from the case of the parishioner, against whom the bill was admitted to be good. And yet by the demurrer to the entire bill, the plaintiff was foreclosed to contest the defendant's title and allegations by the plea. Also if the bill did not contain any sufficient title by the plaintiff, the defendant could have demurred to this without the pleading of his title. And it is further incongruous to plead a title in bar to the plaintiff's demands and by this to make a title in himself to the tithes in question and also to demur to the entire bill for the imperfection of the showing of the plaintiff's title, which without the plea would have been good, and yet by the demurrer upon the plea, the plaintiff was foreclosed to dispute the matter of the plea that was entirely issuable. Query and query again, because it seems utterly irrational and against all practice and experience.

Note [that] the defendant was of the name and kindred of Sir Robert Sawyer, the attorney general, who was counsel for him and greatly pressed the cause. And the reason, which he said, was to compel the plaintiff to show the original lease before the hearing, which the plaintiff did not think reasonable. Note also that though the defendant was rector, which was not denied in fact, yet the plaintiff by such ancient lease that he had or otherwise by lease of the rector himself can be entitled to the tithes of the rectory without prejudice to the right of the defendant as rector, and on account of that a general allegation of title as proprietor should be good. And though the defendant pleaded that he had not made a lease to the plaintiff, yet it was issuable as well as his being rector, to dispute any of which the plaintiff by the allowance of the demurrer was otherwise disabled. *Ideo quaere*, because it seems a strange and incongruous opinion of the three barons and without reason and precedent.[3]

[Other copies of this report: GUL MS. B88–8, p. 6.]

232
Birt v. Humfreys (Ex. 1687)

If a defendant does not demur to the prayer for relief in a bill for discovery and common law relief, the court of equity will hear evidence and grant relief as at common law.

LI MS. Misc. 557, f. 148, pl. 1 [Fr.] (Ward's Reports)

The plaintiff as administrator to J.S. exhibited his bill against the defendants, who were part owners of a ship, and showed that his intestate in his lifetime at the request of one who was master of the ship had sold and furnished to the said master of the ship for the use of the ship divers particular goods such as cloth for sails etc. and also at the request of the said master had done certain work to and for the said ship and the sails of it, which goods sold and delivered were of such a value and what the work done was worth and he deserved so much for it. And he also showed that the master of the ship had not paid for such goods and work but was dead or insolvent. And for this he prayed discovery and relief against the defendants, who were part owners of the ship.

---

[3] This last paragraph was stricken out in the manuscript.

The defendants answered and denied that they ever bought goods or employed the intestate in any work or knew that he furnished any goods or did any work for the ship. And also they swore that they had reckoned and paid the said master for all goods and work for the said ship.

The plaintiff replied generally, and the defendants rejoined, and the plaintiff proved by a witness that some goods were sold and delivered by the intestate to the master of the ship and that they came to the use of the ship and that the intestate had done work for the ship and that the goods in his judgment were worth such a sum and that the intestate deserved for his work such a sum. But the defendants did not examine any witnesses, thinking (as they said to me) that the plaintiff's remedy was at [common] law and not in equity.

And upon the hearing of the cause this day, I for the defendants prayed that the plaintiff's bill should be dismissed, being purely an action at [common] law by *indebitatus assumpsit* or *quantum meruit* and this [was] only in damages, no sum certain being agreed, which the court of equity could not assess but a jury should. And in this case there was not any shadow of equity, the proof being at law, the defendants not having discovered anything by their answers that could entitle the court or the plaintiff to equity.

But the court made a decree for the plaintiff for £14 (being made up of divers particulars for goods and work) without costs and refused to dismiss the bill (though they agreed that the plaintiff had a good remedy at [common] law), inasmuch as the defendant had not demurred to the plaintiff's bill as to relief. And the court took it as a standing rule here and in chancery that if the defendant does not demur to the plaintiff's bill as to the relief that is prayed in a bill that is proper to be exhibited as a bill of discovery but not to be a bill for relief, that the plaintiff should have a decree though the matter is purely an action at law.

And thus in effect no bill should be dismissed at the hearing because the plaintiff has a remedy at law, *quod nota et quaere*, because it seems against practice and reason.

In this case the attorney general [was] for the plaintiff; I [was] for the defendants.

[Other copies of this report: GUL MS. B88-8, p. 13.]

233

Gwavas v. Fountain (Ex. 1687)

Civil contempt of court is not discharged by the death of the king.
A writ of sequestration lies to enforce a final decree in equity.

LI MS. Misc. 557, ff. 150, 166 [Fr.] (Ward's Reports)

Upon a question whether, by the death of King Charles II, the contempt after [a writ of] sergeant at arms [was] awarded and no return was made by him during the life of the king was abated and gone, the court held clearly upon a view of precedents in chancery that such a contempt was not abated and gone but that a prosecution could be [had] upon the return of the sergeant of *non est inventus* according to the law and usage and that though the sergeant at arms in this case took a new warrant from the lord treasurer after the death of the king, yet it was only *in majorem cautelam*.[1] And on account of that the plaintiff's counsel moved strenuously for a sequestration against the defendant being after a decree for a great sum of money, but as to the sequestration, the court [took it under] advisement. But as to the contempt it was held not to be discharged by the death of the king, though no return was made by the sergeant at arms during the life of the king.

And the precedents in chancery produced were Birch v. Maypowder,[2] 21 February 1684, in point; Crew v. Vernon, Cro. Car. 97,[3] that a commission for the examination of witnesses stands in force after the death of the king until notice of it; Wood and Verdon where the order for a sergeant [at arms was made] 18 December 1684, which was during the life of the king, and a warrant upon it for the arrest of Verdon [was issued] 23 February 1684[/85], which was after the death of the king, and arrest after this, and it was held good.

And the arguments and precedents for sequestrations in the exchequer were [as follows:]

1. That it is as great and the same reason that they should be awarded here as in chancery and (as the attorney general urged) greater inasmuch as the Stat. 33 Hen. VIII, c. 39,[4] gave a larger jurisdiction to this court for process for the king, which was concern for his debtor, as all the suitors here are.
2. That this court always grants sequestrations as a[5] mesne process, and it is as reasonable after a decree as before.
3. That without sequestrations after decrees, all decrees would be eluded and rendered ineffectual, and [there would be a] failure of justice.

---

[1] For greater security.
[2] *Birch v. Maypowder* (1686), 1 Vernon 400, 23 E.R. 543, 2 Shower K.B. 467, 89 E.R. 1045.
[3] *Crew v. Vernon* (1627), Cro. Car. 97, 79 E.R. 686.
[4] Stat. 33 Hen. VIII, c. 39 (*SR*, III, 879–892).
[5] en *MS*.

Precedents:

The constant practice in chancery, from the time of lord Coventry before 1640 until this time (because the first sequestration after a decree was by lord Coventry in the Case of Sir Thomas Read[6] who was committed to the Fleet [Prison] and took with him there a trunk or chest with money in it that was sequestered); Zouch and Noy, a case in chancery 1661; Hyde and Petit [in chancery][7] and affirmed in the House of Lords in Parliament in 1666, and then [there was a] great debate and argument in Parliament, and it was held good by the lords in Parliament.

In the exchequer: Hawys and Kett, 10 July 1679, a sequestration [was] awarded upon debate after a decree, though the defendant was also in prison upon the same decree and in a matter [that was] merely personal, see Liber H, f. 54 bis;[8] Miles and Hitchcock, Hilary 35 & 36 Car. II, 12 February 1683[/84];[9] Attorney General ex rel. Sir Samuel Moreland v. Nicholson, 31 October Michaelmas 36 Car. II [1684];[10] Bold v. Sydenham, 31 May 1684; Sir George Curtis v. Sir John Austin; Westrow and Scott, Michaelmas 34 Car. II [1682].[11]

Chief Baron ATKYNS observed that Chief Baron Hale in the case of Sir Robert Croke v. Collett[12] absolutely denied a sequestration after a decree, Collett being in prison in the meantime, and termed it an accumulative execution. But here he held the mischief and inconvenience [to be] great without a sequestration, and thus the court will take it under advisement and will hear counsel [at the] proper term upon this point.

Note that at common law no land was subject to execution for a personal thing or debt, but afterwards by the Statute of Westminster II[13] [they were] subject to an elegit. And in proceedings at common law in personal things, the land was in some manner subject before appearance, as [in] distress for issues, but not in any case after judgment before the Statute gave the [writ of] *elegit*. And this was offered to prove the reasonableness of the distinction that sequestration can be [had] before but not after judgment or decree in imitation of the proceedings at common law.

---

[6] *Russel v. Read*, cited in *Hide v. Pettit* (1667), 1 Chan. Cas. 91, 92, 22 E.R. 709, 710; T. E. Tomlins, *Law Dictionary*, vol. 2, *sub tit.* 'sequestration'; R. North, *Lives of . . . Baron Guildford*, I (1826), p. 420.
[7] *Zouch v. Noy* (1667–1670), 1 Chan. Cas. 91, 185, 22 E.R. 709, 754, 2 Freeman 125, 133, 168, 22 E.R. 1101, 1109, 1135.
[8] *Hawys v. Kett* (Ex. 1679), above, No. 99.
[9] *Miles v. Hitchcock* (1685), PRO E.126/14, f. 289.
[10] *Attorney General ex rel. Moreland v. Nicholson* (1684), PRO E.126/14, f. 208v.
[11] *Westrow v. Scott* (1682–1683), PRO E.126/13, f. 377, E.126/14, f. 21.
[12] *Croke v. Collett* (1667), PRO E.126/9, ff. 287v, 357v.
[13] Stat. 13 Edw. I, c. 18 (*SR*, I, 82).

But note that in the principal case between Gwavas and Fountain, the court awarded a sequestration, which was executed in the usual manner as in chancery.

Upon the argument, JENNER, HEATH, and POWELL, barons, declared their opinion that sequestration of goods and lands after a decree in this personal cause is well awardable in the exchequer upon the mischief and failure of justice in default of it and it is as warrantable here as in chancery and in the inferior courts of Wales where it is generally practiced and [there is] no difference between granting it before or after a decree.

But [note] that no answer was given to the distinction that before the decree it is only a distress but after it is an execution according to the difference at common law, *supra* f. 151.

But Chief Baron ATKYNS was not prepared to give his judgment, but there being a case [in which it was] denied by Chief Baron Hale, in Croke and Collett, and doubted by Chief Baron Mountagu in this very case and never granted, he did not deliver any opinion but deliberated. Yet an order [was] made to award the sequestration.

I [was] for the defendant.

And this sequestration was executed in common form as usually [done] in chancery and [in] other sequestrations. And note [that] afterwards such sequestrations [have been] constantly awarded and practiced.

[Other copies of this report: GUL MS. B88–8, pp. 21, 60.]

[Other reports of this case: 2 Freeman 99, 22 E.R. 1083; 2 Eq. Cas. Abr. 281, 710, 22 E.R. 237, 597.]

[Orders of 1 and 8 Feb. 1687: PRO E.127/16, ff. [47v], [63v].]

[Affirmed on appeal: *Lords' Journal*, XIV (n.d.), pp. 407, 425, 473.]

[This case is cited in Duke of Leeds v. Hawson (Ex. 1700), below, No. 374, and Francklyn v. Colhoun (1819), 3 Swanston 311, 36 E.R. 870.]

[Related cases: Fountain v. Gwavas (Ex. 1676), above, No. 73; Cook v. Fountain (Ch. 1672–1676), 3 Swanston 585, 36 E.R. 984; Cases 273, 500, Nottingham's Reports, 73 Selden Soc. 185, 362; Gwevers v. Earl of Danby (1688), 3 Chan. Rep. 216, 21 E.R. 771.]

234
Berriff v. Beacon (Ex. 1687)

In this case, the heir of a mortgagor was allowed to exercise a right of redemption.

LI MS. Misc. 557, f. 152 [Fr.] (Ward's Reports)

The plaintiff entitled himself as heir at law by descent to the equity of redemption of a mortgage made by his uncle of lands in Essex of the annual value of £50 and more, of which the defendant had a conveyance by lease and release in fee for the consideration of £445 by the defendant sworn to be really and *bona fide* lent and paid to the mortgagor and his order and use with a proviso [for it] to be void upon payment of this sum at the end of eleven months and [with] a clause that if it was not paid at this time, that then upon tender or payment of £5 to the mortgagor or his heirs, they would be barred of all equity of redemption. And he averred the non payment of the mortgage money and tender of the £5 and [that] the mortgagor by the conveyance acknowledged the receipt of the £445 and acquitted and discharged the defendant (who had married the sister of the mortgagor) of it.

And the defendant insisted by his answer that he had expended divers great sums in the building and repairs of the mortgaged premises by direction of the mortgagor and that he had a deed purporting [to show] the agreement of the mortgagor that those expenses should be charged upon the mortgaged premises. And he demanded upon the account more than £1000 to be due to him upon the mortgage. But the defendant could not prove the lending or payment of the £445 upon the mortgage, but by his counsel at the hearing he insisted that in this case against an heir at law, who did not come into the estate as a purchaser or for any consideration paid, the acknowledgment of the receipt and the discharge for the money under the hand and seal of the mortgagor should be conclusive evidence of the receipt and payment of the money.

But upon proof made by the plaintiff which gave[1] great suspicion to the court whether the money was paid or not, notwithstanding the oath of the defendant in his answer (and the tender [?] of the £5, which the court did not attach importance to[2]), the court directed an issue to be tried, what money was really and *bona fide* paid by the defendant for the consideration of the mortgage, and another issue, what sums were expended in repairs by direction of the mortgagor.

And upon the trial, the jury found £325 paid by the defendant as the consideration for the mortgage and, as to the second issue, that nothing was expended in repairs by order or consent of the mortgagor.

And the plaintiff upon it[3] had a decree for an accounting and a reconveyance upon payment of the principal money and interest.

Note that this mortgage was made before 24 June 1677, though the mortgagor did not die until 1682, and during his life he did not question the mortgage or the interest of the defendant, which note.

I [was] for the plaintiff.

[Other copies of this report: GUL MS. B88–8, p. 28.]

[Order of 3 Feb. 1687: PRO E.126/15, f. 56v.]

---

[1] adm^r *MS*.
[2] regard *MS*.
[3] the verdict.

235
Fox v. Charlett (Ex. 1687)

In this case, the court of exchequer ordered the defendant to pay mortuaries to the vicar.

LI MS. Misc. 557, f. 156, pl. 1 [Fr.] (Ward's Reports)

The plaintiff being vicar of Bromyard in the County of Hereford exhibited his bill against the defendant, the relict and executrix of her husband (recently dead), for a mortuary of 10s. The defendant insisted that her husband was a freeman of the borough of Bromyard and that no mortuary was due by custom and insisted upon the Statute of 21 Hen. VIII, c. 6.[1]

The plaintiff made full proof of the payment of mortuaries as well for freemen of the borough as other inhabitants in ancient and modern times by divers living witnesses and also by records in the first fruits office in the taxation of the first fruits that respected mortuaries and also by a terrier in the bishop's court, 1589, which mentions mortuaries due.

And the court made a decree for the plaintiff without any trial at law and did not give any regard to the two books alleged to be ancient and appertained to the borough court there, in which it was mentioned that by ancient custom no mortuary was due by a freeman of the borough. But the modern proofs being to the contrary, a decree [was] made *ut supra*.

And note [that] in this case no notice was taken of the jurisdiction of the court in the case of mortuaries; see above f. 29.[2] And note that the bill did not concern anything but mortuaries.

I [was] for the plaintiff. Williams and others [were] for the defendant.

[Other copies of this report: GUL MS. B88–8, p. 38.]

[Order of 2 May 1687: PRO E.126/15, f. 77.]

236
Coles v. Eyans (Ex. 1687)

In this case, a vicar sued for and recovered tithes.

LI MS. Misc. 557, f. 156, pl. 2 [Fr.] (Ward's Reports)

In an old composition and agreement among the bishop of Lincoln, ordinary, the abbot of Eynsham, impropriator, and the vicar of Charlbury [in] 1495 for explaining doubts and settling the right, it was provided and agreed that the vicar of

---

[1] Stat. 21 Hen. VIII, c. 6 (*SR*, III, 288–289).
[2] *Page v. Lovel* (Ex. 1683), LI MS. Misc. 557, f. 29.

Charlbury and his successors should have always all tithes of corn, grain, hay, and other tithes growing within that part of the parish called Pudlicott. And for the tithes of corn growing there the past three years in three closes called Ash Close, Grove Close, and Chapel Close in Pudlicott, the plaintiff exhibited his bill.

And it was admitted by the defendants that the vicar had at all times received the tithes of hay and other tithes except corn, but never the corn, and that five or six years ago the plaintiff's predecessor sued the occupier of the closes for tithes of corn upon the Statute[1] and upon full evidence a verdict [was given] for the defendant.

To this it was responded by the plaintiff's counsel that the composition and endowment being in full and express words comprehending all kinds of tithes in Pudlicott and [it] being admitted that the closes lay in Pudlicott and all other tithes growing in them [were] paid to the vicar and there not being any proof that the closes were plowed before eight years ago, it was a plain case that the vicar had the right to all tithes.

And the verdict being against this endowment, the court did not wish to put the plaintiff to a trial in so plain a case but decreed for the plaintiff. And a proposition being made that the plaintiff should accept £10 for the time past without costs, and the defendants agreeing to pay it and the tithes in kind for the future, this proposition was accepted and decreed.

I [was] for the plaintiff.

[Other copies of this report: GUL MS. B88-8, p. 39.]

[Order of 2 May 1687: PRO E.126/15, f. 80v.]

237
Lechmere v. Dingly (Ex. 1687)

In this case, the court confirmed an ancient custom for enclosing a certain common and granted an injunction against future disturbance of the enclosed land.

LI MS. Misc. 557, f. 157 [Fr.] (Ward's Reports)

The plaintiffs showed themselves to be seised of divers old houses and lands in Hanley in the County of Worcester in fee and that by custom within this parish time of which etc.[1] the freeholders there had and could at their pleasures enclose their lands in the common fields and hold them enclosed discharged of all

---

[1] Stat. 2 & 3 Edw. VI, c. 13 (*SR*, IV, 55-58).

[1] 'Time of which the memory of man runneth not to the contrary' were the words used to assert a right based on prescription.

commons by others abating the common in the open fields proportionably to the land thus enclosed and that the freeholders at all times acquiesced in such enclosures without claim or pretense of common. And they showed that pursuant to such custom there were divers enclosures made out of the common fields by divers of the freeholders, some by those under whom the defendants claimed and some of those time of which etc., some sixty, fifty, forty, thirty, and twenty years ago quietly enjoyed, and that the plaintiffs around thirty years ago had made enclosures of some of his open lands in Northfield abating the common in the open fields proportionably and that they had been enjoyed until Michaelmas last, at which time the defendant, Sir Edward Dingly, being one of the lords of the manor, and the other defendants freeholders there have thrown open the enclosures of the plaintiffs under pretense of using their commons there, to be relieved against which doings and against three or four actions [at common law] that the defendants have brought against the plaintiffs and to have the enclosures established and for a perpetual injunction was the scope of the bill.

The defendants admitted the enclosures, ancient and modern, but did not admit any such custom for enclosing and justified the breaking of the plaintiffs' enclosures being made, as suggested, in the former times of the usurpation around thirty years ago. And they insist upon their right of common after harvest upon the land within those enclosures as common appurtenant to their houses and lands in Hanley. And also they insisted that they had brought those actions to try the right of their common and of the pretended custom at common law where, as they insisted, those matters are properly triable and determinable and not in a court of equity.

And upon the hearing of this cause this day, in which it appeared fully as well by the depositions of the plaintiffs as the defendants' witnesses that such enclosures, ancient and modern, in this parish had been made and quietly enjoyed without disturbance or claim of common within them by any other freeholders and that almost every freeholder within this parish had some such enclosure (And the plaintiffs' witnesses spoke to the custom and reputation of the custom for such enclosure for seventy years, and the defendants' witnesses agreed with the fact of the enclosure though they did not speak of the custom.) and upon consideration of the reason of the Case of Sir Miles Corbet, 7 Rep. 5b,[2] [in] which there seemed to be such a custom for enclosure, the entire court, that is to say, Chief Baron ATKYNS, JENNER and HEATH, barons, upon consideration of the case and the circumstances of it and the ill consequences of throwing open the enclosures and disturbing those that had been settled and agreed for so long a time and it only [being] for a pique of the defendants against the plaintiffs, the court declared the custom to be good and confirmed and established the enclosures and granted a perpetual injunction.

---

[2] *Corbet's Case* (1585), 7 Coke Rep. 5, 77 E.R. 417.

And in the debate of this case, the case between Dr. Atterbury and the Earl of Nottingham[3] touching the enclosure of Milton (q.v. above f. 62) was remembered. And the court held it to be a common equity for establishing enclosures of thirty or forty years' antiquity and quiet enjoyment without any trial at law, especially as to foreclosing a right of common.

And in the principal case, costs were spared if the defendants acquiesced, otherwise not.

I [was] for the plaintiffs; Levinz and others [were] for the defendants.

[Other copies of this report: GUL MS. B88–8, p. 40.]

[Order of 2 May 1687: PRO E.126/15, f. 76v.]

238
Morse v. Morrice (Ex. 1687)

A principal will be liable where his agent absconded with a bill of exchange so that no protest of it could be made.

It is inequitable for a master's agent to take financial advantage of his principal's apprentice, who was a young person and under his control.

LI MS. Misc. 557, f. 159, pl. 2 [Fr.] (Ward's Reports)

The plaintiff exhibited his bill to be relieved against a bond of £1000 penalty entered into by him to the defendant for the fidelity of the plaintiff's son, who was an apprentice with the defendant, and to be relieved for £300 that the plaintiff had paid to the defendant to be paid to the plaintiff's son at Hamburg, where the son was in the defendant's service and interest by him with one Slater, the defendant's factor there and a partner with him in some trade, for which the plaintiff received a bill of exchange to the defendant struck upon Slater and the plaintiff's son for value received from the plaintiff and to be paid to the plaintiff's son there. And Slater failing and absconding, he took this bill with him and did not pay it, on account of which the plaintiff's son could not protest it, and thus the plaintiff [was] remediless except in equity.

And as for the bill of exchange, the court relieved the plaintiff and decreed the defendant to pay the £300 to the plaintiff, being administrator of his son being a just thing that he should pay it, having received it from the plaintiff. And the protest [was] hindered by the default of the defendant's factor who failed and took it with him until the time of protest was passed, which note. And though it was objected that the plaintiff's son was in trust with Slater and had the bill

---

[3] *Atterbury v. Stafford* (Ex. 1684), above, No. 194.

struck upon him payable to himself and on account of that should have taken care that it should be paid or protested in due time, yet Slater being the factor and principally concerned for the defendant and the plaintiff's son not out of his apprenticeship and a young man and under Slater, it would be unreasonable that the £300 should be lost.

And as for relief upon the bond, the case was that the plaintiff's son during his apprenticeship was sent to Hamburg to Slater to learn the trade there and that Slater had the chief government of all of the defendant's trade and concern there and the plaintiff's son [was] only named in the partnership[1] for the honor and Slater failing, the defendant sustained a great loss by it and did not have any good account of his effects and on account of that he endeavored to repair his loss upon the plaintiff's bond. But the court thought it to be an unreasonable case that the plaintiff should be responsible for the default of Slater, who was a suspicious person when the defendant employed him and had the general[2] management of the concern. And there was not any proof that the plaintiff's son meddled otherwise than with Slater and by his direction. And the court relieved against the bond and decreed it to be delivered up and [decreed a] perpetual injunction.

And the defendant, perceiving the decree of the court, consented to deliver up the bond and pay the £300 without interest and costs, which was accepted.

I [was] for the plaintiff; the attorney general and others [were] for the defendant.

[Other copies of this report: GUL MS. B88-8, p. 45.]

[Order of 28 Apr. 1687: E.126/15, f. 74.]

239

Watkins v. Webster (Ex. 1687)

Creditors of a decedent cannot levy upon the decedent's land where that land was charged by his will with the payment of legacies.

Where land passes by a will and the heir at law conveys it to a purchaser without notice of the contents of the will, the purchaser takes good title.

LI MS. Misc. 557, f. 161 [Fr.] (Ward's Reports)

The case upon the hearing was thus. The plaintiffs were bond creditors of Edward Webster, deceased, the husband of the defendant Grace Webster. And the said Edward was possessed of goods and seised in fee of a brew house of great annual value and thus died, having made his will and by it devised the said

---

[1] society *MS*.
[2] grand *MS*.

brew house to the defendant Grace and her heirs upon condition or trust that she would pay the legacies by this will devised to his children. And in truth the said brew house was not in words subjected to the payment of the debts but of the legacies only to the children. But there was a clause at the end of the will, by which he devised all of the residue of his real and personal estate to the said Grace, whom he made executrix, after his debts and legacies [were] paid. Grace after the death of Edward with her son, who was heir at law of Edward, mortgaged by feoffment the said brew house in fee to Hill for £500. And in this case the court resolved these points:

1. That the brew house was not chargeable by the will with the debts but that it was well charged with the legacies, notwithstanding that the plaintiffs were bond creditors and the legacies only voluntary, and the clause of the residue after debts and legacies paid did not subject the house to the debts.
2. That the mortgage to Hill was good, he not having notice of the will, that is to say of the contents of the will, because he confessed by his answer that he had notice that Edward had made a will but that he never saw nor heard it nor was acquainted with the contents until after his money [was] lent, nor was there any proof to the contrary but only probabilities and presumptions, but before lending he had notice that Edward had made a will.

And the court in this case held that without full notice, Hill would not be affected, having lent his money in good faith, and though it was objected that if Hill did not have notice of Grace's title by the will as it came to pass, that it required her to join. It was answered that she could join with the heir to bar her dower or jointure. And in truth the feoffment did not take notice of the will.

And the plaintiff's bill was dismissed.

I [was] for the plaintiff.

Note the diversity when one purchases under one who did not have any title as heir at law but his title only subsisted by a will, there he should at his peril take notice of the will; but when the vendor is heir at law and thus can have bare title without the will, it can be otherwise.

[Other copies of this report: GUL MS. B88-8, p. 47.]

240

Sambrooke v. Squibb (Ex. 1687)

In this case, a fee farm rent issued out of various rents and demesnes granted by the crown. The king can reserve a rent out of another rent.

LI MS. Misc. 557, f. 162, pl. 1 [Fr.] (Ward's Reports)

The case upon the hearing was thus. [In] 11 Car. I [1635] the king granted the manor of Aldington in the County of Kent, which consisted of some demesnes and divers services and rents of assize and other rents and profits, to Sydenham and Smith, trustees of Edward Sydenham, in fee, reserving the annual fee farm rent of £260 18s. 4½d. payable at Michaelmas and Lady Day with *nomine pene* and remedies for the rents, which were distinctly mentioned in the grant. And all of the particular things granted amounted to the said fee farm rent according to the valuation there mentioned, but in truth they were in all of much greater value. In this manor there was a custom or tenure that the tenants of it, who were of a great number (because many lands in this part of the country were held of this manor by service of court and rents), owed to the courts of this manor to elect from themselves certain reeves, who should collect the rents within their culetts or districts for one year and pay them to the lord of the manor. This manor came to the defendant [John] Squibb, and the fee farm rent under conveyances to the trustees of King Charles II by virtue of the acts for the sale of fee farm rents, 22 & 23 Car. II,[1] came to the plaintiff. And inasmuch as the demesnes and places where the distresses could be taken were not sufficient nor afforded distresses sufficient to pay all of the fee farm rent, the plaintiff exhibited his bill in equity to subject the rents of assize and other profits granted by King Charles I and for or upon which where the persons [were] subject and liable to pay them, no distress could be taken to be subject to the payment of this fee farm rent, otherwise the purchaser of the fee farm rent would be remediless for the greater part of the rent, inasmuch as the desmesnes were not sufficient.

And the court decreed it accordingly, because in truth in judgment of law the fee farm rent issued out of all of the things granted both the rents and the demesnes, and the king can reserve rent out of another rent, and during the time that it was payable to the crown, the prerogative process could issue, but the plaintiff could not have any other remedy but by distress which could not be upon the rents, and otherwise and without those the whole rent could not be recovered. And the court decreed and subjected all of the rents in the hands of the lord of the manor but not in the tenants' or reeves' hands. And the tenants and reeves brought to the hearing were dismissed.

I [was] for the plaintiff.

But query as to the reeves and tenants, because it seems just that the rents should be subjected in whomever's hands they should come.

It seemed [to be] decreed by Chief Baron Hale in the case of the Town of Kettering in Northhamptonshire, where the demesne was not sufficient for the rent.

[Other copies of this report: GUL MS. B88–8, p. 49.]

---

[1] Stat. 22 & 23 Car. II, c. 24 (*SR*, V, 743–745).

241
Chamberlain v. Blagrove (Ex. 1687)

It is a contempt of court to disobey an injunction of which one has notice though it was not officially served.

LI MS. Misc. 557, f. 162, pl. 2 [Fr.] (Ward's Reports)

The plaintiff exhibited a bill to be relieved against a verdict in [an action of] debt for tithes and the same day had an order to have an injunction upon bringing the money into the court and to stay [execution] in the meantime. The defendant and his attorney had notice of the motion but [were] never served with it. And they got execution. And upon motion, an attachment and examination [was awarded], and it [was] adjudged contempt though [they were] never served with the order. See Rule 35.[4] But on payment of costs [the attachment was] discharged.

[Other copies of this report: GUL MS. B88–8, p. 51.]

242
Chitty v. Reeve (Ex. 1687)

In this case, the custom of paying tithes of hops in a certain parish by leaving them standing bound to poles was affirmed by the court. Otherwise, they were to be paid after having been harvested.

LI MS. Misc. 557, f. 164 [Fr.] (Ward's Reports)

The plaintiff was the lessee of Sir Thomas Vernon, who was the lessee of the impropriation of Farnham in Surrey, in which parish there were great quantities of hops growing each year. And it was proved in the cause that the custom was thus for the payment of the tithes of hops, that the parishioner leave the tenth row (if equal), otherwise the tenth pole, standing with the binds uncut for the tithes, and the party who had the right to the tithes in a convenient time come and cut the binds and pick the hops on the ground. And this usage was proved for more than sixty years. And inasmuch as the defendant refused to pay his tithes in such manner but left the tenth pole with the binds cut and the hop poles pulled down and the plaintiff refused to take the tithes in such manner, they being by this means spoiled upon the ground, the plaintiff exhibited his bill for relief, showing that the tithes should be paid according to this custom or in kind, *viz.*, the tenth part as gathered.

---

[4] Rule 35, *Ordines Cancellariae* (1698), p. 35.

And upon the hearing of the cause, the court approved the custom and usage of the payment of the tithes and decreed the defendant to pay the value of the tithes to the plaintiff. And the custom appeared more reasonable and necessary inasmuch as if the parishioners when they gathered their hops should cut the binds of the tithe hops by which they are thrown onto the ground, if they are not gathered within twenty-four hours afterwards, they lose their color and are spoiled, and it is impossible for the owner or lessee of the impropriation to have enough[1] persons to pick and gather the tithes at the same time that the others are gathered by the parishioners.

And the court held that, if the tithe hops were not paid according to this custom and usage, that the tenth part should be paid in kind after the gathering.

I [was] for the plaintiff.

See Rolle's [Abridgment], *Dismes*, 644, letter Y, 3; Godolphin 414; 1 Siderfin 283, 443.[2] And note that at the setting down [of] causes after Trinity term 1688, the deputy [king's] remembrancer's report was decreed with costs for the plaintiff against the defendant. And the court made the decree upon the custom so fully proved without a trial at law, although the custom inasmuch as hops being planted in England within memory, *scil.* the time of Henry VIII, the manner of payment is not capable of [being a matter of] custom, and on account of that as it seems to be paid in kind, *scil.* by measure after [being] picked. See Gee v. Perch, 17 November 1698 and 11 May 1704.[3]

[Other copies of this report: GUL MS. B88–8, p. 55.]

[Other reports of this case: 1 Rayner 67.]

[The decree of 2 June 1687, PRO E.126/15, f. 94, is printed at 1 Wood 251, 1 Eagle & Younge 552. See also orders of 9 June and 12 July 1687: PRO E.126/15, ff. 114v, 222.]

[This case is cited in Bate v. Spracking (1717), Bunbury 20, 145 E.R. 580, 1 Eagle & Younge 736; Bliss v. Chandler (1720), 1 Eagle & Younge 757, 758, 2 Wood 146, 148, 1 Rayner 152; Sneyd v. Unwin (1740), 2 Gwillim 774, 2 Eagle & Younge 84, 85, 2 Wood 403, 404; Knight v. Halsey (1797–1800), 7 Term Rep. 86, 89, 95, 101 E.R. 868, 870, 873, 2 Bos. & Pul. 172, 126 E.R. 1221, 8 Brown P.C. 233, 3 E.R. 554, 4 Gwillim 1531, 2 Eagle & Younge 438.]

---

[1] cy mults *MS*.

[2] *Barham v. Goose* (1617), 1 Rolle, Abr., *Dismes*, pl. Y, 3, p. 644; J. Godolphin, *Repertorium Canonicum* (1680), p. 414; *Ledgar v. Langly* (1666), 1 Siderfin 283, 82 E.R. 1107; *Crouch v. Risden* (1670), 1 Siderfin 443, 82 E.R. 1207, also, above, No. 48.

[3] *Perch v. Gee* (Ex. 1699), Samuel Dodd's Reports, p. 184, 1 Eagle & Younge 633, PRO E.126/17, f. 67v, 1 Wood 386, 2 Gwillim 563, 1 Rayner 87; *Gee v. Perch* (Ex. 1704), Samuel Dodd's Reports, p. 202, 1 Eagle & Younge 660, PRO E.126/18, f. 424v, 2 Gwillim 581, 1 Rayner 97.

243
Lucy v. Newton (Ex. 1687)

An executor must pay tithes due from the testator before paying legacies.

LI MS. Misc. 557, f. 165, pl. 1 [Fr.] (Ward's Reports)

[It was] resolved by the court that tithes incurred and become payable in the life of a testator should be preferred before legacies. And in this case it was more strong inasmuch as the bill was preferred in the lifetime of the testator. And the cause [was] at issue and revived against the defendant executors. And it was held clearly that the executors were liable to the payment of tithes as far as [there were] assets, as this suit is in this court by an English bill, because this suit is not grounded upon the Statute of 2 & 3 Edw. VI[1] for treble damages, which are not recoverable against executors as these causes are, but here in this suit only the duty is recoverable. And without question tithes not paid are a duty due from the testator and should be preferred before any voluntary legacy given by the testator though the duty is not reduced to a certainty in the life of the testator. Otherwise, upon this reason, breaches of trusts or covenants by the testator would be without a remedy, which without question are duties and are recoverable against executors as far as [there are] assets. And the constant practice in this court is to give relief upon English bills against executors for tithes, and this [was] before the Statute of Edw. VI. And the duty was recoverable though not [treble] damages against executors.

Also, in this case it was held that a promise by the testator in his life to one who had married his daughter to give him such a sum in consideration of the marriage without a note in writing according to the Statute against Frauds and Perjuries 29 Car. II [1677][2] did not bind the executrix but she was discharged of it, and if she paid [it], it should not be allowed against other duties demandable against the executors.

I [was] for the plaintiff.

[Other copies of this report: GUL MS. B88–8, p. 56.]

[Orders of 30 May and 6 June 1687: PRO E.126/15, ff. 93, 98v.]

---

[1] Stat. 2 & 3 Edw. VI, c. 13 (*SR*, IV, 55–58).
[2] Stat. 29 Car. II, c. 3 (*SR*, V, 839–842).

244
Acton v. Smith (Ex. 1687)

Mature trees cut down for use as firewood instead of lumber are tithable.

LI MS. Misc. 557, f. 165, pl. 2 [Fr.] (Ward's Reports)

The plaintiff as rector of Bentworth in the County of Southampton[1] exhibited his bill for tithes of underwoods. The defendant showed that the wood was timber, that is to say oak, ash, beech, and aspen of more than twenty years of age, some forty, and some a hundred years, and on account of that insisted to be discharged from payment of tithes being privileged as timber.

And in truth and upon the proof, it appeared that the trees were single trees and not stems and of twelve inches compass around four inches above the stem (which was no more than four inches of timber) and no more. But it was proved that the stems and the butt ends of all and also the bodies of divers of those trees were converted into cordwood for fire and thus used and that the bodies of others were used as poles for hopgrounds in other parishes. And [there was] no proof that any part of the trees was used and employed for timber.

And the court decreed them to pay tithes as firewood notwithstanding the age and quality inasmuch as the use and employment was as firewood and underwood and not as timber. And if any small part had been employed as timber (any of the cordwood being made into laths), yet the court declared that the employment of the greater part as underwood would subject all to the payment of tithes. And thus it was resolved in Franklin and Jones' Case[2] in this court, Hilary term 1685, (above f. 109) and afterwards in an Essex and Suffolk case notwithstanding the Statute of 45 Edw. III, c. 3, for *Sylva Caedua*,[3] and Liford's Case, 11 Rep.,[4] and 2 *Inst.* 642, 643,[5] and the authorities there that said that all timber trees beyond the age of twenty years should not pay tithes and if the bodies are exempt, the branches also are exempt.

I [was] for the plaintiff.

The report was confirmed Thursday 15 May 1690.[6]

[Other copies of this report: GUL MS. B88–8, p. 57.]

---

[1] V.C.H., *Hampshire*, IV (1911), p. 71.
[2] *Franklin v. Jones* (Ex. 1686), above, No. 216.
[3] Stat. 45 Edw. III, c. 3 (*SR*, I, 393).
[4] *Stamp v. Clinton* (1614), 11 Coke Rep. 46b, 77 E.R. 1206, also 1 Rolle Rep. 95, 81 E.R. 354, 1 Eagle & Younge 234.
[5] E. Coke, *Second Institute* (1642), pp. 642–643.
[6] PRO E.126/15, f. 315.

[Order of 16 June 1687: PRO E.126/15, f. 109v.]
[This case is cited in Buckle v. Vanacker (Ex. 1693), Samuel Dodd's Reports, p. 131, 1 Eagle & Younge 570; Abbot v. Hicks (Ex. 1696), below, No. 331; Greenway v. Earl of Kent (Ex. 1706), below, No. 407.]

245
Daniell v. Gore (Ex. 1687)

Lands formerly in the possession of the priory of St. John of Jerusalem are discharged of tithes.

LI MS. Misc. 557, f. 165, pl. 3 [Fr.] (Ward's Reports)

The only question was whether lands pertaining to the priory of St. John's of Jerusalem, which was dissolved by the Statute 32 Hen. VIII, c. 24,[1] and all of their possessions with all privileges given to the king and which by an order *quamdiu [in] propriis manibus*[2] were discharged before the dissolution, should be discharged of tithes in the hands of the owner of the inheritance, as is the defendant. And it was agreed to make a case of this.

I [was] for the defendant.

[It was argued] in favor of the discharge first that the word 'privileges' in the statute [and] order means privilege of discharge, secondly [it was supported by the following cases:] Dyer 277, Bridgman 32, Latch 89, Jones 182, Liber 2, f. 223.[3]

[The following cases were argued] against the discharge: 2 Croke 58, Moore 913.[4]

And note that afterwards, on 10 May 1688, the entire court was of the opinion that those lands *quamdiu in manibus propriis* are discharged of tithes for the reason of the authorities aforesaid. And the plaintiff's bill was dismissed but without costs inasmuch as the defendant himself had paid tithes divers years.

I [was] for the defendant.

[Other copies of this report: GUL MS. B88–8, p. 59, pl. 1.]

---

[1] Stat. 32 Hen. VIII, c. 24 (*SR*, III, 778–781).
[2] *Dum propriis manibus excoluntur*: while it is being worked by their own hands.
[3] *Stathome's Case* (1568), 3 Dyer 277b, 73 E.R. 621, 1 Gwillim 132, 1 Eagle & Younge 59; *Whitton v. Weston* (1628), J. Bridgman 32, 123 E.R. 1179, Latch 89, 82 E.R. 289, W. Jones 182, 82 E.R. 96, also 1 Eagle & Younge 340, 1 Gwillim 410, Godbolt 392, 78 E.R. 231, Benloe 168, 73 E.R. 1031; *Faucet v. Franklin* (1673), LI MS. Misc. 500, f. 223v, pl. 2, 1 Eagle & Younge 501, T. Raymond 225, 83 E.R. 117, 3 Keble 208, 217, 84 E.R. 679, 684.
[4] *Cornwallis v. Spurling* (1604), Cro. Jac. 57, 79 E.R. 48, *sub nom. Quarles v. Spurling*, Moore K.B. 913, 72 E.R. 993, 1 Eagle & Younge 157, 1 Gwillim 224.

[Order of 16 June 1687: PRO E.126/15, f. 106v.]

[This case is cited in Hanson v. Fielding (1725–1727), Bunbury 214, 145 E.R. 651, Gilbert Rep. 225, 226, 25 E.R. 156, 157, 2 Gwillim 663, 664, 1 Rayner 231, 234, 1 Eagle & Younge 812.]

246
Gallop v. Larder (Ex. 1687)

A tender of money due will discharge a debtor from further interest.

LI MS. Misc. 557, f. 166, pl. 3 [Fr.] (Ward's Reports)

The defendant being the mortgagee of the plaintiff's estate for £600 and in possession of it gave notice to the plaintiff to pay his money on a certain day or that he would sue in chancery to foreclose the equity of redemption. The plaintiff provided his money accordingly, and the defendant at this day refused to take it under the pretense that he did not have his attorney's bills and thus could not settle the account. But the plaintiff offered to leave in his hands or with others more than in reason those charges could amount to. And the court debarred the defendant from his interest for all the time after the tender.

I [was] for the plaintiff.

[Other copies of this report: GUL MS. B88-8, p. 61.]

[Order of 16 June 1687: PRO E.126/15, f. 96.]

247
Attorney General ex rel. White v. Lord Bulkely (Ex. 1687–1690)

The person who is to receive fines cannot determine the amount of the fines.

LI MS. Misc. 557, f. 167 [Fr.] (Ward's Reports)

In 12 Car. II [1660] the lord Bulkely was constituted chancellor and chamberlain of the three counties of Merioneth, Carnarvon, and Anglesey in North Wales. And in right of this office, he had the custody of the seal for original writs and claimed the rating and compounding for fines upon all originals for fines, recoveries etc. in those three counties by himself or his deputy. And his office and duty was described, and he [was] made accountable to the king for the profits of the seal (which in truth were only fines and 6d. for each original) according to the Statute 34 & 35 Hen. VIII, c. 26,[1] which in some words seemed

---

[1] Stat. 34 & 35 Hen. VIII, c. 26 (*SR*, III, 926–937).

to exclude him from having any other fees or profits except the £20 *per annum* there mentioned and granted to him in his patent. Afterwards [in] 13 Car. II [1661], the king demised the profits of the seal to the relator [White] for years rendering rent, by color of which the lessee claimed the rating of the fines or to be present at the rating and also to have an account and relief for the making of the writs which was not any part of the profits of the seal. And the defendants agreed to the account for the profits of the seal, that is to say the 6d. for each brief, but not more.

And upon the hearing of the cause, the court declared that it was an unreasonable and illegal thing for the relator to have the rating of the fines of which he himself is the farmer, because if [it were] so, he could assess what sum he pleased. Also the court declared that it was not reasonable for the relator or anyone for him to be authorized to be present at the rating of fines, because it was *quasi* to suspect the chamberlain or his deputy of that [of which there] was not any cause of complaint proved. And the court compared this case to the commissioners of the alienation office, who are indifferent between the king and the people and [who have] no supervisor or controller over them (though it was attempted but without success by one Brunshill five or six years ago under color that less fines than should be were paid).

And it was observed that fines in Wales are five times as great and high as in England, which is the occasion and reason that there are so few fines and recoveries there, in order to avoid the charge of which the course is to have deeds of vouchers, etc.

And as to the money received by the defendant's deputy for writing the writs and for the parchment and materials of them, it was clear that they did not belong to the relator. And there is a clerkship attendant upon the seal and *quasi* a *quantum meruit*. And before the making of the Statute 34 & 35 Hen. VIII, there was a chamberlain of North Wales, who at all times rated the fines, and the writs were written by his clerks, who received the fees now received by them. And they were not restrained by the said Statute, and it was clear that other judges, whose fees are[2] limited by the Statute at this day, received divers others otherwise their offices would have been mean.

And the defendant was decreed to account only for the 6d. for each writ without charge, and the defendant was put at liberty to rate the fines without the presence of the patentee or anyone for him, and the court would consider the instructions for the settling of the fines. And as for pens, ink, parchment, wax, drawing and engrossing writs, the defendant, the lord Bulkely, was to perform them and to have the benefit of it upon the sole payment of 6d. for the seal of each writ without other charge to the relator.

---

[2] son *MS*.

I [was] for the defendant.

And the allowance for the charge in rating the fines (for viewing lands etc.) [was] reserved to the court.

This case in some part [was] altered upon the hearing Monday, 30 June 1690. And the court disallowed the allowance for some of the charges in rating the fines with the consent of the lessee but held that there was reason for allowance, but without consent none could be made, though upon the hearing the decree was that the court upon the return of the report would consider what allowance to make, which implied that some allowance would be made but the amount reserved.

[Other copies of this report: GUL MS. B88–8, p. 62.]

[Order of 16 June 1687: PRO E.126/15, f. 121.]

248
Attorney General ex rel. Lloyd v. Clopton (Ex. 1687)

In this case, after a will had been made, the testator made an inter vivos *gift to a charity, which the court found to be complete and not an alteration to the will.*

The king can sue in a court of equity to have a charity settled without a commission of charitable uses.

LI MS. Misc. 557, f. 168, pl. 1 [Fr.] (Ward's Reports)

The bill or information was to have a charitable use limited by the said Dr. [Isaac] Barrow [formerly bishop of St. Asaph] to be executed. And the case appeared to be thus. Dr. Barrow who had done divers charitable things during the time that he was bishop of St. Asaph made his will in writing [in] December 1679 and died [on] 24 June 1680, of which will the defendants [Martha Clopton and Walter Clopton] were executors. And in it [there was] no mention of the thing in question, but it was proved that after his will [was made] and two or three weeks before his death, he declared his intention of erecting a free school at St. Asaph and endowing it with £10 *per annum* and to give £2 *per annum* for repairs of the almshouses erected by him in St. Asaph and that he called to him the defendant Martha, his sister, and made such a declaration and desired the defendants, his executors, to erect the said school house and to endow it with £10 *per annum* and to add £2 for repairs of the almshouses in perpetuity and to do it with the money due to him from Mr. Anderton of Chester, who owed him more upon security, and with this money to make the purchase.

And [there was] some proof that the defendant Martha agreed to it. And the declaration of the intent was proved by three, though not admitted by the defendants.

And three of the barons, that is to say Chief Baron ATKYNS, HEATH, and POWELL (JENNER dissenting) declared themselves satisfied with the charitable intention and held it to be a limitation and appointment within [the Statute of] 43 Eliz.[1] according to the case [in] Hobart 136,[2] because here the money, the work, and the place was appointed and it was a limitation and appointment in the lifetime of the testator and not an alteration of his will (which being within the Statute of Frauds and Perjuries of 29 Car. II [1677][3] could not be altered without a writing and witnesses). And it was an executed act, *scil.* a complete appointment in his life, and this appointment bound the executor.

And in this case it was held that the bill was proper in this court in the attorney general's name, though [there were] no proceedings before commissioners of charitable uses, because the king can sue in this court or [in] chancery to have a charity settled, and there is no necessity to proceed upon a commission of charitable uses.

And inasmuch as this cause was reheard (because more than a year past, dismission was pronounced), the court decreed the £200 without costs.

I [was] for the defendant.

[Other copies of this report: GUL MS. B88-8, p. 64.]
[Order of 13 June 1687: PRO E.126/15, f. 107.]

249

Luck v. Luck (Ex. 1687)

In this case, bonds by distributees of a decedent's estate to refund payments to the administrator were enforced.

LI MS. Misc. 557, f. 169, pl. 1 [Fr.] (Ward's Reports)

Thomas Luck died intestate without issue. Mary his wife took administration, and, being entitled to one moiety of the personal estate, she gave bond to the ordinary for the distribution of the other moiety but died intestate before any distribution was made. The plaintiff [John Luck] took administration to Mary only and made distribution to several relations of the whole blood to the first intestate in equal degree, but a sister of the half blood was not included within the distribution. And those who had distribution agreed to save the plaintiff

---

[1] Stat. 43 Eliz. I, c. 4 (*SR*, IV, 968–970).
[2] *Flood's Case* (1616), Hobart 136, 80 E.R. 285, or *Collison's Case* (1617), Hobart 136, 80 E.R. 286.
[3] Stat. 29 Car. II, c. 3 (*SR*, V, 839–842).

harmless against every other [person] entitled to the distribution. But the agreement, which was in writing under seal, was imperfect. The sister of the half blood sued in the prerogative court for her proportionable part with the other brothers and sisters of the whole blood and had a sentence against the plaintiff for it. And it was paid accordingly.

For the reimbursing of this, the plaintiff exhibited his bill against the defendants, who had the first distribution, to refund in proportion, which was decreed accordingly, notwithstanding that it was strongly urged by Serjeant *Levinz* for the defendants that the plaintiff, being administrator only to Mary the wife, administratrix, and not to the first intestate was not compellable to pay anything to the sister of the half blood nor could the prerogative court compel such a distribution or payment of anything to the sister of the half blood and that prohibition should have been prayed and the sentence was void, inasmuch as distribution could not be compelled to be made by anyone except the administrator of the first intestate, who the plaintiff was not.

But it was observed by myself that though the plaintiff was not administrator to the first intestate, yet he was to Mary, who had given a bond to make distribution, and the plaintiff was subject to this bond. And in truth he had justly distributed the first intestate's estate, and it should be too harsh that the plaintiff should be compelled by the sentence to make distribution to the sister of the half blood and not be refunded by the others, who had received the actual money that he had distributed to the sister of the half blood.

And the court held it a just and honest thing and compellable upon the bond and decreed accordingly.

I [was] for the plaintiff.

[Other copies of this report: GUL MS. B88–8, p. 67.]

[Order of 22 June 1687: PRO E.126/15, f. 113v.]

250

Attorney General v. Calvert (Ex. 1687)

In this case, the rights of various competing creditors of a common bankrupt debtor were determined by the court.

In this case, a creditor whose equity was prior to that of the crown was preferred over the crown.

LI MS. Misc. 558, f. 2 [Fr.] (Ward's Reports)

The case upon the hearing was thus. Dr. Barbon agreed with Porter for the purchase of the inheritance of Newport House and gardens [were] to be built and wanting money directed the conveyance to be made to Sir James Ward and

Adams, his trustee, Roger Jackson and Meutis [?] by moieties, Ward advancing £3500 and Jackson advancing another £3500. And one Smith, who was trustee for Thomas Price, the goldsmith, he also advanced £2500. And Ward and Jackson covenanted with Smith upon his payment to them of their £7000 to convey to Smith in fee. Price afterwards lent Barbon £500 more in the name of the same Smith, his trustee, upon security of the premises, and Smith covenanted with Barbon by another writing to reconvey to Barbon upon his payment of £7000 which Ward and Jackson and £3000 to Smith with interest, after which Price lent to Barbon £5000 more [. . .] no [?] security in Noel's name (so that Price had £8000 upon this security), after which Barbon borrowed £2000 more from Ward and for his security gave him a statute in the name of [. . .] in trust for him, after which Price lent to Barbon upon the same security £6500 more in the name of Noel in trust for him. After that, that is to say 2 May 1685, Price borrowed £8000 from Calvert, and he and his trustees assigned and conveyed all of their securities to Calvert to be void upon payment of £8000 and interest [on] 3 November 1685. Price after this date of payment became bankrupt and before any commission against him, that is to say 2 December 1685, was found [to be a] debtor to the king by inquisition upon a commission for this purpose out of the exchequer in [the sum of] £10,602 6s. 9d. for so much of the king's money received from one John Price, receiver general of Ireland.

And upon the hearing of the cause, the court decreed the first equity and redemption to Calvert and that he should redeem against Ward and Jackson and before the king and that Calvert should be let in for his £8000 and interest before the king though he had not any estate in [common] law but only in equity, and the king also had an equity but Calvert's equity being prior to the king's should be preferred, which note. And also [it was] decreed that Calvert should be also preferred before the statute to Ward, £8000 of Price's security being before this statute, and postponed the satisfaction of this statute to Calvert's £8000 though Ward had the estate in law in himself by virtue of the first conveyance but by this first conveyance Ward had covenanted upon payment of his £3500 and interest to convey to Price's trustee, Smith, and this covenant and Price's lending £8000 before the statute and Ward's agent's notice of Price's securities for £8000 before the statute though Ward did not know of them postponed this statute. But it was decreed that upon payment of all of the money before the statute, Ward should be let in upon the moiety of the premises upon his statute and should retain it until satisfaction and that after the £7000 and Calvert's £8000 and the charge of the statute upon Ward's moiety for £2000 with interest for all, the king should have all except £6500. The residue of Price's money lent to Barbon and charged upon the premises should be paid. And Barbon [was] foreclosed *nisi* he paid all to all persons by midsummer next.

I [was] for Calvert.

Note that afterwards upon a rehearing in July 1688 as to the statute of £2000 if it should be let in upon all or only upon Ward's moiety of the estate as decreed as above, the entire court decreed that the statute should be let in upon the entire estate before the king would be satisfied any part of this debt and this upon the reason that the statute affected the entire estate in its nature. And Baron ROTHERHAM, who at first doubted, declared that it was clear that the statute should affect the entire estate. And thus it was decreed.

[Other copies of this report: GUL MS. B88–8, p. 78.]

[Calvert v. Attorney General: orders of 7 Nov. 1687 and 4 July 1688: PRO E.126/15, ff. 140v, 222v.]

251

Grascomb v. Jeffreys (Ex. 1687–1688)

In this case, tithes for marshland were ordered to be paid in kind because the alleged modus *was void as too large.*

LI MS. Misc. 558, f. 3, pl. 2 [Fr.] (Ward's Reports)

The plaintiff demanded tithes in kind for marshland. The defendant alleged a *modus* or custom time of which etc.[1] to pay 12d. per acre for all marshland within the parish in lieu of all tithes. And proof was made of this payment for forty and fifty years, and a trial was prayed to be directed upon this *modus* or custom, and [there was] no proof of payment of any tithes in kind or other payment or satisfaction for tithes.

But the court denied the trial and declared the pretended *modus* or custom alleged to be void inasmuch as it was proved in the cause that the marshland was rented for 20s. *per annum* for each acre at this day, which by no means possible or reasonable intention can be a *modus* or custom time of which, because it is almost as great as the annual value of the land itself 400 or 500 years past. And for this reason the court decreed the defendant to account for the tithes in kind and overruled the *modus* alleged without a trial.

And in the same case, the court held that timber trees in hedgerows [are] lopped and usually paid tithes of lops, which tithes of lops are payable as the body of the timber.

I [was] for the plaintiff.

---

[1] 'Time of which the memory of man runneth not to the contrary' were the words used to assert a right based on prescription.

Note that the court usually overrules moduses which seem more great and which by some reasonable intent [?] were equal to the value of the tithes in kind 200 or 300 hundred years ago or more.

But note that this case was ordered to be reheard upon the defendant's motion, and upon the rehearing the *modus* was referred to a trial at law by a Middlesex jury in Hilary term 1687[/88]. Earl Tenham[1] and others [were] in court. But *non constat* that it was afterwards done.

[Other copies of this report: GUL MS. B88-8, p. 82.]

[This case is cited in Chapman v. Smith (1754), 2 Vesey Sen. 506, 515, 516, 28 E.R. 324, 329, 330, 3 Gwillim 847, 857, 858, 2 Rayner 469, 485, 487, 2 Eagle & Younge 141, 147; Pyke v. Dowling (1779), 2 W. Blackstone 1257, 1258, 96 E.R. 740, 741, 3 Gwillim 1166, 1167, 3 Rayner 942, 943, 2 Eagle & Younge 341; Twells v. Welby (1780), 3 Gwillim 1192, 1195, 3 Eagle & Younge 1286, 1290.]

252

Speccol v. Chapman (Ex. 1687–1688)

An interlocutory injunction will not be granted for not answering where it would go to the merits of the cause.

LI MS. Misc. 558, f. 4, pl. 1 [Fr.] (Ward's Reports)

The plaintiff, being the feefarmer of certain mills in Torrington in the County of Devon for multure at which there was a former decree in this court and also for abating handmills to the prejudice of this multure, brought an action on the case against the defendant Chapman for withdrawing and refusing to grind at his mills according to the custom and right. And he had a verdict and damages the last assizes.

And now he exhibited his bill for establishing his right and compelling the defendants to grind all the corn spent ground in their houses in Torrington at the plaintiff's mills there, for which he paid a fee farm rent, and to have the privilege of this court continued to him by the statutes of 22 & 23 Car. II[1] for the sale of fee farm rents notwithstanding the sale of the rent.

And now upon an attachment against Chapman and other defendants for not answering and upon a showing of the verdict, the plaintiff moved for an

---

[1] Christopher Roper, baron Teynham, who fled to France with James II in 1688: G.E.C., *Complete Peerage*, XII/1 (1953), p. 682.

---

[1] Stat. 22 & 23 Car. II, c. 24 (*SR*, V, 743–745); note also Stat. 22 Car. II, c. 6 (*SR*, V, 657–660).

injunction to restrain the defendant Chapman and the other defendants from grinding their corn at other mills until answer or further order.

But the court denied the motion not only against the other defendants but also against Chapman, against whom the verdict was, upon the reason that the grinding is the merits of the cause, which should not be prejudiced by contempt solely for not answering, because such contempt stays only actions at law and not the right or merits of the cause. And being moved again in Hilary term afterwards, the court at first made an order for such an injunction. But afterwards and when the answers were returned and the right denied, they denied any injunction.

I [was] for the plaintiffs.

But note that the decree in truth did not reach the matter now in question because the decree extended only to a horsemill then erected by a person under whom none of the defendants claimed. And the present defendants used handmills in their houses for grinding their malt.

[Other copies of this report: GUL MS. B88–8, p. 83.]

253

Hicks v. Littleton (Ex. 1687)

In this case, the defendants' plea of a fine and nonclaim was a good plea to the bill of discovery to discover assets subject to a recognizance.

LI MS. Misc. 558, f. 8, pl. 1 [Fr.] (Ward's Reports)

The plaintiff exhibited his bill showing that in 1641 the testator Sir William Hicks obtained a judgment in the office of pleas in this court for an £1800 debt against Sir Edward Littleton, the father and grandfather of the defendants, and that the conusor of the judgment was seised in fee at the time of the judgment of divers lands which the defendants had in possession in Staffordshire and other counties and pretended title to them, the certainties and values of which and the title to them, the plaintiff could not discover so that he could subject them to an extent upon the judgment without discovery from the defendants. And he surmised some feigned things to answer for the length of time and prayed discovery of which lands the conusor was seised in fee at the time of the judgment or afterwards.

The defendants[1] answered to part of the bill and showed that they did not claim title to the conusor's lands except those in the County of Stafford. And as to them, they pleaded that before the judgment, the conusor, being seised in

---

[1] plaintiffs *MS*.

fee upon the marriage of Sir Edward, the defendant, and in consideration of it, agreed to settle them in the said marriage, after which the plaintiff's testator sued execution on the judgment and had those lands delivered upon an *elegit* as a moiety of the lands of the conusor and that he was in possession and received the profits of them for several years after the marriage of Sir Edward, the defendant, and during his minority, after which the plaintiff's testator was evicted and ousted by the defendant, Sir Edward, who being in possession the defendant, Sir Edward, levied a fine with proclamations in 1658 or 1655. And afterwards, upon the marriage of the other defendant, Mr. Littleton, another fine with proclamations was levied by the defendants and the lands settled in marriage for a valuable portion, at the time of which fines and five years afterwards and more, the plaintiff's testator was living and no claim was made. And he pleaded these fines and non claims in bar.

And it was held by the entire court to be a good plea in bar. And the plaintiff's title [was] as administrator to the conusee of the judgment, who was a tenant by *elegit*, who was once in possession, and his title was bound by the fine and nonclaim.

I [was] for the defendants.

[Other copies of this report: GUL MS. B88–8, p. 95.]

254
Attorney General ex rel. Barnwell v. Baker (Ex. 1687)

Where a plaintiff admits the truth of a defendant's plea in bar to part of the prayer for relief, the case can proceed as to the rest.

LI MS. Misc. 558, f. 10, pl. 1 [Fr.] (Ward's Reports)

The case [was thus]. Sir Robert Sprignall and [his] son for valuable consideration granted a rent charge of £80 *per annum* for their lives to the defendant Baker and one Ewer (who is dead) by demise and redemise of lands of greater value, after which Sir Robert Sprignall became indebted to Barnwell, who was debtor to King Charles II by bond. And upon an extent upon it, [it] was found that Sir Robert Sprignall was indebted to Barnwell in £140. And upon an extent upon it, the lands of Sir Robert Sprignall, out of which the rent charge issued, were seized by inquisition. And upon it, process issued, and the defendant came in and pleaded his title by demise antecedent to the bond to the king and the seizure.

The attorney general for the benefit and in aid of Barnwell (because he was the relator though not named in the bill) exhibited a bill for discovery [of] the value of the lands and to have relief in equity for all to which the defendant did not have right, and it was in truth to the surplus of the value over the rent charge.

The defendant answered and showed all of the matter. And [it] was questionable upon the answer whether there was a surplus or not.

And the estate was also contingent, depending only on the life of the defendant Sir Robert Sprignall, pending which suit, the attorney general confessed the defendant's plea, and an *amoveas manus* was awarded, notwithstanding which, [there] were proceedings afterwards on the bill and answer.

And this day the cause [was] heard and referred to an accounting. And the court held that the confession of the plea did not hinder or prejudice the remedy in equity upon the attorney [general's] bill, it being a pure equity to have relief for the surplus upon an accounting.

I [was] for Barnwell.

[Other copies of this report: GUL MS. B88–8, p. 100.]

[Order of 14 Nov. 1687: PRO E.126/15, f. 142v.]

255
Earl of Chesterfield v. Lord Holles (Ex. 1687)

A life estate prevents the operation of a collateral warranty to be a bar against remaindermen in fee as heirs to their children and to tenants in tail.

LI MS. Misc. 558, f. 11, pl. 1 [Fr.] (Ward's Reports)

The case briefly was thus. The lord Wootton had four daughters and no son, and upon a settlement [in] 4 Car. I [1628], the lands in question were settled upon lord Wootton for life, remainder to trustees for a term of years for payment of debts, remainder to Lady Mary, wife of lord Wootton for her life, remainder to the heirs male of the body of lord Wootton, remainder to Margaret, one of the daughters, for her life (with the power to limit [it] to any husband for his life), remainder to the heirs of the body of Margaret, remainder to the right heirs of lord Wootton. This Margaret married Sir John Tufton (to whom she limited the estate for his life) and died without issue in the lifetime of Lady Mary, her mother. The plaintiff is the son and heir of another of the three daughters and thus coheir to lord Wootton.

The defendant claimed under a fine levied in 1651 with proclamation by Tufton and his wife. The defendant pleaded it and the collateral warranty by it in bar to the plaintiff's bill.

But the plea was overruled as a plain point in law, that this fine being levied by a tenant in tail in remainder in the lifetime of the life tenant who had an estate in being and in possession did not divest the remainder descended to the other three daughters nor hurt or bar it. But that life estate prevented the effect and operation of the collateral warranty to be a bar against the daughters in remainder in fee as heirs to their sons and to the said tenant in tail, who levied this fine.

I [was] for the plaintiff.
1 *Inst.* f. [*blank*].[1]

[Other copies of this report: GUL MS. B88–8, p. 102.]

256
Ormerod v. Wharton (Ex. 1687)

Where land is bought but the purchaser dies before paying the price, the price is to be paid by the executor if there be assets; where there are no assets, the price is to be paid by the heir or his guardian with reimbursement out of the income from the land.

HLS MS. 1052, f. 8, pl. 28 [Eng.] (Wright's Reports)

Philip Wharton, Esq., bought an estate of the plaintiff and died before he had paid all the purchase money, leaving Mary his sole daughter and heir, whom (being a tender infant) he appointed to the guardianship of Anne Byerly. And [he] left his personal estate to Angellica Magdalena Wharton, his widow, whom he made his sole executrix. The plaintiff exhibited his bill for the purchase money against both heir and executrix. And upon the hearing, the court was of opinion that the executrix should pay the money, she having assets and having received the rents, and not the infant heiress.

This cause was reheard on the 2nd of June following, and it then appearing that the widow had not assets, it was decreed that the guardians pay and the lands stand charged to reimburse them, with their costs.

[Order of 2 June 1687: PRO E.126/15, f. 109v.]

257
Masters v. Allen (Ex. 1687–1689)

In this case, it was held that the power of revocation in issue survived a later conveyance.

BL MS. Hargr. 71, f. 53v, pl. 2 [Fr.] (Dodd's Reports)

Dr. Masters's case in the exchequer upon an English bill [was] about Brome Whorewood's estate. The point was [that] Brome Whorewood had made a lease for ninety-nine years to commence after his death upon trusts with a power of revocation and to alter and change the trusts etc. And then he made a lease and release to J.S. to the use of himself for life, remainder to confirm the lease under and according to the powers and provisoes therein, remainders over. And then he revoked the lease for ninety-nine years. And whether he could was the point.

---

[1] E. Coke, *First Institute* (1628).

Holt and *Trinder* [argued] that he could because the lease and release was in confirmation of the lease for ninety-nine years and the intention appears that it will be confirmed with the powers and [one should] not construe the release [as] a destruction of the power against the intention of the parties.

Levinz and *Pollexfen* [argued] that the power was extinguished and destroyed and he could not confirm the power notwithstanding he confirmed the estate because the power was in privity with the estate, and when the estate was conveyed to the releasor,[1] the power to revoke was gone forever. A power of revocation cannot be annexed to an old estate, but it must be created at the same time, therefore it will not be construed [to be] a new power, and the intention of the party is against the law. If the lease for ninety-nine years be a lease at common law, then the power is void *ab initio* because a power cannot be annexed to common law conveyances. 1 *Inst.*[2] But if it is a lease upon the statute, then [it is] good [because] no powers of revocation existed at common law.

The court [ruled that] it was a lease upon the statute [with] 5s. consideration. But the court inclined that the power of revocation was gone by the subsequent conveyance notwithstanding the intention of the party, which was contrary to the law. [The court] adjourned.

It was argued [again] in Trinity [term] 1688, and the court inclined that it was a new power and referred by appearance[3] to the first lease. And afterwards, in Trinity [term] 1689, [it was] held that the revocation was good and that the release did not extinguish the power but confirmed it or at least created a new power, and a rule [was] given to dismiss the bill.

[Other copies of this report: HLS MS. 537(b), p. 15, pl. 2; Oxf. Brasenose MS. 59, p. 19, pl. 2.]

[Orders of 10 May 1687 and 10 June 1689: PRO E.126/15, ff. 80, 253v.]

258
Brookes v. Hart (Ex. 1688)

Tithes are due for a second crop of clover.

LI MS. Misc. 558, f. 17, pl. 1 [Fr.] (Ward's Reports)

Note [that] by the opinion of the court tithes should be paid of the second crop of clover as well as of the second crop of natural grass without custom or prescription to be discharged of the second crop by making the first into hay. And though clover had been sown for forty years and tithes of the second crop

---
[1] Sic in MS. for releasee.
[2] E. Coke, *First Institute* (1628).
[3] per semblens *MS.*

never demanded or paid, yet they are due of common right there not being anything proved to be in place of or in discharge of them, because in the parish they pay tithes of the first mowing of clover as well as of natural grass in grass cocks without making these into hay.

And the plaintiff had a decree but without costs. And in this case it was remembered that in Hall and Babb's Case[1] in this court, tithes of the second mowing of clover were decreed.

I [was] for the defendants.

[Other copies of this report: GUL MS. B88-8, p. 115, pl. 1.]

[This case is cited in Wallis v. Pain (1738), 2 Comyns 633, 635, 92 E.R. 1245, 2 Rayner 352, 354, 2 Gwillim 749, 751, 2 Eagle & Younge 67.]

259
Andrews v. Child (Ex. 1688)

A temporary heir who loses an inheritance by the birth of a posthumous child is entitled to profits between the death of the father and the birth of the child.

LI MS. Misc. 558, f. 18, pl. 2 [Fr.] (Ward's Reports)

The case upon the hearing was thus. Sir William Child had a lease made by a prebendary to him and his heirs for three other lives (in trust for William Andrews and his heirs) and died, the defendant Sir Laicon Child being his heir and a bailiff being appointed to receive the rents from the tenants, William Andrews died without issue born, but his wife [was] pregnant with a daughter, who was born eight months after his death. Before the birth of which daughter, John Andrews, the brother of William Andrews, was his heir. And the question was who should have the trust of the lease and the rents and profits incurred between the death of William Andrews and the birth of the daughter.

And it was held by the court clearly that John the brother who was heir for this time should have the profits incurred though in the bailiff's hands and not received by him and because[1] no action lies for them, because the court in this case held that the profits followed the trust. And the trust being for John before the birth of the daughter, he shall have the profits. And it was decreed accordingly. But the court held that by the birth of the daughter, the trust for John, the temporary heir as to the lease, was destroyed, *quod nota*.

---

[1] *Hall v. Babb* (1683), 1 Wood 220, 1 Eagle & Younge 541.

[1] per case [?] *MS*.

I [was] for John Andrews.
See Cro. Car. 87.²

[Other copies of this report: GUL MS. B88–8, p. 119.]

[Order of 22 Feb. 1688: PRO E.126/15, f. 163.]

260

Bathurst v. Lord Abergavenny (Ex. 1688)

Where holdover lessees who have paid rent and cut trees are evicted and the wood is converted by the lessor, the lessor must account for the value of the wood.

LI MS. Misc. 558, f. 23, pl. 1 [Fr.] (Ward's Reports)

The plaintiff Bathurst married a wife, the ancestor of whom was lessee of the ancestors of the defendants of a wood in Kent for twenty-one years ending in 1668 by a lease in writing, after which the ancestors of the plaintiff held the wood further paying the same rent of £8 *per annum* and at the end of ten years cut the wood in 1674, after which the plaintiff's wife and the plaintiff continued the payment of the same rent to the defendant's, the lord's, mother (the lord being an infant but now of age) as his guardian and for the benefit of the infant until 1684 when the wood was taken to be cut down. But before the cutting, the defendants discovered that the plaintiff did not have any lease, though he had paid the £8 *per annum* for ten years after the last cutting, and upon this the defendants entered and sold the wood for £120 and refused to make any recompense to the plaintiff for the said rent for ten years or for the wood. And on account of that the plaintiff exhibited his bill to be relieved.

And by the whole court, it was held a case full of equity. And the defendants were decreed to account with the plaintiff for the said wood and the value of it. And the final decree was the [*blank*] of July 1688,¹ by which the defendants were decreed to pay £96 for the value of the wood (allowing £4 for the rent for the half year before the cutting not paid by the plaintiff) with moderate costs.

I [was] for the plaintiffs.

[Other copies of this report: GUL MS. B88–8, p. 129.]

[Orders of 10 May and 12 July 1688: PRO E.126/15, ff. 181v, 219.]

---

² *Kirton's Case* (1627), Cro. Car. 87, 79 E.R. 676.

---

¹ PRO E.126/15, f. 219.

261
Attorney General v. Galliard (Ex. 1688)

A bill in equity for discovery and an account does not lie against a justice of the peace for actions taken in the performance of his official duties.

LI MS. Misc. 558, f. 23, pl. 2 [Fr.] (Ward's Reports)

The plaintiff by his English information showed that the defendant Galliard for so many years was a justice of the peace in Middlesex and Hertfordshire and had convicted divers persons for conventicles and levied great sums of money which were not employed and disposed of in such a manner as the Statute of 22 Car. II, c. [1][1] against conventicles directed nor [was] the third part, which belonged to the king, duly accounted for, but that by confederacy between the said defendant and the constables and officers of South Mimms, who were also defendants, they had converted a great part of this money to their own use. And in order to have discovery and account for this money for the fines and penalties for that which belonged to the king and to the poor persons was the scope of the bill. But in the bill there were some charges for outrageous distresses and levies and for not returning the surplus.

The defendant Galliard answered, pleaded, and demurred to this bill. And for his plea he showed the said Statute of 22 Car. II and the power and directions by it to the justices of the peace for levying, returning, and ordering of the money and the manner of the making of records and that no justice should be questioned or accountable for the part of the king in the exchequer or otherwise but in the quarter sessions and that this Act should be construed most beneficially for the justification and encouragement of those who put it into execution. And he averred that all of the records of the convictions before him were duly returned at the sessions and all of the money levied by any of his warrants which came to his hands [were] duly paid and distributed according to this Act (almost 50s. was paid to the counsel[2] by order of the justices of the peace for advice in putting this Act into execution) and that all of the money paid into the sessions was endorsed on the records. And thus he prayed judgment. And as for the matter contained in the bill which would subject himself to an action of trespass or other tort (as discovery of outrageous distresses and not returning the surplus), the defendant demurred in law.

And the plea and demurrer were both allowed upon debate by the entire court, and the bill was thought to be of a strange nature to call a justice of the peace to account for things done by him as justice who acted pursuant to a statute.

---

[1] Stat. 22 Car. II, c. 1 (*SR*, V, 648–651).
[2] Councill *MS*.

The attorney general and others [were] for the bill. I [was] for the defendant.

And note [that] the constable and officers pleaded and demurred in the same manner, and they were allowed.

[Other copies of this report: GUL MS. B88–8, p. 130.]

262

Atkyns v. Savage (Ex. 1688)

A grant of ingfangtheif does not pass title to the goods of felons.

LI MS. Misc. 558, f. 26, pl. 2 [Fr.] (Ward's Reports)

The plaintiff entitled himself as lord of the seven hundreds of Cirencester in the County of Gloucester to felons' and fugitives' goods within the vill or borough of Tetbury,[1] alleged to be within and part of the hundred of Longtree, one of the seven hundreds. And for his title he alleged a grant made [in] 1 Ric. I [1190] to the abbot and convent of Cirencester of *catallis furum*, and that on 2 May 14 Ric. II [1391] this grant was explained, and there the goods and chattels of felons and fugitives within those hundreds [were] granted by express words. And he alleged the enjoyment at all times until the dissolution of the monasteries. And he showed that the Abbey came to the crown [in] 31 Hen. VIII [1539] and the Statute of 32 Hen. VIII, c. 20,[2] which revived and continued the liberties. And also he showed that on 6 October 6 Edw. VI [1552], the king granted the same liberties, franchises, etc. which the abbot and convent had and enjoyed at the time of the dissolution to Sir Anthony Kingston, from whom they came to the family of Pooles and from them to the plaintiff.

The defendants by their answer denied Tetbury to be within the liberty and franchise of the hundred of Longtree which was one of the seven hundreds, though Tetbury could be within the locality of Longtree Hundred and also denied the right and usage as the plaintiff alleged. And for title to those same, they insisted that King Henry I gave the borough, market, town, and manor of Tetbury to William de Bryosa and the goods and chattels of felons by the name of ingfangtheif and that [in] 15 Edw. I [1287] it was allowed by a judgment in eyre and that the Statute of Quo Warranto 18 Edw. I[3] confirmed this judgment (see Rastall's *Entries* 540[4]) which Statute gave liberty to claim liberties by prescription which lay in grant (if usage was according). And he insisted upon the

---

[1] V.C.H., *Gloucestershire*, XI (1976), p. 265.
[2] Stat. 32 Hen. VIII, c. 20 (*SR*, III, 770–773).
[3] Stat. 18 Edw. I (*SR*, I, 107).
[4] W. Rastell, *Collection of Entries* (1670), 'Quo Warranto', pl. 2, f. 540.

usage and that in the time of Henry VII this borough, liberty, etc. came from the Breons to Maurice, lord Berkeley, and that 25 July 14 Jac. I [1616] those ancient terms of ingfangtheif etc. were explained and *bona et catalla felonum et waiviata* [was] granted in express terms within Tetbury and that [in] 8 Car. I [1632] the lord Berkeley conveyed the premises to Talboys and others in trust for the inhabitants of Tetbury for the maintenance of charitable uses etc., under which grant and title, the defendants claim. And in this grant the mainours and goods and chattels of felons were expressly contained. And the defendants showed which goods of felons they had received within the time of the bill and their value and how disposed and the charges of the prosecution of the felons.

And upon hearing of the cause, the plaintiff showed a record of 49 Edw. III [1375] in the lord treasurer's remembrancer's office in the exchequer from Gloucester which was an allowance upon a claim and in which a grant of Richard I to the abbot etc. of Cirencester of the seven hundreds and ingfangtheif and *catalla furum* were granted under £30 *per annum*, and a confirmation afterwards [in] 14 Ric. II [1390] which explained the former words and the grant of *bona et catalla felonum et fugitivorum*, and an exchequer account contained in a ledger book from the Abbey of 8 Hen. V [1420], and a record from the lord treasurer's remembrancer's office in the exchequer 10 Eliz. [1568], rotulo 155,[5] by which it appeared which goods and chattels of felons within the seven hundreds were claimed and allowed to the abbot etc., Coke's *Entries*, title 'prerogative', f. 439,[6] a confession of those, and a fine levied in 8 Hilary [term] 23 Eliz. [1581] in which felons' goods within the hundred of Tetbury were contained, and thus in a fine from Poole [in] 13 Jac. I [1615] and in an inquisition *post mortem* Poole.

The defendants insisted upon their title and usage to take such goods, of which they proved instances, and [there was] no proof of the deed for the plaintiff. And also they insisted that the word ingfangtheif in the old grants was explained by usage [and] could well pass felons' goods (to which the court agreed, if the constant usage had been thus and no right appeared to the contrary).

But the plaintiff's counsel insisted that the word ingfangtheif will not pass *catalla felonum ex vi termini*, and if not thus, the usage could not gain right without words against the crown. And for authorities that this word ingfangtheif will not pass these goods, these books were cited: 2 *Inst.* 31, at the bottom; Lambarde, *De Priscis Anglorum Legibus*, f. 144; Fitzherbert, Abridgment, title *Prescription*, sect. 27; [YB] 2 Ric. III, 10; Keilwey 139b;[7] the words 'Ingfangtheif' in Spelman and

---

[5] PRO E.368/372, rot. 155.

[6] E. Coke, *Book of Entries* (1614), f. 439.

[7] E. Coke, *Second Institute* (1642), p. 31; W. Lambarde, *Archaionomia* (1644), f. 144; YB Trin. 46 Edw. III, f. 16, pl. 10 (1372), Fitzherbert, Abr., *Prescription*, pl. 27 ; YB Mich. 2 Ric. III, ff. 9, 10, pl. 22 (1484); Pl. 8, Keilwey 139, 72 E.R. 311 (temp. Edw. III).

Terms del Ley; and *Fleta* 47,[8] all which proved that the word ingfangtheif does not go to the title of felons' goods but only to the jurisdiction to judge felons.

And the defendants insisted upon their constant usage and right and that Tetbury is not within the liberty of the seven hundreds and prayed that their title should be determined at law (the king not being concerned in interest). But the court took time to advise.

And afterwards in the same term, it was decreed for the plaintiff to have an account and satisfaction for the felons' goods confessed by them to be received, having allowances for the charges of prosecution and other charges expended by the defendants, but without costs, the defendants having probable cause for a defense.

I [was] for the defendants; the attorney general and others [were] for the plaintiff.

[Other copies of this report: GUL MS. B88-8, p. 140.]

[Order of 21 May 1688: PRO E.126/15, f. 182.]

263
Cave's Case (Ex. 1688)

In this case, the defendants were misjoined as their alleged debts to the plaintiff were purely several and they did not constitute a class.

LI MS. Misc. 558, f. 27 [Fr.] (Ward's Reports)

The plaintiff exhibited an English bill against the defendants being ten or twelve attorneys in the County of Essex who practiced in the county court as attorneys when the plaintiff was sheriff. And the scope of the bill was to discover [with] what appearances and actions they were severally concerned and employed in this court during his shrievalty and what fees were due to him for them from the defendants severally and to be relieved for those against the defendants, showing only for equity that the county court books in which the particulars of the said business were inserted were delivered over to the succeeding sheriff (as in right they must) and on account of that the plaintiff could not have or inspect them.

And in this bill nothing was charged jointly except the combination, which the defendants denied by their joint answer. And they jointly and severally demurred to the residue of the bill showing for cause that it appeared by the plaintiff's bill that

---

[8] H. Spelman, *Glossarium Archaiologicum* (1687), f. 313; J. Rastell, *Les Termes de la Ley*, s.v. 'Ingfangthefe'; H. G. Richardson and G. O. Sayles, edd., *Fleta*, book 1, ch. 45, 72 Selden Soc. 101 (1955).

the demands that the plaintiff had against each defendant was of a several nature and [was a] distinct cause of suit and that one was not concerned for the other and on account of that the plaintiff should not join them in one bill but sue them severally. It is not the same as the case of tithes or executors, etc. where the foundation as a will, etc. is one. But this case does not differ from that where one creditor should join all of his debtors in one bill where the debts and securities for them are separate and of several natures. Also it was shown that the plaintiff's remedy was properly at [common] law for fees, [it] being his fault if he wished to permit them to practice in his court without payment of their fees. And of this opinion was the entire court except for Heath, who seemed at one day to differ. But the demurrer was held good.

I [was] for the defendants.

[Other copies of this report: GUL MS. B88-8, p. 143.]

264

Attorney General ex rel. Sowerby v. Whittaker (Ex. 1688)

A court of equity will enjoin an action at law to recover money paid pursuant to a contract that settled a dispute over duties owed.

LI MS. Misc. 558, f. 28, pl. 1 [Fr.] (Ward's Reports)

The plaintiffs showed that aulnage is due to the king for clothes and that the defendant had not paid his due aulnage but by contrivance with others had procured seals of lesser value than he should to be affixed to his clothes (being a Lancaster clothier). And therefore the relators being officers of the aulnage have stayed the clothes. And the defendant made composition with them and gave to them £30 by way of composition, upon which they discharged the clothes. But inasmuch as the defendant had brought his action against the relators for the £30 as moneys received to the defendant's use, they prayed relief by their bill, to which the defendant by his answer showed that he had paid the full subsidy and duty to the proper officer, who sealed the clothes, and that all was done *bona fide* and without fraud. And he justified his action for the £30.

And upon the hearing of the cause, the court decreed a perpetual injunction against the defendant's action upon the payment of the £30 without costs; *quod nota*. And query the reason because the defendant had not transgressed in any manner.

I [was] for the defendant.

[Other copies of this report: GUL MS. B88-8, p. 144.]

265
Attorney General ex rel. Duppa v. Dean of Winchester (Ex. 1688)

A bill in equity lies to recover customary fees due to servants of the king.
In this case, the evidence was unclear as to whether the fees sued for were due.

LI MS. Misc. 558, f. 28, pl. 2 [Fr.] (Ward's Reports)

The plaintiffs show that time of which etc.[1] there were certain fees called homage fees due to the servants of the kings and queens of England who were in the capacities of the relators amounting in all to £36 6s. 8d. due to be paid by each county, city, vill corporate, cathedral or collegiate church in England when any king or queen of England makes his first entrance into such county, city, vill corporate, cathedral or collegiate church in England the first time after his accession to the crown and that those fees were due to those servants either in their own right or to the king and by his grant and order to the relators. And thus [they] show that [at] such a time the present king after his accession to the crown first came into the cathedral church of Winchester by which £36 6s. 8d. became due *ut supra*. And on account of that, the attorney general and relators pray relief.

The defendants deny the right of the relators or the king and any payment in any time by them or their predecessors.

The relators produced some old papers and rolls by which [it] appeared that such dividend fees among some of the officers had been [paid] in several reigns and some in the time of Charles I and Charles II. But it seemed that the old remedy was by warrant from the lord chamberlain to take into custody the sheriffs or heads of the corporations that refused to pay. And some proof was made of actual payments by some corporations but only by one dean and chapter, and [there was] none of payment by the defendants or their predecessors.

And the court taking this to be a case of concern and consequence took time to consult together but were of opinion that the way of remedy by English bill was proper and the bill here [was] good. But the sole cause of the doubt was whether there was competent proof whether such fees are due of right or have been paid by way of gift and not as droitural fees.

I [was] for the plaintiffs, but no order or decree [was] made.

[Other copies of this report: GUL MS. B88–8, p. 145.]

---

[1] 'Time of which the memory of man runneth not to the contrary' were the words used to assert a right based on prescription.

266
Mullington v. Hacker (Ex. 1688)

In this case, an alleged custom of pro rata tithes for wool was held to be invalid as a matter of law.

LI MS. Misc. 558, f. 29 [Fr.] (Ward's Reports)

In a bill for tithes of wool (among other things), the defendant insisted that his sheep had been pastured within the parish only seven months before the shearing and admitted the shearing within the parish but insisted upon a custom within the parish that in such a case the seventh part of the tithes of the wool only was due to the plaintiff, the lessee of the tithes. And so if the sheep had been pastured in the parish a greater or less number of months, the payment should be of this quantity of the tithes of wool that should be equal to the months pastured, though they are shorn in the parish. And if they are pastured only one month though sheared there, then no tithes are due.

And there was proof of such a usage and reputation of such a custom. But the court rejected this custom as unreasonable and refused a trial upon it, inasmuch as seven months pasturing and shearing within the parish well entitled the plaintiff to the full tithes without showing and proving that tithes had been paid in another parish for the residue of the year, which were not in this case. And the court held that a custom to be discharged of payment of tithes for wool of sheep pastured one month and shorn there without any satisfaction or showing [of] payment or satisfaction in another place is void. And the plaintiff had a decree without trial with costs.

I [was] for the plaintiff.

[Other copies of this report: GUL MS. B88–8, p. 147.]
[Order of 14 July 1688: PRO E.126/15, f. 213.]

267
Attorney General ex rel. Churchwardens of Warnham v. Michell (Ex. 1688)

In this case, title to a certain parcel of land was found to be in the relators contrary to the award of an arbitrator in a pending common law action.

LI MS. Misc. 558, f. 32, pl. 2 [Fr.] (Ward's Reports)

The case appeared to be thus, in Warnham [Sussex] there was a small parcel of land called the Lake Garden, which time of which etc.[1] had been settled and used as a charity for the poor persons of this parish. And about eighty years ago an exchange had been made of this parcel with Sir John Caryll for another parcel of land, part of a messuage and land called Stylers, upon which last parcel four almshouses were erected and constantly repaired at the charges of the parish, and the poor persons [were] placed in them by the parish. And the Lake Garden [was] constantly enjoyed by Caryll and his heirs. And the defendant Michell and Sarah his wife in right of Sarah, daughter and heir of one Raply, who claimed under Sir John Caryll by feoffment made [in] 6 Jac. I [1608], claiming the almshouses and the land upon which they were erected, brought ejectment for them. And at the trial a reference was made by consent to one Machell, being justice of the peace, who upon the hearing of the parties awarded that the almshouses belonged to the defendants and that the relators should deliver the possession of them to the defendants. And the rule for the reference being made a rule of the common pleas where the ejectment was brought and attachment awarded for non delivery of the possession, this bill was exhibited to stay the proceedings and for settling the charity with the parish, the king being *pater patriae* and the relators who consented to the reference only trustees for the parish.

The defendants insisted upon their title at law, claiming and enjoying also the Lake Garden and insisting upon the reference, award, and proceedings. But inasmuch as it fully appeared by the ancient books of the parish and the testimony of the witnesses that the almshouses were erected, repaired, and maintained at the charges of the parish, and [that] the poor persons [were] placed in them constantly by the parish, and that one Raply, under whom the defendants claimed, many years ago being a churchwarden in his accounts to the parish charged the repairs of those almshouses to the parish and claimed amends for trespass in default of repairs of some fences of those almshouses, the court set aside this award and proceedings and decreed the possession and enjoyment with the parish and a perpetual injunction against the suit pending and all others to be brought for the title of the said almshouses by the defendants or any claiming under them.

I [was] for the plaintiffs.

[Other copies of this report: GUL MS. B88–8, p. 151.]

---

[1] 'Time of which the memory of man runneth not to the contrary' were the words used to assert a right based on prescription.

268

Hornely v. Blaythorne (Ex. 1688–1690)

In this case, an arbitral award was ultimately upheld by the equity court.

LI MS. Misc. 558, f. 33 [Fr.] (Ward's Reports)

The defendant being indebted to the plaintiffs, who were brewers, for £58 for beer and ale, the plaintiffs demanded the money or a bond for it. The defendant agreed to give a bond for payment in three months, but the plaintiffs or their attorney prepared a bond with an unusual condition, containing a power of attorney in it for entry of judgment and taking of execution if the money was not paid at the first demand. Afterwards the defendant, being illiterate and in truth the bond and condition not being fully nor truly read to him, sealed it. And this bond was sealed in December but dated in September before, and four days after the sealing, judgment was entered as of Michaelmas term and execution was taken and executed upon the defendant's goods. And upon complaint in the king's bench, the judgment was set aside and attachment was awarded against the plaintiffs and their attorneys for their miscarriage. And the defendant brought his action against the plaintiffs and the officers and others employed in the matter, because by this execution he sustained great damage in his estate and his wife was injured by an assault etc. in the execution and being greatly pregnant miscarried with a dead child.

The plaintiffs here desired the defendant to refer all of the matters between them and the parties concerned in the execution to arbitration. And two arbitrators were elected, and if they could not finish the matter, then it would be referred to the umpirage of Sir Peter Daniel. The arbitrators upon the hearing of the matter could not agree but attended upon the umpire and gave him full information of the matter. And the umpire was also attended by the plaintiffs' agent and someone for the defendant. And he examined all of the matters and awarded the plaintiffs to pay to the defendant £110 on a certain day and that upon payment mutual releases should be given [for matters] up to the submission of all matters between them, which money not being paid, the defendant here sued on the bond of £200 for performance of the award and obtained judgment, which was also affirmed in a writ of error. But in a short time before this affirmance, the plaintiffs here exhibited their bill to have this award set aside as unreasonable, suggesting that the umpire did not hear the plaintiffs nor their witnesses. And upon bringing in the £110 into court, they obtained an injunction until the hearing of the cause.

The defendant pleaded all of the matter of the submission and award and by answer denied the suggestions of the bill and averred all things to be duly observed by the defendant and denied the fraud and practice and showed the truth of the fact and that he was damaged more than was awarded. And the plea was upon argument allowed. The plaintiffs replied generally.

And upon the hearing of the cause [in] the last term before the chief baron [ATKYNS] and Baron JENNER and Baron HEATH, the two barons against the opinion of the chief baron decreed the award to be set aside.

And upon a rehearing of the cause this day, two barons and Baron POWELL affirmed the decree against the opinion of the chief baron [ATKYNS] and the chancellor of the exchequer [BOOTH], who was present in court. The sole ground for the setting aside of the award was that *non constat* to them, though the defendant here could deserve or was damaged as much as was awarded, that is to say £110 and the debt of £53 due to the plaintiffs from the defendant which was also awarded to be discharged. But on the defendant's part, it was urged to be a new and dangerous case to set aside awards made by judges of the party's own choosing who have examined the entire matter under pretense that the full damage was not proved in this case, the defendant relying upon his plea which was allowed and no fraud or practice [being] proved in the case but all was denied by the umpire in his answer (who also was made a party and brought to the hearing). And he said that he believed in his conscience and it thus appeared to him from the examination of the matter and [it was] admitted by the arbitrator elected by the plaintiffs (who also believed it upon his examination) that the defendant was damaged more than was awarded. Also it was insisted by the defendant that the original cause was knavery in obtaining the judgment and all of the proceedings were illegal. And goods of the defendant to the value of £50 or more [were] taken in execution and enjoyed by the plaintiffs without account or recompense. Yet though no fraud, practice, or indirect matter was proved against the umpire or his award, those three barons decreed the award to be set aside and left all the parties to their respective remedies. And notwithstanding this, they ordered that the plaintiffs should pay all of the costs at law and in equity of the defendant concerning this matter out of the money in court and also that the umpire should have his costs out of the said money.

I [was] for the defendant.

Query the reasonableness and consistency of this decree: first to set aside this award for such reasons; second to award costs to the defendant.

Note afterwards in Hilary term 1689[/90] this case was reheard, and the proceedings in it were decried as against all manner of justice, and the plea was held a good bar and the recognizance given by the defendant upon receiving the money out of the court [was] discharged.

[Other copies of this report: GUL MS. B88–8, p. 152.]

269
Attorney General v. Gaynor Jones (Ex. 1688–1690)

A charitable trust for an illegal purpose will be redirected by the crown to a lawful purpose.

I
LI MS. Misc. 558, f. 34 [Fr.] (Ward's Reports)

An English information was exhibited by the attorney general for the king against the defendant showing that one Robert Charnock of Leyland Hall in the County of Lancaster, a priest of the Romish church, intending to settle his lands for such uses or trusts which by the statutes of the realm were declared to be superstitious and illegal by reason of which they would become forfeited to the king, had made divers conveyances of Leyland Hall and Starkey's tenement to the defendant for the uses and upon the trusts aforesaid, by which they became forfeited to the king. But to color the pretenses, the defendant pretended herself [to be a] purchaser for valuable consideration and under pretense of this possessed herself of all of the conveyances and writings, to discover which and the defendant's title and the consideration paid and to be relieved was the information.

The defendants by answer insisted that Charnock was seised in fee of the premises and in 1660 for £500 paid to him by one Grace Bold conveyed Leyland Hall to the said Grace Bold and her heirs to the use or in trust (in effect) for the said Charnock during the joint lives of him and another and afterwards to the use of Bold in fee with the usual covenants in conveyances for freedom from incumbrances, quiet enjoyment, and further assurance. And as to Starkey's tenement, they insisted upon an absolute purchase of it by Bold for £220 paid to Charnock and showed that Charnock died and that after this Grace Bold by will and deed conveyed the premises to the use of the defendant Gaynor Jones for her life and afterwards to other trustees defendants for raising portions for her daughters with other remainders to others. And they insisted upon the conveyances and title and denied [any] fraud or forfeiture by any law.

Upon the hearing of this cause, the court directed a trial upon this issue: whether the lands in question or any part of them were conveyed to the use of Grace Bold in trust and upon what trust.

And the jury at the Lancaster Assizes, as to Leyland Hall, found it to have been conveyed to Grace Bold in trust for the supportation and maintenance of priests of the Romish religion, *viz.* in trust for the supportation and maintenance of the secular priests of the Romish religion in Lancashire. And as to Starkey's tenement, they found it to have been an absolute purchase by Grace Bold.

Upon the return of this verdict, the attorney general and others for him prayed a decree and conveyance for Leyland Hall as forfeited to the king, being conveyed to superstitious and illegal uses. And for authorities, they relied on the statutes of 15 Ric. II, c. 5,[1] [and] 1 Edw. VI, c. 14,[2] and the case of Colonel Gerard of Ince in this court in the time of Chief Baron Hale (but no order or decree of this case was produced, nor [was it] well remembered what it was), and the cases seven or eight years ago in this court between the attorney general and lord Carrington and others touching Sir Thomas Preston's estate (q.v. Liber J, f. 61),[3] and the case between the attorney general and Eyres, a Darbyshire case, which cases (as it was insisted) were the same as this in question.

And the court adjudged and decreed the lands conveyed for such trusts to be conveyed to the king as forfeited for superstitious uses.

The defendants insisted that there was not any forfeiture of the land itself to the king neither by the common law nor by any statute. It cannot be by the common law because those uses were legal and it was the religion at common law. And the Statute of Ric. II made the land conveyed contrary to it to be mortmain in which case the king or lord had it, but that is not this case. And the Statute of Edw. VI did not extend to any lands limited to superstitious uses after this Statute but only before it. (Though Ingleby, a serjeant and of the Romish religion, argued that it was a forfeiture within this Statute, which by construction should be interpreted to look forward as well as backward notwithstanding there were not exact[4] words for it. And thus is the construction upon the Statute of 34 Hen. VIII, c. 20,[5] touching grants in the gift of the crown where [there were] no words [of] prospect, but the construction is so. And he cited the reason of the case [in] Hobart 157 in Colt and Glover's Case, and 10 Rep. 55, and 1 *Inst.* 173.[6])

And the counsel for the defendant insisted that the most that can be made of the trust or use in the conveyance is to make it void, as [in] the case of Croft and Evetts, 4 Jac. I [1606], Moore 784,[7] (which see and it is in point) it was resolved. And in this case, the superstitious use or trust was declared void and the benefit and estate decreed to the heir at law, and it could not be so done, if the land was forfeited to the king, because though the king was not a party, yet the court should *ex officio* take notice of the title of the king arising in a case between subjects. And it was a great authority for the defendant that the land did not belong to the king but the use [was] void, which gave no title at law.

---

[1] Stat. 15 Ric. II, c. 5 (*SR*, II, 79–80).
[2] Stat. 1 Edw. VI, c. 14 (*SR*, IV, 24–33).
[3] *Attorney General v. Lord Carrington* (Ex. 1682), above, No. 143.
[4] proper *MS*.
[5] Stat. 34 Hen. VIII, c. 20 (*SR*, III, 919, 920).
[6] *Colt and Glover v. Bishop of Coventry and Litchfield*, 'The Case of Commendams' (1616), Hobart 140, 80 E.R. 290; *The Case of the Chancellor of Oxford* (1613), 10 Coke Rep. 53, 77 E.R. 1006; E. Coke, *First Institute* (1628).
[7] *Croft v. Evett*, Moore K.B. 784, 72 E.R. 904, also 117 Selden Soc. 342.

And this case was[8] argued divers days in which the attorney general for the king admitted the king's title not to be by any statute (which *Sawyer* for the plaintiff did not admit) but as an unlawful use. And at first the court seemed to be of opinion for the defendant. But afterwards without any overt argument or reasons given, they made a decree for the king that the defendants should convey the land and account for the profits incurred.

Query the reason for it otherwise than upon the aforesaid precedents, and they [were] without precedent.

I [was] for the defendant. See Liber J, f. 61.

Note that afterwards, *scil.* Trinity term, 21 June 1690, upon a demurrer to a bill of review, the court altered the decree and made it to be to such charitable use as the king should direct and refused to reverse the decree and rehear the cause upon the merits but altered it as above. (Query this because it seems that the decree should be either reversed or affirmed and [there should be] no alteration without a rehearing.)

And afterwards upon an appeal in Parliament [in] 1690, this decree thus altered was affirmed[9] (without regard to the aforesaid distinction, which note), and [it was] upon the reason that the king was entitled by [his] prerogative to such a thing that is among *nullius in bonis* etc.

It seems that if the king had such a title, yet there should be an office upon a commission under the great seal found and returned, by which the title of the king could appear, as well as in a case of alienation in mortmain or *contra formam collationis* as [in] Page's Case, 5 Rep. 52b.[10]

I query whether the king being the supreme head of the English church and in ecclesiastical matters and as the popish religion was abolished and the protestant religion established, by which all uses and trusts for the maintenance of the popish religion were become superstitious and illegal, that the king should have the power to convert those superstitious uses into legal uses and by what means he could make them effectual if he should not have the land and interest in it for this purpose and as necessary [for the] conveyance of it and by what means he should have this interest if not by conveyance or office and if by making the superstitious uses void, the same land lasting the continuance of the time for which such uses were limited [. . .] became [. . .][11] the reason of *nullius in bonis* and belonged to the king or by the equity of the Statute of Edw. VI.

[Other copies of this report: GUL MS. B88–8, p. 156.]

---

[8] esteant *MS*.
[9] *Lords' Journal*, XIV (n.d.), p. 560.
[10] *Attorney General v. Page* (1587), 5 Coke Rep. 52, 77 E.R. 133.
[11] ne devene enter: GUL MS. B88–8, pp. 156, 160.

II
BL MS. Hargr. 71, f. 67 [Fr.] (Dodd's Reports)

[It was] resolved upon a bill brought by the attorney general against the defendants that [if] land [be] conveyed to the use of popish priests or in trust for them etc., the use or trust is forfeited to the king and that this is a superstitious use and is unlawful and is forfeited by the common law or by statute. But this forfeiture is not to the personal use of the king[12] nor as an inheritance of the crown but [is] for the king to dispose of to a lawful and good use. There is no law that gives a mistaken charity to the king, but there is a law for the chancery or a court of equity to direct a mistaken charity aright.

But it seems [that] this is by the direction of the king, and thus [it was] decreed in the time of James II. And upon a bill of review brought by Gayner Jones and a demurrer to it, it was resolved again as above this term. See Croft's and Evett's Case, Moore *Reports*, that in such a case, the use will be void and the heir at law will have the benefit of it. But it seems [that] the law is against [this].

Note: [In] Michaelmas [term] 1690, Gayner Jones and Cross brought an appeal in the House of Lords, and upon argument, the decree was confirmed, and the appeal was dismissed.[13]

The fact was that the court of exchequer directed an issue, whether Leyland Hall was conveyed to Grace Bold upon any trust and [if so] what trust, and the jury found that it was conveyed in trust for the support and maintenance of the priests of the Romish religion, *viz.* in trust for the support of the priests of the secular clergy of the Romish religion in the County of Lancaster.

[Other copies of this report: HLS MS. 537(b), p. 22, pl. 1; Oxf. Brasenose MS. 59, p. 30, pl. 2; IU Lilly MS. Parker, 'Cases in the Exchequer, vol. 1', p. 217; IU Lilly MS. Parker, 'Tithes', p. 178; BL MS. Hargr. 70, p. 96, pl. 317; HLS MS. 1162, p. 86, pl. 463; IU Lilly MS. Parker, 'Tithes', p. 61.]

III
MT MS. of Baron Heath, F.3, f. 79v [Eng.]

An English bill for the king set forth that Robert Charnock by lease and release conveys Leland Hall etc. in the County of Lancaster to Grace Bold and her heirs and alleges it was for a superstitious [use] whereby it is forfeited to the king. [The] defendants answer and deny [it]. A trial at law [was] directed, whether [there was] a trust or no trust and [if] a trust to what trust. And the jury found the conveyance to be in trust for the maintenance of the Romish priests in Lancashire.

---

[12] al oeps demesne al roy *MS*.
[13] *Lords' Journal*, XIV (n.d.), p. 560.

And after several arguments, Lord Chief Baron ATKYNS, Baron JENNER, Baron HEATH, and Baron POWELL were of opinion that the title belonged to the king, that the use was a superstitious use and void by the law and statutes of the kingdom, that it was not given to the king by the Statute of Mortmain or of Edw. VI, because that related to superstitious uses before that statute, that the design was a charity but a mistaken charity and so the king as supreme almoner shall direct the charity. In Moore 784, 785, Croft and Evett's [case], there they decreed for the heir at law who was plaintiff in the bill, but in this case no heir is a party. In Baxter's Case[14] money given to the use of Presbyterian ministers [was] adjudged for the king as forfeit. Chelsea College was appointed to maintain nonconformist ministers, [and] the king disposed of it. In [the] case [of] good[s] given to an unlawful use, [they are] *nullius in bonis, ergo* in the king. At the time of 15 Ric. II, c. 5,[15] it was not mortmain at the time of that statute to maintain Romish priests, that was not then unlawful; the unlawfulness is made upon the change of religion, which came since. Adams and Lambert's Case, 4 Rep.,[16] upon the Statute of Edw. VI[17] that only looks back and shall not against the words be construed to have a prospect, though a superstitious and void use, it shall not be taken by equity, as my brother Ingleby said.

According to *Maynard*, the heir at law cannot claim it against the father's feoffment, the trustee [shall] not have it, suppose no heir at law, the king shall have it by escheat. Here no heir at law appears; the court shall lay hold of it for the king.

[Orders of 26 Jan. and 21 June 1688: PRO E.126/15, ff. 169, 207.]

[This case is cited in Attorney General *ex rel.* Boucher v. Portington (Ex. 1694), below, No. 291; Attorney General v. Guise (1692), 2 Vernon 266, 23 E.R. 772; Anonymous (1702), 2 Freeman 261, 22 E.R. 1197; Attorney General v. Burdett (Ex. 1705), below, No. 395; Cary v. Abbot (1802), 7 Vesey Jun. 491, 32 E.R. 198; Mills v. Farmer (1815), 1 Merivale 55, 101, 35 E.R. 597, 613, 19 Vesey Jun. 483, 487, 34 E.R. 596; In re White, L.R. [1893] 2 Ch. 41, 49; Bourne v. Keane, L.R. [1919] App. Cas. 815, 848; G. H. Jones, *History of the Law of Charity* (1969), pp. 82–86.]

---

[14] *Attorney General v. Baxter* (1684), 1 Vernon 248, 23 E.R. 446, 1 Eq. Ca. Abr. 96, 21 E.R. 907.

[15] Stat. 15 Ric. II, c. 5 (*SR*, II, 79, 80).

[16] *Adams v. Lambert* (1598), 4 Coke Rep. 96, 76 E.R. 1079, also Moore K.B. 648, 72 E.R. 815.

[17] Stat. 1 Edw. VI, c. 14 (*SR*, IV, 24–33).

270
Attorney General v. Spooner (Ex. 1688)

In this case of alleged intrusions into crown lands, the defendants pleaded that the crown's rights were barred by statute, and the equity court stayed the suit so that the attorney general could try the issue of title at common law.

LI MS. Misc. 558, f. 36 [Fr.] (Ward's Reports)

The plaintiff exhibited an English information in the nature of intrusion and for an account and to have the possession decreed for certain lands containing 1300 acres and more called Friskney Marshes lying in Friskney in the County of Lincoln, suggesting them to be lands within fifty years gained from the sea and derelict by it and for this reason to appertain to the king by his prerogative royal.

The defendants claimed the lands as their inheritance and denied them to be gained from the sea or to be derelict by the sea within sixty years before the Statute 21 Jac. I, c. 1,[1] and they insisted upon this statute and the constant enjoyment by them and their ancestors and claimed them by divers ancient conveyances and fines, some in the time of Henry VII and Henry VIII and Queen Elizabeth.

And upon the hearing of the cause, it appeared to the court that there were five kinds of land. The first and most distant from the sea were some ancient marshes called the fens. Secondly, some lands called the tofts or the rising ground, adjoining to the fens, and the most distant from the sea except for the fens. And those two sorts of lands were not in question but were admitted to the defendants. But the lands in question were those that lay between the tofts or rising ground and the northmain deeps, which was the sea. And those lands were of three considerations:

1. Certain marshes enclosed forty-five or forty-six years ago.
2. The lands between those enclosures and a certain place called the Hurrheads or the Odds, which extended only a hundred yards in depth by all the breadth of the enclosures next to the sea.
3. The lands from the Hurrheads or Odds until the sea, to which place until the low water mark, is almost two miles, but at the ordinary tides the sea flows almost[2] to the Hurrheads.

And though in the answers the defendants made title to all of the land from the tofts to the sea, yet at the hearing they insisted only upon title to the enclosed marshes and to the lands between them and the Hurrheads, the profits

---

[1] Stat. 21 Jac. I, c. 2 (*SR*, IV, 1210–1211).
[2] prochein *MS*.

and feeding of all which the defendants proved were received and enjoyed by them and those under whom they claimed for sixty years and more without molestation except for one demand and claim made by Sir Peregrine Bertie, patentee of the king, under pretense of letters patent in the time of Charles I. But [there was] no eviction by them or taking of the profits but enjoyment by the defendants and their ancestors. And though it was evident that all of the land between the tofts and the sea was gained from the sea and derelict by it and the enclosures [were] almost forty-six years ago and though the tofts were of such a nature that one of the defendants had one part of them of such a breadth (perhaps [?] one, two, or three acres) abutting upon the land between them and the sea and others of the defendants had other parts of the toft of other breadths and the tofts were unenclosed and each defendant claimed all of the land between the tofts and the sea by the entire breadth of his toft land and this by the custom of the county, yet inasmuch as the defendants had enjoyed the said land thus enclosed for so long a time and under such ancient titles that by anything that appeared to the contrary could be more than sixty years before [the Statute of] 21 Jac. I, in which case the crown was barred by this Statute, the court refused to make any decree or to direct any issue but left the plaintiff to bring a Latin information of intrusion, if he wishes to, in which the defendants could have all legal advantages and defenses. But they did not dismiss the bill.

And in this case in truth, there was a patent granted of the same land to Sir Peregrine Bertie and others in fee under a rent in the time of Charles I. But inasmuch as in so long a time after that there was not any recovery, the heir of the patentee surrendered them to the now king with the intent that the title should be contested in the name of the king, and if any recovery was had, this heir had hope of obtaining a grant of it.

I [was] for the king.

There were thirty-eight defendants but only fourteen [were] brought to the hearing. And the heir of the patentee bore the charges of this suit.

[Other copies of this report: GUL MS. B88–8, p. 164.]

[Order of 5 July 1688: PRO E.126/15, f. 209v.]

271

Earl of Chesterfield v. Bird (Ex. 1688)

Money held by an agent of an agent belongs to the principal and is not part of either agents' estate.

LI MS. Misc. 558, f. 37 [Fr.] (Ward's Reports)

The case was thus. One Harrison was seneschal and collector of all the rents of the plaintiff in Kent and other counties and also was a similar officer and servant to lord Maynard. And the monies received and collected by him which he had not paid over he usually conserved in his lodgings, which he had in the house of the defendant Meres in London, each of which he usually conserved and sometimes entrusted to Meres. And in truth Harrison received £220 of the plaintiff's rents in Kent, which he returned by bills of exchange, and the money due upon those bills was received by Meres (by the direction of Harrison), who had it and also other sums in his custody at the time of Harrison's death. Harrison died intestate, and Dickens, principal creditor, took administration, who died, and Bird, the defendant, was administrator *de bonis non* etc. And he insisted to have all of the money which was in Meres's hands at the time of Harrison's death as part of his estate. The plaintiff demanded the £220 as his own money and no part of Harrison's estate.

And upon the hearing of this case in equity, the entire court held clearly that if my bailiff or servant receive my money and it remain in his custody at the time of his death, yet the money belongs to me and is not any part of my bailiff's estate and should not go to the executor or administrator, and on account of that trover or detinue lies, but the money in such a case should in right belong to me. And the court put it to a trial at law upon this issue, whether the £220 deposited by the said Harrison in the hands of Meres (because in truth Meres received the money in the absence of Harrison by his direction and had it in his custody at the time of the death of Harrison) was the proper money of the plaintiff or not. And the jury found for the plaintiff by direction of the court upon full evidence given that the £220 received in the country was the plaintiff's money and that the £220 received upon the bills of exchange belonged to the plaintiff in property as much as the actual money received from the plaintiff's tenants because it came in lieu and satisfaction of it.

And afterwards there was a decree for the plaintiff to have the money and an injunction against Bird's prosecution of Meres for the same money. And all of the creditors of Harrison by bonds and otherwise were discovered by the answer and their suing of Bird restrained, yet it was held that it was not necessary to make them parties inasmuch as the administrator was a party.

I [was] for the plaintiff.

[Other copies of this report: GUL MS. B88–8, p. 167.]

[Order of 3 May 1688: PRO E.126/15, f. 218v.]

272

Marwood v. Lord Tiveot (Ex. 1688)

The issue in this case was the interpretation of a settlement of land and the dissolving of an interlocutory injunction.

LI MS. Misc. 558, f. 40 [Fr.] (Ward's Reports)

Upon a motion for the continuance of an injunction, the case appeared to be thus. Sir Thomas Spencer of Yarnton in the County of Oxford, baronet, having settled the said manor of Yarnton[1] to the use of himself for life, remainder to Sir Benjamin Maddox and others, trustees, for twenty-one years, remainder to William Spencer, son and heir of Sir Thomas in tail male, remainder to all the sons of Sir Thomas by his wife Jane in tail male successively, remainder to himself in tail male, remainder to the right heirs of Sir Thomas, and the trust of the term for twenty-one years was declared by the same settlement to be for raising £5000 out of the rents of the said manor to be paid in this manner, *viz.* £2000 to the oldest daughter unmarried at the time of his death and the other £3000 by equal parts among his younger children with a proviso to make this term void upon the payment of the £5000 in this manner by the said William Spencer or the issue male of his body, after which William Spencer died without issue (not being ever married), upon which Sir Thomas, not having any male issue but only four daughters, made his will, in which there was this clause 'I declare that I leave my lands of inheritance to descend to my daughters as heirs at law upon the account I die without issue male of my body on Dame Jane my wife and that the lands hereby given and formerly settled upon my wife (because by this will he had devised part of Yarnton to his wife in augmentation of her jointure, which was of other lands) shall not be charged with any portion or sum of money to my daughters by virtue of any former marriage settlement'. And after he died, the eldest daughter married the defendant, the lord Tiveot, and the other three daughters married Marwood, Gerard, and Dormer, the plaintiffs. To these four daughters the entire inheritance of Yarnton descended as daughters and heirs of Sir Thomas. The lord Tiveot claiming the £2000 by force of the settlement prevailed with the trustees to have ejectments brought in their names in order to raise the £2000 for him and the £3000 for the other daughters, against which and to be relieved against this ejectment, the plaintiffs and their wives exhibited their bill, insisting that this term was intended only to raise portions for the daughters when there was living male issue able to inherit the lands, but that never was the intention of the parties nor should the meaning of the settlement be so construed that the

---

[1] V.C.H., *Oxfordshire*, XII (1990), p. 476.

£5000 should be raised when the land itself descended to all of the daughters. And the intention of Sir Thomas thus clearly appeared by his will, that his lands of inheritance were left to descend to his daughters, not to be charged with any portions for them by any settlement. And it was against good conscience for the lord Tiveot to demand the £2000, and on account of that it was prayed that the injunction granted until an answer should be continued until the hearing.

[This] was opposed by the defendant's counsel, insisting upon the term and remedy by it well created to raise the £5000 and that it was not in the power of Sir Thomas after this settlement to discharge the provision for the £5000 though he could have disposed of the manor itself otherwise. But inasmuch as he permitted the inheritance to descend to the four daughters and did not have any power to destroy the term and the trust for the £5000, he insisted upon both and claimed the £2000.

And though the court held it to be a cause fit for consideration, yet they would not continue the injunction but dissolved it, saying that if it is a good cause in equity, they will relieve at the hearing, which note and query.

I [was] for the plaintiffs, but the cause never came to a hearing.

[Other copies of this report: GUL MS. B88–8, p. 171.]

273

Drake v. Young (Ex. 1688)

In this case, the court of equity allowed a bill for discovery and common law relief.

LI MS. Misc. 558, f. 45, pl. 1 [Fr.] (Ward's Reports)

The plaintiff showed that he was possessed of divers goods (mentioning them and their values) and that he lost them and that they came to the defendant's hands who pretended them to be French goods and prohibited to be imported into England[1] and seized and condemned by judgment in this court, when in truth they were not French nor condemned. And upon an allegation of the death of witnesses, the plaintiff prayed discovery and relief.

The defendants answered and showed that the goods were French and, being prohibited to be imported, were forfeited and seized by them and condemned upon an information and a moiety answered to the king.

And inasmuch as the plaintiff made proof that sixteen parcels were seized but only fifteen restored to the plaintiff, who purchased them, and on account of that the plaintiff inferred that, one parcel not being condemned, the defendants

---

[1] Stat. 1 Will. & Mar., c. 34 (*SR*, VI, 98–103).

should account for it to the plaintiff, and upon this, the court put it to a trial at law to try if all the goods seized by the defendants were contained in the indenture annexed to the writ of appraisement and condemned, notwithstanding that the bill was only a declaration in trover. And if the plaintiff had any remedy, it was proper at [common] law by trover, because if any of the goods seized were omitted out of the condemnation, the property in them was not altered, and thus trover lies. Also it appeared to the court that the goods for which the trial was directed were French and prohibited and thus forfeited, and yet the court directed this issue notwithstanding that I, for the defendants, insisted that the bill does not contain equity but is merely an action of trover, which action, if the plaintiff brings and fails in it, the defendants would recover their treble costs being custom house officers. *Quod nota* and query, because it seems a strange case in equity.

[Other copies of this report: GUL MS. B88–8, p. 182.]

[Order of 26 Nov. 1688: PRO E.126/15, f. 230.]

274

Haselrig v. Crew (Ex. 1688)

A decree in the chancery court of Durham is res judicata.

A private person may have prescriptive rights against the jura regalia *of the bishop of Durham.*

LI MS. Misc. 558, f. 45, pl. 2 [Fr.] (Ward's Reports)

The case was thus as appeared by the bill, answer, and proofs. The prior and convent of Durham in the time of Henry VIII were seised in fee of the cell of Monk Wearmouth in the County of Durham and of divers lands pertaining to it, which upon the dissolution of the monasteries in the time of Henry VIII came to the crown. And [on] 18 June 37 Hen. VIII [1545], the king granted to Thomas Whitehead and his heirs the house and site of the said cell and certain lands and things particularly mentioned and all the fishing in the water of the Wear (being a navigable river there) in as ample a manner as it was enjoyed by the last prior or his predecessors holding *in capite* by the fortieth part of the knight's fee. Thomas Whitehead died and the premises descended to William Whitehead, his son and heir, who conveyed them to Robert Widdrington, from whom they descended to John Widdrington, his son and heir, from whom they descended to Robert Widdrington, his son and heir, from whom they descended to Mary and Anne, his daughters and coheirs, which Mary and Anne with Hallman and Brandling their husbands conveyed the premises to George Fenwick and his heirs, from whom they descended to Elizabeth and Dorothy his daughters and coheirs, which Elizabeth was married to Sir Thomas Haselrig, the plaintiff Sir Thomas Haselrig's father, whose heir the now plaintiff is. And the said Dorothy married with the plaintiff Sir Thomas Williamson.

And the plaintiffs by their bill showed that the said priors enjoyed the soil of the said river up to the middle or channel of the water[1] and all profits and advantages pertaining to it and that all of the priors and other parties at all times enjoyed the privileges of beaconage, anchorage, and wharfage of the north side of the said river and also the privilege of laying ballast for ships and the building of quays on the shore there and showed a decree made in the court of wards [in] 14 Jac. I [1616] in a cause there between the attorney general of the said court on behalf of Robert Widdrington at that time a ward of the said king and an infant and owner of the premises by relation of the lessee of the king and Bowes and others at that time lessees of the bishop of Durham claiming the duties of anchorage, beaconage, wharfage, etc. of all of the said river, by which decree the possession of those privileges (being at that time in the ward) was established with the infant and the lessee until altered by the court.

And the plaintiffs insisted upon their right to these five particulars of beaconage, anchorage, plankage, wharfage, and ballast shore, and that they should enjoy them by moieties and complain that they were interrupted by the defendant, the bishop [of Durham], who claimed the inheritance of them, and by French, his lessee, and that an information in the name of the attorney general of the bishop at the relation of French was exhibited in the court of chancery of Durham against the plaintiffs here to settle the right with the now defendants, plaintiffs there, and that an injunction was obtained for this purpose, of which suit the now plaintiffs complain to be against natural right that their inheritance should be drawn in question and determined in the said court of the bishop who is concerned in interest [sic] in the cause; and so [they] prayed removal of this suit by *certiorari* into this exchequer and a stay of all proceedings there and relief.

To this bill, the bishop and his lessee pleaded a decree in the court of chancery of Durham made by Judge Hutton, chancellor of the bishop of Durham, [on] 6 September 2 Car. II [1626], by which the privileges of anchorage, beaconage, and plankage (not mentioning wharfage or ballast shore) were settled and established with the bishop in a suit there between the attorney general of the bishop and the said Robert Widdrington, under whom the plaintiffs claim. And also he pleaded an allowance of a plea in this court for all of the said five privileges in Hilary term 24 & 25 Car. II [1673] to the now plaintiffs' bill.

But this plea to the present bill was overruled [it] being held by the court an unreasonable thing that the now plaintiffs' estate [which was] in question between them and the bishop, should be determined in the court of the bishop

---

[1] filum aque *MS*.

before his chancellor. And it was compared to the Earl of Darby's Case,[2] 4 *Inst.*, Chester, where it was resolved that he being chamberlain of Chester could not sue before his vice chamberlain and a prohibition [was] awarded.

After that the defendants insisted by their answers upon the same things and upon the minutes of a decree made [in] 6 Car. I [1630] by the same Judge Hutton, chancellor, by which it was decreed that wharfage and ballast shore belonged to the bishop. And the defendants insisted that the defendant, the bishop, was owner of the county palatine of Durham and had in right of it *jura regalia*, courts of record, etc. and insisted also that the plaintiffs' title was only to particular things enumerated in the grant from the crown and none of these five particulars were enumerated or passed, and that there were negative words in the particular by which the grant was made that nothing except the things enumerated were purchased. And also he insisted that Fenwick, under whom the plaintiffs claimed, purchased all of the said five privileges in the late times when the estates of the bishop were sequestered and sold, as the estate of the bishop of Durham.

And also he insisted upon the general right that the bishop had within the entire County of Durham to the soil of navigable rivers and all other royal prerogatives there in the same manner as the king had to such privileges out of the county palatine. And also he insisted that the enjoyment that Widdrington had and upon which the decree in the court of wards was founded was under a lease or title which he had in the right of the bishopric.

And upon the hearing of this cause the [*blank*] day of [*blank*] 1687, the court dismissed the plaintiffs' bill as to anchorage, beaconage, and plankage, these being settled by the decree in 2 Car. I [1626] with the bishop. But as to wharfage and ballast shore (which in truth was only one thing), the court directed three issues at law to be tried by a Yorkshire jury at the York assizes.

1. Whether the plaintiffs' soil extended into the river Wear and how far. And it was found to extend to the middle of it.
2. Whether the plaintiffs and those under whom they claim have had a ballast wharf erected on their land [for] time of which etc.[3] And it was found for the plaintiffs.
3. Whether the plaintiffs and those under whom they claim have received the duties and profits for this ballast wharf. And it was found for the plaintiffs.

And in this case the ballast wharf was only of such a nature, that is to say that ships which came to Sunderland to fetch coal emptied their ballast at the said wharf, for which they paid such a sum for which they could agree.

---

[2] *Egerton v. Earl of Darby* (1614), 12 Coke Rep. 114, 77 E.R. 1390; Pl. 10, 1 Eq. Cas. Abr. 137, 21 E.R. 940; E. Coke, *Fourth Institute* (1644), p. 213.

[3] 'Time of which the memory of man runneth not to the contrary' were the words used to assert a right based on prescription.

And in the debate of this case, it was allowed by the court that the owner of land extending into this navigable river within the county palatine could have the privileges of anchorage, beaconage, plankage, and ballast wharf (though they are port privileges) by prescription, which presupposes an old grant. And the court thought that the right of a county palatine (though there are *jura regalia* within it) is not of so great an extent or consideration in law as the case of the king by his prerogative within the realm and that prescription in this case can make a title. But no good title and usage appearing for the three first privileges, [and] the bill was dismissed as to them.

And upon the trial, there being found that the plaintiffs' land extended to the middle of the river and that [for] time of which etc., the plaintiffs and those under whom they claim having ballast wharf upon this land and having received the profits of it, the court made a decree for them for the plaintiffs. And in this case the case between the town of Newcastle and the dean and chapter of Durham in the time of Charles II in this court was remembered where the dean and chapter were owners of the soil where a ballast wharf was on the river Tyne and yet the town prevailed against the dean and chapter for the right and usage of the wharf. And though it was erected upon their own land, yet being a port privilege, upon the trial at bar, it was suppressed by a decree in this court in the time of Chief Baron Hale.

And after the first hearing of this case when the plaintiffs' bill was dismissed for the three points and the three issues were directed to be tried, the now defendants exhibited their [cross] bill to discover the decree made 6 September 2 Car. I [1626] by which the ballast shore and wharfage was alleged to be decreed to the bishop and that the plaintiffs, Sir Thomas Williamson and Sir Thomas Haselrig, had this original decree or an authentic copy of it in their hands and to compel [them] to produce it.

And the defendants to this bill answered to it and showed what paper they had (which in truth was not the original or an authentic copy of the decree), to which answer the bishop replied and examined witnesses.

And the question was whether those examinations should be admitted and read inasmuch as they were to the matter in issue in the original cause, which was alleged by the defendants' counsel to be unprecedented and of dangerous consequence to admit an examination in a cross or supplemental bill for things in issue in the first cause. But after divers debates, those examinations were admitted inasmuch as they went only[4] to the custody of the decree by the defendants and not to the decree or the substance of it.

And afterwards another trial was [had] on the same three issues, and [there was a] verdict against the right of the bishop, after which hearing of both causes, the court made a decree as to wharfage and ballast shore for Sir Thomas Williamson and Sir Thomas Haselrig and awarded costs for them in the entire

---

[4] properment *MS*.

original cause notwithstanding that the bill was dismissed as to three things and relief [was granted] as to two only. And the examinations etc. for the three things were more than those for the two things, which note. And it seemed to me not reasonable to compel the defendants to pay costs to the plaintiffs for the same things to which the plaintiffs did not have (but the defendants did have) right, where in truth the defendants should have their costs for those things for which the bill was dismissed. And at most the plaintiffs should have their costs for the things decreed (if they should have any costs, inasmuch as it was a doubtful case). And the cross-bill was dismissed without costs.

I [was] for the bishop and his lessee.

[Other copies of this report: GUL MS. B88–8, p. 183.]

[Orders of 7 and 14 Feb. 1687: PRO E.126/15, ff. 57v, 68v.]

275
Note (Ex. c. 1688)

A subsequent mortgagee has priority where the first mortgagee afterwards lends additional money secured by the first mortgage having notice of the second mortgage.

MT MS. of Baron Heath, F.3, f. 82 [Eng.]

A. has a mortgage from B. 1st September; C. has another from B. 2nd September; [on] 3 September, B. agrees [that] A.'s mortgage shall be for a further sum; if A. had notice of C.'s mortgage, then [he is] postponed, otherwise not.

276
Attorney General v. Brown (Ex. 1689)

In a suit to set aside a fraudulent conveyance, the transferor, here the debtor's executrix, who in good faith executed the release in issue, must be a party to the suit.

HLS MS. 1052, f. 16, pl. 56 [Eng.] (Wright's Reports)

Wadlow, that kept the Sun Tavern behind the Exchange, had mortgaged his estate there (being a lease for years) to several for as much as the same was worth. Afterwards [he] became indebted to the king and died. The defendant buys in the title of the mortgagees and obtained from Wadlow's executrix a release of her equity of redemption (for which no consideration did appear to be paid). The attorney general exhibited his bill in this court to bring the defendant to an account, suggesting that the mortgages and interest had been paid off by the perception of the mesne profits of the estate and that the release of the equity of redemption was fraudulent. This cause being brought to a hearing [the] 6th of

June, and the plaintiff's side being heard, it was put off upon *Sir Robert Sawyer's* showing for the defendant that the bill was not rightly brought, in regard [that] the executrix ought to have been made a defendant. [It was] ordered that the plaintiff should amend his bill and the attorney general should appoint a relator.

[Orders of 6 June 1689 and 3 Feb. 1690: PRO E.126/15, ff. 261v, 302.]

277

Smith v. Smith (Ex. 1689)

A contingent remainder that will occur within one lifetime is valid.
Leases are devisable.

BL MS. Hargr. 71, ff. 59, 61v, 65 [Eng. & Fr.] (Dodd's Reports)

In the exchequer chamber upon an English bill for an account.

John Betts devises his chattel leases and other personal chattels to John Carolus Smith and the issue male of his body and, if he die before the age of twenty-one years without issue male, then to B.

1. [It was] agreed that [the devise was] void as to personal chattels.
2. Query if [it was] good for the leases.

If a devise be to one for life and, if he die without issue living, [to] J.S., or before twenty-one, it seems that it is good because it is not a direct devise in tail but a tail by implication, which is a collateral limitation and a good executory devise.

A trust of a term was limited in tail and, if [he] die without issue before twenty-one, remainder over; this has been adjudged good [in] Ashe and Sir Henry Massenburgh's Case,[1] in the chancery in the time of North and by the opinion of the judges to whom it was referred. See Child and Bayley's Case;[2] the Duke of Norfolk's Case.[3]

---

[1] *Massenburgh v. Ash* (1684), 1 Vernon 234, 257, 304, 23 E.R. 437, 453, 485, *sub nom.* *Massingberd v. Ash*, 2 Chan. Rep. 275, 21 E.R. 677.

[2] *Child v. Bayley* (1623), Palmer 48, 333, 81 E.R. 972, 1109, W. Jones 15, 82 E.R. 9, Cro. Jac. 459, 79 E.R. 393, 1 Eq. Ca. Abr. 192, 21 E.R. 982, 2 Rolle Rep. 129, 81 E.R. 704.

[3] *Duke of Norfolk v. Howard* (1682), 1 Vernon 163, 23 E.R. 388, 3 Chan. Cas. 1, 22 E.R. 931, 2 Swanston 454, 36 E.R. 690, Pollexfen 223, 86 E.R. 568, 2 Chan. Rep. 229, 21 E.R. 665, 2 Freeman 72, 80, 22 E.R. 1066, 1070, 79 Selden Soc. 904, 922; Samuel Dodd's Reports, p. 42.

On behalf of the plaintiff, Mr. Solicitor General: [Where there is an] estate tail of a term with [a] remainder over, the remainder is void notwithstanding it is upon a contingency within a use. Child and Bayley's Case, [in] Palmer's Cases, Jones, [and] Rolle, see Hilary [term] 31 & 32 Car. II [1680], Gibson and Sanders, Hopkins' Case, Siderfin 137, Hartback and Lee, Easter [term] 29 Car. II [1677],[4] where Child and Bayley's Case was affirmed to be good law.

The Case of the Duke of Norfolk was against the opinions of the three chief justices and the chief baron, and also the case was not an express limitation in tail but only a user upon a collateral limitation. Wood and Saunders's Case.[5] He was never to take nor had anything in him unless [he was] living at the death of [his] father and mother. But in our case, the party took the entire term presently. [In] Sir Henry Massenburgh's Case, the party did not take but upon a contingency, as he took the profits until [he was] twenty-one and, if [he] lived till twenty-one, then [he took] the whole term. But if he died without issue before, then [there was a] remainder over.

Sir R. Sawyer, for the same [side]: It was an express [estate] t[ail] and the contingency is not upon the determination of the tail and there, notwithstanding it is within any short time or time certain, it is void. And so it is said in Palmer's report of Child and Bayley's Case. In the Duke of Norfolk's Case, it was not to begin when the estate was spent but afterwards to determine the very estate. Where the contingency is to vest but upon the determination of the tail, be it within what time it will, it is a void remainder. In the Duke of Norfolk's Case, the whole estate was not granted, but in this case all was given.

Mr. Attorney General: It is not to be construed [to be] similar to an estate tail, but it only describes the mind of the testator. If he died without issue, it makes little [difference] in the case because, if he had given it generally to him or to him and his executors, all [would have] passed. Thus [there is] no difference. By the addition of the issue by this limitation, the remoteness of the remainder is prevented, and the contingency is within one life.

Mr. Finch for the same [side]: [There is] no difference between an express and an implied limitation in tail. The true difference is within what time the contingency will be that makes the remainder good. Lives are resolved to be a reasonable time. Burgess and Burgess's Case.[6] A limitation to a man and his heirs and [if] he dies without issue, remainder over [is] bad because he expects too long.

---

[4] *Huntbatch v. Lee* (1677), 3 Keble 750, 84 E.R. 990.
[5] *Wood v. Saunders* (1669), 1 Chan. Cas. 131, 22 E.R. 728, Pollexfen 35, 86 E.R. 503.
[6] *Burges v. Burges* (1674), 1 Chan. Cas. 229, 22 E.R. 775, Rep. temp. Finch 91, 23 E.R. 49, Pollexfen 40, 86 E.R. 505, 1 Modern 114, 86 E.R. 773, 73 Selden Soc. 43.

The court [said that] the Duke of Norfolk's [Case] seems to be the same case, and it [was] resolved by an appeal in the House of Lords. And Child and Bayley's Case was resolved [on a writ of] error by all of the justices. It is a pure point of law, but it was doubtful what to do. [The court] adjourned.

In Hilary [term] afterwards, [it was] resolved by the barons, them against the chief baron, that the limitation was good because the contingency was limited to happen within so short a time because John Carolus was seven years of age at the time of the devise and it was to happen before his age of twenty-one, which is within fourteen years. [As to] the Duke of Norfolk's Case adjudged in the House of Lords, ours [is] a stronger case because it is within fourteen years [and] this [is] within a lifetime. Sir William Massenburgh's Case [is] not fully the same, but the reason of the judges unanimously for the remainder and contingencies [was that], being to fall within one lifetime, [they were] good.

By Baron LECHMERE: If a man had a lease for years of a house and devised his house, all of the term passes because there cannot be a tenancy at will in a will. It is otherwise if [he] grants his house there at will only. Dyer 307.[7] Leases for years [are] now devisable at law without the aid of any act of Parliament. 50 Ass. pl. 1.[8] The question is the same at law and in equity. It is a certain and near contingency, and the term or time of contingency as to that [is] the same with a fee simple, as [in] Pell and Brown's Case.[9] A perpetuity is where a man has the whole estate and yet [it is] clogged with such a possibility that he cannot dispose of it, but where the possibility is near, there it is good. Pell and Brown's Case against Child and Bayley's Case. In Attorney General and Sandys[10] [it was held that] a term attendant shall not be forfeited nor chargeable by an outlawry etc. The Duke of Norfolk's Case [was] a good but unnecessary resolution because Charles was the party that took the term first after it became a term in gross because before it attended the inheritance.

Chief Baron ATKYNS against: That it is not a good devise upon the contingency nor can there be any limitation of a lease for years after a tail. The common law delights in certainty. There were only four sorts of ownership in land by the common law, *viz.* tenants at will, tenants for years, tenants for lives, and fee simple (he meant this [as a matter] of quantity and not of quality of land, as by copy etc.). Those who have an alterable quality, as leases at will, are at the will of both parties notwithstanding it is otherwise agreed. Secondly, leases for

---

[7] *Fenton v. Foster* (1572), 3 Dyer 307b, 73 E.R. 694.

[8] YB 50 Edw. III, Lib. Ass., f. 321, pl. 1 (1376).

[9] *Pell v. Brown* (1620), Cro. Jac. 590, 79 E.R. 504, Palmer 131, 81 E.R. 1012, 2 Rolle Rep. 196, 216, 81 E.R. 746, 760, Godbolt 282, 78 E.R. 165, J. Bridgman 1, 123 E.R. 1157.

[10] *Attorney General v. Sandys* (Ex. 1666–1669), above, No. 16.

years will go to the executors and not to the heirs notwithstanding it is otherwise agreed. A lessee for years by an executed act cannot grant his term with any remainders. Courts of equity have been guilty of ill things and disturb the repose of the common law. Trusts [are] set on foot by courts of equity against the statute and intention of Parliaments. The change in these cases of leases for years was begun [by] 28 H. 8, Dyer 7,[11] where the judges did not respect the tail although there could be no remainder of a term, but now the common law began to be altered about 10 Eliz. [1568], as [by] Dyer, 6 Edw. VI, 74, 277, 328, 258.[12] [In] Amner and Lodington's Case,[13] they were termed executory devises, but why executory is not clear; and so [also in] Lampet's Case.[14] 28 Eliz. [1585–1586] Matthew Manning's Case, 7 Jac. [1609–1610],[15] calls [them] executory devises. But [they are called] void remainders in 1 Rolle 610, 611.[16] Then came Retorieck and Chappel's Case,[17] and that broke down all. And now comes in the contingency, which was a term never heard of before. And these judges were innovators, as [in] Pell and Brown's Case, etc. But then came Child and Bayley's Case, which disallowed the contingency by ten or eleven judges. A perpetuity of a term is nonsense. But the true reason that [they are] void is that they break the rule of law. Long leases are an abuse of the law and [were] introduced by fraud. 1 [Coke] *Inst.* 45. Gibbons and Somers's Case,[18] Hilary [term] 33 Car. II [1681], common pleas, roll 635, upon a special verdict, and [it was] cited by the chief baron in the Duke of Norfolk's Case. Pell and Brown [was] disputed in Jay and Jay's Case, Stiles.[19] And [it was] adjudged in Child and Bayley's Case, which is confessed [to be] a great authority. The Duke of Norfolk's Case is directly contrary and flatly denied it because was judged by the chancellor, who is not a judge of the law, and [it was] contrary to the opinion of the judges. The common law in chancery is more ancient than equity, but it [is] inferior to the king's bench. The great seal [is] not entrusted with the common law. A point of law can arise collaterally in

---

[11] *Anonymous* (1536), 1 Dyer 7, 73 E.R. 17.
[12] *Anonymous* (1552), 1 Dyer 74a, 73 E.R. 158; *Anonymous* (1568), 3 Dyer 277b, 73 E.R. 620; *Anonymous* (1573), 3 Dyer 328b, 73 E.R. 743.
[13] *Luddington v. Amner* (1584), Godbolt 26, 78 E.R. 17, *sub nom. Amner's Case*, Jenkins 264, 145 E.R. 189; *Amner v. Luddington*, 2 Leonard 92, 74 E.R. 384, 3 Leonard 89, 74 E.R. 559, 1 Anderson 60, 123 E.R. 353, 8 Coke Rep. 96b, 77 E.R. 623.
[14] *Lampet's Case* (1612), 10 Coke Rep. 46b, 77 E.R. 994, *sub nom. Lampit v. Starkey*, 2 Brownl. & Golds. 172, 123 E.R. 880.
[15] *Manning's Case* (1609), 8 Coke Rep. 94b, 77 E.R. 618.
[16] 1 Rolle, Abr., *Devise*, K, L, pp. 610–611.
[17] *Retherick v. Chappel* (1612), 2 Bulstrode 28, 80 E.R. 932.
[18] E. Coke, *First Institute* (1628), f. 45; *Gibbons v. Summers* (1681), 3 Levinz 22, 83 E.R. 557.
[19] *Jay v. Jay* (1651), Style 274, 82 E.R. 706.

an ecclesiastical court, but they are not judges of it. Those in chancery have been too great and made and unmade judges, but where a point of law arises, there they should be assisted by the judges and bound by them in it. The procuring and reviewing of decrees in chancery appertains to the judges, and they do not regard the precedents in chancery. 4 [Coke] *Inst.* 85; 1 Rolle 382; Dyer 201.[20] The last resort is the Parliament and not the House of Lords. And the Lords have nothing to do in appeals but what is new and not more ancient than 1640. In 18 Jac. I, 1621, in the Lords' Journal, pp. 175–208,[21] settles the point; it is called *Style and Collection of the Customs and Privileges of the Lords*; [it is] a book put in by the archbishop. A committee was appointed; and there is a head for precedents for the judiciary, [on] f. 11 it is said for capital offenses, f. 25 for offenses not capital, f. 88 for errors. No[22] writ of error lies immediately from them into the common pleas (181, 188, 196). An appeal [lies] to them from the chancery, but the direction is to the king and his great council, and this is not the House of Peers because it is a petition presented by the lords etc. to the king and his great council. There is but one precedent that they are possessed of, and that is about bribery. In 2 Jac. 1624, [in] Mathews and Mathews,[23] [there was] a petition and appeal from a decree. The lords appointed a committee. The respondent answers that he was informed by his counsel that the usage had been to redress decrees by bill, *viz.* by the legislative power. A second committee [was] appointed, and [it] resolved that the decree ought to be reversed and directed the lord keeper to move the House to grant a commission for that purpose, and accordingly a commission was granted. (Michaelmas and Hilary [terms], 22 Jac. [1624], in the register's office in chancery: all these proceedings [are] there at large.) A commission to the judges is a proper way to reverse decrees. 1 Rolle [Abr.] 382; 1 Rolle's Reports 31; and Vaudry and Pannell's Case.[24]

[Other copies of this report: HLS MS. 537(b), p. 21; Oxf. Brasenose MS. 59, pp. 24, 26, 29; IU Lilly MS. Parker, 'Cases in the Exchequer, vol. 1', p. 215; IU Lilly MS. Parker, 'Tithes', p. 176.]

[Order of 6 May 1689: PRO E.126/15, f. 246v.]

[This case is cited in Lamb v. Archer (K.B. 1693), Samuel Dodd's Reports, p. 156.]

---

[20] *Earl of Worcester v. Finch* (1600), E. Coke, *Fourth Institute* (1644), p. 85; 1 Rolle, Abr., *Chancery*, Z, p. 382; *Chevin v. Paramour* (1561), Dyer 201a, 73 E.R. 443.

[21] This report is mentioned in *Lords' Journal*, III (n.d.), p. 176.

[22] The *MS.* HLS MS. 1169(b), p. 21.

[23] *Mathews v. Mathews* (H.L. 1624) is discussed in J. S. Hart, *Justice upon Petition: The House of Lords* (1991), pp. 48–50.

[24] 1 Rolle, Abr., *Chancery*, Z, p. 382; *Vaudry v. Pannel* (1615), 3 Bulstrode 116, 81 E.R. 99, 1 Rolle Rep. 246, 81 E.R. 464.

278
Doddridge v. Startop (Ex. 1690)

A customary payment of a percentage of the value of the land or of the rental value is a good custom in lieu of tithes in kind.

BL MS. Hargr. 71, f. 68, pl. 1 [Fr. & Eng.] (Dodd's Reports)

[In the case of] Doddridge, parson of Watlington in Sussex,[1] against Stirrupp and others in the exchequer chamber by English bill, [it was] resolved that a custom of 2s. in the pound according to the value of the land or as the same is let for is a good custom, by the whole court, and not tithes in kind. And the parson's bill for tithes in kind [was] dismissed Thursday after the end of this term.

Browne and Chaplin[2] and Bean v. Lee and others[3] [were] resolved contrary.

[Other copies of this report: HLS MS. 537(b), p. 23, pl. 1; Oxf. Brasenose MS. 59, p. 31, pl. 1; IU Lilly MS. Parker, 'Cases in the Exchequer, vol. 1', p. 218; IU Lilly MS. Parker, 'Tithes', p. 179.]

[The order of 10 July 1690, PRO E.126/15, f. 359v, is printed at 1 Wood 283, 1 Eagle & Younge 566.]

[Related cases: Startup v. Dodderidge (1705), 2 Lord Raymond 1158, 92 E.R. 266; 2 Salkeld 657, 91 E.R. 559; Case 87, 11 Modern 60, 88 E.R. 885, 1 Eagle & Younge 666.]

[The case was cited in Browne v. Chaplin (Ex. 1696), below, No. 306.]

279
Paine v. Tape (Ex. 1690–1691)

The assignee of commissioners in bankruptcy can set aside a lease made by the crown after the outlawry of the bankrupt where the outlawry occurred after the bankruptcy because the lease is only a pernancy of profits.

BL MS. Hargr. 71, ff. 68, 74 [Eng. & Fr.] (Dodd's Reports)

Archer was a creditor to Long in 1679. Long became bankrupt [in] 1680. Archer outlawed Long [in] 1682 upon a special *capias utlagatum*. In 1683, a term or a trust of a term for the outlaw was seized. The king thereupon leased to

---

[1] Sic in MS.
[2] *Browne v. Chaplin* (Ex. 1696), below, No. 306.
[3] *Bean v. Lee* (1713), 2 Gwillim 609, 1 Wood 537, *sub nom. Behn v. Lee*, 1 Eagle and Younge 703, 1 Rayner 120, Samuel Dodd's Reports, p. 231.

Archer in 1684 *quamdiu in manibus* etc.[1] Archer assigns to Backer in trust for Tape in 1684. A commission of bankrupts issued against Long in 1687. The commissioners assigned the premises to Paine, a creditor, who brought his bill against Tape etc. and Mr. Attorney [General] to set aside the outlawry and to be relieved against the king and to be let into the premises.

Sir Robert Sawyer on behalf of Tape admits that if Tape's debt [were] satisfied, the court could let in the plaintiff. But he insists that until [it was] satisfied, the court could not retain [the bill]. The great point is whether the assignee of the commissioners may avoid this lease.

First, he cannot avoid it at law. And if it is not void by the Acts of Parliament concerning bankruptcy,[2] no court of equity can avoid it. If this lease had not been made, there would not have been any equity against the king. The king is not bound by the Statute of Bankrupts. (See 2 Syd. 177,[3] which Sawyer denied.) This outlawry was in respect of a contempt, and the king upon it is in [in] the post and came not in merely by the party (as [when] a bankrupt commits treason and then a commission will issue, nevertheless it does not avoid the king). If the king comes in for a debt, he is not bound; *a fortiori* where he comes in in the post. [If] a subject had a judgment and then a commission, [it was] not avoidable until [the Statute of] 21 Jac. I.[4] Between the king and Thomas. An extent in aid after a commission and before an assignment [is] good, and the case of an outlawry is stronger than an extent. If [it is] not relievable if [there is] no lease, neither is it now for it is still in the king's hands. The grantee has only a perception of the profits upon an outlawry. On a mesne process, it is not for the benefit of the party because perhaps the demand is [for] trespass, battery, etc. where it is uncertain what the damages [are]. But perhaps it is otherwise after judgment because then [it is] certain. See Cro. Jac. 179; Yelv. 19.[5]

He is a purchaser within the proviso because the Statute does not say a purchaser under the bankrupt, and if the king comes under the bankrupt and the grantee under the king, then he is expressly within the proviso. If the king come not under the bankrupt, he is not bound by the Statute. And as to the purchase, if [it be] at a first or second hand is not material.

Note that, as I remember, between Rex and Crump and then between Rex and Lechmere, it was resolved in the exchequer that if A. is a bankrupt and, after the commission [issues] and before assignment, the goods are seized by an extent in aid, that it is good and cannot be avoided by commissioners or assignees.

---

[1] So long as in the hands [of the king].
[2] Stat. 13 Eliz. I, c. 7 (*SR*, IV, 539–541); Stat. 1 Jac. I, c. 15 (*SR*, IV, 1031–1034).
[3] *Radford v. Blidworth* (1659), 2 Siderfin 176, 82 E.R. 1319.
[4] Stat. 21 Jac. I, c. 19 (*SR*, IV, 1227–1229).
[5] *Rex v. Twine* (1605), Cro. Jac. 179, 79 E.R. 156; *Soprani v. Skurro* (1602), Yelverton 19, 80 E.R. 14 [this case does not seem to be on point].

After [the end of] this term, Chief Baron ATKYNS and the other two barons (against LECHMERE, [who was] against [them]) [ruled] that the party should avoid this lease in equity or otherwise the Statute of Bankrupts would be avoided, and a creditor will only be helped by this way. And they decreed the grantee to account for the profits and to permit the outlawry to be reversed etc.

Note that the party that had the outlawry was only a creditor for £20 and [was] not capable of suing a commission of bankruptcy. Afterwards, [the court] doubting advised with[6] the justices of the common bench; see below, their opinion of Hilary [term] 1690[/91].

Chief Justice Pollexfen, Powell, and Rokeby signed a certificate as follows:

1. That the bankruptcy made title in the assignee notwithstanding the subsequent outlawry.
2. That by the outlawry, the term was forfeited, and by the inquisition, it vested in the king although the inquisition found only the annual value and not the value of a sale [?].
3. That the grant has words sufficient to pass the term and that, if the term was granted, then the defendant is a purchaser within the proviso of the Statute of Bankruptcy, but if by any course of the exchequer, this grant does not pass the term but only the pernancy of the profits, then Teape is not a purchaser.

And [it was ruled] by the court of exchequer chamber [that] the term does not pass but only a pernancy of the profits, and so [it was] decreed.

[Other copies of this report: HLS MS. 537(b), pp. 23, 28; Oxf. Brasenose MS. 59, pp. 31, 37; IU Lilly MS. Parker, 'Cases in the Exchequer, vol. 1', p. 218; IU Lilly MS. Parker, 'Tithes', p. 179; BL MS. Hargr. 70, p. 97, pl. 318; HLS MS. 1162, p. 87, pl. 464; IU Lilly MS. Parker, 'Tithes', p. 62.]

[Orders of 3 June and 7 Nov. 1690: PRO E.126/15, ff. 338v, 367v.]

280
Sandys v. Pigott (Ex. 1690)

The court of exchequer has jurisdiction to hear suits for accounts for the ecclesiastical revenues of procurations and paschals.

BL MS. Hargr. 71, f. 70, pl. 2 [Fr. & Eng.] (Dodd's Reports)

A bill [was filed] by the archdeacon of Wells against a vicar for procurations and paschals to the value of 9s. And at the hearing, [it was] objected that it is between ecclesiastical persons and for a mere ecclesiastical duty and therefore only

---

[6] Dub:^{r} & advice ove *MS*.

cognizable in the ecclesiastical court. But [it was argued] by the plaintiff that it is in the nature of a pension and is like a mortuary, for which suits are usual. And the court agreed and decreed for the plaintiff, because this court should have jurisdiction in respect that the plaintiff pays first fruits and tenths for those paschals and procurations. Lechmere cited Dr. Parker's Case, archdeacon of London, Hardres 181,[1] who sued the clergy for synodals and pentecosts, and upon demurrer [it was] adjudged good, because if [they are due] by composition, then it is proper in the spiritual court, but [if they are due] by prescription, it is otherwise and only proper in this court as prestation money etc. See 2 [Coke] *Inst.* 491.

[Other copies of this report: HLS MS. 537(b), p. 24; Oxf. Brasenose MS. 59, p. 33, pl. 1; IU Lilly MS. Parker, 'Cases in the Exchequer, vol. 1', p. 222; IU Lilly MS. Parker, 'Tithes', pp. 42, 58, 182; BL MS. Hargr. 70, p. 97, pl. 319; HLS MS. 1162, p. 87, pl. 465.]

[The decree of 5 Feb. 1691, PRO E.126/15, f. 389v, is printed at 1 Wood 284.]

281
Leach v. Hibbett (Ex. 1690)

The issue in this case was whether a judgment creditor can redeem a prior mortgage made by his debtor without payment of a later mortgage which was taken without notice of the judgment.

BL MS. Hargr. 71, f. 71, pl. 1 [Fr. & Eng.] (Dodd's Reports)

By English bill upon a rehearing on a point, the case was thus. Dr. Hibbett lent Hollingsworth £100 and took a mortgage in his trustee's name for a lease for years. Afterwards the testator of Leach recovered a judgment against Hollingsworth, and afterwards Dr. Hibbett lent Hollingsworth £300 more without notice of the judgment and took a mortgage in fee for security to himself. And many years after the forfeiture, Leach's testator brought a bill to redeem.

And [it was] adjudged upon the rehearing that he may redeem the first mortgage without payment of the second, by the chief baron [ATKYNS] and NEVILE and LECHMERE against TURTON. *Quod mirum*, because it is contrary to natural equity and constant practice. The chief baron said that grant the testator [may] recover the judgment, then [he is] entitled to redeem and no act that Hollingsworth [may] make afterwards [can] prejudice the judgment. Note that several authorities [were] cited to the contrary, as Godden and Trafford, and afterwards [it was] reversed [?] in the House of Lords after Michaelmas term 1691.[1]

---

[1] *Parker v. Seabrook* (1661), Hardres 181, 145 E.R. 441.

[1] *Lords' Journal*, XV (n.d.), p. 13.

[Other copies of this report: HLS MS. 537(b), p. 25, pl. 1; Oxf. Brasenose MS. 59, p. 34, pl. 1; IU Lilly MS. Parker, 'Cases in the Exchequer, vol. 1', p. 222; IU Lilly MS. Parker, 'Tithes', p. 183.]

[Order of 27 June 1690: PRO E.126/15, f. 345.]

[Other reports of this case: Anonymous, 1 Freeman 331, 22 E.R. 1237, 89 E.R. 246.]

282

Dummer v. Wingfield (Ex. 1690)

Customary payments may be due in lieu of tithes of wool of sheep pastured in one parish and shorn in another.

LI MS. Misc. 558, f. 104 (Ward's Reports)

The principal case was that Dummer, rector of Hardwick cum Weedon in the County of Buckingham, exhibited his bill against the defendant Wingfield to have an account and to be relieved for tithes of sheep in this parish (among other things) or for the wool or for the agistment tithe for the herbage.

And the defendant insisted by answer upon a custom or *modus* in the parish that, for all sheep depastured in the parish on Candlemas day and shorn within the parish there, tithes in kind of the wool are due, and if sold or removed before shearing out of the parish, then the parson shall have the value of the tithes of the wool paying to the owner of the sheep 4d. per score for each month after Candlemas and before shearing. And for all sheep brought into the parish after Candlemas, whether they are shorn there or not, 4d. per score per month in satisfaction of all tithes of wool and that no tithes of wool shall be paid since[1] the owners did not serve any winter stock. And it appeared that the defendant each year bought in his stock of sheep after Candlemas.

[Other copies of this report: GUL MS. B88–8, p. 209.]

[The order of 10 Feb. 1690, PRO E.126/15, f. 302v, is printed at 1 Wood 273.]

[Other reports of this case: Samuel Dodd's Reports, p. 94, 1 Eagle & Younge 566.]

[This case is cited in Hall v. Filts (Ex. 1708), below, No. 431; Coleman v. Barker (1726), 2 Gwillim 665, 666, 1 Rayner 222, 223, Gilbert Rep. 231, 25 E.R. 160, 161, 1 Eagle & Younge 814.]

---

[1] coment *MS*.

283
Mayor of Coventry v. King (Ex. 1691)

In this case, executors were ordered to pay money plus interest due upon a trust, but court costs were not awarded.

HLS MS. 1052, f. 20, pl. 67 [Eng.] (Wright's Reports)

Costor owed the plaintiffs £20 upon [a] bond, which was assigned by the plaintiffs to the testator of the defendants[1] to be sued, who recovers and receives the money. Upon hearing this cause, the court decreed that the defendants should pay the money with interest, but without costs (because [they were] executors), the barons being all of opinion that this was a trust and not allowing of a detainer in the defendants, on account of £100 due from the City to the testator King, in consideration of his charges when mayor according to an order of that City formerly made to that purpose.

[Order of 9 Feb. 1691: PRO E.126/15, f. 391v.]

284
Attorney General v. Price (Ex. 1691)

In this case, the jury found that insufficient silver was present in the lead ore for the mine to be a royal silver mine.

I
LI MS. Misc. 558, f. 112 [Fr.] (Ward's Reports)

The case was thus, in March 1689 the agents of the Corporation for Royal Mines discovered a rich mine of lead in which a great quantity of silver was contained (as it was alleged) in the defendant Sir Carbery Price's Manor of Llanvihangell Generglin in the County of Cardigan in a common there called Eskyrhir. And the agents of the corporation gained a great quantity of ore out of this mine and worked it as a royal mine. But afterwards Sir Carbery (being a member of Parliament) entered on the mine and took the ore raised by the agents into his possession, upon which divers questions arose in Parliament touching the violation of the privilege of it, and those being accommodated in order to have the right tried at law, the attorney general exhibited in this court an English information against the defendants and moving for an injunction to quiet the possession of the king of the mines, the court *ex assensu Parliamenti* ordered that the

---

[1] The executors of Alderman King.

attorney general should prefer a Latin information in the nature of an action of trover and conversion for such a quantity of ore, which was preferred accordingly suggesting that the king and queen were possessed of 250 tuns of ore containing silver in it to the value of £3000 and that they lost it and that it came to the hands of the defendants who converted it to their own use to the damage etc. And by order of the court, it was to be admitted that their majesties had title and property if it was a royal mine. And the sole question, whether it was a royal mine or not, [was] to be tried by a Middlesex jury. And the trial was in the office of pleas by a jury of knights and gentlemen. And at first it was debated that it should be said in law a royal mine, or where any silver or gold should be found mixed with other metal as the eight judges thought in the Case of the Mines in Plowden's *Commentaries* (which case began on f. 310 and ended on f. 340)[1] or according to the opinion of the three judges in this case who thought that when the silver or gold to be gained out of the mine exceeded the value of the base metal (f. 336) because in such a case all belonged to the king, both the base metal and the gold and silver. And the counsel for the king in this case in question endeavored to define a royal mine to be when the gold or silver (after the expense of refining) together with the remaining base metal not consumed in the refining exceeds the value or price of the metal thus[2] before refining, as for example, [if it is] admitted that a tun of lead made from the ore dug out of this mine was of the value of £10, if out of this tun such a quantity of silver could be extracted which with the remaining lead not consumed in the refining and after the defraying of the charges of the extraction of the silver should be of the value of £11 or exceeding £10, that then it would be said [to be] a royal mine, because by this means the public had an advantage and silver is gained to the realm.

But the counsel for the defendant differed in this definition and relied greatly upon an Act of Parliament made 1 Will. & Mar., c. 30,[3] which declared that no mine of copper, tin, iron, or lead should be afterwards adjudged or reputed to be a royal mine though gold or silver could be extracted out of it, which Act as they alleged determined all pretenses to royal mines in England.

But the cause descending to the proof, it was proved by divers artisans and others for the king that it was a rich mine and that, out of one pound of lead or metal made from the ore of this mine, they extracted twenty-three grains of silver (as some said), nineteen as others, seventeen and thirteen by others, and thus *pro rata* and if it was true first whether this afforded twelve grains out of the pound of metal seemed to all that it was a royal mine or that a royal mine could never exist in England.

---

[1] *Attorney General v. Earl of Northumberland* (1568), Plowden 310, 75 E.R. 472.
[2] insement *MS*.
[3] Stat. 1 Will. & Mar., c. 30 (*SR*, VI, 95).

But on the defendants' part, they produced the assay master of the Tower [of London], Sir John Brattle, and his son and the assay master of Goldsmiths' Hall and other persons, who testified that the ore was not so rich and that one pound of metal or lead gained out of this mine did not produce but three grains of silver and that such a quantity could be extracted out of common lead used for common uses, as for windows, etc.

And upon this different evidence, the jury found for the defendants.

By Scots law, three half pence of silver of a pound of lead [makes a] royal mine in Scotland: Acts, f. 2.[4] But though the court did not disparage the verdict nor blame the jury, yet it being necessary to settle the right of this question, which could not be without the aid and assistance of the court for the indifferent taking and trial of the ore and the court thinking that there was a great art used in the former experiments on one side or the other, there being so great a difference, they awarded a new trial upon payment of full costs.

And afterwards upon another trial at the bar by a Middlesex jury upon the same issue and question in Michaelmas term, there was proved for the king and the relators that 40, 50, 60, 70 grains of silver were extracted out of a pound of lead or metal by the operators employed by the king and the relators. But the same evidence for the defendants was given at this trial, that three grains could not be truly extracted out of a pound of metal. The jury found for the defendants, and the ore imported to make the trials and delivered to the relator for the same intent was ordered to be paid [for] by the relators according to the rate of £8 per tun. And all orders to stay the defendants from working the mines were discharged and liberty [was] given to work them. But the bill [was] not dismissed.

I [was] for the plaintiff.

[Other copies of this report: GUL MS. B88–8, p. 221.]

II
HLS MS. 1052, f. 21v, pl. 71 [Eng.] (Wright's Reports)

The point was what should be esteemed a royal mine? The attorney general and others for the king strongly urged that if the silver refined out of a tun of ore besides the charges together with the remaining lead be of greater value than the lead only of the same quantity of ore would be, in case no silver were refined from it, this is a mine royal and ought to go all to the king; otherwise [it is] no mine royal and belongs all to the lord of the soil.

On the other side Serjeant *Levinz*, Mr. *Finch*, Sir *Francis Winnington*, and Mr. *Jones*, for the defendant, maintained that it was not a mine royal unless the value of the silver in a tun of ore be of greater value than the lead that is in the

---

[4] Act of 1424, c. 13, *Acts of the Parliament of Scotland*, II (1814), p. 5.

same quantity of ore; and here they held that the silver is to be valued exclusive of the lead and not with it. This they said is according to Plowden, in the Case of Mines, f. 328b, and according to the new Statute 1 Will. & Mar.[5] entitled 'An Act for the Repealing the Statute made 5 Hen. IV against Multiplying of Gold and Silver', in the two last paragraphs, the first of which admits that subjects may have mines out of which they may extract gold and silver, but enjoins that they bring such gold and silver to the king's mint, where they are to receive the full and true value thereof; by the other paragraph, it is enacted that no mine of copper, lead, etc. shall be adjudged, reputed, or taken to be a mine royal though gold or silver may be extracted out of the same.

After a long trial at [the] bar, this cause went for the defendant. But upon [a] motion of the attorney general and [the] producing [of] several affidavits, in one of which it was sworn that £12 worth of silver was extracted out of a tun of ore, whereas a tun of lead is not worth above £9, a new trial was granted.

[Orders of 1 and 11 July and 23 Oct. 1691: PRO E.127/17, ff. 306, 308, 323.]

285

Bowater v. Hartley (Ex. 1692)

An oral contract for the sale of land will be enforced in equity where the purchase price has been paid and received.

BL MS. Hargr. 71, f. 80v, pl. 2 [Fr. & Eng.] (Dodd's Reports)

Hartley mortgaged his estate, both freehold and copyhold, to Gulston, who brought a bill to foreclose and had a decree. And before the day, Bowater agreed by parol to purchase it, *viz.* all that Gulston had, for a certain sum and accordingly paid the sum, and he had a conveyance executed by Gulston and Hartley of the freehold. But Bowater did not know until then that any part was copyhold. And then Hartley agreed by parol to surrender the copyhold. (Note [that] the whole estate was [worth] £300 *per annum* and the copyhold was a small parcel of six or seven acres only.) And then he refused, and Bowater brought a bill to execute this agreement. And the Statute of Frauds and Perjuries[1] [was] pleaded and insisted on at the hearing.

The court, *viz.* LECHMERE and TURTON, dismissed the bill. But POWELL was against [the dismissal].

---

[5] Stat. 1 Will. & Mar., c. 30 (*SR*, VI, 95).

[1] Stat. 29 Car. II, c. 3 (*SR*, V, 839–842).

And now upon the rehearing, the chief baron [ATKYNS], TURTON, and POW-
ELL decreed an execution and that Hartley [should make the] surrender. But
LECHMERE was against [it] because it was expressly against the Statute. POWELL
said that the agreement between Bowater and Hartley notwithstanding it was
by parol nevertheless referred to the agreement between Hartley and Gulston,
which was in writing etc. The chief baron and TURTON did not directly allow
this, but they said that it was an agreement executed in part by the payment of
the entire money and the sealing of the conveyance of the freehold.

Note that I was of counsel with Hartley, who had a hard case because Bowater had deceived him and set [him] up for a year.

[Other copies of this report: HLS MS. 537(b), p. 33, pl. 4; Oxf. Brasenose MS. 59, p. 44,
pl. 2; IU Lilly MS. Parker, 'Cases in the Exchequer, vol. 1', p. 228; IU Lilly MS. Parker,
'Tithes', p. 187.]

[Order of 10 May 1692: PRO E.126/16, f. 9.]

286
Wilbraham v. Jackson (Ex. 1693)

A life tenant beneficiary of a trust of a lease cannot surrender the lease.

BL MS. Hargr. 71, f. 85, pl. 1 [Eng. & Fr.] (Dodd's Reports)

Sir Thomas Smith, seised of a bishop's lease of tithes etc. for the lives of A.,
B., and C., granted this in trust for himself for life, remainder in trust for D. for
life, remainder in trust for his executors, and he made D. and F. his executors and
died. D., being beneficiary for life and one of the executors and having the lease
in her custody, delivered it up and took a new lease. And then upon her marriage
with Jackson, she levied a fine of the premises to Jackson and his heirs to Wilbraham etc. upon a *concessit*. And then D. died. And Wilbraham, who after the fine
married F., brought his bill for an account of the moiety of the profits received by
Jackson after the death of D.

And upon a case made, [it was] resolved by three [barons] against LECH-
MERE that he should have [it].

1. [It was] resolved that the surrender was void and was not operative.
2. [It was] resolved that the case of a freehold differs from [that of] a
   chattel because, in the case of a chattel, an executor can grant all. But
   [it is] otherwise in this case because there is only a description of the
   person and she did not take as executor. But [it was said] by LECH-
   MERE [that there is] no difference.

[Other copies of this report: HLS MS. 537(b), p. 37, pl. 4; Oxf. Brasenose MS. 59, p. 59, pl. 3; IU Lilly MS. Parker, 'Cases in the Exchequer, vol. 1', p. 234; IU Lilly MS. Parker, 'Tithes', p. 193.]

[Orders of 26 Jan. and 14 Feb. 1693: PRO E.126/16, ff. 66v, 81v.]

287
Bennett v. Golding (Ex. 1693)

Damages in tort for the loss of mesne profits cannot be recovered after the death of the injured party.

I
LI MS. Hill 49, f. 174, pl. 1 [Fr.]

Bennett, executor of Bennett, formerly rector of Winwick in the County of Lancaster, against Golding and others, tenants of Winwick, and others, their executors.

The plaintiff exhibited his bill in the exchequer showing that the testator was rector of Winwick and lord of the manor there and had many tenants at will there who have entered etc. and under pretense of custom went into chancery and procured an injunction against him by which he cannot have an action at law for the mesne profits and so prayed a discovery of these mesne profits and accounts of it. And it was against all the tenants who were now in being and also against the executors of the others who were tenants during the time that the testator was parson.

The defendants demurred.

And by all the barons with one voice, the bill was dismissed because it was trespass and only personal, dying with the party who was injured or who was injurer, and [was] not within the Statute[1] *de bonis asportatis* in the lifetime of the testator.

II
BL MS. Hargr. 71, f. 86, pl. 1 [Fr. & Eng.] (Dodd's Reports)

The parson demanded the improved rents; the tenants pretended to hold by small ancient rents. The parson entered upon them and brought ejectment; the tenants preferred their bill in chancery, and an injunction [was] granted, and the parson lay under this injunction for three years. And then the bill was dismissed and the injunction [was] dissolved, and then the parson died. And his executor grounded his bill in this court upon this matter to have an account from the tenants of the mesne profits. And upon a demurrer to the bill because it is an action

---

[1] Stat. 4 Edw. III, c. 7 (*SR*, I, 263).

of trespass that *moritur cum persona* etc. and upon argument, the bill [was] dismissed, and the demurrer [was] allowed.

[Other copies of this report: HLS MS. 1169(b), p. 38, pl. 2; Oxf. Brasenose MS. 59, p. 50, pl. 4; IU Lilly MS. Parker, 'Cases in the Exchequer, vol. 1', p. 236; IU Lilly MS. Parker, 'Tithes', p. 194.]

[Order of 6 May 1693: PRO E.127/18, f. 10.]

288
Shaftoe v. Hooke (Ex. 1693)

A judgment creditor has priority over a bond creditor.

BL MS. Hargr. 71, f. 86, pl. 4 [Fr. & Eng.] (Dodd's Reports)

Upon a rehearing, the point formerly resolved 9 February 1692[/93] and now resolved again upon a rehearing was [that] Shaftoe had a decree for a sum certain upon an account against Powell, and it was signed and enrolled. Powell died, having made his will and an executor, who renounced. And then Hooke, being a creditor by a bond took administration *cum testamento annexo*, and Shaftoe brought a bill against him to discover assets and [to] subject them to his decree.

And [it was] resolved that Hooke should not retain [the assets] against him but that the decree should be performed before the bonds. Thus here it was resolved upon a hearing in chancery in Searle and Lane, 5 March 4 Jac. II [1688],[1] and affirmed upon a rehearing 24 November past. There the point was [that] the administrator had paid away his assets to the bond creditors before notice, and yet [it was] resolved that he should take notice at his peril and should pay the decree first.

Note [that] in Shaftoe's Case there was another point that Hooke entered an attachment against the arch[deacon] and took the goods under color of this and then [became] administrator; [the point was] whether he would not be executor *de son tort*. And the court did not resolve this but determined [the case] upon the other point, POWELL doubting.

[Other copies of this report: HLS MS. 537(b), p. 38, pl. 5; Oxf. Brasenose MS. 59, p. 51, pl. 3; IU Lilly MS. Parker, 'Tithes', p. 195.]

[Other reports of this case: *sub nom.* Shafto v. Powell, 3 Levinz 355, 83 E.R. 727; *sub nom.* Stasby v. Powell, 1 Freeman 333, 22 E.R. 1237, 89 E.R. 248.]

[Order of 15 May 1693: PRO E.126/16, f. 99.]

---

[1] *Searle v. Lane* (1688), 2 Freeman 103, 22 E.R. 1086; Cases 31, 84, 2 Vernon 37, 88, 23 E.R. 634, 667; *sub nom. Searle v. Hale*, pl. 4, 1 Eq. Cas. Abr. 332, 21 E.R. 1082.

289
Ward v. Hilder (Ex. 1693)

A statute will not be presumed to recite a falsehood.
Tithes of houses in London can be sued for in the exchequer by a bill in equity.
Impropriators stand in the place of parsons as to the receipt of tithes.

LI MS. Hill 49, f. 175, pl. 6 [Fr.]

In an English bill in the exchequer, the plaintiff showed that he was the impropriator of a church in London. And he demanded the annual sum of 36s. for the customary payment as the tithes upon a house in London against the defendant, the owner of it, or that the defendant should pay to him 2s. 9d. in the pound according to the decree made. 37 Hen. VIII, c. 12.[1]

The defendant answered and insisted upon customary tithes, but it [was] not proved. And it was objected by *Ettrick* and *Dodd*:

1. That there was not any such decree to be found as was recited in this Statute. But to this, the court said that it will be presumed that there was, and though the record could not now be found, decrees have been [. . .] made in this court in affirmance of it, and they will not suffer it to be disputed because a statute will not be presumed to recite a falsehood [and] secondly because it will be of universal inconvenience to order [?] such a dispute.
2. They objected that if this decree should be affirmed, then the Statute had introduced and directed a particular course in which tithes should be demanded and recovered, and this should be pursued because tithes *de jure* were not payable for houses, and when they were made liable and the law directed how they should be demanded, it was exclusive of [any] other remedy, and on account of that the lord mayor and in his default the lord chancellor could imprison [for] the defaults in the payment of tithes. But [this argument] was not allowed; decrees in this court have been frequent, and the Statute does not exclude other remedies than those provided there.
3. They objected that the Statute speaks of parsons, vicars, etc. and their successors, and thus it does not extend to impropriators, Hardres 102,[2] but to such parson etc. who had a successor. But [this

---

[1] Stat. 37 Hen. VIII, c. 12 (*SR*, III, 998–1000); the decree is printed in this edition of the statutes.

[2] *Sheffield v. Serjeant* (1657), Hardres 102, 145 E.R. 402, 1 Eagle & Younge 419, 2 Gwillim 503.

argument] was not allowed because the impropriator is in the notion and language of the law the parson, though he be a mere layman.
4. They objected that the defendant would be charged two times by such an exposition because he would be charged upon the decree of 37 Hen. VIII and also upon the Statute of 22 Car. II, page 75,[3] for the rebuilding of the City of London; there is an express provision that the parson etc. should have all certain [tithes]. But [this argument] was not allowed because this Statute provides only for the preaching minister and not for the impropriator.

And it was only decreed that the defendant should pay 2s. 9d. in the pound after the rate of £30 in the year, as he [the defendant] in his answer had admitted the value of his house to be. He did not accept the offer of the plaintiff to accept the rate of 36s., which had been usually paid but not thus proved for the defendant.

[Other reports of this case: 2 Gwillim 538, Western 103.]

[The decree of 18 May 1693, PRO E.126/16, f. 106, is printed at 1 Wood 305, 1 Eagle & Younge 576; see also order of 11 May 1693: PRO E.126/16, f. 98v.]

290
Webb v. Phillips (Ex. 1694)

Where two persons have an ongoing financial relationship, no cause of action accrues until an account has been stated.

HLS MS. 1052, f. 38v, pl. 111 [Eng.] (Wright's Reports)

The defendant, being indebted to Web, a tailor, for clothes and he to the defendant for some other matters, the defendant brought his action at law. The plaintiff exhibits a bill in this court to be relieved, to which the defendant pleaded the Statute of Limitations,[1] which plea, upon debate, was overruled, because it appeared that the defendant had agreed (though many years ago) that the tailor should work on for him and set off his debt in his bill, and this being to be discounted, no action could arise till the account should be stated.

[Order of 27 Oct. 1694: PRO E.127/19, f. 10v.]

---

[3] Stat. 22 and 23 Car. II, c. 15 (*SR*, V, 725–727); the reference to 'page 75' is an interlinear addition which may be an incorrect copying of 'ca. 15' or it may refer to Stat. 22 Car. II, c. 11, s. 61 (*SR*, V, 680).

---

[1] Stat. 21 Jac. I, c. 16 (*SR*, IV, 1222–1223).

291

Attorney General ex rel. Boucher v. Portington (Ex. 1694)

Depositions taken in a former suit by a party suing in his own right cannot be used in a later suit by the same person suing as a relator.

The crown is not within the Statute of Frauds or the Statute of Limitations.

A charitable trust given to an illegal purpose will be redirected to a legal purpose but will not be forfeited.

BL MS. Hargr. 71, f. 87v [Fr. & Eng.] (Dodd's Reports)

This case was formerly decreed and then reheard. And the court held [that the] depositions [were] irregular in regard that they were examinations in the chancery between Bouchier, the heir at law, and Portington. And the king having granted this estate in fee to the heir at law, the information was as well in behalf of Their Majesties as at the relation of Bouchier etc. And the court held the grant [to be] void and rejected the depositions. But they gave Mr. Attorney [General] liberty to examine, which was done accordingly. And now the cause came to be heard in the exchequer chamber, and it was thus.

Ann Barlow, an old woman, devised several houses in fee to the defendant, Mary Portington, who was (as was sworn) a nun and set up the nunnery in St. Martin's Lane in the time of James II to superstitious uses, *viz.* to God and the Virgin Mary and to pray her soul out of purgatory, as was proved by sworn witnesses. But [there was] no writing of it but only verbal declarations of Portington. And upon this, the questions were:

1. Whether the land should be forfeited, or whether the use should be forfeited and corrected.
2. Whether they could have such a use or trust contrary to the Statute of Frauds and Perjuries.[1]

To the first [question], it seemed to the court that the land, neither the freehold nor the fee simple, was forfeited but remained in the devisee, but the use or trust and profits of the land are either forfeited or rather subject to be corrected in equity and disposed by the king to a lawful use. He can decree a perception of the profits and declare the trust for the benefit of the crown. And they held that therefore no inquisition [was] necessary. Note the Case of Impropriations[2] in the time of Charles I.

To the second [question, it seemed to the court] that such a superstitious use is not within the Statute of Frauds and Perjuries and that the king is not bound by that Statute.

---

[1] Stat. 29 Car. II, c. 3 (*SR*, V, 839–842).
[2] *Attorney General v. Gouge* (Ex. 1633), 118 Selden Soc. 643.

Note [that] there have been divers cases resolved that such an information lies and the land decreed, as Lord Carrington's Case (1682),³ Gaynor Jones' Case, above, which was heard, reheard, reviewed, and affirmed on appeal,⁴ Lawson's Case (1692), and several others.

Note [that] upon a commission, this use was found in Portington's Case and traversed in the chancery and tried in the king's bench before Holt. And upon the trial, a case was made, and [it was] resolved there that he could not have any such trust without a writing. And the judgment [was] to remove the king's hands. Query.

Attorney [General] and Portington, Thursday, 9 May 1694. [It was] resolved upon argument and debate:

1. That the king is not within the Statute of Frauds; where he has any interest, property, or special prerogative, [he is] not bound if [he is] not named. Magdalen College Case;⁵ Lord Berkley's Case. No statute of limitation binds *quia nullum tempus etc.*;⁶ thus of the plenarty. And [it was said] by Lechmere [that] this is [an] unlawful trust, but the Statute is [?] trust declared by him that lawfully may, which in this case is nobody; thus [it is] out of the Statute.
2. The king [is] not entitled in point of forfeiture for there is no forfeiture of a trust of a superstitious use either by common law or by statute. But [it is] given to the king who has a prerogative in point of regulation as supreme head [of the church] and not as a forfeiture. This is a trust that concerns religion [and] thus general, and no public trust shall sink in the land nor a trust upon a charity. Mr. Snell gave land to maintain some persons to teach the liturgy or doctrine of the Church of England in Scotland, and before [it was] disposed, the liturgy was put down there; this was decreed to be a good use here, *viz.* to a college in the University of Oxford.⁷ So [also was] the Case of Impropriations in the late times. And [it was said] by Turton [that the court] may decree the lands, as [in] Gaynor Jones's Case, or regulate or correct the trust.

The General Pardon of 2 Will. & Mar. [1690]⁸ [does] not extend to it for [there is] no forfeiture, offense, or penalty.

---

³ *Attorney General v. Lord Carrington* (Ex. 1682), above, No. 143.
⁴ *Attorney General v. Gaynor Jones* (Ex. 1688), above, No. 269.
⁵ *Warren v. Smith (Magdalen College Case)*, 11 Coke Rep. 66b, 77 E.R. 1235, 1 Rolle Rep. 151, 81 E.R. 394, 2 Bulstrode 146, 80 E.R. 1021, Cro. Jac. 364, 79 E.R. 312 (1615).
⁶ *Nullum tempus occurrit regi*; no time [limits] run against the king.
⁷ *Attorney General v. Guise* (1692), 2 Vernon 266, 23 E.R. 772.
⁸ Stat. 2 Will. & Mar., c. 10 (*SR*, VI, 174–179).

This is an unlawful and superstitious use. See 1 Edw. VI, c. 14,⁹ and Croft's and Evett's Case.¹⁰

The king shall have it not as in point of prerogative for that must be always but as belonging to him in his royal office of king, who is to protect the religion and government. The trust shall not be void. The intention was to give it [away] from the heir and to promote religion, and so it ought to be applied, *viz.* to promote not popery but the true religion. [It was] therefore decreed:

1. The trust [was] for the king.
2. The defendant to convey the estate in law to the king in fee.
3. To be employed for religious purposes.

Note [that] POWELL was for an issue to try the fact, but the other three [were] against him and [were] satisfied with the proof; so this case (according to the Statute) without inquisition or trial [was] decreed. In this case, POWELL said that notwithstanding Sir John Daccomb's Case, a trust of a freehold will be forfeited for treason: Cro. Jac. 513.¹¹

[Other copies of this report: HLS MS. 537(b), p. 40; Oxf. Brasenose MS. 59, p. 52, pl. 5; IU Lilly MS. Parker, 'Cases in the Exchequer, vol. 2', p. 2; BL MS. Hargr. 70, p. 96; HLS MS. 1162, p. 86; IU Lilly MS. Parker, 'Tithes', p. 61.]

[Other reports of this case: 1 Salkeld 162, 91 E.R. 151; 3 Salkeld 334, 91 E.R. 856; Pl. 6, 1 Eq. Cas. Abr. 96, 21 E.R. 906; Case 62, 12 Modern 31, 88 E.R. 1144.]

[Order of 22 Apr. 1695: PRO E.126/16, f. 256.]

[This case is cited in Cary v. Abbot (1802), 7 Vesey 490, 495, 32 E.R. 198, 200; Bourne v. Keane, L.R. [1919] App. Cas. 815, 848.]

292

Dod v. Hesketh (Ex. 1694)

In this case, the court permitted the redemption of a mortgage of a remainder, but the mortgagee was not to be reimbursed for improvements made since the remainder would not vest for many years to come.

LI MS. Hill 49, f. 228v, pl. 2 [Fr.]

The plaintiff exhibited his bill to have execution of a specific agreement. And the case was thus. The defendant, upon good consideration, made a lease to the plaintiff for twenty-one years to begin after the death of one Cooper (who

---

⁹ Stat. 1 Edw. VI, c. 14 (*SR*, IV, 24–33).

¹⁰ *Croft v. Evett* (1605), Moore K.B. 784, 72 E.R. 904, also 117 Selden Soc. 342.

¹¹ *Rex v. Executors of Sir John Daccombe* (1618), Cro. Jac. 513, 79 E.R. 437, also *sub nom. Attorney General v. Carr*, 118 Selden Soc. 475.

had an estate for life) rendering 20s. rent. Then the plaintiff purchased the interest of Cooper in the name of a trustee. The defendant afterwards had occasion [?][1] for £100 and, having notice that the plaintiff had bought the interest of Cooper, by [a deed of] lease and release, he conveyed to the person in trust for the plaintiff the absolute inheritance. But because the defendant urged that it was in value more by £20, the trustee of the plaintiff by a separate defeasance agreed that if he repaid the £100 with all costs and expenses in the title within the year at a certain place, that he would reconvey, and that, if there was a default of payment, that then, upon tender of £20 by the trustee to the defendant, the defendant would make further assurances. The plaintiff purchased [?] the houses, and he erected walls [?] at the expense of £400 to the improvement of the inheritance and made a lease after the year but before tender of the £20 to a stranger for three lives, who had no notice of the defeasance [and] who built to the value of £150.

And upon the hearing of both causes, two points were made: first whether the estate [was] absolute or redeemable, [and] if redeemable, [then] secondly upon what terms.

And the three barons held first that it was redeemable [and] secondly that the defendant should redeem upon the payment of the £100, interest, and costs and that he should not have any allowance for the building because he had an estate for the life of a young [?] man of twenty-two and also [?] twenty-one years after that was sufficient to encourage building, secondly because it was tolerable before and the walls [?] [were] for ornament more than necessity or of convenience and thirdly [because] the lessee should not have any allowance for his building, though he had no notice, but his lessor should indemnify him.

And [Baron] LECHMERE said it was one [with] the case where a man pulled down a brewhouse and erected [?] sumptuous [?] buildings; he should not have allowance.[2] But they agreed that necessary buildings should have allowance to the mortgagee.

And as to the first point, the court and counsel remembered the case of Morgan v. George[3] in this court the other day where a man made such a conveyance [which was] to be void upon payment of the money and absolute upon payment of £10 more; the mortgagor sold his equity for £70, and he came to redeem, and it was received because it was plain that the estate was £60 more valuable than the mortgagee would pay and it was [against good] conscience to take such advantage of men's necessities, but when it approaches the true value, as here, it was pressed to be otherwise.

---

[1] I.e. to sell.
[2] This may refer to the case of *Cole v. Forth* (1672), 1 Modern 94, 86 E.R. 759, *sub nom. Cole v. Green*, 1 Levinz 309, 83 E.R. 422, *sub nom. Greene v. Cole*, 2 Wms. Saund. 228, 85 E.R. 1022.
[3] *Morgan v. George* (1693), PRO E.126/16, f. 155v.

But here the bill of the plaintiff was dismissed with costs. And the defendant upon his bill [was] permitted to redeem as upon a common mortgage, *scil.* [upon] payment of principal, interest, and costs.

And I was of counsel with the plaintiff, and I expected the same decree that the court gave.

[Order of 28 Jan. 1694: PRO E.126/16, f. 243.]

293

Ode v. Halsey (Ex. 1695)

In this case, a penalty in a deed was enforced.

BL MS. Hargr. 71, f. 92, pl. 2 [Fr. & Eng.] (Dodd's Reports)

In this case, the court directed a *quod damnum* for the plaintiff upon a penalty in a deed of which the plaintiff was to have the advantage against the will and desire of the defendant. *Quod mirum.* It was [done] by TURTON and POWELL contrary to LECHMERE, who would have left them to [the common] law.

[Other copies of this report: HLS MS. 537(b), p. 44, pl. 4; Oxf. Brasenose MS. 59, p. 58, pl. 3; IU Lilly MS. Parker, 'Cases in the Exchequer, vol. 2', p. 12.]

294

Sherrington v. Gregory (Ex. 1695)

According to the tax act of 5 & 6 Will. & Mar., a tenant should not deduct from a fee farm rent any greater sum than the tax paid.

BL MS. Hargr. 71, f. 93, pl. 1 [Fr. & Eng.] (Dodd's Reports)

In the case of Sherington and Gregory heard at Serjeants' Inn December 1694 [it was] resolved that a fee farm rent shall pay but in proportion to the land taxed[1] and that the landlord or his tenant shall not deduct 4s. in the pound where the land is not charged so high. Note in this case that the impropriation was not taxed above 18d. in the pound and the deduction of 4s. in the pound out of the fee farm rent was as much or more than the land was taxed. This rectory was the rectory of Barnaby upon Dun in York.

Note [that] this term upon such a bill brought by Sir John Werden[2] and a demurrer upon it, [it was] resolved that [the court would] not examine this matter

---

[1] Stat. 5 & 6 Will. & Mar., c. 1, ss. 3, 4 (*SR*, VI, 427).
[2] *Werden v. Pickering* (Ex. 1695), below, No. 296.

and, upon great debate and consideration, this case of Sherington and Gregory [was] denied. See the breviates.

[Other copies of this report: HLS MS. 537(b), p. 45, pl. 2; Oxf. Brasenose MS. 59, p. 59, pl. 5; IU Lilly MS. Parker, 'Cases in the Exchequer, vol. 2', p. 13.]

295

Bramly v. Philips (Ex. 1695)

It is a reasonable custom for a copyholder for life to have the power to name his successor. In this case, no such custom was found to exist in the particular manor.

LI MS. Misc. 559, f. 6, pl. 3 [Eng.] (Ward's Reports)

The defendant as lord of the manor of Shepshed in the County of Leicester having recovered in an ejectment a verdict for certain copyhold lands parcel of that manor, the plaintiff exhibited his English bill into this court for relief and showed his case to be this, that there is and time out of mind has been within that manor this custom, that the copyholds there have been granted and grantable for three lives by copy of court roll, and that the first taker by such copy has had the power and governance of such estate for three lives, and that upon his surrender in or out of court, the lord has and ought to admit the surrenderee for such other three lives as he should nominate paying a reasonable fine and so *toties quoties*, and that if the first taker dies without any such surrender, that there the other two or, in case of the death of one of them, the survivor of the three has and ought to have a power in or out of court to surrender the estate to such other person or persons as he or they should think fit, and that upon such surrender whether the surrenderer live unto or die before the next court that the lord of the manor has used and ought to admit such surrenderee, his heirs, or assigns unto such copyhold estate for the term of three lives upon payment of a reasonable fine. And the plaintiff made his case within the custom to be the surrenderee of one Bramly, who was the survivor of three lives upon a former surrender and admittance, and that the surrenderer died before the next court and that the surrender was presented by the homage and that he offered to pay the defendant a reasonable fine for his admittance for three lives according to the custom. But the defendant refused to admit him but recovered at law against him, he not having any title at law to defend without admittance.

And at the hearing the last term, it was by two barons against one referred to a trial at law whether there was such a custom or not, with which direction the defendant not being satisfied prayed a rehearing which being granted, and the court being changed and now full (the chief baron and Baron Powys never having heard the cause), it came to be reheard.

And in this case, two points were under consideration, first whether such a custom as the plaintiff pretends to by his bill, being for bare copyholders for life, was good in law, secondly if it was, whether the plaintiff has made probable proof of such custom either to decree it or to send it to a trial at law whether there be such a custom or not within that manor.

As to the first, the defendant's counsel did not insist in point of law that there could be no such custom in law, for it is usual for [a] copyholder for life to have power by custom to name his successor; see 2 Cro. 368, Ford and Hoskins's Case in the manor of Beauminster; Moore 842; 1 Rolle *Abridgment* 108.[1] And by custom a man may be entitled to have a lease renewed for twenty-one years, 2 Cro. 671[2] (manor of Turlex in the County of Bedford). And though the defendant's counsel much insisted on the hardship of such a custom and that such a tenancy for lives was better than a fee simple in regard [that] here no fine was to be paid till the surrender [be] made, which might not be till the last life, whereas in fee simples it is upon every tenant's death, and objected that here is but a bare estate for life and every copyholder for life in England and those upon western estates for lives only and tenants to the church who constantly renew may as well pretend to such privileges in respect of their constant renewals, yet in regard the custom of a manor is the life and soul of copyholds, there does not appear any inconsistency or incongruity in law why there may not be here such a custom as is pretended, to nominate a successor, and the cases of western estates and tenants of churches are not like to this, there being no custom to warrant them, as there is in the North of England where the custom for border service holds place. So as to the first point, the court did not see anything why such a custom as is pretended should in itself be void in law. See Moore 788.[3]

As to the second point, it being proved in the cause on both sides and in effect admitted by the defendant that there had been for many years such an usage in the manor and that the lords had admitted accordingly upon agreement for fines (for there is no pretence of [a] fine certain), the court was not satisfied to decree for the plaintiff without a trial but sent it to be tried in a feigned issue whether there be such a custom as the plaintiff pretends to and the lord bound to admit accordingly wherein the uncertainty of the fine and the constant agreement with the lord for a fine may be considered against the plaintiff's pretences and the lord's admission upon such surrender (as this in question is) without contradiction may be an evidence of the custom, but whether such custom be obliga-

---

[1] *Ford v. Hoskins* (1615), Cro. Jac. 368, 79 E.R. 315, Moore K.B. 842, 72 E.R. 941, 1 Rolle, Abr., *Action sur Case*, pl. N, 24, p. 108, also 1 Rolle Rep. 125, 195, 81 E.R. 376, 427, 2 Bulstrode 336, 80 E.R. 1168.

[2] *Page's Case* (1623), Cro. Jac. 671, 79 E.R. 581.

[3] *Lord Grey's Case* (1607), Moore K.B. 788, 72 E.R. 907.

tory upon the lord or not fit to be tried at law, the uncertainty of the fine, what that shall be, and who shall set it, and after what rule making the difficulty, the case cited, 2 Cro. 368 in the manor of Beauminster, not being like this, for there is a certainty by the homage in case the lord and tenant cannot agree, which is not so here but only a reasonable fine, and that makes a point of law whether there can be such a custom for surrendering and admitting and payment of a fine when it does not appear what fine or who shall set it, in case the lord and tenant do not agree.

Note afterwards in Long Vacation 1696 upon a trial at law at the assizes, there was a verdict for the defendant that there was no such custom obligatory upon the lord and the bill was afterwards dismissed.

[Other copies of this report: GUL MS. B88-8, p. 243.]

[Orders of 6 June and 7 Nov. 1695: PRO E.126/16, ff. 267, 295.]

296

Werden v. Pickering (Ex. 1695)

A bill in equity does not lie to challenge the assessments of tax commissioners.

LI MS. Misc. 559, f. 7 [Eng.] (Ward's Reports)

The plaintiff having a fee farm rent purchased under the crown, title issuing out of the defendant's manor and lands in Cheshire, and the several acts of 4s. in the pound taxes made in the 5th and 6th years of the reign of his now Majesty and of the late queen[1] laying a tax of 4s. in the pound upon all lands etc. and giving the tenants of the lands power to deduct 4s. in the pound out of all fee farm and other rents issuing out of or chargeable upon their estates, the defendant deducted 4s. in the pound out of the plaintiff's fee farm rent of £26 6s. 8d. *per annum* charged upon and issuing out of the defendant's manor. The plaintiff exhibits his English bill to be relieved against the defendant's demand and deduction of 4s. in the pound for his whole rent suggesting that in truth the defendant's estate is worth £104 *per annum* and that that estate instead of being taxed 4s. in the pound was not taxed at, nor did he pay to the taxes above the rate of eighteen pence in the pound, nor ought he to default[2] or deduct more out of the rent than proportionably to what he paid to the taxes, which was 18d. in the pound, and to discover the real yearly value of the defendant's lands liable to the plaintiff's rent, and after what rate he paid to the taxes, and to be relieved against the payment of

---

[1] Stat. 5 & 6 Will. & Mar., c. 1, ss. 3, 4 (*SR*, VI, 427).
[2] defauthe *MS*.

the whole 4s. per pound for the rent, and to pay proportionable only for his rent with what the defendant paid for his land was the bill.

The defendant answered to all the charges in the bill except what tended to discover the true yearly value of his estate and after what rate he was taxed for the same and to state anything of the deduction of 4s. in the pound. And as to them he demurred because the plaintiff ought not to be answered nor relieved the deduction being only such as the several acts well warrant and direct, for the plaintiff of his own showing pays no more than what the acts lay upon him, *viz.* 4s. in the pound.

But the plaintiff's counsel showed that this point had been judicially determined in this court in Michaelmas Term last between Sherrington and Gregory,[3] where the like case was that the tertenants' lands were proved to be taxed and to pay but after the rate of 18d. in the pound and yet he deducted 4s. in the pound for the rent he paid out. And therefore the court decreed that the owner of the rent should not allow more in the pound for his rent than the tertenant was taxed and paid for the yearly value of his land and that this bill was grounded upon that resolution and decree. But I was in doubt whether the court, as this case is, should overrule the demurrer and compel the defendant to discover the real yearly value of his lands in order to let the plaintiff in to an equity for relief.

First it is plain that the acts provide that full 4s. in the pound should be paid for all lands, and for that purpose commissioners upon oath are appointed to see the acts executed and assessors are by a particular oath sworn truly and impartially to rate and assess all lands etc. pursuant to the act. And if anyone was aggrieved, appeals lay to the commissioners and their determination [was] final. And it is hard to found an equity upon the supposed breach of an oath of one authorized and entrusted to assess upon his oath.

Secondly it is to be considered whether, if the king should prefer a bill to be relieved for an undervaluation and undertaxation, the court could relieve, though the plain scope and words of the acts are that the king should have 4s. in the pound of all lands. And it is conceived not.

Thirdly what the consequence might be of such bills' drawing in examination the values of all lands at the instance of persons that have rents charged upon or issuing out of them, there might be [a] multitude of such suits. And the proceedings of the commissioners and assessors upon the acts drawn into an examination against the meaning of the act, for if a question upon the values of lands may be admitted, then whether the taxation was full or short of 4s. in the pound and how much short must be examined which will be difficult, tedious, and chargeable.

---

[3] *Sherrington v. Gregory* (Ex. 1695), above, No. 294.

Fourthly the deduction of 4s. in the pound for the rent is no more than the plaintiff ought to pay, and what equity is there for the plaintiff to be relieved against what the Act of Parliament lays upon him, and if the tertenant does not pay all that he ought, yet that will not raise an equity to the owner of the rent to pay less than the Act requires, for he pays no more than he ought though the other pays not so much.

Fifthly if [the] plaintiff had been taxed separately for his fee farm rent (as he might), he must pay 4s. in the pound, and when the land is taxed, the deduction must be equal as if taxed alone. And there is no ground of equity [that] can accrue or arise to the plaintiff who pays but what by law he ought to pay because another pays less than he ought to pay. And for a court of equity to countenance a fraud to the crown by decreeing that the sum that the crown is defrauded of shall be divided and shared between persons, is like making a decree that a booty taken by thieves shall be equally shared between them.

And upon these reasons above and for that the plaintiff's relief that he seeks is against the words of the Act of Parliament and of dangerous consequence to let in examinations to contradict the values of lands taxed upon assessors' oaths at 4s. per pound and for that this suit was commenced only for relief against the payment of 4s. per pound and to have a deduction less than the Act directs, the whole court was of opinion to allow the demurrer and desired me to deliver the judgment of the court accordingly, which I did at large upon the reasons above on Wednesday the 20th of November. And the demurrer was allowed.

Note afterwards (as was said) the Lord Keeper Somers relieved in the like case, but query that and upon what grounds and under what circumstances if it was so, whether there was not some fraud or contrivance in the matter. And it is hard for a court of revenue to relieve upon a found action of a fraud to the king, as it must be if the king had not his taxes at 4s. per pound out of the lands; by subsequent acts rent and lands [are] to pay proportionably.

[Other copies of this report: GUL MS. B88–8, p. 247.]

[Order of 9 Nov. 1695: PRO E.127/19, f. 361.]

297

Crane v. Hill (Ex. 1695)

A court of equity will grant relief against a common law judgment where the plaintiff at common law who had sold a fee simple afterwards took and set up a superior title or precedent encumbrance to evict his own conveyance.

LI MS. Misc. 559, f. 10 [Eng.] (Ward's Reports)

The case upon the hearing appeared to be thus. The plaintiff Crane was a creditor to the defendant Hill's father and to the defendant for several sums of money, some lent and secured and others for which they were sureties for the said defendant and his father. And the defendant's father having an estate in lands (and amongst others of the rectory of Hales) all of about £300 *per annum* but greatly incumbered with mortgages, judgments, and otherwise and himself living in obscure and privileged places, and the defendant, his eldest son, having little or nothing to live on (though bred at the university) was supplied with some moneys by the plaintiff for his living, for which he gave the plaintiff security by bond and otherwise. And the defendant's father happening to die in Gray's Inn about the 8th of September 1675, his death was made known to the plaintiff but not to the defendant. And before the defendant knew of his father's death, *viz.* on the 10th of September 1675, the plaintiff and defendant entered into a treaty about the plaintiff's purchasing the defendant's father's estate and the plaintiff's interest therein.

And thereupon the 13th of the same September, articles in writing under the hands and seals of the plaintiff and defendant were entered into whereby defendant sold to Crane the plaintiff in fee all his father's estates in Norfolk or Suffolk the plaintiff to find defendant board for a certain time and paying some small sums about £20 and sometime after £30 and after that £40 *per annum* for the defendant's life and to discharge the defendant from all engagements to the plaintiff. And upon this there was only 5s. paid immediately. After entering into these articles, the defendant understood that his father was dead at the time of the articles, and then he considered with himself whether he should perform or stand to the articles or not his father being dead, which he knew not of when he entered into the articles. And an uncle of the defendant's offered to buy the estate of the defendant. But the defendant refused to sell to his uncle but after notice of his father's death upon consideration went on with the plaintiff though upon some better terms the plaintiff having offered to quit all his pretences to the articles or bargain, if the defendant would pay plaintiff what he and his father owed him and save him harmless against their debts for which he was engaged. And thereupon the 13th of the same September, the defendant executed a deed of feoffment to the plaintiff of the whole estate in consideration of the discharge by the plaintiff of a bond of £600 for payment of £300 and two other bonds of £100 apiece from defendant's father to plaintiff and plaintiff's discharge of a book debt of £80 due from defendant to plaintiff and of the payment of an annuity of £30 *per annum* to defendant for five years and of £40 *per annum* after for defendant's life to be secured out of the estate, and by that feoffment grants and conveys the whole estate to plaintiff and his heirs.

And one of the liveries that was made was made upon the glebe, tithes, rights, and dues of the church of Hales. And by this conveyance (which indeed was defective), the defendant was to be saved harmless against his father's mortgages. And a month after all this, *viz.* by lease and release of the 12th and 13th of October 1675, the defendant for the consideration of £735 15s. owned to be paid by plaintiff to him and also for the consideration that the plaintiff should secure to the defendant the said two annuities of £30 for five years and of £40 *per annum* after for the defendant's life unto the defendant, the defendant conveyed to the plaintiff and his heirs all his said father's estate, and amongst the rest by particular and express words the impropriations of Hales and Heckenham in Hales and all glebe, tithes, etc. thereto belonging, with covenants for further assurance, quiet enjoyment, and freedom from encumbrances against himself and all claiming under him. There was the defendant's receipt proved for the £735 15s., and the two annuities of £30 and £40 *per annum* were secured by the plaintiff to the defendant by and out of all the estate conveyed to him. And this lease and release was executed by the defendant to the plaintiff knowingly and willingly and under the deliberation of a month and dictated and fully understood by the defendant as was proved in the cause and a fine levied at [the] same time which mentions not the rectory of Hales, though the lease and release do. There happened to be mesne encumbrances upon the estate by mortgage and judgments, some whereof were paid off by plaintiff, others secured against by him, and others compounded, and amongst the rest old Hill mortgaged part to one Bishop, the benefit of which ought to have come to Roger Cooke, but Crane the plaintiff denying the mortgage and insisting upon himself to be a purchaser without notice (though he after came to have the counterpart of the mortgage by him), the plaintiff paid nothing upon that mortgage, though he did upon others, and enjoyed the estate subject to the encumbrances for fifteen or sixteen years and paid the annuities all the time as they became due. Only the defendant in 1682 gave the plaintiff some trouble in chancery endeavoring to set aside the bargain (but his bill was in truth upon hearing dismissed though that dismission [was] not drawn up).

And afterwards in or about the year 1692, there was brought to the defendant's solicitor's house enclosed in a paper from an unknown person a lease in writing dated the 4th of May 1587, whereby it was mentioned that Sir Edward Clere[1] leased to the defendant's grandfather John Hill, the rectory of Hales with the glebe, etc. and perpetual advowson of the vicarage of Hales for one thousand years rendering 4s. rent yearly to Sir Edward for his life then to Robert his son and the heirs male of Robert, then to the right heirs of Sir Edward. Upon this,

---

[1] See *Cleer's Case* (1611), Ley 43, 80 E.R. 617, PRO Ward 9/90, f. 857v (this reference was kindly supplied by Dr. Neil G. Jones).

the defendant Hill takes administration *de bonis non* etc. of his grandfather and brought his ejectment at law and recovered before Chief Justice Holt, though it no way appeared that ever this rectory was enjoyed by or how it came from the Cleres. And to be relieved against this lease and recovery, the now plaintiff exhibited his English bill.

And the case appearing to be as above, it was by opinion of the chief baron [WARD] and of LECHMERE and POWYS, barons, (*dissentiente* Baron TURTON) decreed for the plaintiff that this lease should be delivered up and that there should be a perpetual injunction against the said lease and verdict and that upon these reasons.

First though the articles of the 10th of September were obtained from the defendant when he knew not of his father's death and so probably not so advantageous terms were made for the defendant as he might have made had he then known his father had been dead or possibly he might not have sold at all, yet those articles were ineffectual for the plaintiff to have had any execution in specie thereupon in any court of equity as well upon the frame of them as the manner of obtaining of them and the smallness of the consideration money paid being only 5s. and had the defendant stopped there, the plaintiff had been remediless thereupon, though it appeared that the plaintiff was an honest creditor and security for the defendant and his father and the plaintiff was in that respect the more excusable in gaining those articles in regard it was in proof that he offered to release them upon receiving what was justly due to him for the defendant's and his father's debts and being saved harmless against his securities entered into for them.

Secondly that when the defendant knew of his father's death and had full consideration of the whole matter, yet he chose to go on with the plaintiff and refused his uncle's offers and thereupon executed the deed of feoffment of the 13th of September in person making thereby something better terms for himself than he had done by the articles.

Thirdly that if both articles and feoffment had signified nothing, yet when the defendant came to London a month after and gave instruction to counsel to draw the lease and release of the 12th and 13th of October, which were perused by and read to him and he had full knowledge of their effect, and willingly executed the same (as was proved in the cause) and the considerations therein were better to the defendant than the articles and feoffment and levied a fine and took a security for his rent charges and received the same several years without further claim and it not being pretended but that the defendant was of full age and sound mind and under no force or surprise when he did all this and having covenanted for quiet enjoyment, freedom from encumbrances, and further assurance and the defendant having both in the feoffment and lease and release expressly conveyed the rectory of Hales in fee and taken it back *inter alia* for security of his rent charges, it must be understood that the defendant did intend to convey that rectory and did take a consideration for the fee simple of it as in possession, and that having so done it is against conscience for himself to set up another title in himself, though as administrator and so in another right, to evict that estate which he before sold and took money for as a fee simple in possession, and the rather for that it does not appear that the defendant paid one penny for that old stale lease, or that one penny of his grandfather's debts remain unpaid or that ever the Cleres had any title to or possession of the rectory of Hales.

And therefore the court looked upon the plaintiff, upon the whole matter, to be a purchaser of that rectory with the other estate for a valuable consideration *bona fide* and without notice of that lease and so relievable within the ordinary rules of equity, which never suffers a man that sells a fee simple in possession to take in and set up a precedent incumbrance to evict his own conveyance. And though Hales rectory was not mentioned in the fine, yet it was in the lease and release which passed the inheritance of it well enough to the plaintiff. And by virtue of his covenant for further assurance [he] may be compelled to levy a fine of it when required. And though the plaintiff might do ill to put in such an answer as he did to Roger Cooke's bill, yet thereby the defendant admits that his estate was mortgaged to Bishop and that the mortgage was due and that the plaintiff took the land charged, though he used ill means to defraud Bishop of the debt, which cannot help the defendant in this case nor make his case better.

So it was decreed *ut supra* and that the plaintiff by his own consent should pay the defendant his rent [in] arrears and the future payments as it shall grow due. And the defendant's agent and solicitor upon those terms submitted to the decree and to deliver up the lease.

[Other copies of this report: GUL MS. B88–8, p. 257.]

[Decrees of 29 Nov. and 7 Dec. 1695: PRO E.126/16, ff. 303v, 420.]

[This report and the order of 7 Dec. 1695 are printed in W. H. Bryson, 'Equity Reports and Records in Early-Modern England' in A. Wijffels, *Case Law in the Making*, II (1997), pp. 73–81.]

298

Cumber v. Atkinson (Ex. 1695)

In this case for tithes, the defendant failed to prove that the land in question formerly belonged to the Cistercian Order and was thus discharged.

LI MS. Misc. 559, f. 12, pl. 1 [Eng.] (Ward's Reports)

The plaintiff sued the defendant for all manner of tithes for three years. Defendant's counsel in discharge offered that the lands were parcel of the Abbey of Fountains and of the Cistercian Order and that the defendant was a jointress and held them for her life and in her own hand. And a question arose whether

[a] jointress for life shall have the privilege of the Order of Cistercians of being discharged *quamdiu [in] propriis manibus*,[1] but that point came not to be spoken to because it was neither alleged in the answer nor proved in the cause (and so not in issue) that the lands were parcel of the abbot of Fountains' possessions nor did it appear (otherwise than by Dugdale's *Monasticon*[2] which was not allowed for evidence) that Fountains was of the Cistercian Order, but it was said that the lands in question were held of the Abbey of Fountains which was not sufficient to prove them to be parcel as they ought, and so a decree passed for the plaintiff.

See Hardres' *Reports*, f. 174,[3] that tenant for life shall not have the privilege of exemption *quamdiu [in] propriis manibus* as [a] tenant in fee or in tail shall.

[Other copies of this report: GUL MS. B88–8, p. 263.]

[Order of 8 Nov. 1695: PRO E.126/16, f. 300.]

[This case is cited in Steyner v. Burgesses of Droitwich (1695), Skinner 623, 90 E.R. 280, 1 Salkeld 281, 91 E.R. 247.]

299

Twitty v. Ewen (Ex. 1695)

Copies of books, other than official records, are not admissible in evidence.

LI MS. Misc. 559, f. 12, pl. 2 [Eng.] (Ward's Reports)

In this case, the plaintiff offered to read a copy out of the register book of the bishop of Sarum, being an old book, but it was denied by the court for the book itself not being a record, a copy of anything out of it cannot be allowed for evidence, but the book itself may, giving an account [of] how it is kept. And this is not like the case of a church book which is in continual use and is the only instance allowed of having a copy proved of anything in a book which is not of record. Copies of entries of judgments in the books of commissioners of excise may and have been allowed because they are the king's books and quasi records and the entries in them by officers upon oath and in a judicial way.

But note afterward copies out [of] bishop's and dean and chapter books being very voluminous and of difficulty to be gotten have been allowed.

[Other copies of this report: GUL MS. B88–8, p. 264.]

[Order of 25 Dec. 1695: PRO E.126/16, f. 300.]

---

[1] As long as [it is being worked in] their own hands.

[2] W. Dugdale, *Monasticon Anglicanum*, V (1848), p. 286.

[3] *Wilson v. Redman* (1660), Hardres 174, 145 E.R. 438, 1 Wood 63, 1 Eagle & Younge 430.

300
Cutlove v. Capon (Ex. 1695)

In this case, certain parish officers were ordered to pay the arrears of the salary of a minister of a church since they had failed to levy the same from the parishioners.

LI MS. Misc. 559, f. 12, pl. 3 [Eng.] (Ward's Reports)

The plaintiff is minister of one of the churches in Ipswich and sued the defendants being portmen and parish officers there in order to have satisfaction made to him for the arrears of the annual sum of £80 which was agreed to be paid to him when he came to be minister there and which was to be raised by [a] tax or rate which the portmen and officers of that parish were by Act of Parliament made in the [*blank*] year of the reign of Queen Elizabeth enabled to make for the maintenance of their minister. And the usage has been that the last rate that was made was yearly collected by the portmen and officers and out of that and the yearly payments for seats and galleries in the church and gifts and benevolences £80 *per annum* had been and ought to be paid to the minister, but that failure had been in six years commencing 1688 and ending 1693, both inclusive, for which years the defendants were the officers and ought to have collected the assessment, the last of which was made in the year 1685 and came to £88 19s., and for which by the Act of Parliament the portmen and officers had power to distrain as for a rent charge by the Act.

And the court (before I was chief baron) decreed that the plaintiff should have his £80 *per annum* made up to him out of the rates, seats, galleries, and gifts, and that each of the defendants during their respective years wherein they were portmen and parish officers should account and severally pay what was received by them, and referred it to the deputy [king's] remembrancer to compute the same. And no exceptions being taken to the report and as the order upon hearing was penned, it was decreed that the respective defendants should make up the £80 *per annum* to the plaintiff for the respective years wherein they were portmen and officers, they having power to have levied the same by distress. And it was their willful default if they did not raise enough, and the minister [was] to be preferred before other [of] the uses they pretended the money unpaid had been employed unto. And this decree was submitted to and observed.

[Other copies of this report: GUL MS. B88–8, p. 265.]

[Orders of 7 May, 25 Nov., and 6 Dec. 1695: PRO E.126/16, ff. 256v, 296, 301.]

301
Attorney General v. Broadbridge (Ex. 1695)

In this case, a tax on a particular ship was calculated and ordered to be paid.

LI MS. Misc. 559, f. 13, pl. 1 [Eng.] (Ward's Reports)

The bill was for an account from the defendants, who had navigated a ship divers years, which was a foreign unfree ship after Michaelmas 1689 divers voyages to and from Newcastle for coals, which by the Act 1 Jac. II, c. 18,[1] for encouraging the building of ships in England, ought to have paid 12d. per ton above other duties. And it was referred to an account, and £53 17s. [was] reported to be due, which this day was decreed to be paid, a moiety to the chest of Chatham and the other moiety to the Trinity House of Deptford Strand, according to the directions of the said Act of Parliament and [the] prayer of the bill.

[Other copies of this report: GUL MS. B88–8, p. 267.]

[Orders of 7 May and 6 Dec. 1695: PRO E.126/16, ff. 262, 297v.]

302
Attorney General ex rel. Mayor of Maidenhead v. Rose (Ex. 1696)

Even though there are royal charters allowing it, the trustees of the Maidenhead Bridge cannot charge a toll for vessels passing under it since the bridge did not aid navigation.

I
LI MS. Misc. 559, f. 17 [Eng.] (Ward's Reports)

The plaintiffs by their bill seek relief against the defendants for a duty or toll of three pence for every barge of the defendants which from April 1689 to Michaelmas 1694 passed laden or unladen upon the river of Thames under Maidenhead Bridge and for title insisted that King Henry VI constituted a fraternity and granted a toll or duty of 2d. *de qualibet nave per pontem illum transeunte onerata cum rebus venalibus*, which fraternity being dissolved in Henry VIII's time, the toll came to the crown. And Queen Elizabeth by her charter under the great seal, dated 7 March 24th of her reign [1582], incorporated divers persons and constituted them and their successors to be bridge masters of Maidenhead Bridge, and confirmed the charter of Henry VI, and granted to this new corporation and their successors (which the now relators are) a toll or duty of 2d. *de qualibet nave sive navicula* (*anglice* a boat or barge) *onerata seu non onerata quotiescumque*

---

[1] Stat. 1 Jac. II, c. 18 (*SR*, VI, 20–21).

transiret per vel subter pontem praedictam. And King James II by his charter under the great seal dated 15 June 1st of his reign [1685] granted to the relators 3d. for every barge laden or unladen passing by or under the bridge, in the same words with Queen Elizabeth's grant only in this is 3d. and in hers but 2d.

And the question upon the hearing this day was whether this toll or duty of 3d. thus granted by this last charter was a legal toll or duty and the defendants compellable to pay the same. The defendants having by answer confessed that during the times in the bill they passed with their laden barges under the bridge two hundred times but insisted that no toll or duty was by law payable for the same. On the behalf of the relators it was urged that they repair the bridge at their own charge, and that the bargemen have this benefit by the bridge that their barges are towed by horses up to the bridge and then by reason of mills they can go no farther on that side but the horses pass over the bridge in order to[2] the towing of the barges on the other side, which passing over the bridge, and the damages which the barges do to the piles of the bridges by running against them and the bargemen's spikes in steering them under the bridge, the plaintiff's counsel insisted was a sufficient foundation for the grant of the toll or duty demanded, it being but a reasonable recompense for the benefit the bargemen receive by the bridge and for the damage which the relators sustain by the barges passing under the bridge laden and unladen, and that there is as much reason for a toll for passing under the bridge as there is for passing over it where there are benefits in both cases, the reason of a toll being a *quid pro quo*.

The defendants' counsel agreed that the crown may grant pontage where the subject has a benefit by it. And in this case the relators have tolls granted them for all carts, carriages, and hackney coaches passing over the bridge (for the last of which there was lately a decree in this court). And these tolls over the bridge have been and are duly paid and are sufficient to keep the bridge in repair. And those tolls are necessary for if there were no bridge those carriages could not pass over the river. And the bridge is much worn by them, and so it is but just that they should pay. But there is not the like reason for a toll for barges that pass upon the river under the bridge, for as to them the bridge was so far from being a benefit to them that it is a nuisance and straitens and hinders the course of the water and weakens the navigation. And it would be hard to make the defendants pay for what is to their prejudice instead of being for their benefit, for as to the benefit of passing their towing horses over the bridge, they would easier be passed over by ferrying if there was no bridge, and that damnification done to the bridge by the running against the piles or by the spikes, these [show] rather that the bridge is a nuisance and impediment than a benefit to navigation, which was upon that river before any bridge was there. And the payment of this toll can

---

[2] Sic in MS.

be no excuse in trespass for damage done to the bridge. And it is clear in law that navigable rivers are the king's highways where his subjects have passage free and that this toll demanded by the relators is in the nature of a toll through which by the law books is called *malum tolnetum* and cannot subsist by grant whatever it might do by prescription, which is not pretended to in this case, it being agreed (and so appearing in the case) that this toll in question nor the former toll of 2d. granted by Henry VI and Queen Elizabeth for passing under the bridge was never paid (at least but by some few persons (and that raption) though demanded for about twenty-five or twenty-six years past. And these books were cited against the toll in question as a through toll and so not good: 22 Ass. f. 58; Fitzherbert, Abridgment, title *Toll*, 1, 2, 3; Cro. Eliz. f. 710; Moore 574;[3] and in the Modern Reports f. 48: Hasborne and Wills,[4] that a toll or duty demanded by custom for passing by such a wharf was judged void; see my reports, Liber 2, f. 96;[5] Siderfin 454.[6] So that in this case here is no legal grant that can establish a right nor prescriptive usage that can support it. And though it was observed by the plaintiffs' counsel and so proved that there is a toll paid for passing under Windsor and Staines bridges upon the same river, yet that might be by prescription or custom time out of mind, which is of another nature and consideration from this which subsists only by a grant within time of memory.

And the court delivered their opinions seriatim that the defendants were not compellable to pay this duty and dismissed the bill with costs.

[Other copies of this report: GUL MS. B88–8, p. 276.]

II

BL MS. Hargr. 71, f. 94v, pl. 2 [Fr. & Eng.] (Dodd's Reports)

Upon an English bill where there was a charter of Henry VI produced that granted 2d. for ships passing Maidenhead Bridge and a charter of Queen Elizabeth for 2d. for all vessels and boats *oneratis vel non oneratis* passing under the bridge and a charter by James II for 3d. apiece but no usage had been with them nor [was there] any benefit to the bargemen but to the contrary [there was] damage, it was resolved by the court that [it was] a *malum tolnetum*, and the bill [was] dismissed.

---

[3] YB 22 Edw. III, Lib. Ass., f. 98, pl. 58 (1348); Fitzherbert, Abr., *Toll*, pl. 1, 2, 3; *Smith v. Shepherd* (1599), Cro. Eliz. 710, 78 E.R. 945, Moore K.B. 574, 72 E.R. 768.

[4] *Haspurt v. Wills* (1670), 1 Modern 47, 86 E.R. 722; this case also reported in other reports, see below.

[5] *Haspurt v. Wills* sub nom. *Hasbert v. Wills* (K.B. 1669), LI MS. Misc. 500, f. 96, pl. 2.

[6] *Haspurt v. Wills* sub nom. *Heshord v. Wills* (1670), 1 Siderfin 454, 82 E.R. 1214.

The chief baron [WARD] cited a toll for passing under Worcester Bridge. But there [it was] said that they could not pass without fixing hooks into the bridge and thus [there was] a benefit.

[Other copies of this report: HLS MS. 537(b), p. 47, pl. 1; Oxf. Brasenose MS. 59, p. 61, pl. 3; IU Lilly MS. Parker, 'Cases in the Exchequer, vol. 2', p. 18; BL MS. Hargr. 70, p. 100, pl. 331; HLS MS. 1162, p. 89, pl. 477; IU Lilly MS. Parker, 'Tithes', p. 63.]

[Order of 3 Feb. 1696: PRO E.126/16, f. 314v.]

303

Attorney General ex rel. Shaw v. Bowater (Ex. 1696)

In this case, arrears of rent were ordered to be paid.
The laches of a tenant of the crown cannot prejudice the rights of the crown.

LI MS. Misc. 559, f. 18 [Eng.] (Ward's Reports)

The bill is to recover a rent of £3 00s. 08d. payable to the lord of the manor of Eltham [in Kent] for divers lands and tenements in Woolwich within and held of the said manor of Eltham, which lands were formerly the estate of Sir Nicholas Gilborne, and after that of Henry Gilborne, his son and heir, and after that of Elizabeth, his daughter and heir of the said Henry and wife of the defendant Aspin and by the said Aspin and his wife sold to the defendant Bowater *pendente lite*, and for the arrears of that rent ever since the restoration of King Charles II [in] 1660, that manor of Eltham having been all that time and for divers years yet to come in lease from the crown to the relator and his father. And the defendant Bowater having confessed by his answer that he purchased and enjoys all the lands and tenements in Woolwich, which were the estate of Sir Nicholas Gilborne and of Henry Gilborne, his son, and it being proved in the case that Woolwich is within the manor of Eltham and that the inhabitants served in juries and offices and paid suit and service to Eltham Manor and it appearing by an ancient survey book of and belonging to this court being an original and taken upon oath the 11th of June 1605 by virtue of a commission out of this court for taking a survey of the manor of Eltham then in the hands of the crown wherein under the head of Woolwich Rents of Assize it is thus entered, 'Sir Nicholas Gilborne, knight, holds divers lands in Woolwich late Mr. Boughton's and pays £3 00s. 08d.' which a memorandum in the margin that Boughton's lands (by old survey) paid 66s. 8d. *per annum*. And it appearing by the proofs in the cause that about thirty years since there was a distress taken in a messuage in Woolwich in the occupation of one John Stakes for the said yearly rent, which was part of the estate of Sir Nicholas Gilborne and after that of Henry Gilborne, and the distress redeemed by order of Henry Gilborne, the court was of opinion and so decreed that there was sufficient evidence that such a rent was yearly due and payable to the lord of the manor of Eltham for the estate of Sir Nicholas Gilborne which came to his son Henry and from him to his daughter and her husband and by them sold to the defendant Bowater, who confessed by answer his having all [of] Sir Nicholas Gilborne's estate in Woolwich, and this rent though it has been long in arrear yet it has been recovered by distress about thirty years since and the laches of the tenant must not turn to the prejudice of the crown, and though Stakes' tenement where the distress was taken for the rent is certain and visible and such where another distress may be taken for the arrear whereby the title at law to the rent may be contested, yet in regard there is great probability that Sir Nicholas Gilborne had a far greater estate in Woolwich liable to that annual rent of £3 00s. 08d., it would be hard to leave the crown to a bare remedy at [common] law by distress upon that tenement of Stakes only, and the Statute of 33 Hen. VIII, c. 39,[7] giving a jurisdiction to the court and creating a remedy by decree as well as upon trials at law where the right appears by the records of the court, as it does here, the court decreed the arrears of that rent for thirty years past to be paid by Bowater, and a commission to set out the lands and tenements liable, or which may be thought most probable to be liable to the payment of that rent and which were formerly the lands of Sir Nicholas Gilborne.

    Query whether such commission issued and what [was] done upon it, but the arrears and growing rent, as it became due, were paid.

[Other copies of this report: GUL MS. B88–8, p. 280.]

[Order of 3 Feb. 1696: PRO E.126/16, f. 313v.]

304

Hawkins v. Chittle (Ex. 1696)

A vicar's lessee is liable to the parson for tithes; however, in this case, it was presumed from past non-payment that the endowment of this vicarage was that the vicar's lessee was exempt from paying tithes to the parson.

LI MS. Misc. 559, f. 19 [Eng.] (Ward's Reports)

    The plaintiff as lessee of the impropriate rectory of Thatcham in the County of Berkshire sues the defendant by English bill for great tithes of corn and hay arising in the years 1692, 1693, and 1694 upon a parcel of land being the glebe of the vicarage there, the defendant holding the same during those years by lease from the vicar. And for the plaintiff it was insisted upon that, though the vicar himself shall not pay tithes of his glebe while he holds it in his own hands, yet

---

[7] Stat. 33 Hen. VIII, c. 39 (*SR*, III, 879–892).

when he leases it, his tenant and lessee shall pay tithes, for which purpose, [see] the case of Griesly cited by the Lord Coke in Blencow and Barksdale's Case, Cro. Eliz., 479 and 579,[1] and Harris and Cotton's Case, Hobart 168,[2] and per Croke *ubi supra*, and Moore 910.[3] If the parson lease his glebe, he shall against his own lease have the great tithes and the vicar the small, and the cases that are put in Rolle's Abridgment, *Dismes*, 655, K, and 656,[4] that where the parson sows the glebe and then leases it or sells the emblements reserving the land, the lessee that severs the emblements shall pay tithes to the parson or, if a parson or vicar sow the land and die before severance, their executors shall pay tithes to the successor were cited for authorities for the plaintiff as to the reason of them that the vicar's lessee should pay tithes, though the vicar himself should not, for that was against the rule that *ecclesia ecclesie decimas solvere non debet*, which holds not in the case of a lessee. But though those cases were held for good law that of common right the lessee of a vicar shall pay tithes to the impropriator and *sic vice versa* where the endowment is not to the contrary. Yet in this case, it being proved that the vicar had formerly leased his glebe for four years together and that no tithes were paid during that time by the lessee, it was held that such nonpayment was an evidence that by the original endowment (whereof usage is the best evidence) the vicar's glebe was to be free from payment of tithes as well in the hands of the lessee as of the vicar himself. And there were two cases in this court, the one Greenwood and Grainger, 16 June 1684,[5] and another Sanders and Ryhall, Hilary 1691[/92],[6] which were so adjudged upon the like grounds and the bills dismissed in both cases as the plaintiff's now was without costs, but without usage not to pay the right was with the plaintiff.

[Other copies of this report: GUL MS. B88–8, p. 282.]

[Other reports of this case: Samuel Dodd's Reports, p. 156, 1 Eagle & Younge 616, 1 Rayner 77.]

[The decree of 20 Feb. 1696, PRO E.126/16, f. 322v, is printed at 1 Wood 356; see also the order of 10 Feb. 1696: PRO E.126/16, f. 316v.]

---

[1] *Blinco v. Barksdale* (1595–1597), Cro. Eliz., 479, 579, 78 E.R. 730, 821; also *sub nom. Blinco v. Backsdale* (1597), 1 Eagle & Younge 134, 1 Gwillim 197, Moore K.B. 457, 72 E.R. 692.

[2] *Harris v. Cotton*, Hobart 168, 80 E.R. 335.

[3] *Blincoe's Case* (1596), Moore K.B. 910, 72 E.R. 990.

[4] *Humfrey's Case* (1598) and *Moyle v. Ewer* (1614), 1 Rolle, Abr., *Dismes*, pl. K, 1–4, pp. 655–656.

[5] *Greenwood v. Grainger* (Ex. 1684), above, No. 193.

[6] *Sanders v. Rial* (1692), Samuel Dodd's Reports, p. 116, 1 Rayner 71, 2 Gwillim 537, 1 Eagle & Younge 570.

305
Stanly v. Hobby (Ex. 1696)

A court on its own motion can dismiss a case because of priority of suit in another court.

LI MS. Misc. 559, f. 20, pl. 1 [Eng.] (Ward's Reports)

The plaintiff, Ann, with her other two sisters, daughters and heirs of the said Philip Hobby, by their next friends and guardians being their uncle by father's and mother's sides having formerly exhibited their bill in chancery to be relieved touching their father's real and personal estates and their mother's dower (she having waived her jointure being made after marriage) and there being two decrees in chancery, the one of the 24th of June 33 Car. II [1681] and the other of Hilary 36 Car. II [1684], made in the case by both or one of which, an account was directed to be taken of the estates *de anno in annum* and security given for it. But the now plaintiff thinking she could better herself in a new suit exhibited her bill in this court to have an account of the same real and personal estates and to be relieved for the same matters for which provision was made by the said decrees or one of them.

The defendant did not plead the former suits or decrees but in a manner submitted to the court insisting upon the merits of the case.

But at the hearing it was considered by the court that, if this court should proceed in this case, it would wholly disturb all that had been settled by the decrees in chancery. And the account being referred in chancery to a master and security given, it would cause an interfering and clashing of jurisdictions between the two courts and set them at variance. So though there was no plea in this case, yet the court thought it altogether improper to make any order in this case in regard [that] all was settled in chancery, whereto the plaintiffs might resort and have full relief.

And so the plaintiff's bill was by consent dismissed without costs.

[Other copies of this report: GUL MS. B88–8, p. 284.]

306
Browne v. Chaplin (Ex. 1696)

In this case, the parishioner alleged a modus decimandi *in lieu of tithes in kind.*

LI MS. Misc. 559, f. 20, pl. 3 [Eng.] (Ward's Reports)

The bill was for tithes of hops and other small tithes within the rectory of Halstead in Essex of a farm of about or little more than £20 *per annum*. The defendant insisted upon a *modus* of 20s. *per annum*, which the plaintiff contested as a *modus* being too big and amounting upon the matter to tithes in kind and therefore cannot be a *modus* time out of mind. The case in this court of Vicaris and Goodyear[1] [*blank*] for the tithes of the rectory of Heythrop in the County of Oxford was remembered where a *modus* of £28 *per annum* was insisted upon and found to be so time out of mind by a verdict, and though it was so found yet it was held unreasonable as being too big and therefore tithes in kind [were] decreed (the rule being ordinarily true that a *modus* is lesser than tithes in kind). Yet the cases of Doddridge and Stirrop (a Sussex case [*blank*])[2] where 2s. in the pound was held to be a good *modus* and that of Edge and Oglander (Hilary 1691)[3] where £8 was held to be a good *modus* for lands of £80 *per annum* being remembered, and the values of the lands being uncertain and changing, it was referred to a trial at law whether there be such a *modus* or not.

Note afterwards 5 December 1698 in the case of Doddridge and Bridger,[4] the defendant was decreed to pay tithes in kind notwithstanding the pretence of a *modus* of 2s. in the pound there being no proof of such a *modus* but that tithes in kind had been paid for want of which proof the court gave that opinion in Doddridge and Stirrup's case, *supra*.

[Other copies of this report: GUL MS. B88–8, p. 285.]

[Other reports of this case: Samuel Dodd's Reports, p. 157, 1 Eagle & Younge 617.]

[Order of 20 Feb. 1696: PRO E.126/16, f. 318.]

307
Wilkinson v. Newsom (Ex. 1696)

In this case, tithes were ordered to be paid.

LI MS. Misc. 559, f. 20, pl. 4 [Eng.] (Ward's Reports)

[In a] bill for tithes, [the] defendant alleges the lands to be parcel of Newburgh Monastery in the County of York and that they came to the crown by the Statute of 31 Hen. VIII[1] at least not by 27 Hen. VIII[2] for that the monastery

---

[1] *Viccaris v. Goodere* (Ex. 1681), PRO E.126/13, f. 307v.

[2] *Dodderidge v. Startop* (Ex. 1690), above, No. 278.

[3] *Edge v. Oglander* (Ex. 1692), 2 Gwillim 536, 1 Rayner 71, Bunbury 301, 145 E.R. 681, 1 Wood 288, Samuel Dodd's Reports, p. 115, 1 Eagle & Younge 628.

[4] *Doddridge v. Bridger* (Ex. 1698), PRO E.126/17, f. 63v.

---

[1] Stat. 31 Hen. VIII, c. 13 (*SR*, III, 733–739).

[2] Stat. 27 Hen. VIII, c. 28 (*SR*, III, 575–578).

was not surrendered till 22 January 30 Hen. VIII [1539] as appeared by a copy proved and so would have the lands discharged by the Statute of 31 Hen. VIII. But in regard that [the] value of the monastery was not proved, it might be under £200 *per annum* and virtually came to the crown by 27 Hen. VIII and so liable to tithes, though there might be a surrender after, as was the case of Mr. Gifford[3] in this court [*blank*] for the Whitefriars in Staffordshire, which was ruled to pay tithes though tithes not used to be paid, and the rather here because it was in proof in the cause that these lands had constantly yielded tithes. And tithes were in this case decreed to be paid.

[Other copies of this report: GUL MS. B88-8, p. 286.]

[Other reports of this case: Samuel Dodd's Reports, p. 158, 1 Eagle & Younge 618.]

[The decree of 20 Feb. 1696, PRO E.126/16, f. 316, is printed at 1 Wood 355.]

308

Stevens v. Martin (Ex. 1696)

Turnips and carrots, though growing in large quantities in fields, are small tithes.

In this case, the court found that, by long usage, the vicar was entitled to the tithes of peas growing in fields.

LI MS. Misc. 559, f. 21 [Eng.] (Ward's Reports)

The plaintiff as vicar of Linton [Cambridgeshire][1] sues the defendants by English bill for small and vicarage tithes, and among others lays claim to the tithes of green peas, carrots, and turnips as well growing and arising within the gardens as within the open and common fields in Linton when and where the peas are set and managed by the hoe. And the question at the hearing was whether the tithes of green peas set and managed by the hoe in the open fields and in great quantities, and of turnips and carrots growing in like great quantities in the common fields are tithable in kind or by composition to the vicar of Linton or to the Master, Fellows, and Scholars of Pembroke Hall in Cambridge, who are owners of the impropriate rectory of Linton or to their lessee (none of which but only the inhabitants are parties to this suit). As to the turnips and carrots (though in great quantities and in open fields), they are as to their nature and quality reckoned [to be] small tithes. And it being proved in the cause that they had been constantly tithable to the vicar and that a constant rate of 4s. per acre

---

[3] *Wightwick v. Gifford* (Ex. 1685), above, No. 212.

---

[1] V.C.H., *Cambridgeshire*, VI (1978), 99.

for sixty years or more had been paid to the vicar for the same and [there being] no proof of any payment to the impropriators or their lessee (at least but lately), that point of the turnips and carrots (though there were many acres of them) was not so much contested by the college. But upon full proof of the usage, it was decreed for the vicar.

But as to the green peas which grew in the fields and whereof there were several acres every year set (not sown) and managed by the hoe, the right of tithes of them was contested by the college and insisted upon as well by common right (that all things primarily and originally are tithable to the parson and nothing to the vicar but by endowment) as from the nature and quality of peas and the place where they grew (*viz.* common and open fields) and from the greatness of their quantities to belong to them and not to the vicar. The plaintiff insisted upon the vicarial right, which his counsel urged was sufficiently evidenced by a long usage, it being proved in the cause that the tithes of peas thus set and managed by the hoe though in great numbers of acres in the common fields were for sixty years past (except about twelve of the twenty last when a vicar being poor left the place, for which that time the lessee of the impropriation took upon him to receive the same in part of a debt due to him) paid to the vicar by and after the rate of 6s. an acre without interruption.

But to oppose the vicar's right, the defendants set up an ancient instrument under seal of the college and of the official of Ely procured at [the] desire of the vicar, dated the 18th of June 1473 purporting to be an agreement between the college and Green, the then vicar, for ending a difference and settling the right of the college and of the vicar and confirmed by the bishop of Ely, wherein there is an enumeration of divers things to belong to the vicar, as a new vicarage house (the old one to go to the college), ten acres of land, the tithes of forty acres *per tota et integra per commune bladorum* 12s. rent, the tithes of three crofts containing several acres *per tota per commune decimarum croci* and 3s. 4d. to be paid by the impropriator, and then follow these words *et omnia et omnimodis oblationes decimas personales, mortuaria extraneorum, [?] et omnes alias decimas minores vizt. lanae, agnorum, laslis [?] et vitulorum lini comab. [?] herbarum et fructum aricarum [?] parcellorum cere, mellis, et per ustrinis* (burials) *infra parochia praedicta pro tota et integra per commune sua et successoribus suorum imperpetuum non obstante quibuscunque rebus aliis de novo imposterum forsan emergendo seu contingendo*, which instrument and agreement as the defendants' counsel urged contained all that the vicar can claim and there are as good as negative words to any other tithable matters not enumerated, and though there be general words of '*omnes alias decimas minores*' yet they are restrained by the '*vizt.*' which reckons up what they were intended to be, and if the vicar should have title to all small tithes, which possibly in the extent of the term may reach carrots and turnips (though they are not enumerated nor [is] corn under the '*vizt.*'), yet it could not by any means extend to peas of any sort or kind in the fields which never were nor could be called small tithes which being added to the last (almost) twenty years enjoyment (and the vicar's enjoyment before, being before this instrument was found out by the college's tenant) the defendants' counsel insisted that the plaintiff had no right to the tithe of the said green peas.

But the court upon consideration of so long and uninterrupted enjoyment by the vicars till within about part of the last twenty years (during which time or most of it, it has been litigious) and that usage is the best expositor of old deeds and rights of vicarages and that there may be a subsequent endowment to that of 1473 which might add this of peas, which may be so intended in regard of the usage, as it has been always understood where the usage is besides (nay even against) the words of an endowment and the vicar's maintenance here being but £28 *per annum* and in a great market town, and the rectory [worth] above £150 *per annum* and the endowment itself extends to all small tithes, which comprehends turnips and carrots, the chief baron [WARD] and two other barons, TURTON and POWYS, (*hesitante* LECHMERE) decreed for the plaintiff as to the peas also, and the rather because it is admitted that the vicar has not the 12s. rent *per annum* and some other small things which by that instrument is allotted to him, which may well be presumed not only in that particular but in others to be altered and changed by some subsequent act or endowment (though not now extant) whereby even the right and title to these peas might be let in, of which the usage is an evidence, and that the '*vizt.*' after the words '*omnes minutas decimas*' does not restrain them to the particulars after the '*vizt.*' according to the reason of Stukely and Butler, Hobart [168].[2] And so it was decreed for the vicar.

But afterwards, 25 February 1696, the cause was heard in the Lords' House in Parliament upon the defendant's appeal from this decree. And the appeal was dismissed and the decree affirmed with £10 costs, not one lord speaking for the appeal or against the right and justice of the decree.[3]

See a similar case, Hardres' *Reports* 328, Brazen Nose College's Case,[4] upon a similar reason, in the time of Chief Baron Hale, that usage without or against an endowment that is ancient prevails.

[Other copies of this report: GUL MS. B88–8, p. 287.]

[Other reports of this case: 1 Rayner 82, Samuel Dodd's Reports, p. 157, 1 Eagle & Younge 616, 2 Gwillim 549.]

[The decree of 20 Feb. 1696: PRO E.126/16, f. 326, is printed at 1 Wood 357.]

---

[2] *Stukely v. Butler* (1615), Hobart 168, 80 E.R. 316.
[3] *Lords' Journal*, XVI (n.d.), p. 104.
[4] *Twisse v. Brazen-Nose College* (1663), Hardres 328, 145 E.R. 481.

[This case is cited in Gumley v. Burt (1724), Bunbury 169, 145 E.R. 636, 1 Eagle & Younge 799, 2 Gwillim 656, 1 Rayner 206; Simms v. Bennett (1760), 3 Gwillim 874, 888, 2 Eagle & Younge 172, 181, 1 Eden 382, 385, 402, 28 E.R. 733, 734, 740.]

309
Clay v. Buckingham (Ex. 1696)

A contingent remainder can descend and be taken by the remainderman's administrator.

BL MS. Hargr. 71, f. 94, pl. 2 [Fr. & Eng.] (Dodd's Reports)

Curtis devised to Anne, his daughter, £2000 to be paid at her age or marriage, and, if she died before her age or marriage, then he gave the £2000 to A., B., and C. equally to be divided. And he made his wife executrix, who married after [his death] Sir Owen Buckingham, and was one of the devisees in remainder. Then the wife died, and Sir Owen took administration, and then Anne died under age and unmarried. And [it was] resolved that this contingent interest remainder was such an interest that should go to the administrator of the wife notwithstanding the contingency did not happen in the lifetime of the wife. Note and see Sheriff and Wrotham's Case, Cro. Jac. 509; Lampet's Case, 10 Rep. Mar. 106.[1]

[Other copies of this report: HLS MS. 537(b), p. 46, pl. 2; Oxf. Brasenose MS. 59, p. 61, pl. 1; IU Lilly MS. Parker, 'Cases in the Exchequer, vol. 2', p. 16.]

[Order of 27 Jan. 1696: PRO E.126/16, f. 315v.]

310
Bowyer v. Gibbs (Ex. 1696)

In this case, a dispute over the payment of tithes of a wood was settled out of court.

LI MS. Misc. 559, f. 22 [Eng.] (Ward's Reports)

The plaintiff Bowyer, as impropriator of Camberwell [Surrey], sues the defendant Gibbs, the tenant of a wood in Camberwell called Parkmans Wood which he holds by lease for years from the Master and Wardens of Dulwich College for tithe wood in and for the years 1691, 1692, and 1693, which the defendant Gibbs pretends to be free from payment of tithes as being parcel of the possessions of the Abbey of Bermondsey one of the greater monasteries being above

---

[1] *Sheriff v. Wrotham* (1618), Cro. Jac. 509, 79 E.R. 434; *Lampet's Case* (1612), 10 Coke Rep. 46b, 77 E.R. 994, also *sub nom. Lampit v. Starkey*, 2 Brownl. & Golds. 172, 123 E.R. 880.

£200 *per annum* and which came to the crown by the Statute of 31 Hen. VIII[1] free and discharged from payment of tithes and insisted that no tithes were due for the same and the tenant and the College exhibited their cross-bill against the plaintiff Bowyer to draw the right of payment of tithes in question and to settle the right by trial at law etc. complaining of a former decree made in this court in the year 1692 wherein tithes in kind were decreed and that decree affirmed upon a bill of review.[2] And the sole question between the parties in this present case was whether the demesne woods of the abbot of Bermondsey, which now belong to Dulwich College whereof Parkmans Wood (now in question) is one, were and are tithe free or liable to the payment of tithes it being admitted on all hands that the common woods (which also belonged to the abbot and were in his possession at the dissolution) not being the demesne did pay tithe and also that the demesne woods themselves when grubbed up and plowed and all other the demesne lands, which the abbot held in his own hand at the time of the dissolution, did and have used to pay tithes to the impropriator, which seemed to be an unusual case that some part of the abbot's demesne which he held in his own hands at the time of the dissolution of monasteries should be tithable and the other part not and that the wood should be free from payment of tithes and the land where the wood grew when plowed should yield tithes. And in this case because it was proved in a former cause in the court of wards in King Charles I's time that tithes had been paid for all the demesne woods as well as other (though there was an inclination then to try it at law) but instead of that in 1642 the masters and wardens take a lease from the plaintiff's ancestors of the tithes of corn and wood at £5 *per annum*, which was held for divers years, but in the articles there was a clause that neither should be bound to their prejudice. But after that time Allen, the master of the College, (*viz.* in 1681 until which time the £5 *per annum* was paid) in the name of himself and [the] wardens take a new lease (the old one being expired) from the plaintiff of the same tithes for the like rent of £5 *per annum*, which was paid several years and then being refused the plaintiff exhibited his bill and had a decree *ut supra*. And after such proceedings Baron LECHMERE and Baron TURTON were for decreeing the tithes without a trial; Baron POWYS was for a trial. And both sides being in court, a proposal was made for accommodation and the parties agreed that the College should pay £6 *per annum* during the life of the plaintiff, who was only tenant for life, and suits to cease. And this agreement was decreed and the cross-bill [was] dismissed without costs.

[Other copies of this report: GUL MS. B88-8, p. 292.]

[The decree of 21 Feb. 1696, PRO E.126/16, f. 327, is printed at 1 Wood 359.]

---

[1] Stat. of 31 Hen. VIII, c. 13 (*SR*, III, 733–739).
[2] *Bowyer v. Barrett* (1692), PRO E.126/15, f. 463v, E.126/16, f. 53v.

311
Tucker v. Hall (Ex. 1696)

A mortgagor may redeem without regard to the mortgagee's having paid for the equity of redemption to the assignee of the crown where the crown's right had been reversed.

LI MS. Misc. 559, f. 23 [Eng.] (Ward's Reports)

The plaintiff in the years 1681 and 1683 made two mortgages, the first of the rectory impropriate of Huish [in Somerset] held by lease for three lives unto one Alice Hinton for securing £1000 and interest at £5 per cent *per annum*, the other of an estate in Sutton Hoasy unto Kett and two others in fee for securing £500 and interest at £5 per cent *per annum*, both these mortgages being forfeited in strictness of [the common] law, the moneys not being paid at the days. The plaintiff was in 1685 accused of high treason in the duke of Monmouth's rebellion in the west, whereof he was shortly after attainted by verdict, and the mortgagees entered and received the profits and assigned to the defendant, who kept the possession and renewed the lease for lives of the rectory changing a life and took it in his own name paying £64 fine for the same. And the estate, interest, reversion, and equity of redemption, which the plaintiff had and which was forfeited to the crown by his attainder, was granted by the crown to Sir Theophilus Oglethorpe under the great seal and by him granted and conveyed to the defendant for six hundred guineas. The plaintiff happened not to be executed (his life being spared by the means of Sir Theophilus Oglethorpe, as was said, but others thought that the hardness or injustice that was used in his trial was the reason of [the] saving of his life). And by application to his now Majesty, he was allowed to bring a writ of error, and the attainder was thereupon reversed in the king's bench, and that reversal affirmed in Parliament,[1] and the king's hands amoved. And now the plaintiff brings his bill to redeem his estates which were mortgaged and to have an account of the profits thereof.

The defendant did not nor could oppose the redemption but insisted upon it that the plaintiff ought to allow the £64 paid for the fine upon renewal of the lease and the 600 guineas paid to Sir Theophilus Oglethorpe for the crown's title by the attainder. As to the £64 fine, the plaintiff agreed to it but denied to do the other insisting that, the attainder being reversed, he has not nor can have any benefit by that grant, so no reason for him to pay for that which is no advantage to him nor necessary for the defendant to buy in his estates by the mortgages [?] being sufficient and he in no danger, he having a large security for his money. And the defendant bought in the crown title (which is now vanished and gone) at his peril and without any necessity.

---

[1] *Lords' Journal*, XV (n.d.), p. 467.

And of that opinion was the court and ordered a redemption without paying the 600 guineas. And in this case, the case in chancery between Peyton and Ayliff[2] was remembered, wherein the now lord keeper gave the same rule upon the redemption of a mortgage by the executors of Sir Robert Peyton, whose attainder was reversed, and the equity granted out by the crown that the executors should redeem without paying the £100 paid for the purchase of the crown's title, in which last cause I was of counsel with the executors in chancery.

[Other copies of this report: GUL MS. B88–8, p. 294.]

[Orders of 23 Jan. and 22 Feb. 1696: PRO E.126/16, f. 320v; E.127/19, f. 429.]

312
Pride v. Monck (Ex. 1696)

Depositions to perpetuate testimony will be allowed in the sound judicial discretion of the court, and the court will preserve the rights of infants where it can.

LI MS. Misc. 559, f. 24 [Eng.] (Ward's Reports)

Lucy Pride and Elizabeth Pride, infants of very tender years daughters and heirs of Thomas Pride, son and heir of Elizabeth Pride, sole daughter and heir of Thomas Monck, who was the elder brother of George Monck, late duke of Albemarle, plaintiffs. Henry Monck and Christopher Monck and others defendants.

20 February 1696[/97]. In the exchequer by English bill.

The plaintiffs entitle themselves as heirs at law to the real estate of George, late duke of Albemarle,[1] deceased, whereof he was seised in fee and settled it in 1669 upon the marriage of his son Christopher (then called earl of Torrington) to the use of the duke for life, remainder to the said Christopher in tail male, remainder to the said Elizabeth Pride, the grandmother, in tail male (her father Thomas Monck being then dead), remainder to his own right heirs, that Duke George and Christopher being both dead, and [there being] no issue of Christopher, and the limitation in tail to the plaintiffs' grandmother being spent by the death of Thomas Pride, the plaintiffs' father, the plaintiffs are become heirs at law to the said Duke George and as such demand his estate, it being alleged in the bill that Christopher was not the lawful son of Duke George, being born while his mother (that was married to Duke George) had another husband living, and by their bill complain that the defendants (the earl of Bath and the earl of

---

[2] *Peyton v. Ayliff* (1693), 2 Vernon 312, 23 E.R. 803.

[1] (d. 1670), D.N.B.; G.E.C., *Complete Peerage*, I (1910), p. 89.

Mountagu (that married the relict of Christopher) and several others being also defendants) had got the settlement of 1669 and other the deeds and evidences of the estate into their hands and threaten to cancel them, and had entered upon the estate and received the rents, and pretend a will to be made by Christopher, and that for want of the deed and evidences they could not maintain any actions at law brought or to be brought, and allege that their witnesses who could prove the deeds and the plaintiffs' pedigree are aged and infirm and live remote and not able to travel and, if they should die before the plaintiffs recover the deeds or obtain a trial at law, they may lose their testimony and estate also, and therefore pray first that their witnesses may be examined *in perpetuam rei memoriam* and their testimony preserved in case of death, secondly that the defendants may set forth the settlement and dates and contents of other writings, thirdly and that the settlement and writings by decree of court may be delivered to the plaintiffs whereby they may be enabled to sue for and recover the estate at law.

The defendants, the two Moncks, (none of the other defendants being served) put in an answer, plea, and demurrer. And for plea to such part of the bill as tends to avoid Duke Christopher's will of the 4th of July 1687 (charged in the bill) and the defendants' legacies thereby, and to set up Duke George's settlement or a title to the plaintiffs as heirs at law to Duke George, and to enable the plaintiffs to examine witnesses *in perpetuam rei memoriam*, and to illegitimate Duke Christopher, they plead that these two defendants (with others) exhibited a bill in chancery against the now plaintiffs' father and grandmother and others to establish the will of Duke Christopher made in July 1687 (which they set forth *in haec verba*) whereby there were several devises of lands and others things made to them and the settlement of 1669 and charging the then defendants' pretenses to avoid that settlement and will and to set up another will of Duke Christopher's made in 1675 and deeds of lease and release made in 1681 in prejudice of the title and pretenses of the plaintiffs' said father and grandmother by the said will of 1687, by which bill in chancery the pretenses of the plaintiffs' father and grandmother as heirs at law to the two dukes were charged, and that bill prayed an examination of witnesses in perpetuity and a discovery of the then defendants' pretenses, and relief, and that the earl of Bath answered and set forth his claim by the will of 1675 and deeds of 1681, and that the plaintiffs' father and grandmother also answered and the grandmother insisted on her title as heir at law to Duke George or by the last remainder in the settlement of 1669 as right heir, and that witnesses were examined in this cause, and further pleaded a bill in chancery by the earl of Bath and others against the plaintiffs' father and grandmother and another bill in the same court against them all to the same effect by the executors and devisees of Duke Christopher's will in 1687 and answers put in to them and examination of witnesses and publication thereof, and further pleaded that the plaintiffs' father (after his mother's death) brought two actions of ejectment for lands in Hertfordshire and Essex, part of the duke's estate, in the king's bench wherein there were two trials at bar and the question was the same that now is, *viz.* whether Christopher was the legitimate son of Duke George or not, and after long evidence in both cases, there were verdicts in both against the plaintiffs' father's pretenses, and that Duke Christopher was the legitimate son of Duke George and by consequence his will or settlement was good and the plaintiffs' father had nothing as heir at law, and further plead that the settlement in 1669 was fully in issue in the cause in chancery and produced and examined to at both the trials and that the same title which the plaintiffs now set up was insisted upon at the said trials and therefore pleaded the said matters in bar to the plaintiffs' bill and insisted that, by the constant practice of the court, the defendants (after the matters in issue and examined to in the chancery causes) ought not upon any [of] the allegations in the bill to be drawn into a new examination and after the proceedings there and in the two trials the matter being found against the plaintiffs' title and they, never having been in possession nor hindered to try their title at law, ought not to be examined to *in perpetuam rei memoriam* unless the title had been affirmed by verdict, and so demanded judgment.

And the demurrer was to the examination of witnesses, because as advised such examination ought not to be admitted unless there had been some impediments, disability, or incapacity in the plaintiffs to try their title at law, which appears not in this case, nor has there been any trial at law which affirms the plaintiffs' title, and so demanded judgment.

The question upon the arguing of this plea and demurrer was whether the matter disclosed in either of them was sufficient to bar or hinder the plaintiffs from examining their witnesses *in perpetuam rei memoriam* or not.

On the defendants' behalf, it was strongly insisted upon by Mr. *Finch* and others of their counsel that it was not of common right and justice that in all cases plaintiffs shall have the liberty to examine their witnesses *in perpetuam rei memoriam*, but that there may fall out, and there has fallen out, several cases wherein plaintiffs have been denied that liberty, and that it will be of dangerous consequence to allow that liberty in all cases without contradiction, and it was stood upon that this was one of those cases wherein it is but just to deny that liberty. For by this plea (which must be taken at this time to be true) it appears that this point of the plaintiffs' right, which is only as heirs at law to their father, grandmother, and Duke George, has been examined to already in chancery by the plaintiffs' father and grandmother under whom they claim in fee and they may have the benefit of those examinations. And it is unreasonable and indeed dangerous for introducing perjury to multiply examinations for the same purpose. And though the depositions in chancery do not directly tend to call in question the legitimacy of Duke Christopher, yet that was the very point in question upon the two trials at bar in the king's bench and verdicts in both cases against the plaintiffs' father, from and under whom they claim by descent in fee, and therefore ought to be concluded by them or at least the plaintiffs ought not to be admitted to perpetuate the testimony of any witnesses after two such trials until the plaintiffs had affirmed their title by some trial at law, to obtain which there appears not any disability, impediment, or incapacity.

And for this purpose, these cases and precedents in the chancery and this court were cited and produced: in chancery, Wednesday, 9 July 32 Car. II [1680], between Charles lord North and Grey and the Lady Catherine, his wife, plaintiffs, and Henry lord Grey and the Lady Katherine Grey, defendants,[2] wherein the plaintiffs by their bill sought a discovery of a deed of settlement by William lord Grey made in 1674 by which the plaintiffs had some estate limited to them or one of them and charged the defendants with having that settlement or some note of it and prayed a discovery and examination of the witnesses *in perpetuam rei memoriam*. The defendants denied the having or knowing of any such settlement or note, and as to the examination of witnesses demurred, in regard the plaintiffs knew the witnesses to the settlement and who could prove the note, and they might go to law, and till their title [be] affirmed at law ought not to examine in perpetuity. The court allowed the demurrer, but the parties being in court agreed to go to a trial at law and the defendant was to waive privilege and, if insisted on, that to be taken to be an impediment to the plaintiffs to try their title. And upon resort to the court, they would make such order for examinations of the witnesses as should be just.

Another precedent in chancery was Thursday 29 January 36 Car. II [1685] between Weston and others, plaintiffs, and Henry duke of Norfolk and others, defendants,[3] by which bill the plaintiffs set forth their right and title to common in Horsham Heath claimed by the defendants and prayed leave to examine witnesses *in perpetuam rei memoriam*. The defendants put in a plea to the plaintiffs' bill and insisted upon their title to the place called Horsham Heath exclusive to any common therein for the plaintiffs and set forth their title and insisted that the plaintiffs ought not to examine their witnesses till their pretenses were asserted by a trial at law, to which they might, if they would, proceed, not being hindered therein by the defendants. In this case, a trial was directed to be had and a stay of any examination till after the trial.

In the exchequer was this precedent, 16 February 34 & 35 Car. II [1683] between James Percy claiming to be earl of Northumberland, plaintiff, and the duke of Somerset and his duchess and others, defendants. The bill set forth the plaintiff's pretense of title and pedigree to the earldom of Northumberland and how derived and prayed leave to examine his witnesses for preservation of their

---

[2] *Lord North v. Lord Gray* (1680), Dickens 14, 21 E.R. 171.
[3] *Weston v. Duke of Norfolk* (1685), PRO C.33/264, ff. 183v, 202v.

testimony, which was granted *de bene esse*, but in Easter term following, *viz.* 28 April, upon a plea and demurrer put in by the defendants to the plaintiff's bill in bar of examination of his witnesses, the plea and demurrer was allowed, and so the bill [was] dismissed.

And it was further insisted upon by the defendants' counsel that, if a man that has a pretense to another estate and has no impediment but that he may try it at law may have his witnesses examined and their testimony preserved, he may stay his trial and depend upon examinations, which are not to be so much regarded as witnesses *viva voce*, and there is more reason for a man that is in possession of an estate and has a pretense hanging over him which his adversary may delay to try till his witnesses be dead, to examine than for one that is not in possession and may try at law when he pleases to be admitted to examine, such examinations being dangerous in regard [that] no publication passes till the witnesses be dead and then they are dispunishable for any perjury they may have committed in their depositions.

Upon consideration of which precedents and reasons, the court took time to consider. And it seemed that it is not so clear and undoubted a rule that every man shall be admitted to examine his witnesses *in perpetuam rei memoriam* as has been pretended to be, but that there may be good grounds (as in the above cases) to deny such examinations. But in this case in question though the matters contained in the plea and demurrer have their weight in ordinary cases where the parties are not under any impediment, disability, or incapacity, yet in this case the plaintiffs being infants of tender years (though they claim under their father in fee simple, whose pretenses being the same with the now plaintiffs as to the pretended illegitimacy of Duke Christopher), the court ought to allow them all just and fitting methods for their defense, and the court is the guardian to infants before them, and if there be two daughters, one under age, demandants in a real action, the parol shall demur till full age, 1 [Coke] *Inst.* 164;[4] so here the court cannot compel the plaintiffs to go to law during their infancy but ought to allow them the liberty of preserving the testimony of their witnesses to be made use of as occasion shall require, and it may be of dangerous consequence in this case to deny it. And the rather in this case because the bill is to preserve the testimony of their witnesses to prove the plaintiffs' pedigree (which never was in question in the former causes) as well as other the merits of the case. And for those reasons, the plea and demurrer were both overruled and the plaintiffs let into their examination of witnesses *in perpetuam rei memoriam* as is usual in such cases of examination.

See Chancery Reports, part 1, f. 174, Cooper and Tregonwell, 1659.[5]

---

[4] E. Coke, *First Institute* (1628), f. 164.
[5] *Cooper v. Tragonwel* (1659), 1 Chan. Rep. 174, 21 E.R. 541.

See 15 and 22 November 1701 where in the like suit by a person of full age claiming as heir at law to Duke George under the plaintiffs here in this cause, the plea and demurrer allowed upon the like reasons in this case urged against such examination. Note the difference between infancy and full age, and by being out of possession and may sue at pleasure and in possession and therefore must defend himself by such examinations not knowing when he shall be attacked.[6]

See Lord Wharton's case a [. . .] and against Attorney General and Marriot's case, Trinity 1706.[7]

[Other copies of this report: GUL MS. B88–8, p. 297.]

[Order of 25 Jan. 1696: PRO E.127/19, f. 435.]

[This case is cited in Attorney General v. Wharton (Ex. 1706), below, No. 405.]

[Related cases: Sherwin v. Clargies (Ex. 1701), below, No. 376, and other cases cited there.]

313

Duke of Shrewsbury v. Steynor (Ex. 1696–1697)

A preliminary injunction will be denied where the defendant denies the entire content of the bill of complaint.

Priority of suit is waived by the party's submitting to the jurisdiction of the court in the second suit before raising the issue.

All of the persons concerned with the same right should be made parties to a suit to settle that right.

LI MS. Misc. 559, ff. 31, 78, 97, 117 [Eng.] (Ward's Reports)

The plaintiffs, being proprietors in fee of several bulliaries of salt water in the pits of Droitwich in the County of Worcester,[1] exhibited their bill against the defendant Staynor (with others) in order to restrain him from digging new brine pits in Droitwich in his own lands there, which if done and proceeded in would destroy the three ancient pits there which have been time out of mind and wherein the plaintiffs claim and enjoy their several bulliaries (being certain quantities of brine for [the] making of salt) and charge that the whole town of Droitwich was anciently belonging to the crown and that the same and the three ancient pits were enjoyed by the crown till granted out in the reign of King John to the Burgesses of Droitwich and their heirs under a fee farm rent of £100 *per*

---

[6] *Sherwin v. Clargies* (Ex. 1701), below, No. 376.
[7] *Attorney General ex rel. Marriot v. Lord Wharton* (Ex. 1706), below, No. 405.

---

[1] V.C.H., *Worcestershire*, III (1913), pp. 73–74, 78.

annum reserved and made payable and which constantly was paid to the crown till the sale of fee farm rents 22 Car. II [1670][2] and since to the purchaser thereof by the proprietors of the three ancient pits and bulliaries only and charge that by custom and prerogative while the same were in the hands of the crown, no person could or might dig or make any new pits for brine or making salt in Droitwich over and besides those three ancient pits and that the proprietors of the several bulliaries of salt water in those three pits (wherein there are in all about four hundred shares or bulliaries) ought by virtue of the grant from the crown and the prerogative and privilege thereby granted to have and enjoy the benefit of the said custom and prerogative, and charged in fact that no person (til the defendant) pretended to dig any new pits there, but that all persons were and ought to be excluded and debarred from so doing, it manifestly tending to the destruction of the three old pits and the several proprietors' shares and bulliaries therein whereby they are disabled from paying the said fee farm rent and the right and custom destroyed, and prayed the aid of the court to restrain the defendant from proceeding in digging any new pits or making salt at Droitwich with any brine taken out of any such new pits, and by the bill charged that the defendant pretended he might lawfully dig new pits and make salt thereat and that such his right was asserted by and upon a trial at law had at the king's bench bar in Trinity term last by a special jury of the County of Worcester upon issues for that purpose directed by the court of chancery[3] upon a bill exhibited into that court by the Bailiff and Burgesses of Droitwich and several proprietors of bulliaries of salt water in the three ancient pits there, wherein there was a verdict in favor of the defendant's right whereby it is found that he might lawfully dig the pits he is now digging of and make and sell the salt made of the brine taken out of those pits, and that the now defendant pretends that the whole Corporation of Droitwich, consisting of the bailiff and burgesses, were and are bound by that trial and by the proceedings thereupon, and that that bill is still depending in chancery and that, while that bill is depending, the defendant ought not to be molested nor have his right again called in question, the now plaintiffs being, as he pretends, bound by the said trial and proceedings, whereas (as the now plaintiffs charge by their bill) the said bill and suit in chancery and the said trial at law in the king's bench were had and carried on by contrivance of the defendant Steiner and other the confederates and were faintly prosecuted and without the privity of the now plaintiffs or of the bailiff and burgesses of Droitwich, and by fraud and combination to give color to the defendant Steynor's pretenses of right to dig new pits, and insisted upon it that the proceedings in that suit did not nor ought to bind the plaintiffs here, who have separate and distinct inheritances in their several bulliaries.

---

[2] Stat. 22 Car. II, c. 6 (*SR*, V, 657–660).
[3] *Stainer v. Burgesses of Droitwich* (1695), 1 Salkeld 281, 91 E.R. 247, 12 Modern 85, 88 E.R. 1181, Skinner 623, 90 E.R. 280, Holt K.B. 290, 90 E.R. 1059.

The defendant Steynor put in a plea to this bill and pleaded the pendency of the bill in chancery and the trial and proceedings thereupon had, and averred that the now plaintiffs as Burgesses of Droitwich were parties in interest to the said former bill and proceedings and ought to be bound thereby, the Bailiffs and Burgesses of Droitwich (of whom the plaintiffs are part) being parties thereunto.

But the now defendant did not answer (nor by his plea did he aver) that the said bill, suit, and proceedings in chancery were adversary and really and *bona fide* prosecuted and that they were not fraudulent or faint, as was expressly charged by the bill, which being an express charge and the thing charged being very possible to be so (as well as it might also not so be), yet being so charged by the now plaintiffs' bill, it ought to have been answered some way or other, either by answer or by averment in the plea, which not being done, the plea did not cover the whole matter charged by the bill. And if the charge in the bill was true, then neither the exhibiting of the bill in chancery nor the trial or proceedings thereupon nor the pendency of the same in chancery undetermined can be a good plea to the plaintiffs' bill, for that would be against the reason of the rule, *non competit exceptio eiusdem rei cuius dissolutio petitur*.[4] And wherever a release or deed is charged to be obtained by fraud, a plea of that release or deed is not good without denying the fraud, and for that reason the plea here was disallowed by the chief baron [WARD] and LECHMERE, POWYS dissenting and TURTON being absent.

And afterward the defendant put in his answer and denied the fraud or faint prosecution and set forth the whole proceedings in chancery and the trial at bar, whereby the equity of the plaintiffs' bill was denied. And the defendant insisting upon his right and title at law (being a fee simple in his lands) and the freedom of his estate from any pretence of restraint from digging new pits either by custom, prerogative, or otherwise, the plaintiffs' motion (grounded upon the nature of the cause contained in the bill and upon several affidavits read of the common usage that none ever dug pits and of the hazard and danger that would ensue to the old pits of letting in fresh water which would spoil them besides the damage that would follow to the proprietors of the old pits by lowering their interest and profits thereby) for an injunction was denied. And though the affidavits after answer put in were admitted by the three other barons to be read *de bene esse*, yet I was against their being read as altogether contrary to practice and experience to gain an injunction upon affidavits after [an] answer put in. But the injunction was denied in regard [that] the answer had denied the whole equity of the bill.

Note that this day [12 December 1696] in the House of Lords the lord keeper spoke to me and Baron Powys about some agreement and settlement to be had touching [the] granting [of] injunctions by the court of chancery or court of

---

[4] A plea of the same matter the dissolution of which is sought is not valid. This maxim also begins *Non valet exceptio*. . . . See *Black's Law Dictionary*.

exchequer in cases of priority of suits in either court, which was occasioned by reason of an English bill brought in the exchequer by the duke of Shrewsbury and others, participants and owners of divers bulliaries of salt water in Droitwich in the County of Worcester, against Steynor (q.v. above f. 31), there being a bill and suit depending in chancery between the Bailiffs and Burgesses of Droitwich, plaintiffs, against the said Staynor, defendant, which had passed into a decree for a trial at law and the equity reserved and still depending in that court, and after that the bill in the exchequer brought to restrain Stayner from digging pits in his own lands etc. for brine, to which bill in the exchequer Staynor pleaded pendency of the suit in chancery. But for faults in pleading it, the plea [was] overruled, and Staynor answered, and [the] plaintiffs, having executed a commission for examination of witnesses, Staynor prayed another (not having examined any) but never took it out but upon motion in chancery and no defense [made] obtained an injunction to the plaintiffs in the exchequer to surcease their prosecution of their suit there in respect of priority of suit in chancery, the plaintiffs in the exchequer being alleged to be burgesses of Droitwich and so parties to the suit in chancery, which injunction stayed the plaintiffs from prosecuting their bill in the exchequer.

And upon that account, it was now agreed between the two courts, that wheresoever there is or shall be priority of suit in either court, that if a bill touching the same matter shall be exhibited in the other court and the party that is entitled to such priority will answer the suit in that other court and not insist upon the priority, or if he shall plead the pendency of the suit in the first court and that plea shall be insufficiently pleaded and for that reason overruled (as it was in this) and the party shall so far submit to it as to answer the bill or not to appeal to parliament for overruling such plea, that, in all such cases or of the like nature, the court where the priority of suit was, will not grant any injunction to the parties to restrain the prosecution of their suit in the latter court, the party entitled to such priority having affirmed and submitted to the jurisdiction of the latter court.

And accordingly, the lord keeper the next day dissolved the injunction upon the grounds above, that Stayner by answering and praying a commission to examine his witnesses in the exchequer had waived and declined the priority of suit in chancery and submitted to the jurisdiction of the exchequer, and if after so doing, he may resort back to chancery and stay the plaintiffs in the exchequer in their suit, it is and would be a means to make a difference between the two courts, which (as his lordship took notice) were under the agreement above, and he doubted not but that the exchequer would observe it as well as the chancery.

And after this injunction was dissolved, Stayner moved the exchequer for a commission to examine his witnesses (not having examined any) returnable next term, which was granted upon hearing counsel on both sides and oath [taken] of not having seen, heard, or known anything of the depositions taken on the other side, and payment of £10 costs, and by consent the cause [was] to be heard next term, it having stood in the paper last term, but stopped by the chancery injunction.

18 February 1696[/97] the bill [was] dismissed *nisi causa* [to the] first Monday of the next Easter term. And then it was absolutely dismissed. See above ff. 31 and 78, and the case and arguments and reasons in my papers of Hilary term 1696[/97] at large there, and my notes upon the trial, and below f. 117, the trial.

[11 May 1697] the plaintiff brings an action of trespass upon the case [in the office of pleas in the exchequer] against the defendant and declares that there are and time out of mind have been in the manor and borough of Droitwich certain salt springs, affording salt water fit for [the] making of salt, which time out of mind have arisen and flowed in certain ancient pits in that borough and time out of mind have been divided and dividable among the proprietors of the salt pits into certain bulliaries or proportions of salt water, and that the proprietors of the salt pits have time out of mind repaired and cleansed the pits, and that the plaintiff[5] 7 April 1694 was seised for her life in two bulliaries of salt water in one of those pits called the Upperwich Pit and ought to have and enjoy the lawful profits thereof, and that within the manor and borough aforesaid there is and time out of mind has been a custom that every [one of] the proprietors of any bulliary have used to take their parts and shares of the salt water out of the old pits within the said manor and borough or some of them and not more nor elsewhere, and that no person *aliquem novum puteum infra burgum praedictum* to draw or gain any salt water out of such new pit to make salt for sale has made or ought to make, that the defendant, being proprietor of one share in the old pits *premissorum satis sciens*, intending to deprive the plaintiff of the profits of her two bulliaries, the 10th of August 1694 did dig or cause to be dug a certain pit within the said borough for drawing salt water out of it and thereby did interrupt and stop the ancient salt springs and in that time did draw and take out of that pit great quantities of salt water (mentioning how much) beyond the plaintiff's bulliaries and quantity of salt water in the old pits belonging to him and therewith made great quantities of salt (showing how much) and sold the same in Droitwich and thereby hindered the sale of the plaintiff's salt to her damage of £40.

The defendant pleaded not guilty. And after a long trial lasting near twelve hours, there was a verdict for the defendant.

The principal point and question in this case was whether there is and time out of mind has been a custom within the manor and borough of Droitwich that the owners of the inheritances of lands within the borough have been and ought to be excluded and restrained from digging any new pits in their own lands within the borough to draw or gain any salt water thence to make salt for sale, or not.

---

[5] Elizabeth Smallbrooke, widow.

There was another question that arose in this case which was whether the defendant in digging his new pit (which is within Moteclose within the borough) did intercept or stop the salt springs flowing to the three old pits or not or prejudice those pits by draining the salt water from the old pits into the new one sunk by the defendant. But as to this, there was not any satisfactory evidence, and so little or no stress was laid upon that.

But the cause depending upon the first point, which was the custom, and in order to come to that, the plaintiff's title to her two bulliaries in Upperwich Pit for her life, and the defendant's title to Moteclose in fee simple and the defendant digging the new pit there and thence drawing of salt water and therewith making salt and selling such a quantity of that salt were all admitted. The plaintiff's counsel being aware how harsh and difficult a thing it was and [it being] scarcely admittable by the rules of law in any case to set up a custom to exclude and restrain the owner of land in fee simple from digging for anything in his own land that may tend to profit and to use his land as he pleases, endeavored to make it out that the manor and borough of Droitwich and the salt springs and pits there and all the soil within the said manor and borough were once the inheritance of King Edward the Confessor and from him came to William the Conqueror and from him to King John, who (as appeared by an ancient charter produced) 1 August 17th of his reign [1215] granted to the Burgesses of Wich (now agreed to be Droitwich) and *heredibus suis villam illam de Wychio quicquid scilt. habemus in eadem villa ad feodum firmum cum saltis et salinis et omnibus pertinentibus et aliis libertatibus et liberis consuetudinibus ad illam partem nostram in eadem villa pertinentibus per £100 sterlingorum nobis reddendum ad scaccarium per manus burgensium* (half at Michaelmas and half at Lady Day) *habendum et tenendum de nobis et heredibus nostris praefatis burgensibus et heredibus suis imperpetuum*, with large words of *adeo libere, honorifice* [?] etc. as the king had or could grant, and therein was a grant of a fair and freedom from tolls with other privileges and then repeats the same words and things again that the burgesses should have and enjoy them *ut supra quicquid habemus* etc. And upon this ground and supposition it was that they relied to make such a custom of exclusion and restraint reasonable, that in regard in no time or age there was any that pretended to dig any new pits within the borough, but that all salt was made out of the brine taken out of the old pits and that they were always sufficient for [the] making of salt to supply the country, that it might reasonably be intended and shall be presumed that the crown, who had the power to make such restraint and exclusion as well while in the crown as by their grants before the charter of King John of any houses or lands in the borough to any others, did make such exclusion and restraint. And though there cannot any such grants be produced, yet in respect there have been all along owners of houses and lands in the borough wherein salt springs have been and that none have dug any new pits till the now defendant and that (as was proved in the cause) it has been by the oldest people living in the borough (some being eighty and above) the constant reputation that none could dig or make any new pits there, and that the fee farm rent of £100 *per annum* has been and is constantly paid by the proprietors of the old pits only, and that digging new ones have and will fall the price and value of the bulliaries in the old ones from £10 *per annum* to 20s. (as also was proved), the plaintiff's counsel relied upon those things for the ground and foundation of such custom to exclude the owners of any ground in the borough from digging new pits and making salt to the wrong or prejudice of the old ones.

And divers witnesses were examined which spoke materially to the usage, that in their times and as they heard from their fathers and other old persons there were only three pits (as now there are) wherein there are and have been about four hundred shares which have been sold and aliened as lands in fee simple and settled upon marriages and in jointures and that each proprietor in the shares (some having more, some fewer) has a separate and distinct property and estate in his share though the pits themselves have always (till a late Act of Parliament[6] made in this reign) been under the government and management of the corporation of Droitwich and taken their bulliaries, being certain buckets or proportions of brine out of those pits by assignment or appointment of such as had the government of them and not otherwise and that each proprietor made and sold his own salt, but yet under some regulations and that none might make salt for sale but those proprietors. And it was proved that there are many salt springs in Droitwich besides those that fed the three pits and that they lay open and visible and that [the] defendant's ancestors, under whom the defendant claims Moteclose, being made acquainted that such springs were there and advised to dig a pit, said he might not do so, being restrained by custom, and that it was never heard of till about eighteen or twenty years ago that any attempt was made to dig any new pits, and then lord Windsor dug a hole, but the corporation stopped it up without giving any recompense, as the witnesses swore (though the point was something doubtful).

And the plaintiff's counsel, to prove Droitwich to belong to the crown, produced Domesday Book[7] wherein mention is made that in Wich *habuit Rex Edwardus* (that is the Confessor) *domos 11, et in quinque puteis habebat Rex Edwardus suam partem, in uno puteo Upwich 54 salinae et 2 hocci reddendi 6s. 8d., in alio puteo Helperic 17 salinae, in tertio puteo Middlewich 12 salinae et duae partes de uno hocco reddenda 6s. 8d. in quinque [aliis] puteis 15 salinae de hiis omnibus habebat Edwardus Rex de firma £52. In ipsis puteis habebat Edvinus Comes 51 salinas et dimidium et*

---

[6] A private act passed in 1688, see *SR*, VI, 155.
[7] PRO E. 31.

de hoccis habebat 6s. 8d. hoc totum reddebat de firma £24. And there were mention made in that book that the king held the manor of Bromsgrove, to which there belonged thirteen *salinae* in Wich and three *salinarii reddentes* such a sum and proportion of salt, the like for Grafton and Tarderbery manor, in effect, and a grant made by Maud, the empress, was stood upon by the plaintiff, by an *inspeximus* whereof, 11 Ric. II pars secunda m. 24, it appeared that she and her son Henry II having founded Bordesly Abbey she grants to the abbot *totam terram de Bordesly et novum puteum de Wych de proprio labore suo ad proprios usus suos sine venditione quam inde faciant*, which the plaintiff's counsel would have to evidence that none should make salt to sell, and then they read the grant of King John *ut supra*.

The defendant's counsel insisted upon it in point of law that the custom was not good, being in restraint of common right and of a fee simple, and that the supposition that the plaintiff's counsel went upon that all this manor, borough, and salt springs and salt pits were once in the crown is not made out and so [is] no foundation for the pretended custom of exclusion, for it appears by Domesday Book that the crown had not all the salt pits or works but that others had some there that were subjects. And they observed that the grant from King John was not of all the manor, borough, or salt pits or springs (whatever the word *salinae* may mean), for though at first the grant is *villam illam de Wychio*, yet it is after restrained by *quicquid scilt. habemus in eadem villa, ad feodum firmum una cum salsis et salinis*, which implies that all Wych did not pass by that grant, and further observed (as was plain) that the fee farm rent (however it may have been paid) is not reserved out of the salt pits only but also out of so much of the other part of the town and the fair, liberties, and privileges, which thereby were granted wherein also there are these words *ad illam partem nostram in eadem villa pertinente*. And they also produced the record of a fine [of] 2 Hen. VI [1424] and another [of] 3 Hen. VII [1488] to make it out that there were then other salt pits in Wych than these three now used and called the old ones whereby there are grants of 14 *salinae aquae salsae in quodam puteo plumbaria et bullaria [?] aquae salsae vocatur Sherevespitt in Droitwich* and a copy of the king's grant of that pit 12 November 35 Hen. VIII [1543] to West, wherein also mention is made of divers *salinarum* in Wych as belonging to others, and a grant [of] 25 February 30 Hen. VIII [1539], whereby the king grants to George Harpur a pit in Middlewich concealed and omitted out of the grant by King John, all which, as they urged, took away the foundation of the pretended custom as grounded upon a supposition or presumption that all Wych was in the crown or granted by King John, but, as they said, to show the foundation of the nonuser of digging pits in Droitwich besides the three old ones, in all probability, it was thus, first either that all the inhabitants in Wich that had any ground there wherein were salt springs were also proprietors of shares in the three pits and so forbore to make any new ones as tending to no profit since there were and might be salt enough made there for ordinary use and to bear a reasonable price, but secondly and principally that the pretense of this exclusion took its rise from a clause which was put into the charter of the corporation of Wych which was renewed 8 November 22 Jac. I [1624], whereby the king, taking notice that he was informed by the humble petition of the corporation *quod salsae et salinae* (in Wich) *consistunt de fontibus et puteis* (not saying how many) *aquae salsae quodque si alii fontes vel putei* should be made, it would be a prejudice and corruption to the old ones, for the better government and benefit of the corporation and for suppression of new pits to be made, the king commands that no other new pit should be dug within the borough or limits under penalty of the king's displeasure and of fine and imprisonment, the fine to be limited by the court of exchequer and levied and that grant to be an authority to the court of exchequer for that purpose, which grant (as was observed) was of too feeble a nature of itself to make such restraint or exclusion in point of law and yet might so far influence the minds and actions of men who might think or be told it was a good restraint or at least that it was more prudent to submit to it than contest it, not to dig any new pits.

And further it was observed by the defendant's counsel that the mere non-user of itself can never be an evidence of or make a right of restraint no more than where A. and his ancestors time out of mind have dug a coal pit or the like and sold the coals and furnished the country thereabout sufficiently and at a reasonable rate can restrain B. that has a coal pit in his ground next to it from digging it and selling the coals, though thereby A. loses the sale of his coals or sustains a loss by abating the price, which none can say will bear an action, for it is for the public good that there be plenty and cheapness of commodities. And though there may be in this case a damage to A., as there may in the principal case be also to the plaintiff and other proprietors of the three ancient salt works by lowering and abating the value and price of their shares and bulliaries, yet it is a *damnum absque injuria* for which the law gives no recompense. And the sole making of salt at the three old pits looks like a monopoly and is not to be favored in law. And all the loss the plaintiff and other proprietors can or do sustain by the defendants or others digging of new pits is only that they cannot sell the salt at the old pits so dear as they could before, which nevertheless is a benefit to the commonwealth and not to be punished in an action but where there is a sufficient and legal ground of exclusion, which appears not to be by custom well founded in this case.

And the defendant in evidence produced witnesses who proved that, in digging for this new pit in Motesclose, they found the ruins of other salt pits and divers utensils for making salt and a tun that would hold five or six hogsheads and timber for ovens to bake salt in and a pit four foot square and eighteen foot deep and form timber and good brine in it, which argues that there have been other pits of later years than the three old ones now used, and that the crown the first year after defendant's digging of his pits received from defendants £40 a week for the duty upon salt and receives now two thirds more for the additional duty. And the defendants read in evidence by consent a verdict obtained at the king's bench bar by a special jury of Worcestershire in Michaelmas term 1695 upon an issue directed out of chancery, wherein the now defendant was plaintiff and Edward Wheeler, George Harris, Richard Smallbrooke, and others, part of the Corporation of Droitwich and proprietors of divers shares in the three old pits, were defendants. And the issue was whether the then plaintiff and now defendant might lawfully dig the brine pit in his close called Motesclose and the brine pit in his close purchased of Hale and others and lying in the borough of Droitwich and thereout draw brine and make salt thereof and sell that salt or not. And a verdict was given for the then plaintiff now defendant which was proved to be very well approved of by the court of king's bench and that it was then said by the court of king's bench that the custom insisted on (which is the same now in question) was unreasonable. And the jury now at the bar after the evidence on both sides fully summed up gave a verdict for the defendant Stayner against the pretended custom conformable to that in the king's bench.

Note the cause of the duke of Shrewsbury and others (q.v. above ff. 31 and 78), having been heard at Serjeants' Inn in Fleet Street the 18th of February before, which endeavored to restrain the defendant from proceeding either in digging any new pit or making or selling of any salt made at such new pit and, after long hearing, the court for the reasons above urged for the defendant in the trial at bar, not being of opinion that they could relieve the plaintiffs, ordered their bill to be dismissed unless cause this term [(Easter, 1697) be shown]. And now the court did the third of this instant May dismiss the bill of the duke and others absolutely but without prejudice to the right, which clause was then put into the dismission in regard the trial at bar above mentioned was not then over, and by order of the 29th of January 1696[/97] in chancery the time for the corporation to procure a trial to prevent the dismission of their bill there to restrain the defendant from digging new pits under pretense of the said custom was enlarged, and they agreed that the action in the exchequer between Smallbrooke and Stayner should be that action wherein the right should be tried. And after this trial, that bill in chancery was absolutely dismissed.

But the main and principal cause why the English bill of the duke of Shrewsbury and other proprietors was dismissed was for want of parties in regard it appeared to the court in the pleadings of the cause that there were some hundreds of proprietors whose interest and right were as much concerned against the defendant Stayner as the plaintiffs were, which were no parties to the suit, and each of them had as much right and as good reason to bring a bill against the defendant as the then plaintiffs had, and therefore all the proprietors ought to have been either plaintiffs or defendants else there might and would be multiplicity of suits and endless contention and a decree or a dismission in this cause or in the cause of any other proprietor could not bind such as were not parties to it. And as to the merits upon the custom and restraint, the court were all of opinion against it, and thought it was determinable at [common] law being matter of law only, the fee farm rent being out of the crown and in a subject and so the owner [is] no more privileged to sue here than any other payer of a fee farm rent purchased from the crown.

See my notes upon the hearing in Hilary term 1696[/97] and upon the trial in Easter term 1697 in the bundles of those two terms.

[Other copies of this report: GUL MS. B88–8, pp. 311, 448, 573.]

[Orders of 18 Feb. and 3 May 1697: PRO E.126/16, ff. 398, 408v.]

314
Harding v. Golding (Ex. 1696)

Matters not pleaded are not in issue and cannot be proved.
Tithes are due for apples that have fallen as well as for apples that have been picked.

LI MS. Misc. 559, f. 32 [Eng.] (Ward's Reports)

In this case, which was a general bill for tithes without charging any fraud, of driving out cows a little before calving time and sheep a little before yeaning time into another parish and letting them calve and lamb in another parish and then bringing them back to the first parish, the plaintiffs by their bill wholly confining themselves to lambs and calves fallen in the first parish, the court rejected the proofs of such fraud, that not being in issue in the cause.

And in this case, the court did not approve of a pretended custom in the parish to pay no tithes of falling apples but only of those gathered as being a dangerous custom and might tend to the defrauding the parson of all fruit, if the parishioner would not gather it but let it fall and the rather because it is usual in cider countries to let their apples fall, which must be tithable.

[Other copies of this report: GUL MS. B88–8, p. 315.]

[The decree of 8 May 1696 is printed at 1 Wood 365, 1 Eagle & Younge 618; see also the orders of 30 Apr. and 22 June 1696: PRO E.126/16, ff. 331, 362v.]

315
Morgan v. Tevell (Ex. 1696)

In this case, an accounting for tithes was settled by the court upon exceptions to the master's report.

LI MS. Misc. 559, f. 33, pl. 1 [Eng.] (Ward's Reports)

In this case, which was a bill for great tithes, the court referred it to the deputy of the king's remembrancer to compute the tithes fallen in the plaintiff's parish. And upon exceptions to the deputy's report that such a part of the tithes fell in such a place which was not in the plaintiff's parish but in another (naming it), the court determined the point upon the proofs before the deputy in which parish that place was without a trial at law that not being prayed or insisted on.

[Other copies of this report: GUL MS. B88–8, p. 316.]

[Order of 30 Apr. 1696: PRO E.126/16, f. 332v.]

316
Chaffin v. Frampton (Ex. 1696)

The deposition of a witness who is later made a co-defendant can be used even though there was no court order for taking the deposition.

A conveyance which was made by an infant who received no consideration or benefit for it and which was not done upon the advice of adult friends will be ordered to be set aside.

LI MS. Misc. 559, f. 33, pl. 2 [Eng.] (Ward's Reports)

The bill was to have a trust preserved and settled for the benefit of the plaintiff's wife, wherein the case appeared to be that Richard Harman for part of a provision for his two daughters, the plaintiff Frances and defendant Joan Weekes, did in 1679 lease to the defendant Durnford and one King (since dead) three closes in Gillingham [Dorset] for eighty-four years in trust to permit the defendant Joan to receive the profits so long or so many of the years as she should live, and after her death in trust for the plaintiff Frances, her executors, administrators, and assigns for the residue of the term. And to have this residue preserved for Frances after the death of Joan (who is still living) was the scope of the bill. And in this case, the plaintiffs having not made the trustee Durnford a defendant at the first hearing but examined him as a witness, they had leave to amend their bill and make him a defendant, which now they have done and brought him to hearing. And the question was whether his deposition taken before he was a defendant should be read at this hearing, there being no order of court for so doing (as is usual, saving just exceptions). And I was doubtful and inclined against it both for the matter and form, the plaintiffs having examined a defendant that is a trustee without order and now he stands both party and witness. But LECHMERE and POWYS (*absens* Turton) were for the reading [of] it, and it was read accordingly.

Another point was this, that the plaintiff Frances and her sister Joan had (upon occasion of a question arising between them and their brother William upon their father's will whereby other lands were devised to them in fee and that difference referred) by conveyances reciting this eighty-four years lease passed away their whole estate therein to their said brother William. But it appearing that the plaintiff Frances was then under twenty-one years of age and that there did not appear to be any consideration for such her conveyance, nor did the defendants insist upon it in their answers but rather to avoid the said lease as either never made or as if copyhold and so not demisable for so long a term, the court held that the said conveyance as it did not bind her in law (being the act of an infant) so it did not bind her in equity there not appearing the least consideration for it nor to be by the advice of friends or as a family settlement which the court declared they would be careful in not to relieve infants in equity for matters which appear to be either advantageous to them or to be done by advice of friends and as a family settlement and agreement, and where possession has gone or enjoyment been for any considerable time after infancy, or disability removed. And in this case, there was a decree for the plaintiffs for preserving the plaintiff Frances's interest after the death of Joan, and that Durnford the trustee, his executors, administrators, and assigns should stand trusted accordingly, and likewise that the heirs, executors, and administrators of William Harmon to whom the said conveyance was made should stand and be possessed of the said leased premises for, (and after [the] death of Joan should convey the same to) the plaintiff Frances, for which purpose the said lease (though cancelled) was set up in equity.

[Other copies of this report: GUL MS. B88–8, p. 317.]

[Order of 4 May 1696: PRO E.126/16, f. 337.]

317

Panton v. Lady Luckin (Ex. 1696)

This case for money damages for breach of contract, which should have been sued at common law, was settled out of court by arbitration.

LI MS. Misc. 559, f. 34, pl. 1 [Eng.] (Ward's Reports)

The plaintiff's bill was to be relieved against the defendant for drawing twenty-nine pictures and an hatchment for the defendant. The defendant denied that she ever employed the plaintiff to do any such thing, but there was some evidence that, after the pictures were brought home, she ordered them to be hung up in the house of her daughter. And because this bill was for nothing but an *indebitatus assumpsit* or a *quantum meruit* and properly and indeed only determinable at [common] law wherein damages must be recovered, and this plainly appearing to be so at the hearing though the defendant might have demurred to the relief, yet in regard [that] the court can make no decree but for damages, I was for dismissing the bill as in justice it ought to be in any man's case that is not *in forma pauperis*, and the measure of justice to poor and rich is all one. But upon the mediation of some of the court, the defendant was willing to refer the matter to Baron Powys, who made an end thereof.

[Other copies of this report: GUL MS. B88-8, p. 319.]

[Order of 7 May 1696: PRO E.126/16, f. 330.]

318

Beer v. Caswell (Ex. 1696)

Clover is tithable in the same manner as hay.
A copy of a book is not admissible in evidence if the original is available.

LI MS. Misc. 559, f. 34, pl. 2 [Eng.] (Ward's Reports)

Upon a bill for tithe of hay in Misterton [Somerset], a question arose whether a *modus* of 3d. for a place tenement to the vicar of Misterton extended to discharge the clover grass growing upon plowed ground (part of such place tenement) from paying tithes to the impropriator, as it does for all hay growing upon meadow or other old ground part of such place tenement. And it was admitted by the court that clover must follow the nature and title of hay, as has frequently been resolved and decreed in this court, and that a *modus* for hay will discharge clover from paying tithes nay even when it runs to seed and is threshed and either bread made of it or hogs etc. fed with the seed, as was resolved in the case of the vicar of Luton in this court [*blank*], which see Liber [*blank*].[1]

But in this case (where there never was but one instance of sowing clover upon arable ground before and that passing *sub silentio*), the doubt arose about the extent of the 3d. whether that covered more than the ancient meadow or ground, though there were no enjoyment by the vicar. Yet the vicar who is endeavored to be entitled by this *modus* being examined, he giving his reasons why he conceived it belonged not to him but to the impropriator and that it extended but to meadow or pasture and not to arable land (and the copy of the bishop's

---

[1] *Pomfret v. Lander* (1680), GUL MS. B88-7, p. 224, pl. 1; Order of 15 Nov. 1680: PRO E.126/13, f. 245v; also 1 Rayner 64, 1 Eagle & Younge 527, 2 Gwillim 530, 756, 2 Comyns 633, 92 E.R. 1245.

register being produced by the plaintiff but not read because it was only a copy whereas the book itself should be here), though the strongest proof was for the defendants, yet the plaintiff offering to try the *modus* as to clover, the court was divided as to the trial, Lechmere and Turton being for dismissing the plaintiff's bill as having the strongest proof. But I [Ward] and Powys were for trying it at law at the peril of costs throughout the cause to be paid by the plaintiff, for though the plaintiff may try it at law in another action, yet where there is but the least semblance of right for a plaintiff and he is willing to try it at law at the peril of costs, the court do not usually dismiss in such cases, for a dismission is an absolute loss of the tithes for the years in question by the bill though he should afterwards prevail as to the right in another suit. And the defendant is the better, if the right be with him, for then he shall have his costs at law as well as in equity in this case, but he shall have no costs at law in an action upon the statute. And trials at law have been awarded by this court upon plaintiffs' bills demanding tithes of lands formerly part of monastery lands though such plaintiffs have not proved in the cause that the lands ever paid tithes. And afterwards the defendants agreed to the trial at law.

[Other copies of this report: GUL MS. B88–8, p. 320.]

319

Cooke v. Haynes (Ex. 1696)

In this case, a debtor was allowed to prove that he had been tricked into executing a bond and to prove repayment of the money borrowed.

LI MS. Misc. 559, f. 35, pl. 1 [Eng.] (Ward's Reports)

[The] plaintiff exhibited his bill against the defendant to be relieved against a bond of £60 penalty dated 10th April 1695 conditioned for payment of £30 to the defendant the 12th of May following upon a suggestion that the said bond was obtained by fraud and that [the] plaintiff was illiterate and that he was told it was only a warrant to enable the defendant to prosecute a suit against one Newman and that there was no money lent upon it and that it was never read to him.

The defendant by his answer swore that at several times he lent the plaintiff the £30 and upon lending the last part of it, he gave up to the plaintiff his former notes and took the bond and swore it to be a just debt and unpaid and that the plaintiff read over the bond twice and well knew what it was and denied all fraud and surprise and other the allegations in the plaintiff's bill which might call the reality of the bond or debt in question.

And it appeared at the hearing that the plaintiff was a literate person and wrote his name to the bond in a very good hand as most men write. And it was proved by a witness to the bond that the plaintiff himself called him to witness it. But because one witness for the plaintiff swore that he heard the defendant in October last say that the plaintiff owed him nothing, and another that in December last he heard the defendant say that he had tricked the plaintiff into the bond and doubted not but he should get his money, and because the defendant had not proved the lending of his money and that it did not appear that the defendant was in a condition to lend so much money, the three other barons sent it to be tried at law upon two issues, first whether the defendant really lent the plaintiff so much money and secondly, if he did, then whether the same be not paid again.

I was content to have the second issue tried if desired by [the] plaintiff, but as to the first I thought it of a dangerous consequence to send a man that swears he lent his money upon a bond to law to prove the money lent when he has a bond for it from a man of full age under no restraint that writes and reads very well when the money is sworn to be lent and to be a real debt and no proof of fraud or surprise and upon the bare surmises in a bill without further proof than here made and against the defendant's answer. For if relief may be had in equity against a legal security upon such pretenses, all creditors by bond may be in a dangerous condition and lose their debts unless they can prove payment of the money which certainly many are not able to do. And it is better to suffer a mischief to one than let in an inconvenience to the public. And it has not been seen that a court of equity has relieved against a bond for payment of money sworn due without manifest proof of some fraud or surprise, which did not appear in this case, further than by the proofs *ut supra*. And though the defendant may be an ill man in other things and might say he tricked the plaintiff into the bond, yet that does not contradict nor invalidate the truth of the debt but only the getting of the security. And that is hard to be believed that a man of age and understanding, as the plaintiff is admitted of all hands to be, should be gained to enter that bond without reason for it. But by the opinion of the three barons, it was sent to a trial *ut supra*.

[Other copies of this report: GUL MS. B88–8, p. 321.]

[Orders of 24 and 28 Jan. 1696: PRO E.127/19, ff. 433, 439.]

320

Attorney General ex rel. Mayor of Huntington v. Mercers Company (Ex. 1696)

In this case of a trust to provide a lectureship, the trustees were found to have the right to select the lecturer, and the unsuccessful plaintiffs were ordered to pay court costs.

LI MS. Misc. 559, f. 35, pl. 2 [Eng.] (Ward's Reports)

The case upon the bill, answer, and proofs appeared to be this, that one Richard Fishborne, a citizen and mercer of London born in Huntington,[1] by his will in writing dated the 30th of March 1625 reciting that he was desirous to do good to the Town of Huntington where he was born and yet was not acquainted nor informed of the state and wants of the said town, he did thereby give and bequeath to the Wardens and Commonalty of the Mystery of Mercers of the City of London the sum of £2000 'upon this trust and confidence that they should therewith purchase lands and hereditaments of the clear yearly value of £100 and bestow and distribute the same to some good and charitable uses in the said town as in maintenance of a lecture or of a grammar school, in erecting and endowing of an almshouse, in any or all these, or such other good and pious uses to have perpetuity and yearly allowance forever, in such manner, form, and proportion as the said Wardens and Commonalty together with the advice of his executor after named should upon information of the state and wants of the said town devise and ordain'. The testator Fishborne died shortly after the will. And in the year 1629 the Mercers Company purchased the manor of Chalgrave, which was of the yearly value of £300 and upwards and cost much above £2000, out of which they allotted £100 *per annum* for Fishborne's charity for Huntington which at first was settled to be £40 *per annum* for a lecture and £60 *per annum* for the poor. But afterwards the proportions were altered by the Company and £60 *per annum* [was] appointed for the lecturer (there being preaching but at one church in Huntington) and £40 *per annum* for the poor, and in those proportions it continued to this day. But the relators, the Corporation of Huntington, now pretending that the right of nominating and appointing who shall be the lecturer belongs to the relators and not to the Mercers Company (though the Company had for some time taken upon them not only to nominate the lecturer but to appoint in what church in Huntington and on what days the lecture should be preached), and that the relators had appointed one Mr. Reynell to preach the lecture, and that he had preached the same ever since the last vacancy to the great satisfaction of the people there, and that the defendants had refused to pay him the £60 *per annum* but had taken upon them to nominate one Mr. Wagstaff to preach the lecture, who (they pretended was not so fit as the other) lived out of town, therefore the relators exhibited this bill and prayed thereby first that the £60 *per annum* might be paid to the minister of the parish (which Mr. Reynell is) so long as he preaches the lecture, secondly that the town's right of choice of the lecturer may be determined, thirdly that the charity may be settled and preserved.

---

[1] V.C.H., *Huntingdonshire*, II (1932), 118, 147.

The defendants by their answer set forth the will and their right and title thereby as they conceived to the appointment of the lecturer and that they had so done ever since the death of Fishborne, and that the charity had been constantly and duly performed (except since the relators gave this disturbance after the removal of the last lecturer), and that they had nominated Mr. Wagstaff, who was ready to have performed the service, who was approved by the bishop, and was hindered by the relators.

And at the hearing of this cause, it was admitted by the relators that the defendants had constantly paid the £100 *per annum* and that nothing was arrear save since the removal of the last lecturer. And the only question was about the right of nominating the lecturer, whether the same belonged to the relators or the defendants. And upon the proofs it appeared that the defendants ever since the gift of the charity have placed the lecturer, and some times altered the church and time, and have frequently refused (though sometimes accepted) the recommendation of the inhabitants of Huntington, nay even contradicted and shown reasons against the recommendations of King Charles I, and that shortly after the gift, and at the first appointment, 1626, refused the request of the same person (Dr. Berd) recommended by the town (as well as the king) by Mr. Bernard, their recorder. And upon the last vacancy of a lecturer that happened, which was in April 1695 (by the resignation of Mr. Sturges), the mayor and aldermen sent a petition or desire to the Company that they would appoint Mr. Reynell, which they declined and chose Mr. Wagstaff.

And no one instance appearing that any lecturer ever was put in by the town but at the most by their representation and desire placed there by the defendants, the whole court was of opinion that there did not appear any right to the relators to have the nomination or appointment of the lecturer and that therefore the bill ought as to that point to be dismissed. And though the special nomination or appointment of the lecturer was not expressly by the will limited to any persons (as it was by another clause in the same will whereby he directed the lecturer of St. Bartholomew's to be chosen in a particular manner and by certain persons) and that it might be thought most reasonable and agreeable to primitive institution for persons to choose their own teachers, yet the relators being a body corporate and but part of the people that are to receive benefit by the lecturer's preaching and instruction, they could no more pretend to the appointment of the lecturer than the defendants in reason could do. And the right of the crown having been acted against in the first nomination of Dr. Berd, and there being no heir nor executor of Fishborne extant, and the trust subsisting in the defendants as an inheritance in fee, the court could not establish the relators' demands and therefore must dismiss their bill, which was done accordingly with costs, the court as to them being divided. And so the rule of paying costs upon dismissions standing where costs are not spared by the court, but (in respect of such division of the court) they were directed to be very moderate though all agreed [that] the relators had no right and that the defendants had done no wrong but executed the trust with all candor and integrity. And the costs were afterwards settled to £27 being taxed at £54.

[Other copies of this report: GUL MS. B88–8, p. 324.]

[Order of 5 Feb. 1696: PRO E.127/19, f. 462v.]

321

Lord Rockingham v. Vyner (Ex. 1696)

A mortgagee in possession must pay any surplus received from the perception of profits to a junior mortgagee.

LI MS. Misc. 559, f. 37, pl. 1 [Eng.] (Ward's Reports)

The plaintiffs' testators and intestates, under whom they claim, being mortgagees of the estate of one Sharesmore at Frolesworth in Leicestershire, sold to one Yarway (or at least mortgaged to him in fee and that mortgage [was] forfeited) for about £3000. And Sir Robert Vyner being a prior mortgagee (derived from the title of Sir Thomas Hyde, whose widow he married) and also a purchaser of the inheritance (but with notice of the plaintiffs' title) and a decree being made formerly that the plaintiffs' testatrix, the Lady Rockingham, and the now Lord Rockingham should redeem Vyner's first mortgage upon payment of what [is] due, and upon a report that that first mortgage was overpaid by perception of profits £2547 18s. 10d. and exceptions to that report by the defendant now coming to be heard, they were all overruled.

And it was decreed:

First that the report should be confirmed.

Secondly that the surplus money received by Sir Robert Vyner and the defendant over and besides what [is] due upon the first mortgage should be paid by the defendant to the plaintiff out of the personal estate of Sir Robert Vyner.

Thirdly that the defendant assign to the plaintiffs the mortgaged premises (besides Husbandman's Pasture, which was an absolute purchase and not liable to redemption by the plaintiffs) to hold till they are satisfied their mortgage money with interest and charges.

Fourthly that an injunction issue to put and keep the plaintiffs in possession accordingly.

Fifthly that the arrears in the tenants' hands be paid to the plaintiffs.

And it was considered in this case that though the defendant never pay the plaintiff the £2547 18s. 10d. towards their debt according to the decree, yet the inheritance and equity of redemption of the plaintiffs' mortgage being in the defendant, that will not go to sink the plaintiffs' mortgage till all their mortgage money be raised out of the profits of the estate.

[Other copies of this report: GUL MS. B88–8, p. 328.]

[Order of 26 May 1696: PRO E.126/16, f. 335.]

322
Attorney General ex rel. Bennet v. St. John (Ex. 1696)

In this case, the accounts of a regiment of the army were settled following an issue to a jury.

LI MS. Misc. 559, f. 37, pl. 2 [Eng.] (Ward's Reports)

Mr. Attorney General having formerly exhibited his English bill or information on the behalf of the officers and soldiers in Colonel Herbert's regiment in Ireland against the defendant, who was agent for the said regiment, to call him to an account for the money received by him for the use of that regiment suggesting that he had not paid what he had received for their use. And upon the account taken and many exceptions put in to the report on both sides and after several days' hearing, it was, by consent of both parties, referred to a trial at bar in this court upon this issue, whether the defendant had paid upon the account of clothing of that regiment to one Potter or any other the sum of £3158 1s. 4d. or any other and what sum and by like consent ordered that if it was found that the defendant had paid that sum for clothing then by consent the bill [was] to be dismissed, but if not so much paid upon that account, then the defendant was to account *de novo* for all the money received by him on account of the regiment as confessed in his answer, and to discharge himself thereof as accountants ought to do. And upon the trial (which lasted eight hours), the jury found that the defendant had paid for the clothing of the said regiment £2758 1s. 4d. and no more, which is less by £400 than the sum of £3158 1s. 4d. And in regard [that] the jury had found expressly that the defendant had paid £2758 1s. 4d. for clothing and no more (whereby the defendant's former account and his books as to the overplus were satisfied, which seemed to be the main design of the trial, to try the credit of the books), yet Mr. Attorney General did not insist upon the strictness of the order and issue but agreed that the defendant should have allowance upon his account for £2758 1s. 4d. under the head of clothing and go to an account for the rest of the items of the defendant's discharge.

Note that afterwards in Michaelmas term 2d [of] Queen Anne 1703 after many references, reports, and exceptions to them relating to the defendant's account, it was decreed that the defendant pay to Captain Bennet, the relator in the cause, who prosecuted for the regiment the sum of £695, so much appearing to be due upon the account to the regiment. And this decree [was] affirmed in Parliament February 1704 with £30 costs.[1]

[Other copies of this report: GUL MS. B88–8, p. 330.]

[Order of 26 May 1696: PRO E.126/16, f. 334.]

323
Chambers v. Briggs (Ex. 1696)

The seizure of a joint debt is void where the process issued against only one of the debtors.
  In an action of assumpsit, all joint obligors must be joined as codefendants.
  Where the crown as a creditor claims through a private person, the crown has no greater rights than the private person; however, once in possession, the crown has greater powers of execution than a private person.
  A prior assignment of a bankrupt's assets is not defeated by a subsequent execution by the crown.
  The date of a seizure under a writ of extent is the date of the inquisition not the date of the writ.
  The crown can release one joint obligor without releasing the other.

I
LI MS. Misc. 559, f. 51 [Eng.] (Ward's Reports)

The case upon the bill, answer, and proofs appeared to be this, that Richard Tapps and Nicholas Crispe, being partners in trade together, were jointly indebted to William Austin in £600 and that Austin was indebted to Augustin Briggs, the king's receiver general of his taxes in Norfolk in £556. An extent issued out of the exchequer against Briggs upon his bond *quoad bona et catalla debita credita et specialitates*, which was in order to find debts in aid of Briggs, and by an inquisition taken 7 September 1693, the debt from Austin to Briggs was found and seized into the king's hands, and that the 8th of September 1693 an extent issued against Austin for the recovery of the £556 *quoad bona et catalla*. And it was in order to find and seize debts due to Austin, and the 11th of the same September, an inquisition was taken, whereby it was found that Tapps (not mentioning or taking notice of Crispe, his partner) was at the time of the taking of that inquisition indebted to Austin by simple contract in £600, which debt was thereby seized into the king's hands. After this, *viz.* 23 November 1693, the commissioners of bankrupts, upon a commission of bankrupts, issued against Austin, assigned the debt of £600 (as a joint debt due and owing from Tapps and Crispe

---

[1] *Lords' Journal*, XVII (n.d.), p. 654.

to Austin) unto the plaintiffs, Chambers and others, for the benefit of them and of Austin's creditors that should come in and seek relief according to law. After this assignment by the commissioners, *viz.* 28 November 1693, another extent issued against Austin for the £556 due from him to Briggs, and by inquisition thereupon taken the 30th of November 1693, both Tapps and Crispe were found indebted to Austin in the £600, which was first seized into the king's hands. And whether that £600 belonged to the plaintiffs as assignees of the commissioners of bankrupts by virtue of the assignment of the 23rd of November or unto the king by both or either of the inquisitions upon the extents against Austin was the question.

This cause depended long in the court and was often spoken to by counsel. And at the setting down of the causes after this term, it was resolved and so decreed by the court that the £600 belonged to the plaintiffs as assignors of the commissioners of bankrupts for, it being a joint debt due from Tapps and Crispe to Austin, the first inquisition that found and seized it as the debt of Tapps only did not in law lay hold upon the joint debt due from Tapps and Crispe, for upon a *scire facias* against Tapps upon the first inquisition, he might safely (as indeed he did, but the attorney general proceeded not) plead *non indebitatus*, as at law he might have pleaded *non assumpsit* to any action that Austin could have brought against him alone if no seizure had been. And here the king, claiming under a subject, is not (in point of entitling himself) in any better condition than the subject was, and he could not have sued Tapps alone, if no seizure had been made. And though it must be admitted that after the king is in completely of a subject's right, he has a larger remedy for recovery of it than the subject had, as in Knight's Case, 5 Rep. 54,[1] and 2 Croke 513, Attorney General v. Death,[2] and Brooke's [Abr.] *Prerogative*, 124,[3] and Hardres' *Reports* 314.[4] Yet that consideration helps not this case where the only question is what was gained by the first inquisition that seized the £600, for if that did not take the whole debt of £600 as it stood a debt from both the partners and vest it in the king (as it was thought it did not), then it remained still a debt due from both the partners, and no part of it [was] affected by the first inquisition. And so the two partners, Tapps and Crispe, remained debtors to Austin for the whole £600 at the time of the assignment to the plaintiffs. And that assignment by virtue of the Statute of 1 Jac. I, c. 15, § 13,[5] vested the debt of £600 from both the partners in the plaintiffs, and then

---

[1] *Knight v. Breech* (1588), 5 Coke Rep. 54, 77 E.R. 137, also Gouldsborough 15, 75 E.R. 965, Moore K.B. 199, 72 E.R. 530, 3 Leonard 124, 74 E.R. 582, 1 Anderson 173, 123 E.R. 414.

[2] *The King v. Death* (1619), Cro. Jac. 513, 79 E.R. 438.

[3] Brooke, Abr., *Prerogative le roy*, pl. 124.

[4] *Gill v. Attorney General* (1662), Hardres 314, 145 E.R. 474.

[5] Stat. 1 Jac. I, c. 15, s. 13 (*SR*, IV, 1031–1034).

the second extent and inquisition of the 28th and 30th November 1693 against Austin came too late.

And in case Tapps, by the first inquisition, should be made liable to the whole £600, why might not another extent for another debt (and an inquisition thereupon found against Crispe) make him liable for the £600 also, and so each made liable to the whole, there not being any remedy by plea to prevent it. See my argument, among my arguments.

And the money, being brought into court by consent of all [the] parties to be delivered out as the judgment of the court should be, was delivered out to the plaintiffs.

[Other copies of this report: GUL MS. B88–8, p. 364.]

II
BL MS. Hargr. 71, ff. 95v, 96v [Fr. & Eng.] (Dodd's Reports)

Upon a bill of interpleader in the exchequer chamber, the point was [as follows]. A. and B. as partners were indebted to C. C. was indebted to D. (who was a debtor to the king) and to divers others. D., upon an extent, caused an inquisition to be found that A. was indebted to C. and seized it into the king's hands. (Note [that] before it was found that C. was indebted to D., the creditors of C. took out a commission of bankruptcy, and the commissioners assigned the debt due from A. and B. And then D. caused a new inquisition to be found, which found and seized the debt due from A. and B. to C.

And upon debate, the court held clearly that, if the first findings were good, then the assignment of the commissioners was void and that, if the first finding was not good, then the assignment of the commissioners was good against the second finding, and that the first inquisition was good. Jones 202, Audley and Halsey, [and] Hardres 314,[6] were cited. And Chief Baron WARD cited the case of the Attorney [General] and Knowles (1683) where Dashwood was indebted to the king; Baker was indebted to Dashwood, Perry and Buckley being partners, and yet upon [the] seizure of the debt of Baker, the king had execution upon the debate. Note [that] there each of the partners could have released or disposed of the whole.

It was insisted to the contrary that C. could not maintain *indebitatus assumpsit* against A. alone, which was agreed to by the court, and as a consequence, the king could not sue A. alone. [The court] adjourned. See Ray. Rep. 6.[7]

[The case was] argued again on 4 May 1696, and these points [were] insisted upon that the teste of the extent binds the debt, that the party becoming indebted

---

[6] *Awdley v. Halsey* (1629), W. Jones 202, 82 E.R. 107; *Gill v. Attorney General* (1662), Hardres 314, 145 E.R. 474.

[7] *Boylestone v. Radcliffe* (1661), T. Raymond 6, 83 E.R. 4.

to the king, the commissioners could not assign, that the king is not within the Statute of Bankrupts,[8] and that the savings in 21 Jac.[9] save this case.

[It was argued] to the contrary that the *teste* of the extent did not bind the debts [and] that the Statute of 21 Jac. does not extend to this case. See below.

Briggs was a receiver of the king and [was] indebted by bond to the king.

[On] 5 July 5 Will. & Mar. [1693], an extent issued upon the bond against Briggs.

[On] 7 September after [that, an] inquisition found Austen indebted to Briggs [for] £556 and seized [it].

[On] 8 September, an extent [was issued] against Austen.

[On] 11 September, an inquisition found Tapps indebted to Austen [for] £600 and seized it.

[On] 23 November, Austen being a bankrupt and a commission [having been] taken out, the commissioners assigned the debt due to him from Tapps and Crisp.

[On] 28 November, a new extent [was issued] against Austen.

[On] 30 November, an inquisition against Tapps and Crisp [found that they] were indebted to him and seized it into the king's hands.

Note [that] the debt in question was admitted to be due from Tapps and Crisp as partners.

The court held:

1. That the second extent and inquisition came too late.
2. That notwithstanding the prosecution was in aid of Briggs, yet [it was] good to the third degree and not after. (Note [that] Powys's Case, 4 [Coke] *Inst.*, and Poultney's Case, Hardres,[10] were cited to the contrary.)
3. That *indebitatus assumpsit* in this case does not lie for Austen etc. against one copartner without the other.
4. That if a copartner die, the creditors can maintain an action against the survivor generally without showing this special matter. (And the chief baron said that it was so adjudged by Hale.)
5. That debts are not bound from the *teste* of the extent.
6. That if two [persons] owe the king money, the king may release one and it does not discharge the other but he shall be chargeable with the whole. Sir Thomas Littleton's Case.[11]

---

[8] Stat. 13 Eliz. I, c. 7 (*SR*, IV, 539–541); Stat. 1 Jac. I, c. 15 (*SR*, IV, 1031–1034).

[9] Stat. 21 Jac. I, c. 19 (*SR*, IV, 1227–1229).

[10] *Auditor Povie's Case*, E. Coke, *Fourth Institute* (1644), p. 11, or perhaps *Lord Powis's Case* (1559), 2 Dyer 170a, 73 E.R. 372; *Attorney General v. Poultney* (1665), Hardres 403, 145 E.R. 519.

[11] *Littleton's Case* (1675), 1 Freeman 391, 89 E.R. 290, 1 Ventris 270, 86 E.R. 180, *sub nom. Gibson v. Thomson*, 3 Keble 451, 84 E.R. 817.

[The case was] argued again by *Pauncefort* for the king [in] Trinity [term] 1696 that if [there be] three creditors and one debtor,[12] each [creditor is] entitled to the whole, the same reason [should apply] where [there be] two or three debtors. It goes to the action but not to the right. See Raymond 7; 2 Saunders 96; 2 Cr. 475; 1 Syd. 5; 2 Rolle 234; 2 Cr. 515; Brooke, [Abr.], *Prerogative*, 124.[13] The king may release one debtor and yet sue another. The king [is] not obliged to such a certainty in his inquisition or information as a subject in his action or declaration. Earl of Devonshire's Case, 11 Rep.[14] He was held to make his account. So also Hardres 191.[15] [The court] adjourned.

Afterwards, in Trinity [term] 1696, it was resolved by all [of the barons] and decreed for the plaintiff that the first inquisition did not seize the debt and the second came too late. See the breviate.

[Other copies of this report: HLS MS. 537(b), p. 48; Oxf. Brasenose MS. 59, pp. 63, 64; IU Lilly MS. Parker, 'Cases in the Exchequer, vol. 2', p. 20; BL MS. Hargr. 70, p. 101, pl. 332; HLS MS. 1162, p. 89, pl. 478.]

[Order of 7 July 1696: PRO E.126/16, f. 348.]

324

Salter v. Salter (Ex. 1696)

In this case to set aside a conveyance on the ground of fraud, the plaintiff failed to prove his allegations of fraud and undue influence.

LI MS. Misc. 559, f. 52, pl. 1 [Eng.] (Ward's Reports)

The plaintiff as brother and heir of Nicholas Salter, deceased, became entitled to an estate at Lyminge[1] in Kent by settlement of his grandfather Nicholas Salter, and wherein Nicholas Salter, the plaintiff's father, had an estate for his life remainder in fee to his son, Nicholas, to whom the plaintiff is heir. The plaintiff by his bill pretended that his title to the Lyminge estate was concealed from him by his father, who told him it was destroyed by a revocation, and thereupon

---

[12] creditor *MS*.

[13] *Boylestone v. Radcliffe* (1661), T. Raymond 6, 7, 83 E.R. 4; *Chester v. Willan* (1670), 2 Wms. Saunders 96, 85 E.R. 768 [this case does not seem to be on point]; *Hingen v. Payn* (1618), Cro. Jac. 475, 79 E.R. 405; *Roberts v. Herbert* (1660), 1 Siderfin 5, 82 E.R. 936; *The King v. Death* (1619), Cro. Jac. 513, 79 E.R. 438; Brooke, Abr., *Prerogative le roy*, pl. 124.

[14] *Earl of Devonshire's Case* (1607), 11 Coke Rep. 89a, 77 E.R. 1266.

[15] *Wilford v. Greaves* (1661), Hardres 191, 145 E.R. 446.

---

[1] Lymage *MS*.

the plaintiff's father under pretense that he had a desire to make provision for his younger children and payment of his debts and offering to settle some houses on Tower Hill upon the plaintiff prevailed with the plaintiff to join with his father in settling the Lyminge estate upon the father in fee that he might make provision as before is said. And by concealing the plaintiff's right and using false and fraudulent suggestions to him, he was prevailed to join in a deed and fine whereby the fee was lodged in the father and the plaintiff disinherited. And the father by will charged the estate with legacies to younger children and payment of his debts. And to set aside that deed and fine *quoad* the plaintiff and by consequence to defeat the payment of his father's debts (amounting to some thousands of pounds) and the younger children's portions was the bill.

But upon the hearing of the cause, it appearing that though the plaintiff was entitled as heir to his brother, Nicholas, to that estate after his father's death, and that possibly he did not know that he was so, yet the plaintiff's father having obtained from him such deed and fine upon deliberation of near half a year, and it appearing that the plaintiff will or does enjoy an estate of a considerable value in Buckinghamshire, which his father (now dead) might have hindered him of, and the father being reputed an honest man though he did obtain that deed and fine from his son yet upon the whole it did not appear to be upon any indirect terms or by any unlawful ways or means but possibly upon the father's desires, and the same being of full age and the settlement had above three years ago and nothing done in the father's life time against it and no other way for the payment of debts or providing for younger children, the court did not think fit to set aside that deed and fine but dismissed the bill. The chief baron [WARD] inclined to have it tried at law upon an issue whether the deed and fine were obtained by fraud or not, but LECHMERE and POWYS did not agree to it, and so the bill was dismissed.

[Other copies of this report: GUL MS. B88–8, p. 367.]

[Orders of 4 Feb. and 1 and 8 May 1696: PRO E.127/19, f. 459v; E.127/20, ff. 5, 29v.]

325
Poole v. Draper (Ex. 1696)

In this case, tithes in kind were ordered to be paid.

LI MS. Misc. 559, f. 52, pl. 2 [Eng.] (Ward's Reports)

The plaintiff as parson of Brailsford in the County of Derby sues the defendant among other things for the tithes of the pasturage and agistment of dry and barren cattle. The defendant endeavors to set up a custom of *non decimandi* for agistment tithes in the hundred of Appletree, within which that parish is, but failed therein, there being many instances of the payment of tithes within the hundred though not within the parish. Rolle's Abridgment, *Dismes*, folio [*blank*] there was a decree for tithes in kind.

See below folio 145[1] [where] such [a] custom [was held] void.

[Other copies of this report: GUL MS. B88-8, p. 368.]

[Other reports of this case: Samuel Dodd's Reports, p. 175, 1 Rayner 83, 2 Gwillim 560, 1 Eagle & Younge 627.]

[Order of 7 July 1696: PRO E.126/16, f. 351v.]

[This case is cited in Browne v. Culworthy (Ex. 1697), below, No. 363; Smith v. Johnson (Ex. 1709), below, No. 437.]

326
Wade v. Smith (Ex. 1696)

The personal estate of a person dying intestate will be shared by those of the half blood equally with those of the whole blood.

LI MS. Misc. 559, f. 61, pl. 1 [Eng.] (Ward's Reports)

A decree was made for the distribution of an intestate's personal estate between the half and whole blood, and the half blood to have as much as the whole according to the late resolution of the House of Lords upon an appeal.

[Other copies of this report: GUL MS. B88-8, p. 397.]

[Order of 10 July 1696: PRO E.126/16, f. 355.]

327
Tayes v. Clarke (Ex. 1696)

In this case, the plaintiff's claim was based on a common law right and the suit in equity was stayed so that the plaintiff could establish his right in an action at common law.

LI MS. Misc. 559, f. 61, pl. 2 [Eng.] (Ward's Reports)

The plaintiff as lessee from the Corporation of Chichester sues the defendants for an account and to have relief against them for certain tolls and duties of wheat meal exported out of the port of Chichester by any not free of the Merchants or Guild there and lays the title by custom or prescription in the

---

[1] *Browne v. Culworthy* (Ex. 1697), below, No. 363.

Corporation of Chichester confirmed and established by the grant of King Edward II [on] 10 March 11 of his reign [1337],[1] whereby the king grants the city to the citizens in fee farm at £36 *per annum* with the liberties and free customs at land and by water *tam amplis modo et forma* as they held the same before except the customs of wools and leather and other customs if any.

The defendants make two defenses. First they say that the inhabitants of Bosham are not liable to pay the duty demanded. Secondly [they say] that Bosham Creek (which is the place where the wheat meal in question was shipped out for the use of the Navy) is not within the port of Chichester.

The plaintiff made proof that for such wheat meal or grain that was shipped out of any part of the port, there had been an ancient duty paid to the city, they repairing the port and creeks there and that the extent of the port was as far as an horn blown at the harbor's mouth could be heard. And some spoke to the place where the meal was shipped to be within the port. But the defendants admit Dell Quay (which the plaintiffs repair) to be in the port but say that Bosham's Creek (where the meal was shipped) is four miles further to the sea and produced an ancient grant made 1 Ric. I [1189 x 1190] whereby the king granted to the marshal Bosham in fee farm free from all exactions, *cum soca et saca thol et them*, and an *inspeximus* 7 Edw. I [1278–1279] whereby it appears that Richard Bigod[2] had liberties there and *quietum de stallagio et theolonio*. But in regard the plaintiff's pretense and defendants' defense were pure matters of law where the plaintiff might help himself if he had right, the court did not think fit to direct any trial but left the plaintiff to pursue his right at law. And if by some trial he did not assert his right before the end of Easter term next, the plaintiff's bill was to be dismissed. And nothing more was done in it that I heard of.

[Other copies of this report: GUL MS. B88–8, p. 397.]

[Order of 29 May 1696: PRO E.127/20, f. 23v.]

328

Attorney General v. Orsell (Ex. 1696)

A person cannot profit by his own fraud though third parties may.

In this case, importers of grain were ordered to account for import duties owed to the crown, they having paid less than was due through fraud.

---

[1] *Calendar of the Charter Rolls*, IV (1912), p. 389; note also *id.*, III (1908), p. 314.
[2] I.e. Roger Bigod.

I
LI MS. Misc. 559, f. 66 [Eng.] (Ward's Reports)

The case upon the bill, answer, and proofs was this. By the Statute for Tillage, 22 Car. II, c. 13,[1] for improvement of tillage etc., there is a duty given to the crown upon the importation of the several sorts of grain therein mentioned when they shall be at the prices therein mentioned at the times and places of importation, *viz.* wheat at 53s. 4d. the quarter or under, 16s. per quarter; when above that price and yet not exceed[ing] £4 the quarter, 8s. per quarter; and when the prices exceed those rates, then the duties payable before that Act (which as to wheat was 4d. per quarter, *Book of Rates*, f. 250[2]). Then the Statute of 1 Jac. II, c. 19, entitled An Additional Act for Improvement of Tillage,[3] was made, which recites the defect of the former law in that no provision was made by it for ascertaining and determining the prices by reason whereof great quantities of foreign corn were imported without paying the duties, for supplying of which defect, it was enacted that, from Michaelmas following, it should be lawful for the justices of the peace in the several counties of England, Wales, and Berwick where foreign corn should be imported and they are thereby enjoined and required at Michaelmas and Easter sessions yearly by the oaths of two or more honest and substantial persons of the respective counties not being merchants nor factors for corn nor any ways interested in the corn imported and each to have an estate of freehold of £20 *per annum* or leasehold of £50 above all reprises and being skillful in the prices of corn (which oaths the justices are enabled to give) and by such other ways and means as to them shall seem fit to examine and determine the common market prices of middling English corn and grain of the several sorts in the said Act mentioned as the same shall be commonly bought and sold in the respective counties into which the same shall be imported and to certify the same with two such oaths made as aforesaid in writing annexed unto the chief officer and collector of the customs residing in the respective ports or havens where the corn shall be imported to be hung up in the Custom House, to which all persons may resort for information. And it is enacted that, after Michaelmas next, the custom and duty of foreign corn and grain imported, 'appointed by the said former act to be paid' shall be 'collected and paid according to the prices contained in such respective certificates and not otherwise', anything in that or in any other former law to the contrary notwithstanding. And it is provided by that last Act that all that is to be done by that Act by the justices in their sessions shall be done and performed in like manner in the City of London in the months of October

---

[1] Stat. 22 Car. II, c. 13 (*SR*, V, 685–686).
[2] *The Act of Tonnage and Poundage and Book of Rates* (1684), p. 250.
[3] Stat. 1 Jac. II, c. 19 (*SR*, VI, 21–22).

and April yearly by the mayor, aldermen, and justices of peace there, and that the persons making such oaths should be no corn chandler, mealman, factor, merchant, or other person interested in such corn so to be imported but to be some substantial house keepers living in Middlesex or Surrey qualified as aforesaid.

And by the bill it was showed that the defendants designing to import divers great quantities of foreign corn into the port of London and contriving how to defraud His Majesty of the customs and duties due for the same by procuring by art and fraud certain quantities of wheat in the neighboring markets of the middling sort of wheat to be bought at above 10s. a bushel thereby reducing the king's duty to 4d. a quarter instead of 8s. and thereupon under pretence of such fraudulent buying to get persons to make oath according to the Act that the common market prices of middling English wheat was above 10s. a bushel (which exceeds £4 a quarter) and thereupon to get the justices of peace to determine that to be the common market price, they the defendants did make that attempt in April 1694 at Brainford market in Middlesex and endeavored to get persons to make such oath but failed and after such failure did in April 1694 go to Croydon in Surrey and there fraudulently gave above 10s. a bushel for wheat which they might have had for under 10s., the common market price at the same market being much under 10s., and yet that the defendants designing as above gave above 10s. a bushel, and procured two persons, *viz.* one Dawberon and one Pullein, both of Croydon, to make oath that the common market price of middling wheat at that market was £4 1s. a quarter, and that under pretext of such oath, the lord mayor and justices of London made their certificate to the Custom House dated the 24th of April 1694 whereby they settled the price of very good middling English wheat to be £4 1s. per quarter. And when that price was settled, then the defendants very shortly after imported into the port of London very great quantities of wheat of the middling sort and paid only 4d. per quarter, when in truth 8s. per quarter was due, the common market price being under 10s. a bushel which is under £4 a quarter. And therefore to discover this fraud and enforce such of the defendants as had taken the advantage of it by importing wheat and paying only 4d. per quarter instead of 8s. to pay the full duty was the scope of the bill, the attorney general thereby waiving all forfeitures and criminal prosecutions and insisting only on the duty due.

The defendants by answer insisted that they ought not to be sued by English bill for the said matters but that the same being of a criminal nature the attorney general ought to proceed at [common] law and not in equity against them but discovered the several quantities of wheat by them imported into and entered in the port of London after the 24th of April 1694 and before Michaelmas sessions following, which amounted to some thousands of quarters for which the duty after the rate of 8s. per quarter came to above seven thousand pounds and by their answer insisted upon His Majesty's late Act of Grace[4] which pardoned all frauds, deceits, etc. before the 30th of April 1695, their supposed offenses being before that time.

And upon issue joined and divers witnesses examined on both sides, the cause came this day to be heard before the chief baron [WARD] and LECHMERE and POWYS, barons. And it appearing by the depositions of divers witnesses taken on the king's part that the defendants did in the last market day of Croydon before the 24th of April 1694 by themselves and agents buy twenty quarters of wheat there and gave for it above £4 a quarter middling wheat, which they might have had for under that price and were not asked above 9s. a bushel for it, but they told the sellers that they asked too little and they would give them above 10s., and the best and highest price for the best wheat that market and since Lady Day before did not exceed 9s. 3d. a bushel but most [was] under that price, *viz.* the middling at 8s. 6d. or 9s. at most, and that the buying at above 10s. by the defendants was looked upon by the country to be a cheat and to serve a turn, and that the defendants did not presently use the wheat by them so bought but laid it up at Croydon and afterwards sold it for less than they paid for it, and that the defendants procured Dawberon and Pullein, the one a grocer and the other a gardener and not qualified as the Act directs, to make the oath upon which the certificate of the mayor and aldermen settling the price of middling English wheat at £4 1s. per quarter was grounded and Pullein himself being examined as a witness swore that he made the oath upon the defendants' buying so and not that it was the common market price, for he neither bought nor sold any wheat at that market and believes the defendants might have had the wheat cheaper than he paid if asked or stood for it. And Sir Robert Clayton, one of the aldermen and justices of London and also one of the commissioners of the customs, being present when this oath came to be made, objected against the prices saying he knew they were not so great at Croydon, he living near it. But the other justices overruled him, and the passing of the certificate upon this oath was opposed but at last passed.

The defendants' counsel seeing the proof of the fact run strong against them (yet *argumenti gratia* but not yielding to the truth of the fact) argued that, if the fact was so, yet that this court upon this bill and in this manner could not relieve the king and insisted upon two things:

First that such relief would be expressly against the Statute of 1 Jac. II, c. 19, which has ascertained the king's duty to be that only which is certified by the justices to the Custom House and that the king has not nor can have any other duty than that, and that, in this case, is but 4d. per quarter, which is paid, urging

---

[4] Stat. 6 & 7 Will. & Mar., c. 20 (*SR*, VI, 607–613).

for reason that the duty pursues the price and the price is by the last Act left to be examined and determined by the justices and that the duty appointed by the first Act shall be collected and paid according to the prices contained in the certificates and not otherwise, which are negatives to all other duties, and that, if the justices in making such certificates have misdemeaned themselves (which is hard to think, being upon their oaths, and having the oaths of two persons positive to the prices), they may be answerable for such their miscarriages, but their certificates are conclusive, this last Act being as much an act that settles the prices as the first that gave the duty, and the duty must be subject to the last Act according as the market prices are thereby settled, and if the method or certificates settled by this last Act should be broken into, it might be an occasion of great uncertainty and mischief both to the king and merchants and the design and purpose of the last Act wholly eluded.

As to this the king's counsel answered (to which the court inclined) that this certificate shall stand as to all persons save the defendants that were parties to the fraud in obtaining it by an ill oath and contrivance. But as to them, they ought not to profit by their own deceit it being the nature of all frauds to make all things void as to the parties to them. And the defendants here shall be in no better a condition than if no certificate at all had been obtained. And if none had been sent into the Custom House, yet the king must not have lost his duty according to the common market prices which could be made out for the duty still subsists according to the rates in 22 Car. II though the ascertaining of the prices is given by 1 Jac. II, and it never could be thought that the Parliament should think that the king should lose his duty if the justices failed to return a certificate or that a certificate obtained upon an ill oath and by a palpable design of cheating, as this was, should deprive the king of his duty honestly due when the corn and grain are really at the prices in the first Act though not so certified.

The second thing the defendants insisted on was that, in case here was a fraud and deceit to the king, it was done before the 30th of April 1695 and pardoned by the last Act of Grace, which pardons all deceits etc.

To this it was answered by the king's counsel, and to which the court inclined, that though the body of the Act pardons all deceits and other things not excepted, yet that both the duty and the fraud in this case are specially excepted, for the exception [at] ff. 501–502 excepts all duties and sums of money given by any Act of Parliament to the king or otherwise due or payable to the king and all concealments, frauds, and offenses by which His Majesty has been deceived and not truly answered for the same, which is full in the case and answers that objection plainly.

Then the defendants, perceiving the inclination of the court against them, went to their proofs that the prices certified were the common market prices of wheat at that time, *viz.* 24 April 1694, and read several witnesses as to the prices of wheat in Brandford [?] market and they exceeded £4 per quarter (but none as to Croydon save by hearsay and belief), and it was made out by proof that there was tampering with two Lowes to have sworn £4 1s. the quarter to have been the common market price of good middling English wheat at Brainford market but being produced durst not make the oath and that therefore the oaths of Daberon and Pullein were made use of.

The defendant Black (though partner in buying the wheat at Croydon and to the fraud yet) not having imported afterwards any wheat so as to take the benefit of it was dismissed. But the other three defendants by the opinion of LECHMERE and POWYS were sent to an account (without any trial at law what was the common market price of middling wheat at that time as the defendants' counsel desired there might be, there being some colorable proof of the verity of prices at Brainsford most under, some above, 10s. a quarter) for what wheat each imported shortly after that certificate and paid but 4d. a quarter for, and to take the account at 8s. per quarter. The chief baron [WARD] inclined first to have a trial to ascertain the common market prices of middling wheat before any decree pass for the making the defendants to account for 8s. per quarter will be either just or unjust as common prices were in the markets, whereof though the plaintiff has made a very probable proof that it was under £4 1s. per quarter, yet it would be much more satisfactory to have the prices ascertained by a jury, especially in so great a cause as this which comes to above £7000 and is a great sum to be settled by a decree upon matter of fact and fraud without a trial. But the other two barons being against a trial, the decree passed referring it to account as aforesaid.

Attorney general, Trevor, Browne, *et al.* [were] for the king. Ettrick, Dodd, Phipps, and Mulsoe [were] for the defendants.

This account was proceeded in for some time but never came to a final decree, the defendants and prosecutor agreeing by leave of the treasury, *ut audivi.*

[Other copies of this report: GUL MS. B88–8, p. 407.]

II
BL MS. Hargr. 71, f. 99, pl. 1 [Fr. & Eng.] (Dodd's Reports)

An English information [was] brought against them for the duty upon corn by them imported, of which they had defrauded the crown by procuring a certificate, oath, and order of sessions according to the Act of 1 Jac. II[5] that wheat was above £4 a quarter when it was under. Note. And upon [the] debate, the court decreed an account. The attorney [general] said in his information he would waive all criminal proceedings. The defendants did not demur but insisted to have the benefit of that and the Act of Pardon[6] by answer. The court were clear that the information was good.

---

[5] Stat. 1 Jac. II, c. 19 (*SR*, VI, 21–22).
[6] Stat. 6 and 7 Will. & Mar., c. 20 (*SR*, VI, 607–613); Stat. 2 Will. & Mar., c. 10 (*SR*, VI, 174–179).

[Other copies of this report: HLS MS. 537(b), p. 51, pl. 3; Oxf. Brasenose MS. 59, p. 66, pl. 3; IU Lilly MS. Parker, 'Cases in the Exchequer, vol. 2', p. 26; BL MS. Hargr. 70, p. 102, pl. 336; HLS MS. 1162, p. 90, pl. 482.]

[Order of 9 Nov. 1696: PRO E.126/16, f. 375v.]

329

Spencer v. Hesketh (Ex. 1696)

In this case, a certain gift to the defendant was found by a feigned issue to a jury not to have been a trust for the plaintiff, though there had been no delivery of the gift.

LI MS. Misc. 559, f. 75 [Eng.] (Ward's Reports)

The plaintiff's wife being the defendant Hesketh's mother by her first husband, and being minded to marry again to one Mr. Lee, and being advised by her friends to add to her former children's portions she having a good estate from their father Hesketh, she having a debt of £500 due to her from her brother, John Grosvenor, a little before she married Mr. Lee caused that bond that was taken in her own name for the said debt to be taken in the defendant Hesketh's name, being her daughter, and declared it should be for her daughter's use and benefit, but kept the said bond all along in her own custody. No interest was paid and she having married the now plaintiff, Mr. Spencer, they exhibited their bill into the exchequer against the defendant, Hesketh, the obligee, and John Grosvenor, the obligor, to the intent that the plaintiffs might have the debt and sue the obligor for the same without release or discharge.

Defendants answer and insist upon the mother's gift.

And the evidence not being full and convincing on either side, the court directed a trial, which was had before me last Westmoreland Assizes, upon this issue, whether the bond at the time it was taken in the defendant's name was a trust for the plaintiff's wife or not. And after a long trial it was found to be no trust. And thereupon the plaintiffs' bill was dismissed. But the plaintiffs being willing to be quiet produced the bond in court and delivered it over to the deputy [king's] remembrancer for the defendant Hesketh's use to be delivered to her upon a receipt for the same, and the plaintiffs to pay costs for the trial and since but nothing before, it being between mother and daughter and a voluntary gift of the mother and not clear till after the trial.

[Other copies of this report: GUL MS. B88–8, p. 438.]

[Order of 19 Nov. 1696: PRO E.126/16, f. 363.]

330
Portman v. Snow (Ex. 1696)

This was a suit involving tithes and customary payments in lieu of tithes; the suit ended inconclusively.

LI MS. Misc. 559, f. 76, pl. 1 [Eng.] (Ward's Reports)

The plaintiff's bill was for the establishing [of] several customary rates or payments or *modus decimandis* for tithe hay and tithe wood, for which and other things the defendant sued them. And upon the defendant's bill, he was relieved for other tithes and several strange pretended customs in the parish as to pay 6d. for a calf where the parson finds the bull, but if he finds not the bull or that the bulling of the cow comes to more than 6d., then nothing and to restrain the parson from fetching his tithes with horses that have shoes on were overruled by the court. And though in the parishioner's bill there were some customary rates not contested by the parson decreed, yet as to hay and wood in regard every owner of a tenement (being above forty in number) had a distinct rate and payment as he pretended for the same, which indeed (if anything) were particular prescriptions and scarce any sum alleged in the bill was ascertained by any proof of the same sum but one different from it, though it was not proved that tithes in kind had ever been paid but annual sums (though not always agreeing). Yet in regard it would tend to multiplicity to send every tenement to a trial (which must be) and the parson being willing for peace sake to accept the annual sums, the court did not think fit, as this case is circumstanced, to send all the prescriptions to trial. But as to the establishment of those prescriptions, no better satisfaction being given to the court concerning them, the court dismissed the bill without prejudice and with moderate costs.

[Other copies of this report: GUL MS. B88–8, p. 439.]

[Other reports of this case: Samuel Dodd's Reports, p. 168, 1 Eagle & Younge 620.]

[Order of 16 Nov. 1696: PRO E.126/16, f. 371.]

331
Abbot v. Hicks (Ex. 1696)

In this case, a custom was proved that all beech trees of whatever age are timber and thus not tithable even though used as firewood.

I

LI MS. Hill 49, f. 234v, pl. 3 [Fr.]

The plaintiff exhibited his bill in the exchequer as parson for tithes of tithable woods. And upon the pleadings and proofs, the question was whether tithes are payable for beech. And upon this question, it was moved whether beech of [. . .] inches is timber and thus excluded [?], being greater than twenty years growth, which was only underwoods in its nature but esteemed timber by custom in this country, being Gloucestershire.

Chief Baron ATKYNS, TURTON, and POWELL thought that it was underwoods in its nature unless custom altered it and that nothing except oak, ash, and elm is woods, *scil.*, timber. Upon this issue, it was directed to try whether by custom here it was timber (because Baron LECHMERE held that [it was] timber) and that for the other demands [?] of the plaintiff, they should be reserved. It was tried [and found] that by custom it was timber, Justice EYRE ruling that it was timber in its nature.

And now it was heard upon the *postea*. And POWELL and TURTON held that it is not timber in its nature and that all the books so hold. They recited some, but [they were] answered [by] 1 Rolle's *Abridgment* 640; 2 *Abridgment* 819; 1 Bro. 94; 2 Leon. 80.[1] But because it was found to be timber by custom, as to this the bill was dismissed, but because it was found that other tithable lands to the value of £40 were proved to be intermixed, the defendant was decreed to account, although if of little value, the greater will [?] have their privilege.

It was agreed in this case that, if one sold growing tithable woods, the vendee should pay the tithes; if it should be sold cut, the vendor should pay: 1 Rolle's *Abridgment* 656, L, § 1, 2.[2] It was decreed in this case that if the plaintiff demises a large thing that is in dispute and also inserts a small, trivial matter [?] that is due and though [. . .] denied, if the large thing be against the plaintiff, he will be dismissed with costs, for otherwise this mixture will be put in by [. . .] cause. But when the demand is general and part be against the parson and the greater part also, if anything of reasonable value be proved against the defendant, this will retain the bill.

---

[1] *Leonard's Case* (1596), 1 Rolle, Abr., *Dismes*, pl. Q, 5, p. 640; 2 Rolle, Abr., *Wast*, pl. [G], 2, p. 819; *Man v. Somerton* (1607), 1 Brownl. & Golds. 94, 123 E.R. 687, 1 Eagle & Younge 172; *Daws v. Mollins* (1584), 2 Leonard 79, 74 E.R. 374, 1 Eagle & Younge 86.

[2] *Ellis v. Drake* (1616), 1 Rolle, Abr., *Dismes*, pl. L, 1, p. 656; *Facey v. Lange* (1631), 1 Rolle, Abr., *Dismes*, pl. L, 2, p. 656.

II
LI MS. Misc. 559, f. 76, pl. 2 [Eng.] (Ward's Reports)

The plaintiff having several years since exhibited his bill against the defendant for tithes of wood and thereby entitled himself to all tithe wood within the parish and charged the defendant that in several years within the space of twelve years last past the defendant had cut down a great wood in that parish consisting of beech wood and other wood and sold [a] great part of it and that it was all or the greatest part of it coaled or used as firewood and that none of it was used as timber it not being so in its nature nor by custom but all of it tithable.

Defendant confesses the plaintiff's title to tithe wood and the selling and cutting of divers great numbers of beech trees and poles which he insisted were all above the age of twenty years and most of them of the age of two or three hundred years, as he believes, and that they were timber and privileged and exempted by the law of the land from payment of tithes.

Upon the hearing of the cause, which was about three years since, the court being of opinion (*viz.* Chief Baron ATKYNS, TURTON, and POWELL against LECHMERE) that beech is not in its nature and by law of the land to be accounted timber but may be so by the custom of the country, they sent it to be tried at law upon an issue whether by the custom of the parish of Whitcomb in the County of Gloucester, beech is accounted timber or not (Atkyns and Powell being both Gloucestershire men). And the court reserved the rest of the plaintiff's demands till after the coming back of the trial. And upon the trial, it was found that beech by the custom of that county was timber. And upon that an order was drawn up that the plaintiff's bill as to all beechwood was to be dismissed, which was opposed by the plaintiffs as to 'all' beechwood, though submitted to as to all beech that was timber, for that he insisted that a great part of the wood though it was above twenty years growth yet it was not timber nor ever had been nor would have been timber, and that it is the quality and not the age either of that or any other sort of wood that is accounted timber that must exempt it from payment of tithes. And there was great and probable proof that a great part of the wood was not nor ever had been timber and that what was felled was for the most part either coaled or used for fuel and very little of that vast quantity cut down as timber. And the court having been divided whether it should be referred to the deputy [king's] remembrancer to take the account of the wood cut down and to sever and distinguish by the proofs taken or to be taken what was or was not timber, as the chief baron and Baron POWYS thought was just to be done, but LECHMERE and TURTON thought otherwise, and that the verdict cleared all beechwood, and MOUNTAGU, the chancellor [of the exchequer], concurring with them, the bill as to all beechwood was to be dismissed.

But the plaintiffs procured a rehearing of the cause upon the same point that was settled three against two, which being granted by LECHMERE and POWYS against my inclination (because the matter could not be more before us than it had been before though not upon a formal rehearing), it came to be heard upon bill, answer, and proofs taken before the first hearing on Thursday the 19th instant. And it fully appeared that the wood was a great wood of above three hundred acres and part cut down one year and part another, and that before [the] defendant cut it down, there was in it little wood besides shrub beech and beech poles, and that all or most that was cut was used for coaling or fuel and very little for timber, and that they grew of themselves and out of their own root and not out of old stools. And though the defendant's proof went to the largeness of some of the trees and to their antiquity, yet there was but little proof that any part (and that but little (neither) of what [was] cut down) was employed as timber. And upon [the] hearing that day, Baron BLENCOWE, being newly come into the court and looking upon a former order made in the cause (which upon this rehearing was set aside) as if it had been in force (which was a mistake), he and Baron LECHMERE and the chancellor [of the exchequer], MOUNTAGU, were of opinion that the bill should be dismissed as to all beechwood and not referred to be distinguished by the deputy [king's remembrancer] what was timber and what tithable.

But Baron POWYS and myself [WARD] were of another opinion and that it was of a dangerous consequence to conclude against such proof as the plaintiff had made that all the beechwood was timber which is not settled so by the verdict nor anyways appears in proof, and it having been of later times (especially) held and so practiced that it is not the age but the quality of the wood that must give it the privilege of timber so as to be exempted from tithes and that as Lord Coke 2 *Inst.* 642 observes that the word *gross bois* signifies such wood as has been or is by the common law or custom of the country timber, for this Act says he extends not to other woods that have not been or will not serve for timber, and it having been held that oak, ash, and elm (which are by law timber throughout the realm) though above the age of twenty years if they be not in their nature timber or fit for timber but are cut down and sold and used as firewood, should yield tithes. Cornwall and Hawkes' Case, Siderfin 18 Car. II [1666], f. [300], Liber 1, 269;[3] and Franklin and Jones's Case, Hilary 1685, Liber K, 109;[4] and Acton and Smith's Case, Trinity 1687, Liber K, 165;[5] and the report confirmed 15 May 1690 (Lechmere then being a baron) warrant this. We were of opinion that it ought to be referred to account and there distinguish the timber from the tithable wood and this could not do wrong to any, for if all appear to be timber,

---

[3] *Cornell v. Haws* (1666), 1 Siderfin 300, 82 E.R. 1118, also 1 Eagle & Younge 450, 2 Keble 1, 90, 833, 84 E.R. 1, 56, 527, 1 Levinz 189, 83 E.R. 362.

[4] *Franklin v. Jones* (Ex. 1686), above, No. 216.

[5] *Acton v. Smith* (Ex. 1687), above, No. 244.

the defendant will be dismissed with his costs for that trouble, but on the other side, if any part of it should be tithable and the bill be dismissed, the plaintiff has lost his right forever, for he cannot recover it in any other suit.

But LECHMERE that day starting a point that it did not appear in the proofs that the defendant had cut down any of the beechwood but that he had sold them which might be standing, and then not he but the buyer that felled them ought to have paid the tithes, I did forbear to deliver my opinion that day, the plaintiff's counsel not being provided then to answer that objection.

And the chancellor [of the exchequer], LECHMERE, and BLENCOWE having declared their opinion as above, the bill was dismissed as to beechwood unless cause this day [be shown]. And upon the proofs it fully appearing that defendant cut a great deal down himself though he sold other standing, I delivered my opinion *ut supra* at large why I could not agree to dismiss the bill as to all beechwood till it appeared that all of it had the privilege of timber (which no ways appeared to me hitherto). And POWYS agreed with me, but LECHMERE and BLENCOWE retaining their former opinion and the chancellor [of the exchequer] not being there, the court was again divided, but because by the order of the 19th the bill was to be dismissed unless cause [be shown] to the contrary this day, and the cause shown being not sufficient because the court divided, the former order became absolute, and at the plaintiff's desire his whole bill was dismissed but without costs, he having other undeniable demands by his bill, which were but small.

That beech is timber in its nature 2 *Inst.* 643; Holliday and Lee's Case, Moore 541; by custom only Rolle's [Abr.] *Dismes*, 640, Let. Q, 5; see Degge, 236; and Godolphin, *verbo* 'tithes', title 'beeches'; see Statute 35 Hen. VIII, c. 17,[6] which appoints standells to be left of oak, ash, elm, asp, and beech, and of those likeliest to be timber where no oak, which seems as if beech was reckoned timber generally by the opinion of the Parliament.

Note in the debate of this case of Abbot and Hicks, the question did not turn whether all beechwood of trees and poles growing of themselves and being above twenty years old should be counted *gross bois* within the Statute of 45 Edw. III[7] (for that came in but incidentally) but only whether the general finding that beech was timber did necessarily conclude that all the beech for tithes, of which the plaintiff exhibited his bill were above twenty years of age and carried the privilege of being timber and so tithe free, which to me did not appear.

---

[6] E. Coke, *Second Institute* (1642), p. 643; *Holliday v. Lee* (1597), Moore K.B. 541, 72 E.R. 745; *Leonard's Case* (1596), 1 Rolle, Abr., *Dismes*, pl. Q, 5, p. 640; S. Degge, *Parson's Counsellor* (1676), p. 160; J. Godolphin, *Repertorium Canonicum* (1680), p. 389; Stat. 35 Hen. VIII, c. 17 (*SR*, III, 977–980).

[7] Stat. 45 Edw. III, c. 3 (*SR*, I, 393).

[Other copies of this report: GUL MS. B88–8, p. 441.]

[The decree of 25 June 1694 is printed at 1 Wood 319, 1 Eagle & Younge 584; see also the orders of 19 and 26 Nov. 1696: PRO E.126/16, ff. 366v, 388v.]

[This case is cited in Greenway v. Earl of Kent (Ex. 1706), below, No. 407; Walton v. Tryon (1751), 2 Gwillim 827, 838–839; Erskine v. Ruffle (1769), 3 Gwillim 961, 969.]

332
Coney v. Horne (Ex. 1696)

In this case, a creditor of a decedent had a decree for the payment of a debt which was proved even though the bond for it was defective and incomplete.

LI MS. Misc. 559, f. 79 [Eng.] (Ward's Reports)

The case upon the hearing appeared to be thus, that the defendant [Elizabeth] Cogger's father became indebted to John Coney, the plaintiff's intestate, in £150 and for securing the repayment thereof (with interest as was proved in the cause), the said defendant's father, William Cogger, became bound in a bond to the said John Coney in this manner: *Noverint universi per presentes me Williamum Cogger* (of such a place) *teneri et firmiter obligari Johanni Coney* (of such a place) *in triginta libre libris bone et legalis monete Angliae*[1] and then on as is usual in bonds till it came to the date, and that was: *dat vicesimus quintus dies* (no month) 1682, with condition for payment of £150 the 25th of December next after the date. And to make this a good debt for £150 and to carry interest and to have it charged upon the profits of his real estate, which by his will he subjected to the payment of his debts, was the bill.

And it appearing to the court that the false Latin and want of date and omission of the interest was merely the mistake and ignorance of one Dyne, that wrote the bond, and that it appeared by the condition that the debt was £150 and that [on] 9 January 1682 Cogger wrote a letter to Coney that Dyne had forgot to put interest into the bond but that he would pay it, the court decreed this debt and interest to be paid out of the rents and profits of Cogger's real estate settled by will for that purpose and that the trustees (who were parties to the bill) should be indemnified for so doing.

[Other copies of this report: GUL MS. B88–8, p. 450.]
[Orders of 23 Oct. 1696: PRO E.127/20, ff. 62, 63v.]

---

[1] Sic in MS.

333
Pyot v. Trafford (Ex. 1696)

A will is to be construed strictly according to the words of the testator.

LI MS. Misc. 559, f. 80, pl. 1 [Eng.] (Ward's Reports)

The said Robert Pyot, the father, being seised in fee of freehold lands in Essex and of copyhold lands in Essex and also in Tring in Hertfordshire and having mortgaged his freehold to Trafford for £600 and made a surrender to the use of his will of his copyhold in Tring but not of his copyhold in Essex, the 4th of May 1689 by will in writing duly attested and executed devised all his freehold lands in Essex and Hertfordshire (not entailed on his eldest son) and all his copyhold lands in those two counties, which he had heretofore surrendered to the use of his will, to the defendant Trafford to sell and thereout to pay his own debt and the rest of the money to be distributed to and among the plaintiffs, being his younger children, and provides that, if any part of it be borough English so that it goes to his younger son, then he provides that such younger son shall have no part of the money. And it was endeavored that the court should have decreed a sale as well of the copyhold lands which were not surrendered to the use of his will as of those for which there was such a surrender. But the court refused that in regard there was a devise only of the copyhold lands which he had before surrendered to the use of his will. And the saving [?] all his copyhold lands in those two counties is restrained and tied up to that expression [?] which he had before surrendered to the use of his will. And the decree was accordingly.

[Other copies of this report: GUL MS. B88–8, p. 451.]

[Orders of 30 Nov and 7 Dec. 1696: PRO E.126/16, ff. 366, 368.]

334
Sutton v. Bradshaw (Ex. 1696)

In this case, the court ordered specific performance of a contract to make leases, the defense of impossibility being held to be invalid under the facts of the case.

LI MS. Misc. 559, f. 80, pl. 2 [Eng.] (Ward's Reports)

The plaintiff's bill was to have an execution in specie of certain articles made between the plaintiff and defendant the 14th of December 1693 touching a lease of divers houses and other things near Clare Market in Middlesex which the defendant claimed and derived title to, from, and under John Hind, who had make a contract and agreement in 1682 with Gilbert, earl of Clare, for taking a lease of the premises for sixty-one years under the fine of £617 10s. and the rents to be reserved and to lay out £5000 in building before Michaelmas 1694. And the earl agrees to make him that lease reserving a peppercorn the first year and for all the rest, the yearly rent or several yearly rents to be apportioned as after mentioned, £250 *per annum* quarterly. And the earl covenanted that upon raising the second floor for encouraging the building and taking of the houses to make leases to such as Hind should appoint for sixty-one years from Lady [Day 16]83 so as the rents to be reserved be not less than 30s. and exceed not 40s. a foot in the front and when £250 *per annum* ascertained in rents the residue to be leased as Hind should appoint for a peppercorn rent. And upon a suit in chancery between John, earl of Clare (now duke of Newcastle), son and heir of Gilbert, and his trustee, plaintiffs, and the now defendant (who stood in Hind's place) and others, defendants, February 1691[/92][2] it was referred to account and to state the rent etc. and when the leases should commence and that the now defendant and his assigns should hold and enjoy the houses and shops built upon the premises for such purposes as occupied and let since the building and that the ground rent should be apportioned as such of the houses and premises in Beareyard (being the place in question) as shall be sufficient to pay the same over and besides the yearly rents to be reserved thereupon. There were several other hearings in the same cause, *viz.* 25th July and 18th of November 1693, but none of these varied or touched upon the apportionment of the rent pursuant to the articles and decree, after which, *viz.* 14 December 1693, the articles in question were made between the plaintiff and defendant whereby the defendant for £1100 secured to be paid to him by the plaintiff upon a mortgage of lands in Bicester covenanted with the plaintiff by the 15th of February next by indenture duly executed to bargain, sell, and assign to the plaintiff the houses and premises mentioned in the earl's articles of the 5th of March 1682 with Hind, and an indenture of sixty-two years to Cawdron and Card and all that Hind and Card had by the articles or indenture. And the defendant covenanted by the 15th of February next to procure Card (Cawdron being dead) to execute to the plaintiff in pursuance of such articles and lease and a decree in chancery made in pursuance thereof such leases of the premises or any of them and for such estate, as Card is enabled by the articles, indenture, and decree in chancery to make to the said Hind or to the defendant there or either of their executors or assigns. And the plaintiff covenants to indemnify the defendant from ground rent and taxes from Christmas next. After this, the plaintiff laid out great sums in and about the premises and expected performance of defendant's covenants and that leases according to the apportioned rents should have been made, but instead thereof the defendant applies to the lord keeper by petition setting forth the decree for apportionment which was 1 February 1691[/92] and the

---

[2] *Earl of Clare v. Bradshaw* (Ch. 1692), PRO C.33/277, f. 248v.

articles of the 14 December 1693 between himself and [the] plaintiff, and that [the] plaintiff insisted to have the ground rents apportioned and distinct leases for each house, which the master had certified he could not do in regard that many of the houses amounting to above £500 *per annum* were untenanted and that such as are let were let only at £275 *per annum* and therefore could not apportion the rents without further directions. Upon hearing counsel for the plaintiff and defendant and for the plaintiff here (who was not otherwise party to the cause then as brought in upon that petition) [the] lord keeper declared that all the houses ought to be subject to the ground rent payable to the earl and ordered the same accordingly.

And thereupon the plaintiff exhibited this his bill in the exchequer to have the defendant execute his covenants in specie and procure such leases with apportioned rents to be made to him as the first articles and decree of 1691 direct, for if every house must be liable to the whole rent of £250, it is impossible for the plaintiff ever to have a tenant.

The defendant insisted upon the last order in chancery and said that all the former orders and decrees terminated in that, and that it was therefore impossible for him to procure leases with apportioned rents to be paid, the chancery having by this last final order or decree determined that no apportionment shall be made but that all shall lie at stake for the whole rent, and therefore [he] insisted that the plaintiff's bill should be dismissed for that a court of equity never decrees an impossible thing to be done, and at most he ought to be left to [common] law for his damages and not to have a specific performance.

But the court, as this case is, decreed the defendant to perform his covenants in specie it being a plain bargain when the articles were made between them. And otherwise the plaintiff can expect to make nothing of the premises for none are so fond to take an house and lie at stake for £250 *per annum* rent. And at the time of that bargain, there was no impossibility in the thing and though there is a subsequent order made by the chancery that says there shall not be any apportioned rent, yet in truth the now plaintiff was no party in that suit but drawn in upon the petition (and as he says at [the] defendant's desire), and he is not thereby made such a party to the cause as to contest it with the true parties. And things must be looked upon to be performed as they were when the agreement was made. And though it may be hard upon the defendant, yet it would be harder upon the plaintiff, for the defendant may procure the earl to ease him touching the apportionment, or he may endeavor to vary the last order, or at least he may repair it in damages. And so the court decreed a specific performance and a *quantum damnificatus* for the time past in nonperformance of the covenants and a baron to settle the leases, but stayed the trial till the leases [be] settled.

Note by this decree the court have not determined what sort of leases shall be made nor whether there will or will not be any apportioned rent but only that the defendant shall perform his covenants in the articles in specie which he entered into for £1100 consideration paid to him and which he undertook to do by a certain time. The leases must be such as the covenant respects, but what they shall be is not determined yet. See 1 Chancery Reports 158, 159, 160, Wiseman and Roper,[3] decree in specie though covenantor at that time had no estate nor power in the lands.

[Other copies of this report: GUL MS. B88–8, p. 453.]

[Orders of 26 Oct. and 12 Nov. 1696: PRO E.126/16, ff. 364v, 365v.]

[Modified and affirmed on appeal: Bradshaw v. Sutton (1698), Colles 25, 1 E.R. 162, *Lords' Journal*, XVI (n.d.), p. 310.]

335
Fanshawe v. Fowles (Ex. 1696)

In this case, the court refused to enforce a long overdue bond against the executors of the obligor's estate.

LI MS. Misc. 559, f. 81 [Eng.] (Ward's Reports)

Simon Fanshawe, Esq., administrator *cum testamento annexo* of Sir Simon Fanshawe, Knight, deceased, plaintiff; Jeffery Cobb executor to his wife, who was executrix to her mother, who was the widow and executrix of Arthur Dean, Esq., deceased, Sir William Fowles, and Williams, executors of the Lady Ann Fowles, who was the relict and administratrix of Sir Lumly Robinson, Baronet, deceased, defendants, 7 December.

The case upon the hearing was to this effect. The 10th of September 1657 Arthur Dean, Esq., deceased, became bound in a bond of £400 to the said Sir Simon Fanshawe for payment of £200 and interest at a day then shortly to come. Arthur Dean died above twenty years ago entitled to the trust of a term of two hundred years and also to the inheritance entailed upon his issue male of divers lands in Suffolk and Essex and much indebted and by his will charged his estate with payment of several legacies to his younger children. The two hundred years lease was looked upon to be a distinct estate from the inheritance. In 1683 this estate was sold by the executor and heir of Arthur Dean to Sir Lumly Robinson and the conveyances were agreed to be executed but were not, only articles wherein it was agreed that £4000, part of the purchase money, should remain in the purchaser's hands for seven years to pay off Arthur Dean's debts that should be discovered in that time. This was all paid out but £1196 5s. 2d. within the

---

[3] *Wiseman v. Roper* (1645–1646), 1 Chan. Rep. 158, 21 E.R. 537.

seven years in debts. In 1692 the plaintiff in order to have his bond debt satisfied out of that money exhibited his English bill against the executors of Dean and Lady Robinson and others, Sir William Fowles having married the Lady Robinson, administratrix to Sir Lumly and guardian to her son (upon whom or for whose use the estate is to be), and the seven years being expired, exhibited their bill against the younger children and legatees and some creditors of the said Arthur Dean (but did not make the plaintiff here a defendant though his bill was depending in the same court) for direction how to pay the £1196 5s. 2d. residue of the purchase money with safety and to be protected for so doing. The now plaintiff attended that hearing and acquainted the barons with his pretenses. But not being a defendant to that bill, the court decreed the money to be paid out to the younger children and legatees of Arthur Dean with a clause to indemnify the plaintiffs in that cause against the now plaintiff, who was no party to the suit. And pursuant to that decree, the money was paid.

And the now plaintiff has carried on his cause against the now defendants to be relieved for his bond debt out of the remaining money or against the defendants or some of them, against whose pretenses these objections were made.

First, that the plaintiff has not made due proof of his bond having only made a probable proof as to one of the witnesses' hands but given no satisfaction whether the other two witnesses be dead or not.

Secondly, that the antiquity of the bond carries a presumption of satisfaction being near forty years old and [there being] no proof or suit or demand till the plaintiff's bill.

Thirdly, that the plaintiff has not well founded his suit having exhibited his bill before he had any administration granted to him, and though an executor may prove at any time and be thereby entitled *ab initio*, yet it is otherwise in the case of an administrator who has no title to to sue till administration actually granted.

Fourthly, that as this case is, that plaintiff cannot affect the money in the assignees' hands without a special reason or agreement for that purpose, for it was the effect of the real as well as personal estate and the lease of two hundred years was said to be only to attend the inheritance and so not personalty howsoever it does not appear to be the effects of Arthur Dean's personal estate, and if it was, yet the estate being sold by the executors of Dean, they and not the assignee of the estate must be answerable to the plaintiff, the sale creating assets at law in the executors' hands which may be recovered at [common] law against them, but not in a court of equity.

Fifthly, it would be hard for the defendants to be compelled in equity in the same court to answer the plaintiff's demands when they have obeyed the decree of this court made [in] 1692 in paying the money otherwise and having a clause in that very decree to be indemnified against the now plaintiff (though that seems a strange clause, the plaintiff being no party) and having releases from the executors and legatees of Dean upon such payment.

Sixthly, Lumly Robinson dying intestate and his wife being administratrix and she being dead and no administrator being *de bonis non* of Sir Lumly, here, there are no representatives to the articles under which the plaintiff would found his demand.

For which reasons, the court could not make a decree for the plaintiff but dismissed his bill without costs.

Note: The plaintiff afterwards appealed to the Lords in Parliament against this dismission, but, upon hearing the 29th of March 1697, the Lords dismissed the appeal and confirmed the dismission, not one lord for the appeal.[1]

[Other copies of this report: GUL MS. B88–8, p. 458.]

[Order of 7 Dec. 1696: PRO E.126/16, f. 381v.]

336

Attorney General ex rel. Mayor of Newcastle-under-Lyme v. Hemings (Ex. 1696)

The court of exchequer has the jurisdiction to hear cases of frauds against public charities.

LI MS. Misc. 559, f. 82 [Eng.] (Ward's Reports)

The bill shows that there were several charities formerly given for the benefit of the said town and the poor of it and that there were also divers annual rents and sums of money and other profits that were and ought to be applied for the good of the town under the power and governance of the corporation and that the defendants in the two late reigns having gotten themselves into the government of the town surrendered the old and took a new charter, but the surrender happened to be void not being enrolled, and thereupon the new charter became void. And upon the Revolution, the old magistrates took upon them the government and found that, during the pretense of the new charter, the defendants had really embezzled or misapplied the charities and other the public stock or revenue of the town. And to have an account of those things and relief therein was the bill.

And upon the hearing, it was by the defendants' counsel admitted that it was a proper bill as to the charities in the attorney general's name but not for the

---

[1] *Lords' Journal*, XVI (n.d.), p. 138.

town revenue, which was an interest in the corporation, and they capacitated to call any member to account for embezzlement or mismanagement. But in regard [that] the town revenue, for which complaint was made, was for the poor and other public uses of the town and in regard of the different pretenses between the old and new corporation as to their rights and jurisdiction by the respective charters, the court held the bill to be well enough to have an account as well of the town revenue as of the charities and sent it to [an] account with directions nevertheless to take distinct accounts of each. And when the report comes in, the court will do right therein.

[Other copies of this report: GUL MS. B88–8, p. 461.]

[Orders of 11 July and 9 Dec. 1696: PRO E/126/16, ff. 349, 388.]

337

Goate v. Browne (Ex. 1696)

A trustee suing in equity to enforce the trust should be joined by the beneficiary as a co-plaintiff.

BL MS. Hargr. 71, f. 97v, pl. 2 [Fr. & Eng.] (Dodd's Reports)

The plaintiff in a bill entitled himself surviving trustee of A., debtor and accountant etc., and then said that [he was] seised in fee of the manor of Walsingham etc. and that a quit rent should issue out of lands held by the defendant etc. and so charged several facts etc.

The defendant demurred because the beneficiary [was] not a party. And the court allowed the demurrer against Chief Baron WARD. And [the court] said that it will be inferred [that he was] seised in trust of the manor because he entitled himself surviving trustee notwithstanding the seisin is substantially charged and not relative [and] secondly that the trustee without the beneficiary should not maintain a bill in equity. WARD [was] against [this ruling] in both points.

[Other copies of this report: HLS MS. 537(b), p. 50, pl. 1; Oxf. Brasenose MS. 59, p. 65, pl. 2; IU Lilly MS. Parker, 'Cases in the Exchequer, vol. 2', p. 23.]

[Orders of 29 Apr. and 12 May 1696: PRO E.127/20, ff. 4, 7v.]

[Related cases: Goate v. Vincent (1697): PRO E.126/16, f. 435.]

338
Williams v. Attorney General (Ex. 1696)

Court costs can be awarded in equity to the crown but not against the crown.

BL MS. Hargr. 71, f. 98v, pl. 1 [Eng.] (Dodd's Reports)

The plaintiff's bill was to have rents granted to those under whom he claimed in Haverfordwest by the crown to be put out of charge. And after many hearings, the court dismissed the bill and ordered that in case the plaintiff gave any further disturbance, he should pay costs although it was insisted that, in the king's case, there were no costs for or against. But Chief Baron WARD and the court [held] that they may give the king costs in equity though none against him. Note [and] query.

[Other copies of this report: HLS MS. 537(b), p. 51, pl. 1; Oxf. Brasenose MS. 59, p. 66, pl. 1; IU Lilly MS. Parker, 'Cases in the Exchequer, vol. 2', p. 26; BL MS. Hargr. 70, p. 102, pl. 335; HLS MS. 1162, p. 89, pl. 481.]

339
Nicholls v. Bigs (Ex. 1697)

Title to a copyhold estate is not complete until admittance.

BL MS. Add. 22609, f. 43 [Eng.] (Wright's Reports)

The plaintiff exhibited his bill in order to recover a copyhold estate. The defendant puts in a plea to the bill, that he had purchased the estate for a valuable consideration of £350 that he had a surrender made and had enjoyed a peaceable possession for so many years. But the plea was overruled, because he had not mentioned in his plea any admittance, for a surrender of a copyhold estate without admittance makes no title in a plea. And Chief Baron WARD said that though a quiet possession for a considerable time may be evidence of a title, yet it is not in itself a title.

[Order of 4 June 1697: PRO E.127/20, f. 159v.]

340
Latus v. Jackson (Ex. 1697)

In this case, tithes in kind were ordered to be paid, but the owners of the tithes settled out of court for a sum of money.

LI MS. Misc. 559, f. 96, pl. 1 [Eng.] (Ward's Reports)

[The] plaintiffs as lessees of the dean and chapter of York sue the defendants, inhabitants of Kirkby Ireleth in Lancashire, for tithes of wool and lamb. [The] defendants set such a custom that the inhabitants of that parish have used time out of mind to meet and rate the sums of money that each should pay for tithe wool and lamb, and the defendants showed the sums rated upon them and offer to pay the same. The court wholly disapproved and disallowed the custom as unreasonable and illegal for the inhabitants to set the value of the parson's tithes and oblige him to take that rate. But the plaintiffs being willing for peace sake to take the sums [given] in the answer as an equivalent for the tithes and not in affirmance of the custom, the court in this case decreed the same, being but one sum apiece to each of the two defendants without referring it to the deputy [king's] remembrancer.

[Other copies of this report: GUL MS. B88–8, p. 507.]

[Order of 28 Jan. 1697: PRO E.126/16, f. 395v.]

341
Attorney General ex rel. Chubb v. Corning (Ex. 1697)

In this case to settle a boundary, the relator failed to prove his case.
The Parliamentary survey of 1649 is not admissible evidence because the parties to the suit were not privy thereto.

LI MS. Misc. 559, f. 96, pl. 2 [Eng.] (Ward's Reports)

There having been an English bill exhibited against the defendants, who are the tenants of the duke of Bolton, for distinguishing the metes and bounds of the king's manor of Bucklawry in Cornwall for the duke's manor of Penryn and a trial at law having been directed to try whether four quillets of land (not worth above 40s. a year) are parcel of the king's or duke's manor, and there having been a trial upon [a] view which passed for the king, but upon the certificate of Justice Rokeby, who tried the cause, a new trial was granted. And at the last Cornwall Assizes (after another view had) a verdict passed for the defendants that the quillets were parcel of the duke's manor. And now a new trial was prayed for the king and relator under pretense that there having been verdict against verdict, one more would be decisive. But the Lord Chief Justice Holt, before whom this last trial was, certified that it was a long and fair trial and to his full satisfaction, whereupon the court thought it not fit for so small a matter to direct another trial and the rather because the chief justice declared that the two surveys, one in the reign of King James I [in] 1611 and the other [in] 1649, being taken when the lord or tenants of the duke's manor were not parties or privies thereto could not in his opinion be allowed in evidence nor were they at either of the trials (which was the main objection used by the plaintiff's counsel for the new trial). And thereupon the court dismissed the plaintiff's bill without prejudice to the king's right. And the king may try it when he pleases in an [action for] intrusion. And in this cause the other three barons rated the costs of the dismission to £40, which had cost [the] defendants above £200. And rather than take that £40, the defendants agreed upon plaintiff's payment of costs to try it again, which I thought but just, unless moderate costs were taxed, but the £40 stood by the opinions of the other three barons.

As to refusal of the surveys, query the law; they seem to be [. . .] probable evidence, the first upon oath and on record in the auditor's office. The Parliamentary survey [of] 1649 has frequently been allowed by judges and in courts both before and after, the Chief Baron Hale always allowed it. It was *quasi* a judicial proceeding and confirmed by the Act [of] 1660.[1] [It was] allowed by Holt [in the] court of king's bench between Bishop Stillingfleet's Executors and Sir Henry Parker,[2] and ever after, and by [the] court of exchequer in the cause between the Queen and Lord Wharton and Marriot.[3]

[Other copies of this report: GUL MS. B88–8, p. 508.]

342

Frankland v. Mason (Ex. 1697)

A person who accepts the benefits of a lease made for him must pay the costs and expenses associated with it.

LI MS. Misc. 559, f. 99, pl. 2 [Eng.] (Ward's Reports)

The case upon hearing was this. The plaintiff is administratrix of Hugh Frankland, who took upon him to be a trustee for the defendant, Simon Mason, then an infant, and by advice of friends bought a lease held of Clare Hall in Cambridge and afterwards renewed it in his own name but in trust for the infant. The plaintiff at [the] desire of the defendant, John Mason, on behalf of Simon, his nephew, the infant, after the death of Hugh Frankland, did in 1684 declare this lease to be a trust for Simon Mason. And in the same writing it was agreed by John Mason on behalf of Simon that there was due to the plaintiff for what

---

[1] Stat. 12 Car. II, c. 12 (*SR*, V, 234–236).
[2] *Stillingfleet v. Parker* (1704), 6 Modern 248, 87 E.R. 995.
[3] *Attorney General ex rel. Marriot v. Lord Wharton* (Ex. 1706), below, No. 405.

her husband had paid and laid out about buying and renewing the lease £495 and that when Simon came of age, he should pay the £495 to [the] plaintiff, and in the mean time the interest of it should be paid to [the] plaintiff by [the] defendant, John Mason, as guardian of Simon and who was to receive and did receive the rents for the infant Simon. And after Simon came of age, it was agreed that the plaintiff should assign the lease to him. And this was negotiated by John Mason for his nephew, Simon, and the plaintiff [was] threatened with a suit if [he] not do this. Simon attained his full age and entered upon the lease and received the rents three or four years but did not pay the £495, nor was any assignment made to the said Simon but offered all along by [the] plaintiff after full age of Simon. But Simon, thinking the lease no bargain after all this [was] done, refused to accept the assignment or to pay the £495. And in order to compel him to do it or to be foreclosed of [the] equity of redemption was the plaintiff's bill.

But at [the] hearing, [the] plaintiff insisted to have the money and not the lease. And it appearing that the first buying of the lease and renewing [of] it was a trust for the infant, and a trust declared upon such terms as above, and the infant's guardian and uncle possessing the lease for the infant and paying some interest during the minority and after, and when the infant attained his full age he did enter upon and hold the leased premises, he had made his election to take the lease and pay the money, which he was decreed to do with interest and costs and also to pay John Mason the costs which he should have from [the] plaintiff in this case.

[Other copies of this report: GUL MS. B88–8, p. 519.]

[Order of 1 Feb. 1697: PRO E.126/16, f. 393v.]

343

Fifield v. Squire (Ex. 1697)

In this case, the defendant proved a prescription for not paying small tithes to the vicar.

LI MS. Misc. 559, f. 100, pl. 1 [Eng.] (Ward's Reports)

[The] plaintiff, vicar of East Dray[ton] Cum Membris [Nottinghamshire] (whereof Ascham is one), sued the defendant for the small tithes of the demesne of the archbishop of York's manor of [*blank*] there for about thirteen years. The defendants insist upon a *non decimando* as to small tithes being the estate of an ecclesiastical person capable of a prescription in *non decimando*. But it was agreed in the cause that these demesne lands paid great tithes to the impropriator and there was competent proof that the lessee of the archbishop had between forty and fifty years ago and since at divers times paid a sum of £4 or thereabouts to the vicar for the small tithes of those demesne [lands], and that the defendant's wife who was the daughter of a former lessee both in her father's time and since had paid that sum or outset it in rent to the vicar for small tithes, and there was proof that about thirty-seven or thirty-eight years ago that the tenant of part of the demesnes paid tithes for conies, etc. kept upon them but that, since and during the time of the bill, the plaintiff had not received anything but upon an action upon the Statute for tithe hemp or flax (which is a small tithe) the plaintiff had obtained a verdict at Nottingham assizes about a year since, which was said by some to be an hard verdict (but it stands unimpeached). The defendant's witnesses were such as had been either servants to the lessee of the whole or tenants to some part of the demesne and proved that they never knew small tithes or anything in lieu of them paid to the vicar or ever demanded but that the demesne lands were esteemed free from payment of small tithes.

The court was something inclined to decree for the plaintiff upon his evidence as being in its nature stronger than the defendant's for payment so long time ago and several times since is more considerable than the defendant's witnesses' evidence, who said they never knew anything paid and spoke only as to reputation and the lessee, who is now dead, paying a yearly sum the servants might not know it and the undertenants might thereby be discharged, and the verdict at law is considerable. And it is but a slight objection to say that what was paid was paid in their own wrong, when the proof went to payments by the defendant's wife while unmarried and had the estate by lease, and by her also when she managed her father's estate. But it being urged that the plaintiff's witnesses upon a trial at law would not be believed and this decree would in effect bind the archbishop [or] at least be a great evidence against his prescription in *non decimando* as to the small tithes (though the great [tithes] were paid, which is not usual), it was sent to a trial at law at the next Nottingham Assizes upon this issue, whether the demesne lands in Ascham be discharged from payment of small tithes to the vicar or anything in lieu of them or not. And at the next Assizes a trial was had and after a long evidence on both sides there was a verdict for the defendant and in favor of the prescription in *non decimando*. And the bill was dismissed the 6th of May 1697.

Note the difference between living and written evidence and the rarity (though not the impossibility) that there should be prescription in *non decimando* for small tithes of the demesne lands when the same lands yield great tithes to the impropriator. Query also the £4 proved paid for small tithes and the recovery upon the trial for hemp which is a small tithe.

[Other copies of this report: GUL MS. B88-8, p. 521.]

[The decree of 11 Feb. 1697, PRO E.126/16, f. 391, is printed at 1 Wood 375, 1 Eagle & Younge 623.]

344
Wyrley v. Ainge (Ex. 1697)

A bill in equity does not lie to set aside a common law verdict for the payment of tithes where the only issue is to reconsider whether tithes were due in kind or not.

LI MS. Misc. 559, f. 100, pl. 2 [Eng.] (Ward's Reports)

The defendant's husband being rector of a parish in Staffordshire and the plaintiff occupier of Haunsworth Hall and lands there, the plaintiff did not set out his tithes, and after [the] defendant's husband's death the defendant brought debt upon the statute and a verdict was [given] for the now plaintiff, but that verdict was set aside as ill obtained. And upon a new trial, the defendant obtained a verdict. And to be relieved against that verdict under pretense that a *modus* of £10 *per annum* only and not tithes in kind are due and to have a new trial was the end of the bill.

But the court dismissed the bill as not having any equity in it, for the defendant who has no continuing interest in the parsonage is not to be drawn into a new contest [of] whether [there be] tithes in kind or a *modus*. But the last trial standing unimpeached, the plaintiff in equity ought not to have any relief against it or the defendant. And for the future the plaintiff will be [at] liberty to defend himself as [he] shall be advised.

[Other copies of this report: GUL MS. B88–8, p. 523.]

[Order of 11 Feb. 1697: PRO E.126/16, f. 399.]

345
Cogger v. Randall (Ex. 1697)

A court of equity will specifically enforce a gift from one member of a close family to another where no third parties will be prejudiced.

LI MS. Misc. 559, f. 100, pl. 3 [Eng.] (Ward's Reports)

Upon the marriage of the defendant, Alice, with one Bowles, her former husband, certain lands in Marden in Kent and an annuity of £10 *per annum* was settled upon Alice (after the death of Bowles, her husband) for her life with remainder to the issue of their two bodies (which the plaintiff, Mary, is). The defendant, Alice, intending to marry with Randall, her now husband, conveyed these lands and the annuity (as was charged by the plaintiff's bill) by deed to the use of the plaintiff, Mary, thereby divesting herself of her estate for life. And this was done by the privity of Randall after the marriage took effect between Randall and Alice. And the bill charged that afterwards Randall and his wife got that deed and destroyed it. And to set up that deed destroyed and to be let into the estate during Alice's life was the end of the bill.

The defendants confess there was such a deed made and that it was destroyed but say it was not the intention of Alice or Randall that Mary should have the estate during Alice's life unless Randall proved unkind to her or that she married with her mother's consent, both which the defendants seemed to deny by their answer, and insist that it was but a voluntary settlement and ought not to be set up in a court of equity. But the defendants did not pretend that the deed had any condition or terms in it or any ways [was] defeasible.

And it being proved that the mother for love to her daughter made the settlement and before she married and with the privity and consent of Randall and that the deed was absolute and that the mother had declared that the daughter was to have it and none could hinder her of it, and the defendants, having destroyed the deed which was made at the desire of Alice and with Randall's privity as aforesaid and to be understood as her present interest and portion and there being competent proof of Randall's harsh and unfitting usage of Mary, and that Mary's marriage was with the privity and approbation of Alice, the court decreed for the plaintiffs and granted an injunction for the possession and an account for the profits from the time of the bill and the old writings of the estate [to be] brought into court to be delivered out to the plaintiffs, for though this settlement was purely voluntary, yet it was by a mother upon her own daughter and in prospect of the mother's changing her condition by taking another husband and putting herself out of the capacity of being kind to her daughter, who had nothing to live on till her mother was dead, and natural love and affection accompanied with the privity of the intended husband and the voluntary destruction of the deed (*in odium spoliatoris*) is sufficient in this case, there being neither creditor nor purchaser concerned. And the parties defendants afterwards submitted to and obeyed the decree.

[Other copies of this report: GUL MS. B88–8, p. 524.]

[Order of 11 Feb. 1697: PRO E.126/16, f. 399v.]

346
Fitzwilliam v. Pitt (Ex. 1697)

When interest is due but the rate is not specified, it will be paid at the legal rate.

In this case, a clause in a will was construed so as to avoid a hardship to one of the legatees.

LI MS. Misc. 559, f. 103 [Eng.] (Ward's Reports)

The case upon hearing appeared to be this. The said George Pitt, deceased, by his will dated the 26th of June 1694 gave to each of his three daughters, the plaintiffs, £5000 apiece to be paid at their respective ages or marriages with approbation of trustees (which first happens) and till then £250 *per annum* each for maintenance. And by his will devised in this manner, that his said three daughters (who were then all unmarried) should have the free use, dwelling, and occupation of the house wherein he then dwelt in Piccadilly in the County of Middlesex and also the free use and wear of all his household goods and furniture in the same house (except his silver plate) for and during so long time of the term of years and estate he had in the same house as his said daughters or any two of them should dwell together in the same house, and shortly after died. Mary and Jane first married, and they and their sister Elizabeth dwelt in the house and so did Elizabeth after her marriage.

By this bill the lord Fitzwilliam and his wife [Elizabeth] demanded her portion of £5000 with interest. And they and the other plaintiffs by the same bill sought relief against the defendants, who since the three daughters' marriages disturbed their living in the house and refused to pay the rent and perform the lessee's covenants in the lease as Mr. Pitt by another clause in his will had directed.

As to lord Fitzwilliam and his lady's £5000, it was owned to be due (they marrying with consent) but the defendants endeavored to have had it done without interest under pretense of some tender that was made of it (at such a time) and refused to be received. But there was no proof of any such tender as could justly cause a cesser of interest. Then they endeavored to have had interest paid only after the rate of £5 per cent *per annum* which the defendants' counsel would have to be the testator's intention in regard it was answerable to the maintenance to each of them till marriage which was £250 *per annum* which is just £5 per cent *per annum* for their respective portions. But it appearing to the court that there was a vast personal estate liable to these portions, and that this portion became due upon the marriage, and that being demanded, one of the executors said if they could not pay it presently (being at a time when the general coin of the kingdom was under a great difficulty and much impaired by clipping, etc.) the plaintiff should have interest for it, the court was of opinion that, as well from the nature of the thing as from the executors' agreement, interest was to be paid from the time of the marriage whereof defendants had notice, and since interest was due and the interest allowed by law being £6 per cent, the court could not in this case abridge it and so decreed payment with £6 per cent *per annum*.

And as to the house, in regard there is no restraint or limitation put upon the daughters' living in the house but only so long as any two of them should dwell together in the same, it did not seem to the court that the marriages of the daughters had determined that devise. For whatever might be the mental intention of the testator whether the daughters should have the use of the house so long only as two of them should be unmarried and dwell in it (thereby to engage cohabitation till otherwise provided for by marriage), yet if literally taken then when two were married, the third unmarried must be (while so) without a house. And it might be as well the testator's intention to continue amity and friendship between his daughters by cohabitation after marriage as before. And the words of the will being general 'so long as any two of them dwell in it' without other qualification or restraint, and there being no disposition of the term in the house to any particular use but to fall into the personal estate in general which being near £200,000 and no proof that the daughters have any other houses for their habitation, the court was of opinion that the daughters that lived in it with their husbands (though they for some time went into the country and visited their friends but left servants in the house) were to be continued so long as two of them shall live there and that the rent and covenants of the lease must be paid and performed by the testator's executors out of his estate and decreed it accordingly.

[Other copies of this report: GUL MS. B88–8, p. 530.]

[Order of 19 Feb. 1697: PRO E.126/16, f. 394v.]

347

Castle v. Cullen (Ex. 1697)

At issue in this case was whether a copy of a copy is admissible in evidence where the original is not accounted for.

In this case for a discovery and accounting for fees, the defendant made discovery, but the plaintiff failed to prove his right to any fees.

LI MS. Misc. 559, f. 104 [Eng.] (Ward's Reports)

The plaintiff entitled himself by letters patents under the great seal of England 30 August 27 Car. II [1675] to the office of water bailiff in the port of Dover and to certain fees and duties (showing what in certain) for goods imported into and exported out of the said port by merchants, as belonging to the said office, and charged the defendant for three years before 1695 that he had upon his own account and for others imported and exported divers goods for which the said fees and duties were payable and ought to have been paid but were not, of and for which goods he prayed a discovery and relief for the fees and duties.

The defendant believed the grant *prout* but denied the right of the fees and duties demanded and if any were due yet not from him in his own right because he was a freeman of Dover, who ought not to pay any such, and made a discovery by his answer of all the goods and merchandises by him imported or exported upon his own or others' accounts during the three years.

The principal proof that the plaintiff relied upon at the hearing to make out the right of the fees and duties was a copy of a table of fees hung up in the town hall of Dover wherein mention was made of some of those fees demanded by the plaintiff, but the table itself was not produced, nor anything charged upon the defendant that he hindered it. But it was sworn by affidavit that some of the jurats of Dover would not let it be brought though it was examined to at the commission for examination of witnesses. And it appeared by the depositions of the plaintiff's witnesses that this which was hung up and called a table of fees was but a copy of another old table and that in 1604 there was an order of Common Council whereby the water bailiffs' fees were adjusted, agreed upon, and hung up. And he that wrote this copy which is now hung up swears he did it about thirty years ago, but by whose order he knows not and believed it a true copy that is now hung up of that old table. And a question arising whether the copy produced by the plaintiff of that copy which was hung up in the town hall which was but a copy of the old table (of the authority of which there is no proof) the order of the Common Council in 1604 or any copy of it not being produced, by the opinion of the other barons, it was read.

But I dissented from it as utterly against all rules of evidence to prove a copy of a copy only and no account given of the original. Besides no fee could subsist by virtue of the order of Common Council which mentions it only to be adjusted and agreed upon. And that is not binding upon the merchants nor establishes a fee to the king's water bailiff.

But afterwards upon the further hearing of the cause, the chief baron [WARD], POWYS, and BLENCOWE (*dissentiente* LECHMERE) dismissed the bill in regard that the plaintiff's remedy is at law, if the fees he demands be legal fees, and if they be not legal, equity has nothing to do in it. And indeed if the court could make a decree for legal fees, yet there did not in this case appear such a right as would justify a decree. And the plaintiff came too early for a decree for fees which are contested not having adjusted his title at law to them by some action for that purpose, which when done he may be proper to have an account and relief for them but not before. And for that reason the bill was dismissed, the plaintiff not praying or desiring any trial at law for ascertaining and adjusting the right to the fees, which if he had, the court would have retained the bill till such action [were] brought. But the plaintiff insisting and relying upon his case as a case in equity only, the bill was dismissed *ut supra*.

[Other copies of this report: GUL MS. B88–8, p. 533.]

[Order of 19 Feb. 1697: PRO E.126/16, f. 397.]

348
Metcalfe v. Preston (Ex. 1697)

The issue in this case was whether a particular contract to pay money in lieu of tithes was reciprocal and binding on both sides.

LI MS. Misc. 559, f. 121 [Eng.] (Ward's Reports)

The case upon the hearing appeared to be this, that one Crawford being vicar of Aveley in Essex [on] 10th July 1691, articles of agreement indented were made between Crawford and Preston beginning and ending thus, 'Whereas the said Crawford for the considerations hereunder mentioned does covenant and agree with the said Preston that the said Preston shall pay or cause to be paid to Crawford £13 3s. for the tithes of three farms (naming them) quarterly by equal portions for four quarters (there mentioned) ending Midsummer 1692, and so to pay the said sum of £13 3s. quarterly as aforesaid during the time that he the said Preston shall hold the three farms, in witness whereof the parties aforesaid have interchangeable set their hands and seals the day and year first above written'. After this Crawford leases the vicarage to the plaintiff, and for some time he received the £13 3s. But afterwards conceiving that the articles were not mutually binding and that the tithes of the three farms were better than the money, he gave notice that he would have his tithes in kind for the time to come. And for the tithes after such notice, he brought this bill.

The defendant insisted upon the articles and offered the £13 3s. *per annum*.

And at [the] hearing this day,[1] I doubted whether these articles were reciprocal to bind both parties the one to pay the other to receive the money, for the defendant in this case says nothing. All proceeds from Crawford,[2] and if the court cannot decree the defendant (in case he should refuse) to pay the money, there is no reason to hold the plaintiff to accept it. And I remembered the case between Baker, vicar of Streatham, and Howland[3] in this court [*blank*] 168[5], where the plaintiff was relieved against such a pretense of composition by articles that he should and would take such a sum yearly but there was no provision to enforce the payment of it. And in the principal case that part of the articles under Crawford's hand and seal was produced only, but proved that defendant sealed one part. And it might be a question how far these articles extended to make a continuing composition. But the other three barons thought the articles [were] reciprocal because the money was to be paid for the tithes of the three farms, which they thought was an obligation upon the defendant to pay it. And so it was

---

[1] 6 May 1697.
[2] Sic in MS. for Preston.
[3] *Baker v. Howland* (Ex. 1685), above, No. 215.

decreed and by consent all [was] to be paid after the bill to the time of the decree. And so the cause was ended by consent.

[Other copies of this report: GUL MS. B88–8, p. 587.]

[Orders of 12 Feb. and 5 May 1697: PRO E.127/20, ff. 109, 132.]

349

Attorney General ex rel. Dongworth v. Tathwell (Ex. 1697)

In this case, the court found that there had been a proper election of a schoolmaster pursuant to a certain will.

In this case, a bill in equity to order the payment of arrears of a salary and to order future payments and to settle the plaintiff's right was allowed.

LI MS. Misc. 559, f. 122, pl. 1 [Eng.] (Ward's Reports)

The case upon the pleadings appeared to be this, that one Edward Burgh of Stow in the County of Lincoln being seised in fee of Stow Hall and of a farm called West Farm in Stow by his will in writing dated the 4th of August 1659 did devise £7 *per annum* to the town of Stow forever for the maintenance of a schoolmaster there, and if that money be not paid (at the times appointed by the will) that then it shall be lawful for the schoolmaster to enter upon West Farm and receive the rents and profits till payments and appoints that the schoolmaster shall be from time to time chosen by the possessors of Stow Hall (being a capital messuage there to which divers lands appertained and were used therewith) and four freeholders in Stow (not saying who by name but generally four freeholders, there being many more in that town). And this £7 being in arrear and unpaid, to have those arrears paid and the duty settled for the future was the end of the bill. The two defendants were owners of West Farm charged with the £7 *per annum* and held it by moieties. Lilly was willing to pay his part. But the defendant Tathwell opposed the relator's pretenses insisting first that the relator was not duly chosen according to the will, secondly that if he was, he has his remedy at law having by the express words of the will power to enter and receive the rents and profits till payment.

As to the first, it was held by the court that the word 'possessors' of Stow Hall must be understood the owners, for otherwise if a tenant at will or for years should live in it, he might be said to be the possessor of it, which cannot be thought to be the devisor's intent, and that such as were owners of the house (though without any of the land belonging to it) must have the election with four freeholders. And it appearing by proof that at the time of the relator's election the defendant Tathwell's husband (though in her right) was owner and lived in the house, and that he with four other freeholders had chosen the relator to be schoolmaster though there was no writing of it (the defendant Tathwell's husband saying that he would have done it in writing but that his wife would not consent). The court held that to be a good election according to the will. And the objection that the relator was then but fifteen or sixteen years old was not regarded because he was licensed by the archdeacon of Stow since and now bishop of Lincoln whereby his fitness and abilities were approved.

As to the second point, it was conceived that the relator has not any title at law, for he once brought an ejectment, but the words of the devise being only to the town of Stow, they were thought to be no such certain persons as could be lessors of the plaintiff in an ejectment. And a difference was taken between this and the case of Jemot and Coling, known by the name of Sir Ralph Bovey's Case, reported in Siderfin and other books,[1] for there the grant was to a certain person of a rent charge and, if unpaid, then for that person, his executors, etc. to enter.

And so upon the whole matter this being a bill as well to settle the right as to recover the arrears, the court decreed the arrears to be paid and the growing duty for the time to come so long as the relator shall continue schoolmaster there and the defendant Tathwell to pay her part (the other defendant having offered his), and declared West Farm chargeable with the £7 *per annum* to the schoolmaster for the future, and referred it to the deputy [king's remembrancer] to compute the arrears.

[Other copies of this report: GUL MS. B88–8, p. 589.]

[Order of 10 May 1697: PRO E.126/16, f. 415.]

350

Tyndale v. Skrine (Ex. 1697)

In this case, the lessee of a rectory failed to prove a custom of giving notice to the owner of the tithes before they are set out.

LI MS. Misc. 559, f. 122, pl. 2 [Eng.] (Ward's Reports)

The bill was for recovery of great tithes for the year 1694 from the defendants, owners and occupiers of land in Bathford in the County of Somerset, of which rectory the plaintiff is lessee under the dean and chapter of Bristol, the impropriators thereof. And the great design by the bill was to establish a custom in

---

[1] *Jennet v. Cooles* (1666–1667), 1 Siderfin 223, 262, 344, 82 E.R. 1070, 1094, 1147, 1 Ventris 193, 211, 217, 86 E.R. 131, 142, 146, T. Raymond 135, 158, 83 E.R. 73, 84, 1 Levinz 170, 83 E.R. 353, 1 Keble 784, 915, 83 E.R. 1241, 1318, 2 Keble 20, 184, 270, 295, 84 E.R. 13, 115, 168, 184, 1 Wms. Saunders 112, 85 E.R. 122.

that parish that the occupiers of land there ought to give notice to the proprietor of the tithes of the setting out of the tithes before the same be set out or the occupiers' corn carried away. And though there were many witnesses for the plaintiff that spoke for a great while that such notice has been given, yet by many of them and by the defendant's witnesses, it was plain that such giving of notice was not of right and duty but of neighborly courtesy or upon rewards given to the parishioners' servants either of money or gloves for coming to give such notice. And it appeared that divers had taken away their corn and hay after tithed by them without any such notice as is pretended, so as well from the nature of the proofs as from the consideration that a trial to be directed whether there be such a custom or no (for without such custom by our law, the parishioner is not bound to give notice of his tithing but may set out the tithe at his peril by the Statute 2 & 3 Edw. VI[1]) will not tend to any establishment because the dean and chapter are not parties. And in regard the tithes in question were not above the value of 23s. and the right of such custom may be tried in an action of debt upon the statute when and as often as the plaintiff pleases, for if notice be due by custom, then the tithing and carrying away [of] the corn or hay without such notice is not such a setting out of tithes as that Act respects, which is as of right and custom ought to have been. And for these reasons the court did not think fit to direct a trial but dismissed the bill, all the other demands thereby being quitted by the plaintiff.

And in this case it plainly appeared that Bathford was formerly called Ford and sometimes Ford *alias* Bathford and that the manor was parcel of the possessions of the Priory of Bath which came to the crown by the Statute of Dissolutions 31 Hen. VIII[2] and that part of that manor *viz.* Oxmead, Westmead, Gattick, Culverclose, and Sheep's Closes had never paid tithes but were reputed the demesne of that manor and as such might be free from payment of tithes as being in the prior's hands so freed at the time of the dissolution though all the rest of the manor did and do pay tithes.

[Other copies of this report: GUL MS. B88–8, p. 591.]

[Order of 18 May 1697; PRO E.126/16, f. 409v.]

351

Williams v. Vicars of St. Mary's (Ex. 1697)

In this case, the court of equity ordered the defendants to allow an agreed deduction from rent due for the defendants' proportion of taxes.

---

[1] Stat. 2 & 3 Edw. VI, c. 13 (*SR*, IV, 55–58).
[2] Stat. 31 Hen. VIII, c. 13 (*SR*, III, 733–739).

The court of equity will take jurisdiction of a case in order to compel discovery of evidence and to prevent a multiplicity of litigation.

LI MS. Misc. 559, f. 123 [Eng.] (Ward's Reports)

The case upon the pleadings appeared to be this, that the defendants, the corporation, the 20th of July 24 Car. II 1672 by indenture under their common seal demised the parsonage impropriate of Laverstock in the County of Wiltshire to the plaintiff's father for an estate or term yet in being, which is come to the plaintiff, under the reserved rent of £44 to the lessors in money and some corn rent and brawn, and also a rent of £16 *per annum* payable to the vicar of Laverstock (which is an augmentation to the vicarage). And in this lease there is an express covenant by the lessee that he, his executors, etc. shall pay all sums of money, taxes, and other charges upon the demised premises during the lease. But there is an endorsement upon the original lease in these words '*Memorandum* that before the sealing of this lease it was agreed that the lessors should pay their proportionable part of the contribution to be laid upon the parsonage as heretofore has been used', and by this endorsed clause the plaintiff insisted that the defendants should allow out of the rent the whole tax of 4s. in the pound imposed by Act of Parliament[1] and charged upon the parsonage for the years 1694 and 1695 which the defendants refusing to do and the plaintiff not paying his rent without such deduction, the defendants ordered one distress for one half year's rent and an action of debt for another half year's rent unpaid to be taken and brought. To be relieved against which distress and action and to have the court make the plaintiff an allowance and deduction for the said taxes of 4s. in the pound upon the parsonage, the plaintiff exhibited his English bill and prayed a discovery if such an endorsement had not been upon former leases surrendered or delivered up to the lessors and then in their custody and whether there had not been an allowance and abatement of taxes by the lessors accordingly, and prayed that the plaintiff might have an allowance of taxes for the future and relief against multiplicity of suits.

The defendants by answer insist upon the express covenants in the lease for the lessee's payment of taxes and that the endorsement extends not to the taxes now imposed but only to ecclesiastical contributions and that not to the whole but only a proportion and that here is no multiplicity of suits nor equity for the plaintiff but pure matter of law which is to be determined by the commissioners according to the express words and provisions made by the acts that lay the taxes or at least upon the trials that shall be upon the distress or action and for

---

[1] Stat. 6 & 7 Will. & Mar., c. 3, s. 3 (*SR*, VI, 511); Stat. 7 & 8 Will. III, c. 5 (*SR*, VII, 8).

the determination of that question or pretense the defendants caused the distress to be taken and action brought.

The plaintiff upon paying all the rent, save what might be due for taxes, to the defendants obtained an injunction till hearing, which was first had the 4th of February last. It appearing upon the proofs in the cause that upon an old lease made 17 Car. I [1641] there was no such endorsement, but upon the lease received [?] after 1660 and about ten of eleven years before on the lease to the plaintiff's father there was such [an] endorsement, but none upon several counterparts which were produced, and that after 1675 and till the year 1681, it appeared by divers acquittances produced by the plaintiff and given by the proctors [the defendants], that several sums yearly were allowed and abated for taxes but after 1681 no allowance of taxes had been made nor indeed demanded by the plaintiff, and it also appeared that the taxes upon the plaintiff for the parsonage were not distinctly laid upon the parsonage but jointly upon the parsonage and two other farms which the plaintiff held of his own so that what the proportion of the taxes upon the parsonage was did not appear nor could be made out. And whether the plaintiff was relievable in this case and in what manner and degree was the question.

The three barons seemed to doubt whether the plaintiff could have an allowance and deduction for taxes by means of the acts of Parliament either before the commissioners or in any remedy taken against him by action or distress in regard [that] the words of the endorsement are as heretofore has been used. And it was proper for him to come into equity to have a discovery of former endorsements upon original leases delivered up to the defendants upon renewals and what has been the former usage in that kind. And they were also of opinion that the word contribution extended to all sorts of taxes, assessments, and other charges upon the parsonage and that the defendants should allow for the whole notwithstanding the words 'proportionable part', which they understood to be all the taxes etc. laid upon the parsonage and laid stress upon the endorsement upon the former lease and the allowance of taxes from 1675 to 1681 and thought this way of relief in equity was proper because it tended to prevent [a] multiplicity of suits. And so [they] declared their opinions and pronounced a decree for the plaintiff that he should have allowance of and deduct out of his rent for the two years in question after the rate of 4s. in the pound for the £44 money rent reserved to the defendants, but not have any allowance for that part of the rent which is reserved in corn and brawn (which was considerable in value though not reduced to a certainty in money) nor for the £16 *per annum* reserved and paid to the vicar, and that this should be without costs.

I did doubt of this manner of relief and also thought the decree pronounced by them [was] not well grounded nor supported by such rules as are usual in case of reliefs in equity.

For first I apprehended that the plaintiffs would and might have good relief at law (in case the landlord ought to allow taxes) upon the clause in the acts of Parliament which give the taxes and gives the tenants power to deduct out of the rents so much of the taxes as are laid upon the land and which ought to be borne by the landlord which all landlords are thereby required to allow. And the plaintiff might and ought to have procured the parsonage to have been distinctly taxed and then he had known what certainty to have deducted. And if the plaintiff upon complaint to the commissioners (who by another clause in those acts have power to hear and determine all questions and differences that shall arise touching any [of] the rates, assessments, or levies or the collecting thereof made to them by any person or persons aggrieved without further trouble or suit in law) could not be relieved by them yet at least having the original lease and the former acquittances for taxes in his own hands and power and having by answer had all the discovery he could, both of the former lease whereon the like endorsement was and of all other matters to enable him to make out his case at law either upon the distress or in the action of debt for rent. And there now at hearing appearing no more to the court than would have done upon a trial at law and the same being a mere question at law and none in equity after such discovery, I thought the plaintiff should have been left to make his defense at law where no doubt he would have had allowance and deduction for taxes according to the purports of the acts of Parliament. And it is not usual to determine matters in law in a course of equity where there is nothing in question but the interpretation or construction of an act of Parliament.

Secondly I was not satisfied that there was any ground to relieve upon the account of multiplicity of suits for there were but two depending, nor could the court settle anything *de futuro*.

Thirdly nor was it clear to me that the word contribution did necessarily extend to taxes of this nature, none such being in being at or before the making of the lease under which the plaintiff claims. And if that word contribution did extend to such taxes, yet it seemed to me, as the endorsement runs, that the lessors were not to pay all the contributions laid upon the parsonage, the words being only their proportionable part thereof, which to me seemed clear not to be the whole. Nor did it appear what part or how much of the former taxes the lessors had paid or allowed, the acquittances being only so much (which were various and different one from the other) for or upon the account of taxes, which might be part only as well as the whole and that ought to have been cleared[2] to the court which was not.

Fourthly I did think it a case something of dangerous consequence for a court of equity to take upon it to give relief in such a case as this touching allowance

---

[2] Sic in MS.

or deduction for taxes which though some said was [a] matter of account, yet it is [a] matter easily and plainly determined at [common] law.

Fifthly I did not well apprehend upon what ground the three barons went to allow only for the £44 money rent whereas the natural and just relief that a court of equity must give (if any) is for the whole taxes laid upon the parsonage. And it being the plaintiff's fault that he did not make that appear distinctly, the court now had no way to distinguish it and so the plaintiff had not brought a case before the court proper for that relief that a court of equity going by rules and not arbitrarily or uncertainly ought to proceed by.

I think no final decree was made in this case, but the parties afterwards agreed among themselves.

See 1 Ventris 223–224, Davenant and Bishop of Sarum,[3] Hale's opinion there touching payments of taxes, where it seemed to be held that a covenant to pay all public taxes assessed upon the land did not extend to a land tax assessed by act of Parliament being a new way of taxing not in use when the covenant was made. And to me that seems a far stronger case that the word tax upon land should not and yet the word contribution (which is at best of an uncertain signification) should extend not only to new sorts of taxes, but even to the whole, when the covenant goes only to a proportionable part.

[Other copies of this report: GUL MS. B88–8, p. 593.]

[This case is cited in Veel v. Blanchard (Ex. 1697), below, No. 355; Walker v. Corbet (Ex. 1705), below, No. 393.]

352

Pierson v. Hockerston (Ex. 1697)

In this case, an alleged local custom as to tithes of lambs was not proved, and the court thought the alleged custom would be unreasonable.

LI MS. Misc. 559, f. 132, pl. 2 [Eng.] (Ward's Reports)

The plaintiff is impropriator of Holbeach in Lincolnshire, and the only question in the case (being a bill for tithes) was at what time lambs by the custom of the parish are tithable. [The] defendant seemed to insist that they are tithable at May Day. [The] plaintiff insisted not till Lammas,[1] and at his desire an issue

---

[3] *Davenant v. Bishop of Salisbury* (1672), 1 Ventris 223, 86 E.R. 150; also 2 Levinz 68, 83 E.R. 453, 3 Keble 69, 84 E.R. 599.

[1] August 1st.

was directed to try whether by that custom tithe lambs are to be set out and paid in that parish at Lammas and not sooner, and it was found against that custom. Indeed the court hardly inclined to send it to a trial in regard of the seeming unreasonableness of it to force the inhabitants not to dispose of their lambs sooner, and the bill was dismissed with costs the 11th November 1697.

[Other copies of this report: GUL MS. B88-8, f. 617.]

[The decree of 21 June 1697, PRO E.126/16, f. 426v, is printed at 1 Wood 380, 1 Eagle & Younge 626.]

353

Fawcet v. Wright (Ex. 1697)

A court of equity will not enforce the penalty aspect of a bond to pay money, nor will it allow a double recovery.

LI MS. Misc. 559, f. 133, pl. 1 [Eng.] (Ward's Reports)

The case upon the hearing appeared to be this, the plaintiff's wife was accused and convicted of receiving the defendant's jewels, which were stolen goods knowing them to be stolen and it being before the late statute[1] which made such receiver an accessory to the felony, the court, where the conviction was, set the less fine in regard [that] the plaintiff gave a bond of £30 to pay the defendant, Wright, (whose the jewels were that were stolen and had not received them again nor any satisfaction for them) the sum of £15. And now [the plaintiff] brought this bill to be relieved against the bond under pretense that the plaintiff's wife was innocent of the fact whereof she was convicted and examined several witnesses to make it appear probable that she was so and further urged that the defendant's jewels were now in the hands of a justice of the peace where he might and would have them again. But that appeared not to the court so that the court rejected the testimony of the witnesses as being an attempt to falsify the conviction, which was not to be endured in a court of equity.

And there being nothing made out of fraud, surprise, or circumvention in obtaining the bond but that it was given freely and voluntarily to the defendant Wright for payment of so much money, the court could not relieve against it otherwise than the penalty by payment of principal, interest, and charges, which if paid by Midsummer, then the bond [was] to be delivered up, if not paid, then the bill [was] to be dismissed. But had it appeared to the court that the defendant would have her jewels again, it would not have been reasonable to let the defendant have those jewels and the bond also given for their value.

---

[1] Stat. 3 Will. & Mar., c. 9, s. 4 (*SR*, VI, 312).

[Other copies of this report: GUL MS. B88–8, f. 618.]

[Order of 5 May 1697: PRO E.127/20, f. 137v.]

354

Knowles v. James (Ex. 1697)

In this case, various rights in a market were determined by a jury.

LI MS. Misc. 559, f. 133, pl. 2 [Eng.] (Ward's Reports)

The plaintiffs claimed the tolls and profits of Shepton Mallet market in the County of Somerset and complained also against the defendants, inhabitants of that town, for setting up pig pens before their houses in that town every market day and taking money for the use of them from persons that brought pigs to be sold at that market and required an account and satisfaction for the same. The defendants did not admit the plaintiff's title to the market and tolls and profits but insisted that the market is a free market and no tolls [are] due and also that by custom they had [the] right to erect and let pig pens upon market days before their houses and take the profits to their own use. A trial at law was directed to try both the plaintiffs' and defendants' pretenses which coming to be tried at the assizes was found too long and sent to the bar which by consent was tried by a Middlesex jury lasting twelve hours, and a verdict passed for the plaintiffs as to some tolls and for the defendants for the pig pens, and decreed the tolls for the plaintiffs and the pig pens for [the] defendants without costs on either side.

[Other copies of this report: GUL MS. B88–8, f. 619.]

[Order of 14 June 1697: PRO E.126/16, f. 422v.]

355

Veel v. Blanchard (Ex. 1697)

In this case, the testator intended that the annuity devised should be paid without any reduction for any tax on the land.

LI MS. Misc. 559, f. 136 [Eng.] (Ward's Reports)

The case upon the hearing appeared to be this. Robert Blanchard, goldsmith, deceased, by his will of the 17th of August 1680 reciting and taking notice that he and others for him were seised in fee and had also some terms for years in being of and in the manor of Hayes and lands in Hayes in Middlesex devised all the said estates and premises to the defendants, the trustees, in trust that in the first place they should pay to the plaintiff Alice (who was the testator's sister) £80 *per annum* by quarterly payments during her life, all to be without any abatement whatsoever, and then limits the trust of the residue for his the testator's wife during her life and then gives all the estate to the defendant [Richard] Blanchard, who was a remote kinsman. From the time of the testator's death (which was shortly after his will) till the year 1689, there were no Parliamentary taxes, after which and all along to the time of the bill, the Acts of Parliament which granted aids and supplies to the crown charged all annuities issuing out of lands with those taxes and gave the tertenants power to deduct taxes. And in some of those acts there is a clause that nothing in that act shall alter or avoid covenants or agreements between landlord and tenants, and in others between landlord and tenant or others. The defendant Blanchard paid the £80 annuity to the plaintiff to the year 1690 without making or claiming any deduction for it. But from 1690 to 1696 he refused to pay it without deduction for taxes. And the plaintiff Alice (not having anything else to live on) was forced to allow him the taxes and upon such deduction gave the defendant receipts in full for the annuity. And to be relieved against such allowance and deduction of taxes for the £80 *per annum* and to have it for the future during her life free from taxes or other abatements, the plaintiffs exhibited their English bill.

And the defendants, the trustees, submitted to the court and to do therein as directed. But the defendant Blanchard insisted upon the right of the deduction of taxes as being both within the words and intention of the Acts which pointed at an equality, and that the tertenants who did not receive all the profits to their own uses but paid [a] great part out to others should not be charged to pay the whole and that it is natural justice [that] it should be so. And if the plaintiff was taxed for that her annuity she must pay it. And it is altogether as fit and just that it should be deducted by the tertenant when he is taxed for the whole estate as if nothing issued out of it. And the case of Brewster and Kidgwell[1] depending in the king's bench upon the same point in effect with this was remembered by Serjeant *Wright* where the extent of the words 'free from taxes' are under consideration, which case though not determined yet he said the court seemed to incline there should be a deduction of taxes notwithstanding those words 'free from taxes'. (But note the court after judged that taxes should not be charged but free from them.) And *Sir Thomas Powys* said it was lately adjudged in chancery between the lady Arran and Crispe that the word taxes generally expressed shall extend to taxes laid by Parliament. 1 Ventris 223.[2]

---

[1] *Brewster v. Kidgell* (1696), Carthew 438, 90 E.R. 853, Holt K.B. 175, 669, 90 E.R. 995, 1270, 1 Salkeld 198, 91 E.R. 177, 2 Salkeld 615, 91 E.R. 521, 3 Salkeld 340, 91 E.R. 860, 1 Lord Raymond 317, 91 E.R. 1108, 5 Modern 368, 87 E.R. 711, 12 Modern 166, 88 E.R. 1239, Comberbach 424, 466, 90 E.R. 424, 466.

[2] *Davenant v. Bishop of Salisbury* (1672), 1 Ventris 223, 86 E.R. 150; also 2 Levinz 68, 83 E.R. 453, 3 Keble 69, 84 E.R. 599.

But upon hearing the plaintiff's counsel in the principal case, the whole court agreed and so decreed that, as this case, is the defendant ought not to deduct the taxes and though he has forced the plaintiff (as was proved in the cause) to give acquittances in full when he deducted taxes, yet that the plaintiff should be relieved against them and pay the money so deducted for taxes to the plaintiff, for this is not an ordinary case. For here the plaintiff devises an estate of a very great annual value in trust to pay £80 *per annum* in the first place to the plaintiff without any abatement so it was the testator's mind [that] she should have it without any abatement, which surely is not so if there be any deduction out of it for taxes. And it must reasonably be understood that in this case the testator intended that the rest of the estate should pay all the charges and reprises out of it. And the word abatement is of a large and comprehensive nature and includes all manner of deductions whatsoever, and the payment to be made of this in the first place is considerable. Moreover, here is an agreement within the statute, the testator agreed it, and the devisee, the defendant Blanchard, agreed to it by accepting the devise as made to him and the plaintiff and paying the £80 *per annum* without deduction for some time. And the plaintiff was refunded by the defendant (as overpaid) in all the time £130 8s. 00d., which [the] defendant [was] decreed to pay the plaintiff.

See above f. 123, a similar case.³

[Other copies of this report: GUL MS. B88–8, f. 631.]

[Orders of 21 June and 1 July 1697: PRO E.126/16, ff. 419, 427.]

[This case is cited in Walker v. Corbet (Ex. 1705), below, No. 393.]

356

Attorney General ex rel. Strode v. Birl (Ex. 1697)

A judgment at common law is res judicata *and will preclude a suit in equity.*

LI MS. Misc. 559, f. 137, pl. 1 [Eng.] (Ward's Reports)

The relator being a copyholder for an estate in being under the crown in eight doles of ground lying in the open and common fields of Shepton Mallet [Somerset] did some years since enclose the same with a mound and stocked it with coneys and converted it to a warren having first had an *ad quod damnum* executed. And because the defendants disturbed the relator in the enjoyment of the warren and killed the coneys, pretending that they had [a] right of common in those doles for their sheep whereas they and the rest of the commoners (who

---

³ *Williams v. Vicars of St. Mary's* (Ex. 1697), above, No. 351.

were all copyholders for lives under the crown) had sufficient common beside and the ground was good for nothing but a warren, and a warren was very useful and profitable to Shepton Mallet (being a market town) and to establish the warren and [to] be relieved against actions at law and judgments thereupon for the defendants against the relator was the scope of the bill.

But inasmuch as upon the hearing of the cause, it appeared that the copyhold which the relator claimed commenced as such but in 1683, and that the warren was made in the late reign against the will of the copyholders and tenants and that it was prejudicial to their right of common, and for that a *quo warranto* was brought in his now Majesty's reign in the king's bench 3 Will. & Mar. [1691 x 1692] against the relator to show by what authority he claimed the warren, and the relator by his plea thereto disclaiming any right or title of warren, and judgment being entered upon that disclaimer, and now read in court, the attorney general's bill was dismissed for would the merits of the cause have allowed any relief, yet so long as this judgment remained in force, this court could not relieve the relator.

[Other copies of this report: GUL MS. B88–8, f. 634.]

[Order of 25 June 1697: PRO E.126/16, f. 424v.]

357

Fleming v. Webb (Ex. 1697)

A testator can direct his executor to pay debts and legacies out of the income from real property.

LI MS. Misc. 559, f. 137, pl. 2 [Eng.] (Ward's Reports)

Richard Webb, the testator, being seised of a real and possessed of a personal estate of good value by his will devised £12 *per annum* to the plaintiffs during their joint lives and gave £100 to the plaintiffs' daughter (who is since dead and to whom the plaintiffs are administrators) and made the defendant Jonathan [Webb] his executor and gave his real estate to the defendant William Webb, and there was a clause in the will that, if the testator's personal estate was not sufficient to pay his debts and legacies, that then the executor was to enter upon the real estate and hold it till the debts and legacies should be paid, and because the plaintiff's annuity and the legacy of £100 were not paid and the defendant, the executor, refused to pay them or enter upon the real estate, the plaintiffs brought their bill. And [they] were relieved and sent to an account, and the report [was] this day confirmed. And the account of the personal estate, which was given by the executor in a suit in chancery and agreed to by the heir there, was allowed in this suit to be the account of the personal estate according to which the account in this suit was settled it being under both their hands and seals.

[Other copies of this report: GUL MS. B88–8, f. 635.]

[Order of 1 July 1697: PRO E.126/16, f. 421v.]

358

Seaman v. Appreece (Ex. 1697)

In this case, a junior mortgagee with notice of and agreement with the negotiations to sell the property that secured his debt was required to join in a conveyance even though he would receive nothing from the sale.

LI MS. Misc. 559, f. 138, pl. 1 [Eng.] (Ward's Reports)

The case upon hearing appeared to be this, that Betts, the defendant, was empowered by the other defendant and others to sell an estate in houses in Norwich for the best price he could get for them, to which houses the defendant, Appreece, laid some claim by a mortgage, which was junior to some encumbrances but senior to others. Pursuant to that authority, Betts sells the houses to the plaintiff for the best price he could get and, before he concluded, acquainted the defendant Appreece with the sum. And he did not oppose but agreed to it. And Betts entered into articles with the plaintiff to procure the defendant, Appreece, to join and convey his estate and interest, who refusing the plaintiff brought his bill to enforce the defendants to perfect the sale and to convey.

[The] defendant Appreece owned the empowering [of] Betts to sell and that Betts acquainted him with the contract with the plaintiff and that he did not oppose it, but insisted that he then understood and was made to believe that there would be enough of the purchase money to pay him, if not all, yet some part of his debt and that since it now appears [that] there will be nothing coming to him, he hopes he shall not be compelled to join and part with his interest for nothing.

But in regard [that] the defendant gave such authority and was so acquainted as above and that the estate was sold to the plaintiff for the full value and that the defendant, Appreece, was shut out by precedent debts from the purchase money agreed for, it was not material what his imaginations or expectations might be, it being just that he should make good his authority and agreement to perfect the sale. And therefore he was decreed so to do and join in the conveyances and to pay costs.

[Other copies of this report: GUL MS. B88–8, f. 636.]

[Order of 2 July 1697: PRO E.126/16, f. 431.]

359

Tilson v. Attorney General (Ex. 1697)

A person who receives the king's money without lawful authority knowing it to be the king's money is accountable for it even though the official account was approved.

LI MS. Misc. 559, f. 138, pl. 2 [Eng.] (Ward's Reports)

The plaintiff's testator [Robert Squibb] was one of the security that Mr. Villiers, one of the tellers of the exchequer, gave for the due performance of his office and paying and answering the money to the king which should be paid in his office of teller. And a bond of £200 entered into by the testator to the king for the purpose aforesaid being put in suit against the plaintiffs, they exhibited their bill to be relieved against it under an allegation that Mr. Villiers had answered all to the king.

And the case upon hearing appeared to be this, that on the 5th of January 1680 there was an exchequer order directed to the said Mr. Villiers to pay out of the king's treasure in his hands to Colonel Gurdon (then designed ambassador to the tsar of Muscovy) the sum of £764. This order was brought to Mr. Villiers's office where both the testator and [the] defendant [Robert] Squibb were fellow clerks and managed the affairs there. But there being no person authorized to receive the money, it was not paid out, but yet was charged and brought into Mr. Villiers's weekly account as if it had been actually paid. But Colonel Gurdon or any for him never had a penny of it. But the defendant Squibb took the money to himself. But it being afterwards discovered that the money was not answered to the use it was first intended, the defendant Squibb by direction of the lords of the treasury paid £464 part of it upon His Majesty's account. And as to the £300 (which was now in question), it was paid by the defendant Squibb to the plaintiff's testator who gave a note under his hand in November 1688 whereby he promised to be accountable to the defendant Squibb for it. And the plaintiff's testator had the custody of the original order for the whole money. And the only question in this case was whether the plaintiffs as executors to their testator should be liable for the £300 to the king and so be liable upon the bond of £200 as far as that went (it being agreed that the bond would reach them) or to the defendant Squibb only upon the testator's note. And it was agreed by the court that if the testator knew the £300 for which he gave the note was the king's money, that then the plaintiffs should not be relieved upon the bond without paying the £300, for in such case the testator became debtor to the crown by the receipt of the crown's money and ought to answer it to the crown. But if he did not know it to be the king's money, then it is not reason to charge him otherwise than upon his note, which the defendant Squibb may put in suit against the plaintiffs when he pleases. But it was affirmed [that] there were no assets liable to that debt to a subject. But the plaintiffs refusing a trial at law offered them whether their testator knew the money to be the king's or not and the penalty of the bond being less than the debt, the plaintiff's bill was dismissed.

Note it seemed clear by this case that there is a dangerous practice in allowing the tellers' weekly or other accounts without vouchers produced, for if this £764 had not been allowed upon Mr. Villiers's account without producing a voucher for his payment of it, there could not have been such a fraud as was after discovered, and whosoever receives the king's money without lawful authority knowing it to be the king's money must be accountable and answerable for it.

[Other copies of this report: GUL MS. B88–8, f. 638.]

360

Berry v. Ladbrooke (Ex. 1697)

The admission to probate of a void will does not create an estoppel so as to create a title under that purported will.

LI MS. Misc. 559, f. 141 [Eng.] (Ward's Reports)

The bill seeks relief for a legacy of £10 given to the plaintiff's wife by the defendant's wife by her will while a married woman. And a power was by the bill charged to be in the defendant's wife for that purpose, or at least some agreement by the defendant to let his wife dispose of that and other legacies by her will and charged that the defendant had paid some other legacies so devised by his wife. Defendant by answer confesses he did by inadvertency prove his wife's will and pay some of the legacies given by her but denies that his wife had any power by any consent or agreement before or after marriage to make any will or dispose of any legacies or sums and hopes such inadvertency shall not oblige him to pay this. And this cause standing upon bill and answer where all the answer is to be taken as true, I held the wife's will void and no way obliging upon the defendant and his payment of other legacies by inadvertency does not create a title to the plaintiff under a will [that is] absolutely void there being no agreement or power to support it. But BLENCOWE and POWYS decreed the legacy without interest and costs, which query.

[Other copies of this report: GUL MS. B88–8, f. 651.]

361

Knight v. Hopkins (Ex. 1697)

In this case, tithes in kind were ordered to be paid, the alleged modus *not being proved.*

LI MS. Misc. 559, f. 144, pl. 2 [Eng.] (Ward's Reports)

The plaintiff being rector of Broughton in the County of Oxford sued the defendants being inhabitants and occupiers of great quantities of lands in that parish (and tenants of the same to the lord Saye and Sele) for tithe corn and hay in the years 1693, 1694, and 1695. The defendants insisted upon a yearly payment of £40 *per annum* in lieu of all tithes of their lands and proved by divers witnesses that the said yearly sum of £40 and no tithes in kind had been paid to five of the plaintiff's next immediate predecessors for the space of forty years and upwards by the now lord Saye and Sele and his ancestors.

But the plaintiff producing into court the counterpart of a lease under the hand and seal of the lord Saye and Sele dated the 14th of December 13 Jac. I [1615] whereby Ralph Taylor, then rector of Broughton, leased the tithes of the lands in question unto the said lord Saye and Sele for three years from the first of May then last and so from three years to three years for eighty years if the said Taylor should so long continue parson there under the yearly rent of £40. And in that lease Taylor covenanted for quiet enjoyment and not to do any act to avoid that lease, which counterpart being proved to be the hand and seal of the then lord Saye and Sele, and that he and his heirs are patrons of the living, and the lands proved to be but about two or £300 *per annum* which makes the £40 *per annum* (being so great a sum) improbable to be a *modus* time out of mind. And it not appearing to be any real composition or agreement upon the enclosure (which, if it had, the court would not have broken into it after so long payment and acceptance by five successive incumbents, Taylor living forty years after the lease and continuing incumbent all that time), the court was fully satisfied that the £40 *per annum* took its rise from the lease, which being expired, tithes in kind are due for what appears to the court to the contrary. And therefore the court decreed tithes in kind for the years in the bill, refusing any trial at law (there being no ground for it) and not regarding the lord Saye and Sele's being no party to this suit the decree not binding the inheritance. And the lord Saye and Sele, if he had thought fit, might have brought on his cross-bill (which is depending in this court) at the same time for hearing or may if he thinks fit bring his bill to establish the £40 *per annum* in lieu of tithes. But as things appeared to the court, they can make no other order or decree in the case, for it is hard to think that if there had been a *modus* time out of mind that the lord Saye and Sele would have accepted a lease of the tithes which would be and be interpreted to be a total destruction of the *modus*.

[Other copies of this report: GUL MS. B88–8, f. 660.]

[Order of 1 July 1697: PRO E.127/20, f. 175.]

362
Attorney General ex rel. Chicheley v. Laycock (Ex. 1697)

In this case, the plaintiff lessee of the crown failed to prove his title in a suit for an account and quiet title, the issue being decided against him by an advisory jury.

LI MS. Misc. 559, f. 145, pl. 1 [Eng.] (Ward's Reports)

The suit was by English information in the attorney general's name at the relation of Sir Thomas Chicheley, lessee from the crown, for a term of years under the yearly rent of £50 of about nine hundred acres of land in the four parishes before mentioned[1] alleged to be derelict lands from [the] Humber, a great navigable river, within thirty years past, and to discover the defendant's title, and to have an account and relief for the profits from the 18th of November 1690 (when an inquisition was taken and the crown title [was] found to those lands as derelict), and to be quieted in the possession thereof.

But at the hearing this day inasmuch as the inhabitants of each of the towns claimed distinct rights of common in distinct parts of those lands and nothing jointly and the bishop of Durham, as lord of the manor of Howden (within which Ellerker is a vill), claimed all derelict lands in that lordship and that there were not any persons defendants at [the] hearing that were inhabitants of South Cave, Bromfleet, or Province or represented the rights of those three parishes wherein it was alleged the derelict lands were, the court could not proceed to make any decree in the cause, but left Mr. Attorney General to bring his informations of intrusion at law in order to try the title at the bar, if he so thought fit. And if he did not do so within a year, the bill by consent was to be dismissed.

Note afterwards in Easter term 1700, 12 Will. III, a trial at [the] bar of the exchequer was had by a special jury of Yorkshire, who by consent had a view before the trial. And after thirteen hours hearing and giving evidence on both sides, a verdict passed for the defendants.

[Other copies of this report: GUL MS. B88-8, f. 662.]
[Order of 18 Nov. 1697: PRO E.126/16, f. 451v.]

363
Browne v. Culworthy (Ex. 1697)

In this case, the defendant was ordered to pay tithes for the agistment of dry and barren cattle.

---

[1] South Cave, Ellerker, Bromfleet, and Province in Yorkshire.

LI MS. Misc. 559, f. 145, pl. 2 [Eng.] (Ward's Reports)

The plaintiff, being rector of Whiston in the County of York, exhibits his bill against the defendant as well in her own right as executrix of her late husband, deceased, being occupiers of Froom Manor within the parish and rectory of Whiston, principally for agistment tithes of dry and barren cattle for five years.

The defendant as to the agistment tithes insists upon a custom in *non decimando* for them within the hundred of Trafford and Tickhill in the County of York, within which hundred the manor of Froom and parish and rectory of Whiston is.

The plaintiff's counsel insisted that the custom alleged is void in law as to agistment tithes, and indeed all customs in *non decimando* [are] void in everything else save for tithe wood, for which thing only (as being doubtful whether tithes were originally due for wood or not) such a custom in *non decimando* has been allowed. And in that sense and under that qualification only, such custom in *non decimando* has and ought to be allowed, but to no other tithable things. And for authority [he] relied upon the case of Hicks and Woodsall in the king's bench Hilary 1696, 4 Modern 336,[1] where the case was that the defendant there libelled below in the ecclesiastical court for tithes of dry, barren, and unprofitable cattle and the plaintiff there prayed a prohibition upon [a] suggestion that the parish wherein the cattle were agisted was within the hundred of Huntspill and Puriton in the County of Somerset, and that within that hundred there was a custom in *non decimando* for dry, barren, and unprofitable cattle. The plaintiff declared upon this prohibition and issue was joined upon the custom and a verdict [was] found for the custom. And upon a motion in arrest of judgment that this was a void custom, the court heard three arguments at [the] bar on each side and took time to deliver their own opinions, which was done *seriatim*, and by all the whole court (*viz.* Chief Justice Holt, Rokeby, Turton, and Eyre, Justices) [it was] held to be a void custom in law as to agistment tithes and a consultation [was] awarded upon the reasons (as was said) that a custom in *non decimando* in an hundred or county holds good only in case of tithe wood in respect of the doubtfulness whether any tithes were originally due of right for wood, and that the books and authorities of *Doctor and Student* 166–167, 362; Rolle's [Abr.], *Dismes*, 653, 654; 2 *Institutes* 644, 645, 653, 654; 1 Rolle's Rep. 22; Brooke's [Abr.], *Dismes*,

---

[1] *Hicks v. Woodeson* (1694), 4 Modern 336, 87 E.R. 429; also 1 Eagle & Younge 592, 2 Gwillim 550, 4 Modern 324, 87 E.R. 422, 3 Lord Raymond 116, 92 E.R. 595, 1 Lord Raymond 137, 91 E.R. 987, 12 Modern 111, 88 E.R. 1200, Skinner 560, 90 E.R. 252, Comberbach 403, 90 E.R. 555, Carthew 392, 90 E.R. 827, Holt K.B. 671, 90 E.R. 1271, 2 Salkeld 655, 91 E.R. 558, Samuel Dodd's Reports, p. 171.

14; 13 [Coke] Rep. 12, 13, etc.² are to be understood in that sense, but some of those authorities as *Doctor and Student*, ff. 167, 362, and 2 [Coke] *Inst.* 645; Brooke's [Abr.], *Dismes*, 14, allow the custom [to be] good even in the case of corn and grain, under this limitation only if there be sufficient for the parson besides [. . .]. See 1 Rolle's Rep. 22: Coke said Wray, C.J., [. . .] *contra*.

But this point in the principal case was reserved for the consideration of the court in case the defendant could make out such a custom within the hundred in this case in question, which was not done, though many witnesses were examined for the defendant none of which came up to the point. But on the contrary, the plaintiff by many witnesses proved divers payments and compositions for agistment tithes in the hundred of Trafford and Tickhill. And so the court (without further consideration of the legality or illegality of the custom in point of law) decreed the defendant to account for and pay the tithes of agistments of dry and barren cattle in question.

See above f. 52,³ such a pretense of custom [was made] but tithes [were] decreed.

As to the case of tithes of wood, it seems to me they are due *de jure* of *sylva caedua*.⁴ If there be not a *jus decimandi*, how can a prescription be good in *non decimando*? See the cases *supra* which allow tithes of wood and Cro. Car. 113:⁵ firewood [is] not discharged of tithes without a custom.

See Rolle's [Abr.], *Dismes*, 637,⁶ etc., which countenances prescription in *non decimando* of wood inasmuch as the right of tithes of wood lies in usage.

See Rolle's [Abr.], *Dismes*, 655,⁷ where [the] court gave judgment against a verdict that found an issue against law.

[Other copies of this report: GUL MS. B88-8, f. 664.]

[Order of 30 Nov. 1697: PRO E.126/16, f. 450.]

[This case is cited in Smith v. Johnson (Ex. 1709), below No. 437.]

---

² C. St. German, *Doctor and Student* (T. F. T. Plucknet and J. L. Barton, edd., 1974), 91 Selden Soc. 300–314; 1 Rolle, Abr., *Dismes*, H. 'Que poet prescriber in non decimando', pp. 653–654; E. Coke, *Second Institute* (1642), pp. 644–645, 653–654; *Porter v. Tike* (1614), 1 Rolle Rep. 22, 81 E.R. 299, 1 Eagle & Younge 224; Brooke, Abr., *Dismes et tenthes spiritualles*, pl. 14; *The Case of Modus Decimandi* (1608), 13 Coke Rep. 12, 77 E.R. 1424, 1 Eagle & Younge 177.

³ *Poole v. Draper* (Ex. 1696), above, No. 325.

⁴ Stat. 45 Edw. III, c. 3 (*SR*, I, 393).

⁵ *Norton v. Fermer* (1628), Cro. Car. 113, 79 E.R. 699, also 1 Eagle & Younge 363, Hetley 88, 110, 117, 124 E.R. 365, 382, 387, Littleton 152, 124 E.R. 182.

⁶ 1 Rolle, Abr., *Dismes*, pl. F, G, p. 637.

⁷ *Earl of Hertford v. Leach* (1635), 1 Rolle, Abr., *Dismes*, pl. I, 2, p. 655.

364

Fitch v. Commissioners of the Navy (Ex. 1697)

An arbitral award that is uncertain will not be confirmed by the court.

At issue in this case was whether a party who contracts for work to be done and owes money on that contract can enforce a performance bond.

A claim for an accounting is cognizable by a court of equity.

The commissioners of the Navy are proper parties to be decreed to perform their contracts specifically by, in this case, executing bills.

At issue in this case was whether interest on claims for accounts accrues when the certainty of the amount due is settled.

Court costs are not paid by the king or by his agents.

LI MS. Misc. 559, f. 146 [Eng.] (Ward's Reports)

The plaintiff having some time since exhibited his bill to be relieved against a bond of £20,000 penalty entered into unto the king for performance of covenants for making and finishing one dry and two wet docks for ships at Portsmouth by a certain time and under certain rates in articles made between him and the commissioners of the Navy on the behalf of the king, and also to be relieved for divers great sums alleged to be due to him for work by him done there both within and without the articles and for his losses in many materials left upon the premises when he was turned out of the work, and for his being turned out, the cause had received several hearings in the court.

And (after several overtures for a reference had proved ineffectual) the court directed seven issues at law to be tried to satisfy the conscience of the court before any decree could be made in the cause. And a time was appointed to try these issues a year since. But then a reference was agreed to by both sides, and by order of the 27th of April 1697 by mutual consent the whole cause was referred to four arbitrators, two chosen by each side to make an end of all or any [of] the matters in variance by a set time, and if all [be] not ended by them, then such not ended was referred to one Thompson, an umpire, so as he made an end by such a day afterwards. The arbitrators met and agreed and settled several things, but differing in others they left them to be determined by the umpire. And what the arbitrators settled they put in writing under their hands and seals. The umpire he proceeded and made his umpirage of the rest under his hand and seal. And both [of] these were delivered into court in order to be decreed.

But the plaintiff, though he well liked the arbitrators' award, yet he greatly objected against the umpirage (though near £2000 was thereby coming to him) as irregularly made and obtained without fully hearing of him and giving him longer time, which was alleged to be promised, and without examining his witnesses before making the umpirage. And therefore he wholly opposed the confirming of the umpirage but desired the arbitrators' award (as far as it went) might be confirmed, that (by the order of reference) being to be conclusive as far as it went.

And the court upon [the] reading of many affidavits on both sides for and against the umpirage did not think fit to confirm or establish the umpirage, there being many reasonable objections against the way and manner of obtaining it. And as to the arbitrators' award, it was agreed that if the same had been clear, certain, and plain as to what in particular had been thereby determined, that the same should and might have been confirmed. But upon perusal and consideration had of it, there manifestly appeared an utter uncertainty in it, for that the arbitrators had taken a view of the whole work, wherein they agreed they set it down and wherein they disagreed they left it to the umpire, and there was some of the same kind of work left undetermined (as to the prices) by the arbitrators because they could not agree [on] the prices (which shows there were different prices for the same kind of work). And the arbitrators' award is altogether silent as to what work in particular and at what places done (the same sort of work being done at several places though not at the same prices), so that it no ways appears what they have certainly determined and what left undetermined, so that the arbitrators' award could not be conclusive nor fit to be decreed in regard of its uncertainty.

And thereupon both the award and umpirage being refused by the court to be decreed, the seven issues formerly directed to be tried were now ordered to be tried at the bar the next term by one or more juries of the County of Middlesex at several days and times, which trials were had the 28th of January [and] the 1st and 4th of February 1697/98, and the seven issues were:

1. What the plaintiff deserved for the work within the articles according to the rates in the articles.
2. What he deserved for the work within the articles in case there had been no articles or agreement for it.
3. What the plaintiff deserved for the work he did which was not in the articles before he was turned out.
4. What the plaintiff was damnified by being turned out before all the work was done.
5. How much the king was damnified by the plaintiff's not having finished the work at the time he was turned out.
6. How much the king was damnified by the plaintiff's insufficient doing of any work within the articles.
7. How much the plaintiff's materials left on the ground and made use of for the king about the work were worth at the time the plaintiff was turned out.

The first of these trials, which was upon the two first issues, lasted eighteen hours; the second, which was upon the third issue, lasted twenty-two hours; and the third trial, which was upon the four last issues, lasted above sixteen hours.

The jury found upon the:

1st issue, that plaintiff deserved	£13,773 4s. 6½d.
2d issue, that plaintiff deserved more than the last	£266 6s. 10d.
3d issue, that plaintiff deserved	£8757 1s. 4d.
4th issue, that plaintiff [was] damnified	£100 00s. 00d.
5th issue, that the king was not damnified anything.	
6th issue, that the king was damnified	£100 00s. 00d.
7th issue, that the materials were worth	£2030 18s. 03d.

After which trials the plaintiff's counsel made two demands upon the cause in equity.

First that the bond of £20,000 may be delivered up and cancelled, for though in strictness of law it was broken the work not being finished by the first of November 1692, which was the time limited for finishing it by the articles, yet in regard [that] it is admitted that the plaintiff has not received so much for his work by some thousands of pounds as the jury has found he deserved for his work and materials, it is but just that he should be relieved against the bond and have it cancelled. And to this the defendant's counsel made no objection. And therefore the bond was decreed to be delivered up, and a perpetual injunction to it.

The second demand of relief made for the plaintiff was that he might have a just and full satisfaction for his work and materials according to the verdicts. But as to this point the defendant's counsel insisted that the plaintiff ought not to have relief in it in equity against all or any [of] the defendants:

First, because the plaintiff's demands are matters purely determinable at law upon an *indebitatus assumpsit* or *quantum meruit* and not in a court or course of equity.

Secondly, if the plaintiff was relievable in equity, yet there can be no decree made in this case to enforce any of the defendants to pay the plaintiff any money for these reasons: first, no such decree can be made against the attorney general, there neither being reason or precedent for it, for though by his office he represents the crown yet he has not the command of money nor [is he] able to pay any; secondly, not against the commissioners of the Navy personally in regard [that] whatever was done or contracted for by them was on the behalf of the king only and nothing upon their own account or in their own right. And a third objection was that in case such a decree as is desired might or could be made, yet that the plaintiff's demands of relief for these things following are not just nor reasonable: *viz.* first, for the allowance of £5 per cent deducted and abated from him for about £10,000 upon account of prompt payment; secondly, nor for any allowance to be made the plaintiff upon the account of discount of tallies, that is for what he was forced to pay or allow for turning the tallies he received (being upon remote funds) into ready moneys, he receiving them as such.

Thirdly, nor for any interest to be allowed to the plaintiff for any moneys that shall be due to him.

Fourthly, nor for any pretense of losses which the plaintiff sustained by losing ships or goods for want of protections or convoys.

Fifthly, nor for any demands of costs of suit in this cause in [common] law or equity.

And upon these points, the cause continued in the paper, and counsel on both sides were heard thereupon several days. And afterwards the court delivered their opinions *seriatim*, wherein they all agreed in these things.

First, that as this case is circumstanced in regard of the plaintiff's being forced into equity for relief against the £20,000 bond put in suit against him (and against which it is agreed he is and ought to be relieved) and with respect had to the articles themselves, which in effect make this case a matter of account depending upon several circumstances and contingencies therein mentioned as referring some rates for work to indifferent men according to the rates given at Portsmouth and for the defendants, the commissioners, and their officers viewing and examining materials and workmanship and for adding to those articles things more convenient or to lessen the charge and for the plaintiff's following their directions, and with respect had to the commissioners' covenant whereby on His Majesty's behalf they oblige themselves (under their public seal though [they be] no corporation) to sign bills upon the treasurer of the Navy to the plaintiff or his assigns by way of imprest for £2500 in tallies and for other payments by bills to be made quarterly according to value of work done and materials laid upon or near the place, to be paid in course according to the custom of the Navy together with the balance of the whole charge by a perfect bill (all imprests deducted) when the whole work done according to the admeasurements, prices, and times agreed on in the articles etc. And also with respect to the proofs in the cause whereby it appeared that the commissioners gave directions for many and great alterations in the design and nature of the work which changed the materials and made a great deal of additional and other work not mentioned in the articles, and the continuing [of] the plaintiff in the work till July 1694 and then turning him out (one third of the work then undone) by which alterations there was a confusion of many of the rates in the articles and an utter uncertainty of price followed thereupon, by all which it became a case in equity. And no breach of any rule of law in this case can happen in regard the court meddles not to make a decree for the king's payment of any money, nor to give uncertain damages (for they are ascertained by the verdicts which all agree to be upon full and fair trials). It was resolved that the plaintiff was relievable in equity and could not be relieved at law for the work and materials not paid for, in regard [that] it may be well questioned whether an *indebitatus* or *quantum meruit* lies against the king or his attorney or the commissioners who acted only for the king (James Graham's Case[1] lately settled in Parliament). And all is now matter of account to compute what remains due (above £20,000 which has been paid to the plaintiff before and since the commencement of this suit upon account of those docks).

Secondly, it was unanimously resolved that the plaintiff was relievable against the commissioners of the Navy, defendants, to enforce them to put in execution all powers they are invested with for payment of money for that service, and one power is to make Navy bills to the treasurer of the Navy for payment of such money as shall appear to be due to the plaintiff for the service aforesaid. For since it is just that the plaintiff should be paid and this court cannot decree the king or the attorney general or the commissioners to pay the money in specie, it not appearing that they have any money in their hands for that purpose, yet it is but just that the commissioners should do all they can in order to have the plaintiff paid. And that is by [the] giving of him Navy bills, which being all they can do, the plaintiff must be content with it, (which he declared himself to be), and that in effect is no more than to compel them to execute their articles in specie.

Thirdly, the court agreed that the plaintiff ought to be allowed upon account for the sum found upon the first issue, (but not the £266 6s. 10d. upon the second issue, it being dangerous to break in upon the king's contracts), and also for the sum found due upon the third issue, and for the £100 upon the fourth issue, and for the materials upon the seventh issue, discounting thereout the £100 found for the king upon the sixth issue. But as to the five per cent discount for prompt payment, or for discount of tallies, or for losses for want of protections or convoys, there being no complaint of the two first in the bill nor proof of any of them in the cause, they were disallowed by the court.

And as to the interest of any of the moneys coming to the plaintiff (except the materials), no interest [is] to be allowed for that till the time of the last verdict all depending in uncertainty till that time and [there is] no reason to pay interest till a certainty, but from there [he is] to have interest. And as to the materials to have interest for the money for them from the time the plaintiff was turned out, in regard [that] he might then have sold them for so much and received interest for his money.

And as to costs, the plaintiff [is] not to have any being relieved against a penalty and his own act. Nor was it known that the king ever paid costs, and [there is] no reason for the commissioners, who acted only for the king, to pay them.

---

[1] *Grahme v. Stamper* (1694), *Lords' Journal*, XV (n.d.), p. 353, also 2 Vernon 146, 23 E.R. 701, Prec. Ch. 45, 24 E.R. 23, 1 Eq. Cas. Abr. 308, 21 E.R. 1066.

Upon the account, there appeared to be due to the plaintiff after all deductions the 25th of July 1698, £4053 19s. 8d. And then the commissioners of the Navy, defendants, were decreed forthwith to make, sign, and deliver to the plaintiff or his assigns bills to the treasurer of the Navy for that sum with interest for the same until such bills be made out, signed, and delivered as aforesaid. And this decree is enrolled of Michaelmas term 10 Will. III, 1698.[2]

See my argument and the trials at large.

But afterwards, *viz.* December 1698, the plaintiff, Mr. Fitch, appealed from this decree to the Lords in Parliament and assigned for cause that he ought to have had allowed and decreed to him these things, being eight in number more than were allowed *viz.*:

First, the £266 6s. 10d. which the jury found upon the second issue that he deserved more for the work within the articles in case there had been no articles or agreement for it.

Secondly, £526 17s. 10d. allowed the commissioners of the Navy for discount of £10,531 1s. 10d. paid him in ready money, though his work was found by the verdict at a ready money price.

Thirdly, £964 8s. 5d. which [the] plaintiff allowed for discount for £10,500 which he received in tallies, his work being found by the juries at a ready money price.

Fourthly, £925 5s. 6d. for the interest of £5934 18s. 5d. from the 20th of July 1694, when he was turned out of the work unto the 18th of March 1696.

Fifthly, £286 2s. 3d. for the interest of £3934 18s. 5d. from the 18th of March 1696 (when £2000 was paid him) to the 30th of May 1698.

Sixthly, and for the interest of £4050 from the 30th of May 1698 until payment of the same.

Seventhly, £231 7s. 7d. for [the] loss of three vessels and goods taken by the French.

Eighthly, and for costs of suit, he having spent therein above £2000 besides the loss of his time and hindrance in his business for above four years.

This appeal was heard in the Lords' House of Parliament on Tuesday, Friday, and Saturday the 7th, 10th, and 11th of February 1698[/99],[3] on the last of which days it was appointed to debate the appellant's demands head by head. And the first head for the £266 6s. 10d. being debated, it was carried by a great majority against the appellant, there not being above four or five for him, so that it was expected [that] the rest would also have gone against him, there being as thought more pretense for that than any other. And thereupon many lords went away. And then the case of interest for his money found due to him for his work

---

[2] PRO E.159/543 (part 2), recorda Mich. 13 Will. III, rot. 151.
[3] *Lords' Journal*, XVI (n.d.), p. 381.

from the time of his being turned out to the time of the verdicts was stirred, and by twenty against nineteen [it was] carried for the appellant that interest should be allowed for that money though it was not reduced to any certainty, which seems to be a case without precedent in the courts below, even between subject and subject, and seemed till this judgment far stronger in the king's case. And as to all the rest of the appellant's demands, the appeal was dismissed and the exchequer decree [was] confirmed with that alteration only, that Navy bills should be also given for that interest added.

And in the debate of this case on Friday, it is said something was offered by one of the lords as if the court of exchequer had gone too far in making the decree, meddling with that wherewith they had no jurisdiction, that is by decreeing anything to the appellant. But upon Saturday, I satisfied that lord that the court had warily proceeded in this case for they had not decreed the king or any of his officers to pay any money to the appellant but only that the commissioners should make good their own contract by the articles and give Navy bills, as they had agreed and were enabled by the king to do, it being a quite different thing for the court to make that decree from making a decree that the king or his officers should pay any money. And that distinction was well approved and allowed, and the jurisdiction and justice of the court in that behalf [was] vindicated.

Note that to prevent the entering of any order or judgment for this interest money allowed by the lords beyond the decree, the treasurer paid him that money which came to about £700 and no order for it was entered in the Lords' House and so no precedent [is] extant to impose interest upon the crown for moneys due upon a contract for work before the certainty of the sum due be settled by a trial at law, there being an account current between the parties as to receipts and payments relating to that work till trial or other adjustment.

January 1699[/1700]: As to the court's power and jurisdiction in decreeing money to be paid out of the receipt and awarding a writ to the treasurer of the exchequer and chamberlains there for that purpose, see the Bankers' Case in Parliament upon a writ of error in Parliament by Williamson v. Attorney General,[4] where such power was asserted and would have justified the court had they made a decree for payment of the money by the crown had the articles been for payment in specie.

[Other copies of this report: GUL MS. B88-8, p. 667.]

[Orders of 28 Oct. and 22 and 30 Nov. 1697: PRO E.126/16, ff. 422, 444v, 448.]

[This case is cited in Bartlett v. Attorney General (Ex. 1707), below, No. 415.]

---

[4] *Rex v. Hornby* (*The Bankers Case*), 5 Modern 29, 87 E.R. 500, Skinner 601, 90 E.R. 270, Comberbach 270, 90 E.R. 472, Carthew 388, 90 E.R. 825, Case 413, 1 Freeman 331, 89 E.R. 246, *State Trials*, XIV (Howell, ed., 1816): cols. 1–114; Samuel Dodd's Reports, pp. 98, 103, 104, 111, 168.

365
Layfield v. Entiknapp (Ex. 1698)

In this case, tithes of lamb were ordered to be paid in kind.

Folger Library MS. V.b.253, f. 67v [Eng.] (Heath's Reports)

In an English bill for the tithe of lambs yeaned in the parish of Chiddingfold in Surrey in bar to this common right claimed by Mr. Layfield as parson of the parish of Chiddingfold, the defendant sets up this custom in his answer, that the parishioners have time out of mind paid threepence a lamb for every lamb yeaned in the parish and sold before St. Mark's day in lieu of the tithes in kind and if [there are] but seven lambs, the parson [is] to have one, and such as [are] not sold before St. Mark's day [are] titheable in kind, or if sold after.

And I [*Heath*] argued that this custom was not a good custom in the manner following. Common right speaks for the parson, and if this custom do not stand in our way, I conceive Your Lordship will decree the plaintiff his tithes in kind. My Lord, I conceive this custom is not good in law upon that objection which, as Mr. Dodd truly affirmed to the disadvantage of his client, came originally from Your Lordship and not from Mr. Serjeant [Heath], and it is this. As Your Lordship has computed it, ten threepences make half a crown, and half a crown may be thought to be the full value of a lamb, which is the tithe in kind, especially at the commencement of this custom, for customs or prescriptions for moduses, though they are laid to be time out of mind, are supposed to have a beginning by consent and composition between the parson, patron, and ordinary, and parishioners, but the memory of the beginning being lost, it is rendered[1] into a custom or prescription. And so I say this custom may be thought at the beginning of it to amount to the full value of the tithes in kind, especially if it be considered, as this custom is laid, the parson is to have threepence for every lamb that is yeaned and sold, though it often times happens [that] the parishioner is to pay the threepences when he has not ten lambs and so the threepences go on still when the parson should have nothing by his common right, because he had not ten lambs. And so upon the whole matter, this extraordinary *modus* may be thought to amount to the full value of the tithes in kind.

My Lord, I have looked upon several books that treat of tithes: Dr. Godolphin; Sir Simon Degge, *Parson's Counsellor*, 310; Rolle's Abridgment, b, sect. 2, Y, 1.[2] And I find a *modus* for a halfpenny a lamb and a penny a lamb. But in none of the books there is a greater *modus* for lambs, much less such an extraordinary

---

[1] runt *MS*.

[2] J. Godolphin, *Repertorium Canonicum; or Abridgment of the Ecclesiastical Laws*; S. Degge, *Parson's Counsellor* (1676), p. 211; 1 Rolle, Abr., *Dismes*, pl. Y, 1, p. 644.

modus as threepence for a lamb. A *modus decimandi* is always less than the tithes in kind or than the value of the tithes in kind.

Selden [in his] *History of Tithes*, chap. 13, p. 409,[3] he says though a layman cannot prescribe in *non decimando* unless he begin in a spiritual person, yet for diminishing the quota in payment only of a less than the tenth, he may prescribe, that is *de modo decimandi*, and to that purpose an immemorial custom of a whole town or manor holds at this day; so he thought a *modus* [is] less than the value of the tithes. Dr. Godolphin's *Abridgment of the Ecclesiastical Laws*, 400, Letter D, 'wood discharged'; Sir Simon Degge, ch. 16, f. 300; Dyer 79, 349.[4] And this is the reason why the temporal courts grant prohibitions upon *modus decimandi*, because they in the spiritual courts refuse to allow of [a] *modus decimandi*, and the reason they refuse to allow them is because these moduses are always less in value than the tithes in kind and the canonists hold tithes in kind due *jure divino*, and so they will not abate of the tenth part. But the common lawyers hold them due *jure divino quoad sustentationem clerici non quoad decimam aut aliquam aliam partem quod est juris positivi*. So it seems a *modus* is less than the tithes or the value.

My Lord Hobart says that a prescription to pay the tenth part of wool and lamb, if the land lay to wool and lamb, is not good; it is not prescriptible because it is the [?] tithe in kind. But, says he, if the owners had not used to pay the tenth part but a less proportion, which is truly a *modus*, it had been good. Hobart 44, Cowper v. Andrews.[5]

Concerning the tithe of houses in the Strand, he says a *modus* is always with an abatement and correction of the tithes in kind. Hobart 11, Dr. Layfield v. Tisdale.[6]

And the pleading of a *modus* is that such a sum of money has been usually paid *in plenam contentationem, satisfactionem, et ponderationem omnium decimarum agnorum*, which implies the *modus* [is] less than the value of the tithes. But now if this *modus* or custom may be supposed to be of the value of the tithes in kind, it will not be good but in effect a prescription for the tithes in kind, which are due of common right and so not prescriptible, as My Lord Hobart says.

---

[3] J. Selden, *Historie of Tithes* (1618), p. 409.

[4] J. Godolphin, *Repertorium Canonicum; or Abridgment of the Ecclesiastical Laws* (1680), p. 400; S. Degge, *Parson's Counsellor*; *Anonymous* (1553), 1 Dyer 79a, 73 E.R. 170; *Parson of Peykirke's Case* (1576), 3 Dyer 349b, 73 E.R. 784, 1 Eagle & Younge 66, 1 Gwillim 136.

[5] *Cowper v. Andrews* (1612), Hobart 39, 44, 80 E.R. 189, 194, 1 Eagle & Younge 240, also Moore K.B. 863, 72 E.R. 957, Godbolt 237, 78 E.R. 138, *sub nom. Hooper v. Andrews*, 1 Rolle Rep. 120, 81 E.R. 372.

[6] *Layfield v. Tisdale* (1614), Hobart 10, 80 E.R. 161.

The custom was 'that, if any inhabitant have five fleeces of wool or above . . . after shearing and binding', he shall pay '*decimam partem inde absque aliquibus visu aut tactu novem partium ejusdem lanae*'. The prohibition [was] denied, because the substance of the prescription is that the true tenth ought to be paid which is not prescriptible, because it is common right. Hobart 107, Wilson v. Bishop of Carlisle,[7] [where it was] adjudged against prohibition.

If a man prescribe to pay to the parson the tenth sheaf as it falls out and the tenth swath, this is not any *modus*, because he does not prescribe to pay another thing than that which is due but a full tenth. Rolle's Abridgment, 648, title *modus*, N, 6; Rolle 651; Croke Elizabeth 609, Austin v. Lucas,[8] there was a *modus* to pay the tenth cheese made from the first of May to August in satisfaction of the tithe of milk that year. [It was] held [to be] a good *modus*, because of common right no tithe [is] due for cheese, but says the book, if it had been the tenth quart of milk, it had been void, because it is what is due. Suppose it had been the value of the tenth part of the milk, that had been void without doubt, so that if the ten threepences with all the other threepences which may happen to be paid according to the custom when there are not ten lambs and no tithe in kind would have been paid may be thought to amount to the value of the tithes in kind, then this prescription for the tithes in kind or the value of them will be void. Suppose the custom had been to pay to the parson the value of the tithes in kind, [it is] sure that had been void, because it savors so much of common right. It had been equipollent to common right, and the logicians say *equipollentia verbis discrepant sensu conveniunt*. And money is the measure, or as My Lord Hobart says *nomos* the law of things, and he that has so much money as the tithes are worth may be said to have the tithes themselves.

And therefore, My Lord, I hope you will not send such an extraordinary *modus* as this is to a trial at law whether the parson have a right to the tithe in kind or to the value of them, which is to make the jury judges of law contrary to the old rule, *ad questionem juris non respondent juratores sed judices*.[9] For to have the value of the tithes in kind or to have the tithes themselves is equipollent, or as the later word is, it is equivalent. And therefore I hope Your Lordship will not make that a custom which is common law and try this custom by a jury to no purpose. It will be *inutilis labor et expensum*. It will be no advantage either to the parson or

---

[7] *Wilson v. Bishop of Carlisle* (1615), Hobart 107, 80 E.R. 256; 1 Eagle & Younge 250, 1 Gwillim 279.

[8] *Barker v. Boswell* (1615?), 1 Rolle, Abr., *Dismes*, pl. B, 6, p. 648; *Austin v. Lucas* (1598), 1 Rolle, Abr., *Dismes*, pl. D, 19, p. 651, Cro. Eliz. 609, 78 E.R. 852, also Moore K.B. 909, 72 E.R. 990, 1 Eagle & Younge 142.

[9] The judges not the jury should decide matters of law. H. Broom, *Maxims*, p. 57 (Kersley ed., 1939).

parishioners, let the verdict go which way it will. *Frustra fit per plura quod fieri potest per pauciora.*[10] And so I hope we shall have your decree for the plaintiffs for tithe in kind of lambs.

And so we had by WARD, LECHMERE, POWYS, [and] HATSELL, though Mr. *Dodd* argued against me and pretended to answer me, but it was not thought so by the court.

Mr. *Dodd* said a penny [is] a good *modus*, 2s. for houses [is a] good *modus* and four nobles; he never knew a *modus* set aside for being too great. *Sed curia contra eum.*

[Other reports of this case: Samuel Dodd's Reports, p. 178; 1 Eagle & Younge 627, 2 Gwillim 560, *sub nom.* Bayfield v. Antecknap, 1 Rayner 83.]

[The decree of 3 Feb. 1698, PRO E.126/17, f. 11, is printed at 1 Wood 383; see also order of 7 July 1698: PRO E.126/17, f. 36.]

[This case is cited in Ekins v. Dormer (1747), 3 Atkyns 534, 26 E.R. 1108, 2 Rayner 425, 427, 2 Gwillim 800, 801; Chapman v. Smith (1754), 2 Vesey Sen. 506, 508, 28 E.R. 324, 325, 2 Rayner 469, 473, 485, 3 Gwillim 847, 850, 857, 2 Eagle & Younge 141, 143, 147; Pyke v. Dowling (1779), 2 W. Blackstone 1257, 1258, 96 E.R. 740, 741, 3 Rayner 942, 943, 3 Gwillim 1166, 1167, 2 Eagle & Younge 341.]

366

Terry v. Dean of Salisbury (Ex. 1698)

The court of exchequer has jurisdiction over disputes over augmentations of ecclesiastical incomes.

BL MS. Hargr. 71, f. 104v, pl. 1 [Eng.] (Dodd's Reports)

In a bill for an augmentation made by the defendants' predecessors, the court clearly resolved that it had jurisdiction, and cited Chappell's Case for the Church of Comb Bassett, in Easter [term] 36 Car. II [1684] in this court, f. 166,[1] and other cases. But in the principal case, [they] dismissed the bill for want of proof and not for want of jurisdiction.

[Other copies of this report: HLS MS. 537(b), p. 57, pl. 1; Oxf. Brasenose MS. 59, p. 73, pl. 1; IU Lilly MS. Parker, 'Cases in the Exchequer, vol. 2', p. 38; BL MS. Hargr. 70, p. 104, pl. 343; HLS MS. 1162, p. 91, pl. 489.]

---

[10] Jenkins 62, 68, 145 E.R. 44, 48. That is done to no purpose by many which can be done by fewer: *Black's Law Dictionary*, p. 799 (4th ed. 1951).

[1] *Hopkins v. Chappell* (Ex. 1684), above, No. 189.

367

Johnson v. Hewett (Ex. 1698)

A surviving devisee takes the entire gift where the other devisee dies in the lifetime of the devisor.

A devise relates to the time of the death of the testator not to the time of the making of the will.

BL MS. Hargr. 71, f. 105, pl. 2 [Eng. & Fr.] (Dodd's Reports)

Henry Johnson takes an assignment in his own and [his] wife's name of a term for years and afterwards made his will [on] 13 March 1684 and devises this term to his wife Alice for life, remainder to his brother William Johnson and dies. Alice survived. William Johnson [on] 15 March 1690 made his will and devises this term to trustees in trust for his daughter Hewett for life and afterwards to his granddaughter, the plaintiff Elizabeth Johnson, and Elizabeth Hall. Then Alice made her will and devises this term to William Johnson in case he paid her executor £30 and directs her executor to assign accordingly and died. Her executor in 1692 assigned to William Johnson. Elizabeth Hall died and then William Johnson died. And the bill was brought against the administrator *cum testamento [annexo]* of William Johnson to compel an assent and against the trustees to assign to the plaintiff. And two points [were] resolved at the hearing:

1. That by the death of Elizabeth Hall in the lifetime of the devisor, all should go to the surviving devisee and not a moiety only, as was insisted upon by the defendants. See Cart. 2.[1]
2. That the devise to the plaintiff was good notwithstanding that William did not have anything at the time of making his will in regard [that] Alice was then living and also in regard [that] Henry Johnson's devise was void because his wife was a joint purchaser with him. Nevertheless the court held the devise good and that it related to the time of the death of the devisor William, that it was clear at the time of his death, and the term [was] in him. And they made a distinction between a chattel and an inheritance. Note [that this was] by all four barons clearly.

[Other copies of this report: HLS MS. 537(b), p. 57, pl. 4; Oxf. Brasenose MS. 59, p. 74, pl. 1; IU Lilly MS. Parker, 'Cases in the Exchequer, vol. 2', p. 40.]

[Order of 26 May 1698: PRO E.126/17, f. 25.]

---

[1] *Davies v. Kempe* (1664), Carter 2, 124 E.R. 789.

368

Hall v. Moore (Ex. 1698)

A writ of sequestration lies against a judgment debtor who is in prison for the debt.

BL MS. Hargr. 71, f. 105v, pl. 2 [Eng.] (Dodd's Reports)

The plaintiff had a decree for £30 tithes and costs and served the defendant therewith and, upon affidavit thereof, had an attachment,[1] and that being in the sheriff's hands, the defendant surrendered himself. And upon a *habeas corpus* at the plaintiff's request, [he was] brought up and committed to the Fleet [Prison] for the said money and costs. And two terms after, the plaintiff moved for and obtained a sequestration notwithstanding the defendant were in custody. And several precedents [were] cited; see one in point upon debate [in] Trinity [term] 31 Car. II [1679], Thursday 10 July, between Roger Howyes, esq., and Richard Warren, gent., plaintiffs and Thomas Kett, defendant,[2] upon great consideration and search of precedents in chancery and perusal thereof.

[Other copies of this report: HLS MS. 537(b), p. 58, pl. 1; Oxf. Brasenose MS. 59, p. 75, pl. 2; IU Lilly MS. Parker, 'Cases in the Exchequer, vol. 2', p. 41; BL MS. Hargr. 70, p. 105, pl. 348; HLS MS. 1162, p. 92, pl. 494.]

[Orders of 12 Feb., 17 May, and 1 June 1698: PRO E.127/20, ff. 225v, 248v, 254v.]

369

Trevor v. Hollingsworth (Ex. 1699)

In this case, a legacy charged on land was ordered to be paid by the grantees of another legatee's heir.

BL MS. Hargr. 71, f. 107v [Eng. & Fr.] (Dodd's Reports)

A., seised in fee, by will charges his lands with £100 to be paid to B. at [the age of] twenty-one and devises the land to C. in fee. C. attempts to make a will and to give this to D., his wife, for life remainder of one moiety to E., his brother and heir, in fee and the other moiety to F., his brother. But he died before the will [was] executed. E., the heir, declared he would make good the will and accordingly by lease and release he conveyed the land to the same uses to which it was devised. And then B., the legatee, attained the age of twenty-one and brought his bill for the £100 against D., who exhibited a cross-bill against B., E., and F. And upon argument, [it was] resolved that E. and F. shall pay two parts of this £100.

---

[1] Order of 17 May 1698: PRO E.127/20, f. 248v.
[2] *Hawys v. Kett* (Ex. 1679), above, No. 99.

[Other copies of this report: HLS MS. 537(b), p. 60, pl. 2; Oxf. Brasenose MS. 59, p. 77, pl. 2; IU Lilly MS. Parker, 'Cases in the Exchequer, vol. 2', p. 46.]

[Orders of 23 Oct. and 8 Dec. 1699: PRO E.126/17, ff. 118, 125.]

370
Attorney General v. City of Oxford (Ex. 1699)

A charter to a municipal corporation should be enforced at common law by quo warranto *and not in equity by injunction where the crown revenue is not concerned.*

BL MS. Hargr. 71, f. 108 [Eng. & Fr.] (Dodd's Reports)

In a charter granted to the city in 16 Car. II [1664], there was a clause that the recorder or town clerk shall not act before [being] approved by the king. Thurston was chosen town clerk and was sworn. The king refused to approve him, [but] the corporation permitted him to act. Upon this the attorney general brought this information against the corporation and Thurston to enjoin him and not to permit Thurston to act and specifically to perform in the said clause in the charter. And after answer and proofs, the cause came to be heard [in] Trinity term, and [it was] resolved this term. The points made were:

1. Whether the corporation accepted this charter, and whether it be any more than a bare charter of confirmation only.
2. Whether, if they did accept it, they are bound to act accordingly.
3. Whether, if they do not, this court shall enjoin and force them to act accordingly.
1. The stronger proof is that they did accept; some said submitted but not accepted.
2. If [they were] entitled before, this acceptance is no surrender of the privilege. 1 Cr. 198, 259; Raym. 439.[1] It only amounts to a confirmation. Littleton, sect. 431. It does not appear [that] they wanted a confirmation. 2 Cr. 121; Littleton, sects. 538, 539; Moo. 631; Dyer 230b.[2] If the corporation had been made by this charter or that they first were empowered by this charter to choose a town clerk, then [it were] good. When sworn to execute the office, [he was] bound so to do, and the prohibitory clause [is] contradictory and comes too late.

---

[1] Perhaps *Lord Brook v. Lord Goring* (1630), Cro. Car. 197, 79 E.R. 773; *Gurney v. Clere* (1591), Cro. Eliz. 259, 78 E.R. 514; *Haddock's Case* (1681), T. Raymond 435, 439, 83 E.R. 227, 230.

[2] *Laughton v. Gardener* (1606), Cro. Jac. 121, 79 E.R. 104; E. Coke, *First Institute* (1628), ff. 305, 306; Case 867, Moore K.B. 631, 72 E.R. 804; perhaps *Anonymous* (1564), 2 Dyer 230, 73 E.R. 509.

3. They will not be enjoined. It is not a matter where the revenue is concerned; [there is] no precedent of such a bill. *'Volumus et intentionem nostram declaramus'* seems [to be] a condition rather than a covenant [and thus a] ground for a *quo warranto* or a *mandamus* or [an] information for a misdemeanor. See 2 Rolle 234; Jones 225, 226; N.B. 63, 200.[3] This court ought not to execute it in specie; [it is] not proper for equity. It is not a contract but concerns government and the duty of the office. If equity should interpose, it would prevent *quo warrantos*; it would make this court the Great Regulator. It is not a case in equity but [one] determinable at law.

[The] information [was] dismissed.

[Other copies of this report: HLS MS. 537(b), p. 60, pl. 3; Oxf. Brasenose MS. 59, p. 77, pl. 3; IU Lilly MS. Parker, 'Cases in the Exchequer, vol. 2', p. 47; BL MS. Hargr. 70, p. 106, pl. 354; HLS MS. 1162, p. 92, pl. 500.]

[Order of 29 Nov. 1699: PRO E.126/17, f. 123v.]

371
Crow v. Crow (Ex. 1700)

Copyhold lands are not covered by the Statute of Frauds.
A court of equity will order copyhold lands to be identified to a legatee.

BL MS. Hargr. 71, f. 108v, pl. 1 [Fr. & Eng.] (Dodd's Reports)

In the exchequer upon an English bill to set out forty acres of [a] copyhold which the ancestor [was] seised of and occupied jointly with the freehold, [it was] resolved:

1. That [if] a copyhold [was] surrendered to the use of the will and then a will was made in writing but not signed or sealed, nevertheless it was good for the copyhold because a copyhold is not within the Act of Frauds and Perjuries.[1]
2. That a commission should issue to set out the copyhold [was] resolved by all [of the court] clearly.

[Other copies of this report: HLS MS. 537(b), p. 61; Oxf. Brasenose MS. 59, p. 78, pl. 1; IU Lilly MS. Parker, 'Cases in the Exchequer, vol. 2', p. 48.]

[Orders of 20 Feb. and 4 Dec. 1700: PRO E.126/17, ff. 127, 194v.]

---

[3] 2 Rolle, Abr., *Prerogative le Roy*, pl. L, 3 and 4, p. 234; *James's Case* (1682), T. Jones 225, 84 E.R. 1229, also 2 Shower K.B. 233, 89 E.R. 908; *Natura Brevium*.

---

[1] Stat. 29 Car. II, c. 3 (*SR*, V, 839–842).

372

Wyne v. Cowper (Ex. 1700)

The issue in this case was whether a grandchild stands in the place of his or her deceased parent for the purposes of the customs of London as to inheritance.

BL MS. Hargr. 71, f. 110, pl. 3 [Eng. & Fr.] (Dodd's Reports)

The plaintiff's bill was for an account of the personal estate of one John Vere, a citizen of London. And upon hearing the cause, the points were as to the custom of London: first if a citizen die and leave a wife and child or children, his estate must be divided into three parts *viz.* one to the wife, one to the child or children, and the third is the dead's part. Now the case was [that] a citizen had a daughter, she married in the life of her father and had a daughter and died; the father married a second wife and then died intestate. Query if this granddaughter shall stand in the place of a child or that the custom does not extend to her. Note [that] no resolution in this common case could be found. The court sent to the mayor and aldermen to certify the custom by the word of the recorder etc. See the breviate. (And it seems to me [she is] out of the custom.)

In this case, it was said that if a freeman give a legacy to any infant in England, although such infant be [in] no way related to the City, yet *quoad,* this legacy, such infant shall be an orphan.

[Other copies of this report: HLS MS. 537(b), p. 62, pl. 5; Oxf. Brasenose MS. 59, p. 81, pl. 1; IU Lilly MS. Parker, 'Cases in the Exchequer, vol. 2', p. 54.]

373

Attorney General v. Basnett (Ex. 1700)

The king holding under an outlawry in debt can redeem a mortgage.

BL MS. Hargr. 71, f. 110v [Fr. & Eng.] (Dodd's Reports)

[It was] resolved that the king under a common outlawry in debt shall redeem a mortgage. The bill brought was *ex relatione tantum* and not *ex parte regis.* And the relator had no lease, and the court would do nothing in it. But the relator alleging that he was about [to get a] lease, the court retained the cause, and then he obtained a lease and brought it into court and had a decree to redeem.

[Other copies of this report: HLS MS. 537(b), p. 63, pl. 1; Oxf. Brasenose MS. 59, p. 81, pl. 4; IU Lilly MS. Parker, 'Cases in the Exchequer, vol. 2', p. 56; Parker 268, 145 E.R. 776.]

[Orders of 27 June and 31 Oct. 1700: PRO E.126/17, ff. 156v, 171.]

374

Duke of Leeds v. Hawson (Ex. 1700)

A judgment debtor in prison for debt is subject to a writ of sequestration under which his goods and lands can be seized for the benefit of the judgment creditor.

A wrongful sequestration can be challenged by a motion upon affidavit rather than by a new bill.

LI MS. Misc. 532, f. [66] [Eng.] (Ward's Reports)

The defendant being decreed upon an account had to pay the plaintiff about £300 which the defendant had received of the plaintiff's rents and for non-payment of which the defendant was committed to the Fleet [Prison] but was allowed too much liberty to go abroad. And notwithstanding this commitment, there was a sequestration awarded against him. And the sequestrators returned what they had sequestered, which were rents of houses and lands in tenants' hands and an empty house. And upon motion to have the rents sequestered paid over by the sequestrators to the plaintiff and an injunction to put [the] plaintiff or [the] sequestrators in possession of the empty house, it was opposed by the defendant's counsel. And upon perusal of the decrees in this court between Gwavas and Fountain[1] and where such sequestrations had been awarded and injunctions [had been] granted for the possession of what estate in lands or houses were in the defendant's own possession and the course in chancery to the like purpose being averred, the court here granted an injunction for the possession of the vacant house and a writ of assistance for the better execution of it.

Precedents in this court:

13 June 3 Jac. II [1687]: Gwavas and Fountain, [a] sequestration [was] awarded for not performing a decree.

8 February 3 & 4 Jac. II [1688]: between the aforesaid parties, writs of assistance to divers sheriffs and an injunction to the tenants in possession to pay their rents to the sequestrators and to put them in possession of the houses and lands in the defendant's occupation.

24 October 4 Jac. II [1688]: between the aforesaid parties, attachments against the tenants for not obeying an injunction.

Between Crossman and Goodridge, Michaelmas 4 Jac. II [1688], a writ of assistance to the sheriff and an injunction to the tenants.[2]

Note [that] if the sequestrators sequester an estate not of the defendant's, the right owner makes affidavit of it, and then the court stays the execution till the examination upon interrogatories and by the court. And when the court receives

---

[1] *Gwavas v. Fountain* (Ex. 1687), above, No. 233.

[2] *Crossman v. Goodridge* (Ex. 1688), PRO E.126/15, f. 162.

satisfaction, they order that sequestration accordingly. Query if the party [be] put to a bill; it seems [he will] not.

[Other copies of this report: GUL MS. B88–9, f. 57v.]

[Order of 7 May 1700: PRO E.127/21, f. 101v.]

375

Hawes v. Mayor of Liverpool (Ex. 1700)

In this case, a second issue to a jury was agreed to by both parties in order to have an impartial jury.

LI MS. Misc. 533, f. [51v] [Eng.] (Ward's Reports)

The cause standing in the paper upon the equity reserved, the plaintiffs prayed a decree that [the] defendants should forever be restrained from demanding or taking from the citizens of London any toll or duty for cheese laden or unladen in the port of Liverpool, both the issues being found for the plaintiffs and against the defendants.

The defendants prayed a new trial by a jury of another county, Hertfordshire being too near to London, which was opposed by plaintiffs, the verdict being upon full evidence and after a long trial, thirteen hours, and [there being] no cause to object against it.

The court declared they did not find fault with the verdict nor did [they] intend to disparage it, yet thought it not proper to conclude [the] defendants' right by this one trial [in] regard it was never seen (as I observed) that where any that are defendants at law come into equity to be relieved against multiplicity of suits only and have a proper and legal defense at law against the plaintiff at law, who may try his right as often as he pleases, that if a verdict happens in such a case for [the] plaintiff in equity, that that shall be conclusive forever against the plaintiff at law and bind his right, who by law may try it as often as he pleases, and the plaintiff in equity has a legal defense at law, and so [it is] n[ot] like the case where the trial passes upon an issue direc[ted] upon a pure case in equity to satisfy the conscience of the court, which may well be conclusive unless the verdict [is] dissatisfact[ory]. And therefore I declared my opinion that I would decree for [the] plaintiffs in this case as desired unless the defendants in some action to be brought by them did not in a year's time evict the plaintiffs at law. And this is the usual decree in such cases. But then the cause of action being like[ly] to arise in Lancashire upon trespass to be brought upon a distress in that county, it would be tried by a Lancashire jury, which plaintiffs were by no means willing to; therefore it was consented to by the plaintiffs and agreed [to] have another trial at bar next Michaelmas term by a Berkshire jury upon the same issues.

[Orders of 14 May and 11 Nov. 1700: PRO E.126/17, ff. 138, 173v.]

376
Sherwin v. Clargies (Ex. 1701–1702)

A bill to perpetuate testimony does not lie where the facts to be proved have already been proved at common law.

Where a defendant who is a member of Parliament puts down his demurrer for argument and then fails to make an argument, the demurrer will be overruled, but it will be without prejudice to the defendant as to a future argument upon payment of costs.

LI MS. Misc. 532, ff. [120v], [134] [Eng.] (Ward's Reports)

[There was a] bill to examine witnesses *in perpetuam rei memoriam*, the plaintiff claiming as heir at law to George, late duke of Albemarle; and the subject matter of the examination was to be to prove the illegitimacy of Christopher, late duke of Albemarle, reputed son of the said Duke George, by proving that the mother of the said Christopher at the time of his birth and many years before had been married to and was the wife of one Radford, and so the said Christopher was not nor could be the lawful son of the said Duke George, which matter had been examined to in chancery and was the subject matter of five trials in ejectment at the king's bench bar brought thither by the plaintiff's ancestors under whom she claims in fee, and upon long examinations of witnesses on both sides, the verdicts went always in affirmance of the said Duke Christopher's legitimacy and against the plaintiff's ancestor's title as heirs to Duke George.

In bar of the said examination, the defendants pleaded the said proceedings in chancery and the said verdicts wherein the plaintiffs' ancestor's title (being the same title the plaintiffs claim) was in question and under examination, and that the plaintiff has no bar or impediment to hinder him to bring his action at law, at least his real action, and the plaintiffs' title having been so often examined into and determined against at law, it is not agreeable to justice or the rules of equity to suffer such examinations to be taken and lie by, wherein there may be perjuries which by the death of the witnesses may become dispunishable and no reason to examine *in perpetuam rei memoriam* when plaintiffs may go to law without impediment but is of dangerous consequence; and thereupon the court allowed the defendant's plea and demurrer in bar of the examinations prayed.

See same case in effect liber M, 24:[1] An examination [was] allowed the then plaintiffs only because they were infants. [There is] no infancy here.

And see my paper of Hilary term 1701[/02] folio [134] where the demurrer of the earl of Montagu and the duchess of Albemarle, his wife, was overruled by the court for want of opening and not upon the merits of the case.

---

[1] *Pride v. Monck* (Ex. 1696), above, No. 312.

Saturday 31 January 1701[/02].

A demurrer put in by the earl [of] Montagu and the duchess of Albemarle, his wife, to the bill of one Sherwin and his wife touching the late duke of Albemarle's estate, and for examination of their witnesses *in perpetuam rei memoriam* standing this day in the paper to be argued, and the defendant's clerk in court having set it down accordingly (which, if not so set down, had been by the standing rules of the court overruled), the counsel for the defendants would not open the bill and demurrer, being, it seems, forbid by the defendant's solicitor so to do, and the court in such case is not to give any rule without being prayed by the plaintiffs' counsel, and they, it seems, having notice from the defendant's solicitor by writing under the defendant's hand and seal (as they said) that the defendants stood upon their privilege of Parliament, refused to pray the demurrer might stand overruled for want of opening. But Sir John Hawles, the king's solicitor general, being of the defendant's counsel and a member of the House of Commons then sitting, moved the court that the demurrer might be overruled, which was ordered accordingly upon his motion, it being the justice of the court in this and all other cases so to do.

See my paper of Michaelmas term 1701, folio 20 [i.e. 120] where the plea and demurrer of Sir Walter Clergies to the same bill were allowed upon the merits of the cause.

Note if the defendant's counsel would have moved the court afterwards for putting the demurrer into the paper again and have it argued, it might and would have so been upon payment of costs for the first day.

But there was after[wards] a complaint in the Lords' House for overruling this demurrer,[2] but [it was] not prosecuted but fell, the plaintiffs in the suit not further proceeding in the cause.

[Other copies of this report: GUL MS. B88–9, f. 99.]

[Related cases: Pride v. Monck (Ex. 1696), above, No. 312; Sherwin v. Clargies (Ex. 1698), PRO E.159/543 (part 2), recorda Mich. 13 Will. III, rot. 17; Earl of Bath v. Sherwin, Prec. Ch. 261, 24 E.R. 126, Gilbert 2, 25 E.R. 2, 2 Eq. Cas. Abr. 171, 243, 522, 22 E.R. 147, 206, 440, 10 Modern 1, 88 E.R. 596 (Ch. 1706–1710); 4 Brown 373, 2 E.R. 253; *Lords' Journal*, XIX (n.d.), p. 39, IU Lilly MS. Parker, 'Cases in the Exchequer, vol. 5', p. 191 (H.L. 1709); Earl of Mountague v. Earl of Bath (Ch. 1693), 2 Chan. Rep. 417, 21 E.R. 704, 3 Chan. Cas. 55, 22 E.R. 963, Nelson 196, 21 E.R. 824; Pride v. Earl of Bath (K.B. 1695), 1 Salkeld 120, 91 E.R. 113, 3 Levinz 410, 83 E.R. 755, Holt K.B. 286, 90 E.R. 1057; Duchess of Albemarle v. Earl of Bath (Ch. 1692), Samuel Dodd's Reports, p. 118, Nelson 196, 21 E.R. 824, 2 Chan. Rep. 417, 21 E.R. 704, 3 Chan. Cas. 55, 22 E.R. 963, 2 Eq. Cas. Abr. 671, 22 E.R. 564, 2 Freeman 121, 193, 22 E.R. 1099, 1155.]

---

[2] *Lords' Journal*, XVII (n.d.), pp. 108, 127.

377

Earle's Case (Ex. 1702)

The executor of a judgment debtor in equity can be proceeded against by a subpoena scire facias *by the judgment creditor.*

LI MS. Misc. 532, f. [200] [Eng.] (Ward's Reports)

There was a decree of this court signed and enrolled three or four years since against Sir Thomas Earle since deceased and whose executor Mr. Earle is, whereby Sir Thomas was decreed to pay to two persons two sums of £50 apiece, and costs of suit were taxed against him also, but he died before any money was paid. After his death, the persons concerned in the cause prosecuted a subpoena *scire facias* against Mr. Earle, the executor, returnable at a certain day reciting the decree and that the money or costs were not paid but the decree abated by the death of Sir Thomas, therefore the executor was required to show cause why he should not perform the decree and pay the money and costs decreed. The executor not appearing at the day nor any cause shown against it, upon oath made of the service of that subpoena *scire facias*, the court made an order that the executor should pay the money and costs out of the assets of Sir Thomas Earle's personal estate, with which order the executor being served, he did not pay the money, and upon affidavit of service of that order, the court awarded an attachment against him.

And *Ettrick* and *Browne* of his counsel moved to discharge the attachment and all the proceedings as erroneous in regard as they urged the proceedings should have been by bill of revivor for as now it is the executor had no opportunity to defend himself nor is there any discovery of assets nor do any assets appear to the court, as they would have done by answer to the bill of revivor.

But upon [the] hearing *Dodd* and *Phipps* for the parties interested, the court was of opinion that the proceedings were regular and the defendant upon appearing to the subpoena *scire facias* had a proper opportunity to make any defense, as by saying he was not executor or had not assets or anything else to defend himself by which, having willfully slipped, the court could do no otherwise than order him to pay out of the assets which the law supposes he has unless he says otherwise. And this way was affirmed by all the clerks to be the practice. However, the court told him, if he would swear he had not assets, the court would help him, but he refused that and owned assets and after[wards] paid the debt.

378
Adams v. Rogers (Ex. 1702)

In this case, the trust in issue was a personal trust and was not a descendible estate.

BL MS. Hargr. 71, f. 111, pl. 2 [Fr. & Eng.] (Dodd's Reports)

On Monday, 9 February, between Adams and Rogers, the case was thus. Dorothy Rogers [was] a servant of the lord Coventry. The lord gave a copyhold to Dorothy for her life, and Dorothy gave a sum to the lord to make it for three lives. The custom of the manor is that the first in the copy can by surrender dispose of the whole. The copy was granted to Dorothy, William, and Edward Rogers for their lives, and it [was] declared [to be] in trust for Dorothy in the copy. Then Dorothy married the plaintiff, Adams, and died without making any disposition of the trust. Her husband took administration and brought his bill against William and Edward to have the estate conveyed.

And upon debate, the court decreed this, because in equity it was, as they said, a personal trust for Dorothy and not for her heir, notwithstanding that it was objected that the trust should go as the land or at least to the heir and not to the administrator because it is of a freehold, but the court said that it was a personal trust for the wife, and the trust could not cease upon the death nor descend to the heir because it was not a descendible estate, and the nominees cannot have it, for [there is] no color for them although they have the legal estate. Query in this case because it seems to me [that] the decree is harsh. See the breviate.

[Other copies of this report: HLS MS. 537(b), p. 64, pl. 1; Oxf. Brasenose MS. 59, p. 82, pl. 3; IU Lilly MS. Parker, 'Cases in the Exchequer, vol. 2', p. 57.]

[Order of 9 Feb. 1702: PRO E.126/17, f. 252v.]

379
Pierson v. Pate (Ex. 1703)

A bill in equity lies to try a suit of mill in order to prevent a multiplicity of litigation.

BL MS. Hargr. 71, f. 113, pl. 1 [Fr. & Eng.] (Dodd's Reports)

Upon an English bill after the end of the term, *scil.* at the setting down of causes in the Temple Hall (Serjeants' Inn Hall being burned down), a bill [was] brought for suit of mill without alleging [it] to be a fee farm or crown mill (as in fact it was not). And it was resolved by all that the bill well lies, and an issue as to the custom [was] directed.

Note that the court said that [there was] no objection in the chancery and that it lies for toll fees etc. and to prevent [a] multiplicity of suits etc. Note that it is contrary to former precedents, but the chief baron [WARD] was positive in it, and it seemed to me that it should well lie.

[Other copies of this report: HLS MS. 537(b), p. 65, pl. 2; Oxf. Brasenose MS. 59, p. 85, pl. 1; IU Lilly MS. Parker, 'Cases in the Exchequer, vol. 2', p. 62; BL MS. Hargr. 70, p. 108, pl. 360; HLS MS. 1162, p. 93, pl. 506.]

[Order of 27 Feb. 1703: PRO E.126/17, f. 312.]

380

Ekins v. Bridges (Ex. 1703)

A deposition taken in a suit that was nonsuited can be used in a later suit between the same parties for the same matter where the witness is dead.

LI MS. Misc. 533, f. [117v] [Eng.] (Ward's Reports)

The plaintiff as rector of Barton Seagrave in the County of Northampton in 1701 exhibited his English bill for tithes against the tenants of Mr. Bridges (but not against him), to which they answered and insisted upon compositions and payments. And after replication, witnesses were examined on both sides by commission in the country taken out by the plaintiff, after which and before any publication had of those depositions, the plaintiff by motion dismissed his bill without the defendants' consent, and in the year 1702 exhibited a new bill in this same court against the same defendants (adding therein their landlord, Mr. Bridges, another defendant) wherein he made the same demands against the tenants, defendants, as he had done by his bill that was dismissed, to which all the defendants answered again and the plaintiff replied. But before any witnesses were or could be examined in this second cause, one Nehemiah Tookey, a material witness for the defendants, the tenants, died. And now *Ettrick* and *Bridges*, of counsel with the tenants, pray that the deposition of Tookey in the former cause that was dismissed might be made use of at the hearing of this second cause saving just exceptions, which was much opposed by *Dodd* and *Browne*, of counsel with the plaintiff, in regard the bill was dismissed and for that no publication ever passed in that cause.

But the whole court considering that it was the plaintiff's own act to dismiss his own bill, and the defendants' witness examined in the first cause dying before any opportunity of examining him again, which was the act of God, it is an hard thing for the defendants to lose his testimony once duly examined, and that only by the plaintiff's act in dismissing his own bill. And the testimony of this witness being material for the tenants could no way be preserved unless a cross-bill, which is hard to put a defendant to where he knew not that the plaintiff would ever proceed further, and if the depositions of this witness were not legally taken, the plaintiff before dismission might, and yet may, object against it, all just exceptions being saved to the plaintiff, and that publication was not passed it was wholly the plaintiff's act and fault in dismissing his bill, whereof he must not take advantage, and the depositions in the first cause being become records of this court, they may be as such ordered to be read and there seems to be no difference in reason in this case between dismission before and after hearing, there being no doubt but that, after a dismission upon hearing, the bill, answer, and depositions not being taken off the file may be and constantly are read as evidence, the dismission being only grounded upon the want of equity for relief and does not destroy what was or might be evidence of fact in the case though possibly not sufficient for relief.

And so the court ordered that the defendants, the tenants, might at the hearing of this second cause make use of the deposition of the dead witness saving just exceptions. But no use [is] to be made of it by defendant, Bridges, who was no defendant in that cause wherein he was examined.

If a witness gives his evidence at a trial *viva voce* and dies, that evidence being proved to be given shall be allowed in any subsequent trial for the same matter. And when a witness is duly examined in a cause and his evidence appears in writing and dies, why shall not that be read upon a question in a future cause for the same thing, though that deposition not published in the former cause only by the means of the plaintiff in dismissing his bill for the reasons *supra*.

Note, at the hearing [of] the cause, the deposition proved wholly insignificant.

[Other copies of this report: GUL MS. B88–9, f. 179.]

[The decree of 26 Apr. 1703, PRO E.126/17, f. 328v, is printed at 1 Wood 416, 1 Eagle & Younge 651.]

[This case is cited in Bosworth v. Limbrick (1777), 2 Rayner 809, 842, 3 Gwillim 1101, 1113, 2 Eagle & Younge 310, 314; Cullimore v. Bosworth (1779), 3 Rayner 934, 938.]

381
Marquess of Carmarthen v. Lord Halifax (Ex. 1703)

A defendant may be granted additional time to answer, plead, and demur to the plaintiff's bill of complaint.

A person cannot sue in equity for an accounting until he has proved his title at common law.

I
LI MS. Misc. 533, f. [118] [Eng.] (Ward's Reports)

[The] defendant not in contempt and being in London prays time till [the] first day next term to answer, plead, and demur without showing any reason for it but from the nature of the bill which is to call the defendant in question for his office of auditor of the receipt of this court and to have account of profits. Time to plead an issuable plea and answer was not opposed by plaintiff's council but only to demur. But the court, being informed that such a motion where [the] defendant was not in contempt was never denied, gave time to answer and plead an issuable plea and demur till last Saturday this term.

[Other copies of this report: GUL MS. B88–9, f. 180.]

II
BL MS. Add. 22609, f. 105v [Eng.] (Wright's Reports)

The plaintiff sets forth in his bill in the exchequer a grant made to him by King Charles II in the year 1676 of the office of auditor of the exchequer after the death of Sir Robert Howard, that Sir Robert Howard died in the year 1698, that the defendant has since got possession of the said office and withholds it from him with the books and records belonging to the same and refuses to account with him for the profits, and therefore prays that he may be put into possession of the said office, books, and records, and that the defendant may discover what profits he has received and account with him for the same.

To this bill, as to all that relates to the possession of the office and the profits of the same, the defendant demurred, but withal [he] answers that he has received in the said office £20. The counsel for the defendant (*Sir Thomas Powys*, Mr. *Cooper*, Mr. *Dodd*, Mr. *Phipps*, and Mr. *Turner*) insisted on these causes of demurrer chiefly that by the plaintiff's own showing, this being an office for life is a freehold and therefore ought to be tried and the title determined at law and not in a court of equity, that the plaintiff might have brought an assize for the office or an ejectment for the house belonging to the office, and having made out his right and title to the office he might have had an action on the case for monies received for his use, but that it is a thing never used to demand the fees and profits before he has evinced his right to the office, by which he is entitled to the same, that the plaintiff has not so much as alleged that he is remediless at common law whereby to entitle himself to the aid and relief of a court of equity, that if this course were allowed, to sue in equity to have an officer of [a] freehold to be put out and another put in without first determining the title at [common] law, there would be no further use of the common law courts, for who would sue at law for lands and inheritances (and freeholds in lands and in offices are the same), if they may begin in a court of equity? etc.

To this the plaintiff's counsel (the solicitor general [*Harcourt*], Mr. *Ettrick*, and Mr. *Brown*) answered that this bill is not merely a suit in equity but an application to the court and to those judges who had the proper powers to give relief, that the Statute 33 Hen. VIII, c. 39,[1] gives a very great and extraordinary

---

[1] Stat. 33 Hen. VIII, c. 39 (*SR*, III, 879–892).

power to the court of exchequer to regulate all matters relating to the revenues of the crown, that this is an office of very immanent concern in the revenue, and therefore in an especial manner subject to the cognizance of this court, that the defendant had in effect overruled his own demurrer, for he had demurred to all that relates to his office or the receipts and profits of the same, and yet he comes afterwards and answers that he has received £20 which being a demurrer and answer to the same thing, the answer, according to the common rule in practice, shall be taken and the demurrer rejected, and where a demurrer is nought and rejected for part, it is so for the whole, that the plaintiff could not bring an assize because he never had seisin of the office, neither could he bring an action on the case for the profits received because he never had possession, etc., to which it was replied that the king's letters patents of grant were a sufficient possession to entitle him to his action on the case, etc.

The barons took time to consider of their judgment till the next day and then allowed the demurrer.

[Orders of 23 Apr. and 2 July 1703: PRO. E.127/23, ff. 20, 84v.]

[This case is cited in Elliot v. Pearne (Ex. 1703–1705), below, No. 384.]

382

Saladine v. Seigmoret (Ex. 1703)

That a plaintiff is an enemy alien is a plea in abatement not a plea in bar.

I
LI MS. Misc. 533, f. [130v] [Eng.] (Ward's Reports)

The plaintiffs exhibited their bill for the discovery of divers letters and other things and divers frauds and trusts touching divers dealings transacted in England between the plaintiffs and [the] defendant and for relief in the premises not charging any particular debt or duty in certain to be due to them.

The defendant put in a plea upon oath in bar of all discovery and relief therein affirming that all the plaintiffs are aliens born out of the queen's allegiance and that two of the plaintiffs at the time of the bill and long before and at the time of the plea were subjects of the French king, then and still the queen's enemy and in open war with the queen, and that they then freely and voluntarily dwelt and traded under the allegiance and subjection of the French king, *viz.* at Lyons in France and not at any other place out of France and the French king's dominions, and then and there were and still are adhering to the queen's enemies. And the whole court overruled this plea.

1. Because it was in bar when it ought to have been in abatement for the disability is but *donec [. . .] communes fuerint*, and like the case

of outlawry, *quousque* when the thing sued for is not forfeited by the outlawry.
2. Here is no disability of enmity shown against one of the plaintiffs whatever may be against the other two.
3. The thing in question and matter of this suit are not forfeited.

Therefore the plea in bar [is] not good, and [it was] so ruled.

[Other copies of this report: GUL MS. B88–9, f. 203.]

II

IU Lilly MS. Parker, 'Cases in the Exchequer, vol. 3', p. 98 [Eng.] (Price's Reports)

[To] a bill to discover dealing and sale of silk between them, [the] defendant pleads in bar that two of the plaintiffs lived in France under the allegiance of the French king and at the time of the bill were alien enemies to the queen of England.

[The] court overruled the plea, the plea in bar not [being] good being entire and no plea to one of the three plaintiffs.

Secondly, the plea ought to be that the plaintiffs were *alienigeni* and born in France under the French king's allegiance and not that they were inhabitants of France and so bound by their local allegiance.

Thirdly, an alien may bring a personal action.

Fourthly, that if the goods of the plaintiffs were forfeited as an alien enemy, there ought to be an inquisition to entitle the queen, and so [there is] no right in the queen until an inquisition [be] found, like the case of an outlawry, for there, upon the outlawry, [the] personal estate is forfeited without an inquisition found, and if sold, though the outlawry was afterwards reversed, there shall be no restitution because there was an absolute property in the queen by the outlawry as in Hoe's Case.[1]

Query [?], for Hoe's Case is directly *contra*.[2]

[Orders of 30 Oct. and 10 and 12 Nov. 1703: PRO E.127/23, ff. 101, 106v, 107.]

383
Attorney General ex rel. Wells v. Brewster (Ex. 1703–1705)

The court of exchequer has jurisdiction over disputes involving rights of a curate appointed by the crown.

---

[1] *Hoe v. Boulton* (1600), 5 Coke Rep. 89, 77 E.R. 191, *sub nom. Hoe v. Belton*, Moore K.B. 468, 72 E.R. 701.

[2] This sentence is in another hand.

A curacy is inseparably incident to the rectory.
A curate serves only during the pleasure of the rector.

I

LI MS. Misc. 533, f. [132] [Eng.] (Ward's Reports)

The plaintiff exhibited an English bill against the defendants and others setting forth that the rectory of St. Botolph's Aldgate came to the crown by the dissolution of monasteries in the time of Henry VIII, that before the dissolution a priest belonging to the priory of St. Bartholomew, whereto that rectory belonged, used to serve the cure and to receive £8 salary or some other sums and £2 for bread and wine for the Communion and this continued to the dissolution. And the king granted it out to such, under whom [the] defendants claim, who covenanted with the crown to pay the curate that £8 and £2 *per annum*. And as the bill surmises the appointment of that curate was reserved to the crown and charged that in fact the crown had all along appointed the curate without disturbance till of late, that the defendants had taken upon them to appoint him, and that they had named Dr. White Kennett[1] who had gotten into possession and obtained license from the bishop of London to preach there, and showed that the queen had appointed the relator to be curate under the great seal who was licensed by the bishop of London to preach there but was opposed and hindered by the defendants, and complained of a verdict in ejectment in the [court of] queen's bench obtained by surprise against Dr. Hollingworth former curate there, who suffered it to pass by default and under color got possession of the pulpit. And to have the right of the crown as to the appointment of the curate settled in this court, and that the relator may be settled curate there and receive the salary, and both queen and relator relieved in the premises was the bill.

[The] defendants demurred and pleaded.

[They] demurred: (1) because [the] matter [is] cognizable at law; (2) because [they] pray relief against a judgment in ejectment.

[They] plea[ded]: pendency of an information for [the] same thing for Savage.

But the plea and demurrer were overruled by the whole court, for as to the first cause of demurrer, it was held that the bill was proper in this court to settle the right of appointing the curate which arises upon the construction of the letters patents, and as this matter relates to the revenue, nor is the right of nomination determinable in the ecclesiastical court, nor has the curate any right to recover the £8 and £2 there, the right of and the obligation to pay it subsisting only by the grantee's covenant with the crown to pay it, and the powers to this court by the Statute Hen. VIII, c. 39,[2] are considerable in this case. And as to the second

---

[1] (d. 1728), *D.N.B.*
[2] Stat. 33 Hen. VIII, c. 39 (*SR*, III, 879–892).

cause of demurrer, the bill is not designed to set aside the said trial but only mentions it, and is no part of the relief prayed by the bill, nor any material part of it.

And as to the plea, it is true that the attorney general did formerly exhibit a bill (which is not dismissed) against the defendants on the behalf of the queen and at the relation of one Savage, who then had the crown title, for settling the right of the nomination of the curate and to have the arrears incurred paid to him. But that curate having resigned his right and title to the queen, and so [is] out of the case. And this bill though it be for the same thing of settling the right of the nomination, yet it is to another purpose and for another person and for the pensions only during the now relator's time, the former bill is become wholly ineffectual and defendants not liable to be prosecuted thereupon, all which appears in this bill.

And so both demurrer and plea [were] overruled.

See Dr. Kennett's plea and demurrer overruled [at] the setting down of causes after Easter Term 1704.

II
LI MS. Misc. 536, f. [12v] [Eng.] (Ward's Reports)

The bill sets forth the crown's right and title to appoint the curate of Aldgate, the impropriation of that parish coming to the crown by the dissolution of monasteries in the time of Henry VIII, the impropriators whereof, *viz.* a prior and convent, having always before appointed the curate with a salary of £8 *per annum* and allowance of 40s. for communions, and the crown having granted out the impropriation to those under whom the defendant claims with a reversion of the appointment of the curate and under a covenant with the crown to pay that salary and allowance to the curate. The bill set forth that the curates, particularly such by name, were placed by the crown and complains that [the] defendant under color of some pretended title from the impropriator had forcibly detained the possession from the relator to whom the queen had granted it, and taken upon him to preach there (though without license) and hindered the relator, and to have the right settled was the bill.

To which the defendant pleaded and demurred but did not answer at all. And for his causes of demurrer assigned, first that he was charged with forcible detainer which is criminous and punishable, secondly that he was charged to pre[ach] without license, which is also punishable both by statute[3] and canon law, thirdly that it is prayed [that] he may discover upon what terms or agreements he came into that curacy, and for plea says there is a bill depending in this court by the attorney general at the relation of one Savage for the same thing, and that the matters of this bill are not properly determinable in this court being of an ecclesiastical nature only.

---

[3] Stat. 2 Hen. IV, c. 15 (*SR*, II, 125–128).

But the court overruled the plea and demurrer in this case in regard [that] there was no answer at all. And it is plain there are many things properly charged which ought to be answered and are not covered by the plea. And though this court meddles not with matters purely of ecclesiastical nature, yet this in question is not so for the crown's right to appoint the curate rises from the letters patents granted of the impropriation and the allowance to the curate subsists wholly by covenant with the crown, none of which the ecclesiastical court can meddle with, all [which] does the curate come in by presentation, [insti]tution, or induction but is a mere donative, nor can any *quare impedit* be brought in this case so that it differs much from other cases of curacy. And the proper remedy is in this court to make the crown's grant effectual it being a court and subject matter of revenue and invested with great powers by the Statute of 33 Hen. VIII, c. 39,[4] nor indeed can the queen or relator be any other way relieved. And as to the word 'forcible' and the parenthesis '(of preaching without license)' and the prayer to set forth the terms and agreements upon which he came in are such things as the defendant is not bound to answer to, yet inasmuch as by the defendant's defect in not answering at all and by the overruling of the plea, the defendant must answer. The court ordered the word 'forcibly' and the words 'of preaching without license' to be struck out of the bill and the setting forth the terms and agreements upon which he came to the curacy to be struck out of the bill, and then he [is] to answer and all without costs.

See Michaelmas 2d of Queen Anne [1703], f. 5, and the judgment of the court, Trinity 1705, among the arguments.

[Other copies of this report: GUL MS. B88–9, ff. 204v, 232v.]

III
BL MS. Hargr. 71, f. 114, pl. 1 [Fr. & Eng.] (Dodd's Reports)

Upon a motion for a sequestration against the Dr. [White Kennett] (who was a Convocation man) for not answering according to an order made for that purpose, three points were debated:

1. Whether he be a proper plaintiff to have it, for the Act about Privilege[5] says 'any person or persons' etc., and the king is not included in it. But the whole court [ruled] that [he was] a proper plaintiff to have it, being a relator.
2. Whether [by] having formerly taken out an attachment and not [having] made an election to proceed, as in the usual form, and not resorting back to the form of sequestration upon the Act of Privilege, [he is precluded]. But the whole court [ruled] against [this].

---

[4] Stat. of 33 Hen. VIII, c. 39 (*SR*, III, 879–892).
[5] Stat. 12 & 13 Will. III, c. 3 (*SR*, VII, 638–639).

3. That a Convocation man's privilege is not taken away by the late Act, for although their privilege be by 8 Hen. VI, c. 1,[6] like the great men and commons etc., yet it is not the privilege of Parliament but [a] like privilege, and like is not the same. And to this point, the chief baron [WARD], BURY, and PRICE [ruled] that the late Act did not extend to members of the convocation, but Baron SMITH was against [them].

These points were resolved upon debate and a week's consideration. See 4 *Inst.* 4;[7] the fourth part of [Prynne's] *Parliamentary Register*, 598, 599.

[Other copies of this report: HLS MS. 537(b), p. 66, pl. 2; Oxf. Brasenose MS. 59, p. 86, pl. 3; IU Lilly MS. Parker, 'Cases in the Exchequer, vol. 2', p. 64.]

IV

BL MS. Add. 35987, f. 110v [Eng.] (Herbert Jacob's Reports)

[This is] a suit in the exchequer by English bill which set forth that one Richard Hollingworth, B.D., grantee of King Charles II of the curacy of Aldgate resigned it to King William III and thereupon King William granted it to William Savage, B.D., for his life, who was put into possession of the desk and pulpit, that William Savage afterwards resigned his grant to Queen Anne and thereupon she granted it to the relator for his life, that the relator upon application to the bishop of London had got a license, that the crown had ever since the dissolution of [the] monasteries (before which the impropriation belonged to the Priory of Christ Church) nominated a curate or chaplain of the said church of Aldgate, and the said Hollingworth, for many years, performed the said cure and received £8 *per annum* of the impropriator, that the defendants Sarah Brewster and Elizabeth Mitchell are heirs at law to Sir Charles Humphreville, late impropriator, and the rectory is descended to them etc., that the defendants, combining to deprive the queen of the patronage, nomination, appointment, and donation of the said curacy or chaplainship, do keep possession of the church and do refuse to admit the relator into the desk pretending they have a right to nominate White Kennett, another of the defendants, and White Kennett pretend to execute the office, that the defendants pretend to have gotten some judgment in ejectment by default upon a demise of a messuage and threaten to take out execution thereupon and to keep possession of the said church and chaplainship and pretend to justify the same under letters patent of King James I whereby the said rectory *inter alia* is granted to Morris and Philips in fee, under whom the confederates claim, that the patronage and donation of the chaplainship or curacy is not granted by the said letters patent, but there is in the said letters patent an exception of the donation, free disposition, and right of patronage of the said church and of all the

---

[6] Stat. 8 Hen. VI, c. 1 (*SR*, II, 238).

[7] E. Coke, *Fourth Institute* (1644), p. 4.

church's vicarages, chapels, and other ecclesiastical benefices whatsoever in the said letters patent contained or belonging or incident to the same, and the crown has ever since been in possession, that therein an express reservation of £10 *per annum* and a covenant by the grantees to pay it, *viz*. £8 *per annum* to the curate and 40s. for bread and wine for the Sacrament and also to indemnify the crown therefrom, that the judgment in ejectment aforesaid ought not to be extended to the church nor be brought to recover the possession of the crown. Therefore the bill prays that the queen's title may be decreed and the defendants' pretenses examined and the relator put into and quieted in his possession and the stipend or salary decreed and White Kennett may account for the profits received since his entry and then be removed from the possession of the church and the judgment in ejectment and all proceedings thereupon may be stayed.

The defendants demurred to the bill as conceiving the matter proper for the courts of common law but not relievable in a court of equity. But the demurrer was overruled and the defendants ordered to answer.

And after answer and proofs in the cause and arguments at large on both sides, now, this term, the barons argued the case *seriatim*.

They considered the case merely as a matter of law upon the letters patent and the execution without relying at all on the proofs in the cause. And therefore I shall state the case as it stands upon the letters patent without going into the proofs or other proceedings in it.

King James I by his letters patent bearing date the 4th of May in the 7th year of his reign [1609] granted to Morris and Philips divers church estates, *viz.* rectories, prebends, vicarages, free chapels, colleges, and collegiate churches, *et inter alia totam illam rectoriam nostram Sancti Botolphi extra Aldgate London necnon omnes decimas, oblationes, et alia proficua et commoditates nostras quaecumque praedictae rectoriae spectanti sive pertinenti (cuidam Georgio Buttenham, armigero, nuper dimisso per particulares annualim redditos sive valoris £22 ultra £10 per stipendium cappellani in dicta ecclesia celebrando et pro pane et vino ibidem annualim allocando) parcellam terrarum et possessionum nuper Priorati Ecclesiae Christi London dissolutae quondam spectantes et pertinentes ac etiam omnia et singula, scil. etc. terras glebales etc. decimas garbarum bladorum granorum et [. . .] lanae, lini, canabis, et agnellorum ac omnes alios decimas quascumque, tam majores quam minores, oblationes, obventiones, fructus, proficua, etc. redditus reservatos super quibuscumque dimissionibus et concessionibus etc. reservationes etc. annuitates annuales solutiones, pensiones denariorum summas solutiones pro decimis vel in satisfactione decimarum seu oblationum etc. proficuum, commoditatum, advantagium, emolumentum, et hereditamentum nostra quaecumque* etc. to the premises belonging or appertaining or reputed or enjoyed as parcel or member thereof and the reversion and reversions of the premises expectant upon any demise or demises for lives or years or otherwise and all rents and yearly profits reserved upon any demise or demises of the premises and the rents and yearly profits of all and singular the said premises except *tamen semper et nobis heredibus et successoribus nostris omnino reservationes omnibus et singulis advocationibus, donationibus, liberis dispositionibus, et juribus patronatus omnium et singularum ecclesiarum, vicariarum, capellarum, et aliorum beneficiorum ecclesiasticorum quorumcumque premissis aut alicui inde parcella spectanta pertinenta incidenta appendenta vel incumben.* to have and to hold the said rectories etc. and all and singular the premises (except for exceptions) to the said Morris and Philips and their heirs to the use of them and their heirs to hold of the king, his heirs, and successors as of his manor of East Greenwich in free and common socage *reddendum inde annualim nobis heredibus et successoribus nostris de et pro praedictae rectoriae Sancti Botolphi extra Aldgate London ac pro omnibus decimis et ceteris premissis eidem rectoriae spectanti et pertinenti £22 legalis monetae Angliae* at the receipt of the exchequer or to the hands of the king's bailiffs or receivers of the premises for the time being at Michaelmas and Lady Day by equal portions yearly forever *pro omnibus exactionibus et demandis et praefatis Fr. Morris et Fr. Phillips pro se, heredibus, executoribus, et assignatis suis ulterius conveniunt et concedunt ad et cum nobis heredibus et successoribus nostris quod ipsi praefati Fr. Morris et Fr. Philips, heredes et assignates suis £8 legalis monetae Angliae capellan. divin. celebran. in Ecclesia Sancti Botolphi extra Aldgate London praedicti pro tempore existente pro stipendio suo de praedicti rectoria Sancti Botolphi extra Aldgate London praedicti annualim exeundo ac pro pane et vino et alio necessario ibidem annualim allocando annualim per solvent. aut solvi facient. ac nos, heredes, et successores nostros acquietabunt, exonerabunt, et indemnes conservabunt imperpetuam in cuius rei* etc.

Baron SMITH argued for the defendants that the bill ought to be dismissed. He said he would consider what the office of a curate is and secondly how this curacy in question stood before and since the dissolution of the monasteries and if it can be distinguished from common cases of curacies.

He took notice that the letters patent granted the rectory and also all tithes, oblations, and other profits and commodities whatsoever belonging to the rectory lately demised to [the] value [of] £22 beyond £10 for the stipend of the chaplain *in dicta ecclesia celebrandi* and for bread and wine *ibidem annualim allocandi* and that then there followed in the grant the general words of all tithes (as before set out in the stating [of] the case) and that then came the exception and the covenant by the grantees (both also before set out).

As to the first point, what the office of a curate is, he said he is but the servant of the impropriator to celebrate divine service for him and is removable by him at pleasure and his salary depends upon the bill of the impropriator or such agreement as he makes with him, and so is Godolphin, *Collection of Ecclesiastical Laws*, 376, and the case of Bott v. Sir Edward Brabalon, Noy 115,[8] where the

---

[8] *Bott v. Brabalon*, J. Godolphin, *Repertorium Canonicum* (1680), p. 376, pl. 56, Noy 15, 74 E.R. 986, 1 Eagle & Younge 160.

impropriator sued in the spiritual court for tithes and the defendant obtained a prohibition upon a suggestion that time out of mind there had been a curate or an incumbent by the appointment of the impropriator, who administers the Sacraments etc., and that by the custom of the parish the curate was to have all the tithes renewing within the parish except *decimis graniorum*, which were paid to the parson, and that every[one] who had so paid the tenths to the curate was discharged against the parson etc. But after a consultation was granted without argument for such, [a] curate cannot prescribe against his master, that may remove him at his pleasure.

As to the second point, how this curacy stood before and since the dissolution of monasteries and whether it can be distinguished from other curacies, he said that that impropriation belonged to the Priory of Christ's Church and that the possessions of that monastery were surrendered to Henry VIII in the twenty-third year of his reign [1531], that while this impropriation was in the Priory, they probably supplied the cure by some person belonging to them then [?], until Henry VIII leased out the rectory, there was no certain salary appointed for the curate as far as can be made [to] appear, that in the thirty-fourth year of Hen. VIII [1542 x 1543] the rectory was leased out and, in that lease, there was a reservation of £8 *per annum* for the curate and 40s. *pro pane et vino*, that it continued thus in all probability until the time of Queen Elizabeth, that that was observable upon these leases, that the lessees covenanted to appoint a curate and to pay him the salary of £8 *per annum*, and that the lord treasurer might in case he saw fit increase the curate's salary, that from all this it appeared that this curacy was all the while it was in the crown under the same circumstances as all other curacies are, and that as to the £8 reserved by the chaplain upon the leases, that was only for his maintenance, for £8 was thought at that time a competent maintenance for a priest, and that appears by the Statute of Pluralities,[9] which makes an acceptance of a 2d.[10] living an avoidance of the first where the first is above the value of £8 and not otherwise.

He said that if this curacy did not differ [?] from any other, then it would follow clearly that the right of nominating the curate is in the impropriator, as it is in all other cases except it be taken from him by the exception. And for that, he cited Dyer 58b,[11] where the case was [that] the king leased a rectory reserving a rent above the value of the benefice, and in the lease was a clause of grant by the king to discharge the lessee *de omnibus et singularibus pensionibus et denaris summis exeuntibus de rectoria*, and the question was in the court of augmentations whether the king or the lessee should be bound to find a curate. And there Dyer says that by the opinion of many, if a common person leases a rectory rendering

---

[9] Stat. 21 Hen. VIII, c. 13, s. 9 (*SR*, III, 293).
[10] sic in MS.
[11] *Taverner's Case* (1545), 1 Dyer 58b, 73 E.R. 128.

rent and there is no clause in the lease that the lessee shall find the curate, the lessor shall do it. But at last it was decreed in this court that the lessee should be allowed £4 towards the stipend of the curate.

As to the exception, he said it had not been made a question but that the words of the execution might be satisfied without extending it to the curacy, nor secondly was it pretended that this curacy was within the exception in express words. But it is excepted that there are words in this exception that will extend to the curacy and that the exception ought to be taken in the largest and most expressive[12] sense the words will bear according to the usual construction in [the] case of [a] grant of the crown.

In answer to which, he said that before the Statute *de Prerogativa Regis*, 17 Edw. II, c. 15,[13] which enacts that where the king grants a manor or lands *cum pertinenciis* that advowsons or *dotes cum accidunt* belonging to the said manor or lands shall not pass unless express mention be made of them in the grant, the grants of the crown were construed as the grants of subjects, and it would have been for the honor of the law if there had been less in the books upon the differences in construction between them. Staunford, in his *Prerogative*, 42, 43,[14] in his exposition upon the Statute, holds that grants of the crown ought to be construed differently from the grants of subjects by that Statute, but unless it be in such cases as are within that Statute, the grant of the crown ought to be construed as a subject's grant.

He said he did not question but [that] the nomination of a curate might have been excepted by proper words, but he did not think it was excepted within the words of the exception, and the words ought not to be strained beyond their natural sense. The words in the exception that are chiefly relied upon are *liberis dispositionibus et ecclesiasticorum beneficiorum* the words free *dispositionibus* to take in the appointment and ecclesiastical benefices, the curacy, the thing to be excepted. It is a rule in [the] expounding of grants that the words of them must be construed with regard to the words that accompany them, and the words advowsons, donations, and rights of patronage cannot be applied to a curacy, for nobody was ever said to be a patron of a curacy, and consequently neither shall the general words 'free dispositions'. He said that the words 'free dispositions' signified no more than presentation, and he cited the case put by Littleton, 14 Edw. IV, 2b,[15] that if a man grants to me *liberam dispositionem ecclesiae suae cum proxime vocaverit*, that is as good and strong as a grant of *proximae presentationis* etc.

[Other copies of this report: BL MS. Hargr. 66, f. 150.]

---

[12] Sic in MS. for 'expansive'.
[13] Stat. 17 Edw. II, c. 15 (*SR*, I, 227).
[14] W. Staunford, *Exposition of the Kinges Prerogative* (1567), ff. 42–43.
[15] YB Hil. 14 Edw. IV, f. 2b, pl. 2 (1475).

V

IU Lilly MS. Parker, 'Cases in the Exchequer, vol. 3', p. 202 [Eng.] (Price's Reports)

A bill [was filed] in the exchequer for the curacy of St. Botolph Without Aldgate, being in the queen's gift, and £8 *per annum* payable to the chaplain by Brewster, the impropriator, that the lord keeper granted to the relator the said curacy.

The defendant [Samuel] Brewster insists that in the right of his wife, who was impropriator of the said rectory as daughter and heir of Sir Charles Humfreville, who claims under a grant made the 25 May 7 Jac. I [1609] to Morris and Phillips and their heirs the rectory of St. Botolph Without Aldgate and all title etc. then in lease to George Puttenham at £22 *per annum ultra £10 pro stipendio capellani* in the said church to be celebrated and for bread and wine to be found, formerly belonging to the Priory of Christchurch, except to him, his heirs, and successors and reserving all advowsons, donations, free dispositions, and right of patronage of all churches, vicarages, chapels, and other ecclesiastical benefices whatsoever part of the premises *spectantes, pertinentes, incidentes, appendentes, et incumbentes* etc. The grantees covenant by the said grant with the crown that they will yearly pay £8 *per annum* to a chaplain *ad divina celebrandum* in the parish church of St. Botolph for his stipend *de rectoria de St. Botolph exeunta* and 40s. in the like manner for bread and wine *et nos et heredes et successores nostros inde acquietos, exoneratos, et indemnificatos conservabunt.*

The attorney general insists that, by the exception, the disposition of the curacy of St. Botolph is in the crown, that Dr. Hollingsworth held this rectory twenty years by grant from the crown dated 18 August 33 Car. II [1681] and [in] 6 Will. & Mary [1694] had a decree in the exchequer against Sir Charles Humfreville[16] for the stipend of £8 and the arrears, being £52.

For the defendant, Mr. *Ettrick*, Mr. *Dodd*, Mr. *Phipps*, Mr. *Broderick*, Mr. *King*, and Mr. *Salkeld* [argued] that several leases have been made of the rectory:

4 February 19 Eliz. [1577], [there was a] lease to Ro[bert] Holliwell for twenty-one years of the rectory at £22 rent. [The] lessee covenants to find at his own charge *convenientem et habilem presbyterum* to do divine service and to repair the chancel.

8 June 30 Eliz. [1588]. [There was a] lease to George Pulman for forty years from the expiration of [the] former lease, [the] lessee to find [a] curate, as before, and pay such salary as the lord treasurer should appoint. This term ended [in] 1638.

13 April 1632. Sir Thomas Reynold and J. Aylworth (who were trustees for Gotts and Bridget, his wife, who had the fee of the rectory) lease [the] rectory for

---

[16] *Hollingworth v. Umfreville* (1694), 1 Wood 332.

thirteen years to Chancey, and [they] except the nominating and appointing [of] the minister and the allowance which the lessee was to pay.

1 April 1647. [There was] another lease of the said rectory by Bridget Gotts [and] Sir Thomas Reynold to Mr. W. Humfreville and Mr. Henry Hardcastle for twenty-one years, except the appointing [of] a minister, which the lessee was to maintain, if Bridget so long lived.

20 February 1656. Sir Thomas Reynold [and] William Humfreville lease to William Cutler and William Latham for eleven years, except the appointing and placing [of] a minister. It was agreed [that] the lessee [was] to name two and the lessor to choose and covenant, [the] lessee to pay [the] curate as [the] lessor should direct.

There were papers purporting [to be] orders from Mrs. Bridget Gott to displace Vyner from the curacy and put in one Gibson and after[wards] Zachary Crofton and Simson and after him Mr. John Maccaness.

For the defendant, it was said that this exception does not reserve the right of the curacy in the crown, it being neither an advowson, donation, *libera dispositio*, or *jus patronatus*. The grant is to Maurice and Phillips as large as Patman then held it, and there the lessee was to find a curate and to pay the curate. Dyer 58b.[17]

It implies [the] lessee [*blank*] being allowed towards the stipend it argues if in the parson's lease there had been an agreement [that the] lessee might name [the] curate.

Hobart 59. The nature of an exception is to restrain part of the thing before granted and not of a new thing not granted.

1 Modern 90[18] [holds] that free chapels were originally colleges, some belonged to the king, some to other persons, and he that was in was entitled as incumbent not stipendiary.

A bishop cannot visit a donative. If [a] bishop does or oblige the minister to take a faculty of preaching, a prohibition lies, but if it be a chapel and the chaplain, there, it may be otherwise. *Ibidem*. [There was] no resolution, and [it] rather enforces that chapelries are visitable by the bishop.

Yelverton 60, Farechild v. Gaire.[19] Chief Justice Popham held that [as to] a donative, the patron was not bound to collate and might receive the profits and sue for the tithes in a vacation in the spiritual court. It was first settled by consent of the ordinary and parishioners. The other four judges [were to the] contrary, that the ordinary could compel [one] to collate, and if not, the patron, but

---

[17] *Taverner's Case* (1545), 1 Dyer 58, 73 E.R. 128.

[18] *Allane v. Exton* (1672), 1 Modern 90, 86 E.R. 756, also 2 Keble 876, 84 E.R. 554.

[19] *Farechild v. Gaire* (1605), Yelverton 60, 80 E.R. 42.

the *rectoria* is exempt from the ordinary's jurisdiction. All the judges held that the church in the execution of the charge is spiritual and a mere layman cannot be collated, as the king may [collate] a layman to a deanery, it being a temporal function, the ordinary cannot correct him for heresy preached but [the] patron by commission may examine and deprive. 33 Edw. III, 103; 13 Edw. IV; 6 Edw. III.[20] [A] grant *de ecclesia* passes [the] advowson, but must now note a donative has not any license.[21]

Godolphin, *Repertorium*, 200, 201. [An] ecclesiastical benefice extends to dignities as well as parochial benefices; it must be spiritual and in its nature perpetual and are either presentative or donative. And a parochial church may be a donative and [be] exempt from ordinary jurisdiction as, where the king founds a church or chapel, he may exempt it from ordinary jurisdiction, and [it] is visitable by the lord chancellor or a subject by [the] king's license; it is visitable by the founder and his heirs. If a donative was an ecclesiastical benefice was a question. And Lyndwood, c. [*blank*] and determined St. Martin Le Grand to be [an] ecclesiastical benefice.

[A] chaplain is not a freehold, but [he is] removable at will *ad nutum rectoris*.

The crown may present by parol because by institution the party is brought before the bishop, which is a sort of record and thereon [is] induction, which is a possession.

These stipends are the acts of the court of augmentations upon granting churches out of the crown. There are four churches in the same grant as this, and the impropriator provides the curates.

Free chapels, as [in] the Tower [of London], are by institution, and donatives are granted for life.

A curacy is no ecclesiastical benefice.

[An] impropriator or appropriator is a perpetual parson, whereas parsons of the gift of a patron are only for life. A curacy is not severable from the impropriation, for it is part of it and [is] granted by the owner, and where [an] impropr[iation] is, a grant of an advowson of it is void.

The bill takes notice of the grant of the curacy to Savage by King William [on] 22 January 1700[/01] and that it was surrendered, but that does not appear.

[A] grant of a rectory and except[ion of] the advowson is good. General grants without usage [are] not good, as grants of tithes in pernancy.

Dr. Hollingsworth's decree does not bind the right, but [it] decreed the stipend to be paid to him who served the cure, and the attorney general was no

---

[20] YB 23 Edw. III, Lib. Ass., f. 108, pl. 8 (1349); YB Mich. 13 Edw. IV, f. 3, pl. 5 (1473); *Plecy v. Ragle* (1332), YB Mich. 6 Edw. III, f. 44, pl. 31.

[21] Sic in MS.

party to it. 3 Levinz 82, Carver v. Pinkley.[22] His continuing so long by leave of the bishop, patron, and dean, it amounts to a new nomination. A debt lies upon a lease made by a stranger. A stipendiary priest or donative or curacy is within the Statute of Conformity,[23] 13 Car. II, c. [*blank*]; and of augmentation, 29 Car. II;[24] and the Statute 31 Eliz., c. [6], against simony,[25] notwithstanding [that] they mention presentations. Cro. Car. 330, Bawderock v. Mackall,[26] presentation [of a] curate to the Tower of London. This case shows [that] curacies are to be augmented and are ecclesiastical benefices and within several acts as within the mischief.

There are many rectories and vicarages in the grant which answer the exception and not to stipendiaries and curacies which are incident to an impropriation and goes along with the church and by the impropriation, the patronage is dissolved, and it remains a perpetual incumbency, and the curacy [is] not severable from [it] no more than a court baron from a manor.

Keilway 48b.[27] In every case of [an] appropriation of a benefice to a religious house, the patronage is gone forever. 2 Leonard, *idem*, 3 Leonard 101, Queen v. Lord Lumley; Hobart 304, *idem*, Hobart 303, London v. Chapel of the Collegiate Church of Southwell; Noy 15, Bolt v. Sir Edward Brabason; Chancery Rep. 1696, Rectory of Hamsteed; Ley's Rep. 14, Stafford's Case; 2 Rolle, Abr., *Parson and Patron*, 337, *idem*.[28]

This case imports the Act of Dissolution[29] vests in the crown in as large a manner as the prior had it or was reputed to have, though originally it was otherwise, as the vicarage was formerly endowed. [Note] that upon the dissolution of [the] monasteries, a stipend was reserved for the curates and the grantee of the rectory provided them and paid them.

3 Rep., in [the] Marquess of Winchester's Case; 3 Edw. III, 74.[30] Hospitallers shall not have a rectory appropriated to be the Templars, though [by] the

---

[22] *Carver v. Pinkney* (1682), 3 Levinz 82, 83 E.R. 588.

[23] Stat. 14 Car. II, c. 4 (*SR*, V, 364–370).

[24] Stat. 29 Car. II, c. 8 (*SR*, V, 849–850).

[25] Stat. 31 Eliz. I, c. 6 (*SR*, IV, 802–804).

[26] *Bawderock v. Mackall* (1633), Cro. Car. 330, 79 E.R. 889.

[27] *Anonymous* (1503), Keilway 48, 72 E.R. 206.

[28] *Regina v. Lord Lumley* (1584), 2 Leonard 80, 74 E.R. 373, 3 Leonard 101, 74 E.R. 567; *London v. Chapter of the Collegiate Church etc.* (1618), Hobart 303, 80 E.R. 447; *Bott v. Brabalon*, Noy 15, 74 E.R. 986, 1 Eagle & Younge 160; perhaps *Attorney General v. Combe* (1679), 2 Chan. Cas. 18, 22 E.R. 825; *Stafford's Case* (1609), Ley 14, 80 E.R. 595, 2 Rolle, Abr., *Parson, Patron*, pl. H, 1, p. 337.

[29] Stat. 31 Hen. VIII, c. 13 (*SR*, III, 733–739).

[30] *Marquis of Winchester's Case* (1583), 3 Coke Rep. 1, 76 E.R. 621; YB Trin. 9 Edw. III, f. 25, pl. 24 (1335).

Stat. 17 Edw. II,[31] all their possessions are translated to Hospitals as the Templars held them because it was an inheritance inseparable annexed in privity.

35 Hen. VI, c. 6.[32] The statute says the Hospital shall hold as the Templars, yet [they] shall not hold in frankalmoigne, because the tenure consists in privity.

Curates are stipendiaries and servants put in by the rector, and there were no licenses for curates till Wycliffe's time.

8 Rep. 82, Vynior's Case.[33] This case is who intended that Vynior's deputation and authority were revocable, and so a curate may be placed or displaced at will.

Hobart 13, Norton v. Simmes.[34] This is compared to the case of a curate that is removable.

4 Rep. 33, Mitton's Case.[35] [A] grant by the queen of a county clerk or shire clerk is void, being incident to the office of a sheriff and cannot be divided from it. [A] grant of [the] office of exigenter in [a] vacancy of [the] chief justice of the common pleas is void. And custody of gaols are incident to sheriffs.

By the exception of [the] advowson, which is the right of patronage, [the] donation is a donative; *libera dispositio* is of a free chapel; *ecclesia* is the rectory; there is no vicar, nor no chapel but a rectorial church, and a beneficed church must be a fixed estate and permanent, which cannot extend to a curacy.

Spellman, *Glossarium*, 'Beneficium'; Fresne, *Glossarium*, 529, 'Beneficium'.[36]

The court of audience gave the judgment for the impropriator and looked on the attempt to be a novelty. The priory served the cure by the monks; it was never presentative nor a donative.

Patronage is *jus disponendi*, and, when appropriated, it is the perpetual gift and cannot be vacant and must find a curate as incident.

There are so many things granted which answer the exceptions in the grant. Fitzherbert, *Natura Brevium*, 32, 33b.

Note [that] the curacy is not named nor grantable not being *in esse* to grant being incorporated in the rectory impropriate. An ecclesiastical benefice is a freehold and not a stipendiary, which is a burden to the crown or the impropriator. Spelman's *Reliquiae*, published by Dr. Gibson: a feudal estate was a lay fee.

If [it had been] a grant to a parson or vicar, which is but for life, saving the naming of the curate, it had been bad, much more such a saving out of an

---

[31] Stat. 17 Edw. II (*SR*, I, 194–196).
[32] *Bishop of Winchester v. Prior of St. John* (1457), YB Pas. 35 Hen. VI, f. 56, pl. 2.
[33] *Vynior v. Wilde* (1609), 8 Coke Rep. 80, 77 E.R. 595, also 1 Brownl. & Golds. 62, 123 E.R. 666, 2 Brownl. & Golds. 290, 123 E.R. 948
[34] *Norton v. Simmes* (1614), Hobart 12, 80 E.R. 163 (re deputy sheriffs).
[35] *Mitton's Case* (1583), 4 Coke Rep. 32, 76 E.R. 965.
[36] H. Spelman, *Archaeologus*; C. Du Fresne, sieur Du Cange, *Glossarium*.

impropriation, which is an inheritance, or a perpetual rectory. The parson or rector before the dissolution of [the] monasteries was answerable for the curate and to see the church well served.

[An] advowson does not pass by a *cum pertinenciis*. To appoint a curate is not a nomination for that a *quare impedit* lies for a nomination, and so it does for a parsonage or vicarage. [It] is a freehold and has institution and induction. 1 Ventris 15, Heath v. Pryn.[37]

The covenant to pay [the] stipend was necessary in behalf of the grantee to be at a certainty [as to] what he was to pay to the curate. Otherwise the ordinary would visit and oblige him to give possibly more for to find a curate or chaplain.

If the crown designed to except [the] chaplain and curate, it might have been as easily expressed as other words and as easily as it is expressed in the covenant that the stipend was to a chaplain to read prayers in the rectory of St. Botolph.

Dr. Kennett said that Dr. Hollingsworth surreptitiously got the grant from the crown where no instance was before. The king never grants by parol and therefore if granted might be found, but [a] patron may because he presents his parson to the bishop to be examined and to be instituted and inducted.

The impropriator has the ordinary right to name a curate, and there are none otherwise in England, it being inherent in his interest.

There were *liberae capellae regis*, which were erected by the kings in their manors and for the service of his tenants. There were *capellae annexae matrici ecclesiae*. What the common law is, but this is the common law of the Church of England.

The parsons did find vicars till they were endowed, and then [they] had the presentations to them, but the alteration must be intended by the consent of the ordinary, patron, and incumbent when [he was] endowed. No pope with all the plenitude of his power ever divided the curacy from the rectory because it was inseparable and as an adjunct, as a shadow to a body, and as transubstantiation in religion is as reasonable.

The consequences are bad, if the gift was in the crown, it being a burden to the crown and the stipend but small to serve a large cure, and the impropriator who does now augment the stipend cannot be supposed to do it if not nominated by him, most grants have this exception, and yet the crown in five hundred such grants does not name any curate, but the impropriator [does].

It will be a mischief to the bishops, who can oversee curates and oblige the impropriator to find a sufficient person, but if the grant or nomination is in the crown, it is visitable only by the lord chancellor.

The stipend of £8 *per annum* to be paid to the chaplain does not argue anything, for it is the same the prior paid, and the king grants it as the prior held it, paying this rent.

---

[37] *Heath v. Pryn* (1669), 1 Ventris 14, 86 E.R. 11.

Sir Edward Northey, attorney general, [argued] for the plaintiff that the queen and the relator, Mr. Wells, who claims the curacy under her grant ought to have the rights decreed and [the] salary or stipend paid.

This stipend was not paid by the prior, but after the dissolution of [the] monasteries, it was settled in the court of augmentations that every church should have a stipend or salary. [By] the leases of 19 and 30 Eliz., the lessee covenants to find [a] curate and to pay him the said stipend. The grant [was] made [in] 7 Jac. I to Morris and Phillips in fee of the rectory of St. Botolph, which was in lease to George Puttenham at the yearly rent of £22 over and above £10 for a stipend for a chaplain and to find bread and wine in the said church. This shows what the value of it was, and the stipend was over and above it, and so [it was] no charge upon the lessee or grantee, and it was the measure for the value by which it was disposed of.

The exception is of the free disposition of all ecclesiastical benefices touching or belonging to the premises or any part thereof. Everything that is of benefit that belongs to the said church and is distinguished from [the] advowson, donation, right of presentation of churches, vicarages, and chapels and the other word, free disposal of all ecclesiastical benefices seem to be appropriated to the several curacies and the stipend annexed.

The curacy is not inseparable from the rectory. The lessees of the crown found curates by covenant, *habilem et convenientem presbyterum* to perform divine service in the said church at his own charge and costs and to pay £22 *per annum* over and besides for twenty-one years, and [there was] another lease after for forty years, which latter lease has a covenant to find a curate and to pay such salary as the lord treasurer shall appoint, except the advowson of the church of St. Botolph and the mesne assignments in 1632, 1647, and 1656 had an exception of appointing the minister, and yet [the] lessee covenanted to pay the salary.

It is not incongruous that one should name and appoint and another [should] pay him.

Curacies are of a new nature and arise since the dissolution of [the] monasteries. That the exception is answered by [an]other part of the grant is not enough, but also the exception takes in the thing in question. It is not a charge to the crown to find a curate since the impropriator pays the stipend. [The term] donation is not confined to donatives but [applies] to the gift of any ecclesiastical benefice.

29 Car. II, c. [8],[38] for augmentation of small vicarages. Curacies were taken notice of; the same relation a patron has to an incumbent, an impropriator has to a curate.

Dr. Hollingsworth's decree is for the duty and the arrears against Sir Charles Humfreville, under whom Brewster claims.

---

[38] Stat. 29 Car. II, c. 8 (*SR*, V, 849–850).

Sir Simon Harcourt, solicitor general: The usage of nominating the curates is not fully proved.

The exception [of] the advowson of the Church of St. Botolph in the lease [of] 1630 is to prevent doubts [about] what is granted, the lease [of] 1646 and [the] 1656 exception of the nomination to the lessor, which shows it was not designed to go in grants.[39]

The placing and displacing [of the] curates by Bridget Gotts and William Humfreville no time nor no authentic instrument under seal.[40]

The usage since the Restoration [1660] is with the crown.

This curacy is separable from the rectory and is capable to be excepted and is so in the most extensive words that can be, which are in favor of the crown, and if they were of a common person, they were sufficient. The grant takes notice of the church, of the chaplain, of the stipend to be paid and by whom, and makes an exception of the free disposal of all ecclesiastical benefices. Plowden, *Com.* [310], the Case of the Mines,[41] in construction of the king's grants.

The construction in cases of the crown, where the grants are taken in the stricter sense, and why should not the same be taken in the largest sense where there is an exception to a grant. There is no onus on the crown when the impropriator pays the stipend.

Mr. *Cooper*: The usage for seventeen years last past is clear with the crown, which does explain what was dark before. If Hollingsworth was under Arden and after[wards] took a grant from the crown, it argues that he took that to be the better title. The exception must be of something granted before, which was the rectory, and it does except the free disposition of ecclesiastical benefices belonging to the premises, that is, to the rectory, and what is that but the church and the stipend.

To argue upon general words of the import of benefices and to apply it to particular purposes or meaning is no true way of arguing. The grant says nothing of *capella annexa* or of the king's free chapel or of vicars perpetual but the disposal of ecclesiastical benefices belonging or incident to the premises.

The covenant is on [the] grantee to pay [the] salary and yet not to name the curate; so did the lessees. They paid the salary and [the] lessor named the curate. There was no need of mentioning the nomination of the curate in the covenant, since it was fully excepted out of the grant.

2 Rolle, Abr., *Parson & Patron*, 334.[42] Abbot, being parson appropr[iate], is patron [of the] vicarage and presents [the] vicarage by name of the parsonage;

---

[39] Sic in MS.
[40] Sic in MS.
[41] *Regina v. Earl of Northumberland* (1567), 1 Plowden 310, 75 E.R. 472.
[42] 2 Rolle, Abr., *Parson, Patron*, pl. [I], 10, p. 338.

this disappropriates the parsonage and [they] are both one parsonage and re-united.

[The] patron has [the] right in the vacation to the rectory but not the profit, as the king held of a deanery of his free chapel or dean and chapter of a prebendary vacant not in abeyance as to the right. [An] advowson is *jus mixtum*, begins by our law by presentment of the laity, and [is] perfected by the law of the church, which belongs to the ordinary.

A deanery [is a] spiritual promotion, not temporal, and the nomination and patronage may belong to the king, yet [it] is temporal.

A donative of the king, as the Tower of London with cure, a parochial church, may be a donative, and [the] parson resign patron no ordinary and visit by patron no ordinary,[43] [a] mere *laicus* [is] not capable of a donative parochial, but [a] clerk *infra sacros ordines* [may be put in] by lay donation and not by admission and institution, yet his function is spiritual.

Com. 496.[44] An abbot appropriate is with cure of souls and differs from another parson, but one is perpetual [and] the other for life.

All bishops in England were donatives in the crown till King John's time. And so they are now in Ireland.

Note [that] if [the] rector appropriate in this case should present to the rectory, who should have the stipend, and if there must be a curate and the second presentment belongs to the queen being new[ly] creat[ed].

The difference between a parson and his vicar of his gift and a parson appropriate and his curate are only in respect of their donation, and, as the vicar may be of the gift of another as well as the parson, so may a curacy.

The crown is *persona mixta* and may grant the rectory to a layman and reserve the curacy. He gives the bishops their temporalties, and he that had the gift of the bishop may be entrusted with a curacy better than a layman. Though [it is] the grant of the crown or the exception in the grant, yet it is to be construed favorably for the crown as far as may be [in order] to answer the intention.

Mr. *Browne*: This grant [of] 7 Jac. and the reservation of [the] £8 *per annum* stipend as a provision for the curate is about the third part of the value, which was the usual reservation for vicars and stipendiary curates.

Ley Rep. 14, Stafford's Case, before.

The king's design was to reserve the curateship (he grants *cappellanum ministrantem*) and grant a stipend of £8 *per annum* and except the disposition of what the chaplain had.

---

[43] Sic in MS.

[44] *Grendon v. Bishop of Lincoln* (1577), 2 Plowden 493, 496, 75 E.R. 734, 737, also Benlow 293, 123 E.R. 206.

A curate is several from a lay rectory, and the impropriator may turn him out at pleasure. The decree of Dr. Hollingsworth is full in the case, being for the stipend and arrears.

In Easter term 1705, the court of exchequer gave their opinion in this case.

Lord Chief Baron WARD [held] for the attorney general and the relator and that the defendant ought to pay the relator the salary of £8 *per annum*. Dugdale, *Monasticon Anglicanum*, 2d vol., 80, [says] that the appropriate church of St. Botolph was appropriated to the Priory of Christ Church, London, time out of mind, that the appropriation being destroyed or determined on the surrender, that then the church becomes presentative and belongs to the crown as[45] donor.

Hobart 307, Winch v. Gerrard; Colt v. Glover.[46] Dyer, Grendon's Case,[47] [was] that the appropriation to an ecclesiastical person if granted to a lay person, he has the church and revenue, if granted to him, but no cure of souls is incident to the layman's grant, and he is only obliged provisionally to find a curate, and [it is] not inseparably inherent.

2 Cro. 218, Britton v. Wade,[48] parson and vicar of the same church, both have cures, one *actualiter*, the other *spiritualiter*. And in the case [of] Parry v. Parker, where [there was] an impropriator and vicar, the bishop shall not destroy or annul the vicarage, for thereby the cure will be lost.

[*blank*] Abr., 202. A cure is not inseparably incident to a rectory in a lay hand; when in [a] prior's hands, he was able to serve the cure, and when in the king's hands, he was *persona mixta*.

The intent of the grant was to save the disposition of all ecclesiastical benefices to the crown. [A] grant of [a] rectory carries the revenue but not the cure, if [there is an] express exception saving the naming of curates to such and such rectories.

Other ecclesiastical benefices is other than are beforenamed. [An] incident belonging or incumbent on the premises, that is on the rector to do.[49] [The] covenant [was] that the grantee pay the salary and the crown nominate. [The] lease [of] 1632 of the rectory has the same exception as the grant [of] 7 Jac.

The king may present by parol. Moore 744; 1 *Inst.* 120.[50]

---

[45] or *MS*.

[46] *Wright v. Gerrard* (1618), Hobart 306, 80 E.R. 449; *Colt and Glover v. Bishop of Coventry* (1612), Hobart 140, 80 E.R. 290.

[47] Dyer 294, note, 73 E.R. 660; *Grendon v. Bishop of Lincoln* (1577), 2 Plowden 493, 75 E.R. 734.

[48] *Britton v. Wade* (1618), Cro. Jac. 515, 79 E.R. 440.

[49] Sic in MS.

[50] E. Coke, *First Institute* (1628), f. 120.

Dr. Hollingsworth claims the curacy by right from the crown, and Sir Charles Humfreville claims the right in him, that the decree being on the grant goes further than the bill, which is not in the case of a decree for tithes.

The remedy is adequate, [the exchequer] being a court of revenue for a revenue granted by the crown and [a] trust in the crown.

Baron BURY, Baron PRICE, and Baron SMITH [held] for the defendant that by the grant of [the] rectory, the curacy was incident, that the words or intent of the exception did not except the curacy, and the reservation of £8 a year was thought a good reservation. The Stat. 21 Hen. VIII says that one having £8 *per annum* takes [. . .] having that salary is according to the contract. [A] curate [has] no fixed right, but is changeable *ad nutum rectoris* and shows how ecclesiastical benefices were construed by the several statutes and canons, how the curacy was inseparably incident, as by many cases.

[The final decree of 3 May 1705, PRO E.126/18, f. 489, is printed at 1 Wood 455.]

[Connected cases: Wells v. Kennett (Ex. 1703), LI MS. Misc. 533, f. [131], GUL MS. B88–9, f. 203v; Hollingworth v. Umfreville (1694), 1 Wood 332.]

384
Elliot v. Pearne (Ex. 1703–1705)

The king may allow colonial governments to make laws for themselves.

A court of equity can make a personal order against a party that is within its jurisdiction though it concerns land outside its jurisdiction.

A person can have a remedy in equity in reference to land without first proving his title at common law where there is an impediment to an action at law, as where the title deeds are not available.

I
LI MS. Misc. 533, f. [135v] [Eng.] (Ward's Reports)

The plaintiffs by their bill seek a discovery and account of and for the profits of a plantation in Antigua and of Negroes left upon it at the death of one John Lingen about the year 1688 and entitle themselves as heirs at law to the said Lingen, who married one Katherine Watts, who was seised in fee of that plantation, and by their bill set forth that by the laws and custom of the province of Antigua that if a man marries a woman seised in fee of a plantation there and they two by deed of feoffment with livery and registered in the courts there do convey the same to any other person in fee, that such conveyance being confirmed under the seal of the province is a good and lawful conveyance in fee and passes such plantation to the feoffee and his heirs as fully and effectually as a fine would do if in England, and that that is the usual and indeed only way for married women to pass their inheritances by and they are and have been always held legal and sufficient and enjoyed accordingly. And then [they] show that the 10th of August 1681 Lingen and his wife by deed of feoffment so executed and registered for £2000 conveyed the said plantation to Rowland Williams, Esquire, and his heirs, and that the 13th of the same August, Williams for £2000 to him paid by the said John Lingen did by like deed of feoffment and so executed and registered convey the said plantation to the said Lingen in fee, and that the said conveyances and estates were confirmed by letters patent under the seal of that province, and show that by like laws and customs all Negroes upon any plantations there do go to the heir and along with the plantation unless in case of debts and charge that divers Negroes and their produce were upon the plantation at Lingen's death, which and the said plantation did by Lingen's death duly come to and descend to the plaintiffs as his heirs at law (showing how they are heirs) and they ought to hold and enjoy the same and the profits thereof, but are disabled so to do by the defendants, who pretending to claim under the said Katherine, the wife and relict of Lingen, have got into possession of all the said premises and have possessed themselves of the said feoffments and letters patent and other the evidences whereby they are disabled to bring any action or try their title at law. And to avoid the plaintiffs' remedy have removed themselves into this Kingdom of England and reside here where no process out of the courts in Antigua can reach them or be effectual. And therefore plaintiffs pray discovery and relief in the premises.

The defendants as to all discovery and relief for the plantation and Negroes and the produce of them do demur and by answer deny one deed charged upon them (but not the letters patent) and admit the custom and right that Negroes go along with the inheritance of the plantation.

And [they] assign for cause of demurrer:

1. That the title by which the plaintiffs claim is insufficient in law being under a married woman without a fine.
2. That this court has not any power to give any relief in the premises to the plaintiffs, it appearing that the matters in question lie and are in Antigua, where this court has no jurisdiction.
3. That the plaintiffs ought to have no discovery or relief in equity till they have affirmed their title at law not having shown anything that disables them in law from so doing.

But the chief baron [WARD], BURY and PRICE barons (*dissentiente* SMITH) overruled the demurrer upon these grounds:

1. That the title set forth by the plaintiffs appears to be such an one as the laws and customs of that province do allow and which there are of the same effect with a fine, which laws and customs being those

of the province and established there and confessed by the demurrer that they are such, this court cannot say they are void in law because not the same as in England, for those laws flowing from the crown and being for the government of that place are as much the laws of that place as our laws here are the laws of England. And the king may appoint them (or give them power to make) such laws for themselves and government and management of their estates as he and they please. Nor is it inconsistent with the customs and usages in some places in England that a married woman may bar herself and issue without a fine, as by deed enrolled in Hastings. Infants at fifteen may make feoffments.
2. That though this court has not power over the estate of the plantation, yet in respect [that] the thing here sought for is a discovery which must be had from the persons of the defendants, and they being here in England the plaintiffs can have it nowhere but from them here, for they are out of the reach and power of the process and courts of Antigua and so to have it here or nowhere. 4 *Institutes* 213, Egerton's Case,[1] trust of a term of lands in Chester, defendant lives out of [the] jurisdiction, suit [was allowed] in chancery here.
3. (Which is in answer to that great objection) that though the plaintiffs have not affirmed their title at law, yet they have shown an impediment why they have not nor cannot do it. And that is because the defendants have gotten into their hands the feoffments and letters patent which are their title at law and without which they can bring no action, and there is a difference in this case where the persons and estate are in different and distinct jurisdictions and where they are both under the same, for if this demurrer stands to all relief and discovery some of the deeds and patents what though the defendants should have denied all (as they have not) does that denial make their demurrer good which without such denial was surely a good cause in equity, and then if the plaintiffs here should proceed for the deeds and patents and prove them in defendants' hands, what relief should he have upon his bill for the mesne profits which they will be entitled to by reason of such detainer of the deeds.

See Liber M, f. 3, Acton and Lawton,[2] as to jurisdiction where defendant lives out of it.

---

[1] *Egerton v. Earl of Derby* (1614), 12 Coke Rep. 114, 77 E.R. 1390; Pl. 10, 1 Eq. Ca. Abr. 137, 21 E.R. 940; E. Coke, *Fourth Institute* (1644), p. 213.
[2] *Acton v. Lawton*, LI MS. Misc. 559.

Note at defendants' desire this plea and demurrer was set down again and came to be argued Tuesday 30 October 1705. And the court took time to consider.

And [they] gave the same opinion Monday 10 December 1705, *viz.* SMITH for and the other three against [the] demurrer.

[Other copies of this report: GUL MS. B88–9, f. 208v.]

II

IU Lilly MS. Parker, 'Cases in the Exchequer, vol. 4', p. 45 [Eng.] (Price's Reports)

[The] plaintiff exhibits a bill to have an account of a plantation in Antigua and of the Negroes and stock and profits, to have possession decreed, and discovery of writings.

[The] defendant pleads to part and demurs and answers to part:

1. [That the] cause was that the plantation had particular laws and customs and ought, being local, to be tried in the plantation.
2. That the title ought to be tried before there could be a bill for the profits.
3. That the plaintiff sets forth a conveyance of the plantation by a feoffment from John Lingham, under whom the plaintiff claims, and his wife and does not allege that they passed a fine, being [that] a married woman cannot convey without it.
4. That, by an Act of the Assembly,[3] all deeds are to be registered and that the deeds the plaintiff seeks a discovery of are registered there.
5. That by an Act of Assembly [in] 1692[4] where there was quiet possession five years and a nonclaim, it was a bar.

And the defendant answers and denies the deeds.

The bill is for that this court has a jurisdiction of causes arising in the plantation, this being one of the Caribby Islands, which were taken and not conquered and by way of occupancy by English subjects, who do not lose their allegiance but carry that and the English laws with them, which they make use of, but where there are acts made by their Assembly and approved of by the sovereign, they are like by-laws and, for any matter of law, a writ of error lies out of the queen's bench, and where there is a colony plantation or colony where the thing is local and the parties live there, the jurisdiction is kept there, but if the matter be local and the party live out of the jurisdiction, it gives jurisdiction here,[5] otherwise [there would be] a failure of justice.

---

[3] Act of 1668, *Acts of Assembly Passed in the Charibbee Leeward Islands* (1734), p. 31.
[4] Act of 1692, *Id.*, p. 80.
[5] there *MS.*

4 *Inst.* 213, Sir John Egerton v. Earl of Derby; 1 Chancery Rep. f. 40, Hil. 14 Car. II, Edworth v. Dacres; 2 Chancery Rep., f. 188, M. 2 Jac. II, Lord Kildare v. Sir Maurice Eustace; 145, Robinson v. Noel; 2 Ventris 358, *idem*; 2 Chan. 249, where [a] bill against proceeding in the fen [?] courts pleaded the Statute of Draining, and [it was] allowed, being [that] it touched the public.[6]

218, East India Company v. Maidston,[7] who accounted in the Indies, and [it was] allowed on an appeal, which being pleaded was overruled.

214, Cartwright v. Pettus,[8] [an] account [for] profit between two joint tenants in Ireland but [who] were in England [was] allowed good, being personal, but bad for a partition.

[It was said] that there lies an appeal from decrees in the plantations to the queen and [privy] council.

31 July 1701. [The] committee of appeals on their report to the lords justices from a decree in the chancery of Barbados, and it was reversed and confirmed by [the] lords justices in council and ordered that the chancery in Barbados should proceed to the merits of the cause and not be[9] bound by the decree made in the chancery in England.

As to the power of foreign plantations, so 3 Modern 159, Sir John Witham's Case,[10] [for] assault and battery and [to] justify [it] by the laws of Barbados. Lord's Cases, the same case.[11] Grotius, *De Jure Belli*, lib. 2, c. 8, s. 6; lib. 3, c. 6, s. 6; Vaughan 290, 291, 402; 7 Rep., Calvin's Case, 20.[12]

---

[6] *Egerton v. Earl of Derby* (1614), E. Coke, *Fourth Institute* (1644), p. 213, 12 Coke Rep. 114, 77 E.R. 1390, 1 Eq. Cas. Abr. 137, 21 E.R. 940; *Edgworth v. Davies* (1662), 1 Chan. Cas. 40, 22 E.R. 684, 2 Freeman 159, 22 E.R. 1129, Nelson 66, 21 E.R. 791, 1 Eq. Cas. Abr. 137, 21 E.R. 940; *Lord of Kildare v. Eustace* (1686), 2 Chan. Cas. 188, 22 E.R. 905, 1 Vernon 405, 419, 423, 428, 437, 23 E.R. 546, 559, 561, 565, 571, 1 Eq. Cas. Abr. 133, 21 E.R. 938; *Robinson v. Noel* (1683), 2 Chan. Cas. 145, 22 E.R. 887, 2 Ventris 358, 86 E.R. 484, 1 Eq. Cas. Abr. 299, 21 E.R. 1059, 2 Chan. Rep. 248, 21 E.R. 670, 1 Vernon 90, 453, 460, 469, 23 E.R. 334, 580, 585, 594; *Brown v. Howard* (1678), 2 Chan. Cas. 249, 22 E.R. 929; Statute of Draining: Stat. 22 Car. II, c. 14 (*SR*, V, 687–689), or Stat. 15 Car. II, c. 17 (*SR*, V, 499–512).

[7] *East India Co. v. Maidston* (1676), 2 Chan. Cas. 218, 22 E.R. 916.

[8] *Cartwright v. Pettus* (1675), 2 Chan. Cas. 214, 22 E.R. 916.

[9] being *MS*.

[10] *Wytham v. Dutton* (1688), 3 Modern 159, 87 E.R. 103, Comberbach 111, 90 E.R. 374.

[11] *Dutton v. Howell* (1693), Shower 24, 1 E.R. 17.

[12] *Craw v. Ramsey* (1670), Vaughan 274, 290, 124 E.R. 1072, 1079; *Anonymous*, Vaughan 395, 402, 124 E.R. 1130, 1133; *Calvin's Case* (1608), 7 Coke Rep. 1, 20, 77 E.R. 377, 401.

As to the objection that [a] married woman join in a feoffment, who knows the custom of Antigua, and it is laid to be the usual way, being registered, as in London [where] married women pass land by deed enrolled.

The answer, though in part, admits the jurisdiction.

Though, regularly, a title ought to be tried before an account for the mesne profits, as in the case of the Lord Halifax and the Marquess of Carmarthen by [a] bill for the profits of the office of the auditor of the exchequer, on [a] demurrer [it was] allowed good because [the] title to [the] office [was] not first tried. Trinity term, exchequer, 1703.[13] But [the] parties being here, how could the title be tried at Antigua. The plantations are partly real, partly personal, and are not so local as land, and so the bill may be both for the title and profit together.

Chief Baron [WARD], Barons BURY and PRICE [were] for overruling the plea and demurrer, and the plaintiffs [were] admitted to except to the answer.

Baron SMITH [was] for admitting the demurrer.

[Orders of 3 and 30 Nov. and 9 Dec. 1703 and 30 Oct. 10 Dec. 1705: PRO E.127/23, ff. 105, 124v, 141, 141v; E.127/24, ff. 200, 225.]

385

Brockman v. Randolph (Ex. 1704)

A demurrer in equity cannot allege new matter.

The owner of a rent out of a manor can have discovery from the owner of the manor to find out the boundaries, rents, and value of the manor.

LI MS. Misc. 536, f. [19v] [Eng.] (Ward's Reports)

The plaintiff as owner of a fee farm rent of £260 *per annum* (anciently reserved to the crown) out of the manor of Aldington in Kent (consisting of a small demesne but of a great many rents of assize and rents services), of which fee farm rent the plaintiff is a purchaser from those that purchased it from the crown, exhibited his bill to be relieved for the said rent and to have discovery of the boundaries and rents and value of the manor surmising that [the] defendant, who is owner of it, is about [the] enfranchising [of] many of the tenants and sinking the rents of assize and rents services whereby his remedy for the rent may be straitened and prejudiced and not enough left to pay it.

---

[13] *Marquess of Carmarthen v. Lord Halifax* (Ex. 1703), above, No. 381.

The defendant set forth a tender of the rent due with a deduction of 4s. in the pound for taxes and sets forth the clause in the Act 1 Anne, f. 232,[1] for the auditors, reeves, and receivers to allow 4s. in the pound for all fee farm and other rents under penalties and demurs to the bill as to discovery of boundaries or rents or value of the manor in regard [that he] may have his rent deducting 4s. in the pound according to the Act.

But the court, *seriatim* delivering their opinion, overruled the demurrer holding that the plaintiff is entitled to have such discovery and that that is sufficient cause for such overruling. And the defendant must not demur upon matter set forth in his answer though it be by Act of Parliament, for every demurrer must be to the imperfections in the plaintiff's bill and not to be supported by anything out of the bill. And they all declared their opinions that the plaintiff is only to allow proportionably for his rent with what the defendant pays for his manor and not 4s. in the pound absolutely, for the clause in that Act, ff. 19 and 20, which gives power for owners of lands to deduct for fee farm and other rents issuing out of their lands, says it shall be proportionably with the owners of the lands tax and that equality is the justice that the Parliament thought was fit between owners of land and rent. And the clause [at] f. 232 goes only to such fee farm and other rents which are in charge before the auditors and receivers and not to those absolutely sold away and out of charge, that clause only enjoining penalties for those rents before auditors alters not the generality of the privilege given [at] ff. 19 and 20, and it has been so ruled in [the] case of Sir William Williams and Dolben.[2] And the defendant here was ruled to answer with costs.

[Other copies of this report: GUL MS. B88–9, f. 237v.]

[Orders of 25 Oct. and 15 Nov. 1705: PRO E.126/18, ff. 534v, 538.]

[Affirmed on appeal: *Lords' Journal*, XVIII (n.d.), p. 197.]

386
Attorney General v. Jeffreys (Ex. 1704)

A general demurrer goes to the entire bill, and, if any part of the bill is good, the demurrer will be overruled.

The actions of commissioners to receive royal taxes can be examined in the court of exchequer.

Goods belonging to the crown are not liable to taxation.

---

[1] Stat. 1 Ann., stat. 2, c. 1, ss. 3, 4, 69 (*SR*, VIII, 89, 90, 145, 146).
[2] Perhaps *Dolben's Case* (1666), 1 Keble 872, 881, 83 E.R. 1292, 1298.

LI MS. Misc. 536, f. 1 [Eng.] (Ward's Reports)

Attorney General versus Sir Robert Jeffreys, Sir Robert Beachcroft, *et al.*, commissioners in the City of London by virtue of an Act of Parliament made in the first year of Her Majesty's reign entitled an Act for Granting to Her Majesty Several Subsidies for Carrying on the War against France and Spain (fo. 447).[1]

By [an] English bill or information of Hilary term 2 Anne [1704], it is set forth that Emanuel Scroop, How, and others therein named, commissioners for the prizes appointed by Her Majesty under the great seal of England the 27th of July last, pursuant to a power by that commission granted to them by a public sale by inch of candle, sold and disposed (pursuant to the power by the said commission given to them) the cargo of the prize ship (called *The Star of the East*) lying in the ward of Lime Street, London, [of the] value £30,000 to divers persons and in several lots and shares, in particular what lots and of what goods and to whom and for what, and that the said persons, the buyers, were obliged to pay the queen the sums of money agreed for the prices thereof according to the usual terms of the sale then published and to be performed by the buyers, and until the goods paid for to the commissioners and the terms of sale performed and an order by the commissioners for their delivery, the goods were to lie in the queen's warehouse in the custody of James Mellifont, Her Majesty's storekeeper, for prizes for securing the payment of the moneys;

That Procter, a broker in London, did about (but no time mentioned) dispose or declare his interest in eight of those lots bought as aforesaid to be in William Lucy, linen draper, who the 25th of January last paid to the receiver of the prizes £573 for the same and had an order from the commissioners of the prizes for delivery thereof and expected to have the goods delivered to him;

That by virtue of the aforesaid Act, 50s. for every £100 value of goods in stock were to be raised throughout England, and a blank sum [?] appointed [?] to be raised on all stocks in the City of London and the commissioners directed to appoint assessors and collectors thereof with [the] usual powers for issuing warrants for levying and, for non payment thereof, for distraining and disposing the distresses for payment of the subsidy;

That the commissioners divided the said sum, (being blank) to be levied upon the City of London into several proportions in each ward, and directed that £760 or some such sum should be levied on Lime Street Ward where the cargo lay, and made Skinner and three others by name to be collectors in that ward for the stocks, which ought to have been collected and paid into the exchequer at the times appointed by the Act;

---

[1] Stat. 1 Ann., stat. 2, c. 17 (*SR*, VIII, 186–202).

But the commissioners (naming Jeffreys, Beachcroft, Chamberlain, and Shepherd), living in that ward combining with the said collectors and others (prayed to be made parties when discovered) designing to ease themselves of that subsidy and the proportions of it in that ward, having great stocks themselves, particularly Chamberlain £15,000, liable to be taxed contriving to assess the same or the greatest part thereof on the said prize cargoes, so ordered it that instead of £760 as first appointed to be assessed on the said ward, advanced the same to £1160, which was £400 more to be applied to what purpose they pleased and towards the £1160 assessed the said cargo of the said prize ship (in or about June last) with £750 for their part thereof and without making the said £400 to issue out of the said ward, the same would have been chargeable above the said £750 but with £40;

That in [the] prosecution of that contrivance, an assessment was made of the said £750 on the said cargo in the hands of Mellefant and that Chamberlain was charged but with £400 stock;

That soon after the confederates took off from the said Mellifant that £750 or part thereof and laid it upon the buyers of the cargo, who had bought the same before or near the time of making that assessment, and continued it till the buyers by appeal procured themselves to be discharged thereof;

That the said commissioners and assessors for the said ward, resolving to ease themselves and to raise the money on the said cargo, at a meeting with other commissioners for London, making about 100, the first of February 1703[/04], set up the former pretended assessment of £750 on the said cargo in the hands of Mellifant (though at [the] first making he had no notice left for him nor was he discharged by any application made by him or any other on his account). And the commissioners, the same instant the assessment was made the 1st of February 1703[/04], signed a warrant for distraining the said cargo without making demand of the tax, and the assessors and collectors came to the warehouse in Lime Street and found Mellifont delivering the goods to the buyers by order of the commissioners of prizes and distrained the same threatening immediately to sell them;

Whereas in truth the said cargoes and goods were not within the jurisdiction of the commissioners for the said tax or subsidy (being Her Majesty's goods) nor had they power to assess or charge the same towards the said subsidy;

And the first assessment being discharged, the commissioners by the said Act had no power so long after appointed by the Act for making the assessment and after the greatest part of the goods [were] delivered to the buyers to assess Mellifant for the same, who was only the queen's servant and had the possession of the goods for the queen till sale and after sale for Her Majesty for securing the money for which [they were] sold;

And Mellifant the 2d of February applied to the commissioners for taxes and offered to swear that the goods so distrained were prize goods and that he had the custody of them only for the queen and offered the queen's counsel's opinion for their discharge, but the commissioners refused restitution;

That the confederates refuse to discover the books and orders and proportion of the ward to the tax;

All which are against equity and tend to the queen's prejudice and lessening her revenue and to ease the inhabitants of the ward from paying their shares and proportions of the subsidy by casting it upon the said cargo and goods belonging to the queen and thereby constraining Her Majesty to pay the greatest part of the subsidy charged upon the said ward;

Therefore the attorney general prays discovery and relief in the premises and the assessment upon the said goods and cargo to be discharged and laid upon the said ward etc.

To which bill the defendants thereto, being two of the commissioners and the three assessors and collectors, put in a general demurrer:

That inasmuch as the information is to call the defendants to an account and to question their proceedings and inquire into the methods of the same as some of them are commissioners by the Act and to put it in execution in London and to levy the money for the service of the crown wherein, as they are advised, they are entitled to the assistance of the attorney general and not to be sued by him, they demur to the information and pray judgment whether they shall be compelled to answer thereto and for causes of demurrer do show:

1. That the matters in the bill for which relief is prayed are concerning the public taxes and assessments in London and charged upon it by the said Act and against the defendants as some of the commissioners and persons acting by virtue of that Act therein acting for the service of the crown.
2. That the bill is brought against the defendants as commissioners of the said taxes.
3. For that it appears by the said Act and the attorney general's own showing that there are several other persons appointed commissioners in London and who acted as such in the execution of the said Act and in this particular case who are not parties to the said bill.
4. That the bill is to enquire into the proportions of the tax set upon a particular ward in London and to know if the same has been duly assessed and collected, whereas by the Act one gross sum is set upon the City and particular charges upon the stocks and personal estates to make up the same, which the raising and collecting of which the commissioners are entrusted as the Act directs.

5. That the bill is to enquire into the stock of some of the defendants liable to be taxed and to question the defendants for a partial execution of the Act and to examine the regularity of their proceedings and the assessments made in pursuance of the Act and to defeat, alter, and avoid those assessments and collections, which ought not to be done in this court.
6. For that the defendants are charged by the bill with altering the assessments after they were made without any regular proceedings or appeal in an extraordinary manner.
7. For that the taxes and assessments and the manner of apportioning, raising, levying, and collecting thereof is by Act of Parliament left to the commissioners, who are thereby made judges of the same, and all matters of difference relating to the taxes or the assessing or levying of the same are by the Act appointed to be finally heard and determined by the commissioners and not elsewhere or by any other judges or persons as advised, and the methods and manner of the determining thereof are set down and appointed in and by that Act, and insist that this court will not intermeddle therein.

For which and other defects, they demur to the bill.

Baron SMITH opens the bill and demurrer at large and holds the demurrer being general is bad; [he] considered [that] the Act holds the queen's prize goods in [a] warehouse and storekeeper's hands not taxable not being sold to any, that the commissioners' proceedings in cases not in their jurisdiction are examinable in this court and the queen [is] relievable. [A] general demurrer confesses all that is well alleged, and what is a proper charge must be answered, and the charge that these were the queen's goods in June, 1703, when the first assessment was put upon Mellifont ought to be answered.

After the buyers charged and then the commissioners discharged Mellifont but after recharged Mellifont upon the fact of the first assessment in June when they were the queen's goods and unsold [was] without question.

Baron PRICE [was] against the demurrer for the same reasons. [The] commissioners met at Lady Day and assessed in May and no assessment after [was] good. Terry and Huntington[2] as to jurisdiction; exceeding jurisdiction takes it away.

I [Chief Baron WARD] delivered my opinion in this case that the demurrer, being to the whole bill and thereby shutting out all answer and examination to

---

[2] *Terry v. Huntington* (1668), Hardres 480, 145 E.R. 557.

or for any [of] the facts and matters charged by the bill and relief thereby sought, ought to be overruled.

It is not to be contested but that the commissioners, acting according to the powers and directions by the Act given them, are not to be called in question for so doing in this court, but if they should act contrary and to the manifest wrong and injury to the crown and against the manifest trust in them reposed by the Act, or if they shall intermeddle with things without their jurisdiction, as by [the] taxing of persons or things not taxable within or by the Act, surely they may be called in question for the same in this court by bill in behalf of the crown or by action at law on behalf of the subject.

And in regard [that] by this bill it is suggested that the defendants both commissioners and assessors, have assessed and by warrant levied the queen's goods, being prize goods in the hands of her servant being store keeper, and that before they were sold, which goods were not then taxable by law, and when they were sold and so by law might be taxable, then yet the commissioners thought fit to discharge the vendees under a pretense as if they had bought them tax free from the commissioners of prizes (which is a fact not admitted but required examination), and then they recharged the queen's officer as for goods in his hands upon the first assessment, which was not good, they then being the queen's own goods, and this last recharge affirming that first irregular assessment, it seems plain that these and some other suggestions and allegations of fact charged in the bill ought to be answered unto in order to receive the judicial determination of the court in the premises, which must all be stifled if this demurrer stands.

And so the demurrer was overruled by the whole court, Baron Bury not being in court when the demurrer was argued and so gave no opinion of it.

[Other copies of this report: GUL MS. B88–9, f. 223.]

[Orders of 21 Feb. and 7 Dec. 1704: PRO E.127/23, f. 171v; E.127/24, f. 34.]

387

Bridges v. Jeffreys (Ex. 1704)

In this case, a jewel, not being paraphernalia and not being subject to a particular bond, passed under the husband's will and not under his widow's will.

IU Lilly MS. Parker, 'Cases in the Exchequer, vol. 3', p. 95 [Eng.] (Price's Reports)

The plaintiff [Edmund Bridges] as administrator to his wife, who was daughter to Sir Thomas Street, claims a breast diamond jewel. Sir Thomas Street [in] 1686 in consideration of marriage to Ro[bert] Row[land] Berkeley's daughter gives a bond [with the] condition that she might dispose by deed or will all the personal estate she was then possessed of or should be. Sir Thomas Street gives her a jewel before marriage and after marriage [ex]changed it for a better

[one]. In 1695, [he] makes his will and gives his wife all his goods, except plate, linen, and jewels, and devised the residue to his executor in trust for the plaintiff's wife. And he died first; his wife survived and made her will and recites Sir Thomas Street's will and the exception and gives the residue to the defendant, [Benjamin Jeffreys].

1. Query if Sir Thomas Street's bond carries any gift or personal estate his wife had from him or any other after the bond and before or after marriage.
2. Whether this jewel being what she wore for [an] ornament where the Lady Street might claim it as a paraphernalia.

[The] chief baron [WARD] and Baron BURY [were] for the plaintiff. Baron PRICE and Baron SMITH [were for the] defendant.

Cro. Car. 343, Lord Hastings v. Douglass; Jones 332, *idem*; Croke agreed with Jones's opinion; Rolle, Abr., *Executors*, 911, *idem*; Moore 213, Viscountess Bindon's Case; 2 Leonard 166, *idem*;[1] 7 December 7 Will. [1695] in the chancery before Lord Somers, Sir John Fort v. Weymouth and Taylor.[2]

21 June 1704. The cause was reheard, Mr. BOYLE, the chancellor of the exchequer, present. He, Chief Baron WARD, Baron BURY, and Baron SMITH, who changed his opinion, [were] for the plaintiff, and Baron PRICE [was] for the defendant.

[Order of 9 Dec. 1703: PRO E.127/23, f. 142.]

388
Archbishop of York v. Duke of Newcastle (Ex. 1704)

The issue in this case was whether payment of something tithable itself could be a valid modus in lieu of a tithe.

IU Lilly MS. Parker, 'Cases in the Exchequer, vol. 3', pp. 153, 167 [Eng.]
(Price's Reports)

[Upon] a tithe bill as farmer of the rectory of Kibburn in the County of York by Baines as lessee to the archbishop [of York], the defendant insists that the several farms were part of the demesnes of the Abbey of Byland, which was one of the great monasteries and of the Cistercian Order.

---

[1] *Lord Hastings v. Douglas* (1632), Cro. Car. 343, 79 E.R. 901, W. Jones 332, 82 E.R. 175; 1 Rolle, Abr., *Executors*, 'Paraphernalia', pl. 9, p. 911; *Viscountess Bindon's Case* (1585), Moore K.B. 213, 72 E.R. 538, 2 Leonard 166, 74 E.R. 447.

[2] *Foach v. Weymouth* (1695), PRO C.33/285, ff. 247, 394v, 395, 395v.

1. They insist upon a *modus* of ten fleeces of wool and two lambs and one half or 18d. for the half lamb at midsummer or after, when demanded, in lieu of a tithe for Bosomworth Farm.
2. A *modus* of six fleeces of wool and three lambs in lieu of small tithes for Cawkerdale farm.
3. The *modus* of eight fleeces and 4s. in money [on] 25th June in lieu of all tithes of Rowland Farm.

Upon the hearing, this was made a case, the plaintiff insisting that the two first moduses are void in law and the last is not true in fact and will try it.

[It was said] that tithe in kind of anything tithable [is] not [a] good *modus* for any other thing tithable. Query.

Moore 911, Gresham v. Lucas, *alias* Dr. Lewis; 909, Sherrington v. Fleetwood; 454, Monday v. Lovice; *idem*, 1 Rolle, Abr., *Disme*, 651, n. 16; Goldsborough 147, Sherrington, as before; 2 *Inst.* 608; 3 Cro. 446, Gresham v. Lucas, *alias* Lewis, same as before; 475, Sherrington, as before; 786, Ingoldsby v. Johnson; Moore 909, Sherington, as before; 2 Lutwyche 1052, Morton v. Briggs; 2 Keble 2, Hutchingson v. Atkinson; 2 Rolle Rep. 38, 62, Mascall v. Price; 1 Rolle 172.[1]

For the defendant, [it was argued] that this land belongs to the Abbey of Byland, which is discharged of tithes. The Stat. 31 Hen. VIII, c. 13,[2] does discharge it in the patentee's hand as it was in the abbot, and if this was a good *modus* in the abbot's hand, it is so now.

3 Cro. 276, Scory v. Baber; 1 Rolle Rep. 120, Hooper v. Andrews; Hobart 39, *idem*; Dyer 149; Hobart 44, *idem*; Moore 863, Hooper v. Andrews, as before; Noy 148, Sharp v. Sharpe; Moore 909; Hutton 58, Pool v. Regineld; Owen Rep. 34; 3 Keble 705, Hud v. Hill; Cro. Jac. 501, Moore v. Bullock; Stat. 31 Hen. VIII, c. 13, for dissolution of monasteries; Cro. Eliz. 206, 216, Nash v. Molyns; Cro. Jac. 607, Gerrard v. Wright.[3]

---

[1] *Gresham v. Lucas* (1596), Moore K.B. 911, 72 E.R. 991, *sub nom. Grysman v. Lewes*, Cro. Eliz. 446, 78 E.R. 686; *Sherington v. Fleetwood* (1596), Moore K.B. 909, 72 E.R. 990, Gouldsborough 147, 75 E.R. 1055, Cro. Eliz. 475, 78 E.R. 727; *Monday v. Lovice* (1596), Moore K.B. 454, 72 E.R. 690; 1 Rolle, Abr., *Dismes*, pl. D, 16, p. 651; *Ingoldsby v. Johnson* (1600), Cro. Eliz. 786, 78 E.R. 1016; *Morton v. Briggs* (1696), 2 Lutwyche 1043, 125 E.R. 580; *Hutchingson v. Atkinson* (1666), 2 Keble 2, 84 E.R. 1; *Mascall v. Price* (1614), 1 Rolle Rep. 38, 62, 176, 81 E.R. 310, 328, 412; E. Coke, *Second Institute* (1642), p. 608.

[2] Stat. 31 Hen. VIII, c. 13 (*SR*, III, 733–739).

[3] *Scory v. Baber* (1592), Cro. Eliz. 276, 78 E.R. 531; *Hooper v. Andrews* (1912), 1 Rolle Rep. 120, 81 E.R. 372, *sub nom. Cowper v. Andrews*, Hobart 39, 44, 80 E.R. 189, 193, Moore K.B. 863, 72 E.R. 957; *Parson of Peykirke's Case* (1576), 3 Dyer 349, 73 E.R. 784, 1 Eagle & Younge 66; *Sharpe v. Sharpe*, Noy 148, 74 E.R. 1110; perhaps *Sherington*

The Stat. 31 Hen. VIII, c. 13, for discharging extends to personal as well as real discharges. And upon this Statute, it was offered for the defendant that this *modus* was a discharge of tithes in kind and that [the] said Act has established it and made it good in law.

It was said that [tithe of] wool and lamb was to be paid at midsummer or when demanded and that this is more than [the] defendant was obliged to do, but ewes upon yeaning and where any labor is done and other care taken, it shall be a cons[tructio]n.

[It was said] that the ten fleeces and two lambs and one half were to be paid whether there was any wool or lamb that year, and it is not said [that] wool and lamb did arise on the farm and they were obliged to pay it whether they had it or not of the land.

How [can] they pay half [a] lamb, for it must be a tithe or none at law, since all *modus decimandi* are intended to be founded on real compositions, and why not eighty fleeces and two and one half lambs as well as land or money or any other thing.

9 November 1704. This day the barons gave their judgment upon the three moduses in this case.

Chief Baron WARD [ruled] for the defendant that the three moduses were good in law, that a *modus* was a real composition, that anything that is valuable is the same as money, if certain and permanent, it extinguishes all tithes in kind, that there is no case in the law which says that things tithable may not be a composition for the tithe of another thing.

Dyer 349, recited in Hobart 39, Cooper and Andrew's Case,[4] where tithe of wool and lamb before the dissolution of monasteries was a discharge by [the] Stat. 31 Hen. VIII, of tithe corn and hay.

Cistercians might prescribe *in non decimando*.

Baron BURY [held] for the plaintiff that all [of] the three moduses were illegal being a tithe paid for a tithe, which must be intended a tithe, which if not showed to the contrary, there being nothing to distinguish it from tithe in kind.

The *modus* is uncertain as to the value of fleeces and lambs, and one half a lamb is against reason.

---

v. Fleetwood (1596), Moore K.B. 909, 72 E.R. 990; *Poole v. Reynold* (1612), Hutton 57, 123 E.R. 1098; *Lord Rich's Case*, Owen 34, 74 E.R. 880; *Huit v. Hill* (1676), 3 Keble 705, 84 E.R. 964; *Moore v. Bullock* (1618), Cro. Jac. 501, 79 E.R. 427; Stat. 31 Hen. VIII, c. 13 (*SR*, III, 733–739); *Nash v. Molins* (1590), Cro. Eliz. 206, 78 E.R. 462; *Wickham v. Cooper* (1591), Cro. Eliz. 216, 78 E.R. 472; *Gerrard v. Wright* (1621), Cro. Jac. 607, 79 E.R. 518.

[4] *Parson of Peykirke's Case* (1576), 3 Dyer 349, 73 E.R. 784, 1 Gwillim 136, 1 Eagle & Younge 66; *Cowper v. Andrews* (1612), Hobart 39, 80 E.R. 189, 1 Eagle & Younge 240, also Moore K.B. 863, 72 E.R. 957, Godbolt 237, 78 E.R. 138, *sub nom. Hooper v. Andrews*, 1 Rolle Rep. 120, 81 E.R. 372, 1 Gwillim 275.

Baron PRICE [held] for the plaintiff for the two first moduses and for the defendant for the third *modus* as being a thing tithable which was to be the composition for another thing tithable and that a tithe is not to be paid for a tithe, as 1 Rolle, Abr., 651.[5]

The third *modus* being wool [and] lamb and 4s. in *modus*[6] were good because the fleeces and lamb might be intended [to be] tithe for them and the 4s. for the rest.

Baron SMITH [held] for the defendant that the three moduses were good. Littleton, sect. 344; Co. Litt. 212b; and Peyto's Case in 9 Rep. 78,[7] [a] forfeiture [of a] condition to pay a sheaf [?] or ring; the condition is performed as much as if money were paid; the acceptance is the foundation.

He agreed that a composition for one sort of tithe [is] not good for another but believed anything tithable is as valuable as money and may be paid for money, and [he] took the wool and fleeces not to be tithes but [a] *modus* for all other tithes.

An issue at law upon all the said moduses [was ordered].

[Other reports of this case: 1 Rayner 99, 100, 2 Gwillim 583, 1 Eagle & Younge 661, BL MS. Hargr. 70, p. 109, pl. 363, 2 Salkeld 656, 91 E.R. 559.]

[the order of 9 Nov. 1704, PRO E.126/18, f. 465v, is printed at 1 Wood 446.]

[This case is cited in Smith v. Johnson (Ex. 1709), below, No. 437; Chapman v. Monson (1729), 2 Peere Williams 565, 569, 24 E.R. 864, 866.]

389

Scamell v. Coppleston (Ex. 1705)

Where a testator makes his brother executor and gives him a legacy, the personal estate that was not specifically bequeathed goes to the executor.

I
LI MS. Misc. 536, p. 8 [Eng.] (Ward's Reports)

The case appeared to be this that Dr. Coppleston[1] of Cambridge in 1689 made his will and gave to his sisters, the plaintiffs, £20 apiece and gave some long leases for years to his brother, the defendant, for twenty years if he so long

---

[5] *Sherrington v. Fleetwood* (1596), 1 Rolle, Abr., *Dismes*, pl. D, 17, p. 651, note also *id.*, pl. D, 16, p. 651, also 1 Eagle & Younge 111, Moore K.B. 599, 909, 72 E.R. 784, 990.

[6] Sic in MS.

[7] T. Littleton, *Tenures*, s. 344; E. Coke, *First Institute* (1628), f. 212b; *Peytoe's Case* (1611), 9 Coke Rep. 77, 77 E.R. 847.

[1] John Coplestone, D.D., died in 1689: J. and J. A. Venn, *Alumni Cantabrigienses*, part 1, vol. 1, p. 394 (1922); W. Sterry, *Eton College Register* (1943), p. 85.

live and then to go to the defendant's son and made the defendant his executor, but did not make any other devise or disposition of his personal estate, which was charged to be very considerable. And the plaintiffs, though they were paid or might be paid their £20 legacies, yet they endeavored by their bill to have the defendant to account for and distribute all the residue of the testator's personal estate not particularly devised away by the will under pretense that it was an undisposed estate and so, as to that, the Doctor was dead intestate and the plaintiffs [were] entitled to their shares of it by virtue of the statute for the distribution of intestates' estates.[2] And there were no other of kin in equal degree to the Doctor but the plaintiffs and defendant, who also was heir at law to the decedent.

And at the opening of the case and upon perusal of the will, the court inclined to allow the demurrer as thinking in this case that the making of the defendant executor, as it was in law, so it ought to be understood in equity, a disposition to him of all the residue of the personal estate not otherwise by the will particularly disposed of, and the rather (as I observed) because the plaintiffs and defendant being in equal representation to the deceased, who gave them all particular legacies (which shows he had them all under his consideration). And why should it not be thought that what he had given the plaintiffs was all that he intended them and that by his making the defendant (who was no stranger but his brother and heir at law) executor, he intended (as well as the law gave) the residue to him. And this sort of proceeding is indeed to suppose that a man must die both testate and intestate and that the making of a man executor (who is in all cases and to all purposes in law the legal representative of the testator as to all personalties) is (as to what is not particularly given away or charged) only a trustee and accountable for that residue of the personal estate unless it be expressly devised to him, which construction breaks in upon the main foundation and principle of the law touching executors and personal estates. And it is a sort of contradiction that a man shall be said to die testate and intestate and to have left an undisposed estate when he has left a legal representative in whom the law vests all not otherwise disposed of, for the rule is true *fortior est dispositio legis quam hominis*.[3] Indeed if anything did appear of the testator's intention that the executor should be only in trust or had a particular legacy given him for his care of pains in the executorship (as it was in the case of Foster and Munt[4] where the executor being a stranger and the [?] money a legacy for his care and pains was decreed by Lord Jeffreys to account to the next of kin in equal degree by way of

---

[2] Stat. 22 & 23 Car. 2, c. 10 (*SR*, V, 719–720).

[3] The disposition of the law is stronger than that of man. E. Coke, *First Institute* (1628), f. 234a; W. Sheppard, *Touchstone*, p. 302.

[4] *Foster v. Munt*, Case 462, 1 Vernon 473, 23 E.R. 598, 2 Eq. Cas. Abr. 433, 22 E.R. 368, 1 Eq. Cas. Abr. 243, 21 E.R. 1020, Samuel Dodd's Reports, p. 78.

distribution for a great residue as an undisposed estate and that decree, being reversed by the late commissioners of the great seal, was affirmed in Parliament[5]), it might be more reasonable, but in this case in question nothing of that or other circumstances appearing to alter what the law has disposed and testator given is to make a new will, which no court can nor ought to do.

But *Hooper*, the queen's serjeant and a great practicer in chancery, affirming there were many precedents of decrees in the like case with this and it being just that there should (as much as might) be an uniform opinion and practice in courts of equity, the court by consent of parties overruled the demurrer without costs on either side, but saving the benefit of the matter, for which the demurrer was, to the defendants at hearing. The defendant was to answer and the cause to be heard next term and then precedents [are] to be produced and the court to determine.

And in July 1705 at setting down of causes, this cause was heard and the court was of opinion that the plaintiffs had no right to more than their legacies and that the executor had [a] right to the residuum.

[Other copies of this report: GUL MS. B88–9, f. 227v.]

II
BL MS. Hargr. 71, f. 115, pl. 2 [Fr. & Eng.] (Dodd's Reports)

The point resolved was [that] Dr. Coppleston, late provost of King's [College, Cambridge], was possessed of a good personal estate and of a long family lease of 1000 years. And he had a brother and three sisters and made his will and gave to his brother the lease for twenty years remainder to his nephew, the son of his brother, and gave £50 apiece to his sisters, and he made his brother executor. And if the legacy of the lease for twenty years barred his brother from anything as executor according to the case of Foster and Munt, above,[6] was the question.

And [it was] resolved that [it did] not but that the brother by being executor took all and [there should be] no proportion or distribution of the personal estate among his sisters.

And in this case was cited the case of Griffith and Knife [?] and others v. Rogers and others, in chancery in Trinity [term] 1703 or 1704,[7] where in his will, he gave all his books to A. except twenty which he gave to his executor and then named an executor, and [it was] resolved that the executor [had] not lost the residue by the devise of the twenty books. See the breviate in the first case.

---

[5] *Forster v. Bernard* (1690), *Lords' Journal*, XIV (n.d.), p. 529.

[6] *Foster v. Munt* (Ch. 1689), Samuel Dodd's Reports, p. 78.

[7] *Griffith v. Rogers* (1704), Prec. Ch. 231, 24 E.R. 112, 1 Eq. Cas. Abr. 245, 21 E.R. 1021.

[Other copies of this report: HLS MS. 537(b), p. 68, pl. 1; Oxf. Brasenose MS. 59, p. 88, pl. 1; IU Lilly MS. Parker, 'Cases in the Exchequer, vol. 2', p. 68.]

[Order of 22 Feb. 1705: PRO E.127/24, f. 87.]

[This case was cited in Packington v. Wyche (Ex. 1709), below, No. 438.]

390

Lennard v. Anger (Ex. 1705)

The court of exchequer will not grant discovery of matters cognizable by justices of the peace.

LI MS. Misc. 536, f. [51v] [Eng.] (Ward's Reports)

The plaintiff exhibited his bill against the defendants for discovery and relief showing that he and others were appointed overseers of the poor for the parish of St. Andrews by the justices of the peace, that the others were to collect the money and deliver it to him and he [was to] pay it out as it ought, that before any money was collected, he, to relieve the poor, advanced out of his own estate £84 which he was to be reimbursed when collected, that upon complaint to some of the justices they thought to put him out from being an overseer and put [the] defendants in but made an order that he should be paid his money out of the first moneys collected by [the] defendants, whom he charged to have received as much or more than would pay him but that they concealed it and refused to pay him though they had it in their hands.

The defendants answered to some very immaterial things in the bill but as to any discovery whether [they had] received money to reimburse him or not and as to all other discovery or relief demurred assigning for cause that this matter was not conusable in this court but before the justices of the peace, and of that opinion were the three barons.

But the chief baron [WARD] held otherwise. For supposing that the justices might examine into the matter and that upon oath (which nevertheless is not clear), yet the plaintiff was proper here to have a discovery at least if not a relief, for if the justices might examine it, they have not a jurisdiction exclusive to Westminster Hall. It is but at best concurrent, for by the law and course of proceedings every subject may have a discovery upon oath from any other in civil causes. And it is an harsh if not an unheard of thing that the pretended inferior jurisdiction of the justices should exclude Westminster Hall in such a case. And where a subject may have discovery or relief in several places, it is his right to have liberty to sue where he pleases and not to be sent and confined to an inferior jurisdiction when the superior may help him. That seems like a denial of justice, and if this court could not relieve the plaintiff, which nevertheless I see no reason why we might not, yet at least he had a right to have a discovery. And the demurrer going to the discovery as well as relief, it ought to be set aside. But it was allowed *ut supra* and the plaintiff paid costs, which to me seemed strange and a bold attempt to impeach the jurisdiction of this court.

[Other copies of this report: GUL MS. B88–9, f. 244v.]

[Order of 21 May 1705: PRO E.127/24, f. 120.]

391

Chetham v. Lamplugh (Ex. 1705)

A bill of review lies only for errors apparent on the face of the record.

Where a party dies after a decree in equity has been pronounced but before it is signed by the judge, the administrator to the deceased party should proceed by subpoena scire facias *rather than by a bill of revivor.*

LI MS. Misc. 536, f. [56] [Eng.] (Ward's Reports)

The said Dr. Lamplugh exhibited his bill in this court against the now plaintiff, then defendant, to be relieved against him for a fraud in procuring the Doctor to lend £1600 to George Packley upon a defective security and to have an account and relief out of the personal estate of Packley come to Chetham's hands or power towards satisfaction of the £1600. The defendant Chetham denied the fraud and, as to the account of the personal estate, insisted by answer upon a stated account between Packley and him of all things to such a time, which was precedent to the bill and but a little before Packley's death, and that upon that stated account, which contained all receipts and payments and allowances to that time, there appeared to be and was due to Chetham above £2500, for [the] securing of which Packley gave Chetham a [confessed] judgment, all which he insisted upon by answer in bar of an account or of any [of] the Doctor's demands to that time.

Upon the hearing of the cause, which was the 21st of February 1698[/99], the court acquitted Chetham of any fraud in procuring or persuading the Doctor to lend the £1600, but (by two barons against the chief baron) the stated account was set aside and Chetham [was] decreed to account for the personal estate of Packley at any time come to his hands or the hands of any other for him with his privity. Chetham's solicitor and the Doctor's attended the deputy [king's] remembrancer, to whom the taking of the account was referred with charge and discharge. But Chetham never after attended though frequently summoned to make good the discharge. Insomuch as the deputy by order proceeded to take the account *ex parte* and made his report 6 June 1702 whereby he reported that by Chetham's answer and by a rental of Packley's estate made in 1687, which was then computed at £448 *per annum*, according to which value he had charged Chetham with the receipt from 1687 to 1693, and they with the £1600 principal money which Chetham received for Packley and some other receipts amounted in all to £3154 15s., no part of which Chetham had brought in any discharges for, though summoned eleven times, that, upon Chetham's counsel's motion 25 June 1702, it was referred back to the deputy to review his report and procure the same to be altered by a week before Michaelmas term 1702, which not being done nor so much as the minutes of that motion drawn up, and Chetham upon his counsel's further motion the 23rd February 1702[/03] had further time given to go back to the deputy and procure an alteration of his report by Easter term 1703 otherwise the report to stand, and the said Chetham not having so much as attended the deputy nor procured any alteration of the report nor put in any exceptions thereto, it was the 28th of June 1703 decreed by the court that the report be confirmed that Chetham pay to the Doctor the £3154 15s. reported due as aforesaid. After the pronouncing and making of this decree, Dr. Lamplugh died intestate, and the now defendant, his wife, took administration to him and also [administration] *de bonis non* of Packley and served Chetham with a subpoena scire facias to perform the decree and with the decree itself.

And Chetham has now brought his bill of review in order to reverse these decrees and proceedings and assigns these errors:

First that it was unjust to set aside the stated account upon the first hearing, no cause being assigned for so doing.

To this it was answered by the defendant's counsel and resolved by the court that nothing can be assigned for error but what is so apparently upon the face of the record and here is no such error appearing, for the court made the decree upon reading proofs in the cause and there might or might not be cause for setting it aside, which upon rehearing or appeal may be looked into but not upon a bill of review, unless an apparent error did appear for setting it aside, which does not in this record appear.

[The] second error assigned was that, in the account taken and reported by the deputy, there is no allowance or deduction made to Chetham for a fee farm rent of £50 nor for any public or parliamentary taxes out of Packley's estate nor for repairs of houses, nor did the decree to account direct the deputy to make Chetham all just allowances as it ought.

To this it was answered that *non constat* there was any fee farm rent or public taxes or repairs, if there had been, Chetham ought to have made them out and what he paid of or for them which he has not done and therefore cannot demand anything justly for them. And if he did not receive all the rents and profits but made the tenants allowances for their payments of them (if any such), then he is not charged with so much as they amount to. But if he paid them, he must make them out. And he has willfully in everything failed. And the order sufficiently provides for his being allowed all the money he paid, laid out, or disbursed upon the account of Packley, and that is comprehensive of all just allowances.

[The] third error assigned was that the final decree [of] 28 of June 1703 was not signed nor enrolled in the life time of Dr. Lamplugh but after his death, and so no *scire facias* but [a] bill of revivor ought to be.

To this [it] was answered that it was against the record to allege that. And if it should be true, yet he being alive when the decree [was] pronounced, it is a decree from thence, and the signing and enrolling after the death (if it was so) does not appear within this record, and is but a perfecting of what was done as to the substance in the life of the party, nor did the death abate the decree, [it] only changed the party plaintiff from the Doctor to his administrator and administrator *de bonis non*, so *scire facias* well lies and not [a] bill of revivor.

[The] fourth error [was] that the court officiously made the decree [of] 28 June without [a] prayer of the plaintiff.

To this [it] was answered that the decree being absolute, that is to say the report confirmed *nisi causa* that day and no cause shown and the cause standing in the paper for judgment of the court, it became of itself absolute. And the court is bound to give some judgment one way or the other, so [it is] no error.

[The] fifth error [was] that it appears by [the] deputy's report that he charged Chetham with the £1600 received by him for Packley and with the annual rents of Packley's estate at £448 *per annum*, which is an uncertain and unwarrantable charge, for there was no proof for such a charge nor ground but only a particular of his estate taken in 1687 and *non constat* that it was true or continued of that value.

But to that it was answered that it was Chetham's own fault if he was surcharged that he did not come in and discharge himself having had so long time allowed and having done nothing. And since it was admitted that Chetham was Packley's receiver of his rents all the time he is charged for and the Doctor a mere stranger and an estimate of the estate being the only way the Doctor had to charge, it was incumbent on Chetham who was privy to all to bring in his discharge and satisfy the charge, for otherwise there could be no proceeding at all when a defendant is refractory and obstinate as he was here, and that contumacy is evident when he stands out eleven summonses and had near a year's time given him upon his own motions to being in his discharges and thereby procure the report to be varied if he could, which he failed in.

Before the court gave any opinion, it was proposed to see if the parties could come to terms amongst themselves, but that not succeeding, the court on Tuesday 13 November 1705 *seriatim* delivered their opinions and unanimously agreed therein, principally for the reasons in the answers to the errors assigned mentioned, and allowed the demurrer to the bill of review. And so that bill was dismissed.

[The] solicitor general, Serjeant Chetham, Dodd, and Phipps [were] for Chetham.

[The] attorney general, Ettrick, and Ward [were] for Lamplugh.

Upon which an appeal was presently exhibited to the Lords in Parliament from the decree and from the allowance of the demurrer also and dismission of the bill of review.

But after a full hearing in the Lords' House in or about Hilary term 1705[/06], the decree was affirmed without a negative[1] and so the whole £3154 15s. [was] charged upon the defendant, for it was his own fault and willful neglect after so many summonses not to come in.

A warning to all others in like case.

[Other copies of this report: GUL MS. B88–9, f. 249.]

[Order of 11 May 1705: PRO E.127/24, f. 105v.]

[This case is cited in Price v. Watkins (Ex. 1707), below, No. 416.]

392

Townley v. Wilson (Ex. 1705)

In this case, the defendants were ordered to account for the tithes of their houses in London.

IU Lilly MS. Parker, 'Cases in the Exchequer, vol. 4', p. 11 [Eng.] (Price's Reports)

The plaintiff [Thomas Townley], as lessee to the dean and chapter of Westminster of the rectory of St. Bryde's in the Liberties of London, exhibits his bill against some of the inhabitants for 2s. 9d. in the pound for tithe of their houses pursuant to the decree and statute of 37 Hen. VIII, c. [12],[1] *anno* 1545.

The defendants insisted on a *modus* or rate tithe before the said statute and produced their Old Books since the year 1640 as an evidence and insisted on the Stat. 22 & 23 Car. II, c. 11,[2] where the building of London is directed and the parishes united.

[In] the Old Books [for] 1640, 1652, 1660, 1666, [and] 1675, all the rates were there rated at 2s. 9d. per pound, but then the houses so called were all under

---

[1] *Lords' Journal*, XVIII (n.d.), p. 75.

---

[1] Stat. 37 Hen. VIII, c. 12 (*SR*, III, 998–1000).
[2] Stat. 22 & 23 Car. II, c. 11 (*SR*, V, 665–682).

value, but that admitted the rate to be 2s. 9d. The parishioners have had leases from the dean and chapter for several years of the rectory and, there being a unity of possession, made what parish rates they pleased and at what rates.

The court were of opinion to decree for the plaintiff the duty or tithe of 2s. 9d. in the pound. The same case had been in this court between Baliol College, who had the rectory of St. Lawrence in the City of London, and the parishioners, which ended in an agreement and an Act of Parliament.[3] But the court left both parties to consider to see if they would agree.

The vicar had [a] £60 a year salary from the impropriator and [a] £60 *per annum* augmentation from the parish.

2 *Inst.* 659, 660, the exposition of the Stat. 37 Hen. VIII; Calthrop's reports 62.[4]

There was after[wards] a decree for the plaintiff that the defendants should account and pay tithes for their houses at the rate of 2s. 9d. per pound.

8 January 1705[/06]. [There was] an appeal to the Lords[5] by the defendants where the cases of grant for St. Dunstan's [and] St. Botolph's Aldgate were cited the 14 Jac. by the name of Ivot's Case [and] Littleton's Rep. 102, 141, Dr. Burgess and St. Magnus London Within.[6] [It was] adjudged [that the] exchequer had a jurisdiction.

[Other reports of this case: 2 Gwillim 635, Western 117.]

[Orders of 10 May and 7 July 1705: PRO E.126/18, ff. 490, 514.]

[This case is cited in Bennet v. Trepass (1723), 2 Gwillim 633, 635, 1 Rayner 168, 172, 1 Eagle & Younge 782, 785.]

393
Walker v. Corbet (Ex. 1705)

The term 'charges and reprises' in the decree in issue included parliamentary taxes.

IU Lilly MS. Parker, 'Cases in the Exchequer, vol. 4', p. 12 [Eng.] (Price's Reports)

The plaintiff is vicar of Avenbury in Herefordshire; the defendant is impropriator. In the year 1652, there was a reference, and the award was decreed in the exchequer to be performed, that the impropriator pay the vicar and his successors

---

[3] Stat. 22 & 23 Car. II, c. 15 (*SR*, V, 725–727).

[4] E. Coke, *Second Institute* (1642), pp. 659–660; *Case Concerning Payment of Tithes in London* (1617), Calthrop 62, 80 E.R. 672.

[5] *Lords' Journal*, XVIII (n.d.), pp. 17, 35, 45, 61, 73.

[6] *Ivatt v. Warren* (1618), Western 88, 3 Gwillim 1054, 3 Eagle & Younge 1203; *Burgess v. Symons* (Ex. 1628), Littleton 102, 141, 124 E.R. 158, 177, 1 Rayner 13, 16, Western 94, 2 Gwillim 433, 434, 1 Eagle & Younge 365, 118 Selden Soc. 565.

£30 a year clear of all charges and reprises. Upon a bill in [the] nature of [a writ] of *scire facias* to execute the said decree, the defendant would have waived it but at length submitted if allowed parliamentary taxes.

Mr. *Ettrick* and Mr. *Edward Winnington* for the defendant: Charges and reprises in the legal sense of them is such charges as yearly are charged upon or issuing out of an estate, as rent [or] corody, though taxes are charges, yet not legally and properly so called.

Terms of the Law [blank], reprises are annual payments out of an estate. The Statute of Games. One is to have so much a year above reprises. Taxes are not considered in that case.

Brooke, Abr., *Quindism*, N, 9.[1] Tax or tallage is a tenth or a fifteenth or other subsidy granted by Parliament, the tenth is of the clergy, the fifteenth [is] of the laity; it was anciently raised out of the personals, now [it] is out of the reals.

Trin. 8 Will. [1696], king's bench, [blank] 295, Brewster v. Kidgell;[2] 2 Levinz 68, Davenant v. Bishop of Salisbury; 1 Ventris 223, *idem*.[3] If this were an ancient covenant, it only discharges ordinary payments as pensions or tenths granted by the clergy and might bind the success[or] by 32 Hen. VIII.[4]

Hilary [term] 1700[/01], chancery, Dyke v. Polehill.[5]

Mr. *Dodd, pro querente*: Clearly [it is] yearly rent of £30 *per annum* above all charges and reprises. 1697, exchequer, Veal v. Blanchard;[6] 1697, exchequer, Williams v. Vicar of Salisbury.[7] [In] the case of Brewster and Kidgell, judgment was given [in] Hilary [term] 9 Will. III [1698] in the king's bench, which case being a rent charge out of which there could be no other charges and reprises but taxes, and it being the clear yearly rent of £30 and the nonpayment of taxes ever since it was granted shows the intent of all parties, which might differ it from a lease of land with those words of 'charges and reprises' and the like.

In Trinity [term] 1705, Chief Baron WARD, Barons BURY, PRICE, and SMITH [ruled] for the plaintiff.

[Order of 1 Mar. 1705: PRO E.127/24, f. 84.]

---

[1] Brooke, Abr., *Quinzime, disme, taxe & tallage*, pl. 9.

[2] *Brewster v. Kidgell* (1696), Carthew 438, 90 E.R. 853, Holt K.B. 175, 669, 90 E.R. 995, 1270, 1 Salkeld 198, 91 E.R. 177, 2 Salkeld 615, 91 E.R. 521, 3 Salkeld 340, 91 E.R. 860, 1 Lord Raymond 317, 91 E.R. 1108, 5 Modern 368, 87 E.R. 711, 12 Modern 166, 88 E.R. 1239, Comberbach 424, 466, 90 E.R. 424, 466.

[3] *Davenant v. Bishop of Salisbury* (1672), 2 Levinz 68, 83 E.R. 453, 1 Ventris 223, 86 E.R. 150, 3 Keble 69, 84 E.R. 599.

[4] Perhaps Stat. 32 Hen. VIII, c. 22 (*SR*, III, 774–775).

[5] Other issues in this case are reported at 1 Lord Raymond 744, 91 E.R. 1398.

[6] *Veal v. Blanchard* (Ex. 1697) above, No. 355.

[7] *Williams v. Vicars of St. Mary's* (Ex. 1697), above, No. 351.

394
Earl of Montague v. Weddall (Ex. 1705)

Money received by an agent by means of a bill of exchange remains the property of the principal.

IU Lilly MS. Parker, 'Cases in the Exchequer, vol. 4', p. 19 [Eng.] (Price's Reports)

The plaintiff exhibits his bill for a bill of £210 drawn by Holright on Walker, a goldsmith. John Weddall, Esq., to whom the defendant [Jane Weddall] was administratrix, was steward to the plaintiff and received his rents in Yorkshire. Mr. Weddall had contracted with Holright to receive these rents and other rents of his own and to return them to London and, if he detained them above a month, to pay interest. By Mr. Weddall's order, he received of the said tenants upwards of £500 and other moneys of other[s] [and] did return three two hundred pound bills, one for £31, another for £10; Mr. Weddall received two of the £200 bills; the other bills were not received; and then the plaintiff sued the defendant Weddall and the goldsmith for the bills of £200 and £10 and £31 in Mrs. Weddall's hands. She insisted on several debts Mr. Weddall owed.

The question was that though the £200 and £10 bills were proved to be the plaintiff's money paid by his tenants, yet whether the same being negotiated by being paid to Holright and then returned by bill to Mr. Weddall, whether the property and nature of the money was so altered that it could not be followed.

Trinity term 1687, the Earl of Chesterfield v. J. Meers and others.[1]

It has been objected in this case that Mr. Weddall being steward had contracted with Holright to receive and return and that the money being negotiated and turned into a bill of exchange and in another name loses its first property and the like, as if A., B., and C. [and] C. is the proprietor of goods but A. has the custody of them and bails them to B., now C. cannot have a[n action of] detinue against B. though he has the property because of the privity of the bailment, but if B. die, C. may [go] against his executor or administrator because the privity of bailment is determined. Rolle, Abr., *Bailment*.[2]

[In] Trinity term 1705, upon the ground of the said precedent, it being a doubtful case, in which Barons PRICE and SMITH hesitated, but after[wards] by the unanimous opinion of the court, [there was] a decree for the plaintiff for the two bills of £200 and £10, and the other bill of £31 [was decreed] for the defendant, without costs on either side.

[Order of 26 Feb. 1705: PRO E.126/18, f. 483.]

---

[1] *Earl of Chesterfield v. Meeres* (1688), PRO E.126/15, f. 218v.
[2] 1 Rolle, Abr., *Bailement*, p. 338.

395
Attorney General v. Burdett (Ex. 1705)

Land given to superstitious uses vests in the crown upon a decree in a court of equity.

IU Lilly MS. Parker, 'Cases in the Exchequer, vol. 4', p. 24 [Eng.] (Price's Reports)

A bill in [the] nature of an information [was exhibited] for the queen for some houses in the Savoy, in King James the Second's time given to superstitious uses to set up a Jesuit school. It was brought in the defendant [Edward] Burdett's name, and the defendant [Mary] Arundell pretended a mortgage for £1600, upon which [there] was an issue directed to try if the £1600 was her money, [and] if it was so, if she had notice [that] it was for a superstitious use. The jury found it not to be her money nor [was it] lent *bona fide* and that she had notice of the superstitious use.

Upon the equity reserved, the court, WARD, BURY, PRICE, and SMITH, decreed an injunction to put the queen in possession and to quiet her there, [and the defendants] to account for the profit received by the defendant, to bring the writings into court, and to convey.

Note it has been the former opinion that lands given to superstitious uses were void and that they reverted to the heir of the donor, as the case in Moore's Rep. 784, of Croft and Evett,[1] was. But in the year 1680, Sir Thomas Preston's Case [and] my lord Carrington,[2] and Gayner Jones' [Case][3] for a popish school in Lancaster, all the said cases adjudged these lands given to superstitious uses to belong to the crown, though not vested in the crown by an inquisition, but [they] may be so in equity.

[Orders of 28 Feb. and 25 Oct. 1705: PRO E.126/18, ff. 474, 539v.]

396
Humphrey v. Betts (Ex. 1705)

The issue in this case was whether tithes are due for turnips fed to profitable cattle.

---

[1] *Croft v. Evett* (Ch. 1605), Moore K.B. 784, 72 E.R. 904, also 117 Selden Soc. 342.
[2] *Attorney General v. Lord Carrington* (Ex. 1682), above, No. 143.
[3] *Attorney General v. Gaynor Jones* (Ex. 1688–1690), above, No. 269.

IU Lilly MS. Parker, 'Cases in the Exchequer, vol. 4', p. 42 [Eng.] (Price's Reports)

The plaintiff [John Humphrey] is rector of Spockenhold in Suffolk[1] and *inter alia* claims tithe turnips which were cut for winter's feed for profitable cattle. There were eight acres of turnips [in] 1702 and nine acres [in] 1703.

For the defendants [William Betts and Thomas Stopher], it was objected that turnips severed from and drawn out of the ground ought not to pay tithe. If it was eaten on the ground, it could be but an agistment for unprofitable cattle, but, for profitable [cattle], no agistment [is] due.

If the [sowing of] turnips is for [the] melioration of the ground, no tithe [is due] for the turnips if [they are] sown after [the] corn harvest. And one acre of turnips [is] as good as three loads of hay, [and] more cows are kept, four cows on £50 *per annum* more. Land that is left fallow, though grass grow on it, no tithe [is due, it] being a melioration, or if one cut grass to soil[2] a horse. [We] agree [that] if [there is a] custom [to] pay tithe turnips, [they are due, but] not otherwise. 1 Rolle, Abr., *Disme*, 645, n. 7, Crawley v. Welt.[3] No tithe [is due] for wood burnt in one's house or wood for inclosure in husbandry nor for pigeons spent in the house, which is the support of those who labor.

Cro. Car. 393, Mead v. Thurman; Jones 357, *idem*; 2 Leonard 27, Perry v. Somes.[4]

Poles cut for hop poles and the bark of them [pay] no tithes.

For the plaintiff, [it was argued] that tithe has been usually paid for turnips cut and severed and used green for cattle.

25 February 9 Will. [1697], Thomas Echard v. Samuel Brown and others.[5] The plaintiff was vicar of Breadfield in Suffolk; [the] defendant had three roods of turnips and fed his cattle; [he was] decreed to account for the turnips severed and drawn from his own land sowed therewith.

22 February 2 Anne [1704], John Solley v. Leonard Reeve.[6] [The] plaintiff [was] rector of Stratton St. Mary in Norfolk; [the] defendant had two acres and a rood of turnips, which he fed his cows with. [It was] decreed that the defendant

---

[1] Sic in MS.

[2] Sic in MS.

[3] *Crawley v. Welles* (1633), 1 Rolle, Abr., *Dismes*, pl. Z, 7, p. 645, 1 Eagle & Younge 382.

[4] *Meade v. Thurman* (1635), Cro. Car. 393, 79 E.R. 943, W. Jones 357, 82 E.R. 188, 1 Eagle & Younge 383; *Perry v. Some* (1588), 2 Leonard 27, 74 E.R. 330, Cro. Eliz. 138, 78 E.R. 395, 1 Eagle & Younge 96.

[5] *Eachard v. Brown* (1698), Samuel Dodd's Reports, p. 179, 1 Rayner 84, 1 Eagle & Younge 623.

[6] *Solley v. Reeve* (1704), PRO E.126/18, f. 403.

account with the plaintiff for the tithe of turnips severed from and drawn out of the ground though fed on the same farm.

And the defendant filed [a] cross-bill to establish a custom of *non decimando* for turnips, but [it was] dismissed because he ought to sue in the name of the parishioners who claim the custom and not in one person's name alone, which cannot bind the rest.

Easter [term] 5 Will. & Mary [1693], Norfolk, Wharton v. Oldfield [is] the same case of turnips.

[Other reports of this case: 1 Wood 471, 2 Gwillim 593, 1 Eagle & Younge 675.]

[Orders of 22 and 23 Nov. and 10 Dec. 1705: PRO E.126/18, ff. 538, 543v.]

[This case is cited in Ringstead v. Redwell (Ex. 1709), below, No. 439.]

397

Snag v. Davies (Ex. 1705)

The terms of a trust can be set aside with the consent of the settlor.

IU Lilly MS. Parker, 'Cases in the Exchequer, vol. 4', p. 44 [Eng.] (Price's Reports)

The plaintiff's bill prays that [the] defendants, the trustees, may be decreed to pay her £500, £200 whereof was given her by her father, the other £300 was given her by her mother, who after[wards] married, and she and her husband are defendants. The £500 were vested in a mortgage in the trustees in trust that the plaintiff have the use of it for life and if she married a husband who would settle £500 in lands to the use of him and her and the heirs of their bodies and if she married one that would not settle so, then she [was] to have the use of the £500 for life and the £500 to go to her children, and, if she died unmarried, the £500 to be [given] to her mother.

The plaintiff is [entered] upon marriage to a tradesman, who has no land, and the money would be more advantageous than land, and so she prays to have the money, the mother and her husband consenting to it and to part with their contingency.

Chief Baron WARD, Barons BURY and SMITH were for decreeing it as prayed, being for the benefit of the plaintiff, which was the intention of the parties consenting and [there being] no children born to take care of, and decreed the trustees to be indemnified.

Baron PRICE was for decreeing the plaintiff the £200 given by her father but not the £300 given by the mother, being a provision for her life and, if she married, to have land settled, and if no land, then her children [are] to have the money, and if children should be born, who could bar them. He did propose that security should be given to leave £300 to the children.

[It was said] that personal estate may be settled and limited so that they be not perpetuities.

1 Chancery Rep. f. 130, Vachel v. Vachel,[1] where books, paintings, medals, etc., were given to several [persons], one after the other upon contingencies.

2 Ventris 347.[2] [There was a] devise [of] £100 to A. at twenty-one years, if [he] die before, [then] to B., [if] B. dies first, then A. dies before twenty-one years, [the] administrator of B. shall have the £100.

249, Broadhurst's Case.[3] Money cannot be entailed, as £300 to three sisters and if either die without issue, then to the survivor. One marries and dies without issue; the husband that was [her] administrator had the £100 because it could not be entailed.

[Order of 5 Dec. 1705: PRO E.126/18, f. 538v.]

398

Sturmy v. Skipwith (Ex. 1705)

A mortgage is the personal estate of the mortgagee and passes to his executor and not to his heir.

IU Lilly MS. Parker, 'Cases in the Exchequer, vol. 4', p. 48 [Eng.] (Price's Reports)

The plaintiff [Thomas Sturmy] exhibited a bill as executor to the Lady Skipwith, who was executrix or administratrix to Mr. Maddison, her first husband, for £400 *per annum* issuing out of the hereditary excise.

Mr. Whitehall was a great banker, and King Charles II [on] 30 April 1677 granted to Mr. Whitehall and his heirs about £14,000 *per annum* out of the hereditary excise upon trust to assign the rent in proportion to his several creditors, in which grant there was a proviso of redemption for the crown and that the assignment made should be enrolled in the auditor of the exchequer or pell office.

Mr. Whitehall owed Mr. Maddison great sums of money. Mr. Maddison died. Mrs. Maddison was executrix; Sir Thomas Skipwith, being counsel for her (and designing to marry her), drew a deed for her [on] 29 April 1673 whereby she conveyed all her estate to trustees for herself and for any husband [that] she should marry and to the survivor of them. In 1674, Sir Thomas Skipwith marries Mrs. Maddison. [In] April 1674, Mr. Whitehall accounted with Sir Thomas

---

[1] *Vachel v. Vachel* (1669), 1 Chan. Cas. 129, 22 E.R. 727, 1 Eq. Cas. Abr. 361, 21 E.R. 1103.

[2] *Anonymous* (1679), 2 Ventris 347, 36 E.R. 478.

[3] *Broadhurst v. Richardson* (1681), 3 Ventris 349, 86 E.R. 479, 2 Chan. Rep. 153, 21 E.R. 644.

Skipwith for Mr. Maddison's debt, and he gave up to Mr. Whitehall his bonds to Mr. Maddison and took new bonds to Sir Thomas Skipwith and his lady (late Mrs. Maddison).

[On] 24 January 1677[/78], Mr. Whitehall, having accounted with Sir Thomas Skipwith to the 25 December before, he assigns £400 *per annum* of the said exchequer rent to Sir Thomas Skipwith and his heirs and to receive the profit from the 25th December before.

The lady, hearing of the assignment to be taken in Sir Thomas Skipwith's name alone, was uneasy, and after[wards] he conveyed the said rent of £400 *per annum* to Walter Rea *et alii* in trust for Sir Thomas Skipwith and his lady and the survivor, but this deed from Sir Thomas Skipwith was dated 24 December 1677, reciting an assignment from Whitehall to Sir Thomas Skipwith [on] 21 December 1677.

Sir Thomas Skipwith did after marr[iage], in the year 1684, make his lady a jointure of £200 *per annum*. And [in] 1694, Sir Thomas Skipwith, designing to alter the uses of the annuity so[1] that his son should have it, would make his lady an additional jointure of £200 or £300 *per annum*, but the lady did not join in any act, nor does it appear [that] she agreed to any such [thing]. She was worth about £4000 to Sir Thomas Skipwith besides this exchequer rent. Sir Thomas Skipwith made the defendant, Sir Thomas Skipwith, who was his heir, his executor and died. The lady survived and enjoyed both jointures and made her will and [made] the plaintiff her executor about the year 1697.

[1.] [The] first question was whether the conveyance from the crown to Mr. Whitehall with a clause of redemption of the said rents was a personal estate, and, if so, if the conveyance from Whitehall to Sir Thomas Skipwith and his heirs of the £400 *per annum* was likewise a mortgage and personal estate in him, and if Sir Thomas Skipwith's conveyance or assignment to Walter Rea and his heirs in trust, as aforesaid, was likewise a personal estate.

The court were all of the opinion that, as it was a mortgage in fee and a security for money in its creation, it was a personal estate and must go to the executor and not the heir, as in the case of other mortgages and the Statute 12 & 13 Will. III, c. 12, s. 15,[2] for appropriating £3700 weekly out of the branches of the excise, f. 419, where £3 *per centum* is to be paid forever out of the hereditary excise to the respective owners of such annual sums in satisfaction of the grant made by King Charles II's letters patent; in the Act, there is a clause of redemption on paying the moiety of the principal money in the respective letters patent to be paid from 25 December 1705. And by the Statute made in the second and third years of

---

[1] and *MS*.
[2] Stat. 12 & 13 Will. III, c. 12, s. 15 (*SR*, VII, 723–729).

Queen Anne, c. 3, s. 1,[3] for the better and more regular paying of the said annuity at the rate of £3 *per centum*, f. 264, that the owners of such annuities, their executors, or administrators may by writing under hand and seal or will assign the said rent and [it is] not to be revocable, there being a memorandum made thereof in the auditor of receipt's office in the exchequer within three months after such assignment or devise, and the owners of the said annuities shall be possessed thereof as of a personal estate, and [it] shall not be descendible to the heir, both which acts do show that it was taken as a mortgage and [a] personal estate.

2. The deed from Whitehall to Sir Thomas Skipwith is dated 24 January 1677[/78], and Sir Thomas Skipwith's deed to Walter Rea is dated 24 December 1677 and recites the deed to him of the 21st December 1677. This antedating looks suspicious, and there is evidence that it was executed after the 24th January 1677[/78]. The date is no material part of a deed, and one may declare upon a writing at a day certain and aver that it was *primo deliberatum* at another day, from which time the deed has its essence. 1 Rolle, Abr., *Faits*, 27, 874.[4]

Then, this deed though antedated by Sir Thomas Skipwith, his son and executor are as much estopped to say it is none of Sir Thomas Skipwith's deed as if he were living or to say that he had no estate then in him. Co. Litt. 47.[5]

Then it was said the bill ought to have set it out specially as it was, but the bill is that [on] 24 January 1677[/78], Whitehall grants to Sir Thomas Skipwith and that after[wards] Sir Thomas Skipwith assigns to Walter Rea, though it had been well so, yet saying it was after[wards] assigned puts it upon the plaintiff to show [that] it was so, of which there is proof.

And the court were all of the opinion that it was antedated, sealed, and delivered after 24 January 1677[/78], but if Sir Thomas Skipwith desired to have the fact tried, he might have it, but it is decreed for the plaintiff that the defendants [Sir Thomas Skipwith and John Rea] are trustees for the plaintiff and that they assign to the plaintiff unless he the first day of next term desires to have [the] said fact tried.

3. That the defendant objected that the deed from Sir Thomas Skipwith to Walter Rea should be enrolled in the auditor of receipts [office] within thirty days; all the court agreed that extended only to the assignment of the first takers or patentees to their creditors and not to any after assignment.

4. That the plaintiff ought to show that the Lady Skipwith was executrix to Sir Thomas Skipwith, that is but an inducement, being [that] she claimed under Sir Thomas Skipwith's assignment to her and the survivor and the heirs of the survivor of them, and whether she was executor or administrator or on an

---

[3] Stat. 2 & 3 Ann., c. 3, s. 1 (*SR*, VIII, 246–247).
[4] 1 Rolle, Abr., *Faits*, pl. Q, 2, p. 27; YB Pas. 20 Edw. IV, f. 1, pl. 1.
[5] E. Coke, *First Institute* (1628), f. 47.

agreement, it was plain that Sir Thomas Skipwith was entitled only in her right, and there is none under Maddison [that] controverts it.

5. That the letters patent from Charles II to Mr. Whitehall were not produced; they were afterwards, and it lay upon the defendants to produce them, since they own them by answer to make good their objections.

6. The defendant Sir Thomas Skipwith has an assignment from the defendant John Rea, who was brother and heir to Walter Rea, who was trustee by Sir Thomas Skipwith's assignment. As it is a personal estate, it belongs to the *cestui que trust* by the deed and not the heir at law, and, by taking such an assignment, it implies the defendant could not depend on his own title.

[It was] decreed by Chief Baron WARD, Barons BURY, PRICE, and SMITH for the plaintiff and that the defendants are trustees for him and must assign unless the defendant will the first day of the next term pray a trial on the said fact of the time of the delivery of the deed of 24 December 1677.

[Order of 11 Dec. 1705: PRO E.126/18, f. 536v.]

[Affirmed on appeal: *Lords' Journal*, XVIII (n.d.), p. 126.]

399

Attorney General v. Smith (Ex. 1705)

A bill of discovery and an accounting for duties due to the crown lies in equity where all penalties and forfeitures for the non-payment have been waived.

LI MS. Misc. 536, f. [58] [Eng.] (Ward's Reports)

The bill suggests that in 1697 a quantity of about two tuns or three of wines was imported in such a ship and changed out of that into another and after came to the defendant's hands being originally imported by [the] defendant and on his account and that the duties were not paid which were due upon the importation, and therefore to have a discovery and relief for the duties (the attorney general on the queen's behalf waiving all penalties and forfeitures) was the bill.

The defendant demurred to the bill (save some small and immaterial part of it, which he answered to) and showed for cause that it tended to bring him within the penalties and forfeitures of the laws [that] where goods are imported duties not paid, there incurs a penalty.

But the court in this case overruled the demurrer, for the importation being in 1697, no remedy or forfeiture lay for the informer. And the attorney general having waived all penalties and forfeitures for the queen and seeking only for the duty which the crown may sue for at law or in equity without taking advantage of any penalty or forfeiture, the defendant is out of danger and ought to answer the duty. And if after discovery the attorney general should prosecute for [the] penalty, the court would grant [an] injunction to such suit, at least upon a bill exhibited for that purpose.

This has all along been the difference that where a bill seeks a discovery of an offense or criminal matter or for anything for which a fine, forfeiture, or penalty is inflicted or the party may be liable to where no original right or duty was in or granted to the crown, there [a] demurrer [is] allowed good. But where there is an original right or duty in or to the crown for which the crown upon discovery or proof may have a remedy at law, that in such case though a penalty or forfeiture be annexed to the nonpayment of it and gives part to an informer, yet if the king's attorney exhibits his information for the duty only (and waives the penalty) before the common informer prosecutes or after the year limited to the informer is expired, that in such case there ought to be an answer, for in such case the duty and not the penalty is to be recovered. Hardres 22, 137, 201;[1] Liber G, f. 58.[2]

[Other copies of this report: GUL MS. B88–9, f. 251v.]

400

Frampton v. Beene (Ex. 1705–1706)

Shares of stock in a corporation can be held in trust.

Where a bankrupt holds shares in a corporation in trust, they belong to the beneficiary of the trust and cannot be reached by the bankrupt's creditors.

IU Lilly MS. Parker, 'Cases in the Exchequer, vol. 4', pp. 52, 70 (Price's Reports)

The plaintiff [Charles Frampton alleged] by [a] bill that William Sheppard and Brag were goldsmiths and dealt much in East India stocks, that the plaintiff paid to Sheppard in May 1700 £3,000 to have so much in East India stock, and that he bought £6,000 of Nunmis Gandy and Robert in William Sheppard's name, and they were transferred to William Sheppard, who gave the plaintiff three notes dated 28 May 1700: 'I promise to transfer to Charles Framton, Esq., or order on demand £1,000 old East India stock, being so much in trust for his account for himself. William Sheppard and Bray'. One is for himself and not Bray.

[On] the 3rd February 1700[/01], William Sheppard failed, and the defendants [Giles] Been and [John] Van Hatton are assignees of the commissioners of [the] bankrupt; William Sheppard has £50,000 worth of old stock, which is in

---

[1] *Protector v. Lord Lumley* (1655), Hardres 22, 145 E.R. 360; *Attorney General v. Mico* (1658), Hardres 137, 145 E.R. 419; *Attorney General v. Anonymous* (1661), Hardres 201, 145 E.R. 452.

[2] *Attorney General ex rel. Thistlethwaite v. Wilson* (Ex. 1675), above, No. 62.

mortgage to the company for £10,000 from the time of the notes to his failing and still has a stock to answer his notes but will not answer his other creditors 6s. 8d. in the pound.

The plaintiff would have Sheppard and [the] commissioner to make a specific transfer of £3,000 stock to the plaintiff or whom he shall appoint. It was alleged to be a trust of so much on the credit of the stock and that it was not allowed by the constitution of the company to declare any trust in the transfer books unless for married women and infants, but Mr. Thoroughgood may declare a trust in the transfer books but [it is] no certain thing but only on the credit of the stock. It is not like the shares in the New River Water nor of so many acres in twenty or the trust of a bond, nor is it a resulting trust, because [it is] not fixed on any certain stock and is no more than a promise to transfer a stock. If it were to pay money, it is as certain a trust as this. But if the plaintiff will redeem or come in with the other creditors, he may, but [I] see no grounds to prefer the plaintiff before other creditors.

The want of making of Brag, who was partner with William Sheppard, a party, it need not, since he was not concerned in the East India stock, though he was in the goldsmith's trade. And if he was the assignee of the commissioner of bankrupts, [he] is before the court.

[It was said] that the plaintiff bought in May and June 1700 £3,000 in East India stocks and [it] was transferred to the defendant William Sheppard and he gave three notes under his hand to transfer £1,000 by each note of the East India stock to the plaintiff, being so much in trust for his account. William Sheppard had great sums in the East India stock and [on] 3 February 1700[/01] became a bankrupt and had then £7,000 in the East India stock in his own name and was not at any time without great sums in his name, from the time of giving the said notes, he had above £50,000 in the said stock in mortgage for £10,000 to the East India Company. The commissioners of [the] bankrupt do assign to the defendant his stock and estate.

It was doubted if the East India stock could be in trust, there being no certainty or mark to distinguish one stock from the other and whether the plaintiff ought to come into the Statute [of Bankrupts] as a creditor or Sheppard and the assignees ought to transfer to the plaintiff, being a *cestui que trust* and not a creditor.

23 January 4 Anne [1706], in chancery, Richard Finch and Dr. Waugh v. J. Higden and Arthur Gaudy.[1] It was decreed that Gaudy, who was trustee for the plaintiff for African Company stocks, and Higden, who was assignee to the bankruptcy of Gaudy, was[2] decreed to transfer to the plaintiff.

---

[1] *Finch v. Higden* (Ch. 1706), PRO C.33/305, ff. 193v, 438.
[2] Sic in MS.

6th December, 4 Anne [1705], J. Walters v. William Sheppard, East India Company, and others, where [there] was a decree about the transfer of stocks.

[It was] decreed that William Sheppard and the assignees of the commission[er] of bankrupts do transfer £3,000 stock in the East India Company to the plaintiff and that the East India Company do allow of the same and give him credit for it and that the plaintiff be decreed to hold and enjoy.

401

Floyd v. Goldsmith (Ex. 1705 x 1706)

A lessor and the lessee of particular tithes may sue jointly for them against the parishioners.

HLS MS. 1082, vol. 1, part B, p. 17 [Eng.]

The plaintiffs join in a bill against the defendants as tertenants of a rectory for not setting forth tithes. They set forth that one Floyd was seised in fee of the rectory and tithes of D. in Surrey, who was father to the plaintiff, and that his father died seised thereof and that the same came by descent or otherwise to him the said Floyd, the plaintiff, and that the plaintiff Rooke was by lease parol or otherwise possessed of the said rectory, etc. under Floyd senior, the father of Floyd the plaintiff, and they when the plaintiff Rooke would desire the defendant to set forth their tithes to him, they would tell him the tithes belonged to Floyd the plaintiff, and when Floyd the plaintiff demanded the tithes, then they used to say the plaintiff Rooke had right to the tithes and so never paid the tithes to the one or to the other, though both the plaintiffs did severally and respectively declare unto the defendants that, if they did pay their tithes to either of [the] plaintiffs, the other would be content therewith. They also set forth that heretofore the plaintiff Floyd did prefer a bill against the defendants in this court for the tithes, which was dismissed for that it did appear [that] the plaintiff Floyd had a right upon the evidence, upon which they both joined in this bill and both pray they may have a decree of this court for the tithes to be paid [to] Floyd or [to] either of them, to which bill the defendant[1] demurred.

> [1.] This bill is so uncertain [that] the court cannot know for whom to judge.
> 2. The title[2] of Rooke does not appear therein, for in it is said he had a lease but does not show it contained or how long it was to continue.
> 3. The plaintiffs had several rights and could not join and should be several parties to several issues.

---

[1] plaintiffs *MS*.
[2] tithe *MS*.

4. If there should be a decree for Floyd (when by this bill it seems Rooke had the right, if any), that would be no bar on an action of debt, 5 Edw. VI,[3] against Rooke.

Serjeant *Darnell*, for the defendants: The bill is so uncertain that the court cannot know for whom to decree, for if you decree for Floyd, the plaintiff Rooke may bring his action at law and this decree is not pleadable to it in bar. Then it appears not that Rooke has still a title, because the lease is or may be determined, so that it is not possible to say how much of the tithes are payable to Floyd and how much to Rooke as this bill is.

Secondly, if you will intend [that] Floyd has a right, then it must be by assignment from Rooke which cannot be, for that at the time of the assignment Rooke had but a right for not setting forth the tithes, and [he] compared it to the case in 1 R[olle] 376,[4] where it is adjudged that a breach of covenant is not assignable because [it is] but a right. Suppose then you should decree for Floyd, how can you hinder Rooke if he bring his action at law. If you should grant an injunction, yet Rooke may have execution, and then after execution is executed, you can only lay Rooke by the heels. Lastly, persons that have rights and titles cannot join, for if the parson have two parts of the tithes and the vicar the third part, you cannot join for setting forth the tithes, but if you join in a lease of the rectory, the lessee may sue, having both rights united in him.

Dodd for the plaintiffs: The parson and [the] vicar, in the case put and that is common experience.[5] Here in our case, it is agreed the right is in one of them and that the tertenants are to pay it. Now when one plaintiff demands the tithes, they will pay the other, and when the other demands the tithes, then they will pay the first. Is not this a plain trick which we set forth so that you are to pay to one of us? We are all parties to the bill, so if you pay either, the other shall be bound by it. Therefore you are safe, and should the other plaintiff sue at law, the court is strong enough to compel obedience.

Phillips [argued] the same and only added it is the common course and, if you pay either of us, you are safe.

Lord Chief Baron WARD: The bill is very uncertain but that can be no reason as this case is to dismiss the bill, for you must answer, and we will overrule the demurrer and we shall consider of the uncertainty of the bill upon making the decree. If the testator does not set forth his tithes, his heir [?] shall be liable, and the like remedy is for the executor of the impropriator for that the tertenants did not set forth the tithes in the time of the testator, the impropriator, and

---

[3] Stat. 2 & 3 Edw. VI, c. 13 (*SR*, IV, 55–58).
[4] *Woodford v. Holland* (1613), 1 Rolle, Abr., *Chancerie*, pl. R, 6, p. 376.
[5] Sic in MS.

that is a settled point now in this court though really heretofore it was otherwise, *quia placitum personalis moritur cum persona*. And the reason why I say this now is so here because the plaintiff Floyd is executor to him by the bill. It seems by the bill that the tithes were not set forth in his time either. There was a case not long unlike this judged in this court. A. purchased lands and sowed the ground, and the parson came to demand his tithes and said that his lands were in another parish. Then the parson of the other parish demanded the tithes of A.; then A. said the tithes were payable to the first parson. Both parsons joined, and it was held well [that] the best way is to join [both][6] rights. When they are for one and the same thing, [it] is allowed in equity. As for what is said that no title is found in the plaintiff Rooke, it [is] shown he had a possession by virtue of a lease and otherwise; only *ex abundanti et firmius* is enough in [an] action on 5 Edw. VI at law. And the three other barons agreed with him to overrule the demurrer.

And Baron SMITH denied the case put by Darnell to be law, of the nonjoinder of the parson and vicar, for he might join in an action at law upon the statute for setting forth the tithes[7] as all tenants in common may upon joint possession and rights, so the joinder is well enough. But suppose A. had lands in two purchases and both the parson [and vicar] join in a bill against A. Is that good? I question it.

Dodd: Yes, that very case has been resolved in this court, which the court did not extremely well like.

Then Baron SMITH went on: The complainants do not so very strictly stand on forms, so that people come fairly at their rights.

I question the case put by my brother Darnell out of R[olle] 376, for here seeing that Floyd is willing that Rooke should be plaintiff and that Rooke is contented Floyd should be paid, I think the defendants are safe enough in paying either, as we shall agree, for there is to be no after reckoning because this decree may be well given in evidence to an action on the Statute of Edw. VI etc.

[The] demurrer [was] overruled.

402

Marshall v. Martin (Ex. 1705 x 1706)

A release is a good plea to a suit for a share of an intestate's estate, but the plaintiff may allege in a reply fraud in obtaining the release.

---

[6] X *MS*.

[7] Stat. 2 & 3 Edw. VI, c. 13 (*SR*, IV, 55–58).

HLS MS. 1082, vol. 1, part B, p. 19 [Eng.]

[The] plaintiffs bring a bill of discovery against the defendant, being administratrix to her husband, who died intestate, to discover his estate that the wife plaintiff, who was the intestate's niece, being his brother's daughter, should have her share on the Statute of Distribution.[1] The defendant pleads that the intestate died about nine or ten years ago and that about nine years since this defendant paid the plaintiff wife, who was then *feme sole*, £20 in full satisfaction of all debts, duties, and demands whatsoever.

[There was a] demurrer. And the question was whether this was a good plea for the plaintiff. It was not the executor's[2] [?]. The plaintiff says in his bill that the intestate's estate was worth £2000 and £20 is not valuable satisfaction for it in a court of equity and this court will not be bound up by a release in this case and it does not appear [that] there was any account stated at the time of the release of the intestate's estate. Lastly it may well be [that] the defendant owed us £20 on some other [thing] than the intestate's account and that our release was not intended to her as in right of the intestate but in her own etc. and we were illiterate and it was fraudulent.

[It was ruled] by the whole court that it was a good plea and it would be of dangerous consequence to set aside a release with one eye open. The plaintiffs' allegation of £2000 is but a flourish but it may be more or less. It is also against an administrator to give an account after nine years. If there was any fraud in obtaining this release, you should reply and show it.

Dodd, for the plaintiff: We cannot reply without leave of the court, for here is an issuable plea put upon us. But the court thought otherwise and gave him leave to reply.

[Orders of 24 Nov. 1705 and 16 Nov. 1706: PRO E.127/24, f. 209v; E.127/25, f. 277.]

403
Landon v. Sheffield (Ex. 1706)

Matters in abatement, such as the plaintiff's lack of capacity to sue, cannot be raised in a plea in bar.

If a defendant deny that a plaintiff is an executor, he must show who is.

---

[1] Stat. 22 & 23 Car. II, c. 10 (*SR*, V, 719–720).
[2] Xs *MS*.

LI MS. Misc. 536, f. [76] [Eng.] (Ward's Reports)

The plaintiff exhibited her bill against the defendants for the discovery of the personal estate of one Silvanus Landon, thereby alleged to die intestate, and styles herself administratrix of the goods and chattels of the deceased in the title of the bill, and in the body of the bill [she] alleges that administration of the goods and chattels of the deceased were legally and duly committed to her as by the said administration under the seal of the prerogative court of Canterbury ready to be produced may appear, and so charging that the defendants had without any right or title possessed themselves of the said intestate's personal estate consisting of many particulars and great values, and charging also several frauds and pretenses upon the defendants touching the intestate and his estate, prays discovery and relief in the premises.

The defendants put in a plea in bar upon their oaths, and taking it by protestation that the deceased did not die intestate but made a will in writing (not saying what nor when nor who [was] executor nor anything else about it), for plea say that the plaintiff has not obtained letters of administration of the goods and chattels of the deceased and that the plaintiff now is not nor at the time of the exhibiting of the said bill was administratrix to the said deceased or his estate nor has nor ever had any letters of administration under the seal of the prerogative court of Canterbury or any other court whatsoever duly granted to her testifying such administration, all which he avers and pleads the same in bar of the plaintiff's bill and the discovery and relief thereby prayed, and prays judgment of the court whether he shall be compelled to make any further or other answer.

1. It seems this should not be pleaded, but the court moved not to be compelled to answer till [the] administration [be] produced.
2. This plea [in] is bar but ought at best (if any plea lies in this case) to be in abatement only, and only so far,[1] as in outlawry, to the disability of the person.
3. Want of a *profert* in court is aided after verdict. Liber 1, [p.] 11.[2]
4. In a *scire facias* to have execution upon [a] testator's judgment, [it] must be shown before, but not mentioned in the *scire facias*. Liber 1, [p.] 298.[3]
5. The defendant shall not abate my bill by saying I am not [an] executor or administrator without showing who is or making some title to the thing in question. If a man entitles himself as son and heir, or as lord of a manor, or by alleging any particular right or title in any bill,

---

[1] quousque *MS*.
[2] *Holmes v. Grove*, LI MS. Misc. 499, p. 11.
[3] *Broyle v. Noblett* (Ex. Cham. 1667), LI MS. Misc. 499, p. 298.

as parson etc, is it enough to come in and plead that I am not such or have not such right and say no more, and so force me to reply and go to issue and then prove my right? And after that how I shall compel or attain to a discovery? This [is] a roundabout way and never practiced.

And the plea was overruled by the court.

[Other copies of this report: GUL MS. B88–9, f. 284v.]

[Order of 9 Dec. 1706: PRO E.127/25, f. 282.]

404

Bendlowes' Case (Ex. 1706)

It is a contempt to call one of the high courts a 'paltry court'.

LI MS. Misc. 536, f. [89] [Eng.] (Ward's Reports)

Upon the occasion of a bill exhibited in chancery by Collingwood against Hindmarsh, it was referred to a master in chancery to examine whether that bill did contain matters which by a former suit in the exchequer upon a bill exhibited there by Hindmarsh against the said Collingwood and others, which had passed into a decree[1] and that affirmed in the Lords' House upon an appeal,[2] had been in question. Mr. Bendlowes, as counsel for Collingwood, and two agents for the said Hindmarsh attending the master, something was said by one of the agents for Hindmarsh that he hoped that the cause should come into the exchequer, where it was depending, by priority of suit. Affidavit was made by those two persons that Mr. Bendlowes thereupon said 'The court of exchequer is a paltry court'. And thereupon, [a] motion was made at the setting down of causes after Easter term for an attachment against Mr. Bendlowes, and though by the standing printed rules of the court,[3] upon the affidavit of two persons of any scandalous words against the court, an attachment shall forthwith issue. Yet he being a barrister at law, the court indulged a day to him and awarded an attachment against him unless he showed cause the first day of this term, when upon his own affidavit that he did not speak those words and of another that was by that he did not hear him speak them but believes he must [have] had they been spoken, Bendlowes by his counsel prayed to have the attachment discharged. But another affidavit by a third person being produced, who proved the speaking of the words, the court did not think fit to discharge Mr. Bendlowes but ordered

---

[1] Perhaps *Everard v. Hindmarsh and Collingwood* (1701), PRO E.126/17, f. 229.

[2] *Hyndmarsh v. Everard* (1702), Colles 241, 1 E.R. 268.

[3] Rule 40, *Ordines Cancellariae* (1698), p. 40.

him to stand committed unless he showed better cause the Wednesday following. And the third affidavit was filed, the intent being to see if he could extricate himself in the meantime, which not being done, upon the motion of his counsel that he was sorry [if] he should offend the court and under protestation of his innocency, the three barons ordered him to be discharged, to which I could not assent it being so high a reflection upon one of Her Majesty's high courts to say it is a paltry one. Had they been against the barons only, I should as much as in me lay have passed by anything that touched me. But the dignity of the court ought to be preserved which is reflected upon as by three affidavits filed on record and by two orders of court may appear. And to have all this passed by *gratis* without examination or censure to me seemed strange and unprecedented and without any provision made for paying the prosecutor his costs to the great discouragement of any that shall pretend to inform the court of any reflection upon it. Which note and query; those three that made affidavits filed [are] triable to indictments of perjury.

[Other copies of this report: GUL MS. B88–9, f. 293v.]

405

Attorney General ex rel. Marriot v. Lord Wharton (Ex. 1706–1708)

A bill of exceptions cannot be allowed after a verdict has been received and the witnesses have been discharged.

I
LI MS. Misc. 536, f. [96v] [Eng.] (Ward's Reports)

After reading many affidavits on either side and [the] relator's bill, and lord Wharton's answer, and the order of the 24 October 1705[1] for the injunction, and of the injunction itself (which was not warranted by the order, that being for quieting such possession in the mines as [the] relator had at [the] time of the bill 'and' three years before, but the injunction itself was 'or' three years before, which was not warranted, but the lord Wharton in court waived that fault and went on as if it had been 'and three years before') and hearing many counsel on either side, Baron SMITH was for awarding an attachment against those that sank and worked in the three new shafts at Grinton How esteeming that to be a breach of the injunction in regard [that] he took it that the relator was in possession of that mine by working it though at a distance from those three shafts.

---

[1] PRO E.127/24, f. 178.

Baron BURY [was] against the attachment as not [being] satisfied [that] the relator had any possession of that mine where the three shafts are sunk and so [there was] no contempt.

Baron Price [was] absent.

[The] chief baron [WARD was] for an attachment against them that spoke disdainfully of the injunction and that shot at such as served it. For though it was not strictly right, yet it was the process of the court and ought not to be disdained, nor the servers of it abused. And he was also for an attachment against such as disturbed [the] relator in working the mines he was working by fitting up trenches which brought water or impediment to the relator's miners or mines in working and where the relator's workmen used at [the] time of [the] bill and three years before to wash ore or carry on works for his mines for that is a necessary incident to the working of [the] mines. But as to the sinking [of] the three shafts by [the] defendants, it being made probable that they are in another manor and sixty yards from the mouth of [the] relator's vein which he is working and that for those sixty yards defendants claim not, but insist that though the same mine or vein that the defendant now works within his own bounds should extend itself after such a distance into the defendant's manor, yet all such part of the mine that lies in [the] defendant's manor belongs to the defendant, and the relator by working the mine in his own bounds is not possessed nor has any possession of or in such part of the mine as is out of his bounds and in defendant's manor, for generally speaking and nothing appearing to the contrary in this case he that has the soil has all the mines in that soil. And working mines in my own soil gives nor makes not any possession of such part of the mine which is in another's soil. And then the relator cannot by the injunction be quieted in the possession of that mine in defendant's manor, whereof he never had any possession.

Had this been in [the] case of a mine in Derbyshire or Cornwall, where by custom the miners dig and follow the mine in and into any man's soil without interruption, in such the working [of] any part of the mine would have been a possession of the whole let it go whither it would, but not so here, for every man has a right to so much and no more of the mine as is in his own soil, unless he can by some good title claim the mines whithersoever they lead.

Now though this injunction is not to settle or determine the title of the mines or boundaries of lordships or any interest or estate in them, but only to quiet a three years' possession in imitation of the statute about forcible entries, yet there must appear to be an uninterrupted possession of the thing in question which is easily determined as to lands or houses. Yet what shall be a possession of a mine is more difficult. It cannot be thought that he that works at one end of the mine is thereby in possession of all of it let it extend itself never so far into another's soil. And therefore I thought as to these three shafts that it did not appear [that] the relator had ever any possession of them. And so the injunction did not extend to them, and therefore as to their sinking and working, [there was] no contempt.

However, I concluded for attachments to go for the other two causes, but therein Baron SMITH and BURY both were against me.

Some overtures were after made between the parties for trying the right of the mines, where the defendant's three shafts were sunk, by ejectment or having issues directed. But after a day or two's consideration, nothing took effect.

After which at the same setting down of causes, the counsel for the lord Wharton (who by his answer to the relator's bill had set forth himself to be but tenant for life, remainder to Philip, his eldest son, in tail) having exhibited his cross-bill in this court in his own name only, and his son [being] no party to it, upon an affidavit of ancient witnesses, naming them, prayed a commission to examine his witnesses *in perpetuam rei memoriam*, which he prayed also by his bill, which was not only a bill of discovery but for relief also (touching the mines and other matters), to which bill the queen's attorney general, and Marriot, the relator, and Sir Solomon Swale (against whom the relator had prevailed upon two trials in ejectment and appeared [as] an amicable defendant) and one Hillary, who is pretended to be lord of Grinton Manor (but claims not the mines), and the parson of Grinton (who is pretended to claim tithes of the mines there), and several others were made defendants, but none [were] served with process but the relator who put in his answer [at the] beginning of last term and no exceptions [were taken] to it, nor had the attorney general been attended with a copy of the bill nor for his answer as [he] ought to be, nor were any other [of] the defendants in contempt for not answering nor [were they] so much as served with process. And whether in this case thus circumstanced, the lord Wharton was entitled to the commission prayed, and against whom it should extend was the question in debate in the court.

And the rules of the court[2] were read where it is provided that, if a bill to perpetuate testimonies be exhibited, and the defendants are in contempt, a commission to examine *de bene esse* shall issue, and if the defendant appears, he may join, and if the defendant answers, the plaintiff may reply. So that in this case in question the attorney general being ready to answer immediately and would have done it sooner if attended, and the relator having answered and there being no precedent that ever a commission to examine *de bene esse* was awarded after answer wherein the whole pretense in the plaintiff's bill was in issue by the general traverse at [the] end of the defendant's answer 'Without that that' etc. and though the time for putting in exceptions was not expired, yet there being an issue between plaintiff and defendant which is sufficient to warrant examinations and if the plaintiff pleases may reply and have a complete issue, the court

---

[2] Rule 34, *Ordines Cancellariae* (1698), p. 33.

did not award any commission to examine *de bene esse* as to the attorney and relator, but did award one as to the other defendants that had not answered, though not in contempt. And the attorney general and [the] relator had the like order to examine *de bene esse* where they were plaintiffs as to such defendants as had not answered though no oath [was] made of ancient witnesses.

But query of what avail such examination will be in regard [that] the issue in tail of lord Wharton is not [a] party to either bill, and Lord Wharton [is] only tenant for life and [it will] serve only for his life, and can neither be read for or against the issue. See Liber M, [f.] 24, Pride and Monck,[3] and [the] cases there cited where examinations *de bene esse* 'may be and have been refused'. And the great question in this case is between the crown and the relator and the lord Wharton as lord of the manor of Swaledale and Helaw.

Note afterwards in Hilary term 1706/07, lord Wharton endeavored to have an information in the Crown Office in the queen's bench to be preferred against the relator and many of his workmen in his mine for a riot supposed to be committed by them in defending the relator's possession and working of his mines and opposing and hindering the lord Wharton's workmen in working of his. But after reading many affidavits on both sides, the court did not think fit to order an information.

[Other copies of this report: GUL MS. B88–9, f. 304v.]

II

IU Lilly MS. Parker, 'Cases in the Exchequer, vol. 4', p. 204 [Eng.] (Price's Reports)

An issue [was] directed to be tried out of the equity side of the court upon a feigned issue and promise: whether the shafts, groves, and pits of lead which were sunk in the moor or waste of Harkaside, whether they were in the manor of Helaugh or in the manor of Grinton in Yorkshire, whether the waste or place where the lead pits were were in Helaugh or Grinton, and whether the waste and moor of West Grinton and Harkaside be in Helaugh or Grinton. If in Helaugh, it is for the defendant; if in Grinton, for the plaintiff.

The jury of Yorkshire gave [a] verdict for the attorney general.

There was a bill of exceptions tendered upon [the] giving [of] a verdict and before it was recorded, that is, between the privy verdict and the verdict in court:

1. That the court admitted as evidence what ancient persons, who were in their lifetime tenants of the manor of Grinton, declared that the River Swale was the boundary between the manor of Grinton and the manor of Helaugh and that the waste and moors of Harkaside, *alias*

---

[3] *Pride v. Monck* (Ex. 1696), above, No. 312.

West Grinton, of the south of the said river was parcel of the manor of Grinton and that the tenants of the manor of Grinton (*ut huiusmodi tenentes*) had common in the waste of Harkaside and West Grinton.
2. That Queen Elizabeth [on] 10 November 41 of her reign [1599] did grant the manor of Grinton to Richard Wiseman and Francis Hitch in fee except *unam mineram plumbi* in the manor of Tremington and Grinton at 40s. rent, which the plaintiff gave in evidence.
3. The plaintiff gave in evidence a lease bearing date 10 August 1696 from King William to George Tushingham of all the mines and veins of lead open or not open in the countries and fields of Grinton, Whiteaside, and Harkaside in the County of York, parcel of the manor of Grinton and late parcel of the monastery of Bridlinton for thirty-one years rendering 20s. rent and the tenth part clear profit.
4. The plaintiff gave in evidence that Sir Solomon Swale, tenant within the manor of Helaugh, being within West Grinton and Harkaside (he then claiming to be lord of the manor of Grinton), that he several times within forty years did dig in the waste of West Grinton and Harkaside and raised much lead there without any interruption from the crown or their farmers or the defendant, the earl, or his ancestors, against which evidence the defendant's counsel did object that it was not legal.

On the defendant's part, it was given in evidence that William the Conqueror was seised in fee of the honour of Richmond in Yorkshire and that the manor of Helaugh was part, which was granted to Allen, earl of Brittain, in fee, that Stephen, brother and heir to Allen, being seised of the said honour, did grant the said manor of Helaugh to be held of the said honour to Walter de Gaunt in fee, that Walter de Gaunt granted to [the] prior and convent of Bridlinton in the County of York the manor of Grinton as part of the manor of Helaugh to hold in frankalmoign, that the manor of Helaugh extended on both sides of the river Swale, and that the tenement of Sir Solomon Swale was held of the manor of Helaugh, to prove which, the defendant's counsel offered in evidence [the following].

[1.] First, they offered an ancient manuscript book out of Cotton's Library, which is established by Act of Parliament,[4] which book purports to be a register of the said honour of Richmond, and a description of the manors, villages, and members thereof, and the genealogy of the earls of Richmond after the Conquest, as Allen and then Stephen, his brother, who died [in] 1164.

---

[4] Stat. 12 & 13 Will. III, c. 7 (*SR*, VII, 642–643); Stat. 6 Ann., c. 30 (*SR*, VIII, 625–627).

The book recites King William's grant by the name *Williamus Cognomine Bastardus Rex Anglie do et concedo nepoti meo Alano Brittannie Comiti et heredibus suis omnes villas et terras quae nuper fuerunt Comitis Edwini in Eborashire cum feodis militum in Richmondshire secundum quod scutagium debuit solvi tam de novo feoffmento quam de veteri secundam pipam scaccarii regis de feodo Gilberti de Gaunt in Swaledale ex utraque parte atque 4 feoda, in baga de feoda in custodia rememeratoris thesaurarii existentes in Eboraco Johann de Brittannia tenet villam de Caterick de domino rege sed per quod servitium non fit mentis in inquisitione predicta Grinton et ibidem una carucata terrae quam prior de Bridlington tenet in puram eleemosinam de antecestoribus Gilberti de Gaunt et nullum fit inde servitium Rith Helaugh Hamell sunt ibi 4 carucatae terrae et Hugo filius Henrici duas carucatas de Gilberto de Gaunt et idem Gilbertus tenet alium dimidium carucatae [blank] Hugo filius Henrici duas carucatas de Gilbert de Gaunt [blank] feoderunt de Richmondshire 1 Edw. II. Dominus Gilbertus de Gaunt tenet in capite de comite Richmond 4 feoda in Helaugh in Swaledale per homagium et redditus scutagii quando currit.*

2. There was offered for the defendant in evidence, which was refused, four ancient rolls of the manor of Helaugh entitled *Extractus Curiae Capit. cum usu frankplegii domini Thomasi Wharton et aliorum dominorum de Swaledale 31 Augusti 1 Elizabethae* [1559], being estreats of the fines and amercements imposed on the tenants of the manor of Helaugh with the several vills and hamlets *ex utraque parte de Swale viz.* Crackpott, Whitaside, Harkaside, Rath, Ruckcross, Raw, and Helaugh and other places and in an extract 12 March 3 Eliz. [1561] of the fines and amercements in Helayne and in the same roll, title [?] Harkaside, for cutting wood there, fines upon several, and in one roll of extracts of the manor of Sir Thomas Wharton, lord Warton, and John Mollineux, lords of the manor of Helaugh in Swaledale 10 June 4 Eliz. [1562] fines and amercements on tenants of Helaugh and 6d. on J. Swale, gent., *quia debuit leetam curiae ibidem et fecit defaltam*, and several fines on tenants in Harkaside *quia non comparaverunt* and for cutting wood there and not cleaning a pool called Geld Pool in Harkaside, that the said book and rolls the barons did refuse to admit as evidence, affirming and adjudging that the said book and rolls ought not to be given in evidence to the jury and because the said exceptions and objections of the defendant's counsel *non constant in recordo et processu in dicta curia scaccarii*, and the counsel prayed the barons' seals to the bill of exceptions, which they did refuse [in] May 7 Anne [1708].

Serjeant Parker, Sir Edward Northey, Cheshire, Ettrick, Lutwyche, Ward, and Johnson [made] objections against the bill of exceptions.

[In the case of] the king against Hayns[5] in the king's bench upon [an] information, [there was] a bill of exceptions and the notes [were] agreed upon in court.

---

[5] *Rex v. Hains* (1694–1695), Comberbach 310, 337, 90 E.R. 497, 513, Skinner 583, 90 E.R. 262, Carthew 320, 90 E.R. 788, Holt K.B. 289, 90 E.R. 1059.

The Town of Newcastle v. Dean and Chapter of Durham, [upon a] trial in the exchequer, a bill was refused because [it was] not demanded and tendered in writing or [upon] notes upon the trial. The Statute of Westminster II, c. 31,[6] requires [that one] must except whilst pleading and put into writing like notes of a special verdict at the same time.

Brownlow, *[Latine] Redivivus*, 129, Verdon v. Dycell,[7] in false imprisonment, justify by warrant of the speaker of the House of Commons, [the] reply [was] that [he] detained him after he had notice of the prorogation, [and he] offered [in evidence] the report of the prorogation, and the votes of the Parliament were given in evidence, and the judge declared his opinion that they were good, and [the] bill of exceptions [was] allowed.

Brownlow, *[Latine] Redivivus*, 131, Michael Phillips v. Elizabeth Chichester,[8] on ejectment in Ireland; Brownlow 134, Hilary term 45 Eliz. [1603], Stidson v. Yeoman,[9] ejectment.

Note that the bill of exceptions was sealed and there was [a] verdict [and] judgment and nothing further.

Brownlow 136, Rouse v. Wright, 15 Car. I [1639]; 1 Lutwyche, Thurston v. Slatford; Goldesborough 137; Statute of Westminster II, c. 31; 2 *Inst.* 426.[10]

[One must] take notes of [a] special verdict which the jury must agree to and draw [them] up afterwards, so must the notes for [an] exception, which [one] may draw up after[wards] in form; [a] bill of exception is to evidence which fact ought to be settled, and if to any other matter, it should be *in scriptis*.

If [there is an] exception upon the trial, the party may accord or allow evidence, or if [it] differ in fact, evidence may be called once again, which, when from the bar, cannot be done.

Easter [term] 1708, in the king's bench, Wright v. Sharpe; 2 Levinz 236, Hilary [term] 31 Car. II [1679], in the king's bench, Enfield v. Hills.[11]

---

[6] Stat. 13 Edw. I, c. 31 (*SR*, I, 86–87).

[7] *Verdon v. Decele* (1683), R. Brownlow, *Latine Redivivus* (1693), p. 129, *sub nom.* Verdon v. Deaele, 2 Shower K.B. 300, 303, 89 E.R. 951, 953, *sub nom. Verdon v. Topham* (1682), T. Jones 208, 84 E.R. 1220.

[8] *Philips v. Chichester* (1680), R. Brownlow, *Latine Redivivus* (1693), p. 131, T. Jones 146, 84 E.R. 1189.

[9] *Stidson v. Yeoman* (1603), R. Brownlow, *Latine Redivivus* (1693), p. 134.

[10] *Rouse v. Wright* (1639), R. Brownlow, *Latine Redivivus* (1693), p. 136; *Thurston v. Slatford* (1700), 1 Lutwyche 905, 125 E.R. 504, also Holt K.B. 299, 90 E.R. 1065, 1 Salkeld 284, 91 E.R. 251, 3 Salkeld 155, 91 E.R. 748; perhaps *Puncheon v. Legate* (1611), 2 Brownlow & Goldsborough 137, 123 E.R. 859; Stat. 13 Edw. I, c. 31 (*SR*, I, 86–87); E. Coke, *Second Institute* (1642), p. 426.

[11] *Wright v. Sharpe* (1708), 1 Salkeld 288, 91 E.R. 255, 11 Modern 175, 88 E.R. 972, Holt K.B. 301, 90 E.R. 1066; *Enfield v. Hills* (1679), 2 Levinz 236, 83 E.R. 535, also 3 Keble 859, 84 E.R. 1054, T. Jones 116, 84 E.R. 1174.

1693, Lord Duke of Grafton v. Chief Justice Holt, Holt v. Bridgman,[12] the exception, [which] was tendered after [a] privy verdict and before [the] verdict [was] affirmed in court, is out of time.

Town of Newcastle v. Dean and Chapter of Durham, in the exchequer, [a] bill of exceptions [was] offered after trial and refused.

For the defendants [were] Sir Thomas Powys, Sir James Montagu, Serjeant Hooper, Serjeant Pratt, Eyres, Lechmere, Harcourt, Bridges, and King.

The law has [a] great regard to bills of exceptions, [a] subjects' right to appeal, and no delay in them more than on writs of error.

A special verdict may be found specially after [the] jury is [gone] from the bar and before [a] verdict, that [a] privy verdict [is] no verdict, for after[wards] the plaintiff may not appear, [the] defendant may confess [the] action, the jury may disagree, and [there may] not [be a] full jury. If judges may seal at any time, why not [a] demand or tender at any time; the jury is not concerned and only the judges.

Writs of error are not *ex debito justitiae* in criminal causes, much less bills of exception. Kel. 15, Sir Henry Vane's Case; Goldsb. 137.[13]

[A] bill of exception not alleged in diminution is [a] distinct record [and] not part of [the] original record. If it must be in writing, [it] cannot intend notes, which is not to be sealed, and exceptions [written out] at length, which must be sealed, are two sorts of writing.

Register 182,[14] writ *ad ponendum sigillum ad exceptionem per* Statute Westminster II, c. 31, recites the case and offer of exceptions: *et exceptiones illas pro eo quod vos illas allocare noluistis scripserit et vos saepius requisierit et petierit sigilla apponere et non sigilla vestra exceptionibus apponere distulistis et adhuc differtis vobis praecipimus si ita est.*

It was said [that] the judges are but ministerial as to the bill of exceptions; the plaintiff is not concerned, nor the jury; it is between the court and [the] defendant.

1702; [an] action against Mr. Clerke in the common pleas, and after [the] plea and demurrer and judgment, [he] prayed oyer of the original, and it was allowed him.

1705; [in the case of the] Warden of the Fleet v. Leighton,[15] before Lord Chief Justice Trevor, [the] defendant pleads in abatement that [the] plaintiff was not warden of the Fleet and in evidence brought a writ of error and the transcript

---

[12] *Dutchess of Grafton v. Holt* (1693), Skinner 354, 90 E.R. 157.

[13] *Rex v. Vane* (1662), Kelyng 14, 84 E.R. 1060, also 1 Levinz 68, 83 E.R. 300, 1 Keble 304, 315, 319, 324, 83 E.R. 960, 967, 969, 972, 1 Siderfin 84, 82 E.R. 985; *Anonymous* (1601), Gouldesborough 136, 75 E.R. 1048.

[14] *Registrum Omnium Brevium* (1595), f. 182.

[15] Note *Regina v. Ford* (1704), Colles 332, 336, 1 E.R. 312, 314.

of a record in a former cause as evidence after judgment, he offered [a] bill of exceptions, and it was allowed of, but [it was] said that it [was] demanded and promised by the court.

1 Leonard 5, pl. 9,[16] a bill of exceptions in [an] information of intrusion.

[There was an] information upon [the] Statute of Recusancy[17] where [the] proceedings against them [were] in the County of Kent, whereas [in] fact [it] was in [the] Town and County of Canterbury, and [the] bill of exceptions [was] allowed.

Bills of exceptions are [allowed] in all civil cases of the crown [but] not in capitals. 1 Ventris 366,[18] in a *quo warranto*, [a] bill of exceptions [was] allowed on a challenge by [the] Statute [of] Westminster II, c. 31, [as] is an auxiliary law to a writ of error to make it good, and [it] is a remedial law and ought to have a liberal and reasonable construction.

The King v. Haynes, in the king's bench on a *quo warranto*, bill of exceptions, and notes taken in court, where [there was] a challenge of the jury [as] not being freeholders, and it was offered in arrest of judgment, [but it was] not allowed, but [it was] error, same as [the] case in Ventris 366.

[On] 23 June 1708, Lord Chief Baron WARD, BURY, and PRICE *seriatim* gave their opinion upon the bill of exceptions that it ought not to be received nor sealed by the judges, being after the privy verdict and after the verdict [was] affirmed at the bar and before it was recorded, yet it was too late offered, the witnesses, being discharged, could not be examined between the privy and public verdict, it being contrary to the Statute of Westminster II, c. 31, which is all in the present time as to the *proponat exceptiones*, the disallowance, and the party who did object writing down the exceptions.

18 Edw. II, Brooke [Abr.], *Assise*, n. 434.[19] It is [a] matter of fact and the exception must be taken presently and written then, being [that] the pleadings formerly were *ore tenus* and not in writing. 11 Hen. IV, 66, 92, 93.[20] The bill of exceptions is looked upon [as] a record from the time of the assise, which shows [that] it must be then tendered. 27 Hen. VIII, 24.[21] [An] exception prayed [was] written and sealed together. The construction of the Statute [of] Westminster II ought to be reasonable and practicable, otherwise all verdicts will be overturned

---

[16] *Lord Paget v. Bishop of Coventry* (1583), 1 Leonard 5, 74 E.R. 5.

[17] Stat. 35 Eliz. I, c. 2 (*SR*, IV, 843–846).

[18] *Rex v. Higgins* (1683), 1 Ventris 366, 86 E.R. 236, also T. Raymond 484, 83 E.R. 253, Skinner 91, 101, 105, 90 E.R. 43, 48, 49.

[19] Brooke, Abr., *Assise*, pl. 435.

[20] YB Pas. 11 Hen. IV, ff. 65, 66, pl. 25 (1410); YB Trin. 11 Hen. IV, ff. 92, 93, pl. 49 (1410).

[21] YB Mich. 27 Hen. VIII, f. 24, pl. 3 (1535).

and proceedings [will be] uncertain. If [they be] not demanded and proposed in time, it is to no purpose. And so the exceptions were rejected.

[The arguments in this case are noted in LI MS. Misc. 536, ff. 94v–97v, 105–120, 159–163; GUL MS. B88–9, ff. 300v–304v.]

[Orders of 9 and 28 May, 19 June, 25 Oct. 1706: PRO E.127/25, ff. 109, 156, 211v, 219v.]

406

Hyde v. Tenison (Ex. 1706)

A court of equity will not specifically enforce an option to renew a lease after the option has expired.

I
BL MS. Hargr. 71, f. 116, pl. 1 [Fr. & Eng.] (Dodd's Reports)

The parson, [Edward] Tenison, rector of Sandwich in Kent, made a lease of the rectory to [John] Hyde for three years and a covenant to renew for three years and thus from three years to three years during the life of the parson if the major part of the parish desired it and he be thereto requested within one month after the expiration of the lease. The lease expires, and the month elapses, and then within two days [the] request [was] made, and [the] parson refused. And a bill [was] brought to compel him to perform the covenant and make a lease etc. And the court dismissed the bill because he did not come within the month, and [they] would not relieve against the two days that had elapsed.

[Other copies of this report: HLS MS. 537(b), p. 69, pl. 1; Oxf. Brasenose MS. 59, p. 89, pl. 2; IU Lilly MS. Parker, 'Cases in the Exchequer, vol. 2', p. 70; BL MS. Hargr. 70, p. 111, pl. 367; HLS MS. 1162, p. 95, pl. 514.]

II
IU Lilly MS. Parker, 'Cases in the Exchequer, vol. 4', p. 114, pl. 2 [Eng.]
(Price's Reports)

The plaintiff's bill was to execute an agreement. The defendant had made a lease of his rectory for three years reserving £140 *per annum* rent, and therein [was] a covenant that if all the parishioners were desirous to renew the lease for three years more and they requested within one month before the end of the three years. The request was made two days short.

It was said to be a voluntary agreement without any consideration and that the defendant could not compel the plaintiff to take a lease. And a court of equity, where the terms of the agreement are not punctually observed and where [there is] no mutual consideration, will not enforce the execution of them. Precedent conditions are not so much regarded in equity but conditions which defeat estates not those who create them. Nor was there any authority for the plaintiff to demand and accept of a lease.

Chief Baron WARD, BURY, and SMITH [were] for dismissing [the] plaintiff's bill. Baron Price came [into the court at] the latter end [of the argument] and gave no opinion, being sick.

[Order of 1 May 1706: PRO E.127/25, f. 92.]

407
Greenway v. Earl of Kent (Ex. 1706)

Tithes are due for all wood that has been cut and corded.

IU Lilly MS. Parker, 'Cases in the Exchequer, vol. 4', p. 54 [Eng.] (Price's Reports)

The plaintiff [Richard Greenway] as rector of Walford in the County of Hereford exhibits a bill against the defendant [Henry, Earl of Kent] for tithe wood from the Chase Valet or coppice wood for the years 1701 [and] 1702.

The defendant submits to pay tithe for the underwood and coppice wood as it was corded and sold to the forge, being allowed for his charges in cutting and cording. And as to the other part of the said bill, he says that there were storers or standels of oaks, which were above thirty years growth, and some old timber trees, that he separated the standels from the underwoods and cut them at several times, that he corded the standels by themselves, and some he sold for building and other uses, and insists they are not tithable.

The court gave their opinions.

Baron BURY, Baron PRICE, and Baron SMITH [held] for the plaintiff that the defendant ought to account for the tithe of all the wood corded and the deputy [queen's remembrancer] to state what timber was sold.

Chief Baron [WARD held] for the defendant that he ought not to account for any timber above twenty years growth.

Baron PRICE argued that these standels of oaks were usually cut with the other coppice wood till of late that they were separated. If the standels are discharged of paying tithe, it must be by the common law or the Statute 45 Edw. III, c. 3.[1] By the common law, all timber was privileged from paying tithe and the tops, crops, bark, roots, and germins from the roots and that all coppice or underwood and *sylva caedua* were tithable as appeared by Lambert's translation of the Saxon laws[2] and by the books which say that the Statute 45 Edw. III, c. 3, is but declaratory of the common law.

---

[1] Stat. 45 Edw. III, c. 3 (*SR*, I, 393).
[2] W. Lambarde, *Archaionomia*.

The Statute 45 Edw. III, c. 3, is to be considered, that gross wood twenty years and upwards, tithe of them being sued for in the spiritual court by the name of *sylva caedua*, a prohibition was to be granted.

Ancient statutes are to be interpreted according to the intent and meaning of them. If construed literally, this case is within the Statute, being gross wood and twenty years and upwards.

Gross wood is not all sorts of wood that is large and above twenty years but is timber and such wood as is usually employed in building and other matters of a high nature. The Statute says that merchants bought it for their profit and to aid the king in his wars, which must be intended [to mean] large timber.

2 *Inst.* 642; Fitz. N.B. 154; 11 Rep., Lyford's Case; Bro., Abr., *Dismes*, 240; Fitz., Abr., *Attach[ment] Sur Prohibition*; Degge 242; Cro. Eliz. 1, Foster v. Leonard; *Reformatio Legum*, 'de decimis', 115; Rastal, 'proh[ibition]', 448; Stat. 35 Hen. VIII, c. 17,[3] that [if] coppice wood [be] cut under twenty-four years growth, there are to be twelve standels in an acre not to be cut till ten inches square within three feet of the ground, if above twenty-four years growth, the standels are to be kept twenty years after, and this was to preserve timber and under a penalty, if any [were] cut otherwise, [with a] proviso not to extend to wood within two miles of the sea or where [there were] dead tops or for the service of the crown.

So that it appears that timber at common law and by the Statute 45 Edw. III was oak, ash, [and] elm, and if, at twenty years growth, they were fit for building, then they were timber; if not for [that] use, [they were] not timber. But timber to be raised in coppice woods and within the Statute 35 Hen. VIII, c. 17, must be ten inches square, as before, or twenty years growth after the wood of twenty-four years growth is cut, so that timber bred in Valets must be distinguished.

The time of twenty years in the Statute 45 Edw. III, c. 3, is not observed and cannot be intended but where the wood is so grown to be fit for timber use.

Cotton's *Ab*. 345, 15 & 17 Ric. II,[4] petition to the Parliament to know at what age wood was tithable and what age *sylva caedua* was to be cut.

---

[3] E. Coke, *Second Institute* (1642), p. 642; A. Fitzherbert, *New Natura Brevium* (1652), p. 131; *Stamp v. Clinton* (1614), 11 Coke Rep. 46, 77 E.R. 1206, also 1 Rolle Rep. 95, 81 E.R. 354; Brooke, Abr., *Dismes*, pl. 3, 4, 14, 18, 19; YB Mich. 9 Hen. VI, f. 56, pl. 42 (1430), Fitzherbert, Abr., *Attachement sur prohibicion*, pl. 1; S. Degge, *Parson's Counsellor* (1681), p. 242; *Foster v. Leonard* (1581), Cro. Eliz. 1, 78 E.R. 267, also sub nom. *Forster v. Peacok*, Moore K.B. 907, 72 E.R. 988, 1 Eagle & Younge 82; *Reformatio Legum* (1640), 'de decimis', p. 115; W. Rastell, *Collection of Entries* (1670), 'Prohibition', f. 488; Stat. 35 Hen. VIII, c. 17 (*SR*, III, 977–980).

[4] R. Cotton, *Exact Abridgement of the Records in the Tower of London* (1657), pp. 345, 349, 355.

The Statute 35 Hen. VIII, c. 17, shows that wood may be cut after twenty-four years, which did not consist with the twenty years in 45 Edw. III, unless those two acts respected several sorts of timber in and out of coppice.

1 Levinz 189, Haws v. Cornwall.[5] If wood is usually cut for fire wood, though it be twenty-five or forty years growth, it shall pay tithe, and so shall pollards, though fifty years of age. Siderfin 300, *idem*.[6]

I conceive the standels here to be *sylva caedua*, which is defined in Linwood's '*Sylva caedua an satur quaecumque incisa repullabat vel ex stirpibus vel radicibus renascatur caedua est quae matura et habilis ad caedendum*'. Linwood, 190, 356.[7]

50 Edw. III, 10.[8] *Sylva caedua* is in the same manner described and said that any woods if preserved will have germins from the roots, and by color of that, the clergy sued in the spiritual court for the tithe of all wood as *sylva caedua*, and from the 17th [year of] Edw. III, when Archbishop Stratford's provincial canon was made to the time of the Statute 45 Edw. III, there were perpetual controversies [as to] what was *sylva caedua* and how far it extended.

Rolle, Abr., *Dismes*, 638,[9] is much to the same purpose.

2 Brownlow 150, Brook v. Cole.[10] Waste was brought for cutting forty standel oaks above twenty years growth, [and] all the judges agreed it was not waste, not being timber, being cut as acre wood, and the parties were used to sell this wood for seasonable wood, and so [it was] not timber and tithe [was] paid for it, which would not have been, if it had been timber.

This case goes far in the case in question and supports Haws v. Cornwall.

Winch, *Entries*, 630, Lob v. Woodnell,[11] a special verdict [. . .] cuts of oaks at twenty-one years growth and being usually cut at that age and no tithe [was] paid, if it was discharged by the Statute 45 Edw. III. I do not find any judgment given.

Doctor and Student 355,[12] custom charged wood under twenty years growth with tithe, custom discharged wood above twenty years, and custom might charge wood above twenty, and if coppice wood above twenty years growth,

---

[5] *Haws v. Cornwall* (1666), 1 Levinz 189, 83 E.R. 362.

[6] *Cornell v. Haws* (1666), 1 Siderfin 300, 82 E.R. 1118, also *sub nom. Cornwall v. Haws*, 2 Keble 1, 90, 833, 84 E.R. 1, 56, 527, 1 Eagle & Younge 450.

[7] W. Lyndwood, *Provinciale* (1679), f. 190 ('*ex stirpibus aut radicibus renascitur*'), f. 356.

[8] *Frankley v. Heyning* (1376), YB Hil. 50 Edw. III, f. 10, pl. 21.

[9] 1 Rolle, Abr., *Dismes*, H-M, p. 638.

[10] *Brook v. Cobb* (1612), 2 Brownl. & Golds. 150, 123 E.R. 867.

[11] *Lobbe v. Woodnett* (1621), H. Winch, *Le Beau-Pledeur: A Book of Entries* (1680), pp. 628, 630.

[12] *St. German's Doctor and Student* (Plucknett and Barton, edd., 1974), 91 Selden Soc. 300–314.

[they] have usually paid tithe and their standels,[13] it is good notwithstanding the Statute 45 Edw. III.

If that be law, that where the timber lies *sparsim* in a great coppice, the coppice brings in the timber to be chargeable if [it is] most[ly] timber and little underwood; the timber privileges the rest.

Degge 243, which cites several cases, which I cannot find.

2 Leonard 79, Davies v. Molyns[14] does support that opinion, and then by the rules, the standels ought to pay tithe with the rest of the wood.

There is a mighty mischief [that] will happen if by this project or experiment of separating the standels that will alter the manner of tithing for [the] law is [that], if a timber tree is privileged, then all its germins which spring from its roots are forever discharged, so if every standel, being privileged in all succeeding falls, then germins will not pay tithes, and in time the wood will be wholly discharged.

If one were to sow a new coppice of oak and at twenty [years] this wood is to be cut, then it is privileged by the Statute 45 Edw. III, c. 3, and consequently all the germins and coppice then after would be tithe free, this being usually a provision for the poor vicars, it will be their ruin and no great advantage to the owners of the wood.

There are some precedents brought to us, which are not much to the purpose.

Trinity [term], 3 Jac. II [1687], exchequer, Acton v. Smith.[15] [The] plaintiff, [the] rector of Bulworth in Hampshire [exhibited] a tithe bill; [the] defendant insisted that the oak, ash, beech, and asp[en] were timber; [it was] decreed that the defendant account for what [was] corded, faggoted, or sold in poles; but what was used for timber [was] to be discharged of tithe; and this was a coppice wood that was then cut, and [the] deputy [king's remembrancer was] to cast up [the] value of the wood not used for timber. This case shows that timber in coppice wood, if sold in cord, pole, or faggot is tithable.

Hilary [term] 6 Will. [1695], Taswell v. Atwell,[16] [a] tithe bill for wood [in] Norfolk, tops and lops of oak, ash, and elm, where the bodies were above twenty years growth, the bill as to the top wood is dismissed.

Trinity [term] 6 Will. [1694], John Abbott v. Sir Michael Hickes,[17] [a] tithe bill, [the] issue [was] if beech be timber in the parish of Whitcombe in Gloucestershire, the cause was reheard, and [there was an] issue finding beechwood

---

[13] there standeth *MS*.

[14] *Daws v. Mollins* (1584), 2 Leonard 79, 74 E.R. 374, 1 Eagle & Younge 86.

[15] *Acton v. Smith* (Ex. 1687) above, No. 244.

[16] *Taswell v. Athill* (1695), Samuel Dodd's Reports, p. 147, 1 Eagle & Younge 590, 1 Rayner 75, 2 Gwillim 537.

[17] *Abbott v. Hicks* (Ex. 1696), above, No. 331.

timber; the bill was dismissed as to beechwood, though it appeared that [the] great part of it was coaled. This argues only that beechwood is timber in that parish, though a very extraordinary issue if timber in that parish, but then being coaled, that did not vary [it].

Trinity [term] 10 Will. [1698], Layfield v. Cooper,[18] [a] tithe bill as rector of Buriton in Hampshire, [it was] decreed [that] no tithe [was due] for the great beech wood, being maiden trees and not stems and that they were timber and useable for timber uses and that the bodies, lops, and tops are privileged. This case only excuses large beech, but why stems should be distinguished, since the stems are privileged as well as the body of the tree or the old tree or [the] maiden tree.

Baron SMITH cited Plowden, *Commentaries*, 470, Molyn's Case.[19] He thought wood [was] not tithable of right, Moore 908,[20] that oak apt for timber under twenty years [growth was] not to pay tithe [was] not [good] law. 8 Rep., Sir Francis B.;[21] the cases, some speak to the ages, others the quality, others the uses.

Baron BURY: This was kept for coppice, cut as coppice, and the standels are not timber or timber kind nor kept for timber.

Chief Baron WARD: 42 Hen. III enumerates all sorts of things tithable, and wood [is] not named till 17 Edw. III.[22]

[It was said] that one may prescribe against as affirmative statute, as the [case of] 9 Hen. VI, 56,[23] as to have the tithe of gross wood, though it is [*blank*]. Custom makes things tithable or not tithable as [*blank*]. Twenty years growth of wood timber kind is privileged and as [an] inheritance is got and is not cut as seasonable wood. 11 Hen. VI, 1b.[24] Lops and tops of trees [are] privileged. Rolle, Abr., 640; Moore 908; Cro. Eliz. 55, same as Moore.[25]

---

[18] *Layfield v. Cowper* (1694), 1 Eagle & Younge 591, 1 Wood 330, Order of 11 July 1698: PRO E.126/17, f. 54.

[19] *Soby v. Molins* (1574), 2 Plowden 468, 75 E.R. 700, 1 Eagle & Younge 60, 1 Gwillim 133.

[20] *Wray v. Clench* (1587), Moore K.B. 908, 72 E.R. 988, 1 Eagle & Younge 91, Cro. Eliz. 55, 78 E.R. 316.

[21] *Sir Francis Barrington's Case* (1610), 8 Coke Rep. 136, 77 E.R. 681.

[22] *Rotuli Parliamentorum*, 17 Edw. III, No. 29, II (1832), p. 142, 1 Gwillim 3.

[23] *Abbot of St. Mary of York's Case* (1430), YB Mich. 9 Hen. VI, f. 56, pl. 42.

[24] YB Mich. 11 Hen. VI, f. 1, pl. 3 (1432).

[25] 1 Rolle, Abr., *Dismes*, pl. Q, 2 and Q, 3, p. 640; *Ranne v. Patison* (1596), Moore K.B. 908, 72 E.R. 988, also 1 Eagle & Younge 133, Cro. Eliz. 477, 78 E.R. 729, Gouldsborough 145, 75 E.R. 1054, and *Broke v. Rogers* (1605), Moore K.B. 908, 72 E.R. 989, also Cro. Jac. 100, 79 E.R. 86, 1 Eagle & Younge 158; *Anonymous*, Cro. Eliz. 55, 78 E.R. 316.

2. Timber kind or nature, as oak, ash, etc., the several statutes 35 Hen. VIII, 1 Eliz., and 13 Eliz.[26] are for other purposes to order timber but do not repeal the Statute 45 Edw. III, c. 3.

If [it is] not timber by nature or kind, though not grown for use, [it] is discharged of tithes.

11 Hen. IV, 89.[27] One sort of wood does not privilege another.

Com. 470;[28] lops of hornbeam above twenty years [pay] no tithe.

2 *Inst.* 643[29] is in opposition to Molyn's Case, Commentaries, and is exploded as if Molyn's Case was not argued and that hornbeam was not timber, but it was adjudged since that it was timber.

Hilary [term] 1699[/1700], Turner v. Colston, rector of Stapleton in Essex.[30] Timber may by time gain an inheritance [status] and, being cut, may lose it.

Molyn's [Case] in Commentaries and Lyford's Case, 11 Rep., differ as to the germins of timber trees cut, one when germins over, the other under twenty years.

Where age and nature of timber agree, that is oak of twenty years growth, [it] is timber.

Waste is no rule as to tithe, though it may be for timber.

If timber at twenty years, [it] may serve for rails and other things as useful, as a beam.

Moore 441, Holliday's Case.[31] Beeches, if rotten, do not pay tithe.

1 Levinz and Siderfin, Hawes v. Cornwall, before; there it is said that timber trees shall privilege itself only, and not others.

This is not fraudulent to separate, but [is] an experiment. If timber and underwood are corded together without distinction, that mixed tithing is good.

Hilary [term] 1 & 2 Jac. II [1686], Franklin v. Jones.[32] Timber and underwood corded together for firewood [pay] no tithe, for there the use not the nature of the wood gave or took away privilege.

He concluded for the defendant as to the standels and stores.

The three barons decreed [the] defendant to account for the tithe and [the] deputy [queen's remembrancer] to report specially what timber there was which was used for building.

---

[26] Stat. 35 Hen. VIII, c. 17 (*SR*, III, 977–980); Stat. 1 Eliz. I, c. 15 (*SR*, IV, 377); Stat. 13 Eliz. I, c. 25 (*SR*, IV, 560–562).

[27] YB Trin. 11 Hen. IV, f. 89, pl. 43 (1410).

[28] *Soby v. Molins* (1574), 2 Plowden 468, 470, 75 E.R. 700, 702, 1 Eagle & Younge 60, 1 Gwillim 133.

[29] E. Coke, *Second Institute* (1642), p. 643.

[30] Note *Turner v. Colson* (Ex. 1680), above, No. 103.

[31] *Holliday v. Lee* (1597), Moore K.B. 541, 72 E.R. 745, 1 Eagle & Younge 138.

[32] *Franklin v. Jones* (Ex. 1686), above, No. 216.

[Other reports of this case: 1 Rayner 161, Bunbury 98, 145 E.R. 609.]

[The order of 31 Jan. 1706, PRO E.126/18, f. 567v, is printed at 1 Wood 479, 1 Eagle & Younge 677.]

[Later proceedings: Greenway v. Marquess of Kent (Ex. 1709), below, No. 444.]

[This case is cited in Walton v. Tryon (1751), 2 Gwillim 827, 832, 835, 837, 2 Rayner 452, 453, 460, 2 Eagle & Younge 123, 1 Dickens 244, 21 E.R. 262, 1 Ambler 130, 131, 133, 27 E.R. 85.]

408

Newt v. Chamberlain (Ex. 1706)

The tithe of a horse malt mill is a personal tithe not a praedial tithe.

IU Lilly MS. Parker, 'Cases in the Exchequer, vol. 4', p. 64 [Eng.] (Price's Reports)

The plaintiff's bill is for tithe of [a] horse malt mill in Tiverton in the County of Devon. The cause was heard in Hilary term.

Chief Baron WARD, Barons BURY, PRICE, and SMITH decreed for the plaintiff to have an account of the tithe.

This is not a personal tithe, which is for the labor deducting the expenses and according to custom, by Statute 2 Edw. VI, c. 13,[1] but is in the nature of [a] praedial tithe. Praedial is the produce of the ground and mixed, which is the produce of cattle which lives on the produce of the earth and what the canonists call [a] mediate and not immediate praedial tithe. 1 Rolle Rep. 405, Jack's Case, 3 Bulstrode 212, *idem*,[2] that [as to] a *modus* for old and new, Lord Coke said tithe must be paid for the new.

Articuli Cleri, 9 Edw. II, c. 5.[3] Tithe shall be paid for new mills. Sir Simon Degge 219[4] said none was to be paid for old mills, which must be a mistake, for Linwood, *de Decimis*,[5] is to the contrary, and there were moduses for old mills, which shows they were payable.

2 *Inst.* 621.[6] Lord Coke seems to say that all mills, as corn mills, fulling mills, iron mills, etc., were personal and that it was never adjudged. 2 Rolle 84,

---

[1] Stat. 2 Edw. VI, c. 13 (*SR*, IV, 55–58).
[2] *Jake's Case* (1616), 1 Rolle Rep. 405, 81 E.R. 568, 3 Bulstrode 212, 81 E.R. 178, 1 Eagle & Younge 257.
[3] Stat. 9 Edw. II, c. 5 (*SR*, I, 171–174).
[4] S. Degge, *Parson's Counsellor* (1676), p. 219.
[5] W. Lyndwood, *Provinciale* (1679), pp. 192, 195, see also below.
[6] E. Coke, *Second Institute* (1642), p. 621.

21 Jac. I.[7] Three judges granted [a] consultation for [a] grist mill and that they were praedial but granted a prohibition for [a] fulling mill. 1 Brownlow 32.[8] If [a] fulling mill, for which [there is] a *modus* or new tithe, if made [into] a grist mill, [it] must pay [tithe] in kind. Rolle, Abr., 1st part, 656,[9] that grist mills now are praedial and shall pay [the] tenth toll dish by [the] custom of the realm. [In the court of] king's bench, 26 Car. II [1674 x 1675], Hugh v. Vizert, that a *modus* [is] good for an old mill, and nonpayment is a good evidence that none [is] due, and [one] may prescribe *in non decimando* for a mill. So was Hall v. Hart[10] in the king's bench lately; tithe of [an] old mill subsists by custom, where [the] tithe is divisible as [a] grist mill, may not be in [an] other mill, that it is paying double tithe corn, it pays to the miller and has but the tenth of the toll, not the corn, and is no more than corn sowed not come up again and pays tithe.[11] Hilary [term] 3 Anne [1705], exchequer, Ross and Windsor,[12] decrees tithe [of] mill, and there is no difference between a water mill, windmill, and horse[13] mill; the trouble and charge is as much in one as the other.

17 February 1706[/07], appeal from the exchequer to the House of Lords, Roger Chamberlain and Francis Plimton, appellants; John Newt, respondent.

The respondent exhibited a bill in the exchequer for the tithe of a horse mill in Tiverton in the County of Devon. He demanded the [tenth] toll dish as a praedial tithe. The appellant answered that none [was] due.

The court of exchequer unanimously agreed and decreed [the] defendant to account for the tenth toll dish notwithstanding [that] the miller had 2d. [a] bushel for grinding.

Upon the appeal, the Lords desired the judges, all that were not of the exchequer, to give their opinion. Chief Justice HOLT, Chief Justice TREVOR, Justice POWYS, Justice GOULD, Justice BLENCOWE, and Justice TRACY [held] that it was a personal tithe. Justice POWELL [held] that it was a praedial [tithe] or partook of the nature of a praedial [tithe].

It was said that it was [a] tithe for the labor and the Statute *Articuli Cleri*, Edw. II, said no prohibition should be granted for [a] new mill and that the Statute 2 Edw. VI, that no personal tithe should be paid that had not been used forty years before the Statute did not repeal *Articuli Cleri* as to the tithe, that if

---

[7] *Anonymous* (1619), 2 Rolle Rep. 84, 81 E.R. 674.

[8] Note, 1 Brownl. & Golds. 32, 123 E.R. 647.

[9] 1 Rolle, Abr., *Dismes*, pl. M, 4, p. 656.

[10] *Hart v. Hall* (1698), 12 Modern 243, 88 E.R. 1292, 1 Lord Raymond 441, 91 E.R. 1193, Holt K.B. 673, 90 E.R. 1272, 1 Eagle & Younge 632.

[11] Sic in MS.

[12] *Ross v. Windsor* (1704), Samuel Dodd's Reports, p. 203, 1 Eagle & Younge 661.

[13] house MS.

canons did not bind as to the tithe, that did not agree with the law. The charge would be great and not answer the labor of the miller, that a new mill had no right to toll and only as they could agree, and that the Statute *Incerti Temporis*, or about 17 Edw. II,[14] that [a] miller not take above [a] 20th or 24th part for toll does not give a right but [says that he] should not take more, and so [there is] no right [of] toll.

It was said for the decree and agreed that personal tithe is not due by law [but] only by custom, and there can be no custom for a new mill. And the Statute 6 Edw. VI expects a custom [of] forty years, which cannot be in a new mill. And the canon law does not oblige them if the mill were not *in feudae* [?] or part of the inheritance. It was agreed that it could not be a praedial tithe, as [a] hand mill, quern, cider mill, and the like, and though [a] praedial tithe must be the produce of the ground and soil and tithe is paid for it to the parson in the field and so [there would be] two tithes, yet this is mixed and partakes of the nature of praedial [tithes].

Register 48,[15] [a] consultation where [there is] a legacy of two quarters of corn, the tithe of a mill.

Linwood 192, *Decima de molendinis est praedialis*, 195. 33 Edw. III, Winchelsea, archbishop of Canterbury, canons. And, as Linwood said, there were old canons before *de proventibus molendinorum decimae fideliter et integre solvuntur.* The notes are *per mensuram granorum tamquam praediales*. So a piscary in a pool [is] praedial, in [a] river or [the] sea [is] personal. Fitzherbert, Abr., *Dam.*, 50; Fitz. N.B. 149; *Reformatio Legum* 115; Madox's *Collection* 28; Fitzherbert, Abr., *Assize*, 435; Selden 228, 225; 2 Spelman 391, 392, 393, 291, 452, 503, 706,[16] are all the tithe of corn mills, are all praedial. Littleton 314; 1 Rolle Rep. 405, Jake's Case; 3 Bulstrode 212, *idem*; 2 Rolle 84; 2 Cro. 523; 1 Brownlow Rep. 32; 1 Rolle, Abr., *Disme*, 656; *Repertoria Canonica* 419, 5 Jac. [*blank*] v. Lax, are most cases that it is praedial, other cases are otherwise, as Sir Simon Degge 260.[17]

---

[14] *SR*, I, 203.

[15] *Registrum Brevium* (1687), f. 48.

[16] A. Fitzherbert, *New Natura Brevium* (1652), p. 125; *Reformatio Legum Ecclesiasticarum* (1640), p. 115; T. Madox, *Formulare Anglicanum* (1702), p. 28; Fitzherbert, Abr., *Assise*, pl. 435; J. Selden, *History of Tithes* (1618), p. 225, 228; H. Spelman, *Concilia*, II (1664), pp. 290–291, 391–393, 452–453, 706.

[17] *Anonymous* (1629), Littleton 314, 124 E.R. 263; *Jake's Case* (1616), 1 Rolle Rep. 405, 81 E.R. 568, 3 Bulstrode 212, 81 E.R. 178, 1 Eagle & Younge 257; *Anonymous* (1619), 2 Rolle Rep. 84, 81 E.R. 674; *Danderidge v. Johnson* (1619), Cro. Jac. 523, 79 E.R. 448, 1 Eagle & Younge 304, 1 Gwillim 354; Note, 1 Brownl. & Golds. 32, 123 E.R. 647; 1 Rolle, Abr., *Dismes*, pl. M, 4, p. 656; J. Godolphin, *Repertorium Canonicum* (1680), p. 419; S. Degge, *Parson's Counsellor* (1681), p. 261.

2 *Inst.* 611.[18] The personal tithe is the clear gain over and above all expenses and that it is doubtful what tithe mills are.

652.[19] If tithe grain is paid in one parish, [it] shall not pay tithe corn for grinding in a mill in the same parish, for that was [a] double tithe.

Sylva caedua [pays a] praedial tithe.

Hilary [term] 1699[/1700], king's bench, Clerke v. Hall, [a] prohibition [was] denied [as to a] new mill.

Trinity [term] 3 Will. [1691], [as to] Hanley Mills, Worcestershire, [it was] decreed [that] tithes [of] mill [are] praedial.

1 Rolle, Abr., 635;[20] honey and wax [are] praedial, wool and lamb [are] praedial and mixed. Alterages by custom [include] wool and lamb as well as oblations. *Garba* extends to wood and faggots and hay though [they] naturally intend corn to be bound.

The Lords reversed the exchequer decree and decreed tithe [of] mill to be personal.[21]

[Other reports of this case: Samuel Dodd's Reports, p. 208, 1 Eagle & Younge 679, 1 Rayner 101, 106, 3 Rayner 1087, 1090, 2 Gwillim 596, 1 Eq. Cas. Abr. 366, 21 E.R. 1107, 2 Eq. Cas. Abr. 731, 22 E.R. 617, 7 Brown P.C. 3, 3 E.R. 2.]

[The order of 22 Apr. 1706, PRO E.126/18, f. 580v, is printed at 1 Wood 482.]

[This case is cited in Carleton v Brightwell (1729), 2 Peere Williams 462, 24 E.R. 815, 1 Rayner 249, 250, 2 Gwillim 676, 2 Eagle & Younge 7; Talbot v. May (1743), 3 Atkyns 17, 18, 26 E.R. 814, 2 Rayner 398, 2 Gwillim 782, 2 Eagle & Younge 93.]

409

Gardner v. Pole (Ex. 1706)

A modus decimandi *that is as large as the tithe itself will be set aside as being only a composition.*

IU Lilly MS. Parker, 'Cases in the Exchequer, vol. 4', p. 114, pl. 1 [Eng.]
(Price's Reports)

A *modus* for 12d. an acre for wet meadow and 8d. per acre for dry was set aside being a composition rather than [a] *modus* by reason of the nearness of the value, it being as much worth as the tithe considering the casualties of floods.

---

[18] E. Coke, *Second Institute* (1642), p. 621.
[19] E. Coke, *Second Institute* (1642), p. 652.
[20] 1 Rolle, Abr., *Dismes*, pl. A, 3; B, 3; C, 1, p. 635.
[21] *Lords' Journal*, XVIII (n.d.), p. 241.

[Other reports of this case: 1 Rayner 103, 111, 3 Rayner 1090.]

[The order of 23 Feb. 1706, PRO E.126/18, f. 556v, is printed at 1 Wood 472, see also order of 6 June 1706: PRO E.126/18, f. 608v.]

[Reversed on appeal: 2 Gwillim 601, 7 Brown P.C. 5, 3 E.R. 4, 2 Eq. Cas. Abr. 734, 22 E.R. 622, 1 Eagle & Younge 675, *Lords' Journal*, XVIII (n.d.), p. 503.]

410

Edge v. Warburton (Ex. 1706)

A court of equity will not grant relief against a penal bond for malfeasance rather than non feasance.

BL MS. Hargr. 71, f. 116, pl. 2 [Fr. & Eng.] (Dodd's Reports)

Sir George [Warburton] made a lease to the plaintiff and reserved a rent. And then there is a covenant from Sir George that the plaintiff might plow forty acres, and if he plowed any more, the plaintiff agreed to pay for each acre £5 *per annum*. The plaintiff plowed sixty acres, and the first rent being [in] arrears, a bond to perform [the] covenants in the lease was put in suit and a judgment and execution issues and more is levied than the first rent but not so much as is due for the rent and the rent of £5 per acre. And upon debate, the court would not relieve against the £5 per acre, for they said it was a malfeasance and not a non feasance and that a settled state (damage or rent) was made in this case between the parties. And upon a recommendation of the court, it was referred.

[Other copies of this report: HLS MS. 537(b), p. 69, pl. 2; Oxf. Brasenose MS. 59, p. 89, pl. 3; IU Lilly MS. Parker, 'Cases in the Exchequer, vol. 2', p. 71.]

[Order of 10 Apr. 1706: PRO E.127/25, f. 69v.]

411

Keble v. Onley (1706)

In a bill for discovery and common law relief, the defendant should make the discovery prayed for and then demur to the jurisdiction.

BL MS. Add. 22610, f. 13v [Eng.] (Wright's Reports)

The plaintiff exhibited his bill in the exchequer against the defendant for printing his copy contrary to the custom used in the trade of booksellers and to have reparations for his damages sustained by the invasion of his separate right and property and prays a discovery of several particulars. The defendant demurs for that the custom as it is laid and showed in the bill is not good in law and because he seeks in a court of equity for satisfaction by way of damages [that] which ought not to be assessed in a court of equity but by a jury at common law in an action etc. Upon debating this case, it appeared that the defendant had not answered as to the discoveries which the bill prayed; the demurrer was overruled, and the defendant [was ordered] to pay costs. The lord chief baron [WARD] said that, where the defendant demurs because the complainant sues for damages recoverable at common law, such demurrer shall not be good unless he discovers what he is put to discover.

[Orders of 1 Feb. and 23 Apr. 1706: PRO E.127/25, ff. 8, 110v.]

412

Packington v. Bailiffs of Droitwich (Ex. 1706–1707)

A judgment against a municipal corporation can be enforced by a writ of sequestration. The court will discharge the levy of sequestrators upon property not in the possession of the judgment debtor.

I
LI MS. Misc. 536, f. [80v] [Eng.] (Ward's Reports)

The plaintiff having by decree of this court of the [*blank*] obtained relief for a fee farm rent of £81 10s. *per annum* clear after all deductions, being the residue of a fee farm rent of £100 *per annum* reserved upon the grant of King John to the Bailiffs and Burgesses of Droitwich of the salt springs and salt works there and other things granted to the said corporation, of which fee farm rent the plaintiff is a purchaser under the crown.[1] And there being £400 found due and in arrear to the plaintiff and that report confirmed and decreed to be paid to the plaintiff and the persons of the two bailiffs and some of the burgesses being served with the said decree and refusing to pay the money and several distringases having been awarded against the said bailiffs and burgesses as a corporation and several issues having been returned against them, a sequestration was this day awarded to sequester the estate and possessions of the corporation, which are the old and new salt pits in Droitwich and several other things for and out of which the fee farm rent is reserved. And this was so awarded, as a reasonable and proper remedy for obtaining the money decreed and the performance of the decree, which respects the future annual payment of the rent, every *distringas* and failure of obedience to perform it being a contempt. And after so many distringases awarded, there are so many contempts. And there is no reasonable difference between a sequestration to be granted against a person and a corporation.

[Other copies of this report: GUL MS. B88–9, f. 289.]

---

[1] V.C.H., *Worcestershire*, III (1913), 77.

II
LI MS. Misc. 535, f. [238v] [Eng.] (Ward's Reports)

[On] 29 June 1704, the plaintiff had a decree against the defendants for £485 8s. 11d. due to him for the arrears of a fee farm rent purchased from the crown by the plaintiff and charged upon the Borough of Droitwich and payable by the defendants. And for non payments of that sum, after other process of contempt, a sequestration issued to four persons to sequester all the lands and tenements, goods and chattels of the defendants, the corporation, into the sequestrators' hands till the defendants discharge their said contempt.

The four commissioners return by a writing under their hands and seals, (but nothing [was] endorsed on the writ nor annexed to it, nor was the commission returnable, but the commission was truly set forth in the return) that they had sequestered as belonging to the corporation one salt work with three pans and [the] brine thereto belonging in [the] possession of Richard Norbury and the like as to other pans and works in four other persons' occupations, naming them.

And upon several affidavits made that the persons, in whose hands those sequestered premises were, refused to yield possession or pay the profits to the sequestrators, the court was moved for an injunction to put the sequestrators into possession and an attachment against the contemners, which was ordered *nisi causa* this day.

Three of the defendants made affidavits and thereby endeavored to excuse their contempts and seemed to make out some titles or pretenses to the sequestered premises in their possessions. And as to them, the court ordered that they should appear to an attachment and be examined upon interrogatories wherein they might set forth their respective titles. And if thereby it appeared that the sequestered premises were the parties' own estates and not belonging to the corporation, they were to be discharged if not otherwise contradicted by [the] plaintiff's proof. Or if they were the corporation's estate but leased to the parties before the sequestration, then the rent only [is] to be liable, for it is a personal contempt only and takes its rise from the decree or sequestration only and affects nothing but what was the corporation's at that time. And the two others that had not made any title or pretense by affidavit (being a mistake only) they were admitted to come in and be examined also.

[Orders of 9 May and 5 Dec. 1706 and 24 Jan. 1707: PRO E.127/25, ff. 118v, 291; E.127/26, f. 85.]

413

Constable v. Agates (Ex. 1707)

A copy of a bond cannot be admitted into evidence where there is no proof that the original was executed.

Personal chattels are liable to be taken in execution by a creditor of the owner.

BL MS. Hargr. 80, f. 9v, pl. 5a [Eng.]

The case upon the plaintiff's bill was thus. The plaintiff, being indebted to three defendants [Norgrade, Newland, and Ireland] in three several bonds, is prosecuted severally to outlawry at the suit of every one of them on the same day. Norgrade has an exchequer lease under the outlawry of certain lands of the plaintiff taken in execution thereupon wherein his interest was an estate for life without impeachment of waste. And being in possession by virtue of this lease, and timber trees growing upon this land to the value of £170 are cut down, Newland finding these trees on the land takes them in execution upon his outlawry as a fruit fallen and separated from the inheritance and become a personal chattel vested in the plaintiff and liable to the executions that were against him. But after he had seized them, he does not proceed to make any sale but suffers them to remain on the land. Hereupon, it was moved in the court of exchequer, where the inquisition upon the outlawry was returned and remained of record, that the plaintiff might be at liberty to sell the trees and bring the money arising by [the] sale into court. [A] rule was accordingly made that he might have liberty, and [the] sale was accordingly made and the money brought.

And the end of the plaintiff's bill is that he should have that money and an injunction upon the defendants to prevent their cutting any more trees. It was said though the plaintiff had such an interest in the land as enabled him, if he had pleased, to fell timber, yet the defendant's claiming only under an outlawry could not do that, for the interest of the crown under which the defendant's is derived is by virtue of an outlawry only to receive the growing profits of the outlaw's land as they arise naturally without meddling with the soil, much less with the inheritance, any otherwise than is necessary for the perception of the accruing profits, that the defendants, having without any right cut down the timber upon the plaintiff's land, should not take advantage of their wrong and of their fraud between them so as to render thereby those profits of the land liable to the satisfaction of their debts, which could not by any legal methods or process have been made so, but that the plaintiff himself should receive the money to his own use, since the defendant under such circumstances of the frauds and wrong ought not to have any benefit thereby.

The bill was thus opened and argued. But upon the plaintiff's proof, there was no other evidence of the trees being cut by the order of Norgrade or of any of the defendants, except only the copy of a bond given them jointly for the indemnity of the workmen. And this copy the court would not suffer to be read in evidence, because there never was any proof that such a bond was ever executed.

So the case on the proof before the court was no more than that Norgrade, being possessed by virtue of a lease under an outlawry of the plaintiff's land wherein the plaintiff's interest was a term for life without impeachment of waste, a stranger cuts down the trees growing upon that land and Newland, the other defendant, finding those trees upon the land liable to his execution, takes them as personal chattels by process on an outlawry obtained at his suit without any fraud that appears between him and the persons who felled the trees or any combination to prepare them in this manner for his execution.

So the court was of opinion that the execution was well made and Newland well entitled to so much of the money in court as was sufficient to defray his debt and damages and dismissed the plaintiff's bill as to that.

And as to that part of the bill which prayed an injunction to stay the cutting of timber, that was likewise dismissed, because there was not any proof of any thing threatened or done on the part of the defendant which might induce a suspicion that any such thing was intended by them.

A letter under a man's hand shall not be taken as an exhibit, unless it be proved to be his handwriting by a witness who has seen him write, and it is not enough for this purpose to prove the man confessed this to be his writing or to make it out by comparison of hands or any other circumstantial evidence which might be proper before a jury.

[Order of 25 Jan. 1707: PRO E.127/26, f. 6.]

414

Haanan v. King (Ex. c. 1707)

A defendant cannot object to the jurisdiction of an equity court after he has pleaded that he ought to account to the plaintiff though not in the manner alleged in the bill of complaint.

BL MS. Hargr. 80, f. 10v, pl. 5b [Eng.]

[A] bill was preferred by the plaintiff to require the defendant to give an account of two certain sums received by A. and B. to the plaintiff's use. The defendant answers that he received those two sums to the use of the plaintiff and two others, his co-partners, and that he ought not to be obliged to account to the plaintiff alone.

The cause coming to a hearing, exception was taken that upon the matter of this bill, the plaintiff was entitled to an *indebitatus assumpsit* at the common law and not to a bill of account in equity, because the sums received to the plaintiff's use were certain and it does not appear that he was to have any allowance or deduction that might reduce the debt to an uncertainty and make it proper for an account.

But it was answered and resolved that if the bill should be taken to be improper, yet the defendant had prevented the benefit of this exception by pleading that he ought to account to the plaintiff and others and not the plaintiff alone, whereby he admitted himself liable to account though not in the manner the plaintiff demanded.

[Note King v. Hannam (1705), PRO E.126/18, f. 625.]

415

Bartlett v. Attorney General (Ex. 1707–1709)

A demurrer lies to a bill of discovery where the plaintiff has not alleged any cause of action against the defendant. Such a person should be examined as a witness.

I
LI MS. Misc. 535, f. [214] [Eng.] (Ward's Reports)

The plaintiff by her English bill as executrix to her husband, who was bound in a bond to the crown with and as surety for one Clarke (who was an officer in the customs) for his true answering, accounting for, and paying to the crown the duties and moneys arising in his receipt, and Clarke being dead insolvent, the bond (which was of a great penalty) was put in suit against the plaintiff, to be relieved against which under pretense of divers suggestions made in the bill of several matters inducing an equity against the crown and praying a discovery of them and particularly whether a new bond was not given by Clarke and others for securing the duties for part of the time for which it was endeavored to charge the plaintiff and for which the plaintiff's husband's bond did not extend to charge him, the bill charging nothing against the commissioners of the customs as in their own right or otherwise than as acting in their places for the service of the crown, nor did the bill pray any relief against the commissioners but only that they might answer the premises, to which bill the attorney general put in a general answer. And the commissioners of the customs by themselves put in a demurrer to the bill and showed for cause that it appeared by the bill that they were made parties thereto and charged therein upon no other account than as commissioners of the customs and that their answer to the bill can be of no use to the plaintiff not being any evidence against the queen nor can the plaintiff by her bill have any relief against these defendants nor does it pray any against them. And this demurrer was allowed by the court for the reasons therein mentioned, it being the common case even between subject and subject to have such demurrers allowed where of the plaintiff's own showing he has no cause of relief against the defendants, in which cases they may and ought to be examined as witnesses. And their answers can be no evidence against the other defendants. And the reason and rule of justice holds alike between the crown and the subject, as it does between subject and subject.

But in this case, I declared my opinion that there may fall out divers cases wherein the commissioners of the customs' answers may be material and wherein relief also may be had against them as where the law or the duty of their places oblige them to that performance or execution of such or such things so that by doing or not doing thereof an equity or cause of relief does arise to the plaintiff, it may be necessary to make them parties either to be compelled to execute their powers (as it was in the case of Fitch against the Commissioners of the Navy, Liber M, [f.] 146,[1] etc.) or else by their nonfeasance to be relieved against the crown on whose behalf they acted and ought to be brought to hearing that the whole matter with all proper parties may appear before the court, for in such case the plaintiff cannot examine them as witnesses but must examine witnesses against them to prove their default. And there the plaintiff's equity arises against the crown. But it is a mischievous case, and it daily increases that when any are sued upon bonds to the crown to exhibit English bills under many pretended and untrue suggestions against all the commissioners and officers of the revenue, several of which are many times absent in divers parts of the kingdom so that for want of all their answers the crown suits are often delayed and sometimes stayed for several years so without making out any just cause but only bare suggestions in their bills. And if anything be made out by affidavit or otherwise, that the commissioners or officers have in their custody anything that may be fit for the plaintiff to have a sight or copy of, the court may and in justice ought to aid the plaintiff in such case and compel the producing of it for the defendants'[2] advantage.

[Other copies of this report: GUL MS. B88–9, f. 340v.]

II
BL MS. Hargr. 71, f. 120, pl. 1 [Fr. & Eng.] (Dodd's Reports)

Clarke in 1691 was made collector of the customs in the port of Boston. Bartlett and others were security for him. In 1698, 10 Will. III, the duties were granted upon coal etc., which by the Act[3] were to be managed by commissioners of the customs, and several clauses for that purpose [were put] in the Act. The

---

[1] *Fitch v. Commissioners of the Navy* (Ex. 1697), above, No. 364.
[2] Sic in MS.
[3] Stat. 11 Will. III, c. 13, s. 8 (*SR*, VII, 602); see also Stat. 6 & 7 Will. & Mar., c. 18, ss. 12–16 (*SR*, VI, 603–604).

commissioners gave Clarke a deputation for that purpose and took security. After Clarke died, the customs were paid, but on this new coal they were unpaid [in the sum of] £2000. Upon this, the bond is sued against Bartlett (*viz.* the widow and executrix of Bartlett), who brought her bill. And whether the bond where Bartlett was security extended to this future duty of coal was the question.

And the chief baron inclined that it did, but he ordered the cause to be adjourned to consider of it.

In the case of Bowdage,[4] the point was the same except that no security was given on the second deputation.

Afterwards, it was resolved that it did not extend to this, and the plaintiff [was] relieved, and a perpetual stay of process [was] awarded.

[Other copies of this report: HLS MS. 537(b), p. 74, pl. 4; IU Lilly MS. Parker, 'Cases in the Exchequer, vol. 2', p. 79; Parker 277, 145 E.R. 779.]

[Orders of 26 Feb. and 10 Dec. 1707: PRO E.127/26, f. 70; E.127/27, f. 33.]

416

Price v. Watkins (Ex. 1707)

Exceptions to the report of a master cannot be made after entry of the final decree.

I
LI MS. Misc. 538, f. [5] [Eng.] (Ward's Reports)

The case upon the bill of review was whether when the court upon hearing directed that the deputy [queen's remembrancer] should make the plaintiff allowance of interest for what should appear to be due upon such an account and the deputy made his report and [the] plaintiff took exceptions to it and it was referred back to the deputy to revise his report and to make it as it should be, and the deputy made a new report wherein (or in the former report) it did not particularly appear that he had made the plaintiff any allowance for that interest, but the account was made up and balanced consisting of divers particulars, the plaintiff took no exceptions to this report and so the court confirmed it and decreed payment, and [the] defendant was taken upon process for not obeying the decree, but going before Baron Price in vacation time upon giving security, he was set at liberty (query that proceeding of court [?] being in execution), but the security was not effectual nor the money paid. But [the] plaintiff brought his bill of review and assigned for error that he had not interest allowed him as was expressly

---

[4] *Bowdage v. Attorney General* (1709), Parker 277, 145 E.R. 779, Samuel Dodd's Reports, p. 218.

directed by the order on [the] hearing. But the court dismissed the bill of review upon arguing the demurrer to it. And thereupon the plaintiff appealed to the Lords in Parliament who upon hearing the cause the 8th of January 1707[/08] dismissed the appeal and confirmed the decree[1] with £10 costs upon the ground that the plaintiff ought to have taken exceptions to the report and that he was too late to have that matter examined into after the final decree was passed.

[Other copies of this report: GUL MS. B88–9, f. 346.]

II
IU Lilly MS. Parker, 'Cases in the Exchequer, vol. 4', p. 135, pl. 1 [Eng.]
(Price's Reports)

[In a] bill of review, to which [the] defendant demurs, [the] plaintiff assigned error in the master's report in not allowing interest for sums of money paid by the plaintiff for the defendant. There were exceptions to the report, and after the decree to confirm the report by default and after [it was] made absolute, by which the plaintiff was to pay the defendant £400 and upwards, all the court [were] of [the] opinion (though Baron PRICE thought the report wrong) [that] yet upon a bill of review, the errors in [the] account were not to be rectified but upon [an] exception to the report, and the plaintiff's laches was not to turn to his benefit.

The case of Price and Button,[2] where [there was] a decree by default on [a] report and [it was] made absolute and enrolled, upon [an] appeal to the [House of] Lords,[3] they would not open the enrollment; though by his own default, it was to his prejudice [of] £1500; staving off defenses and taking advantage after[wards] is a delay of justice, and so the demurrer was allowed.

[In] Lamplugh v. Cheatum,[4] upon a bill of review, [one] would have an allowance of taxes and [a] fee farm rent, [but it was] not allowed.

[Other reports of this case: 2 Eq. Cas. Abr. 175, 22 E.R. 150, Colles 389, 1 E.R. 339.]

[Order of 23 Jan. 1708: PRO E.127/27, f. 37v.]

---

[1] *Watkins v. Price* (1708), Colles 389, 1 E.R. 339, *Lords' Journal*, XVIII (n.d.), p. 404.
[2] *Button v. Price* (1702), Prec. Ch. 212, 24 E.R. 104.
[3] *Prise v. Button* (1702), Colles 246, 1 E.R. 270.
[4] *Chetham v. Lamplugh* (Ex. 1705), above, No. 391.

417
Moulder v. Harris (Ex. 1707)

Tithes of wool are due in the parish where the sheep are pastured and not where they are sheared.

IU Lilly MS. Parker, 'Cases in the Exchequer, vol. 4', p. 127 [Eng.] (Price's Reports)

A tithe bill [was exhibited by Charles Mould] as farmer to the rector of Witney in Oxfordshire and particularly for tithe [of] wool and lamb.

The defendant denies [that] he had any sheep [that] was depastured on his farm, and his answer was disproved, and it appeared that two hundred sheep [were] depastured on the farm, and he took them off the farm to his house out of that parish to shear and sent them back afterwards.

Chief Baron WARD [held] that the bill ought to have suggested the fraud in shearing out of the parish and that the parson of the parish where they were sheared ought to be [a] party, for the wool is due where [it is] sheared by the canon [of] 1305,[1] by which the tithing table is settled. If there be fraud apparent, [there is] no need of [a] suggestion. Twenty days [is] not reckoned as to partial feeding, and [he] would have the bill dismissed or amended.

Barons BURY, PRICE, and SMITH [held] *contra*, that the bill was sufficient, and it was the defendant's fault [that] he did not take notice [of] where the shearing was and did not make it his defense and that tithe [of] wool is by reason of the feeding not [the] shearing, and the shearing is but an evidence of the feeding; it did not appear [to be] any fraud in the shearing, and [there was] no need to show it.

Godolphin, *Repertorium*, 462; *Clergyman's Law* 251; 2 Keble 293; Rolle, Abr., 648; as to fraud apparent, [see] Chancellor of Oxford's Case.[2]

[The] chief baron cited cases against the plaintiff: Tudman v. Jones [and] Nantmell Jones v. Walker, that where shorn must be in the bill.

[There was a] decree [for the] defendant to account for tithe wool.

[Order of 19 May 1707: PRO E.126/18, f. 654.]

---

[1] Archbishop Winchelsey Constitutions of Merton (1305), 4 Eagle & Younge 323, 325.

[2] J. Godolphin, *Repertorium Canonicum* (1680), p. 462; W. Watson, *Clergy-Mans Law* (1701), p. 521; *Weems v. Amerson* (1667), 2 Keble 293, 84 E.R. 183; 1 Rolle, Abr., *Dismes*, pl. C, 1, p. 648; *The Case of the Chancellor of Oxford* (1613), 10 Coke Rep. 53, 77 E.R. 1006.

418

Duke of Devonshire v. Jackson (Ex. 1707)

A view of a jury does not constitute part of the evidence.
A view of a jury is not allowed in a suit sounding in contract.

IU Lilly MS. Parker, 'Cases in the Exchequer, vol. 4' p. 132 [Eng]. (Price's Reports)

The bill being to be relieved on articles of [the] building of Chatsworth in Derbyshire where [the] defendant demands upwards of £4,000, they agreed to come to a trial upon a *quantum meruit*. The duke insisted to have a jury of Derbyshire, which was opposed by reason [that] the plaintiff at law, Jackson, had his election to lay his action and, though it might be removed by the duke on the common affidavit to Derbyshire, yet Jackson offering to give evidence where the action was laid had a right to keep it there.

Secondly, the duke insisted on a view for the jury. All the court [were] against it because if a jury [is] out of another county, [it] cannot be sent without consent, which they could not do. And to what purpose to view walls, which could not inform a jury, and showing other walls or part of [a] building to judge by comparison was giving evidence, which is not to be allowed in [a] view, besides [it would be] the great charge, if not necessary, to send a jury so far, which would be an oppression on a suitor, and besides we never heard of an instance where there was a view on a *quantum meruit* for work done. There are but two sorts of views, either a writ of view, where the defendant may have a view whereby to know the land before he pleads [so] that he may see it, or a view for a jury, which is given by the court and that is either in a real action, as a formedon, assise, etc. or in waste or assise [of] nuisance or diverting a way or watercourse or a *curia claudenda*, but not in an action upon the case or trespass. 2 Rolle, Abr., *View*.[1] And we all agreed against a view.

[Order of 11 July 1707: PRO E.126/18, f. 676.]

---

[1] 2 Rolle, Abr., *View*, pp. 725–731.

419
Attorney General v. Croft (Ex. 1707)

There cannot be a decree pro confesso *where the defendant has not been served with process.*

IU Lilly MS. Parker, 'Cases in the Exchequer, vol. 4', p. 133 [Eng.] (Price's Reports)

[To] a bill for the queen to have Cattens [?] in Yorkshire, being twelve messuages of £350 *per annum*, being Sir Roger Strickland's estate, who was attainted for high treason [in] 1689,[1] the defendant set up [a] mortgage and trust for Ro[bert] Strickland, brother to Sir Roger Strickland.

Robert Strickland is in France and is prosecuted to [a] sequestration.

Baron SMITH was of the opinion that a decree should be against him and the bill taken *pro confesso*.

Baron BURY doubted.

Baron PRICE [held] that a decree should not be against him, nor [the] bill taken *pro confesso*, [but] that the form was to bring the party to the bar and if he did not appear, the bill is read thrice and then the bill is taken *pro confesso*, as was in the case of Sir Samuel Barnardiston.[2]

1 Chan. Rep. f. 204, Dr. Salmon v. Hamburgh,[3] where the defendants had not [the] wherewithal by which they might be distrained, but the Lords directed the chancery that, if they did appear and do several things, the bill should be taken *pro confesso* against them.

2 Chan. Rep. f. 133.[4]

It was said that in real actions upon a grand cape, there was a judgment and [a] writ of seisin if [the defendant] did not appear, but that is but *quousque* he does appear.

The court were after[wards] of [the] opinion that where there was no service, [one] could not by serving [the] clerk in court go so far in [the] contempt [process] as to take [a decree] *pro confesso*.

The court directed issues to be tried.

[Order of 13 Nov. 1707: PRO E.126/18, f. 678(b).]

[Reversed on appeal: 4 Brown P.C. 136, 2 E.R. 91, *Lords' Journal*, XVIII (n.d.), pp. 614, 629.]

---

[1] Note *Attorney General v. Crofts* (Ex. 1697), Samuel Dodd's Reports, p. 172.
[2] *Attorney General v. Barnardiston* (Ex. 1686–1687), above, No. 227.
[3] *Salmon v. Hamborough Company* (1671), 1 Chan. Cas. 204, 22 E.R. 763.
[4] *Denny v. Filmer* (1682), 2 Chan. Cas. 133, 22 E.R. 881, also 1 Vernon 135, 23 E.R. 369, Nelson 64, 21 E.R. 790, 1 Eq. Cas. Abr. 81, 21 E.R. 894.

420
Attorney General ex rel. Gwyn v. Prytherch (Ex. 1707)

In this case, rents of assise were ordered to be paid to the relator.

IU Lilly MS. Parker, 'Cases in the Exchequer, vol. 4', p. 134 [Eng.] (Price's Reports)

The bill was for a rent of assise out of the borough of Builth in the County of Brecon for 15, 15, 2, which was used to be collected by the constables of the inhabitants, but on proof, there was but 2, 5 proved to be paid, which was decreed to be paid him with the arrears, which made £36 and allowed him £14 for costs, which I think was not right to give costs where he had not a decree according to his bill, agreed that rents are usually reserved to the crown from hundreds, manors, parishes, and inhabitants of a vill in one sum and levied by contribution.

[Order of 15 July 1707: PRO E.126/18, f. 674.]

421
Attorney General v. Herring (Ex. 1707)

The issue in this case was whether a defendant must answer to a bill seeking discovery where all penalties resulting therefrom have been waived.

IU Lilly MS. Parker, 'Cases in the Exchequer, vol. 4', p. 135, pl. 2 [Eng.] (Price's Reports)

[A] bill [was exhibited] to discover what malt was made by them [Edmond Herring, Charles Pocock, and others] and what [was] concealed.

The defendants demur, for that is to accuse themselves and make them liable to penalties. It was offered for the demurrer that no person is to charge himself in matters criminal. 1 Chan. Rep. 144, Bishop v. Bishop. Hardres 22, Protector v. Lord Lumley;[1] [one] may have discovery in order to [have] an execution but not to charge himself with a forfeiture.

201, Attorney General v. [*blank*],[2] to discover forfeited goods being imported against the Act of Navigation[3] and [he] allege he waived the forfeiture and would not prosecute, but the attorney general may drop that suit and prosecute criminally.

---

[1] *Bishop v. Bishop* (1640), 1 Chan. Rep. 142, 144, 21 E.R. 532; *Protector v. Lord Lumley* (1655), Hardres 22, 145 E.R. 360.

[2] *Attorney General v. Anonymous* (1661), Hardres 201, 145 E.R. 452.

[3] Stat. 12 Car. II, c. 18 (*SR*, V, 246–250).

137, Attorney General v. Mico,[4] [a] bill [to] discover goods imported, forfeitures,[5] and the corruption of officers. No tithe bill [lies] unless [the plaintiff] waive [the] double penalty. Bill against [*blank*] public revenue, fraud and nuisance, discovery of wines imported for sale, duty on prisage, bill against [a] searcher for bribery, against [an] auditor for false particulars [?]. 2 *Inst.* 657; Hub. 84, Spendlo; Magna Charter, c. 15; Hub. 138; Hardres 144;[6] [a] bill to discover transported cards without paying customs; [the court] allowed good a demurrer for [the] forfeiture.

Easter [term] 13 Car. II, n. 209; [a] bill for French duty by Sir Geoffrey Palmer.

Easter [term] 14 Car. II, n. 100, 153, 154; [a] bill for public money received by several persons.

Trinity [term] 16 Car. II; Sir Geoffrey Palmer, attorney general, [sued] for the arrears of excise; n. 304.

Trinity [term] 17 Car. II, n. 2416; the like for the arrears of [a] wine license.

Michaelmas [term] 20 Car. II, n. 2417; Attorney General [sued] for the arrears of hearth money.

Michaelmas [term] 24 Car. II; Sir William Jones, attorney general, [sued a] bill for the arrears of the law duty, [and there was] no demurrer but [an] answer.

Hilary [term] 33 Car. II, n. 2424; Sir Robert Sawyer, attorney general, [sued] for the like duty against Flatman[7] and the clerks of [the] chancery, which bill charged them by schedules, [and] they demurred. All the *posse* of the chancery bar appeared in the exchequer to argue that it was making them liable to penalties, and the demurrer [was] overruled.

Trinity [term] 34 Car. II, n. 2421; Sir Robert Sawyer, attorney general, [exhibited a] bill for the arrears of the wine licence duty.

Hilary [term] 35 Car. II, n. 214; Sir Robert Sawyer, attorney general, [sued] for the arrears of the aulnage duty.

Easter [term] 2 Will. & Mary, n. 75;. Sir George Treby, attorney general, [sued] for the arrears of the wine license duty; [there was an] answer and not [a] demurrer.

Trinity [term] 5 Will., n. 1703; Sir Edward Ward, attorney general, [exhibited a] bill for the arrears of the wine license duty.

---

[4] *Attorney General v. Mico* (1658), Hardres 137, 145 E.R. 419.

[5] goods forfeiture imported *MS*.

[6] E. Coke, *Second Institute* (1642), p. 657; *Spendlow v. Smith*, Hobart 84, 80 E.R. 234; Magna Carta (1225), c. 29; *Procter v. Darnbrook* (1617), Hobart 138, 80 E.R. 288; *Bowes v. Bore* (1592), Hardres 144, 145 E.R. 423.

[7] *Attorney General v. Flatman* (Ex. 1682), above, No. 140.

Michaelmas [term] 7 Will., n. 39, 774; Sir Thomas Trevor, attorney general, [exhibited a] bill against Moor for duties due for customs; [there was an] answer and not [a] demurrer.

Michaelmas [term] 12 Will., n. 111; Sir Thomas Trevor, attorney general, [exhibited a] bill against maltsters, cider sellers, and other for arrears of excise.

Easter [term] 4 Anne; Sir Edward Northey, attorney general, [exhibited a bill] against brewers and others for arrears of excise.

These instances, where answers [were] put in or where demurrers were overruled, though the discovery made them incur penalties, but the attorney general by bill waiving any advantage of the penalty, have been allowed good.

Hilary [term] 26 & 27 Car. II, Attorney General v. Wilson.

3 February 1704[/05], Attorney General v. Wellington and Girlington; in both these cases, there were pleas and demurrers against answering a general bill of discovery of [a] forfeiture in the king's revenue where the attorney general waived the forfeiture and the defendant desired to look out [for] precedents, and after[wards] the plea and demurrer were overruled.

422

Attorney General v. Weeks (Ex. 1707)

A debtor can be required to make discovery of his assets before any debt is established or admitted.

IU Lilly MS. Parker, 'Cases in the Exchequer, vol. 4', p. 138 [Eng.] (Price's Reports)

An English bill in the attorney general's name against [Michael] Weeks charged him that he was [a] receiver of the impost in the Custom House from 1685 to 1693, that he gave two bonds for £800 each for doing his duty and paying what he received, that he owed the crown £60,000, and he concealed his estate, and to have a discovery of it was the bill.

Weeks demurred for that he did not owe the king anything and was not obliged to discover.

[John] Farrer demurred for that he was but [a] servant or agent.

Chief Baron WARD, BURY, and SMITH overruled both demurrers [and ruled] that Weeks should answer and Farrer [should] answer to the trust.

Baron PRICE [held] *contra* for that though Thomas Weeks gave bonds with special condition, yet without a *scire facias* and judgment, no extent could be had, and allow [that] the bond did affect the land, when the condition was broken so as an accountant having land was bound by relation from the time he was [an] accountant to the time that the account was liquidated and become a debt (Stat. 13 Eliz., accountant or debtor and chargeable; Dyer 224; 7 Rep., Lord Anderson and Sir Thomas Cecil; 3 Rep., Sir William Herbert's Case[1]), by this rule, every accountant and surety to the crown is bound to discover his estate, whether he owes anything to the crown or not.

[Order of 8 Nov. 1707: PRO E.127/27, f. 17v, see also orders of 19 and 28 Feb. 1708: PRO E.127/27, ff. 71v, 95v.]

423

Cary v. Machan (Ex. 1707)

The issue in this suit to set aside a fraudulent or voluntary conveyance was whether the current owner was a purchaser without notice.

IU Lilly MS. Parker, 'Cases in the Exchequer, vol. 4', p. 141 [Eng.] (Price's Reports)

The bill [was] to set up an assignment of a term which was to attend the uses of a settlement and to have satisfaction against [the] defendant [James] Morgan for a fraudulent assignment.

10 October 1693. John Lacy, after marriage to the plaintiff [Mary Cary], for consideration that if he sold her houses to raise money for his use (which was done accordingly), settles the land in question to feoffees to the use of him[self] for life, remainder to the plaintiff for life for her jointure, etc.

10 October 1693. James's mortgage reciting a term of one thousand years in trust which was Mr. Barnard, Ann Lacy, mother of J. Lacy, and James Morgan, the defendants, for £200 to James Morgan paid, they assign the said term to George Penny for the residue of the term upon trust to attend the uses settled by the deed [of] 10 October 1693.

16 February 1671[/72]. James Morgan, the defendant, assigned the said term to Edward Faucet in trust for J. Lacy.

7 March 1701[/02]. J. Lacy and Edward Faucett for £200 assigned the said term to Elizabeth Machan, who had no notice of the former grants.

John Lacy was a papist, and the plaintiff was so, and she turned Protestant, and he, upon that, cancelled the assignment to George Penny and got the second assignment from James Morgan with [the] intent to defraud the plaintiff.

Edward Faucet is son-in-law to the defendant Elizabeth Machan, and she claims as a purchaser for a valuable consideration without notice.

Elizabeth Machan brought an ejectment, and Mary Lacy gave judgment.

---

[1] Stat. 13 Eliz. I, c. 4 (*SR*, IV, 535–537); *Saintloo's Case* (1563), Dyer 224, 73 E.R. 497; *Lord Anderson's Case* (1597), 7 Coke Rep. 21, 77 E.R. 443; *Cecil's Case* (1597), 7 Coke Rep. 18, 77 E.R. 440; *Harbert's Case* (1584), 3 Coke Rep. 11, 76 E.R. 647.

1. The court seems to be of opinion that if Elizabeth Machan was a purchaser without notice, that her title should not be impeached.
2. Whether James Morgan having for £200 consideration made an assignment and that being cancelled by covin and collusion with J. Lacy and made another to Edward Fawcett be not a [*blank*] breach of trust or a fraud whereby Elizabeth Machan becomes a purchaser that is not to be impeached and [*blank*] by reason of that defeat.
3. Whether James Morgan had any trust in him after the first assignment; if not, the second was no breach.
4. Whether the plaintiff's giving judgment in ejectment is not to her prejudice, being [that] she might have set up her assignment to George Penny though cancelled; the court seemed to doubt that, unless she could prove it, [it] was cancelled by collusion.
5. Whether a trial at law whether Elizabeth Machan's mortgage was *bona fide* or the assignment to Fawcett was with the privity of Elizabeth Machan or had notice of the first assignment [or] whether the assignment [of] 10 October 1693 was executed and consideration paid and when and how it came to be cancelled.

[I] query this case, which is adjourned to Hilary term 1707[/08].

Some cases I thought of in the point [are] 1 Chan. Rep. 39; 2 Chan. Rep. 19, 108, 128; 11 Rep., Piggott's Case; 1 Rep., Pelham's Case; 3 Rep., Fermer's Case.[1]

Whether it be a fraud apparent or a deceit by covin and collusion, [a] covenant to make assurance and convey before is a breach.

[Order of 3 Dec. 1707: PRO E.126/18, f. 689, see also order of 3 July 1708: PRO E.126/19, f. 57.]

424

Butterfield v. Perkins (Ex. 1707)

A bill of peace in equity lies to establish a right of common where there are many persons claiming the same right.

---

[1] *Davie v. Beardsham* (1663), 1 Chan. Cas. 39, 22 E.R. 683; *Anonymous*, 2 Chan. Cas. 19, 22 E.R. 826; *Dyer v. Dyer* (1682), 2 Chan. Cas. 108, 22 E.R. 869; *Hobs v. Norton* (1682), 2 Chan. Cas. 128, 22 E.R. 879, also 1 Vernon 136, 23 E.R. 370; *Pigot's Case* (1614), 11 Coke Rep. 26, 77 E.R. 1177, also Moore K.B. 835, 72 E.R. 937, 1 Rolle Rep. 39, 81 E.R. 311, 2 Bulstrode 246, 80 E.R. 1096; *Pelham's Case* (1590), 1 Coke Rep. 3, 76 E.R. 8; *Fermor's Case* (1602), 3 Coke Rep. 77, 76 E.R. 800.

IU Lilly MS. Parker, 'Cases in the Exchequer, vol. 4', pp. 143, 222 [Eng.]
(Price's Reports)

Edward Butterfield and others for themselves and others, the freeholders of Boston Bissett[1] in the County of Buckinghamshire against William Perkins and John Perkins, who claim common, and the warden and scholars of New College, lords of the manor of Dringswick.

The bill is called a bill of peace where all the freeholders of Preston Bissett claim, as belonging to their freehold, common in Dringswick common.

The plaintiffs allege that Dringswick common or wild is about seven hundred acres (formerly called Rockwood Forest), that the several towns part of Tingewick, [i.e.] Barton, Preston Bissett, Chetwode, the Prebend of Buckingham, and Gawcott, they have right of common there and would try the right to have [it] established to prevent multiplicity of actions to try every freeholder's right of common.

It was objected that these suits are not [to be] brought but after some trials have been whereby to assert the right, and then it might be proper to quiet it by an injunction, and here [if there] was no trial for the plaintiffs but always against them, then it will be hard to direct an issue, for, by that, every freeholder's right must be tried by one action. And to try what sort of common, if any, all or any of the freeholders have is too wide an issue.

Sir Thomas Chicheley's Case in Cambridgeshire was cited.

[The case was] adjourned till Hilary term to see precedents.

[At the] setting down of causes after Trinity term 1708, the plaintiff and the freeholders of Preston Bissett claim right of common for all their cattle at all times of the year in Kingswick wild or waste, part of Rookwood Forest, which contains five hundred acres together with other villages, and that at a court of Sir J. Chetwood they made orders for [the] regulation of the common and [the] stinting [of] it.

The plaintiff prays an issue at law to try this right of common.

The defendants oppose it [in] that they are proper parties, all concerned in the right of common, that this common ought to be tried at law and not come to equity in the first instance, that this is no legal common for all their cattle but ought to be restrained to *levant et couchant* or to all cattle that are commonable.

[It was said] for the plaintiff that there are customary commons which are not known by any law and are properly determinable in equity, which are settled by a trial at law.

Tirringham's Case in 4 Rep.,[2] where notice is taken of the custom of shard in Norfolk.

---

[1] I.e. Preston Bissett
[2] *Tyrringham's Case* (1584), 4 Coke Rep. 36, 76 E.R. 973.

The common of Epworth, 1635, the Case of Sir Thomas Chicheley.

21 November 1692, in the exchequer, Roger Steddale and others, inhabitants and tenants of the Manor of Penrith in Cumberland, against the attorney general and the dowager's attorney general, Lancelot Simpson and a cross cause.[3] The plaintiff claims right of common without stint and at all times in the year, that Edward II, being seised of the forest, did grant the common till 44 Eliz. [1601 x 1602], that some lessees of the crown endeavored to enclose. An issue [was] directed [to determine] if the tenants have right of common at all times of the year (except such time as the head jury of the leet do stint the same) upon the said common or which of them; secondly, whether the plaintiffs have sufficient common beside the land enclosed. It was tried before Chief Baron Atkyns and [there was a] verdict against [the] tenant, and they decreed a dismission and injunction to put [the] queen's lessee in possession.

21 February 1702[/03], Andrew Parrott and others, freemen of York v. Ro[bert] Squire and [the] archbishop of York, an issue at law [was] directed:

[1.] Whether the plaintiff and other freemen and inhabitants of York had [the] sole right of common of pasturage in Minefield or Yorkfield when used as pasture from Michaelmas to Lady Day exclusive of the owners.
2. If they had the right of common from the time of reaping or mowing to Michaelmas and from thence to Lady Day exclusive of the owner or farmer.
3. If the tenant has a right to sow corn or grain on it between Michaelmas and Lady Day and to fence it and exclude the cattle from commoning there.
4. If the defendant had any right to sow rapeseed or linseed on the land. And if the jury found any variation in the plaintiffs' or defendants' right, the jury should endorse it on the *postea*.

Upon the trial, the jury found for the freemen upon the two first issues and found that the defendants might sow corn, grain, rapeseed, and linseed between Michaelmas and Lady Day but could not enclose or exclude the commonable cattle. They decreed the freemen to hold and enjoy their common of pasturage and the manner is particularized and exclusive of the farmer, but the farmer [was allowed] to sow but not [to] fence and exclude the cattle, and an injunction [was granted] to quiet [the] plaintiffs' possession and to have costs.

And in this case, it was decreed to try the plaintiffs' right of common and where the right is in Kingswick Wild, part of Rookwood Forest.

[Order of 5 Dec. 1707: PRO E.126/18, f. 689.]

---

[3] *Steddall v. Attorney General* (1692), PRO E.126/16, f. 47v.

425
D'Allone v. Hart (Ex. 1708)

The court of exchequer has jurisdiction for discovery of rents in the Duchy of Lancaster.

LI MS. Misc. 538, f. 32v [Eng.] (Ward's Reports)

The plaintiff [Abel Tassin D'Allone] as holder of several rents in the Duchy of Lancaster to take effect after [the] death of the late queen dowager, who died about Christmas 1705, exhibited his bill in the exchequer against the defendants for discovery of what of those rents the defendants or either and which of them had received and to have relief against them for the same and to be enabled to have a discovery [of] which of them are in charge and to recover the same.

Bellamy answered only and did not plead, and his answer was ruled insufficient, notwithstanding he insisted on the jurisdiction of the duchy court exclusive to the exchequer court for it being a bill of discovery [of] what he had received of the granted rents [and] he did not answer that fully. And Hart pleaded the jurisdiction of the duchy exclusive to the exchequer as well to any discovery as relief, for which reason the plea was overruled. For whatever the exchequer would or might do as to relief, yet certainly [the] plaintiff was proper [in suing] for discovery for he being grantee of the rents, if the defendant had received any of them, upon his discovery by answer, [the] plaintiff may bring an action at law for money received to his use having a title at law to the rents, as well as the grantee of an office may do against any one that receives the profits without title. And a bill to discover such receipt is usual and proper in this court or elsewhere. But if the plea had gone only to relief, it might have borne a further debate, but the plea being both to discovery and relief and being bad as to the discovery, it must be and was overruled as to both, with costs, in both cases. Hardres 171.[1]

[Other copies of this report: GUL MS. B88–10, p. 606.]

[Order of 24 Apr. 1708: PRO E.127/27, f. 119.]

---

[1] *Fleetwood v. Pool* (1660), Hardres 171, 145 E.R. 436 (the exchequer has concurrent jurisdiction with the court of duchy chamber).

426
Lord Howard v. Boomer (Ex. 1708)

In this case, the defendant was ordered to grind at the plaintiff's mill and not to use his own quern.

IU Lilly MS. Parker, 'Cases in the Exchequer, vol. 4', p. 177 [Eng.] (Price's Reports)

The bill was [for] suit to the mill at Rotherham in Yorkshire, [George, Lord Howard] being lord of the manor, from all tenants that owe suit to the lord's court and their undertenants residing in the manor for all corn spent in their houses and the said mill being a prerogative mill which pays a fee farm rent to the crown and that the defendant, having a quern, grinds his own and other men's malt within the said manor.

The plaintiff produced a decree between the plaintiff's father and Joseph Drew and three others upon a bill for suit of the said mill from all the inhabitants, and, after a trial at law, the issue [went] for the defendant [and after] a second trial, [the] issue [went] for the plaintiff, and [there was] a third trial where there was a special endowment that the right of suit of mill was from the tenants who paid suit to the said court and their undertenants being inhabitants. And there was £20 paid of costs that the plaintiff should amend his bill and make it agree with the verdict. And the suit of mill was decreed for the future. [See] Hardres 174, 184,[1] for suits of mill and decrees.

The evidence in this case was the decree for the plaintiff, though [it was] not generally agreed to be conclusive, but as an instance for the custom, [and] several witnesses for the plaintiff, who proved that the plaintiff ought to have suit of mill from the inhabitants, tenants, and undertenants. The defendant's proof [was] that the inhabitants had querns and that strangers sent loaders and carried corn to be ground out of that manor.

It was agreed that a decree for the custom against one or more was an evidence in this case, though he did not claim under him. Secondly, that a proof of a custom that all inhabitants and tenants owed suit is a good proof that the tenants ought to do suit to the prerogative mill.

Chief Baron WARD, BURY, and SMITH decreed the custom as [alleged] by [the] bill and enjoined the defendant to pay and perform it and [decreed] that the defendant do not grind in any hand mill or quern his own corn or the grain of any tenant.

---

[1] *Green v. Robinson* (1660), Hardres 174, 145 E.R. 438; *Mayor of Scarborough v. Skelton* (1661), Hardres 184, 145 E.R. 443.

Baron PRICE was not against the decree but thought there should be a trial at law to bind the defendant's inheritance, the proof being uncertain and the former decree patched up and the defendant not concluded by it.

The cause of South Moller and Turrington in this court, the Case of Loughborough Mills in this court, [and] the case of my Lord Nottingham for Daventry Mill in the duchy are the same with this case.

[Order of 29 Apr. 1708: PRO E.126/19, f. 27v.]

427

Attorney General v. Mason (Ex. 1708)

An accounting will not be ordered where the underlying right is in issue and not yet determined in another court.

IU Lilly MS. Parker, 'Cases in the Exchequer, vol. 4', p. 179 [Eng.] (Price's Reports)

The bill sets forth that the office of the warden of the Fleet [Prison] was an ancient office of inheritance granted by the crown and that the capital messuage and other messuages are appurtenant to it and [he] has the custody of prisoners from the chancery, common pleas, and exchequer, that Anthony Church was warden and after him William Weedon Ford and [they] were admitted into the said office and took the execution. They severally committed several acts of forfeiture, and [in] 9 K[ing] W[illiam] [1697] an inquisition was found upon a commission from [the] chancery that William Weedon Ford was seised in fee of the said office and admitted and suffered a voluntary escape, and he traversed it. And [in] Hilary term 11 Will. [1699], the record was delivered by the lord keeper to the king's bench to be tried by a jury of Middlesex, and [a] verdict was found for the queen against Ford and that the messuage was appurtenant to the said office.

In Trinity term 3 Anne [1704], judgment was given in the queen's bench that the said office should be seized and taken into the queen's hand, and on it [there was] a writ of error in Parliament, and it was affirmed there 29 December 3 Anne [1704][1] and a *capias in manum reginae* was awarded on the said judgment for taking and seizing the said office into the queen's hand, which was executed accordingly, and [that] the queen ought to have an account of the rents, issues, profits, and perquisites and [these] free from any charges or encumbrances made by any warden, the queen not claiming under them but by the right of forfeiture in the crown by a condition in law annexed thereto. [The plaintiff] prays to discover encumbrances.

---

[1] *Lords' Journal*, XVII (n.d.), p. 605.

[There was a] response and plea [by] Gawen Mason that the office of warden of the Fleet is an ancient office of inheritance and [it] descended to Thomas Bromhall, an infant. An Act of Parliament passed [in] 5 Will. & Mary [1693] for [the] sale of [the] said office and thirteen houses belonging [thereto] and the custody of the Palace at Westminster, which were vested in Cavendish Weeden, Esq., Giles Duncombe, Esq., and William Fanshawe, Esq., in fee in trust to be sold. And they being seised the 21 & 22 December 5 Will. & Mary [1693] did sell to the defendant and his heirs, and [it] was enrolled in the common pleas the 7 February 12 Will. [1701].

This defendant pleaded to the said inquisition and denied the seisin of Weedon Ford, to which plea, the attorney general demurred, and [the] issue joined therein was transmitted to the queen's bench and remains [?] there undetermined. And having denied the seisin of Ford and traversed the said inquisition and her majesty's title is not established by any court whatsoever, he[2] prays judgment if he must answer, 3 he offered to show [that] upon executing the said commission that the office was vested in him and that Weedon Ford was not legally deputed or authorized to execute the said office at the time of the forfeiture, which was refused. He denies that there is any *capias in manum reginae* awarded or executed.

Anthony Grindall's plea and answer [was] that at the time of finding the inquisition and time of forfeiture, Gawen Mason was seised of the said office and that he appeared and traversed the said office and to which [there was] a demurrer etc. as before, and he may be double vexed if judgment in [the] queen's bench [be given] for Gawen Mason. [He] answer[ed] that he knows of no *capias in manum* [that] is awarded.

Mr. *Phipps*, Mr. *Turnor*, and Mr. *Ward*, for the defendant [argued] that pending the *monstrans de droit*, [this case] cannot proceed here to an account. Keilway Rep. 201,[4] that where [there was] a traverse to an office and a bill in the exchequer for profit, [the] chancery granted a *supersedeas* to stop the proceedings till [the] traverse [be] determined.

The Statute 2 Edw. VI, c. 8,[5] [was] that offices shall not prejudice leases for years, copyhold, idiots, attainder of treason, ward, rent, offices, profit, and [they] shall keep possession and hold till [it be] determined.

[By the] Statute 21 Jac. I,[6] for informations of intrusion, [one] shall plead [the] general issue, give security, and keep possession.

---

[2] and *MS*.
[3] that *MS*.
[4] *Attorney General v. Eggecombe* (1519), Keilwey 201, 72 E.R. 380.
[5] Stat. 2 Edw. VI, c. 8 (*SR*, IV, 47–48).
[6] Stat. 21 Jac. I, c. 14 (*SR*, IV, 1221).

Sir Edward Northey [argued] *pro querente*.

1. Exception to [the] plea: that the defendant Mason pleads that he was seised at [the] time of the forfeiture but does not say he is now seised, it was answered that he pleads that he was seised and pleaded to the inquisition.
2. That Weedon Ford is said to be seised in fee, to which the defendant does not answer or plead and show his own title and traverse that he was seised in fee, [it was] answered that he pleads and traverses that he was seised.
3. That the queen upon the judgment is in possession of the office and ought to have an account. Sir G. Reynolds, 9 Rep.,[7] that the king is in possession upon an inquisition without any seizure or entry. Stat. 36 Edw. III, c. 13; 8 Hen. VI, c. 16; 23 Hen. VI, c. 17;[8] that if [one] continue [in] possession, [one] must give security, but, that not being done, the queen at common law by the inquisition is in possession, and it belonged to the defendant to plead that he came in the six months and gave security. Stat. 1 Hen. VIII, c. 10.[9] The time is material as to the security and possession, but, as to the traverse of the title, that may be at any time, and so far, the *monstrans de droit* may be regular.

The Stat. 2 Edw. VI, c. 8, as to offices which arise out of the same, that is from lease, copyhold, and other land, as keeper of a park, etc.

Then [there was] no answer to the houses, [as to] why they should not be accounted for. The plea is [that] they are appurtenant to the office. Stamford, 68.[10]

Baron PRICE cited Dowty's Case, 3 Rep., continued [in] 9 Rep.,[11] that where any in possession ought to have a *scire facias* and [the] queen [be] not in possession.

9 Hen. VII, 2, that [one] shall account for profit.

5 Edw. IV, 3,[12] Duke of Norfolk [was] in possession [of] an office.

---

[7] *Sir George Reynold's Case* (1612), 9 Coke Rep. 95, 77 E.R. 871.

[8] Stat. 36 Edw. III, c. 13 (*SR*, I, 374–375); 8 Hen. VI, c. 16 (*SR*, II, 252–253); 23 Hen. VI, c. 17 (*SR*, II, 343).

[9] Stat. 1 Hen. VIII, c. 10 (*SR*, III, 6).

[10] W. Staunford, *Exposicion of the Kinge's Prerogative* (1567), f. 68.

[11] *Attorney General v. Dowtie* (1584), 3 Coke Rep. 9, 76 E.R. 643, cited in *Sir George Reynel's Case* (1612), 9 Coke Rep. 95 at 96, 77 E.R. 871 at 872, 873.

[12] YB Pas. 5 Edw. IV, f. 3, pl. 28 (1465).

4 Rep., Commonalty of Sadlers,[13] as to title by office and *monstrans de droit*. Dyer 170; Stamford 72; 2 Ventris,[14] Woodward sell[s] [a] register's place [which] made [a] forfeiture, Stat. 2 Edw. VI,[15] and [the] king may give [a] place without [an] office to plaintiffs, [the] place [being] vacant. 1 Modern 280,[16] [where the] king's possession or title [is] by office or record, he may traverse or traverse and maintain his own title.

1 Modern 122,[17] seisin [in] law, not [in] fact; 11 Rep., Earl of Devonshire's Case;[18] 2 Modern 121, Plummer v. Whitcott,[19] forfeiture for life, he in reversion shall have it if he pay for the escape; 9 Rep. 98; 2 *Inst.* 382; Dyer 278; 32 Hen. VI, 34; Cro. El. 384; Popham 119; Moore 987,[20] that [where there is a] tenant for life, [the] forfeiture [is for] that life only, but when [there is] a deputy, the whole is forfeited; 3 Modern 146, King v. Lentot;[21] 2 Rolle Abr. 154,[22] tenant at will of [an] office forfeits by [a] voluntary escape and [the] king [is put into] possession [. . .]le be in reversion make [a] claim, then he is [an] officer; 2 Cro. 17, Jones 128, 1 Leonard 219, 202; 2 [Coke] *Inst.* 695; 2 Leonard 122; Stamford 62, 64,[23] [one] cannot traverse [the] title [of the] king without title in him who traverses. In Sir G. Reynold's Case, the awarding [of] seisin is a seisin in the king.

---

[13] *Warden and Commonalty of Sadlers' Case* (1588), 4 Coke Rep. 54, 76 E.R. 1012, also 1 Anderson 180, 123 E.R. 418.

[14] *Lord Powis's Case* (1559), 2 Dyer 170, 73 E.R. 372; W. Staunford, *Prerogative* (1567), f. 72; *Woodward v. Fox* (1690), 2 Ventris 187, 213, 267, 86 E.R. 384, 400, 432, also 3 Levinz 289, 83 E.R. 694.

[15] Stat. 5 & 6 Edw. VI, c. 16 (*SR*, IV, 151–152).

[16] *Rex v. Bishop of Worcester* (1670), 1 Modern 276, 86 E.R. 878.

[17] *Craig v. Norfolk* (1663), 1 Modern 122, 86 E.R. 780.

[18] *Earl of Devonshire's Case* (1607), 11 Coke Rep. 89, 77 E.R. 1266.

[19] *Plummer v. Whitchot* (1676), 2 Modern 119, 86 E.R. 976, 2 Levinz 158, 83 E.R. 497, 1 Ventris 314, 86 E.R. 203, 3 Keble 591, 701, 754, 758, 773, 84 E.R. 896, 961, 992, 995, 1004, T. Jones 60, 84 E.R. 1146.

[20] *Sir George Reynel's Case* (1612), 9 Coke Rep. 95, 77 E.R. 871; E. Coke, *Second Institute* (1642), p. 382; *Gawdy's Case* (1568), 3 Dyer 278, 73 E.R. 624; YB Hil. 32 Hen. VI, f. 34, pl. 30 (1454); *Earl of Pembroke v. Berkley* (1595), Cro. Eliz. 384, 78 E.R. 630, Popham 116, 79 E.R. 1223, Moore K.B. 706, 72 E.R. 854.

[21] *Rex v. Lenthal* (1688), 3 Modern 143, 87 E.R. 92, Skinner 113, 90 E.R. 53, Comberbach 95, 90 E.R. 364, 2 Keble 384, 84 E.R. 240.

[22] 2 Rolle, Abr., *Office*, pl. N, 2–6, p. 155.

[23] *Lady Russell's Case* (1603), Cro. Jac. 17, 79 E.R. 15; *Earl of Derby v. Lord Willoughby* (1626), W. Jones 128, 82 E.R. 68; *Gawton v. Lord Dacres* (1590), 1 Leonard 219, 74 E.R. 201; E. Coke, *Second Institute* (1642), p. 695; *Venables's and Harris's Case* (1586), 2 Leonard 122, 74 E.R. 410; W. Staunford, *Prerogative* (1567), ff. 62, 64.

Cro. Car. 587;[24] 1 Jon. 437, a scire facias on a judgment, and a writ of error [was] brought on the first judgment, it suspends the proceedings on the *scire facias* till the error is determined; Stamford 64,[25] [the] king has possession in law and possession in fact, [the] king [is] in possession in fact if [it is] vacant without entry or seizure. 2 *Inst.* 695.[26]

[As to] a thing in grant, the king is possessed of the right but not [in] fact till it falls into possession. [An] office entitles [the] king to possess by [an] action not [by an] entry, where [a] private person cannot enter but [must] bring his action, the king must have a *scire facias* on the inquisition, and the defendant may traverse and keep possession. Where [the] subject has a possession by entry, the king has [it] by office found or matter of record.

Stamford 54,[27] [the] king has possession in law and possession in fact.

Keilway 151, 42, 157, 200, 201, Edgcomb's Case,[28] where a *supersedeas* from [the] chancery [went] to the exchequer, where [there was] a traverse to an office there and a bill for an account of the profits pending the plea.

2 *Inst.* 695 and 696, [the] king [is] not seised after a year after [an] office found without a *scire facias*. The judgment on a traverse to an office, if [it is] for the pleader, [is] *quod manus domini regis amoveatur et quod ille ad possessionem suam inde cum exitibus restituatur.*

4 Rep., Company [of] Sadlers, where [the] king [was] entitled [to an] action by *scire facias* as to the possession.

Stat. 34 Edw. III, c. 14; 36 Edw. III, c. 13; 8 Hen. VI, c. 16; 23 Hen. VI, c. 17; 1 Hen. VIII, c. 10; 2 Edw. VI, c. 8. It was agreed that [a] party may traverse title at any time, but if the defendant would keep possession on a traverse or *monstrans de droit*, he must take to farm and then traverse and give security in six months, which is not done in this case, and the plea should have averred [that] he had done so.

That the Statute 2 Edw. VI was only to secure the possession of [the] lessees for years or copyhold or those that had offices which arise or related to land, as keepers of parks and the like.

And as to the houses, they are pleaded to be appurtenant to the offices.

The court was of opinion to suspend giving judgment on the plea till the demurrer on the *monstrans de droit* was determined in the king's bench. 2 Saund.,

---

[24] *Meade v. Lenthall* (1640), Cro. Car. 587, 79 E.R. 1104.
[25] W. Staunford, *Prerogative* (1567), f. 64.
[26] E. Coke, *Second Institute* (1642), p. 695.
[27] W. Staunford, *Prerogative* (1567), f. 54.
[28] *Anonymous* (1502), Case No. 8, Keilwey 42, 72 E.R. 200; *Conyngesby's Case* (1509), Case No. 5, Keilwey 154, 72 E.R. 328; *Attorney General v. Eggecombe* (1519), Keilwey 201, 72 E.R. 380.

Jefferson v. Morton, f. 6,[29] in the king's bench, as to monstrans de droit. And [the] cause [was] removed from [the] chancery to the king's bench.[30]

[Order of 31 Jan. 1708: PRO E.127/27, f. 50.]

428
Poole v. Wilshaw (Ex. 1708)

A grandparent, the parent being dead, is not entitled to a distributive part of the estate of an intestate grandchild ahead of his siblings.

I

IU Lilly MS. Parker, 'Cases in the Exchequer, vol. 4', p. 224 [Eng] (Price's Reports)

[A] bill for a distributive part [was] that the plaintiff [Mary Poole], the grandmother, would have the grandchild's estate before the grandchildren.

2 Lutwyche, Burton v. Sharp, 1055; Trinity [term] 13 Will. [1701], king's bench, Blackborough v. Davies, 1 Salkeld 251.[1]

Dr. Lane argued that the grandmother is entitled, there being the same medium between grandmother and grandchildren, the same medium between granddaughter and aunt and so [they] are of equal degree; before the Statute 22 & 23 Car. II, Act of Distribution,[2] the civil law was the rule, and that Act is according to that law. Before [the] Statute 1 Jac. II,[3] the mother carried the whole of her child (Justinian's *Novels* 118) from the rest of her children. The case of [a] grandmother [was] omitted in the Act, and, where [the] Act is silent, [one] must have recourse to the civil law. If [a] mother is dead or removed, the grandmother is *in loco parentis*.

When it is said to those of equal degree, it is intended by civil law, and, if canon law differ from civil law in degree, it is not regarded because [the] canon law degree is in [the] case of marriage only.

---

[29] *Jefferson v. Morton* (1669), 2 Williams Saunders 6, 85 E.R. 540.
[30] Affirmed on appeal in *Mason v. Attorney General* (1710), 4 Brown 133, 2 E.R. 90, *Lords' Journal*, XIX (n.d.), p. 232.

---

[1] *Burton v. Sharpe* (1699), 2 Lutwyche 1055, 125 E.R. 587; *Blackborough v. Davis* (1701), 1 Salkeld 38, 251, 91 E.R. 39, 221, also 1 Lord Raymond 684, 91 E.R. 1355, 1 Comyns 96, 108, 92 E.R. 979, 985, Holt K.B. 43, 90 E.R. 922, 1 Peere Williams 41, 24 E.R. 285, 2 Eq. Cas. Abr. 242, 436, 22 E.R. 206, 371, 12 Modern 615, 88 E.R. 1558.
[2] Stat. 22 & 23 Car. II, c. 10 (*SR*, V, 719–720).
[3] Stat. 1 Jac. II, c. 17, s. 5 (*SR*, VI, 19).

Real and personal estate [are] not distinguished in descents.
1 Ventris 413, Collingwood v. Pace.[4]
The bill [was] dismissed as to the distributive part.

II
BL MS. Hargr. 71, f. 118v, pl. 2 [Eng. & Fr.] (Dodd's Reports)

A. marries the daughter of B. and had issue by her two sons, viz. C. and D., and by another wife one son, E. And he died intestate. F., [the] administrator, divides the estate between D. and E., and then B., the grandmother, brought her bill for a share, supposing herself entitled to it and, as alleged, in equal degree to the intestate with the surviving brothers. And Dr. Lane argued that she was in equal grade and this case was out of the Statute[5] and so *casus omissus* and so to be determined according to civil law. But the whole court was against [him], and [there was] no such usage since the Statute, and [they] dismissed the bill. Note.

[Other copies of this report: HLS MS. 537(b), p. 71, pl. 3; Oxf. Brasenose MS. 59, p. 93, pl. 1; IU Lilly MS. Parker, 'Cases in the Exchequer, vol. 2', p. 77, pl. 1.]

[Order of 6 July 1708: PRO E.126/19, f. 49v.]

429

Lady Campbell v. Lort (Ex. 1708)

In this case, rents were reserved upon two leases, and it was held that they belonged to the plaintiff as heir general of the lessor.

IU Lilly MS. Parker, 'Cases in the Exchequer, vol. 4', p. 240 [Eng.] (Price's Reports)

The cause was heard [on] 29 January 1707[/08], and a case [was] made, viz. Henry Lort had issue, Roger, Samson, John, and William; Roger had issue, John, who was the plaintiff's father; John had issue, the defendant [George Lort, Esq.]. Henry Lort [on] 1 March 6 Car. I [1631] leases [*blank*] in St. Petrox in the County of Pembroke to his third son, John, for ninety-nine years after

---

[4] *Collingwood v. Pace* (1661), 1 Ventris 413, 86 E.R. 262, also O. Bridgman 410, 124 E.R. 661, Hardres 224, 145 E.R. 464, 1 Levinz 59, 83 E.R. 296, 1 Keble 65, 174, 216, 265, 535, 579, 585, 603, 670, 699, 850, 83 E.R. 814, 883, 908, 937, 1097, 1122, 1126, 1137, 1176, 1193, 1280, 1 Siderfin 193, 239, 82 E.R. 1052, 1081, *sub nom. Craw v. Ramsey*, Vaughan 274, 124 E.R. 1072, 2 Ventris 1, 86 E.R. 273, T. Jones 10, 84 E.R. 1122, Carter 185, 124 E.R. 905, 2 Keble 601, 84 E.R. 378, *sub nom. Foster v. Ramsey*, 2 Siderfin 23, 51, 148, 82 E.R. 1235, 1251, 1304, 1 Eq. Cas. Abr. 213, 21 E.R. 998.

[5] Stat. 22 & 23 Car. II, c. 10 (*SR*, V, 719–720); note also Stat. 1 Jac. II, c. 17, s. 7 (*SR*, VI, 19).

his death, reserved £10 rent to his son Roger in tail male, then to Samson in tail male. And [at the] same time, [he] grants the same lease to John of Thurston and Woodsend in the same manner at the rent of £3 13s. 4d. and some reservation.

The question is if the reservation be good or is void, being [that] Roger, Samson, and William are dead without issue male, though the rent has been paid all along till the death of Sir Gilbert Lort, who was brother to the plaintiff and [who] died about ten years.

The rent reserved is incident to the reversion, and where the reservation is general, it goes as the law directs, if [the] reservation to [the] lessor and his heirs [is] good or to a privy in blood, not to a privy in estate or to a stranger.

1 And. 273, Harcourt v. Peel.[1] [A] tenant for life with a power to make leases makes a lease [and] reserved rent to [the] lessor for life, remainder to whom the reversion belonged, and [it was] a good reservation.

Dyer 45, n. 1.[2] [A] lease for years reserving rent to [the] lessor for life is good if rendering rent generally, and [if] nobody [be] named, it shall be to him and his heirs, but where [a] reservation for life is not to his heirs, it goes no further, but where [a] lease is so long as the term continues, it is a good lease.

Co. Litt. 47.[3] Reserving rent to [a] lessor for life is good; if general, it is to him and his heirs; if to one and his executors or assigns, it is but for life being incident to the reversion, but reservations to one, his heirs, and assigns goes to the reversioner. 3 Cro. 217; 2 Leonard 214; 1 And. 261; 2 Rolle, Abr. 450; 12 Rep. 36, Richmore v. Bulcher.[4]

If it be a reservation to [a] lessor and his assigns annually during the term, it is but for [the] life of the lessor. Latch 99, 255, 264; 2 Rolle, Abr. 451, Sury v. Brown; 3 Rep. 832; 5 Rep. 111, Pain v. [*blank*]; Com. 171, Hill v. Granger; 2 Saunders 370, Sacheverell v. Frogat; Cro. Car. 288, Bland v. Inman.[5] [A] lease reserving [a] rent to [the] lessor, his executors, administrators, and assigns during

---

[1] *Harcourt v. Pole* (1591), 1 Anderson 273, 123 E.R. 469.

[2] *Anonymous* (1539), 1 Dyer 45, 73 E.R. 97.

[3] E. Coke, *First Institute* (1628), f. 47.

[4] *Richmond v. Butcher* (1591), Cro. Eliz. 217, 78 E.R. 473, 2 Leonard 214, 74 E.R. 488, 1 Anderson 261, 123 E.R. 462, also Owen 9, 74 E.R. 861, 2 Rolle, Abr. *Reservation*, pl. N, 3, p. 450, 12 Coke Rep. 36, 77 E.R. 1318.

[5] *Surry v. Brown* (1623), Latch 99, 82 E.R. 294; *Sury v. Cole* (1624), Latch, 44, 255, 264, 82 E.R. 266, 373, 378, also Noy 96, 74 E.R. 1062, *Shurey v. Brown* (1625), 2 Rolle, Abr., *Reservation*, Pl. N, 7, p. 451; *Mallory v. Payn* (1601), 5 Coke Rep. 111, 77 E.R. 228; *Hill v. Grange* (1556), 1 Plowden 164, 75 E.R. 253, also 2 Dyer 130, 73 E.R. 284; *Sacheverell v. Froggatt* (1671), 2 Williams Saunders 361, 85 E.R. 1150, also 2 Levinz 13, 83 E.R. 430, T. Raymond 213, 83 E.R. 112, 1 Ventris 148, 161, 86 E.R. 101, 109, 2 Keble 798, 819, 833, 839, 84 E.R. 504, 517, 527, 531, Hetley 105, 124 E.R. 378; *Bland v. Inman* (1632), Cro. Car. 288, 79 E.R. 853, also 2 Rolle, Abr., *Reservation*, pl. N, 6, p. 450.

the term, that shows that the intent was not that the rent should determine with the lessor's life being to hold during the term.

Hobart 130, Oates v. Frith.[6] [A] father and son make a lease for years to begin from the death of the father reserving rent to the son (who was heir to the father); [it was] not good, being not reserved to the heir, and [he] cannot have it on the reservation, being a stranger to the land and had nothing in it. And the reservation ought to be to the father and his heir. The father could not demand it but might release and [the] heir have it after[ward].

The word heirs and the words *durante termino* do carry the reservation farthest.

Cole and Sury and Sury v. Brown. The reservation to [the] lessor during the term carries the rent to the heirs. And it was adjudged in Sacheverel's case for the plaintiff that the reservation during the term to the lessor goes to the assignee of the reversion during the term.

Dalison 13.[7] [A] lessor may reserve rent after the term is ended.

Hardres 89, Cother v. Essex Meyrick.[8] A tenant in tail, being to him and the heirs male of the body of the grandfather, lease for years reserving rent to him and his heirs, the reservation went to the heirs male of the grandfather not to the lessor's right heirs. The rent goes with the reversion and is in [the] Statute 32 Hen. VIII,[9] and [the] reservation was during the term.

Michaelmas [term] 8 Jac., in the king's bench. Sir James Skidmore[10] reserved rent to issue in tail, though the lessor [was] not named, [it] is a good reservation. Rent is incident to the reversion and goes to the heir in borough English where [there is a] general reservation or [the] heir on the part of the mother.

Easter [term] 4 Jac., Co. Ent. 124, in the king's bench, Hill's Case.[11] [The] husband leases [the] wife's land reserving rent to him and his heir; [the] rent goes to the wife, who has the inheritance.

10 Car. I, Cumberford's Case.[12] [A] tenant in tail leases for years reserving rent to him and his heirs; it is good; it goes to the heir, who has the reversion.

The case of Cother and Meyrick was [that a] tenant in tail male had sons by two wives, [the] first son makes a lease for twenty-one years reserving rent to him and his heirs and died without issue and had two sisters, who were his heirs at law. The land went to the second son. If rent goes to the second sister or half

---

[6] *Oates v. Frith* (1614), Hobart 130, 80 E.R. 280.
[7] Case 24, Dalison 13, 123 E.R. 235.
[8] *Cother v. Merrick* (1657), Hardres 89, 145 E.R. 395.
[9] Stat. 32 Hen. VIII, c. 28 (*SR*, III, 784–786).
[10] Cited in *Cother v. Merrick* (1657), *ut supra*.
[11] E. Coke, *Book of Entries* (1614), f. 124.
[12] *Cumberland's Case* (Wards 1634 x 1635), cited in *Cother v. Merrick* (1657), *ut supra*.

brother and if [it be a] good lease by [the] Statute 32 Hen. VIII, the rent [goes] with the reversion and [the] heir expounded *secundum subjectam materiam.*

Where the reservation is general to [the] lessor or lessor and [his] heirs, judges will construe them in favor of the rent and reversion; where the reservation is to [the] lessor and [his] heirs special, [it is] otherwise, and there the intention is manifest, as [in] Oates and Frith's case.

Where the reservation is to a person capable, it shall go according to the reversion.

If [a] reservation [is] restrictive as to a man and his heirs male, there it could not go with the reversion but must be void, but if [it is] to a man and his heirs general, then the construction will be to heirs in gavelkind or borough English or heirs general.

[In] Oates and Frith, the son was a stranger to the land and wanted privity. Where reservations are general during the term and to his heirs, [it] shall go with the reversion; if special or to [an] improper person, there [it] follow[s] the words; if [the] estate of [the] lessor is [a] particular estate and [the] reservation [is] general, there the law construes it to go with the reversion, but if it be a reservation to a particular person, it shall go no further.

Dyer 45.[13] [A] lease reserving rent to a son, [the] heir shall not have it, but if rent is reserved and not any [one is] named during the term, [it goes to the] lessor and his heirs, because it is for the term.

Cro. Car. 288, Bland v. Inman. A., a husband lessee for one hundred years, and B., his wife, assign the lease to C. reserving during the term rent to A. and B. and the survivor; A. dies; it is a void reservation to B., who had no interest in the term and [was] a stranger and did not seal, and [it was] good only for A.'s life and void as to the survivor, and this is an express reservation that it shall not be during the term, but for the husband and wife's life.

On 22 November 1708, the court held the rents [to have been] well reserved upon the two leases and that they belonged to [the] plaintiff as heir general of the lessor.[14]

[Orders of 29 Jan. and 22 Nov. 1708: PRO E.126/19, ff. 8, 80v.]

[Note the related case of Lady Campbell v. Lady Buckly (Ex. 1714), below, No. 468.]

---

[13] *Anonymous* (1539), 1 Dyer 45, 73 E.R. 97.

[14] This last paragraph is in a different hand from the rest of the report.

430
Streper v. Carter (Ex. 1708)

A court of equity will not relieve against a penal bond to enforce the resignation of a vicarage even where the bishop refused to accept the resignation that had been tendered.

I
BL MS. Hargr. 71, f. 119, pl. 1 [Eng. & Fr.] (Dodd's Reports)

The plaintiff gave bond of £500 to resign a vicarage (of £30 *per annum*) upon request after ten years. The defendant after the ten years requested, and the plaintiff went to the bishop of Hereford to desire him to accept a resignation and tendered one etc. But the bishop refused to accept, pretending those bonds [to be] void and [that he] could not in conscience accept of the resignation, upon which the bill was brought. And upon [the] hearing, [there was] proved non residency, dilapidations, and disorderly etc. and the court gave him three months to resign and in default dismissed the bill. And [they] went principally upon the refusal of the plaintiff for, at his peril, he must procure the bishop to accept etc. And [they] lay no great weight upon the proofs.

[Other copies of this report: HLS MS. 537(b), p. 72, pl. 1; IU Lilly MS. Parker, 'Cases in the Exchequer, vol. 2', p. 77, pl. 2; BL MS. Hargr. 70, p. 112, pl. 370; HLS MS. 1162, p. 96, pl. 516.]

II
IU Lilly MS. Parker, 'Cases in the Exchequer, vol. 5', p. 100 [Eng.] (Price's Reports)

[A] bill [was filed] to be relieved against a bond for [the] resignation of the church of King's Pyon in Herefordshire after ten years upon request to the defendant; the plaintiff sealed an instrument, which the bishop refused.

Serjeant *Lloyd*: That bonds of resignation are good in [common] law is not questioned, being so determined, but courts of equity have restrained them.

23 November 1701, Hilliard v. Stapleton,[1] in chancery, [on] a bond for [the] resignation, of a great penalty, [there was a] decree to acknowledge satisfaction and a perpetual injunction against the bond and to enter into a new bond to the patron of [*blank*] to oblige [the] clerk to his duty.

2 Chan. Rep. 186, Dunston v. Sanders.[2]

20 February 1708[/09] [?], Hodgson v. Thornton,[3] to resign when [the] patron's son comes of age and is qualified, [there was an] order to consult the bishop as to that.

---

[1] *Hilliard v. Stapleton* (1701), 1 Eq. Cas. Abr. 86, 21 E.R. 898.
[2] *Dunston v. Sandys* (1686), 2 Chan. Cas. 186, 22 E.R. 904, also 2 Chan. Rep. 398, 21 E.R. 698, 1 Eq. Cas. Abr. 86, 21 E.R. 897, 1 Vernon 411, 23 E.R. 552.
[3] *Hodgson v. Thornton* (1702), 1 Eq. Cas. Abr. 228, 21 E.R. 1009.

Mr. *Ettrick*: That bond must be to good purposes and not £500 to force a resignation.

Mr. *Ward* [cited] Cro. Jac. 249, Jones v. Lawrence.[4]

Owen's Reports 12.[5] [A] resignation must be free and voluntary and not compulsive; [it] must be pure and *simpliciter*. [The] bishop is the only judge whether he shall accept of the resignation.

Serjeant *Birch*: That the plaintiff does not reside, that the vicarage house is out of repair, that he does not do his duty, and that he is a drunken disorderly man, that being bound he must procure the bishop to accept of a resignation, it being a lawful act which may be performed. 1 Cro. 180, Babington v. Wood,[6] bonds of resignation, that it was policy to take them. Jones 220, *idem*, Hutton 111, *idem*; Cro. Jac. 248, Jones v. Lawrence; 1 Rolle, Abr., 411, Cary's Case, Degge 51, 52.[7] Where [the] condition must be performed, 5 Rep., Lamb's Case; 3 Cro. 864, Moor v. Moor, 645; Co. Lit. 209; 1 Levinz 191, Butcher v. Lane.[8] [The] plaintiff knew [that] the bishop would accept the resignation, otherwise [he was] not bound. This puts greater power in the bishop than the crown can do. An honest man is as good as his word, but this is a trick between the bishop and [the] plaintiff.

Mr. Dodd and Mr. Turner [were] for [the] defendants. Sir Simon Harcourt [was] for [the] plaintiff.

Chief Baron [WARD], BURY, and LOVELL were for dismissing the bill. PRICE, *contra*, was not satisfied how the practice in chancery was in those cases, but [they] made a provisional decree that [the] plaintiff should resign by Lady Day, and the court reserved the consideration of costs if he comply.

Some cases [that] I thought of on the subject [are] the oath against simonical contracts, the Statute 31 Eliz., c. 6,[9] against corrupt presentations and resignations, contracts *ex turpi causa* [*blank*] nor gratuity.

---

[4] *Johns v. Lawrence* (1610), Cro. Jac. 248, 274, 79 E.R. 213, 235.

[5] *Gayton's Case* (1591 x 1592), Owen 12, 74 E.R. 863.

[6] *Babington v. Wood* (1630), Cro. Car. 180, 79 E.R. 757.

[7] *Babington v. Wood* (1630), W. Jones 220, 82 E.R. 117, Hutton 111, 123 E.R. 1137; *Johns v. Lawrence* (1610), Cro. Jac. 248, 79 E.R. 213; 1 Rolle, Abr., *Condition*, p. 411; S. Degge, *Parson's Counsellor* (1676), pp. 51, 52.

[8] *Lamb's Case* (1599), 5 Coke Rep. 23, 77 E.R. 85, *sub nom. Lamb v. Brownwent*, Cro. Eliz. 716, 78 E.R. 950; *More v. Morecomb* (1601), Cro. Eliz. 864, 78 E.R. 1090, Moore K.B. 645, 72 E.R. 813; E. Coke, *First Institute* (1628), f. 209; *Butcher v. Vane* (1666), 1 Levinz 191, 83 E.R. 363, also *sub nom. Butcher v. Vale*, 2 Keble 118, 84 E.R. 75, 1 Siderfin 313, 82 E.R. 1127.

[9] Stat. 31 Eliz. I, c. 6 (*SR*, IV, 802–804).

15 Hen. VII, 8.[10] [The] bishop [is to] judge of sufficiency and, in *quare impedit*, shows the cause specially.

Articuli Cleri.[11] There must be a reasonable cause of a refusal when [one is] admitted as *persona idonea* and [the] plaintiff empowers [the] patron to deprive him.

Linwood 55.[12] Resignation to the patron is void; no resignation without [the] bishop's acceptance [is] good where [there is] cure of souls.

Owen's Reports, Grayter's Case; Noy 22, Pascal v. Clark, there [a] bond [was] adjudged [to be] simony; 1 *Inst.* 17, presentment freely.[13]

2 Chancery Reports 8vo 398, Darston v. Sanders.[14]

Tothill 26, Wood v. Berry,[15] bond to resign, distinction about simony; Michaelmas [term] 3 Car. I [1627], Snell's Case, a voluntary bond [and a] decree against it or for procuring [a] marriage. The acceptance by a bishop is a judicial act, to which a condition cannot be annexed.

2 *Inst.*,[16] on [the] Statute Articuli Cleri, where the civilians were heard in this case.

431

Hall v. Filts (Ex. 1708)

In this case, the issue was whether a parson should have agistment tithes for sheep after their lambing, being then unprofitable cattle.

HLS MS. 537, part 2, p. 173, pl. 2 [Eng.] (Eden's Reports)

The case was [that] several of his parishioners had bought in about November some considerable numbers of sheep and after the lambing, but, before Easter before the shearing about three weeks or a month, they sold them again. And the question was if the parson should have agistment tithes with relation to their feeding after their lambing, being that time in respect of him unprofitable cattle.

---

[10] YB Pas. 15 Hen. VII, f. 6, pl. 2 (1500).
[11] Stat. 9 Edw. II, st. 1 (*SR*, I, 171–174).
[12] W. Lyndwood, *Provinciale*.
[13] *Gayton's Case* (1591 x 1592), Owen 12, 74 E.R. 863; *Pascal v. Clark* (1617), Noy 22, 74 E.R. 992; E. Coke, *First Institute* (1628), f. 17b.
[14] *Dunston v. Sandys, ut supra.*
[15] *Wood v. Berry* (1630), Tothill 26, 21 E.R. 113.
[16] E. Coke, *Second Institute* (1642), pp. 599–638.

Ettrick, Phipps, Bridges, and *Ward* upon the hearing argued he should. And *Ettrick* cited a case in Sir Robert Atkyns's time between Dummer and Wingfield,[1] where the case was [that] the cattle were bought in after shearing and sold before lambing time and there [they] decreed the parson to have agistment tithe and, as Mr. Baron Lechmere then said, the wool has unprofitable cattle[2] for the time to come. And [it was said] by *Ettrick* [it was] sold away about three weeks before shearing time, and the parson where [it was] shorn could not claim by ecclesiastical law except [where the sheep were] fed a month in his parish.

[Chief Baron] WARD: There is a difference when [the sheep are] so disposed of by way of defrauding the parson and when not.

[Baron] PRICE: He has paid [tithe of] lamb; they cannot be called unprofitable. Yet if they had paid [tithe of] wool too, they had been more profitable. The court inclined against Dummer and Wingfield's Case, but [ordered] that it should be made a case [for a jury].

[Other reports of this case: 2 Gwillim 606.]

[The decree of 1 July 1708, PRO E.126/19, f. 56v, is printed at 1 Wood 510, 1 Eagle & Younge 690.]

432

Kirton v. Manwaring (Ex. 1708–1710)

Corruption of blood and forfeiture of lands are separate punishments for treason.

A person who has been granted lands forfeited by a traitor can redeem a mortgage of them.

I

IU Lilly MS. Parker, 'Cases in the Exchequer, vol. 4.', p. 225 [Eng.]
(Price's Reports)

[Upon an] English bill, [it was shown] that Roger Whitley for £1200 consideration did make a lease to Joshua Horton for three lives, *viz.* Ann, Joshua, and Joseph Horton of Cotton Hook etc. in Chesterton in the County of Chester, that Joshua Horton did reconvey the said lease to Sir J. Manwaring in trust for Roger Whitley to secure £600, part of the said sum, and Joshua Horton was indicted for high treason on the Statute 8 & 9 Will.[1] for preventing counterfeiting the coin of the kingdom, and there was [a] special verdict found, he escaped and

---

[1] *Dummer v. Wingfield* (Ex. 1691), above, No. 282.
[2] Sic in MS.

---

[1] Stat. 8 & 9 Will. III, c. 26 (*SR*, VII, 269–271).

died, and judgment was given. In the said Act, there is a proviso that the treason or felony by the said Act should not make any corruption of blood to any of the heirs of such offender or [his] wife, her dower or interest.

Joshua was bound for the postmaster and forfeited his bond, and the same had [been] extended and [was] in the hand of the crown. And the defendants Elizabeth and George [Cookson] are tenants to the crown. The Lady Manwaring is executrix to Sir J. Manwaring, who had the said £600 mortgage in trust for Roger Whitley. Samuel Harris is administrator to Sir J. Manwaring.

[On] 26 July 5 Anne, 1706, the queen made a lease under [the] exchequer seal to the two plaintiffs [Anthony and John Kirton] in trust for Sir Salathiel Lovell of the said leasehold for the lives of the said grantees, which grant recites that the said Joseph Horton [on] 8 April 1690 was attainted of high treason and that an inquisition was found [on] 1 June 1 Anne, 1702, and the said lease was found, and the rent was £13 13s. 4d.

The bill offers to redeem the queen's interest and the said mortgage and to have an account of the profit of the farm ever since the grant [and to find] that the land is in the crown by the Statute 32 Hen. VIII[2] without inquisition or office for high treason.

The answer of John Horton, son, and [*blank*] by [his] guardian is no evidence against them, and so, in the king's bench in Ackleston and Betty's Case,[3] it was adjudged.

Secondly, if the inquisition is sufficient as a ground for the title of the lease without a copy of the record and attainder, that it may appear that it is the same with the record recited in the inquisition and grant.

It was said that no more than an inquisition was produced in the Lord Powis's Case,[4] the same in Sir Roger Strickland's [case],[5] that the heir may plead to the inquisition that there is *nul tiel record* as set forth in the inquisition as to the attainder.

Sir Edward Northey, for [the] defendant: The Act has an exception that no corruption of blood [occurs], and so [one] can forfeit but for his life and not injure the heir.

---

[2] Stat. 32 Hen. VIII, c. 4 (*SR*, III, 750); note also Stat 26 Hen. VIII, c. 13, s. 4 (*SR*, III, 509).

[3] *Eccleston v. Petty* (1689), Carthew 79, 90 E.R. 650, 3 Modern 258, 87 E.R. 170, 1 Shower K.B. 89, 89 E.R. 469, Comberbach 156, 90 E.R. 402, Holt K.B. 222, 90 E.R. 1021.

[4] Perhaps *Lord Powis's Case* (1559), 2 Dyer 170, 73 E.R. 372.

[5] *Attorney General v. Crofts* (Ex. 1697), Samuel Dodd's Reports, p. 172. See also *Attorney General v. Croft* (Ex. 1707), above, No. 419, 4 Brown P.C. 136, 2 E.R. 91, *Lords' Journal*, vol. XVIII (n.d.), pp. 614, 629.

3 Rep. 10, Dowty's Case; Hale's P.C. 8; attainder in felony is corruption of blood. 1 *Inst.* 391, 392; 1 Rep., Alton Woods Case; 3 *Inst.* 47;[6] saving against the words of the judgment is bad, but saving to a thing which is implied is good, as a forfeiture which is implied in the judgment.

Secondly, forging deeds is [a] felony without clergy [with] forfeiture of life and goods and land, but [one] shall not lose [her] dower or [is there a] disinherison of the heir.[7]

Stat. 8 Eliz., c. 3,[8] transporting of sheep; [the] second offense [is a] felony, but [there is] not corruption of blood or loss of dower.

Stat. 31 Eliz., c. 4;[9] embezzling [the] queen's ordnance is [a] felony, [but it] extends not to corruption of blood or loss of dower; only [the] offender forfeits for his life.

3 Jac., c. 4,[10] felony [for] not taking the oath; [but there is] not [a] loss of dower [or] disherison of the heir or corruption of blood.

3 *Inst.* 47; where there is [a] sav[ing of] corruption of blood or [a] saving [of the] right of the heir, [it] saves his inheritance and prevents corruption, yet it is a forfeiture for life by [the] Statute 26 Hen. VIII[11] notwithstanding the [s]aving; by the avoidance of the corruption of blood, the inheritance is impliedly saved.

It is convenient when new felonies are made that there be such savings of the wife's dower and the heir's inheritance as former acts had them. 11 Rep. 1, Lord Delaware's Case.[12]

A person attainted of treason or felony can have no heir by reason of the corruption of the blood. An alien can have no heir. Escheat to the lord [occurs] where [there is no] tenure upon [an] attainder of felony for want of [an] heir.

Serjeant *Banister*, for the plaintiff: [The] Statute 33 Hen. VIII[13] gives [a] forfeiture in high treason, and [a] saving [of the] corruption of blood takes the estate forfeited out of the crown by implication. There ought to be express words as saving the blood and inheritance. Statutes 8 Eliz. and 3 Jac. What estate Horton had [was] for[14] another life, which is a special occupancy, but this he leased to

---

[6] *Attorney General v. Dowtie* (1584), 3 Coke Rep. 9, 76 E.R. 643; M. Hale, *Pleas of the Crown* (1678), p. 8; E. Coke, *First Institute* (1628), ff. 391–392; *Attorney General v. Bushopp* (1595–1600), 1 Coke Rep. 26, 76 E.R. 64; E. Coke, *Third Institute* (1644), p. 47.

[7] Stat. 5 Eliz. I, c. 10 (*SR*, IV, 443–445).

[8] Stat. 8 Eliz. I, c. 3 (*SR*, IV, 487).

[9] Stat. 31 Eliz. I, c. 4 (*SR*, IV, 801).

[10] Stat. 3 Jac. I, c. 4 (*SR*, IV, 1071–1077).

[11] Stat. 26 Hen. VIII, c. 13, s. 4 (*SR*, III, 509).

[12] *Lord de la Warre's Case* (1596 x 1597), 11 Coke Rep. 1, 77 E.R. 1145.

[13] Stat. 33 Hen. VIII, c. 23 (*SR*, III, 863–864) (treason); note also Stat 26 Hen. VIII, c. 13, s. 4 (*SR*, III, 509) (forfeiture for treason).

[14] had Horton for *MS*.

Manwaring in trust for Roger Whitley till he paid £600, then in trust for Horton, which certainly may be forfeited, and the saving of the corruption is but the blood and honor and not the estate, which is forfeited.

Mr. *Dodd*: [The] Statute 25 Edw. III[15] [gives a] forfeiture of [the] inheritance for high treason. 26 Hen. VIII and 33 Hen. VIII, and [they] forfeit all their lands, the forfeiture by the attainder, it goes to the crown and prevents special occupancy and thus is a term to pay money, and the equity of the term is forfeited and prevents occupancy. The crown is likewise in possession by inquisition, and [the] heir must plead his title to the inquisition. This is a forfeiture to the crown not an escheat to the lord for want of [an] heir by tenure.

Mr. *Turner*: The corruption of blood [is] saved; [it does] not give or save any estate by implication against an express forfeiture.

Stat. 1 Jac. I, c. 11,[16] marrying a second wife with a saving as before saving dower or inheritance is not of any weight here, where there is neither dower or inheritance to be had.

The special occupant, though it should be [the] heir, yet is not an heir to other intent; it is not assets in his hand; [he] shall not have his age as heir at law; no debt [lies] against him as heir.

The trust is to Horton till he fails to pay and then to Sir J. Manwaring till [he be] paid.

Mr. *Page*: Restitution is partial of blood and not estate; if *de integro*, then blood and estate. Hardres 405, Attorney General v. Sir George Sands; 12 Rep. 1, Ford v. Shelton.[17]

Mr. *Ward*: The statutes which have the saving is not upon account of the corruption of blood, but what [it] saves is not the disinherison of the heir or dower.[18] The king cannot be disseised by implication. Descendible freeholds are not in favor of the heir. The queen has the term by forfeiture not the inheritance, which the saving would help.

Sir Edward Northey: The corruption of blood saved is the same in treason and felony. Statute 25 Edw. III, forfeiture [of] escheats; this is not by implication but a saving for the heir. The heir in tail before the Statute forfeits only for life, and the heir after[wards] entered. If [there be a] forfeiture for life, [there] must be an office, but if he die, [the] heir enters without an office.

This is a descendible fee, a special occupancy which the heir has against the general occupancy.

---

[15] Stat. 25 Edw. III, st. 5, c. 2 (*SR*, I, 319–320).

[16] Stat. 1 Jac. I, c. 11 (*SR*, IV, 1028).

[17] *Attorney General v. Sands* (1665–1669), Hardres 405, 488, 145 E.R. 520, 561, also above, No. 16; *Ford and Sheldon's Case* (1606), 12 Coke Rep. 1, 77 E.R. 1283, also *sub nom. Attorney General v. Hoord*, 117 Selden Soc. 345.

[18] Sic in MS.

The term of ninety-nine years is a mortgage and not a resulting trust, but the equity of redemption is so. Com. 487, Nicolls v. Nicolls,[19] upon forfeiture and trust. 2 Rep., Sir B. Cholmley's Case;[20] [the] grant [was] void.

Serjeant *Cheshire*: [A] saving prevents [a] forfeiture of the estate but does not make a restitution by implication. If [there was a] forfeiture for life, Horton, the heir, may enter.

Oldham v. Pickering, king's bench; the Statute of Frauds has made a general occupancy a freehold, and so a special occupancy is so where no debt [is] to be paid. 2 Salkeld 464; Carthew 376; 1 Ld. Raymond 96.[21]

Mr. *Ettrick*: Saving and forfeiture is the same law, if [the] money [be] paid, then [the] lease is void and nothing [is] forfeited; if not, then [it is] in trust.

1. What estate or interest had Joseph Horton at the time of the attainder; had he a fee determinable on three lives or an equity of redemption of the mortgage lease made to Sir J. Manwaring in trust for Mr. R. Whitley?
2. Whether the son upon the death of J. Horton has the right of redemption or [is he] entitled by special occupancy?
3. What is forfeited and what interest the queen has by the attainder and whether the office or inquisition [is] necessary to entitle the queen?
4. What operation the saving in the Statute 8 & 9 Will. as to the corruption of blood has in this case, and whether it supersedes the forfeiture?
5. What is granted by the exchequer lease to the plaintiff, and if [it is] well granted?

Hardres 419, Barrington v. Attorney General and others; Hardres 488;[22] [a] trust of [an] inheritance [is] not forfeited for felony, but [a] trust of [a] term is. A lease in trust [is] liable to the king's debt, though after[wards] aliened, [a] matter of account is forfeited; [a] power of revocation [is] subject to the king's debt; [if a] husband and wife purchase in fee and the wife survives, [it is] liable to the debt of the king.

---

[19] *Nichols v. Nichols* (1574), 2 Plowden 477, 75 E.R. 711.

[20] *Cholmley v. Hanmer* (1597), 2 Coke Rep. 50, 76 E.R. 527.

[21] *Oldham v. Pickering* (1696), 2 Salkeld 464, 91 E.R. 400, Carthew 376, 90 E.R. 819, 1 Lord Raymond 96, 91 E.R. 960, 3 Salkeld 137, 91 E.R. 738, Comberbach 388, 475, 90 E.R. 545, 600, Holt K.B. 503, 90 E.R. 1176, 1177, 12 Modern 103, 88 E.R. 1195.

[22] *Barrington v. Attorney General* (1665), Hardres 419, 145 E.R. 527; *Attorney General v. Sands* (1668), Hardres 488, 145 E.R. 561.

That an inheritance in trust or [a] term in trust [is] not forfeited for felony if it attend the inheritance where [the] fee is forfeited to the king, it is by escheat for want of an heir, and where [there is] no tenant in law, but [it is] otherwise for treason by [the] Statute[s] 26 Hen. VIII and 33 Hen. VIII.

That the attainder of a felon may be avoided or falsified by the heir by his plea without going to a writ of error and the escheat of the land once vested may be divested by matters *ex post facto*. If [a] principal [be] attainted and [the] heir to the principal reverse his attainder, the heir of the accessory may plead to the attainder; if [the] principal [be] pardoned, he may avoid the attainder by plea. 3 *Inst.* 232; Dyer 35; 6 Rep. 13, Arundel's Case.[23] If [there is] an indictment for treason or felony and the indictment does not lay down the true time and is found guilty generally, a feoffee or lessee who may be prejudiced by such finding may falsify the time not the offense. 3 *Inst.* 230. If [one] attainted by confession prejudice the lessee, he may traverse the felony; if [it be] by verdict, then [one] must traverse the time not the offense. Com. 390;[24] the earl of Leicester, attainted by confession, admitted by special plea, [and] falsified the attainder, [it] being void and *coram non judice*.

1 Levinz 202, Gery v. Bearcroft; 1 Saunders 260, Took v. Glascock; Vaughan 193, Holden v. Smallbrook; Vaughan Rep. 202; 1 *Inst.* 41, no occupant against the king; Littleton, sect. [*blank*]; 2 Rolle, Abr., *Occupant*, 151; 4 *Inst.* 125; 5 Eliz., c. 11; 18 Eliz., c. 1; 5 Eliz., c. 1.[25]

[On] 16 May 1709, judgment was given in this cause.

Baron PRICE was of [the] opinion against the plaintiff, that he ought to be dismissed, the lease [was] made by Roger Whitley to Joseph Horton and his heirs for the life of Joseph, Anne, and Joshua, that he had a descendible freehold title, right, or estate, and that upon his death, his son was entitled thereto by descent, though not called an inheritance, yet [it] was of the nature of a fee, that the son did not claim as a purchaser nor by special limitation but by descent, and though it be called a special occupancy, yet it is very improperly so called, yet it is a descendible right.

---

[23] E. Coke, *Third Institute* (1644), p. 232; *Anonymous* (1564), 2 Dyer 235, 73 E.R. 519; *Cases of Pardons* (1587), 6 Coke Rep. 13, 77 E.R. 272.

[24] *Earl of Leicester v. Heydon* (1571), 1 Plowden 384, 75 E.R. 582.

[25] *Geary v. Bearecroft* (1667), 1 Levinz 202, 83 E.R. 368, also Carter 57, 124 E.R. 822, 1 Siderfin 346, 82 E.R. 1148, 2 Keble 148, 250, 285, 84 E.R. 93, 156, 177, O. Bridgman 484, 124 E.R. 702; *Took v. Glascock* (1669), 1 Williams Saunders 250, 260, 85 E.R. 298, 307; *Holden v. Smallbrooke* (1668), Vaughan 187, 124 E.R. 1030; E. Coke, *First Institute* (1628), f. 41; T. Littleton, *Tenures*, sect. 56; 2 Rolle, Abr., *Occupant*, 'Special', p. 151; E. Coke, *Fourth Institute* (1644), p. 125; Stat. 5 Eliz. I, c. 11 (*SR*, IV, 439); Stat. 18 Eliz. I, c. 1 (*SR*, IV, 607–608); Stat. 5 Eliz. I, c. 1 (*SR*, IV, 402–405).

Co. Lit. 8, heirs [*blank*] makes an inheritance in feoffment and grant. Littleton, sec. 739; Co. Litt. 41, 239, 388; 10 Rep. 95; 1 Saunders 260; 2 Levinz 138, Baxter v. Deuxwell;[26] Vaughan's reports, Holden v. Smallbrooke, 201, which shows it [to be] a descendible interest and that occupancy special is improper.

Secondly, that by the attainder of Joshua Horton on the Statute 8 & 9 Will., about coin[ing] for high treason, the estate was forfeited to the crown, that the proviso or saving in the Act [is] that it should not extend to [the] corruption of blood to the heir or loss of dower.

Hale's P.C. 8 and 3 *Inst.* 47, saving the corruption of blood is preserving the descent, and saving the land to the heir is preventing the corruption of blood and though by 2 *Inst.* 37; 3 *Inst.* 21, 212; 1 *Inst.* 392,[27] by the attainder of felons of felony or treason, the blood is corrupted, and corruption of blood in felony was on account of the want of an heir and a tenant to do the lord service, and so [it] escheated to the lord and to the king for a year and a day to prevent wreck and destruction, yet [the] Statute 25 Edw. III gave the forfeiture of escheats to the king that by corruption of blood would have come to the lord and though [*blank*] Statute 5 Eliz., c. 11, as to clipping, has made a forfeiture for life and says corruption of blood, [the] Statute 5 Eliz., c. 14,[28] against forgery, saved corruption of blood and disinherison of the heir, and [the] Statute 3 Jac., c. 4, is saving corruption of blood and disinherison of the heir, they are unnecessary expressions, for by saving of the corruption of blood was the same as saving the inheritance or disherison of the heir is the same as corruption of blood, so that the descent is saved and the right of the heir. And so [he] concludes [that] the heir is entitled.

And though it was seized into the king's hand on the attainder, that being but a forfeiture for life, when that was determined, the heir may enter without any *monstrans de droit* or petition, and this had but a forfeiture for life the heir unless in the inheritance is reserved for him and [*blank*] this being the queen's suit by her farmer, who sues to have a possession decreed, seeks a remedy against the subject and not the subject against the crown. And [he] was of [the] opinion to dismiss the plaintiff's bill.

Baron BURY [held for a] judgment for [the] plaintiff.

The queen [is] entitled by inquisition or office; it cannot be taken out without a traverse or *monstrans de droit*.

---

[26] E. Coke, *First Institute* (1628), ff. 8, 41, 239, 388; T. Littleton, *Tenures*, sect. 739; *Seymor's Case* (1612), 10 Coke Rep. 95, 77 E.R. 1070; *Took v. Glascock* (1669), 1 Williams Saunders 250, 260, 85 E.R. 298, 307; *Baxter v. Doudswell* (1675), 2 Levinz 138, 83 E.R. 487, also 3 Keble 475, 486, 498, 84 E.R. 832, 836, 843.

[27] E. Coke, *Second Institute* (1642), p. 37; E. Coke, *Third Institute* (1644), pp. 21, 212; E. Coke, *First Institute* (1628), f. 392.

[28] Stat. 5 Eliz. I, c. 14 (*SR*, IV, 443–445).

The escheat upon corruption of blood belongs to the king before the Statutes 25 Edw. III, c. [2], and 26 Hen. VIII, c. 13, [and] 33 Hen. VIII, c. 2.

Note where the king was lord, otherwise he had but a year and a day, and the lord had the escheat.

The saving in the Statute 8 & 9 Will. as to the corruption of blood is saving the inheritance and the dower, not such an estate as this determinable freehold is, and thus [it] is not called an inheritance.

10 Rep., Seymour's Case, distinguishes what an inheritance [is], what a freehold; a fee is either absolute or determinable. The determinable [ones] are carved out of estates of inheritance by a proviso or condition or so long as he has heirs of his body or [a] tenant in tail conveys in fee by deed and fine; it is a base fee as long as there are issue. And what is [a] determinable fee? What may continue forever or have a continuance, but a fee determinable on one, two, or three lives is not such a determinable inheritance within the Act.

There may be a remainder at law limited upon this estate but cannot on a determinable fee, as it is in Chudleigh's Case, 1 Rep.,[29] so that this is not within the saving.

Chief Baron WARD: The Statutes 25 Edw. III, c. [2]; 26 Hen. VIII, c. 13; 33 Hen. VIII, c. 20, have given all estates of persons attainted for high treason to the crown by way of forfeiture. This estate is called a descendible freehold, right estate, or special occupant.

Co. Litt. 41. It is good to insert the word 'heirs' to prevent occupancy. The lessee has such an interest in him that he might alien or sell and so may forfeit.

By the attainder in treason, the estate is forfeited.

By attainder in felony, there is corruption of blood and escheat to the lord.

[The] Statute 25 Edw. III makes the estate in fee which should escheat forfeited; 26 Hen. VIII, [c. 13], forfeits [the] estate tail; 33 Hen. VIII, c. [20], forfeits uses, right, [and] trust, and the crown is adjudged in possession on such attainder without office.

The saving in the statute is not to [the] inheritance and extends only to cases of felony not high treason.

Hale's *Pleas of the Crown* 8; 3 *Inst.* 47; 2 Levinz 138: nothing is saved but what comes by corruption of blood, not what comes by forfeiture; by the corruption of blood, the interest which descends from any collateral relation, the name and reputation of the family, is saved, but the estate of the father, which would otherwise descend, is forfeited and vested in the crown by forfeiture, so that nothing can descend to the heir. Though corruption of blood is implied in the judgment of high treason, yet that is not the only thing implied; there

---

[29] *Chudleigh's Case* (1589–1595), 1 Coke Rep. 113, 76 E.R. 261.

is forfeiture of land likewise, which takes place before the corruption of blood, which relates to the escheat not [the] forfeit[ure].

Hub. 345, 346, Sheffield v. Ratcliff.[30] The estate tail is vested in the king upon the attainder of high treason as a forfeiture and not by corruption of blood. 248. The right of [a] tenant in tail is bound and his heirs, there being no saving.

Com. 489, Nichol's Case; 560, Walsingham's Case; Dyer 332; and Doughty's Case in 3 Rep.;[31] the forfeiture is by attainder, that office does not give title but finds it.

If the estate had come to the crown by corruption of blood, then by a pardon of the corruption, there must be a restitution of the estate and it being forfeit, descent is prevented.

[An] estate tail reverts to the crown on [the] attainder of [the] tenant in tail; the estate vests that the king may have the reversion, but if [it] reverts to the subject, the tail is forfeited to the king.

That the case in Bracton, liber 2, c. 9; Com. 556.[32] [Where there is a] lease for three lives, an assize of *mort d'ancestor* lies, which makes it a fee. Fitzherbert, *Natura Brevium*, 195.[33]

Special occupancy prevents general occupancy. [The] Statute of Frauds and Perjuries[34] takes notice of special occupancy. Corruption of blood in [the] case of forfeiture does not save the heir as to the father but as to collateral relations.

If a person is entitled by attainder and also by office, it is a double title by matter of record, and [one] must traverse and not enter [a] special occupancy against the crown.

[There was a] decree [for] an account and redemption.

Note [that] this case was Baron Lovell's case, and [the] plaintiff [held] in trust for him. Baron Lovell's argument [was] not spoken, [it] being his own case.

The proviso in the Statute 8 & 9 Will., upon which Horton was attainted, [was] that [it] should not extend to corruption of blood or loss of dower, thus no forfeiture does incur. 3 *Inst.* 47. On [the] Statute 8 Eliz., c. 3, felony for transporting sheep [has the] same proviso etc. which has no notice of the inheritance, and thence Lord Coke infers that, by implication, the inheritance is saved, but

---

[30] *Lord Sheffield v. Ratcliffe* (1625), Hobart 334, 80 E.R. 475, also 2 Rolle Rep. 501, 81 E.R. 943, W. Jones 69, 82 E.R. 36, Godbolt 300, 78 E.R. 176.

[31] *Nichols v. Nichols* (1574), 2 Plowden 477, 75 E.R. 711; *Attorney General v. Walsingham* (1569), 2 Plowden 547, 75 E.R. 805; *Carew's Case* (1574), 3 Dyer 332, 73 E.R. 752; *Attorney General v. Dowtie* (1584), 3 Coke Rep. 9, 76 E.R. 643.

[32] *Bracton On the Laws and Customs of England* (S. E. Thorne, ed., 1968), vol. 2, pp. 90–93; *Attorney General v. Walsingham* (1573), 2 Plowden 547, 75 E.R. 805.

[33] A. Fitzherbert, *New Natura Brevium* (1652), pp. 486–490.

[34] Stat. 29 Car. II, c. 3 (*SR*, V, 839–842).

it was never so adjudged, nor is he positive, for he advises that in [a] new felony, [there] should be [a] saving of the heir's inheritance, as [the statute] 3 Jac. I, c. 4, does not extend to [the] disherison of the heir. [Statute] 5 Eliz., c. 14, second forgery felony, [has a] proviso to save heirs' inheritances. [Statute] 31 Eliz., c. 16, embezzling [the] king's stores, [has a] proviso not to disinherit the heir. [Statute] 1 Jac. I, c. 11, marrying [a] second wife, [has] the same [proviso]. [Statute] 3 Jac., c. 4, serving [a] foreign prince, [has a] proviso not to disinherit the heir. Thence he infers that they necessarily save [the] inheritance by express words and every statute but 8 Eliz., c. 3, has [a] saving [of] inheritances as well as corruption of blood in all new felonies.

[The] blood of attainted felons is corrupt at common law, and land returns to the lord for want of an heir to do the service, and [it] is no forfeiture but an escheat for want of the heir to do service. Lord Hale's *Pleas of the Crown*, f. 8,[35] saving of blood is saving the inheritance, but all these are in felony, not in treason.

1. All the judges agreed that in doubtful cases, construction [should be] for the crown [*blank*] by implication or intendment. 5 Rep. 56.
2. [In] cases of high treason, the condition to the king [is] *de novo* by the statute and is good against [the] lord as well as [the] tenant and his heirs, which differs from felony and is from treason committed not conviction, as in felony. Statute 26 Hen. VIII, forfeiture for high treason.

[Statute] 33 Hen. VIII, c. 2, is forfeiture for high treason, saving the rights of all but [the] heirs of [the] attainted [person]. [Statute] 5 & 6 Edw. VI, c. 11,[36] forfeiture for high treason, [the] estate real and personal [is] forfeited and actually vested in the king.

The convict here might have sold or incumbered and so may forfeit if he had made [a] feoffment in fee. Dyer 347, Weston's Case,[37] where two statutes clash, [a] construction [was] made that both may stand by attainder of treason; inheritance [is] forfeited, and [there is] corruption of blood. But, by this Statute, inheritance is forfeited, but corruption [of blood] is saved, whereby may inherit [a] collateral heir, as to [an] honour etc.

That the estate of Horton is not inheritable nor descendible; it is not dowable. 1 *Inst.*, 239: it is [a] bare freehold and, forfeited, lies waste; 6 Rep. 37, Dean and Chapter of Worcester;[38] 1 *Inst.* 41. If [an] implication did save [the] inheritance, it must be such as the wife is dowable in.

---

[35] M. Hale, *Historia Placitorum Coronae*, pp. 354–370.
[36] Stat. 5 & 6 Edw. VI, c. 11 (*SR*, IV, 144–146).
[37] *Weston's Case* (1576), Dyer 347, 73 E.R. 780.
[38] *Dean of Worcester's Case* (1605), 6 Coke Rep. 37, 77 E.R. 307.

If [the] heir is [a] special occupant, [there can be] no occupant against the king. 1 *Inst.* 41. But [there] could be no occupant, for the freehold was in the king by forfeiture before the father died, and [tenure] cannot be in abeyance.

That there was a lease to Manwaring for ninety-nine years by [a] mortgage which prevents the occupancy and the equity is forfeited. Cro. Jac. 512, Sir J. Daccomb's Case, [a] lease for years [was] forfeited. Coke, First Report, Adams v. Lambert.[39] [A] trust of the profit of land is [of] the land and not [a] trust to attend the inheritance as[40] condition[s] of redemption are. Trusts are forfeited by attainder [of the] *cestui que trust*. Hardres 495; Raymond 122,[41] [the] king cannot be [a] trustee for another. [If the] king [be] in possession, [the] profit belongs to him, and [he] is entitled by record and not [*blank*]. Staunford 56.[42]

[The] judgment [was] for [the] plaintiff, as before.

II

IU Lilly MS. Parker, 'Court Proceedings', p. 135 [Eng.]

J.S. being seised of an estate for three lives is attainted of treason for counterfeiting the king's coin upon the Statute of 8 & 9 of Will. III, c. 26,[43] wherein there is a proviso that no attainder upon that Act shall work any corruption of blood or loss of dower. The late king, supposing this estate to be forfeited upon this attainder, makes a grant thereof to Baron Lovell, and the estate being in the possession of A., mortgagee upon a mortgage forfeited, the baron prefers his bill in the exchequer to redeem suggesting this title.

Now the question was whether the clause of the Statute whereby the corruption of blood is saved does not likewise prevent the forfeiture of the estate, and of this opinion was Baron PRICE, but the chief baron [WARD] and BURY [were] *contra* and accordingly made their decree for a redemption.

And upon an appeal in the House of Lords,[44] the decree was confirmed by the opinion of all the other judges except POWELL. They said that the corruption of the blood and the forfeiture of goods and lands were distinct parts of the

---

[39] *Rex v. Exors. of Daccombe* (1618), Cro. Jac. 512, 79 E.R. 437, also *sub nom. Attorney General v. Carr*, 118 Selden Soc. 475; *Adams v. Lambert* (1602), 4 Coke Rep. 96, 78 E.R. 1079, also Moore K.B. 648, 72 E.R. 815.

[40] or *MS*.

[41] *Attorney General v. Sands* (1668), Hardres 488, 145 E.R. 561; *Whaley v. Anderson* (1665), T. Raymond 120, 83 E.R. 65, also 1 Siderfin 260, 82 E.R. 1093, 1 Keble 329, 874, 905, 909, 933, 83 E.R. 976, 1293, 1311, 1314, 1328.

[42] W. Staunford, *Les Plees del Coron* (1557), book 3, chap. 36, f. 196b.

[43] Stat. 8 & 9 of Will. III, c. 26 (*SR*, VII, 269–271).

[44] *Horton v. Kirton* (1710), 4 Brown 141, 2 E.R. 95, *Lords' Journal*, XIX (n.d.), p. 53, *sub nom. Lovell's Case*, 1 Salkeld 85, 91 E.R. 80.

punishment of treason and so taken notice of by several statutes concerning treason, whereof some save the forfeiture, some the corruption of blood, and some both. They agreed that in the case of an attainder of felony, the forfeiture of the estate to the lord is in law only an escheat for want of a tenant and is therefore only a consequence of the corruption of the blood, whereby the felon is rendered incapable of holding any lands that for this reason the saving of the corruption of blood in felony might prevent the forfeiture, which is only an effect incident to that corruption of blood, which works an incapacity of the person. But in the case of treason, the lands of the traitor are given to the crown as a forfeiture and not as an escheat, and therefore, the loss of lands is in this case not barely the effect and consequence of the incapacity of the person wrought by his attainder and corruption of blood as it is [for] felony but is a distinct felony[45] given to the king that he may have all the satisfaction which the traitor is capable of making either in his person or goods for an offence committed so immediately against his person or government.

[Orders of 18 May, 5 July, and 8 Nov. 1708: PRO E.126/19, ff. 31, 49, 71.]

433

Atkins v. Wayland (Ex. 1709)

A contract to convey is not subject to stamp taxes but an arbitral award is.

BL MS. Hargr. 71, f. 119v, pl. 1 [Fr. & Eng.] (Dodd's Reports)

Atkins treated with Wayland for a grant or assignment of a tucking mill in Salisbury for nineteen years etc. The heads were put in writing as to time, purchase money, yearly rent to be paid, repairs, taxes, etc. And [they] covenanted and agreed to execute articles or deeds to perfect it. And this agreement or contract was put in writing and signed and attested, but [it] was not on stamped paper. And it was opposed to be given in evidence upon a bill brought by Atkins to have an execution of this agreement. And [it was ruled] by the court that it was not necessary to be on stamped paper for it is but an evidence of an agreement and futurity to be performed, and thus it was resolved here in 1707 [in a case] between White and Lawes.[1]

In Michaelmas [term] 1710, [there was] an award in writing signed by an umpire pursuant to a rule of court and the court inclined that it was a notarial

---

[45] Sic in MS. for punishment.

[1] *White v. Lawes* (1707), PRO E.126/18, f. 657.

act and obligatory and it should be stamped, and on account of that, it was not read.

[Other copies of this report: HLS MS. 537(b), p. 72, pl. 3; Oxf. Brasenose MS. 59, p. 93, pl. 4; IU Lilly MS. Parker, 'Cases in the Exchequer, vol. 2', p. 78, pl. 2.]

434
Robinson v. Collet (Ex. 1709)

A modus *of tithes for cherries does not extend to the tithes for the herbage of the land.*

I
HLS MS. 1169, part 2, p. 139, pl. 3 [Eng.] (Eden's Report)

[To] a bill of tithes for cherries and agistment of pasture, a *modus* was pleaded to pay 2s. in the pound of rent reserved, if let, in discharge of tithes of the cherry orchards and the agistment of them through the whole County of Kent; if not let but if sold, then the buyer [was] to pay 2s. a pound for so many pounds as he gave for them.

Turner and Phipps [were] for the plaintiff; Dodd and another [were] for the defendants.

It was insisted upon by *Turner* that a *modus* of paying [?] 2s. in the pound of the rent reserved in discharge of the tithes was an ill *modus* [. . .] because of the uncertainty because it may rise and fall and there may be fraudulent leases made or a great fine paid and so less rent, whereby the parson might be defrauded or suffer [. . .] of Sir John Collet in his own hand, and so the *modus* did not extend to it, and that they had laid the *modus* to extend to the agistment too, which was a different tithe, and the nature of the *modus* was only to cherries and could not extend to it.

Dodd, for the defendant: In the case of houses, it has been good, as in Grant's Case, 11 Rep.,[1] and if let by fraud, [it is] no letting at all; if [it is] let fairly [?], then [it is] within the *modus* and by him, though [it was] objected [that] the *modus* [was] not laid to extend [to] when in his own hands, it then must pay according to the valuation of them.

The court: This *modus* cannot extend to the agistment. Had the *modus* been for the ground, it had, but being only for cherries, it can extend no further, as it was said by [Baron] LOVELL that a *modus* extinguishes only the payment of tithes

---

[1] *Graunt's Case* (1613), 11 Coke Rep. 15b, 77 E.R. 1165, also 1 Gwillim 259, 1 Eagle & Younge 222.

and not the right of them. [Chief Baron] WARD [was] to the contrary. And so is it in my lord Hobart[2] and so adjudged in Noel and Hicks' Case[3] that payment of tithes in kind shall never revive again, and an old orchard may have a *modus* but a new [?] one cannot. The court inclined [to hold] the *modus* bad, but I could not hear the rule made, but I suppose it was that they would consider of it.

N.B. *Turner* cited that 2s. a pound of the rent was not a good *modus*: Atkill and Chapman in 1699 in this court,[4] and Goreman and Withers (1702), and in the last case, a case [was] mentioned which was Dodderidge and Stafford,[5] which was [in] Trinity [term] 1690, and Hobart 10 and 11,[6] and Rolle's [Abr.], 651, title *Disme*.[7]

II
BL MS. Add. 22610, f. 33v [Eng.] (Wright's Reports)

The plaintiff, being vicar of Chalk in Kent, exhibited his bill in the exchequer for tithes of a certain ground, being a cherry orchard. The defendant pleaded a *modus* of 2s. in the pound if the cherry trees be let, according to the rent, and if the cherries be gathered by the owner and sold, then 2s. in the pound out of the profits. The court were clearly of opinion that this *modus* for the cherries was not [a] discharge for the herbage, if mowed or fed with dry beasts. And [the court] decreed for the plaintiff. Otherwise it would have been, if the *modus* had been laid to arise from the ground, for that would have discharged the herbage and cherries and all other product of the ground. See the case of Cowper and Andrews in Hubbard, p. 39,[8] for the force and nature of a *modus*.

[Order of 11 July 1709: PRO E.126/19, f. 136v.]

---

[2] *Cowper v. Andrews* (1612), Hobart 39, 80 E.R. 189; see below.
[3] *Nowell v. Hicks* (1601), 4 Gwillim 1570, 3 Eagle & Younge 1201, E. Coke, *Second Institute* (1642), p. 653.
[4] *Athill v. Chapman* (1698–1699), PRO E.126/17, ff. 83v, 110.
[5] Perhaps *Doddridge v. Startop* (Ex. 1690), above, No. 278.
[6] *Leifield v. Tysdale*, Hobart 10, 80 E.R. 161.
[7] 1 Rolle, Abr., *Dismes*, p. 651.
[8] *Cowper v. Andrews* (1612), Hobart 39, 41, 80 E.R. 189, 1 Eagle & Younge 240, also Moore K.B. 863, 72 E.R. 957, Godbolt 237, 78 E.R. 138, *sub nom. Hooper v. Andrews*, 1 Rolle Rep. 120, 81 E.R. 372, 1 Gwillim 275.

435

Lay v. Beamont (Ex. 1709)

A devise to the heir of a living person is valid.
Since a will must be in writing, a deposition to explain the will cannot be considered.

IU Lilly MS. Parker, 'Cases in the Exchequer, vol. 5', p. 131 [Eng.] (Price's Reports)

This was a bill on the will of Colonel Sprot, who devised his real estate to trustees for twenty-one years to pay his debts and legacies and then to his cousin John Sparks for ninety-nine years if he so long lived, remainder to [his] first son in tail male etc., remainder to Jonathan for ninety-nine years if he lived, then to [his] first son in tail male, and [the] remainder to the heirs male of Richard and Elizabeth Lay in tail male.

John and Jonathan Sparkes died without issue male; the plaintiff Elizabeth [Lay] was aunt to Colonel Sprot and had issue then living, the plaintiff Thomas and others.

[The issue was] whether this was a good limitation to the son of the plaintiff Elizabeth, the mother then living, for which was quoted Noy 43;[1] 4 Modern, Goodright v. Cornish;[2] 1 Modern, Pybus v. Mitford, 2 Levinz 78, *idem*;[3] 2 Rep., Cholmley's Case;[4] 4 Modern, Tipping v. Cosins;[5] 2 Levinz 230, James v. Richardson;[6] Syderfin 153,[7] where [to] one *en ventre sa mere* [is] a good devise; Moor 593, Clark v. Day.[8]

---

[1] *Payne v. Ferrall*, Noy 43, 74 E.R. 1012.

[2] *Goodright v. Cornish* (1694), 4 Modern 255, 87 E.R. 380, also 1 Salkeld 226, 91 E.R. 200, Holt K.B. 227, 90 E.R. 1024, Comberbach 254, 90 E.R. 461, Skinner 408, 90 E.R. 181, 12 Modern 52, 88 E.R. 1159, 1 Lord Raymond 3, 91 E.R. 898, 1 Eq. Cas. Abr. 189, 21 E.R. 980, 2 Eq. Cas. Abr. 337, 22 E.R. 287.

[3] *Pybus v. Mitford* (1673), 1 Modern 98, 121, 159, 86 E.R. 761, 780, 800, 2 Levinz 75, 83 E.R. 456, also 1 Ventris 372, 86 E.R. 239, 3 Keble 129, 239, 316, 338, 84 E.R. 634, 697, 741, 754, T. Raymond 228, 83 E.R. 119, 1 Freeman 351, 369, 89 E.R. 262, 275, 3 Salkeld 337, 91 E.R. 859.

[4] *Cholmley v. Hanmer* (1597), 2 Coke Rep. 50, 76 E.R. 527, also Moore K.B. 342, 72 E.R. 617.

[5] *Tippin v. Coson* (1694), 4 Modern 380, 87 E.R. 455, also Comberbach 312, 90 E.R. 498, Carthew 272, 90 E.R. 761, Holt K.B. 731, 90 E.R. 1303, 1 Lord Raymond 33, 91 E.R. 918.

[6] *James v. Richardson* (1678), 2 Levinz 232, 83 E.R. 533, also T. Jones 99, 84 E.R. 1166, Pollexfen 457, 86 E.R. 610, 3 Keble 832, 84 E.R. 1039, T. Raymond 330, 83 E.R. 172, 1 Ventris 334, 86 E.R. 216, 1 Eq. Cas. Abr. 214, 21 E.R. 998, 1 Freeman 458, 472, 89 E.R. 343, 353, Samuel Dodd's Reports, p. 60.

[7] *Snow v. Tucker* (1663), 1 Siderfin 153, 82 E.R. 1027.

[8] *Clerke v. Day* (1593), Moore K.B. 593, 72 E.R. 779, also Cro. Eliz. 312, 78 E.R. 564, *sub nom. Lilly v. Taylor*, Owen 148, 74 E.R. 965.

The court decreed the plaintiff [to be] at liberty to affirm his title at [common] law[9] [and decreed] the lease and all obstacles to be removed.

Secondly, it was objected against [the] reading [of] the deposition for explaining the will and that the Lords in the Lord Falkland and Mr. Lytton's Case,[10] on Sir William Lytton's will, they blamed the reading of it in chancery, and yet in the case of Nicolas v. Nicholas before lord Somers, it was allowed, where [there was] a devise of land to a wife and [there was] proof that it was intended in bar of dower, though [it was] read, yet [it was] not admitted against a will. The Statute of Wills and Frauds and Perjuries[11] says that wills must be in writing, so it was passed over.

[Long v. Beaumont: Order of 24 Feb. 1709: PRO E.126/19, f. 93.]

436

Crispe v. Mickleburgh (Ex. 1709)

In this case, the question was in which parish the tithe of barren cattle was due.

IU Lilly MS. Parker, 'Cases in the Exchequer, vol. 5', p. 171 [Eng.] (Price's Reports)

[Crispe exhibited a] bill of tithe of barren cattle in Micklefen Common in the Parish of Kingham in Norfolk.[1] The defendant lived in Kirby Cane and had land there and in Stockton and Golderston Parish, and [it was said] that there were many commons together without division and the cattle strayed from one to the other and [the] defendant put and drove his cattle into Micklefen.

[The defendant was] decreed to account for [the] tithe of the cattle put in; the proof was full that this common was in Ellingham and that the defendant put in his cattle, and, if they had by way of common of vicinage come there, yet [he] must pay tithe to the parson in whose parish the common is, but, if it had been uncertain or not known in what parish a common is, there, by the Statute 2 Edw. VI, c. 13,[2] [he] must pay to the parish where the owner of the cattle lives. 2 *In.* 651; 1 Modern 216, on the said statute.[3] By [the] canon law, no tithe [is due] unless depastured thirty days, [but] not for every trespass.

---

[9] See *Darbison ex dem. Long v. Beaumont* (1713), 1 Peere Williams 229, 24 E.R. 366, Fortescue 18, 92 E.R. 743, 3 Brown P.C. 60, 1 E.R. 1177, 1 Eq. Cas. Abr. 214, 21 E.R. 999, 2 Eq. Cas. Abr. 331, 22 E.R. 282.

[10] *Viscountess Falkland v. Lytton* (1709), 3 Brown 24, 1 E.R. 1152.

[11] Stat. 29 Car. II, c. 3 (*SR*, V, 839–842).

---

[1] Sic in MS.

[2] Stat. 2 Edw. VI, c. 13 (*SR*, IV, 55–58).

[3] E. Coke, *Second Institute* (1642), p. 651; *Anonymous* (1676), 1 Modern 216, 86 E.R. 838.

[The][4] decree [was] reversed in the House of Lords [on] 10 February 1709[/10],[5] and [the] plaintiff's bill [was] dismissed without prejudice to his right to the *modus* of 2d. per acre for the five acres in Ellingham; so King *et al.* and Fox, Michaelmas [term] 6 W. & M.; so Plummer's [?] MS. reports 97; Salkeld 169.[6]

[Other reports of this case: 1 Rayner 115.]

[The order of 21 July 1709, PRO E.126/19, f. 136, is printed at 1 Wood 517.]

437
Smith v. Johnson (Ex. 1709)

A custom of not paying tithes for barren cattle is void as a matter of law.

I
HLS MS. 537, pt. 2, pp. 134, 140 [Eng.] (Eden's Reports)

The case was [that] the Doctor [Smith] as rector of the rectory of Wearmouth [Durham] preferred amongst others his bill against some of his parishioners that lived within the ward or hundred of Easington for tithes and among other things for tithe of barren cattle. The defendants in their answer pleaded a *non decimando* throughout the whole ward of Easington for tithe of such cattle and alleged further that the Doctor as rector etc. had a sufficient sustentation and maintenance besides. Upon this, the question was whether a *non decimando* for tithe of all barren cattle within a hundred or ward were good or not.

It was argued by *Sir Simon Harcourt, Phipps, Turner*, and *Lutwyche* that it was not good. They argued that this was the same with Hicks and Woodington's Case, 4 Mod. 336,[1] which was a case as express as could be in point. Indeed if the tithe[2] had subsisted by custom, there they might have pleaded such a *non*

---

[4] This last paragraph is in a different hand.
[5] *Mickleburgh v. Crisp* (H.L. 1710), 1 Rayner 117, 3 Rayner 1091, 2 Brown 444, 1 E.R. 1053, 2 Gwillim 604, 1 Eagle & Younge 693, 2 Eq. Cas. Abr. 732, 22 E.R. 618, *Lords' Journal*, XIX (n.d.), p. 63.
[6] *Rex v. Fox* (1694), 1 Salkeld 169, 91 E.R. 156.

[1] *Hicks v. Woodeson* (1694), 4 Modern 336, 87 E.R. 429; also 1 Eagle & Younge 592, 2 Gwillim 550, 4 Modern 324, 87 E.R. 422, 3 Lord Raymond 116, 92 E.R. 595, 1 Lord Raymond 137, 91 E.R. 987, 12 Modern 111, 88 E.R. 1200, Skinner 560, 90 E.R. 252, Comberbach 403, 90 E.R. 555, Carthew 392, 90 E.R. 827, Holt K.B. 671, 90 E.R. 1271, 2 Salkeld 655, 91 E.R. 558, Samuel Dodd's Reports, p. 171.
[2] title *MS*.

decimando, but where [it is] due of common right, there it was not allowable. Palmer 37; Littleton's Reports 152.³ The *Doctor and Student* meant the same difference in his last chapter.⁴ And they agree [that] one parish cannot make such a prescription, and there is no difference when several make the prescription and when one only. They said indeed this difference [is] from Hicks's Case, as they have alleged, that Dr. Smith had a sufficient maintenance besides. But that [is] a trifling reason, for who shall be judge what [is] a sufficient maintenance; besides what [is] a sufficient maintenance to one person may not be to another person succeeding him, nor what [is] a sufficient maintenance at one time to the same person a sufficient one at another. They cited indeed 1 Rolle, *Abridgment*, 653.⁵ But my lord Rolle takes notice of Chief Justice Coke's opinion⁶ to the contrary [. . .]. And what difference the case of wood [is] from the rest of them is that it is not a thing, though annually increasing, that yields an annual profit and is annually renewing. So [it is] not within that rule that makes tithes due of common right. And this [is] the reason given by the court in Hicks and Wooderson's Case, which is entered Trin. 6 W., rot. 404.⁷ That of a sufficient maintenance was indeed mentioned by the counsel who argued it, as it is mentioned in 4 Modern. But the court (according to Lutwyche [who was] then present) laid no weight upon it, as it is likewise there reported, and so left it to the other side to answer upon Hicks and Woodeson's Case.

WARD, in the same time, remembered two cases of this nature decreed according to Hicks' Case, and that case [was] cited in one or both of them, the one a case out of Yorkshire, which was Brown and Godfellow's Case,⁸ and upon [an]other out of Derbyshire, which was Pool and Draper's Case.⁹ And so the court was inclined, but, however, heard on the defendants.

And on behalf of the defendants, Mr. Serjeant *Parker* argued that it was the old and constant opinion that there may be such a custom extending to a country as the *lex loci*, and so is the *Doctor and Student*, c. 47. And though the chapter there is principally about tithe wood, yet it is there laid down generally. And so [it] seems to be Brooke's opinion: Brooke's Abridgment, tit. *Dismes*, 14.¹⁰ And

---

³ *Aldresh v. Ray* (1619), Palmer 36, 81 E.R. 966, also 1 Eagle & Younge 310; *Norton's Case* (1628), Littleton 152, 124 E.R. 182, also Cro. Car. 113, 79 E.R. 699, Hetley 88, 100, 117, 124 E.R. 365, 382, 387, 1 Eagle & Younge 363.

⁴ C. St. German, *Doctor and Student* (T. F. T. Plucknett and J. L. Barton, edd., 1974), 91 Selden Soc. 300–314.

⁵ *Barham v. Goose* (1617), 1 Rolle, Abr., *Dismes*, pl. H, 8, p. 653.

⁶ *Anonymous* (1614), 1 Rolle, Abr., *Dismes*, pl. H, 9, p. 653.

⁷ *Hicks v. Woodson*, PRO KB.27/2103, rot. 404.

⁸ *Browne v. Culworthy* (Ex. 1697), above, No. 363.

⁹ *Pool v. Draper* (Ex. 1696), above, No. 325.

¹⁰ Brooke cites *Doctor and Student*.

so 1 R[olle's] Abridgment [*Dismes*] 653, H,8 and 9. And there he speaks generally. And according to him, tithe wood [is] due of common right, but by custom there he must claim it as due by custom, as in [the] case of tithe claimed of lead ore, there he must claim it by custom. And wherever anything [is] claimed as due by custom, the defendant may, by way of defense, deny the custom and not to be obliged to plead as in this case a *non decimando* by way of discharge of himself. And besides if tithe wood [is] due only by custom, he may deny the custom of that parish as well as the custom of a county. He cited Sewer and Bikner's Case, 1 Rolle 654, H,12,[11] and the objection that ewes [are] not properly mulgible and of little value etc., as in 4 Modern 338. Yet [it was said] by him [that] whether properly milked or no, since we do milk them and make a profit of them, the parson ought to share in it. And in our case here, [there] are other parts of his parish which [are] no part of Easington Ward, and this being only a *non decimando* for a particular thing, [it] ought to be allowed. He argued that there might as well be a *non decimando* in this case as in the case of wood. And as to the objection that tithe wood [was] due only by custom, [it was said] by him they were due of common right. And the Statute of *Sylva Caedua*[12] was made upon a complaint that the tithes were extended to all sorts of trees and wood and not made upon a complaint that no tithes [were] to be paid at all for wood, but only that it was carried so far.

And as to the objection that [it was] not due of common right because [there was] no annual profit, [it was said] by him [that] there arises in that case as much annual profit to the parson as in several others which are yet allowed to be *de communi jure* and which are two or eight years agrowing (as flax or hemp). And here [there] is an annual increase, and he has the benefit of every year's increase in time, though not yearly.

And besides in [the] case of tithe wood, he may be paid a tenth part, but now he cannot have it in specie of this case. And this being such a thing that he cannot have a tenth of but only money in lieu of it, if any thing [be] tithable not of common right, it must be this. And when there is a full and ample maintenance besides, that might be the consideration of this place being dis[. . .] because there was a sufficient recompense. And this [is] but a reasonable construction. And [he said] that this *non decimando* should prevent in this case as well as for wood (or any other tithe).

Cheshire of the same side [argued that] the question whether a *non decimando* for pasturage and agistment of cattle be allowable when the parson has such an ample provision besides, which is in the judgment of the court whether sufficient or no. He makes common law and common right to be synonymous. And though

---

[11] *Sewell v. Bickner* (1616), 1 Rolle, Abr., *Dismes*, pl. H, 12, p. 654.
[12] Stat. 45 Edw. III, c. 3 (*SR*, I, 393).

the reason of a custom does not appear, yet if [it is] not unreasonable, it is enough [if] it is of common right for the church to have tithes for all things renovant and to have tithes of things not renovant by custom; and certainly if they may be entitled to things not due of common right, certainly they may be likewise by custom abridged, as in [the] case of lead ore, especially in some particular place. And if anything [is] not of common right, it should appear to be this case. And that there may be a *non decimando* in a country, he cited 2 *Inst.* 645, 653,[13] where My Lord Coke lays down his opinion generally. 1 R[olle's] R[eports] 22; Sir Simon Degge 263.[14]

As to Hicks and Woodeson, it is not there suggested that there was a sufficient maintenance, and therefore upon it, necessarily, a consultation ought to go. Such a custom indeed as this will not be good for a particular town or person and gen[eral] in all customs no particular person can be assigned a private act will be presumed, and why not there. So there may be other reasons, as suppose now this hundred [is in] the demesnes of the crown and the king being capable of a *non decimando*, his alienees became so entitled too. Or it may be presumed that this was anciently a forest and so the crown [is] entitled and so the patentees. Why may it not likewise be reasonable likewise to construe that in consideration, the parson had tithes by the custom of the minerals, as there are many in that parish, that by the same custom, those of the ward should be discharged of those kind of tithes. And so [he] concluded.

Ettrick [was] of the same side. He apprehended this may differ from Hicks and Woodeson's Case. There the parson had only a few moduses to live upon. He cited Kidden and Edwards in Rolle's *Abridgment* 674.[15] And he said that tithes were always paid for underwood, as apprehended by the Statute of *Sylva Caedua*, and therefore [they] cannot be said due by custom but must have been due of common right, as much as this or any other. Besides how can they say they are due by custom when an Act of Parliament makes them due. But they say the reason why wood did not pay at right [was] because [it was] not renovant every year. That can be no reason because there is an annual increase and thus no profits [are] annually received; yet there is a profit by the yearly increase had one time or other, for if in [the] case of wood [it] becomes due from the severance, as in [the] case of corn and tithe lead, and if corn [is] never severed, no tithe [is] due; now if due only by custom, a custom in such case would be suggested, and it is never suggested in a bill in this court nor is it in a libel in the spiritual court. And he mentioned an attempt by Sir William Smith by [a] bill in this court for

---

[13] E. Coke, *Second Institute* (1642), pp. 645, 653.

[14] *Porter v. Tike* (1614), 1 Rolle Rep. 22, 81 E.R. 299, 1 Eagle & Younge 224; S. Degge, *Parson's Counsellor* (1676), p. 263.

[15] *Kidden v. Edwards* (1639), 1 Rolle, Abr., *Dismes*, pl. H, 13, p. 654.

the parson of Elland to compel (as I apprehended) several [persons] either to cut their wood or to pay according as the tithes would be, but it was the only attempt he ever knew. ([Query] the case.)

Dodd [said] now they would differ tithe wood from our case. And first they say that tithe wood [was] not due of common right but by custom or canon (which was the canon of Stratford,[16] which, according to Turner, was obligatory *in omnes recipientes*). We say it is due of common right, for if [it is] due by custom, why may not it be allowed in [a] parish or vill as [in] a county or hundred, which only consists of more of them.

Secondly, they say that tithe wood is due by a canon. [It was said] by him [that] tithe herbage and tithe milk stand upon a canon and the canon [is] the same to milk as wood. And the contest before *Sylva Caedua* was only when tithes should be paid for wood. And there have been some late resolutions by way of exposition upon that Act, as the Earl of Kent's Case,[17] which he owned had exceedingly perplexed him how to determine upon that Statute. And he seemed not to be satisfied with it. It seemed to have been in this chief baron's time and why a parish cannot and a hundred [can be] preserved in such [a] *non decimando*. He cannot see the distinction. Indeed the reason is said to be that in a parish etc. a great man may at one time or other overpower the parson and obtain it but that such a thing cannot be supposed in [the] case of a whole hundred etc. Now a tenth of herbage cannot be paid in this case, and this custom now is for people to pay what no Act of Parliament has [...][18] it [...].[19] But it was the discretion of the court in such cases as a parson could have no benefit in specie that he must have an equivalent, so in [the] case of calves or lambs, when less than a tenth, it is turned into money. But now wood may be taken in kind, but this could not be paid in kind and therefore orig[inally] [he] could not be said to have it in kind. And he takes it that it was the intent of the law in so proving payment in this case that the parson should have a reason supporting and subsisting. But when a custom interferes against such payment of it and turning [it] into money, he thinks it must give way to such custom, this [is] only for necessity. And when [there is] no necessity, he thinks it ought to be carried no further, especially when [there is] no usage. But to the contrary in Hicks and Woodeson's Case, there was but one or two parsons in the hundred and there was set forth no sufficient maintenance besides. But in our case [there] are several in the hundred and, as we have

---

[16] John Stratford, archbishop of Canterbury from c. 1333 to 1348. W. Lyndwood, *Provinciale* (1679), pp. 187–191 (bk. 3, tit. 16, ch. 3, and bk. 5, tit. 18).

[17] *Greenway v. Earl of Kent* (Ex. 1706), above, No. 407; note also *Greenway v. Marquess of Kent* (Ex. 1709), below, No. 444.

[18] sum'd *MS*.

[19] too *MS*. [?]

att[ested], sufficient maintenance; in such [a] case, he thinks customs may run upon them.

To the contrary, *Phipps* [argued] that the gentleman on the other side had gone against [?] two established maxims of the law, (1) that the church cannot lose its right without a recompense, (2) that no layman or laymen can prescribe in a *non decimando*. And what they go upon principally is the *Doctor and Student* which, though it should warrant what they say, can be no great authority, there being no precedent resolution taken notice of to warrant it. And what seems to weaken it the more is a reason there given.

(2) That by [the] not demanding of [it] in that time, it must be looked upon as a remitting of it. And that surely can be no reason, for the successor is at no prejudice by the laches of the predecessor and the church always has the privilege of infancy. And for that reason, the Statute of Limitations[20] does not prejudice the [suc]cessor, but that he has his five years notwithstanding [that] his predecessor [be] absolutely barred. They have cited likewise Br[ooke, *Abr.*] tit. 'Dismes'. But he took notice that it was laid down generally there, which is certainly bad, and he cannot see [that] it can be applied to this only. And as to the tithe wood, what it was before the Statute, it does not appear but that it was then de[. . .]ed for which reason the Act was made.

(3) To settle it, and because there has been such an Act of Parliament to settle it, for that reason, there is no occasion to mention a custom in entitling a man's self to these tithes. And the reason that is given for the *non decimando* prev[iously] in this case [was] because the parson has a sufficient maintenance. Besides it is a very wild one, for who shall judge. If the court is judge of it, then it will be requisite [to know] what family etc. the parson has, and the parson at that time may be a single man, and then the successor may perhaps have a great family, so that it will be a most difficult matter for a court to judge what is and what may be a sufficient maintenance.

And as to what Mr. Serjeant Cheshire agreed, *viz.* that such a custom as this would be good in a hundred, he thinks there is as much reason for its being bad in a hundred, as it will affect and turn to the prejudice of more ministers.

As to his objection of presuming it [to be] within a forest, [it was said] by him [that] if within a forest, it shall be paid to the parson except [it be] in no parish and then indeed it shall be paid to the crown. Then [he] said indeed that [a] *non decimando* stands upon the same reason as a *modus*, but he says in [the] case of a *modus*, there is supposed a consent between [the] parson, patron, and ordinary, the persons concerned, and a recompense still. But there is no satisfaction in this case; he loses all. Whereas in the other, he has what the parson, patron, and ordinary thought reasonable for him.

---

[20] Stat. 21 Jac. I, c. 16, s. 2 (*SR*, IV, 1222).

As to woods being renewable, what grows every year cannot properly be called renewing. And thus he concluded.

[It was said] by WARD [that] it is in the Canon *Etiam si non est annuatim renovans*.

Turner [said that] it is admitted that a particular person or parish or town cannot make any such prescription. He takes it there cannot be a *non decimando* except [there be] a sufficient maintenance for the parson besides. And [it was said] by him [that] a prescription must be perpetual and must not be to rise and fall, as, in this case, the profits are more or less according to the manner the lands are employed. Then besides, in this case, it appears there is a competent maintenance for all the parsons in all the parishes in the hundred, for it must be throughout the hundred or not at all.

As to the cases that have been cited, most of them are grounded upon [the] Doctor and Student's Case, and the main treatise there is upon tithe wood. But then they say [?] well [one] cannot differ this case from tithe wood, for they say tithe wood [is] due of common right and that no custom [is] set forth in this or the spiritual court. But he said, though not in this court, yet he believed and he thought he had read they did in the spiritual court. But however we say, it is due by [a] canon which must be obeyed if received as the law of the land.

And though Sir Thomas Parker objected that that must be a rational reception in a legislative way, yet [it was said] by him a canon may be received generally in the kingdom and not in particular places, as the canon that the parson shall choose the clerk (or churchwardens), yet that [is] not received generally but that the parishioners in many places choose by custom.

As to the presumption that it was the crown's land, it shall pay when it comes out of the crown; so [also] when disforested, as the Marquess of Worcester's Case. And thus [he argued] for the plaintiff.

Lutwyche [argued that] as to what Mr. Serjeant Cheshire said of an Act of Parliament as having been presumed to support customs, he thinks Acts of Parliament were never presumed to support customs of this kind. And as to what was said of presuming that the parson had tithe lead in respect of this, [it was said] by him that [it] ought to have been alleged, and so that of a forest and [it] ought to have been proved. And [it was said] by him the reason of tithes payable in this case is [. . .] the grass which as it would be hay and so [be] tithable, he is now deprived by cattle which yield nothing of [a] tithable nature, and to the same effect with the rest.

It was adjourned for the opinions of the court.

The court now gave their opinion for the Doctor, [with Baron] Lovell dissenting.

LOVELL: There may be a custom of *non decimando* gen[eral] in a county, as in 2 [Coke] *Inst.* and in the *Doctor and Student*. And yet he thinks this is a stronger case because this [is] not a *non decimando* generally but only as to barren and unprofitable cattle. He thinks it may have a very reasonable commencement in point of construction. But he said he would only give a general opinion and that, if the custom [be] established by a trial, it might be fit to consider it further.

PRICE: He thinks it neither a just nor legal custom and that it cannot be so, not by the rules they would go upon to make it good, for he thinks:

1. It does not sufficiently appear upon the answer that there is a sufficient maintenance besides for the parsons.
2. It does not appear [that] there are more parishes, but suppose it had appeared so, the question could be whether it was a good custom or not, and [it was said] by him [that] he cannot differ this from Hicks and Woodeston's Case in 4 Modern, and [it was said] by him there it was only insisted upon by the counsel as to the maintenance (the court give their opinion without taking any manner of notice of the insufficiency) and that that was a solemn authority and [there were] no opinions to the contrary, for he thinks they have no ground to support them. Indeed they have mentioned four authorities, but all in effect only are and that scarcely to be called so, for Brooke, Coke, and Rolle [are] all founded upon that saying of the *Doctor and Student*. [He said] that he has a great respect for the *Doctor and Student*, yet that can be no great authority. The book does not contain any determination but [is] only by way of argument, nor does it refer to any. And Brooke refers to the *Doctor and Student*, and indeed he goes so far [as] to question whether agistment be tithable or no. And 2 *Inst.* refers after the same manner. But My Lord Coke himself [was] not of that opinion as appears by Coke's *Abridgment* where [it is] said to the contrary by Coke. And it is further manifest [that] he was so by 1 Rolle's Reports 22. It is Coke that Wray said so and so but that it seemed to him to the contrary. And so it is in the case of Easter term, 12 Jac. [1614], in 2 Bulstrode, Russell v. [Backhurst].[21]

So those authors they have insisted upon are answered by themselves. And Rolle is only an abridgment of the case, not his own opinion, as appears [in] his 2 Reports 122,[22] and he thinks it must be allowed that agistment [is] a custom of common right and [there is] a great division between tithe wood and this. And indeed he does take it [that] there may be a *non decimando* of tithe wood, and so are the latter opinions notwithstanding the opinion of Coke and Dodderidge in Rolle, *supra*.

---

[21] *Russel v. Backhurst* (1614), 2 Bulstrode 285, 80 E.R. 1126, 1 Eagle & Younge 236, 1 Gwillim 270.

[22] *Earl of Clanrickard v. Lady Denton* (1619), 2 Rolle Rep. 122, 81 E.R. 699, also Palmer 37, 81 E.R. 967, 1 Eagle & Younge 306, 1 Gwillim 360.

And he is [of the] opinion that tithes for wood [are] due by custom, and really [there is] a great deal of ground to believe that; so is the *Doctor and Student* 355.

And as to pl[ead] a custom of *non decimando* in discharge of it, what need is there [of] a custom to destroy it where a custom [is] necessary to set it up. He believes the custom might arise from tithes not being payable for timber and so at length to prevail generally. And so he concluded for the plaintiff.

BURY: In Hicks and Woodeson's Case, it is not alleged [that] the parson had a sufficient maintenance. But there it is indeed but only for this parish and the prescription for a *non decimando* in two hundreds, but [they] do not say there is a sufficient maintenance for all the rest. And we are not to suppose the two hundreds [are] only one parish, and therefore he thinks they do not so much as even bring themselves within the case of the *Doctor and Student*.

And as for a general prescription of a *non decimando* without laying a sufficient maintenance, though that may legally commence, yet it does not follow that it is a good prescription. He thinks [there is] no case resolved where they may prescribe but in the case of wood, but that on the other hand, Hicks and Woodeson's Case [is] a positive resolution that they may not. And so he concluded that [it was] not a good prescription.

WARD: First, whether there can be such a custom; second, whether they have brought themselves within that custom. It is said that time out of mind there has been a custom in the hundred that the owners, tenants, and farmers of any lands [and] tenements in those hundreds have been and used to be discharged from payment of tithes of or for any tithe of barren and unprofitable cattle, for the agistment thereof. And [he] said further that the custom [is] more reasonable for that the rector of Wearmouth had a sufficient maintenance.

Now, one man or parish cannot prescribe, but if a hundred though only one, perhaps two, yet by the collectiveness of the hundred, they may. But the reason in the first case is because a layman cannot and as not being capable of receiving tithes in pernancy, but then if one parish in that hundred pays tithes, there is an end of the custom.

They ought to have shown that every parish had a sufficient maintenance. But then they say that it is an odd sort of tithe and can hardly be said due of common right, and so such a custom may run and prevail upon it. He mentioned F.N.B. 53.9, but then [he] said that book [is] denied for law in Cro. Eliz. 413, 446; Moore 454.[23]

---

[23] *Hoe v. Taylor* (1595), Cro. Eliz. 413, 78 E.R. 655; *Grysman v. Lewes* (1595), Cro. Eliz. 446, 78 E.R. 686, also Moore K.B. 911, 72 E.R. 991, 1 Eagle & Younge 112, 1 Gwillim 165; *Monday v. Lovice* (1595), Moore K.B. 454, 72 E.R. 690, 1 Eagle & Younge 118.

He seemed to mention a case (but I did not hear it well) of a *modus* of paying a penny for every milk cow whereby [there was a] discharge of tithes of milk cows and of tithe of barren cattle. And it was adjudged a *non decimando* of the barren cattle and that, as it was said, it could only extend to the tithes of the milk cows. He mentioned the Duke of Newcastle's Case and the Archbishop of York's Case[24] that a *modus* of tithes of one kind could never discharge the tithes of another (but [it was said] by Hutton in the same case that [it] was never determined but sent to a trial).

But N.B. WARD cited it as an authority, and [it] seemed to be a case in his own time.

He wondered what reason there could be why a hundred could prescribe in a *non decimando* and why a parson could not. It may [. . .] indeed because it is supp[. . .] hundred will be certain that all the parsons in it have a sufficient maintenance. As to the *non decimando* in Rolle of the milk ewes, that is by him because not mulgible that not such as used to give milk that [. . .] the only ones looked upon to be mulgible, as appears by the *Laws of Edward the Confessor*[25] and the old law.

Yet wherever [there is] a custom of *non decimando*, nobody can show that there was a sufficient maintenance set forth.

He is of opinion that tithe wood became due by Stratford's Canon as appears by the Canon *Etiam si non renovantur*. But N.B. afterwards he argued as if [it was] due by custom, and for that reason [he] took that the c[. . .] of the petition against that canon concludes always as accustomed to be paid. (And this seemed to me much the better opinion.)

That the ch[urch] may be entitled [is] very plain [?], but then you shall not notwithstanding take all away from them by custom (but that upon the reason of particular maxims). But why a hundred shall prescribe more than a single man or parson he cannot see. He took notice of Hicks and Woodeson's Case, and therefore he thinks it [is] not a good custom. But if it could have been good, it is not so laid as to make it one because they have not shown that all the parsons have a sufficient maintenance.

And thus with PRICE and BURY [he held] that [it was] bad.

II

IU Lilly MS. Parker, 'Cases in the Exchequer, vol. 5', p. 167 [Eng.] (Price's Reports)

[Dr. J. Smith exhibited a] bill for tithes as rector of Bishop's Wearmouth in the County of Durham against the defendant Hodson, and [he] insists upon a *non decimando* for barren cattle in the Hundred of Easington in Easington Ward

---

[24] *Archbishop of York v. Duke of Newcastle* (Ex. 1704), above, No. 388.
[25] 'Leges Edwardi Confessoris' in B. Thorpe, ed., *Ancient Laws*, vol. 1 (1840), pp. 442–464.

and that the said parish is parcel thereof and that the rector had in the said parish sufficient [income] to maintain him[self].

The question upon the point being whether [it was] a good custom or not.

[Sir] *Simon Harcourt*, Mr. *Phipps*, Mr. *Turner*, and Mr. *Lutwyche* [argued] that it was a bad and illegal custom, that it is not laid in the defendant's answer, that there was sufficient [income] to maintain the ministers in all the parishes in the hundred or ward to say that the plaintiff had sufficient [income] in his parish is not enough for the whole hundred.

Michaelmas [term] 6 Will. & Mary, in the king's bench, Hicks v. Woodson, 4 Modern 336, *idem*, a prohibition where the hundred of Huntspill in the County of Somerset had a custom *in non decimando* for barren cattle and that the parish of Hulspill was part of it, and the issue was tried, and [it was] found for the plaintiff, and in arrest of judgment:

1. That it was a void custom.
2. That it was not showed [that] there was a sufficient maintenance for the minister besides those tithes.

1.That it was against common right and no custom [is] good to discharge a layman *in non decimando*; [it is] otherwise in ecclesiastical persons; agistment is the profit of the land; *non decimando* gives every person a right to prescribe so, and then the parson has nothing. 1 Rolle, Abr. 654, Kiddes v. Edward,[26] a miller for two hundreds [was] exempt from tithes of corn for mills for work because [there is] no discharge without [the] consent of [the] parson, patron, and ordinary. Tithes [were] due before the Council of Lateran. 2 Bulstrode 285,[27] [the] whole country may be discharged having [a] reasonable beginning, as *Doctor and Student*; Littleton 152; 2 *Inst.* 653.[28] Prescription *in non decimando* [was] denied in the Weald of Kent and in Michaelmas 12 Jac. allowed in the Weald of Sussex, 1 Rolle, Abr., 653.[29] Tithe wood is by custom and usage and not of common right and not an annual profit or growth, as corn, but are destroyed by cutting and [there is] a small profit. 13 Rep. 13.[30]

Stat. 45 Edw. III, c. 3, Statute of *Sylva Caedua*, that wood above twenty years [is tithable does] not imply [tithes] should be paid [where] under.[31] 2 *Inst.*

---

[26] *Ut supra.*

[27] *Ut supra.*

[28] *Ut supra.*

[29] *Porter v. Tike* (1615), 1 Rolle, Abr., *Dismes*, pl. H, 10, p. 653, also 1 Eagle & Younge 224, 1 Rolle Rep. 22, 81 E.R. 299.

[30] *Case of Modus Decimando* (1608), 13 Coke Rep. 12, 77 E.R. 1424, 1 Eagle & Younge 177 (Weald of Kent).

[31] Sic in MS.

645, prescription in [a] county for wood or anything else *in non decimando* is good, but not so in a hundred, which is uncertain, allowed not good in a parish, and how can a county be exempt from tithe? All prohibitions on this head showed that the parson had sufficient [maintenance], which intended an agreement and provision and [that he] had *uberiores decimas*.

By custom or prescription, they are discharged of tithe, if reasonable and just, [there is] no need to enquire [of] the beginning. [The] clergy demand by custom tithe against common right, as in sea fish, [*blank*] rabbits, etc., and why not to be discharged by custom where none have been usually paid. Cro. Car. 264; Rolle, Abr., 642, 646.[32]

[The] parish or parishioner must show what recompense the parson has in [the] county [and] cannot imagine a combination. *Doctor and Student* 167; 13 Rep. 13. Wood for fencing hedges [is] discharged of tithe, if [they] pay corn to [the] rector [and it is a] good custom in [the] parish, but in a county, [it is] good without consideration. 1 Saunders 141; Rolle, Abr., *Dismes*, pl. 14; March 15; 1 Rolle Reports 22.[33] Prescription *[in] non decimando in villa* [*blank*], it is too particular, but [it is] good in [a] county or hundred because it is the custom of the place or *lex loci*.

[The] discharge of a hundred in [the] case of wood has been adjudged, but nothing else may be intended to be grounded on a composition.

Tithe wood [is] of common right; else why did [they enact the] Statute of *Sylva Caedua*, which shows and confines to what wood tithe [is due]. Ro., Abr., 638; 2 *Inst*. 643.[34] Tithe[35] is generally of right and not on [a] custom.

There ought to be sufficient maintenance showed.

[There is] no instance of *non decimando* but in wood for [a] county or hundred. Tithe wood [is] not of common right. Why [the] canon of Archbishop Stratford [in] 17 Edw. III that tithe shall be paid of *sylva caedua*, [the] petition to Parliament that tithe not [be] paid for wood, and [why was there] ordered [a] prohibition where tithe wood has not been usually paid? *Doctor and Student*, 164, 169.

[The] ecclesiastical court says [that] tithes [are] due of common right for everything as clay and gravel, but [the] common law says only from annual profit

---

[32] *Anonymous* (1632), Cro. Car. 264, 79 E.R. 830; 1 Rolle, Abr., *Dismes*, pp. 642, 646.

[33] *Croucher v. Collins* (1668), 1 Williams Saunders 141, 85 E.R. 151, also 1 Eagle & Younge 469, 2 Keble 319, 84 E.R. 199, 4 Gwillim 1576; Case 36, March 15, 82 E.R. 391 (tithe of mills); *Porter v. Tike* (1614), 1 Rolle Rep. 22, 81 E.R. 299, 1 Eagle & Younge 224, 1 Rolle, Abr., *Dismes*, pl. H, 10, p. 653.

[34] 1 Rolle, Abr., *Dismes*, pl. H-M, p. 638; E. Coke, *Second Institute* (1642), p. 643.

[35] Libel *MS*.

not from the renewing yearly as wood [*blank*] but not annual profit, and if not due by annual profit do arise by custom,[36] but custom *[in] non decimando* is not good, and so a consultation [lies].

Doctor and Student 342. Tithe wood before the Statute 45 Edw. III for *Sylva Caedua*. [*blank*] 346, 348, 349, 355; Rolle, Abr., *Dismes*, 642, 653; 2 *Inst.* 645; 1 Rolle, Reports 22, Porter v. Tyke; Littleton 152, Norton's Case; Linwood 104; Selden 409.[37]

A discharge [was] from [the] parson, patron, and ordinary before [the] Statute 13 Eliz., c. 10.

Godolphin's *Repertorium*, 'Tithes'; 2 Bulstrode 285, Russell v. Bakehurst; 2 Rep., Bishop of Winchester's Case; 2 Ric. II, *Rotuli Parliamentorum* 4; 2 Rolle, Reports 122, 17 Jac. I, Lord Clanricard v. Denton.[38]

Serjeant *Parker*, Serjeant *Cheshire*, Mr. *Ettrick*, Mr. *Dodd*, and Mr. *Ward* [argued that] if the whole county prescribe or by custom to be quit of tithe, tithe of barren cattle is *ad valorem*, not in kind, not due of common right, tithe wood is by canon or custom and not of common right as tithe is set up by custom, so [it] may be lost by custom. Sir Simon Degge 263; Brooke, Abr., *Dismes*.[39] Agistment by custom cannot intend combination where a hundred, not like [a] parson and [a] parish.

[It was] adjudged by the court to be an ill custom.

[Other reports of this case: Samuel Dodd's Reports, p. 221, Bunbury 1, 145 E.R. 574, 1 Rayner 121, 2 Gwillim 606, 1 Eagle & Younge 692, 705.]

[The decree of 14 July 1709, PRO E.126/19, f. 144, is printed at 1 Wood 514; see also order of 19 May 1709: PRO E.126/19, f. 118v.]

---

[36] Sic in MS.

[37] C. St. German, *Doctor and Student* (T. F. T. Plucknett and J. L. Barton, edd., 1974), 91 Selden Soc. 300–314; 1 Rolle, Abr., *Dismes*, pl. S, 3, and S, 6, p. 642; *Porter v. Tike* (1614), *id.*, pl. H, 10, p. 653; *Norton's Case* (1628), Littleton 152, 124 E.R. 182; W. Lyndwood, *Provinciale*; J. Selden, *Historie of Tithes* (1618), p. 409.

[38] J. Godolphin, *Repertorium Canonicum*; *Russel v. Backhurst* (1614), 2 Bulstrode 285, 80 E.R. 1126, also 1 Eagle & Younge 236, 1 Gwillim 270; *Wright v. Wright* (1596), 2 Coke Rep. 38, 76 E.R. 501, also Cro. Eliz. 475, 511, 78 E.R. 726, 760, Moore K.B. 425, 72 E.R. 672, 1 Gwillim 167, 1 Eagle & Younge 167; *Rotuli Parliamentorum*, III (1767), p. 43, no. 47; *Earl of Clanrickard v. Lady Denton* (1619), 2 Rolle Rep. 122, 81 E.R. 699, also Palmer 37, 81 E.R. 967, 1 Eagle & Younge 306, 1 Gwillim 360.

[39] S. Degge, *Parson's Counsellor*; Brooke, Abr., *Dismes et tenthes spirituelles*, pl. 14, 18, 19.

438
Packington v. Wyche (Ex. 1707–1709)

Where an executor is given a legacy to pay the testator's debts, the executor acts as a trustee for the heirs at law for any surplus from the legacy after paying debts and legacies.

I

IU Lilly MS. Parker, 'Cases in the Exchequer, vol. 4', p. 144 [Eng.] (Price's Reports)

The bill is to call the defendant to an account for the rents and profits of the plaintiff Hester [Packington]'s real estate and to set aside some pretended accounts and assigns errors by bill in those accounts. Sir Herbert Perrott, the father of Hester, [in] 1682 made his will and gave to his wife, who after[wards] married the defendant [Sir Cyril Wyche], £200 *per annum* out of his estate in Pembrokeshire for thirteen years upon trust to pay all his debts and legacies which he owed in law, conscience, or equity and to that end did devise the said rent and by the said will gave an augmentation to his lady for a jointure and devised that an almshouse should be built. He gave £10 in hand and £80 more he was to give, which he had left with his wife, ordered the tithe of Wellington to be settled for a maintenance or £500 whereby the interest might be applied to the almshouse, and made his wife sole executrix. She proved the will. Sir Herbert Perrot died in July 1683. Lady Perrot married the defendant and died [in] October 1690. [On] the 4th November 1690, Lady Hester, being just of age, did sign an account and owned herself indebted [for] £197, though [she] did not sign the account. [On] the 6th January 1690, [an] account was stated and signed by Lady Hester but not by Sir Cyril, which carried on the first account and rested £298 9s. 10d. Another account [was] dated [*blank*] 1697. A third account, which takes notice of all the former accounts and continues it and makes Hester debtor [for] £1199 4s. 4d., which accounts are [. . .][1] all accounts and [the] plaintiff ought not to be chargeable with it, and if it be an account from the beginning, it opens the other two accounts.

1. The plaintiffs demand an account of the copyhold estate in which Sir Cyril Wyche and his lady received and also to have £160, which they charge for the repairs of that copyhold, which they charge as jointure; if it be allowed not [as] jointure, then it is fit [that] the repairs should be allowed.

2. The accounts were in great sums, and, being just of age and under the power of a sort of a parent, it has fraud apparent in it, there being no voucher or particular, and he not signing it, it was not mutual or reciprocal.

Wheeler and Brain, a case Mr. Phipps cited, [was] that a guardian made an account with his ward at twenty-five years of age and a balance [was] due to him

---

[1] altom [?] *MS.*

and [there was] a conveyance to secure it, there being no voucher, and the power of the guardian, it appeared to be fraudulent, and the deed [was] set aside, and an account [was] decreed.

3. There was £80 left in the lady's closet by Sir Herbert Perrott and is taken notice of in the particular under the Lady Perrott's hand of what money was left and the charge instead of £80 is £161 for building the almshouse that ought to be charged on the executor and not the heir, the personal estate appearing to be in money £690 besides stock and goods.

4. That the residuum of the personal estate after debts and legacies [are] paid ought to be distributed, the Lady Perrott being executrix and was not residuary legatee, that was waived by the plaintiff because there were no particular legacies left [to] her which would have implied that that legacy was as much as was designed [for] her and the rest [was] to be distributed.

5. The £200 which was given for thirteen years to the Lady Perrott was upon trust to pay all his debts and legacies, and to that end he gave the said rent charge, which is a plain resulting trust for the benefit of the heir, and that my Lady had it the better to enable her to pay his debts and legacies and [it] could not be designed as a bounty or gift to his wife, to whom in the next clause in his will, he gives an additional jointure or an augmentation. It was said that Sir Henry Perrott knew his personal estate to be more than[2] would pay his debts and this was a gift with a trust, not on a trust, and it was silent as to the surplus, which it intended for the heir or any else would have been expressed, and there is nothing by implication that can result to the heir, and there is no undisposed interest, it being given to the wife.

Gellingham v. Mellish,[3] 6 November 1691, before [the] Lord Chancellor. A. had issue, B. and C.; he devises land to C. upon trust to pay his debts and made him executor; A. dies; B. calls C. to an account for the estate after payment of the debts, being an undisposed residuum, but [it was] adjudged [that] it was a gift with a condition to pay the debts and that the residuum was given and could not be a resulting trust. 1 Chan. Rep. 196, Nutt and Crump,[4] where a gift to the same purpose [was made].

It was answered that this case differs being a provision for a younger child that was not provided for, and so [it was] a full gift. A gift to A. and B. to pay debts was a resulting trust.

---

[2] that *MS*.

[3] *Gillingham v. Melvish* (1691), Samuel Dodd's Reports, p. 108, *sub nom. Cunningham v. Mellish*, 2 Vernon 247, 23 E.R. 759, Prec. Chan. 31, 24 E.R. 17, 1 Eq. Cas. Abr. 273, 21 E.R. 1040.

[4] *North v. Crompton* (1671), 1 Chan. Cas. 196, 22 E.R. 759.

It was said, as to the copyhold, that it was a part of the jointure and the will explains it, where it is to make a provision for a wife unprovided for or for children on [the] payment of debts. Courts of equity help the want of a surrender, but here there is a large provision for the wife without it.

The defendant did not oppose going to an account from the foot of the second account of the 6th January 1690[/91] and that it was not so loose as was suggested because the same agents were in the Lady Perrott's time as were in the Lady Packington's, that the Lady Wyche managed it and that Sir Cyril, his lady, and daughter went to Herefordshire and sent to the Pembrokeshire agent to account, and this must be with the lady's privity.

Pen's Case, after several accounts made and stated, would not open it but sent it back to see if there were any errors in the face of it. The plaintiffs objected that Mr. Wyche was examined as to the account and [his deposition was] not read, no rent roll or book of account or acquittance [was] produced, that such accounts as these are not capable of being falsified; if [a] mortgagee kept such an account, [it] would not be admitted.

[The case was] adjourned to Hilary term to consider and [to] see precedents in the point of the trust.

21 June 1708. Present: Chief Baron Ward, Baron Bury, and Baron Price.

1. Baron PRICE was of [the] opinion that the term of thirteen years of £200 *per annum* out of the estate in Pembrokeshire for [the] payment of debts and legacies, after [the] debts and legacies are paid, is a surplus and undisposed estate and is an implied trust or a resulting trust for the benefit of the plaintiff Hester, the heir at law, it being first given to the Lady Perrott, his wife and executrix, by his will dated 21 June 1682. Nevertheless, to the intent and on trust that she might be supplied with money to pay his debts and legacies and to which end and purpose, he devised to her a lease for thirteen years to begin within six [months] after Sir Herbert Perrott's decease. He devised to his wife and executrix all his manors and lands in Wallington, Moreton, Pipe, and Burghill in the County of Hereford for her life for an augmentation to her jointure and made her executrix; that she might be supplied is intended; that she having the personal estate which is first to be applied to the payment of debts, £200 *per annum* shall be the supply if deficient.

It shows the intention, upon trust, and to which end that the debts were to be paid and then the augmentation is a recompense or satisfaction for her pains as executrix. This was a compensation or a recompense to her for the trouble of her execution of the will. [The] trust charged upon land is governed by the intention of the parties.

2. That where there is a doubt between [an] heir and [an] executor, it shall be construed in favor of the heir.

3. That the general words which precede in a will are controlled and expounded, qualified, and restrained by the latter words.

4. That a surplus or undisposed land or interest in land must descend to the heir, where it is a real estate, and to the executor, where it is a personal estate, as a representative.

In [the] construction of wills, the courts of equity have gone a great way as, where an executor is made by will, it is a trust to pay debts, and the residuum, though not expressed, goes to him, but if a legacy is given [to] the executor, then it is determined that the executor is but a trustee, and the estate is to be distributed as to the residuum upon [the] construction that the devise of part is a control of the construction as to the residuum and that the testator could never intend the executor to have the residuum, that is the whole, when he devised to him the part of it.

Foster v. Munt,[5] which was so decreed by Lord Chancellor Jeffreys, upon a rehearing by the commissioners, the decree was reversed, and upon an appeal to the House of Lords, the decree of the commissioners was reversed.

The next advance that has been made in equity where there is a devise of the rents and profits of land to pay debts and legacies or portions, when the debts and legacies are paid, the residuum shall attend the inheritance, and if a portion is to be raised out of land and the portionee died and the mother takes administration and the portion not being raised, it was decreed for the heir against the administratrix.

Easter [term] 1 Jac. II [1685], the Case of the Lady Pawlet,[6] and [it was] affirmed in the House of Lords, and yet the disposition or provision for a child out of the profits is as much a personal estate as much in the power of the portionee to be disposed of as if it had been ready money or security given for it but yet in favor of the heir at law and for [the] preservation of the inheritance against the administratrix, it was so determined against a mother.

The next progress of the court was, where lands are given in fee for life or for years upon trust to pay debts and legacies by a will after debts and legacies are paid, the surplus or residue is a resulting trust for the benefit of the heir, who has the inheritance.

2 Ventris 359, Michaelmas [term] 34 Car. II [1682],[7] where it is reported as a rule that where one has the inheritance and he by deed or will gives or devises a

---

[5] *Foster v. Munt* (1687), 1 Vernon 473, 23 E.R. 598, 2 Eq. Cas. Abr. 433, 443, 22 E.R. 368, 378, Samuel Dodd's Reports, p. 78.

[6] *Lady Pawlett v. Lord Pawlett* (1683–1685), 1 Vernon 204, 321, 23 E.R. 415, 496, 2 Freeman 93, 22 E.R. 1079, 2 Ventris 366, 86 E.R. 489, 2 Chan. Rep. 286, 21 E.R. 680, 1 Eq. Cas. Abr. 267, 21 E.R. 1036.

[7] *Anonymous* (1682), 2 Ventris 359, 86 E.R. 485.

term for payment of his debts, which being done, the profits of the estate answering more, the residuum does result for the benefit of the heir.

2 Ventris 349, Easter [term], 32 Car. II [1680],[8] a devise of land to pay debts and gives the residue of the personal estate to his executor, though it looks like a legacy, yet shall [it] be applied to pay the debts, and what is deficient is to be paid out of the real estate.

Upon construction of these trusts devised to executors by way of resulting trust, if anything is given to the executor for his pains or trouble, it is a ground for a resulting trust, being an inference that the testator did not design the executor [to be] both.

1 Chan. Cases 196, North v. Crompton. A devise of all his real and personal estate to his executor to be disposed of for [the] payment of his just debts and legacies and gives to his heir at law £200; [it was] adjudged and decreed by the Lord Keeper Bridgman with the assistance of Twisden, Wilde, Raynsford, and Wyndham that this was a devise in fee, being to pay debts; second, that there was no implied trust for the heir of the surplus, for, if there were, the devisee had no benefit, and it was in vain to devise £200 to the heir if he had intended the surplus to the heir.

3 Will. & Mary, 1691, Callingham v. Mellersh,[9] before the Commissioners, a devise of land to Thomas Mellersh in fee in trust to be sold for the payment of debts and legacies within one year after his decease, because there was no devise of the surplus nor the executors had nothing for their care and pains in the executorship, that the overplus shall go to the executor not to the heir at law.

10 February 6 Anne [1708], in Chancery, Ralph Docksey v. Elizabeth Docksey,[10] [a] devise of land to the defendant in fee to be sold for payment of his debts and legacies and that the defendant and the plaintiff, his heir at law, were to exchange some land by the will; it was resolved that there was no implied or resulting trust in the defendant, the executrix, for the benefit of the plaintiff, the heir, for that it appears by the words of the will, as also by the proof, that such implication is contradicted and that it was the intention of the testator that this should be a beneficial devise to the defendant; it appeared that the exchanged land should be sold, otherwise, there could be no fee, and without a fee in the defendant, she could not exchange, that the defendant brought a fortune, had no jointure or dower but £1000 four years after, which could not be a provision, that

---

[8] *Anonymous* (1680), 2 Ventris 349, 86 E.R. 480.

[9] *Cunningham v. Mellish* (1691), 2 Vernon 247, 23 E.R. 759, Prec. Chan. 31, 24 E.R. 17, 1 Eq. Cas. Abr. 273, 21 E.R. 1040, Samuel Dodd's Reports, p. 108.

[10] *Docksey v. Docksey* (1710), 2 Eq. Cas. Abr. 415, 430, 506, 22 E.R. 352, 366, 429, 3 Brown P.C. 39, 1 E.R. 1163.

the testator declared [that] he designed it wholly for her, and that he had given his heir as much as he designed.

But in all these cases, if there had been any devise to the executrix, it would have made a resulting trust.

These precedents were brought for the defendant, but the reason why they were not adjudged resulting trusts makes for the plaintiffs.

The plaintiffs' precedents were [as follows].

25 January 1682[/83], 34 & 35 Car. II, in the exchequer, Edward Cooke v. William Gwavas and Elizabeth Cobb,[11] by English bill. John Cook by will [of] 28 July 1671 gave all his personal estate to Robert Cooke [and] the defendants Gwavas and Cobb to their disposition, whom he made executors and the same day made a lease of his manors and land to Robert Cooke and [the] defendant Gwavas for five hundred years in trust to pay his debts and four years after to attend the inheritance. It was adjudged that the defendant should not take the personal estate as legatee but as executor and [it] should be applied to pay the debts in ease of the lease of five hundred years. And after debts paid, the five hundred years should attend the inheritance and that they should not wait for the expiration of the four years being to be construed a trust for the heir's benefit, in whom the inheritance was vested of the trust estate, and it was then decreed by Chief Baron Mountagu, Sir Edward Atkyns, Sir William Gregory, and Sir Thomas Street, barons. The reason of this case was that each of the executors had a legacy and that the lease and will were the same and calculated for the same purpose and while the executors had their legacies and all their charges and troubles borne out of the estate, the rest was an implied trust for the heir (which seems to be a hard decree against an express legacy of the personal estate and a gift of the four years).

3 July 9 Will. [1697], Earl of Bristol and Rachel, his wife v. Edward Hungerford and others,[12] at the rolls [court] and [on] appeal to the Lords. Sir William Bassett [on] 21st September 1693 by [his] will appointed Sir Edward Hungerford and J. Hill executors and empowered them to sell all his real estate for payment of his debts and if any surplus remained, the same should be deemed part of his personal estate and gave each of his executors £100, who insisted that the surplus belonged to them, but the sister and heir of the testator demanded the surplus after debts and legacies paid as belonging to her by way of an implied trust or resulting trust by reason [that] the executors had each of them legacies, and [it] was so adjudged. And this decree as to the surplus was affirmed in the House of Lords.

---

[11] *Coke v. Gwavas* (1683), PRO E.126/14, f. 39v.

[12] *Earl of Bristol v. Hungerford* (1697), 2 Vernon 524, 645, 23 E.R. 938, 1021, Prec. Ch. 81, 24 E.R. 39, 1 Eq. Cas. Abr. 44, 142, 245, 272, 21 E.R. 862, 944, 1021, 1040.

And these precedents go no great way for the plaintiff because the real estate when sold was to be deemed a personal estate and then distributive by the defendant, the executrix, being [that] they had legacies, but the decree was founded upon the ground that it was a real estate to be sold and the executors having recompense.

Though it be said that no implication is against a wife, [in] the case of the Lady Pawlet, before, who was a mother, it was so adjudged, and that was a mother against a son, and this [is] a mother against a daughter.

It was said that a devise of the augmentation was of an estate for life and that did not savor of the personalty and could not be intended [as] a recompense to the executrix for her pains, but since the augmentation is given her as wife and executrix, it is as good a compensation as [the] granting in North v. Crompton's case [of] £200 to the heir was a bar to the heir to have the resulting trust of a real estate to be sold for payment of debts, and [in] all the cases where lands were to be sold or estates in fee or for [a] term of years under a trust or legacy [given] to [an] executor, [it] was allowed [as] a recompense.

Though these constructions of wills and raising of uses where they are not expressed may seem hard and is an occasion to mislead men in the disposition of their estates, yet since courts of equity have made so many solemn resolutions, it will be very mischievous to deviate from the same and [I] am of [the] opinion upon the whole case that the £200 *per annum* for thirteen years was but a calculation of what number of years (as in Boraston's Case[13]) would pay the debts and legacies and since a trust was coupled to it and [an] augmentation given, I must conclude that there is a resulting trust for the benefit of the plaintiff.

Secondly, I think the devise being general of all his manors and lands in Moreton, Wellington, Pipe, and Burghill in Herefordshire will not carry the copyhold estate, [it] not being expressed, though when a wife is not provided for or children or debts, though no surrender to the use, yet [they] have passed, but here is a jointure and an augmentation and [it] need not the help of a construction.

I think the defendant ought to account for the profits of the copyhold since the title belongs to the plaintiff.

Thirdly, as to the almshouse, there is £161 for building the almshouse, which is charged on the plaintiff and ought not to be, being there was £80 left in the house for that purpose and £10 paid on an agreement. And if the executrix will of her own head build further than directed, she must suffer; it was said to be accounted for and allowed it was in the account [in] 1689 when the plaintiff Hester was under age and not in any other.

---

[13] *Hynde v. Ambrye* (1587), 3 Coke Rep. 16, 76 E.R. 664, 1 Eq. Cas. Abr. 190, 194, 21 E.R. 980, 984.

Fourthly, as to the repairs of the copyhold, the plaintiff ought to be chargeable with it if [the] defendant accounts for the rest and other repairs belong to the defendant.

Fifthly, the account must be general, only [being] regulated by the special directions herein given, and [the] plaintiff and defendant [are] to be examined upon interrogatories.

Baron Bury [held] that the devise of [the] £200 annuity for thirteen years was chargeable with the debts and legacies and the residue is a bounty to the wife [and] that the augmentation is of another nature from the term [and a] further bounty.

The design of the will was that the wife should have his personal estate and [it was] not to be applied in ease of the real [estate]; the debt was inconsiderable and so were the legacies.

The defendants precedents are not to the purpose. Cook and Gwavas is the same as Foster and Munt, named before. The case of leases differs from disposition by will; wills are a consideration in themselves, but leases without consideration do carry resulting trusts in their own bowels, and for that reason, the four years of the five hundred years attended the inheritance, not being for any consideration.

The Lady Pawlet's case was upon a deed of settlement, and the trust might well result, being for no consideration.

1. That the defendant was not accountable for the annuity of £200 *per annum* for thirteen years.

2. That the copyhold did pass by a devise of all his land to his wife, and the defendant should not account, since the same was not taken notice of by the former account.

3. That the defendant shall account for the £80 that was for the almshouse and nothing more.

4. That the defendant should not go to a general account, but where particular things in an account are objected against in order to open an account, he shall proceed only upon them and none other, there being [that] no fraud appears in the account.

Chief Baron Ward: There is a disposition of the party and disposition of law. The case of realty goes to the heir and in personality to the executor. The construction of wills is favored.

That the devise of £200 *per annum* for thirteen years is to supply what the personal estate is short or defective in to pay debts and legacies and it being to begin six months after, that the executrix might see how far the personal estate would go.

[There is] a difference between disposing of a term and creating a term by deed or will for a particular purpose.

Hughes and Hughes Case[14] in the common bench. It was a question whether, a person dying intestate, the ordinary had the disposal of the residuum. 1705 in the exchequer, Scammell v. Cobleston;[15] [one] had a lease for years and gave it to his brother for life, the residue to his brother's son, and made him executor, and gave £20 to each of his sisters and [his] nephew, though the brother's son was executor, yet the devise to him was not construed [to be] an implied trust for the sister where a distribution, but they were to have their legacy and no more; this was a testamentary disposition. [In] Foster and Munt, a stranger was executor and not a brother's son, otherwise it would vary the case, if heir sued and recover[ed], but [the] heir may sue the executors and be refunded.

To which end in the will does confine it to the trust expressed in the will; it shall not be construed [to be] a bounty.

If [the] testator designed more than to pay debts and legacies, he would say so. [In] Cook and Gwavas, the personal estate at the disposition of the executor, that is according as the law does direct them, and the four years [is] to attend the inheritance, being [a] legacy given.

1. [He] agreed that the thirteen years of £200 [was] to be accounted for by [the] defendant.

2. The copyhold did pass by the general words to his wife, and [the] defendant should not account for it, since it was not offered in the account.

3. That the defendant ought not to charge the plaintiff with £161 for building the almshouse.

4. That the defendant must go to a general account, and [the] plaintiff and defendant [are] to be examined on interrogatories.

[On] 7 December 1708, Serjeant *Jekyll* moved for a rehearing and cited a case, 1 Chan. Rep. 98, Gore v. Blake,[16] as a case in point for Mr. Wyche, and [a] rehearing [was] allowed.

II
HLS MS. 537, part 2, pp. 97, 111, 125 [Eng.] (Eden's Reports)

Upon a motion for a rehearing in this case by *Joseph Jekyll*, the court said that by the practice of the court, though a petition for a rehearing was signed by counsel, yet that a rehearing was not [granted as] of course without [a] motion, as in chancery, nor was it only a motion of course, but [they were] most commonly denied. And my Lord Chief Baron [WARD] said [that] when he was attorney general, he signed but two, and both [were] denied, and he thought then [that] there

---

[14] *Hughes v. Hughes* (1666), Carter 125, 124 E.R. 867, 1 Levinz 233, 83 E.R. 384.
[15] *Scamell v. Coppleston* (Ex. 1705), above, No. 389.
[16] *Gore v. Blake* (1668), 1 Chan. Cas. 98, 22 E.R. 712, 1 Chan. Rep. 263, 21 E.R. 568.

was good cause for both. But in this case because the petition suggested a precedent, which was Gore and Blake's Case, in Chancery Cases 48 and Chancery Reports 263, and which was not mentioned in the former hearings, and because that Baron BURY in the court's resolution differed in opinion from [Chief Baron] WARD and [Baron] PRICE, the only three barons at that time, the court allowed a rehearing. *Sir Thomas Powys*, Mr. *Parker*, and Mr. *Ward* defend[ed] the motion.

N.B. Upon this motion, it was said by my Lord Chief Baron, *Sir Thomas Powys*, and *Sir Joseph Jekyll* that the *Chancery Cases* [were] written by a learned hand, *viz*. Sir Anthony Keck, and who is generally thought to have written them.

The case was this. Sir Herbert Parrot in 1682 made his will and therein made his lady, the defendant's mother, executrix of all his personal estate, goods, and chattels. And afterwards by another clause, [he] devises to his 'dear wife and executrix' (as he expressed himself), her executors, administrators, and assigns a rent charge of £100 *per annum* for thirteen years to commence six months after his death 'nevertheless with this trust and confidence that she pay my debts and legacies which I shall owe in law, equity, or good conscience, and to the end she may be the better enabled, I give and grant to her the said rent'. In another clause, he devises to her about £100 *per annum* in augmentation of her jointure.

Sir Herbert died in 1683. The personal estate happened to be sufficient. His lady afterwards married Sir Cyril Winch,[17] the defendant's father, and this rent charge was looked upon as part of her personal estate and a jointure accordingly. Sir John Packington afterwards married Sir Herbert's daughter and heiress, and now [they] prefer their bill to have an account of the profits received of that rent charge.

The case had several hearings, and at last by the opinion of [Chief Baron] WARD and [Baron] PRICE against the opinion of [Baron] BURY, it was agreed [that] the defendant should account. Upon that and upon Baron Lovell's coming upon the bench, the defendant, upon the case of Gore and Blake, in Chancery Cases 96, petitioned for a rehearing, and [it was] granted. See above.

And now it was argued for the defendant by *Sir Joseph Jekyll, Sir Edward Northey*, Mr. *Ettrick*, Mr. *Dodd*, and Mr. *Guidot* that this was a beneficial devise to his lady and no trust resulted to the heir.

It was argued:

[1.] [That] a devise imports a bounty and thereof needs no consideration. It is in its nature a bounty and so in [the] case of a legacy. And if I devise a personal thing, the ecclesiastical court [is the] proper judge to determine this, and that which entitles a jurisdiction of equity as in this court is when an account is

---

[17] Sic in MS.

wanted, as in this case. And that what falls incidentally in the way to be questioned must be determined.

Now the clause by which he devises it to her for thirteen years certainly gives her a legal interest. And the question then [is] whether the subsequent words 'nevertheless' etc. will let in an equitable one so [as to] alter the other which is the legal one. And it was argued by them [that] it did not for the clause 'nevertheless' etc. is only a charge upon it, as if a man makes an executor and gives him a good estate provided he pay his debts and legacies, certainly he shall have the estate after the debts [are] paid, that they were only a sort of a drawback of the bounty and a *sub modo* annexed to it.

2. That there might be a difference when such a devise is to the wife and when to a stranger, because, in this first case, it carries the consideration of love and affection along with it.

3. That it was unnecessary to have devised it to her if he had no[t] designed it a beneficial one, for they themselves show that the personal estate was sufficient and there could not be much alteration in its increase or the debts upon it. Sir Herbert died within a year after the making [of] his will.

4. And that it was the constant opinion of the family that he left it so.

5. That the defendant's father settled a jointure accordingly, it being looked upon by both sides at the time of the treaty as part of her personal estate.

6. That its being given to her, her executors, administrators, and assigns did not look like a trust; these proceeded from a personal confidence and the testator could not foresee who might be her executors, administrators, or assigns.

7. He made her executrix of all his personal estate, goods, and chattels, and there was no other chattel but this, and mak[ing] her executrix imports a consideration.

8. If he had not designed her [to have] it for her trouble and pains, it would have been very easy to have given the surplus to the heir, and Sir Herbert being a circumspect [and] prudent man, it is a great argument [that] he did not design [that] his heir should have it.

9. It being for a certain number of years, it looks as if he had calculated what might be sufficient to supply her to pay his debts and to be a reward to herself. And if he had designed [it] to his heir, he would not have limited any time, for he seems very desirous of paying his debts, as they allow on the other side. And if this should have happened not [to have been] sufficient, the heir must have had it and particular sum of his debts unsatisfied, and if he thought it had been sufficient, he would rather have limited no time, and so if too much that the heir as soon as the int[. . .] of the will part sooner or later might have it.

10. [To the] objection that [it was] an augmentation, [it is] answered that [it] was an augmentation of her jointure and not for her trouble as executrix.

They cited North and Crompton's Case, 1 Chancery Cases 196,[18] and one Gillingham and Melish's Case, decreed in 1691,[19] which case, as I apprehended, was one having two sons devises an estate to the younger for paying debts and legacies, whom he made executor after the debts and legacies [be] paid; the heir presents his bill, and [it was] decreed [that] his bill should stand dismissed.

They cited Gore and Blake's Case, upon which the rehearing was, which was upon the order, A. by his will, whereof he makes B. his executor, devises that B. shall take the rents and profits of his lands of inheritance for fifteen years in trust to pay debts and legacies, and, after the expiration thereof, [he] devises over to a stranger. There [it was] decreed, and the court [was] clear of opinion, [that] the executor should have it. And as for the objection that [it] was devised over and so the heir could not be intended to have it, [it is] answered that [that] can make no difference, for if there is the less left, there is the more reason [that] he should have it. And the order is that the court [was] clearly of [this] opinion, and my Lord Ch[ancellor] Hyde in that case had the advantage of Mr. Baron Turner. And the query in the book [is] but the query of the reporter.

To the contrary, it was argued by *Sir Thomas Powys*, Mr. *Phipps*, Mr. *Ward*, and Mr. *Parker* that it was no beneficial devise but [that] a trust resulted to the heir when the debts [were] satisfied, it being for that end only drawn out of the inheritance.

As for the objection that it is to her executors and assigns, [it is] answered [that] all trusts are generally given so. And the words 'nevertheless' etc. [are] an express trust, and he says it is to that end [that] he gives and grants it.

They insisted upon having an augmentation of her jointure by the same will. And [they] cited Foster and Monk's Case,[20] where [it was] resolved that, where a man makes an executor, it is a gift of his personal estate because it imports a consideration, yet if he has a particular sum given him by the will, it excludes him from having any further surplus, but the surplus shall undergo distribution as if he had died intestate.

[As to the] objection [that it was] not necessary because his personal estate [was] sufficient, [it was] answered [that] he, when he made his will, could not foresee how long he should live; he then was building a hospital and designed to pay his uncle's debts, which he thought himself obliged in conscience to pay, so

---

[18] *North v. Crompton* (1671), 1 Chan. Cas. 196, 22 E.R. 759; also 1 Eq. Cas. Abr. 272, 21 E.R. 1040.

[19] *Gillingham v. Melvish* (1691), Samuel Dodd's Reports, p. 108, *sub nom. Cunningham v. Mellish* (1691), 2 Vernon 247, 23 E.R. 759, Prec. Chan. 31, 24 E.R. 17, 1 Eq. Cas. Abr. 273, 21 E.R. 1040.

[20] *Foster v. Munt* (1687), 1 Vernon 473, 23 E.R. 598, 1 Eq. Cas. Abr. 243, 21 E.R. 1020, 2 Eq. Cas. Abr. 433, 443, 22 E.R. 368, 378, Samuel Dodd's Reports, p. 78.

that it was impossible to know how much he should be indebted at his death. But by his words, he seems very intent upon paying his debts, and he did this by way of precaution. The term was never to come in[to] play except the personal estate [be] insufficient. They cited 2 Ventris 349, 359; 2 Chancery Cases 115 and 84.[21] They had formerly cited one Cook and Gwavas's Case formerly but did not mention it now. A case between Doxy and Doxy[22] [was] cited but not put and one Hungerford's Case.[23]

As to the case of North and Crompton, the heir appears to be excluded for the same reason [as] the executor in Foster and Monk's Case because he had £200 devised to him and the executor must have had the estate in that case or nothing.

As to Gore and Blake, that differs from ours:

1. It appeared [that] the heir was to be excluded because the estate [was] devised from him and a stranger [?] preferred to him.
2. The remainderman.
3. The devisee could not have it because he [was] to have nothing until the expiration of the fifteen years, but if not for these express words which exclude Sir Thomas Packington seemed to argue as if he,[24] and so did Baron Price. And for this, see 2 Chancery Cases 84.

As to Gillingham v. Mellish, there no legacy [was] given to the executor as in our case.

N.B. As to the surplus devised to the executors in Gore and Blake's Case, as it is in 1 Chancery Reports 98, it was not so upon the order.

For the defendant, [they] replied as to 2 Ventris 349, that [is] only that the personal estate [is] to come in aid of the real estate; as to that [case at] 359 that [it is] both anonymous and anomalous [and] too short and general to have any weight laid upon it.

As to Cook and Gwavas's Case, which had formerly been cited and which I apprehended to be this: Cook, by deed indented bearing the same date with his

---

[21] *Anonymous* (1680), 2 Ventris 349, 86 E.R. 480; *Anonymous* (1682), 2 Ventris 359, 86 E.R. 485; *Culpepper v. Aston* (1682), 2 Chan. Cas. 115, 22 E.R. 873; *Popley v. Popley* (1681), 2 Chan. Cas. 84, 22 E.R. 858.

[22] *Docksey v. Docksey*, 2 Eq. Cas. Abr. 507, 22 E.R. 429 (Ch. 1708); 3 Brown P.C. 39, 1 E.R. 1163 (H.L. 1710).

[23] *Countess of Bristol v. Hungerford*, 2 Vernon 645, 23 E.R. 1021; *Earl of Bristol v. Hungerford*, Prec. Chan. 81, 24 E.R. 39, 1 Eq. Cas. Abr. 244, 272, 21 E.R. 1021, 1040, 2 Vernon 524, 23 E.R. 938 (1705–1709).

[24] Sic in MS. It appears that some of the original text was omitted by the copyist of this manuscript.

will, raised a term of five hundred years in A. and B., whom he had made his executors, for the satisfaction of his debts etc., and by his will [he] made A. and B. and another his executors, and [he] devises [that] the trust of that term should attend the inheritance after four years, and [he] gives it [to] them as executors in the meantime and to dispose of as such, and it seemed there being a surplus within the four years, the heir might [hold] them to account. Query [?] as to the case itself. But they answered [that] if that trust was upon a deed which imported no bounty as a will did and, according to *Dodd*, the court [was] not unanimous in that case and everybody [was] not satisfied with it.

The court were now divided. WARD and PRICE [were] for the plaintiffs; BURY and LOVELL [were] for the defendants.

LOVELL: The opinion [*blank*] (as has been argued on behalf of the plaintiff) but what he relies upon that the words are 'nevertheless' etc. with this special trust and confidence that he laid a weight upon the words 'this special trust and confidence' and for that reason takes [it] not to be a general trust but a special one.

As to Gore and Blake's Case, he agreed that [it] differed from ours:

1. In that he devised the land from the heir so that in that case he had no consideration for him, and
2. That the devisee could not claim anything but was excluded until the fifteen years expired but upon the words *supra* of opinion for the defendants for it is only a special charge upon it.

N.B. It was 'upon trust and confidence' in most of the briefs made that take notice of it.

PRICE: He thinks that 'nevertheless' etc. [is] a restr[iction] to the est[ate] first given, *viz.* she should have it only upon such and such terms etc. and that by the words for that end a trust [was] engrafted to the estate, that it could never be designed a beneficial devise, that the reason why [it was] not to commence until six months after his death was that he might calculate the debts etc. and show whether she might have occasion for it or no. He took notice of the building [of] the hospital and the uncle's debts which he designed and these uncertainties why this aid [?] given. And [he held] to the same effect with the counsel for the plaintiffs.

[To the] objection if he had intended it for the heir, it might have been easily devised to him by devising [?] the residue, [he] answered [that] the same objection may be made on the other side why he could not have devised the residue to his executor if he had designed it, and it is a rule in chancery that everything [is] to be construed in favor of the heir. And [he] gives North and Crompton's Case and Gore and Blake the same answer had been before given them, only that as to the obj[ection] in consid[eration] Gore and Blake's Case [it is] better to give him that little than none at all, that that is making a will and not construing it.

BURY: He thinks the words 'nevertheless' etc. [are] only a charge so far as to pay etc. and that is not to be thought he would [put] her to so much trouble without giving her something to make her amends. As for the augmentation, it was for the augmentation of her jointure and not for her trouble as executrix. It was that having had experiences of her goodness etc., he thought he had not already given her a jointure such as she deserved. And [he] gives Cook and Gwavas, the same answer the counsel had given it, and [he] cited Gillingham and Mellish's Case.

WARD: He took the same difference as before between Gore and Blake's Case and this he relied upon the words for which [*blank*] and that he gave it [to] her only as executrix because he gives it to his wife and executrix [. . .] through the will. And [he] cited Ventris 359, which though anonymous yet the gentleman [?] being a learned gentleman [?] would never have published it if not thought fit by him, and that he knew it to be equity. And [he] argued as Price and the other counsel had argued before. And so [he held] for the plaintiff.

And the court [being] thus divided, another rehearing [was] ordered before the chancellor of the exchequer and themselves.

N.B. The chief baron [WARD], upon citing Foster and Monk's Case in his argument, expressed himself dissatisfied with it and, upon that occasion, cited a case where yet they would have carried it further, which was Scavill and Thompson's Case[25] before himself in the exchequer, which was this, the plaintiffs' father devised £20 apiece to them being three sisters and makes the defendant, their brother, executor and likewise gives him a legacy. They come and prefer a bill for distribution upon Foster and Monk's Case, but [it was] dismissed. And now he said it is almost become the same to die with a will and making an executor and dying intestate, which [is] against the reason of the old common law.

He likewise in his argument cited Cook and Gwavas, as I took it to be, and said this as part of the case. The plaintiff's father devised to his daughters so much apiece for their portions issuing out of his hands to be paid at such a time it seemed that, as he put the case, one of them before the time had disposed of her part and after the disposal died, and the question's [were] (1) Whether they could dispose of it. (2) Whether the assignee could have it she dying before the time. And it seemed [that] the court was of opinion that she might dispose of it and if she had lived so long [it would have been] good, but having died before her time, her administrator should not have had it if undisposed nor, having assigned, her assignee because every construction and [*blank*] in a court of equity for the benefit of the heir and she dying before the time it should sink back into the estate from whence it came. But always if out of the personal estate because equity does not consider the executors so much as the heir.

---

[25] *Scamell v. Coppleston* (Ex. 1705), above, No. 389.

N.B. It seemed to be either [. . .] or Gillingham and Mellish. Query the second case and which it is.

The case that was adjourned before the chancellor of this court and the barons of it because of the court's being divided was this term [Easter term, 8 Anne, 1709] argued and decreed for the plaintiff. LOVELL and BURY [were] of the same opinion as formerly, and PRICE, WARD, and [the] chancellor [of the exchequer, SMITH, were] for the plaintiff. I was not at the argument by the counsel, but the court gave their opinions as following.

LOVELL: (I was not [present] at the beginning of this.) As to the objection of the rule that the heir shall not be disinherited by ambiguous or doubtful words, he made a difference between a devise to a stranger and when to a [. . .] or wife. He thinks that in the latter case, it did not at least so fully take place.

He observed that in this case, she is bound to pay what he owes in law, equity, or good conscience. And this follows immediately the clause 'nevertheless' etc. And there are many cases where a remedy [is] taken away both in law and equity and yet a right remains, as where one [is] barred by the statute of limitations.

But what he principally relied upon was what he had formerly relied upon, *viz.* 'nevertheless with this special trust and confidence' etc., for he was of [the] opinion that in this case, it was not a devise upon or in trust but an estate given only with a trust. And he took this to be a stronger case than any that had been put on the one side or the other. And so [he] concluded for the defendant.

PRICE: As to the intent of the will, he took notice that he had proceeded very naturally in it, and in the first place [he] provided for the payment of his debts and legacies, in the second place for his wife by an augmentation of her jointure, and thirdly for his daughter by leaving her all the rest of his estate.

But now as to the clause upon which the question arises, he observed [that] it consisted on [. . .] parts: First, he gives [a] £200 rent charge with a clause of distress to his wife that nevertheless with this special trust and confidence etc. And now what estate goes to the wife? An estate given to one to pay debts and legacies must be for life, and had it been for [the] paying of money, it would have carried a fee. Hammond's [?] Case, 3 Co. So that by this, an estate for life or in fee would have passed. But now what follows is coupled to this estate nevertheless etc. And now he cannot perceive any difference between in trust, upon [a] trust, and with [a] trust so as to give an estate for life with [a] trust as long as construing a trust in a court of equity he thinks there is no reason to make any such distinction as had been made.

Now as to the second part of the clause 'to the end, intent, and purpose that she may be the better enabled' etc., he gives to his wife for thirteen years to commence six months after his death, so this has overturned the first limitation by adding an express one. And it is to this purpose, having debts and legacies which he designed should be paid, that they might be the more certainly so. Suppose it had been inserted to the intent to pay debts and legacies; suppose he owed £1000 and to the intent and purpose to pay it, [he wrote] I give my wife etc. for thirteen years, will any construe this that it carries any more than a trust to pay the £1000.

If he had intended it for her, why did he not expressly give it to her, and though the same objection [may be] made why not to the heir, if so intended, but he says there was not so much reason to make that express in favor of the heir as of the wife, for besides the natural resulting of it to the heir, yet there is afterwards a general devise to her.

And he says [there is] a great difference between an estate given to trusts and when a charge upon an estate only [is] so given; the latter is always under the direction of a court of equity.

He likewise mentioned Boraston's Case[26] for that was adjudged upon a calculation supposed there; he thinks that comes very near our case and answers the reason of the limitation of a term certain, *viz.* thirteen years, and besides in our case, there was buildings, alms houses, etc. going forward which made his debts etc. more uncertain and more necessary to be provided for against all uncertainties.

He said likewise it could never be designed as a bounty to her because he had left nothing, debts besides.

He then took notice of some rules of courts of equity.

1. That wherever [there is] any controversy between an heir and an executor, the heir [is] always to be most favored.

2. That where any consideration [is] given to the heir, executor, or trustee, it bars their having any advantage by implication or construction because of the evidence, that it is that the intent of the devisor was to the contrary.

3. That though executors, in construction of law, have the personal estate, yet if any legacy [be] left [to] them etc., it makes them only trustees, and [. . .]ts. He cited several cases in pursuance of them.

1. My Lady Pawlett's Case,[27] which was this. A term was created by My Lady's husband and in his lifetime to raise portions for their two daughters which were to be paid them at the age of twenty-one years. One of them died before she came of that age so as to be entitled to her portion. And My Lady, her mother, took out administration to her. And in law she was entitled to it (or rather in law [she] would have been entitled to it). And [she] preferred her bill for the

---

[26] *Hynde v. Ambrye* (1587), 3 Coke Rep. 16a, 76 E.R. 664, 1 Eq. Cas. Abr. 190, 194, 195, 21 E.R. 980, 984.

[27] *Lady Paulet v. Lord Paulet* (1685), 1 Vernon 204, 321, 23 E.R. 415, 496, 2 Freeman 93, 22 E.R. 1079, 2 Ventris 366, 86 E.R. 489, 2 Chan. Rep. 286, 21 E.R. 680, 1 Eq. Cas. Abr. 267, 21 E.R. 1036.

daughter's portion. And [the case] coming up into the House of Lords, it was there dismissed. He mentioned 2 Ventris 359, where the rule of resulting uses [was] laid down, and though [it was] objected [that it was] anonymous, yet it is afterwards supported by Culpeper's Case. He then cited:

2. Cook v. Guavas, in this court, which was [this]. Cook created a term for 500 [years] in M. and others for the payment of his debts, which was by deed bearing date the same day with his will. And he provides that four years after the payment of his debts, the term should attend the inheritance. He then in his will comes and makes Guavas and others his executors but not all the same persons that the deed had made trustees of the term and gives several legacies to those, his executors, and several others and devises all [of] his personal estate to his executors to be disposed by them as executors and so [to] have it only as such. And in this case, it was decreed [that] the whole personal estate should be applied to the payment of the debts in discharging of the lease, that though the term was to attend the inheritance only after four years, yet that four years should likewise attend, as no such limitation [was] made. See above.

But one, they say, was a lease by [a] will and the other by a deed, that the will carries a bountiful consideration along with it which the deed does not. He cannot see any such difference that the[re] was a consideration to raise the trust, and a peppercorn [is] a sufficient consideration etc. Then they objected [that] the court [was] divided in that case, but he said [that] it was only said so; they did make it appear.

N.B. By this, I suppose that the four years was given to the trustees, who most of them being executors, to have to dispose of as executors and only as such.

N.B. [Baron] BURY in putting the case afterwards said [that] they were excluded from the personal estate and the four years by legacies [was] given them in the will upon the reason in Foster and Monk's Case.

3. Earl of Bristol and Hungerford's Case, in the House of Lords. The earl devised these lands to be sold for the payment of his debts, and [he] willed that the surplus of the money should be deemed and construed as part of his personal estate. He made Sir Edward Hungerford and one Hill his executors but left in his will a £100 apiece to them. And upon that [it was] decreed notwithstanding his willing of it to be deemed his personal estate that it should result and go to their heir at law.

He mentioned likewise Cranmer and Southampton's Case, which see [in] Sir Bartholomew Shower's Cases in Parliament.[28] And [he] said [that] the author of the other side went upon the same ground. And in Gore and Blake's Case, the

---

[28] *Wood v. Duke of Southampton* (1692), Shower 83, 1 E.R. 58.

heir was disinherited, and all [was] given to a stranger. In North and Crompton, in the same book, there was £100 given to the heir which excluded him.

As to Gillingham and Mellish's Case, that was a devise or disposing of an estate to Mellish and his heirs for payment of debts, and upon a bill (as above) it was decreed for Mellish. But he said [that] that differed from ours, for there was a disposal of the inheritance to a trust, and there was no recompense given to Mellish for all his trouble, and for that reason it was construed [to be] no resulting trust because no other satisfaction [was] given [to] him. So upon the whole, he continued still [to be] of his former opinion, which was for the plaintiff.

BURY: He is of [the] opinion [that] this devise of the £200 ought to be construed as a beneficial one but with this charge annexed, *viz.* the payment of debts and legacies. [It is] objected [that] it is only a trust, and if the word 'only' had been in, it had been indisputably so, and that as it is, it is tantamount and just the same. But he thinks as this it is not a general trust and that it ought not to be construed as if 'only' had been inserted.

He took notice (as [Baron] Lovell had done) that Sir Herbert Parrot does own and say in his will that there is something due by him in conscience that he trusts her with the payment of it, which, as he takes it, makes his intent appear that she should not be accountable for the remainder, for then this private trust (and which was only so) must be made known. And [. . .] a court of equity will not [?] make allowances for such payments as [one is] not compelled to pay in law or equity, as she was in this case obliged to, so that he takes it upon the surface of the will [that] she should not be accountable for the surplus.

And as to Cook and Gwavas's Case that had been mentioned, he said in that case Cook gave to Gwavas and the other executors several legacies so that the reason which ruled in that case was the same with Foster and Monk's Case decreed in the House of Lords. And he observed [that] the deed which created the term was not to all his executors and did make them all and only trustees so that they were to take the four years without any respect to them had as executors, by which, as I apprehend, he inclined to the difference between a deed and a will and that the first did not in itself import the consideration [that] the latter died. As that a trust shall result as well in the case of a deed as a will, he agreed, and so was My Lady Pawlett's Case, above, and which indeed was the reason in Cook and Gwavas's Case; for there being no limitation during the four years, it must of course go to the heir.

And he observed that in the Earl of Bristol's Case, Sir Edward Hungerford and Hill have £100 apiece given [to] them.

And he took notice of the rule laid down in Culpeper and Aston's Case and said [that] he wondered [that] it should be laid down so. Therefore the case had nothing in it to warrant it, and he took notice that it was there that all lords

[. . .] to pay debts should result without distinction, which the rather weakened it, as he thought.

He did not seem entirely satisfied with Foster and Monk's Case but that he submitted to it as being decreed by the House of Lords. And then he objected to Ventris 349, 359, and he thinks not one precedent that came up to them. And he took notice that Mr. Justice Ventris was a good lawyer and a very ingenious man but that his credit would have been nevertheless if his *Reports* had not been printed especially the second part of them. And so he concluded as of his former opinion.

WARD: It is a rule [that] if a testator subjects his estates to pay debts and legacies by way of disposing of the estate or by way of charge, yet there will be a resulting trust unless there be plain and express terms to the contrary. And he thinks [that] the case in question falls under this rule. And [it was said] by him [that there is] another rule in [the] case he binds himself and [his] heirs to pay etc. Let the personal estate be never so small and the real estate never so great, yet a court of equity will make the personal estate come in discharge of the real one. And though the heir has no equity against the creditors, yet he has against the executors.

He said [that] the devise was to the intent to pay debts and legacies and that nobody can know what condition he was in at the time of making the will, and therefore this was a provision against all accidents. And he cannot think that Sir Herbert, by the frame of this will, had any intent to give her this as a beneficial devise. And he did not see indeed any difference in trust upon or with trust and though [it is] not said only as upon yet [it is] all one.

He expresses himself in his argument dissatisfied with Foster and Monk's Case, as above. And [he] mentioned Scavill's Case, as above.

He said [that] he could not well see why legacies should not exclude the executor, for it might be only prudence in some cases to give him a legacy that he might be sure of something and be entitled to come into average with the rest of the legacies, where if no such was given, he would perhaps have nothing at all for his pains, and not with a design to exclude him from the remainder if there was any. He talked something as if there might be a difference in making a relation and a stranger executor with such [a] legacy given [to] him. Query [?][29] of such devise and how Foster and Monk's Case, whether in case of a stranger or relation.

And as to [the cases in] Ventris, he said [that] he could not be of the same opinion with the gentlemen of the bar who objected against them that they were anonymous, for if that was a sufficient objection, it would throw [out an] abundance of the cases in our law books.

---

[29] Qu. *MS.*; perhaps *quia*, because.

And [it was said] by him [that] in equity we must be guided and governed by the rules and reasons of other cases.

And [it was said] by him *arguendo* [that it is] now settled that a moiety in fee is but a personal estate and [it is] always for the benefit of the executors.

And he concluded that he was of his former opinion for the plaintiff.

SMITH, the chancellor of this court. He mentioned the not commencing within six months as a reasonable time whether any occasion for it or no. And the augmentation of her jointure follows after and that there is apparent reason why he should rather have given it expressly to her rather than [to] the heir, if he had designed it [for] her. And he thinks the precedents generally go in favor of the heir, Sir John Packington, as far as they are parallel to this case. And so he concludes with WARD and PRICE for the plaintiff.

N.B. But it was told [to] me by [Baron] Bury's clerk that Smith, baron of this court and now chief baron of Scotland, was of [the same] opinion with Bury and Lovell.

[Order of 9 Dec. 1707: PRO E.126/18, f. 681; order of 30 May 1709: PRO E.126/19, f. 153.]

[Affirmed on appeal: Wych v. Packington (1712), 3 Brown P.C. 44, 1 E.R. 1166, 2 Eq. Cas. Abr. 507, 744, 22 E.R. 429, 632; *Lords' Journal*, XIX (n.d.), p. 448; LI MS. Misc. 503, p. 281.]

[This case is cited in Countess of Bristol v. Hungerford (1709), 2 Vernon 645, 23 E.R. 1021; Roper v. Radcliffe (1712), 9 Modern 181, 187, 88 E.R. 387, 390.]

439

Ringstead v. Redwell (Ex. 1709)

Tithes are due for turnips that have been harvested but not for turnips eaten by cattle without being harvested.

I

IU Lilly MS. Parker, 'Cases in the Exchequer, vol. 4', p. 214 [Eng.] (Price's Reports)

The plaintiff [Thomas Ringsted, vicar of Tolden in Norfolk] demands by bill the tithe of turnips sowed either in the open fields or [in] enclosures, and the defendants insist that no tithe [of] turnips was ever paid for fifty years and none is due, that they feed their cattle upon the turnips, that the turnips were not sowed till the corn was off, and that the cattle eat the tops and dig the apple out of the ground and scooped it, and that in order to plow it, sometimes they plowed the turnips into the ground, sometimes they pulled it up and threw it for their cattle to eat, and sometimes for muck, and if it was eaten on the ground or carried off, if eaten by unprofitable cattle, it was under the pay and allowance of herbage or agistment; if it was eaten by profitable cattle, there was no agistment due.

The plaintiff says that it appeared that the defendant had five, ten, seventeen, and more acres of turnips in a year, and some they eat the tops in the ground, and others they severed and pulled up and carried to other ground to feed their cattle promiscuously, some profitable, some unprofitable. If they had been sold, [they were] agreed to be tithable, but as pulled up and severed, they are of a distinct nature as to their tithe and not like the case of stubble or wood for hop poles or hedging nor grass or tares cut green to feed cattle.

Michaelmas [term] 1705, Humphrey v. Bett and Stopher,[1] which were turnips drawn or pulled up for feed of profitable cattle, though it was said to be for amelioration of the ground, and [the defendants were] decreed to account for [the] turnips.

25 February 9 Will. [1697], exchequer, Thomas Echard v. Samuel Brown,[2] the plaintiff, vicar of Bredfield in Suffolk, [sued] for three roods of turnips, and [the defendant] fed his cattle and [was] decreed to account for the tithe, it being pulled and drawn up and severed from the place they grew.

22 February 2 Anne [1704], John Soley v. Leonard Reeves,[3] [the] plaintiff, rector of Stratton St. Mary in Norfolk, [sued] for the tithe of two acres of turnips, which were pulled up and drawn out of the ground and severed and with which he fed his cows.

Easter [term] 5 Will. & Mary [1693], Wharton v. Oldfield, [there was the] same decree for turnips.

Cro. Car. 393, Mead v. Thurman,[4] tithe tares on headlands.

[it was] decreed that tithe [of] turnips is due and [the] defendant is to account for the profits.

II
HLS MS. 537, part 2, pp. 101, 139 [Eng.] (Eden's Reports)

Upon a motion for altering the words of an issue directed in the equity side, it appeared to have been decreed upon debate there that turnips severed from the land whatsoever use applied to should pay tithes but, if eaten by cattle before [being] severed, it seemed they should not. But query about this. I am not positive what the difference is. And see the decree drawn up. It seemed to have been decreed last term.

This was the case above p. [101]. And it was as before as I apprehended, for after the decree it was referred to the master to examine how much etc. [was] so

---

[1] *Humphrey v. Betts* (Ex. 1705), above, No. 396.

[2] *Eachard v. Brown* (1697), 1 Rayner 84, Samuel Dodd's Reports, p. 179, 2 Eagle & Younge 623.

[3] *Solley v. Reeve* (1704), PRO E.126/18, f. 403.

[4] *Mead v. Thurman* (1635), Cro. Car. 393, 79 E.R. 943, also W. Jones 357, 82 E.R. 188.

employed. And upon reading the decree before the report, it appeared by it that upon a day given to produce precedents and upon precedents being produced that it had been decreed that turnips drawn or severed from the land and employed to the feeding of cattle profitable or unprofitable should pay tithes, and though so spent in the same parish. But [it was argued] by Bridges, one who took exception[5] to the report, [that] if they had been eaten so upon the ground, tithe had not been due, *scil.* before the severance. And so the court seemed to admit.

It seems [that] tithe shall be paid if eaten by barren cattle. Query.

[The order of 2 July 1708, PRO E.126/19, f. 53v, is printed at 1 Wood 510, 1 Eagle & Younge 690, see also order of 30 June 1709: PRO E.126/19, f. 135v.]

440

Bagnall v. Yates (Ex. 1709)

The issue in this case was how a sequestrator should account for income received from a rectory during its vacancy.

HLS MS. 537, part 2, p. 105, pl. 11 [Eng.] (Eden's Reports)

One Edwards, being rector of [the] rectory of Donnington, resigned and, after an almost six months vacancy, the plaintiff, Bagnall, was presented, instituted, and inducted. And during the vacancy, the bishop had appointed the defendant sequestrator (having put in one during the vacancy to supply the care). And now the plaintiff, being entitled by 28 Hen. VIII, c. 11,[1] to the profits during the vacancy, preferred a bill against the defendant that he may account.

The court doubted the bill did not lie. And WARD and PRICE inclined much against. And WARD said he had known it denied. It is the same now as it was before the Act except that the ordinary shall restore the profits to the successor, but the ordinary as before appointed the sequestrator, and the sequestrator only accounts to him in his court etc. He is to allow those deductions etc. and which he is judge of, but the Act provides he shall give the overplus to the next successor and to be allowed those things, so that it seems he is to take the first account and the next successor to be bound by it and to allow him as he has thought fit to allow the sequestrator. But the court said they would notwithstanding consider of it. See the Statute. And query, because it seems [that] this might be prejudicial to the successor.

---

[5] Execucion *MS*.

---

[1] Stat. 28 Hen. VIII, c. 11 (*SR*, III, 666–667).

441

Anonymous (Ex. 1709)

In a bill for tithes, every answer gives discovery even though the defendant pleads a modus. Therefore, any objection to the discovery must be made before a decree after an issue to a jury.

Executors are compellable to make answer upon interrogatories for what came to their hands since their answer.

HLS MS. 537, part 2, p. 122 [Eng.] (Eden's Reports)

In a bill for tithes, the defendant, though he pleads a *modus*, always sets forth a discovery. After [he] pleads a *modus*, the plaintiff proceeds and, upon an issue directed, a decree in favor of him [is made], and he now, by *Dodd*, moves that the defendant, as to some things discovered in his answer, might be examined upon interrogatories and they will abide by it. But the court refused and said that the plea of a *modus* differed from all other pleas, *ut antea*, that if they had any exceptions[1] to the discovery, etc., they then ought to have taken them, for the court would not compel him now to be examined upon interrogatories unless he himself would consent. Indeed if exception[2] had been taken in due time and by consent [it was] referred to any upon interrogatories after the issue of the cause, there well enough because [it was] by consent. It was urged by the counsel for the motion, and the court allowed it, that executors [are] compellable to make answer upon interrogatories for what came to their hands since their answer. But they said as to anything that ought to have been set forth in the answer, if not set forth, it shall not be supplied by interrogatories.

But N.B. query if they may not be examined upon interrogatories for discovering of what the land [was] sown with, etc., pending the suit and since answer; it seems by the practice in the case of executors [that] they may.

Upon denying the motion, [it was said] by *Dodd* [that] we must then have a supplemental bill.

[Chief Baron] WARD: You may have that if you will.

But query if a supplemental bill will lie to relieve them against a neglect of their own. It seems a supplemental bill is proper to discover, etc., what has come to an executor's hands and such like since [the] answer. But query if it will help them against a neglect of their own.

---

[1] Execucions *MS*.
[2] Execucion *MS*.

442

Kempen v. Duke of Devonshire (Ex. 1709)

Executors who are merely nominal executors should not be made parties defendant.

HLS MS. 537, part 2, p. 138 [Eng.] (Eden's Reports)

A bill was preferred against these four as executors of the late duke upon a promise of that late duke. And now it was moved [that] all but the duke should be struck out of the proceedings for an issue was directed upon the bill. It was opposed because the duke might afterwards insist upon his privilege.

And [it was argued] by *Dodd*, who opposed it, [that] we shall be in a great measure disappointed of our costs if we let go the others.

But [it was argued] by *Parker*, who spoke as for himself in the cause, [that] we are all privileged as well as the duke.

[It was said] by *Dodd* one of the other is his steward and lives separately in a house of his own etc.

[It was answered] by *Ettrick* he is with the duke and in his house the most part of the day.

And the court thought fit that they should be struck, they being [in] no way concerned but only nominal executors; they said there was a cause in the court which afterward went up into the House of Lords, wherein one Croft was thus in and would have been struck out, but they said they then refused it, because he was then concerned in the cause, but had he been as in this case no way concerned, they would have let him out. And in this case, the issue will be as well tried etc. if the duke [is the] only party as if all [are] and the end [will be] as well answered.

443

City of York v. Thomson (Ex. 1709)

The statute against the sale of offices forbids an officer to make payments in gross for his office but not payments out of the profits of the office.

LI MS. Misc. 538, f. [85], pl. 2 [Eng.] (Ward's Reports)

The plaintiffs by their bill allege themselves to be entitled by prescription or at least by some contract or instrument to the annuity or yearly sum of £50 *viz.* £40 of it payable to the corporation and £10 to the recorder of York, by the prothonotary of their court of record in the City of York to enable them to pay an annual fee farm rent of £40 to the crown, and charge that the defendant, being by them duly constituted prothonotary of that court many years since, he did for several years pay the same, as his predecessors had always done, but of late years has refused and has got into his hands an instrument in writing under his hand and seal whereby he had covenanted to pay the same so long as he should continue in that office, and therefore to compel him to pay the same was the bill.

The defendant pleads the Statute of 5 & 6 Edw. VI[1] against sale of offices and shows that the said court was a court for the administration of justice and the office of prothonotary was an office within that court and he [was] such an officer there, and that, when he was appointed prothonotary, he was required to pay and give an instrument to the plaintiffs to pay them £50 *per annum* so long as he continued in that office, which was the terms he came into that office and the consideration for the same and that all was done against the form of that statute and [was] void.

And it seemed that the allegations of the bill were fictitious only to avoid the statute and that the defendant's coming into the office was directly against the statute and was sworn by the defendants to be so, and that though it was held in the case of Godolphin and Tudor[2] in the Lords' House that if an officer grants a deputation of an office to one and obliges him to pay him £50 *per annum* out of the profits of the office that that is not against the Act, yet it was there holden (as the case here was) that if it be generally to pay £50 *per annum* in gross and not out of the profits of the office, that that is against the Act. And so here the court allowed the plea but with liberty to the plaintiffs to reply to it if they pleased.

[Other copies of this report: GUL MS. B88–10, p. 655.]

444

Greenway v. Marquess of Kent (Ex. 1709)

A rehearing may be refused because of the movant's laches.
Tithes are not due for timber though it be used for firewood.

LI MS. Misc. 538, f. [103v], pl. 2 [Eng.] (Ward's Reports)

[The] plaintiff obtained a decree for tithe wood, some of which being oak and ash above twenty years growth. By the opinion of Bury, Price, and Smith, the three barons, against the opinion of the chief baron [Ward], it was referred to the deputy remembrancer to compute the values. And upon his report thereof, the cause was heard and the defendant's exceptions to the said report were overruled and the report [was] confirmed and [the] decree [was] pronounced for payment, which not being drawn up and signed in regard of defendant's privilege of Parliament for some time, and Baron Lovell now sitting in court in the absence

---

[1] Stat. 5 & 6 Edw. VI, c. 16 (*SR*, IV, 151–152).
[2] *Godolphin v. Tudor* (1704), 1 Brown 135, 1 E.R. 468.

of Baron Smith in Scotland, the defendant moved for a rehearing of the whole cause *ab origine* upon a petition signed by considerable counsel that in their opinion the cause was fit to be reheard. But in regard [that] the cause was originally heard so long ago as the 31st of January 1705[/06],[1] and that decretal order signed by the three barons that pronounced it and entered in the book as usual[2] and the hearing on the report had in June 1709, and the execution overruled (in my absence), the court did not think fit to grant a rehearing after such agitation and proceeding in the cause, which otherwise and had it been asked in [a] reasonable time notwithstanding the signing and entry of the first decree (which is only in effect an interlocutory judgment *quod computet*, upon which no writ of error lies) might and possibly would have been granted. And the decree being against the defendant, if he had been dissatisfied with it, he was at liberty all along to have prayed a rehearing. And therefore for the length of time and defendant's submitting to the account and travailing so long in it, the rehearing was refused and [the] defendant [was] left to his appeal or bill of review as he pleased. But he did not think fit to bring either, though in my opinion he might and ought to have had relief by appeal thinking the decree against law as to the oaks, ash, and elms above twenty years growth let them be put to what use they please.

It was said that by the usage in that country all wood cut and corded and used for firewood pays tithe notwithstanding its age. But query that custom, for it is against law to compel a man to pay tithe of what is or has been timber by law or custom though it be used for or as firewood.

See my argument at large in this case.

It was said [that] the defendant would not appeal because he would not disoblige the clergy. Query that reason.

[Other copies of this report: GUL MS. B88–10, p. 692.]

[Order of 8 July 1709: PRO E.127/28, f. 46.]

445

Attorney General ex rel. Burton v. Bishop of London (Ex. 1710)

The court of exchequer cannot compel a bishop to grant a person a license to preach. For this reason, the question of who had the right to elect a curate was moot in this case.

---

[1] *Greenway v. Earl of Kent* (Ex. 1706), above, No. 407.
[2] This order is printed at 1 Wood 479, 1 Eagle & Younge 677; note also Bunbury 98, 145 E.R. 609, 1 Rayner 161.

LI MS. Misc. 538, f. [109] [Eng.] (Ward's Reports)

The queen's attorney general at the relation of Littleton Burton, clerk, and the inhabitants of Hammersmith, plaintiffs. Henry, lord bishop of London, Philip Dwight, clerk, vicar of Fulham, and Michael Hutchinson, clerk, defendants.

This cause was begun to be heard on Thursday the 26th of January 1709[/10], and was further heard Monday the 6th of February following, and the court gave their opinions therein the 14th of February 1709[/10].

And the case upon the hearings appeared to be to the effect following, *viz.* in the year 1631 the inhabitants of Hammersmith (which is a vill or hamlet in the parish of Fulham in the County of Middlesex and distant from the parish church about a mile) had a desire at their own costs and charges to erect a chapel of ease in Hammersmith, and for that purpose applied to the then bishop of London (Dr. Laud), who was lord of Fulham Manor and patron of a prebend in St. Paul's, London, the corps of which is the rectory impropriate of Fulham, and unto the then vicar of Fulham, who and whose successors have the cure of souls throughout the whole parish of Fulham, and thereupon at their great costs and charges erected a very handsome and convenient structure upon a piece of ground (a very small part whereof was the waste of the lord's manor and the residue of the ground whereon the chapel was built) and the chapel yard for burial and other uses made (being very much bigger than the waste) was either purchased or given by all or some of the parishioners for the uses and purposes aforesaid, which chapel and yard being so erected and made, there were articles of agreement in writing under the hands and seals of the then vicar of Fulham and of divers of the principal inhabitants of Hammersmith in the behalf of themselves and the rest of the inhabitants, reciting the erection of the chapel at the costs and charges of the inhabitants of Hammersmith by the consent of the bishop and vicar of Fulham and the intention of having it consecrated and the reservation of the right of the vicar and church of Fulham. And for avoiding of all differences and controversies in time to come, it was agreed:

1. That the inhabitants of Hammersmith perpetually for the time being should 'find and maintain' at their own costs and charges a curate to officiate the cure in the chapel and at their own charges repair and maintain it and that the vicar of Fulham should be discharged from finding a curate or contributing thereunto, and yet the inhabitants of Hammersmith shall be perpetually liable to the reparations of Fulham Church as formerly.

2. That Hammersmith inhabitants shall resort to Fulham Church at Easter and receive the sacrament there and at all times shall have liberty to come thither and that all tithes and duties from Hammersmith inhabitants shall be reserved and paid to the vicar of Fulham.

3. That all fees and duties for marriages, christenings, churchings, and burials in the chapel or in Hammersmith shall be accounted for and paid to the vicar and church of Fulham as if done in the church or parish of Fulham.
4. That if any sermon on any [of] those times or occasions be preached, it shall be by the vicar of Fulham or by his consent.
5. That for the securing [of] the vicar's duties, it is provided that the curate and churchwarden of Hammersmith side shall weekly bring to the vicar a note of all marriages, christenings, burials, etc. had at Hammersmith and the duties for the same, and to be registered at Fulham.
6. That the vicar of Fulham shall be forever free from exercising his ministerial function in the chapel unless what and when he pleased and to have a pew in the chapel.

Shortly after the making of these articles, it appeared by the register book of the bishop of London that the 7th of June 1631 an act of consecration of the chapel was there entered to be done that day, which took notice of the Hammersmith inhabitants' petition to the bishop for the consecration, and that the ground where the chapel stands was given part by the bishop and [the] rest by the inhabitants, and took notice also of the articles and the saving of the rights of the vicar and church of Fulham, the bishop did therefore consecrate and set apart the chapel for the use of the inhabitants of Hammersmith, in which act or instrument of consecration, there is a clause whereby the bishop does 'reserve' to himself and successors bishops of London 'the power and authority of choosing and nominating' a fit presbyter to be curate of that chapel, and also to him or his vicar general and successors the power and authority of approving, admitting, and licensing the presbyter so chosen and nominated curate from time to time. And in that instrument, the bishop took notice that by the articles no provision was made for any certain stipend or sum for the curate. It is therefore thereby provided that the inhabitants of Hammersmith shall from time to time at their proper costs and charges maintain or sustain the curate by the bishop and his vicar general's successor's authority to be appointed as aforesaid, by paying to him the yearly sum of £30 at least quarterly without deduction in respect of anything as to [the] vicar or church of Fulham.

In the entry of this instrument or act of consecration, under the *his testibus* there are mention made of the names of several of the inhabitants of Hammersmith, who were parties to the articles, but none of them subscribed their names but were only named by the notary public that drew up that act, that they were witnesses to that act of consecration (which whether they were or not does not otherwise appear than by the said entry). In a book said to be the book of Dr.

Duck,[1] the bishop's vicar general, which refers to a parchment book as the original (which original is not extant), there was an entry made that the 13th of July 1631, one Dent was admitted upon the bishop's nomination to be curate of that chapel. And it appeared in the pleadings in this cause that between the consecration of the chapel and the death of Mr. Wade which happened in November 1707 there had been four curates of that chapel, *viz*. Dent who came in in 1631, Knight who came in 1647, Fowler who came in 1648 and continued till 1662, and Wade who came in in 1662 and continued till November 1707. And then the question came who should have the election of the curate (for it was agreed by all that the admission and licensing of the curate to preach must be by the bishop of the diocese). The bishop he claimed the election either as ordinary or as patron in virtue that part of the chapel and its yard were upon the waste of the manor whereof he is lord or thirdly (which he most relied on) in virtue of the instrument of consecration whereby the bishop reserved to himself and successors that power of choosing and nominating the curate, which he would have extend and be understood to be by the consent of the inhabitants as implied under the words at the end of the instrument of consecration of *his testibus*.

The inhabitants (that is the greater part (though not of the chief) of Hammersmith inhabitants) claimed the election by the right of building and repairing of the chapel and donors of the far greatest part of the ground on which the chapel was built and in virtue of the said articles by which they were obliged to find and maintain the curate in all times whereby and by the vicar's being discharged of the cure, they conceived the right of election was in the major part of the inhabitants not affected by any [of] the pretenses of the bishop by the instrument of consecration or otherwise. [On] the 2nd of December 1707, the now bishop of London grants a license to the defendant Hutchinson *ad peragendum officium curati in capella de Hammersmith in precibus communibus aliisque ministeriis ecclesiasticis ad dictum officium pertinentibus durante bene placito*.

[On] 5 February 1707[/08], there was a vestry of the inhabitants at the chapel where it was agreed that Hutchinson should have the pew and gallery money (which by the way is the curate's whole profit) for some years. And it appeared by entries in the chapel books that Hutchinson is there mentioned or owned to be the present minister of that chapel by a great majority of inhabitants then present, *viz*. 25 out of 28. And a further agreement is entered there that in regard [that] Hutchinson laid out some money in building a gallery that, if he ceased to be curate there before he was reimbursed, what remains should be secured and paid to him or his representatives out of the profits of that gallery, and this was in July 1708. And it further appeared in the cause that the relator Burton, who had

---

[1] Arthur Duck (d. 1648): *D.N.B.*; B. P. Levack, *The Civil Lawyers in England* (1973), p. 225.

officiated in the chapel for Mr. Wade, continued so to do under Mr. Hutchinson till November 1708 when he set up for himself under an election by the major part of the inhabitants of Hammersmith after due notice given of the time and place for such election, for which time of serving the cure under Hutchinson he recovered against him upon a *quantum meruit* in the common pleas. But there did not appear [that] the inhabitants had made any election of curate till that of Burton's, nor that the bishop had ever elected Hutchinson otherwise than by getting him the license aforesaid.

And now this bill setting forth the erection of the chapel at the costs and charges of the inhabitants of Hammersmith and the aforesaid articles and that it was consecrated and that the right of electing a curate of right belonged to the inhabitants, who had chosen Burton, and that he ought to be admitted curate there with all the profits to that curacy belonging but that the bishop refused to admit him and give him a license to preach but on the contrary had admitted Hutchinson (though not elected by the inhabitants) who pretends to have served the cure there and had received the profits thereof to the damage and prejudice of Burton and the inhabitants and therefore prayed a discovery of the articles in the defendants' hands and of their respective pretenses to the election of the curate and that the right to the election of a curate, which is in the nature of a charity and religious endowment and of public concern for the inhabitants might be as it is proper to be settled in this court according to the purport of the articles and that the bishop may be enjoined to remove Hutchinson and he and the vicar confirm Burton to be curate upon the foot of the right of election by the inhabitants and that Hutchinson may account to Burton for the profits received and that Burton may be established in possession by the decree of this court and the right of the election by the inhabitants settled and the plaintiffs otherwise relieved was the scope of the bill.

The defendants by their answer insist upon the bishop's right of choosing, admitting, and licensing the curate upon the beforementioned pretenses and that plaintiffs' pretenses are not sufficient nor true so as to induce any relief to be granted to them.

The plaintiffs examined divers aged and other witnesses, some whereof remember Dent's and others Knight's, Fowler's, and Wade's coming in to be curates and that they were all elected by the inhabitants, and that by what some of them have heard from their parents and others and the common and constant reputation all along that the elections and the right thereof was in the inhabitants. And it appeared by the bishop of London's certificate dated the 26th of November 1662 that Wade was therein styled curate of Hammersmith and had taken the oaths before him and yet the bishop's license to Wade to preach and perform divine service in Hammersmith chapel and elsewhere in the diocese of London during pleasure was not granted till the 2nd of December 1662 so that before the bishop's license (which is no election) Wade is named curate, which might well be by the election of the inhabitants beforehand. And in the bishop's book of entry of licenses it appears that Wade *iam admittendus ad peragendum officium curati in capella de Hammersmith* took the oaths and [there was] not a word anywhere that Wade was elected or appointed by the bishop to be curate but only admitted (for so he must be though elected by the inhabitants). And these witnesses and observations were made and offered to call in question the truth of that entry in Dr. Duck's book that Dent was admitted by the nomination of the bishop.

The defendants observed that two of the curates came in when there were no bishops and contend the fact of Wade's coming in by the election of the inhabitants upon the credit of one Hall that was chapel clerk in some part of Wade's time and of one Mary Hancock, who testify that about eighteen years ago Wade told them apart that Alderman Bard and two or three others of the inhabitants went to the bishop to nominate and license Wade as one acceptable to the inhabitants and that, if he refused and nominated another, there would little to be had or that they would starve him and thereupon the bishop nominated and licensed Wade. Walker said thereupon the bishop consented to Wade's nomination by the inhabitants so that it seemed doubtful whether those two depositions or either of them extended to the bishop's nomination or only Wade's admission.

The court after consideration had upon the nature of the cause and of the relief prayed by the bill and after hearing divers counsel of each side dismissed the bill upon the ground that the court could not grant the relief prayed by the bill in regard [that] the plaintiff Burton was not capacitated to serve the cure in the chapel not having a license from the bishop to preach in the diocese, nor was it in the court's power to compel the bishop to grant him one or to do any other ecclesiastical act to capacitate him to serve the cure there nor to compel the vicar to confirm him nor Hutchinson to pay him any of the profits. And this was thought sufficient cause to dismiss the bill without entering into the right of election whether it does belong to the inhabitants or the bishop, those inhabitants that inclined for Hutchinson against Burton refusing to renounce the inhabitants' right of election.

But in my own opinion, I inclined to think that the right of election did belong to the inhabitants from the consideration of their erecting the chapel and their obligation by the articles forever to find and maintain the curate at their own charges, which in my apprehension according to the reason and resolutions of Adams and Lambert's Case, 4 [Coke] Rep. 104,[2] and the Statute of [1] Edw. VI,[3] upon which that case is founded, extends plainly to the choosing of the

---

[2] *Adams v. Lambert* (1602), 4 Coke Rep. 104, 76 E.R. 1091, also Moore K.B. 648, 72 E.R. 815.

[3] Stat. 1 Edw. VI, c. 14 (*SR*, IV, 24–33).

curate where there is no express power of election given to any other. For where a man is to find it necessary implies he must have the choice and must do it at his peril and that the inhabitants must perpetually repair the chapel and that the vicar of Fulham is to be discharged of the service of the cure in the chapel and enjoy all the ecclesiastical rights arising in it and from the consideration that all the inhabitants are also to be liable to the payment of tithes and duties to the vicar and remain liable to the repairs of and the duties and rights to the vicar and church of Fulham, so that the curate has nothing for his maintenance that encroaches upon the church or vicar of Fulham nor indeed but what arises by the profits of pews and seats in the chapel erected at the charges of the inhabitants, who therefore set a rate upon them to be paid by every inhabitant that is placed in them. And I cannot apprehend that the reservation in the act or instrument of consecration, whereby the bishop did reserve to himself and [his] successors the power of choosing, nominating, and admitting of the curate, can confer any such power to the bishop which was not in him before, that being only the words of the bishop and not of any grant or concession of the inhabitants, who though some of their names come under the *his testibus* yet never signed it. Nor am I moved by any [of] the entries in the bishop's or vicar general's books in favor of the bishop's pretenses but rather incline to the testimony of those witnesses who prove the elections to have been always before this last vacancy by the inhabitants, for the ecclesiastical officers may enter what they please in their books and acts of consecrations without the privity of other persons and it is too hard to say such entries should conclude them, especially where opposed by so many living witnesses. And though this contest is about the choice of an ecclesiastical person and the serving of a cure and that this court has not any coercive power (as this case is and as courts of law have in cases of quare impedits depending before them) against the bishops to revoke or grant licenses, yet it is not inconsistent that inhabitants, or the major part of them, may have a right of electing their minister as well as they have in the choice of lecturers in parishes, which is daily practice and as societies of law, etc., as Gray's Inn, Lincoln's Inn, etc., do and always have done and as originally the people did.

From this dismission, Burton appealed to the House of Lords, upon the hearing of which appeal, the Lords took into consideration the right of election, and upon debate, the appeal was dismissed and the dismission confirmed by a majority of one only, as that the right of election was in the bishop and not in the inhabitants, all the bishops voting on that side.[4]

[Other copies of this report: GUL MS. B88–10, p. 701.]

---

[4] *Attorney General ex rel. Burton v. Bishop of London*, Case 76 (1710), Colles 399, 1 E.R. 343, *Lords' Journal*, XIX (n.d.), p. 137.

[Order of 24 Jan. 1710: PRO E.127/28, f. 110.]

[Related cases: Burton v. Bishop of London (1711), Colles 403, 1 E.R. 345, *Lords' Journal*, XIX (n.d.), p. 304; IU Lilly MS. Parker, 'Practice of the Exchequer, ca. 1691–1763', pp. 288–293 (argument of counsel); Hutchinson v. Burton (Ex. 1710), below, No. 446.]

446

Hutchinson v. Burton (Ex. 1710)

A court has the power to reinstate a nonsuited lawsuit if the plaintiff pays the defendant's costs.

In this case, the plaintiff failed to show good cause why a former preliminary injunction that had been dissolved should be reinstated.

I

LI MS. Misc. 538, ff. [145, 148v] [Eng.] (Ward's Reports)

There was heretofore a question [that] arose between these two persons, which of them was the lawful curate of the chapel of Hammersmith in the parish of Fulham in the County of Middlesex. The plaintiff claimed under the bishop of London's appointment and the defendant under the election of the inhabitants of Hammersmith. The defendant and the inhabitants of Hammersmith were the relators in a bill exhibited in this court in the attorney general's name on their behalf,[1] which was to have the defendant's right to be curate established against the now plaintiff and the bishop of London and the vicar of Fulham, who were parties thereto.

And the now plaintiff exhibited his bill against the now defendant and some of the inhabitants of Hammersmith setting forth his title and complaining of disturbances [and] prayed he might be established in his possession. In the first cause, witnesses were examined on both sides, but the first cause was only brought to hearing and dismissed and that dismission appealed from to the Lords in Parliament, who affirmed that dismission.[2] And the now plaintiff proceeded no further than answer in his cause, and for want of prosecution, the now plaintiff's bill was before the hearing of the first cause dismissed with costs to be taxed as the Act for Amendment of the Law[3] in that case directs. The now defendant notwithstanding the affirmance of the dismission by the Lords and after the dismission of the now plaintiff's bill sets afoot again his pretenses to the

---

[1] *Attorney General ex rel. Burton v. Bishop of London* (Ex. 1710), above, No. 445.

[2] *Attorney General ex rel. Burton v. Bishop of London*, Case 76 (1710), Colles 399, 1 E.R. 343, Lords' Journal, XIX (n.d.), p. 137.

[3] Stat. 4 & 5 Ann., c. 3, s. 23 (SR, VIII, 460–461).

curacy and enters into the chapel the last long vacation partly by force and reads prayers and preaches there and with a great number of loose people and by the aid and assistance of some of the defendants, the inhabitants, [according] to the now plaintiff's bill, and some others continue and detain the possession of the chapel, pretending that notwithstanding the Lords' affirmance of this court's dismission, yet the title between the now plaintiff and defendant to the curacy is not determined or settled.

Whereupon the now plaintiff's counsel moved to set aside the order of dismission of the now plaintiff's bill, in order as they said to continue an injunction formerly granted for quieting him in the execution of his pastoral office in the chapel, which being opposed by the now defendants' counsel, the court took into consideration whether, first, they could set aside the dismission of the now plaintiff's bill since the said Act of Parliament has enacted that, when a plaintiff's bill is dismissed upon his own motion or for want of prosecution, it shall be with full costs to be taxed. And the court ordered precedents to be searched in this court and the chancery whether since the Act any orders have been [made] for setting aside dismissions fairly obtained, at least in another term. For if it may be done so, the defendant must lose his full costs which the Act entitles him to. For then if there be no dismission, there can be no costs given by the court.

And upon Friday 10th of November 1710, the court was informed that there are multitudes of precedents in chancery (some produced) since the Act, that upon payment of costs the court retained the bill. For though by the retainer the costs by the Act are lost, yet since the plaintiff by retaining the bill has put the defendant to costs, unless the plaintiff will consent to pay the costs out of pocket, the court will not retain the bill. And so in the principal case it was here ordered that the bill should be retained, the plaintiff consenting and submitting to pay the costs to be taxed, and if the defendant will not procure his costs to be taxed (which he seemed unwilling to and said he would not), it is his own fault and that [is] not to hinder the retaining, but if taxed and not paid by the plaintiff, the order for retaining the bill to be discharged, and [the] former order of dismission to stand.

But as to the renewing of the injunction, it not appearing now to the court that any or what injunction had been granted, the court left the plaintiff to move for that as he should be advised.

[On] Friday 17 November, the plaintiff's counsel produced an injunction granted July 1708 directed to Burton and others to permit the plaintiff Hutchinson to exercise his sacerdotal office in the chapel as he had done for almost two years before and at the time of exhibiting the bill and not to disturb him therein *quousque* the court should otherwise order, which injunction was granted upon [the] filing [of] the plaintiff's bill upon affidavit of disturbance but before any answer came in or time for answering out. In February following after [the] answer came in, [the] defendant moved to dissolve the injunction, the answer being come in, whereby he set up a right to himself to be curate in opposition to the plaintiff's. And upon hearing counsel on both sides, it was ordered to be dissolved unless cause [be shown on] such a day in Easter term, and no cause being shown, it was actually dissolved. And now plaintiff's counsel prayed, upon affidavits of some disturbances in the chapel by others hindering [the] plaintiff from preaching there, that the injunction should be revived.

But upon debate the chief baron [WARD], BURY, and LOVELL, (*dissentiente* PRICE) denied the motion as the case now stood in court in regard [that] the injunction was granted before answer and that after answer upon hearing counsel on both sides, it was dissolved, so that to renew this injunction granted before answer and after answer dissolved upon the merits of the case, at least without hearing the defendants' answer and the reasons of dissolving the injunction (none of which was produced or made out to the court), it was not not reasonable to renew that injunction so dissolved, but if anything was to be done for the plaintiff it must be upon matters appearing upon [the] plaintiff's bill and defendants' answer whereof nothing was offered to the court nor was a new injunction moved for but only the old so granted and so dissolved as aforesaid to be renewed.

Upon this denial to renew the old injunction 29 November 1710, the bishop of London and Hutchinson and [the] vicar of Fulham petition the Lords in Parliament setting forth what their lordships had done by commanding the sheriffs of Middlesex to suppress the riots and tumults which happened while the appeal was depending in Parliament and that in favor of Hutchinson's title Burton's appeal was dismissed, and yet that after that Burton had by violence got and kept possession of the chapel assisted by a rabble of people who defiled the chapel, and refused Hutchinson to serve the cure there, and therefore prayed their lordships would interpose their authority in this case and that the force might be removed so that Hutchinson whose right was made to appear upon the appeal might be enabled to serve the cure in the chapel or to that effect.

But in this petition no notice was taken of any [of] the proceedings in the exchequer after the dismission of the appeal. But upon the debate in the House and to [. . .]id the question of meddling with an original matter, some notice was taken that there was then a bill depending in that court between the two litigants.

And thereupon the House sent for me to give an account thereof, which I did as before is set forth touching the retaining of Hutchinson's bill and not granting the motion for the renewing [of] the injunction that was granted upon the forms of the court upon affidavit before answer and dissolved upon the merits upon hearing counsel on both sides and till this motion acquiesced in, and nothing of a new motion made for an injunction upon the merits, with which reasons and causes the Lords were very well satisfied, and that the Court could do nothing upon their Lordships' confirming the court's dismission, that not giving any direction or jurisdiction to the court, but that thereupon the parties were wholly out of court and no order could be made thereupon. It was hinted by some lords that resort might be had to the court for granting an injunction upon the merits on consideration of [the] bill, answer, and affidavits of the disturbances. I said the court would do right upon proper application made to them.

I told My Lord Keeper and some lords privately that I thought a writ *de vi laica removenda* was the most proper and speedy way to remove the force which could not be denied. But it was expected that at the setting down of causes after this term, an injunction would have been moved for, but instead thereof the plaintiff's counsel moved to dismiss his bill with costs, which was granted, and he exhibited his bill in chancery, and so the court was rid of the cause.

The injunction first granted being before answer and [the] defendant not [being] in contempt was intended by the court only to continue the plaintiff in that bill in such quiet possession of the chapel as he had at the time of the exhibiting of his bill and three years before, as usual in like cases the courts of equity in such cases following the reason of the statutes against forcible entries and detainers[4] where no possession is to be changed if the party has been in it by the space of three years or more. But here the party wanted something of three years. Yet because divine service and preaching was so necessary to be had in the chapel and the plaintiff had the bishop's license to preach, which the defendant Burton had not, and the principal cause wherein the attorney general at Burton's relation was to be sped and heard suddenly, the injunction was granted but not ordered or understood to be as the clerk drew it up to permit the plaintiff quietly and peaceably *peragere officium suum sacerdotale* in the chapel there being no precedent of such an injunction. And if [it be] good in this case, why not in any case where a contention arises between two ecclesiastical persons contending the right to the church and service of the cure? And how the bishops and ecclesiastical persons would like of such injunctions in matters purely ecclesiastical, as this case is, and where nothing of lay fee or interest is concerned (as in cases of right of patronages or proceedings thereupon there may be) may be thought upon.

[Other copies of this report: GUL MS. B88–10, pp. 803, 819.]

II
HLS MS. 537, part 2, p. 176 [Eng.] (Eden's Reports)

Burton exhibits a bill against Hutchinson, who had been put in by the bishop of London to the curacy of Hammersmith, and Burton [had been put in] by the inhabitants. And upon the hearing, it was dismissed, and it [was] confirmed

---

[4] Stat. 31 Eliz. I, c. 11 (SR, IV, 809–810).

by the House of Lords. Hutchinson in the same time had exhibited a bill to have an injunction to quiet his possession; he had been in possession two or three years, and [he] had it without the words 'till answer or further order'. After that an answer [was] put in, and Hutchinson apprehended no further occasion for his bill and injunction. The other side [obtained] a dismission and dissolution.

And now Burton and others disturbed his possession by force and arms. He moved to retain his bill. And upon great debate, it was retained notwithstanding the dismission. And now [it was] moved to revive the injunction. And by WARD, BURY, [and] LOVELL, [it was ruled] that it could not [be] and that he might have [a writ of] *vi laica removenda*. But query their reason.

[Baron] PRICE [said] that it might. He said [that] injunctions to quiet possession were granted of course and without opposition where [there was] three years possession in imitation of the Statute of Forcible Entry[5] but very often sooner, if [there was] occasion, as in this case, and he saw no reason why the injunction might not for the very same reason be revived as the bill [was] retained. And as to the objection by Ward [and] Bury that the order [was] not right, he said it was as it ought to be and they dislike[6] in such case upon their going to a trial at law or a hearing. Query as to the matter of the injunction and as to the learning of them.

III

IU Lilly MS. Parker, 'Cases in the Exchequer, vol. 5', p. 1 [Eng.] (Price's Reports)

Attorney General at the relation of Burton *contra* Hutchinson and *e contra*, Michaelmas [term] 1710 in the exchequer, [was a] bill to establish the relator's right to the chaplain's or curate's place in Hammersmith in Middlesex under [the] pretense that the inhabitants had built and endowed [?] the chapel and ought to choose their chaplain; the defendant was placed in by the bishop of London and had his license.

Upon [the] hearing [of] the cause, the bill was dismissed, and on appeal, the dismission was affirmed by the Lords.

Mr. Hutchinson exhibits his bill pending this cause to quiet his possession upon the common affidavits of [. . .] three years possession, [and he] had an injunction.

After the former cause was dismissed, Burton moves to dissolve the injunction on [the] coming in of Burton's answer and then moves to dismiss Hutchinson's bill. And when that was done, he entered [?] on the chapel and, by a mob, kept out Hutchinson, who moved to revive the bill to quiet his possession, which

---

[5] Stat. 31 Eliz. I, c. 11 (SR, IV, 809–810).
[6] disl' MS.

being done, he moved to revive the injunction to quiet his possession upon fresh affidavits of a continued disturbance.

Baron PRICE said that since Burton's bill, which owned Hutchinson's possession and desired to have his right established and he put in possession, was dismissed, his right was at an end. And since [there] were disturbances, there was reason to revive the bill and injunction to quiet the possession. It was an incident to the reviving of the bill. It was the province of courts of equity to quiet possession till the right is tried, and, though the right was determined against the intruder, yet he kept a wrongful possession. And [he] thought the bill should be revived and the injunction, for though these sorts of injunctions are granted upon three years possession and the possession they had at the time of the bill, yet where there are particular cases and the possession is doubtful, they are granted *toties quoties* they have occasion and do not confine it to the answer coming in but till the right is determined. Otherwise, men may intrude and keep possession. It may be without force [?] and without right, and, if with force, an indictment for riot and forcible entry or a *vi laica amovenda*, which removes or punishes the force but does not alter or secure the rightful possession.

Chief Baron WARD, BURY, and LOVELL, barons, though they agreed to revive the bill and [held] that the possession was an illegal possession and against their own determination, yet [they] would not revive the injunction.

(The denial of this motion occasioned the filing of a bill in the court of chancery by the bishop of London and Mr. Hutchinson, and the court, on 7 May 1711, established the bishop's right of nomination and decreed that Mr. Hutchinson should be quieted in the possession of the curacy, and the decree [was] affirmed in the House of Lords on appeal;[7] see the cases in Parliament, MSS. 'Practice of the Exchequer', 288.[8])

[Orders of 8 Nov. and 31 Dec. 1710: PRO E.127/28, ff. 207v, 212.]

[Related cases: Burton v. Bishop of London (1711), Colles 403, 1 E.R. 345.]

447

Dummer v. Barret (Ex. 1710)

A deposition taken without notice to the other party will be suppressed.

A deposition taken to perpetuate testimony cannot be used where the witness could have later been examined in the usual course but was not.

A deposition cannot be taken by a baron of the exchequer more than fifteen miles from London but should be taken by a commissioner.

---

[7] *Lords' Journal*, XIX (n.d.), p. 304.
[8] IU Lilly MS. Parker, '1691–1763, Nov. 29, Practice of Exchequer', p. 288.

LI MS. Misc. 538, ff. [119v, 123] [Eng.] (Ward's Reports)

[On] the 20th of May 1709, the plaintiff upon affidavit of the age and infirmity of one Inler his witness, and filing his bill obtained an order to examine him *in perpetuam rei memoriam*, and on the next day and before any subpoena taken out against the defendant and without any notice to the defendant, procured him to be examined before a baron, after which the plaintiff served the defendant with a subpoena to answer returnable the first day of next term being [the] 4th of June when the defendant appeared and put in his answer the 23rd of June. And the witness lived near six weeks after that and then died, in which time the plaintiff might but did not reply. And the plaintiff having obtained an order to publish this deposition *nisi causa*, the court this day suppressed the deposition as being wholly irregular, first for want of notice by subpoena or otherwise to the defendant who might have cross-examined the witness if he pleased, the benefit of which was lost, but chiefly because the plaintiff might have replied and examined his witness in chief he not dying in near six weeks after the answer came in. And in such a case as this it would be very dangerous and of evil example to allow of depositions taken *de bene esse* only to be used at the hearing, when the witness lived so long after answer put in that he might have been examined in chief if the plaintiff had thought fit to reply. And though it may be a prejudice to the plaintiff to lose the benefit of that deposition, yet that being the effect only of the plaintiff's laches, it must not redound to the defendant's prejudice that he shall lose the benefit of the cross-examination.

[On] 22 May 1710, Mr. Attorney General [*Montagu*] and others pray to suppress the deposition of one of the plaintiff's witnesses taken before Baron Smith in Scotland, who though he is one of the barons of this court and chief baron of Scotland, yet in regard the examination was in Scotland in a cause depending in this court in England, and notice given in the office here by the plaintiff to the defendant of such examination in Scotland, yet the court thought such notice was not sufficient to justify an examination at such a distance, nor indeed at any distance above fifteen miles from London, but that in all such cases the witnesses ought to be examined by commission. And therefore the court suppressed that examination and deposition and very much questioned the power of taking such examinations in Scotland by the chief baron there who, though he be a baron of this court, yet he is not so in Scotland as to things in this court. And though England and Scotland are united into one kingdom, yet the laws and the execution of them and their respective jurisdictions by the articles of the union remain distinct,[1] as before. The court also thought that an examination before a baron

---

[1] Stat. 6 Ann., c. 11, art. 18 (SR, VIII, 571).

in his circuit or house in the country [would] not [be] good, but it ought to be by commission. Liber 1, [p.] 212.[2]

[Other copies of this report: GUL MS. B88–10, p. 721.]

[Order of 29 June 1710: PRO E.127/28, f. 183v.]

448

Wright v. Elderton (Ex. 1710)

In this case, tithes were not due for turnips sown as a second crop.
The rector of a parish has the general right of tithes.
A vicar's right to tithes comes from his endowment.
Usage of receiving tithes is the best evidence of an endowment.

LI MS. Misc. 538, f. [155] [Eng.] (Ward's Reports)

The plaintiff's bill was to be relieved (*inter alia*) for the tithes of a winter crop of turnips sown upon the same land which had that year borne a crop of corn whereof the impropriator had received the tithe in kind or a composition of 4s. or 5s. an acre for the corn. It appeared not in the cause what the endowment of the vicarage was nor that it was of all small tithes, and therefore the usage was to be observed in that as in all other cases where the endowment was not extant (nay in many cases usage prevails against the very words of the endowment). And in this case, it appeared that when the inhabitant sows his land with turnips as a first and summer crop, there the vicar has had the tithe of that crop, but there never was any instance of the vicar's having the tithe of any turnips sown after a crop of corn received from the same land in the same year the inhabitants alleging that such winter crop of turnips were sown principally for the meliorating and improving the land for a crop of corn the next year. And it was proved [in] the cause that for above fifty years that vicars never had any tithe or composition for such winter crop of turnips though such [were] sown all the time, and though it did not appear that the impropriator ever received the same (which might be conceived to be by reason the [ti]thes of corn the next year would be thereby meliorated), yet in regard [that] the vicar never had the same in [a]ny time, and that not having any usage for him but against him, though the parishioner might not have any just [ex]cuse against the impropriator who has the general and [co]mmon right to tithes and the vicar only a partial right confined to those tithes and species of tithes and times, [p]laces, and manner of tithes which in the

---

[2] *Place v. Mounson* (Ex. 1666), above, No. 8.

endowment or the usage, the court (*dissentiente* Price) dismissed the plaintiff's bill *quoad* the winter crop of turnips in that case.

And in this case, was remembered the case [of] 20 February 1705[/06] in this court, Barry, vicar of Fulham, against Bridges, lessee of the impropriator[1] there, where was the very same case with this; the vicar had the tithe of turnips sown for the summer crop and pretended to have the tithes of the winter crop also, but never having had them, the court offered him a trial at law to try whether he had a right to them [or] not, but he declined the trial and chose as to them to be [d]ismissed and was so. And this being the same case went upon the same reason (however, Price that now differed was then of another opinion) for it is no necessary conclusion [wi]thout evidence that the vicar should generally have either all small tithes or the tithes of all turnips in all places and at all times throughout the parish because he has them for the first summer crop to which only the usage (which is the only evidence of the endowment as to turnips) is confined and the general right to all tithes not in the endowment remains in the impropriator. And whether the impropriator receive them or not, if the vicar make not out a title to them, the court in justice cannot make a decree for him, for a *non decimando* as to such a thing or for such a time is not incongruous, because he having no general right, the impropriator may have them.

These things to me seem to subsist and be settled by the reasons and authorities in law and by the practice and precedents of the court:

1. That a rector, impropriate or not impropriate, has the general and common right within his parish and tithable places thereof to the tithes customary or other rates for all tithable things any ways due by law or custom in such parish.
2. That no vicar (as such only) is or can be entitled to any tithes but to such only and in such places, times, and manners as are limited by their respective endowments, or by usage time out of mind or for a long time, which is the proper evidence of such endowments where they are not extant.
3. That where an ancient endowment is extant and it does not thereby appear that such or such tithes great or small do belong to the vicar, yet where the vicars for the memory of man, or a very long time, have constantly and all along without interruption had and received such tithes not mentioned in such endowment such usage has prevailed against the endowment upon presumption of some subsequent endowment or title to them. Hardres 328, 329.[2]

---

[1] *Barry v. Bridges* (Ex. 1706), PRO E.126/18, f. 566v.

[2] *Twisse v. Brazen-Nose College* (1663), Hardres 328, 145 E.R. 481, 1 Rayner 36, 2 Gwillim 514, 1 Eagle & Younge 439.

4. That ancient and other words in an endowment have been by construction extended beyond the common and strict sense and proper signification and import of them to carry tithes and duties which by usage the vicars have for long time received, as for example the word *altaragium*[3] has been construed to carry great tithes of corn or grain or the like where the vicar has used to receive them and had no other words in his endowment that could possibly extend to them, and so the like in many other instances.

5. That where there has been an usage in a parish for a long time that the vicar has received one species of small tithes either in one part of the parish or under one sort of husbandry or management but has never received any tithes for the same species in another part of the parish or under another sort of husbandry or management, when there have been such species of tithes there, that the vicar in such case cannot be said to have a right to such species of tithes throughout the parish or in any other manner than according as the usage has been it not being of common right that he should have all small tithes but such only and at such places, times, and manner as his endowment (which usage is the only evidence of) does entitle him to. And few vicarages were endowed *de omnibus minutis decimis* it being evident in fact that there are many, very many, if not far the greater part of the impropriations in England, the owners whereof, even bishops and other ecclesiastical persons as well as laymen and their lessees, receive many, and in some places all, the small tithes allowing the vicar only a stipend. And if by presumption [that] only the vicars must be intended to have all small tithes because they have some, such construction will shake many impropriations, which are become the inheritance of multitudes of laymen and the chief part of many ecclesiastical persons' revenues.

[Other copies of this report: GUL MS. B88–10, p. 783.]

[The decree of 23 July 1709, PRO E.126/19, f. 149, is printed at 1 Wood 518, 1 Eagle & Younge 694; see also order of 8 Dec. 1710: PRO E.126/19, f. 250.]

[Other reports of this case: Samuel Dodd's Reports, p. 224, 2 Gwillim 607, 1 Rayner 119.]

---

[3] Altarage, offerings made upon the altar, small tithes: C. T. Martin, *Record Interpreter* (1949), p. 184.

449

Anonymous (Ex. 1710)

Upon a bill for discovery and relief, if the defendant denies the plaintiff's right, the discovery need not be made until after the right be established.

HLS MS. 537, part 2, p. 153 [Eng.] (Eden's Reports)

A bill was [brought] to establish a toll and to seek discovery and relief. And the answer denied the right to the toll and made an insufficient discovery. Afterwards and upon exception[1] and argument upon it, it seemed to be the opinion of the court [that] where the right was denied, they were not obliged to discover, and that of tithes was a particular case. Query where the common right [is] against the defendant, but in other cases, it is enough to deny the right, for then they must go to [common] law and settle that, and then it will be proper to oblige them to a discovery. And it being opened as if a *nomine poena* attended the non p[ayment], [the] chief baron [WARD] questioned if [they were] at all obliged but then denied that there was any *nomine poena* in the case but as [a] fine. [It was ruled] by the court [to] let them go on to a hearing and agree to be examined upon interrogatories as to the quantities and values etc. And thus it was.

450

Anonymous (Ex. 1710)

The issue in this case was whether when a Protestant mortgagor redeems against a Roman Catholic mortgagee, the mortgagor pays the double land tax.

HLS MS. 537, part 2, p. 174 [Eng.] (Eden's Reports)

[In a case] where there was a Protestant [who] mortgaged lands to a Roman Catholic and the mortgage [was] forfeited and upon redemption and [it being] sent to an accounting, [the] question was whether he [the mortgagee] should be allowed only to [pay the] single land tax or the double land tax, for by the Act,[1] [it] is double for the papists.

The attorney [general] and the solicitor [general argued] that he ought not to be allowed anything that fell upon them by reason of any personal default of

---

[1] execucion MS.

---

[1] Stat. 4 Will. III & Mar. II, c. 1, s. 34 (*SR*, VI, 366).

his own, as if he should burn an house upon the premises down etc. But No. denied [?] he should [because] it was the mortgagor's fault [that] he did not redeem; his was the first.

But it seems [that] if [the] mortgagor [was] a Roman Catholic, [it would be] otherwise. Query if the [case was] not thus. But as Mr. Solicitor [General] put it to Howe at the Rolls the same day, it was *ut supra*, and Howe [was] very clear in [his] opinion with him.

451

Canning v. Clark (Ex. 1710)

Tithes are debts that are senior to debts due upon simple contracts.

BL MS. Add. 22610, f. 37v [Eng.] (Wright's Reports)

The plaintiff, being an impropriator, sued the defendant by English bill in the exchequer for certain tithes due in the time of a person deceased, whose administrator he is. [The] defendant answers that he has not assets above such a sum, out of which there are certain debts to be paid, *viz.* so much due upon [a] bond and so much upon [a] simple contract, beyond which he has no assets. The only question was whether monies due for tithes should be preferred in payment before simple contracts. And it was strongly urged that they ought, because tithes savor of the realty and tithes are now become a debt by the Statute of Edw. VI[1] etc. And the court decreed accordingly, that tithes are to be preferred in payment before simple contracts.

In debating this case, that of Orde v. Gifford[2] was mentioned, a case that has been depending in this court for five or six years last past, where the question was whether money due for tithes is to be preferred to a debt due upon [a] bond, and the point has not been yet determined.

[Orders of 21 Feb., 4 May, 6 and 15 June, and 27 Nov. 1710: PRO E.126/19, ff. 174v, 195, 213, 215v, 240v.]

---

[1] Stat. 2 & 3 Edw. VI, c. 13 (*SR*, IV, 55–58).
[2] *Ord v. Giffard* (1703–1707), PRO E.127/22, f. 165v; E.126/18, f. 464; E.127/26, f. 118.

452
Bernard v. Jenkins (Ex. 1711)

The children of a deceased uncle do not take equally with their uncles by representation as to the estate of their intestate cousin.

BL MS. Hargr. 71, f. 123, pl. 2 [Eng. & Fr.] (Dodd's Reports)

A bill [was] brought for the distribution of the nephew's estate. The court held that if [there were] three uncles and one died before the nephew, the intestate, and left issue, and then the nephew died, that the issue of the uncle would not come in for a share for [they were] not in equal degree with the uncles. And they will not carry the representation in collaterals further than uncles and aunts, and not to their children. But if the uncle had died after the nephew, then it had been an estate vested in him, and his executors should come in for his share. Raymond 496.[1]

[Other copies of this report: HLS MS. 537(b), p. 77, pl. 1; Oxf. Brasenose MS. 59, p. 98, pl. 3; IU Lilly MS. Parker, 'Cases in the Exchequer, vol. 2', p. 89, pl. 1; BL MS. Hargr. 70, p. 116, pl. 383; HLS MS. 1162, p. 98, pl. 529.]

[Order of 23 Jan. 1711: PRO E.127/28, f. 247.]

453
Wall v. Theedam (Ex. 1711)

The children of a decedent's deceased sisters share per capita including those of the half blood.

BL MS. Hargr. 71, f. 123v, pl. 1 [Eng.] (Dodd's Reports)

The bill was brought by the administratrix to have the account stated and to be directed in the distribution. Dr. [Samuel] Wall had two sisters, Elizabeth and Susanna; both died in his life time. Elizabeth left issue, Johanna Theedam, Mary, and Dorothy. Susanna being on the half blood left issue, Samuel Sumpter. And [it was] resolved that the widow shall have one moiety and that the four children of the deceased sisters should have the other moiety equally among them, each a fourth part, and not that Susanna's child should have as much as Elizabeth's three children, for all the old stock are gone, but if Susanna had survived, then she should have had an equal share with her sister Elizabeth's three children.

---

[1] *Carter v. Crawley* (1683), T. Raymond 496, 83 E.R. 259.

[Other copies of this report: HLS MS. 537(b), p. 77, pl. 3; Oxf. Brasenose MS. 59, p. 99, pl. 1; IU Lilly MS. Parker, 'Cases in the Exchequer, vol. 2', p. 90, pl. 1.]

[Order of 28 June 1711: PRO E.126/19, f. 298v.]

454
Freke v. Sundry (Ex. 1711)

An unsecured debt cannot be used to set off a secured debt in the absence of a specific agreement to that effect.

BL MS. Hargr. 71, f. 123v, pl. 3 [Eng.] (Dodd's Reports)

The court would not allow the plaintiff to discharge a bond debt due from the plaintiff by setting off simple contract debts due from the defendant without there were a special agreement. And an issue [was] directed for that purpose.

[Other copies of this report: HLS MS. 537(b), p. 77, pl. 5; Oxf. Brasenose MS. 59, p. 99, pl. 3; IU Lilly MS. Parker, 'Cases in the Exchequer, vol. 2', p. 90, pl. 3.]

[Order of 9 Feb. 1711: PRO E.127/28, f. 254v.]

455
Gibson v. Taylor (Ex. 1711)

A widow does not have dower rights in a leasehold or in the profits therefrom.

BL MS. Hargr. 71, f. 123v, pl. 4 [Eng.] (Dodd's Reports)

A. purchased a tenement in fee and took an assignment of a term standing out to a trust in trust to attend the inheritance and after makes a mortgage and dies. His executrix gets the mortgage and receives the rents. The heir at law brought his bill to redeem and to have an account of the profits and that the mortgage money might be paid out of the assets. The widow and executrix insisted to retain a third part of the profits for her dower. And [it was ruled] by the court:

1. She cannot do it for the term protects against dower, though it be not a term in gross but to attend the inheritance.
2. She had not recovered dower at [common] law.

Note [that] she is dowable because of the freehold and inheritance, but the profits [were] disposed of by the term. See My Lady Radnor and Vendibende's Case, Shower's *Reports*,[1] and the case there cited.

---

[1] *Countess of Radnor v. Vandebendy* (1697), Shower 69, 1 E.R. 48.

[Other copies of this report: HLS MS. 537(b), p. 78, pl. 1; Oxf. Brasenose MS. 59, p. 99, pl. 4; IU Lilly MS. Parker, 'Cases in the Exchequer, vol. 2', p. 91, pl. 1.]

[Order of 23 Jan. 1711: PRO E.127/28, f. 256v.]

456
Collingwood v. Bendlowes (Ex. 1711)

Where a mortgage is assigned without the privity of the mortgagor, the mortgagor, upon a bill for redemption, need not pay any sums payable under the assignment.

BL MS. Hargr. 71, f. 124, pl. 2 [Eng. & Fr.] (Dodd's Reports)

Foster lends £250 on a mortgage of an *interesse termini* of Holy Island in Northumberland to commence eight years after; no interest is paid by the mortgagor. Foster six years after assigns over his mortgage to one Collin Collingwood and receives both principal and interest. And three or four years after, the mortgagor brings a bill to redeem, and whether the mortgagor shall pay interest for the sum paid by Collin Collingwood to Foster or only interest for the principal then due was the question. And by three [barons] against PRICE, [it was ruled] that he should not pay interest for the money paid to Foster but only for the principal then due because the mortgagor [was] not [a] party to the assignment nor [was] the account settled by a court of equity. Note that it was an *interesse termini* and the mortgagee or his assignee could not enter etc.

[Other copies of this report: HLS MS. 1169(b), p. 78, pl. 3; Oxf. Brasenose MS. 59, p. 100, pl. 2; IU Lilly MS. Parker, 'Cases in the Exchequer, vol. 2', p. 92, pl. 1.]

[Orders of 13 Feb. and 29 June 1711: PRO E.126/19, ff. 260, 298v.]

[Affirmed on appeal *sub nom.* Potts v. Everard (1713): *Lords' Journal*, XIX (n.d.), p. 585.]

457
Attorney General ex rel. Barnardiston v. Butterworth (Ex. 1711)

The issue in this case was whether a bond for mesne profits covers such profits before the date of the bond.

LI MS. Misc. 538, f. [227] [Eng.] (Ward's Reports)

In April 27 Car. II [1675], an inquisition was taken upon an extent issued out of this court against [the] defendant Butterworth upon four bonds each of [the] penalty of £2200, which he entered into to the king, by which inquisition it was found that Butterworth at the times of the entering into of the said bonds and at the time of taking the said inquisition was seised of divers lands in Lancashire some in fee others for his life of the yearly value of [*blank*], which were all seized into the king's hands to be there held till the debts should be satisfied, some that the relatrix claims, and, having paid the crown's demands, obtained a lease and grant of those several debts and also of the extended premises from King Charles II and were in possession for some time and leased them to [the] defendant Butterworth under a yearly rent, which for seven years he duly paid, but, refusing to pay longer, some under whom [the] relatrix claims brought ejectments and, a fault being found in the grant by reason of a variance in it from the inquisition, those under whom the relatrix claims obtained another grant of the extended premises and of all the arrears of the rents and profits thereof *a tempore captionis earundem* into the hands of the crown, some years after which the defendant Holt claiming title to the premises by a pretended deed, said to be a trust for Butterworth made in [a] time precedent to the bonds, pleaded the same in discharge of the seizure and prayed upon giving security to perform the order of the court upon the determination of his plea touching the mesne profits of the premises there having several [writs of] *levari facias* issued before for the levying [of] the issues and profits of the lands *a tempore captionis earundem* into the king's hands to such a time mentioned in the writ, to which process the grantee was entitled by his grant in his aid and for his benefit. And £80 was levied as part of the mesne rates, there being divers other great sums incurred and leviable by like process. And in that respect the court, ordered that the security that should be given upon [the] putting in of that plea should be £1000, there being great arrears not levied. And thereupon the plea was received and further process [was] stayed till the determination of that plea or otherwise as the court should direct. And [the] defendant Butterworth was bound in that recognizance with Holt, the plea being a good plea at law as pleaded, though never insisted upon till then though made so long ago and the possession under the crown's grantee's lease and title submitted to and rents and profits answered and levied for divers years before by the process of this court without pretense of such title and the defendant Butterworth, for whom this lease was a trust, having been in possession and received the rents and profits and bound in the recognizance for the mesne profits. Yet the attorney general for the queen and [the] relatrix, without replying *per fraudem* or otherwise to the plea, exhibited his English bill or information against both the defendants.

And upon [the] hearing of the cause, it plainly appeared that the lease pleaded was fraudulent and, as such, the court set it aside and ordered [that] an account should be stated of the mesne rates of the premises in order to put the recognizance in suit for the recovery of them. And a question being moved how far backwards the state of the mesne rates should be computed and against whom the recognizance should be put in suit for the recovery of them, PRICE and LOVELL, barons, were of opinion that the recognizance should not be made use of for any mesne rates incurred before the giving of the recognizance though thereby all process for levying of them as well as what should incur after was stayed and that the recognizance should not be made use of against Butterworth but against the pleader Holt only, for whom (as they said) Butterworth was only a surety, though it plainly appeared in the cause [that] Butterworth was in possession and received all [of] the mesne rates all along and Holt was but his trustee.

But BURY and the chief baron [WARD] were of a contrary opinion and that the security ought to extend as well for the past arrears as for what shall incur after till the determination of the plea. For it is just and reasonable in itself as well as the constant practice and experience in the court that in all cases where a pleader gives security upon [the] putting in of his plea and thereby obtains a stay of the crown's process, that such security (especially in such a case as this is) must and ever hitherto has been made use of to make good all that might and could have been levied, if such security had not been given and process stayed, and the contrary never yet heard of for certainly the profits of the lands seized ever since the seizure have belonged to the crown and its grantee, and the crown might have maintained an information of intrusion or a suit for the mesne profits or levied them by *levari facias* and no process for the crown has been or ought to be stayed but upon security to make good all that could have been levied by such process. For otherwise the crown is rendered very insecure if the security shall extend only to the mesne rates incurred after the security whatever the arrears incurred before should be, for as to them that process that by law might and ought to have levied is stayed, for though if the plea prevails there is no loss to the crown. Yet where the plea does not prevail (as it did not in this case) the crown then has in effect lost all the mesne rates incurred before the security, for many times the lands are extended at such a yearly value that over and above the yearly rates for which such process must issue there may be nothing to be had above them for they must be levied *pro rata et juxta ratum temporis* and not otherwise. And this may be a precedent dangerous to the just rights of the crown, who is entitled to all the mesne rates incurred from the seizure and yet deprived of levying such as are incurred before security, which possibly were by negligence not looked after. And the experienced counsel and practicers were also of that opinion. And as to the exempting [of] Butterworth as being surety, he must, as all sureties do, undergo the sale of their principals, and in this case he himself was most concerned having received the profits all along.

So the court being divided, I [WARD] proposed that the chancellor [of the exchequer] should be desired to come to court as in like cases of the court's being divided has been usual and never opposed.[1] But the attorney general, for what

---

[1] *See* Bryson, *The Equity Side of the Exchequer*, pp. 44–45.

reason I could not understand, thought fit to give his consent in court and had it so entered that he did agree to take the account of the mesne rates incurred only since the security. And so it was ordered *me dissentiente*.

But in my opinion, it is a dangerous precedent for an attorney general to consent in effect that the securities in such a case should extend only to mesne rates incurred after the security and not before be they never so great and the crown never so long delayed or the matter concealed, but etc.

Note, a conveyance at law well pleaded and not replied unto [will be] set aside upon a bill in equity for the crown wherein the conveyance appeared and was proved to be fraudulent and a trust for the crown's debtor.

[Other copies of this report: GUL MS. B88–10, p. 858.]

[Orders of 15 May and 18 Nov. 1711: PRO E.126/19, ff. 283, 320.]

458

Cary v. Attorney General (Ex. 1711)

The issue in this case was whether a bill of interpleader lies where one of the competing claimants has not reduced his claim to a sum certain.

LI MS. Misc. 538, f. [232] [Eng.] (Ward's Reports)

Dodd, for [the] plaintiff, moves for an injunction upon bringing 2000 and odd pounds into court to stay two suits against him for that money, the one brought at law by the administrators and the other by English bill by the attorney general for the crown for the same money, Cary being only the hand that has it but claims no title to it, but is willing that such of them as have right to it should have it. And for that purpose he has brought his bill of interpleader and that upon bringing the money into court he may be at quiet, and [he] made the usual oath that he takes not part with either of [the] parties. And upon opposition to the motion, the case appeared to be thus. Colonel Coddrington the father and son, to whom William Coddrington is executor, were successively governors of Antigua and took and received many prizes and moieties for prizes due to the crown several years since, as charged by the attorney general's bill, and but lately discovered and for which the attorney general exhibits this bill against the plaintiff Cary for that money which was the estate and effects of the last Colonel Coddrington, who was as well executor of his father as also liable for prizes to the crown, and so follow that estate in the hands of [the] plaintiff as the estate of the son and assets of the son in [the] plaintiff's hands and liable to the crown. The administrators sue at law.

And the court was divided [as to] whether an injunction to stay both suits on [the] bringing in [of] the money or no, PRICE and LOVELL [were] against it because it does not appear that the crown has any claim against the Coddringtons but merely by allegation without any matter of record or office to charge them or either of them as accountants or otherwise, so that, till the crown's demand is reduced and established to a certainty, the attorney general's bill cannot affect the plaintiff nor the money or estate in his hands nor is a cause of interpleader or to stay the administrator's action.

But the chief baron [WARD] and BURY held that the attorney general is in a proper way to pursue the Coddringtons' personal estate in any person's hands to make it liable to the crown for what shall be due to it in the event of that suit. For whatever accountant to the crown dies, the crown may by law upon a *diem clausit extremum* seize his goods in specie and, if anybody has taken them, may pursue him for it. And this case admits no other pursuit but by bill, for every man that takes the king's goods even by wrong he is liable to account for the same upon a Latin or English information. [The Earl of] Devonshire's Case, 11 [Coke] Rep. 89a.[1] And it is contrary to law or reason to pretend that when an English information is depending that that is not a proper demand and prosecution though the debt or sum wherewith the accountant shall upon the upshot be found chargeable with, is not beforehand reduced to a certainty upon record, for that notion destroys in effect all informations, the exhibiting of which makes a *lis pendens*. And it is hard to say that the attorney general's information is not to be regarded as a proper suit for the crown unless there be some record of its demand, for by that at one stroke the crown's suits for moneys received *in pais* or for any part of the revenue cannot be maintained till some record be had, the consequence whereof is dangerous to the crown and never before objected to. And it is the first time that the merits of the cause between the two contending parties is looked into by the court or taken notice of by the plaintiff in the interpleading bill, his part being only to be at quiet and let him be free from each of their pretenses upon producing into court the matter in demand and leave it to those who [have the] right.

Query therefore the sense of denying the injunction and leaving an innocent man to be torn to pieces and subjected to two several suits without [a] remedy. For if the administrators should recover against the plaintiff at law, who can make no use of nor give in evidence for his defense anything of the crown title, and the attorney general carry on his suit and make it a cause of relief for the crown, the plaintiff may, nay must, be charged again for the same money though he claims no title to it but as in all like cases exhibits his bill of interpleader between the two claimers that he may be safe, which is the usual and natural equity and course in like cases.

[Other copies of this report: GUL MS. B88–10, p. 879.]

---

[1] *Earl of Devonshire's Case* (1607), 11 Coke Rep. 89a, 77 E.R. 1266.

459

Corporation of Warwick v. Lucas (Ex. 1711)

Where court costs are awarded to a defendant and the defendant dies before they are taxed, the defendant's administrator can have them taxed and paid.

LI MS. Misc. 538, f. [233], pl. 1 [Eng.] (Ward's Reports)

The plaintiffs exhibited an English bill for tithes against William Lucas. And the court thought fit upon [the] hearing to send it to a trial at law upon the Statute of 2 & 3 Edw. VI.[1] But the plaintiffs did not think fit to proceed to trial but rather to have their bill dismissed with moderate costs, which upon [a] hearing was done, and [it was] ordered by consent to be dismissed with moderate costs to be taxed by the deputy [queen's] remembrancer. But before the costs were taxed, the defendant died. And whether the costs were lost in this case or should be paid to the administratrix of William Lucas was the question, it being alleged by [the] plaintiff's counsel that by the rules of a court of equity that, if the party that is to have the costs die before [the] taxation of them, the costs are lost, and the like of costs in an ejectment where costs are to be paid by rule of court.

But the whole court was of opinion in this case that the administratrix was entitled to have the costs taxed and that the plaintiffs ought to pay the same by reason of the plaintiffs' consent to have their bill dismissed with moderate costs. And the judgment and direction of the court for the same and on producing the administration ordered the taxing of the same accordingly.

[Other copies of this report: GUL MS. B88–10, p. 883.]

[Orders of 23 May and 5 July 1710: PRO E.126/19, ff. 191, 221.]

[This case is cited in Aldermen of Bury St. Edmunds v. Evans (1739), 2 Rayner 364, 377, 2 Gwillim 757, 765, Comyns 643, 653, 92 E.R. 1249, 1253, 2 Eagle & Younge 72, 77.]

460

Harding v. Hoblyn (Ex. 1711)

In this case, the defendants were found in contempt of court for assaulting commissioners who were attempting to execute a writ of sequestration.

LI MS. Misc. 538, f. [233v] [Eng.] (Ward's Reports)

The defendants being charged by the affidavit of one Tubb for assaulting and beating him and others in the execution of a sequestration awarded for sequestering and seizing the goods and personal estate of Richard Hoblyn, the

---

[1] Stat. 2 & 3 Edw. VI, c. 13 (*SR*, IV, 55–58).

defendant Grace's husband, for the contempt of him and his wife in not appearing to the plaintiff's bill and answering the same directed to the said Tubb and others, the defendants appeared and upon their examinations denied the contempt charged upon them by Tubb's affidavit. And the plaintiff desiring a commission for examination of witnesses to prove the same, the court awarded it accordingly. And the defendants filed interrogatories and examined witnesses on their own behalfs without any order of court for that purpose, which is against the 33rd standing order and rule of court.[1] The plaintiff by six or seven plain and full witnesses proved the contempt of the defendants in assaulting and beating the commissioners and other persons whom they took to their assistance in the execution of the said sequestration and rescuing the goods seized and sequestered. And though the defendants' examinations were irregularly taken contrary to the standing rules of the court, yet the court did not suppress the same as might have been done but permitted the same to be read, which being altogether immaterial as to the matter of the contempt (though they contained about two hundred sheets) pretending to draw in question the property of the goods which at first they were offered to put in their claim to but refused it, the goods being in [the] defendants' house and possession, the court adjudged the defendants to be in contempt and to stand committed till they satisfied the court touching their misdemeanor and paid the prosecutor his costs according to the 40th standing rule of the court.[2] And the defendants being in Cornwall, the court awarded process to fetch them into the court to make fine to the queen for their contempt. And the recognizance given upon the contempt to be sued [. . .] by that 40th rule the affidavit of one person for the beating and abusing of any in the executing or serving the process or order of the court is sufficient for bringing the party into contempt and no examination in that case to be allowed.

In this case, a question was started that if there be three or more that make affidavit of the fact in order to have an attachment, whether, though they all tend to prove the fact that one of them only was beaten, the others may be again examined upon the commission as witnesses to prove the contempt. But that not happening to be the fact in this case, the court gave no opinion in it but thought the testimony of such as were witnesses only to prove the beating of the others should not be lost but either their affidavits or examinations should be made use of. Therefore it may not be necessary to produce the affidavits of more than one person to prove the beating and reserve the testimony of the others to be examined as witnesses in case the party denies the contempt upon his examination.

[Other copies of this report: GUL MS. B88–10, p. 885.]

[Order of 23 Feb. 1711: PRO E.127/28, f. 227.]

---

[1] Rule 33, *Ordines Cancellariae* (1698), p. 38.

[2] Rule 40, *id.*, p. 40.

461
Stewart v. Worsely (Ex. 1711)

A pernor of profits in equity cannot commit waste.
  In this case, it was the testatrix's intention that the land in question not be plowed.
  Even if the plowing of the land in question be not waste at common law, it would be prejudicial to the remaindermen and it was enjoined.

LI MS. Misc. 538, f. [236v] [Eng.] (Ward's Reports)

The case upon the bill, answer, and proofs appeared to be this, [on] 22 October 1692, Sir Nicholas Steward and [*blank*] his wife being, or one of them being, seised in fee of a messuage and farm called Tarrant Hinton in the County of Dorset consisting of 320 acres of arable, thirty-one of meadow, twenty of pasture, and of five hundred acres of downs being pasture for sheep, of which downs 250 acres, called East Down solely appertained to that farm, and in the other 250 acres called West Down other persons intercommoned with their sheep together with the sheep of the owners or tenants of the said farm, and being so seised by deed and fine conveyed the same to the defendant Smith and one Lane (since deceased) and their heirs to the uses and upon the trusts following, *viz.* of Sir Nicholas for his life then to the use of the trustees and their heirs in trust to dispose, convey, and settle the same as the lady during her life by deed or will with three witnesses should during coverture or being sole dispose or direct and in default thereof to stand seised in trust for the lady and her heirs. The lady by her will or writing purporting to be her will (and according to the power and trust in the deed) dated the 12th of June 1699 dire[cts] that the trustees shall stand seised in trust to permit the defendant Worsely to receive the rents, issues, and profits of the premises for eight years next after the death of her and of Sir Nicholas, if the defendant lives so long, and made the defendant Smith executor and died in the life time of Sir Nicholas, who, surviving her, died about two years since. And by the same will she devised and directed [that] the trustees should after the said term of eight years was determined permit and suffer the now plaintiff during his life to receive the rents, issues, and profits of the premises, and after his death to permit and suffer the first and other sons of the plaintiff in tail male to receive the rents, issues, and profits of the premises successively, and in [the] failure thereof the plaintiff and his heirs in tail general to do the like.

Four days after the date of the will, *viz.* the 16th of June 1699, the lady by a writing under her hand and seal but without any witnesses to it made it her request to the trustees to take security from the defendant Worsely and all others that they should permit to receive the profits of the trusted premises, not to cut timber, or commit waste by [the] plowing of [the] land which ought not [to] be plowed or broken up during the time they shall receive the profits thereof.

Presently after the commencement of the term for eight years, Worsely entered upon the premises and prepared to plow fifty acres of the East Down by [the] burnbeaking of it first, which is a term and way used in that county and in the west of England of cutting and getting off of the sward of the grass ground pretty thick and burning it in heaps upon the land and spreading it thereupon and then to plow and sow the land with such grain as shall be thought fit. And [the] defendant Worsely giving out that he would burnbeake and plow all the rest of East Down and the trustees not having taken any security from him as the lady desired, the plaintiff exhibited his bill against the defendants to restrain the defendant Worsely from burnbeaking or plowing any more, he being only a pernor of the profits in equity not having any estate in law in him, such burnbeaking and plowing being a manifest destruction to the land and in effect a total deprivation to all others that come after him from making or receiving any profit from the land and render the keeping of sheep upon those downs which go there and are used in a course of husbandry necessary for maintaining the arable part of the farm with the folding of them and comprestring the land with the sheep's dung, which otherwise cannot be managed to the reasonable and usual benefit of the farm, and as being against the lady's intent and to the ruin of the farm as to all succession.

The defendant, Smith, submitted to the direction of the court. But the defendant, Mr. Worsely, by answer confessed the conveyances, will, and note, before set forth, but insisted upon his right that he may burnbeake and plow alleging that it is no waste nor prejudice to the farm nor more than what a pernor of profits in his condition may lawfully do, and that if the land be plowed three years and laid down with grass [se]eds sown upon it, it will come to grass and be better than at first, and that some of this was formerly plowed.

Pending the suit, the defendant plowed eighteen acres of the fifty, to which the injunction formerly granted did not extend to restrain, but in effect by consent had leave to plow them eighteen acres for this crop with wheat. And the cause coming finally to be heard this day (after [a]ll overtures of accommodation between plaintiff and defendant, Worsely, who are near relations, proving ineffectual) after long debate and hearing the proofs and counsel on both sides, the court *seriatim* delivered their opinions. All the four barons agreed that the injunction formerly [gran]ted for restraining the defendant from burnbeaking or plowing any more of the downs (except the said eighteen acres and that for this crop only) should be continued during the said term of eight years, and that principally upon these grounds and reasons.

First that as well by the common and reasonable import of the words 'rents, issues, and profits' of the farm to be taken by Mr. Worsely, who has no estate in law in the said farm but is a mere pernor of the profits of it in equity, as by a reasonable and equitable construction of the will, no more was or can be supposed or intended nor have than the common and usual profits arising by the common and usual management of the farm as it was at and before the time of the commencement of the defendant's interest of eight years.

Secondly because it appears to be the lady's intent and meaning and is the import of the will that the plaintiff and his children successively for their interests after the determination of the defendant's term of eight years (which is determinable sooner by his death) should have the profits of the farm in as full and ample manner as the defendant was to have them, which is impossible to be so if the downs should be plowed up, for then the whole herbage and feed for sheep (the constant use the downs were always put to) must necessarily be destroyed, for grass w[ill] not grow in many years after plowing, the strength and heart of the ground being worn out and exhausted by plowing, and thereby not only the future profits but also the course of management of that farm in keeping sheep upon the downs for the fold of them upon the arable land of the farm would be lessened and inverted, such keeping downs for sheep for such folding being the constant method of managing like farms throughout the whole country.

Thirdly that though this plowing should not prove in strictness of law to be waste for which the defendant could be punished as such, yet in regard [that] the plaintiff is not in a capacity to maintain such action and is by such plowing equally prejudiced and the act done by the defendant as equally prejudicial to the inheritance as if it was in law waste, the defendant ought not in such case be allowed to do an unwarrant[ed] thing prejudicial in the necessary consequence to the plaintiff but to be restrained from it in equity. For where there is [a] tenant for life, remainder for life, remainder in fee, though the remainderman in fee cannot bring an action of waste against the first tenant for life, yet he may have an injunction in equity against him to stay waste. And this plowing here is in equal mischief and therefore ought to have equal relief with waste and may well be called destruction. And though no great stress is to be laid upon the lady's desire to her trustee for taking security not to commit waste by plowing land which ought not to be plowed, that sufficiently explained h[er] intentions that nothing should be done by any pernor of profits to the injury of the farm. And when the desired security should be taken, she certainly intended the thing should not be done, and there is no way to restrain it but in equity.

Fourthly as it is apparent in the nature of the thing that the plowing is a manifest wrong to the far[m], so it appears by many witnesses to be so. And what the defendants chiefly aimed at by his witnesses was to show that, if these downs were plowed three years and laid down with seed grass, that the grass will soon return and be better pasture than before and an advantage to the farm, the herbage now being worth not above 8d. or 12d. an acre. But the plaintiff's witnesses proved that it would be 40s. a year by damage to the reversioners to have the fifty acres plowed and though sown with seed grass that will last but three years and then worsted after. But considering that the defendant has but a term and that determinable upon his life and so but an uncertain and contingent interest which may soon determine after plowing, and that the court has no power to enforce the defendant to sow it with grass seeds, nor is he [in] any way obliged to do so, but that the plowing up [of] the downs is a manifest prejudice of the farm in succession and the supposed [r]ecompense at best but contingent and arbitrary, the court continued the injunction *ut supra*.

Ettrick, Stevens, and others [were] for the plaintiff.

Serjeant Pratt, Dodd, Turner, and Ward [were] for the defendant.

From this decree the defendant appealed to the Lords in Parliament, which was heard the 4th of March 1711[/12] and [the] appeal [was] dismissed and [the] decree [was] affirmed without a question or so much as one negative.[1]

[Other copies of this report: GUL MS. B88–10, p. 897.]

[Orders of 25 Oct. and 29 Nov. 1711: PRO E.126/19, ff. 322, 324v.]

462

Mathews v. Hayter (Ex. 1712)

In this case, the defendant was ordered to pay tithes in kind.

LI MS. Misc. 539, f. [3v] [Eng.] (Ward's Reports)

The plaintiff, vicar of Steyning in Sussex, entitled to all tithes, great and small (except corn and grain only), sues the defendant for the tithes of hay and other small tithes for three years ended 1706 arising upon three farms, called Nash Farm, Dixon's Farm, and Staplefield Farm. [The] defendant insisted upon a *modus* of £3 10s. 00d. for Nash's Farm, which was of the yearly value of about 75n. at this time and upon another *modus* of £3 6s. 8d. for the other two farms, which he alleged to be parcel of a great farm or demesne of the manor of Wappenthorne [of the] value £60 *per annum*, and then insists thus, for which farm or manor or demesne lands belonging to it, there has been time out of mind paid and payable to the vicar a *modus* of £3 6s. 8d. in lieu of all tithes due to the vicar yearly. The vicar's tithes if paid in kind for all came to £4 3s. 6d. yearly or near thereabouts. There was not any proof that ever any tithes was in memory of any man living paid in kind, but by reputation these moduses had been esteemed due, and [there was] some proof that the last of them had been paid and receipts had been given by one or two of [the] plaintiff's predecessors in the years 1692, 1693, and 1694, none earlier or later being produced and they only for the *modus* of Wappenthorne lands in Steyning and the first for Wappenthorne and

---

[1] *Worsley v. Stuart* (1712), 4 Brown 377, 2 E.R. 255, *Lords' Journal*, XIX (n.d.), p. 393.

Staplefield. [There was] no proof of payment of [a] *modus* for Nash Farm save only by hearsay.

And in this case, the court unanimously decreed the defendants to account for his tithes notwithstanding such pretense the moduses being so near to the value of the tithes in kind. The court looked upon [them] to be rather compositions than moduses time out of mind, being so big and large. And as to the *modus* of £3 6s. 8d., it was so uncertainly alleged in respect of Dixon's and Staplefield, which were said to be parcel of a great farm or demesne of the manor of Wappenthorne, for which farm or manor or demesne land belonging to it that *modus* was paid, so that there was no certainty for what it was, for which reasons the court decreed *ut supra* without any trial at law but without prejudice.

[Other copies of this report: GUL MS. B88–10, p. 921.]

[Order of 19 May 1712: PRO E.126/19, f. 364.]

463

Hilton v. Lambton (Ex. 1712)

The use of navigable rivers is free to the general public.
The operation of a ferry cannot obstruct navigation on a navigable river.

LI MS. Misc. 539, f. [75] [Eng.] (Ward's Reports)

[The] plaintiffs have [a] right to a ferry over the river Wear in Durham, which for convenience they manage with a rope from one side to the other across the river, which rope hanging high would not permit the keels carrying coals down the river to the staiths for exportation to pass under the rope without striking their masts etc., which was a work that required two men to do. And therefore the defendants cut the rope that obstructed navigation down the river. And upon affidavit made of the long possession and use of that rope, the plaintiffs prayed an injunction to quiet them in such possession of it as they had at the time of their bill and three years before.

And day being granted to the defendants to show cause against the injunction, upon reading many affidavits whereby it appeared that the rope hanging across the river where the ferry was much obstructed the freedom of the navigation of that great navigable river, which is free for all to navigate upon of common right, and that though the owner of the ferry may use a rope across the river yet that must not hinder the navigation down the river nor bring a charge or trouble upon those that do not use that ferry, it being sworn here that the plaintiffs demand a sum for passing under their rope, which seems to be unwarrantable, navigable rivers being, like common highways, free to all, and so no injunction was granted but [the] former order [was] discharged.

[Other copies of this report: GUL MS. B88–10, p. 960.]

464

Conning v. Menzies (Ex. 1712)

A freeman of London can devise over the orphanage part of his children where a son dies before twenty-one and where a daughter dies before twenty-one or marriage.

I
LI MS. Misc. 539, f. [80] [Eng.] (Ward's Reports)

The case upon hearing appeared to be thus, one George Conning (who was not a freeman of London) upon his marriage with the defendant Elizabeth for himself and the said Elizabeth, and another trustee for her entered into articles before marriage that in [the] case of his death his personal estate should go and remain in the same manner and to such persons as a freeman of London's personal estate should go by [the] custom of London in case of his death, and that [the] defendant Elizabeth and such child and children as should be born between them should have their shares and parts of it as in [the] case of a freeman. George Conning by his will gives all his personal estate in moieties, *viz.* one moiety to his wife, the defendant, the other moiety to A. his only child between them (being a son), and if that son died before twenty-one, then that moiety to go to the plaintiffs. The testator died, and after him the child died before twenty-one. And whether this devise over was good by the custom of London or that the defendant, the mother, as administratrix to the child should have it was the question.

And the court having ordered a case to be made and signed by counsel of both sides and that it should be referred to the court of aldermen of the City of London to certify (by the mouth of the recorder) what the custom of London was in that case where a freeman dies leaving only one child and a wife, whether in such case he might devise the orphanage part of the child (in case of his death before twenty-one) to any other or not.

And this day *Sir Peter King*, recorder of London, produced a certificate under the hands of the lord mayor and all the court of aldermen and of himself and thereby as also by himself *ore tenus*. It was certified that by the custom of London a freeman thereof having one only child under the age of twenty-one years being a male, or under twenty-one years and before marriage being a female, such freeman may by the custom devise over such part of his estate which by that custom is to come to such child or orphan, in case such child being male shall die before twenty-one or female before twenty-one or marriage, to any person whatsoever. And the court, taking themselves to be bound by this certificate that the custom is so, decreed the defendants to account for the child's orphanage part devised over to the plaintiffs (being near of kin to the testator), notwithstanding the defendant's administration to him, and to be examined upon interrogatories for discovery thereof since answer but without costs, the articles of agreement before marriage setting the parties to it, in the same condition in equity as in case of a freeman of London though he was none.

Note, as this case is certified, if the only child being a son shall marry before twenty-one and die before that age and leave wife and children, yet by this custom such wife or children are excluded from having any part or share of the husband and father's orphanage part, which may seem an hard case upon the son that if he marries and dies before twenty-one his part may be devised away, and yet if the female orphan marries under twenty-one, her orphanage part cannot be devised over. And yet by the custom they both have their shares vested in them, for by the custom and it is commonly accepted that a freeman's will cannot alter the proportions settled by the custom, which is in [the] case of [a] wife and child or children a third to the wife, a third to the children, and a third called the death's part to be disposed as the freeman pleases by will or to go to his legal representatives.

See 1 Levinz 227, Hamond and Jones.[1] 1 Chancery Reports 199, May 5th, 23 Car. II [1671], in Pate and Hutton's Case,[2] Lord Keeper Bridgman decreed the devise over in case of the death of an orphan son before twenty-one to be void and that his part should go to his administrator. 2 Ventris 341, in Phesant's Case,[3] the devise over [was] not good, being only a possibility and a thing not vested in himself.

And the saying of Wild, recorder, in Hamond and Jones's Case, 1 Levinz 227, went only to the custom that the father might devise over the part of one of his children dying before twenty-one among the surviving children, but says nothing further, and that made a query; the recorder in the principal case was of counsel for the plaintiffs here. And afterwards he assured me they had multitudes of cases and precedents which justified their certificate above. I perceived the distinction between [a] son and daughter seemed to be that the son could not marry before twenty-one without the city's consent no more can the daughter, and if she did so, yet her part [is] not devisable over. And why should the son's be, and his wife and children [be] defeated?

[Other copies of this report: GUL MS. B88–10, p. 975.]

---

[1] *Hamond v. Jones* (1667), 1 Levinz 227, 83 E.R. 381.
[2] *Pate v. Hatton* (1671), 1 Chan. Rep. 199, 22 E.R. 760.
[3] *Phesant v. Pheasant* (1670), 2 Ventris 340, 86 E.R. 475.

II
BL MS. Hargr. 71, ff. 122v, 124 [Fr. & Eng.] (Dodd's Reports)

Upon the marriage of Coning, the testator, he by deed reciting that he was not a freeman of London yet covenanted that his wife and the issue by her should have such shares as if he had been a freeman. He had issue, one son, and made his will and devised one moiety of his estate to his wife and the other to his son, but if the son died before twenty-one, then he devised that moiety to his nephew and his brother. And he died. [Then] the son died before six years of age. The wife, having proved the will and taken administration to the son, insisted that the devise of the orphan's share over was void and that it ought to go according to the Act of Distributions.[4]

Upon debate, [it was] agreed that the indenture or deed made the testator *quasi* a freeman to this purpose that by the custom the wife had one third, the child one other third, and the rest was testamentary, that the testator's share was well devised to the wife and son, and that of that share, the devise over was good. But as to the devise over of the son's share, the court doubted and ordered a case to be made but inclined against the devise. See 2 Ventr. 341; 1 Levinz 227.[5] See the breviate.

Upon a treaty of marriage by an unfreeman, it was agreed that his estate should go as if he were a freeman. He had one child. The father devises that if this child (being a son) should die before age, that his share should go to the plaintiff etc. And upon hearing the cause and a reference to the lord mayor and aldermen, Sir Peter King, the recorder, certified the custom to be (having a writing signed by the mayor and aldermen) that if a citizen have a son or a daughter, he may devise that part of such only child, if a son and [he] die before twenty-one, if a daughter and she die before age or marriage, to J.S., and the court decreed accordingly.

But the chief baron [WARD] seemed dissatisfied with the custom and objected [that] suppose the son were married and had children and died before twenty-one, what should become of them? But sure that was not the present case, for perhaps the custom might then be for the benefit of his wife and children, but the case in question was upon a single point of a son dying unmarried before twenty-one. See 1 Rolle 557[6] [and] my notes.

[Other copies of this report: HLS MS. 537(b), pp. 76, 78; Oxf. Brasenose MS. 59, pp. 98, 100; IU Lilly MS. Parker, 'Cases in the Exchequer, vol. 2', p. 87, 91.]

[Order of 17 Nov. 1712: PRO E.126/20, f. 17.]

---

[4] Stat. 22 & 23 Car. II, c. 10 (*SR*, V, 719–720).

[5] *Phesant v. Pheasant* (1670), 2 Ventris 340, 86 E.R. 475; *Hamond v. Jones* (1667), 1 Levinz 227, 83 E.R. 381.

[6] 1 Rolle, Abr., *Customs of London*, pl. N, p. 557.

465
Keddington v. Simpson (Ex. 1713)

A parishioner can contract with his parson to retain tithes for one year but not for a longer period of time.

LI MS. Misc. 539, f. [133] [Eng.] (Ward's Reports)

The plaintiff being lessee by deed of the tithes of a rectory from the rector exhibited his bill for tithes due to him from the defendant within the time of his lease. The defendant put in his plea to the bill and pleaded that, before the making of the plaintiff's lease, the plaintiff's lessor had made an agreement or composition with him by parol that upon such terms the defendant should for three years have and retain his tithes to his own use. And *Ettrick* endeavored to make it out that such parol agreement for three years to retain his tithes was good and prevented the plaintiff's title by his lease. The court, as the law stands, admitted the agreement to retain for one year good but no longer, and this being for three years was void.

The authorities cited by *Ettrick* were Yelverton 94, 95; 2 Croke 668; Rolle's [Abr.], title *Grants*, 63, N, 18; 2 Leonard 29; Hetley 107, 122; Noy 121; 2 Brownlow 11.[1] But none of these maintain a parol retainer longer than one year, and it has been often ruled in this court that it is not good longer than where made only for one year. Besides this is not a matter for plea, or if it was, it was not formally pleaded, and so it was overruled as a plea (though he had answered to quantities and values) and to stand for an answer with liberty to except and defendant to pay 20s. costs.

See Ludlam and Moore, above, f. [129v].[2]

[Other copies of this report: GUL MS. B88–10, p. 1101.]

[Further proceedings: *sub nom.* Keddington v. Adamson (Ex. 1716), 2 Gwillim 611, 2 Wood 47; *sub nom.* Keddington v. Bridgman, 1 Rayner 132, Bunbury 2, 145 E.R. 574, 1 Eagle & Younge 709.]

---

[1] *Hawkes v. Brothwith* (1606), Yelverton 94, 95, 80 E.R. 64, also Cro. Jac. 137, 79 E.R. 119, Hobart 176, 80 E.R. 322, 1 Eagle & Younge 165; *Wheatley v. Low* (1623), Cro. Jac. 668, 79 E.R. 578; 2 Rolle, Abr., *Graunts*, pl. G, 18, p. 63; *Woodward v. Bugg* (1588), 2 Leonard 29, 74 E.R. 331, 1 Eagle & Younge 99, also 3 Leonard 257, 74 E.R. 669, Owen 103, 74 E.R. 931, Cro. Eliz. 188, 249, 78 E.R. 444, 504; *Stone v. Walsingham* (1628), Hetley 107, 122, 124 E.R. 379, 392, 1 Eagle & Younge 367, also Littleton 155, 124 E.R. 184; *Small's Case* (c. 1607), Noy 121, 74 E.R. 1085; *Robotham v. Trevor* (1611), 2 Brownl. & Golds. 11, 123 E.R. 786.

[2] *Ludlam v. Moore* (1713), LI MS. 539, f. [127]; GUL MS. B88–10, p. 1084, also Samuel Dodd's Reports, p. 232.

466
Beale v. Hacking (Ex. 1713)

The executor of a defendant must pay court costs that had been taxed against his decedent. Court costs are taxed as a matter of course without any order for them.

LI MS. Misc. 539, f. [133v] [Eng.] (Ward's Reports)

The testator's bill was dismissed, and thereupon the defendant to that bill had £62 costs regularly taxed after which and before they were paid or the testator served with any process for the same, the testator died and made the defendant here his executor. And by motion in court a subpoena in the nature of a *scire facias* was awarded to the executor to show cause why he should not pay those costs so taxed in [the] testator's life and not paid. The executor at the return of the subpoena *scire facias* comes and puts in a formal Latin plea that there was not any record in the court which warranted or manifested the taxation of those costs. And upon the defendant's counsel's motion in court, that plea was set aside as a novelty and frivolous, for, upon the dismission of a plaintiff's bill, the costs go of course without any order or decree for them, and they being taxed by a bill that is the foundation of the subpoena, and the executor if [he does] not pay upon affidavit, an attachment issues, if he shows not good cause against it, which never was by any Latin plea, especially of *nul tiel record*, in such a case. And the executor perceiving the opinion of the court, agreed to pay the costs forthwith being so advised by Sir Peter King, recorder of London, his counsel.

[Other copies of this report: GUL MS. B88–10, p. 1106.]

467
Buckingham v. Pycroft (Ex. 1713)

A bill in equity lies to recover for dilapidations to a parsonage from the former parson's executor.

BL MS. Hargr. 71, f. 124v, pl. 1 [Eng. & Fr.] (Dodd's Reports)

The plaintiff is incumbent of the rectory of Ditchingham in Norfolk, and the defendant is executor of Mr. Pycroft, the last incumbent. The bill in equity is for dilapidations in the time of the testator. In the testator's will, there is a devise of lands subjected to the payment of debts (the personal estate not being sufficient). And upon [the] hearing, the court held jurisdiction and directed an issue to try the amount of the dilapidations; the equitable assets showed a bill necessary. But as to the jurisdiction, the court did not seem to difference it. Note there was cited a bill dismissed for dilapidations in Chief Baron Mountagu's time, and a demurrer [was] allowed in a former time. But in the present case, Chief Baron WARD [was] strongly for the bill and [the] jurisdiction; it was argued that no action at [common] law lay, *quod mirum*. And see Degge 97; 3 Levinz 268, 413; Lutwyche 118.[1] See the breviate.

[Other copies of this report: HLS MS. 537(b), p. 78, pl. 4; Oxf. Brasenose MS. 59, p. 100, pl. 3; IU Lilly MS. Parker, 'Cases in the Exchequer, vol. 2', p. 92, pl. 2; BL MS. Hargr. 70, p. 117, pl. 385; HLS MS. 1162, p. 99, pl. 531.]

[Orders of 24 Feb. and 17 Nov. 1713: PRO E.126/20, ff. 33v, 97v.]

[This case was cited in Bankes v. Rye (Ex. 1686), above, No. 224.]

468
Lady Campbell v. Lady Buckly (Ex. 1714)

A jointress is not compellable to produce deeds unless the heir first confirm her jointure.
An infant cannot waive a penalty given by statute.
Discovery will not be ordered where it may result in a forfeiture for committing waste.

IT MS. Mitford 32, p. 345 [Eng.]

[A] jointress [is] not compellable to produce deeds unless the heir first confirm her jointure.

The end of the bill was to discover and have produced to the use of the infant all the deeds and writings relating to a certain estate, formerly belonging to Sir T. Lort, the defendant's first husband, to whom the infant plaintiff is heir at law, and likewise to have an account of waste already done by the defendant (being jointress of the said lands) and to have an injunction to stay waste for the future.

To the first part of the bill the defendants plead that the lady is seised for life by [a] settlement made by Sir T. Lort precedent to the marriage and insist that, as a jointress and purchaser for valuable consideration, she is not compellable by the course of the court or any court of equity to produce the deeds relating to the estate unless the plaintiff do first confirm to her her jointure and the infant in this case not being in a capacity to confirm or to be decreed to confirm, therefore etc.

[An] infant cannot waive a penalty given by statute.

---

[1] S. Degge, *Parson's Counsellor* (1676), p. 79; *Jones v. Hill* (1690), 3 Levinz 268, 83 E.R. 683; *Okes v. Ange* (1695), 3 Levinz 413, 83 E.R. 757; *Kingford v. Lloyd* (1695), 1 Lutwyche 117, 118, 125 E.R. 62.

To the other part of the bill praying [an] injunction and account of the waste offering to waive the double penalty given by the statute,[1] the defendant demurred and showed for cause that there were others in remainder that ought to have been parties to the suit and also that the infant could not waive the penalty given him by the statute nor would the court oblige him by decree so to do so the defendant might be doubly charged.

All the court held that the defendant, being a jointress, was not compellable to produce the deeds nor to bring them into court to be kept for the infant's use (though the plaintiff did not desire sight of them), unless the plaintiff did in the first place confirm her jointure, for by so doing she might discover some dormant entail which might destroy her jointure and, till that was secured, no court of equity would compel her. Now the plaintiff in this case being an infant, his confirmation would neither bind him nor, in case he died, those that should claim under him, therefore the court allowed the plea.

As to the demurrer, the court likewise allowed it for that, since the infant has the inheritance, he may have an action of waste afterwards notwithstanding he should now waive the double forfeiture, for such waiver would not bind him. And as to the account of what is past, he has his remedy for the trees felled by action of trover.

Query why the demurrer was allowed as to granting the injunction, for an injunction is often granted to stay waste where no action of waste lies as in case of an intermediate remainder for life interposing between the particular estate in possession and the inheritance, as was said by Baron BANISTER.

[Orders of 26 Jan. and 12 Feb. 1714: PRO E.127/30, ff. 74v, 128v.]

[Related cases: Lady Campbell v. Lort (Ex. 1708), above, No. 429.]

469

Fellon's Case (Ex. 1714)

In this case, the issue was whether a married woman is liable for court costs in a suit to enforce her own rights.

IT MS. Mitford 32, p. 347 [Eng.]

Mr. *Littleton* moved to discharge her [Mary Fellon] out of custody, [she] being taken up and imprisoned for costs of suit by attachment out of this court. And [he] produced an affidavit that she was a married woman and that her husband was in jail (but [it was] not said for these costs). His motion was opposed

---

[1] Stat. 6 Edw. I, c. 5 (*SR*, I, 48).

by [*blank*] who said the costs were given upon the dismissal of a bill brought by her and her husband in this court for her jointure and thereupon an attachment was taken out against both as is usual and, the husband not being found, the wife was arrested.

Chief Baron WARD, PRICE, and BURY thought she ought to be discharged, as a married woman in the eye of the law has not [the] wherewith[al] to pay.

But BANISTER said he thought that not the reason why in many cases married women are discharged out of custody, for if so, then it would extend to all cases which it is certain it does not, as in battery against husband and wife, where she is found guilty, she may be taken in execution, and this attachment is an execution.

And the clerks being asked of the practice said they took it that where the suit is for the wife's right, she is liable to costs, whereupon the deputy [queen's remembrancer] was ordered to inquire how the practice is in chancery.

Index of Persons and Places

[These references are to case numbers, not page numbers.]

Adams, Dorothy Rogers, 378
Albemarle, duke of, Christopher, 376
Albemarle, duke of, George Monck, 312, 376
Aldington, Kent, 240, 385
Aldwells, nr. Ludlow, Shrops., 104
Annandale, earl of, 45
Antigua, 384
Appletree Hundred, Derbyshire, 325
Arlington, lord, Henry, 198
Ascham, Notts., 343
Ashbury, Berks., 35
Ashley Farm, 97
Ashton, John, 222
Aspin, Elizabeth Gilborne, 303
Aspinwall, Edward, 187
Aspinwall, Eleanor Ireland, 187
Astly Manor, Worcs., 69
Austin, Sir John, 131
Austin, William, 323
Aveley, Essex, 348
Avenbury, Heref., 393

Barbon, Dr. Nicholas, 250
Barkham, Sir Edward, 115
Barlow, Ann, 291
Barnaby upon Dun, Yorks., 294
Barrow, Dr. Isaac, 248

Barton, Bucks., 424
Barton Seagrave, Northants., 380
Bateman, Sir William, 55, 188
Bath, earl of, 312
Bath Priory, Somerset, 350
Bathford, Somerset, 350
Bax, Mary, 180
Belchamp St. Paul, Essex, 202
Benion, Sir George, 31
Bennet, Simon, 141
Bennet, Sir Henry, 198
Bentworth, Hants., 244
Berkeley, lord, 198
Berkeley, lord, Maurice, 262
Berkeley, Robert Rowland, 387
Bermondsey Abbey, Kent, 310
Bertie, Sir Peregrine, 270
Betts, John, 277
Blanchard, Robert, 355
Bloxham, Oxon., 169
Bold, Grace, 269
Bosomworth Farm, Yorks., 388
Boston, Lincs., 415
Boston Bissett, Bucks., 424
Botham, Sussex, 327
Botham's Creek, Sussex, 327
Boulton Mill, 25
Brailsford, Derbyshire, 325

Brain, Henry, 101
Brainford, Mddx., 328
Brattle, Sir John, 284
Brebendend, Bucks., 424
Bridlington Monastery, Yorks., 405
Bristol, 74, 101
Brockhalls, Yorks., 123
Bromfleet, Yorks., 362
Bromhall, Thomas, 427
Bromyard, Heref., 235
Broughton, Oxon., 361
Bryosa, William de, 262
Bucklawry, Cornwall, 341
Builth, Brecon, 420
Burgh, Edward, 349
Burghill, Heref., 438
Burwell, Francis, 122
Butler, Katherine Hill, 180
Byerly, Anne, 256
Byland Abbey, 388

Cadiz, Spain, 117
Camberwell, Surrey, 310
Carteret, Sir George, 171
Caryll, Sir John, 267
Cattens, Yorks., 419
Cawkerdale Farm, Yorks., 388
Chalgrave Manor, 320
Chalk, Kent, 434
Challinor, Thomas, Abbot, 29
Charlbury, Oxon., 236
Charlton, Sir Job, 104
Charnock, Robert, 269
Chase Valet, Heref., 407
Chatsworth, Derbyshire, 418
Chelwood, Bucks., 424
Chesterton, Cheshire, 432

Chichele, Sir Thomas, 73
Chichester, Sussex, 327
Chiddingfold, Surrey, 365
Chigwell, Essex, 100
Child, Sir William, 259
Christ's Church Priory, 383
Church, Anthony, 427
Cinque Ports, Kent, 154
Cirencester, Glos., 262
Cirencester Abbey, Glos., 262
Clare College, Cambridge, 342
Clare, earl of, Gilbert, 334
Clare Market, Mddx., 334
Clayton, Sir Robert, 328
Clere, Sir Edward, 297
Cleveland, earl of, 61
Cockersand Abbey, Lancs., 102
Coddrington, William, 458
Cogger, William, 332
Cold Ashton, Glos., 95
Comb and Harnham, Wilts., 189
Comb Bisset, Wilts., 189
Constantinople, Turkey, 191
Cooke, Lucy, 229
Cooke, Roger, 297
Coplestone, John, 389
Cottington, Sir Francis, 54
Cotton Hook, Cheshire, 432
Cricklewell, Brecon, 82
Crispe, Nicholas, 147, 323
Crofton, Zachary, 383
Croydon, Surrey, 328
Croxden Monastery, Staffs., 29
Cullier, Augustine, 127
Cullier, Robert, 127
Cuddington, Bucks., 75
Culverclose, Somerset, 350

Index of Persons and Places

Cutler, William, 383
Curtis, Anne, 309

Dallum, Anne, 107
Dalton, Robert, 143
Daniel, Sir Peter, 268
Darcy, George, 147
Darcy, Sir William, 147
Datchet, Bucks., 5
Datchet St. Helens, Bucks., 5
Dean, Anthony, 115
Dean, Arthur, 335
Dean, Jane Barkham, 115
Dean, Sir Drue, 115
Dean, William, 115
Delaval, Isabell, 228
Deptford Strand, Kent, 301
Ditchingham, Norfolk, 467
Dixon's Farm, Sussex, 462
Dover, Kent, 347
Doyly, Sir William, 52, 183
Drax, Yorks., 123
Drew, Joseph, 426
Dringswick, Bucks., 424
Droitwich, Worcs., 313
Duncombe, Giles, 427
Dunke, Thomas, 195

Earle, Sir Thomas, 377
Eashington, Co. Durham, 437
East Drayton Cum Membris, Notts., 343
East Meon, Southampton, 157
Ellerker, Yorks., 362
Ellingham, Norfolk, 436
Eltham, Kent, 303
Elwes, Sir John, 124
Eskyrhir, Cardigan, 284

Falmouth, countess of, 198
Fanshawe, Sir Simon, 335
Fanshawe, William, 427
Farnham, Surrey, 242
Faucett, Edward, 423
Faversham, Kent, 154
Fenne, John, 171
Fenwick, George, 274
Fishborne, Richard, 320
Ford, Somerset, 350
Ford, William Weedon, 427
Forton, Lancs., 102
Fountains Abbey, Yorks., 298
Fowlston, Yorks., 176
Frankland, Hugh, 342
Freeman, Sir Ralph, 16
Friskney, Lincs., 270
Frolesworth, Leics., 321
Froom Manor, Yorks., 363
Fulham, Mddx., 445, 446
Furness Abbey, Lancs., 143

Gandy, Nunmis, 400
Gattick, Somerset, 350
Gaunt, Walter, 405
Gawcott, Bucks., 424
Gawdey, Sir Dennis, 92
Gedney, Lincs., 185
Gerard, Lucy Cooke, 229
Gilborne, Elizabeth, 303
Gilborne, Henry, 303
Gilborne, Sir Nicholas, 303
Gillingham, Dorset, 316
Golderston, Norfolk, 436
Goring, lord, 115
Gotts, Bridget, 383
Greenville, Bernard, 220

Gregory, Jane, 217
Gregory, Oliver, 120, 167
Gregory, Robert, 217
Grimstone, Sir Harbottle, 115
Grinton, Yorks., 405
Grosvenor, John, 329

Haddenham, Bucks., 75
Hales, Norf., 297
Halstead, Essex, 306
Hamburg, Germany, 238
Hammersmith, Mddx., 445, 446
Hamswell Manor, Glos., 95
Hancock, Mary, 445
Hanley, Worcs., 237
Hardcastle, Henry, 383
Hardwick cum Weedon, Bucks., 282
Harkaside, Yorks., 405
Harman, Richard, 316
Harris, Samuel, 432
Hartington Manor, Beds., 61
Hartlebury, Worcs., 113
Harvey, Sir Daniel, 191
Haunsworth Hall, Staffs., 344
Haverfordwest, 338
Hayes, Mddx., 355
Helaugh, Yorks., 405
Heneage, Sir Thomas, 127
Henley, Oxon., 46, 133
Hicks, Sir William, 253
Hill, Alice, 180
Hill, John, 297
Hill, Katherine, 180
Hill, Mary, 180
Hill, Sarah, 180
Hind, John, 334
Hinton, Alice, 311

Hitch, Francis, 405
Holbeach, Lincs., 352
Hollingworth, Richard, 383
Holliwell, Robert, 383
Holy Island, Northumberland, 456
Honiton, Devon, 126
Horton, Joshua, 432
Howard, Sir Robert, 381
Howden, Yorks., 362
Hudson, Thomas, 222
Huish, Somerset, 311
Humphreville, Sir Charles, 383
Hyde, Sir Thomas, 321

Ipswich, Suffolk, 300
Ireland, Sir Gilbert, 187
Iron Acton, Glos., 141

Jackson, Roger, 250
Johnson, Henry, 367
Jowles, Chrysagon, 53

Kennett, White, 383
Kettering, Northants., 231
Kibburn, Yorks., 388
Killigrew, Sir Henry, 2
King, Sir Peter, 464, 466
Kingham, Norfolk, 436
King's College, Cambridge, 389
King's Mill, Cambs., 172
King's Pyon, Heref., 430
King's Sutton, Northants., 124
Kingston, Sir Anthony, 262
Kingston-upon-Thames, Surrey, 222
Kingswick, Bucks,, 424
Kirby Cane, Norfolk, 436
Kirkby Bellars, Leic., 56

Index of Persons and Places

Kirkby Ireland, Lancs., 340
Knoyle, Wilts., 54

Lacy, Ann, 423
Lacy, John, 423
Lake Garden, Sussex, 267
Landon, Silvanus, 403
Langibby, Monmouthshire, 216
Langley, barony of, 45
Latham, William, 383
Laverstock, Wilts., 351
Leach, Sir Simon, 225
Leake, Lincs., 204
Leyton Hall, Lancs., 269
Lingen, John, 384
Lingen, Katherine Watts, 384
Linton, Cambs., 308
Littleton, baron, 156
Llanvihangell Generglin, Cardigan, 284
Lloyd, John, 18
London, City of
    Blue Boar Inn, Holborn, 199
    Curriers Alley, 222
    Fleet Street, 71
    Gray's Inn, 297
    Lime Street Ward, 386
    Little Tower Hill, 138
    Newport House, 250
    St. Bartholomew's Priory, 383
    St. Botolph's Algate Church, 383
    St. Bryde's Church, 392
    St. Dunstan's in the West, 70
    St. Martin's Lane, 291
    St. Paul's Cathedral, 445
    Savoy, 395
    Spittlefields, 58
    Sun Tavern, nr. Exchange, 276
    Tower Hill, 324
    Tower of London, 138
Longcroft, Essex, 202
Long Sutton, Lincs., 211
Longtree, Glos., 262
Lort, Henry, 429
Lort, Sir Gilbert, 429
Lort, Sir T., 468
Lovell, Sir Salathiel, 432
Lucas, William, 459
Luck, Thomas, 249
Lucy, William, 386
Ludlow, Edmund, 23, 54
Lyminge, Kent, 324
Lyons, France, 382

Maccaness, John, 383
Maddox, Sir Benjamin, 272
Maidenhead Bridge, Berks., 133, 302
Mansfield Mills, Notts., 149
Marblethorpe St. Marys, Lincs., 114
Marden, Kent, 345
Marshland, Norf., 64
Martin, Thomas, 229
Massonn, Ferdinando, 220
Masters, Richard, 159
Maynard, lord, 271
Mellifont, James, 386
Micklefen Common, Norfolk, 436
Middleton Keynes, Bucks., 194
Misterton, Somerset, 318
Molemills, Devon, 60
Molineux, viscount, 143
Monck, George, 312
Monke, John, 222
Monks Wearmouth, Co. Durham, 274
Moreton, Heref., 438

Morris, John, 199
Mould, Flintshire, 227

Nappier, Sir Nathaniel, 97
Nash Farm, Sussex, 462
Newburgh Monastery, Yorks., 307
Newcastle, duke of, John, 334
Newcastle-upon-Tyne, Northumberland, 301
Newnham Mills, Cambs., 172
Noel, Sir Martin, 66
Norbury, Richard, 412
Norwich, Norfolk, 358

Oglethorpe, Sir Theophilus, 311
O'Neal, Daniel, 198
Ossulston, lord, 198
Ottery St. Mary, Devon, 126
Oxmead, Somerset, 350

Packley, George, 391
Palmer, Sir Roger, 54
Parkmans Wood, Surrey, 310
Parton Manor, Cumberland, 106
Parton Pier, Cumberland, 106
Paul, Anthony, 154
Paul, Cornwall, 105
Pawlet, William Lambert, 97
Peckham, Margaret, 195
Pelham, Sir Nicholas, 115
Pembroke College, Cambridge, 308
Penington, Isaac, 19
Penn, George, 141
Penny, George, 423
Penryn, Cornwall, 341
Pepwall, John, 95
Perrott, Sir Herbert, 438

Pet Down, Wilts., 134
Piccadilly, Mddx., 346
Pipe, Heref., 438
Pirton Manor, Staffs., 186
Pitt, George, 346
Player, Sir Thomas, 171
Plowden, Edmond, 143
Plymouth, Devon, 3
Pointz, Sir John, 141
Pollard, John, 202
Pollard, Peter, 202
Pollard, Sir Lewis, 60
Poole, Sir Henry, 183
Portsmouth, Hants., 364
Powell, Jane, 209
Preston Bisset, Bucks., 424
Preston, Sir Thomas, 143
Price, John, 250
Price, Thomas, 250
Pride, Thomas, 312
Province, Yorks., 362
Pudlicott, Oxon., 236
Pulman, George, 383
Putney, Surrey, 229
Puttenham, George, 383

Rea, Walter, 398
Reynardson, Jacob, 227
Reynold, Sir Thomas, 383
Robinson, lord mayor of London, 10
Robinson, Sir Lumly, 335
Rochester, Kent, 154
Rockwood Forest, Bucks., 424
Rotherham, Yorks., 426
Rowland Farm, Yorks., 388

Sadler, Sir Robert, 69

Index of Persons and Places 693

St. Asaph, Flint, 248
St. Bartholomew's Priory, London, 383
St. James Priory, Bristol, 74
St. Omers, France, 143
St. Petrox, Pembrokeshire, 429
Salisbury, Wilts., 433
Sandwich, Kent, 154, 406
Sandys, Freeman, 16
Sandys, Sir George, 16
Sandys, Jane Freeman, 16
Santen, Luke, 200
Saunderson, Lady, 13
Savage, William, 383
Sawyer, Sir Robert, 92
Scroop, Emanuel, 386
Selsden Manor, 25
Shackshoone, 219
Sheep's Close, Somerset, 350
Sheppard, William, 400
Shepshed, Leic., 295
Shepton Mallet, Somerset, 354, 356
Shrewton, Wilts., 134
Smith, Edward, 86
Smith, Sir James, 141
Smith, Sir Jeremy, 92
Smith, Matthew, 86
Smith, Sir Thomas, 286
Smith, William, 199
Somerset, Sir Charles, 101
South Cave, Yorks., 362
South Mimms, Herts., 261
South Molton, Devon, 60
Sparke, Arthur, 11
Sparks, John, 435
Sparks, Jonathan, 435
Spencer, Arnold, 36
Spencer, Jane, 272

Spencer, Luke, 36
Spencer, Sir Thomas, 272
Spittlefields, London, 58
Spockenhold, Suffolk, 396
Sprignall, Sir Robert, 254
Squibb, Robert, 359
Staines Bridge, Surrey, 46, 302
Staplefield Farm, Sussex, 462
Stapleford Tawney, Essex, 103
Steep, Southampton, 157
Steyning, Sussex, 462
Stockton, Norfolk, 436
Stockton, Yorks., 221
Stoke College, Suffolk, 202
Stow, Lincs., 349
Stow Hall, Lincs., 349
Stowell, Sir John, 16
Streatham, Surrey, 215
Street, Sir Thomas, 387
Strickland, Robert, 419
Strickland, Sir Roger, 419
Sutton Mills, Notts., 149
Sutton Poole, Devon, 3
Swale, Sir Solomon, 405
Sydenham, Edward, 240

Talbott Inn, Southwark, 120
Talgarth, 145
Tapps, Richard, 323
Tarrant, Dorset, 23
Tarrant Hinton, Dorset, 461
Tatwick Manor, Glos., 95
Taylor, Ralph, 361
Terrington, Norf., 64
Tetbury, Glos., 262
Thatcham, Berks., 304
Thorley, Isle of Wight, 135

Tiverton, Devonshire, 408
Tolden, Norfolk, 439
Tomkins, Sir Thomas, 179
Tookey, Nehemiah, 380
Torrington, Devon, 252
Trafford and Tickhill, Yorks., 363
Tring, Herts., 333
Tufton, Margaret Wootten, 255
Tufton, Sir John, 255
Turnor, Sir W., 17
Tushingham, George, 405

Uttoxeter, Staff., 29

Vanlore, Jacoba, 27
Vanlore, John, 27
Vanlore, Mary, 27
Vanlore, Maurice, 27
Vanlore, Sir Peter, 27
Vanlore, Susanna, 27
Varnish Hall, Essex, 177
Vennard, George, 189
Vera Cruz, Spanish West Indies, 117
Vere, John, 372
Vernon, Sir Thomas, 242
Vyner, Sir Robert, 171

Walford, Heref., 407
Waller, Sir Thomas, 154
Wallington, Heref., 438
Walmesly, Richard, 143
Wandsworth, Surrey, 229
Wappenthorne, Sussex, 462
Ward, Sir James, 250
Warnham, Sussex, 267
Watlington, Sussex, 278
Watts, Katherine, 384

Wearmouth, Co. Durham, 437
Webb, Richard, 357
Webster, Edward, 239
Weddall, John, 394
Weeden, Cavendish, 427
Weekes, Joan, 316
Weld, Humphrey, 143
Wells, Somerset, 280
West Farm, Stow, Lincs., 349
West Grinton, Yorks., 405
West Harnham, Wilts., 189
West Malling, Kent, 220
Westmead, Somerset, 350
Westminster, 53
Weston, Anne, 213
Weston, Elizabeth, 213
Whaddon Farm, 97
Wharton, Philip, 256
Whiston, Yorks., 363
Whitcomb, Glos., 331
White, Griffith, 209
White, Jane Powell, 209
White, Thomas, 209
Whiteaside, Yorks., 405
Whitehaven, Cumberland, 106
Whitehead, Thomas, 274
Whitehead, William, 274
Whitelocke, Sir Bulstrode, 46
Whitley, Roger, 432
Whorewood, Brome, 257
Widdrington, John, 274
Widdrington, Robert, 274
Widnes, Lancs., 173
Williams, Rowland, 384
Williamson, Sir Thomas, 274
Winchester Cathedral, 265
Winchester, John, marquess of, 97

Windsor Bridge, Berks., 302
Winnington, Sir Francis, 120
Winter, George, 101
Winwick, Lancs., 287
Wiseman, Richard, 405
Withers, Richard, 158
Witney, Oxon., 417
Wootton, lady, Mary, 255
Wootton, lord, 255

Wootwich, Kent, 303
Worden, Elizabeth Blondell, 144
Worden, James, 144
Worden, Mary, 144
Wyndham, Sir Edmond, 158

Yarnton, Oxon., 272
York, City of, 210
Young, John, 189

Subject Index

[These references are to case numbers, not page numbers.]

A

Account, writs of, 33
Accounts
    Accrual of, 290
    Accrual of interest, 364
    Collectors, 12
    Destruction of, 111
    False, 12
    Generally, 50, 364
    Interest on, 364
    Suits for, 160
Acts of Parliament, *See* Statutes
Ademptions, 195
Administrators, *See* Decedent's estates
Admiralty
    Prizes, 63, 386, 458
    See also Navy
Aequitas sequitur legem, 229
Agents, 238, 271, 364, 394, 422
Almshouses, 267, 438
Altarages, 185, 448
Answers
    Bishops, by, 24
    Corporations, of, 90
    Election of remedies, 49
    Failure of, contempt of court, 42
    Guardians, by, 22
    Incompetent persons, 22
    Jurisdiction raised, 425
    Limitations, statute of, 37
    Oath, under, 42
    Parties, defect of, 178
    Peers, by, 24
    Release, 31
    Sufficiency of, 21
    Women, married, 42
    See also Pleading
Appeals, *See* Procedure
Appearances, *See* Procedure
Arbitration
    Awards
        Stamp tax on, 433
        Uncertain, 364
    Generally, 267, 268, 317
Army, 132, 322
Assault, 460
Assignments
    Defeated in bad faith, 108
    Generally, 188
Assumpsit, indebitatus, 202, 232, 317, 323, 414
Attorney-client privilege, 68
Attorney general, bonds, suits on, 11
Attorney's fees, 211
Aulnage, 94, 142, 264

B

Backgammon, gambling at, 208
Bailments, 394
Bankruptcy and bankrupts
    Commissioners assignments of, 200
    Crown debts, 200
    Crown not bound, 279
    Farmers, 119
    Generally, 84, 119, 196, 250, 279, 323
    Graziers, 119

Priorities, 279
Shares of stock, 400
Sureties, 415
Trustee bankrupt, 400
Bequests, *See* Wills
Boats, tolls for, 46, 133, 302
Bonds, *See* Contracts; Creditors; Penal bonds
Booksellers, 411
Boroughs, *See* Cities and towns; London, City of
Boundaries, 341, 385
Bridges
   Maidenhead Bridge, 133, 302
   Staines Bridge, 46, 302
   Tolls, 46, 133, 302
   Windsor Bridge, 302
   See also Rivers

C

Catholicism
   Roman Catholics, 143, 269, 291, 395, 423, 450
   Superstitious uses, 143, 269, 291, 395
   Tithes
      Cistercian lands, 29, 102, 136, 197, 298, 388
      Premonstratensian lands, 102
Chancery, court of
   Cursitors, 4
   Six clerks' privilege, 59
   See also Equity
Charities
   Almshouses, 267, 438
   Chatham chest, 301
   Commissioners of, 248
   Dulwich College, 310
   Election of schoolmaster, 349
   Exchequer jurisdiction, 336
   Gifts to, 248
   Illegal purposes, 143, 269, 291, 395
   Lectureships, 320
   Redirected, 269, 291

Rights barred by recovery, 229
Schools, 229, 248, 310, 349, 395
Stow school, 349
Suits in equity, 248
Trustees of, 320
See also Churches
Cheshire land, 93
Churches
   Altarages, 185, 448
   Augmentation of income, 189, 366
   Bishop's leases, 286
   Chantry rents, 202
   Chapels, 445, 446
   Crown appointments, 383
   Curates, 383, 445, 446
   Dilapidations, 32, 148, 162, 430, 467
   Disorderly behavior, 430
   Disturbances of, 446
   Ecclesiastical fees, 91
   Election of curate, 445, 446
   Enclosures, 194
   Endowments, 64, 185, 304, 448
   Exchequer jurisdiction, 148
   Forcible detainer of, 383
   Glebes
      Generally, 134
      Tithes from, 193
   Impropriators, 231, 289
   Leases of, 189, 286, 406
   Lessees of, 242
   Licenses to preach, 445
   Mortuaries, 169, 235
   Nonresidency, 430
   Paschals, 280
   Penal bonds, 430
   Pension out of, 56, 150
   Prebends, 189
   Procurations, 280
   Rectories
      Generally, 56, 75, 176, 231, 297, 311, 351
      Pensions, 135, 192
   Rectors, 35, 383

Subject Index 699

Resignation of vicarage, 430
Salaries of ministers, 300, 383
Sequestration of, 155, 440
Sequestrators, 224
Simony, 176
Tithe leases, 286
Vacant, 155, 440
Vicarages, 32, 77, 162
Vicars, 32, 134, 445, 446
See also Tithes
Cider, 314
Cities and towns
  Alienation of land, 170
  Burgage tenure, 170
  Charters, 370
  Chichester, 327
  Cinque Ports, 154
  Liverpool, port of, 375
  Newcastle-under-Lyme, 336
  Portsmouth docks, 364
  See also London, City of,
Civil law, decedent's estates, 428
Civilian lawyers, 100
Clothes, 94, 142, 264
Colonies of the king, 384
Common pleas, court of, 267
Complaint, bills of
  Accounts in exchequer, 12
  Amended, 90, 276
  Discovery, bills of, allegations of, 41
  Execution of decree, 393
  Intrusion against crown, 16
  Peace, bills of, 424
  Prayer for process, 90
  Right, petition of, 163
  Sufficiency of, 379
  Titles alleged, 230, 231
  Waste, for, 230
  See also Discovery, bills of; Pleading
Contempt of court
  Affidavits of, 404
  Answer, failure to, 42
  Assault of court officer, 460

  Attachment for, 241, 252, 374, 377, 404, 412
  Costs not paid, 469
  Crown, death of, 233
  Decree taken for confessed, 227
  Imprisonment for, 42, 227, 460, 469
  Injunctions, 252, 405
  Insult to court, 404
  Not proved, 405
  Order, notice of, 241
  Proof of, 460
  Sequestration, 26
  Women, married, 469
Contracts
  Abatement of price, 182
  Account, to make, 166
  Assignments of, 36
  Bonds, 410
  Composition for aulnage, 264
  Consideration
    Failure of, 219
    Illegal, 208, 218
    Lacking, 215
    Proof of, 207
  Construction of docks, 364
  Convey, to
    Enforced, 69, 112, 166, 172, 285, 334, 358, 364, 406, 433
    Generally, 98, 182, 187, 285
    Oral, 201
    Part performance, 201
  Conveyances, tithes already paid, 129
  Damages for breach, 317
  Debts, not, 187
  Earnest money, 201
  Enforceable against crown, 364
  Enforced, 45
  Gambling, 208, 218
  Harsh, 334
  Illegal, 208, 218
  Impossible, 334
  Insurance, 117
  Interpreted, 128, 182, 448

Land, to buy, 187
Lease to be made, 334
Malfeasance, 410
Marriage, consideration of, 243
Mills, 172
Mutuality of, 348
Options, 406
Oral
  Generally, 98, 112, 243
  Part performance, 285
Performance bonds, 364, 410
Performance not adequate, 364
Performance, specific, 69, 112, 166, 172, 285, 334, 358, 364, 406, 433
Purchasers without notice, 186
Recital of consideration, 207
Releases, 159
Rents reserved, 36
Rents to be paid, 69
Sales, tithes payable, 216
Stamp tax, 433
Tithes, compensation for, 215
Women, married, by, 199
See also Creditors; Penal bonds
Conveyances
  Administrators, by, 17
  Altered, 177
  Bona et catalla, of, 65
  Burgage tenure, 170
  Church prejudiced by, 56
  Common recoveries, 229
  Consideration lacking, 223, 316
  Contracts to convey
    Enforced, 69, 112, 166, 172, 285, 334, 358, 364, 406, 433
    Generally, 98, 182, 285
    Oral, 201
    Part performance, 201
  Copyholds
    Admittance, 339
    Complete, when, 339
    Generally, 18, 19, 371
  Covenants of title, 17

Crown grants, 158, 220
Decedent, to, 256
Defeated by revocation, 257
Destroyed, set up, 89, 345
Enforced, 177
Entails, leases of, 115
Execution presumed, 187
Fairs, of, 79
Family settlements, 223
Fee farm rents, of, 220
Felons' goods, 262
Feoffment, by, 170, 209
Fine and nonclaim, 123, 253
Fine with proclamations, 255
Fraud, 81, 297, 324
Fraudulent
  Generally, 1, 119, 227, 276
  Purchaser without notice, 423
Gifts, 195
Grantee defrauded, 297
Jointures, 89, 98
Infants, by, 316
Ingfangtheif, 262
Leases
  Generally, 201, 257, 342
  Options to renew, 406
  Post office, of, 198
Markets, of, 79
Mortgage, of, 456
Mortgagee forced to, 358
Negligence, 81
Patents interpreted, 383
Penalty enforced, 293
Power of revocation, 257
Purchasers, *bona fide*, 54, 158, 190
Purchaser without notice, 75, 239
Remainders barred, 225, 229
Rents, of, 95
Set aside, 316
Spendthrift, by, 223
Surrender, death of, 295
Surrenders of copyholds, 170, 295
Surrenders of leases, 286

Subject Index

Tithes already paid, 129
Trusts, of, 65
Undue influence, 324
Variation of oral, 223
Voluntary, 223
Wales, in, 247
Women, married, by, 384
See also Mortgages; Trusts; Wills
Copyholds, *See* Property
Copyright, 411
Corporations
  Answers of, 90
  Charters, 370
  East India Company, 55, 227, 400
  Maidenhead Bridge, 133, 302
  Misnomer, 214
  Municipal, 412
  Process against, 90
  Quo warranto, 370
  Royal mines, 284
  Sequestration against, 412
  Shares of stock, 400
  Stock transfer, 55
  See also Charities; Cities and towns; Crown; London, City of
Costs
  Agents of crown, 364
  Awarded, 86, 139, 148, 157, 187, 198, 202, 214, 230, 241, 242, 260, 266, 268, 274, 284, 292, 308, 320, 329, 330, 331, 341, 342, 352, 377, 390, 411, 416, 420, 459
  Computed after death, 459
  Computed without order for, 466
  Crown, to or by, 338, 364
  Decedents, against, 466
  Enforced, 368
  Executors, against, 283, 466
  Exemplary, 5
  Generally, 3, 29, 318, 376
  Not assessed, 47, 54, 77, 78, 83, 98, 121, 134, 135, 147, 149, 166, 173, 182, 193, 201, 204, 213, 216, 218, 220, 232, 245, 248, 258, 262, 264, 305, 310, 331, 335, 351, 354, 360, 389, 394, 464
  Paid upon reinstatement, 446
  Payable by whom, 197
  Relators, against, 31
  Waived, 236, 237, 238
  Women, married, against, 469
  See also Procedure
Counsel, advice of, 223
County palatine of Chester, 93
County palatine of Durham, 274
Courts
  Priority of suit, 305
  See also individual courts by name
Creditors and debtors
  Absconding debtors, 297
  Accounts
    Accrual of, 290
    Generally, 50, 364
  Accrual of interest, 364
  Agents, 394
  Assignments
    Crown, to, 51
    Generally, 171
  Attachment of debt to executor, 80
  Bonds
    Blank, 84
    Consideration, failure of, 219
    Defective, 332
    Discharged, 52
    Distributees, of, 249
    Fidelity, 359
    Forfeited, 432
    Gambling debts, 208, 218
    Generally, 11, 86, 238, 239, 268, 283, 288, 329
    Laches, 335
    Penal, 39, 353, 410
    Performance, 364
    Released, 108
    Relieved against, 335
    Scriveners' errors, 332
    Void, 208, 218

Co-debtors, 28
Collectors of crown debts, 28
Contracts not debts, 187
Contribution, 203
Co-obligors, 414
Crown
　Accounts, 359
　Bankrupts' debts, 200
　Bonds of debtors to, 422
　Debtor, as, 163
　Generally, 28, 30, 227
　Lessee of ejected, 51
　Priority of, 132, 250, 323
　Releases by, 323
　Sureties, 415
Debtors
　Deceased, 180, 357
　Joint debtors, release of, 323
　Judgment debtors, 33, 281, 288, 377
　Executors of, 377
　Preference of creditor, 55
　Realty of, 357
Debts
　Due executor, 80
　Gambling, 208, 218
　Husbands, of, 53
　Setoffs, 454
　Tithes senior, 451
Deceased debtors' realty, 357
Decedent, of, 332
Distress for rent, 88
Equity of redemption, 23
Exchange, bills of, 238, 394
Executors
　Bonds of, 66
　Cum testamento annexo, 288
　Executors, of, 222
Exoneration, 50
Fines to, 17
Fraud, 159, 276, 319
Fraudulent conveyances 1, 119, 227
Grants to, 18
Indemnity, loss, none, 52

Inquisitions, 323
Interest
　Accounts, on, 364
　Generally, 246
　Legal rate, 346
Joint debts, 323
Joint liability, 28
Judgment debtors, 33, 281, 288
Junior creditors' rights, 321, 358
Legacies of land, 239
Limitations, Statute of, 50
Marshalling, 281, 321
Mortgagees, junior, 321, 358
Outlawry, 373
Personal chattels of debtor, 413
Preference of creditor, 55
Principal's property, 394
Priorities
　Generally, 250, 275, 279, 281, 288, 323
　Crown, of, 132
　Tithes, of, 451
Profits from land, 321, 413
Protests of bills, 238
Realty of deceased debtor, 357
Redemption of debtor's land, 120
Releases
　Bad faith, 108
　Generally, 159, 323
　Presumed, 161
Rent charge, 139
Rent due to crown, 30
Salvo jure regis, 28
Security for debt, 18
Setoffs, 454
Shares of stock, 400
Statutes, 17, 120
Sureties
　Generally, 84, 415
　Bankrupts, of, 415
Tender, 246
Tithes superior to legacies, 243
Tracing of assets, 458

Trusts for married women, 53
Usury, 346
See also Accounts; Bankruptcy and bankrupts; Decedent's estate; Executions; Mortgages; Penal bonds; Process; Taxes
Crimes
   Accessories to, 353
   Conventicles, 261
   Corruption of blood, 432
   Counterfeiting, 432
   Disturbance of churches, 446
   Embezzlement, 238, 336
   Escheats, 16
   Fraud, 328
   Gambling, 208, 218
   Murder, 16
   Pardons, 63, 328
   Perjury, 176
   Receiving stolen goods, 353
   Riots, 446
   Sale of offices, 443
   Simony, 176
   Suicide, 158
   Treason
     Forfeiture for, 19, 23
     Generally, 311, 432
   See also Contempt of court; Forfeitures; Fraud
Crown
   Accounts to, 359
   Agents of, costs not paid by, 364
   Almoner, supreme, 269
   Amoveas manus, 51
   Ancient demesne, 46, 133
   Bankruptcy
     Debts of bankrupt, 200
     Effect on crown, 279
   Bonds to, 11
   Church, head of, 269
   Colonies, 384
   Costs not paid by, 338, 364
   Creditor, as, 132, 250, 323
   Curate appointed by, 383
   Death of, contempt discharged, 233
   Debtors of, 422
   Debts due to, 28, 227
   Decrees against, 364
   Discovery from, none, 163
   Equity of redemption, 373
   Estoppel against, none, 220
   Excise tax leased, 40
   Forfeitures
     Generally, 16, 19, 23
     Superstitious uses, 143, 269, 291, 395
   Goods not taxed, 386
   Grants by
     Fairs, 79
     Generally, 36, 220
     Markets, 79
   Information of intrusion, 16
   Laches, none, 303
   Lancaster, duchy of, 425
   Leases
     Bankrupts, 279
     Generally, 412
     Tolls, of, 327
   Lessee of
     Ejectment, writ of, 51
     Generally, 362
     Injunction, 51
     Tithes, 7
     Marshes, 270
   Mills of, 60, 149, 172, 426
   Mines, silver, 284
   Mint, 214
   Mortgages of excise, 398
   Pardons, 63, 328
   Pater patriae, 267
   Piers, 106
   Ports, 3
   Post office, 198
   Priority as creditor, 132, 250, 323
   Privilege from discovery, 163
   Prizes, 63, 386, 458
   Purprestures, 3, 106

Releases by, 323
Rent due to, 30, 36, 443
Rents reserved, 240
Rights not barred by acquittance, 28
River shores, 362
Sale of crown goods, 28
Salvo jure regis, 28
Seacoast, 3
Silver mines, 284
Statutes
    Frauds, 291
    Limitations, 291
Sureties of bankrupts, 415
Tenants' laches, 303
Tithes, 7
Toll by charter void, 302
Treason, forfeiture for, 19, 23
See also Army; Navy; Prerogative; Taxes
Customs, *See* Property; Taxes; Tithes

D

Damages
    Mesne profits, 287
    Moritur cum persona, 287
    Survival, no, 287
Debtors, *See* Creditors
Decedent's estates
    Ademptions, 195
    Bonds
        Defective, 332
        Generally, 66, 86, 249
    Conveyances from, 17
    Costs against decedent, 466
    Costs due to, 459
    Covenants of title, 17
    Creditors, beyond, 239
    Damages in tort, 287
    Death pending suit, 391
    Debts of, 332
    Decrees against, 13
    Devisees, surviving, 367
    Dilapidations, liable for, 32, 467
    Discovery of, 151, 159, 402

Distributees' bonds, 249
Distribution of, 151, 159, 326
Executors and administrators
    Archdeacon attached, 288
    Assign leases, to, 33
    Capacity denied, 403
    Constructive trust, 217
    Contingent remainders, 309
    Costs against decedent, 466
    Costs collected by, 459
    Creditor, as, 288
    Cum testamento annexo, 288, 367
    De bonis non, 199, 271, 297, 335, 391
    Debts of testator, 78
    Debts to be paid by, 32, 33, 139, 174, 283, 346, 438
    Debts paid from realty, 357
    Decedent's bonds, 335
    De son tort, 288
    Dilapidations, 32, 467
    Discovery from, 41, 402
    Discovery by, 232
    Equity of redemption, 54
    Executor, of, 78
    Fraud by, 217
    Fraudulent conveyances, 276
    Legatees, 107, 389, 438
    Mesne profits, 33
    Mortgagee, of, 57, 122, 398
    Mortgages, 122, 199, 234
    Mortuaries, 169
    Nominal, 442
    Payment of price of land, 256
    Personal assets, 80
    Personally bound, not, 17
    Powers of suspended, 178
    Probate of will, 153
    Redemption, suit for, 96
    Releases of, 402
    Repairs to be made, 438
    Revivor, bills of, 377
    Subpoena *scire facias*, 377
    Suits against, 57, 181

Suits by, 153
Tithes, to pay, 243
Trust, in, only, 107
Trustees, as, 222, 316, 438
Trusts, 195
Waste, 66
Felons' escheats, 16
Forfeitures of trusts, 16
Fraud, 159
Gifts by decedent, 195
Heirs
   Disinherited, 225
   Equity of redemption, 57, 122, 234, 398
   Payment of price of land, 256
   Profits, 259
   Temporary, 259
Inheritances of naturalized persons, 27
Insufficient for debts, 195
Inventories of, 195
Land
   Charged, 239
   Purchasers without notice, 239
Legacies
   Charged on land, 369
   Payable, 184
   Tithes superior to, 243
Legatees liable for debts, 180
Mesne executors, 78
Mesne profits, 287
Money in agent's hands, 271
Mortgages, 57, 122, 122, 234, 398
Mortuaries, 169
Personal property, half blood, 326
Probate of void will, 360
Rents reserved upon leases, 429
Residual personal estate, 389
Sale of land, price paid by whom, 256
Suits against decedent enforced, 33
Survival of damages, 287
Tithes payable before legacies, 243
Trusts
   Debts to be paid, 222
   Felon beneficiary, 16
   Generally, 195
   Personal, 378
Women, married, 144
See also Descents and distributions; Wills

Decrees, judgments, and orders
   Appeals, stayed pending, 178
   Breach of, 405
   Common law
      Relieved against, 75, 81, 85, 209, 226, 241, 297
      Res judicata, 356
   Confessed, taken for, 227, 377, 419
   Consent, by, 128, 138, 168, 310
   Contempt of court, 241
   Crown
      Against, 364
      Not bound, 7
   Default, by, 227, 377, 419
   Discovery of, 160
   Durham chancery court, 274
   Enclosure of commons, 168
   Enforcement of, 13
   Infants, against, 177
   Modified, 195
   Office of pleas, in, 253
   Parties to, 168
   Party dies before signing, 391
   Pro confesso, 227, 377, 419
   Res judicata, 274, 383
   Scire facias, 13
   Wales, council of marches, 175
   See also Executions; Process
Deeds, *See* Conveyances
Delegates, court of, 178
Demurrers
   Common law relief, 181, 383
   Discovery, to, 41, 411, 415, 422
   Entire bill, goes to, 386
   Forfeiture alleged, 48, 140, 399, 421, 468
   Generally, 45, 231
   Jurisdiction, to, 384, 411

Misjoinder, 149, 263, 337, 401
New matter alleged, 385
No cause of action, 415
Oral contract alleged, 98
Overruled for lack of argument, 376
Parties, defect of, 153
Penalties
    Alleged, 38, 39, 44
    Waived, 62, 140, 399, 421, 468
Pleas, to, 402, 427
Prayer for common law relief, 232
Res judicata, 383
Review, bills of, 416
Speaking, 385
Title at common law lacking, 384
See also Pleading; Procedure
Descents and distributions
    Cousins, 116, 452, 453
    Executors, 107, 122, 389, 438
    Grandparents, 428
    Half blood, 249, 326, 453
    Heirs, generally
        Disinherited, 225
        Equity of redemption, 57, 122, 234, 398
        Joint tenants, 47
        Payment of price of land, 256
        Profits, 259
        Survivorship, 47
        Temporary, 259
    London customs, 372, 464
    Naturalized persons, 27
    Orphanage part, 464
    Widows, 453
    See also Decedent's estates; Wills
Devises, *See* Wills
Dilapidations, 32, 148, 162, 430, 467
Discovery, bills of
    Accountants to crown, 422
    Accounts, 198, 210, 347, 381, 384, 415
    Action pending, 41
    Agents of debtors, to, 422
    Answer insufficient, 449
    Assets, of, 148, 169, 253, 288, 422
    Boundaries, 385
    Commercial dealings, 382
    Commissioners to aid, 5
    Common law relief, 181, 232, 273, 410, 449
    Corporations, by, 90
    Crown privilege, 163
    Decedent's estate, 151, 159, 402, 403
    Deeds, of, 93, 468
    Demurrers to, 41, 411, 415, 422
    Documents, 382
    Encumbrances, 160, 427
    Fees due, of, 263
    Forfeitures, of, 16, 468
    Generally, 39, 45, 73, 351
    Goods seized, of, 386
    Interrogatories, records disclosed, 10
    Justices of peace, to, 261, 390
    Lancaster, duchy, rents, 425
    Lands liable to payments, 202
    Lands, value of, 254
    Manors, of, 385
    Mesne profits, 287
    Muniments of title, 47
    No cause of action, 415
    Not required, 31
    Orders of court, 274
    Perpetuate to, 405
    Pleas in bar, 35, 253, 425
    Prisage, 58
    Profits, mesne, 93
    Records of parties, 10
    Rent due, 5, 385, 425
    Self-incrimination, none, 38, 39, 44, 62, 140, 399, 421
    Settlements, 312
    Tithes, for, 35, 231
    Tolls, of, 46, 449
    Transfer, fraudulent, 119
    Trusts, 382
    Waste, 468

Subject Index

See also Equity; Evidence; Pleading; Procedure
Docks at Portsmouth, 364
Domesday Book, 313
Dulwich College, 310
Durham, chancery court of, 274
Duties, *See* Taxes

E

East India Company, 55, 227, 400
Ejectment, actions of
   Generally, 51, 295, 297, 376
   Relieved against, 81, 85
Election of remedies, 49
Enemy alien, 382
Equitas sequitur legem, 229
Equity
   Accounts, 50, 277, 280, 305, 327, 336, 349, 362, 364, 372, 362, 364, 372, 374, 381, 399, 414, 427, 440
   Arbitral awards, 268
   Assignments, 171, 188
   Bad faith releases, 108
   Bonds
      Consideration illegal, 208, 218
      Relieved against, 52, 353, 359
   Boundaries, 341
   Cancelled lease set up, 316
   Charities settled, 248
   Common, right of, 424
   Common law
      Action stayed, 202, 264, 267, 290
      Courts, perjury in, 176
      Execution, 200
      Judgments, relief against, 75, 81, 85, 208, 209, 218, 226, 241, 297
      Relief granted, 232
      Verdicts, 344
   Consideration, failure of, 219
   Contribution, 203
   Criminal convictions, 353
   Crown, lessee of, 51
   Damages in contract, 317

   Deeds, destroyed, set up, 345
   Dilapidations, 467
   Discovery, 151, 159, 351
   Double recoveries, 353
   Equitas sequitur legem, 229
   Evidence, loss of, 56
   Executors to pay tithes, 243
   Fees of servants of king, 265
   Fraud, 324, 353, 391
   Future payments ordered, 349
   Gambling debts, 208, 218
   Gifts enforced, 345
   Harshness, 40, 334
   House to be rebuilt, 162
   Impossibility, 334
   Instruments set up, 89
   Interpleader, 323
   Intestate's estate, 151, 159
   Jurisdiction lacking, 317
   Jurisdiction over persons, 384
   Jurisdiction waived, 414
   Land, foreign, 384
   London customs, 9
   Marshalling, 281
   Multiplicity of suits, 219, 351, 375, 379
   Municipal charters, 370
   Overreaching, 297
   Payments of arrears, 349
   Peace, bills of, 424
   Penalty enforced, 293
   Penalties, relief from, 353
   Perjury, 176
   Perpetuation of evidence, 376
   Possession decreed, 89
   Pretium affectionis, 83
   Quiet possession, 446, 463
   Quiet title, 284, 362
   Relief against distress, 88
   Rent, suit for, 45, 179
   Rent due to crown, 30
   Scrivener's errors, 332
   Specific performance, 166, 285, 334, 358, 364, 406, 433

Surprise, 92, 353
Tax assessments, 296
Trusts, 151, 164
Undue influence, 324
Verdicts at common law, 344
Windfall to party, 40
See also Contracts; Discovery; Trusts;
  Wills
Estates, See Property
Estoppel, probate of void will, 360
Evidence
  Account books, 56
  Affidavits, 313
  Ancient deeds, 170, 299
  Ancient records, 186, 235, 265, 405
  Commissioners to hear, 169
  Contempt of court, of, 460
  Contract actions, view of jury, 418
  Copies
    Bonds, 413
    Books, 299, 318
    Copies, of, 347
  Court records, 170, 202, 263, 299
  Custom, proof of, 426
  Decree, former, 426
  Depositions
    Admissible, when, 25
    Baron of exchequer, before, 447
    Co-defendants, 316
    Commissioners, before, 447
    Cross-examination, 8
    De bene esse, 380, 447
    Nonsuited case, from, 380
    Notice of, 8, 226, 447
    Perpetuation of testimony, 312, 447
    Predecessor in title, of, 20
    Quashed, 8
    Records in court, as, 380
    Scotland, taken in, 447
    Suits, in former, 291, 380
    Suppressed, 72, 226, 447
    Testator's intent, 435
    Timeliness, 72

  Witness dead, 380
  Destruction of, 111
  Domesday Book, 313
  Exceptions, bills of, 405
  Exceptions to report, 416
  Exchequer records, 235, 313
  Handwriting proved, 413
  Loss of relieved, 56
  Matters not pleaded, 314
  Objections to, 405
  Original not accounted for, 347
  Past performance as, 131
  Perjury, 176
  Perpetuation of, 376
  Presumptions, 56
  Proof of consideration, 207
  Quiet possession as, 339
  Records
    Ancient, 127, 186, 235, 265, 405
    Courts, of, 202, 235, 263, 299, 313, 426
    Domesday Book, 313
    Private, 150
  Res judicata, 376
  Survey of 1649, 341
  Testator's intent, 435
  Usage, as, 95, 131, 187, 193, 308, 448
  View of jury as, 418
  Witnesses
    Dead, 380
    Interested, 187
    Old and infirm, 447
    Parties as, 415
  See also Discovery, bills of; Procedure
Exchange, bills of, 238, 394
Exchequer
  Accountants of crown
    Discharged, 52
    Generally, 31, 67, 247
  Accounts, 12, 92, 112, 167, 198, 322, 359
  Acquittance by, 28
  Army accounts, 322

Subject Index 709

Auditors, 163, 198
Augmentations of church incomes, 366
Bonds, 11
Chancery privilege, 59
Charities, 336
Cheshire land, 93
Chimney money sued for, 38
Church revenues, 280
Collectors
   Generally, 12, 28
   Tolls, of, 46
Crown appointments, 383
Crown mills, 60
Crown revenues, 381
Debtors to crown, 93, 148, 151
Decrees of lower court, 175
Election of remedies, 49
Escheators, 67
Exchequer leases, 413
Executors to pay tithes, 243
Fines, how rated, 247
Farmers of the excise, 31
Fraud in, 359
Insult of, 404
Jurisdiction
   Generally, 148
   Objection to, 43, 82
Jurisdictional amount, 38
Justices of peace, 261, 390
Lancaster, duchy, rents, 425
Latin plea in equity, 30
Licenses to preach, 445
London
   Mayor of, 67
   Tithes, 70, 71, 289, 392
Mittimus of fines, 227
Moneys in, 167
Municipal charters, 370
Peer's poll money, 167
Pipe roll, 12
Pleas, office of
   Generally, 4, 253, 284

   Subpoenas, 11
Post office fees, 198
Privilege to sue, 4
Receivers, 52
Rent due to crown, 30
Schedula auditorum, 30
Supersedeas to, 4
Tallies, 163, 167, 171, 198
Tax commissioners, 386
Tellers' weekly accounts, 359
Treasurer, lord, 163
Treasury bills, 171
See also Equity; Officers; Pleading; Procedure; Process; Taxes; Tithes
Executions
   Assault during, 268
   Attachments, writs of, 368
   Bill of complaint, 393
   Bonds, blank, 84
   Common law stayed, 200
   Crown, by, 51, 323
   Deceased defendant, against, 33
   Distress for rent, 11, 30, 88, 90
   Executor's assets, 80
   Extents, writ of
      Bankruptcy, 200
      Generally, 55, 196, 254, 432
      Mesne profits, 457
      Rent due crown, 30
      Seizures under, 323
   Inquisitions, 323
   Levy against third party, 412
   Outlawry, writs of, 55, 279, 413
   Personal chattels, upon, 413
   Redemption of debtor's land, 120
   Revivor, bills of, 33
   Sequestration, writs of
      Corporations, against, 412
      Generally, 99, 233, 368, 374
   Subpoenas *scire facias*, 13, 33, 377, 391, 466
   Timber seized, 413
   Women, married, against, 469

Wrongful, 374
See also Contempt of court; Creditors; Process
Executors, *See* Decedent's estates

F

Fences destroyed, 203
Ferries, 463
Fleet Prison, 99, 227, 368, 374, 427
Forfeitures
    Discovery of, none, 38, 39, 44, 62, 140, 399, 421, 468
    Enforced, 293
    Equity of redemption, 23
    Inquisitions of, 382, 427
    Murder, for, 16
    Outlawry, by, 53
    Suicide, for, 158
    Superstitious uses, 143, 269, 291, 395
    Treason, for, 19, 23, 432
    Waived, 48, 62, 140, 399, 421, 468
    Warden of Fleet Prison, 427
    Waste, for, 468
    See also Crimes; Mortgages; Penal bonds
Fraud
    Bonds, 319
    Constructive trust, 217
    Conveyances, fraudulent, 1, 119, 227, 276, 423
    Customs not paid, 44, 328
    Generally, 81, 196, 217, 324, 328, 359, 402
    Grantee, against, 297
    Prisage avoided, 221
    Release pleaded, 31
    Repayment, 319
    Tithes of wool, 417
Frauds, Statute of
    Copyhold land, 371
    Generally, 223, 291

G

Gambling, 208, 218
Gifts
    Charity, to, 248
    Delivery of, 329
    Enforced, 345
    Generally, 195
Grants, *See* Conveyances

H

Hedges destroyed, 203
Heirs, *See* Descents and distributions; Decedent's estates; Wills
Houses
    Generally, 190, 346
    Purprestures in ports, 3
    Tithes of, 289, 392
    Waste, 88

I

Injunctions
    Future disturbances, 237
    Generally, 374
    Lessee of crown, 51
    Preliminary, 106, 252, 272, 313, 351, 446
    Quia timet, 413
Insurance
    Contraband goods, of, 117
    Contracts of interpreted, 117
Interest, legal rate of, 346
Interpleader, bills of, 323

J

Judgments, *See* Decrees
Jury trials, *See* Procedure

K

King's bench, court of, 268
King, *See* Crown

Subject Index   711

L

Laches, 104, 303, 444
Lancashire clothes, 142
Lancaster, duchy of, 425
Land, *See* Conveyances; Property
Leases, *See* Conveyances; Property
Legacies, *See* Wills
Limitations, Statute of
   Account, action of
      Accrual of, 290
      Generally, 50
   Crown not bound by, 220, 291
   Decrees, enforcement of, 56
   Enclosure presumption, 168
   Equity, pleaded in, 50
   Exoneration, 50
   Laches
      Crown none, 303
      Generally, 104, 444
   Mortgage, release presumed, 161
   Presumptions
      Generally, 168
      Payment, of, 335
      Usage as, 193
   Tithes, 15
   Trusts, 37, 174
London, City of
   Aldermen, 9
   Aldermen's court, 464
   Chamber of, 171
   Clothworkers Company, 9, 10
   Custom House, 328
   Customs of
      Attachment of debt, 80
      Generally, 9
      Inheritance, 372, 464
   Great Fire of 1666, 188, 222
   Liverymen, 9
   Mayor, Lord, 9, 10, 67
   Orphanage part, 464
   Prisage exemption, 58
   Recorders, 464
   Sheriffs, 200

Tithes, 70, 71, 289, 392
Tower of London, 138
Trinity House, 301
See also Prisons

M

Manors, *See* Property
Market places, 79, 354
Marshalsea Prison, 227
Mills
   Allocation of water, 172
   Crown, of, 60, 149, 172, 426
   Custom, 60
   Customary, 6, 82
   Duty to grind, 6
   Generally, 252, 379
   Horse malt mills, 408
   Operation of, 172
   Parties to litigation, 149
   Rights lost, 6
   Suit of, 25, 82, 104, 126, 149
   Tucking, 433
Mines and minerals
   Alum, 147
   Extent of mines, 405
   Lead
      Generally, 210, 284, 405
      Tithes of, 7
   Royal, 284
   Salt, 313, 412
   Silver, 284
   Tin, tithes of, 14
Mint, the, 214
Monmouth's rebellion, 311
Monster, 219
Mortgages
   Assigned, 456
   Copyhold lands, 18
   Equity of redemption
      Contract to buy, 199
      Creditors, judgment, 120
      Crown, by, 373
      Devised, 66, 141

Generally, 23, 37, 54, 57, 61, 199, 207, 220, 281, 292, 311, 456
Heir of mortgagor, 234, 455
Land tax payable, 450
Ordered by court, 81
Party to suit for, 96
Process, service of, 183
Release presumed, 161
Released, 34, 276
Roman Catholic mortgagee, 450
Traitor's land, 432
Whom, by, 281
Foreclosures of, 18, 61, 147, 246, 285, 342
Fraudulent, 276
Generally, 17, 115
Improvements by mortgagee, 199, 292
Mortgagees
Death of, 57
Junior mortgagee forced to convey, 358
Lessor, 147
Possession by, 321
Priority of, 275
Personalty of creditor, 122, 398
Priorities, 281
Profits from land, 321
Purchasers, bona fide, 54
Release presumed, 161
Remainders, of, 292
Secured land sold, 358
Mortuary fees, 169

N

Navy
Docks at Portsmouth, 364
Prizes, 63, 386, 458
Stores, 171
Treasurer of, 171
Victualling of, 92
See also Ships
Negligence, 81
Negroes in Antigua, 384

Nuisances
Purprestures
Houses in ports, 3
Piers, 106
Tower of London, to, 138

O

Oaths, answers under, 42
Obligations, *see* Contracts; Nuisances; Torts
Officers
Accountants to crown, 458
Almoner, 158, 269
Archdeacons, 280, 288
Assault of, 460
Assay masters, 284
Attorneys
County courts, of, 263
Fees of, 211
King's bench, of, 268
Auditors of the exchequer, 163, 198, 381
Bailiffs of towns, 412
Bishop of Durham, 274
Bonds of, 39
Bridge masters, 46, 302
Chamberlain of North Wales, 247
Chancellor of the exchequer, 227
Chief baron of Scotland, 447
Chief justice of king's bench, 166
Clerks
Exchequer, in, 167
Court, of, 469
Collectors
Customs, of, 415
Generally, 171, 202, 271, 323, 386, 422
Commissioners, 203
Commissioners in bankruptcy, 200
Commissioners of customs, 415
Constables, 261, 420
Court criers, 166
Cursitors in chancery, 4

Subject Index 713

Custom house, of, 273
Debtors to crown, 132, 359
Escheators, 67
Excise officers, 31, 163
Exegenters, 39
Fees of, 247
Governors of colonies, 458
Justices of peace, 261, 390
King's remembrancer, 11, 195, 227, 242, 300, 315, 329, 331, 340, 391, 407, 416, 459, 469
Navy
    Commissioners of, 364
    Treasurer of, 171
Overseers of the poor, 390
Parish officers, 300
Payments for office, 443
Portmen, 300
Postmaster, 198
Prothonotaries, 443
Receivers, 171, 202, 271, 323, 386, 415, 422
Recorders, 370, 372, 443, 464
Reeves, 240
Seneschals, 271
Sequestrators
    Church, of, 440
    Generally, 224, 412
Sheriffs
    Accounts destroyed, 111
    Generally, 263, 374, 446
    London, of, 200
Six clerks in chancery, 59, 140, 220
Storekeepers of crown, 386
Sworn clerks in chancery, 140
Tally cutters, 163
Tax commissioners, 386
Tellers of the exchequer, 167, 359
Town clerks, 370
Treasurer, Lord, 163
Warden of Fleet Prison, 427
Water bailiffs, 347
See also London, City of
Orders, *See* Decrees

P

Pardons, 63, 328
Parliament
    Members' franking privilege, 198
    Privileges of, 284, 376
    See also Statutes
Parsons, *See* Churches; Tithes
Parties
    Administrators, 178
    Assignees, 188
    Bishops, 11, 24
    Contract suits, 364
    Co-plaintiffs, 149
    Corporations, 90
    Defect of abates suit, 403
    Defendants
        Abroad, 183
        Co-defendants, 323
        Representative, 203
    Depositions used against, 25
    Died pending suit, 391
    Enemy alien, 382
    Executors, 153, 403, 442
    Fraudulent conveyance suit, 276
    Incapacity of, 22, 403
    Informers, 399
    Misjoinder
        Generally, 263
        Suits for tithes, 401
    Misnomer, 214
    Navy commissioners, 364
    Necessary, 229
    Nominal executors, 442
    Nonjoinder
        Generally, 203, 276, 313
        Tithes suit, 396
        Trust beneficiary, 337
    Numerous, 424
    Peace, bills of, 424
    Peers, 24
    Redemption, suits for, 96
    Relators
        Generally, 63, 276, 291, 373

    Liable for costs, 31
    Representative, 203
    Review, bills of, 25
    Tithes, suits for, 224
    Witnesses, as, 187
    See also Answers; Decedent's estate; Officers; Persons; Women, married
Penal bonds
    Generally, 39, 84, 353
    Mesne profits, for, 457
    Performance bonds, 364, 410
    Relieved for bad faith of debtor, 111
    Resignation of vicarage, 430
    See also Contracts; Creditors; Forfeitures
Penalties, *See* Forfeitures; Penal bonds
Pensions, *See* Churches; Property
Perpetuities, 115, 277
Personal property, *See* Property
Persons
    Aliens, 382
    Ambassadors, 191, 359
    Apprentices, 219, 238
    Archdeacons, 288
    Attorneys, 211, 263, 268
    Bakers, 126
    Bankers, 163
    Bargemen, 302
    Barristers, 404
    Bastards, 376
    Bishops, 11, 24, 274
    Booksellers, 411
    Brewers, 268
    Bridge masters, 46, 302
    Curates, 383, 445, 446
    Factors, 238
    Farmers, 119
    Fishermen, 105
    Graziers, 119
    Guardians, 22
    Impropriators, 231, 289
    Incompetents, 22
    Infants, 173, 177, 183, 312, 316, 372, 468
    Informers, 399
    Mariners, 219
    Masters of ships, 232
    Merchants, 238
    Millers, 172
    Monsters, 219
    Naturalized, inheritance by, 27
    Orphans, 372
    Painters, 317
    Parliament members, 11, 24, 198, 284, 376, 444
    Paupers, 164, 267, 390
    Peers
        Answers by, 24
        Privileges, 198, 284, 376
        Process against, 11
    Prebendaries, 189
    Rectors, 35, 383
    Roman Catholics, 143, 269, 291, 395, 423, 450
    Scriveners, 332
    Servants, 191
    Spendthrifts, 159, 223
    Suicides, 158
    Tailors, 290
    Tenants in ancient demesne, 46, 133
    Tinners, 14
    Vicars, 32, 445, 446
    Watermen, 229
    See also Agents; Bankruptcy and bankrupts; Corporations; Creditors and debtors; Crown; Decedent's estates; Officers; Parties; Women, married
Pictures and hatchments, 317
Pleading
    Abatement, matter in
        Auter action pendent, 73, 383
        Better writ, 403
        Misnomer, 214
        Priority of suit, 305, 313, 427
    Admission of plea, 254

Subject Index 715

Amendment allowed, 153
Auter action pendent, 73, 383
Cross-bills, 274, 396
Enemy alien, plaintiff as, 382
Estoppel, crown, 220
Fraud, 402
Infants, by, 177
Interpleader, bills of, 458
Jurisdiction waived by, 414
Latin pleas in equity, 30
Letters testamentary, of, 153
Misjoinder, 382
Misnomer, 214
Necessary for proof, 314
Pleas in bar
   Admitted in part, 254
   Allegations needed, 339
   Demurrers to, 427
   Discovery, to, 425
   Generally, 197
   Jurisdiction, to, 93
   Respondeat ouster, 50
Priority of suit, 305, 313, 427
Releases, 402
Replies
   Generally, 197
   Fraud, of, 402
Res judicata
   Chancery court of Durham, 274
   Common law judgment, 356
   Facts already proved, 376
   Generally, 56
   Priority of suit, 305, 313, 427
Respondeat ouster, 50
Sufficiency of, 76
See also Answers; Complaint, bills of;
   Demurrers; Discovery, bills of;
   Limitations, Statute of
Ports
   Portsmouth docks, 364
   Purprestures in, 3, 106
   See also Cities and towns; London, City
      of; Rivers

Post Office, 198
Powers of attorney, 188
Precedents searched for, 30, 41, 44, 62, 70,
   89, 368, 424, 438, 446, 469
Prerogative, *See* Crown
Prerogative Court of Canterbury, 86, 249
Prescriptive rights, 136
Principal and agent, 238, 271, 394, 422
Priority of suit
   Generally, 305, 427
   Waived, 313
Prisage, *See* Taxes; Wine
Prisons
   Escapes, 427
   Fleet, 99, 227, 368, 374, 427
   Marshalsea, 227
Privileges
   Attorney-client, 68
   Parliament, member of, 444
   See also Exchequer; Forfeitures
Prize ships, 63, 386, 458
Procedure
   Accountings, 242, 254, 300, 315, 328,
      357, 391, 407, 416, 439, 450
   Affidavits, 284, 374
   Appeals
      Generally, 177, 277, 308
      Lower courts, from, 175
      Orders suspended, 178
   Appearances
      Compelled by process, 11
      Generally, 90
      Peers, by, 11
      Refusal to make, 227,
      Voluntary, 16
   Argument on demurrer, 376
   Cases stated, 286
   Certificate of custom, 372
   Certiorari, 274
   Commission to set out land, 202
   Commissioners
      Contribution, to decide, 203
      Discovery, to aid, 5

Generally, 169
Common law judges consulted, 279
Confirmation of arbitration, 364
Continuance denied, 226
Co-plaintiffs, 149
Dismissal, priority of suit, 305
Election of remedies, 49
Error, writs of, 268
Exceptions, bills of, 405, 416
Injunctions
  Future disturbances, 237
  Generally, 374
  Lessee of crown, 51
  Preliminary, 106, 252, 272, 313, 351, 446
  Quia timet, 413
Joinder of actions, 149
Jury trials
  Exceptions, bills of, 405
  Generally, 2, 34, 52, 60, 89, 132, 136, 138, 141, 169, 171, 177, 200, 208, 210, 219, 234, 251, 270, 273, 274, 284, 295, 313, 318, 319, 322, 327, 329, 331, 341, 343, 347, 354, 362, 364, 375, 395, 418, 424, 426, 427, 431
  Special verdicts, 2
Motions to quash, 374
New trials, 176, 177
Nonsuits, 380, 446
Outlawry, 53
Pleas of fine and nonclaim, 253
Rehearings, 250, 256, 257, 268, 285, 288, 295, 387, 438, 444
Reinstatement of case, 446
Reports by king's remembrancer, 242, 254, 300, 315, 328, 357, 391, 407, 416, 439, 450
Review, bills of, 25, 76, 92, 269, 310, 391, 416
Revivor, bills of, 20, 33, 56, 377, 391
Sequestration, pre-judgment, 26
Stated accounts, 391
Stays of proceedings, 327

Subpoena *scire facias*, 13, 33, 377, 391, 466
Time to respond extended, 381
See also Arbitration; Decrees; Evidence; Executions; Parties; Pleading; Process
Process
  Amoveas manus, 254
  Assistance, writs of, 374
  Attachment, 241, 252, 288, 374
  Capias in manum, 427
  Co-defendants, 323
  Corporations, against, 90
  Death of crown, 233
  Distringas, 11, 30, 88, 90
  Extent, writs of
    Bankruptcy, 200
    Generally, 55, 196, 254, 432
    Mesne profits, 457
    Rent due crown, 30
    Seizures under, 323
  Habeas corpus, 368
  Habeas corpus ad respondendum, 227
  Injunctions
    Future disturbances, 237
    Generally, 374
    Lessee of crown, 51
    Preliminary, 106, 252, 272, 313, 351, 446
    Quia timet, 413
  Laches, 104
  Letters to peers, 11
  Levari facias, writs of, 227
  Outlawry
    Bankruptcy, 279
    Generally, 55, 413
  Prayer for, 90
  Returns of, 233, 374
  Sequestration, 26, 99, 152, 233, 374, 368, 412, 419, 460
  Sergeant at arms, 233
  Service
    Agent, 183
    Necessity, 419

Subject Index 717

Subpoenas
  Generally, 11, 90, 104
  Scire facias, 13, 33, 377, 391, 466
  Venditioni exponas, 55
  Venire facias, 11
  Waived, 16
  See also Executions; Procedure
Property
  Ancient demesne, 46
  Annuities
    Generally, 213
    Taxes charged to, 355
  Assignments of, 36
  Antigua, in, 384
  Boundaries, 341, 385
  Brew houses, 239
  Burgage tenure, 170
  Chantry rents, 202
  Cheshire, in, 93
  Common, 424
  Commons
    Enclosed, 134, 168
    Generally, 226, 356, 362
  Contracts to sell
    Generally, 98, 182, 201, 285
    Enforced, 69, 112, 166, 172, 285, 334, 358, 364, 406, 433
  Converted, 260
  Copyholds
    Conveyances of, 18, 339
    Fee, in, 157
    Forfeited, 19
    Generally, 230, 333, 356, 371, 378
    Rents out of, 202
    Security for debt, 18
    Succession, 295
  Copyrights, 411
  Crown
    Copyhold, 356
    Intrusion into, 270
    Leases, 279
    Rents reserved, 240
  Customary land, 170
  Dilapidations, 32, 148, 162, 430, 467
  Discontinuances, 209
  Disseisin, nonpayment of tithes, 123
  Dower rights, 455
  Downs, 134
  Durham, in, 274
  Ejectment, 51
  Enclosures
    Forced consent, 211
    Generally, 134, 168, 194, 237, 356
  Encumbrances, discovery of, 160, 427
  Entails
    Barred, 209
    Generally, 144, 156, 173, 255, 429, 435
    Lease, of, 115
    Remainders defeated, 225
  Escheats, 16, 432
  Estates, nonfeasance, 123
  Fairs, 79
  Felons' goods, 262
  Fences, 203
  Fens, 270
  Forfeited
    Generally, 16
    Superstitious uses, 143, 269, 291, 395
    Treason, for, 19, 23
  Gavelkind, 139
  Hedges, 203
  Houses, 88, 190, 346
  Improvements by mortgagee, 199, 292
  Ingfangtheif, 262
  Inherited by naturalized person, 27
  Inns, 199
  Jewels, 83, 353, 387
  Jura regalia, 274
  Leases
    Bankrupts, 279
    Devises of, 206, 277
    Dower rights, 455
    Entailed, 115
    Fraudulent, 1
    Generally, 187, 277, 342, 410

Life tenant of, 286
Mortgaged, 66
Pensions, 127
Rents reserved upon, 429
Survivorship, 40
Waste, 260
Lessees
  Holdover, 260
  Post office, of, 198
Liberties, 36
Life estates, 255
Lord's escheat, 16, 432
Manors
  Customs of, 170, 295
  Fines in, 121
  Generally, 69, 385, 405
  Markets, 79
  Mills, 6, 82
  Quit rents discoverable, 5
  Rents in, 240
  Succession to copyhold, 295
Markets, 79, 354
Marriage settlements, 345
Marshes, 131, 226, 270
Meadows plowed up, 461
Nuisances, 3, 106, 138
Occupancy, special, 432
Offices as, 427
Paraphernalia, 387
Parks, 113
Pasture plowed up, 461
Pensions, 56, 112, 127, 135, 150, 159, 186, 192, 213, 355
Perpetuities, 115, 277
Profits of, 259
Port privileges, 274
Possession
  Decreed, 89
  Presumed in good faith, 187
Prescription, by, 136, 274
Pretium affectionis, 83
Prize ships, 63, 386, 458

Profits
  Mesne, bonds for, 457
  Pernor of, 461
Purchasers
  Good faith, 158
  Without notice, 239
Purprestures
  Houses, 3
  Piers, 106
Redemption proceeds, 57, 122, 234, 398, 455
Remainders
  Barred, 209
  Charitable, 229
  Contingent, 225, 277, 309
  Generally, 230, 255
  Mortgages, of, 292
Rents
  Apportionment of, 130, 131
  Arrears of, 147
  Assise of, 420
  Charge, 88, 97, 139, 254
  Copyhold, out of, 202
  Discoverable, 5, 385, 425
  Fee farm, 130, 131, 240, 252, 294, 296, 443
  Frank, 202
  Generally, 69, 95, 179, 186, 188, 303, 334
  Manors, in, 240
  Quit rents, 5, 337
  Reduced for taxes paid, 351
  Reserved, 36, 240, 351, 429
  Rivers, of, 36
  Seck, 45
  Sequestered, 374
  Tithes of, 70, 71, 75
Reversions
  Crown, in, 7
  Generally, 429
River shores, 362
Rivers, 36, 274
Salt pits, 313

Seacoast, 3
Security for debts, 18
Settlements, family, 85, 89, 115, 144, 156, 173, 177, 209, 225, 272, 312, 324, 329, 346, 397, 423, 429, 435, 461, 468, 469
Superior titles to, 297
Surrendered, 286
Survivorship, 47, 367
Tenants, joint, 47
Trust to pay debts, 332
Void will creates no title, 360
Walls, 292
Warranties, collateral, 255
Wood converted, 260
See also Churches; Conveyances; Forfeitures; Mills; Mines and minerals; Mortgages; Timber and wood; Tithes; Trusts; Waste; Wills

Q

Queen, See Crown
Quo warranto, writs of, 370

R

Real property, See Property
Records, See Evidence
Rectors, See Churches; Tithes
Remedies, See Procedure; Process
Res judicata
    Chancery court of Durham, 274
    Common law judgment, 356
    Facts already proved, 376
    Generally, 56
    Priority of suit, 305, 313, 427
Review, bills of, 25, 76, 92, 269, 310, 391, 416
Revivor, bills of, 20, 33, 56, 377, 391
Rivers
    Ferries over, 463
    Generally, 36, 274
    Humber, 362
    Obstruction of, 463
    Ouse, Hunts., 36
    Public, free to, 463
    Purprestures in ports, 3, 106
    Stour, Essex, 36
    Swale, 405
    Thames, 46, 133, 302
    Wear, Co. Durham, 274, 463
    See also Bridges; Ships

S

Salt pits, 313
Schools, See Charities
Sheriffs, See Executions; Officers; Process
Ships
    Generally, 232
    Maidenhead Bridge, 302
    Mariners, 219
    Masters of ships, 232
    Prizes, 63, 386, 458
    Star of the East, 386
    Taxed, 301
    Tolls for, 46, 133, 302
    Trinity House, 301
    See also Bridges; Navy; Rivers
Silk, 382
Stannaries, tithes sued in exchequer, 14
Statutes
    Frauds, of, 223, 371
    Interpretation of, 19, 189, 289, 432
    See also Limitations, Statute of
Suicide, 158
Superstitious uses, 143, 269, 291, 395

T

Taverns, 276
Taxes, Tolls, Customs, Duties, and Fees
    Anchorage, 274
    Ancient demesne tenants, 46, 133
    Assessments of, 296
    Aulnage, 94, 142, 264
    Ballast shore, 274
    Beaconage, 274
    Charge on annuity, 355

'charges and reprises' as, 393
Chimney money, 38
Contraband, 117
Crown goods exempt, 386
Customs for exports, 44
Deductions from rents, 351
Discovery of, 46, 58, 263, 449
Duties due to town, 210
Duty for cheese, 375
Exchequer jurisdiction over, 386
Excise
   Generally, 62, 112
   Hereditary, 398
   Lease of, 40
Export fees, 347
Fines, 247
Fraud, 44, 221, 328
Grain, on, 327, 328
Granted to towns, 327
Homage fees, 265
Import duties, 328, 347
Land taxes, 450
Leases of, 94
Liverpool, port of, 375
Maidenhead Bridge, 302
Market tolls, 354
Paid by whom, 294
Parliamentary taxes, 355, 393
Plankage, 274
Prisage
   Assessed, how, 101
   Bonds for, 84
   Cinque Ports, 154
   Due, when, 74
   Exemption from, 154
   Fraud, 221
   Generally, 399
   London exemption, 58
Salt duties, lease of, 128
Ships, on, 301
Stamp tax, 433
Tolls
   Bridges, 46, 133
   Charter for void, 302
   Exports, on, 327
   Void tolls, 302
   Wharfage, 274
   See also, Crown; Mills
Timber and wood
   Generally, 244, 413, 468
   Tithes of
      Generally, 103, 157, 230, 310, 330, 331, 363, 407, 444
      Upon sale, 216
   Waste, 260
Time limits, *See* Limitations, Statute of
Tithes
   Accrued, when, 15
   Agistment (herbage), 77, 123, 282, 325, 363, 396, 431, 434
   Apples, 314
   Arrears of, suit for, 78
   Barren cattle, 436, 437
   Barren ground, 134
   Beech trees, 331
   Calves, 314
   Carrots, 308
   Cattle, 204, 205
   Cherries, 434
   Cistercian lands, 29, 102, 136, 197, 298, 388
   Clover, 110, 124, 258, 318
   Coleseed, 64, 185
   Common law action for, 241
   Composition for, 129, 215, 409, 465
   Computed, 315
   Conies, 77, 343
   Contracts to compound for, 348
   Copyholders in fee, 157
   Corn, 29, 113, 185, 236, 304, 350, 361, 448, 462
   Crown, eggs for, 125
   Custom of time of, 352
   Customary, 7, 308, 331
   Customs, local, 242
   Debts, as, 243

Decrees for, 368
Delivered, where, 100
Discharged, 29, 157, 310
Discovery of, 35, 231
Eggs, 125
Endowments of, 304, 448
Firewood, 244
Fish, 105, 205
Flax, 343
Fleeces, 388
Food for animals, 110
Foreigners, by, 204
Fowl, wild, 125
Generally, 307, 380, 459
Glebe as compensation, 134
Glebes, of, 304
Grain, 102, 113, 236, 462
Grass, 124, 258
Harvest, after, 242
Hay, 29, 110, 118, 123, 236, 304, 318, 330, 350, 361, 462
Hemp, 343
Hops, 48, 242, 306
Hornbeams, 103
Hospitalers' land, 102
Houses, 289, 392
Lambs, 91, 114, 137, 145, 314, 340, 352, 365, 388, 417
Land discharged of, 102
Lands of lesser abbeys, 212
Leases of, 75, 231, 286, 340, 361, 401
Lessees of
   Crown, of, 7
   Generally, 350
   Vicars, of, 193
London, in, 70, 71, 289, 392
Lops, 251
Lost by enclosure, 134
Madder, 109
Marshland, 251
Meadows, 409
Milk, 100
Mills, 408

Minerals, 7
Modus decimandi, 59, 113, 114, 194, 251, 278, 282, 306, 318, 330, 340, 344, 361, 365, 388, 392, 409, 434, 462
Non decimando, 314, 325, 343, 350, 363, 388, 396, 437
Nonpayment not disseisin, 123
Notice of setting out of, 350
Oysters, 205
Paid by vendor or vendee, 331
Paid in kind, 113
Papal bulls not valid, 102
Pasturage, 114, 118, 145, 204
Payable before legacies, 243
Payable by vendor or vendee, 216
Peas, 308
Pembroke College, 308
Personal, 408
Pigeons, 87
Pilchards, 105
Plaintiff not entitled, 35
Pleaded, how, 21
Premonstratensian land, 102
Prescription against, 136
Prescription, discharge by, 157
Prescription for, 343
Priority over debts, 451
Pro rata custom, 266
Rents, 70, 71, 75
Saffron, 124
Second crops, 258
Sequestered, 155, 224
Sheep, 134, 282
Standing in fields, 242
Stannaries, 14
Statutory discharge, 29
Suits for
   Collector, by, 224
   Generally, 42, 231, 401
   Limitation of, 15
Templar's lands, 245
Tin, 14

Turnips, 308, 396, 439, 448
Usage as evidence of, 193, 448
Verdict at common law, 344
Vicarage, lost, 77
Vicar not to pay, 134
Woad, 124
Wood and timber, 103, 157, 216, 230, 244, 251, 310, 330, 331, 363, 407, 444
Wool, 15, 114, 137, 145, 146, 266, 282, 340, 388, 417
See also Churches
Tolls, *See* Taxes
Torts
  Assault, 460
  Contribution for, 203
  Moritur cum persona, 287
  Trover, actions of, 273
  See also Nuisances
Towns, *See* Cities and towns; London, City of
Trinity House, 301
Trover, actions of, 273
Trusts
  Beneficiaries
    Common recovery by, 229
    Co-plaintiffs, 337
    Deceased, 195
    Felons, 16
  Breach of, 85
  Charitable, 229, 248
  Constructive, 85, 217
  Debts of settlor, for, 222, 332
  Enforced, 173, 174
  Equity jurisdiction, 151
  Escheats of, 16
  Felons' goods forfeited, 16
  Fine and nonclaim, 37
  Forfeited
    Felons' goods, 16
    Outlawry, by, 53
  Fraudulent conveyances, 119

Generally, 115, 141, 272, 283, 286, 316, 329, 461
Heirs, temporary, 259
Laches, none, 174
Land, given to executor, 222
Lease, of, 40, 286, 342, 432
Life tenant of, 286
Limitations, Statute of, 37, 174
Personal, 378
Power of revocation, 257
Redemption proceeds, 57
Remainders, 286
Resulting, 223
Revocable, 397
Shares of stock, 400
Spendthrift, 159, 223
Suits to enforce, parties to, 337
Superstitious uses, 143, 269, 291, 395
Terms not alterable, 164
Woman, married, 53
See also Charities; Decedent's estates; Forfeitures; Property; Wills

U

Usury, *See* Creditors and debtors

V

Venue of jury trial, 418
Vessels
  Generally, 232
  Maidenhead Bridge, 302
  Mariners, 219
  Masters of ships, 232
  Prizes, 63, 386, 458
  Star of the East, 386
  Taxed, 301
  Tolls for, 46, 133, 302
  Trinity House, 301
  See also Bridges; Navy; Rivers
Vi laica removenda, writs of, 446
Vicars, *See* Churches; Tithes

W

Wales, council of marches of, 175
Wales, court of great sessions, 209
Warrens, 77, 356
Waste
    Dilapidations, 32, 148, 162, 430, 467
    Discovery of, 468
    Distrainor, by, 88
    Enjoined, 461
    Executor, by, 66
    Forfeiture for, 468
    Houses, 88
    Leases, 260
    Pernor of profits, not by, 461
    Pleading, 230
    Remaindermen, harm to, 461
    Timber, 260
    See also Property
Widows, *See* Women, married
Wills
    Ademptions, 195
    Alterations of, 248
    Ambulatory, 367
    Augmentation of jointure, 438
    Contracts to make, 98
    Date of, 367
    Debts
        Paid from realty, 357
        To be paid, 37, 66, 222, 332, 438, 467
    Devises
        Annuity of, 355
        Distributive, 213
        Equity of redemption, 141
        Generally, 122
        Heir of living person, 435
        Implication, by, 66
        Interpreted, 34, 228
        Leases, 206, 277
        'Mortgaged lands', of, 34
        Orphanage part, 464
        Payment of debts, 37, 66, 467
        Redemption of land, 66
        Repugnant, 206
        Surviving devisee, 367
    Election of schoolmaster, 349
    Evidence of not allowed, 435
    Execution of, 248
    Generally, 37, 316
    Harshness avoided, 346
    Heirs
        Joint tenants, 47
        Survivorship, 47
    Interpretation of, 34, 141, 165, 191, 206, 213, 228, 272, 333, 346, 349, 355, 387, 438, 461
    Land charged, 239
    Legacies and bequests
        Ademption, 195
        Brother, to, 389
        Charged on land, 369
        Executor, to, 389, 438
        Generally, 195
        Interpreted, 165, 191
        Ordered to be paid, 180
        Servants, to, 191
        Specific, payable, 184
    Nuncupative, 57
    Paraphernalia of widows, 387
    Priority among creditors, 37
    Probate
        Void will, of, 360
        Where, 86
    Redemption of land, 66
    Revocation by later will, 2
    Tenants, joint, 47
    Trust to pay debts, 222, 332, 438
    Void, 360, 435
    Women, married, 360, 387
    Written only, 435
    See also Decedent's estates; Descents and distributions
Wine, 58, 74, 84, 101, 154, 221, 399
Women, married
    Answers to bills, 42
    Contracts by, 199
    Costs payable by, 469

Devise to wife, 66
Land in Antigua, 384
Paraphernalia, 387
Property of, 144
Servants of, 191
Settlements, family, 85, 89, 115, 144, 156, 173, 177, 209, 225, 272, 324, 329, 346, 397, 423, 429, 435, 461, 468, 469
Trusts for husband's debts, 53
Widow's share, 453, 455
Wills of, 360, 387

Wood, *See* Timber; Tithes